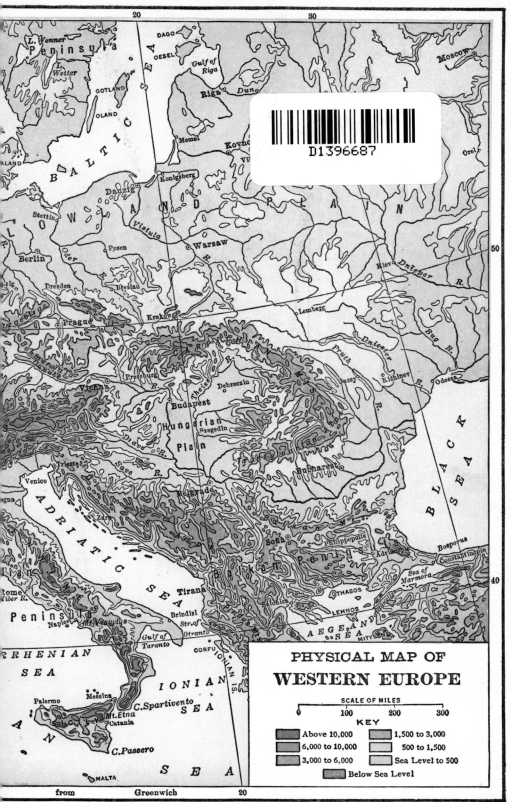

PHYSICAL MAP OF
WESTERN EUROPE

SCALE OF MILES

0   100   200   300

KEY

Above 10,000	1,500 to 3,000
6,000 to 10,000	500 to 1,500
3,000 to 6,000	Sea Level to 500
Below Sea Level	

From Ferdinand Schevill, *A History of Europe*, Harcourt, Brace and Company, Inc.

A History of Europe

from the Reformation to the Present Day

FERDINAND SCHEVILL

PROFESSOR EMERITUS OF MODERN HIS-
TORY IN THE UNIVERSITY OF CHICAGO

NEW AND REVISED EDITION

HARCOURT, BRACE & WORLD, INC.

New York and Burlingame

CONTENTS

SECTION I

Preliminary Survey

SECTION II

The Reformation and the Religious Wars from 1500 to 1648

CONTENTS

SECTION III

The Absolute Monarchy from 1648 to 1789

SECTION IV

Revolution and Democracy

I. FROM THE FRENCH REVOLUTION TO WORLD WAR I (1914)

SECTION V

Revolution and Democracy (continued)

2. AGE OF THE WORLD WARS

LIST OF MAPS

LIST OF MAPS

FOREWORD

THE NEW version of this book does not differ greatly from its predecessor. It offers in Chapter 45 a fuller account of World War II, in Chapter 46 a broadened treatment of the Cultural Trends of the Twentieth Century, and in Chapter 47 the story of the "cold" war of the Postwar World. During the five years since the issue of the last edition there rose into the general consciousness of mankind a subtle but definite sense of a change of outlook of world-wide scope. It may be summarized as a growing recognition that an epoch of history has ended and that a new epoch has arisen to replace it. Close observers of the world scene are in substantial agreement to call the new epoch the Global Era. So impressed is the author with the effected transformation that he is tempted to change the title of his book from "A History of Europe from the Reformation to the Present Day" to "A History of Europe from the Reformation to the Global Era." However, since the altered title might convey the mistaken impression that a new or at least a substantially remodeled text is herewith submitted to the public, he has resolved to abide by the original title.

In the hope of providing the student with a measure of guidance amidst the rapid changes of a monstrously confused world, the author proposes to trace the train of thought that led him to his conviction that an entirely new historical epoch has dawned on mankind. When, a generation ago, he first undertook to recount the story of Europe beginning with the Reformation, this small continent or, as it more truly is, this mere western termination of the Asiatic land-mass, had ever since the Reformation so manifestly been the leading center of creative activity on earth that the unfolding of this activity for the last four hundred years was certain to prove as enriching an experience as might be encountered, in any area of man's struggle through the ages.

The four centuries that have rolled around since our starting point constitute what is commonly called Modern History, and the leading dramatis personae of Modern History are the great states which arose within the compass of Europe and which by reason of their might gained the designation of the great powers. In war and peace alike they dominated the world situation. A circumstance notably contributory to their domination was that they served as champions and carriers of the civilization which had been slowly maturing among them from even before the Reformation and which, to distinguish it from other, chiefly Oriental, civilizations based on very different assumptions, has been called Western civilization. To whatever regions of the earth the great powers penetrated by reason of their organized might they took their civilization along with them, until in the course of the nineteenth and twentieth centuries it had effectively girdled the globe.

A significant result of the universal spread of Western civilization was that the diverse peoples of the earth were brought into closer touch and to a better understanding of one another. While this drawing together may be declared to have opened the possibility of some kind of future political association, an early realization of this prospect was defeated by the stubborn persistence of the ancient competitive rancors among the great powers. These continued incurably to fester until in the first half of the twentieth century they reached frightening twin peaks in two savage wars of world-wide scope.

At the close of the first of these wars there was a considerable shake-up among the great powers but no substantial change of system. On the termination, however, of the much more ferociously fought World War II, the traditional system went completely to pieces. It did so because in the course of the inhumanly prolonged and exhausting struggle most of the great powers shrank so visibly in might and stature that they fell to a rank very little above that of their admittedly minor European neighbors. Towering head and shoulders above them stood the two giant survivors of the conflict, the United States of America and the Union of Socialist Soviet Republics (identical in point of authority with the single state of Russia). An aspect of the transformed power picture that immediately leaps to view is that the two survivors stand on ground which lies outside the original bounds of Europe; and this aspect imposes the inescapable conclusion that Europe has been definitely and irretrievably deposed from that thousand-year-old domination which is the subject matter of this book.

It is beyond dispute that from World War II onward the power struggle in the world will pivot on the United States and the U.S.S.R., with Europe wooed by each in turn but no longer capable of aspiring to a leading role. It is equally clear that the main issue between the two giant contestants will be the creation of a world government prepared to give effective expression to the cultural fusion of all the peoples of the earth, a fusion for which Western civilization has cleared, and is still engaged in clearing, the way.

Such is the tremendous and terrifying prospect looming before the living generation of men. While it is undeniable that it has its origin in the earlier European developments, it is also true that it so definitely marks a break with the European past that a history like the present one, focused throughout its length on Europe, cannot with any show of reason be expanded to include the unknown vicissitudes of the new power rivalry. Both historical logic and the artistic unity to which every literary product of man instinctively aspires uncompromisingly demand that this, and for that matter every general history of Europe, come to its terminus with the supersession of Europe by its two non-European heirs.

From this reading of the power revolution that has convulsed the world stems an educational conclusion which is fairly evident but has not yet been generally recognized. It runs to the effect that the eclipse of Europe should be formally acknowledged by conceding to the post-war world a separate and distinct college course. Indeed, without awaiting the judgment of the experts, the issue is already in process of being solved in this sense. Within the year a half-dozen world histories have been published which make the era of the World Wars their starting-point and the problem of world unity as presently contested between the United States and Russia their primary subject matter. Guided by a no longer avoidable global viewpoint, they concern themselves with tracing the current development toward or away from unity in every country of our round earth.

There is even noticeable a beginning trend to let this narrowly contemporary kind of history replace altogether the older kind, with its story of slow growth through many centuries, to which this book belongs. But this trend by every valid kind of educational norm is surely an aberration and may confidently be expected before long to be recognized as such. For without a deeper rearward view of the origin and development of European society and civilization, the student, narrowly restricted to a purely contemporary outlook, will be faced with innumerable riddles of politics and culture for which no solution is available from the material under this hand.

There remains the obligation of an explanatory word on the last chapter of the new version. It carries the title of the Postwar World (1945-1950) and plainly trenches on the Global Era which, as set forth in the foregoing analysis, lies beyond the scope of this book. However, the author is strongly persuaded that this intrusion is justified. For, far from attempting to present in this chapter a detailed history of the five years in question, he limits himself to treating a single but absolutely determinative event of these years, the so-called "cold" war. That war, called cold, but steadily and tragically gathering heat, marks the transition from the old and vanishing epoch to the new and global epoch and binds them together into a meaningful whole. Moreover, it establishes beyond the possibility

of a doubt that the cold war is the result of the clash of two absolutely
incompatible ideologies or, as it may more simply be put, between two
absolutely incompatible ways of life. There is no question in the author's
mind nor can there, in his opinion, be any question in an intelligent
reader's mind that the recognition of this incompatibility is the indispensable pre-condition for all clear thinking about the Global Era, through
the massed confusions of which it is the hard and cruel lot of the living
generation to find its way.

APRIL 15, 1951

A HISTORY OF EUROPE

1 CONCERNING HISTORY IN GENERAL AND THIS HISTORY IN PARTICULAR

AN INDISPENSABLE PRELIMINARY measure for every present-day historian is to explain to his readers what he means by history. For it cannot have escaped even superficial observation that history has become a very elastic word with wholly indeterminate boundaries. It is hardly an exaggeration to say that there are today as many definitions of history as there are historians and that in effect every historian writes his own kind of history.

History a very elastic word

This extension of the bounds of history is a development of relatively recent date. The English historian, Edward Freeman, who lived in the second half of the nineteenth century, was still able to proclaim narrowly and dogmatically that "history is past politics." Not content with stating his position, he rode into the lists against all adversaries and fought hotly for his definition on the double ground that it alone accorded with the honorable tradition of his craft and that its abandonment would bring about an intolerable confusion. And indeed the facts were so indisputably on his side that no one dreamed of denying that the European predecessors of Freeman as far back as the revivers of historical studies in the Renaissance had accepted history as substantially concerned with politics. More impressive still, the ancient historians from Herodotus to Tacitus, whom early nineteenth century historians still looked up to as unapproached masters and whom they attempted as far as possible to imitate, had proceeded on precisely the same theory. It could not be challenged that an ancient tradition gave its sanction to the view that history was bounded by politics and that the bursting of its boundaries would infallibly open an era of experimentation and uncertainty.

History traditionally concerned with politics

And yet neither Freeman nor the long line of historical writers stretching in a shadowy column behind him as far back as Herodotus, father and fountainhead of history, could stop the movement that leveled the old barriers. Like all movements of great energy it had been secretly at work some generations before men became aware of its existence. Undeniably it was tied up with the whole modern complex; above all, it resulted from the observational and scientific influences that had given birth to the new physics, chemistry, and biology, to the new critical philosophies, and to the new naturalistic phases of art and literature.

Modern research assembles vast bodies of new material

3

Beginning more particularly with the eighteenth century, man's innumerable activities involving his social and legal as well as his political institutions, his life on the farm and in the city, his relation to his group and the relation of social groups to one another, together with a score of other matters shedding a novel and amazing light on the issue of his destiny, had begun to receive an increasingly profitable attention.

The old barriers of history are swept aside By the middle of the nineteenth century this new material, all of it strikingly illustrative of the persistent human struggle to make the earth a better place in which to live, had reached immense proportions and could no longer be ignored by scholars who, calling themselves historians, were obliged to take the ground that nothing appertaining to man might remain foreign to their sympathy. To be sure, the vigor inhering in the accepted practice of history was such that a conservative group continued to insist that only political data were relevant to the historian's business and that it was for economists, sociologists, and other new-fangled specialists, but not for the honorable craft of the historians, to utilize the new material. But with each new decade the membership of the conservative school fell off until we come to the memorable fight made by Freeman. In spite of its having the appearance of a vigorous offensive, it was, regarded in the perspective of nineteenth century development, no more than a last-ditch rally fought under that most irrational and pathetic of slogans: "The old guard dies but does not surrender."

A new historical orientation begins With the dawn of the twentieth century what we may call the traditional or Old History had definitely lost its hold and something groping and different, which we may call the New History, had begun to take shape. Since there had been no systematic preliminary debate among historical writers as to the constitutive elements of the New History, the victory of the innovators did not fail to result in the confusion which Freeman and his adherents had so confidently foretold. It has continued to the present day, not, however, without a gradual clearing of the atmosphere. In spite of each historian feeling free to follow an independent course, there have latterly begun to rise into view two leading aspects or forms of the New History, of each of which it may be said that it represents a promising escape from the reigning anarchy.

Of two emerging forms of the New History the first is a history of civilization Of these two emerging forms the first is of a more comprehensive and revolutionary, the second, of a more narrow and conservative nature. What the champions of the first form propose to do is so to broaden the concept of history that it shall embrace nothing less than the sum of man's activities and become a record of civilization. The proponents of this trend enjoy a wide contemporary support. They have gathered under their banner all those advanced elements of opinion which, impressed with the recent accelerated drawing together of the world under the influence of science, communications, and machines, look forward to the achievement in the not too distant future of an effective political expression of these unifying processes. Civilization, in spite of the immense diversity of its aspects, constitutes a spiritual whole, according to this historical school, and the confidently expected climax of its uninterrupted unfolding is the world state.

For all their agreement on a vastly extended survey, the followers of the civilization trend have developed some very important differences. **Differences among historians of civilization** This was inevitable since, after the innumerable cultural data had, as a first step, been assembled, they had, as a second and concluding step, to be brought into an intelligible relation, that is, they had to be subjected to interpretation. Interpretation signifies the adoption of a principle, in accordance with which the progressive unification of mankind might be represented as having been effected; and such a principle defining a continuous development depends primarily on the purpose or end ascribed to the unifying movement. While one historian of civilization declared that the end of humanity's age-old endeavor was a democratic society in which every individual shall achieve his highest development in freedom, another historian favored as a goal a society in which freedom is sacrificed in the interest of equality and security. Besides these two perhaps most commonly envisaged ends, many another purpose, projected at one time or another by the world's dreamers and thinkers, has had its quota of supporters.

The point to which to hold fast among these conflicting interpretations is this: regardless of his particular integrating formula, the historian of **Agreement among historians of civilization** civilization has his eye uninterruptedly on the movement of society, and specifically of our Western society, as a whole and is inclined to minimize and even to rule out entirely the activities of the individual entities called states. By this procedure he effects a complete break with traditional history, which, identified with politics, was exclusively concerned with the successes, failures, and conflicts of governments.

The natural unwillingness of some minds to subscribe to so complete a departure from tradition as is represented by the type, history of civilization, accounts for the second type of history which is visibly rising out **The second type of the New History is a broadened political history** of the reigning confusion. This type still undertakes to trace the activity and destiny of states, that is, it adheres to tradition; but it does not do so without imposing two important modifications on the practice of the past.

The first of these modifications springs from a new conception of the nature of politics. Quite usually the older historians regarded politics as **The second type broadens history by placing politics in a social setting** an autonomous activity of governments, which were conceived as dwelling substantially in a vacuum. We are now much more acutely aware of the social setting within which political movements take place. It is this setting, constituting what we may call the nursing-ground of politics, which the followers of the second type of history insist on bringing to the fore. In this manner the old-style history is completely transcended, since the New History, its offspring, regards politics not as a self-operating activity, but as conditioned by geographic, economic, intellectual, and all the other forces at work in society. In short, in distinction from the older practice, politics is closely integrated with the social-economic developments within the particular group which the state is intended to serve.

The second modification imposed on the traditional history is a consequence of the recognition that the contentious states of the Western world are united by a common culture. While these states are still treated as the separate units they are, each pursuing stubbornly its particular set of interests, they are viewed as sharing a common culture, by which, in spite of their often ferocious struggles and hatreds, they have achieved a high measure of spiritual and intellectual unity. This community of thought and, to a large extent, of institutions, is never lost sight of. However, as it is not central to this type of history, which continues to make politics its organizing principle, the common culture must be treated, sometimes in connection with a particular national group at the precise moment at which that group has made an important cultural contribution, more often and more systematically in separate chapters summing up the cultural conquests of successive periods.

Each of the two emerging types of the New History has its advantages and disadvantages. The civilization type unfolds a panorama as wide as the world itself and as deep as the perspective of the ages of mankind. This is an alluring prospect but runs the risk of crowding the record with such an abundance of every variety of data as to cause it to take on the character of an encyclopedia of general information. Hardly less objectionable is the unifying end or purpose, when it is too dogmatically imposed and is made to point the cultural creativeness of man toward an unalterable and predetermined goal pursued through all his centuries of struggle. Thus narrowly inspired, interpretation becomes a subjective mania and the constitutive facts of history are distorted in the interest of a theory until they lose what to every lover of life is their most precious quality—their uniqueness.

The second or politico-social type enjoys perhaps less favor at the present moment than the rival type, because, instead of underscoring the forces making for human solidarity, it organizes its materials around the contentious sovereign states which visibly dominate the scene. The leading difference between the two types appears at this point. For it is these very states, each constituting a distinct unit, which the historians of civilization are disposed to ignore on the ground of their being the chief obstacle to that world union envisaged as the end of desire. To be sure, the politico-social type proposes not only to make due acknowledgment of the operation, at the side of the struggling governmental entities, of a

The second type takes due account of cultural developments

Advantages and disadvantages of the civilization type of history

A leading difference between the two types is their evaluation of the sovereign states

common culture, but also to insist that the divided states are, by virtue of that culture, bound together in an ideal unity. But it does not forecast as certain the transformation of the ideal unity into a real or political unity. Rather it takes the neutral position that the competitive states and their common culture are in so unstable an equilibrium that confident prognostication regarding the final adjustment of their relationship is out of the question.

For the book in hand the author has resolved to adopt the second or politico-social form for the persuasive reason of its realism. Historical study should under all circumstances start with the actualities; and the actualities of Europe in the Modern Age, with which continent and period this book is concerned, bring us face to face with sovereign states involved in an unceasing struggle for power. This is a constant element, we might even say *the* constant element, of Modern History. It operates with undiminished energy at the present moment, and to suppress or even to minimize it gravely distorts the European picture. Undesirable at all times, distortion is particularly to be avoided in the case of beginners of college age, for whom this book is intended. As already stated in the general description of this type, the power struggle among the contentious states will not appear in isolation. It will be accompanied first, by the social-economic development within each state, and second, by a description of the cultural movement constituting the common possession of all the members of the European family.

The present book conforms to the second type

In this connection it may not be overlooked that a history in order to achieve its character as an accredited literary form must be not only an assemblage of pertinent, tested facts but also an interpretation of their significance. The present history will therefore have an underlying interpretive principle. Although it should be sought primarily in the text, with which the principle is closely fused, a preliminary indication regarding it may not be unwelcome. It is here submitted, in connection with a swift concluding statement on the author's proposed plan of periodization.

The present book molded by an interpretive principle

As this is to be a History of Modern Europe beginning with the Reformation, it falls within the frame-work of west-European or Occidental civilization. Occidental civilization dates from the settlement of barbarous tribes of Germanic stock on the soil of the Roman empire of the west. From this event there followed in due course a fusion with the older populations on the ground and the absorption of such of their institutions as had survived the decline of the once vital Greco-Roman civilization.

This history concerned with Western civilization

As is the case with all civilizations, the outstanding feature of Occidental or Western civilization is change. A civilization may be likened to a living organism in that, like any such organism, it runs through the many phases of which birth, adolescence, maturity, and decline are the leading aspects. The first or childhood phase of Western civilization may be thought of as covering approximately the eight centuries from 500 A.D. to 1300 A.D. This period has been called the Middle Ages, a term utterly without meaning for the present generation but incapable of being displaced, owing to its having become mortised into every European language.

First phase of Western civilization: the Middle Ages

The salient feature of the Middle Ages was that throughout the centuries they embraced, western Europe possessed a common religious culture set forth in the first place, and afterward fostered and developed, by the Roman Catholic church. The core of this culture was the idea of God. It ruled the minds and hearts of men, persuading them that they lived under divine guidance in a divinely ordered universe.

The most notable feature of the Middle Ages is religious unity

Toward the end of the Middle Ages the dominant religious culture was for the first time effectively modified. There followed the second phase of Western civilization, commonly called the Renaissance and extending from 1300 to 1500 or 1550. All dates giving the beginning and the end of a period should be understood to be approximate, and the proposed periods themselves should not be taken too seriously. Other periods than those accepted for this book and quite as pertinent to the ruling facts could be easily devised. The term Renaissance is as unsatisfactory a description of the second phase of Western civilization as the Middle Ages is of its predecessor, but we are obliged to accept it because it, too, is so deeply imbedded in usage that it is futile to attempt to supplant it.

The second phase of Western civilization: the Renaissance

In the Renaissance men began slowly to adopt a new attitude toward life in consequence of new activities in which they had begun to engage in the later medieval centuries. These activities were the natural outcome of the love of barter, knowledge, and adventure apparently inborn in man. The effect of novel activities cumulatively engaged in throughout the Renaissance was that man explored, traveled, and traded on an ever enlarging scale, that he made over the inherited law and government to suit the altered politico-social situation, and that he developed a hesitant skepticism regarding the dominant church and its supernatural teachings. In sum, man exhibited a growing confidence in his own energy and intelligence. Or, to say the same thing in more philosophic language, he began to emancipate himself from the theocentric or divine world, which had enveloped him in the Middle Ages, and to lay the foundations of an anthropocentric or purely human world.

Significance of the Renaissance

Out of this situation the next phase of Western civilization developed with irresistible logic. It is called the Reformation and extends from 1500 to 1648. Narrowly considered, the Reformation was a revolt against the Catholic church and the restraints imposed by the church on the adventurous spirit of man. To be sure, there were reactionary theological aspects to the Reformation which gave it something of the character of a throwback to the Middle Ages, but they were of a strictly temporary nature. Viewed in its proper historical perspective, the Reformation continued the work begun by the Renaissance of breaking down the barriers to thought and enterprise erected by the Middle Ages and of launching man upon the task of replacing the divine order, identified with a dominant church, with a secular order projected by man's intelligence and accommodated to his proud new view of himself as the lord of creation.

The third phase of Western civilization: the Reformation, 1500-1648

The most conclusive proof that, in spite of the theological din with which the age resounded, the Reformation was an era of rapid secular change is supplied by the rise of the great European monarchies. Dominated by rulers more or less absolute, the emerging monarchies are identified with the great national stocks settled on the soil of Europe. Each monarch already in the Reformation drew his strength to a certain extent from that sentiment of nationalism which was destined to gather momentum through all the succeeding generations. The thesis, on which the present history rests and with which it must stand or fall, is that it was the rise of the national states and their ensuing struggle for power which has to a very important degree determined the evolution of Western civilization down to our day.

The rise of the great monarchies during the Reformation

In no case may it be overlooked by the reader that the Reformation constitutes the point of departure for this book. The statement is not invalidated by a Preliminary Survey, which briefly reviews the first and second phases of Western civilization, the Middle Ages and the Renaissance. The Preliminary Survey is intended to serve as an introduction or portal leading to the third or Reformation phase, which is the effective start of our enterprise.

Our starting point the Reformation

The Reformation was followed by a period which, from the politico-social viewpoint adopted by us, we shall call the Absolute Monarchy. It extends from 1648 to 1789. Viewing the period purely as a phase of culture, we might call it the Age of Natural Science and Reason. Regardless of the angle from which we view it, it marked such an increase of the secular energies of men that the belief seemed justified that men might by their unaided strength bring the forces of nature and society under their control. More and more their attention swung from the Hereafter with its promised rewards and threatened punishments to the immediate Here with its agitating problems and its narrowly earth-bound but passionately alluring prospects.

The fourth phase: the Absolute Monarchy, 1648-1789

The last phase of European evolution dates from the French Revolution of 1789 and continues to the present day. While the historical formula to which this book subscribes may be satisfied to call it the Age of Revolution and Democracy, the civilization school of historians will

prefer some such designation as Science and Technology Revolutionize
Industry and Communications. Regardless of the label chosen, the feature of the period bearing on the interpretive formula underlying this
book is that the movement of secularization, begun hesitatingly in the
Renaissance, has been pushed to its last consequences. We are in this
period confronted with a progressively human and natural world, which
men are resolved to shape to their needs and purposes with no other aid
than their native resources of mind and heart.

The most recent phase: Revolution and Democracy

And here we may ask: Is it possible or even likely that with his strictly
limited powers man will succeed in reaching the goal he has in this his
latest phase set for himself? This book, a history and not a prophecy,
leaves the matter undecided. It contents itself with the affirmation that
Western civilization has from the start been characterized by aspiration
and movement and that it has passed and will continue to pass through
many phases.

The uncertain future of Europe and of civilization

What the reason may be for this uninterrupted and recently greatly
accelerated movement of Western civilization is open to debate. It is at
least a stimulating suggestion that a civilization unfolds according to an
inner law and that consequently it passes through an appointed cycle like
any biological organism. But it may also be true that the inner law which
determines the behavior pattern of Western civilization is referable to
Western man himself. Restless, inventive, and daring beyond the man
of any other civilization, it may be that he with his particular sum of
gifts is the key to the multiple changes through which the occident has
passed, and that the triumphs and failures alike of Western civilization
are the fruit of his peculiar genius.

The riddle of cultural change

Section 1

Preliminary Survey

2 THE FIRST OR MEDIEVAL PHASE OF WEST-EUROPEAN HISTORY

THE MOST MEMORABLE feature of the first or medieval phase of west-European history is that it represents an attempt by the peoples of western Europe to live together as a single religious community. They had one and all adopted Christianity in the form promulgated by the Roman Catholic church, to which they believed the guidance of the Christian flock had been divinely intrusted. The authoritative Christian church is therefore the leading institution of the medieval period. *The church the leading medieval institution*

While the church asserted and exercised spiritual control because through it alone mankind might hope to attain to salvation, it did not claim to rule its subjects in purely secular matters. These pertained to the civil states which had been set up with great sovereigns at their head, such as the emperor, who ruled both Germany and Italy, and the kings of France and England. However, as these and all other sovereigns found their power disputed by the great barons, the chief civil rulers were, generally speaking, in a somewhat depressed position, since the authority which was theoretically theirs had been appropriated, at least in part, by their vassals, great and small, constituting the feudality. The sovereigns and their barons, taken together, were the apex of the feudal system. This system, of which the people were the base, is as characteristic, if not as important, a feature of the period as the universal church. *A second characteristic institution: the feudal system*

To these two outstanding features, which rise into view and take definite shape as soon as the Middle Ages are well under way, was added at a somewhat later time a form of civil association which could not be harmonized with the feudal system and which caused it gradually to disintegrate. This revolutionary institution is the self-governing commune or town. In an effort to reduce the Middle Ages to their absolutely essential elements, we shall take up these three institutions in turn and shall begin with the leading institution, the church. As the keystone of the medieval arch, the church serves to unify the period and to give to it its abiding significance. *A third characteristic institution: the self-governing town*

THE CHURCH

Whoever considers the church must first direct his attention, however

Spiritual care of the church briefly, to the origin and spread of the Christian religion. Its founder was Jesus of Nazareth, whose simple teachings, greatly elaborated by his followers through several generations, gradually won increasing adherents throughout the extent of the Roman empire. These teachings affirmed the eternal damnation of mankind because of the sin of disobedience of our first parents, Adam and Eve, the redemption effected after thousands of years by God's sacrifice of himself upon the cross in the person of his beloved son, Jesus Christ, and the resurrection of Christ as a pledge of immortality and a symbol of eternal life. The teachings themselves and their extraordinary implications are too involved to be rehearsed in detail in such a sketch as this. It may under no circumstances, however, be overlooked that Christianity is a dualistic faith, that is, it makes a clear-cut distinction between spirit and matter, and, identifying matter with evil, fixes attention on the divine spark alight in each of us, the soul. To the soul it offers such safe guidance during our perilous earthly pilgrimage that, when the hour of death comes, the soul will mount to its reward in heaven and be eternally reunited with the Father.

An unescapable consequence of this central teaching was that the earth

The goal of the soul is the Hereafter was held to be a mere testing-ground of the soul, a temporary abode and vale of tears, and that the heavenly Hereafter was pictured as the soul's true goal and home. Perhaps more uncompromisingly than any religion known to history Christianity inculcated contempt of this life and exaltation of the life beyond the grave, the life eternal. In short, Christianity was a religion which invited its worshipers to fix their attention, not on the ephemeral rewards and pleasures of this world, but on the abiding glories of the world to come.

The early Christians assembled for worship in separate communities

Triumph of the Christian church in the fourth century held together by a common organization called the church. After a few hundred years of intermittent persecution by the supporters of the ruling pagan faith, the church had succeeded in gaining so many adherents that, by an edict of the year 313, the Roman empire at last renounced persecution and gave it legal standing. Shortly after, the reigning emperor, Constantine the Great, assumed the protection of the new faith and in 325 presided over the first General Council of the church held at Nicaea in Asia Minor. Thus elevated to a position of authority, the church embarked with such success on the policy of suppressing its many religious rivals that, before the fateful fourth century had closed, it had become enthroned in exclusive majesty throughout the Roman world.

When the northern barbarians, the German and Slav tribes, overwhelmed the Roman empire, the church did not, like the empire, go to pieces. By courageous missionary activities extending over many centuries it proved its amazing vitality by gradually drawing the heathen conquerors within its fold. Consequently the world which slowly emerged from the barbarian chaos was Christian, theoretically one in faith and church. Actually, however, owing to ecclesiastical disputes which cannot be examined here and which have proved incapable of settlement down to our day, Europe witnessed the establishment of two Christian churches, one of the east and the other of the west. The eastern church, organized under the patriarch of Constantinople, embraced in the main the Mediterranean areas of Greek speech and is known as the Greek Orthodox church; the western church, called Catholic, dominated the Latin areas, employed Latin as its official language, and acknowledged the bishop of the great metropolis on the Tiber as its head. As the developments with which we shall concern ourselves in this book belong to the area dominated by the Latin church, it is the western or Latin church with which this account is alone concerned.

Two Christian churches, one of the east, the other of the west

While it is true that the church owed its influence in the first place to the fact that it was the official organization of believing Christians, its towering authority resulted from the conviction that it was instituted by Christ himself and hence had a divine origin. According to the gospel of St. Matthew, Jesus had appointed the Apostle Peter as his successor by addressing him with these words: "Thou art Peter and upon this rock I will build my church." In the course of his missionary voyages Peter had come to Rome, the mighty capital of the empire bearing its name and, after establishing a Christian community there, had served as its first bishop. Since that event Peter's successors, called popes, had been acknowledged as heads of the church which, founded by Christ himself, was the sole and divinely appointed means for bringing salvation to mankind. When an early Christian father pronounced the judgment, "Outside the church there is no salvation," he succinctly stated its claim and defined its function.

The church the divine instrument of salvation

In these circumstances it was the primary duty of the church to keep its members ever mindful of its holy office by surrounding them with evidences of its solicitude and love. To this end it gradually evolved a number of important measures: it drew up a creed containing the essential articles of the Christian faith; it framed a succession of prayers adapted to the many different circumstances of the human lot; and it established a body of rites and services of which the most solemn and impressive was the mass. Above all, however, it provided, as the effective means of that salvation which was held to be the central concern of every child born into the world, the Seven Sacraments. These, constituting what is often called the sacramental system, contain so much of the teaching and prac-

The kernel of the church the sacramental system

tice of the church that an acquaintance with them illuminates not only the overshadowing importance of the church throughout the medieval centuries, but also the utter dependence of its members on its divine authority. For, through the sacraments, the individual Christian was watched over by the church from the cradle to the grave, and solely through them could he hope to become the recipient of the divine grace whereof the church was the exclusive dispenser.

In dealing with the Seven Sacraments we may begin with *ordination*.

The Seven Sacraments: Ordination Ordination was reserved for the clergy and was administered by a bishop by the laying on of hands. It conferred upon the candidate for priesthood the sacerdotal character with the authority and power to administer the other sacraments except confirmation, which, like ordination, was reserved to the bishops. Ordination drew a sharp dividing line through the Christian body since it marked off the clergy, specially called to the service of God, from the multitude of common men, the laity.

Baptism By the *sacrament of baptism* the newborn infant was received into the membership of the church. The holy water on its brow signified that its share in the guilt of Adam's fall was washed away and that it had become a Christian and the child of God.

Confirmation When the boy and girl reached the age of about twelve years, they received, after due instruction in the creed and customs of the church, *confirmation* (that is, confirmation of their membership in the church) from the bishop, who rubbed holy oil and balsam on their foreheads.

Penance If a believer yielded to temptation and sinned, as, being human, he was only too likely to do, he could receive pardon by the *sacrament of penance*. This consisted of four parts: (1) He must feel sincere contrition for the sin he had committed. (2) He must confess his sin orally to a priest. (3) He must receive absolution from a priest. (4) He must render satisfaction for the wrong he had done by performing the particular penance, e.g., a pilgrimage or almsgiving, which the priest might see fit to impose.

Extreme unction At the hour of death the priest stood by the bedside and by anointing the dying man with holy oil strengthened his soul for the journey to the other world. This rite was called the *sacrament of extreme unction*.

Marriage The *sacrament of marriage* bound husband and wife in lawful Christian wedlock, held to be indissoluble by human power. Only the church which made the marriage could annul it, and even the church could do so only in case a holy ordinance had been overlooked at the time the marriage was celebrated.

The Holy Eucharist Finally, there was the *sacrament of the Holy Eucharist*. This developed from the Lord's Supper as described in the gospels and involved the consecration of bread and wine by the priest, its miraculous transformation into the body and blood of Christ, and its proffer in this consecrated form to the Father in renewal of Christ's original sacrifice upon the Cross. The change of substance effected at the altar is called transubstantiation and is the central mystery of Catholicism. It was the sacrament of the Lord's Supper, which, dignified with an elaborate chanted ritual and made impressive with candles, incense, and gorgeous vestments, finally evolved into the magnificent service called the mass.

Conceding that the spiritual guidance of the faithful, disclosed in the sacramental system, was the chief function of the clergy, we must not overlook other duties of a more mundane sort which devolved on it. When we recall that to the clergy fell exclusively the government of the church, and that the church on its material side consisted of innumerable houses of worship, clerical residences, landed estates, and property of every conceivable kind, we are bound to admit that its worldly activities were neither few nor slight. To meet its innumerable obligations, spiritual as well as administrative, the clergy had been obliged to provide an elaborate organization which extended from the parish priest at the foot of the ladder of advancement to the pope at the top. *The government of the church*

The parish, served by the priest, was the territorial unit of administration. A larger or smaller number of parishes were assembled into a diocese, at the head of which stood a bishop. A variable number of dioceses constituted a province, over which one of the bishops enjoyed authority under the title archbishop. The succession—priest, bishop, archbishop— culminated in the pope, the unchallenged head of the church, residing in his appointed capital, in ancient and venerable Rome. *The clerical hierarchy of priest, bishop, archbishop, pope*

Rome, as the hub of a vast administrative wheel, harbored an almost endless variety of officials, some attached to the papal chancellery, others to the papal law courts, and still others to the papal treasury. The most distinguished group of these central officials was the college of cardinals. Appointed by the pope, the cardinals were associated with him in governing the church, and upon them on the death of the ruling pope devolved the responsibility of electing his successor. *Function of the cardinals*

At the side of the above-mentioned officials on whom fell the burden of church government, there had, in response to the renunciatory and ascetic spirit of the age, grown up another group of churchmen, whom we must accept as a highly characteristic feature of medieval Christianity. I refer to the monks and nuns. The monks and nuns were organized in a great variety of orders which had been founded by men and women animated by a passionate religious fervor. Some of the more popular monastic orders spread rapidly over the face of Europe, reached a large membership, and achieved through the free offerings of the faithful a towering position measured in terms of prestige, lands, and houses. The oldest and most famous of the orders was that of the Benedictines, founded by a dedicated spirit, St. Benedict, as early as the sixth century *The monastic orders a characteristic expression of medieval piety*

(529 A.D.). However, the Cistercians, Carthusians, and others, who sprang into existence at a later time, hardly, if at all, lagged behind the Benedictines in riches, popularity, and power.

In the thirteenth century the two famous orders, the Franciscans and Dominicans, came into being, fashioned in the heat of a great religious revival and pledged to ideals somewhat different from those of their monastic predecessors. The older orders—all organized more or less on the Benedictine model—emphasized the life of studious contemplation of divine things in seclusion from the world and its temptations. The Franciscans and Dominicans, on the other hand, sought out the crowded centers to dispense among the poor and heavy-laden the offices of Christian charity. Dedicated, like their predecessors, to poverty, chastity, and obedience, the three obligatory monastic vows, and seeking their living, at least at first, from door to door, they were distinguished from the older monks under the name of begging brothers or friars (from Latin *frater,* i.e., brother).

The heads of monasteries were called abbots or priors. They and their flocks were usually subject to the jurisdiction of the bishop in whose diocese they resided. But occasionally individual abbots and, in the case of the begging friars, the orders themselves had sought and obtained from the pope the right to be responsible only to him.

The officials of the church from pope to priest and including the monastic orders constituted a sharply defined class or caste of medieval society called the clergy. The respect felt for the clergy is indicated by the circumstance that everywhere in medieval Europe they took the highest rank and were called the first estate. The remainder of the inhabitants of a medieval state constituted the laity, which fell into two classes, an upper class, embracing the nobility and called the second estate, and a lower class, composed of all the rest, the commoners or third estate. Neither in practice nor theory did the laity have anything to do with the government of the church, which was reserved exclusively to the first estate, the clergy.

In the light of this brief review of the authority and government of the church, we should be prepared to agree that its place in medieval society was very different from what it is at present. In fact, the church was a state, so much greater than the various civil states, at the side of which it played its part, that it completely overshadowed them. In consequence of this pre-eminence the church had acquired from the civil authorities a body of privileges known as immunities. The leading immunities were exemption from civil taxation and the right for the members of the clergy to be amenable only to law courts conducted by the church.

By reason of his legal immunity a member of the clergy, on being charged with an offense, was haled before an ecclesiastical tribunal and

---

The begging friars: Franciscans and Dominicans

Abbots and priors answerable to either bishop or pope

The clergy the highest medieval class or first estate

The church functions as an independent state

judged by ecclesiastical judges in accordance with ecclesiastical law. This, commonly called canon law in distinction from the civil law of the secular courts, was composed of acts of church councils and decisions of the popes. So great in a world dominated by the church was the importance of the canon law that it enjoyed at the very least the same consideration and prestige as the civil law.

The two systems of canon law and civil law

In certain important matters, such as marriage and divorce and the proving of wills, the ecclesiastical courts possessed authority also over the laity. From these various practices and regulations it came about that throughout Western Europe the individual clergyman, by being answerable in all respects to ecclesiastical authority, was exclusively the subject of the church, while the individual layman by owing obedience to two rulers, the church and the civil state of his residence, was amenable to each in certain exactly specified matters.

The layman or citizen subject to both church and state

Another important function of the church by virtue of which it met the definition of a state was that it levied taxes. Since the church owned immense estates, for which it had obtained immunity and paid no contribution to the civil powers, it enjoyed a considerable income. This income, of the nature of rent, constituted its basic revenue. However, its rents were not large enough to meet the great expenses of its far-flung organization. In consequence the church had, in every country in which it was established, gained the further right to levy a tax, called tithe, amounting in theory to one-tenth of the annual yield of the soil, although in practice it usually came to a good deal less.

The church lives by (1) rents and (2) tithes

If we further consider that, since the church undertook to direct the steps of its erring followers, it very naturally assumed control of their education and conducted all educational enterprises from the grammar school to the university, we add another significant item to the influences by which it counted in the affairs and overwhelmed the imagination of the faithful.

The church in charge of education

Let no one imagine even for a moment that law courts, taxes, and education represented unlawful usurpations of the church. In the confusion of the early Middle Ages, when the young states of Europe were only just taking shape and were too weak to stand firmly on their feet, all the social services which the church cared to assume fell to its lot without a struggle, because it was the strongest and, in some extreme cases, the only institution of any kind that in the general dissolution of society continued to operate.

The social services of the church not usurpations

However, in measure as the civil states gained strength, as they indeed tended to do from an early time, the vast power of the church would be felt to be excessive and a conflict would be inevitable. Consequently the Middle Ages resound with the struggle between church and state which, in spite of its spontaneousness and vigor, was in sharp opposition to the

Theoretic equality of church and state

accepted theory of their relationship. For Christian theory affirmed that church and state derived equally from God, who had created them both for the service of his creatures, intrusting to one the rule of the souls of men and to the other the rule of their bodies. At the head of the two complementary institutions God had placed the pope and the emperor, endowing them respectively with the spiritual and material authority over mankind. But as, in point of fact, pope and emperor, instead of working in harmony, were involved in a struggle as constant as it was vehement, certain particularly vigorous popes, like Gregory VII, Innocent III, and Boniface VIII, had been moved to brush the older equalitarian theory aside in favor of the view of the dependence of the emperor and all civil governors whatever on the pope, conceived as the only true spokesman and representative of God.

The later papal theory of church superiority   In this manner the later papal theory, formulated at the time of the greatest power of the church, came to be that since civil as well as ecclesiastical authority had been divinely committed to the pope, the emperor and, of course, all other civil rulers as well held their thrones subject to their retention of the pope's favor. Owing to the considerable expansion of civil power in the course of the fourteenth century, this extravagant claim was vigorously assailed and had again to be abandoned.

The clergy charged with vices and abuses   Since the clergy were the most exalted and wealthiest class in Europe— the first estate—they paid the usual price of power by more than ordinary exposure to temptation. All through the Middle Ages serious charges of corruption were preferred against them. Occasionally popes and bishops inaugurated a reform. In spite of these praiseworthy efforts, the abuses persisted or cropped up again. Human nature is weak and frail even under surplice and cowl.

The abuse and sin of simony   The chief abuse was perhaps simony, which is the buying and selling of church offices. The church officially condemned simony as a sin, but many clergymen and even popes were nonetheless guilty of it. So long as abbacies and bishoprics produced huge revenues, it is easy to see how ambitious men should crave their possession even at the price of bribery.

Other abuses: worldly living and excessive fees   A charge leveled particularly against the upper clergy was that they lived in a state of pride and worldliness entirely out of keeping with humble followers of Christ and the apostles. Many rode to hunt and even war and lived in splendid palaces amid an unbroken round of festivals. As for the lower clergy, the accusation most frequently directed at them was that they squeezed excessive fees out of their parishioners for marriage, burial, and other necessary services.

Prevalence of carnal vices   That these and other charges were made does not establish them as true; but it may be accepted as proved that individual ecclesiastics of all ranks were guilty of gross carnal vices. The literature of the later Middle

Ages is in substantial agreement in laying fleshly excesses particularly at the door of the monks and friars.

The shortcomings of the clergy were scourged by ardent and upright priests all through the Middle Ages, sometimes even by incumbents of the highest ecclesiastical positions. It did not derogate from the church to make public acknowledgment that some of its ministers were unworthy, for the personal conduct of clerics was conceded to be a field of permissible criticism. But it was different with criticism which gnawed at the organization and doctrine of the church, because these represented God's own handiwork stamped with a holy and unalterable character. Such critics were blasphemers and against them the church was armed with formidable weapons. She branded them as heretics and launched her excommunication against them, thereby excluding them from her fold and enjoining on all true believers to shun intercourse with them as spreaders of a deadly infection. There she left them, for an ancient scruple forbade her to shed blood; but at this juncture, her partner and more often her subordinate rather than partner, the state, stepped in to seize the heretic as a public enemy and put him to death, usually by fire.

Criticism of doctrine and organization of the church constitutes heresy

In spite of this rigorous repression heresy and heretics were not uncommon in the Middle Ages. Even in that period of overshadowing ecclesiastical power an occasional hardy spirit was moved to assert his individual convictions. Of these isolated heretics, who were perpetually cropping up at odd corners of Europe, there is here no need to speak, although they hold a not unhonored place in the intellectual history of the period.

Persistence of heresy in spite of ferocious persecution

More dangerous than the scattered individual heresies were the mass heretical outbursts. They often affected a wide area and jeopardized the very existence of the church. Of these collective heresies, that of the Albigensians, belonging to the beginning of the thirteenth century, spread over much of southern France. The Albigensians went the length of attacking the core of Catholicism, the sacramental system. When the excommunication with which they were visited proved ineffective, Pope Innocent III, in 1208, preached a crusade against them and crowned his victory, won only after a savage carnage, by setting up a special tribunal called the Inquisition. This was charged with inquiring into the opinions of the survivors and with punishing in an exemplary manner every minute departure from orthodoxy. After extirpating the Albigensian heresy, the Inquisition was retained as a convenient tool of ecclesiastical repression and was destined to acquire an unenviable reputation for severity and bigotry.

Collective heresies: the Albigensians

In spite of the rigor with which the Albigensian rebellion was repressed, other movements of protest raised their heads from time to time. In the fourteenth century John Wyclif inaugurated a heretical agitation

in England, which taught that the individual needed no clerical mediator between himself and God and which it took several decades to
stamp out. Shortly after, John Hus began a similar movement of protest against priestly domination in Bohemia. Although Hus, in 1415,
paid for his audacity by being burned at the stake, the heresy which he
started continued to agitate his country for several generations after his
disappearance.

*The hereti-
cal move-
ments of
Wyclif and
Hus*

By such movements of concerted revolt, and by many other signs as
well, it was in the course of the later Middle Ages becoming clear, not
only that the church no longer enjoyed its old unquestioned authority
but that new ideas and forces were coming to the fore, sure to alter the
whole medieval inheritance and outlook. What these agencies were and
what particular conditions were bringing them to the front will engage
our attention when we take up the next phase of Western civilization,
commonly called the Renaissance.

*New ideas
and forces
presage the
passing of
the Middle
Ages*

FEUDALISM

The troubled and confused aspect which, in sharp distinction from the
firm and admirable order of the church, is presented by civil society in
the Middle Ages, has received the name of feudalism. Feudalism is very
difficult to define with anything approaching accuracy. It will serve the
purpose of this swift review if we take it to be the sum of the economic,
social, and political institutions representing the first effort of the youthful society settled on Roman soil to rise above an unmitigated barbarism.

*Feudalism a
complex of
rude insti-
tutions*

Under the feudal system European society, in spite of a bewildering
mass of local variations, presented itself to view in rarely simple terms.
Essentially there were but two classes: the rulers who possessed the soil
and the ruled who tilled it. Land was the outstanding form of wealth and
land determined the structure of society. The rulers bore arms and had
the pride of an hereditary caste of warriors; the ruled, disarmed and
forbidden to acquire arms, were attached to the soil as an hereditary
caste of peasant-serfs. Governments of the modern type, maintaining a
well-regulated administration over a large area, did not exist. Substantially each petty lord, though theoretically subject to an overlord and
ultimately to the king, was master over his own acres, with the result
that for all practical purposes Europe was made up of thousands of
loosely associated little lordships.

*Two main
social classes
under feu-
dalism: the
rulers and
the ruled*

The social-economic unit of feudal society was the type of farmstead
called in England the manor. The manor or unit-estate was worked
co-operatively by the peasants, who dwelled together in the village and
were governed either in person or by deputy by their military lord and

*The agricul-
tural unit is
the manor*

master. This great personage resided in the outskirts of the village in the manor-house or castle.

Carefully weighing these several data, we may think of the early Middle Ages as effecting, owing to the influx of numerous German and Slav tribes of a nomad and semi-nomad type, the re-agrarianization of the Roman empire. Under the impact of peoples on a lower culture level the ancient and notable Roman city culture, already in precipitate decline before the coming of the barbarians, suffered a final and complete eclipse. The downward plunge to a rude agrarianism proceeded on the whole according to a simple formula: a select warrior class forcibly took title to the soil, permitting the rest of the population to work it in return for a rental payment, which, in the absence of money, took the form of personal services and natural products. The development in its sum signified that a warrior class dominated society as a privileged nobility, while the peasants, at the mercy of their masters, were depressed to the status of serfs. Serfs had customary rights which varied bewilderingly from region to region and, often enough, even from village to village. While these rights raised them above the level of slaves or chattels, they did not preserve them from being ferociously exploited by their masters. *The Middle Ages signify an agrarian society*

Feudalism is the word which embraces the indicated enormous complexities. While it defines the relations between the arms-bearing landlords and their peasant-serfs, it more particularly takes account of the mutual obligations of vassal and lord, that is, of the complicated legal relations obtaining among the rulers themselves. In short, feudalism signifies a primitive agrarian society together with the experimental and fluctuating political, economic, and social institutions to which such a society necessarily gives birth. *Feudalism re-summarized*

THE RISE OF THE TOWNS

During the first five centuries of the Middle Ages the rude civil order called feudalism characterized all western Europe. Around 1000 A.D. a new civil element made its appearance, which not only gravely shook the feudal structure but also produced a state of mind which ultimately undermined even the far more imposing institution of the church. We refer to the rise of the towns. Originating in the birth or, it is more accurate to say, the gradual intensification of trade and industry, the towns represented an association of men engaged in the production and multiplication of the conveniences of living and in defending themselves with all the strength at their command against a nobility established on the soil and instinctively hostile to traders only too plainly *Around 1000 A.D. urbanization again sets in and modifies agrarian feudalism*

bent on freeing themselves from the political control of a tyrannical warrior caste.

The springing up of towns all over the face of Europe gradually
changed the familiar agrarian picture. By imperceptible stages the lords
in their scattered castles found themselves face to face with burgher
groups which exceeded them in wealth, culture, and ultimately even in
military power. Confronted with this phenomenon, the feudal warriors
did not, of course, promptly vanish from the scene or even noticeably
reduce their pretensions; but relatively they lost ground, both economically and politically, in the face of the steady advance of the town-
dwellers, themselves armed behind tall, battlemented walls and in command by their courageous enterprise of constantly increasing material
resources and an ever-expanding mental outlook.

With the multiplication of towns and of the many novel activities
in which the townsmen engaged medieval society in the twelfth and
thirteenth centuries reached its climax. There are many people of our
own day, especially philosophers and artists, who uphold the opinion that
that climax represents such a harmony of the forces of life and art as
has been only rarely achieved by man. However, impressive as the flowering of the Middle Ages in the first age of the towns may have been,
it is not the concern of this book. Our purpose goes no farther than to
indicate (1) the political and (2) the cultural contribution of the towns
within the framework of the later Middle Ages.

And first the political contribution. On finding itself opposed by the
existing feudal order and obliged to fight for its life, the town boldly
developed a political principle of its own, the principle of self-government. Wherever a town sprang up, there also, sooner or later, will be
found a movement intent on self-help and aiming at independence.
By means of charters wrung from their lords, the towns gained their
earliest liberties, which, with the aid of later, more comprehensive grants,
they strove to enlarge whenever the occasion served. Some towns, notably
those of Italy and Germany, succeeded finally in becoming free republics, detached or all but detached from the feudal state in the midst
of which they had sprung up. In other countries, such as England and
France, the new urban units consciously and unconsciously helped to
build up the power of the king. They put their strength behind the king
because under him the peace of the land, so necessary to their well-
being, was more likely to be secured than under a turbulent nobility,
to which war was hardly more than the periodic intensification of their
favorite sport, the hunt.

Without any question the towns served as the leading historical agent
in the gradual process of replacing the loose feudal regime with the
royal centralized state. Although, exactly like the landlords, with whom

Margin notes:

Rapid ad-
vance of
the towns
after
1000 A.D.

Urban so-
ciety carries
medieval
civilization
to its
climax

The towns
promote
self-govern-
ment

they locked horns, the rising townsmen thought only of themselves and of their selfish interests, they achieved results beyond their immediate calculation because they represented economic and social forces which, in the long run, were bound to replace the reigning anarchy called feudalism with a more effective government. The replacement, as we shall see in due course, took the form of the centralized monarchy. This revolutionary institution must therefore in last analysis be charged to the account of the towns.

The towns promote the centralized monarchy

The cultural contribution made by the towns is no whit less significant. By living together within the narrow confines of the town wall, large numbers of men were brought into close contact, quarreled with one another over conflicting interests or worked out common plans, and, to an extraordinary degree, stimulated their wits through the constant necessity of action in the face of new situations. Some townsmen, in the capacity of enterprising merchants, gained wealth and experience by seeking profits and adventure in neighboring towns or distant countries, while others, engaged in weaving cloth, tanning leather, or forging weapons, rose in honor and authority by turning out a constantly improved product.

The new activities of the towns-men signify an enlarged experience

Living experimentally and rewarded for their hardihood with constantly increasing riches, the townsmen tended to break through the crust of custom not only in matters affecting their material and political welfare but in mental and spiritual matters as well. How could it have been otherwise? When men acquire the habit of freely applying their minds to the immediate concern of earning a living, they will unescapably be moved to apply them also to the higher interests represented by philosophy and religion. Let us agree that philosophy and religion everywhere and always represent an attempt by man to give emotional and intellectual expression to his most pressing problems and experiences. It follows that if a primitive, relatively fixed agricultural society, such as that which preceded the rise of the towns, develops a religion and philosophy in tune with its general outlook, a commercial and mobile society like that produced by the urban movement is sure to wax critical of its inheritance and to set about the formulation of an ideology of its own. That such a development is attended by a vast cultural ferment will be disclosed by the following, our Renaissance chapter.

The urban movement calls for a corresponding mental outlook

We cannot bring to a close this hurried enumeration of the outstanding features of the medieval landscape without calling attention to a development which is older than the towns, but to which the towns imparted considerable stimulation. While Europe was religiously and ecclesiastically a single unit—a feature which we have agreed lends to the Middle Ages their special distinction—it embraced many different peoples, who refused to be merged into an undifferentiated mass and

The single Christian family of Europe composed of many separate nations

who, stubbornly retaining their inherited characteristics, clung, above all, to those symbols of their separateness, their respective languages. It must therefore never be lost from view that Europe, in spite of its spiritual unity, was composed of many different groups, who never ceased going their several ways. To call these groups nations within the meaning attached to this word at the present time would be to misrepresent the situation; but it cannot be denied that they are nations in the making. Certainly the medieval historian is obliged to recognize that within the, on the whole, remarkably unified Christian community he is already confronted with Italians, Frenchmen, Englishmen, Germans, and all the other national units which have increasingly dominated the scene in the most recent centuries.

The townsmen the carriers of nationalism

It is a fact, however, that, while throughout the Middle Ages the nations were already on hand, they had not yet developed that competitive passion which was destined to manifest itself so powerfully at a later day and which we commonly call nationalism. Neither the church with its Christian-universal outlook nor feudalism with its exaltation of a ruling warrior class had an immediate concern with the nation. Clergy and nobles may even be said to have been fundamentally antinational, since, as privileged and exploiting orders, they were separated from and raised above the working masses. Such was not the case with the rising order of the townsmen, for they sprang from the common people, among whom, if anywhere, we must look for the nation. Not at once, it is true, but gradually the towns developed something akin to a national sentiment. In any case with the rise of the towns the nations of Europe assumed a more definite character and from the close of the Middle Ages, as we shall have abundant occasion to learn, played a steadily increasing part on the European stage.

3 THE SECOND OR RENAISSANCE PHASE OF WEST-EUROPEAN HISTORY

THE SECOND STAGE of west-European civilization has received the name of the Renaissance, i.e., the Rebirth, owing to a view the present generation is obliged to reject that its outstanding and decisive feature was the recovery of classical literature and art. The period is much more correctly conceived as a continuation of, not a break with, the preceding period, which went through a gradual transformation under the impact of a large variety of influences. Among these the recovery of ancient literature and art played an indeed important, but far from exclusive, role. As with the Middle Ages, the term Renaissance is so firmly lodged in general usage that it will have to be here retained. It covers the period from 1300 to 1500 and for some parts of Europe may be said to extend to 1550 and even to 1600. There is, of course, at all times an overlapping of periods, since the many diverse sections of Europe have never moved forward on an unbroken front. *The Renaissance not a sharp break with the Middle Ages*

Having followed the plan of characterizing the Middle Ages by means of its three most salient features, we shall adopt the same course in regard to the Renaissance, except that in view of its leading directly up to the Reformation, our formal point of departure, we shall treat the Renaissance with a little more fullness and discuss it under nine heads or aspects. The general drift of the period was a rapidly spreading secularization or worldliness. There was as yet little or no conscious revolt against the unworldly teaching of religion and the church. However, the towns had been coming to the front and had pushed their citizens into activities passionately concerned with the earth, its manifold problems, and its material returns. Consequently, the world, in the Christian sense of that word, had begun to occupy a much larger place in the thought and actions of men than had been the case in the Middle Ages. So decisively did this shift of emphasis flow from the towns that it would not be extravagant to represent the Renaissance as an essentially urban movement and to regard the nine aspects, under which we propose to examine it, as so many facets flashed by the expanding life of the townsmen. *The Renaissance a worldly movement to be examined under nine heads*

DEVELOPMENT OF COMMERCE AND INDUSTRY

Since the towns, which, as we have learned, began to raise their heads

Commerce and industry a pre-Renaissance phenomenon around the year 1000, lived from the first by commerce and industry, the development taken by these activities in the Renaissance is, and can be, nothing more than a later chapter of town history. In now taking this matter up, it will not be possible to draw a dividing line between trade before and trade after 1300. The commercial movement is continuous and will be so treated here; we shall, however, attempt to bring out the sharp intensification of the production and exchange of goods characteristic of the period under consideration.

When the town movement began, it was the Italian communes which

The Italian towns: their Roman tradition came most rapidly to the front. This was, in the first place, owing to their ancient Roman tradition. In the days of the Roman empire Italy had been a country of large and busy towns, which, with the German invasions, had shrunk till they appeared as no more than ghosts of their former selves. These shriveled towns had but to respond to the new opportunities to put themselves on the road to revival.

There was a second and far more important reason than the Roman

Favorable position of the Italian towns tradition for the pre-eminence achieved by the Italian towns. Italy lay in the center of the Mediterranean basin which, during both the Middle Ages and the Renaissance, continued to be the most populous and civilized area of the European world. To the west and north of Italy lay the relatively backward societies of Spain, France, England, and Germany, while to the east there lay, first, the Greek or Byzantine empire, still, though in patent decline, a highly civilized state, and second, a group of Arab emirates, often hostile to each other but held loosely together by the bond of their common Moslem faith.

Since the Arabs had taken over much of the culture of the Greeks, they

High level of near-eastern culture dwelt on approximately the same level of civilization as their Byzantine neighbors. Like them, they were industrious and skillful artisans as well as busy traders who spun the threads of an ambitious commerce all the way to the remote regions of India and China. Within the compass of both the Byzantine and the Arab areas conveniences and luxuries were to be found of which backward and impoverished Europe had lost the very knowledge. The nobles of the near east wore garments of silk and brocade, their ladies bedecked themselves with ropes of pearls and many-colored jewels, while the houses of the enterprising Moslem merchants of Syria and Egypt and the Christian churches and palaces of Constantinople were hung with glowing tapestries and enriched with ornaments of gold and ivory expressive of a cultivated society and a refined taste.

Although, as the crusades amply proved, the near east loomed vaguely as a region of fabulous riches to the whole backward body of western Christendom, it appealed particularly to the Italians. For not only did the peninsula lie within the range of Arab and Byzantine influence, but its southern tip, together with the island of Sicily, had served for generations as an Arab-Byzantine battleground, thus bringing to the Italians an immediate knowledge of eastern politics as well as an acquaintance with eastern arts and wares. To the Italian folk the near east was the Levant, Land of the Rising Sun, and they turned to it with envy and admiration in their eyes. *Italy in contact with Arabs and Byzantines*

In these circumstances the Italian merchants became the natural middlemen between east and west. In the cities lying directly on the coast, such as Amalfi, Pisa, Genoa, and Venice, enterprising individuals formed companies of merchant adventurers who sailed their galleys to Alexandria, Jaffa, Acre, and Constantinople to fetch back the silks, the jewels, the gold chains, the carved ivory, and, above all, the dyes, spices, and slaves obtainable in the markets of the Levant. That slaves were for a long time one of the most profitable commodities handled by the medieval traders throws a penetrating light on the primitive and predatory character of the age. The other eastern wares, however, were without exception luxuries of small bulk, and could, on being landed on the Italian wharves, be loaded on horseback to be carried to the Italian inland and thence over the Alpine passes to France and Germany. Then, from the beginning of the fourteenth century, by which time the galleys had become larger and the sailors more experienced, the oriental goods could be transported by an unbroken water-route past the straits of Gibraltar to the cities of the English channel and the North sea. *The precious eastern wares*

In short, the Italians utilized every available avenue of land and water to spread the eastern wares throughout the west. As their merchants penetrated Europe, they would stop at one town after another, displaying their goods and causing the rude natives to gape with wonder over the marvels spread before their eyes. Desires before undreamed of were excited in their breasts, desires which, to satisfy, they were obliged to offer in exchange their crude gold and silver coins and such raw products, native to the north, as linen, wool, leather, and furs. These, carried back to Italy and refined by Italian industrial skill, would then make up the cargo with which the galleys returned to the Levant to complete the circle of exchange. *The western goods offered in exchange*

The multiplied international trade was bound to produce changes in innumerable directions. It gradually altered even the physical aspect of Europe, since, to serve the convenience of the traders, the old Roman roads had to be revived, new highways to be traced, and bridges to be thrown across streams and rivers. Trade also fathered a new code of *Legal and technical advances made by commerce* economic and legal customs. As the merchants needed to be safeguarded in life and goods, treaties to this effect were signed between neighboring governments; and from these treaties there sprang in the course of time a rudimentary system of international law. Finally, numerous technical advances contributed each one its share toward placing business on a sounder foundation. Thus, the merchants learned to form partnerships based on written contract; they set up banks as aids and stimulants to commerce; they invented bills of exchange to facilitate the transfer of credits between places geographically separated; and they used their influence to replace the debased and unreliable medieval coinage with a sounder and more stable currency.

Trade fosters industry and both adopt the gild organization The most important single consequence of the ever-increasing east-west exchange of goods was that it powerfully stimulated the industrial arts. If the west felt an irresistible longing for the precious eastern luxuries, it would imperatively have to give to the east goods of its own of an approximately equal value, and these, owing to the difficulties and expense of transportation, could not, at least to any large extent, be raw products. Soon, therefore, the original merchant associations or merchant gilds, as they were called, were everywhere supplemented by the associations or craft gilds of the woolen and linen weavers, the armorers, the leather-workers, the furriers, and the many other occupational activities. The uninterrupted expansion of both trade and craft gilds signified a growing urban population as well as a steadily increasing productivity and wealth.

Importance of the gild Every town was economically dominated by its gilds, which, in their two fundamental types of merchant and craft gilds, monopolized its entire business. We should not fail to note, however, that the gild was more than an economic unit, for it served religious, social, and even political ends as well. Indeed some gilds, wholly non-economic, satisfied purely social and religious purposes, somewhat in the fashion of our modern fraternal orders. Nonetheless the most powerful gilds were the economic ones, and so great was their power that they were usually able, or a combination of the wealthiest of them was able, to take over the town government. Thus lifted into the view of men, the gilds fostered a swelling civic pride, of which the most conspicuous outward signs were their meeting places or gild halls. These, together with the municipal center or town hall, constituted the most expressive physical features of each rising community, furnishing by their size, harmony of parts, and beauty of detail a remarkably accurate measure of the community's importance. In short, he who would know well the town of the medieval and Renaissance periods must thoroughly familiarize himself with its organic cell, the gild.

To complete the picture we must familiarize ourselves with the leading town areas of this period. They become intelligible on the basis of the general conditions of exchange just sketched. In Italy the northern half of the peninsula, because of the proximity of the Alpine passes, behind which lay the markets capable of absorbing eastern wares, far outstripped the south in the development of town life. Milan, Genoa, Bologna, Verona, Padua, are the names of some of the members of this unusually brilliant galaxy of towns. But they were outshone by Venice and Florence, which in the course of the Renaissance gained an undoubted primacy among Italian cities. The greatness of Venice resulted from its serving as the chief distributor of the spices and other specialties of the east; Florence owed its ascendancy to its becoming a leading center for the manufacture of textiles, first, of wool and, later, of silk.

Leading cities and city areas of Italy

The leading city area of southern France was the valley of the Rhone. This was matched and presently outstripped in northern France by the Marne-Seine group of towns. In this group Paris gained an early eminence, ending in complete ascendancy. The town movement was still young when the German cities along the river Rhine all the way from Strasburg to Cologne came to the front. Their commerce was favored by one of the most fruitful valleys of Europe as well as by a fairly easy connection via the Alpine passes with the Italian cities.

Leading town areas of France and Germany

In their favorable situation lay also the explanation of the rise of the Flemish towns, which served as the seaports of the rich Rhine hinterland. A further advantage accrued to them from the proximity of England, one of the main sources in the Middle Ages of the supply of that invaluable staple, wool. By importing this article on a large scale the Flemish cities, such as Ghent, Ypres, and Bruges, developed a textile industry which presents an interesting northern counterpart to the textile industry of Florence.

The Flemish towns

The English cities lying across the channel from Flanders developed no equivalent industry and for a long time remained industrially inferior. But being favorably located for commerce, several of them, and more particularly London on the broad-backed Thames, became flourishing emporiums.

The English towns

A last town area to consider embraced the German settlements along the coast of the North and Baltic seas. In addition to exploiting the profitable herring fisheries of their waters, they acted as middlemen by conducting the native products of Russia, such as leather, wax, and furs, and of Scandinavia, such as iron and tar, into the stream of world trade. Lübeck, Hamburg, and Bremen, lying conveniently at the mouths of navigable rivers, stood forth as leaders in this area. In order to overawe the kings and other rulers of the north they persuaded a considerable number of smaller towns either on or near the sea to unite with them in a great federation called the Hanseatic league. During the fifteenth

The northern German towns united in the Hanseatic league

century, when the Hanseatic league was at its height, it dominated politically and economically the basin of the North and, even more effectively, of the Baltic sea all the way from Novgorod in Russia to London and Bruges. At Bruges in Flanders the two greatest streams of European commerce, coming respectively from the Mediterranean and the Baltic, coalesced, making Bruges a leading world emporium until supplanted in the sixteenth century by Antwerp.

THE REVIVAL OF LEARNING

New experience gives rise to new ideas

With the townsmen caught in the toils of trade and industry, journeying into far countries to make acquaintance with strange climes and peoples, struggling to dominate the prevalent feudal confusion, and courageously trying their hand at self-government, the world in which they lived began to assume a new form, making it indispensable for them to bring their inherited ideas and institutions into conformity with the reality about them.

The medieval church teaches other-worldliness

We have already seen that medieval Europe lived its life under the shelter of religion and the church. The core of the teaching of the church was that the body of man, as well as the earth of which it was a part, was under the curse of Adam and invited the scorn of the true Christian. The only thing of value was the soul, which, having come from God, would be unhappy here below until it had been reunited with the Father. Houses, lands, feasts, and finery, as empty possessions, as things seen, counted less than the dust of the fields against the unseen treasure of the spirit. If this is an extreme, ascetic statement of the church's teaching, it nonetheless communicates the essential attitude toward the problem of living which the church drove home to the faithful. This may be said to have been that man was in tune with the divine will if he resolutely rejected this world for the better world to come. His best hope of being saved was to be other-worldly.

The earth-bound activities of the townsmen

At a relatively early time the townsmen, engaging in activities which conferred pleasure in themselves as well as highly welcome material benefits, began to entertain doubts touching the invariable applicability to them and their affairs of the purely idealist doctrine of the church. They were glad to be alive, they frankly enjoyed the colorful garment in which the earth was clothed, and they delighted in the improved material position resulting from their increased resources. Since the church was an elastic institution, extremely responsive to the society which it served, an immediate clash over the new tendencies was avoided. We cannot fail to see, however, that during the later Middle Ages the burgher mind began to receive a cast abhorrent to fundamental ecclesiastical principle.

Long before this cleavage was threatened, in the full Middle Ages, the church had inaugurated an educational movement which greatly strength- ened its foundations. In the eleventh and twelfth centuries the clergy rapidly increased the monastery and cathedral schools, originally called into being for the training of priests. At the same time it fashioned for them the curriculum of the so-called Seven Liberal Arts. Three of these arts, grammar, rhetoric, and logic, constituted the *trivium* and served as the foundation on which rested the *quadrivium* of the four arts of arith- metic, geometry, astronomy, and music. In point of fact the whole cur- riculum turned largely about Latin, the one indispensable feature of an education, the chief aim of which was, and long continued to be, to prepare a clerical aspirant for his profession. In the early thirteenth cen- tury this theologically inspired educational movement came to an amaz- ing flowering in a new institution, the university. In the course of a few generations universities sprang into being in all the leading countries of Europe. But both in the renown of its teachers and in the number of its students the university of Paris outshone all the others.

The medie- val school system cul- minates in the uni- versity

The universities brought about a genuine and remarkable intellectual awakening. They were able to do this by having come into possession, although unfortunately in faulty Latin translations, of most of the works of Aristotle, the most adventurous and encyclopedic of the great Greek minds. Among the many books of Aristotle the university professors were particularly drawn to his treatise on logic, in which they sensed an instrument happily adapted to give the added authority of reason to the teachings of Christianity originally received by faith alone. To this task they set their minds and by degrees produced a Christian philosophy, which, from its sponsors, called schoolmen or *doctores scholastici,* has received the name of scholasticism. The crown and apex of the scholastic thinkers was St. Thomas Aquinas (d. 1274). In his great work, the *Summa,* he was considered to have solved the philosophic problem of the age. His solution consisted in bringing about so subtle and convincing an adjustment between the articles of faith, on the one hand, and the demands of reason, on the other, that the Christian religion was held to have acquired a rational foundation without any impairment of its character as divine revelation.

Medieval philosophy aims to harmonize faith and reason

Although scholastic philosophy continued to show signs of consider- able vitality in the generations after Aquinas, it had with this master passed its climax and in its average representative was inclined, instead of seeking to enlarge the mental vista of the age, to fall back on the dialectic exercises which were the proving-ground of the Aristotelian logic. The result was that the universities lost touch with the intelligentsia of the towns engaged in wrestling with their own pressing group of problems. Although perhaps but dimly aware of the fact, the burghers

Scholasti- cism out of touch with the town movement

wanted intellectual sanctions for the worldly ways of living to which they had increasingly succumbed. And when they could not get them from the learned schoolmen, perpetually engaged in spinning dialectic cobwebs, they took them from the only other authority available, the ancients.

Therewith we are confronted with the intellectual movement some-times called humanism, and sometimes the Revival of Learning. The first thing to note is that, generally speaking, it took place outside of and even in conflict with the universities. It was in simple fact a by-product of town life. To lend authority to this assertion it will suffice to point out that the Revival of Learning had its origin and reached its climax in the great towns of Italy, more particularly in Florence.

The Revival of Learning an urban movement

The first conscious champion of humanism was Petrarch (1304-1374). Of Florentine ancestry, he had spent much of his youth at Avignon on the Rhone, where his father was an unimportant hanger-on of the papal court. On returning to Italy to prepare himself for a legal career, Petrarch developed such a passion for literature that he made the bold decision to give up the profitable law and devote his life to unprofitable letters. He succeeded in becoming the most famous poet of his time, celebrated, above all, for the long sonnet sequence in which he poured out his troubled love for the lady of his worship, Madonna Laura.

Petrarch, humanist and poet

His place in the history of thought Petrarch owes, not to his poetry, but to his pioneering in behalf of classical literature. Owing to the cir-cumstance that Greek had become an unknown language to the peoples of the west during the long mental twilight of the Middle Ages, classical literature in Petrarch's day was limited to the literature of Rome. What caused the Latin works, belonging to a civilization which had disap-peared many centuries ago, to have a vital appeal for Petrarch and, through Petrarch, for his contemporaries was a very simple circumstance. They were the free expression of an urban society engaged in wrestling with the always bewildering problems of the human lot. For the rising urban classes of Italy, who, after an interval of over a thousand years, were repeating all the experiences of their Roman predecessors, the ancient writings carried an invaluable lesson.

Petrarch, an intellectual pioneer

A warning is in order at this point against overstating the case for the champion of classical literature. Petrarch's praise has sometimes been sung so extravagantly as to give the impression that he rescued the ancient authors from oblivion. Nothing could be farther from the truth. Not only was the Latin language, as we are aware, the cornerstone of the medieval curriculum, but the Latin writers, particularly Virgil, served as the basic texts for learning an unfamiliar speech. Taken up, however, with philosophical and theological thought carrying the Christian hall-mark, the schoolmen made no effort to penetrate to the spirit of the

Petrarch's service defined

ancients, who with their ready pagan acceptance of the earth dwelt in a realm incomprehensible and even hateful to ascetically minded men. Petrarch, therefore, did not so much recover the ancient books as he unsealed his mind to their message, and, arising in his place, proclaimed that message to his countrymen.

Prompted by his better understanding of the ancients, Petrarch became the advocate of a reform of the traditional curriculum of the schools. Its core, according to him, was still to be Latin; henceforth, however, Latin was no longer to be taught as a tool for empty dialectical disputes but as an avenue to a fresh and genial outlook on life. As this prized geniality was admirably expressed by the word *humanitas,* the Revival of Learning has often been identified with humanism, and Petrarch has been called the first humanist. On account of his concomitant strong distaste for the logical or dialectic character of medieval education, he has also been acclaimed as the first modern man. Petrarch and education

On the immediately practical side Petrarch set himself, as his main object, the task of improving the manuscripts of Virgil, Horace, Livy, Cicero, and the other Latin poets, historians, and philosophers, whose texts, owing to the carelessness of many generations of medieval scribes, had become exceedingly corrupt. He also aimed to establish libraries, by which the precious manuscripts could be made accessible to the studious, and to discover valuable lost works of the ancients among the dusty shelves of forgotten monasteries. In support of these various labors he mobilized an enthusiastic following of scholars who devoted a vast energy to the recovery, correction, and multiplication of the classical remains. Petrarch inaugurates a new era in classical scholarship

Although the west was no longer acquainted with the Greek language, Petrarch was dimly aware of the wisdom and beauty of Greek literature. Within a generation after his death a number of scholars from the Greek east had been drawn to Italy as teachers; and in the first half of the fifteenth century these scattered forerunners were followed by a voluntary influx, due to the gradual conquest of the Byzantine empire by the Ottoman Turks. When, in 1453, Constantinople, the Greek capital, itself fell before the Asiatic onslaught, still greater numbers of scholars turned their footsteps toward Italy, taking with them as their most precious possession such books and art treasures as they succeeded in saving from the wreck of their world. In this way the treasure house of Greek literature, immeasurably richer than that of Rome, was again made accessible to the western seeker after knowledge; and a steadily growing body of humanists, engaged in reaping the fruitful fields of classical philology, history, and philosophy, might be encountered in every great center of Italy. Recovery of the Greek language and literature

By the middle of the fifteenth century the prospect of a new intellectual culture, based on antiquity, had seduced the whole educated world of the

peninsula. Not only leading laymen associated with government or trade,
The new learning penetrates the upper classes but many members of the clergy as well shared in the general enthusiasm. Not infrequently the highest churchmen, including cardinals and
popes, assumed the patronage of the new learning and steeped themselves in the philosophic speculations of the Greeks much as if these
speculations were an integral part of the Christian outlook. Thus by
gradual stages the other-worldliness of the Middle Ages made way for
the avowed worldliness of the Renaissance, and a glad affirmation of this
life became the characteristic attitude of the upper, educated classes of
society.

Of the blithe temper of the period and of its happy expression in the
The spread of pagan sentiments arts we shall presently learn more; but one disturbing concomitant of the
humanistic liberation belongs here and must not escape our attention.
It should not surprise us to hear that the continued occupation of the
humanists with the pagan world threatened in the long run to estrange
them from Christianity. To be sure, this had not been the case with
Petrarch for the reason that he was still too close to the Middle Ages to
lose his awe for the faith of his fathers. But after a hundred years of
Cicero and Seneca, of Plato and Thucydides, the inherited faith no longer
loomed so large as formerly, and almost imperceptibly many humanists
became infected with religious skepticism. At the same time their departure from orthodoxy no longer produced any particular commotion.
Too many churchmen were themselves tarred with the same stick to
provoke interference; the Inquisition, once so prompt to punish the
slightest evidence of Christian backsliding, lost its vigor; and a religious
toleration came to prevail, at least in the upper clerical circles, which was
in the sharpest possible contrast with their uncompromising orthodoxy
of the past.

The immediately preceding paragraphs have listed outstanding aspects
Main char- acteristics of later, fifteenth century humanism of the Revival of Learning in the generation or two following Petrarch.
They were found to be: first, the broadening and deepening of classical
learning by the recovery of Greek literature; second, its wide diffusion
through the upper levels of society, both lay and clerical; third, the spread
by its means of a skeptical religious temper. Stated in this generalized
form the later or fifteenth century humanism will remain vague and in-
distinct unless particularized by reference to individuals and their contribution.

Among the men who specialized in both Latin and Greek scholarship
and whom we may think of as pioneer classical philologists were
Leonardo Bruni (d. 1444) and Poggio Bracciolini (d. 1459). Enamored
also of ancient philosophy and history, they published works which
greatly stimulated interest in these purely secular fields. Bruni also wrote
on education. This with Petrarch had become and ever since had re-

THE CHURCH OF SAN LORENZO AT FLORENCE. By Brunelleschi (d. 1446). The church marks the return to classical principles of architecture. (Alinari)

THE MEDICI CHAPEL. By Michelangelo (d. 1564), who designed the chapel and carved the sculpture. The chapel is an example of later or High Renaissance architecture. (Alinari)

BRONZE EQUESTRIAN STATUE OF THE LEADER OF MERCENARIES, COL-
LEONI, AT VENICE. By the Florentine sculptor, Verrocchio (d. 1488). An expressive
embodiment of the self-assertion of the Renaissance. (Alinari)

THE RAISING OF DRUSI-
ANA BY ST. JOHN THE
EVANGELIST. Fresco by
the Florentine painter, Giotto
(d. 1337), in the Church of
Santa Croce at Florence.
(Alinari)

THE VIRGIN WITH THE
CHRIST-CHILD AND SIX
ANGELS. Altarpiece by the
Florentine painter, Botticelli
(d. 1510). (Alinari)

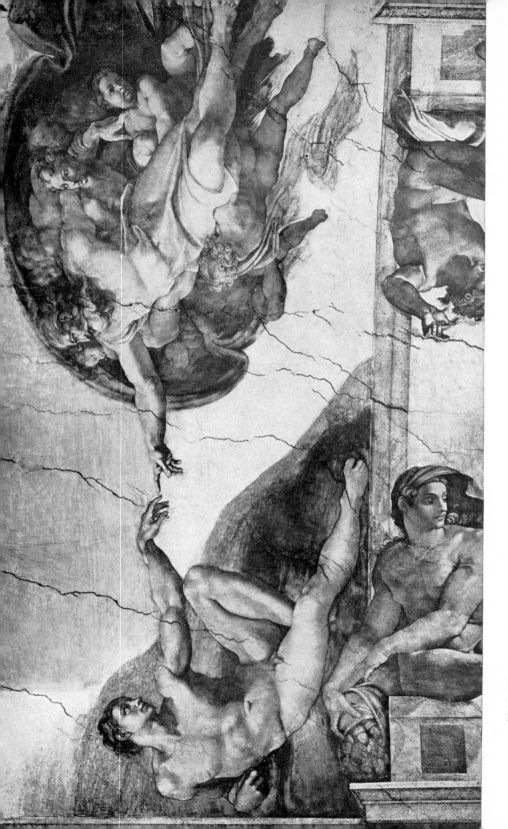

THE CREATION OF ADAM. Fresco in the Sistine Chapel at Rome by Michelangelo. A magnificent expression of the energy and passion for beauty characteristic of the Renaissance. (Alinari)

mained a passionate humanist concern, because the innovators recognized that their cause would not be established unless they succeeded in supplanting the dry scholastic with a classically inspired curriculum. Several humanists, among whom Vittorino da Feltre (d. 1446) and Guarino of Verona (d. 1460) figured most prominently, even founded model humanist schools. They were consciously and definitely organized around the new classical studies; but it is noteworthy that, like all truly successful pedagogues of the age, Vittorino and Guarino were moderate-minded men and retained Christian instruction as an essential feature of their program. It was, after all, only a relatively small group of extremists that completely broke away from the ancient Christian moorings.

The philologists Leonardo and Poggio; the educators Vittorino and Guarino

For no revived intellectual interest was a greater passion manifested than for history. The conviction that at once arose that it must no longer be constructed on hearsay and rumor but be based on authentic material led to the birth of a critical school, of which Lorenzo Valla (d. 1457) was a leading exponent. His great achievement was to demonstrate that the Donation of Constantine, a document of the eighth century on which the papacy rested its claim to temporal power, was a deliberate forgery. The excellent philologists, Bruni and Poggio, both of them Florentines, proved their already mentioned interest in history by composing histories of their native city. These works would without question be more highly regarded today, had their authors not been so excessively imitative of the worshiped classical exemplars. However, in the next generation the classical bondage was at least partially cast off and a Florentine historical school came to the front which stands on its own feet and presents itself to view as the earliest group of distinctly modern historians. Its pre-eminent names are Guicciardini (d. 1540) and Machiavelli (d. 1527). The former wrote a *History of Italy,* the first ever to be composed which covered the whole peninsula; and Machiavelli has to his credit not only a penetrating *History of Florence* but also a study of the theory and practice of tyranny called *The Prince,* which is regarded to this day as the unrivaled treatment of the subject.

The revival of history; from Valla to Macchiavelli

So slowly did the Revival of Learning make its way across the Alps that at the beginning of the sixteenth century it was still substantially an Italian phenomenon. The other Europeans gazed therefore with disquieting amazement, above all, at the brilliant succession of the Renaissance popes. These latest pontiffs lived in sumptuous palaces among scholars and artists and seemed to have completely lost touch with the Christian tradition of humility and poverty. The more the other nations, especially of the Teutonic north, pondered the problem, the more they became convinced that it constituted an intolerable scandal. By the year 1500 it was clear that a storm was brewing which might have ominous consequences for the hitherto united Christian family.

The cultural chasm between Italy and the rest of Europe

THE RISE OF THE NATIONAL LITERATURES

Emergence of the native languages and literatures

Since during the Renaissance men were stirred with new ideas, they were bound to give them expression in literature as well as in architecture, sculpture, and painting, constituting the so-called Fine Arts. If we turn first to literature to inquire what novel turn it may have taken under Renaissance stimulus, we become aware that the situation is involved in a certain confusion. As we have repeatedly noted, the town dates from approximately 1000 A.D. Since its unfolding was a continuous movement, the Renaissance in many fields of activity signified no more than a new stage of something that had sprung to life in the Middle Ages. Were we therefore to declare that an important feature of the literary history of the Renaissance was that the awakened townsmen favored their native tongues and that the French, Italian, Spanish, English, and German languages, which had thus far been regarded as unimportant compared with Latin, now became vehicles of literary expression, this would be essentially true; but it is also true that the movement is older than the Renaissance since it goes back to the Middle Ages.

The native tongues cultivated first by the nobles

On looking into the emergence of the European vernaculars in the medieval period, we learn that they were in the first instance cultivated by knights and nobles moved to give voice to the ideals of their class embraced under the name of chivalry. Without any doubt whatever some of the nobilities of Europe, above all, the French and German, gave notable utterance in epic poems and lyric verse to the specific thoughts and sentiments which governed their lives.

Enrichment of French and English literature

In these circumstances we must be content with noting that the vernacular literatures of Europe, brought to birth under nobiliary auspices in the later Middle Ages, became more definitely and solidly established under burgher influence in the Renaissance. As the detailed proof of this statement is beyond our scope, we shall have to confine ourselves to a few indications. For the area of French speech, the great chronicler, Froissart (1339-1410), and the highly original poet, Villon (1431-1484), may serve to attest the enrichment experienced by French literature in this period. Crossing the channel to England, we encounter the towering figure of the poet Chaucer (1340-1400). With his incomparably animated *Canterbury Tales,* Chaucer became the fountainhead of the great stream of English literature.

In Italy the first great writer to employ his native tongue was Dante (d. 1321), a citizen of Florence. His *Divine Comedy* is one of the masterpieces of world literature; but it owes little to the Renaissance, for it is saturated with the thought and feeling of the Middle Ages. Dante was followed by Petrarch (d. 1374), who, as we have learned, was both poet and humanist and in both respects a man of the new age. Even more completely committed to the Renaissance was Boccaccio (d. 1375), author of the hundred gay, agitated, and often licentious tales familiar under the name of the *Decameron*. Boccaccio was also a humanistic scholar, who followed in the footsteps of his good friend, Petrarch, though far behind the master.

Bloom of Italian literature: Dante, Petrarch, Boccaccio

After these three brilliant inaugurators of a native Italian literature there was a painful decline. It may fairly be ascribed to the humanists who with their fanatical exaltation of classical literature and its Latin medium brought it about that the native literature fell once more, at least for a time, into disrepute. Latin became practically prescriptive for all the higher levels of expression. But let our final, summary word be that in the Renaissance the native European languages and the literatures that derived from them experienced, with unimportant setbacks and exceptions, a notable development.

Setback of Italian literature owing to the humanist preference for Latin

THE FINE ARTS

Since the Fine Arts registered, on the whole, a more steady forward movement in the Renaissance than literature, they may fairly be expected to yield fuller information regarding the temper and achievement of the age. They cannot, however, any more than any other Renaissance manifestation, be understood without some knowledge of artistic production in the preceding medieval period. Let us begin by agreeing that architecture, sculpture, and painting reached a most impressive level in the Middle Ages. It is architecture that may be said to have been *the* art of the period, for in the Gothic cathedral it created one of the great monuments of all time. From both an engineering and an esthetic viewpoint the Gothic cathedral, still surviving in many imposing examples throughout the west-European area, commands an admiration which no building of later times enjoys in the same degree. Although sculpture and painting also flourished, they were cultivated in agreed subjection to the work of the architect. The close interdependence of the Fine Arts in the Middle Ages gives them a unity which they never again attained and which, in last analysis, they owe to the fact that they were alike employed in the service of the church and inspired with an identical religious purpose.

The great achievement of the Fine Arts in the Middle Ages

When with the fourteenth century a more secular spirit began to gain ground, the Fine Arts experienced a gradual transformation which carried them forward into their Renaissance phase. As we have no other aim than to illustrate the new development by selected examples, we shall direct our attention to Italy and, more particularly, to the single

Renaissance art can be best illustrated by its Florentine developmen⁴ city of Florence. Our choice is hardly open to debate since in this period not only did Italy hold the European van in every branch of the Fine Arts, but within Italy Florence was indisputably the leading creative center.

With the scholars from the time of Petrarch passionately extolling antiquity, the artists, in their turn catching the classical infection, were moved to accommodate their practice to the principles disclosed by the still abundant Greco-Roman remains. It was not until about the year 1400 that the effect of their enthusiasm made itself felt. The case for architecture can be best illustrated by the famous innovator, Filippo Brunelleschi (1377-1446). A Florentine by birth, he went as a young man to Rome to study the temple and theater remains of the ancient capital at first hand. On returning to his native city, Brunelleschi deliberately abandoned the reigning Gothic style with its massive piers, its flying buttresses, and its soaring vault of stone, for a style featured by the conscious resumption of the fundamental element of classical construction. This was the column-and-lintel or column-and-arch characteristic of the ancient temple. Applied to the kinds of building that were in demand in the rising cities—churches, town halls, private palaces—the graceful column crowned by a Doric, Ionic, or Corinthian capital gradually insinuated a classical quality of proportion and taste into the rudely constructed medieval town. (See Church of San Lorenzo, opp. p. 36.)

Agreed that Renaissance architecture made its appearance in Florence in the first half of the fifteenth century, let us note that it promptly made its way throughout Italy and that, once established, it confronts the observer with the usual phenomenon of development. The relatively simple forms of Early Renaissance structures ripened in the course of two or three generations to the fullness of High Renaissance; and of the High Renaissance phase the best Florentine representative is Michelangelo (1475-1564). The classical elements introduced by Brunelleschi—column, pilaster, cornice, pediment—are all present in Michelangelo's Medici Chapel (opp. p. 36), with the addition of a precision of detail and a harmony of proportions that reveal a long and loving study of ancient models. Since, however, the classical forms became a general Italian possession, it happens that the richest display of buildings of the High Renaissance is encountered not in Florence but in such other centers as Venice and Rome. Probably it is Rome that gives us the clearest view of an evolution that ranges from that clean example of Early Renaissance, the Palace of the Chancellor (la cancelleria), to the sumptuous Farnese Palace, which sounds the full, deep tone of the High Renaissance.

In the course of the Renaissance the average Italian town took on something of a pseudo-classical appearance. The other European countries followed the Italian example, although often at the remove of several generations and invariably with certain modifications imposed in each instance by the national genius. There are therefore French, Spanish, German, etc., Renaissances, which in their sum register the sweeping conquest of Europe effected by the classical revolution inaugurated by Brunelleschi. More remarkable even than this triumph is the fact that the new style retained its popularity for centuries and that it has continued to be favored for great public buildings down to our own day.

The long reign of classical architecture throughout the Western world

On turning to sculpture we encounter a similar situation. The Florentine, Donatello (1386-1466), a contemporary and friend of Brunelleschi, was the pioneer in this field. Although he, too, fell in love with antiquity and closely studied such classical remains as were available for his art, he had the good sense to regard nature as a more vital source of inspiration than the ancient models. Consequently he initiated a school of sculpture which, in spite of its absorption of classical elements, owes its admirable freshness to its closeness to nature. Enamored of the life about him, Donatello loved to present children at rest or at play and to fashion the heads and figures of contemporaries in their most characteristic aspect.

Renaissance sculpture originates with Donatello

Donatello thus became the herald of the new secular influences that were abroad and the first of a long line of Florentine sculptors who dipped for inspiration into life itself. They are still honored as artists who have rarely, if ever, been excelled. The fame of Luca della Robbia, Verocchio, and Michelangelo—to name only a few of the outstanding successors of Donatello—shines with undiminished luster after four hundred years. Michelangelo (1475-1564), last in this succession of artistic royalty, marks a departure from the Donatello tradition. As close to reality as the earlier master, he achieved a peculiar and unique grandeur by merging the individualized form, which was the objective of his immediate sculptural ancestors, with the ideality, that is, the generalized form, which is the revealing hallmark of the ancient Greeks. (See the "Moses" at Rome; the Tombs of the Medici at Florence, pictured opp. p. 36.)

Florentine sculpture culminates in Michelangelo

Important as were the architecture and sculpture of the period, they did not reach the significance of painting, which was the leading Fine Art of the period. So decidedly is this the case that every Italian town of any importance could boast its own succession of painters, who constituted a local group or "school" with a distinct and individual manner of expression. The richness and variety of Italian painting are owing to these schools, which we cannot here undertake even to enumerate. We shall have to content ourselves with a succinct statement about the Florentine school, followed by an even more succinct word about the neighboring school of Venice.

Abundance and variety of Renaissance painting

Giotto
founder of
Florentine
painting

Like the other Fine Arts, Florentine painting reaches back to the Middle Ages. In the days when the poet Dante was alive, a contemporary and friend of his, Giotto by name (1266-1337), founded the Florentine school. Gladly subordinating himself to the church in the still prevalent medieval manner, he produced an imposing succession of religious works in which we still recognize one of the major achievements of the Middle Ages. (See "Raising of Drusiana," opp. p. 36.)

Three
painting
techniques:
fresco,
tempera, oil

The kind of work for which Giotto was chiefly engaged was to cover the walls of churches with scenes from the life of Christ and the saints. For these large-scale undertakings he employed a technique that consisted in the artist's tracing his original charcoal design on a smooth plaster wall and then, after covering the wall with a fresh coat of plaster, in filling the outlined design with color and letting the plaster and paint fuse in the process of drying. From the practice of applying the paint to the *fresh* plaster the method received the name of *fresco* painting. In spite of its perishable character, fresco painting continued to flourish after Giotto's day and was not finally abandoned till late in the Renaissance. At the side of the fresco style Giotto and his successors also practiced painting on specially prepared wooden boards. In this kind of painting the colors were mixed or, as the phrase went, were "tempered" with a medium of yolk or white of egg. Hence the name *tempera* for this method. Not until late in the fifteenth century did the Florentines or the Italians in general borrow from the artists of the north of Europe (Flemings and Germans) the practice of carrying their colors in the thick oil medium, which has remained the favored technique of painting down to our day.

Masaccio
the realist

The first Florentine painter to depart from the religious tradition of Giotto and his medieval successors and sound the secular note characteristic of the Renaissance was Masaccio (1401-1428). Like Donatello, the sculptor, who was his contemporary, Masaccio turned for inspiration to life, to nature, and imposed a vigorous realism on the Florentine school. As he died at a very early age, his claim to fame rests mainly on the single fresco series of the Brancacci chapel at Florence.

The great
names of
the Floren-
tine school;
Botticelli

There is so much human penetration and such a rich variety of thought and feeling in the work of Masaccio's successors that they have elicited an extraordinary admiration through the ages. Notable among them are Fra Filippo Lippi and Fra Angelico. Shortly after their departure from the scene the school reached its culmination in three artists so great and so individual that it is almost to do them a wrong to give them the hardly more than bare mention which is their lot here. The oldest of the three was Botticelli (d. 1510). Joining to the spirited naturalism of his school a strong mystical vein, he produced paintings so winning and tender and at the same time so strangely disturbing to the heart and mind that for a group of special devotees he is, if not the greatest, certainly the most beloved of the Florentines. (See "Virgin, Christ-Child, and Six Angels," opp. p. 36.)

The two remaining Florentines, the greatest by all but general consent of the whole succession, were Leonardo da Vinci (1452-1519) and Michelangelo (1475-1564). Besides painting, each practiced as many other arts as at one time or another happened to excite his interest. In short, they were universal geniuses, a type not uncommon in the Renaissance and greatly admired by that strenuous age. *Two painters who were universal geniuses*

By natural preference Michelangelo was not a painter at all but a sculptor. It is his statuary, generally on a titanic scale, which most powerfully conveys his particular message. Yet he would be bold indeed who would not put this sculptor's Sistine Chapel frescos at Rome on a level with his best marbles. (See "Creation of Adam," opp. p. 37.) A single glance will show that the close and gracious naturalism of his painter-predecessors has been superseded. Michelangelo sought, in painting as in sculpture, to express himself not so much in particular as in generalized human forms, somewhat in the manner of the ancient Greeks. Together with Leonardo he carried the Renaissance at the exact moment at which it reached its summit from a close realist to a harmonized idealist manner of expression. *Michelangelo painter of the Sistine Chapel frescos*

Leonardo da Vinci so plainly excelled in painting that we must consider it to have been his favorite field of work. His greatest paintings are the "Last Supper" at Milan and a portrait at Paris called the "Mona Lisa." Besides painting, however, it was not so much its sister arts that drew his attention as it was science, which in its many departments of physics, botany, geology, and mechanics exercised a fascination which plunged him into exciting speculations about them during all the days of his life. Some of these speculations are indicative of intuitive and reasoning powers of rarest worth. Thus he forecast the much later discovery of the geologic ages of the earth and suggested the first steps leading to two such recent inventions as the airplane and the submarine. *Leonardo da Vinci painter and scientist*

In conclusion, the painting of Venice merits a word, if for no other reason than for the sharp contrast it presents to that of Florence. The difference in artistic approach between the two towns is partly a matter of underlying temper and partly a matter of political and economic security. Not only were the Florentines, like all seekers of an unattainable perfection, an essentially restless people, but they were perpetually disturbed by the recurrence among them of political and economic crises. Venice, on the other hand, from an early time dominated a field of commercial enterprise which brought material satisfactions and was attended by a political stability which was the envy of every other Italian government. Its school of painting admirably reflects these happy condi- *Venetian painting contrasted with Florentine painting* tions. Inhabitants of an untroubled paradise, the Venetian painters excel in brilliant color and project a world of aristocratic manners wherein grace and elegance exercise an unchallenged sway.

Titian sums up the Venetian school
Titian (1477-1576), the culmination of the school, reveals all that it is and also all that it is not. Whether we look at his many brilliant portraits of contemporaries ("Emperor Charles V," "Pope Paul III," "Man with the Glove") or at his richly robed Holy Families beyond the reach of either grief or want, we are transported into a world of material well-being and social magnificence untouched by as much as a breath of medieval earnestness, where none but secular and sensuous values reign.

Raphael the representative Italian in whom all schools meet
For former generations, but hardly any longer for ourselves, the greatest painter of the culminating Renaissance was Raphael (1483-1520). By birth he belonged to a small Umbrian town but, owing to travel and an unusually facile spirit, he succeeded in absorbing the influences of several neighboring schools and in becoming, far beyond any contemporary artist, a representative Italian. If we add that in his last phase he worked at Rome under the eye of the pope, we have a further explanation of the great reputation he achieved in his day. At the same time he exhibited such amazing skill of composition in his great frescos in the Vatican palace and wove such a winning grace about his many Madonnas that we are easily persuaded of his abiding merits. The "Sistine Madonna" and the "Madonna of the Chair" are among his best altarpieces, while any one of his Vatican frescos as, for instance, the Mystery of the Eucharist, called "La Disputa," will supply evidence of a power of composition rarely equaled and never excelled. Since Raphael probably embodied the Renaissance spirit at its human best, we mav with him appropriately conclude this swift survey of the Fine Arts.

INVENTION AND SCIENCE

Science and invention in the Middle Ages
The Middle Ages did not particularly distinguish themselves in respect either of science or invention. This should cause no surprise, for science and invention are not likely to flourish in a conservative society averse to experimentation and immobile by principle, if not altogether so in fact. With the coming of the Renaissance, which signified movement, the immobility ended. However, mobility operated so languidly that its effects only gradually made themselves felt.

Gunpowder ineffective without improved weapons
Turning first to invention, we note the sporadic appearance, in the course of the fourteenth century, of gunpowder. It was probably invented at several places in Europe independently. Only gradually put to use in warfare, it did not greatly affect military tactics till well into the fifteenth century. One invention has a way of leading to another; and it is this accumulation that reshapes a traditional situation. Thus

before gunpowder could revolutionize warfare it was necessary to provide muskets and artillery, and these inventions did not achieve a desirable effectiveness till after much painful experimentation.

As soon as the new weapons had become militarily serviceable, they set important social and political changes in motion. The feudal lord owed his ascendancy, on the one hand, to his moated castle, and, on the other hand, to his possession of an expensive equipment of horse, lance, and armor. In measure as the new weapons came into action they invalidated both the castle, the walls of which the artillery could easily breach, and the nobleman's armor, which was not proof against a musket bullet. The loss of the baron was the gain of his overlord, the king. If in the course of the fifteenth century the feudality began to decline before a strengthened monarchy, of which we shall presently hear, gunpowder and the military changes which followed in the wake of gunpowder have much to do with the altered situation. *Gunpowder and improved weapons deprive the nobles of their military pre-eminence*

A still more significant invention, doubtless one of the most far-reaching in the annals of the human race, was printing. So long as books were written laboriously by hand, they were necessarily few in number and expensive, a prerogative of kings and princes, lay and ecclesiastical. With the rise of populous towns the problem of a simpler and cheaper method of making books and spreading information became urgent, and was met, as was the case with gunpowder, not with a single invention, but with a long interlocking series of them. *Printing involves a series of inventions*

The ancient Greeks and Romans wrote on papyrus made from a reed of that name which grew in the valley of the Nile. The memory of their practice still lives on in our word paper. When, during the Middle Ages, Egyptian papyrus became unobtainable, men resorted to parchment prepared from the skins of animals, preferably of sheep. To supersede the handwritten book it would be necessary to replace the costly parchment with some cheaper substitute and indefinitely to multiply the individual handwritten letter by its equivalent in movable type. By a succession of small steps both these replacements had been successfully mastered toward the middle of the fifteenth century. By that time a linen paper, made of the fiber of flax, had come into use; and in 1454—the great event deserves to be precisely dated—the first book printed on linen paper from movable type dropped from the press. This first printed book, still extant in a few priceless copies, is a Latin Bible. It was issued from the press of John Gutenberg of the city of Mainz on the Rhine. Gutenberg added the last link in a long chain of improvements representing the work of many generations. He may have invented movable type, as is often claimed; but whether he did or not, he deserves to be accorded the honor of having been the first to combine the inventions of many predecessors into the practical art of printing. *The invention of linen paper and movable type the most important steps leading to printing*

Printing promotes a mental and social revolution

Within a few decades printing had spread from the Rhine to all the countries of Europe. Books, once a rarity, were multiplied as by magic, and, sold for a small price, carried both the old medieval and the new humanistic learning far afield. Not only did the proud and barricaded scholarship of the universities now become more accessible, but an enormously potent engine for the promotion of his program was put into the hands of every innovator and reformer. Though it would be a mistake to think of the European masses as now promptly taking to reading and gaining a new outlook, it is certain that the middle classes, the true carriers of the Renaissance, greatly strengthened their position. By way of immediate evidence we may cite the fact that, within the space of a few decades of the new art, the books printed in Latin, the vehicle of a limited group of scholars, were greatly outnumbered by those published in the various European vernaculars. Plainly, whoever wished to be widely read was obliged henceforward to circulate his ideas in the language of the street and home.

Science during the Renaissance moves slowly

If invention during the Renaissance moved at a very deliberate pace, science cannot be said to have moved any faster. Humanist culture was so exclusively directed toward literary and esthetic interests that science suffered a relative neglect. Even so, however, it was far from overlooked, since the ancients themselves, especially the Greeks, had accumulated an important body of knowledge in many fields, more particularly in geography, mathematics, astronomy, and medicine, and all this had again been made accessible.

Advance of geography and cartography

In the case of geography the merchants, sea captains, and travelers of the Renaissance gradually added to the knowledge communicated by the Greeks their own firsthand information about the coasts and waters of the Mediterranean. Then came the amazing Portuguese and Spanish discoveries, with the result that in the course of a few generations geographic knowledge had penetrated to the ends of the earth. This exciting enlargement called for maps to make the vast new knowledge available not only for captains with vessels to steer across the perilous seas but for the intellectually curious as well. In this manner was called into existence the profession of map-makers or cartographers, who gathered in their drafting-rooms the scattered bits of information supplied by scores of voyagers and recorded them in regional or world maps of steadily increasing accuracy.

Absorption of the mathematics of the Greeks and Arabs

Of mathematics there is much less to report, since this, the most abstract of the inventions of man, did not advance till the succeeding period beyond the arithmetic and geometry of the ancients, with something added from the Moslem world. This addition was a rudimentary algebra together with the far more important Arabic numerals, which already toward the end of the Middle Ages had begun to displace the clumsy numerals in use among the Romans and taken over by their medieval heirs.

One of the fields of science most successfully cultivated by the Greeks was astronomy. The last of the great Greek astronomers was Ptolemy, who lived at Alexandria in Egypt in the second century after Christ. He taught that the earth was round and calculated its circumference at an astonishingly close approximation to the true figure. His further doctrine was that the earth was the stationary center of the universe and that the sun, moon, planets, and stars revolved around it. To support this hypothesis he promulgated an elaborate theory of celestial mechanics, which constituted what was called the Ptolemaic system.

Astronomy the Ptolemaic system

So firmly rooted in educated belief were the Ptolemaic teachings that it was not till near the close of the Renaissance that they were challenged. The challenger was a native of Poland, Copernicus (1473-1543) by name. On the strength of wide reading among the earlier Greek astronomers with theories at variance with those of Ptolemy and with the aid of such imperfect observation of the heavens as his rude instruments permitted, he propounded a revised astronomy with two outstanding propositions. The first was that not the earth but the sun was the center of the planetary system; the second that, instead of being stationary, the earth not only revolved around the sun in the course of a year but once every twenty-four hours revolved also about its axis.

Copernicus formulates a new astronomy

Because the Ptolemaic or geocentric system enjoyed the endorsement not only of scholars but also of the church, Copernicus, in fear of a trial for heresy, long hesitated to announce his heliocentric view. Indeed it was not till the year of his death (1543) that his epoch-making treatise, *De Orbium Coelestium Revolutionibus* ("Concerning the Revolutions of the Heavenly Bodies"), was issued from the press. Not greatly noticed at first, its teachings filtered very slowly into the European consciousness. This chilly reception of the correction of an established but erroneous theory proves, if proof is needed, that scientific investigation did not yet enjoy much favor and that a main obstacle to its advance was the too great authority enjoyed by the ancients.

The Copernican astronomy slow to win recognition

The way in which the ancient learning both helped and retarded science may be further illustrated by the developments in medicine. When, in the thirteenth and fourteenth centuries, the remarkable medical science of the Greeks, culminating in the work of Galen, was again made accessible to the west, both theoretical and practical medicine scored a decided advance. It was presently halted, owing to the blind worship which the new leaders of thought, the humanists, entertained for the ancients. Their attitude caused them to swear by the written word as the sum of wisdom and to decry experimentation and innovation as a kind of sacrilege. The result was that medicine came to be regarded as a body

Greek medicine helps and later hinders medical advance

of facts contained in existing books and incapable of being enlarged by fresh discoveries.

Not till the sixteenth century was the subjection of medicine to stupid authoritarianism seriously threatened. The man who more than any other cleared the path for this advance was the Fleming, Vesalius. In 1543 he published his anatomical treatise, *Fabrica Corporis Humani* ("Structure of the Human Body"), which ventured to challenge the findings of Galen himself and took the ground that more important for knowledge of the human body than any book are the facts as established by the trained physician in the dissecting room. It was of course an accident that the work of Vesalius appeared in the same year as that of Copernicus. We are, however, free to bracket the two publications and to advance the claim that with them science had begun to liberate itself from the dead hand of authority by exhibiting the gains bound to result from an observational and experimental approach to its various fields of study.

Vesalius throws off the Greek yoke with an independent work on anatomy

THE RISE OF AN INDIVIDUALIST ETHICS

It is difficult for a modern man to realize to what an extent the Middle Ages were a period of classes and class discipline. Whether you were a cleric, a knight, a merchant, a craftsman, or a peasant, you lived out your life in the spirit of class loyalty and in strict submission to the established customs of your group. In case you were injured in your rights you appealed for justice to the court which functioned for your social level. There were therefore ecclesiastical, baronial, municipal, and peasant (manorial) courts, to which the individual was amenable according to his status. Above the various civil courts was the court of last resort, the court of the king, but it did not always function because the king was frequently without power. Each class was distinguished by a style of dress peculiar to itself, had its own manners and amusements, and in many instances developed its own dances, songs, and other forms of self-expression. In sum, so authoritative was the class code that the individual was bound and dominated in every concern of life by a multitude of meticulous prescriptions.

The class system of the Middle Ages

With the coming of the Renaissance the stout barriers of custom began to give way, and scattered individuals, particularly such as had enjoyed the advantages of travel or study, were prompted to abandon their group allegiance in the hope of a greater measure of personal freedom. The great merchant of Venice or Florence chafed at the numerous restrictions imposed by his fellows of the gild of merchants regarding buying and selling, and nursed the conviction that, under a freer system, he would much more rapidly mount the ladder of success. Encouraged

Break-down of the medieval class code

by such thoughts, he favored an economic policy of untrammeled enterprise, just as his contemporary, the humanist, enamored of classical
literature and advocating a new educational program, desired to cut
loose from the intellectual and moral restrictions imposed by church and
university. Whenever you bring a Renaissance situation under intimate
observation, you are likely to discover that the men who figure as leaders
are liberating themselves from the fetters of the past and aiming at a
fuller life.

From the point of view of social conduct the Renaissance is therefore
an age of emerging individualism, the essence of which is freedom. Freedom—what a seductive battle cry! It has sounded through all the succeeding centuries and continues in our day to make itself heard with all
its original persuasiveness. The amazing galaxy of fifteenth and sixteenth century personalities, more brilliant perhaps and more sharply
defined than those of any other epoch, may be accepted as the first fruits
of the achieved emancipation.

Individual-
ism means
freedom
from
inherited
trammels

Since individualist practices point to an individualist ethics, it will help
our understanding to characterize the outstanding feature of the individualist code. By a policy of minute and rigorous control the medieval
class regime taught men to find their happiness in service to the group
to which they belonged. The Renaissance, on the contrary, with its
individualist trend tended to ignore and sacrifice the group in favor of
its most energetic and highly endowed members. Consequently it sanctioned an ethical system which exalted and honored the gifted and successful individuals without looking too closely into the methods they
employed.

Individualist
practices
foster an
individualist
ethics

Two types of social conduct were thus brought into confrontation
with each other. If the pagan-individualist type came to the front in the
Renaissance, the older medieval, or, as we may term it, the Christian-
socialist type, was by no means driven from the scene. In fact it is evident that both have continued to exist side by side, often enough in open
discord, down to the present generation. The irrepressible conflict is
complicated by the circumstance that the modern man, as the historical
heir of two ethical codes, most often tries to combine them both in his
single person. The inevitable consequence is a disturbing inner conflict.
Certainly it will not do to make out that men and women in our day
adopt and tenaciously cling to one or the other of the two systems, seeing that in practice they pay a disconcertingly sincere homage to both.

Two sharply
opposed
ethical codes

Making every possible allowance for a situation varying from place to
place and from class to class, we are still forced to admit that the Renaissance ushered in, at least for an upper social level, a new moral code. Its
main elements can be distinguished without any difficulty. They are: a

The main
elements of
individual-
ism

strong individual assertiveness, a spontaneous rejection of inherited trammels, and an ethical and, by implication, an esthetic practice in harmony with the new libertarian attitude toward the problem of living.

THE RISE OF CAPITALISM

A feature of our period which we may not overlook is that it fostered a new form of economic organization which is the germ of modern capitalism. In considering the growth of the town we noted that the expanding economic life centered around the gild. The gild was an admirable institution in its way and for its time. It was organized with reference to the town market in such a way that each gild enjoyed the monopoly for its particular product within the limits of the town. In return for this favor conceded by the town government the gild assumed the obligation to furnish the consumers a sound article at a fair price. Although competition was not entirely eliminated among the members of the same gild, it failed to become an important factor in the commercial situation, owing to the prevailing Christian system of ethics with its ideal of a decent living on a basis of approximate equality for all the members of the organization. An equally characteristic feature of the gild economy was the attempt to eliminate the middleman, the mere trader, by requiring whoever produced an article to display and sell it in his shop.

Medieval economy is town economy

Fashioned for purely local ends, the gild became ineffective as soon as a lively export trade developed. This called for foresight and initiative, that is, for the promoter and enterpriser who was free to arrive at independent decisions and who was unhampered by the minute regulations concerning buying and selling which governed the gilds. As soon, therefore, as a foreign trade of considerable dimensions put in an appearance, such, for instance, as the Italian trade with the Levant during and after the crusades, it eluded the control of the gild and was appropriated as his particular preserve by the merchant endowed with a special genius for business. Though the risks involved in these distant enterprises were enormous, the profits, correspondingly large, produced riches undreamed of by the stay-at-home craftsmen and shopkeepers. The expanding foreign trade gave rise, first, in the towns of Italy and later, throughout the west, to a relatively small body of merchant princes and capitalists who towered head and shoulders over the rest of the community.

Foreign trade appropriated by the merchant-adventurer

The form of organization adopted for foreign trade on a wholesale scale was the merchant company. We can grasp the need for this business novelty by considering the case of a Venetian trader who desired to import a cargo of spices from Alexandria. He could not from his own limited resources supply the ships, the wages of a large number of seamen, and the articles of the outbound voyage which were to be sold on

Rise of the merchant company

the Egyptian market. He would have to find partners who would share in the prospective profits in proportion to their contribution to the enterprise. Formed in the first instance for a single voyage, the association, if successful, might take on a permanent form. Because of the greater measure of trust among blood relations it came about that most early merchant companies possessed a family character. Before long this feature was abandoned and any reputable person able to contribute capital was accepted into the partnership.

As the merchant companies took advantage of every opportunity of profit that arose, they engaged also in financial operations, without which, **Rise of** owing to the bewildering coinage situation, no trade in goods was pos- **banking** sible. All early trading companies without exception did also the business of banks; the trading companies of Florence, for instance, often enough entered on their banking career as humble pawnbrokers and only gradually extended their action to cover the full range of the banking field. Even before the close of the Middle Ages they had won for their city a financial pre-eminence like that of London or New York in our day.

That with the Renaissance money had become king, more particularly, of course, in Italy, is illustrated by the company of the Medici. **The Medici** Substantially a family bank, which had accumulated its huge capital **bank** under the leadership of several generations of eminent merchants, it engaged in the manner typical of early capitalism in trade and credit operations on a growing scale. By the second half of the fifteenth century the Medici bank operated a branch establishment in every important center of Europe. On the strength of its money power the family was able gradually to insinuate itself into the government of Florence with the result that the head of the bank finally emerged as the ruler of the city.

A similar, if more tardy, development in the regions north of the Alps, particularly in Flanders, prepared the way for the subjection of the whole **Capitalism** economic life of Europe to the power of money; for, while capitalism **undermines** originated with the export trade, it was not long before it invaded and **the gild** overwhelmed the inherited gild economy. The exporter with connections **economy** in every market and commanding ample resources could buy the raw products, such as wool or leather, much more cheaply than the local gild. Thereupon, by supplying the individual gildsman with the raw product he required, and by contracting at the same time for his annual output, the export merchant could bring the gilds more or less under his control. As early as the fourteenth century the flourishing cloth manufacture of Florence was so completely in the power of a relatively small group of great promoters, who merely bought up the cloth for export without themselves producing a single yard, that the gild system no longer squared with its original principle. In the altered circumstances the masters of the Florentine wool gild leave the impression of having been reduced to a body of small shop-foremen, while their journeymen and apprentices look for all the world like a proletariat of modern wage-earners.

The decline of the gilds occurred somewhat later in Flanders and, later still, in England. The decline signified an economic revolution which was bound to end by crowding the socialistic gilds entirely from the scene and by establishing a competitive, capitalist order of society. Nor does it admit the least doubt that this was a fated development, for it harmonizes with all the forces abroad in the Renaissance: with the enlargement of the world and its markets; with the new individualist ethics inviting every man to make the most of his talents; and with the replacement, of which we shall presently hear, of the town as the economico-political unit of society with the nation ruled by an autocratic sovereign.

The rise of a capitalist society

THE VOYAGES OF DISCOVERY AND EUROPEAN COLONIZATION

Already in the Middle Ages, during the first period of town expansion, the traders, especially of Italy, began those sea voyages which ended in their becoming thoroughly acquainted with the whole Mediterranean basin. Owing to the slight tonnage of their ships, which were as yet chiefly galleys propelled by rowers, and owing also to their fear of the unknown ocean beyond the straits of Gibraltar, they hesitated to advance beyond the great middle sea which was their immediate domain. In these circumstances the exploration of the Atlantic fell to the lot of the Atlantic states. The leader of the movement was Portugal.

Early voyages limited to the Mediterranean

In the first half of the fifteenth century a brother of the king of Portugal, Prince Henry, called the Navigator, took up the idea of exploring the near-by coast of Africa. Its inhabitants were Mohammedans and pirates, who, on this double count, had for centuries been regarded by the Portuguese with stubborn aversion. When Prince Henry, a pious Christian gentleman possessed of ample means, turned to exploration, he was largely moved by the hope of bringing these infidels into the Christian fold; but he was also animated by the idea, which had been popularized by the Ptolemaic system, that it was possible to sail around Africa and establish a direct connection with the Indies, home of the precious spices and other hardly less precious products of the fabulous orient.

Prince Henry the Navigator

The first reward of the prince's efforts was the discovery of the Azores and Madeira Islands. With the vessels at his command, which only gradually became larger and better equipped, progress along the coast of

Africa was slow. However, when Henry died in 1460, his mariners had penetrated almost to the equator. The voyages, continued after his death, carried the Portuguese ships farther and farther down the coast, until in 1486 Diaz succeeded in rounding the southernmost point of the continent, which received the name of the Cape of Good Hope. Twelve years later, in 1498, Vasco da Gama crowned almost a century of heroic effort by sailing across the Indian ocean to Calicut in Hindustan.

Progress of Portuguese discovery

Since, beginning with the voyage of Vasco da Gama, the Portuguese were able to acquire the spices, silks, and other luxuries of the orient at low cost in the countries which produced them, and since they were able to bring them without breaking cargo to the western markets, the European trade in these commodities was put on a new foundation. The Italian cities, with Venice at their head, unable to buy and transport as cheaply as Portugal, suffered a heavy blow. Although the Adriatic metropolis did not at once feel the effects of the new situation, its heyday was over and its decline had set in.

The spice trade revolutionized

The startling discoveries inaugurated by Prince Henry aroused the emulation of all the hardy spirits throughout the maritime world. Since the Portuguese had devoted themselves to the task of reaching the Indies by rounding Africa, why should not the attempt be made to reach the same goal by sailing west over the Atlantic? If the Ptolemaic theory was correct, it was impossible to miss the Indies by that route. Pondering the idea, a bold skipper, Christopher Columbus (1446-1506), a native of the Italian city of Genoa, became more and more persuaded of its feasibility. Much derided by cautious stay-at-homes and long unable to find the necessary financial sponsors, he at last secured the support of a woman of vision, Queen Isabella of Castile. Supplied by her with three small caravels, on August 3, 1492, he set out from Palos, a port of western Spain. Over two months later, on October 12, when all his companions, save himself, had already despaired of success, he touched land in the small island group of the Bahamas. Before turning his prow back to Europe he discovered also the large neighboring islands of Cuba and Haiti.

Christopher Columbus sails west

Owing to his undercalculation of the earth's circumference, Columbus believed that he was on the fringe of the desired spice lands, the fabled Indies; and the name Indians, which he gave to the western aborigines, has clung to them to this day. On his return to Spain he was cordially acclaimed by court and people. Queen Isabella raised him to the rank of admiral, conferred a patent of nobility on him, and invested him with the viceroyalty of the new lands.

Columbus' mistake about his discovery

In three subsequent voyages Columbus learned nothing which led him to correct the impression that he had reached the outskirts of Asia and the Indian spice lands. A choleric man by nature, with more enemies

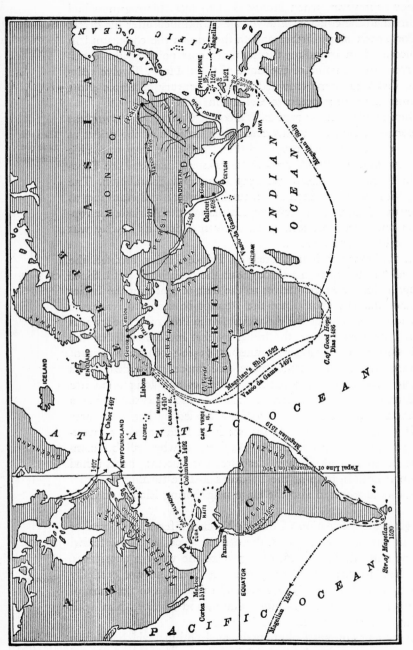

Voyages of Discovery

Note to the Student: Observe the land route followed by the famous Venetian traveler, Marco Polo, the first European who penetrated into China (13th Century). Trace the Portuguese voyages, noting the culminating stages, Diaz at the Cape in 1486 and Vasco da Gama at Calicut in India in 1498; also follow Columbus on his voyage of 1492, and Magellan's great circumnavigation, 1519-1522.

than friends, he experienced many strange vicissitudes, of which perhaps the strangest is that in the course of his third voyage (1498-1500) he was arrested and sent back to Spain, a prisoner in irons. On the dismissal of the charges against him, he was equipped for a fourth voyage, during which he sighted the American mainland. On his death in 1506, near Valladolid, he fell into temporary oblivion; and by the decision of an obscure German cartographer, the world which Columbus had, so to speak, called out of the void [1] was named, not after him, but after a relatively unimportant traveler and geographer, the Florentine, Amerigo Vespucci. The later voyages of Columbus

In consequence of these startling successes discovery became a passion, especially among the Portuguese and Spaniards. Though the seas were wide and perilous, every adventurer's soul felt a personal summons to strike out into the unknown regions, whence fame and riches beckoned. Voyage soon followed voyage, each new enterprise adding its mite to the rounding-out of the world's geography. In 1497 John Cabot, a Venetian in the employ of Henry VII of England, reached Cape Breton Island, off the coast of North America; and in 1499 Pinzon, who had accompanied Columbus on his first voyage, skirted the shore of Brazil. Thus the great continental mass behind the curtain of islands discovered by Columbus slowly hove in view, and it became clear that this mass was neither India nor China. Multiplied discovery

A fitting climax of this multiplied endeavor was reached when Magellan, a Portuguese in the Spanish service, attempted in 1519 to reach Asia by a passage to the south of the American continental barrier. Having successfully rounded South America, he was the first European ever to furrow the Pacific. In 1522, after a journey of three years, his ship, happily named *Victory,* reached its European starting-point. Magellan himself did not live to see this triumphant conclusion, for he was killed upon the Philippine Islands. But no one will dispute that to him goes the honor of having been the first man to circumnavigate the globe. Magellan circumnavigates the globe, 1519-22

As the discoveries originated largely in man's commercial instincts, they were promptly utilized for purposes of trade. But that is not the whole story. Both Portuguese and Spaniards undertook also to Christianize the new regions and to settle them with colonists from the homelands. They thus committed themselves to a policy of Europeanization. However, it became apparent before long that Europeanization would be successful only in the savage and sparsely inhabited continents of North and South America. In the thickly settled regions of Asia, especially in India and China, where the natives boasted a civilization, Different treatment of Asia and the Americas

[1] It may be noticed in passing that the Northmen, proceeding from Iceland, had discovered America in the tenth century and called it Vinland. But as their discovery was not followed up, it had no results for Western civilization and does not detract from the well-earned fame of Columbus.

which, if different, was quite the equal of that of Europe, both Christianization and colonization encountered insurmountable obstacles. In consequence we note a difference: Asia remained, as it began, a field of commercial exploitation; the Americas, on the other hand, were gradually planted with settlers and Europeanized.

In this work of colonial appropriation Portugal and Spain, as first upon the ground, had an advantage over the other European states. For a moment they even dreamed of excluding all third parties and sharing the immense booty between themselves. Appealing to the pope to serve as arbiter, after much haggling they agreed (1496) on a division of the New World based on the meridian which lay three hundred and seventy leagues west of the Cape Verde Islands. All the newly discovered lands to the east of this meridian were to belong to Portugal, all to the west thereof to Spain. But this arrangement, so immensely profitable for the partitioning powers, could not be maintained. In the long run, even as between Portugal and Spain, each power was likely to hold only what it could actually lay its hands on; and both together would find it impossible to shut out determined rivals. Sooner or later England, France, and, very likely, other countries would join in the scramble for the new possessions, and, in view of the resources at their disposal, were almost certain to effect a lodgment.

The fierce colonial rivalry among the European powers is one of the most important interests of the Modern Period and will play no small part in this history. For the present, however, we shall merely associate the various European powers with the main regions to which in the first instance they directed their enterprise. By means of a chain of fortified trading posts planted along the coast of Africa and the southern shore of Asia the Portuguese succeeded in dominating for a long time the adjacent waters and their profitable trade. Their leading area of settlement, however, was Brazil in South America, to which they could lay claim because it lay to the east of the meridian agreed upon with Spain. Brazil was successfully settled with sufficient numbers of Portuguese to make it gradually Portuguese in speech and manners.

The Spaniards located their chief colonial centers at the following points: (1) The West Indies, whither Columbus himself had directed the stream of immigration; (2) Mexico, which was won for the Spaniards by the daring adventurer, Cortez; (3) Peru, acquired by the equally undaunted Pizarro; (4) the Philippine Islands, secured by Magellan. With the West Indies, Mexico, and Peru as outlying bases of action, Spain surrounded and gradually occupied the whole region of Central and South America (except Brazil), while by means of the Philippine Islands she acquired an important foothold in Asiatic waters.

The northern countries of Europe entered late, and with only gradually

Attempt of Portugal and Spain to monopolize the new lands

Colonial objectives of Portugal

Main colonial objectives of Spain

increasing vigor, into the struggle for the new islands and continents. The little which Henry VII of England did to secure a share for his nation in the great extension of the world is of importance only by reason of consequences which he did not foresee. In 1497 he fitted out John Cabot, a Venetian, who, as already noted, reached the coast of North America. After Henry's time English enterprise slumbered, to be directed on its revival toward the discovery of still another passage, a hoped-for passage by the waters of the northwest, to that goal of all desires, the spice lands of Asia. By this route it was hoped to repeat the feat of the Portuguese and Spaniards, who had reached Asia by following respectively a southeasterly and a southwesterly course. Although, owing to the far projection of North America into the Arctic sea, the English plan was doomed to failure, it had the effect of keeping alive the English interest in the North American coast. Not till the early seventeenth century, however, did the English fully realize their opportunities and set about the systematic colonization of the Atlantic seaboard. *England establishes an American claim*

The French proved even more lax than the English in colonial enterprise, and it was not till the reign of Henry IV (1589-1610) that they seriously undertook to carve out a conquest for themselves. They then hastened to undo, as far as possible, the consequences of their neglect by settlements in Canada, and, later, in Louisiana; that is, in the great basins respectively of the St. Lawrence and Mississippi rivers. *The claims of France*

Colonial success was in every instance dependent on the support of a strong home government. By grasping this fact we have the explanation why Germany, where the feudal lords had reduced the central sovereign to impotence, shared neither in the voyages of discovery nor in the colonial prizes which the discoveries brought. In the case of Italy, too, it was its unhappy political atomization which explains its failure to share in the Asiatic and American spoils. These vast potential benefits were reserved for the united and the strong. *Germany and Italy do not share in the colonial movement*

THE AUTOCRATIC MONARCHY

It remains to discuss the characteristic political development of the Renaissance period. Already during the Middle Ages the rising towns, as we are aware, had flung a challenge at the feudal system; but the baronage had not been dislodged and remained a powerful factor in the general situation. Under the constitutional conceptions of the Middle Ages the monarch was himself a baron, though a baron-in-chief, to whom was conceded an honorary and strictly limited headship over his fellow-barons. He was *primus inter pares* (first among equals). Himself steeped in feudal conceptions, he frequently failed to understand that the town *The political alliance between towns and monarch*

movement offered itself as a means for strengthening his position against the nobility. In the long run the fact could hardly escape him, while, regardless of his far- or shortsightedness, the cities would be only too eager to give him their support against a baronage whose lawless habits constituted an intolerable interference with trade. Throughout Europe it comes to this: The towns and the monarch had a common enemy in the feudal nobility and were, therefore, natural political allies.

Decline of the monarch's power in Italy and Germany

Owing to special circumstances belonging to medieval history, Germany and Italy constituted the Holy Roman Empire and had the same monarch, the emperor. Confronted in Germany with the great landed nobility and in Italy with the pope supported by the towns, the emperor was in the course of the twelfth and thirteenth centuries so badly beaten in both countries, but more particularly in Italy, that he was reduced to impotence. In Italy the towns and such great nobles as had survived the rise of the towns became substantially independent, while in Germany the largest of the barons acquired a power approximating to sovereignty. In the Renaissance this medieval decision against the emperor became irrevocable. In Italy he all but completely disappeared from the scene; in Germany, though he made a feeble, belated effort to strengthen his hand by favoring the towns, he remained so weak that he conveys the impression of being hardly more than tolerated by the great dukes and prelates, the real masters of the land.

The monarchs of Spain, France, and England lean on the towns

In Spain, France, and England, on the other hand, the feudal monarchy in this same period traveled the opposite road and steadily waxed in strength. In these three countries, for reasons that need not be examined here, the king was not exposed to the combination of circumstances which sapped the vigor of the emperor. Consequently, he was able to profit, as the emperor was not, from the rise of that urban element which was opposed to the barons and was busily engaged in increasing the wealth of the country. When the king needed money, as he constantly did since the jealous nobles would concede him nothing beyond the meager terms of their feudal contract, he found that the easiest way to get it was to apply to the men with the moneybags, his doughty burghers. As the burghers naturally asked for a return favor, they received it, on the one hand, by enlarged municipal charters and, on the other, in the form of a concession of national scope: they were admitted to the feudal assembly of the realm.

The towns enter the feudal parliament

The feudal assembly or parliament was originally composed of clergy and nobles and constituted the national council of the king. When to clergy and nobles, who in feudal law were regarded respectively as the first and second estates, the representatives of the towns were added, these, having gained a foothold within the feudal frame, received the designation of the third estate. It was at the approximate dividing line between the Middle Ages and Renaissance that this advance in political status was won by the towns of the three great states of France, Spain, and England.

To the bonds of a financial and constitutional order created between the townsmen and their king a powerful emotional element was presently added in the rise of nationalism. As one of the decisive influences in the history of modern Europe, nationalism cannot be too closely scanned by the student. Although not entirely lacking in the medieval period, it became clearly manifest as a political factor only in the Renaissance. From the Renaissance it has grown steadily until, like a slowly developing motif in an orchestral piece, it has mounted to a thundering climax in the contemporary period. Nationalism is a sentiment based on community of language, religion, and customs and is historically connected with the social order created by the towns. Latent and unimportant in the period of unchallenged feudalism, it first came actively to the front in the Renaissance. The most common occasion for its emergence was the invasion of the country by an armed outsider and the suffering imposed thereby on all classes of the population alike. *Rise of nationalist sentiment*

Spanish nationalism was born in the struggle against the Mohammedan Moors, who had conquered the Christian Spaniards in the eighth century; and it expanded and became consolidated in the long-continuing, ferocious wars which threw the invader back across the straits of Gibraltar. Similarly, French nationalism, as the name of Joan of Arc eloquently attests, was the child of the English invasion and the Hundred Years' War. Again, the English largely achieved their own powerful group consciousness in the same struggle. We must guard against exaggerating the new sentiment manifested among these three peoples, since so long as the baronial class held aloof from the third estate, considering itself a breed infinitely superior to the common run of men, a sentiment, binding all classes together, can hardly be said to have existed. However, there is no denying that the towns, which in their first phase had been animated by nothing more than a purely municipal patriotism, became the champions of the broader sentiment and, in measure as they prospered, spread among the people of the same speech a more generous love of country. But as the head of the country was the king, as, in fact, he visibly embodied the nation, it followed that the increasing patriotic sentiment redounded to his benefit. *Nationalist sentiment helps the king*

In this manner developments connected with the towns and their activities came to the aid of the king in his struggle with the nobles. To the nobles, as rivals of the royal power, must be added the clergy, who in the medieval period had acquired a body of rights and immunities amounting in their sum to a substantial independence of the state. To complete the picture of the difficulties of the medieval monarch let us recall that at the height of the Middle Ages the pope, as overlord of the *The royal power and the church* clergy throughout Europe, had gone the length of declaring that every sovereign held his dominion by the pope's grace as a papal fief. It was indisputable that if ever the king was to become the effective head of a united people, the vast clerical pretensions would as imperatively have to be reduced as those of the nobility. In fact the only conceivable way by which a united nation could be created was by the subjection of all classes alike to the laws emanating from the king. Wherever, therefore, the national unification movement was inaugurated, a struggle with the church followed as logically and inexorably as with the nobles.

It must now be clear that the plan of every active sovereign of the
Renaissance was to strengthen in every way the monarchy centered about
his person. The statement defines the royal program pursued alike in
Spain, France, and England; and though its execution exhibits considerable variation in each country, there is noticeable a broadly identical procedure. Without necessarily disturbing the numerous judicial tribunals
inherited from the feudal regime, the king confirmed his position as
court of final appeal and head of the national system of justice; he
multiplied the officials who looked after the royal interests in the provinces, thereby building up a royal administration; he increased his income by subsidies from the towns which he tried to make fixed and
regular; and with his enlarged means he laid the foundation of a permanent armed force dependent on no one but himself. The royal measures
had in reality a more tentative character than is indicated by the above-
recited, over-definite statements. Sometimes, as, for instance, in England
during the Wars of the Roses, it seemed as if the monarchy, instead of
winning its cause, was on the point of going down before the feudal
lords. However, in spite of setbacks, the tendencies here indicated continued to operate and ended by producing that novel political phenomenon, the autocratic monarchy.

Measures by which the king increased his power

As a result of this political evolution, before the close of the Renaissance, the kings of Spain, France, and England had acquired a formidable stature; and though they long continued to be engaged in the difficult process of extricating themselves from feudal bonds, it may fairly
be said of them around 1500 that they had become the heads of a centralized organization which enabled them to exercise a power undreamed
of by their medieval predecessors.

Spain, France, and England become strong monarchies

The nine heads under which we have attempted to familiarize ourselves with the Renaissance are so many paths by which Western man
ventured into new fields. If we hold fast to the idea that he was carrying forward a movement of civilization, the foundations of which had
been laid in the Middle Ages, his many activities during the new period
become amazingly unified. For, viewed in this organic manner, the

The Renaissance summarized

Renaissance signified in substance a breaking away from childhood with its innumerable, inevitable bondages. Surely it is not merely fanciful to see in the man of the Middle Ages essentially a child, a timid stay-at-home, clinging to his familiar patch of earth and disinclined to look beyond the narrow limits of his hearth and parish. Besides, the church, which led him like a mother by the hand, bade him make as little as possible of this life of tribulation but to feast his eyes on the vision of the life to come. There was in consequence something repressed and passive about the Middle Ages. By the hundreds and thousands both men and women sought the seclusion of a cell, voluntarily renouncing life before its natural close. Yet within other thousands and tens of thousands a spark gleamed and a sap stirred which would not be extinguished or suppressed. And when in due time the child became a youth, Western civilization entered upon a new and higher stage. Here lies the significance of the Renaissance, here is the reason why the nine aspects, under which we have examined the movement, exhibit with the often wanton breaking of customary bonds also the courageous testing of new opportunities. The Renaissance triumphantly affirmed that the special characteristic of Western civilization was to be experimentation and love of danger in a degree beyond that of any other civilization of which there is record. From this position it followed that Western civilization would refuse to submit indefinitely to inherited ecclesiastical authority, and that by combining curiosity with enterprise it would impose on itself the obligation of perpetual self-renewal.

The Reformation
and the Religious Wars

FROM 1500 TO 1648

THE EUROPEAN STATES ON THE EVE
OF THE REFORMATION

THE EMERGENCE IN Spain, France, and England of
the strengthened monarchy, of which we have just heard, is in striking Desirability
contrast with the increased political disintegration in Germany and Italy. of a detailed
This contradictory phenomenon suggests the necessity of a detailed sur- survey of
vey of the whole European political situation at the beginning of the Europe
sixteenth century. As politically disorganized Italy was at that time the
cultural leader of the western world, it is fitting that we should begin
our survey with the Mediterranean peninsula.

ITALY

The central fact of Italian political history during the Middle Ages
was that the emperor, sovereign of both Germany and Italy, lost his hold Italy breaks
on the peninsula. He suffered defeat because he represented feudalism away from
the Holy
and thwarted the growth of Italian city life, but also because, as a Ger- Roman
man, he signified the domination of Italy by a foreigner. The conflict Empire
of the towns with the emperor persuaded them to join forces with the
pope, who feared the emperor on ecclesiastical grounds, and the combination of towns and pope proved too much for the imperial strength.
With the death in 1250 of Emperor Frederick II, of the house of Hohen-
staufen, the sun of the Holy Roman Empire may be said to have set in
Italy. Nor did the occasional reappearance of an emperor in later centuries alter the situation—Italy had thrown off the imperial yoke.

The immediate result of the fall of the Empire and the victory of the
towns was an extraordinary confusion. Scores of towns of the highly The Italian
developed trading area of northern and north-central Italy became free political
chaos
republics and, having no more to fear from the emperor, engaged in
violent conflict with one another over markets and boundaries; in the
inaccessible mountains of the Alps and Apennines occasional feudal lords
continued to maintain themselves against the expanding towns; the central area, with Rome as capital, was claimed by the pope as his temporal dominion; and finally, the spacious south, including the island of
Sicily, constituted the kingdom of Naples (officially called the kingdom
of Sicily).

CORSICA
(To Genoa)

SARDINIA
(To Aragon)

ADRIATIC SEA

DALMATIA

SAVOY

Geneva

Milan

Turin

Pavia

Genoa

Mantua

Modena

Ferrara

VENICE

Venice

Pisa

Florence

FLORENCE

Siena

SIENA

STATE OF THE CHURCH

Rome

Benevento

Naples

NAPLES

MEDITERRANEAN SEA

Palermo

SICILY
(To Aragon)

ITALY
IN THE
RENAISSANCE

SCALE OF MILES

0   50   100   150   200

The most promising elements, both politically and culturally, in this complicated situation were the north and north-central towns. They had won their independence and overflowed with vigor. Unfortunately, however, like the Greek cities of antiquity, neither could they keep the peace with one another nor maintain an indispensable minimum of internal harmony. Consequently a double movement was soon manifest among them: the large towns swallowed up their small neighbors, and all towns, large and small, becoming a prey to domestic faction, tended to fall under the rule of some bold adventurer who seized the government by military force. Thus in the course of the Renaissance the city-state of Milan came to embrace all Lombardy, while Venice and Florence, as powerful as they were restless and ambitious, achieved a position of corresponding eminence in the provinces respectively of Venetia and Tuscany. Around 1450 the towns of Milan, Venice, and Florence exercised such sway that only the State of the Church, dominated by the pope, and the kingdom of Naples could be compared with them. These five outstanding states ruled the politics of Italy; and while some ancient lords, such as the dukes of Savoy and Ferrara, survived as representatives of the older feudal order, they brought little effective power to bear on the situation. Let us take a closer view of the five leading states.

Emergence of five leading states

Milan

Even before Milan acquired the control of Lombardy by subjecting the neighbor-cities to her rule, her local government had undergone the typical transformation from free republic to military despotism. It was the penalty the citizens had to pay for being unable to bring their local difficulties to an amicable settlement. The first despot was a member of the local house of the Visconti, which by its bold and unscrupulous conduct succeeded in making its power permanent. In sign thereof a ruler of the house took the title duke and converted his state into a duchy. In 1447 the last Visconti died without male heirs. Thereupon the city reasserted its freedom, but, lacking the energy to carry out its purpose, it was in 1450 obliged to accept a new despot, the *condottiere* (leader of mercenaries), Francesco Sforza. Like the Visconti rulers before him, Sforza fastened his power on the state. The second ducal line set up a brilliant court at Milan and entered with zest into the political rivalries of the peninsula.

The ruling houses of Visconti and Sforza

Venice

From early medieval times it was clear that the city of Venice was destined to play a large role not only in Italy but throughout the Medi-

terranean area. A sea-city, planted among the islands of the Adriatic
lagoons, she was secure from attack by land, while her position at the
very center of the Mediterranean world imposed upon her, as it were by
a decree of nature, the part of intermediary in the steadily mounting
commerce between east and west. Not only did her alert merchants
succeed in almost completely monopolizing the rich trade of the Levant,
but in order to make their position impregnable they built up a colonial
empire in the eastern waters. At its height this empire included the
long Dalmatian coast line, the large islands of Corfu, Crete, and Cyprus,
and a vast body of small islands of the Aegean sea, which in their sum
made up an unbroken chain of posts stretching all the way across the
waters of the eastern Mediterranean. When the poet Wordsworth, reviewing the medieval greatness of Venice, began a sonnet to her with
the words, "Once did she hold the gorgeous east in fee," he said no more
than the bare truth.

Venice founds a maritime empire

But their colonial empire did not suffice the ambitious traders of the
island-city hailed Queen of the Adriatic. Desiring to secure the passes of
the Alps, indispensable for their trade with Germany, they began an
expansion movement on the continent; and at the very time when
neighboring Milan was consolidating her rule in Lombardy, the Vene-
tians set up the banner of their patron saint, St. Mark, throughout the
northeastern province of the peninsula, the province of Venetia. Already
deeply involved in the politics of the eastern Mediterranean, the City
of the Lagoons by this acquisition became enmeshed also in the territorial rivalries of Italy.

Venice becomes an Italian land power

Venetian domestic government constitutes a unique Italian instance.
The explanation of this uniqueness is that the merchants, who had built
up the wealth and greatness of the city, were firmly resolved that the
political control should not pass from their hands. In this purpose they
were aided by the circumstance that, pre-eminently commercial, Venice
never developed a numerous industrial proletariat. In consequence of
the weakness of the common people the merchants succeeded not only
in gradually eliminating the democratic features originally embodied
in the Venetian constitution, but also in setting themselves up as a
dominant hereditary oligarchy. It was in 1297 that they carried the
culminating measure in this development. Called "Closing of the Grand
Council," it declared that the government should be vested permanently
in the citizens who in that year were members of the Grand Council and
in their descendants.

The Venetian government a merchant oligarchy

Naturally the limited number of families thus exalted above their fellow citizens thenceforth designated themselves as noble. Although in
this manner a body of hereditary nobles seated in the Grand Council
became the masters of Venice, the actual administration rested not with

the Grand Council but with the various commissions which the Grand
Council appointed. Of these commissions the so-called Ten so completely overshadowed the others that the Ten may be regarded as the
real rulers of the state. The nominal ruler, however, was the duke or
doge, who, chosen for the term of his life, was held in check by an
elaborate system of constitutional restrictions. In view of her prosperity,
political stability, and, last but not least, her brilliant contribution to
the culture of the Renaissance, Venice may be regarded as probably the
most successful merchant oligarchy in European annals.

Leading political institutions: the hereditary Grand Council, the Ten, and the doge

Florence

The Italian city which economically matched and culturally far outstripped Venice was Florence. In political stability, however, the Tuscan
town made but a poor showing compared with its Adriatic rival. The
explanation lies in the circumstance that Florence, though by no means
eschewing trade, developed primarily as an industrial center and became
densely populated with workingmen engaged, above all, in the manufacture of woolen cloth. At a relatively early time the gilds, around
which the economic life of the town revolved, took over the government
of the city. In point of fact, however, a few large and powerful merchant gilds of bankers and wholesalers acquired the lion's share of the
government, held the lesser or craft gilds in submission by various devices, and effectively kept the common workers from exercising either
economic or political influence by forbidding them to organize.

Florence an unstable merchant republic

In spite of these inner rifts and because of its exceptional passion for
political liberty, Florence retained a republican form of government
longer than any city of Italy. In the long run, however, the class divisions proved disastrous. In the first half of the fifteenth century a local
family of merchants and bankers of the name of Medici succeeded in
organizing a political machine, which, while respecting the established
forms, took over the government by underground manipulations. The
Medici system was much like that of a present-day American city "boss,"
with, of course, the considerable difference that the Medici bosses succeeded in making their control hereditary. It was a Medici ruler of the
third generation, Lorenzo by name, who first openly asserted his power.
This Lorenzo (d. 1492), called the Magnificent, was an intelligent and
gifted statesman, besides being a poet and a patron of poets, philosophers,
and artists. But even he so far continued to respect the vigorous republican tradition as to refrain from taking a title such as prince or duke.

Merchant rule replaced by the Medici

The State of the Church

How the pope, head of western Christendom, slowly built up a tem-
Uncertain poral dominion around the city of Rome is an impressive chapter of
control by medieval history. For us it will suffice to note that the gradual failure
the popes of the imperial power in Italy clinched the papal claim to territories
of their which extended from south of the river Tiber in an northeasterly direc-
temporal tion all the way across the Apennine mountains to the Adriatic sea. The
dominion papal dominion proved difficult to rule, as it was made up in part of
small hill-towns bent on independence, in part of feudal lords securely
ensconced in inaccessible castles. Even when, at the height of his power,
the pope issued commands to all the monarchs of Europe, his control of
his immediate dominion was most precarious; and when, at the beginning of the fourteenth century, he abandoned Rome for Avignon, entering on what is known as the Babylonian Captivity (1305-1377), his
rule over the State of the Church broke down completely. On the return
of the popes to Rome, in the last quarter of the fourteenth century,
they resolutely took up the plan of at last reducing their Italian dominion to submission. They met with such resistance on the part of hill-
towns and feudal barons that more than a hundred years passed before
the battle was won.

The determination of the popes to consolidate their temporal dominion
The political and to play a role like that of the other Italian rulers was an outstand-
aim of the ing feature of their policy during the fifteenth century. This frank bid
Renaissance for worldly power should not cause us the least surprise. The Renaissance
popes had dawned over Italy and the Renaissance signified, in essence, a passionate turning to earthly values. On the side of politics it prompted state-
building, that is, a more effective organization of government; and with
all the world intent upon this matter it was not possible for the popes,
themselves temporal sovereigns since the early Middle Ages, to remain
politically unconcerned.

But this was not the only effect the Renaissance had on the Roman
The cultural pontiffs. Steeped in the atmosphere of their age, they took up humanism
aspect of and gloried in the patronage of literature and the arts. Certainly from
the Renais- Nicholas V (d. 1455) to Leo X (d. 1521) we encounter a succession of
sance popes popes who are so characteristic of their time that we may think of them
as constituting a distinct Renaissance series. Considered as a body, they
desired to enjoy life on the same terms as any other Renaissance despot;
their chief political concern was to consolidate their Italian state; and in
order to acquire the means wherewith to maintain a splendid court, to
build palaces and churches, and to exercise a liberal patronage of scholars

and artists they did not scruple to lay heavy financial burdens on clergy and laity alike throughout the vast extent of the Catholic church.

Although the Renaissance popes often appear in a most agreeable personal light, it is also true that some of them, mastered by their worldly passions, fell into degrading excesses. The worst of them was without any doubt Alexander VI (1492-1503), a Spaniard of the family name of Borgia. Without crediting all the ferocious scandal which circulated concerning him in his own time, it remains undeniable not only that he indulged himself in every sensual pleasure but also that he monstrously abused his power by employing it to advance the fortunes of his many illegitimate children. The most famous of these was his son, Caesar Borgia. As gifted and courageous as he was morally debased, Caesar entertained the impudent idea of acquiring the State of the Church with the consent of his father as his personal possession. Not impossibly he might have carried through his audacious project, had his father not died prematurely. *Alexander VI and Caesar Borgia*

Like and yet very unlike Alexander were his successors, Julius II (1503-1513) and Leo X (1513-1521), the latter a son of the Florentine ruler, Lorenzo the Magnificent (Medici). The special political merit of Julius II was that he at last completed the reduction of the State of the Church to papal obedience, while both he and Leo X are memorable as lavish patrons of the arts. Two actions of Julius II will always be held in esteem: he laid the foundations of the new St. Peter's at Rome and, drawing Michelangelo and Raphael into his service, he commissioned the former to paint the Sistine chapel frescos, the latter the Vatican frescos, and thus sponsored two of the noblest monuments of the whole Renaissance period. *Pope Julius II*

Compared with the forceful Julius, Leo X presents himself to view as a cultured, easy-going voluptuary. He is sufficiently characterized by his cheery invitation to his intimates, on the occasion of his elevation to the chair of St. Peter, to help him to "enjoy the papacy." Although he was a pope not very different in worldly outlook from his immediate predecessors, it was perhaps not entirely an accident that the protest against the Renaissance papacy, which in recent decades had been gathering momentum in northern Europe, came to a head during his reign. *Pope Leo X*

The Kingdom of Naples

The southernmost of the Italian states was structurally so different from the others that, except geographically, it hardly seemed to belong to the peninsula. It was a feudal state governed by a king set over a body of unruly barons and, besides Naples, the capital, hardly boasted any city of note. Consequently the urban movement, which had in- *A feudal survival* wardly and outwardly transformed the Italian north, had left the south-ern kingdom essentially unaffected, permitting it to retain its medieval social and political organization right through the Renaissance. In fact the Renaissance hardly made itself felt in the south except in the field of letters.

The disputed Neapolitan succession leads to the French inva-sion of 1494

If the kingdom constituted a conservative, relatively unchanging me-dieval society, its size gave it such power that it counted heavily in Italian politics. After having been held by a succession of three dynasties the crown passed in the fifteenth century to still another dynasty, which hailed from Aragon in Spain. However, as certain French relatives of the immediately preceding dynasty put forth a claim to Naples, based on ties of blood, there followed a long and cruel conflict between the house of Aragon, in possession, and the French pretenders of the house of Anjou. In 1481 the last Anjou pretender died, leaving all his claims to the crown of France. For over a decade the claim was permitted to slumber. Then, in 1494, the reigning French king, Charles VIII, be-thought himself of his Neapolitan rights and made them the basis of an invasion of Italy. That invasion, as we shall see, changed the face of the peninsula and, to a not inconsiderable measure, also of Europe.

GERMANY OR THE HOLY ROMAN EMPIRE

Revival of the ancient Roman Em-pire under the name of the Holy Roman Empire

What determined the history of Germany in the Middle Ages more than any other one thing was that by the coronation of its king, Otto I, as emperor, it became involved in the attempt to revive the Roman Empire. The event took place at Rome in 962 A.D. An earlier attempt at revival had been made some hundred and sixty years before by the great Frank king, Charlemagne, whom the pope had crowned at Rome as Roman emperor in the year 800. However, under Charle-magne's feeble successors this attempt suffered complete shipwreck. When Otto I made a second attempt at revival on a more limited scale, he had a better success. The Roman Empire, which he brought again to life, lasted for many centuries but, owing to its close association with the church, it came, with a queer note of extravagance to our modern ears, to be designated as the Holy Roman Empire.

The Holy Roman Empire, composed originally of Germany and Italy, is reduced to Germany alone

For several generations after its creation, the Holy Roman Empire presented itself to view as the leading European power. Never, however, in spite of its pretension to European paramountcy, did it comprise more than the central area made up of Germany and Italy. Then, when in the thirteenth century, following the crushing defeat of the house of Hohen-staufen, Italy in effect repudiated the imperial connection, the Holy Roman Empire became substantially restricted to Germany. Thenceforward the Holy Roman Empire and Germany may be regarded as interchangeable terms.

Viewed in his original role of German king, the emperor figured in Germany as a distinguished sovereign of the limited feudal type. But his long and losing fight in Italy reacted disastrously on his position in Germany. For, on finding him engaged to his full strength in Italy, his German vassals had obliged him to pay for the military help he demanded with ever increasing political concessions to themselves. At about the time that he lost Italy outright (1250), he had been reduced, so far as Germany was concerned, to a puppet ruler. A hundred years later the great feudal lords resolved to perpetuate their triumph in a constitutional document. From its official seal (*bulla*) it has received the name of the Golden Bull (1356). **Decline of the emperor's power**

The domestic situation defined by the Golden Bull is illuminating, especially in the matter of the emperor's dependence on the great lords. Elected in the past by the whole baronage, he was now made the nominee of a select body of the seven greatest princes of the realm. Of this number, three, the archbishops of Mainz, Trier, and Cologne, were ecclesiastical princes, while four, the king of Bohemia, the duke of Saxony, the margrave of Brandenburg, and the count palatine of the Rhine, were lay lords. On the demise of an emperor these seven, who assumed the expressive title of electors, met and elected a new emperor. The successful candidate became and, properly, took the title, German king. However, looking on himself from the day of his election as also the Holy Roman emperor, he exercised the greatly reduced rights still pertaining to that office. He did this in spite of the theory by the terms of which he was not supposed to be invested with the Roman title till he had been crowned in Rome at the hands of the pope. **The seven electors**

Another feature connected with the Golden Bull was that the traditional legislative and administrative dependence of the emperor on the feudal assembly, called the *Reichstag* or diet, was confirmed and strengthened. The diet was composed of two houses, an upper house of the seven electors and a lower house of the lesser barons, lay and ecclesiastical. But as, in the period after the Golden Bull, those cities which had won self-government under the designation of free imperial cities were constituted as an additional house, the German Reichstag in its final form was composed of three houses. **The diet or Reichstag of three houses**

By this constitution the German king whom, in accordance with universal practice, we shall always designate emperor, was incapable of taking any action without the consent of all three houses; and as two of the houses were made up of feudal magnates bent on playing the master in their respective territories, it was clear that the emperor was sure to be kept in close bondage. He was in point of fact left without **Impotence of the emperor** army, navy, administration, and taxes and became no better than a graven image draped for merely decorative purposes in the mantle of royalty. While the *form* of a united Germany was maintained, to all practical intents the rights of sovereignty had been taken over by the members of the three houses, called the estates of the realm. Thus Germany was broken up, or at least entered on a phase preliminary to being broken up, into several hundred little sovereignties.

The German nationalist movement of Maximilian's time fails

Toward the end of the fifteenth century, as a result of the breath of nationalism which had begun to stir in Europe, an attempt was made to revive the power of the emperor. The nationalist sentiment was strong enough to create a party of constitutional reform within the Reichstag itself. Putting its strength behind the young and popular Maximilian, who had mounted the German throne in 1493, it developed an ambitious program. Owing however to the persistent separatist tendencies, the program in the long run came to nothing. True, a few measures were adopted which gave Germany a superficial appearance of unity. The old feudal right of private warfare was abolished by a proclamation of perpetual internal peace; a supreme national tribunal was established as a court of last resort under the name *Reichskammergericht;* and a tentative step was taken toward a national administration by dividing the country into ten districts (*Kreise*) to serve as a frame for future military and financial measures. But as the emperor was endowed neither with an army nor taxes nor officials of any kind, Germany remained, as before, impotent, unrespected, and disorganized to the point of chaos.

Emperor Maximilian, 1493-1519

The Emperor Maximilian (1493-1519) belonged to the house of Hapsburg, established in the old east mark of Bavaria, called Austria. Possessing a mobile mind and hospitably disposed to the cultural influences emanating from Italy, he continued nonetheless to be so greatly dominated by medieval dreams of chivalry that his contemporaries, perhaps with derisive intent, called him "the last knight." Driven by contradictory emotions, he steered an uncertain and quixotic course and by a long string of failures proved himself one of the poorest politicians that ever lived.

Greatness of the house of Hapsburg due to two marriages

In partial correction of these fiascos a matrimonial program, projected by Maximilian's father and extended by the son, succeeded in the course of two generations in raising the house of Hapsburg to a leading position in Europe. In 1477 Maximilian himself was joined in wedlock to Mary of Burgundy, heiress of the Netherlands, one of the busiest and wealthiest areas of Europe. Then, in 1496, the son of this union, Philip, married another and even greater heiress, Joan, daughter of Ferdinand and Isabella of Spain. The oldest-born of this latter match, Charles by name, represented the junction of three great reigning houses and in due course entered upon possession of Austria, the Netherlands, and Spain. (See genealogical table at head of Chapter 5.)

In 1519 "the last knight" ended an inglorious career. When thereupon the electors raised Charles, who took the title Charles V, to the imperial dignity, it may have seemed to superficial observers as if the dimmed glories of the Holy Roman Empire were about to be brilliantly renewed. But if Charles's reign, which was destined to be filled with the uproar of the Reformation, proved that he was a powerful monarch, it also proved that he was strong, not by reason of any power conferred on him by Germany and the imperial office, but solely because he commanded the immense resources represented by the lands of which he was master by right of inheritance. Pre-eminent among these was Spain.

Emperor Charles V

SPAIN

While the Spanish people were still in an early formative stage, they suffered the crushing blow of being conquered by the Mohammedan Moors from across the straits in Africa. The event occurred in the eighth century. The victory of the followers of Allah and his Prophet was so complete that only in the shelter of the northern mountains did scattered Christian groups manage to maintain themselves in freedom. Before long, however, these groups took courage, advanced against the enemies of both their country and their faith, and slowly pushed them southward toward their African homeland.

Gradual liberation of Spain from Moslem rule

On the liberated territory a number of Christian states took shape which, though gravely hampered by jealousy, on the whole tended to act together against the hated infidel. In the course of time, the Christian states, possessing alike a feudal and military character, were reduced in number either by conquest or matrimonial alliance. The result was that by the second half of the fifteenth century two of them, Castile and Aragon, dominated the situation. It was now only necessary for Isabella, heiress of Castile, to marry Ferdinand, heir of Aragon, for the country's lost unity to be substantially restored (1479).

Union by marriage of Castile and Aragon

Owing to the emergence along the Atlantic coast of the state of Portugal, the fusion into a single political unit of all the states of the peninsula was made difficult to the point of improbability, because the inhabitants of Portugal gradually developed a national consciousness of their own. However, as Portugal comprised less than one-fifth of the total Iberian area, the peninsula was not prevented from becoming preponderantly Spanish.

Portugal

The states of Castile and Aragon owed their greatness to the fact that by accepting as their mission the expulsion of the Moors from the peninsula they served as rallying-points for the national and religious sentiment

of the Spaniards. Therefore no sooner had Ferdinand and Isabella become a royal pair than they turned their combined arms against Granada,
the last foothold maintained in the peninsula by the Moors. In the year
1492 they completed the difficult work of conquest. It was a triumph such
as only a few sovereigns have ever tasted, for it meant the final disappearance of a power which had exercised a hateful, alien rule for almost
eight centuries.

The conquest of Granada

But if the state of the Moors vanished, the Moors themselves did not.
In certain sections, chiefly along the southern coast, they constituted a
leading urban element, while agriculture too, in which they had distinguished themselves by the introduction of an efficient system of irriga-
tion, gave a livelihood to many thousands of their faith and blood. Nor
should their contribution to philosophy, science, and art be overlooked.
The religious and racial situation of the country was still further complicated by the presence in most towns of flourishing communities of
Jews. In an effort to propitiate these two alien groups they had originally
been treated with great liberality. In fact, they had even been endowed
with formal charters guaranteeing their separate rights.

The Moors and Jews of Spain

During the long-drawn-out war for the conquest of Granada a wild
Christian and national fanaticism flared up among the Spanish people
which demanded nothing less than the forcible conversion of both Jews
and Moors to the ruling faith or, in lieu of conversion, their expulsion
or death. Clergy, nobility, and common people shared this fiery intolerance, which reached the height of its expression in an institution with an
evil fame, the Inquisition.

The rising tide of Christian intolerance

The Inquisition took the form of a central governing committee, with
branches in all the provinces of Spain, charged to ferret out heretics and
infidels to the end either of bringing about their conversion or, in case
of refusal, of visiting an exemplary punishment upon them. Avowedly
a Christian institution, it pursued a policy which was quite as much
political as it was religious, since its purpose was to consolidate the state.
The mainly political character of the Spanish Inquisition is put beyond
dispute by the fact that it was subjected to the crown and that the pope's
control was entirely eliminated.

The Spanish Inquisition

At the head of the institution was the Grand Inquisitor, and under the
first incumbent, Tomás de Torquemada, who held the office from 1483
to 1498, some two thousand persons suffered death by fire and some
tens of thousands were sentenced to prison terms and money fines. Rather
than submit to an uncontrolled tyranny innumerable families of self-
respecting and well-to-do Jews and Moors fled the country. It is undeniable that Protestants have frequently exaggerated the horrors of the
Spanish Inquisition. However, Protestant and Catholic scholars alike are
agreed concerning the economic and intellectual injury suffered by Spain

Organization and work of the Inquisition

THE UNIFICATION
OF FRANCE

Fiefs resumed by the crown
in the time of Louis XI and
Charles VIII.

SCALE OF MILES
0   50   100   150   200

THE UNIFICATION
OF SPAIN

SCALE OF MILES
0   50   100   150   200

through the suppression of the two racial elements which constituted the most alert groups of the peninsula. It may also not be overlooked that the Spaniards developed a settled intolerance and a narrow national pride which made them the people of Europe perhaps least responsive to the expansive forces inherent in Western civilization.

The succession passes from Ferdinand and Isabella to Charles
Queen Isabella, a resolute, gracious, and deeply religious woman, who died in 1504, was survived twelve years by her husband Ferdinand, a remarkably capable but harsh and unscrupulous ruler. Owing to the death of their only son, the crown was destined to pass to their daughter Joan, who in 1496 had been married to Philip of Hapsburg, son of Emperor Maximilian. As Philip died in 1506 and Joan was adjudged insane and therefore unfit to rule, the successor of the famous unifiers of Spain was the oldest issue of the Hapsburg marriage, Charles. When on the death of Ferdinand in 1516 Charles assumed the crown, he was but sixteen years old.

The king and the cortes
To understand Charles's role in Spanish history we must grasp the constitutional position to which he fell heir. In medieval times, the monarchy, both in Castile and Aragon, had exhibited the usual feudal character, that is, the sovereign had ruled in either kingdom with the advice of a baronial assembly, called the *cortes*. As early as the thirteenth century the commoners of Castile, the larger and more important of the two kingdoms, had risen to such consideration by charters of self-government issued to their towns that representatives of the towns were admitted to the cortes. Unfortunately the promise contained in this broadening of the parliamentary system was not realized, for the long-continued struggle with the alien Moors so violently inflamed the national sentiment that it rallied enthusiastically around its visible symbol, the king.

The movement of royal centralization
In consequence of this popular favor the king of Castile was able to extend his administrative and judicial system, to maintain a permanent armed force, and to insinuate his tax-gatherers into the towns, although there was no abrogation of the constitutional custom that the taxes had to be authorized by the cortes. The movement toward centralization was subtle and imperceptible but inevitably led to the exaltation of the king, whose person served as the focus of the constantly multiplying administrative activities. In short, although the cortes of Castile—and the cortes of Aragon as well—continued to function with all their traditional rights apparently intact, there fell across them the constantly lengthening shadow of the king.

During the reign of Ferdinand and Isabella there took place so memorable a territorial expansion that it may under no circumstances be overlooked. If it was Castilian Isabella, who, by putting her faith in Columbus, acquired a title to the new world beyond the Atlantic, it was her Aragonese husband who pushed Spanish influence in the opposite direction, that is, eastward into the Mediterranean. Not that Ferdinand was the originator of this policy, for long before his time his ancestors had spread their power from the Balearic Islands to Sardinia and Sicily, until at length (1435) a member of the royal line had mounted the throne of Naples.

Enormous expansion of Spanish power under Ferdinand and Isabella

In this eastward thrust was implied a possible control of Italy which Ferdinand, one of the most grasping sovereigns of his day, was not likely to overlook. In consequence, when Charles VIII of France tried to seize Naples for himself (1494), he at once encountered a most lively opposition from neighboring Spain. We shall presently look into the Franco-Spanish conflict which ensued; but in connection with this summary of Spanish territorial growth we may anticipate the outcome by noting that Ferdinand more than held his own against his French rival. In 1504 he acquired the kingdom of Naples for himself. And shortly before he died he took over (1512) the southern or Spanish section of the small mountain kingdom of the Pyrenees known as Navarre.

Ferdinand challenges the attempted French control of Italy

FRANCE

So successful was the French monarchy in initiating a process of consolidation at the expense of the feudal barons that, as early as the thirteenth century, it stood out as the most effective government in Europe. Then, in the fourteenth century, began the Hundred Years' War with England, during which France was so badly beaten that the royal power was reduced to a shadow. The abasement of the country at length brought about a great national revival. Led by the heroic maid of Orléans, Joan of Arc, the French people began the task of driving the English invaders back across the channel. For the fighting masses as well as for Joan herself the natural head of the movement of liberation was the king; and though the king, Charles VII (1422-1461) was a man of low capacity and despicable character, he played the role assigned to him by fate and thus substantially restored the prestige and power of his office. By 1453 the English had lost every foot of their French conquest except the port of Calais.

The French monarchy and the Hundred Years' War

Theoretically the French king was, even in the Middle Ages, the source of all authority. In practice, however, his power was limited not only by the great nobles and the church, but also by the Estates General. This was the feudal assembly composed originally of clergy and nobles and strengthened, since the beginning of the fourteenth century, by the addition of representatives from the towns. Since the Estates General bear an undeniable resemblance to the Spanish cortes, the German Reichstag, and the English parliament, it becomes clear that all the

Powers of the Estates General

European states boasted a somewhat similar political structure and developed constitutionally along parallel lines. True, the Estates General convey a rather feeble impression compared with the English parliament; nevertheless, without their consent the king could not collect the *taille,* the tax on land or property constituting his chief revenue.

In 1439 the Estates General, under pressure of the national struggle, divested themselves of their right to vote the land tax and from that moment their fate was sealed. Assured of a regular income, the king created a permanent armed force and was soon beyond the control of his subjects. From the earliest days of history a secure revenue and a standing army have been the foundation of absolute monarchy. If the French people did not protest against the constitutional turn taken under Charles VII, it was, as already indicated, owing to the fact that at the moment no sacrifice seemed too great to purchase liberation from the English yoke. However, almost as much as to the presence of an English army on French soil the monarchy owed its increased power to the conviction of the townsmen that a strong king was the surest means of enforcing the peace of the land against the lawless feudal lords.

It was under Charles's son and successor, Louis XI (1461-1483), called the Spider, that the menace of the great lords which periodically threatened to destroy the monarchy, was so effectively met that the edifice of absolutism was fortified beyond the possibility of destruction. Louis was a conspicuous example of the new order of ruler just coming to the front, whose game was to spin a web as elastic as a spider's (hence his nickname) and to gain his cause by diplomacy rather than by war. He was aided in his purpose by the feudal custom of escheat, under which a fief reverted to the crown on the failure of male heirs. In this manner, on the death (1477) without a son of Charles of Burgundy, Louis acquired Burgundy (the duchy) and Picardy, while by the death (1481) of the duke of Anjou, he laid his hand on the rich patrimony of Anjou, Maine, and Provence. When Louis's successor, Charles VIII (1483-1498), married Anne, the heiress of the duchy of Brittany, he acted in strict accord with his father's policy of absorbing the great semi-independent fiefs by means other than war. The addition of Brittany to the crown practically completed the process of French territorial unification.

In measure as the power of the great nobles diminished, the power of the king grew, chiefly by the multiplication of the instruments of government at his command. He distributed his administrative agents more generally through the land and established beyond challenge the ascendancy of the royal courts of ultimate appeal, called *parlements.* As the Estates General had, in essence, abdicated their power by the perpetual grant of the taille, they were rarely called together after the middle of the fifteenth century and gradually lost prestige. Nor did the church escape the general trend. In 1438, in the Pragmatic Sanction of Bourges, the autonomy of the Gallican (i.e., the French) church had been asserted as against the exclusive control over it claimed by the pope. With the loosening of the papal hold on the French church inaugurated by the Pragmatic Sanction, the way was cleared for the waxing ecclesiastical influence of the king. Accordingly, the king refused to authorize the levy of certain papal taxes, such as the annates; furthermore, he increasingly appointed bishops to office without regard for the claims either of the pope or of the cathedral chapters, which in earlier times had exercised that right.

The constitutional development indicated by the above-enumerated measures is not limited to the reign of Charles VII or Louis XI but extends over the remainder of the fifteenth and continues into the following centuries. Exactly as in Spain the movement, if slow, was sure and its meaning clear—it signified the coming of one-man power, the system of absolutism. *The goal of the king is absolutism*

ENGLAND

The later medieval history of England is dominated by the conquest effected in 1066 by William of Normandy, who became King William I. By this event England gained the benefits of a strong monarchy and was spared some of the worst excesses of feudal self-will. Neither William nor his successors, however, dispensed with the assembly of barons, lay and ecclesiastical, known as the parliament. *Government vested in king and parliament*

By taking advantage of certain difficulties in which some of William's successors became involved, the parliament gradually increased its powers, more particularly under John I, whom it obliged to sign (1215) the famous document, the Magna Charta. By Magna Charta the royal wings were definitely and effectively clipped. *Magna Charta, 1215*

Toward the end of the thirteenth century, in 1295, the parliament was expanded by the admission of representatives of the towns (boroughs). Thus strengthened, it organized in the course of time in two houses. The first house was made up of the great barons, lay and ecclesiastical; the second, of the representatives of the boroughs together with the representatives of the smaller holders of fiefs, called knights. *Lords and commons*

The parliament of two houses proved so effective an organization of the social classes interested in putting a check on the monarchy that the king might have been obliged to renounce most of his royal prerogatives, if a number of sweeping national upheavals had not come to his aid. The earliest of these was the Hundred Years' War with France, which, by inflaming the national sentiment, tended to redound to the *Constitutional development interrupted by the Hundred Years' War*

benefit of the king, the country's natural head in a conflict with a foreign foe.

In spite of brilliant triumphs won in the field, the Hundred Years' War ended disastrously (1453), for the English lost all their gains across the channel except Calais. To make a bad matter worse, under the weak Henry VI (1422-1461) they became entangled in the long civil struggle familiar under the name of the Wars of the Roses. On the surface this was a struggle between two rival claimants to the throne, the house of Lancaster (red rose) and the house of York (white rose). Essentially, however, it was a struggle for loot and power among rival bands of unruly nobles. When the war ended with the victory of Henry Tudor at the battle of Bosworth (1485), England was an exhausted country ready to welcome a dictatorial ruler, provided he brought the domestic peace she passionately longed for.

The long civil war prepares the way for absolutism

The Wars of the Roses were such an upflare of baronial arrogance as England had rarely, if ever, known. The new sovereign, Henry VII (1485-1509), signalized the advent of a new house, the house of Tudor, though through his mother he could claim Lancastrian descent. As he prudently married a princess of the house of York, he could urge the appeasement of the civil brawls on the ground of the convergence in him and his queen of the two rival royal strains. Even with these precautions Henry was repeatedly disturbed by pretenders, who obtained a following among the people by a false claim of a Yorkist origin. All such crises he met with subtlety and adroitness, with traits, in a word, that are rather a modern than a medieval political specialty.

The accession of Henry VII of the house of Tudor

Naturally Henry's political penetration would prompt him to utilize the general exhaustion for the establishment of a strong monarchy of the kind just then triumphantly emerging in France and Spain. Of such a program there would be two outstanding opponents: the great nobles who had made the crown their plaything during the Wars of the Roses and the parliament, which in an earlier period had firmly established its right to a substantial share in the government.

Henry resolves to strengthen the monarchy

In a lifetime of narrowly concentrated effort Henry put a curb on both of his opponents. By a law (Statute of Livery and Maintenance), which deprived the nobles of the right to keep under arms great bodies of retainers, he extinguished the centers of provincial resistance to the royal will. To make assurance doubly sure he established an extraordinary court, the court of Star Chamber. It sat in London under his eye and visited punishment on the recalcitrant nobles as well as on all other malefactors whom the local courts were too feeble to bring to justice.

Henry curbs the nobles by the Star Chamber court

In curbing the parliament Henry took a far less drastic course because the parliament was an integral feature of the English constitution and well entrenched in the affections of the people. With shrewd self-restraint he even adopted a policy of ostensible co-operation with the rival institution. Although he owed his throne to his having been victor in a civil broil, that is, to the fortunes of war, he stirred the representatives of the nation to an enthusiastic response when he requested them to legalize his accession by a formal resolution. Throughout his reign he scrupulously observed the ancient custom by which the king could raise no taxes except with the consent of parliament. Then, with his supplies obtained, he husbanded the returns like a miser in order not to be obliged to demonstrate too frequently his dependence on a popular body. In the last thirteen years of his reign he took counsel with his parliament only twice and, partly out of gratitude for his re-establishment of the domestic peace, it showed no disposition to bring him under control. Henry and the parliament

No doubt the legal claim of parliament to be associated with the king in governing England remained intact. Nonetheless, from failing to appear regularly in London, the parliament tended to fall into oblivion, leaving the king to occupy the national stage alone. All facts considered, it may be safely asserted that Henry Tudor renewed the prestige of the crown and created, certainly not a royal absolutism, but a strong monarchy pointed in that direction. Henry creates a strengthened monarchy

The predecessors of Henry Tudor, although chiefly occupied with the conquest of France, had not failed to concern themselves with the subjugation of the three smaller states nearer home, Wales, Ireland, and Scotland. Their success, while frequently checked, had on the whole been notable. In the thirteenth century the principality of Wales had been brought definitely under the English crown. A hundred years earlier, during the reign of Henry II, Ireland had been invaded and reduced to at least a semblance of vassalage. The characteristic feature of the Irish situation was that the natives were split into numerous autonomous clans incapable of acting together except on rare occasions. Even in these unpromising circumstances the Irish resistance to English rule was vigorous enough to make the English hold on the western island an uncertain, fluctuating affair. Henry VII, cautious by nature and fully occupied with the English domestic situation, contented himself with holding the coastal section around Dublin, called the English Pale, and relegated the task of a sweeping reconquest of the island to his successors. England encroaches on Wales and Ireland

As for Scotland, wars with it had been frequent throughout the Middle Ages, but the Scots and their king had thus far successfully maintained their independence. Without doubt the Hundred Years' War, which had kept England occupied in France for several generations, had favored the northern neighbor. With the Hundred Years' War at an end, it became probable that England would scan the situation beyond the Tweed somewhat more narrowly. The effect of such unsolicited interest would be to prompt the alarmed Scots to draw closer to France. In fact, England and Scotland

the tendency of Scotland and France to stand together was a factor with which Henry had constantly to reckon.

This dangerous position between the French hammer and the Scottish anvil partly explains why Henry VII felt little inclination to renew the traditional struggle with the French monarchy. But it is also true that he had no love of military adventure for its own sake. Of course he did not and could not fail to take a hand in the politics of Europe; and it was natural that he should usually align himself against France. However, as soon as serious conflict or embarrassing expense threatened, he quietly withdrew.

Henry's policy of peace

On the whole, Henry held to the view that his safest policy was to maintain good and even intimate relations with Spain; and in 1501 he gave expression to this opinion in the fashion of the time by arranging a marriage between Arthur, prince of Wales, and Catherine, daughter of Ferdinand and Isabella. When Arthur died shortly after the ceremony, his widow was retained in England with a view to a later marriage to the king's second son, afterward Henry VIII.

Henry seeks the support of Spain by a matrimonial alliance

In a commendable effort to detach Scotland by friendly means from her traditional ally across the channel Henry, in 1502, gave his daughter, Margaret, in wedlock to the Scottish king, James IV. Briefly, the first Tudor was a man of peace. If he kept a sharp lookout toward France he was content, in the main, with such diplomatic measures for keeping France in check as amicable relations with Spain and Scotland.

Henry seeks to bind Scotland to England by a matrimonial alliance

THE INVASION OF ITALY BY CHARLES VIII OF FRANCE AND THE RISE OF THE EUROPEAN POWER SYSTEM

At the end of the fifteenth century there occurred an event which profoundly affected the relation toward each other of all the European states just passed in review. We refer to the invasion of Italy by Charles VIII of France in 1494. Although Charles pretended that he invaded Italy in the interest of his rightful claim to the kingdom of Naples, he was mainly prompted by personal ambition born of the fact that the French monarchy had become so strong that it overflowed like a brimming cup. The invasion astonished the world by proving that Italy, home of humanists and artists and focus of the new culture of the western world, was politically too feeble to offer more than a show of resistance to the new centralized type of monarchy. Had her five most important states stood together, there might have been a different tale to tell; but their incurable jealousies made a united front impossible. Charles marched the whole length of the peninsula without meeting serious opposition, drove the Aragonese incumbent, a relative of King Ferdinand, from the throne of Naples, and crowned himself king.

Charles VIII of France invades Italy (1494) and conquers Naples

That act ended his triumph. King Ferdinand was not the man to let a rival appropriate a garden which he coveted for himself, and, allying himself with as many of the offended Italian states as could be persuaded to join him, he obliged the French king to beat a precipitate retreat. In 1495 Charles stood again on the soil of France with nothing but a few martial memories to show for his lavish expenditure of blood and money.

Charles VIII loses Naples

However, the French king had proved that Italy would fall an easy victim to a strong neighbor with a will to conquer. On the death in 1498 of Charles, his successor, Louis XII, inherited his Italian ambitions; and when, after a reign of seventeen years, Louis was succeeded by Francis I (1515-1547), the new king adopted the same warlike policy. It would be tedious to follow in detail the many Italian campaigns of Louis and Francis and mortally dull to trace the fluctuations of their shifty diplomacy. Let it suffice that France's rival, Spain, was ready to move heaven and earth to hinder the consummation of the French designs, and that in the battle of the two towering contestants the pigmy states of Italy were at first their pawns and, ultimately and inevitably, their victims.

Charles's Italian ambitions taken over by his successors

Although France and Spain were, on the whole, well matched, the scales tended from the first to incline in favor of the latter. As early as 1504 the issue over Naples was settled by its unconditional cession by Louis XII to King Ferdinand. In compensation for this loss the French king hoped to be left in possession of the duchy of Milan, on which he had fixed his eye as more desirable than Naples because nearer to France, and which he had seized (1499) immediately on coming to the throne on the pretext, dearly beloved by the monarchs of his day, of an hereditary claim. But Ferdinand was not minded to leave Louis in possession of Milan either, and in 1512, with the aid of some of the Italian states, succeeded in driving him out. Thereupon the new king, Francis I, on the very morrow of his accession to the throne, returned to the attack and once more gained a lodgment in the Lombard duchy (1515). Shortly after, Ferdinand ended his acquisitive days (1516), leaving the quarrel with France over Italy to his grandson and heir, Charles. How the poor Italian bone was worried by Francis and Charles all the days of their life we shall learn in a later chapter.

The struggle in Italy turns around Naples and Milan

Long before the struggle between France and Spain over Italy was brought to a settlement, it had become plain that the peninsula was a doomed land. Helpless before the might of the two western monarchies, the small Italian states wasted their resources in a frenzied scramble for individual preservation. Their abasement before the invaders availed them nothing, for so long as they failed to create an effective confederation, they were bound one after the other to lose their independence.

Political and cultural decline of Italy

With their liberty gone the Italians would inevitably lose also the intellectual zest which had made the Renaissance such a brilliant national episode. There is no denying that the political knock-out effected by the invasions was attended by a general cultural decline. Hardly noticeable at first, by the middle of the sixteenth century it was apparent to all the world.

In this tragic decline of a whole people the fate of each of the five
Fate of the leading states calls for a passing word. Naples, as we have already heard,
individual became a Spanish dependency as early as 1504. After having been tossed
states about for some decades between France and Spain, Milan went ultimately the same way as Naples. While the republic of Venice and the State of the Church did not, in a technical sense, lose their sovereignty, they were too feeble to play an independent role and followed a shifty policy of turning alternately for protection from France to Spain and from Spain to France. Loss of effective independence was also the lot of Florence; but in the course of its adjustment to the altered peninsular circumstances it experienced so many remarkable vicissitudes that, for their sake and, more even, for the sake of the unique contribution made by this state to the culture of the Renaissance, we shall pass these vicissitudes in brief review.

We have already traced the political fortunes of Florence to the rule
Florence of Lorenzo de' Medici, called the Magnificent. On the heels of Lorenzo
and the Magnificent's death in 1492 came the invasion of Italy by Charles
Savonarola VIII. Taking advantage of the general disturbance of the peninsula, the Florentines rose against Piero, the youthful heir of Lorenzo, drove him and all his family to flight, and again set up a republic. The renewed republic lived for a time in the shadow of the austere Dominican friar, Girolamo Savonarola, and under his hypnotic influence reverted, to a certain extent, to the manners and outlook of the Middle Ages. The flaming religious zeal of Savonarola was directed to two objects, the reform of the loose morals of his fellow citizens and the purification of the Catholic church from the corruption into which it had fallen. While he achieved a measure of very temporary success in respect to the former purpose, he made not even temporary headway with the reform of the church. When we recall that at this time Alexander VI, the Borgia of evil fame, was pope, we shall have no difficulty in agreeing that the feeble and isolated friar was foredoomed to failure in his attempt to cleanse the church of its accumulated abuses. After four years of devoted Christian labor on Savonarola's part, his enemies, civil and ecclesiastical, had grown so strong that they compassed his downfall and burned him at the stake on a trumped-up charge of heresy (1498).

It is a notable fact that the restored Florentine republic was organized on a more democratic basis than its predecessor, destroyed by the Medici.

However, a broader democratic regime would not of itself prove of avail against the situation created by the permanent presence in Italy of the two foreign powers, France and Spain. Obliged to lean on one or the other, the Florentine republic threw in its lot with France. The result was that when King Louis XII went down to defeat (1512), the republic promptly collapsed. With the help of victorious Spain the Medici now returned to the city; and although they were, after fifteen years, again driven out (1527) and the republic again set up, the chances of the new attempt to safeguard the liberty of the Florentines had not improved. Putting their faith in Spain as consistently as the republic had put its faith in France, the Medici, after a memorable siege of Florence, again brought the city under their yoke (1530).

Twice driven from Florence, the Medici twice return

As it had by now become clear that it was useless to kick against the pricks, the citizens grudgingly accepted their native masters, who in their turn accepted the mastery of Spain. In 1532, with the consent of their Spanish protector, the Medicean rulers transformed the conquered Florentine republic into a duchy. Before a generation had passed, the duchy, still under Spanish protection, had expanded into the grand duchy of Tuscany. However, it was not the original Medici line which achieved this honor. On becoming extinct in 1537, the original line was succeeded by a younger branch, which continued to reign in Tuscany till its own extinction in the eighteenth century.

The Florentine republic becomes a duchy ruled by the Medici

During the last passionate attempts of the Florentines to maintain their republic in the midst of an Italy and a Europe in which tyranny was riding to a general triumph, there lived among them for several years as secretary of their government, one of the most penetrating political minds of any age. He was Niccolo Machiavelli; and his importance for the student of history is that he embodied his observations of the political changes of his day in a remarkable treatise called *The Prince* (1516). In this work Machiavelli recognized that the day of republics was, at least for the time being, over, and that the present and the immediate future of Europe belonged to the absolute monarch for the convincing reason that only under him could the state be solidified and the contentious social classes be brought under a common law. In particular he noted that the large successful rulers of his time, such as Ferdinand of Aragon and Louis XII of France, as well as their small Italian counterparts, such as Caesar Borgia, pursued their policy of aggrandizement with complete lack of scruple and that, to gain their end, they indulged in every form of deceit and violence. A policy of this unethical sort has ever since been called Machiavellian, although Machiavelli, far from inventing it, merely described what was going on in his day.

Machiavelli, the theorist of despotism

Besides the effects for Italy of the long struggle for Italian supremacy between France and Spain, there were effects of the greatest importance for Europe in general. To see them in proper historical perspective it is necessary to revert to the Middle Ages and to the idea of the single Christian family which that period cherished. Put forth originally by St. Augustine in his work, *The City of God*, the Augustinian idea in its developed form envisaged a Christian world-state committed to a program of peace and justice under the double guidance of pope and emperor.

Passing of the medieval political ideal

The project of a united Christian commonwealth failed in the course of the Middle Ages and was replaced by an actuality of separate and independent states engaged in stark rivalry with one another for the possession of lands, commerce, and other evidences of material well-being. During the Renaissance these competing civil entities finally and completely disengaged themselves from their medieval chrysalis with the result that the Franco-Spanish conflict over Italy took a form in which there was no longer traceable the smallest vestige of medieval ideology. The wars between France and Spain were not and never pretended to be other than a naked power struggle.

Europe falls into jealous sovereign units

It is therefore plain that toward the end of the Renaissance Europe had become endowed with a new political system which, since it continues to this day, may properly be called the modern system. It is distinguished by an unlimited competition among its component parts, logically culminating in the shock of war. However, even when war is accounted a legitimate tool, it is undoubtedly a weapon of destruction; and the Modern Period which, just beginning to dawn, was dedicated to commerce and industry and the multiplication of wealth, was sure to develop, at least at intervals, a strong aversion against an indiscriminate indulgence in war.

War a legitimate but destructive tool of policy

To conduct their profitable enterprises the burgher classes, with whom the control of society was coming to rest in constantly increasing measure, required peace; and therefore as soon as the patriotic intoxication which war released had evaporated, they welcomed the treaty of peace which muffled the din of battle and at the same time cleared once more the highways and opened the markets. Treaties of peace, though primarily political in character, usually contained also commercial provisions or, in their stead, were supplemented by express treaties of commerce. To be sure, each new war canceled the treaties of every kind existing between the belligerent states; but on the termination of the conflict new treaties, which were the old treaties modified in accordance with the issue of the recent struggle, were promptly negotiated.

War counterbalanced by treaties of peace and commerce

To secure the precise execution of treaties and to maintain profitable relations among sovereign states there were gradually developed two special administrative services, a diplomatic service for political matters and a consular service for commercial affairs. Placed under the super-

Emergence of a diplomatic and a consular service

vision of the department of state or foreign office, the two services, taken together, constituted the administrative machinery for maintaining and developing the relations among states according to current agreement and traditional practice.

The sum of all the treaties negotiated among sovereign states for any end whatsoever may be thought of as constituting the raw material for the formulation at a later and more reflective day of a body of international law. Although in the sixteenth century this development had not yet begun, it is evident that the mere multiplication of treaties would serve to bind Europe into a single, more and more compactly organized commonwealth. Undeniably, however, so long as each sovereign state, large or small, insisted that it had an inalienable right to bring every difference of opinion or interest to the arbitrament of war, the delicate and infinitely complicated organization of the European states would be periodically exposed to anarchic disorganization. In view of this situation the time was bound to come when advanced and humanitarian thinkers would search the mass of international treaties and practices for an underlying principle or principles which would serve to lift the conduct of states to a higher moral level than mere self-interest. Whenever that moment should come international law in a technical and theoretic sense would have seen the light of day. *Treaties serve to bind the European states together*

Although this emerging modern system comprised all states, great and small alike, only the powerful states, powerful in last analysis because of their military and naval strength, figured in the system as great powers. With them during the last four centuries has rested the control of Europe and, in measure as Europe has expanded overseas, the control of the rest of the world. However, as each great power has been unceasingly engaged in the attempt to outstrip its rivals, there has developed the curious phenomenon called the balance of power. *The great powers and the balance of power*

Balance of power comes into play when one great power, either by reason of its actual resources, or by an alliance with other powers, or by attaching to itself a group of lesser client states, achieves a position which points to or seems to point to domination. Automatically its opponents draw together in order to redress the scales—a complicated diplomatic operation touching which enlightening evidence was supplied during the Franco-Spanish wars. Whenever in the struggle for the Italian prize France was in the ascendancy, there was an immediate rush on the part of the other powers of Europe to come to the aid of Spain. Whenever Spain was in the lead the rush was the other way. *How the balance of power operates*

To the reflective reader it must now be reasonably clear that with organized diplomatic and consular services and with multiplying international treaties supplemented by the principle of balanced power Europe should be conceived as a single commonwealth. Such unity as this commonwealth possessed was, however, under constant challenge and on occasion was completely nullified by the claim of each member-state to an unlimited sovereignty culminating in the right of war. Before a more effective commonwealth than this was possible the individual European citizen would have to learn to think in terms of Europe rather than in terms of the country of his particular allegiance. That time in the sixteenth century was still far away. Indeed it may be doubted if even yet, in this, the twentieth century, it has dawned for more than a small and widely scattered band, the hopeful vanguard of a new political order.

Europe a single but imperfect commonwealth

5 | THE GERMAN REFORMATION TO THE PEACE OF AUGSBURG (1555)

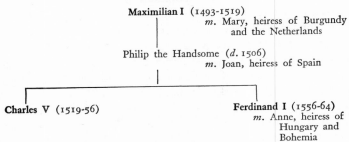

THE HOUSE OF HAPSBURG

Maximilian I (1493-1519)
m. Mary, heiress of Burgundy
and the Netherlands

Philip the Handsome (*d.* 1506)
m. Joan, heiress of Spain

Charles V (1519-56)

Ferdinand I (1556-64)
m. Anne, heiress of
Hungary and
Bohemia

WE HAVE LEARNED that Germany, in the course of a long series of medieval happenings, had become effectively identified with the Holy Roman Empire, called the Empire for short. We have also learned that the Empire was a loose federation of several hundred semi-sovereign states, and that in the reign of the Emperor Maximilian (1493-1519) it experienced something of a national awakening which, however, did not in any essential respect strengthen the feeble central government. The national awakening was itself an effect of the stimulation that came to all sections of Europe alike with the Renaissance. Only a somewhat detailed analysis of the particular stir which the Renaissance brought to Germany will enable us to grasp the origin of the great sixteenth century movement of religious revolt called the Reformation. *The Renaissance a forerunner of the Reformation*

By way of introduction to both Renaissance and Reformation let us examine the implications of the unshaken domination in Germany, and almost alone in Germany, of the church. We are aware that the deep Middle Ages were so thoroughly dominated by the church that its head, the pope, was able to proclaim the theory that, since all power came from God and he himself was God's earthly vicar, all government, civil as well as ecclesiastical, was of right vested in his person. True, the doctrine of papal supremacy in this, its extreme form, never enjoyed general acceptance and hardly, if at all, hindered the European monarchs from asserting their independence in the civil field. Nonetheless, during the Middle Ages the church was so generally free from interference by the state that *The popes exercise powers which prejudice the rights of civil rulers*

91

it succeeded in placing itself in all essential respects outside the national frame. When we further consider that the pope, as head of the church, exercised a very substantial control over each national ecclesiastical establishment, we shall agree that he rose in every country to a co-ordinate position with the monarch, since he exercised sovereignty in the monarch's territory, chiefly by laying taxes on ecclesiastical property and by controlling the higher ecclesiastical appointments.

Decline of the pope's power in the absolute monarchies

When, during the Renaissance, powerful monarchies developed in France, Spain, and England, they undertook to challenge the pope's power exercised within their boundaries. In each instance they scored successes, which, if incomplete, showed that the wind had veered and was now no longer filling the pope's sails. Thus, in France, King Charles VII issued (1438) a royal ordinance, known as the Pragmatic Sanction of Bourges, challenging the papal pretensions to control the French church; and, letting the deed follow the boast, he and the rulers after him took over the nomination of the French bishops and abbots. In this way they successfully usurped a power to which the popes had never ceased to pretend. In Spain, under Ferdinand and Isabella, the crown took over (1482) the right to nominate to bishoprics and forbade appeals from the Spanish ecclesiastical courts to Rome; while in England by the repeatedly renewed statutes of Provisors (1351) and of Praemunire (1353), a similar anti-papal policy had taken shape. The former measure denied the pope's claim to appoint to English clerical dignities, the latter forbade the carrying of judicial appeals outside the realm, that is, to the pope.

Abuses of papal power in Germany

In Germany, where, in distinction from the western monarchies, the crown instead of growing stronger had, especially during the long reign of Emperor Frederick III (1440-1493), become steadily more feeble, a concordat, signed at Vienna in 1448, had confirmed the pope in the very rights the western monarchies had denied him. Consequently the popes of this century still exercised the same extensive powers in Germany as in the Middle Ages. Not content with this advantage, they, or at least some of them, adopted practices which, even when authorized by custom, aroused general indignation. They accepted money from candidates to office, which was the sin of simony; they taxed the clergy by a frequent levy of tithes on the pretext of a crusade against the Turks which never materialized; and they unflinchingly exacted annates or first fruits. The impost called annates involved the surrender of one-half of his revenues during the first year of office on the part of each new episcopal incumbent.

The German Reichstags of the second half of the fifteenth century never ceased voicing their condemnation of these abuses by detailed complaints dispatched to Rome. Quietly pigeonholed on their arrival, they proved no more effective than if they had been messages from another

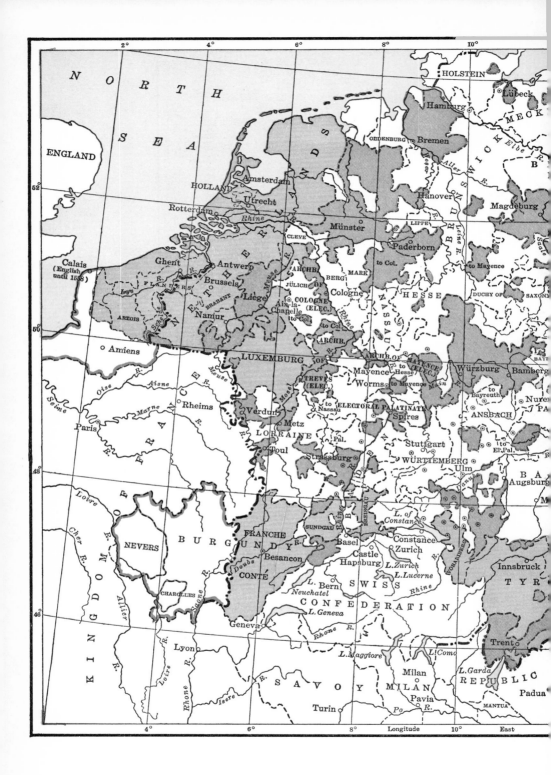

GERMANY

on the Eve of

THE REFORMATION

0   20   40   60   80   100

SCALE OF MILES

━━ ∙ ━ ∙ ━ Boundary of Holy Roman Empire

━ ━ ━ ━ ━ Boundary of the States of the Empire

Hapsburg Territories

Ecclesiastical Territories (Archbishoprics, bishoprics, abbacies)

NOTE TO THE STUDENT:

1) Locate the territories of the seven electors (four of them lay lords, three of them ecclesiastical lords). 2) Note the numerous territories (lavender) held by bishops and abbots. 3) Note that the territories at the southern and western periphery (Milan, Savoy, Swiss Confederation, Netherlands) had already practically broken away from the Empire. 4) Note that the Burgundian territories which fell to the house of Hapsburg by marriage are largely Empire, that is, German fiefs; however, Artois and Flanders are French fiefs. 5) The territory left white in southern and western Germany is the main region of political atomization and is divided among many scores of small princes and free cities.

planet. In this connection it is necessary never to forget that this was the period of the Renaissance group of popes who, in the main indifferent to spiritual matters, desired money and ever more money to satisfy their political ambitions and their sumptuous patronage of the arts. Since such men were likely to have an easy conscience where their revenues were concerned, they agreed to every shifty measure for filling the treasury which their unscrupulous financial advisers might suggest. One of these measures was the sale of indulgences. While it would be excessive to say that indulgences "caused" the Reformation, they undoubtedly were the occasion of its outbreak. Repeated complaints of the German Reichstags dispatched to Rome

Who would understand what is meant by an indulgence must be willing to have a look at the rather abstruse world of medieval theology and, more particularly, to scan the sacrament of penance.[1] The sacrament of penance dealt with acts of sin which God was ready to forgive the sinner on contrition and confession. Absolution by the priest was evidence of the divine forgiveness. However, before the forgiveness was complete in all respects, the sinner was obliged to "satisfy," that is, to pay the temporal penalty he had incurred by reason of his sinful act. The usual form of payment was a deed of Christian charity classifiable as a good work. Indulgences and the sacrament of penance

It is here that the indulgence comes in. An indulgence is a remission of the temporal penalty by means of the Treasure of Grace, defined as the sum of the merits of Jesus Christ and the great company of saints and martyrs. The Treasure of Grace came into existence because the founders and confessors of the Christian faith offered much more satisfaction (that is, submitted to much heavier penalties) than was required by the few sins they may have committed. All good works in excess of the amount required to balance each individual account are called works of supererogation and comprise the Treasure of Grace. It is administered by the pope, who may at his discretion apply it to the benefit of others lacking in good works. The document declaring the remission of the temporal penalty by a draft on the unexhausted and inexhaustible treasure of the church is called an indulgence. An indulgence a draft on the Treasure of Grace

Conceding that the theory of indulgences offers serious intellectual difficulties to many people of our day, we may yet agree that it so closely conformed to the ruling ecclesiastical ideas that it would have aroused no criticism had it not in its practical application lent itself to abuse. In the Middle Ages the popes issued indulgences with a certain restraint and conscientiously applied the financial returns to approved Christian ends, such as the spread of the faith by either a peaceful mission or a fighting crusade. However, with the coming of the Renaissance the sale of the papal certificates acquired the character of a device for raising taxes. In The abuse of indulgences

[1] See p. 16.

order to stimulate their sale they were consigned to licensed vendors who offered them to the public of every country of Europe, except those from which the vendors were excluded by a strong civil power. Because the pope had more authority in Germany than anywhere else, the hawkers spread themselves with particular freedom over German territory without letting themselves be discouraged by the often bitter criticism they aroused.

Complicated nature of the anti-papal and anti-clerical sentiment

In view of indulgences and the other indicated abuses it is not difficult to understand that the pope, and the German prelates as well who cooperated with the pope, encountered a rising tide of indignation. But unless we understand that this indignation was also fed by considerations of a political and economic order, we shall fail to grasp the complicated nature of the tidal wave which, presently bursting all bounds, swept over the country.

The anti-papal sentiment has both a religious and a national root

By a remarkable combination of circumstances it happened that at the beginning of the sixteenth century the critical attention of the Germans became riveted on the pope and the church from several directions at once. While some groups, the simply and honestly pious of every social level, were quite as much offended, on account of the sumptuous manner of their life, with the great native dignitaries as with the pope and car- dinals, other groups, constituting the growing mass of politically inspired men, directed their enmity exclusively at the distant head of the church. Animated by the new sentiment of country, they saw in him an outsider exercising more influence in their land than the national government of emperor and Reichstag. This body of eager nationalists was recruited largely from the rising burghers; and the burghers were further excited to hostility to Rome by the taxes annually raised in Germany and dispatched across the Alps.

The anti-papal sentiment has also an economic root

To the town dwellers of an age whose expanding economic enterprise called for capital, the steady stream of gold and silver pouring out of Germany caused a veritable nightmare. In raising their voices to stop the movement they found sympathizers among all classes, including even numerous members of the lower clergy. It would be vain to try to decide which of these several motives figured most vigorously in the mounting anti-clerical sentiment. Admitting that the situation was complex, as human situations always are, we would seem to be justified in summing it up by saying that, given the papal and clerical abuses in general, the Renaissance spirit, which reflected the waxing assurance of bold and ambitious townsmen, was certain to protest against them, and that the protest, once launched, would receive reinforcement from the religious, political, economic and every other field of human interest.

Turning from these various discontents to the contemporary intellectual movement of Germany, we are confronted with the phenomenon of

humanism. Originating in Italy and taking the form of a passionate
search among the remains of antiquity for a new foundation of life and How
knowledge, humanism spread gradually to the other regions of Europe German humanism
and, of course, also to Germany. But, as was only natural, the German differs from
humanists reshaped the Italian model in accordance with the national Italian
temperament and outlook. So completely had the Italians identified them- humanism
selves with the new learning that they became scornful of their medieval
heritage. A few of them even carried their pagan enthusiasms so far that
they actually abandoned Christianity. The Germans felt no such inclination. While they might be stimulated by antiquity, they would not be
overwhelmed by it as had been the Italians, to whom it signified a return
to their national tradition. The Christian faith, on the other hand, had
been the introduction of the Germans to Western civilization. It had
taken possession of their souls and, as an unexhausted force, claimed their
sincere devotion. They, therefore, put their own interpretation on the
intellectual stimulus emanating from Italy and, without shutting their
ears to its classical message, preferably directed its energies into purely
Christian channels.

In accordance with this preference the German humanists focused their
attention, first, on the Christian Fathers and, ultimately, on the Bible. German humanism
In measure as they saturated themselves with the sources of Christianity directed to
they became aware of the chasm yawning between the simple practices the sources
of the apostolic age and the splendor of the ecclesiastical establishment of of Christi-
their own time. We are not to imagine that no sooner had they begun anity
their studies than they were persuaded that the church was an unnatural
growth. Themselves steeped in its imposing traditions, they continued to
yield it a willing obedience. Nonetheless, their accumulation of fresh
knowledge about so many phases of the Christian past gradually produced a viewpoint which was very different from the unquestioning belief and submission of their forebears.

The German humanists were a relatively small body of men who
served the usual provocative function of an intelligentsia. Since, after Humanism
some delay, most universities opened their doors to them, the ascendancy gets a foot-
of the inherited scholastic system was gradually shaken. When men like hold in the
Rudolfus Agricola (d. 1485) and Konrad Celtes (d. 1508), who had gone universities
to Italy to imbibe the new learning at its fountainhead, returned to their
native land, they were received with enthusiasm by swarms of students
who crowded to their lectures. Under these circumstances the familiar
battle of conservatives and liberals was soon joined all along the line and
early in the sixteenth century led to a memorable incident. Its central
figure was Johann Reuchlin, in whom we encounter a typical expression
of German humanism.

Like most of the humanists of his time, Johann Reuchlin (1455-1522)

Johann Reuchlin, a typical German humanist

had made firsthand acquaintance with the new intellectual movement by travel and study in Italy. An acknowledged master of both Latin and Greek, nonetheless, by a preference which he shared with most of his countrymen, he turned enthusiastically to the Fathers and from them to the Bible. But no sooner had he plunged into the Christian origins than he became persuaded of the necessity of knowing Hebrew. Not only had this language been neglected, but, owing to the aversion felt in the Middle Ages for the Jews, it was under a general and severe taboo.

The quarrel over Hebrew studies

In 1506 Reuchlin performed an important scholarly service for all Europe by publishing a Hebrew grammar and lexicon. It immediately aroused a storm of reprobation among the old-time schoolmen, whose main German stronghold was the university of Cologne. As this university was in the hands of the Dominican order of friars, identified since the thirteenth century with the scholastic system, the professors sounded the alarm and in violent language put themselves on record against the lifting of the Hebrew ban. At the signal the stalwarts of the old regime gathered under the Dominican banner, while the friends of the new learning rallied around Reuchlin. It was a miniature war, in which the combatants denounced each other in fiery pamphlets, and which culminated in a series of trials for heresy wherewith the exasperated Dominicans attempted to crush the bold champion of Hebrew studies. Appeased only to flare up again, the combat dragged along for ten years and, though tiresome in detail, had the considerable merit of focusing attention on the issue of the freedom of the mind from traditional ecclesiastical control.

The "Letters of Obscure Men"

What usually determines the victory in an intellectual conflict is the swing of educated public opinion. And public opinion, veering slowly toward Reuchlin, was finally almost stampeded into his camp by the *Epistolae obscurorum virorum* ("Letters of Obscure Men," 1515-1517). The work was the product of a group of gay and emancipated spirits, champions of the new learning, and was as telling a satire as the young and impertinent have ever aimed at their grave and stodgy elders. The *Letters* pretended to be communications addressed by students and admirers to one of the Cologne standpatters. The fun lay in having the supposed correspondents reveal by intimate exchanges, composed in an exaggerated version of the grotesque Latin current among schoolmen, their secret viciousness and abysmal ignorance. To be sure, much of the humor was in the nature of rude horseplay; but it did its work and fairly buried the old learning under a tempest of inextinguishable laughter.

Erasmus, the prince of humanists

Although he sympathized with Reuchlin and smiled with characteristic malice at the broad humor of the *Letters,* Desiderius Erasmus (1467-1536) had no hand in their composition. In this remarkable scholar we meet the greatest figure of the humanistic circles of his generation not only in Germany but throughout Europe. Though born at Rotterdam, and therefore a Dutchman by birth, he lived in turn in almost every country of Europe; and not only did he profess himself a cosmopolitan but actually became one by successfully suppressing in himself every distinct national trait. Like all humanists, north and south of the Alps alike, he employed the Latin language as his medium of expression. This tongue was still the language of the educated, whether of the old or the new type, and enabled him to make himself heard throughout the extent of Christendom. In his deepest intent he was a scholar, rarely competent in both the classical and Christian fields and establishing himself as preeminent in each alike by his editions of the ancients and the Fathers. But he was also a reformer and chiefly to this activity owed his wide reputation. His vast indignation over the evils of his age prompted him at times to abandon his study and hold up to ridicule what were to him the false idols of the market place.

Erasmus's most important contribution to Christian, as distinct from classical, scholarship was the publication of the New Testament in Greek, accompanied by a new Latin translation of his own. In this work he exposed the numerous errors of the Latin version of the New Testament which the church had stamped with its approval and incorporated in the official version of the Bible called the Vulgate. The Vulgate dated back to the fifth century and was regarded by conservative theologians as sacred and untouchable. *The Christian scholarship of Erasmus*

While the New Testament of Erasmus is a good illustration of the attempt of northern scholars to put Christian learning on a sound foundation, regardless of what tradition might be upset and whose withers might be wrung, it reveals the equally important attitude of this group toward the Scriptures as the supreme fountain of faith. "I long," Erasmus wrote in explanation of his occupying himself with this fundamental Christian document, "that the peasant should sing the Scriptures to himself as he follows the plow, that the weaver should hum them to the tune of his shuttle, and that the trader should beguile with them the weariness of his journey." This is the quiet evangelical note sounded by him and Reuchlin and the whole body of northern humanists firmly and steadily, but with no frenzied hostility against the prevailing ceremonious ecclesiasticism. Magnified by the succeeding generation to a vast cry, it became the trumpet blast which brought down the walls of Jericho. *The evangelical tendencies of Erasmus*

We have noted that, though Erasmus was in the main a dedicated scholar, his feet were sufficiently planted in the world for him to speak out against its evils. His sharp intelligence put him, in the literary satire, in possession of a weapon which he wielded unsparingly and to the delight of critics and reformers the world over. In his most famous production in this kind, the *Praise of Folly* (1509), he presents Folly as a woman adorned with cap and bells and proudly assembling about her *The "Praise of Folly"* her numerous earthly subjects. Her merry discourse becomes a fierce lashing of the sordid customs of monks, the ignorance of schoolmen, the venality of the clergy, the ambition of kings, and the gross superstition of the masses, in sum, a biting exposure of all the evils of the age.

The humanists do not accept the Lutheran revolt

The Europe which cheered to the echo this attack on its religious, social, and political inheritance was already, even though it might not be conscious of the fact, in the throes of a revolution. To the humanists, champions of the new outlook, the name of Erasmus became a battle cry; and when presently Martin Luther made his appearance and went a step farther by flinging his challenge directly at the church, he counted, not unnaturally, on Erasmus's support. He proved himself mistaken, not only in the single Erasmus but, to a considerable extent, in the whole older generation of humanists; for, though they regarded Luther at first not without favor, as soon as he broke definitely with pope and church, they drew back in alarm. They adopted this course partly because they were timid scholars with a temperamental aversion for the heat and dust of the arena, in greater measure, however, because, as they viewed the situation, they had preached not revolt but reform.

Erasmus in his own opinion and in that of his opponents

More particularly Erasmus, the honored chief of the humanists, had always cherished, futilely perhaps but earnestly, the ancient dream that the spread of sound knowledge would by its own corrective action eradicate the evils from which the world was suffering. His whole lifework was, on its moral side, an advocacy of reasonableness and toleration; and, instead of joining the ranks of violence and revolution, he consistently and resolutely backed away from the Lutheran movement. Protestant writers, who, on this account, have often angrily berated Erasmus as a white-livered knave, fail to do justice to his fundamental conviction that the only reforms which are ever worth while come through gradual enlightenment. Nevertheless, there is a modicum of truth in the pithy summary of the situation credited to a Catholic contemporary: Erasmus laid the egg; Luther hatched it. To bitter, partisan Catholics, Erasmus was no less a criminal than Luther.

Martin Luther turns from law to religion

Martin Luther was born November 10, 1483, in a village of Thuringia at the foot of the Harz mountains. His ancestry for many generations back had been hard-working peasants, and much of peasant sturdiness and simplicity, with much of peasant obstinacy and superstition, remained characteristic of this son of the soil to the end of his days. By personal sacrifices his parents managed to send young Martin to school and later, to the university of Erfurt, where he prepared himself for the law; but in the year 1505, during a thunderstorm which overtook him on the highway and filled him with wild terror, he made the vow to become a monk.

It was a characteristically medieval act inspired by a sense of sin and the need of salvation. Luther joined the Augustinian order of friars, devoting himself with the greatest earnestness to his new duties. In 1507 he was ordained a priest and in due time became a doctor of theology. To crown his labors he was called to a professorship at the university of Wittenberg. This was an institution recently founded by the Elector Frederick of Saxony at the seat of his government. Luther immediately became a leading professor, largely because in the spirit of the new learning he based his instruction not so much on the medieval schoolmen as on the living Christian sources, the Fathers and the Bible.

Luther becomes a professor of theology at Wittenberg

These externals do not touch the inner problem which agitated Luther throughout his early manhood nor do they explain how it happened that he rebelled against the church. To him, as to every sincere Christian, the supreme concern, before which all else shrank to nothingness, was the question of salvation. The medieval church had worked out a solution which was an adjustment between faith and good works; that is, it advocated as the best means to the end in view complete surrender to God's love together with the conscientious performance of the many holy acts (works) enjoined by the sacraments. Neither one way nor the other sufficed by itself to reach the goal. You traveled each way in turn according to the need of the hour and, so proceeding, at last met with your reward.

Luther's inner agony over the question of salvation

Luther tried the traditional Catholic combination, or, according to his Catholic critics, committed the error of trying works too exclusively. His choice left him crushed by an agony of doubt touching his future fate until the certainty came to him like an illumination from on high that God accepted all who confidingly surrendered their individual will into his hands. Not by works but by faith, and faith alone, did sinful man win his way to peace and forgiveness. In this the friar originated nothing new and never claimed he did. He derived his doctrine, in the first instance, from St. Augustine, the great Latin father, and somewhat later, from the impetuous Apostle Paul, in whom Luther discovered a remarkable spiritual kinsman. Faith had therefore the highest authority behind it, as the church for its part in no way denied. Only faith as the one and only road to salvation—that was not a position which a good Catholic, heir of an unbroken and authoritative tradition, could accept.

Luther accepts faith as the only road to salvation

Luther was still far from seeing the many implications of his doctrine concerning faith, he was still searching his two great exemplars, St. Augustine and St. Paul, when there occurred the event which flung him into the center of the world's interest and inaugurated the movement which Catholics call the Protestant revolt and Protestants the Reformation. In 1517 a Dominican friar, Tetzel by name, appeared on the confines of Saxony to sell indulgences, and Luther came forward to protest against the abuses with which they had become tainted. He showed his still con-

Luther challenges a vendor of indulgences

servative viewpoint in that he raised no objection whatever against the theological doctrines on which indulgences were based.

We have seen that indulgences were letters of pardon issued by the pope, and that, rightly or wrongly, the Germans had come to suspect that they were a financial device to minister to the scandalous luxury of the Roman court. Apparently Luther's protest against the particular indulgence offered by Tetzel was inspired by a report that, among other exaggerations, the Dominican salesman did not scruple to lure purchasers by fraudulently telling them that his certificate remitted not only the penalty but the sin itself. Luther's protest took the form of Niney-five Theses concerning indulgences, which, in the scholastic manner still prevalent, he proposed to defend against any and all opponents. Composed, according to usage, in Latin, they were affixed by him to the door of the castle church of Wittenberg on October 31, 1517. They produced a tremendous reverberation, were translated into German, and in a few weeks known throughout the land. Since they were, in the main, abstrusely theological, their popularity can be accounted for solely on the ground that they sounded an anti-papal note and therefore appealed to a sentiment which, as we have seen, had become widely current in Germany.

The reverberation caused by the Ninety-five Theses against indulgences

That Luther was surprised by the tumult he had raised is certain, for he was still at the time a good Catholic and not consciously hostile to either the church or the pope. His thoughts, born of a long inner conflict, had revolved solely about the question of salvation, and he had not yet faced the historical issue of the evolution of the church. However, since the Ninety-five Theses loosed a torrent of discussion, he was swept on into investigations he had hitherto neglected and moved to broaden the basis of his criticism. The three years from 1517 to 1520 constitute an extraordinarily important interlude when there was still some hope that a compromise might be effected which would restrain the audacious friar from taking an irrevocable step. But Luther's native impetuosity was as inimical to long-drawn-out debate as to spineless formulas framed skillfully to evade the issue. Besides, the Catholics who broke into the discussion were as unrestrained as himself and, with flint striking steel, caused sparks to fly in every direction.

The critical period from 1517 to 1520

A debate, into which Luther permitted himself to be drawn at the university of Leipzig with a certain Dr. Eck (1519), proved particularly decisive for his revolutionary development. In the course of his argument with this violent papal partisan he arrived at the conclusion that the papacy, instead of having been instituted, as claimed, by Jesus himself, was the product of a long historical process. At this point his rising wrath against the Roman supremacy was fed with additional fuel by the attitude adopted toward the German tempest by the reigning pope, Leo X. It was an attitude typical of the cultured Italian gentleman of the Renais-

Luther turns against the pope

DESIDERIUS ERASMUS. By the German painter, Hans Holbein (d. 1543). (Alinari)

MARTIN LUTHER. By the German painter, Lucas Cranach (d. 1553). (Bettmann Collection)

HENRY VIII OF ENGLAND. *(top left)* By the German painter, Hans Holbein (d. 1543). (Bettmann Collection)

FRANCIS I OF FRANCE. *(top right)* By the French painter, Jean Clouet (d. 1572). (Bettmann Collection)

EMPEROR CHARLES V. By the Venetian painter, Titian (d. 1576).

THE SURRENDER OF BREDA. By the Spanish painter, Velásquez (d. 1660). The Dutch general presents his key of the town, in sign of surrender, to his Spanish opponent. (Anderson)

BURIAL OF COUNT ORGAZ. By the Greco-Spanish painter called El Greco (d. 1614).
Below the actual burial, above the reception of the count's soul in heaven. (Anderson)

sance, for Leo mildly wondered why the faithful in Germany were showing such excitement over "a squabble of monks." That was to what the
attack of Augustinian Luther on Dominican Tetzel reduced itself in
Leo's mind. Nevertheless, as head of the church, he was sensitive to every
attack on its authority and by characteristically cunning diplomacy tried
to lure Luther to Rome. But the agents whom he dispatched to this end
to Germany were arrogant and unskillful, and their attempts at a reconciliation were wrecked on the friar's rock-like stand.

When, after three agitated years, Luther had clarified his views on the
church, he took a decisive forward step and in a series of ringing pam-
phlets [2] advanced straight to the attack on pope, clergy, and sacraments. **Complete break with the pope**
Leo X did not misread the new onslaught and, abandoning negotiations,
issued a bull declaring Luther a heretic. The friar met the challenge with
a dramatic counterblast (1520). Amid a concourse of applauding Wit-
tenbergers he consigned the papal document to the flames and, to leave
no doubt as to the revolutionary meaning of his act, he threw in the
books of Canon Law which recorded all the immunities and privileges
accumulated by the church in the Middle Ages. The breach was complete. It remained to be seen for which side the German people would declare.

Germany had just passed through the throes of an imperial election.
In January, 1519, the Emperor Maximilian had been gathered to his **The accession of Charles V**
fathers and, after a particularly agitated campaign, the choice of the seven
electors fell on the king of Spain, who assumed the crown under the
name of Emperor Charles V. The new emperor did not owe his election
to his possession of the Spanish throne. He owed it primarily to his being
the head of the house of Hapsburg and the most powerful prince of Germany. In the year 1520 he left Spain for the Low Countries to travel
thence to Aachen, where he received the German crown with the usual
elaborate ceremony. Then he summoned a diet to the city of Worms on
the Rhine. Many matters demanded the diet's attention but all were overshadowed by the conflict which raged around Luther. The Wittenberg
professor had just been condemned by the pope. It was incumbent on emperor and Reichstag to declare their stand in regard to the papal sentence.

The sovereign who confronted his German subjects for the first time
at Worms was a youth twenty-one years old. He had passed his life in **Charles summons Luther to Worms**
the Netherlands and in Spain, where he had been brought up as a good
Catholic who might acknowledge the existence of abuses in the church,
but who, in the main, gave it an unhesitating allegiance. Therefore he,
personally, was prepared to dispose of Luther without more ado. But

[2] These pamphlets, containing the gist of early Protestantism, are very important. They
bore the titles: *Address to the Christian Nobility of the German Nation; On the Babylonian
Captivity of the Church; Concerning Christian Liberty.* They have been made accessible in
English by Wace and Buchheim under the title *Luther's Primary Works.*

there were certain considerations which could not be overlooked. So large a section of the German princes and people were secret or open supporters of Luther that to condemn him unheard might bring on civil war. Accordingly, Charles agreed to have him summoned to Worms for a public hearing under a special pledge of safety. Luther's friends besought him not to walk into the lion's mouth, reminding him of the fate of Hus at Constance. "I would go even if there were as many devils there as tiles on the house-roofs," he answered. As the devil and his cohorts were to him an indubitable reality, it was a characteristically fearless reply. On April 17, 1521, he appeared before the diet.

Luther before the diet of Worms, 1521

The scene is one of those historical spectacles which bring an involved and confusing conflict to a dramatic focus. The friar, whose audacity had given voice to the latent opposition of a people, was confronted with his supreme civil judge, the emperor, who sat upon a throne surrounded by a brilliant gathering of ambassadors, princes, and bishops. As Luther let his eye travel over the faces of the throng, he encountered all gradations of expression, ranging from deep devotion, through the many shades of indifference, to fierce hatred. Would he recant the heresies he had uttered? That was the question put to him by the emperor. If he had answered affirmatively, he might have won both forgiveness and an ample material reward. But he insisted that he should be proved wrong out of Holy Writ. He made this the crucial issue, having in the course of his troubled cogitations persuaded himself to place the authority of the Bible above the traditional authority of pope and church. "Here I stand. I cannot do otherwise. So help me God. Amen."

Permitted to depart, Luther finds safety in Wartburg castle

If the friar did not utter these precise words, they concisely state that right of private judgment which, for the moment at least, he claimed and which was to become the common basis of the many later forms of Protestantism. To cow him was out of the question, especially as Worms was seething with his partisans. Permitted to depart in accordance with the imperial promise, he was seized on the highway by servants of his prince, the Elector Frederick of Saxony, and carried secretly to the castle of Wartburg in the Thuringian forest. There let him lie concealed, was the thought of his protector, until the crisis was over and he might once more show himself without danger.

Reasons why Charles was averse to Luther

It did not take Charles long to come to a decision. He had nothing but abhorrence for a movement which threatened the authority of the church and the unity of Christendom. Moreover, his attention at that moment was fixed less on Germany than on Italy, where the predominance won by his Spanish predecessors had again been challenged. In dealing with this sovereign we must never forget that he had interests in the most widely separated regions—in Spain, the Netherlands, Germany, Italy, and America. In Italy, more particularly, the king of France had recently renewed the Franco-Spanish struggle for peninsular ascendancy with the successful seizure of Milan (1515).

From the vantage point of Milan, whence the king of France threatened the Spanish control of the peninsula, Charles was firmly resolved to oust his rival. In such an enterprise the aid of the pope could not be dispensed with. But unless Charles was prepared to back Leo X's bull against Luther, Leo would refuse to help the emperor against France. Accordingly, on May 26, 1521, Charles published the Edict of Worms, which, not without a measure of deceit, he had wrung from the Reichstag and which pronounced the ban of the empire against the heretic, that is, declared him an outlaw. Full of hope that he had disposed of a dangerous religious crisis, Charles abandoned Germany to give his attention to the French war and the reconquest of Milan.

Luther condemned by the Reichstag

But the Lutheran movement had already acquired too great a momentum to be stopped by an imperial fiat. If Charles could have remained in Germany to attend personally to the execution of his decree against the heretic, or if the civil power in Germany had not lain substantially with the princes, who, from the nature of the case, were divided in their sympathies, the history of the Reformation might have been different. As it turned out, Charles remained away from Germany for the next decade, and the princes and imperial cities, even if they had wished to act against Luther, could not do so in the face of the strong popular support behind the belligerent friar. For to many of his countrymen he had become, since the scene at Worms, a messenger straight from heaven. Consequently the hostile decree remained a dead letter, and the party behind Luther, encouraged by the vacillation of the central government, grew so strong that, by the time Charles saw fit to return to Germany, it dared to defy him as well as the pope.

The edict against Luther not executed

Let us now look into the measures carried through by the followers of Luther wherever they gained the ascendancy. As always when considering Germany, it is imperative to remember that the decisive role fell to the princes in effective possession of sovereignty. As soon as a prince went over to the new faith, his first act was to appropriate the monastic and other ecclesiastical property. He thereby greatly increased his revenues and magnified his importance. Without any question the lure exercised by the rich lands of the church was for many a prince the determining factor in his conversion. However, regardless of the motives of his action, on a prince turning Lutheran he assumed the responsibility of giving the new faith an organization effective for his dominion. He thereby became its patron and master. Consequently the German Lutheran church, although apparently self-governing, was never really free and independent, since it was in last resort controlled by a secular overlord.

The new or Lutheran church organized under princely patronage

Other changes carried through by the reformers belong more particularly to the realms of doctrine and worship. On the monasteries being
seized by the state the monks and nuns resumed their civil condition
and in many instances married. Friar Martin Luther himself set an
example by renouncing his vows and marrying (1525) Catherine von
Bora, a former nun. Many characteristic medieval practices, which, falling under the general head of "works," had invited Luther's criticism,
were formally condemned and abandoned. Outstanding among them
were pilgrimages to holy shrines, the adoration of the Virgin and the
saints, and, of course, indulgences, with the attack on which the revolt
had begun.

At the same time a new religious service was devised. The impressive
mass, declared to be idolatrous, was more and more simplified until it
had been stripped to an irreducible nucleus of prayer, song, and sermon.
Since the priesthood was no longer held to be a privileged class called to
mediate between God and man, the communion in both bread and
wine, instead of in bread alone, was conceded to the laity. Finally,
Latin was dropped from the service and replaced by German.

With an unparalleled ferment gripping the country, visionaries and
fanatics with a cure for every ailment of society rose to the surface and
found willing converts. Not only religious panaceas but political and social as well were shouted from every pulpit and platform. Such sweeping
radicalism has attended every great upheaval in history and has regularly
proved the greatest enemy of the cause of reform. Since it was reform
that Luther wanted, a limited religious reform, he felt no sympathy
whatever for the extremists who preached the indiscriminate destruction
of all the institutions inherited from the past.

In these circumstances it was inevitable that Luther should, before long,
have applied the brakes and done his best to defend himself against the
charge that he was heading a general revolution. In attempting to plumb
his mind we should always remember that, overwhelmingly concerned
with the strictly Christian problem of salvation, he regarded social and
political problems as relatively unimportant and refused to give them
serious consideration. His exclusively religious outlook made him anxious to detach his movement from every issue save his own and from
every leader save himself. It is possible that this narrow decision saved
the Reformation; but it is more than possible, it is all but certain, that
the former friar's extremely limited contacts with life sapped the vigor
of the German upheaval by turning it too soon and too exclusively into
the single channel of a moderate and exclusively religious reform.

The first place at which the seething German kettle overflowed was
Wittenberg itself. Fanatics, calling themselves prophets, appeared in the
town, inviting the people to rise in their might and apply the ax to the

Leading changes effected by the Lutheran church

The new Lutheran religious service

Revolution grips the country

Luther adopts a moderate position

Catholic images and altars. Luther lay concealed in Wartburg castle, where he was turning his enforced leisure to account by translating the Bible into German. So serious in his eyes was the Wittenberg situation that he rushed to the rescue and successfully rallied the townsfolk to his banner. The prophets fled to spread their iconoclastic preachments through the land. Wittenberg, saved, became the citadel of the true, the moderate Lutheranism (1522). Luther drives the "prophets" from Wittenberg

Simultaneously another revolution, involving a purely political and economic program, broke out among the petty knights of the Rhine region. This order of small landlords, theoretically directly under the emperor, had been ruined by the capitalistic development of the rising towns and was in consequence threatened with absorption by the more powerful princes. Infected by the revolutionary virus, they tried to improve their status by indiscriminately attacking their more prosperous neighbors, particularly the hated bishops and abbots. In a short war (1522-1523) they were crushed, not by the emperor, but by the Rhenish princes, lay and ecclesiastical—another indication, if one were needed, as to who exercised the effective political power in Germany. Uprising of the Rhenish knights

Shortly after, a far greater disturbance than that of the knights shook society to its very foundations. Since the social ferment was spreading to every class, it was clear that the humble tillers of the soil would not remain immune. Serfs, attached to the manors of the nobility and the church, they had in recent decades frequently registered a protest against their hard lot by rising in insurrection. Not only had all their past rebellions been cruelly suppressed, but their burdens had been multiplied by increased rents and services as well as through the seizure by the lords of the woods and pastures once owned by the villagers in common. With the expansion of trade, characteristic of the Renaissance, the old medieval simplicity was passing, and we need not think of the lords as necessarily harder of heart than their forebears if they tried to meet the higher cost of living by squeezing a larger return from their peasants. An economic adjustment attends every period of change, bringing an unusual pressure to bear on all classes alike. Depressed state of the peasants

Such considerations do not alter the fact that the peasants dwelt in a deepening gloom, into which the wild hopes aroused by the Reformation fell like a ray of light. What finally stirred them to action was the prospect held out by the innumerable itinerant visionaries that an unexampled era of social justice was about to dawn on the world. Resolved to speed its realization, they rose against their masters in successive waves till all the country between the lake of Constance and Thuringia was in violent commotion. By the spring of 1525 armed hordes of peasants were wandering over the land, killing the lords who ventured to resist them, The peasant revolt of 1525 burning castles and monasteries, and confidently predicting the golden age which was to rise, phoenix-like, from the ruins they had wrought.

Coolly considered, the great peasant insurrection was a midsummer madness and never had a remote chance of achieving success. The numerous bands of marauding rebels were unco-ordinated; they were poorly armed; their leaders were insignificant men, all of them ignorant and deluded, some few vile and ready to betray the cause. They put forth several programs, some of which, like the famous Twelve Articles, demanded the restitution of the appropriated common lands, the abolition of excessive rents and services, and other perfectly reasonable items, while even the most extravagant were extravagant only for the sixteenth century and would sound like commonplaces on the lips of a present-day preacher of reform. Of course the outraged princes with their panicky following of nobles and clergy were in no mood to listen to demands for justice accompanied by a regime of violence, fire, and murder. They put an army into the field, resolved to settle the issue by the sword. The showing of the peasants was lamentable. Their undisciplined phalanxes dissolved in a wild scramble for safety, leaving the individuals to be butchered by the thousands by the ruthless conquerors.

Luther's attitude toward this great upheaval is illustrative of his determination to keep clear of extremes. While the peasant movement was still no more than the rumbling of a distant drum and before the era of violence had set in, he issued a pamphlet which was, in the main, a call to the lords to do justice to their offended serfs. But the battle once joined, a battle in which the peasants threatened the existing order of society, he sided with the princes without hesitation. If, in the light of his set purpose, his decision can be readily understood, it was unpardonable that in a second pamphlet on the peasant movement he should have given free rein to his hot temper and in language of unsurpassed coarseness have spurred on the princes to trample their adversaries in the dust.

The ferocious crushing of the peasant uprising put an end to most of the visionary hopes entertained in connection with the Reformation. That in itself was perhaps no loss; but it was a check of grave consequence to a promising development that Luther, by committing himself and his movement to the victorious princes, broke with those popular forces which alone would have been able, not only to renew Germany politically, but also to assure the periodic freshening of the stream of the Reformation itself.

While Germany was seething with these troubles, its absentee ruler, Emperor Charles V, was occupied with his many other interests, and chiefly with the war with France. In fact, war with France was a leading feature of his reign and often for many years together prevented him from giving more than casual attention to the German problem. There

Crushing defeat of the peasants

Luther at first for and finally against the peasants

With the crushing of the peasants the Reformation turns conservative

The four wars of Charles V with Francis I

were in Charles's time four wars between France and Spain, all concerned with Italy as the prize. They befell as follows: first war, 1521-1526; second war, 1526-1529; third war, 1536-1538; fourth war, 1542-1544. Toward the end of his life Charles conducted a fifth war against France which will be treated at the close of this chapter and which differs from the others inasmuch as it was precipitated less by the Italian than by the German situation.

The first two wars were really a single war of almost a decade since only a brief and insincere peace intervened between them. The details of all four contests need not long detain us. Suffice it that, in spite of the ever renewed efforts of the French king, each conflict ended regularly with Charles in the ascendancy. In 1525, at Pavia, in northern Italy, a great battle was fought which proved a French disaster and led to the capture of the king. He was carried a prisoner to Madrid and there signed a peace (1526), by which he surrendered all his pretensions to Italy and, in addition, ceded the duchy of Burgundy, once held by Charles's Burgundian ancestors, to his Spanish rival. Released on the strength of a solemn oath that he would execute the peace, Francis nonetheless renewed the struggle as soon as he had crossed the Pyrenees and again touched the soil of France.

Defeat and capture of the French king at Pavia (1525)

The French king was encouraged to take this stand by the sudden friendliness of Pope Clement VII, Henry VIII of England, and other lesser potentates, chiefly of Italy. These rulers, alarmed by the completeness of Charles's victory, feared his European ascendancy would prove overwhelming and swung instinctively to the weaker side to redress the balance. But the allies were neither energetic nor harmonious and failed to break Charles's grip on the situation.

The pope, alarmed by the magnitude of Charles's victory, turns against him

The emperor was therefore free to single out the vacillating pope for vengeance. In the spring of 1527 a combined army of Spaniards and Germans descended upon the Eternal City and took it by assault. The Spaniards were mercenaries, the Germans largely Lutherans, and between them the famished hordes, breaking every bond of discipline, put the ancient capital of Christendom to such a sack as no words are adequate to describe. To superstitious anti-Catholics the catastrophe assumed the character of a divine punishment visited on the papacy for its innumerable misdeeds, while even the Catholic faithful were inclined to regard the cruel pillage as a not unfitting return for the selfish political game so passionately pursued by the long succession of Renaissance popes.

The sack of Rome (1527)

As for Clement VII, a member like his predecessor, Leo X, of the Florentine house of Medici and as unspiritual a man as ever wore the triple crown of St. Peter, the thought borne in on him as, from the near-by castle of St. Angelo, he stared at the ruin wrought by the im-

The Peace of Cambray 1529

perial army, was that he had lost the game and must come to terms with the all-powerful Charles. He opened negotiations, and although his French ally did not at once abandon the conflict, a general peace was at length arranged by the Treaty of Cambray (1529). In return for a reconfirmation of the French withdrawal from Italy coupled with the payment of a large money indemnity, Charles agreed to give up his claim to the duchy of Burgundy. Italy was his: such was the upshot of the ten years' struggle.

As soon as peace was assured Charles visited the peninsula in order to **Charles,** set the Italian house in order. He set up his court at Bologna, where he **master of** was visited in turn by the pope and all the petty Italian princes. With **Italy, is** one foot planted in the kingdom of Naples and the other in the duchy **crowned** of Milan, he straddled the peninsula like a colossus and overawed the **emperor at** pigmy powers at his feet. True, whenever in the years ahead France saw **Bologna** fit to revive the ambition which first drew her to Italy, the pope and his Italian fellow rulers did not fail to rattle their chains in mute sympathy with the French designs. But it is clear that already by 1529 fate, in the matter of the Franco-Spanish combat over Italy, had pronounced in favor of Spain. To put the final touch upon his victory, Charles yielded to medieval precedent and had himself crowned emperor by the pope. The great pomp occurred at Bologna, in the month of February, 1530.

Encouraged by an unprecedented triumph, Charles, after an absence of **The affairs** almost a decade, resolved once more to look into the affairs of Germany. **of Germany,** For that span of years the outlawry of Luther decreed at Worms had **1521-1530** remained unexecuted. Only the emperor himself could have enforced it. If, in his absence, the divided princes should show hesitation, the friar and his followers were sure to remain unmolested. In a Reichstag held at Speyer in 1526, their paralysis was publicly revealed by a declaration, according to which the German estates, that is, the princes and free cities, were given the right to act in matters of faith as each could answer to God and to the emperor. It was a qualified recognition of the new Lutheran church. Three years later (1529) Charles had become reconciled with the pope. With his fortunes at their zenith he sent a peremptory command to a new Reichstag, again convened at Speyer, to revoke the concession of 1526. As the Catholic princes, lay and ecclesiastical, still commanded an easy majority in the Reichstag, the behest was complied with and Luther and Lutheranism again outlawed.

It was now made apparent that the decade of liberty enjoyed by the **The reform-** Lutherans had stiffened their resolution. At the risk of incurring the **ers are called** emperor's displeasure they drew up a document, wherein they avowed **Protestants** that their duty to God and conscience took precedence over their duty to their earthly overlord. On the strength of this protest against the renewed condemnation of their faith the reformers were for the first time welded into a party under the name of Protestants. It was a designation destined in the years to come to serve as the common label for all the groups that successively fell away from the Roman obedience.

It was a decidedly tense situation which Charles confronted at a Reichstag, called to meet him at the city of Augsburg (1530). Though his mind was even more completely made up than at Worms, he was, as then, persuaded that he would at least have to grant the opposition a hearing. Asked to put their position in writing, the Protestants commissioned Melanchthon, a friend and fellow worker of Luther's but less averse than he to compromise, to formulate the strict essentials of the new faith. In a document which received the name of the Confession of Augsburg, Melanchthon made a conservative statement of the new tenets. So greatly did it appeal to his co-religionists that it became and has remained to this day the creed of the Lutheran church.

The Confession of Augs-burg, 1530

True to his assumed role of judge, Charles listened to the Protestant defense and then, supported by the Catholic majority, firmly announced his decision. The innovators were given a respite of six months before action would be taken to bring them back by force into the Catholic fold. Would the movement collapse in the face of this threat? Thoroughly aroused, the Protestant princes called a meeting at the little Thuringian town of Schmalkalden. The outcome was a league for mutual protection (1531). It meant the resolution to stand by the Protestant cause, if necessary by meeting force with force.

A Protestant league of defense formed at Schmal-kalden

Just as a religious war seemed unavoidable, an incident occurred which adjourned it. It was precipitated by the Mohammedan Turks, who, since their conquest of Constantinople in 1453, had built up an imposing empire around the eastern Mediterranean. Bent on the conquest of Europe, they had begun to push westward up the valley of the Danube, and in 1529 had appeared before the city of Vienna. Only the unflinching valor of its citizens had on that occasion saved the capital of Austria and the eastern gate of Germany from capture.

Germany threatened by the Turks

Nothing daunted, Sultan Solyman resolved two years later to renew the attack on a larger scale. As the Turks once more moved up the Danube, the whole German people spontaneously and breathlessly faced eastward. In need of united support Emperor Charles prudently decided to adjourn the threatened action against the Lutherans. In 1532 he signed a truce with them, wherein he agreed to refer the religious differences between the Protestants and Catholics to a General Council of the church. Such a Council had long appeared to him as the likeliest means of restoring the unity of Christendom, especially as the Protestants had frequently declared and now repeated that they were prepared to submit their case to a body which a section of Christian opinion had from the earliest days regarded as superior to the pope.

Civil war adjourned by the truce of 1532

Marching against the Turks with a united Germany behind him, Charles was able to make such a display of power that the Turks retired without venturing a battle. On his return from the campaign he found that other interests of his wide dominions demanded his attention. Spain and his Italian provinces had long suffered from the depradations of the Mohammedan pirates established along the Barbary coast of Africa and ever ready to co-operate with their Turkish co-religionists at the eastern end of the Mediterranean. From numerous coves and harbors they pounced upon the Christians ships and dragged off crews and passengers into degrading slavery. Unless Charles V was prepared to see the Mediterranean effectively closed to Christian trade, he would imperatively have to make an effort to punish and repress these pests.

To this end the emperor, in 1535, organized a vast maritime expedition which scored an important triumph by capturing Tunis, the main pirate stronghold. Before he could follow up this blow with more and heavier blows, his whole situation underwent an unhappy change. The mighty Ottoman ruler, Sultan Solyman, whom the pirates regarded as their overlord, came to their aid with ships and subsidies, while the king of France, prompt to take advantage of any difficulty besetting his hated rival of Spain, sought to ally himself with these two adversaries of Charles V. In the year 1535, the very year of Tunis, Francis and Solyman signed a treaty of mutual assistance. It was by no means an easy step for the French sovereign to take, for the tradition of Christian solidarity against the Mohammedan unbelievers was still vigorous in every European breast. But necessity overleaps every barrier, and his particular necessity, as Francis saw the situation, was at all costs, even at the cost of honor, to reduce the swollen power of Spain.

The result of these machinations was that hardly had Charles V scored his Tunis triumph, when he was called back to Europe to engage in a new war (1536-38) launched against him by King Francis, this time with Mohammedan naval support in the Mediterranean. Directing his energies, and with the same success as before, toward a land attack upon the French, the emperor was obliged to treat the struggle at sea as of less account. This choice enabled the pirates, aided by the sultan, once more to ride the waves at will. Wherewith is disclosed the political predicament that Charles faced for the remainder of his life. At the conclusion, in 1538, of the new French war, his third, he felt free once more to fall upon the corsairs. But no sooner was he involved again along the African coast than he found himself challenged by Francis in a fourth war waged from 1542 to 1544. It profited the French king no more than its predecessors, for when the Treaty of Crespy ended the conflict, he had again to forswear all claims to the great prize of Italy, which constituted, as from the beginning, the leading object of his policy.

Marginal notes:

Charles's Mediterranean problem

Charles V captures Tunis (1535) and is confronted by an alliance between the French king and the Moslems

Francis I wages two new wars against Charles V with Mohammedan help

This rapid summary of wars which shook the whole structure of Europe will once more make clear that Charles, owing to the vast extent of his dominions, had too many irons in the fire. He was an intelligent and conscientious ruler, unusually restrained for so powerful a man. Although he had a temperamental preference for adjourning an important decision, to a program once adopted he held fast with the silent stubbornness of a tenacious nature. This trait will explain why, on his return to Germany in 1544, when, much as in 1530, he was for the moment disembarrassed of all his other difficulties, he took up the Lutheran schism, resolved by hook or by crook to put it at last out of the world.

Charles again faces (1544) the Lutheran issue

Back in 1532 the war which threatened between Catholics and Lutherans had been avoided by referring the religious differences to a General Council of the church, regarded from the Middle Ages as the supreme ecclesiastical tribunal. Ever since that time Charles had been tireless in his effort to persuade the pope to convene such an assembly. Owing to the fact that the Councils of the past had regularly attempted to assert themselves against the pope, the Holy Father was averse to the imperial proposal and employed every device at his disposal to block it. The African campaigns, the French wars, even the Schmalkaldic league were welcomed by a succession of popes as means of escape from the emperor's demands.

The Council of the church proposed as a remedy for the religious schism

However, by 1545 Charles had triumphed over all his obstacles and Pope Paul III, accepting the inevitable, at last summoned a Council to meet in the Alpine city of Trent. It was too late. By 1545 the Protestants had completely broken with their past and were no longer willing to find their way back to the Roman church on any terms. In the face of their refusal to recognize the Council, Charles resolved to take the final step and settle the issue on the battlefield.

Accepted at last by the pope, the Council is rejected by the Protestants

Just before the outbreak of hostilities Luther died (February, 1546). With little or no understanding of political issues and inclined to regard human affairs exclusively from a theological angle, the Wittenberg reformer has in these untheological times lost something of the glamour which he possessed for the earlier generations of Protestants. Nevertheless, his simplicity and rude, vibrant sincerity still set him apart among the born leaders of men, lending him an authority which his gift for music and poetry tends to enhance. He was no mean performer on the lute, while the hymns which he contributed to the new church have a solemnity and strength unsurpassed among Protestant productions. Present-day opinion inclines to the view that Luther was still largely a man of the Middle Ages. Though this can hardly be disputed, he nonetheless made an impressive contribution to modern mentality. For, by appealing from pope and church to the Bible as the supreme Christian authority, he asserted the right of private judgment in the two all-

Final estimate of Luther and his work

important fields of faith and conduct. True, this right was not so firmly declared as not again to be denied at a later time by both Luther himself and the other Protestant leaders. But, once proclaimed, it could never again be blotted from the memory of men. Slowly gaining supporters, it served to fortify that individualism which was born in the Renaissance and which was bound to lead in the course of time to the challenge of one and every traditional authority.

The first war of religion in Germany, usually called the Schmalkaldic war, broke out in the year of Luther's death (1546). The Protestant forces, commanded by the leading evangelical princes, John Frederick of Saxony and Philip of Hesse, acted without plan or energy. An additional difficulty resulted from an internal Protestant division. While some of the Protestant princes weakly remained neutral, Maurice of Saxony, a cousin of the Elector John Frederick, actually turned traitor and, in return for the promise of his relative's electorate, gave military help to Charles. In consequence Charles was able to outmaneuver his opponents and to end the war with one stroke at the battle of Mühlberg (April, 1547), in which he crushed the Saxon army and took the elector himself prisoner. At once all resistance broke down, leaving the emperor master of the situation.

What now? Charles peremptorily ordered the Reichstag to re-establish Catholicism with a few trifling concessions to the Protestant position. These were to continue in force until the Council of Trent, which, under orders from the pope, had taken an adjournment, should reconvene and render final judgment. But the religious rift had gone too far to be closed by either force or argument, and the very Protestant prince who had helped Charles defeat his fellow Protestants took advantage of the incurable situation. This was Maurice of Saxony whom Charles, according to their bargain, had made elector of Saxony in place of Maurice's defeated and imprisoned cousin. A deft intriguer, Elector Maurice first secretly united the disgruntled Protestants around his person, and then, to make success more sure, won the support of the French king for his projected rising. The French king was no longer Charles's life-long adversary, Francis I, who had died in 1547, but his son, Henry II.

For once in his life Charles must have let himself be lulled to sleep by deceitful words. For when, in 1552, the Elector Maurice, having spun his complicated web, was ready for action, the emperor was completely taken by surprise. So suddenly did Maurice with his army pounce upon him that only by precipitate southward flight across the Alps did he save his life. Almost overnight and without a battle the sweeping victory of 1547 had been turned into an equally sweeping defeat.

Reluctantly admitting his discomfiture, Charles empowered his brother

The Schmalkaldic war, 1546-47

An insurrection against victorious Charles secretly prepared by Maurice of Saxony

Surprise and defeat of Charles, 1552

Ferdinand to sign the preliminary Peace of Passau (1552), which permitted the re-establishment of Protestantism on the pre-war basis. Then, The Peace
with the German civil war composed, he directed his restored strength of Passau
(1552) and
against France. In aid of his Lutheran allies, Maurice and his Protestant the attempt
co-conspirators, Henry II had invaded Germany from the west and had to retake
seized the three bishoprics of Metz, Toul, and Verdun. Metz was a Metz
fortress on the Mosel river and the key to western Germany. As, in
Charles's view, Metz must under no circumstances be left in French
hands, he organized an expedition which tried to retake the fortress
but failed (January, 1553). France was not to be dislodged from the new
vantage ground. The conquest effected in 1552 marks the beginning of
an era of French encroachment on territory under German sovereignty,
destined to continue uninterruptedly for several centuries.

His failure at Metz, in connection with the collapse of his German
program, deeply discouraged the emperor. He withdrew from Germany, Charles
first to the Netherlands and thence to Spain, with the fixed, pessimistic abandons
the conduct
resolve to throw off the burdens of office. Not till 1556 did he fully of German
execute his purpose. From the time of his departure from Germany he affairs to his
left the conduct of German affairs entirely in the hands of his younger brother
brother Ferdinand, who, more than two decades before, had been desig- Ferdinand
nated by the electors as Charles's successor in the imperial office. The
first task confronting Ferdinand was to convert the preliminary arrangements of Passau into a definitive religious peace. At a Reichstag held
at Augsburg in 1555 this was accomplished in a document known as the
Peace of Augsburg.

To every reflective student the most memorable feature of the Peace of The Peace
Augsburg is without doubt its abandonment of the unity of the church, of Augsburg
(1555)
the central concept of medieval civilization. By the side of the old breaks with
church an imperial law for the first time recognized a heretical de- the principle
parture from Catholicism called Lutheranism and theologically defined of a single
by the Confession of Augsburg of 1530. church

For the student of the German political development the importance
of the legalization of the new faith lies in its marking a fresh victory of The Peace
the territorial principle over the central power. It will be recalled that of Augsburg
a victory for
when Lutheranism first arose it was not doubted for a moment that decentrali-
Emperor Charles had the right to deal with it, in close co-operation zation
of course with the Reichstag. By failing to carry through his policy, he
greatly lowered the imperial prestige. The proof is furnished by the fact
that the Peace of Augsburg succinctly declared that religion was not a
national but a territorial issue; and it confirmed this principle by giving
to every state represented in the Reichstag the right to choose between
Catholicism and Lutheranism and to impose its choice upon its subjects.

Clothed in the Latin formula, *cuius regio eius religio* (religion pertains to the territorial government), this privilege of choice between two

legal religions must not be confused with modern individual toleration, with which it had nothing to do. The conceded choice pertained only to rulers and not to their subjects. These latter, if Catholic, might be evicted from Protestant regions and vice versa. Indeed a fresh wave of intolerance may be said to have inundated Europe with the coming of the Reformation, since the theological fury of the Lutherans reacted on the Catholics and made them more stiffly doctrinal than they had been in the immediately preceding generation. It would be difficult to prove that Lutheranism or any other form of Protestantism directly and intentionally promoted toleration in the modern sense. Yet it is clear that indirectly and in the long run Protestantism favored a more liberal attitude, since by emphasizing the right of private judgment it tended so greatly to multiply dissident faiths that in the end the idea of a religious uniformity enforced by penalties had to be given up as unrealizable. In 1555 individual toleration was still so far from the comprehension of men that not a voice was raised in its behalf.

With Lutheranism legalized it was easy to settle the question of

former ecclesiastical property within the Lutheran territories. To all such property already seized at the date of the Treaty of Passau (1552) the church was obliged to surrender title. However, as nothing was said in the Treaty of Augsburg concerning property seized after 1552, there was the prospect of renewed wrangling wherever a Lutheran prince seized Catholic property within his dominions after that crucial year.

Another and much more serious ambiguity sprang from the issue of

the prince-bishops. A prince-bishop was a bishop who was also a temporal ruler, and backward Gemany was endowed with a goodly number of these feudal survivals. With regard to such outmoded dignitaries the Lutherans contended that they had the same right of choice between the two faiths as the secular princes, while the most the Catholics would concede to them was the right of choice for their own persons. As, in the Catholic view, the bishoprics themselves were inalienably Catholic, the bishop who turned Protestant was under the obligation at once to resign his office in order to permit a Catholic successor to be appointed in his place.

It was the Catholic view that was laid down in an article of the peace

called the Ecclesiastical Reservation; and although the Protestants clamorously voiced their objection to the article, it was duly incorporated in the treaty. Since within a few years after the Peace of Augsburg had been signed a considerable number of bishoprics passed, in spite of the Ecclesiastical Reservation, into Protestant hands, the Catholics nursed a serious and fairly justified grievance against their rivals. This and other difficulties led to the renewal of the religious struggle. Instead of being a peace, as it claimed to be, the Augsburg agreement settled nothing satisfactorily and was at best a truce.

Charles V saved himself the humiliation of putting his signature to the Peace of Augsburg by abdicating his crown, a step which, long meditated, he finally took in 1556. Two years later the man who had overshadowed Europe died, a religious recluse, in a modest house attached to a Spanish monastery. *Sic transit gloria mundi.* Ever since Charles's accession to the empire, his brother Ferdinand had exercised rule in the strictly Austrian lands; and as early as 1530 he had been named as Charles's successor to the empire. Thus Ferdinand became the founder of a second, a younger Hapsburg line, established in the German territories of the house. The older line was continued by Charles's son, Philip, who was endowed with Spain (and her colonies), the Netherlands, and the Italian possessions. Henceforth until the extinction (1700) of Philip's male progeny, we have to reckon with a Spanish and an Austrian branch of the house of Hapsburg.

Abdication of Charles and division of his heritage, 1556

6   THE SPREAD OF THE REFORMATION TO THE SCANDINAVIAN COUNTRIES AND TO SWITZERLAND

THE MOVEMENT OF revolt inaugurated by Luther spread rapidly through the northern, the Germanic, area of Europe and even made threatening inroads on the Latin countries, Spain, Italy, and, more particularly, France. However, no matter where it appeared, it regularly met with resistance, though of a varying degree of intensity. In some countries, such as Italy and Spain, Protestantism was promptly and thoroughly suppressed; in others, such as France, it waxed strong enough to oblige the monarch to come to terms with it; and in still others, such as Sweden and Denmark, it won the civil government to its side and completely replaced the old faith. These Protestant vicissitudes will now be passed in review. In the present chapter we shall limit ourselves to an examination of the conditions under which the new faith established itself in the Scandinavian countries and in Switzerland.

The Reformation spreads throughout Europe

Nowhere was the success of the Reformation more sweeping than in the Scandinavian north. Toward the end of the Middle Ages the three Scandinavian countries, Denmark, Norway, and Sweden, had become united under one king by virtue of an agreement called the Union of Kalmar (1397). The concentration was more effective in name than in fact, since the king's residence in Copenhagen gave the government a Danish slant, which aroused frequent resistance in Norway and an almost uninterrupted opposition in Sweden.

Denmark, Sweden, and Norway united by the Union of Kalmar (1397)

In the sixteenth century the reigning Danish sovereign, King Christian II, resorted to the oft-tried method of force to reduce the recalcitrant Swedes to obedience. He excited a country-wide revolution (1521) which, under the guidance of a Swedish nobleman, Gustavus Vasa, met with complete success. As a result Gustavus Vasa was invited by his Swedish countrymen to assume the kingship in place of the deposed Christian II. He thus founded (1523), together with the independence of his country, a royal house, the house of Vasa, destined to be identified with some of the most brilliant pages of Swedish history.

Sweden wins independence from Denmark (1523)

Norway was not moved to follow the example of Sweden and to proclaim its independence. In fact, it fell even more completely than before under Danish rule, continuing in this state of subjection until the beginning of the nineteenth century.

Norway in
continued
dependence
on Denmark

Although the Swedish war for independence was in its origin a political and not a religious struggle, the disturbance which it caused throughout the Baltic area inevitably favored the spread of heretical religious opinions. Swedish and Danish theological students, on returning from Wittenberg in Germany, preached the Lutheran innovations to willing listeners in town and castle and, before long, drew, not only many burghers, but also numerous nobles as well as occasional members of the old royal family of Denmark and of the new royal family of Sweden to their side. While it would be invidious to deny that conviction played a part in these conversions, greed and ambition were, at least so far as the princes and nobles were concerned, the really decisive factors.

Protestant-
ism spread
by students
from
Wittenberg

Precisely as in Germany, the ruler who adopted Lutheranism stood to gain the immense Catholic properties, to which he would automatically fall heir in case Catholicism should be abandoned. Also again as in Germany, a Scandinavian ruler could contemplate the spoliation of the Catholic church without fear of a popular revolt because the church had fallen into disfavor with the people, owing to its wealth and to the consequent offensive ostentation of the great prelates. The only opposition of any weight likely to develop was that of the nobles, and their protest could be silenced by the shrewd proffer to them on the part of the prince of a share of the ecclesiastical booty.

Greed the
chief motiv.
power of
rulers and
nobles

The statements of the preceding paragraphs present no more than a very generalized picture of the politico-religious agitation that shook Scandinavia in the crucial period when Lutheranism was gaining a solid foothold in Germany. It was hardly so much a question in the northern countries of an irresistible popular movement as of revolutionary measures passionately championed by a small but compact group of religious enthusiasts and resolutely carried through by a ruling class with a sharp eye for its material advantage. However, without any question at all the rising national sentiment contributed in an important degree to the success of Protestantism. In the Scandinavian lands, as everywhere else, the medieval universality was losing ground, and a national church divested of foreign influences made a powerful appeal to the patriotic emotions nursed more particularly by the rising burgher class.

Main factors
in the
victory of
Lutheranism

We may summarize the religious revolution in Scandinavia in the following terms: By the year 1527 Lutheranism had become established as the state church of Sweden; then, in the succeeding decade, Denmark, together with dependent Norway, also broke conclusively with

Scandinavia
the only
conquest of
Lutheranism
outside
Germany

Rome and brought its religious thought and organization into conformity with the Lutheran Confession of Augsburg. Scandinavia—Sweden, Denmark, Norway—represents the one considerable conquest made by the Lutheran form of Protestantism outside of Germany.

Turning next to Switzerland, we must, in order to grasp the crisis created by the Reformation, have at least a general knowledge of the political situation. The Alpine region familiar to us as Switzerland was in the Middle Ages an integral part of Germany. The central Swiss uplands were inhabited by sturdy peasants and herdsmen who had succeeded in preserving a considerable measure of their original Germanic freedom. Consequently when, in the course of the thirteenth century, certain of the neighboring feudal lords attempted to bring them into subjection in order to saddle them with novel dues, they offered resolute resistance. The most powerful member of the aggressor group was the count of Hapsburg; and when, in 1273, Count Rudolph of Hapsburg was elected emperor and had the good fortune of practically perpetuating his successors in the imperial office, the threat to the freedom of the mountaineers was greatly increased.

At the start of the conflict the uplanders met the feudal thrust in a purely local and sporadic way. The first notable step toward better coordination of their efforts was taken in 1291. In that year representatives of the three cantons of Schwyz, Uri, and Unterwalden, bordering on the picturesque lake of Lucerne, came together to form a loose defensive league. This league may be regarded as the nucleus of the future republic named in common parlance, as it expanded, after one of the original members of the confederation (Schwyz). The amazing thing drawing general attention to the Alpine struggle, which continued through many generations, was that in an age when the horseman was held to be a fighting-man immeasurably above the foot-soldier and noblemen regarded as a special human breed not to be mentioned in the same breath with peasants, the mountaineers proved themselves more than a match for the high-born aggressors and drove them in engagement after engagement from their valleys. Some of the earlier encounters rapidly took on a legendary form and, associated with such reverberating names as Arnold of Winkelried and William Tell, lit a flame in the bosoms of the defenders that steeled their solid squares of pikemen unyieldingly to stand their ground against every assault of the enemy.

For over two hundred years following the formation of the nuclear federation of the three cantons, the counts of Hapsburg clung to their dream of conquest, only to have it shattered on something stronger than dream, on the iron will of the mountain men to be free. In the last decade of the fifteenth century Count Maximilian of Hapsburg, identical with the well-known Renaissance sovereign, Emperor Maximilian, made

The beginnings of Swiss independence

A Swiss Confederation formed in 1291

The Swiss Confederation wins complete independence in 1499

a last effort to reduce the Swiss to obedience. When this effort also proved vain, Maximilian accepted the decision of fate. In a treaty signed at Basel in 1499, he acknowledged the freedom of the Swiss from all claims of the house of Hapsburg and, for good measure, threw in their independence from the German Reich, to which they had hitherto belonged.

From an early time the success of the three original cantons so fired the enthusiasm of the neighboring communities of peasants that they asked to be admitted to the alliance. Before long, the only two large towns of the region, Zurich and Bern, followed suit. As a result of these voluntary adherences, just before the above-mentioned last struggle with Emperor Maximilian the Swiss Confederation had increased from the original three to ten cantons. Two decades later, by the time of the Lutheran revolt, the number of cantons had risen to thirteen. Steady territorial expansion of the Swiss Confederation

In the matter of organization, however, the expanding state never got beyond the phase of a loose association for defense against present and prospective enemies. The central authority of the Confederation was a diet composed of representatives from the thirteen constituent cantons. Owing to the unwillingness of the cantonal governments to divest themselves of their sovereignty, the function of the diet was restricted to the single matter of peace and war. On this feeble federal foundation the very successes of the Confederation put an almost impossible burden. In the course of their victories the Swiss had conquered from the Hapsburgs and other neighboring lords considerable territories. These conquests, called common bailiwicks, it fell to the lot of the Confederation to administer as federal property. All would go well regarding this common property so long as there was peace and concord among the thirteen federal units. However, once let them be split by a passionate difference of opinion, a struggle for control of the common bailiwicks would follow which would subject the weak central government to an intolerable strain. The Confederation a loose union of sovereign states

The test of the Swiss union came with the Reformation. The movement of reform was first championed in Switzerland by a native son, Ulrich Zwingli by name. He was born in a village not far from the lake of Constance on January 1, 1484, and was therefore only a few weeks younger than the stormy petrel of Wittenberg. He came of an influential burgher family and received an excellent schooling, crowned by attendance at the universities of Vienna and Basel. In both of these institutions humanism had come to the fore, and Zwingli devoted himself, not only to the study of the classics, but quite as enthusiastically, in accordance with the familiar Erasmian precedent, to the mastery of the sources of the Christian faith. Zwingli, the Swiss reformer

Ordained a priest in 1506, Zwingli was launched on his ecclesiastical

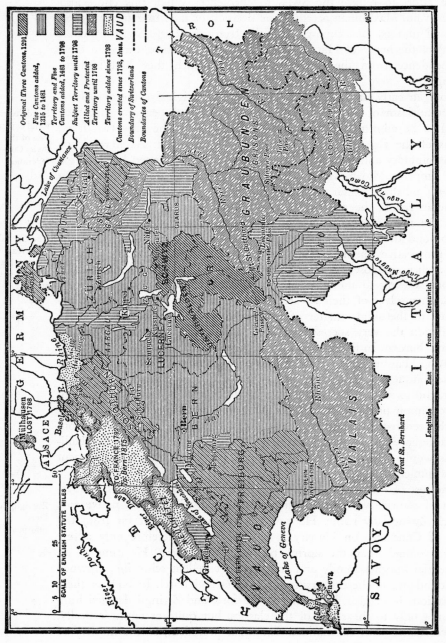

The Swiss Confederation from its origin (the Three Cantons, 1291) to the present day

career by having a country parish committed to his care. An even, balanced temper saved him from the religious crisis that darkened the early manhood of Luther and gave him a joyous confidence in the intellectual promises of humanism. At the same time, in his capacity of free-born Swiss, he made acquaintance with the democratic system of government, becoming imbued with that virile patriotism which is the product of political responsibility.

Zwingli, humanist and citizen

Humanism and democracy, conceived as twin lodestars, shaped Zwingli's labors and determined his fate. They explain why he began his public career not as a religious but as a social reformer. He first rose into wider view among his countrymen by his denunciation of the long-established mercenary system, which induced the Swiss to sell their services to any European ruler with money to pay the price. Zwingli's idea was that the sons of freedom should be too proud to fight for any cause but their own. Although this early agitation was not crowned with success, it showed the inborn mettle of the man.

Zwingli begins as a social reformer

So far as ecclesiastical abuses were concerned, Zwingli was, like Erasmus, at first content to let them be driven from the world by ridicule. Then, with a certain abruptness, he inaugurated (1519) a policy of direct action, moved, it may be, by the example of Luther, although he always insisted on his complete independence of the German reformer. It is, however, true that, with certain exceptions, of which we shall presently hear, he identified himself with most of the doctrinal positions of his Saxon contemporary.

Zwingli becomes a religious reformer

When it came to the issue of the kind of government to be given to his church, it will at once be conceded that Zwingli strictly followed a line of his own. We have seen that when in Germany the rule of the church by pope and clergy was rejected, the control of the new, the Lutheran, church was vested in the princes, the representatives of the civil power. As a result the Lutheran church became identified with the state and subjected to the hereditary ruler of the state. In Switzerland, where the civil power was exercised by magistrates elected by the people, a new and reformed church would have to operate with their sanction; and, in conformity with the ruling democratic practices, the new church, when established, would have to endow the individual parish units with as large a measure of self-government as possible.

Zwingli an advocate of democratic church government

To this plan Zwingli, the born republican, subscribed enthusiastically, thus favoring a form of church government much more responsive to popular currents than that of Germany. From his general position it also followed that Zwingli, far from feeling any aversion for politics as Luther did, regarded political activity, not only as the sacred duty of the free citizen, but as the indispensable concomitant of all healthy self-expression in religion.

Zwingli's ideal was a citizen active in both state and church

As already said, Zwingli did not actively take up religious reform till
1519, in which year he was called to take charge of the great central
church of Zurich, the largest and most thriving community of the whole
Confederation. Luther had recently hurled his bolt against indulgences,
and Zwingli, joining the attack, was, much like the German friar, moved
before long to broaden his criticism. In a surprisingly short time he had
freed himself from the bonds of ecclesiastical tradition and, breaking
every connection with Rome, steered straight for independence. By 1525
his persuasive tongue had so completely swept the Zurich townsmen off
their feet that he was enabled with their ardent support to set up a new,
a Reformed church.

Zwingli begins his reform activity at Zurich

That, administratively, the Zwinglian church was to the Lutheran
church just emerging in Germany as republicanism is to monarchy has
already been remarked. In point of doctrine the two faiths, although
at first almost identical, developed gradually a number of differences.
Of these by far the most important regarded the Holy Eucharist or
Lord's Supper. For the Catholic church the Holy Eucharist was, in
effect, the central mystery of Christianity. Luther, after first question-
ing the Catholic teaching, in his later, conservative period ended by
reverting, or all but reverting, to it. The Catholic position, briefly stated,
was that the bread and wine of the communion-table are, by a miraculous process called transubstantiation, changed into the actual body and
blood of Christ. The doctrine finally adopted by Luther is called, not
transubstantiation but consubstantiation, and, except for professional
theologians, may be admitted to be so close to the Catholic teaching as
to be not readily distinguishable from it.

Catholic transubstantiation and Lutheran consubstantiation

To a certain humanist tendency in Zwingli, a tendency which
prompted him to test everything by the evidence of reason and the senses,
transubstantiation and its Lutheran relative, consubstantiation, were of a
piece with every other medieval superstition, and he contemptuously
tossed them on the scrap heap together with fasts, pilgrimages, adoration
of the saints, and other so-called works. So sweeping an elimination
of mystery from life and faith enraged Luther, who, instinctively hostile
to rationalism of every kind, had consistently refused to identify himself
with the humanistic movement, except insofar as its positions happened
to accord with the deep, religious demands of his nature.

Zwingli rejects both transubstantiation and consubstantiation

It was natural that, so long as Protestantism was weak and exposed
to attack, efforts should be made to draw the Lutheran and Zwinglian
movements into an alliance. In 1529 when Charles V, having just brought
his war in Italy to a triumphant conclusion, was preparing to return to
Germany to stamp out heresy by force, the outlook for the reformers
became suddenly bleak. In consequence Philip of Hesse, a Lutheran
leader addicted to political intrigue, prudently enough urged the closing

Philip of Hesse acts as conciliator between Luther and Zwingli of the Protestant ranks. As an indispensable preliminary measure, he brought Luther and Zwingli together in a conference at his city of Marburg in order to give them an opportunity to iron out their several doctrinal differences.

Matters went smoothly enough until the Lord's Supper was broached. On this rock the meeting suffered shipwreck because Luther would not make the slightest concession to Zwingli's rationalism. Zwingli, for his part, though ready to retain the Lord's Supper as a feature of his church service, refused to regard it as other than a purely symbolic act commemorative of an actual occurrence recorded in the gospels. Thus, on the inflexibility of the two Protestant champions, the plan of consolidating their movements came to naught. Failure of the Marburg Conference, 1529

It was fortunate for the schismatics that Emperor Charles, on coming to Germany, found himself diverted from his anti-Protestant purpose by the alarm caused by a threatening Turkish invasion. As the Turks had to be attended to first, Charles was obliged to adjourn his projected slaying of the dragon of heresy, and thus the Luther-Zwingli rift brought neither faith any immediate harm. From the failure at Marburg the Lutheran and the Swiss Reformed churches went, and have continued to this day to go, each its own way. Two separate churches

From Zurich, its center, the Zwinglian movement spread into the adjoining Swiss areas, particularly into the towns, which, here as elsewhere, proved to be the chief carriers of Protestantism. When Bern adopted his cause (1528), it looked to the sanguine Zwingli as if all Switzerland must ultimately fall like ripe fruit into his lap. But the five innermost (or forest) cantons, representing the original nucleus of Schwyz, Uri, and Unterwalden plus the two neighbors, Zug and Lucerne, clung stubbornly to their ancient faith. The Swiss Confederation divided between Protestantism and Catholicism

Exactly as might be expected, it was over the conquered territory, the so-called common bailiwicks, that the religious quarrel between the two parties finally came to a head. Dominating the federal diet, the five forest cantons planted their officials in the common bailiwicks and suppressed the preaching of Protestantism by force. Against this violence Zwingli, hesitatingly backed by the Protestant cantons, protested so vigorously that civil war could not be avoided. In the first clash in 1529, Zwingli, by expeditious action, won a bloodless victory and carried his point, which was that the common bailiwicks should be conceded a free choice between the two rival faiths. However, when the dissatisfied Catholics renewed the struggle in 1531, the Zwinglian forces were completely routed at Kappel (October 11) and the resolute Zwingli himself slain. Religious war: defeat and death of Zwingli (1531)

The defeated Protestants were obliged to sue for peace, which, signed before the year was out at Kappel, cleared the atmosphere. The issue of

the common lands was of course settled, in the main, in the Catholic
interest. However, the authority of each separate cantonal government
to adopt the religion of its choice was freely recognized. The Kappel
solution of the Swiss religious conflict closely resembles the one afterward
found by Germany and laid down in the Peace of Augsburg (1555)
under the formula *cuius regio eius religio:* that is to say, Switzerland,
like Germany, a weak federation, was obliged to leave the thorny religious issue to the local governments. Consequently each canton was
given the right to choose between Catholicism and Protestantism, thereby
giving to the religious map of Switzerland the same checkered appearance as marks Germany and characteristic of both these countries down
to our own time. A constitutional by-product of the religious division of
the Swiss was that the already feeble central government became still
more feeble and so remained till well into the nineteenth century.

THE STRENGTHENING OF THE REFORMATION UNDER THE LEADERSHIP OF CALVIN AND THE COUNTER-REFORMATION OF THE CATHOLIC CHURCH

THE STRENGTHENING OF THE REFORMATION UNDER THE LEADERSHIP OF CALVIN

TOWARD THE MIDDLE of the sixteenth century the Protestant movement experienced an enormous strengthening and enlargement. The story takes us to the city of Geneva, which, located at the western end of the lake of the same name, had at the beginning of the sixteenth century a form of government suggestive of the transition from medieval to modern conditions. Although the city, an active community of merchants, had acquired a measure of self-government, it was still subjected to its original feudal lord, the bishop of Geneva. Since, in the course of the previous century, the most powerful secular lord of the neighborhood, the duke of Savoy, had insinuated himself into the government as the lieutenant, in civil matters, of the bishop, the town enjoyed the perilous luxury of a threefold rule. {.marginnote Threefold government of the city of Geneva}

The unstable equilibrium represented by this system was destroyed by the duke of Savoy, who, abetted by the bishop, tried to bring the town completely under his thumb. His bold action aroused the resistance of the citizens. They attacked the two high-born conspirators with so much vigor that they drove them both from the town. By 1536 Geneva had become a free city republic, recognizing no superior under heaven. {.marginnote Geneva becomes a free republic, 1536}

The victory of the Genevans could not have been achieved without the help of the near-by Swiss cantons and, particularly, of the large and war-like canton of Bern. Since Bern was Protestant, it introduced Protestant preaching into Geneva and largely under the Bernese influence the citizens were persuaded to adopt the Reformation. They took this decisive step (1536) immediately after gaining their civil independence. The double revolution had hardly been effected when a certain John Calvin appeared upon the scene. {.marginnote Geneva becomes Protestant, 1536}

125

John Calvin, a Frenchman by birth, saw the light of day at Noyon, in Picardy, on July 10, 1509. He received an excellent education in the classics, chiefly at the universities of Paris and Orléans. Originally intended for the church, he switched at Orléans to the law, to which study, it may well be, he owed that order and precision which are the characteristics of his ripened thought. Throughout his life he remained devoted to classical literature and warmly advocated its predominance in the school curriculum.

Calvin, his training as a classicist and legist

Though a son of the sixteenth century might love the classics and devotedly pursue the law, he could not, more especially if he had the passion for righteousness which distinguished Calvin from birth, avoid being sucked into the whirlpool of contemporary religious debate. While still a student at the university Calvin came into touch with the circles in France which were nursing the seeds of the Reformation; and when the government of Francis I made one of its sporadic attacks on heresy, which brought many leading men to the stake, Calvin was obliged to seek safety in flight (1534).

Calvin driven into exile

The exile settled in the Swiss city of Basel, which some years before had adopted the Zwinglian reform. Here he published in 1536 his famous treatise *Christianae Religionis Institutio* ("The Institutes of the Christian Religion"). *The Institutes,* greatly enlarged in subsequent editions, represented the most scholarly attempt that had yet been made to reconstruct the original church of Christ on the basis of the evidence supplied by the New Testament and the Fathers. A work of profound learning, *The Institutes* was at the same time a precise exposition of the elaborate additions to the apostolic structure made by the medieval church. No book had yet come from the Protestant camp combining so much historical information with such invincible logic.

His great work: "The Institutes" (1536)

In the course of a journey undertaken not many months after the publication of his great work, Calvin chanced to stop for a night's rest at the city of Geneva. The Protestant faith, only recently adopted, was still an exceedingly frail plant. This weakness was owing to the fact that the citizens, having turned Protestant largely on grounds of political expediency, had not felt the uplifting force of a great moral experience. The leading preacher of Geneva, Farel by name, was aware of the evils of the situation and struggled bravely to overcome them. When the news was brought him that the famous young author of *The Institutes* had arrived in town, he called upon him at his inn and warmly solicited his aid in the great work of evangelization that still remained to be done. Enamored of the quiet life of the scholar, Calvin at first refused; but Farel plied him with such vigor that he at last agreed to make the sacrifice and dedicate himself henceforth to a life of action.

Calvin settles in Geneva, 1536

The work on which Calvin now entered lasted, with the exception of a short setback and exile, till his death in 1564. By sheer force of will and ascendancy of genius he soon made himself the commanding figure within the city walls and, with the consent of the citizens, ruled their destinies like a dictator. His plan, one of the most audacious ever formed by man, was to realize in Geneva the original church of Christ as outlined in *The Institutes*. It was the reconstructed evangelical edifice which was and remained his central concern. *Calvin plans to realize the true church of Christ at Geneva*

While Calvin fully recognized the need of a civil government operating at the side of his church, he was not so much concerned with the precise form of this government as with the circumstance that its officials should be imbued with the sense of their Christian mission. He was therefore prepared to accept the democratic regime recently established at Geneva, provided it would assume the obligation to work in close association with his church to the end of producing as nearly perfect a Christian commonwealth as possible. Instead of separation of church and state, a relatively recent ideal which had not yet anywhere risen into view in the sixteenth century, he demanded the same co-operation between the two leading institutions as had characterized the Middle Ages. According to him the state, which governed temporal man, and the church, which ministered to his immortal spirit, could not disjoin their labors if God's great purpose in regard to man was to be realized. This, a theocratic doctrine, does not differ from that of the great scholastic teachers. Precisely like them, Calvin held life to be worthless in itself and valuable only when lived under God with a constant view to salvation. *Calvin's theocratic ideal similar to that of the scholastics*

On one point, however, Calvin and the scholastics differed, and the difference digs an unbridgable chasm between him and them. The medieval teachers exalted the Catholic church as the divinely created instrument of salvation. This elaborate edifice, intermediary between God and man, the French reformer cleared from the scene with a single sweep of his arm, thus bringing the individual face to face with God. The church, in his view, the real but invisible church, was the body of true believers throughout the world. They were gathered for practical purposes in separate units or congregations and were guided by clergymen who preached and prayed. But these guides were only guides and could not by any power vested in them promote to the smallest degree the salvation of the sinner. *Distinction between the medieval theocratic ideal and that of Calvin*

Although Calvin's theocratic ideal may not be passed over, it was not so much by it as by other features of his system that he impressed himself on the contemporary world. What we may call his three major contributions belong to the respective fields, first, of church government, second, of morals, and third, of theology. *His three major contributions*

Beginning with church government, we note that, although relatively indifferent to the form of civil government, from the first Calvin insisted for his church on the democratic principle. He did this because democracy was, in his view, the system of the primitive church, in which every believer was equal to every other and the neighborhood group constituted a natural, self-governing unit. By its emphasis on religious democracy Calvinism made a popular appeal which was absent from Lutheranism, committed by the Wittenberg reformer to the control of the secular princes. It was this democratic kernel which was largely responsible for the winning by Calvinism of the middle classes in so many European countries, thereby enlisting on its side the most powerful carriers of modern as distinct from medieval civilization.

Calvinism identified with the democratic principle

A second memorable feature about Calvinism is the extraordinary emphasis it placed on conduct. According to the Genevan leader the conversion of the individual to the reformed faith ought infallibly to mean a life lived on a plane of high endeavor in the consciousness of God's active and incessant grace. Hence the true Christian turned his back on frivolity and self-indulgence and went about his daily tasks and conducted himself among his fellow men with dignified austerity. Calvin is the first Puritan and his Genevan code of morals the source and model of all Puritanical codes whatever.

Calvin, the father of Puritanism

Aware of the frailty of the flesh and familiar with human backsliding and misdemeanors, Calvin was unwilling to trust to exhortation alone to hold sinners to the narrow path. He was a man of grim resolution and a convinced believer in the value of drastic punishment. He therefore created at Geneva as the executive organ for his moral code a commission, called consistory, made up of six ministers and twelve elders. The consistory was in substance an ecclesiastical and moral police and was empowered to arrest and bring to trial any man, woman, or child charged with failure to comply with the Genevan standard of conduct.

Supervision of morals by the consistory

The records of the consistory, which still exist, show that children were whipped for being disrespectful to their parents, men pilloried for blasphemy, and money fines and imprisonment meted out for dancing, card-playing, the singing of profane songs, and non-attendance at church. Of course, heresy and blasphemy were regarded as particularly heinous offenses and in several instances led to the infliction of the death penalty by either the sword or the fagot.

Punishments meted out by the consistory

The third feature of Calvinism destined to be historically important belongs to the province of theology. It touches the Genevan leader's conception of God. Calvin made the might and majesty of the Creator so unapproachable and all-inclusive that they overshadowed the universe. No system has ever been set forth which reduced man to such total insignificance, made him so entirely a helpless worm.

Calvin's conception of God

From this conception of God's majesty it followed for Calvin that man could not contribute so much as an atom's weight to his own salvation either by the good works recommended by the Catholic church or by the faith extolled by Luther. God alone could save and his saving was an act of pure mercy. But since God is eternal and omniscient he must know and has willed, even before a soul is born, whether it shall be saved or lost. Familiar under the name, sometimes of election by grace, sometimes of predestination, this teaching has proved a rock on which the waters of discussion have dashed themselves to spray for many centuries down to the present hour. Calvin's doctrine of predestination

To men of a different temper from the austere Calvin, to tender-minded men throughout the ages, the doctrine that man is as utterly unimportant and God as implacable as predestination implies has proved exceedingly repugnant. Such men predicted, even in Calvin's lifetime, that discouragement would seize upon the adherents of his creed and that something akin to fatalism would paralyze their wills. Rarely has a prophecy been more completely disproved by the facts, for history reveals that the Calvinist form of Protestantism is associated with a remarkable display of human energy. What the doctrine of election by grace may have to do with an unexampled activism is a psychological mystery beyond the scope of this book. Calvinism an activist, not a fatalist, faith

From the foregoing it will be seen that Calvin advocated a far more radical and thoroughgoing reform than Luther. The difference between the two men may be summed up as follows: Luther was content to lop off from the Catholic church what he considered to be its historical excrescences; Calvin went back to the origins of the church in order to rebuild it from the foundations. Now it need hardly be said that, in measure as the Protestant movement spread from country to country and the resistance of the Catholic church grew more vigorous, the struggle between the contending parties became more heated and uncompromising. We shall presently examine the extraordinary steps the Catholics took to meet the Protestant challenge. The corresponding phenomenon among their opponents was to turn away from Lutheranism as too mild a doctrine and to rally to Calvinism as a more truly fighting faith. This transfer of allegiance occurred even in some sections of Germany, although the German Protestants, in the main, contented themselves with Lutheranism, especially as with the Peace of Augsburg (1555) it had by winning legal recognition reached safe ground. But in such countries as France, the Netherlands, and Scotland, where Protestantism met with fierce resistance on the part of the constituted authorities, both clerical and civil, Calvinism completely supplanted Lutheranism and ended by winning, in the case of Scotland and the Dutch Calvinism supplants Lutheranism section of the Netherlands, a sweeping victory, while, in the case of France, it achieved at least a partial success.

THE COUNTER-REFORMATION OF THE CATHOLIC CHURCH

The papacy steadily opposed to reform

The reform movement, of which Luther, Zwingli, and Calvin were the leading champions, could not have achieved the resounding success it did, if it had not appealed to a conviction, which had been gathering strength for over a century, that the church was corrupt in head and members. To all criticism of this kind the popes not only had turned a deaf ear, but by a resourceful diplomacy had nullified every attempt to produce a reform by constitutional means. Two General Councils of the church were held respectively at Constance (1414-1418) and Basel (1431-1449) with the express purpose of remedying the situation. Their labors came to nothing owing to the opposition of the papcy, which unflinchingly resisted any infringement on its authority by a usurping parliament.

Moral obtuseness of the Renaissance popes

Issuing with unshorn powers from the conciliar crisis, the Roman pontiffs plunged into the Renaissance and, in the spirit of the age, gave themselves wholeheartedly to worldly interests and schemes of temporal power. While many of the Renaissance popes by befriending humanism and patronizing the arts gave evidence of great cultural refinement, it is also true that, almost without exception, they proved themselves morally so obtuse that the general laxity of clerical manners and the scandalous financial practices under their eyes failed to disturb their equanimity. Such popes were not able to cope effectively with the northern revolt when it occurred, because they had no comprehension of its moral fervor. They continued to loiter in the pleasant gardens of the Renaissance and refused to face the hard realities beyond the Alps.

The papacy breaks with the Renaissance

With the spread of the Protestant disaster a gradual change took place. Some of the more sensitive members of the papal court took alarm and raised their voices in favor of reducing criticism by removal of the most flagrant scandals. Reaching before long the college of cardinals, the reform sentiment registered in 1534 a first, if partial, success in the elevation to the papal chair of Paul III (1534-1549). Although this pope was undoubtedly a characteristic son of the Renaissance, still he was genuinely disturbed by the evils of the church and, intermittently at least, considered the problem of their cure. Thus for a few decades the issue trembled in the balance until, with the election of Pope Paul IV (1555-1559), the papacy definitely and forever renounced its Renaissance past and took up the question of saving what was left of the universal church. Under these circumstances began that famous movement of church reform by church action commonly known as the Counter-Reformation. Although the Counter-Reformation did not acquire its full momentum until the popes had put themselves at its head, the movement had begun to gather energy long before the middle of the sixteenth century. Any attempt at a systematic presentation of its gradual unfolding must start with the ecclesiastical reforms carried out in Spain on the initiative of Ferdinand and Isabella. These sovereigns intrusted the regeneration of the church to the learned and devoted Cardinal Ximenes (Eng. pron. zĭ-mė-nēz), who in a lifetime of courageous service cleansed the Augean stables of the Spanish clergy. This great man renewed the spiritual life of the monastic orders, brought the parochial clergy back to a sense of their obligations as guides and comforters of the people, and established schools and seminaries which, obligatory for all candidates for the priesthood, put an end, to a large extent, to the clerical ignorance so vigorously scourged by the humanists.

The Catholic reform begins in Spain under Ferdinand and Isabella

It is true that the Spanish revival identified itself with medieval scholasticism and was distinguished by a rigorous orthodoxy. It is also true that it shaped for itself as its mightiest weapon the Inquisition and practiced a fierce intolerance. However, in spite of the starkly conservative character of the movement, Spain experienced a genuine religious renewal. So great was its energy that it poured at last over the national boundaries and sent an electric current through the whole paralyzed body of the church.

Dynamic character of the Spanish revival

One of the outstanding accompaniments of every religious revival in the Middle Ages had been the voluntary association of men and women in monastic orders dedicated to religious exercises or to social service. Not only in Spain but in the other Catholic countries as well, in measure as they caught the Spanish spirit, this medieval phenomenon was repeated, with the result that organizations animated with the purest Catholic zeal came into being and multiplied rapidly. As early as 1524 a handful of earnest ecclesiastics at Rome founded the order of the Theatines. Influenced by the Spanish example but also no doubt by the chilling blasts that blew from Wittenberg, they held that, above all, the parochial clergy must be aroused to a new sense of duty. The Theatine order was planned, therefore, and rose to fame as an association of priests, who, turning away from idleness, ignorance, and self-indulgence, pledged themselves to the highest ecclesiastical ideals.

Early evidences of Catholic revival: the Theatines

Far more widely effective was a new order of begging friars, the Capuchins. Founded some two years after the Theatines, the Capuchins practiced simplicity and kindliness and, moving freely among the common people from whom they sprang and whose language they spoke, they became an important link in the chain of influences that kept the Italian masses loyal to the church. Both of these orders were before long completely overshadowed by the Jesuits.

The Capuchins

The Jesuits, or Society of Jesus, as the order is officially called, were

founded by Ignatius Loyola. Loyola was a Spanish nobleman, who, as
was natural in one of his birth, followed the profession of arms until,
during convalescence from a wound received at the siege of Pampeluna
(1521), he chanced to read certain holy books dealing with the lives of
Jesus and the saints. His high-strung nature was so fired with this reading that thenceforth he knew no other ambition than, in imitation of
the early martyrs, to dedicate his life to the church.

Loyola, the knight, turns to the saints

The earliest actions of the convert were wildly extravagant and ineffective. He eventually saw that he needed to put himself in possession
of a solid body of knowledge, and at thirty-three years of age began the
study of Latin, philosophy, and theology. While attending the university
of Paris, he made the acquaintance of some kindred spirits who in 1534
solemnly bound themselves to him and to one another in the service of
Christ and the church.

Loyola seeks an education

The group of seven companions (for that was the original number),
welded into a unit by the inspired leadership of the Spanish nobleman,
presently departed for Venice in the hope of crossing the sea to the Holy
Land. When the outbreak of a new war with the Turks made the plan
impossible, they contented themselves with taking the road to Rome to
obtain the papal endorsement of their society. In 1540 Paul III officially
authorized the order and at the same time approved its purpose and
organization as outlined in Loyola's petition.

Founding of the Jesuits, 1540

The Society of Jesus experienced an almost phenomenal growth. Before it had celebrated its fiftieth anniversary it boasted thousands of
members attached to hundreds of colleges and houses distributed
throughout Catholic Europe. With rare consistency this enormous establishment remained dedicated to the founder's leading purposes, which,
as recited in the original charter of 1540, were three: (1) mission work
throughout the world but, more particularly, in Protestant lands; (2)
preaching and directing the conscience; (3) education of the young.

Rapid expansion of the order and its three aims

Turning first to the mission work of the Jesuits, we learn that the
dedicated enthusiasm of the members carried them to the ends of the
earth. Thus Francis Xavier (pron. zā'-vi-er) had an extraordinary success in the far east among the Japanese, while the conversions effected
by Father Marquette among the Hurons and Iroquois loom large in
American colonial history. Very numerous were the Jesuits who labored
as missionaries in European lands threatened by Protestantism. Some
particularly bold spirits even ventured among peoples already fanatically
Lutheran or Calvinist. If Poland, Austria, and Bavaria, hanging on the
brink, were saved for Catholicism, the thanks of the church are due
mainly to the Jesuits. Their usual practice in Protestant lands was to
single out for attention ruling families and officials in the highest walks
of life. It was to this procedure that they owed the conversion, in the

(1) Jesuit missionary labors

seventeenth century, of the elector of that country, Saxony, which had been the cradle of the Reformation, and of the Scottish Stuarts on the British throne.

By their preaching and confessing, the second of their above-listed activities, the Jesuits gave proof of their intellectual energy and subtlety or, as their Protestant enemies would have it, of their trickery and dishonesty. So successfully did they exhort the faithful from the pulpits of their churches and so delicately did they direct the lives of their followers from the confessional that they were in eager demand in an age in which men were deeply perturbed by the prevalent religious differences. Practically without exception the Catholic sovereigns of Europe promoted Jesuits to the service of their private chapel, enabling them by this intimate intercourse to wield a wide, though indefinable, political influence. **(2) Jesuit work in pulpit and confessional**

In was in their third field, the field of education, that the Jesuits won their greatest distinction. Aware that youth is the impressionable age, they gave their attention to the multiplication of schools and colleges, and by their zeal and energy brought their instruction to a high degree of excellence. It was to a certain extent by championing better educational methods that Protestantism had won its victory, especially among the upper classes. To this Protestant educational movement the Jesuits opposed their own, carrying it out on a much more comprehensive and unified plan. By the seventeenth century the Jesuit colleges, established in Italy, France, the Spanish Netherlands, and Catholic Germany, had fairly outstripped all rival institutions, while in Portugal and Spain the order had gained a complete monopoly in the educational field. **(3) The Jesuits as educators**

Devotion, no matter how well sustained, cannot by itself explain the remarkable achievements of the Jesuits. Their success may in no small part be ascribed to a form of organization, which, although only gradually perfected, was implicit from the start in Loyola's conception. As was natural for a former soldier, Ignatius took the army as his model. Through gradations of authority culminating in a commander-in-chief or general, he fused his followers into a co-ordinated group held together by an iron military discipline. **The Jesuits organized as an army**

A youth on being accepted as a Jesuit novice learned as his first lesson complete subordination. As an aid to this end he was obliged to shape his life by the *Spiritual Exercises,* a devotional book composed by Loyola himself and marvelously adapted to the suppression of every trace of an individual will in the interest of the order. After a two years' course the novice became a *scholastic.* Scholastics took the course in arts and on graduation were permitted to qualify as teachers in their turn. Specially endowed scholastics, and only such, were invited to study theology. After a thorough training they might hope to become priests and to be elevated **Jesuits classified according to training and ability** to the rank of *spiritual coadjutors*. Individuals found to be unsuited for the profession of either teachers or priests were classified as *temporal coadjutors* and served the order to the best of their ability as laymen. They represented the lowest Jesuit rank, with the scholastics and spiritual coadjutors set above them in the order named.

The inner governing group and the supreme general

Although the above-listed three classes embraced the bulk of the membership, they had no claim to the government of the Society. This was reserved to the *Professed of the Four Vows,* a limited body selected from the spiritual coadjutors and composing the Society in the strict sense of the word. All Jesuits of whatever grade took the three vows, sanctioned by monastic usage, of chastity, poverty, and obedience, but the Professed added a fourth vow (hence their name) of special and unalterable obedience to the pope. Even the Professed, however, were not so much a consulting parliament as a military staff. They might advise the supreme general, whom they elected to office for life, but they were absolutely at his will and pleasure, once he had been installed in office.

Significance of the fourth vow

In the fourth vow resides the special significance of the order for the political history of the Counter-Reformation. The Jesuits conceived of themselves as and, in fact, were the militia of the pope and first, defensively and finally, offensively waged perpetual war with heretics and infidels for the glory of the church—*ad maiorem gloriam ecclesiae.*

There remain for consideration three agencies with which the church completed its armament in preparation for the war with its enemies. They are the Inquisition, the Council of Trent, and the Index.

The Spanish Inquisition

We have learned that the Inquisition, conceived as a special board for the investigation and suppression of heresy, was intermittently employed throughout the Middle Ages, sometimes locally by the bishops, sometimes more universally by the popes. In the fifteenth century the spread of humanism somewhat discredited violence in matters of faith and caused the Inquisition to decline in authority. It experienced a revival when the Spanish government, faced with the problem of the Jews and Moors, petitioned the popes for its resumption. In consequence, under Ferdinand and Isabella, the famous Spanish Inquisition was set up, but it should be noted that it remained in all essential respects independent of Rome and operated as much in the civil as in the ecclesiastical interest.

Creation of the Roman Inquisition

When Pope Paul III began to look about in order to strengthen the Catholic defenses, he was greatly struck with the repressive work done in Spain. In 1542 he issued a bull establishing a papal Inquisition endowed with universal authority. A board of cardinals sitting at Rome was empowered to try heresy cases and pass sentence, acting at the same time as a court of appeal from inquisitorial courts to be set up in the various European territories. As heresy, besides being a sin, was also accounted a crime, the inquisitors were privileged, in consonance with the practice of criminal courts throughout Europe at that time, to put the accused to torture in order to extract a confession of guilt. This circumstance, together with the fires which were presently lit at Rome, explains why the Roman Inquisition soon spread a terror hardly inferior to that connected with its Spanish exemplar.

Although it was the ambition of Paul III and his successors to give the new institution a jurisdiction as wide as that of the church itself, they did not achieve their purpose. The Spanish government politely notified Rome that in the future, as in the past, it intended to do its own heresy-hunting, and almost all other Catholic states answered in the same vein. Not that these governments were averse to persecution or, as we shall see, failed to practice it, but they were averse to increasing the pope's power by authorizing an infringement of the national jurisdiction.

The Roman Inquisition excluded from many Catholic states

In point of fact the new Roman Inquisition never exercised any notable activity outside of Italy. Over Italy, however, it was completely effective and had no small part in stamping out, not only the new seeds of heresy, but also some of the fairest spiritual plants which had grown up under the shelter of humanism. It will not do to explain the gradual cultural eclipse of Italy on the single ground of the Spanish political conquest. The eclipse was caused even more by the fact that the Italians, tiring of their perilous Renaissance audacity, succumbed also spiritually to Spain.

Crushing effect of the Inquisition in Italy

It will be remembered that the Lutheran schism had no sooner made its appearance than a General Council of the church was proposed as the natural and certain remedy. Emperor Charles V was won over to the plan and from an early date importuned the pope to call together the parliament of Christendom. But the pope hesitated. The Councils of Constance and Basel, sitting in the first half of the fifteenth century, had threatened papal control by championing a policy which would have lowered the pope to the rank of a constitutional sovereign. It was only with the greatest difficulty that the pontiffs of the conciliar age had defeated the plans of their opponents and preserved the power which they considered to be theirs as the divinely instituted successors of St. Peter.

The popes oppose the calling of a General Council

Stubborn as was the opposition of the popes of Luther's day to Charles's policy of a General Council, Charles was a very powerful man and could not be consistently flouted. Sometimes he was almost omnipotent and on such occasions the pope had to make at least a show of acquiescence. In these circumstances Paul III in the year 1542 reluctantly issued the call for a Council to meet in the city of Trent on the southern slope of the Alps. Changing his mind, he adjourned it before even a single session had been held. In 1545 Pope Paul III once more, and in 1551 Paul's successor, went through the same comedy, except that the sessions were at least formally opened and a limited amount of business transacted. When,

The popes repeatedly summon and adjourn the Council of Trent a little past the middle of the century, Emperor Charles V was defeated by the German Protestants, he reached the conclusion that his conciliar remedy for the heretical poison was a failure and, resigning the imperial crown, retired to Spain to die in monastic seclusion.

Simultaneously with the disappearance of Charles V from the scene the whole Catholic outlook underwent a dramatic change. The spirit of reaction triumphed, the policy of conciliation was rejected, and under Jesuit inspiration the church drew its ranks closer together, committing its destinies into the hands of its traditional leader, the pope. No longer fearful of a Council under these altered circumstances, Pope Pius IV (1559-1566) issued a new call which resulted in the famous and concluding session of Trent of 1562-1563. With the trouble-breeding Protestant question eliminated from discussion, for these stalwart prelates met to the battle cry of "no compromise," the Council was able to perform a notable work of strictly orthodox reconstruction.

In response to the new moral fervor animating the clergy the Council began by correcting some outstanding clerical abuses. It enforced episcopal residence, condemned pluralism (the practice of holding several ecclesiastical benefices at the same time), and established seminaries to bring the clergy to a higher educational level.

Then the Council rolled up its sleeves to attack the basic issues between itself and Protestantism, the issues of doctrine. Without a trace of equivocation it took its stand on tradition, reaffirming the labors of the scholastic doctors and restating in terms of strict historical continuity every doctrinal position the Protestants had attacked. Of course the Lutheran formulation of justification by faith was condemned and the efficacy of good works explicitly affirmed. By laying a formal anathema on every slightest variation from Catholic orthodoxy every possibility of a present or future compromise between the old and the new faith was destroyed. In short, *The Canons and Decrees of the Council of Trent,* under which name the official acts were published, constitute a declaration of war. From a purely military viewpoint they have the merit of precisely staking off the ground which the Catholics were prepared to defend in the current and continuing struggle with their opponents. In that wearing fight the Protestants were to learn that the lack of a common doctrinal ground, resulting from their bitter differences of opinion, was a tremendous handicap.

A result of the Council, surprising in view of the reluctance of the popes to call it together, was that the papacy emerged from the sessions with added prestige, for, though not in express words, the Council disposed of the ancient constitutional issue whether the final authority in the church rested with the pope or with the general assembly of Christendom. Though the papal absolutism had become established in the Middle

---

The final session of the Council of Trent, 1562-1563

The Council corrects abuses in the church

The Council condemns every Protestant variation from orthodoxy

Victory of papal absolutism

Ages, it had frequently been challenged, especially by the Councils of the fifteenth century. Even in the Council of Trent there was a party of bishops who took their stand on the old platform of conciliar supremacy. But the papalists, ably assisted by the new champions of the pope, the Jesuits, won an undisputed victory. It would hardly be an exaggeration to say that the Council of Trent in effect surrendered the ancient conciliar claim and affirmed the absolutism of the pope in matters of both faith and government. In proof of this statement let the fact be adduced that the next ecumenical council did not meet till the nineteenth century (1870), and then only to add the final touch to the pope's supremacy by the declaration of his infallibility.

Before adjourning, the Council of Trent empowered the pope to draw up a list of forbidden books (*Index Librorum Prohibitorum*). The commission to which the work was intrusted issued its first list or Index in 1564. By additions from time to time an attempt was made to keep abreast of new publications as they fell from the press. The Index was arranged in three categories, the first of which listed tainted individuals, so-called heresiarchs, who were condemned *in toto;* the second named individual dangerous works; the third indicated forbidden passages within books otherwise unobjectionable. Wherever, as in Italy, the Index became effective, it must have contributed to the darkening of the intellectual skies. But many Catholic countries, doubtless to the advantage of the free play of ideas, refused to enforce it; and even a learned Jesuit was found, who, a white crow in a black flock, significantly hinted that the best way to discredit bad books was to write better ones.

The Index of Forbidden Books

In summing up the renewal effected by the Roman church, we are fully justified in speaking of it as a Reformation since it improved the manners and morals of the prelates, gave birth to new and highly disciplined orders, and raised the level of learning and devotion in the priesthood. But it is also clear that by breaking with the spirit of criticism and reverting to the medieval tradition the Counter-Reformation turned its back on humanism and the Renaissance. Of course it might be argued that Protestantism had preceded Catholicism in declaring war on the Renaissance by reviving theological controversies and by resting its case ultimately not on human reason but on blind faith. Regardless of the exact degree of responsibility for the phenomenon incurred by each of the two hostile Christian groups, around the middle of the sixteenth century the promise of a liberated human spirit implied in the Renaissance was wiped out by a troubled period of religious warfare.

Reformation and Counter-Reformation temporarily extinguish the Renaissance

By that warfare, blindly and passionately conducted, Western civilization seemed to be permanently deflected from the line of advance traced

by the Renaissance. If this proved not to be the case, if the great interrupted adventure of the fifteenth century was, after an interval, resumed,
the credit for that resumption belongs to neither Catholicism nor Protestantism but rather to those scattered individuals who, servants of the
human spirit rather than of any church, were content to tend the sacred
flame outside the warring camps.

The Renaissance marches on

8   SPAIN UNDER EMPEROR CHARLES V AND HIS SON, PHILIP II: HER WORLD EMINENCE AND HER DECAY

RULERS OF SPAIN

Ferdinand (of Aragon) *m.* Isabella (of Castile)
d. 1516   d. 1504

Joan (*d.* 1555) *m.* Philip of   Catherine *m.* { 1 Arthur, prince of Wales
Hapsburg (*d.* 1506)   2 Henry VIII of England
Charles I (1516-56) *m.* Isabella of Portugal
(Emperor Charles V)

Philip II (1556-98)

Philip III (1598-1621)

Philip IV (1621-65)

WHEN THE GRANDSON of Ferdinand and Isabella, who in 1516 mounted the throne of Spain as King Charles I, was, three years later, elected to the empire and became Emperor Charles V, his Spanish subjects had cause to mourn rather than to rejoice at this increase of dignity; for, having duties henceforth in Germany, the monarch could no longer give an undivided attention to his Spanish task. In fact his interests, which, besides Spain and Germany, embraced also the Netherlands and Italy, obliged him to abandon a narrowly national viewpoint and to broaden his policy till it assumed continental dimensions. — *Charles not merely a Spanish monarch*

Charles was by nature neither exceptionally energetic nor unusually ambitious. Even as a young man he was taciturn, wary, and patient. However, having once made up his mind to pursue a particular course, he was inclined to stick to it with stubborn tenacity. When a series of remarkable coincidences put him at an early age in possession of a large part of Europe, far from having his head turned by the abundant favors of fortune, he faced his responsibilities with, on the whole, extraordinary deliberation and elaborated a policy characterized by a very creditable self-restraint. — *Character of Charles*

Having examined the actual policy pursued by Charles in the chapter dealing with the German Reformation, we may here sum it up as signifying a conception of himself in the capacity of arbiter (not master) of the states of Europe, which were conceived to be held together by a single faith, whereof the Roman church was the divinely appointed custodian. — *His conception of himself as arbiter of Europe*

139

This view signified the revival of a medieval dream which Charles succeeded in bringing nearer to realization than any emperor since the Saxon Ottos. Nonetheless, in the end his dream failed, most conspicuously, no doubt, in Germany, where Charles experienced the bitter sorrow of having to concede the protection of the law to a hateful heresy.

Since for the support of a policy that covered all Europe the emperor depended largely on Spanish resources and Spanish soldiery, the conclusion seems justified that his failure to identify himself exclusively with the particular interests of Spain was hurtful to that country. Moreover, he left a perilous heritage to his son Philip, who, without becoming emperor, identified himself as fully as ever his father had done with the Catholic faith. As we shall see, he did not hesitate to stake all the resources of Spain on the struggle against the rising tide of Protestantism. While, by championing the Catholic church, father and son gave their country a universal significance it might otherwise have missed, the fact remains that they put a burden on the Spanish state and people under which, in the end, they disastrously broke down.

Philip pursues a universal Catholic rather than a national Spanish policy

The reigns of the emperor and his son, covering almost the whole sixteenth century, constitute an extraordinarily brilliant episode, during which the history of Europe seems to revolve around Spain. With Philip's demise (1598) there was an eclipse so sudden as to bewilder the observer and so deep as to have remained substantially unbroken to our own day. We are forced to conclude that beneath the surface splendor a dry rot was quietly at work which, when it at last broke through the crust, produced catastrophe. An examination of the domestic situation, to which we shall turn first, will bear out this hypothesis. Beginning with the reign of Charles (1516-1556), we shall examine the internal developments of Spain to the end of discovering what light they may throw on the amazing Spanish collapse.

The brilliance of the two reigns followed by darkness

We have learned in an earlier chapter that Charles inherited a growing royal power which, exercised against the lawlessness of feudalism, had been the source of considerable social benefits. But, strong monarch that Charles was, in both of his still separate kingdoms of Castile and Aragon he had in each case to reckon with a parliament or cortes, which not only controlled the purse but also insisted on being consulted in all legislative matters.

Charles a constitutional ruler

In Castile, the real heart of Spain, there occurred early in Charles's reign a constitutional crisis. Angered by the sovereign's too arbitrary procedure, the cities of Castile, constituting the most active element represented in the cortes, revolted with the general plan of gaining more consideration for their wishes. As the movement was poorly co-ordinated, the royal forces were able to stamp out the fire (1522) so completely that Charles was left in a position enabling him to dictate the terms of peace.

Revolt of the cities of Castile (1522) and triumph of absolutism

In consequence, some cities were, by way of punishment, deprived of their right of representation in the cortes, while all of them had to admit a royal representative (*corregidor*) in their midst and to accept other serious curtailments of their municipal liberties. It was a set-back for self-government from which it never recovered. True, the cortes of Castile was not deprived of its right to meet periodically and vote the taxes. Henceforth, however, it showed no initiative and, lacking self-confidence, became completely subservient to the executive. In short, following the rout of 1522, the once proud Castilian cortes degenerated to a royal rubber stamp.

The cortes of Aragon proved itself to be made of sterner stuff than its Castilian counterpart and obliged Charles strictly to respect its traditional rights. It was not reduced to subservience till the reign of Charles's successor, Philip II. In the year 1591 this monarch seized a convenient pretext to overrun Aragon with a Castilian army and by this means to break, if not exactly the Aragonese constitution, at least the will of the Aragonese deputies to use the cortes against the royal pleasure. Undoubtedly the movement in Spain throughout the sixteenth century was toward absolutism and away from constitutional practices. The steady expansion of the arbitrary power of the crown may be safely interpreted as a decline of public health. *Taming of the cortes of Aragon by Philip II*

Another cause of deterioration, already noticeable under Charles and cumulatively effective under his successors, carries us into the field of economics. The Spaniards were not a numerous people nor was their country rich in natural resources, save in minerals like iron, zinc, and copper still but sparingly used in that day. Besides, owing perhaps to the warm climate, they were characterized by a certain physical indolence. When the trans-Atlantic discoveries under Ferdinand and Isabella and the projection of Spain into world politics under Charles lifted the country into the leading place in Europe, the necessity arose of increasing the national productiveness if the rapidly rising expenses of the government were to be successfully met. *The mediocre resources of Spain*

Now the peninsula was a land of agriculture and sheep-raising with few and relatively unimportant manufactures. Instead of the country experiencing in the wake of its territorial expansion a broadening of its economic activities, they continued much as before, with the single exception of sheep-raising. While this activity increased, it had then and has always had the drawback of involving a very destructive use of land. Besides, the increase of pasture meant a contraction of the land devoted to crops. This in its turn brought about the decrease and impoverishment of the peasantry to the sole advantage of the great land-owning nobles. After the middle of the century economic production declined in prac- *Territorial expansion attended by economic stagnation*

tically every department, even including sheep-raising, and the impoverishment of the country became manifest to every observer.

The material decay may in large measure be ascribed to an unbelievably inept system of taxation. Since the clergy and nobles, the two privileged classes, were tax-exempt, the task of finding the national revenue
fell almost exclusively upon the towns; and the method of taxing the
urban population was to lay a burden of ten per cent on every commercial transaction. This sales tax, called *alcabala,* had the inevitable
effect of depressing trade, since it shut off the very air by which the
urban classes lived.

Stupid taxation throttles trade

The sad story of Spanish manufactures furnishes another instance of
governmental stupidity. The demand of the Spanish colonists beyond the
seas for manufactured articles should have been the occasion for a lively
expansion of industry. But the blank ignorance on the part of the government of the laws of political economy led it to burden the rising industries of silk and woolen textiles with so many regulations that they
were suffocated under a mountain of red tape. A stationary or declining
productiveness, on the one hand, and ominously growing government
expenses, on the other, define a situation which obliged the monarch to
become so extortionate as gradually to drain away the wealth of the
country.

Stupid regulations throttle industry

For a time, it is true, the government was able to deceive itself regarding the uninterrupted economic enfeeblement. The gold and silver mines
of Mexico and Peru poured a stream of bullion into the country which
everybody fallaciously took for wealth and which did indeed enable the
government to hire mercenaries and purchase military stores, that is, to
engage in expenditures imposed by the exigencies of foreign policy. However, economically considered, all such expenditures must be set down
as pure waste. In the long run the Spanish bullion regularly passed into
the hands of the commercial and industrial peoples, such as the Dutch
and English, who were able to supply the goods which the Spaniards
wanted but which either through native indolence or ignorant government measures they failed to create. In fact the paradox might be ventured that the abundance of American metal poured into the Spanish
coffers was, instead of a blessing, a curse, since it had the evil moral
effect of confirming this southern people in the delusion that a nation
can become rich without work.

The mirage of American gold and silver

From this recital of the maladies of Spain the Inquisition must not be
omitted. Established, as we have seen, under Ferdinand and Isabella, it
retained its tragic effectiveness under Charles, who never wavered in his
support of its main purpose. That purpose was to persecute the two alien
groups, the Jews and the Moors, which in the course of the Middle Ages
had been incorporated in the Spanish body politic, until every trace of

*The Inquisi-
tion directed
against Jews
and Moors*

infidelity had disappeared from the land and the nationalist dream, "one people, one king, one faith," had been realized. When we recall that trade and industry were largely in the hands of these same Jews and Moors, their systematic extermination provides us with a further explanation of Spain's economic decline.

The fierce intolerance indicated by the Inquisition was shared by all classes alike, from the great nobles to the humble peasant-serfs. The victims of the inquisitorial courts were openly and ceremoniously destroyed by fire in public executions called *autos-da-fé* (acts of faith), and to these gruesome spectacles the whole population crowded as to a merry-making or a bullfight. The descendants of the Moors, who after accepting Christianity were called Moriscos and continued to be regarded as insincere converts, proved a greater problem than the Jews because of the nearness of their Moslem relatives across the straits of Gibraltar. Against them the royal vigilance was never for a moment relaxed. Occasionally the fanatic treatment to which they were subjected caused them to break forth in an armed rebellion. This may to a certain degree have eased their tragic fate, since, instead of perishing individually and over a long period by rack and fagot, they fell in multitudes on a single day by the avenging sword. "Autos-da-fé" and wars of extermination

When in the course of Charles's reign, the Lutheran opinions gained a foothold here and there, the Inquisition, rejoicing at the discovery of a new group of enemies, threw itself upon the Protestant heretics and so thoroughly eradicated them that Protestantism never again raised its head in any form in Spain. Not in many pages could one exhaust the ills, moral, economic, and intellectual, which flowed from the fierce system of oppression represented by the Inquisition. Suppression of the Protestant heresy

The last thirteen years of his rule Charles spent away from Spain closely occupied with German affairs. His failure to quell the Protestant movement broke his spirit, and he resigned his many crowns. Spain with Italy and the Netherlands went to his son Philip, Germany to his brother Ferdinand. Philip II (1556-1598) found himself on his accession at the head of territories not much less extensive than those which Charles had governed; and as he did not become emperor he could, following his accession, reside uninterruptedly in Spain and identify himself in speech, dress, and manners with his Spanish countrymen. In consequence his policy, even though it was not so much dedicated to Spanish as to universal Catholic interests, aroused so little opposition that he came to be regarded by his people, as his father never had been, as a truly national king. Philip II an out-and-out Spaniard in feeling and manners

Every historical personage has two aspects, depending on whether he is viewed with favor or disfavor. To his devoted Spaniards Philip II was a circumspect and estimable ruler; for the other peoples of Europe,

more particularly of the Protestant north, he was the fiercest tyrant and
the most persistent enemy of light the age produced. The modern historian cannot identify himself with either of these views. He sees in
Philip a severe, formal, and narrow-minded man, who was animated by
the Catholic fervor traditional among his people and his family, and
whom the sad experiences of his father filled with an instinctive horror
of religious diversity. Hence his guiding thought was to maintain the
Catholic faith by repression of heresy through the Inquisition, where he
had the power; by war, where war was the unavoidable alternative.

The character of Philip II

Contemporary Protestants shuddered as they identified Philip with the
Inquisition. While from their standpoint their aversion was fully justified,
it should not be forgotten, especially as it throws a penetrating light on
this age of religious conflict, that there was not a feature of his reign of
which he was more proud than of the Inquisition since, by means of it,
he was doing God's will and securing the triumph of the divinely instituted Roman Catholic church.

Philip and the Inquisition

However, apart from this one spark of religious enthusiasm, Philip's
joyless nature was as foreign to elation as is that of the typical head of
a bank. He passed his days and his nights over state affairs. Every document had to go through his own hands. Historians who have examined
his papers declare it incredible that so much matter should have been
read or written by one man in one lifetime. In fact, work was his failing,
for work with him degenerated into a rage for minutiae and ended by
enfeebling his grasp of essentials. Out of business hours this ogre of the
Protestant mythology was a tender and devoted husband and father.
Even his worthless son, Don Carlos, whose mysterious death in prison
has been the occasion of violent and frequent defamation of the royal
name, he is now admitted to have treated with an exemplary forbearance.

Philip a puritan of Catholic persuasion

This limited and mediocre ruler loomed like a titan on the stage of
European politics for the single reason that he became the representative of a party of world dimensions in a clash of world importance. At
the very time that Philip succeeded to the throne of Spain the Counter-
Reformation had at last organized its forces and was prepared to take the
offensive against Protestantism, which had thus far met with little or no
systematic opposition. Without doubt it accorded with Philip's fanatical
devotion to the church to put himself and his country at the service of
this cause. But here again a judicious observer will demur from the
emotional Protestant view which presents Philip as the evil-minded and
persistent aggressor in the Catholic-Protestant conflict of the second half
of the sixteenth century. Such an observer will readily agree that the
struggle was as much forced on Philip by the logic of events as determined by his own Catholic impulses. Nothing will lend better support to
this position than the narrative account of his reign, to which we shall

*Philip's world posi-
tion owing
to his iden-
tifying him-
self with the
Counter-
Reformation*

now turn. It will show that he slipped into the role of Catholic champion gradually and under the unescapable pressure of circumstances.

On Philip's mounting the throne it looked as if the chief concern with him, as with his father, would be the purely political program of maintaining the Spanish hegemony in Europe by a close watch on France. Within a year of Philip's accession, the French king, Henry II, showed that he, for his part, nursed the same ambition as his predecessor, Francis I, for, in conjunction with Pope Paul IV, he began (1557) a war, the chief object of which, as on all previous occasions, was to wrest Italy from Spanish control.

The Franco-Spanish war of 1557-59

In this new struggle fortune again, as so often before, decided in favor of the Spaniard. True, France gained some successes; above all, she captured Calais from the English, who had come into the struggle on the side of Spain. But after suffering two capital defeats in the English channel area, one at St. Quentin (1557) and the other at Gravelines (1558), she agreed to come to terms. By the Peace of Cateau-Cambrésis (1559), except that France was permitted to retain Calais, no territorial changes of note were carried out. The real import of the treaty may be said to have been that France once more acknowledged the Spanish domination of Italy.

The Peace of Cateau-Cambrésis again underscores the ascendancy of Spain (1559)

As the admission of defeat ran counter to the trend of French ambition, we may be sure that Henry II would have returned to the attack as soon as the occasion served, if the wheel of fortune had not now taken an unexpected whirl. When the Peace of Cateau-Cambrésis was signed, France was already simmering with heresy and rebellion; and Philip, for his part, was morbidly aware that throughout his Netherland heritage Protestant opinion had gained a powerful foothold. By these domestic developments the two kings were temporarily diverted from their political rivalry and moved to concentrate their attention on the problem immediately under their eye. Thus Cateau-Cambrésis marks an epoch. It rings down the curtain on the long struggle between France and Spain, a struggle chiefly over Italy, which had begun more than half a century before, in 1494, with the famous expedition of Charles VIII; and it inaugurates an era of religious wars which cover the rest of Philip's reign.

Cateau-Cambrésis the end of one and the beginning of another epoch

The origin and development of the Protestant movements in France and in the Netherlands will be taken up in later chapters devoted to these countries. Here, where we are considering Spain, it will suffice to indicate the consequences which followed from Philip's mobilizing of the Spanish resources against the Netherland heretics. Let us clearly understand that the Netherlands or Low Countries were not a part of Spain, and that their association with that country was due to the circumstance that through a turn of luck, good or ill, depending on the reader's viewpoint, they owed allegiance to the same sovereign. There was therefore

Netherlands and Spain separate countries with the same ruler no reason why the Spanish state as such should concern itself with the local happenings along the shores of the North sea; and as a matter of fact it did not do so. But Philip, the absolute ruler of Spain, saw fit to employ his Spanish soldiers and revenues to solve a problem that had arisen in another and distinct territory under his scepter.

When, in the course of the decade following Cateau-Cambrésis, the Netherland situation culminated in an armed rising against Philip, the whole contemporary world was sympathetically aroused. In the eyes of the pope and the Catholics, Philip was doing nothing less than fighting their battle, while for the Protestants, whether in Germany, France, or England, the Netherlanders were heroes defending an European cause. Naturally both combatants took advantage of the wide appeal made by the struggle to summon all available help to their side. In this the rebels were, on the whole, more successful than the Spanish ruler, of whose excessive power even Catholics, nay, at times even the pope, continued to be fearful. Intermittently, it is true, but, after all, with much self-sacrificing fervor the Protestants of Germany and France, and most effectively of all, the English Protestants, came to the aid of the hard-pressed sailors and merchants of the Netherlands.

When we take up this struggle in our Netherlands chapter we shall see that it was, in large part at least, the help furnished the rebels by outsiders that balked every effort of Philip to reduce them to obedience. Slowly and reluctantly Philip swung to the opinion that he would never master the situation in the Lowlands until he had punished the leading supporter of his enemies. In what we may call the second phase of the conflict in the Netherlands he turned furiously on Elizabeth of England.

The gist of Philip's enlarged plan was to gather an irresistible navy in the harbors of Spain, an irresistible army on the coast of Flanders, and by an accurately timed co-operative action to overwhelm the island-kingdom in order to make it incapable of giving further help to continental Protestantism. By 1588 the great stroke had been prepared and was inaugurated by the dispatch of an immense fleet, called the Invincible Armada, against the English coast. In our English chapter we shall recount how the Armada proved a miserable fiasco, largely by reason of the superior skill and audacity of the English seamen.

Philip bore his defeat with dignified resignation. He spoke unaffectedly of the deep grief it caused him "not to be able to render God this great service." And as soon as his exhausted means permitted he returned to the attack. But the English, made confident by success, not only parried every blow, but themselves now took the offensive by ravaging the Spanish coast and capturing the treasure-ships which brought to Spain the silver of America.

The dispatch of the Armada may be set down as the climax of the

Philip's war in the Netherlands interests every country of Europe

Philip is drawn into a war with England

Failure of the Invincible Armada, 1588

The English assume the offensive

general struggle over the issue of religion. Not that Philip ever weakly renounced his purpose or that there were not later ferocious wars involving the two embroiled faiths. However, in the light of the failure of 1588 a number of statements bearing on Philip and the Catholic-Protestant rivalry may be safely ventured: (1) Philip's championship of the Catholic cause had come to a disastrous end; (2) the Netherland rebels and the Protestant north in general had been made safe from overthrow; (3) Spain's brief rule of the seas passed into history to be succeeded by the sea-rule of the Netherlands and England. The consequences of Philip's failure against the Netherlands and England

It gives us the measure of Philip's difficulties and helps explain his failure in his war with Protestantism to recall that he was heavily engaged at the same time on another, the Mediterranean, front. Here he had to meet the naval power of the Turks and their corsair allies of the African coast. We are aware that this same Mohammedan combination had troubled the Emperor Charles, and that, even though he occasionally carried the war to Tunis and Algiers, both his ships and shores continued to be exposed to the depredations of the pirates. With Philip's advent the situation changed, if at all, for the worse because of the uninterrupted attention he was obliged to give to the developments in northern Europe. Philip's Mediterranean difficulties

At length, in 1571, Pope Pius V persuaded Philip to join hands with Venice, still a considerable naval power commanding the remnants of a colonial empire in the eastern Mediterranean, in a resolute effort to set a term to the audacity of the Mohammedans. The pope himself made a contribution of money and ships, and Philip, for once liberating himself from the administrative red tape which so often choked his activities, with unusual speed assembled a great fleet in the waters of Sicily at Messina. The supreme command over the allied forces was intrusted to Don John of Austria, the handsome and chivalrous half-brother of the Spanish king and his complete counterpart in temper and demeanor. War against the Turks by Philip, Venice, and the pope

When all was ready, Don John sailed his fleet eastward, resolved to throw himself upon the enemy with the least possible delay. On sighting the Mohammedan fleet in the gulf of Lepanto, off the western coast of Greece, the enthusiastic prince poured into his men his own unconquerable spirit. Conspicuous in a suit of white velvet trimmed with gold, he had himself rowed between the lanes of galleys, crying exhortations to his men: "Christ is your leader. This is the battle of the Cross." In the combat that followed (October 7, 1571) the young commander's dash and courage contributed notably to the outcome, which was the greatest victory at sea thus far ever won by any Christian force over the apparently invincible Turks. Of the two hundred galleys engaged on either side a squadron of only forty Turkish vessels managed to escape. The rest with all their men and armament were either sunk or captured. It The battle of Lepanto, 1571

was a by no means minor source of satisfaction to the victors that 12,000 Christian rowers, forcibly pressed for this menial service, were freed from Moslem slavery.

Great was the exultation of the Christian allies, and justified the self-congratulation of the Spaniards who had made the main contribution to the triumph. It may not be overlooked, however, that its consequences fell short of expectations. Torn violently apart through jealousy, by failing to follow up their success the victors permitted the Ottoman sultan to rebuild his fleet and resume the unchallenged domination, at least of his home waters. After his one magnificent spurt Philip returned to his familiar bureaucratic jog-trot and starved his navy in so shortsighted a manner as to incapacitate it for further offensive fighting. In 1573 his disgusted Venetian allies signed a peace with the Turks in which they surrendered Cyprus to the Moslems; and though the war between Spain and the sultan dragged on for some years, no further battle of consequence took place.

Expectations aroused by Lepanto not realized

The Algerine corsairs, hitherto always open or secret allies of the Turks, continued to be a pest that weighed heavily on the commerce of Spain and Italy. Perpetual vigilance toward them was a fixed necessity of the situation. However, an indisputable benefit resulting from Lepanto was that the Turks renounced an active policy in the western Mediterranean and henceforth gave only sporadic encouragement to their African brothers in the faith.

The African corsairs an unabated evil

Perhaps the most unqualified success associated with the reign of Philip II was his winning of Portugal. The acquisition of this kingdom had, in the interest of peninsular unification, been an ancient object of the Spanish kings. They had, however, wisely refrained from the attempt to effect a union by force of arms. Frequent marriages between members of the two reigning houses had fostered a dynastic intimacy, of which Philip took full advantage when, in 1580, the death of the childless king of Portugal opened up the question of the succession. While there were aspirants to the Portuguese crown with as good or a better claim than Philip, the Spanish ruler was close at hand with an irresistible army and, by acting swiftly, took possession of the throne before the opposition could gain momentum.

Philip acquires Portugal, 1580

Owing to the considerable trade and numerous colonies of Portugal, its subjection to the Spanish ruling house greatly strengthened the Spanish position in the world. However, it was not long before Philip discovered a fly in the ointment. Conscious of their separate nationality and intensely proud of their achievements during the Age of Discoveries, the Portuguese accepted the yoke of the Spanish king unwillingly and never ceased to exhibit evidences of restiveness. True, they organized no systematic rebellion against their first Spanish master, but, quietly nurs-

The union not to the liking of the Portuguese

ing the precious memories of independence, they adjourned action till the decline of Spain had run its destined course.

Some forty years after Philip II's death the Portuguese at length revolted and won back their freedom under a new royal house, the house of Braganza (1640). Thus ended in disaster what in Philip's lifetime was celebrated as the successful consolidation of the peninsula.

The union again severed, 1640

On turning to the domestic situation under Philip we find there is little to add to the story already told of the country's ills, except to say that they became steadily more deep-seated and incurable. In the face of the waxing absolutism the cortes of both Castile and Aragon, although they continued to be summoned from time to time for a formal session, paled to helpless, constitutional wraiths; the Inquisition completely dominated the social and intellectual life, acting on the plan promptly to pounce upon and extinguish every spark of dissidence or originality as soon as it appeared; and the productiveness of both city and countryside declined until to a visitor from the busy industrial north the Spanish people gave the impression of a nation of idlers and beggars.

Intensification of the domestic evils under Philip II

Nor is this the end of the tale. In measure as misery spread, the taxes did not decline but mounted, owing to the high-flying foreign policy of the sovereign and his ceaseless embroilments with enemies in every part of Europe. Up to the very last year of his life Philip was engaged in sucking up, as with a sponge, the wealth of Spain, with the result that when the ruler died, who in the eyes of the credulous was, owing to the bullion of America, as fabulously rich as Croesus, there was not enough money in the treasury to meet the most immediate wants of the royal household. The Inquisition, absolutism, insane administrative and economic measures, and a spendthrift Catholic imperialism may be confidently named as the ills which engulfed Spain in her ruin.

Spain exhausted and bankrupt at Philip's death

The successor of Philip II, his son Philip III (1598-1621), was an incapable, deeply religious man, the tool and puppet of his favorites. In 1609 he was forced to lower his pride so far as to sign a truce for twelve years with the Netherland rebels, thereby virtually acknowledging their independence. Thus did the seeds sown by the emperor and his son come to maturity under their successors.

Philip III comes to terms with the Netherland rebels

During the long reign of Philip IV (1621-1665) the shadows still further deepened. In consequence of disasters suffered in the Thirty Years' War and its aftermath, the wretched country sank definitely to the second and third rank among European powers. How in the course of the Thirty Years' War France resumed the struggle for the supremacy in Europe, interrupted by her religious difficulties, and how, under the leadership of the great Cardinals Richelieu and Mazarin, she completely reversed the decision of Cateau-Cambrésis (1559), we shall learn in due time. Let our last word on this swift review of Spanish glory and decay

Accelerated decline under Philip IV

be that by the middle of the seventeenth century the decline of Spain was patent to the most superficial observer.

Spain shares
in the
Renaissance

The early identification of Spain with the Inquisition and its complete identification, under Philip II, with the Counter-Reformation would seem to impose the conclusion that Spain can have had no part in the cultural movement liberated everywhere else in Europe by the Renaissance. Nothing could be more erroneous than such a deduction. In spite of the protective wall erected by the medievally minded state and church of Spain around the country in order to shut out the Renaissance spirit with its worldly aspirations and audacities, that spirit managed to leap the barrier and make a place for itself in the ultra-conservative society of the peninsula. For evidence it will suffice to point, in letters, to Cervantes (d. 1616), in painting, to El Greco (d. 1614) and Velasquez (d. 1660). Nor do they appear alone, as our review of the culture of this period of European history in Chapter 13 will amply show.

9

TUDOR ENGLAND: FROM THE ACCESSION OF HENRY VIII TO THE DEATH OF ELIZABETH

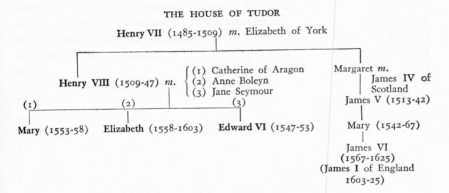

THE HOUSE OF TUDOR

Henry VII (1485-1509) *m.* Elizabeth of York

Henry VIII (1509-47) *m.* { (1) Catherine of Aragon
(2) Anne Boleyn
(3) Jane Seymour

Margaret *m.*
James IV of Scotland

(1) (2) (3)

Mary (1553-58) Elizabeth (1558-1603) Edward VI (1547-53)

James V (1513-42)

Mary (1542-67)

James VI
(1567-1625)
(James I of England
1603-25)

IT WAS DURING the pacification effected by the first Tudor monarch, Henry VII, a pacification in the course of which the civil rage loosed by the Wars of the Roses was gradually spent, that the Revival of Learning gained its first foothold in England. English travelers and scholars, returning from the continent and, more particularly, from Italy, communicated their humanistic enthusiasm to their countrymen until first, the university of Oxford and, later, the sister institution at Cambridge became active centers for the promulgation of the new ideas. While the literature of the ancients was taken up with avidity, in accordance with the tendency generally exhibited among the peoples of northern Europe, a preference was entertained for the Christian learning which centered about the Bible and the Fathers. *The English universities centers of the Revival of Learning*

Throughout the Germanic area, let us recall, the Renaissance was a return to the sources of Christianity rather than to those of antiquity, and England was no exception to the rule. On account of his devotion to both classical and Christian learning the great Dutch scholar, Erasmus of Rotterdam, was given an eager welcome when, in 1499, he paid a visit to the circle of the Oxford humanists. We have already made acquaintance with Erasmus as the leading representative of northern scholarship. During the six visits he paid his English friends between the years *Erasmus in England*

151

1499 and 1517 he gave and received a stimulus which had the happiest consequences for the cause of letters. Innumerable as were the famous Dutchman's English contacts, his best friends as well as the leaders of the English movement were Colet and More. Hence a review of their intellectual interests will serve as the best possible introduction to the prevailing mood of English humanism.

After travel in Italy, John Colet (1466-1519), the son of a wealthy London merchant, settled at Oxford. Here he soon distinguished himself by lectures on the New Testament which combined a sound learning with the deep sentiments of Christian piety. It is significant of his reforming fervor that, like so many contemporary scholars of the continent, he was drawn to the Apostle Paul, in whose direct, concentrated faith he detected an unconscious protest against the theological elaborations of the medieval church. His deep enthusiasm made him a master of pulpit eloquence. Chiefly because of his fame as a preacher, he received a call to the capital, to London, to serve as dean of St. Paul's cathedral.

John Colet, scholar and preacher

Not content with his exacting new duties, Colet resolved to found at his own expense and personally to conduct St. Paul's school for boys, dedicated to the principles of humanism (1512). In the new institution Latin and Greek, taught in a fresh way, replaced the barren studies of the schoolmen. At the same time Christianity was incorporated in the curriculum, not as a round of mechanical ceremonies, but as a spiritual message pointing to right living in this world as the proper approach to the life eternal.

Colet founds St. Paul's school

A similar moral passion informed the thought and life of Sir Thomas More (1478-1535), friend and intimate of both Colet and Erasmus. Brought up in the humanistic circle of Oxford, he became a barrister and, choosing a public career, was at an early age elected to the House of Commons. His distinguished qualities did not escape King Henry VIII, who drew him into his service and, advancing him from post to post, raised him in 1529, on the disgrace of Cardinal Wolsey, to the office of Lord Chancellor, the highest dignity in the realm under the sovereign. His service in this capacity and his tragic end belong to the political history of England to be presently taken up.

Sir Thomas More, humanist and public servant

Concerned at this juncture exclusively with More's place in the English Renaissance, we may agree that his fame rests chiefly on a single volume, the well-known *Utopia*. Originally written in Latin and published in 1516, the *Utopia* is composed of two parts to meet a clear-cut double purpose. Part One is a sweeping criticism, social, political, and religious, of the England of his day; Part Two unfolds the picture of an imaginary commonwealth, Utopia, the region of Nowhere. In Utopia the wrongs and abuses of contemporary society are remedied and men live together in conditions of work and friendship enabling them to enjoy life to the

More's "Utopia"

utmost. Both before and after More there have been sensitive souls who, tormented by the sufferings of humanity, have projected a new and better world to live in. In his particular projection More sketched a communistic society in which private property, considered the root of all evil, is abolished and the simple economy is conducted without the use of money. Only goods rated as necessary are produced, and their distribution is so controlled that every member of society gets an equal share of them. The Utopians are dispersed over their country in small, self-governing groups, each group being made up of a limited number of families which, while living in separate houses, take their meals together in common dining halls. Every grown person is obliged to work at either farming or a craft, though for no more than six hours each day; and each such person employs his free time, not in sports and games, which are taboo, but in the cultivation of virtue by the reading of good books. While several religions flourish and are tolerated by the government, they are all united in the worship of a divine creator.

Exactly as in Germany the English humanists helped prepare the way for social and religious reform; and, also like the German humanists, when the movement called the Reformation came, they protested against its violence as well as against its theological tendencies. Generally speaking, they repudiated the Reformation either in part or altogether. The outstanding difference between the English and the German Reformation is that, instead of the English Reformation being carried through under the leadership of a religious enthusiast, it was, at least in its earliest phase, championed by the ruler of the land. Animated by little or no interest in religious reform as such, the ruler was chiefly moved to score a political victory over the pope. Indeed it is doubtful whether King Henry VIII did anything whatsoever for the Reformation considered as a religious movement. He did, however, most certainly promote it indirectly by withdrawing his country from the Roman allegiance. How that withdrawal was brought about is the kernel of Henry's reign.

The English Reformation in its first phase a political rather than a religious movement

HENRY VIII (1509-1547)

Henry VIII mounted the throne in 1509 in succession to his father, Henry VII, from whom he inherited an authority hardly short of absolutism. He was not yet twenty years old, a youth of attractive presence, skilled in gentlemanly sports, such as riding and tennis, condescending with all people, free-handed and fond of pageantry, and altogether the idol of his nation, which received him with acclamations of joy. Not least exultant over his coming to power were the English humanists, for Henry had been brought into the circle of the new learning by his tutors and was reputed to look upon it with favor.

The accession of Henry VIII, 1509

The joy of the humanists over the accession of Henry did not last long. The king, to be sure, distinguished various members of the learned group by offices and emoluments, but he soon showed that he did not seriously share their reforming zeal, and that he was bent on following his own lead. Beneath the king's smooth exterior appeared a stubborn will which, with the passing of the years, he tended to indulge with less and less restraint. A despot by nature, Henry became ever more despotic by habit and success and, as he grew older, developed a physical grossness which canceled every trace of his early youthful charm.

Breach between Henry and the humanists

Throughout his reign Henry's main purpose was to make himself and his country a decisive factor in European politics. His father had sat quietly at home, perfecting the administration and amassing a considerable treasure. The son saw at once that, with France and Spain holding each other in check and engaged in permanent enmity over Italy, there was a remarkable opportunity for an ambitious sovereign who felt free to throw his weight into the scales for either party. It is true that the French-Spanish controversy only peripherally touched the interests of England. Still, an English ruler of the sixteenth century could not forget that, less than a hundred years before, a warlike predecessor had been crowned king of France, and that from the port of Calais on the French coast, the last stronghold on the continent which floated the English flag, a descent could still at almost any time be made on Paris.

Henry free to choose between France and Spain

That Henry kept a sharp lookout across the channel requires neither apology nor explanation. Nor is it difficult to understand that in the ever renewed wars between France and Spain Henry should have inclined to throw in his lot with Spain, since by this means he might hope to be rewarded with some of the lost French territory. However, though leaning by preference toward Spain, contingencies might arise which would make it advantageous for him to comport himself as the ally of France. In that case he would probably have to content himself with a handsome subsidy of money paid by the French court.

Henry shapes his policy with a sole view to his advantage

Such in outline was Henry's foreign policy, modified, however, by one factor—Scotland. His predecessor had inaugurated a policy of reconciliation with Scotland, which he had hoped would lead in the course of time to a union of the two kingdoms. In this expectation he had married his oldest daughter, Margaret, to the Scottish king, James IV. But matters did not progress as favorably as he had planned. The enmity between Scots and English was bred too deep in the bone to be easily eradicated; and the Scots, suspicious for centuries of their more powerful southern neighbor, had looked so steadily toward France for aid and protection that they could not be easily persuaded to abandon the habit.

Continued enmity between England and Scotland

In the past a war between England and France had very generally also brought Scotland into the field with the object of making a diver-

sion in favor of France along the English border. This traditional alliance, which caught England between two fires, suffered no change during the reign of Henry VIII. Consequently the king was obliged to
wage frequent war with Scotland. But only in moments of intense resentment did he forget what we may call the Tudor policy of reconciliation
and ultimate union between England and Scotland.

Henry VIII frequently at war with Scotland

After these general remarks we can dispense with following in detail
the intricate game which Henry played upon the diplomatic chessboard
of Europe. He joined the pope and Spain in the Holy League of 1512,
the object of which was to drive France from Italy. When Emperor
Charles V in 1521 renewed the war against France, Henry again fought
shoulder to shoulder with Spain, until the great victory of Pavia and the
capture of the French king frightened him with the specter of a universal Spanish domination and drove him for a time into the arms of
France. Late in his reign, in 1543, he joined the emperor once more in
an attack upon Francis I, in which the chief English success was the
capture of Boulogne. During these wars Scotland was very troublesome
and several times invaded England, though with small effect, since at
Flodden (1513) and again at Solway Moss (1542) her armies were crushingly defeated. To sum up, we may say that Henry won small profit for
England from his diplomacy and wars, but that he had the purely personal satisfaction of playing a conspicuous role in international politics.

The record of Henry's wars

The favorite adviser of Henry in the early period of his reign was
Thomas Wolsey. Wolsey was a commoner by birth. Taking orders as a
priest, he rose rapidly by virtue of his talents from post to post, until
the king's favor won for him the archbishopric of York. At the same
time Henry made Wolsey head of the civil administration by appointing
him Lord Chancellor (1515). No public man in his day accumulated
more offices and power.

Wolsey, churchman and statesman

As Lord Chancellor, Wolsey won honor by an able and zealous administration. On first taking office he resolved, under prompting from the
humanists, to remove some of the abuses of the English church. He was
still engaged in examining the problem when, in 1517, Luther drew the
question of a radical reform of the church into the open by publishing
his theses against Indulgences.

Wolsey in favor of moderate reform

Henry, despot and natural lover of authority in every form, followed
Luther's attack upon the papacy and Catholic doctrine with instinctive
aversion. In fact, such was his resentment that he did not disdain to
descend into the lists in person against Luther, and in 1521 published a
vehement pamphlet, wherein he defended both the sacraments and the
papal supremacy. In return the gratified Leo X conferred upon Henry
the title—still employed by English sovereigns—of Defender of the Faith.

Henry attacks Luther and becomes the Defender of the Faith

So close was the understanding between pope and king in Henry's early days. In another ten years the wind had veered and couriers were speeding from Rome, not with messages of friendship but with bulls of excommunication. This radical and dramatic change was brought about by the peculiar circumstances of Henry's marriage and his suit for divorce.

Henry's marriage calls for close consideration. The reader will remember that Henry VII, in pursuance of his plan to strengthen himself against his immediate neighbor, France, had resolved to draw close to Spain. An outcome of this political intimacy was a contract of espousal, by which Arthur, prince of Wales, was married to Catherine, daughter of Ferdinand and Isabella. Shortly after the ceremony Arthur died. But as the desire for the alliance continued as before, the idea naturally occurred to the families concerned to marry Arthur's widow to his surviving brother, Henry.

Marriage of Catherine of Aragon to Arthur, prince of Wales

Unfortunately the plan ran counter to an ancient ordinance of the church, which forbade a man to marry his deceased brother's wife. In this dilemma Pope Julius II, when appealed to, had recourse to his dispensing powers, which enabled him to make an ordinance inoperative in a particular case. He issued what is called a papal dispensation, on the strength of which the marriage took place in 1509, the year of Henry's accession to the throne.

Marriage of Catherine and Henry based on a papal dispensation

Now it will be readily understood that if the pope, as Luther was affirming every day with increasing violence, was an impostor, the exercise of the dispensing power was a usurpation, the law remained inalterably the law, and Henry's marriage was illegal. In addition, therefore, to the natural inclination of a despotic mind to uphold the cause of authority everywhere and at all times, Henry had a very personal reason for wanting to see Luther put down and the sovereignty of the pope raised above reproach and challenge. In this way it happened that Henry crossed pens with Luther and became the Defender of the Faith.

Why Henry supported the pope

But time brings about surprising changes. Only a few years after Henry had appeared as the champion of the pope, his attitude toward his marriage altered. After having for almost two decades shown much attachment to his queen, he began to discover reasons for wanting a divorce from her. The queen had given birth to several children, but only one child, Mary, had survived infancy. What made the situation precarious was that, owing to Queen Catherine's advanced years, she was not expected again to become a mother. Even if Princess Mary had not been a very sickly child, the king might reasonably feel that he was playing a risky game to stake the succession on one fragile life. On dynastic grounds, therefore, Henry felt troubled and desired to marry again.

Henry desires divorce on dynastic grounds

Henry had also an incentive to action of a more personal nature. The aging Catherine had lost her charm for him, and he was now madly infatuated with her young and charming maid of honor, Anne Boleyn. In 1527 he first whispered to his confidant, Wolsey, the word divorce.

Henry desires divorce on personal grounds

Questions of marriage and divorce belonged, as we are aware, to the exclusive competence of the church; and because marriage was a sacrament, the church refused to countenance divorce save in certain exceptional circumstances. Henry believed or professed to believe that his case was exceptional in that the dispensation, on which his marriage was based, was legally defective. He wanted the reigning pope, who was the worldly minded Medicean prince, Clement VII, to acknowledge that defectiveness, thereby automatically canceling his predecessor's dispensation and rendering the marriage null and void.

Henry requests the pope to annul the dispensation

This course Wolsey, who had meanwhile, in addition to his other dignities, become cardinal and papal legate, undertook with all his might to urge upon Pope Clement VII. The pontiff hesitated to comply, partly from conscientious scruples, partly because he did not dare offend the powerful Charles V, who as head of the Spanish house naturally stood by his aunt, the English queen. Clement would examine, he would not pronounce. In 1529 he agreed to send to England Cardinal Campeggio, who, together with Cardinal Wolsey, already on the ground, was empowered to hold a legatine court and ascertain the facts. The king put aside his dignity so far as to appear before the two cardinals like a common suitor. Even this self-humiliation profited him nothing, for the pope, still proceeding on his original plan of delay, suddenly transferred the case to Rome.

Reasons for the pope's delay

Furious at this crumbling of his hopes, Henry let fall the weight of his displeasure on the head of Wolsey. He stripped him of all his civil honors and exiled him from London. Still unappeased, he had just ordered his arrest as a measure preparatory to his execution, when the cardinal was stricken ill and died (1530). At the last he cast a regretful backward look upon his life, using to his attendants words which Shakespeare employed almost literally in his play, *Henry VIII:* "Had I but served my God with half the zeal I served my king, He would not in mine age have left me naked to mine enemies."

Disgrace and death of Wolsey, 1530

Almost any other man would now have given up, but Henry had the kind of will which grows terrible with opposition. If the pope could not be got to act in what the king considered a just cause, he would repudiate the pope altogether and establish the English church on a purely national basis. Further, he would no longer permit the church to function as an independent power, but would reduce it to subjection to the state, which meant, of course, himself. The officers of a church cut off

Henry resolves to be divorced without the pope's consent

from Rome, on the one hand, and dependent on the king, on the other, could be trusted to settle the divorce question as the king desired.

Upon this plan Henry proceeded, but not without frequent pauses in order to give the pope time to reflect upon the dangers he was running, for the royal quarrel with the papacy was a matter of policy, not of conviction, and the king would have avoided it at any cost short of the sacrifice of the divorce. As the pope remained deaf to both the threats and the pleas of Henry, the anti-papal enactments succeeded each other without interruption until every cable binding England to Rome had at last been slipped. Let us tabulate the leading steps of the process.

Henry reluctant to break with the pope

The assembly of the English clergy is called Convocation. In 1531 Convocation was summoned and a decree wrested from it, declaring Henry to be head of the English church. Owing to the qualms expressed by many of the members, the qualifying phrase was added, "as far as the law of Christ allows." The next year the king destroyed the legislative independence of the clergy by requiring them to permit him to revise their statutes and to adopt no new laws without his consent.

Submission of the clergy

By these measures Henry had established his authority over the English clergy. His next act was to repeal the laws by which Rome possessed a foothold in England. As these laws, being acts of parliament, could be repealed only by parliament, this body was by mingled threats and persuasion moved to bow to the royal will. In 1532 parliament abolished the payment to Rome of First Fruits, which, the first year's income of ecclesiastical benefices, constituted the chief revenue the pope drew from England. The next year parliament renewed in a sweeping form a statute of the fourteenth century prohibiting the taking of any legal case outside the kingdom. By this enactment the English ecclesiastical courts acquired the right to pronounce, and pronounce finally, upon the king's suit.

Submission of the parliament

And now further delay was neither necessary nor possible. In February, 1533, Cranmer, a creature of Henry's and half a Protestant at heart, was made archbishop of Canterbury and primate of England; and three months later Cranmer pronounced the desired divorce in his own court. Henry had already without waiting for this action married Anne Boleyn and now proceeded with her public coronation as queen of England (June 1, 1533).

Divorce pronounced by an English ecclesiastical court

When the pope heard of these startling occurrences he at last recovered his power of unambiguous speech and fulminated at Henry a decree of excommunication (July, 1533). But Henry was now secure and could meet the pope's wrath as an equal. In 1534 he had parliament pass a culminating act, the Act of Supremacy, by which the last traces of connection with Rome were removed and the king confirmed in the title,

The Act of Supremacy, 1534

already voted by the clergy, of Supreme Head of the English church, to which title there was now attached no qualification whatever.

Thus, while the English church became national by being cut off from Rome, it also lost its independence and became subject to the crown. Naturally there were many who regretted these changes. If they thoughtlessly crossed Henry's path, they were not likely to escape with their lives. His marriage with Anne Boleyn, the Act of Supremacy, and the other crucial measures could be criticized only at the risk of death. When Sir Thomas More, the humanist, although he had been Lord Chancellor for three years following Wolsey's disgrace and although he was the foremost living Englishman, refused to take the oath involving acquiescence in these high-handed measures, he was convicted of treason and hurried to the block (1535). *Henry forcefully suppresses opposition; execution of Sir Thomas More*

From the first it was an interesting question how far Henry would depart from the traditional Catholic system and approach the Protestant position. In his personal outlook he was as much a Catholic after as before the separation. The sole distinction between Henry then and Henry now was that he had taken, as regards England, the pope's place at the head of the church. To a certain extent, however, he could not fail to be influenced by the Reformation, for the pope and the Catholic world had solemnly repudiated him, and at the height of the struggle with the pope he had fallen under the influence of a counselor, Thomas Cromwell by name, who entertained strong Lutheran sympathies. A number of minor changes, redolent of Lutheranism, were therefore carried through. Every church was ordered to provide itself with an English Bible for general use, indulgences were condemned, pilgrimages forbidden, and a few miraculous images destroyed. The single definitely radical innovation adopted was the suppression of the monasteries. *Henry makes a limited number of Protestant concessions*

We have repeatedly noted that monasticism was the feature of the church which chiefly invited the ridicule and criticism of the humanists. It followed that, wherever the Reformation was victorious, monasticism was the ecclesiastical institution which was first thrown overboard. Doubtless there was much exaggeration in the tales of depravity circulated by Erasmus and other virulent enemies of the orders. Still, where there was so much smoke it is safe to assume there was some fire. Even during the chancellorship of Wolsey, long before the policy of separation was entertained, a number of smaller monasteries had been discontinued on the ground that they no longer rendered a recognizable service. *The issue of the monasteries*

When, after the separation from Rome had become an accomplished fact, Thomas Cromwell presented to the king a plan of monastic suppression on a large scale, Henry readily gave his consent. Without any question he was chiefly persuaded by the immense material advantages accruing to the royal exchequer from the proposed confiscations. To prepare *The suppression of the monasteries, 1536* the ground for his measure Cromwell sent partisan agents through the land to investigate the monastic houses. Although their reports grossly exaggerated the delinquencies of the monks, they served the purpose of the unscrupulous minister, since on being presented to parliament, they moved that body, outraged by the thought of so much wickedness, to adopt the desired legislation.

Disposal of the monastic wealth

In 1536 a bill was passed ordering the suppression of all, save a few of the richest monastic establishments. By bringing pressure to bear on the abbots of the exempted institutions Henry managed by degrees to subject them to the same doom. Before many years had rolled by the English monasteries had become a thing of the past. But the vast wealth of the confiscated houses and lands did not, to any large extent, remain in possession of the crown. A part of it was used to meet Henry's immediate necessities; another part was distributed among greedy noble-men and courtiers; and still another part was honorably dedicated to the support of schools and churches.

The English people accept the royal policy

As far as it is possible to ascertain the attitude of the English people toward the ecclesiastical changes inaugurated by Henry, it would seem that in their majority they consented, though somewhat hesitatingly, to the separation from Rome. They took this stand because in England, as everywhere else, the prestige of the papacy had in recent generations been seriously impaired. However, although they rallied behind the newly created national church, they were, like Henry himself, essentially conservative and Catholic in spirit. Apart from a small band of reformers influenced from the continent, they had no desire for any radical change in the familiar features of the church. Therefore the suppression of the monasteries went beyond their wishes and in the backward counties of the north, where attachment to tradition was particularly strong, led to a dangerous revolt, known as the Pilgrimage of Grace (1536). Henry, as might be expected, put down the insurrection with vigor. But taking the hint which it conveyed, he refused to go farther along the path blazed by the Lutheran princes of Germany.

Henry's doctrine remains Catholic

For the rest of his life Henry was content to stand fast, force the acknowledgment of his supremacy on his subjects, and keep both the service and the doctrine of his church free from the taint of Protestantism. From time to time, in order to remove all doubt, he condescended to inform his subjects what they were authorized to believe; and these pronouncements, such as the Ten Articles of 1536 and the Six Articles of 1539, contained very little to which a strict partisan of Rome might not have set his name. The Six Articles in particular were eminently Catholic. They upheld the sacrament of the mass, auricular confession, and the celibacy of the clergy. For good measure, they made diversity of opinion punishable with death.

Under such a regime there was no peace in England either for supporters of the pope or for adherents of Protestantism, and both these groups were vehemently persecuted. Thomas Cromwell himself, though his fall was coupled with other causes, could not be saved by a long record of faithful, if shifty, service when his support of the religious radicals became obnoxious to the king. In 1540 he was charged with treason and beheaded. The only safety for Englishmen lay in acceptance of the system which their masterful sovereign had imposed and which was substantially Catholic, except for the separation from the venerable capital of Rome and the suppression of the monasteries. **Execution of Cromwell, 1540**

A personal page in Henry's history demands at least passing recognition. It presents the story of his marriages. His ferocity and ruthlessness, which often did him good service in the field of politics, stand out in appalling nakedness in the tenderer associations of the family. We have already followed the tragedy of Catherine of Aragon to the coronation of her coquettish rival, Anne Boleyn. Anne Boleyn gave birth to a daughter, Elizabeth, and not long afterward was executed on the charge of unfaithfulness (1536). The next wife, Jane Seymour, died in childbed, leaving a son, Edward. The fourth wife, a German princess, Anne of Cleves, did not suit Henry at all and was married only to be immediately divorced (1540). As the fifth wife, Catherine Howard, proved unfaithful, her head too was severed by the ax (1542). And so room was made for a sixth wife, Catherine Parr, who managed by dutiful submission to outlive the royal Bluebeard. **Henry's six marriages**

Henry died in 1547. Before his death he had been granted by parliament the right to regulate the succession by will. Accordingly, he devised the crown to his son Edward, with the provision that it should pass, on the failure of Edward's blood, to his daughters Mary and Elizabeth, in the order named. As Edward was a boy only nine years old at his father's death, Henry had provided that a council of regency should govern during his son's minority. At the head of the regency he put Edward's maternal uncle, the duke of Somerset. **The succession as regulated by Henry**

EDWARD VI (1547-1553)

Henry was hardly dead when the council of regency met and, without regard to Henry's wishes, in effect resigned its powers to Somerset, who was authorized to assume the title protector. This measure was of decided consequence because Somerset leaned toward the reforming party. As a majority in the council held similar opinions, Somerset had no difficulty in inaugurating an era of Protestant legislation, especially as he was heartily seconded in his policy by Cranmer, the archbishop of **The Protector Somerset pursues a Protestant policy**

Canterbury. We have therewith touched upon the real significance of the rule of the protector. The English church, which Henry had zealously kept free from theological innovations, was now definitely launched upon Protestant waters.

The Protestant changes enumerated

In case we admit that it was impossible to keep the English church, following its initial breach with the Catholic world, exactly where Henry had left it, we shall incline to defend Somerset against the charge of precipitate change which is frequently made against him. In any case his decision was, while keeping the church national and uniform, to swing the door wide open to Protestant influences. English was therefore substituted for Latin in the services; priests were allowed to marry; the use of holy water was discontinued; and all images were removed from the churches. To lend dignity to the conduct of the new services in English, there was published in 1549 the First Book of Common Prayer. It vindicates the sobriety of Somerset's policy, since Archbishop Cranmer, its chief author, modeled it closely on the ancient services of the church.

The agrarian crisis produced by sheep-raising

But Somerset's fall was at hand. Not because of discontent with his religious innovations, at least not in a marked degree, but, owing primarily to prolonged economic misery, the peasantry of England rose in the summer of 1549 and threatened civil war. The troubles among the English peasants, who were freemen, bore little resemblance to the situation which had provoked the German peasants, held in galling serfdom, to wage the bloody war of 1525. Instead of being bound to the land and laden with services, the English peasants were so little bound that they found themselves in large numbers driven off the land altogether by a procedure known as enclosure. The great English landlords had discovered that, owing to the steady demand for wool in the markets of the continent, their returns were larger from sheep-raising than from agriculture. Therefore, by letting their lands run to pasture and enclosing them, with perhaps the addition of the common lands of which the whole village had once had the use, they drove thousands of peasants from the soil and reduced them to the greatest misery.

Defeat of the peasants and fall of Somerset, 1549

This conversion of agricultural land to pasture was not new in Somerset's day. It had been going on for several generations, and many were the laws by which the government had tried to stop the movement and give protection to the tillers of the soil. But economic changes have frequently proved stronger than legislative acts, and the peasants had not been relieved. When in 1549 they rose, Somerset, who had a heart that beat for the oppressed, did not hesitate to declare his sympathy with them. The rest of the council, members to a man of the landlord class, waited until the army of the government had scattered the insurgent hosts and then proceeded to rid themselves of the traitor in their midst. In October

Somerset was arrested and deposed. Although he was allowed to live for a while, his opponents did not feel secure until his head had been severed from his body. He was executed in 1552.

The leader of the landlord party in the council which had brought about the overthrow of the protector was Warwick, better known by his later title of duke of Northumberland. He became Somerset's successor as governor of the kingdom, without, however, assuming the title of protector. He was a clever, unscrupulous, ambitious man without any particular religious convictions. However, he became an enthusiastic advocate of Protestantism on learning that a majority of his colleagues in the council favored that opinion. Not content with Somerset's relatively moderate program, he allied himself with the religious radicals and gave free scope to their passions. Now first occurred violent scenes of iconoclasm in England, when the people, incited by the so-called "hot gospellers," entered the churches and indiscriminately broke altars, statuary, and stained glass windows. Now, too, came persecution of orthodox Catholics, although the government never entirely lost the tolerant quality impressed upon it by Somerset.

Northumberland introduces radical Protestant measures

In 1552 there was issued the Second Book of Common Prayer, which was again largely the work of Cranmer but differed from the earlier edition in the more Protestant color of many of its passages. It was followed by a confession of faith which goes under the name of the Forty-two Articles of Religion. Therewith the reconstruction of Henry's national church along Protestant lines was completed. An Act of Uniformity imposed the reformed church upon the nation.

The Book of Common Prayer and the Forty-two Articles of Religion

The Protestant revolution of Edward's reign was, as we have seen, the work of Somerset and Northumberland. Nevertheless the king, who, as is frequently the case with feeble children, was a boy of remarkable precocity, followed the religious changes with intense sympathy. When he was twelve years old the German reformer, Bucer, wrote of him: "No study enjoys his favor as much as the Bible." His favorite diversion was a theological discussion, which he would follow with a countenance whence every touch of childish grace had been banished by an unnatural austerity.

The boy king

Such a boy was only too likely to exhaust prematurely his small treasure of vitality. Early in 1553 Northumberland perceived that Edward was dying. By Henry's will the succession would now fall to Mary, who, like her Spanish mother, was a devout Catholic. With his Protestant record, Northumberland had everything to fear from her; wherefore, in order to secure himself, he played upon the young king's Protestant conscience with such skill that he persuaded him to devise his crown away from his sisters Mary and Elizabeth upon his cousin, Lady Jane Grey, who

Edward VI changes the law of succession

could trace her lineage back to Henry VII.[1] In Northumberland's eyes Lady Jane not only had the advantage of being a Protestant likely to sympathize with his religious measures, but as he had lately married her to one of his own sons, Guilford Dudley, he might hope through these young and inexperienced people to perpetuate his power.

Death of Edward, 1553
It was a base intrigue without a vestige of legality. When Henry VIII arranged the succession by will, he had acted in accordance with an express permission granted by parliament; Edward, having been accorded no such power, signed an utterly worthless document. Northumberland was still elaborating the details of his plot when, on July 6, 1553, Edward breathed his last.

MARY (1553-1558)

Public sentiment declares for Mary
Edward had hardly expired when Northumberland hopefully proclaimed Lady Jane Grey. He was quickly disillusioned. The mass of the people saw through his scheme and rallied around Mary, their lawful sovereign. They hailed Mary gladly, because not only their sense of law and justice, but also their religious prejudices designated her as queen. For the majority of the people still leaned strongly toward the ancient Catholic usages and had little or no sympathy with the radical Protestantism carried through in Edward's reign. From Mary they expected the return of the mass and the other beloved practices from which they were not yet weaned in their hearts.

Downfall of Northumberland and Lady Jane Grey
The Lady Jane Grey was, in consequence of this unhesitating devotion of the English people to their rightful sovereign, crowned only to be deposed again. Northumberland, deserted by his followers, gave himself up and was beheaded. His death was a fit punishment for his misdeeds. Unfortunately Lady Jane, the unwitting tool of an ambitious man, paid the same penalty. It is true that Queen Mary felt compassion for her and delayed the execution. But a rebellion of the following year exasperated her to such a degree that in sudden alarm she gave her consent to her young cousin's death.

It seems likely that if Mary had adopted a moderate Catholic policy, taking her stand upon the platform of her father, Henry, her measures would have accorded with the wishes of her people. But Mary had noth-

[1] GENEALOGY OF LADY JANE GREY

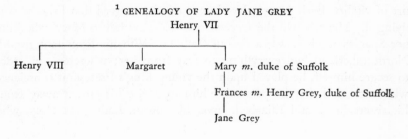

Henry VII

Henry VIII   Margaret   Mary *m*. duke of Suffolk

Frances *m*. Henry Grey, duke of Suffolk

Jane Grey

ing about her suggesting compromise. Her Spanish blood called upon her to be faithful, above all things, to her faith. She therefore planned nothing less than a return of England to the pope's fold—a full Catholic restoration. And that was a delusion. For, however much the English people were attached to the ancient worship, the Act of Supremacy, proclaiming the English independence of Rome, had the nation almost solidly behind it. Mary plans a full Catholic restoration

The first acts of Mary's reign left no doubt about her policy. The parliament, obedient to a word from the throne, sweepingly rescinded the religious legislation of Edward's reign, thereby bringing the church back to its condition at Henry's death. The mass was again celebrated in the Latin language, altars were set up, and the married clergy were expelled from their livings. Protestant legislation rescinded

So much was probably acceptable to the nation. But doubtful and impolitic measures followed. Urged on by Mary, the parliament next abolished all the legislation pertaining to the pope and ended by voting the unconditional return of England to the papal obedience. To crown this policy Cardinal Pole, an Englishman with royal blood in his veins, who had been sent to England as the legate of the pope, in November, 1554, extended absolution to the nation and formally received it back into the papal fold. England returns to the Catholic fold

Even so, England had not yet been quite brought back to the religious status that obtained when Henry began his memorable conflict. There were still the confiscated monastic lands. Mary in her honest zeal would gladly have restored them to the ancient orders. But here the parliament, made up largely of landholders who had profited by the spoliation of the church, showed itself intractable. The monastic property not restored

If the uncompromising Catholic policy of Mary alienated many sympathizers, she hurt herself still more in popular estimation when she rejected marriage with one of her own countrymen and accepted the proffered hand of her kinsman Philip, son and heir of Charles V. Such a union could not but inspire vague fears of a foreign domination; and although every provision was made in the marriage contract to insure the independence of England, the country was nevertheless drawn unescapably into the Spanish system. The marriage took place in the summer of 1554. While it is true that Philip proved himself afterward in his Spanish realm to be an unbending autocrat and fanatic, it must be set down to his credit that during his occasional visits to England he maintained an attitude of tactful reserve. Mary marries Philip of Spain, 1554

Although the religious persecutions which gave the finishing stroke to Mary's declining popularity and won for her from bigoted Protestant enemies the title of "Bloody Mary" date from about the time of her marriage, they cannot be fairly ascribed to her Spanish consort. If Mary Religious persecution under Mary

persecuted, the incentive was chiefly furnished by her own fiery enthu·
siasm. It was she who prompted the parliament to re-enact the old ferocious statutes against heresy, and it was she who urged the bishops to
carry them out. Soon the prisons were filled with the Protestant leaders
of Edward's time, and soon, too, the fires of persecution were lighted
over the realm.

In agreement with innumerable earlier instances the staunchness of
the victims in death contributed more toward establishing their cause
than could have been done by an army of fanatical preachers. It was
even as Bishop Latimer said to Bishop Ridley at the stake: "Master
Ridley, play the man; we shall this day, by God's grace, light such a
candle in England as I trust shall never be put out." But the persecution
struck a more prominent, if not a more noble, victim than these two,
in the person of the deposed archbishop of Canterbury. This was the celebrated Cranmer, who had served under two kings. Cranmer, a perfect
embodiment of the religious vacillation of the age, flinched when the
trial came and denied his faith. But in the face of death his courage
came back to him. He thrust his right hand into the flame, and steadying
it there, said resolutely: "This is the hand that wrote the recantation;
therefore it first shall suffer punishment."

The Protestant martyrs

If Edward's violent Protestantism made his reign detested, Mary's violent Catholicism produced much the same result. She was at bottom a
quiet, tender woman, whose intolerance was an attitude of the age
shared by Catholics and Protestants alike. She suffered from her unpopularity, as she suffered also from her marriage. She loved Philip, but Philip
cared little for her and did not much trouble to hide his indifference to
the sickly and ill-favored woman, twelve years older than himself.

Mary's unhappy marriage

To crown her misfortunes, she allowed her Spanish husband to draw
her into a war with France, in which Philip won all the honor and Mary
suffered all the disgrace by the loss of the last French foothold remaining
to England from its former large possessions across the channel, the port
of Calais (1558). Doubtless the loss of Calais was for England a benefit
in disguise. She was thereby cut off from the continent and directed to
her true sphere, the sea. But to Englishmen of that day the capture
seemed an insufferable dishonor. No one felt it more keenly than Mary.
"When I die," she is reported to have said shortly before her death
(November, 1558), "Calais will be found written on my heart."

Loss of Calais and death of Mary

ELIZABETH (1558-1603)

Elizabeth, Anne Boleyn's daughter and Mary's younger half-sister, succeeded to the throne on Mary's death and inaugurated a reign which
proved to be one of the most memorable in English annals. Under her,

Protestantism was firmly established in England; the great Catholic sea-power, Spain, was challenged and defeated; and in the poetry of Shake-speare and his contemporaries the national spirit achieved a more exuberant expression than ever before or since. To the greatness which England won in the sixteenth century, Elizabeth has lent her name. She grew into a legend for her people, a figure endowed with every conceivable virtue. This legend the modern historian is obliged to subject to critical analysis. The result is a far less glamorous queen but a much more human and credible woman. *The glorious reign of Queen Elizabeth*

Elizabeth had few of the graces of womanhood and many of its customary weaknesses. Her vanity was so great that, though a very plain-featured person, she conceived herself to be a beauty of a particularly rare type. She could not live without flattery and flirtations and, accepting the compliments of the courtiers for true coin, allowed herself to be persuaded to dance and sing in her maladroit manner before a brilliant court of gentlemen and ladies, who could hardly hide their amusement behind their handkerchiefs. Her manners were rude, especially at the council board, and her ministers were frequently annihilated by language which would have done honor to the camp and the fishmarket. However, while failing to meet the feminine ideal of her own and most other times, Elizabeth certainly possessed the virtues which men with characteristic self-esteem have presumed to call masculine. She had an inflexible will and an exceptional intelligence. Above all, she loved her country to the point of completely identifying herself with its interests. Her statesmanship, supreme of its kind, took the form of consistently promoting, though less by martial than by diplomatic means, the greatness of England. *Elizabeth as woman and statesman*

One of the qualities by which she rendered England perhaps her greatest service her contemporaries would have been quick to condemn if they had been more clearly informed about it: she was lukewarm in matters of faith. Regardless of our theoretic view of this state of mind, we can hardly do other than agree that in the England of that day, shaken by religious passions, the sovereign's religious tolerance was an undisguised blessing to the commonwealth. By reason of it Elizabeth was delivered from the destructive radicalism of both Edward and Mary and, being unusually disinterested, was peculiarly fitted to play the part of mediator between antagonistic positions. In this connection let us not forget that the sixteenth century was the century, not only of the Reformation, but also of the Renaissance. Elizabeth had been brought up to read Latin and Greek and was not unacquainted with the living languages and literatures of the continent. It is, therefore, not so very strange that, like Shakespeare, Jonson, and the poets of her time generally, she gave more heed to the voices coming from Italy than to the *Elizabeth's relative indifference in matters of religion* solemn pronouncements of Luther and Calvin. We come closer to her particular outlook, if we think of her as a creature rather of the Renaissance than of the Reformation.

Elizabeth ruled with the Privy Council

The chief organ of Elizabeth's government was the Privy Council, the advice of which she regularly heard before she arrived at a decision. In this body was gathered the best political talent the country boasted. It is no small credit to Elizabeth to have exhibited such discernment in the choice of her ministers. Most prominent among them was William Cecil, Lord Burghley, who devoted a life of exemplary service to advance the twin causes with which England came to be identified, Protestantism and sea-power.

Elizabeth and the parliament

Although Elizabeth was willing to consult the Privy Council, which was a body of her own choice, she was not inclined to grant much political influence to parliament, composed of the representatives of the people. Parliament remained, therefore, what it had been under the other Tudors, an obedient recorder of the royal will. During the queen's life the undivided sovereignty of England may be declared to have rested on her shoulders.

Elizabeth steers a middle course in matters of religion

As might be expected, the leading question of Elizabeth's reign proved to be the question of religion. Edward had followed a policy of radical Protestantism and Mary a policy of radical Catholicism. Both had failed. In the circumstances Elizabeth resolved to steer a middle course and inaugurated it by casting off the papal yoke which her predecessor had re-assumed. She was the more moved to this measure as in the view of the papacy, which had never consented to Catherine of Aragon's divorce, she was an illegitimate child and therefore ineligible to the throne. Accordingly, when her first parliament assembled in 1559, she had it pass a new Act of Supremacy, asserting the English independence from Rome and declaring the sovereign the highest authority in religious as well as in civil matters. There followed a new Act of Uniformity, which imposed upon every minister the form of worship laid down in a new Book of Common Prayer. The new book was nothing but the Second Prayer-Book (1552) of Edward's reign with a few revisions.

The pope's long delay in excommunicating Elizabeth

Elizabeth's plan was to make the re-established national church a rallying-ground for average men and women averse to the zealotry of either party. Such was her politic and shifty moderation that for a time even the pope nursed the hope of her return to the Catholic church. Not till he had waited more than ten years for this to happen, did he lose patience and issue a bull excommunicating and deposing her (1570).

From that moment Elizabeth became definitely pledged to the Protestant cause and was forced into a more active hostility against Catholicism. As a result severe measures were passed against adherents of the pope, but never in ungoverned passion or without recognition of varying degrees of culpability. Catholics who refused to attend service in the national church were visited with money fines, while heavier fines, culminating in imprisonment, were inflicted for saying or attending mass. Finally, those Catholics whose enthusiasm led them to engage in political plots were repressed by special treason bills authorizing the seizure and execution of conspirators and sufficiently elastic to strike down any inconvenient Catholic partisan. Under this repressive legislation a considerable number of Catholics were put to death, and all of them, by the system of fines, were gravely molested. However, compared with the contemporary persecution in Spain, France, and the Netherlands, Elizabeth's measures may fairly be said to have borne a moderate imprint.

The persecution of Elizabeth more political than religious

A church built on these foundations must have met the wishes of a majority of Englishmen, for they gave it their adherence in increasing numbers, accepted its worship and government, and gradually forgot the Latin mass. Proceeding in her deliberate manner, Elizabeth could, therefore, gradually complete her structure by new legislation. The most important of these supplementary acts is a confession of faith bearing the name of the Thirty-nine Articles of Religion (1563). Like the Book of Common Prayer, the Articles were based upon an enactment of Edward's time and mark a considerable departure from Catholic doctrinal tradition. The Acts of Supremacy and Uniformity, the Book of Common Prayer, and the Thirty-nine Articles are still in our own day the essential pillars of the Anglican or English national church. It may, therefore, claim Elizabeth much more truly than Henry as its founder.

Elizabeth's enactments create the historical Anglican church

Throughout Elizabeth's reign the Roman Catholics steadily decreased in numbers. But as they diminished, there rose into prominence another body of religious opponents. These were the Protestant radicals, who were dissatisfied with what they called Elizabeth's half-measures and who clamored for a thorough-going Protestant revolution. These radicals, it soon developed, were of two kinds, Puritans and Separatists. The Puritans were the more moderate opponents, who, while accepting the national church and attending its services, hoped to eliminate from it certain ceremonial features, such as the elaborate vestments of the clergy, which they despised as "Romish" trappings. Their demand for what they called a purer worship won them as a nickname, in the first instance, the party designation of Puritans.

Protestant radicals: the Puritans

The Separatists (sometimes called Brownists, after their founder, Robert Browne) were radicals of the most uncompromising sort. The national church with its bishops, its surplices, its ceremonies, was hardly better in their eyes than the Roman church, and they refused to attend it. As their propaganda spread, they were sharply persecuted, while the Puritans, who in the main yielded obedience and worshiped as demanded by the law, were left comparatively undisturbed.

Protestant radicals: the Separatists

On turning to the foreign developments of Elizabeth's reign we are at
once struck by the fact that they are so intimately associated with her
religious policy that we are forced to conclude that one is incomprehensible without the other. Exactly as in matters of religion, the whole
tenor of her conduct in the foreign field was caution, a daring caution,
if one may venture the expression. In consequence, she remained for a
surprisingly long time on reasonably good terms, not only with the pope,
but also with Philip of Spain. However, in measure as her Protestant
policy took a more definite shape, a coolness sprang up between her and
the two champions of Catholicism, which the bull of excommunication
of 1570 converted into open hostility.

Caution the chief note of Elizabeth's foreign policy

Turn as Elizabeth would in her shifty manner, there was after 1570
no way by which she could avoid being identified with the general Protestant movement. With the closing of the ranks effected by the Council
of Trent (1563), the Catholic Counter-Reformation, waxing stronger
every day, became more resolutely set on winning back the lost ground;
and unless the Protestants closed their ranks in their turn, it was only
too likely that their cause would be sent down to defeat. The outstanding
fact of the last quarter of the sixteenth century is that inexorably Catholicism and Protestantism were drawn into a world struggle, in which
Philip of Spain presented himself as the zealous champion of Rome and
Elizabeth, with characteristic manifest reluctance, became the paladin of
the newer faith.

Circum-stances impose on Elizabeth the cham-pionship of Protestant-ism

Every event of Elizabeth's reign contributed to precipitate the inevitable struggle, notably the queen's relations with Scotland and Scotland's sovereign, Mary Stuart. Scotland and England had been foes for
centuries. We have seen that Henry VII, with a view to a better understanding and possible union of the two countries, had married his daughter Margaret to James IV. But war was not thereby averted. James IV
and James V both sympathized with France and both died fighting
England, the latter (1542) when his successor, Mary, was but a few
days old.

The con-tinued ten-sion between England and Scotland

As Scottish Mary grew to womanhood, owing to her descent from
Henry VII she came to be regarded as a possible eventual successor to
the English throne; and when in 1558 Elizabeth, the last direct heir of
Henry VIII, assumed the scepter, the opinion was generally entertained
that, unless Elizabeth married and had children, the crown would in
due course devolve on the Scottish queen. Nor should it be overlooked
that, for uncompromising Catholics, Mary Stuart had a claim that took
precedence even over that of Elizabeth, since for them the daughter of
Anne Boleyn was an illegitimate child. From this delicate situation
sprang the instinctive aversion Elizabeth and Mary had for each other

Mary of Scotland Elizabeth's eventual successor

and the long drama of their rivalry, ending in Mary's death upon the scaffold.

When Mary succeeded to the throne of Scotland, she was, as has been said, a child in arms. Her mother, another Mary, of the French family of Guise, assumed the regency and, in order to withdraw her child from a threatening English control, sent her to France, where she was soon betrothed to the heir of the throne, who bore the title dauphin. Thus, in spite of all the Tudors had been able to do, the interests of France and Scotland had become more closely knit than ever. *Queen Mary sent to France and betrothed to the dauphin*

Mary of Guise, as Scottish regent, soon met with the difficulties which beset every government in her time. Toward the middle of the century the voices of the Reformation began to be heard in the land. Conversions grew apace, and presently the struggle between the old and the new faith was joined with the customary vehemence. But nowhere was it so brief and nowhere was the victory of the new teachings so decisive. Scotland was still a backward, feudal land, where the chief power rested with a lawless nobility. The clergy, too, had considerable wealth and power, but the religious indifference and luxurious living of the prelates had undermined the affections of the people. So slight was the hold of the church on Scotland that a few years of proselyting by a band of Calvinist preachers, whose most eminent representative was the fiery John Knox (1502-1572), sufficed to draw the common people to their side. When the nobility, lured by the bait of the rich church lands, threw in their lot with the preachers, the success of the Reformation in Scotland was assured. *The Scottish people turn Protestant*

The French gentlewoman who held the regency of Scotland viewed these developments with consternation. She had lost her hold on the country and could think of no other way of getting it back than with the aid of French troops. At her request France sent soldiers, who had seized a number of important places and were on the road to repressing the Protestant movement altogether at the very moment when Elizabeth gave a Protestant turn to English affairs by establishing her national church. In the conviction that the most effective way to drive the French from Scotland was to aid the northern Protestants, Elizabeth sent men and ships to their support. Her forces succeeded in bringing the French to terms. By the Treaty of Edinburgh (1560) the invaders from across the sea agreed to abandon Scotland. *The regent supported by French troops, the reformers by English troops*

As at this juncture the regent fell ill and died, and as Queen Mary was still in France, the Protestant party found itself in complete control of the situation. It called a parliament, which, dominated by the followers of Knox, abolished the papal supremacy, forbade the mass, and laid the foundations of a new church (1560). *The Protestants win control, 1560*

The Scottish church that thus came into being only a year after Eliza-

The national
church of
Scotland
erected
according to
a Calvinist
blueprint

beth had set up her Anglican establishment was based, like it, on independence from Rome. This feature apart, however, it bore little resemblance to its southern neighbor. John Knox, its guiding spirit, had sat at
the feet of Calvin at Geneva, and was resolved to model the new creation, as nearly as the difference between a small city-state and an extensive kingdom permitted, according to Calvin's theory of church organization. In consequence, each individual congregation governed itself
democratically, that is, it was ruled by the pastor in connection with
elected laymen called presbyters or elders. The individual congregations
in their sum constituted the national church. Its government was intrusted to a body called the general assembly and made up of delegates
from the constituent congregations.

The national
church is
Presbyterian

Together with these self-governing features the doctrines and worship
of Geneva were taken over by the new institution practically without a
change. Because of the important place conceded to the presbyters the
new church came to be known as the Presbyterian church (or kirk) of
Scotland.

Queen Mary
returns to
Scotland,
1561

Up to the time of this religious revolution the absent Queen Mary had
not concerned herself much with events in rude and far-away Scotland.
By the accession (1559) of her husband, Francis II, to the throne she had
become queen of France; and ever since the death of Mary Tudor (1558)
she had, supported by a good part of the Catholic world, looked upon
herself as also the rightful queen of England. But the year 1560 perceptibly darkened her outlook. Her ailing young husband, Francis II,
died, and Elizabeth made herself tolerably secure on the English throne.
All that was left to Mary was Scotland, and in 1561 she suddenly abandoned France and sailed for home.

Mary's
difficulties

When Mary returned to the country of her ancestors, she was only
nineteen years old and no better than a stranger. If we add that she was
confronted by a lawless nobility, and that, as a Catholic, she was an
object of intense suspicion to her Protestant subjects, we have the elements of a situation that a better and wiser woman than Mary might
not have been able to meet.

The person
and qualities
of Mary

Although Mary proved unequal to her royal task, she was a person of
admirable gifts. To grace of body and spirit she joined a nimble wit and
a keen intelligence. Brought up at the French court, a brilliant center
in her time of Renaissance influences, she had been imbued from childhood with the joy of living. Even before she had become queen of
France, she was the ruling spirit of a bright circle, for which the hours
revolved amid dancing, music, and poetry. Her contemporaries never
tired of praising her beauty. But, better than formal beauty, she possessed an indefinable charm which appealed to the chivalry of men and
which has raised up partisans for her down to our day.

Thus endowed, Mary would be a great queen on the single condition that she would subordinate her impulses to her duty as a sovereign. And here it was that she failed. Her cousin Elizabeth, who did not fail in this particular, proved herself thereby, if not the better woman, at least the greater queen. Comparing the two cousins, who inevitably force a comparison upon us, standing as they do on the stage of history flashing challenge at each other, we are moved to subscribe to the familiar judgment: Elizabeth was first a statesman and then a woman; Mary was first a woman and then a statesman.

Mary and Elizabeth compared

Mary began well enough. She made no difficulties about the Presbyterian kirk, merely reserving to herself as sovereign the right of Catholic worship. For four years Scotland enjoyed an unusual degree of peace. But in the year 1565 Mary married her cousin, Lord Darnley, and by that event she and all Scotland were plunged into troubles involving a succession of climaxes unique in history.

Mary marries Lord Darnley, 1565

Lord Darnley, who was hardly more than an overgrown boy, turned out to be proud, loutish, and dissolute. He was no sooner married than he let himself be used as the tool of the party of nobles opposed to Mary. They represented to him that if he did not enjoy full authority with the queen, it was due to one of Mary's foreign secretaries, an Italian, David Riccio. Darnley, egged on by the nobles, resolved to rid himself of his rival. One night while Mary was sitting at supper, the conspirators burst into her room, fell upon Riccio, and, in spite of the queen's frantic efforts to save him, dragged him from the chamber and stabbed him to death at the door (1566).

The murder of Riccio, 1566

Much of what followed is uncertain. It may be accepted as certain, however, that such love as Mary may still have had for her husband was turned to hate. She planned revenge. For the moment Darnley and his friends held the reins and she was forced to resort to dissimulation. By feigning an affection she did not feel, she brought her husband to his knees before her, separated him from her enemies, and re-acquired control. Thenceforth she took few pains to hide her loathing for the wretched prince. In February, 1567, the house where Darnley was staying, just outside the walls of Edinburgh, was shattered by an explosion of gunpowder and Darnley was found dead in the wreckage the next morning.

The murder of Darnley, 1567

It is established beyond doubt that the murder of Darnley was the work of the earl of Bothwell, a dare-devil nobleman of evil repute in love with the queen. It is suspected but has not been proved that the queen was his accomplice. Whether guilty or not, by what followed the murder Mary compromised her reputation beyond the possibility of rescue. Not only did she permit Bothwell's trial for the death of her husband to degenerate into a judicial farce, but shortly after the murderer's acquittal she married him.

Mary marries Bothwell, her husband's murderer

The revolt against Mary

Obliged to defend her hasty nuptials, Mary alleged that in marrying Bothwell she had not acted on her own volition but had yielded to violence. The apology has little inherent probability and was rejected with scorn by her subjects. Filled with horror and resentment, they revolted against her; and although she rallied repeatedly from defeat, by the year 1568 she found herself without further resources.

Her flight to England, 1568

Despairing of success without English help, Mary crossed the border to appeal to Elizabeth. It was a grievous error of judgment, for she became her cousin's prisoner and won her release only after nineteen years by laying her head upon the block.

Mary's son succeeds as James VI

Before we take up Elizabeth's conduct, let us take note that, tragic as Mary's fate was, her country was the gainer by her downfall. Her infant son was crowned king as James VI, while her half-brother, the earl of Moray, assumed the regency. Moray represented the Protestant party, and his rule meant religious peace for Scotland on the basis of the unqualified triumph of the Presbyterian church.

Reasons for Elizabeth's harsh treatment of Mary

It is not difficult to account for the harsh policy which Elizabeth adopted toward her royal cousin. Imperative considerations of state left no other course open. Looking out from London over Europe she beheld an alarming situation. She saw Philip II in arms against the Netherlands, resolved, if necessary, to drown Dutch Protestantism in blood; in France she took note of a civil war, in which the Catholic party, in order to achieve its end, did not balk at such revolting measures as the massacre of St. Bartholomew; she was in frequent peril of her life through the plots of her own Catholic subjects who aimed to raise Mary to the throne; and she saw a threatening general concentration of the whole Catholic world for a supreme blow against the Protestant schismatics.

Threat of war between England and Spain

Under these conditions her conduct could not but be regulated primarily with reference to the Catholic movement now plainly mounting to a climax. By the beginning of the eighties, Philip, through his famous general, the duke of Parma, had gone far toward reducing the Netherlands to subjection, while through his alliance with the French Catholic party he so dominated France as to be reasonably sure that that kingdom would not strike him from the rear. He could therefore concentrate his attention upon the dangerous and elusive Elizabeth.

Unofficial war on Spain by English adventurers

In measure as the blow from Spain became more imminent, the patriotism of Elizabeth's subjects mounted, causing them to rally with increasing fervor about the throne. Refusing to stand on guard waiting for the Spanish attack, adventurously inclined spirits, such as John Hawkins and Francis Drake, fittted out ships at their own expense and, ranging the Spanish main as pirates, plundered his most Catholic majesty's treasure fleet or set fire to his trans-Atlantic settlements. While Philip and Elizabeth, cautious spirits both, slow to decide for war, were still protesting friendship in official notes, their subjects had already engaged in combat on their own account. Not till, in 1585, the queen went the length of giving open, armed aid to the revolted Netherlands, did Philip decide to show his hand. He prepared against England the greatest armament his means permitted.

It was the rumor of Philip's invasion of England, coupled with the renewed activity of the English supporters of Mary, that cost the unfortunate queen of Scots her life. Probably it no longer had much value for her, since, grown old and gray behind prison walls, she knew herself beaten. Elizabeth's ministers succeeded in convincing her that Mary was party to a conspiracy which a man by the name of Babington had directed against the life of the sovereign; and though hypocritically feigning reluctance, she signed her cousin's death warrant. With the Spaniards about to descend on the country it was dangerous, nay, suicidal, not to destroy every Catholic nucleus and rallying-point within the kingdom. That at least was the settled view of Burghley, Walsingham, and the strict Protestant group which dominated the Privy Council. In February, 1587, Mary was executed at Fotheringhay as a sacrifice to Protestant and national security.

Execution of Mary, 1587

Immediately after Mary's execution the war between Spain and England came to a head. Philip, having at length got together over one hundred ships, known to fame as the Invincible Armada, dispatched them (1588) toward the English coasts. The purpose of the Armada was to sail to the Netherlands and put itself at the disposal of the duke of Parma, commander of the Spanish forces in that area. Supported by an irresistible navy, this general would then undertake the invasion of England.

The Spanish plan of campaign

The island-realm was thoroughly alive to its danger. In the face of the Spanish enemy religious differences were forgotten and replaced by a flaming national enthusiasm, uniting all parties. Without any doubt the Armada, more than all the repressive legislative acts put together, weakened the English Catholic ranks, for, from the day the war began, to be a Catholic meant to be a friend of Philip, and not many Englishmen cared to expose themselves to so revolting an imputation. A navy filled with the spirit which is ready to do and die was put at Elizabeth's disposal. With such leaders as Lord Howard, Sir Francis Drake, and Sir Martin Frobisher, many of whom had gained fame by fighting the Spaniards unofficially on all known seas, the English were not likely to fail for want of bravery or skill. Nor were they likely to fail for want of ships. They mustered even more vessels than the Spaniards, which, although not so large as the galleons of the enemy, by virtue of their speed, the size and number of their guns, and the capable seamanship of officers and men might hope to prove themselves superior to the enemy.

The English preparations against the Armada

Hardly had the slow-sailing Spanish fleet appeared in the English
channel (July, 1588), when the more expeditious English vessels fell upon
its rear and flank. The injuries suffered by the Spaniards during the running sea-fight lasting eight days forced them to lie off Calais for repairs.
Here a number of fireships sent among them drove them from their
shelter into the arms of the English lying in wait outside the port, and in
the ensuing combat they suffered so much additional damage that the
expedition lost its last breath of offensive vigor. Finding the channel
blocked behind him, the discouraged Spanish admiral tried to make for
home by the coast of Scotland. But he encountered storms even more
devastating than the English enemy. His ships were shattered miserably
by waves and rocks, and only an insignificant remnant ever returned
to Cadiz to tell the story of the great disaster.

England was safe, and more than England, the cause of Protestantism
in the Netherlands and throughout Europe. The English admirals now
transferred the scene of action to the Spanish coasts, and soon the dis-
heartened Philip sued for a peace which his triumphant foe would not
allow. As for Elizabeth, the defeat of the Spanish Armada was the climax of her reign. Thenceforward her people identified her with the national triumph and worshiped her as the embodied soul of England.

The queen's private life, it is true, went into slow eclipse. She was old,
childless, and lonely. Her last attachment, of which the earl of Essex was
the object, brought her keen disappointment and sorrow. Essex had been
put at the head of an army destined to subdue Ireland, just then agitated
by one of its frequent risings; but as he mismanaged his campaign and
came home without leave, he was dismissed in disgrace. Full of resentment, he now engaged in a treasonable plot, which ended in his arrest
and execution (1601).

Elizabeth's relations with the handsome earl were hardly as romantic
as the legend which gathered around Essex would have us believe. In
fact she was not romantically inclined, or rather, let us say, such romance
as she may have been endowed with by nature was suffocated at an early
age by the accident which raised her to the throne. Obliged from that
moment to regard marriage, not as an end in itself but as an affair of
state, she deftly fished, with herself as bait, in all the matrimonial waters
of Europe only to remain single to the last. Her resolution not to marry
was not the least benefit she conferred on her country. For, if she had
married a foreign prince, she would have bound England to the interests of some other country; and, if she had had children, she would have
deprived James, son and heir of Mary Stuart, of the succession and so
have delayed or even rendered impossible the union of England and
Scotland.

Passing in review the whole Tudor period from the accession of Henry

VII in 1485 to the death of Elizabeth in 1603, the observer is struck by the amazing transformation effected in English society, material well-being, and intellectual culture. Under the vigorous Tudor leadership the national sentiment was so greatly stimulated that it welded the people into a single political entity. Ranged behind Elizabeth, her unified people constituted the real secret of her strength. Overflowing with confidence, thousands of Englishmen ventured upon the seas in search of fortune and, on being thwarted by the maritime preponderance of Spain, began a buccaneering attack which in due time dragged their reluctant government into a life-and-death struggle with the world power of Philip II. If at Elizabeth's death England had not yet replaced Spain as the leading colonial power, at least a way had been cleared which the succeeding generations would have only to follow with energy in order to achieve that eminence. In short, the English, who, in view of their island position, had hitherto rather strangely neglected the sea, discovered that the sea was their true element, opening the possibility, not only of adventure and colonial expansion, but of an enriching trade with all the peoples scattered over the face of the earth. Already by Elizabeth's time a rapidly expanding commerce had greatly increased the wealth of the country and raised the standard of living, especially among the gentry and merchants, while the court was distinguished by a splendor and luxury which recall Renaissance Italy and signify a complete break with the frugal tradition of the Middle Ages.

Upsurge of England under the Tudors

However, proud navies, a growing merchant fleet, abundant trade, and a splendid court are only material manifestations of the underlying human spirit, which is the real achievement of any age. The Tudor spirit was the English version of the energy which spread through the occident with the Renaissance and which signified the seizure of the earth as an unrivaled field of opportunity. Emboldened by this fresh faith, men conceived of themselves as gods with no perceptible limit to the possibilities of self-realization. By way of evidence we have but to look at the literature of the age, particularly at its drama. For the drama became the chosen medium to express the visionary hopes that poured like a spring freshet through the minds of men. In the plays of Marlowe, Shakespeare, Jonson, and their peers we have the abiding imaginative expression of "the spacious times of great Elizabeth."

The age of Elizabeth expresses its indomitable energy in literature, especially the drama

10 THE REVOLT OF THE NETHERLANDS AND THE FOUNDING OF THE DUTCH REPUBLIC

BURGUNDY AND THE NETHERLANDS

The Nether-
lands be-
come inde-
pendent of
Germany

THE SECTION OF Europe known as the Netherlands or Low Countries lies at the mouth of the Rhine and Meuse rivers and in the Middle Ages belonged in the main to Germany. As, however, the western coastal area, called Flanders, was ruled by a count who owed allegiance to the French king, it followed that France had an interest in the region and kept a watchful eye on it. The Lowlands belonging to Germany were divided among many lords, such as the duke of Brabant, the count of Holland, the count of Hainault, and the bishop of Liége, who, in the manner of their kind, aimed to become increasingly independent of their suzerain and who, owing to the steady decline of the imperial fortunes, succeeded to a large extent in their object. By the fifteenth century the authority of the German sovereign over these territories and their local rulers had become quite shadowy.

The Nether-
lands pre-
eminently a
region of
self-govern-
ing towns

There were other reasons than the German ruler's enfeeblement for the growing independence of the Netherlands. Favorably located on the sea and possessing rivers that permitted an easy penetration to a populous hinterland, they had developed the most flourishing trade and industry to be found anywhere in northern Europe. These activities gave birth to prosperous towns which through charters wrung from their feudal masters enjoyed a considerable measure of self-government. Hence a spirit of communal independence was abroad in the land which, while able to flout the weak and distant emperor openly, was strong enough to impose respect on the powerful local counts and dukes. In short, the towns of the Netherlands, teeming with commercial enterprise, had largely freed themselves from the dead weight of feudalism.

Rise of the
Burgundian
state

Still another cause for the gradual failure of imperial authority in the Netherlands requires mention. It has to do with the remarkable political experiment inaugurated in the fourteenth century by the duke of Burgundy. The duke, a younger member of the French reigning house enfeoffed by his king with the duchy of Burgundy, conceived the ambitious project of adding the prosperous Low Countries to his French duchy. His plan may be summarized as an attempt to build up at the expense of both France and Germany a powerful independent state lying between them.

Several dukes of Burgundy in succession pursued this policy, employing as their means a combination of marriage, treachery, and violence, until toward the middle of the fifteenth century the family seemed to be within sight of the goal. Then Duke Charles of Burgundy, called the Bold, overreached himself and perished in battle against the Swiss (1477). He left as his sole heir a young daughter Mary. Taking advantage of her helplessness, Louis XI of France seized the duchy of Burgundy on the ground that it had, with the death of the last male duke, escheated to the French crown. The other Burgundian lands, however, constituting the Netherlands proper, were kept intact by Mary's marriage with Maximilian of Hapsburg. From Mary and Maximilian the Netherlands passed to their son Philip (d. 1506), and from Philip to his son, Charles. Charles ruled them to his abdication in 1555.

Breakup of the Burgundian state at death of Charles the Bold, 1477

EMPEROR CHARLES V

Charles, heir of the house of Burgundy, was, as we are aware, heir also of the houses of Spain and Austria and the dominating figure of his age under the title of Emperor Charles V. Born and brought up in the Netherlands, he always retained an affectionate regard for this territory, although in his later life, owing to the exigencies of his great position, he paid it only occasional visits. In view of his considerable political intelligence it is not surprising that he should have tried to round off his Netherlands possessions territorially and to bring them into an effective federation.

Emperor Charles V a native of the Netherlands

In both these respects the success of Charles was notable. By acquiring Friesland and certain other minor lordships he brought the provinces under his control to the number of seventeen. At the same time he tried to draw them more closely together by strengthening the embryonic federal institutions his predecessors had called into being. As the central government for the united Netherlands he set up three councils, of which the Council of State was the most important; he raised Brussels, centrally located in the province of Brabant, to the dignity of federal capital; and he provided that the common interests of the provinces, especially in so far as they concerned taxation, should be provided for by a common parliament. This parliament, called the States General, was made up of delegates from the provincial parliaments and was therefore more provincially than federally inspired.

Charles welds the seventeen provinces into a confederation

Although by these measures Charles did much toward consolidating the seventeen provinces, he at best overlaid and in no sense destroyed the older system of self-government native to this area. In consequence, each province retained its local government, composed of its own local administrators and a legislative body called the Provincial Estates, while the chartered liberties of the many flourishing towns remained as exuberant as ever, practically constituting them municipal republics.

Persistence of local self-government

Speaking summarily, we need not hesitate to call Charles's rule of the provinces a success. The life of the Netherlands was based on commerce and industry, which prospered so prodigiously that this small territory easily maintained the reputation it had won in the Middle Ages of being the beehive of Europe. Its busy cities, such as Lille, Valenciennes, Antwerp, Ghent, Bruges, Amsterdam, and a score of others, were the wonder and envy of the rest of the world, not only because of their wealth, but also by reason of the high culture level of their citizens. Charles drew heavily on their resources for the support of his Spanish and imperial program, scrupulously respecting, however, the constitution by collecting and spending only such monies as had been previously authorized by a vote of the States General.

The prosperity of the Netherlands under Charles

While the Netherlanders registered a measure of discontent at being obliged to contribute to imperial undertakings which were not their immediate concern, they always remained devoted to the sovereign whom they regarded as their countryman. This devotion flared up magnificently and for the last time when, in 1555, at his capital of Brussels, Charles abdicated the rule in favor of his son Philip. Not improbably the loyalty displayed on that occasion owed some of its fervor to the suspicion with which the inhabitants regarded the new sovereign who, brought up in Spain, was a stranger to these coastal lands.

Abdication of Charles, 1555

From one source, however, from the Reformation, a deepening shadow had, long before his abdication, begun to fall across the land. The religious agitation which centered about Luther was disrespectful of landmarks and at an early point in its history invaded the Low Countries. Charles, whose dependence upon the German princes forced him, as we have seen, to a dilatory policy toward Lutheranism in Germany, was not the man to hesitate where he had the power to act. In the Netherlands therefore the Protestant heresy was from its first appearance met by a relentless hostility, which waxed more and more fierce as Charles's reign unfolded.

Charles attempts to suppress Lutheranism

The Inquisition, with its record of triumphs in Spain, not unnaturally appealed to the Spanish monarch as the best way of meeting heresy everywhere. Accordingly, it was established in the Netherlands, special inquisitors being appointed for each of the seventeen provinces and the civil authorities being held to a strict execution of the sentences imposed by the churchmen. Confiscations, imprisonments, burnings at the stake, became common occurrences. The edicts of Charles against heresy

Charles establishes the Inquisition

finally went so far as to impose the death penalty on persons found in possession of forbidden writings or proved to have as much as discussed the Holy Scriptures.

The Protestants in the Netherlands were for a long time no more than a fraction of the population, but Charles's rigor did not exterminate them. To the original Lutherans were presently added Anabaptists and other extravagantly revolutionary sects, who found the mobile society of the Netherlands a fertile soil for the propagation of their tenets. Then, from the middle of the century, the faith of Calvin, destined to give the Protestantism of the northern Netherlands its peculiar mold, found admission, by way of France, into all the leading cities.

Many Protestant sects in the Netherland

The Inquisition, therefore, gathered a rich harvest. Contemporary speculation placed the figure of its victims during Charles's reign at fifty thousand. This is doubtless a gross exaggeration. But it testifies to Charles's intolerance and establishes his partial responsibility for the disaster which overtook his successor. However, as Charles was regarded by the Netherlanders as one of themselves and as his reign was in other respects happy, his policy of persecution did not during his life arouse any notable resistance.

The Inquisition fails to achieve its object

PHILIP II

Such was the country and such were the questions which were agitating it when the cold, bigoted, and Spanish-bred Philip took up the reins of government. The old heartiness which had obtained between ruler and ruled vanished almost over night to be succeeded by a deepening chill, of which the first manifestation was the severe curtailment by the States General of Philip's demand for money. If, after this exhibition of the democratic resolution of his subjects, there remained a single existing institution of the Netherlands which continued to enjoy his favor, it was the Inquisition.

Philip supports the Inquisition

In view of the abundantly ferocious provisions of the Inquisition, Philip felt no need of increasing its authority. On the other hand, he was unwilling to mitigate its severities, even in the face of a growing opposition. Unmistakably an opposition was beginning to make itself felt. The uninterrupted flow of blood was getting on the nerves of the Netherlanders, and voices began to be heard in favor of a more humane and rational treatment of the current heresies. As Philip sealed his ears to all such appeals, the discontent seized upon ever widening circles of the population.

Growing opposition to the Inquisition

While he was still residing in the provinces made over to him by his father, Philip became (1556) king of Spain and had to meet the problems peculiar to that monarchy. Of these the greatest was the long-standing feud with France. Charles's last war, precipitated in large part by the help conceded by Henry II of France to the German Protestants, had re-

A new war
between
France and
Spain (1557-
1559);
England
sides with
Spain

cently (1556) been brought to an unsatisfactory close. With so many matters unsettled between them, both Philip and Henry were ill inclined to
peace and looked forward to an early resumption of the conflict. Accordingly, in 1557 a new Franco-Spanish war broke out, in which, as on several previous occasions, England took part on the Spanish side. On this
occasion the decisive reason for England's Spanish partisanship was that
the English sovereign, Mary, was the wife of Philip, and that Philip
was able to persuade her to cast her lot with him.

The victory
of Spain
sealed by the
Peace of
Cateau-
Cambrésis,
1559

Philip's well-trained armies won two brilliant victories over the French
forces along the Netherlands border, the first at St. Quentin (1557), the
second at Gravelines (1558), thereby disposing the French to come to a
settlement. It was effected in the Peace of Cateau-Cambrésis (1559). As
Queen Mary died during the negotiations, Philip refused to concern himself further about allied England and paid, at least in part, for the favorable terms conceded by the French by leaving in their hands the port of
Calais, the last English possession on French soil, which had been captured by the French in a surprise attack.

Cateau-Cambrésis is a European landmark. It closed for the present the
long rivalry between France and Spain; it confirmed Philip in the possession of Italy and the Netherlands; and it assured the Spanish ascendancy in Europe for another generation. With this feather floating from
his cap, the proud victor resolved to end his residence in the Netherlands
and to return to his native Spain. Leaving behind as regent his half-
sister, Margaret of Parma, he sailed away (1559) never to return.

Philip's departure rapidly brought the domestic crisis to fever heat.
While the government had been nominally intrusted to the Regent
Margaret, a well-liked and intelligent woman, the real power was
vested in the Council of State and fell, within the Council, into the hands
of a single individual, Cardinal Granvelle, a trusted servant and confidant of Philip. What Philip expected of Granvelle was strictly to carry
out the orders received from Madrid; and as these insisted on maintaining every established measure no matter how hateful, the harassed cardinal was soon the object of a general aversion.

The great nobles were particularly vociferous against Granvelle, in
part no doubt on public grounds, but also because they saw in him the
personal favorite, whose political omnipotence signified the destruction
of that influence in the administration exercised in the past by them.
The most prominent members of this powerful class were Prince William
of Orange and the Counts Egmont and Hoorn. Drawing together in
their common disappointment, they became the nucleus of an active
opposition party.

The waxing discontent seized also upon many members of the lesser nobility and burgherdom. These latter, the real bearers of the peculiar urban civilization of the country, were exacerbated by a long list of ills which they did not hesitate to bring to Granvelle's notice with the request that they be forwarded to the king. Naturally, they protested against such a breach of the constitution as the quartering on their cities during the recent war and afterward of Spanish troops. However, what excited them more than all other causes put together was the grievance, now a generation old and borne with less and less patience, of the Inquisition and its ferocious punishments.

All classes opposed to the Inquisition

Repeatedly the great nobles, acting as spokesmen for the country, undertook to send emissaries all the way to Spain to plead with Philip for a change of system. They did not gain much, although the Spanish troops were at last withdrawn and the hated Granvelle was dismissed (1564). Thereupon the lesser nobles, among whom there was an impoverished, madcap, and avowedly Protestant element, took the bit between their teeth and resolved to stage a more effective protest of their own. Forming a league among themselves directed at the abolition of the Inquisition, which operated, as they put it, "to the great dishonor of the name of God and to the total ruin of the Netherlands," on April 5, 1566, they proceeded in a body to the palace of the Regent Margaret at Brussels to put their petition in her hands. At a banquet held by the petitioners some days later they were informed that one of the regent's courtiers had slightingly referred to them as beggars (*gueux*). Amid a scene of frenzied excitement they adopted the slur as their party name and assumed as honored badges the beggar's wallet and wooden bowl.

The protest of the "beggars," 1566

The open demonstration of the "beggars" set the match to the tinder-heap and the whole country flamed up in spontaneous rebellion. The prisoners of the Inquisition were forcibly released and the inquisitorial courts dispersed. Coming out of their hiding-places, the Protestants gathered in fields and public squares to listen to the addresses of fanatic preachers. At length the excitement culminated in a form of madness. The Catholic churches were invaded, their pictured windows and saintly images were broken, their crosses and altars were shattered to fragments. The ruin of art wrought by these iconoclasts was incalculable. It was weeks before the fury spent itself, and months before the government, rallying the propertied elements about it, succeeded in repressing the insurgents.

The "iconoclastic fury" of 1566

It is possible that the abolition of the Inquisition, coupled with the proclamation of the religious tolerance which public sentiment demanded, would have made the pacification permanent. But religious compromise was foreign to the rulers of that day and seemed nothing less than mortal sin to a man like Philip. He planned revenge. One of his best generals was the duke of Alva. Soldier and bigot, he was the typical

Philip plans revenge and punishment

Spaniard of the day, animated with blind devotion to his king and faith. This man of iron was appointed to supersede the Regent Margaret and to ferret out and punish the participants in the late rebellion.

The coming of Alva, 1567

In 1567, accompanied by 10,000 Spanish veterans, Alva made the long trip from Spain to Brussels via the Mediterranean, Italy, and the Alps. The Spanish troops were the best in Europe and had proved their invincibility on many a battlefield. They were bound for the Netherlands, which country, though Philip was its sovereign, was, we should never forget, not a Spanish province but a separate dominion. Alva's coming was therefore an invasion and terror flew before him. As it did not require much intelligence to foresee a period of coercion and violence, William of Orange, with a host of those who felt themselves compromised by the recent events, crossed the border into safety.

Alva sets up the Council of Blood

Alva did not long leave the anxious Netherlanders in doubt as to the meaning of his coming. He set up a special council, called the Council of Troubles, for the discovery of all those who had taken part in the late excesses. Operating at Alva's pleasure, the new governing body soon received from the people the more ominous name of the Council of Blood. It signified a redoubled Inquisition, freed from the delays of law and the promptings of human pity. Hundreds perished at its order; thousands from among the best of the land fled the country. Among the more illustrious victims of the executioner were Counts Egmont and Hoorn, whom neither their Catholic faith nor their conspicuous services to the king could save. As the greatest men within the reach of Alva's arm they were sent to the block as a warning to their countrymen.

William of Orange identified with the Netherlands

Against this paralyzing tyranny one man did not cease to protest— Prince William of Orange. William belonged to an ancient German family, which had its seat in Nassau in western Germany. At an early age he had inherited from a cousin the tiny principality of Orange on the Rhone, which he never thought it worth while even to visit. However, as he did not scorn the title inhering in his French possession, it has become inseparably attached to his name. His connection with the Netherlands sprang from the fact that he was possessed of large estates there, chiefly in Holland and Brabant, and that he had been drawn by his early patron, Emperor Charles V, into the service of the provinces.

William, leader of the revolution

Suspicious from the first of Philip's policy, William passed gradually from secret to open opposition, to take his stand at last on the platform of his country's liberties. Although brought up a Catholic, he disapproved strongly of the Inquisition. Throughout his life he never ceased pleading for tolerance, a plea to which all parties alike of that passionate age were deaf. Passing by degrees over into the Protestant camp, he cast his lot at last with the Calvinist faith. He made this choice because Calvinism was adopted as its religion by the Dutch element of the Netherlands, with which, as the struggle developed, William chose ever more closely to identify himself.

The fame of William rests on his risking life, wealth, and happiness in the cause of an oppressed people. As a general he was mediocre; even as a statesman, though he played the political game as skillfully and subtly as any of his contemporaries, he has many a superior among the great names of history. Clearly his chief distinction is his stout, courageous heart. Sometimes almost singlehanded and at best with but the divided support of his little people, he braved the world power of Spain and through defeat piled on defeat persisted in his purpose. **Character of William**

In the spring of 1568 William, having turned all his available possessions into money and having summoned the most daring exiles around him, began gathering an army for the purpose of invading the Netherlands. His resolution was tantamount to a declaration of war against Philip. To fill the provinces with his own spirit of resistance became William's supreme object, and gradually, although not without grievous disappointments and delays, he succeeded. As a result a small people challenged the greatest power of Europe and, after a dramatic struggle of eighty years (1568-1648), issued from the fight as victor. No more uplifting war than this has ever been waged. **William levies war on Philip, 1568**

The first campaign proved the complete superiority of both Spanish generalship and Spanish soldiery. William's army, largely composed of ill-paid mercenaries, was defeated and scattered. Alva, in consequence, made light of the invasion. It had not been supported, as William had hoped, by an internal rising. To all appearances the country, crushed under the Spanish heel, had fallen into a torpor. **Failure of the invasion of 1568**

A greater aid to the rebellion than William's military effort was Alva's own folly. Not only did he continue to suspend a pitiless terror over the country, but, in perpetual need of funds to pay his soldiers, he resorted to an extortionate taxation. When he at length attempted to introduce the Spanish alcabala, the so-called Tenth Penny, consisting of the levy of ten per cent upon every commercial transaction, including the purchase of daily necessities, he awakened passionate resentment. Though the tax was soon abandoned because it proved uncollectable, the whole urban population was henceforth solidly arrayed against this reckless representative of military despotism. **Alva's measures arouse resentment**

At last the rebels scored their first notable success. If Spain held the land in her iron grasp, she could not in the same unchallenged way hold the sea, peculiarly the element of these coast dwellers. Ever since William had given the signal for resistance, freebooters, proudly calling themselves "beggars of the sea" in imitation of the first brotherhood of the enemies of Spain, had done great harm to Spanish trade. At length, rendered bold by the battle with wind, wave, and foe, they swept down **The sea-beggars seize Brill, 1572** upon their native coast and, braving the terror of Alva's soldiery, stormed the small port of Brill (April 1, 1572).

A score of towns, located mostly in the northern provinces, felt suddenly encouraged to drive the Spaniards out. To his dismay Alva found his power limited to Brussels and the south. In order to hold the advantage gained, the province of Holland now elected William the Silent stadholder or governor. Together with the neighboring province of Zeeland, Holland from this time forth became the heart of the resistance.

Thrown into the fiercest mood by this new phase of the struggle, Alva prepared to win back the lost ground. Malines, Zutphen, Naarden, and many other towns which he recaptured were delivered over to the unbridled excesses of the Spanish soldiery. In 1573, amidst scenes of revolting horror, Alva retook Haarlem, after it had resisted him for eight long months. Therewith the war entered upon a stage in which oppressors and oppressed thirsted for each other's blood and neither sought nor gave quarter.

The exhausting struggle at length shook even Philip's faith in his agent. In December, 1573, the man who six years before had come to the Netherlands to sow the dragon-teeth of war took his departure amidst the curses of both friend and foe.

The outstanding event of the governorship of Requesens (1573-1576), Alva's successor, was the siege of Leyden (1574). When, owing to the failure of provisions, the city was on the point of surrender, William, who had made futile efforts to succor the inhabitants, resolved on an extreme measure: he ordered the cutting of the dykes built to protect the land against the invasion of the sea. As the water rushed over the fields, the "beggars of the sea" pressed on in their ships, sailing past trees and houses till they reached the walls of the city. For the drowning Spaniards there was no alternative but retreat. Thus was Leyden saved. Wishing to reward the inhabitants for their heroism, William founded a university in their midst which rapidly rose to the front rank and has made the name of Leyden illustrious in the intellectual annals of Europe.

With the sudden death of Requesens in 1576 came a notable extension of the revolt, to understand which we must direct a glance at the peoples inhabiting the seventeen provinces. Acquired by the house of Burgundy in a drive for political power and subjected to a partial centralization, the Netherlands nonetheless lacked the main qualification for a successful union in modern times, the consciousness of a common nationality. The seven northern provinces, of which Holland and Zeeland were the chief, together with the two central territories of Brabant and Flanders, were overwhelmingly inhabited by a people of Teutonic stock. The southern provinces, such as Namur, Hainault, and Artois, were mainly inhabited by Walloons, a Celtic people using the French language. The

Margin notes:

The province of Holland makes William stadholder

Barbarous excesses of the war

The recall of Alva, 1573

Siege and relief of Leyden, 1574

The two main stocks of the Netherlands

population of the Netherlands was therefore predominantly Teutonic, though with a notable Celto-French admixture.

Directing our attention to the Teutonic group, we note that in its turn it fell into two sections. The inhabitants of Flanders and Brabant were Flemings, while the people of Holland and the adjoining provinces were Dutch. The differences between Flemings and Dutch in speech, customs, and mentality were inconsiderable and would, under favorable circumstances, have proved no obstacle to close political association. Nationalism, as we are aware, was as yet a relatively new force in the world. Certainly it had thus far hardly made itself felt in the area under consideration nor had it interfered with the Burgundian-Hapsburg program of uniting Walloons, Flemings, and Dutch in a single state. However, brought to life by religious and economic differences, nationalism might yet prove a force that would have to be reckoned with. Flemings and Dutch distinct members of the Teutonic group

Up to 1576 the revolt had been confined to the northern or Dutch provinces, which had steeled their rebel spirit by immersion in the Calvinist faith. From a purely political standpoint the grievances of the central and southern provinces were as great as those of the northern provinces, but as the former clung, in the main, to the Catholic faith, they never gave up the hope of an ultimate accommodation with their Catholic ruler, Philip. For a brief moment, however, following the death of Requesens, north, center, and south, Dutch, Flemings, and Walloons—in a word, a united Netherlands—presented a single and unbroken front to the oppressor. The revolt up to 1576 restricted to the Dutch

The occasion for this display of a united purpose was furnished by the general horror inspired by the Spanish soldiery. Left on the death of Requesens without a leader and without pay, the Spaniards indulged in a wild orgy of theft, murder, and pillage. The "Spanish Fury," as the mutinous outbreak was called, reached its peak at Antwerp. In this, the greatest trading city of the Atlantic seaboard, some seven thousand inhabitants were put to the sword, while property of untold value was carried off or wantonly destroyed. The "Spanish Fury," 1576

At these outrages a vast indignation against Spanish rule swept the whole country. In an agreement of November, 1576, called the Pacification of Ghent, representatives of all the seventeen provinces declared that they would not rest until the foreign troops had been withdrawn from the land and all the old liberties restored. The Pacification of Ghent

This, the most auspicious moment of the revolution, held out a promise which was never realized. True, the successor of Requesens, Don John of Austria, who in 1571 had won the famous victory of Lepanto, found himself so isolated that, when he died in 1578, he had made no headway against the united opposition. However, with the coming of Alessandro Farnese, duke of Parma (1578-1592), the situation gradually changed. Advent (1578) and policy of the duke of Parma

Son of the former regent, Margaret, and a nephew of King Philip, this Italian prince possessed military and diplomatic gifts of a high order and may without hesitation be accepted as one of the foremost men of his time. Faced with a total revolt, he was resolved to proceed with the greatest caution and to employ either force or cajolery according to the situation.

Parma's immediate aim was to break up the solid front represented by the Pacification of Ghent. This was not particularly difficult, since in those days a partnership between Catholics and Protestants was regarded by both parties with insurmountable suspicion. Aware of this situation, the clever duke took his residence in the French or Walloon provinces, in the midst of a solidly Catholic population, and by offering important concessions soon won them over to his side. By January, 1579, he had succeeded in persuading Artois, Hainault, and Douay to sign the Union of Arras. By its terms they undertook to defend the Catholic religion and, in return for a guarantee of their ancient political rights, to renew their allegiance to Philip.

Parma separates the Catholics from their Protestant allies

As soon as the Union of Arras had created a rallying-ground for Catholicism, it became necessary for William of Orange, in his capacity of rebel leader and chief opponent of Parma, to draw the Protestants together into a counter-league. This was effected in the same year (1579) at Utrecht, where the northern provinces established a union in their turn. Holland and Zeeland, as the main centers of the rebellion, led the way but were joined by their immediate neighbors, finally five in number, Utrecht, Gelderland, Overijssel, Groningen, and Friesland.

The Union of Arras confronted with the Union of Utrecht, 1579

The Union of Utrecht was substantially a declaration of independence, although the sovereignty of Philip was not definitely renounced till two years later. The state thus brought into existence officially took the name of the Seven United Provinces, but before the world it became known under the more compact title of the Dutch republic. The articles of the Union of Utrecht served as the constitution of the newborn state. That this constitution established nothing more than a very loose federation will appear when we note that, while creating a certain amount of central machinery to handle the common interests, it left the sovereignty of the seven constituent provinces substantially intact.

The Union of Utrecht marks the birth of the Dutch republic

The reluctance of the provincial governments to surrender their power is best illustrated by the central executive they authorized. Instead of intrusting the executive to a single person, they vested it in a collective group, the Council of State. In the same spirit of jealous provincialism the seven constituent provinces made it impossible for the central legislative body they created under the name of the States General to impose taxes except with the consent of the seven Provincial Estates. The paralyzed federal executive and legislature were so little capable of sustained

The feeble federal institutions

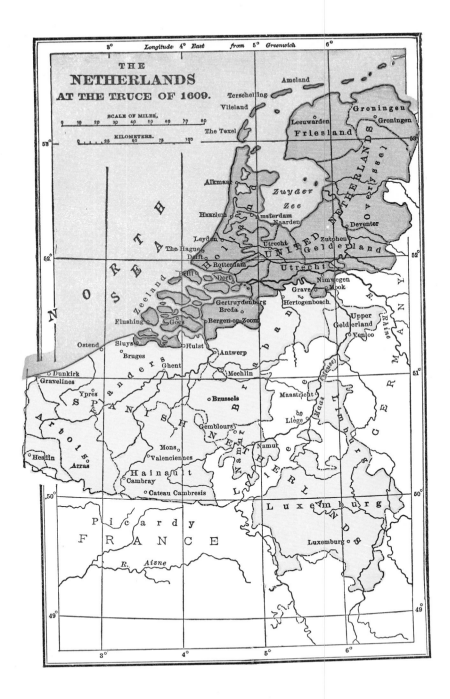

THE
NETHERLANDS
AT THE TRUCE OF 1609.

SCALE OF MILES.
0 10 20 30 40 50 60 70 80
KILOMETERS.
0   25   50   75   100

Longitude 4° East   from 5° Greenwich   6°

Ameland
Terschelling
Vlieland
The Texel

Groningen
Groningen
Leeuwarden
Friesland

N O R T H   S E A

Alkmaar
Zuyder Zee
Haarlem
Amsterdam
Naarden
Leyden
The Hague
Delft
Rotterdam
Dort
Gertruydenberg
Breda

H O L L A N D

U N I T E D   N E T H E R L A N D S

Utrecht
Zutphen
Gelderland
Utrecht
Nimwegen
Grave
Mook
Hertogenbosch
Upper Gelderland
Venloo

O v e r   I j s s e l
Deventer

Zeeland
Flushing
Goes
Bergen-op-Zoom

B r a b a n t

R. Rhine

Ostend
Sluys
Bruges
Hulst
Antwerp
Ghent
Mechlin

Dunkirk
Gravelines
Ypres

F l a n d e r s

S P A N I S H   N E T H E R L A N D S

Brussels
Maastricht
Liège
Gemblours

Maas (Meuse)

L i m b u r g

G E R M A N Y

Mons
Valenciennes
Hainault
Cambray
Cateau Cambresis

Namur
Namur

N a m u r

Luxemburg

Hesdin
Arras

P i c a r d y
F R A N C E

R. Aisne

Luxemburg

action that often the very existence of the state was threatened. During the early years, however, the personal ascendancy gained by William of Orange, who was stadholder of the two leading provinces, Holland and Zeeland, and who exercised a broad influence in the other five provinces as well, served somewhat to overcome the shortcomings of the federal constitution.

With the creation of the Unions of Arras and Utrecht, expressive of the irreparable division of the Netherlands into a Catholic and a Protestant section, the war entered on a new phase. Parma, firmly planted in the Walloon south, faced William of Orange, solidly established in the Dutch north. Between them lay the two rich Flemish provinces of Flanders and Brabant, which long hesitated to come to a decision, and which, courted and assaulted in turn by both sides, might fall either way. By slow degrees the skill of Parma, backed by the resources of Spain, tipped the scales in favor of the Catholics. In his cunning way, sometimes by a successful siege, sometimes by negotiations, the duke penetrated into the doubtful middle area and even threatened the seemingly secure north. To all the world and, more particularly, to Philip II it appeared that only William's leadership and resolution stood between Parma and ultimate success. Often the prayer must have risen to the Spanish king's lips that some happy chance might rid him of his enemy. *The struggle between William and the duke of Parma*

At last, since fate seemed reluctant to act, Philip resolved to come to its assistance. In 1580 he published a ban against his rebellious subject, offering gold and a patent of nobility to whoever "should deliver this pest to us, dead or alive." It was William's death-warrant. Many abortive attempts had already been made upon his life, when a Burgundian, Balthasar Gérard by name, one of those unflinching religious fanatics in whom the age abounded, pierced his breast with a bullet. The murder occurred on July 10, 1584, as the prince was descending the stairway of his palace at Delft. The victim's last thoughts turned toward the struggle in which his country was engaged. "Lord, have pity on my soul," he breathed, "and on this poor people." *The murder of William, 1584*

While William's death did not break down the resistance of the Dutch, as Philip had calculated, it greatly encouraged the Catholic faction. Parma was able to occupy most of the disputed area of Flanders and Brabant, climaxing his successes with the capture (1585), after a long and memorable siege, of the great port of Antwerp. It only remained now to turn against the north and conquer the two key provinces of Holland and Zeeland. *New successes of Parma; capture of Antwerp, 1585*

If, in the face of so many misfortunes, Holland and Zeeland were able to continue their resistance, it was for the single reason that, as from the beginning of the conflict, they still commanded the adjacent waters with

their ships. Their dead leader had held that independence could not be
finally won save with the help of foreign powers, and during the last
years of his life he had directed passionate appeals for aid to France and
England. Elizabeth had occasionally sent secret encouragement in the
form of money, but in her cautious way had refused openly to commit
herself. As for France, she was too torn by civil war to venture on any
action beyond her boundaries.

William's
theory of
the need of
foreign aid
to win
independ-
ence

There was no chance of effective help from any quarter except Elizabeth, and the Dutch, at the end of their tether, at last made her a pressing tender of the young republic. Characteristically, she declined the
dangerous honor. Nevertheless, she could no longer with due regard to
her own safety refuse to grant substantial help. The relations of Spain
and England had long since entered a troubled phase, owing to the unofficial war made by Sir Francis Drake and other English freebooters on
Spanish trade and the Spanish colonies. Philip II had a just grievance
against Elizabeth's government. If ever he gained the necessary freedom
of action by the recovery of the Low Countries, it was certain to go hard
with the island realm. Ungenerous as Elizabeth was where others were
concerned, she had a sharp eye for her own interests. In December, 1585,
she signed a treaty with the Dutch, whereby she promised to send 6,000
soldiers to their aid.

Elizabeth
comes to
the aid of
the Dutch,
December,
1585

When the Englishmen came, under the command of the earl of Leicester, the queen's favorite, they did perhaps more harm than good, for
Leicester seemed to consider it his chief business to create divisions
among the Dutch themselves (1586-1587). His entrance in the struggle
nonetheless marks still another phase in the war of liberation, for, angered
by the open intervention of Elizabeth in the Netherlands, Philip resolved
to bring down on her an exemplary punishment. Deliberately he began
to assemble all his resources for a direct attack on England.

Philip's
attack
diverted
from the
Dutch to
the English

Against this dissipation of the Spanish strength the duke of Parma
entered an energetic protest. He wanted Philip to adjourn action against
England until the Dutch resistance had been definitely broken. Determined to have his way, Philip refused to listen to his capable adviser
and in the year 1588 sent his Invincible Armada against the English
coasts. We need not again recount the disastrous termination of that
enterprise.

Immediately after this failure a Protestant, Henry of Navarre, succeeded to the French throne (1589). Alarmed at the new peril to the
Catholic faith, Philip resolved to move heaven and earth to save the
neighbor kingdom for the Roman church. In this manner fate, or chance,
or a too unbridled ambition led him to expend his power on enterprises
which carried him far afield and obliged him to relax his grip upon the

Netherlands. His exhausting wars, on the water against England, on the land against the Huguenot king of France, drained Spain to such an extent of both money and men that inevitably the war against the Dutch was pursued with less and less vigor. When, in 1592, the duke of Parma died, worn out even more by his disappointments than by his great labors, the last chance of conquering the rebel provinces may be said to have slipped through Philip's fingers. Philip's strength further diverted by his war on Henry of Navarre

The respite they enjoyed, owing to the wars waged by Spain against England and France, was fully utilized by the Dutch. They found in John of Oldenbarneveldt, trained in the school of William of Orange, a statesman not unworthy of the master. As chief official of Holland, the province which was the real backbone of the republic, and as a representative of the great merchant class, he was enabled to impress that unity of purpose on the nation which it ran the risk of losing on the passing from the scene of William of Orange. The statesman, John of Oldenbarneveldt

To supplement the diplomatic work of Oldenbarneveldt there gradually rose to the front, in the military field, William's son and heir, Maurice of Nassau. Only seventeen years old at his father's death, he exhibited such intelligence and dedicated himself to the study of war with such wholehearted zeal that at the age of twenty-one he was made captain-general and admiral of the republic. Aware of the decline of the Spanish monarchy through the dispersion of its strength, he boldly took (1590) the offensive and was soon able not only to clear the Dutch soil of the enemy by successful siege operations but also occasionally to defeat the hitherto invincible Spaniards in the open field. At the same time the Dutch fleets, riding the waters more triumphantly than ever, drove the Spanish merchantmen like frightened gulls before them. Rise of the soldier, Maurice of Nassau

Thus matters stood, with the Spaniards fighting with their backs to the wall, as Philip II neared his end. He tried to open negotiations with the enemy. Too proud to acknowledge defeat, he made no headway toward an accommodation. On his death in 1598, his successor, Philip III, persisted in his father's wasteful and impracticable course. Only when utterly exhausted, did he humble himself sufficiently to agree (1609), not to a final peace, but to a Twelve Years' Truce. The Twelve Years' Truce, 1609

Incomplete arrangement that the truce was, it contained a veiled acknowledgment of the Seven United Provinces as a free and independent state. At the same time it confirmed the hold of Spain on the ten central and southern provinces. They figure in history after 1609 as the Spanish Netherlands. When the Spanish branch of the house of Hapsburg failed in the year 1700, its Netherland possessions, as we shall see in due time, were transferred to the Austrian Hapsburgs and became the Austrian Netherlands. After further extraordinary vicissitudes the Vicissitudes of the ten Catholic provinces

Austrian Netherlands became, early in the nineteenth century, the kingdom of Belgium. In this manner the seventeen provinces, over which Emperor Charles V and his son, Philip, had ruled as a single federation, became eventually two distinct European states.

Futile renewal of the war by Spain at close of the truce

If the truce of 1609 was not the end, it was the beginning of the end. When it expired (1621), the Thirty Years' War was raging in Europe; and although Spain tried to make the confusion serve her purpose and again attacked the Dutch, the firm resistance of the hardy little nation rendered the second effort at subjugation even more vain than the first. When the Peace of Westphalia (1648) put an end to the long German war, the king of Spain at last declared himself ready for the great renunciation and signed a peace with the Dutch republic which was an unqualified acknowledgment of its independence.

STADHOLDERS OF THE HOUSE OF ORANGE-NASSAU

William I, the Silent (d. 1584)

Maurice (d.1625)　　Frederick Henry (d. 1647)

William II (d. 1650) m. Mary, daughter of Charles I of England

The domestic issues: the feeble federal government

Returning to the landmark of the Twelve Years' Truce, let us briefly take note of some of the internal problems agitating the new state. That Maurice of Nassau and John of Oldenbarneveldt, to whose excellent teamwork the recent triumph had been largely due, developed a dangerous rivalry after 1609 was owing to their taking opposite sides in these domestic issues. The first issue, with which we are already familiar, concerned the unsatisfactory federal machinery. The most important federal feature was the national parliament, called the States General, but the States General could not free themselves from subordination to the seven Provincial Estates, representative of the constituent provinces. Was this subordination of the national to the several local governments sound and should it be permitted to continue?

The domestic issues: domination of the republic by the province of Holland

Another disturbing issue was caused by the superiority in resources of the single province of Holland with its many flourishing municipalities, such as Amsterdam, Haarlem, Leyden, and Rotterdam, over the other six provinces put together. Under these circumstances Holland was usually able to impose its decision on the rest of the country. The preponderance of Holland was so generally recognized that people throughout Europe commonly thought of Holland as synonymous with the Dutch republic.

Still another problem arose from the circumstance that the control in the great municipalities rested exclusively in the hands of the leading merchant oligarchs or "burghers," for it was they alone who possessed the franchise. As Oldenbarneveldt was identified with Holland, on the one hand, and with the burgher oligarchy, on the other, it followed that, when Maurice of Nassau challenged Oldenbarneveldt's control, he sought the support of the other six provinces and at the same time courted the disfranchised and disgruntled masses throughout the republic.

The domestic issues: the "burghers" in effective control

While the above-mentioned issues were serious, it was reserved to the passions released by differences of religious opinion to produce civil war. The Reformed church of Calvin had been made the sole legal religion of the country; the older Catholic faith, although after a time no longer persecuted with fire and sword, was denied the right of public worship. But the dominant and domineering Calvinists were themselves not an unbroken unit. In the days of Maurice and Oldenbarneveldt a sect arose among them, which refused to subscribe to the doctrine of predestination with its many harsh implications and which, because of a remonstrance issued on this head, became known as the Remonstrants.

The domestic issues: rise of a Calvinist sect, called the Remonstrants

When the strict constructionists answered the Remonstrants with a prompt and vigorous counterblast, they received the name of Counter-Remonstrants. The quarrel, abstruse and irrelevent to our present-day way of thinking, rocked the country and led to the demand for a synod of the Dutch church to decide the issue. Such an assembly Oldenbarneveldt, who was identified with the tolerant party of the Remonstrants and who feared the rock-ribbed intolerance of the fierce Calvinists, opposed with all his might. Under the circumstances an appeal to force was unescapable.

Oldenbarneveldt identified with the Remonstrants

Before the threatened civil war had fairly begun, Maurice of Nassau by a quick stroke disarmed the opposition. He arrested Oldenbarneveldt, who, tried on trumped-up charges of treason, was found guilty and beheaded (1619). Thereupon a national church synod, assembled at Dort (Dordrecht), condemned the lax views of the Remonstrants, and imposed the most unbending definition of predestination on the Dutch Reformed church.

Victory of Maurice of Nassau (1619)

Thus Maurice and the groups behind him, forming what was called in his family's honor the Orange party, had triumphed, while the burgher oligarchs went into temporary eclipse. Had Maurice been recklessly ambitious—which he was not—he might now quite probably have overthrown the constitution of 1579 and made himself king. But he died (1625), like his father before him, a mere stadholder. His titles and honors passed to his younger brother, Frederick Henry, who, as the new head of the Orange party, proved himself as capable as and even less ambitious than Maurice. In the nature of the case the Orange party with its acknowledged single head had a monarchical tinge, while the defeated burgher oligarchs, strong through their ascendancy in the prov-

Dutch domestic history a seesaw between the Orange and the republican parties

ince of Holland, formed what was called the republican party. Through many succeeding generations, in fact as long as the Dutch republic lasted, these two parties struggled with each other for the control of the state with the result that sometimes one, and sometimes the other, exercised authority to the exclusion of its rival.

The most important, if not the only, explanation of the great place in the history of Europe filled by the Dutch republic in the sixteenth and seventeenth centuries is its amazing commercial expansion. It was as if the heroic effort against tyranny had released an unmeasured energy. In spite of their exhausting war with Spain, the Dutch steadily increased the number of their merchant vessels and undertook with them a profitable commerce with all the countries of the world. They became the leading carrier nation of Europe. In this capacity they controlled the North sea, penetrated the Baltic sea, and were gradually emboldened to challenge the Spanish and Portuguese monopolies in the West and East Indies respectively.

Dutch commercial expansion

In 1601 the Dutch East India Company was founded. Its charter, issued by the government, granted the members, in return for the risks they assumed, a monopoly of the far eastern trade. It was owing to the success of the East India Company that an extensive Dutch colonial empire was gradually built up in the Malay archipelago.

The Dutch East India Company

When industrial Flanders was reoccupied by Spain, many manufacturers, being Protestants, emigrated to Holland, where they created linen and woolen works employing thousands of workmen. Not to be overlooked in this record of business enterprise is the Dutch herring industry. From of old a leading occupation of this seaboard people, it provided and continued to provide a livelihood for a considerable percentage of the population. It was the wealth won in the herring trade that gave rise to the saying that the great city of Amsterdam was built on the carcasses of herrings.

Industrial activities

During the first half of the seventeenth century the general upward swing of Dutch prosperity suffered no interruption. Not till the second half of the century did the powerful neighbors of the republic, France and England, enter upon a more active competition with the Dutch. To clear the path for their own advance they adopted commercial and political measures which inaugurated a gradual Dutch decline. These measures will be examined in due time.

Dutch decline dates from the rise of France and England

An intense cultural activity kept pace with and gave dignity to Dutch material expansion. The university of Leyden became a leading intellectual and scientific center of seventeenth century Europe; and a school of painting arose which endowed the west with some of its most notable artistic treasures. At Haarlem lived and worked the great Frans Hals

The notable Dutch culture

(d. 1666), at Amsterdam the even greater Rembrandt van Rijn (d. 1669), while throughout the republic we encounter vigorous representatives, such as Jan Steen, Gerard Ter Borch, Jan Vermeer, of that earth-born spirit of realism which has given enduring pictorial expression to the life of the people in home and tavern, in field and on water.

11 THE REFORMATION AND THE CIVIL WARS IN FRANCE

THE HOUSES OF VALOIS AND BOURBON

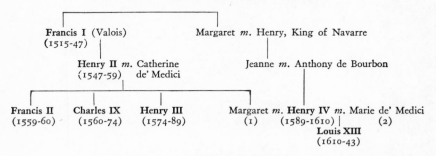

A SWIFT RECAPITULATION of what has already **Again the** been said touching the general French situation will help our under- **growing** standing of the Reformation developments in that country with which **absolutism** this chapter is concerned. We have seen that the king had so increased **of the** his power that he had come to overshadow in a very decisive manner **French king** his two medieval partners, the clergy and the nobles. Nonetheless they retained certain traditional powers, which, especially in the case of the nobles, were so extensive that, as shall hereafter appear, the crown continued to be threatened by this feudal class far into the seventeenth century.

In regard to the relation of king and church an important milestone **The French** had been reached in the Pragmatic Sanction of Bourges (1438). The **church falls** leading purpose of the Pragmatic Sanction was to affirm that the French **into depend-** (or Gallican) church was largely independent of Rome, and particularly **ence on the** so in the matter of the appointment of the great prelates, the bishops and **king** abbots. The power of which the pope was deprived was gradually absorbed by the king so that the Gallican church fell into increasing dependence on the crown. In 1516 this transfer of power was confirmed by Pope Leo X, who signed a Concordat with King Francis I, wherein he reserved to himself nothing more than the formal induction into office of the bishops and abbots whom the French king saw fit to nominate. The Concordat of 1516 is an important milestone in the growth of the power of the French king.

With the steady consolidation of the power of its king France was bound to play an ever larger part in the affairs of Europe. A decisive step in this direction was taken when, in 1494, Charles VIII undertook his celebrated invasion of Italy. We have seen how this bid of France for the control of Italy was challenged by Spain and how it led to a long series of wars between the two countries. They reached their climax in the first half of the sixteenth century when Charles V was king of Spain and Francis I king of France. By a succession of four wars fought in the course of his reign Francis I attempted to dislodge his adversary from Italy, only to be obliged to admit on each occasion that he was unable to do so. Having already in connection with the reign of Charles V treated the European aspect of the reign of Francis I, we shall in this chapter concentrate on French domestic developments during this king's rule.

Once again the rivalry of France and Spain over Italy

FRANCIS I (1515-1547)

Even before Charles VIII had by his invasion of 1494 intensified the interest of his countrymen in Italy, the Renaissance influences identified with Italy had leaped the Alps and won disciples on French soil. The immediate contact with Italy established by Charles VIII (1483-1498) and his successor, Louis XII (1498-1515), greatly promoted a movement which, under Francis I (1515-1547), reached a climax.

The Renaissance comes to France

Francis was a liberal patron of both humanistic scholarship and the plastic arts. In his day the new learning gained a foothold at the university of Paris as well as at other French university centers. A really great scholar came to the front in the person of Budé (Budaeus, 1467-1540). Second only to Erasmus in his command of Latin and Greek, he held aloft a torch which lighted the way for the younger student generation.

Spread of classical learning; the great Budaeus

During his frequent sojourns on Italian soil the art-loving Francis sought the friendship of such leading painters as Leonardo da Vinci, Titian, and Andrea del Sarto, and rejoiced not a little at his success in persuading some Italian artists to settle in France. By this means a direct Italian impulse was communicated to the French followers of the arts, which led them to break away from the older Gothic inspiration and to found schools of architecture, sculpture, and painting of a distinct Renaissance character. The literary and artistic initiative of Francis, who was a gay, light-hearted worldling, counted for much in the cultural transformation of his country but should not be exaggerated. On the whole, our judgment must be that France, like Germany and England, had reached a stage of social and mental development which prompted it of its own initiative to absorb the stimulating influences from beyond the Alps.

Gothic art gives way to Renaissance art

When the Reformation followed on the heels of the Renaissance, King Francis became greatly puzzled. Prizing social merriment, refinement of dress and habitation, and the other circumstances of a pleasant, mundane

existence, he lacked the moral seriousness which would have enabled him to understand the deep indignation at the bottom of the Reformation protest. As for the theological subtleties raised by the reformers, they lay wholly outside the circle of his mind. Personally unaffected by the stir connected with the Lutheran crisis, he did not honor it with his attention till he made the disconcerting discovery that the religious agitation had a political side and involved him in difficulties with the pope and with the fervently Catholic element of his people. Then at times he would strike out at the reformers from what were clearly not motives of religious enthusiasm but cold reasons of state.

The Reformation in France, as everywhere else, developed from small beginnings. The new learning, its forerunner, had spread a certain vague longing for the reform of both state and church. At the opening of the sixteenth century, exactly as in every other country of Europe, some of the bolder spirits began to cast their protest against existing conditions into more precise terms. One of these bolder spirits was Jacques Lefèvre (1450-1537). After studying in Italy and occupying himself eagerly with the classics, he made the swing toward Christian learning so characteristic of northern scholarship. In 1512 Lefèvre published a translation of St. Paul's Epistles with a commentary, wherein he set forth the doctrine of Justification by Faith and a number of other positions afterward identified with Lutheranism.

When one of Lefèvre's pupils, Briçonnet by name, was promoted to the bishopric of Meaux, he summoned his old master and other kindred souls about him and with their help made the town of Meaux the center of the movement of religious reform in France. On the appearance, after 1517, of Luther's writings, they were welcomed, at least at first, as corroborative of the position of the Meaux circle toward the ecclesiastical abuses of the day. Only when Luther took a radical course and broke entirely away from the church did his Meaux sympathizers hesitate, for in their majority they were, like the humanists of Germany, firmly opposed to separation.

Nonetheless some of the more fiery representatives of the younger French generation accepted the leadership of Luther with the result that the Reformation gradually gained a foothold here and there. Alarmed at the spread of heretical opinions, the theological faculty of the university of Paris undertook to combat them. The theological faculty was known under the name of the Sorbonne; and the Sorbonne, having for centuries been one of the foremost watchdogs of orthodoxy, was only running true to form in raising the hue and cry against the latest religious agitation.

In order to be effectively repressive the heresy hunters of the Sorbonne would have to have the civil authorities on their side. In sixteenth cen-

tury France that meant the king. However, owing to the cultured tolerance of Francis I, he could not be persuaded to act until an unfortunate
turn in his political fortunes put him more or less at the mercy of the
theological doctors and their immense following among the orthodox
clergy and population. The unhappy political event was his capture at
the battle of Pavia (1525) and his incarceration in Spain as the prisoner
of Charles V.

The captivity of Francis (1525) helps the orthodox cause

During the captivity of Francis his mother acted as regent. An intelligent woman, above all, a devoted mother, she saw the necessity of meeting the crisis by marshaling a united France behind her; and when she
discovered that the powerful clerical element was not to be had save at
the cost of a persecution of the innovators, she gave her consent. The first
systematic repression of heresy occurred therefore at this time. On the
return of Francis from Madrid he withdrew his support from the orthodox and again permitted the reformers to spread their doctrines under an
unofficial form of toleration.

Circum-stances of the first systematic persecution

This swing between persecution and toleration characterized the reign
of Francis to the very end. It is not uninteresting to note in passing that
in one of these periods of persecution, in 1534, there was banished from
France a young man who was destined to make the world resound with
his name—John Calvin. On the whole, the severity of repression grew
with the progress of the years. For, although Francis continued to be
personally reluctant to punish the heterodox, in connection with his lifelong struggle against Spain he needed the help of the pope and the financial backing of the French clergy, and he could get them in no other way.

Oscillation between persecution and toleration

The climax of this repressive violence was reached in the famous Waldensian massacre. The Waldenses were a Christian sect of peasants and
mountaineers who dwelt on the slopes of the western Alps. Largely because they lived unnoticed in their remote upland valleys, they had been
left in undisturbed possession of certain opinions and practices, which
had originated with one Peter Waldo as far back as the twelfth century.
Characterized by evangelical and anti-clerical features very much like
those of Lutheranism, the Waldensian teachings drew the fire of the increasingly intransigent supporters of Catholicism. They besieged Francis
to destroy the Alpine nest of corruption and would not yield ground
until the king had signed an order to that effect. In 1545 the snow-capped
Alps witnessed a cruel scene. Three thousand villagers were butchered,
hundreds were dragged from their homes to wear out their lives in the
king's galleys, and many other hundreds were driven into exile.

The Waldensian massacre, 1545

HENRY II (1547-1559)

Francis was succeeded by his son, Henry II (1547-1559), who had little
in common with his engaging, if somewhat soft and frivolous, predecessor. If Francis persecuted from political necessity, Henry did so from
deliberate choice. He had a somber streak in his character, indicative of
the shadow which the approaching Catholic reaction was casting before
it. On the day of his coronation he took with gusto the traditional oath
that he would exterminate from the kingdom whatever subjects of his
the church saw fit to denounce.

Henry II a
persecutor
by choice

True to his word, Henry II labored throughout his reign to put an end
to heresy. He went so far as to desire to set up the Inquisition with its
vigorous machinery of courts, prisons, and police. But here he met with
opposition from his supreme law courts, the *parlements*. These, ten in
number at the time, divided the territory of France among them. Having
in the past extended their jurisdiction to heresy on the ground that heresy
was quite as much a civil felony as a dereliction from the faith, they
resisted the attempt to have their power clipped by a rival ecclesiastical
tribunal.

Establish-
ment of the
Inquisition
resisted by
the parle-
ments

Hence the Inquisition was never established in France. However, the
parlements, and more particularly the leading parlement, the parlement
of Paris, urged on by the zealous king, did such thorough work in in-
flicting death and confiscation of goods on suspected persons that it is not
easy to see how an Inquisition manned by clerics could have been more
energetic. When the existing organization of the parlement of Paris no
longer sufficed to handle the business, a special criminal section, popularly called *Chambre Ardente* (Court of Fire), was instituted and soon
won an ominous reputation as an instrument of persecution.

Religious
persecution
conducted
by the parle-
ments

Neither the thoroughness nor the ferocity of the parlements availed to
suppress the enemy. The printed words of the exiled Calvin at Geneva
had a magical effect on the Protestants of his native land, while in his
person they found a leader ever ready to hearten the wavering ranks. In
spite of the risks involved, dozens of preachers who had studied under
Calvin's guidance secretly entered France as missionaries. By, or a little
past, the middle of the century they had achieved the startling success
of giving the whole French reform movement a uniform Calvinist cast.

Steady
growth of
the Calvinist
faith

It was the artisan class of the urban centers which supplied the main
body of Calvinist believers. Noteworthy, however, was the fact that conversions grew apace also among the nobility, particularly among the
small nobles of the countryside. To the French followers of Calvin there
came to be applied the term Huguenots, which no one has ever been able
to explain in an entirely satisfactory manner. Presently an underground

The French
Reformed
church born
in 1559

organization of the Huguenot congregations was effected, and in 1559 the congregations succeeded in holding their first national synod. The most important act of the synod was to adopt a confession of faith prepared by Calvin himself. In the teeth of the law and its alert orthodox watchdogs the French Reformed church had become a fact!

If Henry was largely occupied with fighting Protestantism, he did not on this account neglect the foreign interests of France. As the heir of his predecessors he found himself involved in the ancient rivalry with Spain over Italy. As stubbornly determined to contest the issue as his father Francis, he made as little impression on his stalwart adversary. In 1559 he signed the Treaty of Cateau-Cambrésis, which solemnly acknowledged the Spanish mastery of the peninsula. *Henry II at war with Spain over Italy*

Nonetheless the wars of Henry brought certain not unimportant advantages to his country. It will be remembered that, fiery Catholic though he was, he did not scruple to join with the German Protestants in their struggle (1552) against Emperor Charles V, and that he was enabled, by virtue of his intervention in the German civil war, to occupy the three border bishoprics of Metz, Toul and Verdun. *Henry acquires three border bishoprics, 1552*

Furthermore, though in the war (1556-1559) which ended in Cateau-Cambrésis he was repeatedly defeated by the forces of Philip II of Spain, he scored a triumph over the English, who had joined the war as Philip's allies, by capturing the port of Calais. *Henry acquires Calais, 1558*

The acquisition of Calais and the three bishoprics is an interesting indication that French political ambition, balked of its Italian objective, had uncovered a more promising field of expansion toward the east and north. However, before the monarchy could take further advantage of this discovery, it became involved in civil broils and was obliged to give up an active foreign policy for many a year. *Successful French expansion toward the east and north*

When Henry signed with Philip of Spain the Treaty of Cateau-Cambrésis, it was with the resolve to adjourn the conflict with Spain until he had settled the baffling problem of the Reformation. In a close Catholic partnership with Philip he planned to extirpate heresy, root and branch. The new alignment was signalized by the marriage of his daughter Elizabeth with the Spanish king. At a tournament, which was a feature of the sumptuous nuptial celebration, Henry rode into the lists against the captain of his guard. A chance splinter from his antagonist's lance entered his eye, and he died before he could realize his dream of purging his realm of the heretical poison. *Death of Henry II, 1559*

FRANCIS II, CHARLES IX, HENRY III, AND THE HUGUENOT WARS

On the death of Henry, his son, Francis, who was but sixteen years old and physically and mentally ailing, succeeded to the throne. When the power in an absolute monarchy, such as France had by this time become, is not exercised by the sovereign, it is inevitably seized by some ambitious man or faction. The situation at the court of the boy-king has therefore an unusual interest.

Francis II, 1559-60

The wife of the sickly Francis was a queen in her own right, Mary of Scotland. Although a woman of parts, she was only a little older than her husband and too inexperienced to assume control in his name. Her presence on the throne, however, smoothed the path for the ambition of her two uncles, brothers of her mother and heads of the noble house of Guise. The older was Francis, duke of Guise; the younger was a churchman, Cardinal Lorraine. They seized the power in the name of the king and, because they were ardent Catholics, continued Henry II's policy of Protestant persecution.

French factions: the Guises

There were those, however, who looked with jealousy upon the rule of the Guises and called it usurpation. They were the princes of the house of Bourbon, a younger branch of the royal family. The head of the house was sovereign of what was left of the ancient kingdom of Navarre in the Pyrenees and was known as King Anthony. His younger brother was Louis, prince of Condé. They contended that, as princes of the blood, they had a better right to rule for the feeble king than the family of Guise, and presently attracted to their cause whoever held a grudge against the ruling clique.

French factions: the Bourbons

In this way the Bourbon princes came to head a party of "malcontents," ready to seize every opportunity to rid themselves of the Guises. In casting about for supporters they could not fail to observe that the Guises were held in particular aversion by the persecuted Huguenots. Out of this common enmity there grew an intimacy and an alliance. Anthony in a faithless, vacillating manner, Condé more firmly, accepted the Reformed faith. Since many "malcontents"—high-placed courtiers and noblemen for the most part—followed the example of the Bourbon princes, it came to pass that French Protestantism became inextricably involved with political intrigue at court.

The Bourbons seek the support of the Protestants

Between the rival court factions of Bourbon and Guise, and belonging to neither, stood a person not highly regarded at first but destined to become famous, Catherine de' Medici. She was a Florentine princess, widow of Henry II and mother of the young king. Protestant contemporaries came to look upon her as an incarnate fiend, but one of her chief antagonists, who afterward became King Henry IV of France, judged her more leniently and more objectively. He once silenced an over-harsh critic by asking what she was to do, an anxious mother, torn hither and yon by the fierce party feuds and with no adviser in whom she could trust.

Catherine de' Medici, the queen-mother

In this apology of the great king lies in all probability the key to Catherine's career. She was, above all, a mother, a mother of royal children, for whom she desired to preserve the throne of France. Doubtless, too, after she had once tasted the sweets of power, she clung to them with selfish tenacity, as men and women will. Armed only with her woman's wit she plunged into the conflict of parties and, like other rulers of her time, intrigued, bribed, and prevaricated to keep herself afloat. Only a very biased person would ascribe to her a code of political conduct essentially different from that of Philip of Spain or Elizabeth of England. *Catherine an unscrupulous opportunist*

Out of these factions around the throne grew the intrigues which led to the long religious wars in France. It is futile to try to put the blame for them on one or the other side. Given a weakened royal executive, the implacable religious temper which marks the society of the sixteenth century, and a horde of powerful, turbulent, and greedy nobles, and civil war is inevitable. We can notice only a single incident indicative of the impending catastrophe. A Protestant rising against the dominant faction was planned for March, 1560. Getting wind of it, the Guises pounced upon their adversaries before they were ready, scattered them to the winds, and by way of warning hanged those they succeeded in catching to the battlements of the king's castle at Amboise or drowned them in sacks in the river Loire. *The dominant Guises on the alert against their enemies*

But the downfall of the Guises was at hand. In December, 1560, King Francis died, and his widow Mary, finding her role in France at an end, returned to her Scottish kingdom. Thus the props on which the power of the Guises rested broke under them. The successor of Francis was his brother Charles IX, a weakling like his brother and a minor only ten years old. In these circumstances Catherine de' Medici assumed the regency and for the first time held the reins in her hands. *Catherine regent for the boy-king, Charles IX*

Desirous of maintaining the authority of the crown and conscious of the difficulty of her position between Guise and Bourbon, Catherine resolved on a policy of balance and moderation. Calling representatives of both factions into her council, she attempted to conciliate the estranged Bourbon party by an order to the parlements to put an end to religious persecution. Then, in January, 1562, she went the length of conceding to the Protestants a limited right of worship. *Catherine adopts a policy of toleration*

Here was a change of policy inviting us to hail in Catherine the first official promoter in France of religious liberty. However, her good intentions came to naught, were bound to come to naught among men who, like the Protestants and Catholics of the sixteenth century, were passionately set on realizing their own religious system without the abatement of a jot or tittle. While the Catholics were embittered by the extent of Catherine's concessions, the Huguenots grumbled at the remaining limitations. Among the more fanatical followers of the two parties conflicts spontaneously flared up which frequently led to terrible excesses. *The passionate temper of the age defeats toleration*

One of these conflicts, the massacre of Vassy (1562), precipitated the
inevitable war. The duke of Guise was passing through the country with
a company of armed retainers, when he happened, at Vassy, upon a
group of Huguenots assembled in a barn for worship. Sharp words led
to an encounter, and before the duke rode away thirty persons lay dead
upon the ground and almost two hundred had been wounded. Fierce
indignation seized the Protestants throughout France; and when the
duke of Guise was received by Catholic Paris like a hero returning from
a successful war and Catherine confessed herself unable to call him to
account, the prince of Condé, leading figure of the Huguenots, issued an
appeal to his followers and took the field.

Thus were inaugurated the religious wars of France. They were not
brought to a conclusion until 1598 by the Edict of Nantes, and in their
consequences they continued to trouble the country well into the next
century. For our purpose it is sufficient to look upon the period from
1562 to 1598 as one war, though it is true that there were frequent sus-
pensions of arms supporting themselves upon sham truces and dishonest
treaties. The war, like all the religious wars of the century, was waged
with inhuman barbarity, and incendiarism, pillage, massacre, and assassination blot every stage of its progress. Protestants and Catholics alike
became beasts of the field and vied with each other in their efforts to turn
their country into a desert.

When the Treaty of St. Germain (1570), which once more confirmed
to the Protestants a limited measure of toleration, temporarily closed the
chapter of conflicts, many of the original leaders had passed away. King
Anthony of Navarre had been killed (1562) in battle against his former
friends, the Huguenots, whom he had deserted with characteristic lack
of scruple; the duke of Guise had been assassinated (1563); and Condé
had been treacherously slain after surrender in the field (1569). The official head of the Huguenot party was now Anthony's young son, King
Henry of Navarre; but for the present the real leadership devolved on
the worthy and gifted admiral of France, Gaspard de Coligny.

The new leader was one of the few high-born noblemen who had
joined the Huguenot ranks for reasons other than political rancor. While
fighting with conviction for the religion of his choice, he never forgot, in
the wild broils of partisanship, that he was a Frenchman and owed a
duty to his country. He belonged to the great family of Châtillon, was
allied through his mother with the still greater family of Montmorency,
and without going to sea held, anomalously enough, the purely honorary
post of admiral of France. By reason both of character and ability Coligny rose well above all the faction leaders of his time.

The outstanding feature of the Peace of St. Germain was that it expressed the attitude of a group of moderate men desirous of smoothing

the way to a genuine pacification. To them it was only too clear that the bloodshed, which was draining the country of its strength, ruined both parties and brought profit to none except to the enemies of France. For the time being King Charles himself, who was now of age and ruled in his own name, inclined to the same view. And yet so persistent were the suspicions and animosities that the attempt to put an end to the excesses of the past precipitated the most horrible of all the incidents of the war, the massacre of St. Bartholomew.

Genuine attempt to pacify France after St. Germain

After the Peace of St. Germain, Coligny joined the court and, being a man of unusual force of character, rapidly acquired great influence with the king. The young monarch seemed to be resolved to restore peace to the country, to enforce strictly the terms of the recent treaty with its provision of a limited right of worship for the Protestants, and to weld the opponents together by turning their united strength against Spain, regarded by all factions and classes as the leading enemy of France. To fortify his policy Charles IX arranged, as a preliminary step, a marriage between his sister Margaret and young Henry of Navarre. Joyfully responding to the invitation of the king, the Huguenots poured in swarms into Paris to attend the wedding of their chief, which was celebrated on August 18, 1572.

Marriage of Henry of Navarre and Margaret, sister of the king, 1572

The wedding seemed to inaugurate a period of national harmony based on religious toleration and the ascendancy of Coligny in the councils of the king. That was more than the extreme Catholics under the leadership of the Guises could bear. Besides, Henry, the present head of the house of Guise, bore a grudge against Coligny, whom, under the distortion common to extreme partisanship, he regarded as the instigator of his father's murder in 1563. He found an ally in the queen-mother, exasperated beyond endurance by finding herself supplanted by Coligny at the council-table of her son. Together they hired an assassin, who on August 22 fired at Coligny, as he was leaving the king's palace, and wounded him severely in the arm. The young sovereign, who hurried to the bedside of his councilor, either felt or shammed a deep indignation. "Yours the wound, mine the sorrow," he said and swore to bring the assassin and his hidden accomplices to justice.

The attempted assassination of Coligny, August 22

What followed was long enveloped in mystery but is now reasonbly clear. Since the failure of the attempt on Coligny's life would be followed by an investigation, and since Queen Catherine and the Guises could not permit themselves to be pilloried before the world as the patrons of assassins, they resolved to get rid of Coligny and his whole Huguenot following by a comprehensive massacre. The conspirators did not dare launch their project without the consent of the king. It was the work of the mother to wring his approval from the son, who was as unsteady as a weather vane. The king, the queen-mother, and the Guise faction must

The improvisers of the massacre of St. Bartholomew

accept responsibility for the improvised crime. They were its moral per-petrators. Their active agent was the passionately Catholic population of Paris.

Story of the
massacre of
August 24
On the day following the attempt on Coligny's life the details of the proposed massacre were carefully worked out. Accordingly, at the earliest dawn of August 24, which was the feast of St. Bartholomew, the bells rang from all the church steeples of Paris. At the signal such Catholic residents of Paris as had been initiated into the project slipped from their beds, attacked the houses which had been previously designated with a chalk-mark as harboring Huguenots, and slaughtered as many of their opponents as they could get into their hands.

The victims
of the
massacre
The wounded Coligny was the first victim of the bloody orgy, Duke Henry of Guise presiding in person at the butchery of his antagonist. The young bridegroom, Henry of Navarre, was spared the same fate by temporarily renouncing his faith. That day the streets of Paris ran with blood and, for many days after, the provincial towns, encouraged by the example of the capital, indulged in similar excesses. The victims of the savage explosion numbered some three thousand in Paris and probably more than double that number in the rest of France. We reach some understanding of the ferocity of the religious divisions of the time when we hear that at the news of the massacre Pope Gregory XIII ordered a solemn *Te deum* to be sung and that the somber Philip of Spain burst into his only recorded laugh.

Henry III,
1574-1589,
and the
question
of the
succession
War with all its dreary concomitants straightway flamed up again. In 1574 Charles IX succumbed to disease and was succeeded by his brother, Henry III (1574-1589). A new element of interest was introduced into the struggle only when it became clear that Henry, who was the last male survivor of the reigning Valois line, would leave no offspring. This opened the question of the succession.

The Holy
League
rejects a
Protestant
succession
By the law of the realm the crown would have to pass upon Henry's death to the nearest male relative, who was Henry of Navarre, head of the collateral branch of Bourbon. But Henry, converted to Catholicism in 1572 in order to save his life, had long ago relapsed and was the enemy of the faith of the vast majority of his future subjects. When his succession became probable, Henry of Guise and his orthodox followers formed what they called a Holy League. It pledged itself to maintain the interest of the Roman church at all hazards, to crush Protestantism utterly, and never to suffer a heretic on the throne of France.

The
Huguenots
organize as
an independ-
ent power
The Huguenots showed a spirit hardly less narrow and selfish than that of their opponents. They organized themselves as a self-governing republic, practically independent of the kingdom. It was plain that party was counting for more and more, country for less and less, and that the

outcome of the wasteful civil strife would be the ruin and disruption of France.

In consequence of the growing bitterness, Henry III found himself in an all but untenable position. As head of the state he was pledged to the interests of the country and in a weak, shambling way was inclined to pursue a policy of reconciliation and peace. But the League, headed by Henry of Guise, and the Huguenots, under Henry of Navarre, would have no peace except on their own terms. Trying to steer a middle course, the king was gradually deserted by all except the handful of men who refused to share in the madness of partisan fury. In the new turn of the civil struggle three parties, each championed by a leader of the name of Henry, disputed the control of France. The three ruling factions

The new phase, called the War of the Three Henrys (1585-1589), steeped the country in such confusion that men soon practiced every lawlessness without punishment. King Henry, an effeminate dandy with a fondness for lapdogs and earrings, was so generally flouted that he was unable to maintain even the appearance of authority save by handing over the reins to the masterful Henry of Guise. War of the Three Henrys, 1585-1589

In December, 1588, the indignant king resolved to put an end to his humiliation. Inviting Henry of Guise to an interview in the royal castle at Blois, he treacherously had him dispatched by his guard. Cowardice and rancor could go no farther. The League turned in horror from the murderer, while the all but solidly Catholic population of Paris clamored noisily for his deposition. Murder of Henry of Guise, 1588

In his despair the royal culprit fled to the enemy camp, to the camp of Henry of Navarre. With the aid of his Huguenot subjects he was advancing on his hostile capital, when a fanatical Dominican monk gained admission to his presence and slew him with a knife (August, 1589). With him the house of Valois came to an end. The war was now reduced to an issue between Henry of Navarre, the rightful claimant to the crown, and the League, which would have none of him. Murder of Henry III, 1589

HENRY IV (1589-1610)

The new sovereign, Henry IV, first king of the house of Bourbon, was a brave soldier, an intelligent politician, and a courtly gentleman. He had his faults, springing from a sensuous and mercurial temperament, but, intensely human as they were, they actually helped endear him to his followers. Character of King Henry IV

Henry IV was confronted on his accession by the disconcerting fact that his Huguenot followers were only a small part of the French population. The attachment of the Catholic majority he knew could only be won slowly, and force, he suspected from the first, would be of no avail.

Therefore, he undertook patiently to assure the Catholics of the loyalty
of his intentions in order to win their recognition. If the League could
only have found a plausible rival for the throne, Henry might have been
easily displaced. But his claim was incontrovertible and his claim was his
strength.

It was also in Henry's favor that the fanatic League had made an alli-
ance with Spain, a foreign power and leading enemy of France. The
Spanish intimacy brought it about that many Catholic patriots, who hated
Spain more than they hated their Huguenot fellow countrymen, rallied to
Henry's banner. In the circumstances no one thought of disarming. King
Henry won a number of engagements, notably the battle of Ivry (1590).
But the League, still managed by the Guise faction in the person of the
late leader's younger brother and supported by the resources of Philip of
Spain, could not be beaten into submission.

For four years Henry waited for his subjects to acknowledge him as
their king. When they did not do so, he took a step which it is not difficult to understand. The universal misery caused by the endless struggle
wrung his heart; he was in constant alarm lest the League or Philip II
or both in agreement should impose on France a Catholic ruler of their
own choice; and finally, with his bubbling southern vivacity Henry, who
was a typical son of Gascony, did not at the bottom of his heart feel
sympathetic with the austere Calvinists constituting his immediate following. In the light of such considerations, it could not have caused him
much heart-burning to conclude that, since nothing short of his conversion would reunite and restore France, he should have to abandon
an unpopular cause. His much-quoted remark: "Paris is well worth a
mass," reveals by its flippancy his purely political appraisal of the situation. In July, 1593, after cautious preliminary negotiations with the Catholic clergy, he solemnly abjured the Huguenot faith and was readmitted
to the Roman communion.

The effect of the king's action was electric. Cities and provinces made
haste to recognize him, the League fell apart, and the civil broils came
to an end, except for a few lingering fires. By February, 1594, Henry
could proceed with his coronation at Chartres, and when, a month later,
he approached Paris, the gates were thrown open and he was received
like a savior by those same Parisians who in their intense Catholic
fervor had, during his apostasy, spewed him out of their mouths.

To complete the work of unifying the country two things remained
to be done: to punish Spain for interfering in the domestic affairs of
France and to give the Huguenots the security to which they were entitled if they were ever to become contented citizens. As soon as he felt
reasonably secure on the French throne, Henry declared war on Spain
(1595), bringing the united Catholic and Protestant forces of the country

into the field against the ancient foe. Since, as a sequel to the revolt of
the Netherlands, the Dutch and the English were already at war with
Philip, Henry naturally allied himself with these two peoples.

Beset by three governments, Philip soon saw the necessity of giving up
his far-ranging schemes and notified Henry of his willingness to treat. **The Peace**
The result was the Peace of Vervins (1598), in which Henry received **of Vervins**
formal recognition as king of France and the relations between the two
countries were re-established on the terms laid down in the Treaty of
Cateau-Cambrésis (1559).

With the country at peace with its neighbors Henry could turn to the
Huguenot problem. In April, 1598, he issued from the city of Nantes, **The Edict**
where he was temporarily residing, an edict by which he hoped to satisfy **of Nantes**
his Huguenot subjects. The edict granted to the Protestants, still, it **(1598)**
should be remembered, a very small minority of the nation, a considerable body of rights classifiable as religious, civil, and political.

In the matter of *religious* rights, the Edict of Nantes authorized Protestant worship at two places in each bailiwick (*bailliage,* an administrative **Religious**
division approximately equivalent to an American county) as well as, **and civil**
with certain restrictions, in the castles of Huguenot noblemen. As a con- **rights con-**
cession to the uncompromising Catholic fervor of the Parisians the re- **ferred by**
formed service was expressly excluded from the capital. When it came **the Edict**
to the *civil* rights conceded by the Edict, the Protestants did very well
indeed, for they were guaranteed the protection of the law and declared
eligible to public office.

So far the settlement was intelligible and intelligent and, in spite of its
restrictions, far more liberal than any solution found anywhere else up to **The exces-**
that date. However, in the sections dealing with *political* rights conces- **sive political**
sions were made to the Huguenots which to a citizen of our day must **rights con-**
appear amazing and which, in point of fact, were incompatible with the **ferred by**
interests and even the existence of the monarchy. Not only were the **the Edict**
Huguenots permitted to hold political assemblies in which they might
legislate for themselves like an independent power but, as a guarantee of
the execution of the treaty, they were put in possession of a certain number of fortified towns, of which La Rochelle was the most important. By
these concessions the Huguenots were constituted as an armed minority
within and yet outside the state.

It was highly doubtful that the Edict of Nantes, especially its political
provisions, would stand the test of time. Owing to the great authority **The Edict**
which Henry enjoyed in all circles as the pacifier of France, it was not at **of Nantes**
once challenged. Nonetheless the tension between Catholics and Protes- **produces**
tants continued unabated, reminding us that in that age intolerance was **only a**
an emotion as spontaneous as the love of kin or the fear of fire. There- **superficial**
pacification

fore, no sooner had the strong hand and balanced temper of Henry been withdrawn than the religious passions burst once more into the open.

But that was as yet some years off; and while life smiled at him, Henry gave himself with zeal to the task of utilizing the peace in order to heal the many wounds of his country. One of his earliest concerns was the royal finances, which were in hopeless disorder. Since for years taxes had been only intermittently collected, the debts of the crown had reached alarming proportions. By putting a friend of his Huguenot days, the duke of Sully, in charge of the treasury, he had the satisfaction of seeing how by the vigilance of this enlightened servant the royal debt was gradually reduced and the annual deficit converted into a surplus available for further debt reduction.

Henry's work of reconstruction: the finances

Personally Henry was much interested in agriculture and did all in his power to encourage this fundamental activity, then as now a leading source of French prosperity. In addition, he improved communications by building roads; he encouraged new industries, especially the manufacture of silk; and he made a modest beginning in the direction of a colonial empire by furthering French enterprise in the basin of the St. Lawrence.

His agricultural, commercial, and colonial activity

For all these domestic labors Henry did not fail to keep a sharp eye on Europe and the international situation. As to all his immediate predecessors, so also to him the house of Hapsburg, reigning through its two branches in Spain and Austria, appeared as a power which threatened France by too closely enveloping it. In the period following the Peace of Vervins Henry therefore cultivated the friendship of all the small neighbor states—the Dutch, the Swiss Confederation, the still independent states of Italy, such as Venice and Tuscany, dwelling under the shadow of Spain, and the German Protestant princes fearful of their Catholic emperor—until he exercised a kind of informal protectorate over them. When he had thus fortified France with a ring of political outposts, he considered the time to be ripe once more to summon the house of Hapsburg to the field.

Henry prepares to renew the conflict with the house of Hapsburg

A quarrel over the succession to a small German state on the lower Rhine furnished him with the welcome pretext to inaugurate a war against the Austro-Spanish combination. While still engaged in making preparations for the campaign, he was, on May 14, 1610, laid low by the dagger of a fanatic who had become persuaded that Henry was a secret traitor to the Catholic cause.

Murder of Henry, 1610

THE AMAZING CARDINAL RICHELIEU

No sooner had the strong pillar of domestic order fallen than France was threatened with the resumption of the dissension from which she had just recovered. Henry's successor was his son Louis XIII (1610-1643), a lad but nine years old. The situation demanded a regency, and in the **Regency of** hope of avoiding the quarrel of factions that had followed on the death **Marie de'** of an earlier Henry, of Henry II, the regency powers were concentrated **Medici** in the single person of the young king's mother, Marie de' Medici. A Florentine like the former regent, Catherine de' Medici, Queen Marie was Henry's second wife, to whom he had been joined (1600) on the grant of a divorce from Margaret of Valois, his bride of the stormy period of St. Bartholomew.

The new ruler of France was a large, coarse-featured woman without distinction of either character or intelligence and therefore wholly in- **Renewed** capable of consistently asserting her authority. In consequence, in spite of **outbreak of** her formal supremacy, the crown became the football of favorites and in- **factions** terested groups. Perhaps without her knowing it, but no less successfully for all that, Marie was exploited by some of her Italian countrymen constituting her personal following. This situation naturally enough aroused the resentment of the great French nobles who, regarding the foreign interlopers with aversion, never ceased plotting against them.

Among the turbulent nobiliary elements the Huguenot aristocracy constituted a specially dangerous group, since they had been permitted by **The danger-** the Edict of Nantes to maintain an army and hold several fortified towns. **ous Hugue-** On meeting with less consideration from the regent than they felt to **not nobility** be their due, they rose in arms against her. While they craftily let themselves be again brought to terms by a shower of honors and pensions, they continued to suspend the threat of a new religious war over the country.

If France was saved from this confusion, it was due, and solely due, to one man, Armand Jean du Plessis, known to fame as Cardinal Riche- **Richelieu** lieu. When Richelieu entered the royal council to become before long, by **saves the** the natural ascendancy of his intellect, the leading minister (1624), the **state** authority of the queen-regent had already been replaced by that of the king; but under the king, who had much more of his mother than of his father in him and was dull and slothful, the affairs of the realm had not been in the least improved. Richelieu, therefore, found himself confronted by a confused and difficult task.

Only the unique authority which Richelieu succeeded in accumulating enabled him to meet and master the situation. As a boy he had been **Richelieu,** destined for the church, and at an amazingly early age he had, by reason **cardinal** of his noble birth and the favor of the king, been made bishop of Luçon. **and prime** On his diplomatic talents making themselves felt, he was honored by the **minister** pope with the cardinal's hat. Thus it happened that when he became the king's chief minister, he united in his person a sum of dignities that raised him above attack so long as he enjoyed his sovereign's support. This support, to his honor, Louis XIII gave to the fullest possible extent.

While Richelieu lived, he retained, in spite of innumerable intrigues and conspiracies, the power in his hands and was the real ruler of France.

Richelieu was one of those rare statesmen who can form and carry

Richelieu's
three main
aims

through with an iron will a policy adjudged by him to be in conformity with the needs of the country. His program, which dovetails nicely with that of Henry IV, falls into three sections. In the first place, endowed with Henry's tolerance, he would accept the Edict of Nantes so far as its main provisions were concerned. These were the articles guaranteeing the Huguenots their civil and religious rights. The political rights, however, which made them almost independent of the state, Richelieu was determined ruthlessly to destroy. His second aim was to clip still further the wings of the turbulent nobility; and his third, to overthrow for the greater glory of France the power of the house of Hapsburg.

Richelieu first attacked the problem of the Huguenots. Ever since the

Siege and
capture of
La Rochelle,
1628

death of Henry IV they had become restless and hung on the horizon like a thundercloud ready to burst at any moment. Richelieu proceeded cautiously, treated with them as long as negotiation was feasible, and suddenly, when the opportunity came, invested their chief town, La Rochelle, with an army. A long siege followed, wherein the endurance of the beleaguered citizens proved no match for the skill of the tireless cardinal, who conducted the operations in person. In vain did the English fleet, sent by King Charles I at the solicitation of the Huguenots, try to relieve the town. In 1628 La Rochelle, having lost 16,000 inhabitants through hunger and pestilence, surrendered at discretion.

The next year the remnant of the Protestant forces in the south was

Richelieu
confirms the
Huguenots
in their es-
sential rights

disarmed and Richelieu was master of the situation. And now his remarkable moderation came to light. The average ruler of the time would have compelled the beaten minority to conform to the religion of the majority or else be slaughtered or banished. Not so Richelieu, who cherished a toleration far in advance of his time. Confirming to the Huguenots the civil and religious rights granted by the Edict of Nantes, he mercilessly canceled their right to have an army and hold a number of fortified towns. They were no longer to be an *imperium in imperio* (a state within the state), but French citizens subject to the laws of their country.

The turbulent nobles intrenched in the provinces, where they consti-

Richelieu's
measures to
tame the
nobility

tuted to a certain extent the local government, gave the cardinal much food for thought. In his view they had become an anomaly in a sovereign state aspiring to exercise an exclusive authority. They carried on a veritable private warfare by their dueling habits and defied the authorities from behind their fortified castles. Hence Richelieu waged war upon duels and castles, declaring by edict that castles used against the crown would be destroyed and duelists punished with death.

Nonetheless, the great cardinal must not be credited with miracles. Battlemented castles and public duels did, from the time of Richelieu, gradually become things of the past, but less, on the whole, because Richelieu frowned on them than because of the great change which time was effecting in the manners of the upper classes. Social attitudes were gaining the ascendancy which persuaded the nobles to surrender their crude medieval independence for the pleasures and luxuries associated with the more urbane forms of the new age. Regarding the feudal strongholds more particularly, it is not recorded that Richelieu troubled himself to destroy many of them. More usually they were voluntarily abandoned in favor of newly built, villa-like country houses better suited to the softer manners of this and especially the succeeding century. *The new age casts discredit on the ancient feudal manners*

With the measures directed at the still towering prestige of the nobility there went hand in hand an effort to create a centralized administration, over which the nobles should have no power and which should be responsible exclusively to the king. That this was no new idea originating with Richelieu becomes clear when we recall that the French kings had been engaged in strengthening their hand for many generations. However, in spite of their growing power, the royal officials had not yet been able consistently to make their power felt throughout the area subjected to the crown. *Richelieu the advocate of a centralized administration*

Following a lead taken by former rulers but again abandoned, Richelieu appointed royal agents, called *intendants,* whom he dispatched to the provinces to take charge of police, justice, and finance. He selected the intendants exclusively from the commoners (the third estate), on the ground that commoners might be expected faithfully to carry out the orders of the government and to keep aloof from the intrigues of the local nobles. The intendants set the coping-stone on the historical structure of French administrative centralization, which, however, far from inventing, Richelieu merely brought to a new effectiveness. *The royal "intendants"*

In the face of this increase of the royal power, what became of the Estates General and the parlements, two institutions which had thus far, in some sort, shared in the government of France and which the king regarded as his more or less dangerous rivals? That their position would be impaired by Richelieu's policy of making the king the exclusive arbiter of French destiny was highly probable. Although the Estates General, composed of the three estates, clergy, nobles, and commoners, had not succeeded in achieving a place in the French political system remotely comparable to that occupied in England by the parliament, they had been irregularly consulted as late as the sixteenth century and had served to maintain a certain amount of valuable contact between the king and his people. Summoned in 1614, during the regency of Marie de' Medici, the three groups of representatives had quarreled *The feeble Estates General* impotently with the government and among themselves. They had then been dismissed by the regent, not to be summoned again for one hundred and seventy-five years.

Richelieu shelves the Estates General

For this shelving of an ancient institution Richelieu was largely responsible since, owing to his suspicion of everything that might challenge the omnipotence of the king, he carefully refrained during his control from issuing a call for a new session. In this way he set an example which was followed by the rulers after his day, until the breakdown of absolutism in the following century forced a resort to the barely remembered institution which had proved such a feeble prop of the popular liberties.

Richelieu and the parlements

The parlements, supreme courts of justice, as we have learned, could not be shelved like the States General since they were the apex of the national system of justice. Nor did Richelieu desire to shelve them, although he firmly refused to acknowledge, as an infringement on the king's powers, the right they claimed to refuse to register, that is, to absorb into the corpus of the national laws, an edict issued by the monarch of which they disapproved. To this attitude, too, the rulers after Richelieu clung till the overthrow of the whole inherited system by the French Revolution. In sum, Richelieu exalted the royal prerogative until the power of the crown seemed to depend on itself alone and the king appeared as an irresponsible agent ruling by divine right.

Richelieu and the Thirty Years' War

With the Huguenots pacified and the selfish nobility held in check, Richelieu could take up with vigor his foreign plans, looking to the humiliation of the house of Hapsburg. It was a most convenient circumstance that Germany was convulsed in his time with the religious conflict known as the Thirty Years' War. With the instinct of a statesman Richelieu felt that if he interposed to help the German Protestants against the Catholics, represented by the emperor and Spain, he would sooner or later acquire some permanent advantages for France. That he was helping Protestants against Catholics did not disturb him in the least, since he was a Frenchman first and a Catholic afterward. His gradual interference, developing from occasional subsidies of money to the recruitment of large armies, finally secured to his king the balance of power in the German war and made France in effect the dictator of Europe when the Peace of Westphalia (1648) ended the struggle. Richelieu did not live to see this result (he died in 1642), but the advantages which France secured in that document may be written down to the great minister's energetic conduct of the government. Our concluding word on Richelieu may well be that he more than any other single individual welded France into a solid political unit and prepared the way for her supremacy in Europe.

12
THE THIRTY YEARS' WAR

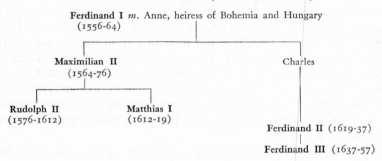

THE HOUSE OF HAPSBURG (AUSTRIAN BRANCH)

Ferdinand I *m.* Anne, heiress of Bohemia and Hungary
(1556-64)

Maximilian II
(1564-76)

Charles

Rudolph II
(1576-1612)

Matthias I
(1612-19)

Ferdinand II (1619-37)

Ferdinand III (1637-57)

THE PEACE OF Augsburg of 1555 must undoubtedly be construed as a victory for German Protestantism. But it was also, since it took the control of religion out of the hands of the central authority, the emperor, and gave it to the princes, a victory for the principle of decentralization. The significance of such a development in a Europe whose states were becoming daily more compact through the opposite movement of centralization must not be overlooked. Weakened and disunited Germany would draw the covetous gaze of her stronger neighbors and would henceforth be exposed to their attack. {The Peace of Augsburg a victory for (1) Protestantism and (2) decentralization}

Admittedly a victory for Protestantism, the Peace of Augsburg did not prove to be a final settlement of the religious conflict. Unfortunately, it left many important matters in suspense. For instance, it recognized Lutheranism without extending any rights whatever to the followers of Calvin. This is explicable on the ground that at the time of the peace Calvinism had hardly as yet penetrated into Germany. Then, a little past the middle of the century, a number of princes and free cities adopted it in place of Lutheranism. Not only did such converts fail to enjoy the protection of the law, but they were faced with the enmity of Catholics and the even more vindictive enmity of their Protestant rivals, the Lutherans. {Defects of the Peace of Augsburg: failure to recognize Calvinism}

Even more important as a source of continued disturbance were the features of the peace dealing with church property, and, more particu-

larly, the article called the Ecclesiastical Reservation. The position of the
Catholics, affirmed with constantly increasing vehemence, was that all
appropriations of Catholic property since the conclusion of the Preliminary Peace of Passau (1552) were illegal. Refusing to be intimidated, the
Protestants continued to secularize monasteries and to appropriate bishoprics where and whenever the opportunity offered. In consequence a
vast mass of land and buildings in the actual possession of Protestants
was angrily declared by their adversaries to be unlawfully held.

The
Protestants
charged by
the Catholics
with illegal
land seizures

That these venomous disputes did not precipitate a new civil war till
over half a century had passed is fairly remarkable and may be ascribed
to a variety of causes. In the first place, the immediate successors of
Emperor Charles V, Ferdinand I (1556-1564) and Maximilian II (1564-
1576), were moderate men, who did their utmost to mediate among the
factions. Their peaceful policy was seconded by the leading Lutheran
princes, inclined by the natural conservatism of successful men to rest
content with what they had won. Besides, these princes entertained the
hope that without war, by gradual infiltration into all classes of society
and through all districts, Protestantism might make a clean sweep of
Germany.

Reasons
why a new
civil war
was so long
adjourned

And, really, for some years following the Augsburg settlement the outlook for Protestantism was brilliant. It possessed youth and confidence,
and, in the Lutheran form at least, had acquired a legal sanction. Continuing to mount, like a tide, until it had covered the whole center and
north of Germany, it at last threatened the great bishoprics along the
Rhine and the hitherto staunchly Catholic dominions of Austria and
Bavaria in the south. To a dispassionate observer it might have seemed
not improbable that the Roman church, undermined in these, its last
strongholds, would soon altogether disappear from Germany.

Continued
advance of
Protestantism well
into the
sixteenth
century

This final Catholic catastrophe never took place. For one thing, the
dominant Lutherans, in distinction from their Calvinist relatives, were
too self-satisfied and unenterprising to make the best of their opportunities; and in the second place, in the very nick of time the Catholic
revival reached Germany and reinvigorated an apparently dying cause.

How
Catholicism
was saved

We have already taken note of how the Counter-Reformation, slowly
gathering strength, steadied the wavering Catholic ranks throughout the
world. It did not make itself felt in Germany until the last quarter of the
sixteenth century, when Rudolph II (1576-1612) was emperor. Breaking
away from the conciliatory policy of his immediate predecessors, Rudolph
resolved to put the Catholic church again in the saddle and to make use
to this end of the Jesuit order. Operating from the court of Vienna as a
center, and also from that of Bavaria, whose ruling family was, if possible, even more fervently Catholic than the Hapsburgs, the devoted followers of Ignatius Loyola gradually radiated in every direction. Their

The
Counter-
Reformation
gathers
strength in
Germany

churches multiplied, and their schools, conducted with energy and intelligence, were crowded with pupils. Before long the Protestant advance was checked all along the line, and an energetic Catholic propaganda began to score triumphs in those doubtful regions, chiefly of the south, where Protestantism, having but recently gained a foothold, was still feeble.

By the beginning of the seventeenth century the tension between the religious parties was nearing the danger point and every new incident increased the probability of a rupture. A glance at the affair of Donauwörth will show us from what quarter the wind was now blowing over Germany. Donauwörth, on the upper Danube, was a free imperial city and, as such, enjoyed representation in the Reichstag. It had declared for Protestantism, but the town council with unusual liberality had authorized Catholic worship while forbidding public Catholic demonstrations. In spite of this prohibition some Catholic zealots organized (1606) a religious procession, which was broken up by a riot. In hot indignation the Catholics appealed to Emperor Rudolph, who, maintaining that Catholic rights had been curtailed, put the city under the ban of the empire. At the same time he commissioned Duke Maximilian of Bavaria to occupy it with an armed force. Not content with carrying out the imperial orders, the duke, regarding Donauwörth as conquered territory, forcibly reconverted it to Catholicism.

Increasing tension: the Donauwörth incident, 1606

This decidedly high-handed act greatly excited the more radical Protestant elements, chiefly adherents of Calvinism. They came together for conference and in 1608 formed a Protestant Union to hinder a repetition of the Donauwörth outrage. Thereupon Duke Maximilian, considering himself threatened by this move, joined with other Catholic princes, chiefly prince-bishops, in a similar association which took the name of the Catholic League (1609). When people among whom no love is lost begin to go about armed, the chances of a bloody clash become excellent. Nevertheless, so general was the dread of civil war, that peace was preserved for another decade.

Formation of a Protestant Union and a Catholic League, 1608-1609

The occasion that finally precipitated the long-expected conflict was furnished by Bohemia. Bohemia was a kingdom which in 1526 had come into possession of the house of Hapsburg, partly through inheritance and partly through election by the Bohemian diet. Its inhabitants were Czechs and Germans, the Czechs, a Slav people, being decidedly in the majority. In the fifteenth century Bohemia had risen into European prominence through John Hus, who initiated a reform movement in the church and met a heretic's death at the stake (1415). The wild rebellion of the Hussites, as the reformer's followers were called, was put down only after a tremendous struggle lasting several decades.

Bohemia the home of the reformer, John Hus

When, a century after Hus's death, Luther lifted his voice in Saxony,

his words raised an answering echo across the Bohemian border. Slowly
but surely the movement of reform spread through the land. The Hapsburg rulers made no serious effort against it till Emperor Rudolph II
came to the throne. Devoted son of the church, he tried to put the Reformation down; but, crotchety and more than half insane, he only botched
matters and was in the end constrained to grant the Protestants a limited
toleration in a charter issued in the year 1609.

Rudolph concedes toleration, 1609

Both Rudolph and his successor, Emperor Matthias (1612-1619), carried out the terms of the charter grudgingly and by a number of irregular
acts kept the Protestants in an inflamed state of mind. On May 23, 1618,
resolved to get rid of the Hapsburg dynasty and to give themselves a
ruler of their own faith, they rose in revolt against Matthias. The emperor resided at Vienna and was represented at Prague, the capital of
his Bohemian kingdom, by a body of governors. These the insurgents
attacked, invaded their castle residence, and summarily tossed two of
them, with a secretary thrown in for good measure, out of the window
into the moat below.

The revolt at Prague, May, 1618

It was a fall of some sixty feet, but, wonderful to relate, beyond the
shock to their bones and the more enduring shock to their feelings, it
had no evil consequences for the victims. The rebels crowned the day's
work by setting up a revolutionary government at Prague. While their
act was no more than a local Bohemian occurrence, in its consequences
it set fire to the inflammable German house and precipitated the struggle
known as the Thirty Years' War.

A revolutionary government set up in Bohemia

Whoever closely studies the Thirty Years' War will be struck by the
fact that it is really not so much a single war as an aggregation of
related wars. It therefore falls naturally into different periods, designated
by the issue which was uppermost at the time. Five such periods are
clearly distinguishable: the Bohemian Period (1618-1620), the Palatine
Period (1621-1623), the Danish Period (1625-1629), the Swedish Period
(1630-1635), and the French Period (1635-1648). These divisions indicate
how the struggle, beginning in Bohemia, spread like a contagion until
it embraced all Europe.

The Thirty Years' War falls into five periods

THE BOHEMIAN PERIOD (1618-1620)

The rebels at Prague had hardly set up their government when they
appealed to the German Protestants for help. The Lutherans of the north
denied them even their sympathy, while the Calvinists, inhabiting chiefly
the south and constituting the leading element of the Protestant Union,
offered advice but little help. The fact was that the Bohemians were in
rebellion, and rebellion is a matter which men with something at stake
will always handle with caution.

The Bohemian rebels appeal to the German Protestants

Among the members of the Union there were a few flighty, sanguine characters, who were bent on striking, through the Bohemian situation, a blow at the Hapsburgs and Catholicism. Chief of this band was the president of the Union, the Elector Frederick. He ruled over the region which, loosely strung across southern Germany, was called the Palatinate and boasted as its capital the city of Heidelberg, located on the Neckar not far from its confluence with the Rhine. The Elector Frederick was a Calvinist, a fact which helps explain his readiness to take the offensive against Catholicism. From the first he gave the Bohemian rebels secret aid. At the same time he attempted to commit the Protestant Union to an active policy. In this purpose he frankly failed. The Union would not go beyond a few temporizing measures. After a while, paralyzed by fear, it decreed its own dissolution (1621). Its story is an unbroken record of shilly-shallying incompetence. *Frederick of the Palatinate supports the rebels*

Meanwhile hostilities had begun between the emperor at Vienna and his rebellious subjects at Prague. They had not advanced far when the incapable Matthias died (March, 1619), and the Hapsburg dominions passed to a better man, Ferdinand II. Ferdinand had been brought up by the Jesuits and filled by them with their devotion to the church. He was small and feeble, with a hooked nose, weak eyes, and thin hair, plainly not a captain of men who shakes the world with his great projects. Nevertheless, where his convictions were involved this frail sovereign proved himself more immovable than men of a more heroic mold. *The accession of Ferdinand II*

Having raised an armed force and secured his capital, Vienna, against attack by the Bohemian rebels, Ferdinand set out for Frankfort, where the assembly of German electors was convened, after the usual fashion, to name the successor of Matthias. Although three of the seven electors were Protestants, the electoral college so far accepted the time-honored ascendancy of the house of Hapsburg as to raise Ferdinand to the imperial dignity. *Ferdinand elected emperor, 1619*

With the German crown in his possession, the Hapsburg ruler felt that he must next strain every nerve to recover Bohemia. The case seemed to him the more urgent as almost at the same moment that he was acclaimed emperor at Frankfort, the Bohemian struggle had entered a new and more dangerous phase: the rebels had made an offer of the crown to the Elector Frederick. Frederick hesitated, torn between anxiety and hope, but in the end, spurred by his ambitious wife, who was a daughter of James I of England, set out for Prague. On November 4, 1619, he was crowned king of Bohemia. *Frederick of the Palatinate crowned king of Bohemia*

In the course of his preparations for a vigorous campaign, Ferdinand naturally approached the Catholic League for aid. This organization, which was destined to play a very considerable role in the Thirty Years' War, was, in distinction from its rival, the Protestant Union, most effi-

ciently managed by its president, Maximilian, duke of Bavaria. Maximilian proved himself in the course of the war to be the most capable
of the princes of Germany. Brought up, like Ferdinand, by the Jesuits,
he shared the new emperor's devotion to the church but tempered it
with a political intelligence which was foreign to the imperial dreamer
and bigot. From the moment of his accession to his Bavarian duchy,
he had prepared for the coming German crisis by laying up money and
drilling an army. Thoroughly aroused over what he considered the Elector Frederick's usurpation, Maximilian did not require coaxing to put
his forces at Ferdinand's disposal.

Maximilian of Bavaria, head of the Catholic League

In the year 1620 there followed the campaign which decided the fate
of Bohemia. Was the country to remain Protestant under its new king,
Frederick, or was it to be won back by the Catholics and handed over to
Ferdinand? If the Protestants had had a different champion, their outlook might have been more brilliant. Frederick was a man of small intelligence, and such spirit as he boasted was pumped into him by his
vivacious spouse, the Electress Elizabeth. A further handicap was that
he was politically isolated. The Protestant Union, in spite of his appeals,
did next to nothing for him, while among the Lutherans one man, the
powerful elector of Saxony, actually went the length of co-operating with
Ferdinand.

Frederick left without support by the Protestants

The forces of the League, controlled by Maximilian but under the
immediate command of the very capable General Tilly, penetrated into
Bohemia without encountering opposition till they came within sight
of the towers of Prague. On the White Hill, to the west of the town,
they ran into Frederick's army. The ensuing battle was a crushing defeat
for Frederick, who fled for his life all the way across Germany to find an
asylum in Calvinist Holland. The Jesuits had mockingly foretold that
he would prove but a winter king, a man of snow destined to vanish at
the first ray of the sun, and they were right.

Battle of the White Hill, 1620

Followed by an army of priests and Jesuits, Ferdinand took possession
of Bohemia, confiscated the immense estates of the rebellious nobles, and
proscribing every shade of Protestantism, imposed the Roman faith as
the sole religion of the country.

Triumph of Catholicism

THE PALATINE PERIOD (1621-1623)

The Bohemian episode was closed and lovers of peace hoped that the
war would now end. They were disappointed chiefly because the elated
Catholics could not resist the temptation to make the most of their victory. The war entered a new phase when the emperor outlawed the
Elector Frederick and commissioned his two Catholic allies, Duke Maxi-

Seizure of the Palatinate

milian and the Spaniards—these latter operating from the Spanish Netherlands as their base—to take possession of the Palatinate.

This was an indisputable provocation since the Palatinate was recognized Protestant territory. But Ferdinand and Maximilian reckoned with the incurable divisions among the Protestants, wherein they were fully justified by the event. Although the Protestants loudly voiced their indignation, when it came to helping the Elector Frederick to defend his inheritance against the adversary they backed away. Before long the Palatinate had been completely overrun by Catholic armies.

Victorious beyond his dreams, the emperor now undertook to reward his leading supporter. He transferred (1623) the electoral dignity from Frederick to Maximilian, duke and henceforth elector of Bavaria, and in addition made over to him that part of the Palatinate (the upper Palatinate) which was contiguous to Bavaria. At the same time the Catholic army drove the Protestant preachers out of every section of the Palatinate and imposed the Catholic faith on the inhabitants.

The continued Protestant disasters at last alarmed the other Protestant powers of Europe, such as England, the Dutch, Sweden, and Denmark, and started a correspondence among them in favor of a concerted intervention. In any such movement the leadership would naturally fall to England, first, because, since the days of Elizabeth, England had been the strongest bulwark of the new faith, and second, because the reigning sovereign, James I, was, as we have seen, the father-in-law of the Elector Frederick. James, to be sure, had not encouraged Frederick's disastrous Bohemian ambitions. But when his son-in-law, in addition to Bohemia, lost also his inherited territories, he could not fail to be disturbed.

Wisely wishing to avoid war, James developed a plan to compose the German troubles in close association with the great Catholic power, Spain. In furtherance of this policy he tried to effect an Anglo-Spanish alliance to be clinched by the marriage of his son and heir, Charles, to a Spanish princess. The Spaniards willingly negotiated in order to keep the English king from actively interfering in the German struggle. However, as soon as the rewards of victory reposed safely in Catholic hands, the Spanish court made it plain to the duped James that it had no interest in either a matrimonial or a political alliance.

At this discovery James fell into a rage and made up his mind that only war would readjust the German balance. To this end he planned a great Protestant alliance. But here, too, as in so many of his measures, he was the victim of either ill-luck or his own unusual ineptitude. His possible allies were the Dutch, Sweden, and Denmark. As to the Dutch, the Truce of Twelve Years having just expired (1621), their war with Spain had been resumed. Consequently that country, fully occupied with its own problem, had no resources to spare for a German venture. The case

Marginal notes:

The Protestant paralysis continues

Maximilian rewarded; the Palatinate Catholicized

Proposed intervention by the Protestant states of Europe

The Spanish plan of James I of England

James turns unsuccessfully to the Dutch and to Sweden

of Sweden was similar. Gustavus Adolphus, the very capable ruler of Sweden, was involved in difficulties with Russia and Poland, which constituted as great a burden as his shoulders could for the time being bear.

James persuades Denmark to enter the lists against the Catholics

There remained Denmark, whose king, Christian IV, declared himself willing to strike a blow for Protestantism, provided James would supply him liberally with money. This James agreed to do, but as he had foolishly involved himself in a quarrel with his parliament—a quarrel which under his son led to civil war—he could not lay hold of the funds he had promised. The upshot was that James, after pushing the Danish king into a conflict with triumphant German Catholicism, left him without support.

THE DANISH PERIOD (1625-1629)

Advantage at first with the Danes

With the entrance into the war of Christian IV in the role of champion of threatened Protestantism, the scene of action was transferred from southern to northern Germany. Tilly, still in command of the army of the League, moved against Christian, but the Dane had for a time the advantage of position and numbers.

Creation of an imperial army

Just as King Christian thought he had the situation well in hand, a second Catholic army appeared and threatened his flank. Raised in the name of the emperor, the new force, under the command of Wallenstein, was the first *imperial* army to make its appearance in the war. The army of General Tilly, it must always be remembered, belonged to the Catholic League. Wallenstein was a Bohemian nobleman who, having remained faithful to Ferdinand in the crisis of 1618, had been rewarded with immense estates taken from the defeated rebels.

Wallenstein's army maintained by forced contributions

Irked by his sovereign's military dependence on the League, Wallenstein had counseled Ferdinand to raise an army of his own. On the emperor's pleading his lack of means to support an army Wallenstein offered a plan by which the army would prove to be self-supporting. According to this plan Wallenstein, as head of the new force, would oblige the magistrates of the region or regions which the army happened to be occupying to furnish him with the supplies and ready money of which he stood in need. It was at best a system of regulated robbery and, had he known any other way of getting what he wanted, the legal-minded and scrupulous Ferdinand would never have given his consent to the proposal.

The harrying of Germany by the armies

Wallenstein at first exercised some restraint upon his men. In measure, however, as the country grew poorer and it became harder to obtain a regulated support, the general seized what he needed without first stopping to ask permission. Naturally the other armies in the field were not slow to imitate Wallenstein's example, with the result that there now began that awful harrying of Germany, the cold facts of which remain frankly incredible. And at this time the war may be said to have no more than begun, for it was destined to drag on for some twenty additional years. More than one writer has declared that the survival of Germany from its interminable agony constitutes one of the major endurance tests recorded in history.

At this point we may inquire how the armies of the seventeenth century were recruited, equipped, and organized. When the time came for a ruler to raise an army, his first measure was to commission a group of officers, who through recruiting agents radiating over the land signed up volunteers to the required number. In consequence, an army was not unlike an international congress, for many peoples, costumes, and languages were represented in its ranks. The pay of both officers and privates was liberal, and the cost of an army rose, at least in salaries, to a relatively much higher figure than today. Owing to the great cost and the difficulties of collecting the necessary food, an army rarely exceeded 20,000 men. They would be distributed about equally among infantry and cavalry. The artillery was in process of development and was yet far from being the decisive factor it afterward became.

The army of the seventeenth century a mercenary army

The infantry was in part armed with muskets, as yet rude and ineffective. However, as generals still largely counted on winning battles by the push of solidly massed men (the ancient phalanx idea), the more usual weapon of the foot-soldier was a pike, some eighteen feet in length. In preparation for a battle the cavalry was drawn up on the wings, while the infantry, with the clumsy and ineffective artillery corps in front of it, held the center. All this looks very primitive from a present-day point of view. Nonetheless it should not be overlooked that great advances were made in this period, chiefly under the stimulus of Gustavus Adolphus of Sweden. He increased his artillery pieces, turned them to better use in battle, and developed in his troops a greater mobility both on the march and under fire.

Equipment and tactics of armies during the period here considered

Returning to the Danish War, we note that Christian IV proved no match for the combined forces of Tilly and Wallenstein. A single campaign settled his fate. In 1626 Wallenstein defeated Christian's lieutenant, Mansfeld, at the Bridge of Dessau, and in the same year Tilly crushed Christian himself at Lutter. Not only was the king obliged to retire from Germany, but he was pursued into his own dominions and had finally to take refuge in the Danish islands. He had every reason to be thankful when, in the year 1629, the emperor signed the Peace of Lübeck with him, whereby, in return for his abandonment of the German Protestants, he got back his Danish territories.

Christian IV crushed by Tilly and Wallenstein

Even before the Peace of Lübeck was signed, Wallenstein, in the name of the emperor, had overrun the whole Protestant north. Nothing seemed to be able to stop him. Capable, unscrupulous, and ambitious—the type

Wallenstein
plans to
make the
emperor
supreme in
Germany

of the successful military adventurer—he began to nurse designs so vast and intricate that even yet they have not been entirely unraveled. In the main, his plan appears to have been to overawe the princes, both Catholic and Protestant, and once again to make the emperor the real master of Germany with himself the master of the emperor.

Such a plan was sure to have anything but easy sailing. In the first

Wallenstein
meets with
difficulties
from the
emperor and
the princes

place, scrupulous-minded Ferdinand soon showed that he had no taste for the part of conqueror, for which Wallenstein had cast him. Furthermore, all the princes, regardless of whether they were Protestant or Catholic, constituted themselves a solid mass in opposition to the man who had the audacity to try to diminish their political stature.

If we survey the German situation in the year 1629, the Catholic suc-

cess seemed to be complete. In the Bohemian and Palatine stages of the war the Protestant Union had been scattered and south Germany occupied; in the following Danish stage, the victorious Catholic soldiery had occupied north Germany and had pushed its way to the shores of the North and Baltic seas. Within the length and breadth of the land there was no force able to resist triumphant Catholicism.

It was now or never, if a decisive blow was to fall on the Protestant

enemy. Accordingly, in March, 1629, Emperor Ferdinand published the Edict of Restitution, by which the Protestants were dispossessed of all church territories seized by them since the Preliminary Peace of Passau of 1552. The measure was a revolution. At a stroke of the pen two archbishoprics, twelve bishoprics, and hundreds of monasteries were reappropriated by the Catholics. After having up to this point cajoled the Lutherans in order to keep them quiet, the emperor at last removed the mask. He no longer pretended that it was merely the radicals, the Calvinists, with whom he was at war. The enemy was Protestantism in general. The Edict of Restitution marks the peak of the Catholic tide.

The policy laid down in the Edict of Restitution meant the seizure of

Dismissal of
Wallenstein
on demand
of the
princes,
1630

territory from every Protestant prince and city in the land and could be carried through only by force. But within a year of its publication the emperor committed the fatally inconsistent act of depriving himself of the strong army which alone had made the Edict of Restitution possible. In the year 1630 a meeting of the electors was held at Ratisbon (Regensburg), where the long-repressed indignation of the German princes against Wallenstein found a voice. He was pictured as a ravening wolf; his army exhausted the country, weighing on Catholic and Protestant alike; his imperial plans were revolutionary; his personal ambition was dangerous and boundless. A unanimous cry went up for his dismissal which the timid emperor lacked the stamina to face. Repudiating the political implications of Wallenstein's action, he discharged his able lieutenant together with his army at the very moment when the Edict of Restitution had for the first time welded the Protestants into a solid mass and just as a new and threatening power appeared upon the scene.

THE SWEDISH PERIOD (1630-1635)

In July, 1630, Gustavus Adolphus, king of Sweden, landed on the Baltic coast at the head of an army. We have seen that some years before, when James I of England attempted to create a great Protestant combination, Gustavus had declined to be a party to it. His excuse was that, engaged in securing his position in the Baltic area against the Poles, he would first have to bring the Polish war to a close.

Gustavus Adolphus lands in Germany, July, 1630

When Wallenstein won his sweeping victory over Denmark, the king of Sweden was filled with apprehension. He entertained the ambition of securing for himself the first place on the Baltic, of converting, in fact, the Baltic into a Swedish lake; and here was Wallenstein reviving the defunct empire and unfurling its eagle banner along the shore of the northern sea. Gustavus felt his security threatened and made up his mind to enter the war.

The invasion prompted by Swedish national interests

There was more, however, than the safety of Sweden to the king's intervention. Although he was an ardent Protestant and had sympathized from the first with his fellow believers of Germany, it was not till the Edict of Restitution had disclosed the Catholic designs that he felt action in behalf of the defeated cause to be imperative. Admitting that the usual mixture of motives prompted the Swedish intervention in the German civil war, we may agree that Gustavus acted, in the main, in order to safeguard the interests of his country. But it is also true that he desired to rescue German Protestantism from the destruction with which it was threatened. The abiding historical significance of his intervention is that he succeeded in doing so.

The invasion prompted by religious considerations

Gustavus is the outstanding figure of the Thirty Years' War and succeeded during his brief presence on the stage in bringing into the barren struggle something of an epic movement. His first concern on landing in Germany was to secure the alliance of the Protestant princes, whose salvation, together with the safety of his Swedish kingdom, constituted, as we have seen, the double object of his coming. Here he at once ran into difficulties. On account of the Edict of Restitution, the Protestant princes had, it is true, little or no affection left for their emperor. But they naturally hesitated about allying themselves with a foreigner and aiding him in getting a foothold in their native land.

Gustavus and the Protestant princes of Germany

While Gustavus was in turn coaxing and threatening them, help came to him from another quarter, from France. The French government, since 1624 in the extremely capable hands of Cardinal Richelieu, had

Richelieu not prepared to intervene in Germany till 1629 followed the German developments with close interest, but, owing to domestic troubles with the Huguenots, had thus far been unable to interfere. By the year 1629 the Huguenot difficulties had been ironed out and Richelieu became free to step out more confidently.

Richelieu in alliance with Sweden, 1631 Though a great prelate of the church, Richelieu was, above all, a Frenchman eager to advance the power and influence of his country. Clear in his mind that the strong Germany planned by Wallenstein was not to the advantage of France, he resolved not only to aid the successful plot which at Ratisbon had compassed the fall of Wallenstein, but to welcome with open arms every avowed or prospective enemy of the emperor. Expressing therefore from the first his approval of Gustavus's German enterprise, he presently (January, 1631) concluded the Treaty of Bärwalde, wherein he agreed to pay the king of Sweden a considerable annual subsidy toward the prosecution of the war. It was a measure preliminary to entering the conflict in person.

Tilly storms and sacks Magdeburg, 1631 The first operations of Gustavus were directed to the reduction of the strongholds of Pomerania and the neighboring areas for the purpose of acquiring a secure base on the Baltic sea. While he was thus engaged, Tilly, who since Wallenstein's dismissal was again the leading general of the Catholics, took by storm the great Protestant city of Magdeburg on the Elbe. In the course of the assault a fire started, and when the flames had spent their fury only the cathedral was discovered standing among the blackened ruins.

Alliance between Gustavus and the Protestant princes Fear and horror now caused Protestant sentiment to veer vehemently toward Gustavus. When, following the destruction of Magdeburg, Tilly undertook to invade Saxony, its ruler, who was the traditional head of the Lutherans, put an end to his long indecision. Together with his neighbor, the elector of Brandenburg, and followed by many minor princes, he made an alliance with Sweden.

Defeat of Tilly at Breitenfeld, 1631 By these arrangements the position of Gustavus in northern Germany became so secure that he could march southward and seek out Tilly for a decisive encounter. In September, 1631, a great battle took place at Breitenfeld, near Leipzig, in which Swedish generalship and discipline astonished the world by completely crushing the veteran army of Tilly.

Gustavus master of northern Germany The victory of Breitenfeld laid all Germany at the feet of Gustavus. Never was there a more dramatic change. The Catholics, who a year before had held the reins in their hands, were now in exactly the same helpless position in which the Protestants had been. Gustavus, received everywhere by the Protestant common people as a deliverer, marched without opposition straight across Germany to the Rhine.

In the episcopal town of Mainz the Swedish king took up his winter quarters. It was natural that, under the stimulus of a triumph exceeding all expectations, his plans should have undergone a measure of revision. With Sweden safe and German Protestantism rescued, his expedition had secured its original objects. There is no doubt that he now played with the idea of establishing himself permanently in Germany as the head of its Protestant territories. But he did not get far with this project, for he had too practical a mind not to know that as long as southern Germany, above all, as long as the great Catholic strongholds, Bavaria and Austria, were unconquered, he could not hope to reorganize Germany according to his personal wishes.

Gustavus entertains the idea of becoming the head of Protestant Germany

In the spring of 1632 Gustavus again took the field, driving straight at the two centers of Catholicism. At the river Lech, Tilly tried to block his passage into Bavaria. Again signally defeated by his more versatile opponent, the veteran general received a wound from which he died. Bavaria became the prize of the great Swede, who entered its capital, Munich, in triumph.

Gustavus occupies Bavaria, 1632

The next objective of Gustavus was Vienna, residence of the emperor. Some months before the situation had taken its present extremely critical turn, Ferdinand had found his way back to the one man capable of saving him, to Wallenstein. Since his dismissal Wallenstein had been sulking on his Bohemian estates. When Ferdinand's ambassador besought his aid, he allowed himself to be persuaded to collect another army on conditions which, by securing him against a new dismissal, made him effectively a dictator. On Wallenstein's now floating his standards to the wind the adventurers of all nations and creeds that made up the mercenary armies of that era once again joyously responded to the call.

Wallenstein assembles a new imperial army

In the summer of 1632 Wallenstein and Gustavus, the two leading generals of their day, took the field against each other. After long, futile maneuvering around Nuernberg, the two armies met for a decisive encounter at Lützen, not far from Leipzig (November, 1632). After the trumpeters had sounded the hymn of Luther, "A Mighty Fortress is Our God," and the whole army had knelt in prayer, Gustavus ordered the attack. The combat was long and furious, but the Swedes won the day; they won, but at a terrible cost. In one of the charges of horse, the impetuosity of Gustavus carried him too far into the ranks of the enemy and he was surrounded and slain.

Battle of Lützen and death of Gustavus, 1632

With the death of the king of Sweden the war degenerated into a scramble for the meanest material advantages. Gustavus's achievement had been that he had turned back the Catholic tide and saved the German Protestant cause. But he left Germany in hopeless confusion. The rage between Protestants and Catholics, now more implacable than ever, was inextricably involved with the territorial greed of the German princes. And as if such degradation were not enough, the German

Degeneration of the war

neighbor powers now took advantage of the impotence of the nation to appropriate whatever lands they could seize.

On the death of Gustavus, Wallenstein became the leading figure of the German scene. A soldier not without large views, he evolved a plan of German pacification on the basis of toleration for the Protestants. Since he was persuaded that he could never win the emperor and his Jesuit councilors to such a program, he opened secret negotiations with his Protestant adversaries, thus formally committing treason. This was too much for a group of his subordinate officers. Secretly encouraged by Ferdinand II, they entered into a conspiracy against the general's life, and in February, 1634, in the Bohemian town of Eger, put an end to him and his plan of pacification.

Wallen-stein's treason and murder, 1634

Meanwhile the Swedes did not relax their efforts to retain the dominant position which Gustavus had won for them. The political direction fell into the capable hands of the chancellor, Oxenstiern, who ruled in the name of Gustavus's infant daughter, Christina, while the military interests were, on the whole, very creditably handled by various generals whom Gustavus had trained. Nonetheless, in September, 1634, the Swedes were signally defeated by the Catholics at Nördlingen and had to evacuate southern Germany.

The Swedes driven out of southern Germany, 1634

With fortune smiling once more on the emperor, he resolved to make a gesture in the direction of peace. Having been taught by the recent disaster to moderate his demands, he declared to the elector of Saxony, still the recognized head of German Protestantism, his willingness to sign with him a treaty of peace, which should be based on a disavowal of the Edict of Restitution and on the settlement of the issue of the appropriated Catholic lands by a compromise. Accordingly a document was drawn up by the two principals which in May, 1635, at the city of Prague, received their respective signatures. Such was the longing for peace in the exhausted country that, in spite of the treaty's shortcomings, more particularly its failure to recognize Calvinism, it was, before many weeks had passed, accepted by nearly all the German princes and free cities.

The emperor attempts to pacify Germany by the Treaty of Prague, 1635

Had Germany been left to itself peace might now have descended on the land already tormented by seventeen years of civil warfare. Unfortunately, the decision between peace and war no longer lay in German hands. It now rested with those foreign powers whom the divisions of the Germans had drawn across the border. Securely ensconced in the heart of the country, the Swedes mocked at the idea that the war could be concluded without the satisfaction of their territorial demands. And they were fortified in their position by a new turn in the policy of France.

Sweden demands territorial compensation

To the very end of holding the Swedes to their German plans Richelieu

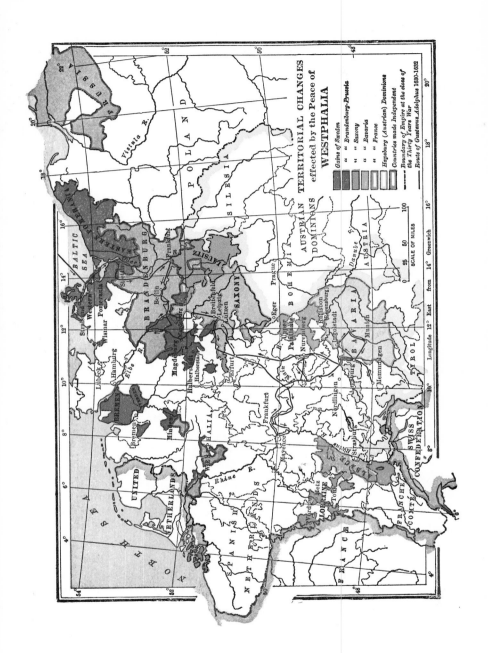

TERRITORIAL CHANGES
effected by the Peace of
WESTPHALIA

Gains of Sweden
  "   "   Brandenburg-Prussia
  "   "   Saxony
  "   "   Bavaria
  "   "   France
Hapsburg (Austrian) Dominions
Countries made Independent
------ Boundary of Empire at the close of
       the Thirty Years War
——— Route of Gustavus Adolphus 1680-1682

SCALE OF MILES
0   25   50   100

Longitude 12° East   from   14° Greenwich   16°   18°   20°

at this time (April, 1635) changed from a passive to an active participant in the war. No longer content with money-aid to the Swedes, he promised to put an army in the field which should harass the imperialists on their Rhenish or western front. At the same time, as an indication that he regarded the two branches of the house of Hapsburg as essentially a single power, he issued a declaration of war against Spain.

France
becomes
an active
participant
in the war,
1635

THE FRENCH PERIOD (1635-1648)

The war now entered a new and last phase, characterized by the effort of the allied powers of France and Sweden to effect a permanent lodgment in Germany. That religion was no longer an issue of great consequence is sufficiently indicated by the circumstance that of the two invaders of Germany one was Protestant, the other Catholic. They and the German princes still bandied the word religion when they believed something to be gained thereby, but their intimate thoughts turned solely about territory and power.

The war
henceforth
concerned
with the
acquisition
of German
territory by
Sweden and
France

From year to year, following Richelieu's decisive step of 1635, France fell with increasing weight into the scales, chiefly owing to the broad outlook and concentrated resolution of the great cardinal. Taking in with statesmanlike vision the whole European scene, he sought the friendship and help of every state, great or small, capable of being mobilized against either of the Hapsburg houses, although we may agree it was the Spanish branch which he honored with a particular aversion. His most immediate object was to weaken the hold of Spain on the Spanish Netherlands, since from this vantage-ground a perpetual threat was suspended over the French capital. At the very time (1635) that he drew closer to the Swedes, he entered also into alliance with the Dutch, who in 1621, when the Twelve Years' Truce expired, had renewed their war of independence. Thus in its last phase the Thirty Years' War was less a German conflict than an immense international struggle for supremacy between the house of Bourbon and the two branches of the house of Hapsburg.

From an-
other angle
the war is a
world
struggle
between the
houses of
Bourbon and
Hapsburg

The fighting in Germany during the last or French Period took the form of a forward thrust across the Rhine, on the part of France, and a steady movement southward from its Baltic base, on the part of Sweden. The object of the allies was to crush the emperor between them. It remains a matter of astonishment that that sovereign, exhausted as he was and but ill-supported by the German princes and people, should have made so stubborn a resistance.

The Franco-
Swedish
plan of
campaign

In the early years the emperor even won some notable successes. But in campaign after campaign the French and Swedes fastened on his flanks, and with each new campaign he found it more and more difficult to shake the enemies off. The German people, meanwhile, overrun by a

soldiery which had grown insensible to every appeal of justice and pity,
was ground gradually to dust. The cities fell into decay, the country became a desert. In view of the certainty that the product of labor would
become the booty of marauders, nobody cared to work. The only profession which afforded a semblance of security was that of the soldier,
and soldier signified robber and murderer. Armies became loose bands
organized for pillage and marched up and down the country, followed
by immense hordes of starved camp-followers, women and children, who
hoped, in this way, to get the sustenance which was no longer obtainable at home.

Accumulated disaster finally brought the emperor to terms. The forces
The French
and Swedish
victories
bring the
emperor to
terms
of France had been growing gradually stronger and at last, under the
leadership of the fiery prince of Condé and the gifted strategist, Turenne,
penetrated far into southern Germany. The honors of the last campaigns
rested chiefly with them, though their allies, the Swedes, did not lag far
behind. When the emperor was at last persuaded that these strangers
could not be turned from the gates, he accepted the decree of fate. It was
not Ferdinand II who bared his head to receive the blow. He had been
succeeded, on his death in 1637, by his son, Ferdinand III (1637-1657).
On opening negotiations with the two victor powers, he brought them,
after wearisome delays, to a successful conclusion in 1648, in the Treaty
of Westphalia.[1]

The Peace of Westphalia is, from the variety of matter which it treated,
one of the key documents of modern times. First, it determined with
what territorial concessions in Germany, France and Sweden were to
be persuaded to retire from the war; second, it laid a new basis for the
peace between Protestants and Catholics; and third, it authorized important political and territorial readjustments within Germany.

As to the first point, Sweden received the western half of Pomerania
and the two secularized bishoprics of Bremen and Verden. By these possessions she established herself as guardian at the mouths of the rivers
Oder, Elbe, and Weser and came into substantial control of the whole
German seaboard. Victorious France was confirmed in the possession
of the bishoprics of Metz, Toul, and Verdun, provisionally held ever
since 1552, and received, in addition, the greater part of Alsace. The
acquisition of Alsace carried with it the inestimable advantage of a foothold on the upper Rhine. It should be noted, however, that the free city
of Strasburg and a number of other minor Alsatian towns and lordships
were excluded from the cession.

When the German religious issues came up for discussion, far and

---

[1] The Peace of Westphalia receives its name from the province of Westphalia on the
lower Rhine, embracing the two cities of Münster and Osnabrück. Münster served as the
headquarters of France and the Catholic states, Osnabrück of Sweden and the Protestant
states.

away the most pressing question was of course whether the Protestants were to be permitted to retain the church properties seized after the signing of the Preliminary Peace of Passau. The Catholics, it will be remembered, had always held that these seizures were illegal; and by the Edict of Restitution of 1629 the emperor had peremptorily ordered their surrender. In the peace negotiations the Protestants took the position that they should be restored to all the property they had held in 1618, the year when the war broke out. They agreed at last to compromise on the year 1624. The compromise signified that such former Catholic possessions as were held by the Protestants on the first day of January of 1624 were to remain Protestant, and that all property held by the Catholics on that day was to remain Catholic. The arrangement settled the question of the disputed lands, in the main, in the Protestant interest. However, it also represented a concession to the emperor, since it sanctioned the Catholic restoration carried out after 1618 in the kingdom of Bohemia. *The dispute about church lands settled, in the main, in favor of the Protestants*

The issue of Calvinism was brought to rest by the only conceivable solution. Calvinism was given the same legal standing as Lutheranism. *Calvinism legalized*

Our third head embraces a variety of political and territorial changes within Germany. The princes were conceded a number of new sovereign rights, among others, the right of forming alliances with each other and with foreign powers. Therewith the decentralization of Germany became complete and the component states of Germany won in effect their independence. If the emperor was weak before, he was henceforth no more than the honorary president of a congress of sovereign powers. *New measures of German decentralization*

A word needs to be said of four of the larger constituent states of Germany: the Palatinate, Bavaria, Saxony, and Brandenburg. The Palatinate, confiscated by the emperor in the early stages of the war, was restored in a reduced shape to the son of Frederick, ex-king of Bohemia, who had died in the course of the long war. At the same time this son was recognized as an eighth elector, for Maximilian of Bavaria was not disturbed in possession of the electoral dignity transferred to him in 1623. Maximilian was also permitted to retain the upper Palatinate. From this time on enlarged Bavaria aspired to leadership in southern Germany. *The Palatinate and Bavaria*

The leadership of Protestant north Germany had, ever since Luther's day, been exercised by Saxony. In consequence of the Treaty of Westphalia the Protestant leadership passed to the elector of Brandenburg. This prince received additions of territory—eastern Pomerania and four secularized bishoprics—constituting a possession so considerable as to enable him by gradual stages completely to overshadow Saxony. *Saxony and Brandenburg*

In 1648 Germany lost the last vestige of its claim to be considered an effective European state. It was broken into about three hundred separate free cities and principalities, some of the latter no larger than a good-sized game preserve. Of Germany's three hundred component units only the four above-named electorates, together with of course Austria, possessed sufficient power to command a measure of respect. With Germany itself no longer of any political consequence such German developments as call for attention after 1648 center about its five most considerable territories.

Complete impotence of the Empire after 1648

As a last curious detail of the Westphalian treaties it may be added that the Swiss Confederation and the Dutch Netherlands (Seven United Provinces), once members of the Empire but long since practically independent, were formally endowed with sovereign status.

The Swiss and Dutch independent

Germany, after her insufferable crisis, lay insensible and exhausted. While the contemporary stories of the ruin wrought by the war abound in the usual exaggerations, it is certain that the country took more than a hundred years to recover in a moral and material sense from its disasters. From their disruptive political effect it did not recover till the nineteenth century. We may accept as substantially true that most of the accumulated wealth and, more important still, the ethical and intellectual treasure assembled by a long succession of generations had disappeared in the long agony. The generation which survived the war grew up without schools, almost without pastors and churches, and to its mental and material degradation it added, owing to the prolonged rule of force, a disdain for all simple and honest occupations. Although reliable statistics are not available, it is probably safe to assume that the population declined to half its pre-war size.

Crushing effect of the war on Germany

Our final comment in connection with the Peace of Westphalia may well be directed to the great issue of religious toleration. From the appearance of Luther religion had become a leading source of both domestic and foreign conflict. Europe had fallen into two camps, Catholicism and Protestantism, which opposed each other with all their might. In the Peace of Westphalia, which gave legal expression to the stalemate of the Thirty Years' War, the two opponents recorded their conviction that their quarrel was as futile as it was cruel, and that, since neither adversary could annihilate the other, it was the part of good sense to ground arms. Almost imperceptibly men's *minds* had grown more tolerant, even if the *laws* maintained as tenaciously as ever the old exclusive viewpoint.

Growing conviction of the futility of religious warfare

The best proof of the improved state of the European mind toward the middle of the seventeenth century is offered by the practical application of the Peace of Westphalia. The toleration therein granted was merely of the old kind: each prince or free city of Germany could choose among the legally recognized religions without any obligation of tolerating dissidents. Nonetheless, persecution was henceforth the exception rather than the rule. It would be an exaggeration to say that the principle of toleration exercised an unquestioned ascendancy after the Thirty

Gradual diffusion through Europe of the principle of toleration

Years' War either in Germany or anywhere else in Europe or that wars for religion's sake entirely ceased. But it may be asserted, without fear of contradiction, that toleration had by the time of the Peace of Westphalia won a standing among a limited body of liberal-minded men. During the next one hundred and fifty years the concept filtered slowly, in consequence of the literary labors of numerous high-minded champions, through the upper strata of society and became in the era of the French Revolution the common possession of Western mankind.

13 LEADING CULTURAL TRENDS IN THE PERIOD OF THE REFORMATION AND COUNTER-REFORMATION

Activities of the man of the Renaissance recalled

WE HAVE LEARNED in an earlier chapter dealing with the Renaissance that its cultural trends may be summed up as prompting the European man gradually to break away from his medieval heritage with its social order based on feudalism, with its economic scarcity of goods, and with the emphasis, in religious matters, on man's sinful nature and God's marvelous plan for his redemption. Proceeding to details, we took note of how Renaissance man engaged in trade on an ever enlarging scale, recovered the literature and learning of the ancients, multiplied his economic activities by resting them on individual enterprise and capital, crossed the perilous seas to discover Asia and America, and did a score of things besides, which revealed to him the earth, the heavens over the earth, and finally himself.

The Reformation a reactionary and a liberating movement

Then, from the new ground gained, Luther challenged the authority of the church and precipitated the great struggle of the Reformation and Counter-Reformation. Judged by its purely intellectual content, the Reformation had undoubtedly a reactionary flavor, since it once more brought theological controversies to the fore. On the other hand, by attacking the prestige of the great institution which had sanctioned the medieval way of life, it promoted the liberation of the human spirit by asserting, though often with many reservations, the novel right to private judgment.

The Reformation did not smother the Renaissance

In the view of certain modern critics by no means moved by Catholic partisanship, the Reformation proved to be, on the whole, a misfortune for Europe since it put an end to the broad humanitarian promise implicit in humanism and particularly implicit in the northern humanism, of which Erasmus was the acknowledged head. A better-balanced and more sober judgment would seem to be that the religious revolution did indeed apply the brakes to some of the liberating tendencies of the Renaissance; but that it signified a reversion to the Middle Ages is a contention in palpable contradiction with the facts. In this chapter we propose to marshal the evidence which proves that the expansive forces of the Renaissance, considered in the mass, continued steadily to gather

234

strength behind the theological controversies which filled so much of the foreground of the age's consciousness. We shall show conclusively that Europe continued, although with a certain slowing-up of pace, its onward march along the paths cleared for it by the enterprising spirits who first broke through the medieval barriers.

SCIENCE

Because of the undisputed pre-eminence of science in our time, historians have come to the front who are inclined to evaluate the successive stages of Western civilization by the progress of science alone. Although the application of a single measuring rod is not in accordance with the fundamental position of this book, we may admit that science is so determining a feature not only of our present intellectual outlook but of our whole contemporary existence that we must give the closest scrutiny to its unfolding through the centuries.

The growing importance of science

In our survey of Renaissance culture (Chapter 3) we learned that science was not held in high regard in that strenuous age. In the succeeding period to be treated here it rose greatly in esteem with the result that memorable forward strides were made in almost every one of its divisions. Developments in geography may be first considered. So abundant were the data that continued to pour in from the numerous seafarers and the professional observers who often went along with them on their voyages that by the time of the Thirty Years' War the main land masses of the earth had been located and their contours drawn with reasonable accuracy. An immediate consequence was that the cartographers, stimulated by the uninterrupted flow of material, turned out progressively more attractive and elaborate maps, atlases, and globes. The most famous cartographer was a man, the latinized form of whose Flemish name is Mercator (1512-1594). He invented the projection maps, still called by his name, which represent spherical surfaces on a flat page.

Geography and cartography

Hand in hand with the assembling of geographic information went the notation of the many strange plants, animals, and minerals encountered over the face of the earth. The effort to master this material and to co-ordinate it with the data already in hand led to the closer staking-off of the fields of botany, zoology, and mineralogy. Ever the first step toward bringing order out of disorder is classification, and consequently the best efforts of the botanists, zoologists, and mineralogists of the Reformation period were all of a classificatory nature. A leading naturalist thus occupied was the German Swiss, Conrad Gesner (1516-1565). He produced both a *Catalogue of Plants* and a *History of Animals* based

Emergence of botany, zoology, and mineralogy

on principles of classification, partly inherited and partly evolved by himself, which were not superseded for several generations.

We have learned of the great advance in medicine associated with Vesalius's *The Structure of the Human Body* (1543). Specifically it represented a triumph in anatomy and stimulated study through dissection in the laboratory. One of its effects was to cause the related study of physiology to be more intensely pursued, and it led, after some generations, to the notable discovery of the circulation of the blood from the heart to the arteries and thence to the veins and back again to the heart. It was in 1628 that this discovery was published to the world by the English physician, William Harvey.

Dissection leads to the discovery of circulation of the blood

The improved knowledge of body structure redounded to the advantage in the first instance not of general medicine but of surgery, as the case of the Frenchman, Ambrose Paré, suffices to illustrate. Living in the second half of the sixteenth century, Paré published a surgical work (with remarkable illustrations) which advocated an entirely new method of treating gunshot wounds and amputations. He had acquired his novel understanding in a genuine, if revolting, laboratory, the battlefields of the French civil war.

Paré and surgical advance

Important as these advances were, they were slow to affect that department of medicine, called therapy, which deals with the treatment of disease. A stubborn traditionalism moved the physicians to cling to the remedies and procedures of the ancient authorities and accounts for the long persistence of many superstitious practices, such as cupping (blood-letting). These practices offer reasonable ground for the suspicion that the doctors may have been a leading cause of the disconcertingly high European death rate.

The stubborn conservatism of physicians

When it comes to the persistence of ancient superstitions, the medical practices of the day were far from constituting an isolated instance. Well-known universal superstitions of the Middle Ages were the false sciences of alchemy and astrology. In spite of the advance of true science in this period, they continued to maintain their footing among the upper classes, which had been addicted to them from far back in the Middle Ages. Many a learned man who should have known better persisted in devoting himself to the conversion of baser metals into gold; and there was hardly a monarch who did not make a practice of consulting an astrologer before committing himself to any important undertaking.

The persistence of superstitions

Even more general, and far more dangerous because frequently arousing the common people to spontaneous violence, was the belief in witchcraft. Again and again it sufficed for the word to be passed around that a lonely and unloved old woman was a witch for her to be haled before a judge and condemned to death, often enough by fire. This madness was more prevalent among the Protestants than among the Catholics.

Persistence of belief in witchcraft

Not till the eighteenth century did it disappear, which goes to show how gradually, after all, science, which is reason directed by evidence, gained authority over settled habit and tradition.

Far and away the most decisive advance made by science in this period was in the related fields of mathematics, physics, and astronomy. The heliocentric theory of Copernicus proved to be tremendously exciting to the imagination. But before its validity would be generally recognized it would have to be demonstrated mathematically. It therefore stimulated a furious pursuit of mathematics, in the course of which the west-Europeans for the first time went beyond the inherited geometry of the Greeks and the inherited algebra of the Arabs. *Interdependence of mathematics, physics, and astronomy*

Outstanding among the mathematical advances were the adoption of the decimal point and the invention of logarithms. The latter great contribution derives from John Napier, a Scotsman, and was given to the world in the year 1614. The French philosopher Descartes (d. 1649) was also a mathematician, and invented a combination of algebra and geometry which he called analytical geometry. An invaluable simplification may be attributed to the adoption in this period of a new system of mathematical symbols, including such signs as $+$, $-$, $\times$, $=$ and so familiar to us that we are inclined to think of them as almost as old as the world. *Progress in mathematics*

When all is said it is the remarkable development of physics and astronomy, the Siamese twins of science, which lends a special luster to this period. For, apart from striking advances particular to each field, it was from the concern with both of them that there finally emerged that creation crucial for the whole modern development, a sound scientific method. *Co-operation between physics and astronomy*

To follow the story through from the beginning let us go back to Copernicus. His presentation in his *De Revolutionibus* was lacking both in observational data and in mathematical underpinning. The man who made a beginning toward at least swelling the meager data was Tycho Brahe, a Dane (1546-1601). With liberal support from his king he erected a better-equipped observatory than Europe had ever seen and, with the aid of numerous assistants, gathered vast heaps of data concerning the movements of all the heavenly bodies. True, he failed to turn them to satisfactory account, but when a man of greater genius came along they yielded the happiest results. This newcomer was a German, John Kepler (1571-1630). The special talent of Kepler was mathematics and it enabled him to derive from Brahe's observations, supplemented by his own, the three laws of planetary motion which bear his name and which furnish a sound mathematical foundation for the Copernican hypothesis. *Tycho Brahe and John Kepler, astronomers*

We come next to an even greater genius, undoubtedly one of the leading figures of all time, the Italian, Galileo Galilei (1564-1642). It

is interesting to note that Galileo was an expert writer and musician, that
is, an artist, and that it never occurred to the men of his age to question
his scientific reliability on the ground of his parallel artistic endowment.
Like his contemporaries and even his successors far into the eighteenth
century, he did not narrowly specialize in science but devoted himself to
mathematics, physics, and astronomy much as if they constituted a single
body of subject matter. Very early in his career he became interested in
the phenomena having to do with falling bodies, that is, with matter
in motion. Tradition credits him with having made his first experiments
by dropping objects of different weights from the Leaning Tower of
Pisa, thereby proving their equal speed (making allowance for the difference due to the resistance of the air) and incidentally refuting the
still almost slavishly worshiped Aristotle. In the end he discovered and
formulated the laws of falling bodies as they stand to this day.

Galileo the physicist

As an astronomer Galileo's fame springs largely from his construction of the first practical telescope. The fundamental idea of the lens
had long been common property and there is evidence that a telescope
had been put together in Holland before 1609, the year Galileo completed
his instrument. While it magnified objects by no more than three diam-
eters (a second telescope of his construction was many times as powerful), he had now only to sweep the heavens with it to make the most
amazing discoveries. He saw ten times more fixed stars than had ever
been seen before by man; he traced the mountains and the valleys on the
moon's surface; he discovered the moons of Jupiter and the ring of
Saturn.

Galileo the astronomer

Long before these wonders had revealed themselves to him, Galileo
had become persuaded of the truth of the Copernican theory. He had,
however, suppressed his convictions from fear of the papal Inquisition.
When the new evidence persuaded him openly to avow himself a
Copernican, the clash with the dread institution followed as promptly
as thunder follows lightning. He was summoned to Rome and, probably
before torture was administered, although tradition carries a different
story, disavowed his Copernican belief. He was permitted to spend the
remaining years of his life on his estate near Florence under ecclesiastical supervision but free to continue his work in the related but religiously
less compromising field of physics.

Galileo and the Inquisition

Although a tireless observer and laboratory worker, Galileo had the
philosophical turn of mind that caused him to give much attention to
the general theory of science. Indeed it was his philosophical inclination
that accounts for what we may call his crowning achievement, the
formulation of a method under which science continues to operate to
this day. This method, according to Galileo, consists of four parts: (1)
observation brought to the highest possible development by prolonged

Galileo de-scribes the scientific method

special training; (2) the isolation of phenomena in laboratories for the purpose of experimentation; (3) the use of steadily improved precision, that is, measuring instruments such as scales, barometer, telescope, etc.; (4) the scientific hypothesis as an avenue for penetrating into the unknown, but conscientiously treated as pure hypothesis until fully confirmed by the evidence. Let us be clear in our minds that Galileo did not invent the modern scientific method. He merely *described* the method which he and his contemporaries and more immediate predecessors had been using with more or less consistency and completeness. The service which he rendered the natural sciences by mapping out a precise course for them can hardly be exaggerated.

A contemporary with a no less passionate interest in scientific method than Galileo was the Englishman, Francis Bacon (1561-1626). He was not in any way influenced by Galileo, of whose work, whether practical or theoretical, he seems to have had no knowledge. Bacon's point of departure was medieval philosophy, against the method of which he reacted violently because it began with general propositions, from which it descended to particulars by a process of logical deduction. In his *Instauratio Magna* ("The Great Renewal") Bacon proposed the opposite method. Instead of beginning with general propositions, the searcher for knowledge was to start modestly with experience, that is, with particular objects or events, in order, on the strength of accumulated instances, to rise at last to general conclusions. He thus advocated the abandonment of deductive processes in favor of the method of induction.

The scientific method of Francis Bacon

There can be no doubt that Bacon's attack on medieval philosophy and the deductive method did much toward clearing the path for modern science. But the claim that he formulated the correct method of science must, in spite of his advocacy of induction, be rejected. The true method was formulated by Galileo and is, as an examination of its four component elements puts beyond dispute, a happy combination of induction and deduction.

The two methods compared

An advance from which the whole world ultimately benefited may well conclude these scientific data. That it came about at the prompting of the papacy, certainly no champion of science, gives it added piquancy. It was in 1582 that Pope Gregory XIII lent his authority to an, after all, relatively slight correction of the so-called Julian calendar in general western use since Roman times. To re-establish the true solar year the calendar was advanced ten days and a leap-year arrangement adopted to maintain the New or Gregorian calendar's accuracy. Protestant countries did not adopt the Gregorian calendar till after the passing of some generations. England did not adopt it till 1751; Russia, an Orthodox Christian country, waited till 1922.

The New or Gregorian calendar

PHILOSOPHY

The birth of modern philosophy　　The rapid increase of knowledge together with the elaboration of a sound scientific method accelerated the decline of scholastic or medieval philosophy already begun before the Reformation. Since medieval philosophy was inseparably tied up with Christianity, since indeed it was erected on Christian foundations, the idea began to gain ground that the time had arrived to develop a new, a modern philosophy, which did not rest on revealed, but on what might pass as scientifically established, truth.

Giordano Bruno　　The philosopher who, influenced by Copernicus and modern science, first broke violently away from scholasticism was the Italian, Giordano Bruno (1548-1600). Beginning life as a Dominican friar, he fled from the monastery and spent the rest of his life as a hunted wanderer over the face of the earth. His intense contemplation of the Copernican universe turned him away from all specific religious creeds and made him what we may loosely call a pantheist. But he did not succeed in systematizing his thought in the time at his disposal, for the Inquisition, which had started in pursuit on his escape from the monastery, at last caught up with him, and he perished at Rome at the stake.

Descartes the rationalist　　The first effective systematizer of a philosophy based on neither ancient nor scholastic philosophy and therefore properly identifiable as modern was the Frenchman, Descartes (1596-1650). He went even beyond Bruno in his devotion to science, for one reason because by his time there was much more science to be devoted to. His self-surrender to science and mathematics can be gathered best from his *Discourse on Method*. The starting-point of his philosophy was a sweeping skepticism, that is, he rejected everything handed down from either the classical or Christian past, including the two concepts, common to both, of the soul and God. At the end of this process of elimination there remained a complete blank, except for the mental activity that had produced the blank, the act of doubting. And since doubting is a form of reasoning, and reasoning implies a reasoner, Descartes arrived at his fundamental proposition, the famous *Cogito ergo sum* (I think, therefore I am).

The substance of Descartes' philosophy　　By this proposition Descartes proclaimed more emphatically than any predecessor of any period whatever the supremacy of reason. With it as his point of departure and with logical deduction as his tool, he accounted for all things embraced within the world of our experience. He did more. Spinning his argumentative web finer and finer, he ended by solemnly affirming the leading conclusions that have comforted suffering man from the beginning of time and which in point of fact constitute the essential truths of Christianity: God, the immortality of the soul, spirit and matter as two distinct substances.

In the face of these affirmations of Descartes' philosophy, it would seem that orthodox Christian theologians, whether Catholic or Protestant, might well have hailed Descartes as an ally. Further, his reliance on reason should have gained the favor, particularly of Catholics, as scholastic philosophy operated with the same intellectual tool. There were, however, two aspects to the philosophy of the Frenchman that made him forever inacceptable to orthodox Christians of whatever church. He exaggerated and exalted reason far beyond the permissible Christian measure, and worse, far worse, in constructing his rationalist system he totally ignored the central Christian position that the Christian religion has a divine origin.

Why orthodox Christians rejected Descartes

A follower and yet not a follower of Descartes was a Jew of Amsterdam, Spinoza by name (1632-1677). While accepting the Frenchman's rationalism, he rejected his dualism, that is, mind and matter as distinct realities. The kernel of his philosophy was that there is but one reality, one substance, which may be conceived as God but which is also Nature. This pointed to the pantheism to which already Bruno had inclined before Spinoza. For God, according to Spinoza, was immanent in all things, in matter as well as in thought; he was, in short, the Nature that envelops us in every direction and of which our human species is an inseparable part. Though persecuted as unorthodox by his own people, Spinoza was in his ethical, as distinct from his philosophical, outlook a lineal descendant of the old Hebrew prophets and was inspired by their stern concept of righteousness. This gave to the ethical system which he elaborated a severity and loftiness that has won it a small but distinguished band of supporters through all the subsequent ages.

Spinoza the pantheist

THE FINE ARTS

Italy

Having in our Renaissance chapter followed the movement of the Fine Arts in Italy well into the sixteenth century, we are aware that they swung through a cycle of development that registered no sudden break at the coming of the Reformation. Such leading figures as the Florentine, Michelangelo, and the Venetian, Titian, did not disappear from the scene till past the middle of the sixteenth century, by which time the Early Renaissance had reached its natural culmination in the High Renaissance.

The Renaissance develops in stages

Michelangelo and Titian are themselves the expression of that culmination for Florence and Venice respectively. But approximately from

the time of their death we note a decline in all the Fine Arts, in archi-
Peak and decline of the Renaissance tecture, sculpture, and painting alike. Among the causes were certainly Italy's political enslavement by Spain and her intellectual enslavement by the Inquisition. But it may also be that the creative energy of the Italians had run its natural cycle. Be that as it may, there was after 1550 a decline accompanied by occasional spurts of revival which did not, however, check the general downward course.

The decline proceeds unevenly The situation is therefore involved in some confusion. Turning, for example, to painting, we note that the school of Venice continued to show extraordinary vitality long after 1550, as the great works of Tintoretto (d. 1594) and Veronese (d. 1588) abundantly show. In Florence the decline was more precipitate. The busiest native painter after Michelangelo's final departure for Rome was Giorgio Vasari (d. 1574), who, while devoted to Michelangelo and a slavish imitator of that master's powerful and agitated forms, failed completely to bring them to life. Though an artist of small stature, Vasari proved himself—and his merit in this respect can hardly be exaggerated—a great historian. He has to his credit the first history of the Fine Arts in Italy ever written. By universal consent it is still, after four centuries, rated a masterpiece.

Building history of St. Peter's at Rome Sculpture exhibited the same hesitant decline, and so did architecture, as is convincingly shown by the single example of St. Peter's at Rome. Planned as a replacement of the old St. Peter's, which went back to the fourth century and was despised as too humble a structure to express the magnificence of the Renaissance popes, it was laid out in the High Renaissance by Bramante (d. 1512) in the form of a Greek cross. Its decisive and overwhelming feature, erected over the intersection of the equal arms of the cross, was to be a cupola majestically dominating the Eternal City. Owing to the great expense, St. Peter's remained in process of construction throughout the sixteenth and well into the seventeenth century. When the supporting walls had got far enough along for the cupola, this master-feature was intrusted to Michelangelo, who all but brought it to completion before his death. Dark days followed. An uncomprehending age changed the Greek cross of the ground plan to a Latin cross by lengthening the eastern arm by two bays and providing a high elaborate façade which practically smothers the cupola as seen from the front (see opp. p. 244).

The High Renaissance slides into the Baroque The historical significance of the final stages of the construction of St. Peter's is that the feeling for quiet dignity and noble proportions characteristic of the High Renaissance has given way to a pompousness and theatrical grandeur marking a new period of taste. The new period is called the Baroque and may be accepted as the last phase of the Renaissance. But its pretentiousness is not the whole story of the Baroque. That it sometimes achieves a genuine majesty a glance at the square of

St. Peter's with its double colonnade, obelisk, and fountains will prove to the most skeptical mind (see opp. p. 244). The projector of this astounding decoration was Bernini (d. 1680), and his purpose plainly was to create an approach so magnificent that the worshiper was made instinctively aware that he was entering the central temple of his faith.

France and Spain

In France and Spain, both strongly under Italian influence, the Fine Arts passed through the normal development from Early to High **The** Renaissance, tapering off to the Baroque. Obliged to be selective, we **amazing** shall fasten on Spain and, even so, shall entirely omit the relatively **El Greco** unimportant developments in Spanish architecture and sculpture. Though Spain had a medieval and Early Renaissance school of painting, the earliest definitely outstanding painter belongs to the High Renaissance. He is Domenico Theotocopuli (d. 1614), and by birth he was not a Spaniard at all but a Greek. To this circumstance he owes the name El Greco, by which he is commonly known. Trained in Crete, his home, and at Venice, close to Titian, he migrated in early manhood to Spain and so saturated himself with its peculiar religious spirit that no native practicer of any art form has ever more intimately expressed the tormented Spanish soul. To view El Greco's paintings is to be confronted with the Counter-Reformation sometimes in its intense asceticism, at other times in its ceremonial elaborateness and splendor. (See "The Burial of Count Orgaz," opp. p. 101.)

A very different aspect of Spanish life and painting is exhibited by Diego Velasquez (d. 1660). Endowed with not as much as a trace of **Diego** mysticism, Velasquez was an energetic realist, whose work has a defi- **Velasquez** niteness of outline and a three-dimensional solidity that has rarely been equaled. Add that he was a master of color and, above all, of pictorial design, and we understand why he will ever be bracketed with the world's greatest exponents of his art. (See "The Surrender of Breda," opp. p. 100.)

Germany and the Netherlands

On turning to northern, to Teutonic Europe, we become aware at once that the Fine Arts were hardly touched by the influences radiating **Dürer and** from Italy and that they took their development from native precon- **Holbein** ceptions under the inborn energy of the race. In Germany we can trace a steady advance in painting beginning in the Middle Ages and continuing into the High Renaissance. In the latter period we encounter a distinguished group of artists, among whom Dürer (d. 1528) and

Holbein (d. 1543) are the acknowledged leaders. Refusing, like the rest of their countrymen, to be fired with the enthusiasm of the Italians for classical subject matter, they lingered contentedly among the medieval religious themes of Virgin and saints. (See Dürer's "St. Jerome," opposite.) Their modernism, for they were also modern, shows itself in the carefully observed intimate details of life and nature woven into their work. Plainly they responded to the world about them with quickened senses. Their keen perceptions explain why both men, but Holbein in particular, practiced portraiture, wherein they achieved the highest eminence. (See Holbein's "Erasmus," opp. p. 100.)

The fading-out of German art Since Dürer and Holbein had no notable successors and all the arts in Germany rapidly declined after their time, it might be argued that the Reformation acted as a check on artistic expression. This may be so; but in the case of Germany, exactly as in the case of Italy, the effect of the depressing political and economic conditions should not be overlooked.

Rise of the Flemish school of painting The close relatives of the Germans, the Netherlanders, both Flemish and Dutch, made not only a greater but also a far more unbroken contribution to painting. The people of Flanders, called Flemings, brought both architecture and painting to an impressive flowering in the later Middle Ages. That means that they stamped these arts with a characteristic Gothic imprint. Then, in the first half of the fifteenth century, a change took place comparable to the early Renaissance in Italy but with no attendant inclination to absorb the classical influences so alien to these dwellers by the North sea. The brothers Hubert (d. 1426) and Jan Van Eyck (d. 1440) gave to the altarpieces they continued to provide such a novel strength of drawing associated with such an abundance of finely noted realistic detail that they were promptly hailed as pathfinders and leaders. As, in addition, they perfected, although they did not invent, the technique of oil painting, which only in the next century spread to Italy, they were enabled to give their canvasses a hard and lustrous surface that has kept them to this day as fresh as at their birth.

Its apex is Breughel The Flemish school culminated in Peter Breughel (d. 1569). He delighted equally to present the changing seasonal aspects of his homeland and the boisterous games and festivals in which its lusty villagers violently cast off their cares and tribulations. (See "Winter Landscape," opp. p. 380.)

Even before Breughel died Italian influences had rather surprisingly begun to invade the Flemish area and ended by seducing the artists with the smooth surface charm of the southland. This led to a decadent period of hollow imitation from which Flemish painting was rescued by the genius of Peter Paul Rubens (1577-1640). His vast artistic appe-

ST. PETER'S CHURCH AND COL-
ONNADE AT ROME. The façade
and the colonnade belong to the seventeenth century and have the sumptuous
baroque character. (Anderson)

CUPOLA OF ST. PETER'S SEEN
FROM THE REAR. By Michelangelo.
It is unfortunate that the view of the
cupola from the front is obscured by
the high façade erected in the century
after Michelangelo. (Alinari)

ST. JEROME IN HIS STUDY. Engraving by the German artist, Dürer (d. 1528).

THE SUPPER AT EMMAÜS. By the Dutch painter, Rembrandt (d. 1669). With the feeling for living values characteristic of the Dutch school the artist presents the Bible story in terms of contemporary life. (Giraudon)

WILLIAM SHAKESPEARE. From the First
Folio Edition of his plays (1623).
GALILEO GALILEI. From a contemporary
painting.

FRANCIS BACON. From an old engraving.
RENÉ DESCARTES. From an etching after
the Dutch painter, Frans Hals.

(All from Bettmann Collection)

tite enabled him to absorb the classical myths, the allegory, the suave line, and the harmonious proportions of the Italians without the loss of the Flemish energy which was his birthright. His pupil, Van Dyck (d. 1641), became the most popular portrait artist of his day; and no wonder, for he gave his sitters a uniform aristocratic distinction without troubling over much about such deeper matters as character and personality.

A false Italianate tendency rc deemed by Rubens and Van Dyck

The Dutch achieved artistic expression later than the Flemings but, having found themselves, were apparently never even tempted to surrender to the Italian influences that in the long run overwhelmed their neighbors. Dutch painting began and ended to all intents within the limits of a single century, the seventeenth. Averse, as a Calvinist people, to the adornment of their churches, the Dutch, generally speaking, eschewed religious subjects. That avoidance turned them, with their powerful attachment to the world in which they lived, to portraiture, city scenes, house and tavern interiors, and common happenings of every kind on land and water.

The stay-at-home Dutch

Such men as Jan Steen (d. 1679), Gerard Ter Borch (d. 1681), and Jan Vermeer (d. 1675) reproduced contemporary life with such exactitude and zest that they make us direct participants therein after the lapse of three hundred years. However, the two greatest names are those of Frans Hals (d. 1666) and Rembrandt van Rijn (d. 1669), the former chiefly a portrait painter (see "Descartes," opposite), the latter so universally gifted that the mere listing of his merits is a serious undertaking. Certainly he got effects with a dramatic chiaroscuro, that is, with a light-and-dark technique, as have not been achieved before or since. In the "Supper at Emmaus" (opposite) we are struck with the way in which the light radiates from the figure of Christ and how the high enclosing space is constructed of alternating planes of light and shade. While Rembrandt was a Dutchman exceptional in that he did not, like his fellow artists, avoid religious themes, he showed his close kinship to the school from which he sprang by projecting his Christian scenes against the homely native setting of which he had immediate knowledge. The "Supper at Emmaus," though steeped in religious feeling, is a supper among Dutchmen in a Dutch inn.

Dutch painting cu minates in Hals and Rembrand

MUSIC

Folk music is always and everywhere a spontaneous growth but music as an art springs from conscious cultivation. Western art music owes its origin to the Christian church, which cultivated it systematically throughout the Middle Ages as an adornment of the service of the mass. First came simple Plain Song, which was then gradually elaborated by

Ecclesiastica music culminates in Palestrina

the invention of harmony and counterpoint. These efforts reached their fullest development in the High Renaissance under the inspiration of the Italian, Palestrina (d. 1594). With this genius, Catholic ecclesiastical music achieved the noblest expression it has ever attained.

Already in the Middle Ages secular music began to be practiced and under the secular influences abroad in the Renaissance made rapid progress. As might be expected from the primacy in the arts enjoyed by Italy, it was in that country that two new musical forms were developed outside the boundaries of the church and almost at once leaped to great importance. They were the oratorio and the opera. The oratorio exhibited a persisting inclination toward religion by devoting itself to the presentation of a sacred theme involving a spiritual conflict; the opera, wholly worldly, consisted of a musical accompaniment to a purely secular drama, usually a love tale. While the oratorio long continued to confess its ecclesiastical connection, among other respects, for instance, by being performed in churches, the opera frankly and from the first abandoned itself to entertainment on a purely worldly level and in sign thereof was performed in specially constructed buildings called opera houses.

It was around the year 1600 that, following a period of experimentation, the opera and oratorio came to birth. It will cause no surprise to learn that the city of Florence took a leading part in the creation of these novelties, though it is true that Rome, Naples, Venice, and other Italian towns shared actively in their development. This went on uninterruptedly throughout the seventeenth century largely because both forms, but especially opera, firmly established themselves in the affection of all the peoples of Europe. By the close of the period here under consideration secular music had made great forward strides. But it had as yet hardly done more than cast off its swaddling clothes. The great conquests of music both in respect of technique and range of expression belong to the eighteenth and nineteenth centuries.

Development of secular music: oratorio and opera

The vogue of Italian opera

THE NATIONAL LITERATURES

The forward movement noted in the Fine Arts and Music is equally characteristic of the National Literatures. As it was France, Spain, and England that particularly distinguished themselves in this department, we shall confine ourselves to indicating the development in these three countries.

The three literary leaders

The outstanding contribution to French literature in this period was made by the two sharply contrasted and yet complementary figures of Rabelais (d. 1555) and Montaigne (d. 1592). Rabelais' name is associated with the vast, disordered mock epic called *Gargantua and Panta-*

France: Rabelais and Montaigne

gruel, dealing satirically, and often with offensive brutality, with the struggles and delusions of mankind. At the same time the work, being a Renaissance product, sparkles with as much zest of living as has ever been crowded between the covers of a book. Montaigne lives on by reason of his immortal *Essays,* in which he communicates an attitude more classically inspired and hence more temperate and restrained than that of Rabelais, and which has always been admired as a noble expression of man's intellectual freedom. Since both Rabelais and Montaigne voiced their impatience with the barren religious dogmatism which threw such a spell over many members of the contemporary intelligentsia, we may safely conclude that a cantankerous theology was not, after all, the sole mental pabulum of the leading European minds.

When, later, in the days of Richelieu, religious pettifogging began to go definitely out of fashion, French literature took a fresh start, and in the dramas of Corneille (*Le Cid,* 1636) sounded the characteristic Renaissance theme of the self-assertion and heroism of man. There followed on the heels of Corneille the great outburst of literature connected with the reign of Louis XIV. It lies outside the range of this chapter, but that it was a delayed expression of Renaissance energy hardly admits of doubt. *Corneille, founder of French classical drama*

Spanish literature, like Spanish art, offers a problem to the student only because we are reluctant to concede that Spain was at all affected by the Renaissance. But as soon as we agree that in Spain, too, the Renaissance found admission, though always in subordination to dominant religious ideas, we have smooth sailing. The great figure of Spanish letters is Cervantes (d. 1616), a writer of romances, of which far and away the most original and famous is *Don Quixote.* In this story of the adventures of an extravagant, half-mad knight attended, for purposes of contrast, by a dry, over-sober servant, Sancho Panza, the author aimed a dart, compact of humor, satire, and pathos, at the moribund but still lingering chivalry of the Middle Ages and drove it, a contemptible wraith, out of the world of living men. *Spain: Cervantes*

The theater enjoyed a remarkable popularity in Madrid and elsewhere in Spain. It was supported by a succession of capable dramatists, among whom Lope de Vega (d. 1635) and Calderon (d. 1681) hold the leading place. Owing to the taboo clapped by the ever watchful Inquisition on all intellectually contentious matter, the Spanish drama unfolded vigorously but within a narrow range, for it rang the changes to weariness on the two hackneyed themes of love and honor. *The Spanish theater*

Richer and far more widely ranging was the literature of Spain's chief adversary, England. And it was, above all, in the drama that English literature scaled the heights. The drama enjoyed a short but intense development, for it was born, flowered, and died within the reign

of two sovereigns, Elizabeth and James I. If it was Christopher Marlowe
(d. 1592) who in such plays as *Tamburlaine* and *Dr. Faustus* first
sounded the majestic note to which the drama was destined to be keyed,
it was William Shakespeare (d. 1616) who carried it to a unique
climax. In an incomparable succession of tragedies (*Hamlet; Othello;
King Lear; Macbeth*) and comedies (*Twelfth Night; Much Ado About
Nothing; As You Like It; The Merchant of Venice*) he climbed the
heights and plumbed the depths of life in a manner so memorable and,
we may add, so unrivaled that he shines as a star of the first magnitude
not only over England but over all the world.

*Spenser,
Bacon*   We are sometimes inclined to forget that Shakespeare made his appearance amidst a galaxy of lesser but still brilliant luminaries, such as
Ben Jonson, Webster, and the usually inseparable collaborators, Beau-
mont and Fletcher. While these, too, are exponents of the reigning
literary form, the drama, other forms did not fail to find followers.
Edmund Spenser (d. 1599) wrote the delicate *Faerie Queene,* a curious
mixture of epic and allegory, and Francis Bacon (d. 1626), the statesman whose contribution to science has already been mentioned, inaugurated for his country the long succession of profound or witty commen-
tators on life with his *Essays.*

*The short
Puritan
eclipse*   However, even as these writers were lifting their triumphant voices,
there slowly rose and gathered round them the somber mists prophetic
of the Puritan eclipse, which in the succeeding generation blotted the
theater from view and caused Shakespeare himself to become for a time
hardly more than a myth. The victory of Puritanism went far toward
smothering that free and untrammeled expression which is the soul of
art. The reign of religious repression, however, was short-lived, and
long before the seventeenth century had come to a close English literature was again on the march with all its native vigor.

Milton   In conclusion, John Milton (1608-74), whose life-span and production
lies in both the Renaissance and Puritan periods, imperatively calls for
mention. Beginning life as a Renaissance lyricist (*L'Allegro, Il Penseroso,
Lycidas*), he became the chief Puritan poet and won a place among the
immortals with his noble Christian epic, *Paradise Lost.*

SOCIAL-ECONOMIC CHANGES

European Colonization

*The earliest
colonizing
states:
Spain and
Portugal*   In turning next to the vast social-economic changes of the Reformation period, let us begin with the colonial movement. As a result of the
conditions under which the transoceanic discoveries took place, Spain
and Portugal were the only two European states that succeeded, in the

From Hyma's *Europe from the Renaissance to 1815*, courtesy of F. S. Crofts & Compa

EUROPEAN COLONIZATION
AROUND 1700

British Possessions   Spanish Possessions

French Possessions   Portuguese Possessions

Dutch Possessions

first instance, in building up colonial empires. First on the ground, they actually succeeded for a time in their monopolistic plan of dividing the new world between them.

From their earliest fortified outposts in the West Indies, Mexico, and Peru, the Spanish adventurers, supported by the armed power of their government, radiated in every direction until the vast area lying between the Gulf of Mexico and the southern tip of South America came substantially into their hands. They settled at important points bodies of their own people sufficient in number not only to keep the natives in subjection, but also to assimilate them gradually to Spanish speech and culture. While Emperor Charles V and his son Philip II were with an enormous political and military apparatus asserting their primacy in Europe, their Spanish subjects, a picturesque company of sea-rovers, soldiers of fortune, gold-seekers, and adventurers of every sort, laid the foundations of an empire beyond the Atlantic, beside which the mother-country shrank to Lilliputian dimensions. *The vast colonial empire of Spain*

In contrast to the Spanish procedure, Portugal was content largely with commercial enterprise. With the momentum supplied by Prince Henry the Navigator and his successors, it claimed and held for its own particular advantage the fortified route around the Cape of Good Hope to India and the Spice Islands (Moluccas), and by jealously monopolizing this trade harvested enormous profits. *Portugal tries to monopolize the spice trade*

At one point, however, Portugal departed from its commercial policy. By planting a chain of settlements along the Brazil coast, the kingdom engaged in the territorial game of Spain and no doubt greatly annoyed its larger neighbor by driving a wedge between the northern and southern settlements of Spanish South America. *Portugal colonizes Brazil*

Though trouble often threatened between the two Iberian rivals, it was in general avoided by each sticking to his own vast and well-marked zone. Besides, for a period of sixty years (1580-1640) Portugal was ruled by the king of Spain and the rivalry between the ancient competitors was for that span of time suspended. When in 1640 Portugal reasserted its independence, the European situation had become so profoundly altered that, instead of Portugal and Spain crossing swords with each other, the two declining kingdoms had their hands full, and more than full, defending their too vast possessions against the youthful impertinence of the English, French, and Dutch. *The Dutch, English, and French enter the colonial race*

It was in the days of Philip II that the colonial monopoly so long maintained by the Spaniards and Portuguese began to give way. The two peoples owed the control which they had exercised to their command of the sea, and when this command broke down—the failure (1588) of the Invincible Armada supplies us with an approximate date —the English, Dutch, and French were prompt to take advantage of the decline of their Iberian antagonists. The problem for the three

The three
assailants
invade the
claims of
both Portu-
gal and
Spain

assailants was to penetrate either into the Portuguese sphere of the east or into the Spanish sphere of the west in order to seize and, if possible, keep whatever of value came to hand. As the Dutch were fighting for their lives with Philip, it is not surprising that they took the lead in this invasion. Behind them followed the English, and behind the English the French, slowed up by their disastrous religious wars, which were not wholly terminated till the days of Cardinal Richelieu.

With sound commercial logic the Dutch threw themselves first upon the oriental trade, in which they had long been interested, since, though the spices were brought in Portuguese bottoms to Lisbon, they were distributed over Europe from the Netherlands, notably from Antwerp. In the first phase of Dutch expansion numerous merchant-adventurers made their way into Asiatic waters in competition with one another and at their own risk; but when this was found to lead to disorder and sometimes to mutual destruction, the Dutch government took action. It consolidated the various existing enterprises under the name of the Dutch East India Company (1601) and then granted this company a monopoly of the eastern trade.

Shortly after the creation of the East India Company the Dutch fleet drove the Portuguese navy from the waters of the eastern archipelago. At the same time it cleared the paths of the Atlantic by administering a signal defeat to the Spanish navy near Gibraltar. By these two victories the Dutch acquired an effective, though constantly challenged, mastery of the oriental route and bit by bit picked up the Portuguese outposts and commerce in the far east.

Not content with this triumph, the Dutch presently organized (1621) a Dutch West India Company which, while cruelly raiding the Spanish settlements in America, won its greatest glory in wresting, though only for a time, a part of Brazil from its Portuguese masters. Nor was this all. Taking advantage of a North American claim which owed its origin to a voyage, under Dutch auspices, of the famous seaman, Henry Hudson, the West India Company promoted colonial enterprise along the majestic American river to which Hudson had given his name, and in 1626 founded, on the strategic island of Manhattan, the settlement of New Amsterdam.

In a word, the Dutch roamed the seven seas and when, at the signing of the Peace of Westphalia (1648), their republic achieved its unqualified independence, it had also reached the acme of its maritime power. It had supplanted Spain as mistress of the seas and had created a carrying trade which introduced the Dutch flag to every known port and made the Dutch metropolis, Amsterdam, the focal point of the world's commerce.

Aware of the potentialities of the eastern trade, Queen Elizabeth had chartered (1600), a year before its Dutch rival, an English East India Company. But the Dutch pursued their opportunities with more unflagging vigor and, having ousted the Portuguese from the East Indies, refused to split their profits with their neighbors from across the channel. Successful in crowding the English competition out of the islands where the spices chiefly grow, they organized the islands as a colonial dominion with its capital at Batavia on the island of Java.

The Dutch give their eastern islands a colonial government

The success of the Dutch obliged the English East India Company and, later, a similar French concern to give up the East Indies as a field of exploitation. The best the two rival companies could do was to edge their way into the Portuguese trade with the Asiatic mainland, more particularly with the vast peninsula of India. In this way the English and the French gradually built up their respective Indian (mainland) interests, which in the eighteenth century came into fatal conflict.

The English and French directed to the mainland (India)

The successful pre-emption of the eastern spice trade by the Dutch prompted England and France to seek compensation by turning westward. They were the more readily persuaded to this course since they had already in the Age of Discoveries established vague claims to certain coastal areas of North America. It also weighed with them that Spain, a power still to be reckoned with, was not likely to interfere with projects so far north of actual Spanish interests.

France and England turn to North America

It was not till the beginning of the seventeenth century that the two powers seriously went about the task of securing for themselves some part of the American seaboard. As though propelled by an identical impulse, both moved almost simultaneously. In 1608 the great French explorer, Champlain, founded Quebec as the first permanent settlement of France in the New World. By this act he staked off the huge basin of the St. Lawrence as prospective French territory. The year before (1607) a company of English adventurers, chartered by James I, landed on the Atlantic coast in a vast but ill-defined region named Virginia (in honor of Elizabeth, "the Virgin Queen") by the famous buccaneer, Sir Walter Raleigh. They cast anchor off the mouth of a river, which in the reigning sovereign's honor they called the James, while to the settlement they planted on the river they gave the name of Jamestown.

The earliest French and English settlements

While this colony was with difficulty getting a firm foothold on Virginian soil, King James's persecution, in the interest of the Anglican church, of the radical Protestants called Puritans, assumed serious proportions and drove many of them to consider the advisability of deserting their native land. In 1620 a small vessel, the *Mayflower,* brought the first group of these refugees to the inhospitable shore of Massachusetts.

Establishment (1620) of the Puritan colony of Plymouth

There, amidst incredible hardships, they established the colony of Plymouth.

From these two slender beginnings, Jamestown and Plymouth, there sprang a relatively rapid development which enabled the English to plant settlements at many additional points along the Atlantic coast. The consequences of this expansion might even then have been foreseen. Inevitably the time would come when English colonial enterprise would clash, on the one hand, with the claims of the Dutch centered at the island of Manhattan, and, on the other hand, with the claims of the French, radiating in all directions from the basin of the St. Lawrence. And though during the period considered in this chapter conflict was avoided, it was nonetheless certain that the future would bring a lively struggle among the three vigorous northern nations for the possession of the magnificent colonial prize represented by the North American continent.

Certainty of a future struggle for North America

The Commercial Revolution

From the colonial expansion here indicated there flowed great commercial consequences for Europe. Most immediately apparent was a change in the goods brought to the European market. During the Renaissance, Europe chiefly imported from the orient spices, silks, and objects of art which, essentially luxuries, were neither heavy nor of great bulk. As soon as European ships could make an unbroken journey from India, it became possible, on the one hand, to import such quantities of spices that their price was reduced sufficiently to bring them within the reach of the common man, and, on the other hand, to carry bulky goods like rice, sugar, tea, and coffee. Gradually these articles, unknown in the older, simpler days, became so firmly incorporated in the European diet that they rose almost to the level of necessities with the demand for them experiencing an unbroken increase.

Europe flooded with Asiatic products

As compared with these numerous and cherished eastern or Asiatic articles, the products furnished by the Americas were at first few. In fact the gold and silver of the mines of Mexico and Peru constituted for a long time the only notable importation. However, sugar became a very important product of the West Indies as soon as the transplanting of African slaves to American soil secured to the European enterprisers a reliable supply of plantation labor.

America provides gold, silver sugar

From approximately the beginning of the seventeenth century tobacco, which with the more useful, if not more esteemed, potato, represents the most famous contribution from America's native herbarium to European civilization, leaped into prominence as an item of American importation. The tobacco habit spread among the Europeans with something of the speed of a contagion. Conclusive witness of the fact was

Tobacco and the importation of African slaves

the steadily increasing volume of the American tobacco trade. Exactly as in the case of sugar, the intensive cultivation of tobacco called for the importation of African slaves on an ever increasing scale. Consequently not only did the nefarious slave trade climb to ever greater heights but "black flesh" came to be listed as one of the leading articles of American commerce.

American gold and silver, if indicative of the rather undiversified character of early commerce, had the startling effect of setting European economy almost on its head. Europe was only just emerging from the system of barter and exchange in kind, and the sudden influx of specie greatly hastened the decline of this primitive system. It did more. Flowing in unexampled quantities into Europe, especially after the middle of the sixteenth century, exactly like any other overproduced commodity it declined in value, causing a rapid appreciation of all articles measured in terms of money. No one could remember that any such amazing inflation had ever occurred before. Having not yet taught themselves to think scientifically about economic processes, men were a good deal dazed and manifested considerable social unrest. Particularly grave were the disturbances among the lower orders, the wage-earners, until in response to an inevitable adjustment, wages had been advanced sufficiently to meet the increased cost of living. *A price revolution resulting from the influx of bullion*

All these phenomena taken together—the new quantity wares, first from the east and, later, from the west, the influx of American bullion, the more general use of money in place of barter and services, the universal rise in prices—have been often represented as constituting a Commercial Revolution coincident with the invasion by Europe of Asia and America. It is a serviceable suggestion, provided we are not led to regard the Commercial Revolution of the sixteenth and early seventeenth century so much in the light of an isolated event as the inevitable outcome of the whole economic readjustment inaugurated in the Renaissance and continuing during the Reformation. Taken in that large sense, the Commercial Revolution is inseparable from another contemporary movement, the spread of capitalism. *The changes summarized as a Commercial Revolution*

New Aspects of Capitalism

Before attacking the developments proper to this particular head a clarifying word on the terms "capital" and "capitalism" seems to be called for. Capital in its most primitive sense is nothing more than "savings"; it follows that originally (and fundamentally to this day) every man is a capitalist to the exact extent of such "savings" as he commands. The economic system called capitalism is another matter. It comes into existence when the savings of a single man or of a group of *Capital and capitalism differentiated* partners is employed in a commercial or industrial enterprise with a view to profit. This first stage of capitalism is followed by the second stage when production and distribution are vastly increased and call for a proportionate increase of the capital investment. It will be seen at once that the system is capable of a practically unlimited expansion.

The earlier, Renaissance phase of capitalism

In treating of capitalism during the Renaissance (Chapter 3) we noted that it was heralded by such outstanding features as these: the coming of the merchant-adventurer and the merchant company; the breakdown of the medieval town economy by reason of the displacement of the town market by a market of national and, ultimately, of world scope; and the beginning of the dissolution of the characteristically medieval institutions, the gild and the manor. All these tendencies continued to make themselves felt in the era of the Reformation, strengthened and accelerated by the contemporary Commercial Revolution.

The increasing concentration of capital illustrated by figures

The expanding transoceanic trade was taken over by the merchant-adventurers, already brought to the front during the Renaissance. Either they themselves constituted a temporary merchant company or they were fitted out by a permanent merchant company, which to all practical purposes was also a bank. The merchant and enterprising element in European society therefore grew very rapidly, as did also the capital which it commanded. Just prior to the Age of Discoveries the largest European merchant company and bank was probably that of the Medici of Florence. Its resources have been calculated at $8,000,000. By the first half of the sixteenth century much larger bank resources are encountered. The Fuggers of Augsburg in southern Germany, for example, operated with a capital calculated at about $40,000,000.

The center of trade and finance shifts to the Atlantic coast

While the formidable Fugger figures reflect the larger dimensions of the Reformation world, they signify much more, since they also attest that the center of world trade and finance had, with the Discoveries, moved across the Alps to southern Germany. Before the middle of the sixteenth century the center shifted again, this time to the Netherland seaboard and, more particularly, to Antwerp. This Flemish city, favorably located on the Scheldt, at a point where important river, sea, and land routes converged, assumed around 1550 an unchallenged trade and financial primacy. It lasted till toward the end of the sixteenth century, when Antwerp suffered an eclipse through its conquest by Spanish troops and its enforced return to Spanish obedience (1585). Antwerp was then replaced as the center of world trade by the near-by Dutch metropolis of Amsterdam. Amsterdam, in its turn, was succeeded, but not within the period here considered, by London on the convenient estuary of the Thames.

By the time business had reached the development indicated by the ascendancy of Antwerp and Amsterdam, the form in which the original merchant companies had been cast was found to be no longer serviceable. The old companies had been largely family partnerships, which, subject to sudden dissolution through death or withdrawal, lacked that security and permanence which capital instinctively seeks. To replace the family partnership, the joint-stock company was invented. It was based on negotiable shares (shares that could be bought and sold in the open market) and had the double advantage that it guaranteed continuous operation and that its conduct could be intrusted to a manager of outstanding talent responsible to a board of directors. The merchant company replaced by the joint-stock company

After 1600 all the great trading companies, as, for instance, the Dutch and English East India Companies, were joint-stock concerns. The negotiability of shares gave birth to that eminently modern institution, the stock exchange. At the same time the small size of the individual shares made it possible for men with relatively trifling savings to become stock-holders and so contribute their part toward turning the ever mightier mills of capitalism. Birth of the stock exchange

By the first half of the seventeenth century it had become clear that it was the Dutch, the English, and, to a somewhat less extent, the French, who were taking full advantage of the new economic opportunities. The Latin countries, Italy, Spain, and Portugal, had been left behind, as was also Germany, where fatal internal divisions precipitated the destructive Thirty Years' War and hung a black pall over the country for several generations. Economic ascendancy of the Dutch, English, and French

It is therefore to the group of three peoples around the English channel and the North sea that we must turn if we would study at close range the social transformation that had been brought about in Europe by the middle of the seventeenth century. Among these peoples capitalism had become most firmly rooted, and among them, as leading representatives of the system, had come to the front a body of men called burghers in Holland, bourgeoisie in France, and middle or upper middle class in England. Descended from the merchant-adventurers of an earlier age, they had become differentiated by a process of progressive economic specialization: they participated in the commerce of their day as wholesalers, bankers, shipmasters, transportation agents, and manufacturers. In these capacities they employed thousands of clerks, seamen, stevedores, and other wage-earners and wielded a tremendous, if indefinable, social influence. Growing importance of the capitalist class

That this socio-economic influence could at need be converted into political power was conclusively proved first, in the case of the Dutch republic, and afterward, during the Puritan Revolution, in England. In the following century, in the great upheaval of 1789, it was proved also in France. That the established governments of the three countries under consideration did not find it easy, with their lingering feudal and eccles- The capitalist (or burgher) groups aspire to political power iastical traditions, to adjust themselves to the demands of the rising business class was no more than to be expected. The point to note is that in every instance they either in the course of time came to terms with the representatives of capitalism or else lived to see themselves overthrown by revolutionary action.

But let us guard against exaggerating the importance of the bourgeoisie in the seventeenth century. It was at this time still in process of formation and from long habit looked upon itself as inferior to the landed gentry. Besides, the landed gentry often had the advantage of a political experience which the bourgeoisie lacked. And the representatives of "big" bsuiness faced another, by no means insignificant, rival in the "little" business men (shopkeepers and craftsmen) organized in the gilds. To the new-rich, who were large-scale merchants and capitalists, the gilds, with their charters, their privileges, and their precise regulations touching every phase of production and sale, represented so many economic shackles which would have to be got rid of if enterprise was ever to become truly free. The heads of the gilds, however, the so-called masters, wished to retain a system which underscored their importance and were generally influential enough to gain their point. A first breach of the gild system occurred among the Dutch. An even larger breach followed in England.

In England the so-called *free contract* system came into vogue and gradually, without destroying the gilds, reduced them to hollow shells. By this system, also called the *domestic* or *putting-out* system, the capitalist gained control of production by buying the raw product, let us say, wool, and *putting it out* among individual workmen on terms mutually acceptable. Plainly such individual workers, even if they owned their tools and used their homes as workshops, were wage-earners, much reduced from the status and dignity of medieval gildsmen. But as the new system, conducted by trained and responsible specialists, produced more and cheaper goods than the gild system with its conservative attachment to time-hallowed methods and with its elaborate restrictive regulations, it was destined to win out everywhere, though in the seventeenth century it was victorious as yet only in England.

The advantage gradually acquired by England over the continent in all departments of manufacture (an advantage patent even to casual observers by the eighteenth century) must be ascribed, in the main, to the new system. It put at the disposal of the English capitalists a mass of free labor entirely unprotected by the gild or any other form of workingman organization. In most of the continent, in sharp contrast to England, the gild system, although showing many evidences of decay, continued to weigh upon production until the coming of that hurricane

The free enterprise tendency opposed by the gilds

England develops a capitalist system of production

Persistence elsewhere of the gild system

called the French Revolution. Destructive of innumerable vested interests, the French Revolution brought to the ground also the long-since hollow edifice of the gilds.

EMERGENCE OF INTERNATIONAL LAW

We have learned that the Europe of the seventeenth century still recognized that it possessed an ideal unity, of which the leading expression was a common culture. But we are also aware that, politically, Europe had become a congeries of sovereign states engaged in an unrestrained struggle with one another for commercial profits, territory, and power. As in this struggle war figured as a means to which each sovereign state was free to resort at its pleasure, the later history of Europe unfolded amidst an almost uninterrupted succession of wars. *Sovereignty culminates in the right of war*

Nonetheless, large bodies of men, more particularly artists, scholars, and philosophers, regarded war with aversion. They recognized that it was inherent in the idea of sovereignty and that its reign could not be broken until some principle had been discovered which would rank higher than sovereignty and to which there was some prospect that sovereignty might be subordinated. In the Middle Ages Christianity had been such a principle, but it had never been really effective in banning war; and from the time of the Renaissance, with its anti-Christian worldliness, the pacifist implications of Christianity had suffered a gradual further enfeeblement. *Peace requires a principle superior to sovereignty*

The credit for first propounding a principle at least mitigative of the excesses of sovereignty and at the same time not out of tune with the contemporary situation in Europe belongs to the Dutchman, Hugo Grotius (1583-1645). In 1625 Grotius published his famous treatise, *De Jure Belli et Pacis* ("On the Right of War and Peace"). According to this work, there is a law of nature which is superior to the vaunted sovereignty of states. To arrive at what the author rather grandiosely called the law of nature, he deduced from the records (treaties, laws) the practices in peace and war of the most civilized nations. Plainly, with this rather makeshift "law of nature" he did not nor could he hope to abolish war. And in point of fact he aimed at nothing more than to limit wars to such as might be conceived of as "just." At the same time he aspired to have the occupations of peace regarded as so much more rational an expression of human nature than war that war would gradually lose the prestige it owed to having been rated throughout the ages of the world as the highest form of sovereignty. *Grotius and his makeshift law of nature*

War did not lose its prestige and peace remained the same precarious possession of European mankind after Grotius as before. Nonetheless, the Dutch humanitarian thinker has a considerable achievement

to his credit: he founded the science of international law. Taken up by
Grotius innumerable devotees after the founder's day, it has swollen to a vast
founder of body of material bearing on the intercourse of nations. Not even yet,
the science
of inter- after three centuries of endeavor, have the successors of Grotius suc-
national law ceeded in mastering the problem presented by the claim of every independent state to an unlimited sovereignty. However, they have kept
alive the issue of a better world order, and such progress as may have
been made in that direction must, at least in large measure, be attributed
to the many men who, following the lead of Grotius, have labored in
the field of international law which he staked off.

The Absolute Monarchy
FROM 1648 TO 1789

14 THE STUARTS AND THE PURITAN REVOLUTION

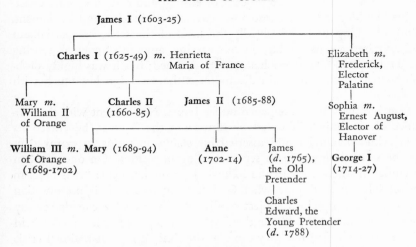

THE HOUSE OF STUART

James I (1603-25)

Charles I (1625-49) *m*. Henrietta Maria of France

Elizabeth *m*. Frederick, Elector Palatine

Mary *m*. William II of Orange

Charles II (1660-85)

James II (1685-88)

Sophia *m*. Ernest August, Elector of Hanover

William III *m*. Mary (1689-94) of Orange (1689-1702)

Anne (1702-14)

James (*d*. 1765), the Old Pretender

George I (1714-27)

Charles Edward, the Young Pretender (*d*. 1788)

WHEN ELIZABETH DIED in March, 1603, she was succeeded by the son of Mary Stuart. He had been king of Scotland almost from his birth under the name of James VI. Among English monarchs he figures as the first of that name.

Accession of the house of Stuart

James's accession opened the prospect of that union between England and Scotland for which several far-sighted statesmen beginning with Henry VII had carefully prepared the ground. However, the plan still encountered opposition. So deep-rooted were the long-standing antagonisms of the two nations that they refused to consolidate their institutions and fortunes, though James himself gave his ardent adherence to the project. In consequence, Scotland kept its own parliament, laws, and officials, and the accession of James did little more for the present than give England and Scotland a common sovereign.

Scotland and England acquire a common sovereign

It was unfortunate that at a time when the sovereign exercised enormous power the crown should have descended to a man like James. He had an ungainly figure, a shuffling gait, distasteful personal habits, and was obstinate, weak, and cowardly. A person less royal to look upon

Character of James

261

had not sat upon the English throne in many a century. He had crammed himself with a considerable stock of knowledge, which had not matured into wisdom and which his vanity prompted him to exhibit on every occasion in order to hear himself acclaimed by the flattering courtiers as the British Solomon.

James heir of the strong Tudor monarchy

All this would have merely exposed him to more or less amiable ridicule if he had not made himself dangerous by holding the most exaggerated idea of his royal office. It was he who first carried into English political discussion the theory of the divine right of kings. The English constitution, which was the product of custom and certain specific enactments like Magna Charta, vested the government in king and parliament. While the king was undoubtedly the head of the state, the parliament had exercised a considerable, though varying, amount of control. During the Tudor period its power had greatly declined; but it was highly probable that it would rise again the moment the sovereign lost touch with the nation.

James arouses opposition by his excessive claims

That is exactly what happened under James. Not content with the substance of absolutism inherited by him from the Tudors, he craved its open acknowledgment and asserted his claims in terms so extravagant that he seemed almost to be set on rousing opposition. On one occasion he edified his hearers with the following pronouncement: "It is atheism and blasphemy to dispute what God can do; . . . so it is presumption and high contempt in a subject to dispute what a king can do, or say that a king cannot do this or that." The Tudors, as has been said, held this identical theory; but they came at the time of a great national crisis and acted, in the main, in close accord with the people. Should the first Stuart undertake to act against the people and their real or supposed interests, it might well be that he would find his power challenged and the nation prepared to fall back on that older conception of the role of parliament which the Tudor absolutism had supplanted.

The favorable foreign situation at James's accession

The accession of James occurred amid circumstances which augured a happy reign. The defeat of the Spanish Armada had placed the independence of England beyond question, and subsequent events on the sea and in the Netherlands had so weakened Spain as to remove all danger from that quarter. In consequence, James wisely enough negotiated with Spain a treaty of peace (1604).

The domestic situation turns about religion

In domestic affairs the chief interest revolved around the Anglican church established by Elizabeth on the foundation of the Acts of Supremacy and Uniformity (1559). By the time of her death her creation had acquired an air of permanence. The Catholics were a waning group and the Puritans, influenced but not yet dominated by Calvinism, demanded certain concessions, based chiefly on their aversion to the use of the surplice, to kneeling in service, and similar externals. It must be remembered that they were as yet, in overwhelming majority, friendly to the national establishment, accepted the religious headship of the sovereign and the episcopal form of government, and merely advocated the simplification or purification, as they called it, of divine service. If James would know how to conciliate them, the religious troubles of England might be accounted as over.

But James did not know how to conciliate the Puritans. Shortly after his accession, in 1604, he called a religious conference at Hampton Court for the purpose of discussing a Puritan document, called the Millenary Petition from the fact that almost a thousand clergymen had signed their names to it. Unfortunately he lost his temper during the debate and flared up wildly against the petitioners. He declared that they were the enemies of episcopacy—which was not yet the case—and affirmed with unnecessary emphasis that that system of church government had his unwavering support.

James against the Puritans

His personal spite becomes explicable when we remember that he had been brought up in Scotland, where he had made the acquaintance of the Presbyterian system. By this system the church was withdrawn from the control of the king and was put in the hands of the ministers of religion and the people. Having made the pleasing discovery that in England the sovereign ruled the church through bishops whom he appointed, he was jealously on the lookout against the importation of Presbyterian ideas. He went the length of identifying episcopacy with monarchy and formulated his opinion in the epigrammatic assertion, "No bishop, no king."

Why James hated the Puritans

Acting on the unjustified assumption that the English Puritans were Scotch Presbyterians in disguise, James dismissed the Millenary petitioners gruffly. Shortly after he issued a proclamation ordering every clergyman who refused to meet exactly and literally the prescriptions of the Book of Common Prayer to be removed from his living.

James orders the Puritan clergymen to be ejected

Toward the Catholics, whom James to his credit regarded with a tolerance much in advance of his time, he initiated a temperate but unsuccessful policy. He began by lightening some of their burdens of persecution; but when, owing to the pressure brought to bear upon him by his Protestant subjects, he faltered in his resolution, a group of disappointed and desperate Catholics resolved to destroy the whole Protestant government —king, Lords, and Commons—by one gigantic stroke.

James and the Catholics

The conspirators heaped gunpowder in barrels in the cellars beneath the parliament buildings and set November 5, 1605—the day of the opening in state of a new session—for the crime. Suspicion, however, had been awakened by hints thrown out by some of the participants in the plot; and luckily, on the eve of the planned disaster, Guy Fawkes, the hardiest of the conspirators, was discovered keeping watch among the explosives. While he and his associates were hunted down and executed with all the

The gunpowder plot 1605

barbarity characteristic of the period, a much more regrettable consequence of the plot was that the English people were confirmed in that
intense distrust of the Catholic faith which long remained the leading
article of their religious and political creed.

Such was the relation of James to the religious question—the ritualistic

wing of the national church was vigorously sustained, the Puritan or
reform wing was opposed and actively repressed, and the Catholics, not
without a decent reluctance, were persecuted and crushed. Even so, the
religious situation might not of itself have provoked a crisis, if James had
not created a second difficulty by antagonizing his parliament. To understand this new development we have but to recall to mind that he wished
to plant the practical absolutism of the Tudors on a solid foundation of
absolutist theory.

The quarrel began almost immediately. James needed money, partly

owing to the mounting costs of government, partly because he was extravagant. The required revenues had, of course, to be voted by parliament; and if that body had been managed after the Tudor fashion, it
might have granted supplies as readily as in the days of Henry or Elizabeth. But James's talk about a monarch being above the law had aroused
suspicion and moved the parliament to ask, as a return favor, for a redress
of grievances. The king, thereupon, in a huff, began to help himself to
funds by arbitrarily increasing the impositions (or rates) on certain
articles of import and export. When a merchant, named Bates, refused
to pay the imposition on a consignment of currants from the near east,
he was tried and sentenced by the judges.

In this manner James triumphed. But the victory added only a small

amount to his revenue, did not settle his financial difficulties, and exasperated the parliament so greatly that it prepared to oppose every demand, reasonable or unreasonable, which the king might make. On the
angered James dissolving one parliament, he found its successor still more
unwilling to bow to his dictation. Out of what was originally a simple
matter of supplying revenue for the crown's legitimate outlay had grown
by James's arrogance an issue, at the core of which was the all-important
question as to who had the last say in matters of taxation: king or
parliament.

Over impositions and related revenue issues James quarreled with his

parliament throughout his reign, with the result of an increasing irritation on both sides. In the year 1621 the wrath of the Commons reached
the point of a savage attack on the whole administration, culminating in
the impeachment of the highest official of the realm, the Lord Chancellor.
This was none other than the philosopher, Francis Bacon, one of the
greatest Englishmen of the period. By taking fees from suitors while
their cases were still pending in his court, Bacon had become technically

guilty of bribery. His excuse was that the acceptance of gifts was a long-established custom of his office. With a disarming candor he avowed that the practice was indefensible. Bacon was fined and dismissed from office, the sentence being declared by himself "just, and for reformation's sake fit"; but he would not have been attacked at all if the parliament had not been bent on vicariously striking the king through his leading official.

Bacon's trial took the form of an impeachment, in itself an ominous sign that the parliament was raising its claims as the best answer to the king's attempt to exalt his own position. Impeachment was a means by which, in earlier times, the parliament had exercised control over the king's advisers. It had become obsolete under the Tudors, when the humbled parliament had been obliged to abandon all influence upon the royal ministers. The revival of impeachment at this juncture meant that the parliament was furbishing up the old weapons with which it had once held the monarchy in check. An impeachment was a somewhat complicated process. The House of Commons appeared at the bar of the House of Lords to present to it the offender against the commonwealth, and the House of Lords, after listening to the charges, declared them founded or unfounded, pronouncing sentence accordingly. *Significance of the revival of impeachment*

The unpopularity caused by his harsh treatment of the Puritans and his violent quarrel with the parliament was increased by the foreign policy of James. We have remarked that shortly after his accession he had concluded peace with Spain. His general program was to further the cause of religious peace in Europe by maintaining a close relationship with his late enemy. *James's foreign policy*

Such a policy was not to the taste of his Protestant subjects and would depend for its success on the willingness of Spain to meet him half-way. This Spain refused to do, for, when the Thirty Years' War broke out in Germany in 1618, the Spanish government immediately came to the help of the emperor and the Catholics. James, for his part, did not budge, although Frederick of the Palatinate, whom the Bohemian Protestants raised to the kingship of their country, was married to his daughter Elizabeth. *Outbreak of the Thirty Years' War*

When Frederick was driven from Bohemia, James continued inactive and not till Frederick had been outlawed (1620) and driven from the Palatinate, too, did he bestir himself; even then he did no more than make an appeal to Spain to help restore his son-in-law to his inheritance. That power was delighted to find him so docile, made temporizing proposals, but too thoroughly approved of the Catholic success in Germany to do anything to check it. *Attempt of James to act concordantly with Spain*

Thus matters dragged on until the year 1623, when the young and handsome duke of Buckingham, who was the king's all-powerful favorite, proposed to take a last step to bind Spain to England in a close

The plan of Buckingham
alliance and to secure the settlement of the Palatinate question without war. He developed the plan of a secret journey with Charles, the prince of Wales, to Madrid in order personally to present the case of his master. By an impetuous attack he hoped to persuade the king of Spain to affiance his daughter to the English heir and at the same time to sign the desired treaty of alliance. It was a plan as harebrained as it was impolitic, but James, teased and wheedled by the two young men, at last gave his blessing to the enterprise.

Failure of the plan followed by a martial policy
After many adventures Charles and Buckingham arrived at Madrid, but they did not have the triumph they had anticipated, for their hosts skillfully avoided making any commitment. Utterly disgusted, they came back resolved to persuade James to give up his passive for an active policy; and so vigorously did they work on him that he at last consented to essay the reconquest of the Palatinate by war. This turn met with the approval of his countrymen, but the parliament, still suspicious of James, voted inadequate supplies. Consequently the expedition into Germany proved a disastrous failure. In the midst of this crisis the distracted king died (March, 1625).

CHARLES I (1625-1649)

Character and views of Charles I
The new king, Charles I, was outwardly very unlike his father. His face, familiar to us from Van Dyck's many portraits of the English royal family, was handsome and his manner kingly. Unfortunately he was liberally endowed with the obstinacy of the Stuart family and shared his father's inflated views of the royal prerogative.

Charles continues to antagonize Puritans and parliament
The two main difficulties created by James bore immediate and dangerous fruit in the new reign. By antagonizing the Puritans, James had driven them into open opposition to the national church; and by quarreling with parliament he had raised the question as to who controlled taxation. Determined to follow in his father's footsteps, Charles succeeded in an incredibly short time in arousing such opposition to himself that the Commons, who had been servilely docile under Elizabeth and had, even while protesting, been deeply respectful under James, plainly put the question: Who was sovereign in England, parliament or king?

Puritan fervor fired by Catholicizing tendencies
Shortly after his accession Charles married Henrietta Maria, a sister of Louis XIII of France. This marriage with a Catholic, extremely unpopular on its own account, was made doubly so by the suspicion, only too well founded, that Charles had entered upon an agreement with Louis to relax the penal laws against the English Catholics. When parliament assembled, it at once showed signs of restlessness. They mounted to a storm on the discovery that a small party of churchmen, closely associated with the court, was advocating views that savored of Romanism.

Not only did these so-called High churchmen defend an elaborate, ritualistic service but they also attacked some of the teachings of Calvin and, in particular, his doctrine of predestination. As the king shared their views, he naturally sided with them, while they reciprocated by adhering to his theory of the royal prerogative.

To the Puritans, whose fervor and numbers were steadily increasing, the association of king and Romanizing clergymen looked very much like the alliance of popery and tyranny. Maintaining that the church of England was, in the realm of doctrine, Calvinist, they were carried away by their feelings to the point of declaring that the High churchmen were innovators engaged in a plot to carry England back to Rome. Heatedly opposed to Charles on ecclesiastical grounds, the Puritans naturally joined forces with those individuals and groups who resented the king's political claims. Thus it came about that the absolutist and High church parties had no sooner united than the two oppositions, Puritan and parliamentarian, fused in their turn. With this ominous division of his people into two camps Charles was confronted from the very beginning of his reign. *Fusion of the Puritan and parliamentary oppositions*

In view of the strained relations between king and parliament, it is intelligible why the parliament took a most unusual course with regard to the chief revenue of the crown, called Tonnage and Poundage. Tonnage and Poundage was the name given to the customs dues on wines and merchandise commonly voted at the beginning of each reign for the whole period of the sovereign's life. Partly from occupation with other business, partly from desire to bring pressure to bear upon the king, the parliament now failed to make the usual life grant. However, Charles, who could not carry on the government without Tonnage and Poundage, continued, through his officials, to collect it. *The quarrel over Tonnage and Poundage*

With the heavens darkening over him by reason of these domestic infelicities, Charles invited additional criticism by his extraordinary mismanagement of foreign affairs. The war with Spain furnished the occasion. Since it was he who had forced it on his father, he was bent on prosecuting it with vigor. Inclined to give him support, for the war with Catholic Spain was popular, the parliament did, however, expect that the money which it granted would be spent in giving the Spaniards a sound beating. With characteristic lack of judgment Charles intrusted the conduct of the war to the duke of Buckingham, his father's as well as his own favorite; and the duke, a handsome, dashing, and romantically minded individual unfit for weighty affairs of state, reaped nothing but disaster. *Mismanagement of the war with Spain*

We have already noted that the first campaign, directed toward the immediate object of contention, the Palatinate, was a complete failure. Nothing daunted, Buckingham resolved to level a blow directly at Spain

by an expedition to Cadiz. It ended in an ignominious retreat (1625).
Thereupon the Commons refused to make additional grants until the
blundering duke had been removed. As the king resented as an impertinence the attempt to dictate to him in the matter of his advisers and
angrily dissolved the parliament (1626), the threatening deadlock became
definite.

The Commons demand the dismissal of Buckingham

In the year 1627 matters grew worse. The king, not content with the
unsuccessful war with Spain, allowed himself to be dragged into a conflict with France in behalf of the French Huguenots, who were being
besieged by Richelieu in La Rochelle. As no money could be had from
the angered parliament, Charles adopted a perilous device: he asked
first for voluntary gifts; and when the nation failed adequately to respond, he levied a forced loan. On a citizen's refusing to pay his quota,
the government would bring pressure to bear by quartering troops on
him. In order to spread a general terror, it even threw some of the more
conspicuous parliamentary critics into prison. Not only were these measures dangerous, but the sums thus extorted brought no blessing. An
expedition under Buckingham's command set out to relieve La Rochelle.
It failed as miserably as had the attack on Cadiz. Thus fresh disgrace
was added to the disgrace already incurred in the war with Spain.

War with France; failure to relieve La Rochelle

The new parliament, which Charles, hard pressed for supplies, was
obliged to call in 1628, was filled with the utmost wrath against the government. Before granting another penny, it insisted that the wrongs of
the nation be redressed; and in a document called the Petition of Right
it enumerated the most outstanding grievances. The Petition of Right
declared gifts, loans, and taxes not voted by parliament illegal; it insisted
that no freeman should be imprisoned without cause shown; and it condemned the quartering of troops upon householders. As there was no
other way of getting money, the king had to swallow the bitter morsel.
The Petition of Right, celebrated as a renewal of Magna Charta, was accepted by him and became the law of the land (June, 1628).

The king accepts the Petition of Right, 1628

Unfortunately the Petition of Right did not settle all questions at issue
between sovereign and legislature. In the first place Charles continued to
collect Tonnage and Poundage, although it had not yet been voted, on
the ground that it belonged to the sovereign by right of custom. Sec-
ondly, he persisted in showering favors upon the High church element
and in supporting the obnoxious Buckingham. Proof of the fiery passions engendered by the party strife was offered soon enough. While a
new expedition to La Rochelle was being prepared at Portsmouth, a
fanatic patriot, John Felton by name, assassinated the hated duke (August, 1628).

Murder of Buckingham, 1628

The parliament had no sooner met in the following year (1629) than
it reopened the combat. Vehemently the members complained that the

king was collecting Tonnage and Poundage, though the duty had not been voted; and they were no less wroth at his continued support of the ritualistic churchmen. In mingled alarm and disgust, Charles determined to break up their session; but before his command to adjourn was read in the house, resolutions expressing the general indignation were put, and, while the speaker was forcibly detained in his chair, carried by acclamation. The resolutions declared that whoever introduced innovations savoring of popery into the national church, and whoever paid or advised the payment of Tonnage and Poundage, was an enemy of the English people. *The session of 1629; breach between king and parliament*

Thus, over the two questions of the ceremonial character of the church and the control of Tonnage and Poundage, war had been virtually declared between king and parliament. All prospect of an amicable settlement had disappeared. Either the king would impose his system and crush parliament or the parliament would do the same by the king. *The constitutional alternative*

For the next eleven years (1629-1640) the victory, or seeming victory, was with the king for the reason that by not summoning the parliament he gave it no opportunity to contest his pre-eminence. In this proceeding custom played into his hands, since a king was not obliged to summon parliament at stated intervals. In point of fact the kings of the past had hardly ever summoned parliament except for the specific purpose of a money grant. The position of Charles was now and had always been that he was acting within his rights as defined by the constitution, and that it was not he, but the parliament, which had broken with English law and tradition. *Charles governs without the parliament*

It should be clear, however, that Charles's plan of getting along without the parliament necessitated extreme economy and therefore an immediate termination of the expensive wars with France and Spain. Before the end of 1630 Charles had made his peace with both these powers. His outlook was now, on the whole, not unhopeful. Tonnage and Poundage, although condemned by the Commons, was regularly paid into the exchequer by a people not yet ready to renounce their king; and Tonnage and Poundage, with a number of other revenues appertaining to the crown or scraped together by hook or by crook, was found to be sufficient or almost sufficient for ordinary current expenses. *Charles makes peace with France and Spain, 1630*

Charles's chief advisers during this eleven years' interlude of personal government were Thomas Wentworth, for civil matters, and William Laud, for ecclesiastical affairs. As the king himself was still hedged about with something of divinity, all the unpopular measures carried in church and state during this period were laid at the door of these two men, who, as the years came and went without a parliament, became the target of a wild, unreasoning animosity. *Wentworth and Laud, chief advisers of the king*

Laud was identified with the drift in the English church toward dignity and ceremony. It was precisely because of this attitude of the inflexible churchman that the king honored him with his favor. In the
year 1633 Charles showed his attachment to Laud's principles by appointing him archbishop of Canterbury. This made him primate of England and enabled him to enforce his and the king's ecclesiastical views.

*Laud arch-
bishop of
Canterbury*

By means of visitations which brought every parish of the kingdom
into line and by penalties imposed by the ecclesiastical court, the Court
of High Commission, controlled by him, the fiery archbishop obliged
every Anglican minister strictly to adhere to the prescribed forms. Indeed
he did not hesitate to favor the return to partially abandoned features of
an older time. At his instigation the communion table was assigned a
fixed position in the east end of the church, and by being surrounded
with an iron railing was given, at least in Puritan eyes, something of the
appearance of a Catholic altar. As part of the same policy the Declaration
of Sports was issued authorizing and encouraging games on Sunday. To
the strict Sabbatarianism of the Puritans the re-establishment of the frolic-
some medieval Sunday was a tremendous moral shock. The consequence
of these measures was to drive the remaining Puritan ministers from the
church and to bring about the final estrangement of the Puritan clergy
and population from the national establishment.

*Ecclesiastical
measures of
Laud*

Wentworth was a man of far greater intellectual powers than either
Laud or Charles. His theory of government was that a king who governs
well is better than a babbling, distraught parliament. The natural corollary to this position was that the executive power should be strong, efficient, and large-minded, and that it should steer its course without fear
or favor. It was a theory of enlightened despotism, designated by Wentworth with the name of "thorough." Admitted to the Privy Council,
Wentworth uniformly encouraged the king to keep up a bold front.
However, he cannot be made responsible for all the measures, many of
them ill-advised, which followed the dissolution of 1629. As early as
1633 he was sent as Lord Deputy to Ireland and was for many years out
of immediate touch with English politics.

*The
enlightened
despotism of
Wentworth*

Certainly Wentworth cannot be charged with the great blunder committed in connection with ship-money. We have seen that Charles's system left him in constant need of funds. So slim were his revenues that he
could not even maintain a navy large enough to enforce respect for the
English flag upon the waters of the channel. The legal remedy for the
inconvenience would have been to call a parliament and ask for supplies,
but that step Charles refused to consider. He hit upon a subterfuge. In
former times monarchs had, when the country was in danger, ordered
the ports and seaboard counties to furnish ships. In issuing such an order
in 1634 he therefore had a measure of legality on his side. It was against

*Charles
resorts to
ship-money*

precedent, however, when in the two following years he ordered the *inland* counties to contribute money to the same end.

Although a navy might be good in itself, Charles's way of getting it was a piece of very sharp practice. Indignation swelled like an advancing tide, and when a country gentleman, John Hampden by name, chose, rather than to pay his assessment, to suffer arrest and trial, he made himself the hero of the hour. When the case came up in court, the judges by a bare majority decided against Hampden; but so general was the disaffection following upon his trial, that it required only an occasion to show that the loyalty which had bound England for ages to her sovereign had suffered fatal impairment.

The test case of John Hampden

That occasion was furnished by Scotland. We are aware that the northern kingdom had established the Presbyterian kirk. Resting on the combined action of clergy and laity, it was virtually an independent institution free of control by the monarch. Such a system displeased Charles, as it had his father before him, and he resolved to impose on it the episcopal and ceremonial features of the Anglican church.

Charles resolves to modify the Scottish church

The measures of the king, gradually introduced, culminated in 1637 in the imposition on the Scottish kirk of a new service book fashioned largely on the English Book of Common Prayer. At once a hurricane was loosed. The Scottish people, radical Presbyterian Protestants almost to a man, not only refused to bow to the royal decree but answered it with a solemn National Covenant, which every Scotsman rushed to sign. The Covenant pledged him to offer the utmost resistance to any attempt to force religious innovations on the kirk. The unanimity and enthusiasm of the people gave them an irresistible power. In the face of it Charles was moved to open negotiations; but on discovering that he must either completely reverse his policy or fight, he chose the latter.

Charles encounters united Scottish resistance

There followed the campaign of 1639 against the Scottish Covenanters, known as the First Bishops' War, in derisive reference to the bishops, whom Charles planned to set over the northern establishment. The campaign was a miserable fiasco. Owing to lack of funds, the king led northward an undisciplined rabble. When he came upon the Scots, he found himself compelled to sign a truce.

Failure of his war on his Scottish subjects. 1639

Between his Scottish and his English subjects, whom he had alike alienated, the position of Charles was now thoroughly humiliating. In order to avenge himself upon the Scots, he required effective money help from England, and effective money help from England involved calling a parliament. In one direction or the other he had, therefore, to make concessions. Charles fought a hard battle with his pride. Finally, feeling that the Scottish matter was more pressing, he summoned the English parliament (1640).

Charles summons parliament

Thus the long period of government without a parliament had come to an end. When, however, the parliament, known as the Short Parliament, instead of voting money for the enslavement of the Scots, began to remind the king of the nation's grievances, Charles flamed up as of old and dismissed it. Once more, in spite of his lack of funds, he conducted a campaign, known as the Second Bishops' War, against the Scots (1640). When the second campaign failed even more completely than the first, he had to acknowledge himself finally and irrevocably beaten.

The Short Parliament and the new campaign against Scotland, 1640

In November, 1640, Charles summoned another parliament, which he knew would have him at its mercy. It has received the name of the Long Parliament and is the most famous legislative body in English annals. It sat, though not without an important interruption, for two decades, witnessing, and itself initiating, the transformation of England.

The Long Parliament, 1640

The Long Parliament had no sooner assembled than it took the government into its own hands. The king's innings were over and it was now the turn of his offended rival. Burning for revenge, the Commons turned first upon Laud and Wentworth and ordered them both under arrest. Wentworth, who had lately been created earl of Strafford, was impeached for treason. When the case against him threatened to break down owing to insufficient evidence, the parliament simply legislated him out of the world by a bill of attainder.[1] The dismayed king reluctantly signed the act, which on May 12, 1641, sent the most energetic defender of the throne to the scaffold. The aged Laud was spared for the present. In 1645 he, too, paid with his life for having aroused the relentless hostility of the Puritans.

The parliament turns against Strafford and Laud

At the same time the Commons threw themselves on the accumulated grievances of the past. As the Scots, who had invaded the northern counties, would not leave England till their expenses had been made good to them, Charles, to get money, had to accept every proposal. Filled with exultation, the parliament resolved to leave the swollen power of the king no leg to stand on. The special courts, such as Star Chamber and High Commission, which had supported the tyranny of Charles and Laud, were abolished. Star Chamber, it will be remembered, had been created by the first Tudor in order to curb the lawlessness of the feudal nobility. Charles had chiefly employed Star Chamber as a tool to punish the too free expression of Puritan opinions.

The king is stripped of authority

In a devastating succession of acts parliament condemned the king's position relating to Tonnage and Poundage; declared ship-money illegal; and provided against the future elimination of the legislature by the Triennial Act, which made it obligatory on the king to summon parliament at least once every three years. As a crowning measure it decreed that the present parliament should not be dissolved without its own con-

The acts offensive to the king enumerated

[1] "An impeachment followed, in some sort, legal rules; a bill of attainder was an act of power for which no reasons need be given" (Gardiner).

sent. Although Charles was obliged to accept these to him intolerable decrees, everyone who knew him was convinced that he would attempt to annul them at the first opportunity.

That opportunity dawned for the king on the appearance in the ranks of the Commons of the first serious division. Admirably united on the *political* measures at issue between them and the sovereign, the Commons ran into difficulties from the moment they proceeded to debate the *ecclesiastical* settlement. The consequence of the Laudian tyranny and the concomitant growth of a vengeful Puritanism was that a decisive majority of the Commons desired to destroy episcopacy and all its works. No sooner, however, had this project been bruited than it was found that a minority, cherishing a sentiment of loyalty toward the church of their youth, deprecated sweeping changes. Alarmed at the wild agitation which was rocking the country, they registered a conservative reaction and prepared to defend not only the remaining rights of the king but, first and foremost, the national church. *The Commons split over the religious issue*

The emergence of a royalist and Episcopalian party within the Commons not only delighted the king but moved him to resume his former policy and to engage in plots against the parliament. These maneuvers the parliamentary majority resolved to crush by a frank disclosure of them to the nation. It drew up (December, 1641) the Grand Remonstrance, wherein it enumerated article by article the abusive and deceitful acts which had caused Charles to lose the confidence of the people's representatives. The Grand Remonstrance passed the Commons by only a small majority. That fact clearly indicated that at the close of its first year of power, parliament was almost evenly divided touching the further measures to be taken. *The Grand Remonstrance, December, 1641*

This knowledge was enough to spur the incautious king to the attempt to overawe the Commons by a display of force. On January 4, 1642, he marched at the head of his guard to Westminster Hall, the meeting-place of the parliament, and entering the House of Commons, attempted to seize the five leaders, Pym, Hampden, Hazelrigg, Holles, and Strode, in order to bring them to trial on the charge of treason. Forewarned, the intended victims had fled and the king was balked. London rose clamorously to express its indignation and, fearing an attack, the king and royal family withdrew into the country. *The king's attempted "coup d'état"*

The dramatic invasion of the House of Commons by the king was tantamount to the declaration that rather than continue to wear the yoke of the Puritan majority he would resort to violence. That diplomatic relations were not at once broken off blinded no one to the fact that the die had been cast. On August 22, 1642, Charles, unfurling the royal banner at Nottingham, bade all loyal Englishmen rally to their king. The parliament in its turn gathered an army and prepared to take the field. *The civil war begins 1642*

The parties thus about to engage were at first rather evenly matched. The king's party, known by the proud name of the Cavaliers, held most of the northern and western counties. The adherents of parliament, derisively dubbed Roundheads by their opponents because many of them, in order to show their contempt for the fashionable curls of the Cavaliers, cropped their hair close, held the south and east, with London for their center. Neither side was prepared for war; but the fact that the slashing, fox-hunting country gentlemen crowded into the king's service gave the royal side at first the advantage.

The country divided between Cavaliers and Roundheads

In the early campaigns the armies of the parliament suffered many reverses. On one occasion London, the chief parliamentary stronghold, almost fell into the king's hands. It was not till the year 1644 that the parliament began to develop anything resembling an efficient army. Simultaneously there rose into prominence the man who was destined to overthrow the king and bring the war to a conclusion—Oliver Cromwell.

Early successes of the king

Oliver Cromwell is one of those surprising characters who sum up a whole period of their nation's history. He was a country gentleman of the east of England, whose life had become bound up in the Puritan cause. With moral firmness and religious enthusiasm he combined an unusual measure of practical good sense, which enabled him to see things exactly as they were. When everybody else was in consternation over the victories of the king, he went straight to the core of the military problem with which the Commons, wherein he sat, was vainly wrestling. He thus expressed himself to his cousin, John Hampden: "Your troops are, most of them, old, decayed servingmen and tapsters. Their troops are gentlemen. Do you think that the spirit of such base fellows will ever be able to encounter gentlemen? You must get men of spirit or else you will be beaten still."

Oliver Cromwell

Cromwell's sound judgment had discovered the thing needful and his love of action urged him to go about it without delay. He took the field and gradually collected about himself a special cavalry troop of men of his own mind—earnest Puritans who had their hearts in the cause; and his troop soon won for itself the grim title of Cromwell's Ironsides.

Cromwell's Ironsides

In the campaign of 1644 Cromwell's Ironsides first prominently showed their mettle. On July 2, 1644, at Marston Moor, near York, was decided the fate of the northern counties, and here for the first time Cromwell's troopers broke the charge of the hitherto invincible royal cavalry commanded by Prince Rupert, the king's nephew. When night descended upon Marston Moor, the king had lost his hold upon the north. At the battle of Newbury, which took place a few months later, it is probable that the king himself would have been captured, if Cromwell had not been thwarted by a sluggish and incapable superior.

The tide turns and the king is beaten, 1644

That winter Cromwell fiercely denounced in parliament the lax method of carrying on the war which had hitherto prevailed. As a result a sweeping military reform was voted. By means of two ordinances, the Self-denying Ordinance and the New Model, the army was completely reorganized. By the Self-denying Ordinance all members of parliament were obliged (with the exception of Cromwell) to surrender their commands in favor of men exclusively concerned with the conduct of the war; and by the New Model the army was adequately financed from national revenues and put on a strictly professional basis. The spring of 1645 found Sir Thomas Fairfax at the head of the reformed forces and the fiery Cromwell in command of the horse. *Army reforms, 1644*

The effect of the change made itself felt at once; the campaign of 1645 proved decisive. At Naseby, in the heart of England, the king made his last formidable effort. The gallant Rupert plunged, as so often before, through the squadrons of horse opposed to him, but his reckless pursuit took him miles away from the battlefield. Before he could return, Cromwell had broken the king's left and center and won the day. For almost a year the king still held out, vainly hoping for relief from this or that small circumstance. In May, 1646, judging that all was over, he surrendered to the Scottish army in possession of the English north. *Complete defeat of the king, 1645*

How had the Scots been drawn upon the scene? Aware of the king's continued secret opposition to the Presbyterian system, they had followed with sympathy the struggle of the English Puritans. In September, 1643, yielding to the solicitations of the parliament, they had signed a treaty of alliance and taken the field. In return for their help against the king, they had exacted a grave concession: the parliament was obliged to promise to reorganize the English church on a Presbyterian basis. *Conditions of the alliance between England and Scotland*

Since the outbreak of the civil war, the situation in the parliament in respect of the religious settlement had suffered a change insofar as the Episcopalian minority had surrendered its seats and deserted to the king. Hence the Puritans were now in unchallenged control; and as a religious solution other than episcopacy had to be found, many looked with favor on Presbyterianism. Before long, a majority had been definitely won for this faith, but a minority of the Commons, calling themselves Independents, voiced a protest on the ground that the possibilities of tyranny under a Presbyterian establishment were every whit as great as under Episcopalianism. What the Independents desired was the authorization of free, congregational units under an act of toleration covering all Protestant sects. The project was frankly repulsive to the Presbyterians, who were as little inclined as the displaced Episcopalians to tolerate the slightest departure from their system. *The religious situation in the parliament: Presbyterians versus Independents*

Though the Independents were at first no more than a handful in the Commons, they enjoyed an influence out of proportion to their vote through the circumstance that they commanded the backing of Cromwell

The Independent minority supported by Cromwell and army and the army. As a result, the Presbyterian majority was obliged to proceed with caution, especially so long as the war continued and the troops had to be kept in good humor. But no sooner had the battle of Naseby been won and the enemy been scattered than the quarrel asserted itself with irrepressible vehemence.

The king's calculation When the king surrendered to the Scots he was well informed of these differences of opinion among the victors, and hoped, in his shifty way, to find his profit in them. Let the army, representing the Independents and their idea of tolerance, only fall to quarreling with the majority of parliament, representing the Presbyterians and their system of religious uniformity, and his turn would come.

The Second Civil War, 1648 Herein Charles calculated both well and ill. In the year 1647 the Scots, after trying in vain to bring him to a settlement with themselves, surrendered him, on the payment of their campaign expenses, to the parliament. When the Commons now tried to impose a Presbyterian settlement on him, the watchful army plucked him from the hands of parliament and negotiated with him on the basis of an Independent program. Thereupon the Scots resumed negotiations on their own behalf, and in their anger with the anti-Presbyterian army plotted with the king to invade England in conjunction with a new royalist rising. As a result of these intrigues, of which Charles was alike the cause and the manipulator, a second civil war broke out in the summer of 1648 with the Scots perversely fighting for the king.

Victory of the army over the king and the Scots In spite of Scottish support, the Stuart trickster fared as ill in the new struggle as he had in the old because the army had become an irresistible power. In a brief campaign Cromwell scattered the invading Scots like chaff, while Fairfax suppressed the unimportant rising of their allies among the English royalists.

Pride's Purge; the army overrides the parliament Unquestionable masters of the situation, Cromwell and his friends resolved to tolerate no further negotiations with "that man of blood," Charles Stuart, but to bring him to his trial and death; and when the Presbyterian majority, incurably addicted to compromise, again resumed negotiations with the monarch, the army leaders no longer scrupled to attack the parliament. On December 6, 1648, they stationed a troop under the command of Colonel Pride at the door of Westminster Hall with orders to exclude one hundred and forty-three Presbyterian members from the Commons. The "Rump" (some 60 members) that remained was no longer a truly representative body and continued its enfeebled existence at the mercy of the army.

With the army in complete control the trial of the king could have begun at once, except for the fact that the army leaders desired to give their proceedings the appearance of legality. They had the servile Rump pass an act redefining treason in such manner as to embrace the mis-

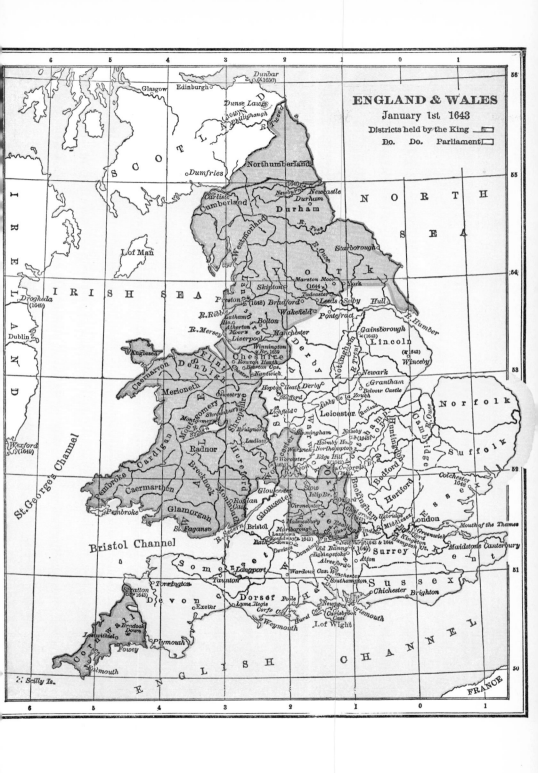

ENGLAND & WALES
January 1st 1643

Districts held by the King
Do. Do. Parliament

deeds of the king, and followed this up with the creation of a special High Court of Justice. Its sentence was a foregone conclusion. It found the king guilty of treason as defined for this particular occasion. On January 30, 1649, Charles was executed on a scaffold erected in front of his palace of Whitehall. He had never been shaken in the conviction that the right, during the whole course of the civil war, had been with him, and he died, not without dignity, in that belief. *Trial and execution of the king, January, 1649*

The violent events connected with the civil war had destroyed the historical English government. King and Lords had disappeared, the Commons were a fragment. The power now lay exclusively with the army, and the question on everyone's lips was whether the military leaders would be able to build a new constitution grounded in sound principles and acceptable to the country. *The army in complete control*

For eleven years the army and, more particularly, Cromwell attempted with unquestionable zeal and sincerity to make their ideal of government a reality. That ideal was born of the conviction that every man must indeed be a follower of Christ, but that he should be allowed to worship Christ after his own fashion. In consequence, Cromwell and his friends desired a government of upright Puritan men which tolerated every belief save popery. Unfortunately for the men in power the vast majority of contemporary Englishmen were either Episcopalians or Presbyterians and, in addition, convinced adherents of the monarchical system. *The eleven-year struggle to realize the Puritan ideal*

THE COMMONWEALTH

On the death of the king, the Rump voted that England was a Commonwealth without king or Lords, and appointed, provisionally, a Council of State to act as the executive branch of the government. *The Commonwealth*

There was pressing work ahead for the young republic. In Ireland, which had been in rebellion since 1641, the rebels refused to recognize the new government, while, in Scotland, Charles, the oldest son of the dead sovereign, had been proclaimed king. In the clear recognition that the Commonwealth could not live with Ireland and Scotland ranged against it, Cromwell was dispatched to reduce the neighboring kingdoms to submission. *Ireland and Scotland refuse to recognize the Commonwealth*

In an irresistible campaign of the year 1649, Cromwell crushed the Irish, not scrupling to break the spirit of resistance by two bloody massacres at Drogheda and Wexford. Thereupon he set up a rule of force more rigorous than Ireland had ever experienced and at the same time elaborated a plan for the confiscation of vast tracts of land for the benefit of the conquerors. *Ireland conquered*

This done, the victor turned to Scotland. At Dunbar (1650) Cromwell's soldiers, whose tempers were like the steel with which they smote, scattered the Scottish army; and when a second army, with King Charles in its midst, struck across the border in the hope of stirring up an English rebellion, Cromwell, starting in pursuit, met it at Worcester and won the crowning victory of his life (1651). After many romantic adventures Charles effected his escape to the continent. The Scots were let off with a peace, wherein they aligned themselves politically with the victorious Commonwealth. With their Presbyterian church Cromwell was too wise to meddle.

Cromwell brings the Scots to terms, 1651

With peace re-established throughout the British Isles, the question of a permanent government became more pressing than ever. Everybody clamored for a settlement and the termination of the long disorders. Only the Rump was in no hurry. Not only did the fifty to sixty members who composed it cling to office, they even planned to perpetuate their power. With the characteristic impatience of soldiers the army grew ever more restive over the long delay. Despairing of good from so selfish a body, Cromwell at last resolved to have done with it. In April, 1653, he invaded the Rump with a detachment of troops and ordered the members to disperse. "Come, come," he shouted in indignation, "we have had enough of this. It is not fit you should sit here any longer." The last fragment of the old constitution had vanished from the scene.

Cromwell dismisses the Rump, 1653

A new, freely elected parliament, would have been the normal solution of the difficulties which now confronted Cromwell. But such a parliament would immediately have called back the Stuarts; and Cromwell was ready to exhaust every possibility before he would admit that the Puritan cause had failed. In conjunction with a number of officers he therefore *nominated* an assembly of Puritan partisans who were to discuss the bases of a new government. Undoubtedly well meaning, the nominees were inexperienced and crotchety. The town wags, greatly amused at their provincial manners, called them Barebone's Parliament, from a certain worthy member whose excessively evangelical name of Praise-God Barebone invited an inevitable ridicule. Luckily, after a few weeks, a group among the nominees recognized its own unfitness and brought about the end of the session (December, 1653).

Barebone's Parliament, 1653

The victorious officers thereupon came forward with a plan of their own. They drew up a constitution in forty-one articles, called the Instrument of Government, which placed the chief power in the hands of Oliver Cromwell under the title of Lord Protector. By the new constitution the Lord Protector, together with a Council of State, was to exercise the executive power, while a parliament of a single house, from which all partisans of the Stuarts were excluded, was to perform the legislative functions of government.

The Protectorate, 1653

The Instrument of Government came nearer to being a workable scheme than anything that had been tried since the outbreak of the civil war. It must not be overlooked, however, that it was grounded on the disfranchisement of the royalists and that such success as it achieved was owing to the fact that it placed in control a man of extraordinary gifts.

Qualified success of the Protectorate

The five years (1653-1658) of Cromwell's rule as Protector were beset with innumerable difficulties. His very first parliament insisted on revising the Instrument of Government. As that was tantamount to calling the whole settlement in question, Cromwell in high dudgeon dissolved it (January, 1655). There were frequent attempts upon his life, royalist risings, and even a number of republican conspiracies. With its one-man rule the Protectorate was as offensive to the strong republican element which had come to the front in England as it was, for other reasons, to the adherents of the Stuarts.

The domestic difficulties of the Protector

In the year 1657 Cromwell called a second parliament and with this he got along more smoothly for a while. The traditional English conservatism came to the front in this assembly and it tried to get back to the forms of the old constitution. It created a second house to take the place of the abolished House of Lords and proposed to make Cromwell hereditary king. But Cromwell, who already exercised a virtual kingship as Protector, wisely declined a title repugnant to the republican sentiments of his army adherents. When this same parliament assembled for a second session and attempted to limit the powers of the executive, Cromwell reproachfully dismissed it (February, 1658).

Parliament proposes to make Cromwell king

Cromwell's bitter experience with his successive parliaments must have convinced him, if he stood in need of proof, that the nation was not with him. Disguise the fact as he might, his rule rested upon the army and was a military despotism.

Cromwell's military despotism

In all this time the great principle of toleration, which Oliver had mainly at heart, made no progress. His original plan, laid down in the Instrument of Government, was to give to all Christians, except such as adhered to "popery or prelacy," the protection of the law. That meant state support for the whole diversified body of Protestant sects. He even conceded the *private* use of the Book of Common Prayer; and, while excluding the Catholic mass, he greatly relaxed the penalties in force against the Catholics. But he could not extinguish the fierce religious fires that, in accordance with the temper of the times, kept flaring up all over the country. Long before his life came to a close he had gained the bitter conviction that the government of his beloved Puritan Commonwealth rested on no single principle that had taken root in the nation.

Failure of the limited Cromwellian toleration

At best but moderately successful at home, Cromwell accumulated triumph on triumph abroad. From 1652 to 1654 there was a war with the Dutch, caused by English jealousy of the immense commerce of the rival republic. In a measure passed by the Rump in 1651, and known as the Navigation Act, the English jealousy found vigorous expression.

War with the Dutch, 1652-54

Since this act declared that foreign ships were permitted to bring to England only such goods as were produced in their own country, the Dutch, who were carriers for the whole world, were dealt a severe blow. In the course of the war that followed, the English navy cleared the channel of the Dutch fleet, thus enabling Cromwell to sign (1654) a peace, which, apart from a few concessions to the Dutch, signified the enforcement of the Navigation Act.

Cromwell makes war on Spain

Soon after, in 1655, Cromwell engaged in a war with Spain, finally joining in an alliance with France against the common foe. By the seizure of Jamaica England gained a firm foothold in the West Indies, and by defeating, in conjunction with the French, the Spanish forces in the Netherlands, the English army was enabled to occupy Dunkirk,[2] one of the best ports in Flanders (1658). Not since the days of Elizabeth had England held so lofty a position in the councils of Europe. Cromwell's arm reached even to the Alps, and at his command the duke of Savoy ceased persecuting the Protestant peasants and herders of the upper Alpine valleys.

Death of Cromwell, 1658

Thus to the end the Protector held the rudder firmly. But his health was broken by his great responsibilities and on the third day of September, 1658, he passed away. It had been his "fortunate day," the day of the great victories of Dunbar and Worcester, and was to his mind, heavy with the disappointments of office, perhaps no less fortunate in that it put an end to tribulation.

A year of anarchy following Cromwell's death

Cromwell's death was followed by a year of anarchy. As the Commonwealth was founded on the power of the army and not on the consent of the people, its continuance depended on the army's finding a successor of the same mettle as the great Protector. But that was impossible. Cromwell was succeeded in the protectorate by his inoffensive and incapable son, Richard. In May, 1659, Richard resigned an office calling for powers which he did not possess. Thereupon the Rump came back, arrogantly insisting that it was the true and authentic English government. At the same time the generals, who with the death of their leader had lost their cohesion, quarreled with the Rump and with each other. Clearly the only way out of the intolerable confusion was to call back the son of the dead king. The people themselves were more than willing, but to insure success a resolute man at the head of an armed force would have to take the enterprise in hand.

General Monk brings back the Stuarts, 1660

The savior wanted was found in General George Monk, one of Cromwell's most capable lieutenants and his representative in Scotland. At the head of his army Monk marched to London, and, re-calling the Long Parliament, obliged it to dissolve after issuing writs for a new election. With the way thus cleared, Charles Stuart from his exile in Holland

---

[2] Dunkirk was held only till 1662, when Charles II sold it to France.

issued a general pardon and, when the new parliament met, was enthusiastically invited to mount the throne of his ancestors. The new parliament declared that "the government of this kingdom is, and ought to be, by king, Lords, and Commons." When Charles entered London on May 28, 1660, the houses emptied their inhabitants upon street and square who cheered the repatriated king like a conquering hero.

CHARLES II (1660-85)

Charles II was one of the most popular monarchs England has ever had. As has happened before and since in history, his popularity was owing not so much to his virtues as to his vices. In this connection we should never forget that the Restoration signified a sweeping general reaction. Not only did it mark the abandonment of the republican political experiment but also a sharp revulsion against the austere and somber scheme of life which the Puritans had imposed upon society. Like one who had long dwelt in darkness, the Englishman of the Restoration threw himself greedily on color, splendor, and distractions. The restored monarch had lived long in France, where his self-indulgent nature had drunk its fill of the gaiety and licentiousness which characterized the sumptuous court of Louis XIV. Upon his return to England he became the advocate of contemporary French manners and, making profligacy fashionable, added to his constitutional function of sovereign the far more congenial role of master of the revels. The country, out of sorts with the Puritan ideals, applauded, admired Charles's witty sallies and studied courtesy, and joined the dance and sounded the pipe around the "Merry Monarch" of an England passionately resolved to be likewise merry.

Character of Charles II and of his age

Charles, though endowed with a good deal of natural sagacity, had little mental energy and not the faintest particle of that rectitude which we define as character. His pleasures went before everything else. When a conflict threatened with either ministers or parliament, he was in the habit of giving way with the jocose fling that whatever happened he did not care to start again upon his travels. Intelligent, supple, and unencumbered with either the obstinacy or the principles of his father, he succeeded in making himself both popular and secure.

Charles's political opportunism

No sooner was the monarchy restored than the desire seized the victors to be revenged upon their Puritan adversaries. The king's general pardon issued from Holland was subject to parliamentary revision, and the parliament, far more vindictive than the sovereign, resolved to punish all who had been instrumental in bringing Charles I to death. Thirteen regicides were executed, and a revolting vengeance was wreaked upon the body of the great Cromwell. Dragged from the tomb, it was for the length of a day suspended with iron chains from the gallows.

The vengeful reaction; punishment of the regicides

Such scenes apart, the Restoration was far less violent than similar reactionary occurrences in history, owing, in the main, to the lack of rancor

**The revolu-
tion not
in vain**

of the king. Yet, to the defeated and dejected Puritans, whose leading
survivor was the poet Milton, it looked as if the return of Charles had
closed on them the gates of paradise and rendered vain both the civil
and religious struggle of the past generation. Such, however, was not
quite the case. As the Petition of Right and most of the early enactments
of the Long Parliament had received the royal assent, they remained in
vigor, thereby substantially reducing the royal prerogative.

**Possibility
of a new
conflict
between
king and
parliament**

To prove that the situation had definitely changed, it suffices to point
out that no king ever again disputed the right of parliament to control
taxation. Nevertheless, the royal power was still so great that an energetic
monarch might feel encouraged to carry through a personal program in
the teeth of parliamentary opposition. In that case a new conflict would
be unavoidable. But that so unenterprising a reveler as Charles II would
undertake and, having undertaken, would sustain such a conflict was
highly improbable.

**The Cavalier
Parliament,
1661-1679**

The Cavalier Parliament, as Charles's second parliament, convened in
1661 and allowed to hold power for eighteen years, was significantly
called, exuberantly expressed the reaction which had taken hold of the
country. It was more royal than the king. One of its earliest acts was
to vote that no one could lawfully take arms against the sovereign.
Thereby it propounded the doctrine of non-resistance and defined the
late civil war as a rebellion. The most pressing issue which confronted
it was the question of religion. During the last twenty years every conceivable form of Protestant dissent had sprung into existence, and Presbyterians, Congregationalists (Independents), Baptists, and Quakers disputed the ground with Anglicans and Catholics.

**The Cavalier
Parliament
passionately
Anglican**

Were all these denominations to be tolerated or was England to go
back to a uniform national church? In the Cavalier Parliament—a body
of royalist reactionaries—there was only one opinion: the church of England and nothing but the church of England. It undertook, therefore, to
restore the historical church and persecute every deviation from it with
relentless severity.

**A new Act
of Uniform-
ity; the
Dissenters**

In the year 1662 the parliament imposed a new Act of Uniformity on
the re-established church. By its provisions the Prayer Book was made
obligatory, and two thousand clergymen, who would not bend their
necks to the yoke, were ejected from their livings. Among the dismissed
ministers were many zealous men of all denominations, who together
with their followers were henceforth classed together as Dissenters.

In the religious history of England this final ejection of the Puritan
element from the church marks a notable milestone. It will be remembered that the Puritans in general had not wished to separate from the

national church. They had desired rather so to modify its forms that it might include or "comprehend" them. From now on all hope of comprehension was given up. Accepting their exclusion from the national church as an irrevocable fact, the Dissenters henceforth directed all their efforts toward acquiring toleration for their various distinct forms of worship.

The Cavalier Parliament was the last body in the world to give ear to a request for religious liberty. As in its opinion the proper way to treat Dissenters was to suppress them, it developed a highly perfected system of persecution. Already in 1661 it had enacted the Corporation Act, providing that no man could hold office in a corporate town unless he took the sacrament according to the church of England. In 1664 the Conventicle Act was passed, by which the meetings (conventicles) of Dissenters for religious purposes were punished with fines culminating in transportation to the colonies. A year later (1665) there followed the Five Mile Act, by the terms of which no dissenting minister was allowed to live within five miles of any corporate town.

It is probable that the Cavalier Parliament would not have insisted on the national creed with such vehemence, if it had not been persuaded that toleration granted to Dissenters would open a loophole for the Catholics. And just then the suspicion against Catholicism was stronger in the land than ever because of the machinations of the king and his intimates in its behalf. Indeed with each passing year the atmosphere of the court became more markedly Catholic. Before long many courtiers, with the king's younger brother, James, duke of York, at the head, openly avowed their return to Rome. Charles himself was restrained from taking the same step by nothing more noble than his fear of what might happen to him at the hands of his people.

A monarch who identified himself so little in religious matters with his people was not likely to serve them in the foreign field. In fact, his guidance of England was of a piece with his superficial character. Disliking the bluff, republican Dutch and admiring the sumptuous Louis XIV of France, he permitted this question of taste to play a large part in determining his public conduct.

We have noticed the growing commercial rivalry between the Dutch and the English. The Navigation Act, passed in 1651 by the Rump, and the war that followed gave ample evidence of it. When to conflicting colonial claims in the East Indies and along the American coast was added the animosity created by the re-enactment (1660) of the obnoxious Navigation Act, war could not long be averted. For three years (1664-1667) the adversaries engaged each other upon all the seas. When peace was signed, the Dutch were obliged to cede their American colony with its capital of New Amsterdam. Renamed New York in honor of the duke of York, brother of the king, it soon gave evidence of commanding one of the most favorable commercial sites in the western world.

This was the time of the ascendancy of France in European politics.

Charles leans by preference toward France

The leading fact of the general situation was that Louis XIV was planning to extend his territory and power at the expense of his neighbors. The logical policy for England, as the rival of France, would have been to support the victim against the aggressor; but it was the peculiarity of Charles that he looked at the situation from a personal rather than a national angle. Since he led a riotous and disordered life, flinging fortunes away on entertainments and mistresses, he was in perpetual financial straits. To get money, therefore, and ever more money became his great object in life; and Louis XIV, who was not without a shrewd streak amid his lavishness, was perfectly willing to oblige his brother of England, if he could by this means buy England's support or, at least, neutrality in the conflicts he anticipated.

The Treaty of Dover, 1670

The French king began his systematic aggression in the year 1667 by invading the Spanish Netherlands. After taking a few towns he was forced to desist, chiefly because of the energetic protest of the Dutch, supported by Sweden and temporarily, owing to public pressure, by Charles himself. No wonder that the haughty Louis resolved to have revenge on the Dutch. By the Treaty of Dover (1670) he persuaded Charles by means of an annual grant of money to become his ally against the Dutch; and Charles, in his turn, stipulated to avow himself a Catholic, as soon as the moment was propitious, and to call on Louis for military aid in case his subjects, on the news of his conversion, rose in revolt.

Charles publishes and withdraws his act in favor of the Catholics

When, in the year 1672, all the necessary preparations had been made, Louis and Charles fell suddenly like two highwaymen upon the Dutch, engaging in what in England is known as the Second Dutch War of the Restoration. Just as the war was about to break out, Charles, not yet daring to go the whole length of announcing his return to Rome, published a decree of toleration, the so-called Declaration of Indulgence, which suspended the execution of all penal enactments against both Catholics and Dissenters. The measure nullified the laws of England by an arbitrary royal act. The outcry was general; and when parliament met, it so vehemently insisted on the king's withdrawing his Declaration that the weak-kneed Charles gave way (1673).

The Second Dutch War of the Restoration, 1672-74

With his retreat from his religious position the war against the Dutch lost its interest for Charles. He therefore deserted his ally and made peace with the enemy (1674). Thus the treason hatched out in the Treaty of Dover came to nothing, except insofar as it involved the Dutch in another heroic struggle for life and liberty. So stubborn was their defense under the stadholder, William III of Orange, that Louis XIV, baffled and discouraged, finally followed Charles's example and brought the war to an end (Peace of Nimwegen, 1678).

Though triumphant in the matter of the Declaration, parliament was not satisfied with its victory. Thoroughly suspicious of the pro-Catholic policy of the court, it added (1673) a crowning act to its intolerant religious legislation, the Test Act. The Test Act provided that all persons holding civil or military office under the crown must agree publicly to receive the sacrament according to the national church. In consequence, only avowed adherents of the church of England could henceforth hold office; and no less a person than the duke of York, the king's brother and prospective successor, had to resign the post of Lord High Admiral because he was a Catholic. **The Test Act, 1673**

Unfortunately the specter of Catholicism, aroused by the king's secret cabals, continued to stalk through the land, leading at times to outbreaks which would have been ludicrous, had they not been so profoundly tragical. The most famous of these outbreaks belongs to the year 1678 and is known as the "Popish Plot." A certain Titus Oates, a discredited adventurer and confessed scoundrel, told a rambling story before a magistrate to the effect that he had discovered a conspiracy on the part of the Catholics to institute in England a second and more terrible massacre of St. Bartholomew. Although Oates's story was palpably absurd, it won general credence; and as a result of the frantic agitation which seized the country a score of prominent Catholics were executed on false and trumped-up charges. At the same time a corollary was added to the Test Act by which Catholics were barred from sitting in either house of parliament. **The "Popish Plot," 1678**

Charles died in the year 1685 after a reign of twenty-five years. On his deathbed he received first, privately, the sacrament according to the church of Rome. Then, keeping up his lifelong comedy to the last, he died, as it were, publicly and a second time according to the prescriptions of the Anglican church, of which he was the official head. **Death of Charles, 1685**

The reign of Charles is marked by an advance in the political life of the nation which merits attention. The gushing loyalty of the early years of the Restoration did not last. Gradually impaired by the Catholicizing tendencies of the court, it was seriously undermined when, owing to the absence of a direct heir, it became apparent that the crown would pass to the king's Catholic brother, James, duke of York. A party, called Whigs, arose which proposed to exclude the king's brother from the throne on the ground of religion. A second party, called Tories,[3] stood staunchly by the principle of legitimate succession. By adroitly taking ad- **Whigs and Tories originate over the succession issue**

[3] These names were originally taunts, flung by excited orators at the heads of their opponents. Tory is derived from the Irish language and signifies robber. Whig comes probably from Whiggam, a cry with which the Scotch peasants exhorted their horses. Applied as a party name, it was intended to convey the idea of a rebellious Scotch Covenanter.

vantage of the extreme violence of the Whigs, Charles managed to arouse
a strong royalist sentiment in the country, which made him more powerful at the close than at any time during his reign. While he undoubtedly,
in connection with the succession issue, scored a personal triumph, the
historic import of the controversy lies in its bringing into existence for
the first time two opposed parliamentary parties, each with a definite
program and something like a permanent organization. For over two
hundred years after their appearance the Whigs and Tories (later under
the names of Liberals and Conservatives) were destined to dispute the
government of England between them.

JAMES II (1685-88)

James II, who succeeded his brother Charles, was not only an open
and avowed Catholic, which, of course, raised an impassable barrier between him and his subjects, but he was resolved, if possible, to bring
England back to the Roman fold. Sincere and honest, he scorned to
resort to the political trickery of his predecessor. He was cordially acclaimed on first mounting the throne but by a succession of rash and ill-
judged measures was, with extraordinary rapidity, reduced to a state of
icy isolation.

*Sincere
Catholic
character of
James II*

As James was a Catholic among suspicious and embittered Protestants,
he would have been wisely inspired at the very least to let sleeping dogs
lie. But his conscience forbade him to feign a neutrality he did not feel.
Overriding the Test Act, he at once put his coreligionists into important
positions in the military and civil service. Soon after, in 1687, he published, in imitation of an earlier act of his brother's, a Declaration of Indulgence suspending all penalties against Catholics and Dissenters alike.

*Catholic
measures
of James*

James justified his action in these matters by the *dispensing power* inhering in the crown, which was supposed to confer the right to suspend
the execution of a law. Regardless of the general discontent, he published,
in 1688, a second and more sweeping Declaration of Indulgence which
he ordered to be read from all the Anglican pulpits. By this measure he
mortally offended the Anglican clergy, the main supporters of obedience
to the king's will and backbone of Tory opinion throughout the country.
An overwhelming majority of ministers refused to communicate the royal
order to their flocks, and seven bishops went the length of presenting a
written protest to the king. James's answer was an order that legal proceedings be taken against them. Immense excitement gathered around
the trial of the seven bishops, which occurred in June, 1688.

*James mor-
tally offends
the Anglican
church*

Meanwhile other irregularities and violences of the king had added to
his unpopularity. In the year of his accession, the Protestant duke of
Monmouth, an illegitimate son of Charles II, had invaded England with

a small force. He was defeated, captured, and executed. James might have been satisfied with this success. He preferred to institute a general persecution. He sent into the west, among the people who had supported Monmouth, the savage Judge Jeffreys for the purpose of ferreting out the adherents of his nephew. The mockery of justice engaged in by Jeffreys is known as "the Bloody Assizes." This ferocious official was not satisfied until he had executed three hundred and twenty victims, mostly poor peasants, and had transported eight hundred and forty unfortunates to the West Indies. The odium of these misdeeds fell, of course, upon the king.

Rebellion of Monmouth and "the Bloody Assizes," 1685

The distressing situation was for a time put up with by the people because the next heir to the throne, James's daughter Mary, who was a child of his first marriage and the wife of William of Orange, was a Protestant. The nation looked forward to her succession with the more pleasure as her husband, too, was, through his mother, of Stuart blood. When, however, James's second wife gave birth, in June, 1688, to a son, who by English law would take precedence over Mary, consternation seized the whole people. The son, it was foreseen, would be educated in the Catholic religion and thus the Catholic succession would be perpetuated. As the birth of the son and the trial of the seven bishops befell at the same time (June, 1688), England was filled with excitement from end to end. Forgetting their differences, a group of Whig and Tory leaders sent a secret letter inviting William of Orange and his wife Mary to come to England's rescue.

Birth of a Catholic successor, 1688

In November, 1688, William landed in England, and joyously and spontaneously the people of all classes rallied around him. When some of James's officers went over to the enemy and the whole army wavered in its allegiance, the wretched king could no longer close his eyes to the fact that he stood alone. Suddenly and utterly discouraged, he sent his wife and infant son to France and, shortly after, followed in person. History does not report a revolution which was more swift and bloodless.

The bloodless revolution of 1688

When parliament met, it was confronted by the difficult task of harvesting the fruits of the popular success. Declaring that the throne had become vacant through desertion, it offered the succession conjointly to William and Mary. By this act it committed itself to the view that the king did not rule by hereditary divine right but was the choice of people and parliament. Henceforth a king of England could boast no better claim to the crown than a statute of the realm.

Parliament regulates the succession

With the succession disposed of, the victorious parliament proceeded to complete the edifice of its power. Throughout the seventeenth century the conflict had raged between king and parliament over their respective spheres of control. The Petition of Right (1628) was the first act which had effectually clipped the wings of the monarchy. The Long Parliament

Review of
the long
controversy
between
king and
parliament was engaged in completing the work of royal subjection, when the civil war intervened and buried the issue beneath the din of arms. At length the flood of loyalty, once again set in motion by ten years of military rule, brought Charles II back to the throne without, however, restoring him to the ample prerogative of his grandfather, James I. The only means of tyranny left in his hands was the claim that, as a divinely appointed king, he was above the laws and could suspend their execution at his pleasure. While Charles II, a cautious man, had invoked this traditional right only occasionally, the infatuated James had erected on it a sweeping Catholic policy.

The Bill of
Rights, 1689 This last remaining loophole of arbitrary rule the parliament now proceeded to stop up by means of a Bill of Rights (1689). By this measure the royal dispensing power was declared abolished and the king was in every respect subjected to the law. Further, the Bill of Rights enumerated and condemned all the illegal acts of James II and formally excluded Roman Catholics from the throne. We may say summarily of this famous measure that it terminated the long constitutional struggle by giving the victory and the fruits thereof to the parliament. With the Bill of Rights England entered on a new era, the era of parliamentary government.

The Tolera-
tion Act,
1689 If the revolution of 1688 closed the long political conflict by seating the parliament in the place of power, it also led to a measure which pointed the way toward a solution of the religious troubles. Almost simultaneously with the Bill of Rights, parliament passed a Toleration Act conceding to the Dissenters the right of public worship. Though the intolerant legislation of Charles II's reign was not repealed, non-Anglican Protestants henceforth enjoyed at least *religious,* if not as yet *political* liberty. To the adherents of the pope, however, the current Anglican bigotry refused to make the slightest concession. Against them the penal laws continued in full force. Nonetheless, by mollifying the strong Puritan element of the population the Toleration Act distinctly promoted the religious pacification of the kingdom. Together with the Bill of Rights it defines the historical significance of what has ever since been called the "Glorious Revolution."

15 THE ASCENDANCY OF FRANCE UNDER LOUIS XIV

THE HOUSE OF BOURBON

Louis XIV (1643-1715), *m.* Maria Theresa, oldest daughter of Philip IV of Spain
|
Louis, the dauphin

Louis, duke of Burgundy

Louis XV (1715-1774)

Philip, duke of Anjou, who, as Philip V, became founder of the Spanish line of the house of Bourbon

THE WORK OF Richelieu cleared the way for the supremacy of France in Europe. By destroying the political privileges of the Huguenots, by reducing the power of the nobility, and by discontinuing the Estates General he had freed the royal authority from its last bondages and made it absolute. At the same time the great minister had engaged France in the Thirty Years' War and had reaped for her the benefits of the Peace of Westphalia (1648). At this point, just as France was about to assume a dominant position, she was threatened once more and, as it proved, for the last time under the old monarchy, by civil war. The work of Richelieu summed up

Richelieu's king, Louis XIII, died only a few months after him, in 1643, leaving behind a five-year-old son, in whose name the queen, Anne of Austria, assumed the regency. At the same time the post of leading minister, which had been occupied by Richelieu, fell to the confidant of the regent, another churchman and an Italian by birth, Cardinal Mazarin. Trained under the eyes of Richelieu, the new minister tried faithfully to carry out his predecessor's program. Although he won fresh and startling successes in the foreign field, he gained them by such reckless expenditures that the financial confusion, already grave under Richelieu, became intolerable. Regent Anne of Austria and Cardinal Mazarin

At last the parlement of Paris resolved to make itself the spokesman of the popular discontent by protesting against the excessive taxes imposed by the government in order to meet the cost of its participation in the Thirty Years' War. It will be remembered that it was an issue of taxation which led to the civil war in England, just then coming to a close with the complete defeat of the self-willed king. Doubtless the parlement was The parlement of Paris challenges the government on the issue of taxation encouraged to resist financial oppression by the English example. But it did not stop to reflect that it was not suited either in respect of its personnel or its functions to play a truly popular role; for the parlement was not only a supreme court, that is, a judicial body, but its officials were irremovable and hereditary, that is, they constituted a privileged, secondary nobility, officially called *noblesse de robe*.

In spite of these drawbacks, the parlement in January, 1648, boldly opened the struggle with the monarchy by demonstrating against a fresh series of tax edicts. Encouraged by the acclaim of the Parisians, the members thereupon took the further step of drawing up a sweeping reform program which aimed at nothing less than the conversion of France into a constitutional monarchy. To Regent Anne and her minister Mazarin this meant a revolution to which they would submit only under duress. In consequence a civil war resulted, known in French history as the Fronde.

Aim of the parlement is constitutional monarchy

The Fronde lasted five years (1648-1653) and ended in the complete triumph of Mazarin chiefly for two reasons. The first has already been indicated in the fact that the parlement, being neither a legislative nor a representative body, was not the natural rallying-point for the French people in a constitutional struggle. It never furnished more than a half-hearted leadership and in a surprisingly short time permitted the control of the movement to slip into the hands of the nobles.

Defeat of the Fronde, owing (1) to the parlement

Here lies the second and leading reason for Mazarin's success. For, since the turbulent nobility cared not a straw for either the people or constitutional government and fought only to recover its ancient power, the citizens, rather than see the return of feudal disorder, rallied once more around the throne. In short, if Mazarin came out on top, it was because, as soon as the revolution was deflected from its original purpose, the nation, left to choose between king and nobles, declared unequivocally for a single master.

Defeat of the Fronde, owing (2) to the nobles

The Fronde turned out to be the last rising of the nobles against the crown. Henceforth they accepted the loss of their power as a class with traditional political rights. However, they retained their landed estates and their immunity from direct taxation; and as further, certain important posts, such as the officer positions in the army, were reserved exclusively for them, they remained far and away the leading group of French society. They crowded to the court of the king, where they were transformed from rough feudal warriors into a soft, pleasure-loving, decorative aristocracy. But let there be no doubt regarding their continued influence. They had the ear of the king and by indirect, if no longer by direct, methods continued to play an important part in shaping French policy.

The nobles continue to play an important role after their defeat

The Fronde was only a few months old when Mazarin authorized the Peace of Westphalia (1648), which, by ending triumphantly the war with the Austrian branch of the house of Hapsburg, brought immense advantages to France. However, as the Spanish branch of the Hapsburgs was unwilling to accept Mazarin's terms, the war between France and Spain continued after, as before, 1648.

Owing to the embarrassments caused by the Fronde, the French were for a number of years obliged to stand on the defensive in their war with Spain. Under these circumstances the Spaniards regained much of the lost ground. But as soon as the Fronde was broken, the energetic cardinal pushed the fight with fresh vigor and soon forced his proud neighbors to come to terms.

Borne down by foreign wars and internal revolution, Spain was in fact at her last gasp. On signing (1659) with France the Peace of the Pyrenees, she signed away with it the last remnant of the supremacy which she had once exercised in Europe. France, the victor, took the place of Spain and signalized her triumph by acquiring a number of Spanish territories. These were Roussillon, lying on the north or French slope of the Pyrenees, and Artois, which gave the monarchy a more favorable boundary toward the Spanish Netherlands.

With the glory of the Peace of the Pyrenees still lingering in the skies of France, Mazarin's life turned to its setting (1661). The skillful Italian will always be remembered among the great ministers of his adopted country. On his disappearance from the scene the young king, Louis XIV, assumed the government in person. When he announced with quiet assurance that he would henceforth be his own prime minister, the courtiers could hardly conceal their smiles. However, he kept his word, and while he lived the government rested squarely on his shoulders.

Louis XIV is said to have boasted once: *l'état c'est moi* (I am the state). Even if he never employed this exact phrase, it expresses admirably the spirit of his reign, for he held himself to be the absolute head of the state, source of every authority exercised throughout the country. No wonder that even his ministers were in his view no better than clerks who met with him in various Councils to receive his orders. Of these Councils the most important was the Council of State. He chose the sun as his emblem, because he was pleased to imagine that, as the earth drew its sustenance from the central luminary, so the life of France emanated from his person. *Le roi-soleil* (sun-king) was the title given him by idolizing courtiers. Absolutism, that is, monarchy strengthened by the ruin of the feudal powers, had existed in France and Europe long before Louis XIV; so had the theory of divine right, which had been invoked by sovereigns as far back as the Middle Ages. Nevertheless, divine right acquired a new glamour when, as happened under Louis, the sovereign carried his absolutism to a completeness never before attained.

Significance
of Versailles,
the king's
official
residence
Louis spared no pains to minister to his own exaltation. It is here that Versailles comes in, the palace or rather the royal city which he built for himself fifteen miles to the southwest of Paris. By withdrawing to Versailles, he removed himself from contact with the common herd and lived, like a pagan divinity, amidst acolytes and worshipers. It is remarkable to what degree Versailles aroused the admiration of the world. That was not so much because of its, after all, gaudy and theatrical splendors as because, first, it symbolized the new absolutism, envy of all the other monarchical governments in the world, and second, because it served as his stage to a ruler who, to borrow the words of a contemporary, undoubtedly was "the greatest actor of majesty that ever filled a throne."

Louis
builds his
system on
Richelieu's
foundations
Important as the ceremonial element was in Louis's conception of his office, he was also possessed by a sense of duty, obliging him to attend strictly and regularly to business. To his unflinching acceptance of responsibility must be added, if we are to do him justice, a strong predilection for order and harmony in all the concerns of life. It was this particular inclination that enabled him to make important additions to the haphazard government edifice which had been put together during several previous generations. Administrative centralization had been effected, in principle, by the royal agents of Richelieu's invention, the intendants. The next step was to rearrange and energize the central departments destined to serve as the brains of the system.

The minis-
ters of state,
Lionne and
Louvois
Of incalculable value in this work were the devoted officials trained in the school of Richelieu and Mazarin. One of them, Lionne by name, was largely responsible for the effective organization of the foreign office with an unequaled staff of diplomats. Another was the tireless Louvois. Serving as minister of war, Louvois (d. 1691) created a standing army of 100,000 men, a figure far in excess of anything seen in Europe since the distant days of the Roman empire. By drilling and uniforming the soldiers and by creating a system of arsenals and depots of supplies under government management he raised the national preparedness far above that of his country's neighbors and rivals. Military historians are agreed that Louvois created the European standing army in its elaborate modern form.

Colbert,
minister of
finance
An even more important collaborator of the sovereign than Lionne and Louvois was the controller general (minister of finance), Jean Colbert (d. 1683). On being put, in 1661, at the head of the French treasury, Colbert found himself flung into an Augean stable choked with the accumulated refuse of the previous half century. He began by eliminating the prevailing graft and establishing a system of strict accounting. By these simple measures he succeeded, without the aid of new taxes, in freeing the government of its burden of debt and in actually accumulating a surplus. The minister might even have proceeded to a reduction

of taxation, if, after a few years of a welcome peace, the country had not been again plunged into war. War became the very breath of Louis's nostrils and long before his end threw the country back into the financial abyss from which Colbert had rescued it.

Much more than a capable minister of finance, Colbert was also an economic thinker and planner. With a science of political economy not yet in existence, Colbert took an important step toward its creation when he decided that the question of revenues was inseparably tied up with the whole problem of production. A properly inspired minister of finance, according to him, will always regard his leading function to be the increase of the national wealth. Colbert therefore undertook deliberately to foster agriculture, manufactures, and commerce. His system, often called Colbertism, except for the severer logic of its application, hardly differs from that of such a predecessor of his as Sully. Moreover, it is substantially identical with the policy, which, under the name of mercantilism, dominated all the European states in this and the following century. The economic policy of Colbert identifiable as mercantilism

It will serve our purpose to say of mercantilism at this point that it favored home industries by imposing a heavy tariff on imported manufactures and that it encouraged exports in the hope of creating a favorable balance of trade. It redounds to the credit of the mercantilist Colbert that he succeeded in stimulating the manufacture of certain articles suited to the French genius, such as silks, brocades, laces, furniture, and glass. Moreover, aware of the value for merchants and farmers of easy communications, he gave France an excellent system of roads and canals. Finally, he unfolded a considerable colonial activity in Canada, India, and the West Indies. True, his commercial companies (East India Company, West India Company), formed on the Dutch model, were not an unequivocal success; and even many of the manufactures which he called into existence by means of special privileges disappeared when France plunged deeper and deeper into war. But fair-minded critics will incline to ascribe these and other failures in the economic field less to Colbert and his system than to the unfortunate militarism of his lord and master, Louis. Appraisal of Colbert's economic achievements

While the king took pleasure in ample revenues and was of course by no means averse to bourgeois prosperity, he was, nonetheless, particularly eager for military fame, beside which every other kind of reputation seemed to him to be of little value. Though only twenty-two years old at Mazarin's death, he was already the cynosure of Europe. In simple truth he could regard himself as the leading power of the western world. It was therefore in no way unusual that, in measure as he found his neighbors to be no match for him, he began to be tempted by the thought of making himself their master. Accordingly, in 1667 he inaugurated a career of conquest, which we shall now undertake to follow, through Louis resolves on a career of conquest its showy rather than substantial successes, to its tragic and depressing close.

Four great wars largely filled the rest of Louis's life. They were:
Louis's wars
enumerated (1) a war with Spain for the possession of the Spanish Netherlands, commonly called the War of Devolution (1667-1668); (2) a war with the Dutch (1672-1678); (3) the War of the Palatinate or of the League of Augsburg (1688-1697); (4) the War of the Spanish Succession (1701-1714).

Louis
resolves
to expand
northward When Louis, in the year 1667, surveyed the political situation and, noting his own resources and the weakness of his neighbors, resolved on a career of conquest, he must have debated with himself where to deliver the first blow. He decided finally to extend French territory toward the north. Spain, intrenched in the Spanish Netherlands, seemed moribund. Besides, from a purely military viewpoint, France needed to be strengthened, most of all, on this side.

The Spanish
Netherlands
invaded In 1667 Louis suddenly invaded the Spanish Netherlands. The fact that he tried to justify his action by reference to the claims of his Spanish wife, daughter of Philip IV, to these territories, only added hypocrisy to violence. His magnificent army, brought to an unrivaled pitch of perfection by the labors of Louvois, seized without difficulty several border towns. Decadent Spain was unable to offer effective resistance. If the Dutch, frightened at the prospect of such a neighbor as Louis, had not bestirred themselves, Louis might have overrun the whole of the Spanish Netherlands.

Louis
checked by a
combination
of three
powers The Triple Alliance of the Dutch, England, and Sweden, formed by the rapid ingenuity of the republican patriot, John de Witt, at that moment the controlling member of the Dutch government, bade Louis halt. He was still at the beginning of his career and not yet stubbornly set on having his way regardless of consequences. In answer to the threat of the Triple Alliance, he declared himself satisfied with a frontier strip and abandoned the struggle. The Peace of Aix-la-Chapelle (Aachen) formally secured him in his bold acquisition (1668).

Louis
isolates the
Dutch and
then falls
upon them,
1672 For the next few years Louis seemed to be dominated by a single thought—revenge on the Dutch. The Dutch had been the soul of the Triple Alliance; the Dutch were the leading obstacle to his northeastward expansion. According to his plan the Dutch were to be cut off from all their friends and allies and then be attacked unawares. The preparatory diplomatic campaign was a masterpiece. Sweden and the emperor were lulled into security by special treaties; Charles II of England was by a generous bribe even persuaded to become Louis's ally (Secret Treaty of Dover, 1670). In the spring of 1672 everything was ready. While the combined French and English fleets engaged the Dutch fleet in the channel, the French army, led by the famous generals, Condé and Turenne, in-

NORTH SEA

Hamburg

ENGLAND

London
Thames R.

Amsterdam
Ryswick • Utrecht
Nimwegen

Calais
ARTOIS
1659

FLANDERS
SPANISH NETHERLANDS

Aix-la-Chapelle

English Channel

La Hogue

Rouen

Rocroi

Rheims
1648

Verdun
1648

Metz
1648

LORRAINE 1766

Blenheim

GERMANY

Rhine R.

Strassburg
1648

Danube R.

Versailles • Paris

Orleans

Seine R.

ALSACE
1648

FRANCHE
COMTE
1678

SWISS CONFEDERATION

Nantes

Loire R.

F R A N C E

La Rochelle

Saône R.

Lyons

SAVOY

MILAN

PIEDMONT

TYROL

VENICE

ATLANTIC OCEAN

Bordeaux

Dordogne R.

Garonne R.

Rhône R.

ORANGE
Avignon

GENOA

Pyrenees

Marseilles

ROUSSILLON
1659

SPAIN

MEDITERRANEAN

SEA

CORSICA
1768

SARDINIA

ACQUISITIONS OF
LOUIS XIV and LOUIS XV

Acquisitions of Louis XIV
Acquisitions of Louis XV

SCALE OF MILES
0   50   100   150   200

vaded the territory of the Seven United Provinces by following the course of the lower Rhine.

**Reinstate-
ment of the
house of
Orange**

In a few weeks most of the provinces, owing to the decay into which the too secure de Witt had permitted the army and fortresses to fall, were in the hands of the French. At this crisis, one of those savage panics, to which men are but too unfortunately prone, took possession of the Dutch people. A frenzied mob fell upon and murdered de Witt, and would be satisfied with nothing less than the triumphant reinstatement of the house of Orange, which, some twenty years before, in the eternal seesaw between the Orange and the burgher parties, had been excluded from the public service. In an outburst of enthusiasm William III of Orange was re-established as stadholder and made supreme commander on sea and land.

**Character of
William III
of Orange**

William III, hardly twenty-one years of age, was a man of no more than average endowment. But he was sprung from heroic stock, and the responsibility for a nation's safekeeping, laid on him in a stern crisis, brought out his best qualities. The English ambassador invited him to. look about him and submit, urging that it was easy to see that the Dutch were lost. "I know one means of never seeing it," he replied. "To die on the last dyke." It was this spirit that now steeled the temper of the little people and enabled them to emulate the deeds of their ancestors against Spain.

**The Dutch
war becomes
general;
England
abandons
her French
ally, 1674**

Before Louis could possess himself of the heart of the Netherlands, the city of Amsterdam, the Dutch had, at the order of William, cut the dykes and restored their country to the original dominion of the waters. Louis was obliged to retreat; his opportunity was lost. Moreover, the fear of France had by now become general and, before many months had passed, Spain, as well as the emperor and a large number of German princes, had rallied to the cause of the Dutch. In the year 1674 the position of Louis was still further weakened. In that year the angry state of English feeling forced Charles II to abandon Louis and to make peace with the Dutch.

**The Treaty
of Nim-
wegen, 1678**

In this manner the isolated Louis found himself obliged to face a great continental coalition. Although the superiority of the French army both in organization and leadership enabled him to win every pitched battle with his foes, he was glad enough to end the war when peace was offered. By the Treaty of Nimwegen (1678) he had to acknowledge his failure in his main purpose, for the Dutch did not lose a foot of territory. However, he was permitted, in recognition of his military successes, to incorporate with France the Franche Comté (Free County of Burgundy), a detached eastern possession of the king of Spain.

The second war, too, although it had roused an European alliance against Louis, had brought him the prize of a new province. Louis was now at the height of his glory. The adulation of his court became more and more slavish, until the flattered monarch imagined he was no longer bound by ordinary human restraints. Bent on continuing his aggressions, even though peace now reigned, he submitted the interpretation of the Treaty of Westphalia, an international instrument, to a national, that is, to a French law court; and on the strength of a one-sided verdict he occupied a number of districts of the German border with an armed force. His most considerable acquisition made in this breathing-spell between two wars was the Alsatian city of Strasburg. Seized (1681) in open disregard of the public law of Europe, it was promptly incorporated in France.

Louis seizes German border districts, including the city of Strasburg, 1681

The same highhanded treatment was accorded to a group of his own subjects, the Huguenots. Since the suppression of their political privileges by Richelieu they had proved themselves faithful subjects of their king, content with the civil and religious liberties guaranteed them by the Edict of Nantes. However, the Catholic hierarchy had never ceased to protest against the presence of a tolerated heretical minority among the orthodox majority of the subjects of the king. Unable to bring such prudent statesmen as Richelieu and Mazarin to their point of view, they achieved a better success from the moment they began to deal with Louis.

Continued protest of the Catholic clergy against the toleration of the Huguenots

Even Louis hesitated at first to take vigorous measures against the Huguenots. However, surrounded by Catholic zealots and under the influence of Jesuit confessors, he adopted gradually a policy of petty annoyances expressive of his aversion for the dissident minority. The next, more serious step was a succession of encroachments which deprived the Huguenots of their printing-presses, schools, and temples. When, finally, the king authorized the seizure of their children in order to hand them over for training to Catholic priests and teachers, the royal protection guaranteed by treaty had become a mockery.

Gradual resumption of persecution

By the early eighties it remained only to apply the last indignity in the form of a forceful conversion of those who still clung to their faith. Rude soldiers were quartered in the homes of Huguenots until their occupants murmured their willingness to be confessed by a priest. When, in 1685, his councilors reported to Louis that all or nearly all the Huguenots had returned to mother church, Louis revoked the Edict of Nantes on the ground that it no longer served any useful purpose. By a unique mixture of hypocrisy and violence approximately one million people had been deprived of their religious rights, and, insofar as they did not succeed in winning security for their persons and property by accepting Catholicism, had become outlaws.

Revocation of the Edict of Nantes, 1685

The responsibility for the suppression of the Huguenots rests squarely on the shoulders of Louis and the Catholic clergy of France. The outraged Protestants, however, were inclined to throw most of the blame on

Madame de Maintenon. A highly gifted woman brought up as a Hugue-
Madame de Maintenon and her influence on Louis not, she had become a convert to Catholicism and, like many another convert, distinguished herself by a passionate devotion to the church. She
came into contact with Louis by her appointment as governess of the
royal children and by the natural ascendancy of her character gained a
remarkable influence over him. When his first wife, Maria Theresa, a
Spanish princess, died, he married Madame de Maintenon (1683) and at
the same time gave up his loose and libertine habits in favor of her
severe and impeccable moral code.

The woman who could work this miracle with an habitual rake was
Her share in Huguenot persecution unimportant naturally credited with an inordinate influence over his policy. The suspicions of the Huguenots, already ill-disposed to her as a renegade from
their faith, are therefore comprehensible. However, when we remember
that the policy of persecution considerably antedates Madame de Maintenon's ascendancy, we are obliged to declare that her share in the
Huguenot tragedy has been exaggerated. She figures in it with certainty
only in the last act.

The tragedy of the Huguenots brought loss and sorrow not only to the
The Huguenots strengthen the enemies of France immediate victims. The heaviest loser was France itself, for several hundred thousand active and resolute people, chiefly of the artisan class,
escaped across the border and carried their industry, their culture, and,
above all, their unflinching spirit to the neighbors and enemies of France.
Many settled among the Dutch, the English, and the Germans; not a
few sought refuge in the English colonies of North America.

The seizure of Strasburg and the Revocation of the Edict of Nantes
William of Orange organizes an anti-French coalition befell in a period of nominal peace. They spread such a feeling of insecurity among the neighbors of France that William of Orange resolved
to prepare for the worst by a new coalition. By 1686 he had persuaded
Spain, the emperor (Austria), and a large number of German states to
join him in a league of mutual protection.

The war between Louis and this new combination had already become
England joins the coalition against Louis inevitable, when a turn of the wheel of fortune brought England into
the fold of the allies. In 1688, James II, who, like his brother, Charles II,
cultivated friendly relations with France, was overthrown by the "Glorious Revolution" and William of Orange became king of England. As
the temper of the English people had at the same time become thoroughly anti-French, William found no difficulty in persuading them to
join Europe against the French monarch. Thus in the new war—called
the War of the Palatinate from the double fact that with his usual boldness Louis put forth an unfounded claim to the Palatinate and that the
war began with a terrible harrying by fire and sword on the part of
the French of that Rhenish land—Louis was absolutely without a friend.

This third war (1688-1697) is, for the general student, thoroughly un-memorable. Battles were fought on land and on sea, and, generally speaking, the French proved their old superiority at least on land. However, they were no longer strong enough to reap any benefit from their successes. In 1697 all the combatants from mere exhaustion were glad to sign, on the basis of mutual restitutions, the Peace of Ryswick.

The War of the Palatinate was the first war by which Louis had gained nothing. That and the circumstance that England had now definitely joined the ranks of his enemies should have served him as a warning that the tide had turned. And indeed he must have felt less secure than had once been the case, since he gave a most anxious consideration to the problem of the Spanish succession just then looming over the horizon. The king of Spain, Charles II, had no direct heir. At his death, which might occur at any time, the vast Spanish dominion—Spain and her colonies, Naples and Milan, the Spanish Netherlands—would fall no one was sure to whom. The younger or Austrian branch of the house of Hapsburg naturally put forth a claim; but Louis believed that his descendants had a still better title in right of his first wife, who was the oldest sister of the Spanish king. The issue was so involved on account of a long succession of treaties and renunciations that even at this day no scholar would venture authoritatively to declare who, in a strictly legal sense, was the heir of Charles II.

Old enough to have grown cautious, Louis approached his chief adversary, William of Orange, as soon as the Peace of Ryswick had been signed, with the very sensible proposal to come to some arrangement with him over the Spanish inheritance by which war might be averted. Accordingly, the two leading sovereigns of Europe pledged themselves to a plan of partition as the most plausible settlement of the threatening difficulties. When, however, on the death of Charles II, November, 1700, it was found that the Spanish king had made a will in favor of Philip, duke of Anjou, one of Louis's younger grandsons, Louis, intoxicated by the prospect, forgot his obligations and threw the Partition Treaty to the winds. He sent young Philip to Madrid to assume the rule of the undivided dominion of Spain. The house of Bourbon now ruled the whole European west. "The Pyrenees have ceased to exist," were, if we may believe the historian Voltaire, the exultant words with which Louis announced his resolution to his court.

It was some time before Europe recovered from the shock of its surprise over this bold step and nerved itself to resistance. The hoodwinked and angered William was indefatigable in arousing his own two peoples, the Dutch and English. By 1702 he had succeeded in creating the Grand Alliance, the reconstituted coalition of the previous war. Before the conflict had fairly begun, however, William, the stubborn, lifelong enemy of Louis, had died by a fall from his horse (March, 1702). In the new and supreme struggle against the ambition of Louis, a struggle familiar under the name of the War of the Spanish Succession (1702-1714), it is not purely fanciful to imagine his indomitable spirit marching with and heartening the hosts of the allies.

War of the Spanish Succession: the combatants compared

In the new war the position of Louis was much more favorable than it had been in the preceding struggle. He commanded the resources not only of France but also of Spain; his soldiers carried themselves with the assurance of troops which had never been beaten; and his program, both military and civil, sprang from his single initiative. The allies, on the other hand, were necessarily divided in council and interest. What advantages they had lay in these two circumstances, which in the end proved decisive: they possessed greater resources of money and men and they developed superior commanders. The brilliant generals of Louis's youth, men like Condé and Turenne, had long since died, and their successors, with the exception of Vauban, the inventor of modern military engineering, and the intrepid Villars, were all, like Louis himself, without a spark of fire and originality. In the highest commands, where France was weak, England and Austria, on the other hand, proved themselves particularly strong. Each developed, England in the duke of Marlborough, Austria in Eugene, prince of Savoy, an inspired leader and strategist.

The War of the Spanish Succession a world struggle

Not even the Thirty Years' War had assumed such proportions as did the struggle in which Europe now engaged. It was literally universal and raged, at one and the same time, at all the exposed points of the French-Spanish possessions, that is, in the Spanish Netherlands, along the upper Rhine, in Italy, in Spain itself (where the Hapsburg claimant, the Archduke Charles, strove to drive out the Bourbon king, Philip V), on the sea, and in the colonies of North America. The details of this gigantic struggle have no place here. We must content ourselves with noting a few striking military actions and the final settlement.

Blenheim (1704), the turning of the tide

For the first few years the French showed their strength by maintaining an offensive, which aimed at nothing less than the termination of the war by the capture of the Austrian capital, Vienna. In 1704 this overdaring plan led to a great catastrophe. Securely planted on the upper Danube, the French were proceeding eastward when to their great surprise they were confronted with the combined armies of Marlborough and Eugene. Against all expectations the two audacious generals had brought their forces, one from the lower Rhine, the other from Italy, to throw a barrier across the French advance. In the resulting battle of Blenheim the two commanders administered a crushing defeat to France. Not only did it put an end to the long chain of French victories but it demoralized both army and government.

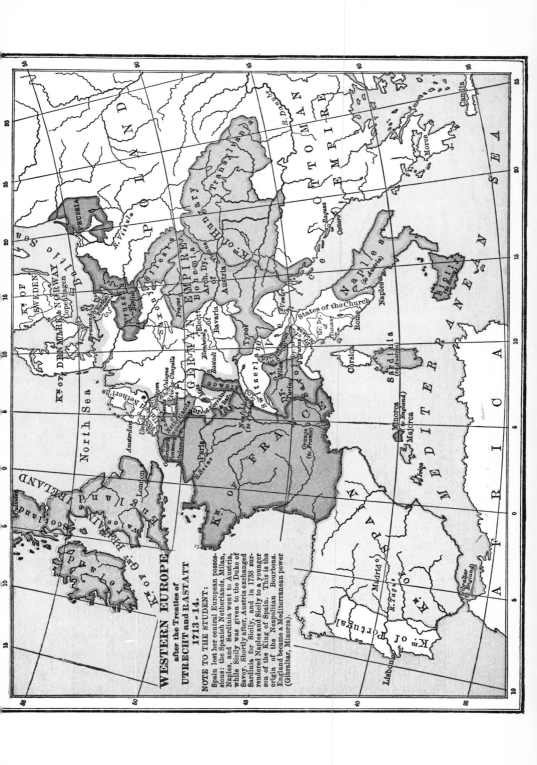

WESTERN EUROPE
after the Treaties of
UTRECHT and RASTATT
1713-14.

NOTE TO THE STUDENT:

Spain lost her central European possessions: the Spanish Netherlands, Milan,
Naples, and Sardinia went to Austria,
while Sicily was given to the Duke of
Savoy. Shortly after, Austria exchanged
Sardinia for Sicily, and in 1788 surrendered Naples and Sicily to a younger
son of the King of Spain. This is the
origin of the Neapolitan Bourbons.
England became a Mediterranean power
(Gibraltar, Minorca).

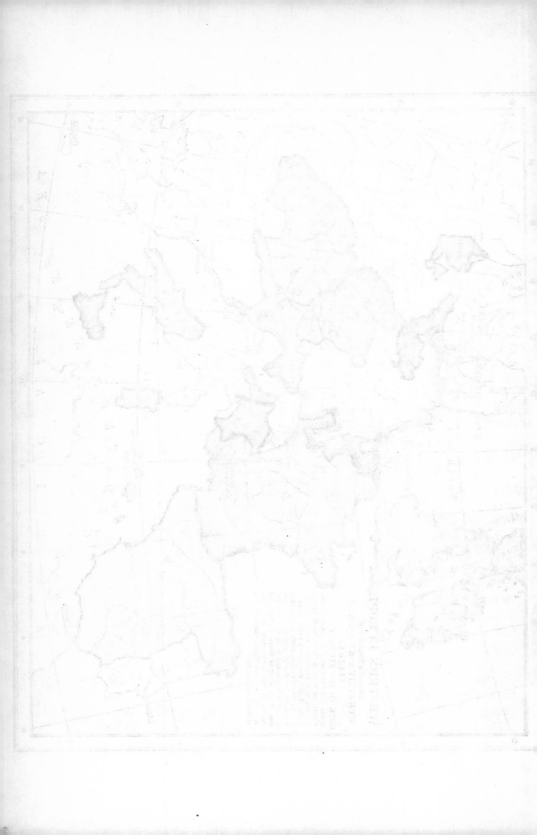

Following up their success at Blenheim, the allies scored triumph on triumph. In 1706 Marlborough won a splendid victory at Ramillies, in the Netherlands, and in the same year Eugene defeated the French at Turin and drove them completely out of Italy. The victories of Oudenarde and Malplaquet, won in 1708 and 1709 respectively, seemed to complete the discomfiture of France, for they exhausted the country and cleared the road to Paris.

The road was never taken, for a number of unexpected happenings completely changed the general European situation. In 1710 the Whig ministry, which had supported Marlborough and advocated the war, was shaken by certain English domestic developments. Gradually Tory ministers, strongly in favor of peace, displaced their Whig rivals. On Marlborough's no longer receiving adequate support from home his activity in the field was paralyzed. In 1711 the English cabinet, now wholly Tory, opened secret negotiations with Louis. No sooner had this step been taken than an event at Vienna put an end to what little harmony still existed among Louis's enemies.

In April, 1711, the head of the Austrian branch of the house of Hapsburg, Emperor Joseph I, died. In default of a direct male heir, he was succeeded by his brother, Charles VI. As Charles was also the candidate of the Grand Alliance for the Spanish throne, his accession to the crown of Austria held out the prospect of the reunion of the vast Hapsburg dominions in one hand, as in the time of Charles V. As such a development did not accord with the interests of the two sea-powers, England and the Dutch, they were moved—and we have seen that England at least needed no spurring—to come to an agreement with the French behind the back of Austria. The exhausted Louis eagerly seized the hand unexpectedly held out to him. In 1713 the Peace of Utrecht ended the War of the Spanish Succession.

In the Peace of Utrecht it was agreed that the vast Spanish empire was not to be kept intact. The most important part of the settlement was the disposition made of Spain itself. Louis's grandson was recognized as king of Spain together with Spain's transoceanic colonies under the title, Philip V. While it was stipulated that the crowns of France and Spain should never rest on the same head, there was no denying that a Bourbon now sat on the Spanish throne and that in the main Louis's policy had triumphed.

Of course the Hapsburg claimant could not be overlooked. To Emperor Charles VI was given the bulk of the Italian possessions of Spain (Milan, Naples, Sardinia), together with the Spanish Netherlands (henceforth Austrian Netherlands).

The Dutch claimed and received a string of border fortresses, which they were authorized to convert into a military barrier against France.

England acquired a clear title to certain contested possessions in the New

Gains of the
Dutch and
of England
at Utrecht
World, Newfoundland, Nova Scotia (Acadia), and Hudson Bay. It also acquired two Spanish strongholds, the island of Minorca and the rock of Gibraltar. These two Spanish prizes made England the gatekeeper of the western entrance to the Mediterranean sea.

Emperor Charles VI refused at first to accept the Peace of Utrecht, in

Delayed rec-
ognition of
Utrecht by
the emperor
the making of which he had not had a hand. He resolved to continue the war, but, deserted by his allies, he was no match for Louis. In 1714 he was obliged to give way and in a separate document, signed at Rastatt, to confirm the Treaty of Utrecht.

Not long after the Treaties of Utrecht and Rastatt, Louis XIV died

Louis's
death, 1715
(September 1, 1715). The material prosperity of his early years had vanished and in its place his failing eyes rested upon a famished peasantry, an impoverished middle class, and a government breaking down under its burden of debt. The disastrous end was the answer of fate to an excessive ambition. When his little five-year-old successor, his great-grandson, was brought to his bedside, the dying man said to him with great seriousness: "Do not imitate me in my taste for war."

The political and military predominance of Louis XIV in his time is

The Age of
Louis XIV a
period of
general
French
ascendancy
only a part of the extraordinary influence that radiated from him over Europe. He overshadowed everybody and everything so impressively that the whole period may very properly be called the Age of Louis XIV. His absolutism, his magnificent palace at Versailles, his royal bearing, the manners and fashions of his courtiers became an object of slavish imitation throughout Europe and contributed almost as much as the French victories in the field to the contemporary ascendancy of France.

The contribution to this ascendancy of the French people themselves

The bril-
liance of the
Fine Arts
under Louis
must under no circumstances be overlooked. When all is said, it was, after all, their achievements and not the military triumphs of the monarch which have survived and continue to this day to count in the cultural life of Europe. A spurt of national energy, which had manifested itself with the first flush of the Renaissance in the sixteenth century, came to its natural flowering in the reign of Louis. Richly creative, it took possession of every art. Architecture, sculpture, painting, and music were alike fructified and reached a high level of excellence. They owed much in each instance to the inspiration of Italy but were in the end regularly given the peculiar imprint of the national genius. Speaking summarily, we may say that the Fine Arts of Louis's age breathe a spirit somewhat too grandiose, ornate, and overwhelming for the simpler taste of the present generation. That does not alter the fact that the French creations in each of these arts were in Louis's day greatly admired and widely copied throughout Europe.

It is generally agreed that the French genius touched its highest level in the related realms of language and literature. Such lucidity, elegance, and nervous strength were given to the French language in the course of the seventeenth century by the labors of scores of inspired masters that it gained an ascendancy, as a tool of expression, over all the other languages of Europe. Of course the ascendancy was aided by the political prestige of Louis, by the social prestige of his court, and by the artistic prestige of the architects, sculptors, and painters who co-operated to produce the wonders of Versailles. In consequence French now began to replace Latin as the language of diplomacy. It gained an even wider empire when it was adopted as the speech of polite society through the length and breadth of Europe.

Perfection and diffusion of the French language

Doubtless the most important single factor in diffusing the French language was, however, the rich new literature in both prose and poetry to which the French people gave birth. Among the masterpieces in prose are the works of the mathematician, Pascal (d. 1662), above all, his *Provincial Letters,* an attack in the grand manner on the Jesuits; the *Fables* of La Fontaine (d. 1695), who followed in the footsteps of the ancient Aesop; and the sermons and histories of the eloquent Bishop Bossuet (d. 1704).

High quality of French prose

However, the literary expression of the period touched its peak in the poetic drama. While French drama saw the light before Louis's time, in the period of Richelieu, through the work of Corneille (*Le Cid,* 1636), it did not achieve maturity till Racine (d. 1699) produced his severe and lofty tragedies (*Phèdre*) and Molière (d. 1673) his vivacious comedies (*Le Malade Imaginaire, Tartuffe*) with their penetrating exposure of human pretentiousness and sham.

The theater of Racine and Molièr

16 BALTIC AFFAIRS: THE RISE OF RUSSIA AND THE DECLINE OF SWEDEN

THE RISE OF RUSSIA

THE HOUSE OF ROMANOV

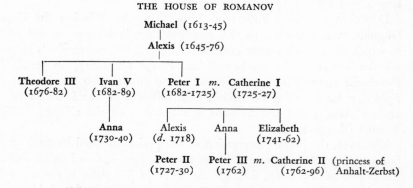

Michael (1613-45)
|
Alexis (1645-76)

Theodore III (1676-82)   Ivan V (1682-89)   Peter I *m.* Catherine I (1682-1725) (1725-27)

Anna (1730-40)   Alexis (*d.* 1718)   Anna   Elizabeth (1741-62)

Peter II (1727-30)   Peter III *m.* Catherine II (princess of (1762) (1762-96) Anhalt-Zerbst)

Russia outside the range of Western civilization   IT WAS NOT till the sixteenth century that Russia swung decisively into the ken of Europe. During the Middle Ages the Russian people, who constitute the easternmost branch of the Slavs, spread slowly over the great east-European plain. Throughout that time they remained steadily outside the pale of west-European civilization.

Major influences in early Russian history: (1) conquest by Northmen; (2) adoption of Christianity   In this early period of their history they experienced successively three influences from without of enduring significance. In the ninth century they were conquered by a band of Germanic Northmen under a leader, Rurik by name, who gave them a military organization and a taste for conquest. Predatory expeditions under Rurik's successors brought them into contact with the Byzantine empire which, putting the same spell on them as the Roman empire of the west had put on the barbarous German tribes, persuaded them (in the tenth century) to give up paganism and adopt the Christian religion of the eastern or Greek Orthodox type.

(3) Conquest by Asiatic Tartars   While they were digesting this Mediterranean influence and slowly raising themselves from barbarism, they were (in the thirteenth century) overrun by a wild Asiatic people, the Tartars, and subjected to a crushing servitude. The military spirit of the Northmen, the cultural effects of Greek Christianity, and the harsh rule imposed by Mongolian Tartars constitute the main ingredients from which was brewed the early Russian destiny.

After two hundred years of Tartar subjection, that is, toward the middle of the fifteenth century, there occurred a national revival championed by a Russian chieftain of the Moscow era. The Tartar yoke was gradually shaken off and the prince of Muscovy, as leader of the movement, was enabled to adopt a title indicative of complete liberation: he called himself tsar of Russia.[1]

Liberation under the prince of Muscovy

Although the first tsars present themselves to view as autocratic rulers of an Asiatic order, they were not so irresponsible that they were not obliged to reckon with two rival agencies. One of these was the body of nobles (boyars), who fed upon a tradition of military prowess, the other was the clergy of the Russian Orthodox church, which possessed an almost magical influence over a downtrodden and superstitious peasantry.

The tsar, the nobles, the clergy

Toward the close of the sixteenth century the extinction of the first dynasty led to civil disturbances which, taken advantage of by the neighboring Slav kingdom of Poland, almost brought about the renewed ruin of the barely resuscitated state. From this evil epoch, known in Russian history as "the Time of Troubles," the country was saved by a popular assembly which, prompted by the instinct of self-preservation, conferred (1613) the crown on a leading boyar, Michael Romanov. Michael was the first ruler of the dynasty which maintained an uninterrupted ascendancy in Russia for three hundred years.

Accession of the Romanov dynasty, 1613

The most pressing business of the new dynasty was to drive back the western invaders, the Poles, who had attempted to extend their rule all the way to Moscow. Between Russia and Poland, both of them countries of the vast east-European plain, was interposed the flat expanse of the Ukraine, held by loosely organized bands of warlike Cossacks. Hardfighting frontiersmen though they were, the Cossacks, who were squeezed between two great states and were protected by no natural barriers, were not strong enough to preserve the independence which was their goal. In 1667 the Tsar Alexis, the second ruler of the Romanov line, had become strong enough to oblige Poland to accept a division of the Ukraine, by which the Russian boundary was pushed westward to the left bank of the river Dnieper. The treaty was an indication that Polish eastward expansion had come to an end and that it was to be replaced by the westward expansion of Russia.

The Ukraine; the westward movement of Russia begins, 1667

Even more important than the partial conquest of the Ukraine was the fact that Tsar Alexis glimpsed the idea that the time had come to put an end to the intellectual stagnation of Russia by multiplying its contacts with Europe. Unable, however, to break away from the tradition enthralling him and his people, he stood irresolutely in his tracks, looking at Europe, as it were, across an impassable stream. It was his son Peter who built the first bridge between Russia and the occident.

Tsar Alexis looks toward Europe

[1] The origin of the word tsar is in dispute. It may be derived from **Caesar**.

Tsar Peter is that rare and stirring combination, autocrat and revolutionary in one. Together with an older brother, Ivan, he was proclaimed tsar in 1682. As the two lads were too young to rule, a regency was established under an older sister, Sophia. Peter, a wide-awake and masterful youth, accepted this situation until 1689, when, having reached the age of seventeen, he took the government into his own hands and relegated Sophia to a nunnery. As the co-tsar, Ivan, was a feeble, half-witted creature, he did not, during the few years he continued to live, interfere with Peter's exclusive control.

In order to grasp Peter's epochal activity it is necessary to have in mind the chief factors of the situation. At the young tsar's accession the Russians were still essentially an Asiatic people, connected with Europe solely by the two bonds of race and faith: they were Slavs and Christians. Their state was of vast extent, comprising the great plain lying between the White sea in the north and the Caspian sea in the south and extending across the Ural mountains into northern Asia. In fact by a spontaneous eastward movement of the Russian peasantry, comparable to the westward movement of the American pioneers in the nineteenth century, Russia in the person of the tsar had already by Peter's accession established a loose control over the thinly populated mass of sub-Arctic Siberia.

In the opposite direction, however, toward the west, Russian action had been hampered, as we have seen, by rival Poland. Nor was that all. Sweden blocked Russian access to the Baltic sea; and the vast Mohammedan state, the Ottoman empire, either owned or controlled all the land surrounding the Black sea. Enormous as Russia was, embracing an area greater than that of all the west-European states put together, it suffered from being a land-locked empire without an approach, except by the usually ice-bound White sea, to the oceans which are the open highways of the world.

It was this distinctly inland character of Russia which is the explanation of its long delay in establishing contact with European civilization. The country's prolonged isolation accounts also for the existence of a government so peculiar and indigenous that, although of the absolute type, it was looked upon by European visitors as having little or no resemblance to the absolute governments with which they were familiar. A curious mixture of Byzantine autocrat and Mongolian khan, the tsar was the product of a tradition very different from that which had produced Louis XIV of France.

Nevertheless, if an Asiatic as distinct from an European despot, the tsar was not without checks upon his power. The assembly of the boyars still counted for something; the patriarch, head of the Russian church, exercised the authority emanating from a numerous and richly endowed

Margin notes:

Accession of Tsar Peter, 1689

Russia already a vast state at Peter's accession

Russia shut off from the Baltic and Black seas

Russia an absolutism of a peculiar type

clergy; and the *Streltsi*, a sort of national militia, had acquired a great, if indeterminate, power because, in addition to being the main organized force of the state, they had been endowed with a number of special privileges. Existent checks on the tsar's power

From the very outset of his rule Tsar Peter set himself, in the main, three aims and clung to them to the end of his life with an incomparable tenacity: (1) He resolved to clear the path for European influences and not to rest until he had brought his country within the circle of Western civilization. (2) He planned to open a direct road to the west by gaining a foothold on the Baltic and Black seas. (3) He determined to rid himself of the restraints put upon him by boyars, patriarch, and Streltsi, not so much because they seriously hampered his action as because they were the symbols of a hateful past, which he was minded to obliterate. Peter's three aims

Peter is a difficult person for a modern man to understand. At one time he seems to be no better than a common murderer; again he strikes us as an inhuman monster in the grip of revolting violences and sensualities; on a third occasion we are prepared to hail him as one of nature's noblemen. Thus strangely compounded, his life was full of the most dramatic contradictions. With barbarian eagerness he appropriated every western institution and invention that appealed to his understanding, surrendering himself completely to their sway. Certainly his distinguishing characteristic was an indomitable energy: his life burned at a white heat. The character of Peter

Peter's first chance to initiate his foreign program came in the year 1695. The Emperor Leopold was at that time waging war against the Turks, who were manifesting unmistakable symptoms of their approaching collapse. Peter at once recognized that the embarrassment of the Mohammedans was his chance to establish himself on the Black sea. In 1696 he conquered the port of Azov. The future now opened more confidently to him and, as a preliminary to further measures, he determined to visit the west and study the wonders of its civilization with his own eyes. Peter's first conquest, Azov, 1696

Peter spent the year 1697-1698 in travel through Germany, Holland, and England. The journey, undertaken with a large suite of his semi-Asiatic countrymen, was purely a voyage of instruction. Throughout its course Peter was indefatigable in his efforts to get at the bottom of things, at western administrative methods, at the sources of western wealth, at the systems of western trade and manufacture. "My part to learn," is the motto encircling the seal which he had struck for this voyage. In Holland he hired out for a time as a common ship-carpenter, ships having been a passion with him from his boyhood. In addition, he attended surgical lectures, visited paper mills, flour mills, printing presses, in short, was untiring in his efforts to assimilate, if not the underlying principles, at least the more obvious features of Western civilization. The uncouth Peter, a Peter's journey of instruction to Europe giant towering to the height of six feet and six inches, was the joke of the day among the courtiers and dandies, but intelligent observers paid a ready respect to the tireless worker, who balked at no drudgery to fit himself for the task of drawing his backward people into the European family.

Revolt of the Streltsi

The tsar had reached Vienna on his return trip when he heard that the Streltsi had revolted. He set out posthaste for home; and although order had been restored before he reached Moscow, he took a fearful vengeance. Over a thousand of the luckless guards were executed with unimaginable tortures. In his savage fury Peter, splashed with blood, presided in person at the butchery. Sovereign and executioner—such a combination of offices in one hand clearly exhibits the chasm that then yawned between Europe and Russia. However, there was method in Peter's madness. The Streltsi, a privileged national militia, were the spokesmen of the discontent aroused in Russia by the policy of Europeanization, and Peter felt that in striking at them he dealt a blow to the forces of conservatism.

Peter creates an army

The Streltsi were completely disbanded. In their place the tsar created an army on the European pattern, which before the close of his reign had become an efficient instrument of war. As the assembly of the boyars was, like the Streltsi, a center of narrow Russian nationalism, he rid himself of its influence by the simple device of not calling it together.

Peter's reforms

With the opposition trampled in the dust, Peter's reforms crowded thick and fast. Every barrier was leveled to facilitate the invasion of western influences. He invited western peasants, mechanics, and shipwrights to settle in Russia. He introduced western dress by making it obligatory for the court. He discouraged the wearing of beards, an ancient, almost a religious practice of his people. Armed with a pair of shears, occasionally with his own imperial hand he would practice the barber's art on his recalcitrant subjects.

Peter becomes head of the Russian church

By such measures Peter clashed with many cherished habits, and the clergy, the most powerful of the associations representative of the national tradition, became increasingly suspicious of his policy. As their discontent was a danger to the throne and a hindrance to reform, the tsar resolved to bring them into dependence on himself. When the patriarch died in 1700, Peter committed his functions to a Holy Synod of his own appointment. In this way he became the head of the church as he already was the head of the state.

The inevitable clash with Sweden

Following his return from the west, Peter was more desirous than ever of gaining an outlet on the Baltic. Azov, on the Black sea, was worth little to him as long as the Turks held the Dardanelles, the bottle-neck opening to the Mediterranean. Peter's paradise, the west, it was clear, could be reached more conveniently by the northern route. But the enter-

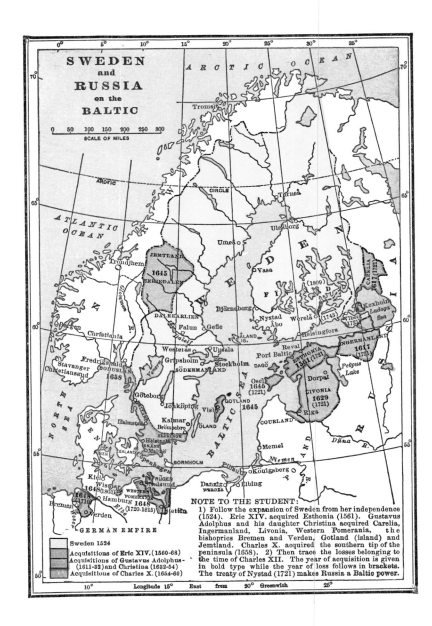

SWEDEN
and
RUSSIA
on the
BALTIC

0 50 100 150 200 250 300
SCALE OF MILES

ARCTIC OCEAN

Tromsö

ARCTIC CIRCLE

ATLANTIC OCEAN

Torneå

Troudjhem

JEMTLAND
1645
HERJEDALEN

Umeå

Vasa

Uleåborg

(1809)

CARELIA 1617 (1721)

DALEKARLIEN

Björneborg

Nystad Werelä (1743)

Kexholm

Ladoga Sea

Wiborg 1721

Falun Gefle

Åbo

Helsingfors

Christiania

ÅLAND IS.

Westerås Upsala

Reval

Port Baltic

INGERMANLAND

1617 (1721)

Fredrikshald
Stavanger BOHUSLÄN
Christiansand **1658**

Gripsholm
SÖDERMANLAND Stockholm

DAGÖ

ESTHONIA
1561 (1721)

Peipus Lake

Göteborg

Osel
1645
(1721)

Dorpat

Jönköping Visby

GOTLAND **1645**

LIVONIA
1629
(1721)

Kalmar
Halmstad Brömsebro ÖLAND
BLEKINGE
SKÅNE

COURLAND

Riga

Helsingborg
Malmö

Memel

Düna R.

VEN ZEALAND

Copenhagen

BORNHOLM

Niemen R.

Kiel
Wismar
1648(1803) WESTERN POMERANIA
1648
(1719)
Hamburg **1648**
(1720-1815)

STRALSUND
RÜGEN
WERDEN

Pillau Königsberg

Danzig Elbing

Bremen Verden

Stettin

Elbe

Weser

GERMAN EMPIRE

Longitude 15° East from 20° Greenwich 25°

NOTE TO THE STUDENT:
1) Follow the expansion of Sweden from her independence (1524). Eric XIV. acquired Esthonia (1561). Gustavus Adolphus and his daughter Christina acquired Carelia, Ingermanland, Livonia, Western Pomerania, the bishoprics Bremen and Verden, Gotland (island) and Jemtland. Charles X. acquired the southern tip of the peninsula (1658). 2) Then trace the losses belonging to the time of Charles XII. The year of acquisition is given in bold type while the year of loss follows in brackets. The treaty of Nystad (1721) makes Russia a Baltic power.

Sweden 1524
Acquisitions of Eric XIV. (1560-68)
Acquisitions of Gustavus Adolphus- (1611-32) and Christina (1632-54)
Acquisitions of Charles X. (1654-60)

prise was far from easy. At every point within the possible reach of Russia the Baltic coast was held by Sweden; and Sweden, the leading power of the north, was prepared to resist with energy any attempt to displace her.

THE DECLINE OF SWEDEN

THE HOUSE OF VASA

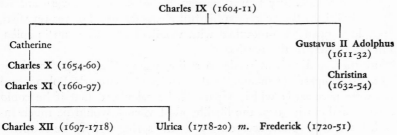

Charles IX (1604-11)

Catherine

Charles X (1654-60)

Charles XI (1660-97)

Gustavus II Adolphus (1611-32)

Christina (1632-54)

Charles XII (1697-1718)   Ulrica (1718-20) *m.* Frederick (1720-51)

The rise of Sweden to the position of the leading Baltic power dates from the heroic time of Gustavus II Adolphus (1611-1632). In his early years Gustavus successfully extended the Swedish territory along the eastern shore of the Baltic. One of his first acts was to take (1617) from Russia the small foothold (Ingermanland) Russia had on that sea. On plunging into the Thirty Years' War, in which he met his death, he won such successes in Germany that his daughter, Christina, who succeeded him, was enabled to demand, as her share in the German booty, western Pomerania and the land at the mouth of the Weser and the Elbe (Treaty of Westphalia, 1648). Rise of Sweden to the position of leading Baltic power

For the remainder of the seventeenth century Sweden took rank with the great powers of Europe. Unfortunately her greatness was the result not of her wealth, population, and culture, but solely of her military prowess; and as history abundantly shows, a purely military greatness rests on shaky foundations. A weak, unmilitary ruler, or a military adventurer who overstrains the bow, will suffice to produce a collapse. The fatal flaw in Sweden's greatness

Although the immediate successors of Gustavus were rulers not without gifts, they and their predecessors had offended so many of their neighbors that their situation was always precarious. Denmark to the west, Brandenburg-Prussia and Poland to the south, and Russia to the east, had all paid for Sweden's greatness with severe losses and nursed a corresponding grudge against her. The many enemies of Sweden

The opportunity for revenge patiently awaited by these enemies seemed at length to have arrived when in the year 1697 Charles XII, a boy of fifteen, came to the throne. The youth and inexperience of Charles appeared to mark him as an easy victim, and Denmark, Poland, and Russia formed a league against him to recover their lost territories (1700). Accession of Charles XII and the league against him

At once the allies learned that they had made their reckoning without the host. Charles XII turned out, in spite of his youth, to be the most warlike member of a warlike family—a perfect fighting demon. Aside, however, from his unflinching courage and his Spartan code of conduct, he lacked every virtue of a ruler. Of a proud and obstinate nature, he shaped his policy in accordance with a childishly romantic notion of fame and honor. He was Don Quixote promoted to a throne, and though he could fight with admirable fury against windmills, he could not govern and he could not build. In the year 1700 his full character was not yet revealed, and people stopped open-mouthed with wonder as he went up in splendor, like a rocket, in the north.

Character of Charles XII

Before the coalition was ready to strike, young Charles gathered his forces and fell upon the enemy. As the armies of Denmark, Poland, and Russia were necessarily widely separated, he calculated that if he could meet each of them in turn, the likelihood of victory would be much increased. He laid his plans accordingly. In the spring of 1700 he suddenly crossed the waters from Sweden and besieged Copenhagen. The king of Denmark, unprepared for so bold a step, had to give way and sign with Charles the Peace of Travendal (August, 1700), in which he promised to remain neutral during the remainder of the war.

Charles's campaign: defeat of Denmark, 1700

Hardly was the ink of his signature dry before Charles was off again like a flash. This time he sailed to the gulf of Finland, where Tsar Peter with 40,000 men was besieging Narva. Charles, at the head of only 8,000 men, advanced straightway to the attack, and his well-disciplined Swedes soon swept off the field the improvised army with which Peter had replaced the recently disbanded Streltsi.

Charles defeats Peter at Narva, 1700

Free to turn upon his last and most hated enemy, Augustus the Strong, king of Poland, Charles now moved southward and in the course of another year signally defeated Augustus's forces.

Charles in Poland

Thus far the war had been managed admirably. Charles might have gained a favorable peace from Poland and gone home. But passionately stubborn, he was set on humiliating Augustus, whom he regarded as the instigator of the anti-Swedish alliance and whom he was determined to drive out of Poland altogether. The attempt necessitated getting Poland into his hands. The plan proved so difficult to execute that it led to the undoing of his first successes and, finally, to his ruin.

Charles bogs down in Poland

Poland was at this time in a condition hardly better than anarchy. The nobles were the ruling power of the state, each individual nobleman having in effect become a sovereign in his own right. The only remaining witnesses of an earlier unity were a diet, which never transacted any business, and an elected king, who, having been deprived of power, was impotent.

The anarchy of Poland under an impotent elected king

In the year 1697 the nobles, who, like their kind throughout Europe, were class- but not nation-minded, went the length of electing to the kingship a German, Augustus the Strong, elector of Saxony. When in the course of the Northern War, as the struggle against Charles XII was generally called, King Augustus met with repeated reverses at the hands of Charles, the majority of the Polish noblemen were glad rather than sorry, for Augustus had engaged in the war without their consent. However, when Charles began to harry Poland with an armed force and, in addition, insisted on forcing a monarch of his own choosing on the country, a national party gradually arose and gathered round Augustus, who, although a foreigner, was the legally elected king. *The Poles give half-hearted support to King Augustus*

For many years following his brilliant opening campaign Charles hunted Augustus over the marshy and wooded plains of the Slav kingdom. Always in victorious pursuit, he never quite succeeded in catching up with his quarry. Even the capture of Warsaw and the elevation to the Polish throne of his own candidate, the Polish nobleman, Stanislaus Leszczynski, did not bring the issue to a close. Finally, in 1706, Charles desperately plunged after Augustus into Saxony, whither Augustus had withdrawn in the hope of escaping further molestation. There Charles forced Augustus to sign a humiliating peace. Its most important article was the resignation by Augustus of the Polish crown. *Charles obliges Augustus to abdicate the Polish crown, 1706*

The vindictiveness of its sovereign was destined to cost Sweden dear. While Charles was chasing a mere will-o'-the-wisp, the practical Peter was making solid use of his time. The lesson of Narva had not been lost on him. He reconstructed his army on the model of the victorious Swedes; at the same time, taking advantage of the long absence of Charles XII in Poland, he slowly wedged his way into the Swedish territory along the Baltic coast. To show his confidence in the future, he founded in 1703, on the banks of the Neva, a new capital and boldly named it St. Petersburg. *Peter gets a foothold on the Baltic; founding of St. Petersburg, 1703*

Not till 1708, when he had, as he thought, finally disposed of Augustus of Poland, did the king of Sweden deign to take notice of the systematic Russian aggressions. Then, to let the tsar feel the full weight of his sword, he set his army in motion toward the heart of the Russian dominion, toward Moscow. *Charles invades Russia, 1708*

Long before headlong Charles could reach that distant capital, his ranks had been thinned by the rigors of a Russian winter and decimated by disease. When the plodding Peter at length came up with Charles at Poltava (July, 1709), the Swedes fought with their accustomed bravery, but their sufferings had undermined their strength. And now Narva was avenged. The Swedish army was literally destroyed. Accompanied by a few hundred horsemen, Charles barely succeeded in making his escape to Turkey. *Charles defeated at Poltava, 1709*

The verdict of Poltava was destined to be final. Sweden stepped down from her proud position, and a new power, Russia, henceforth ruled in the north.

Triumph of Russia

The sultan of Turkey received the famous Swedish fugitive hospitably and offered him Bender (on the Dniester) for a residence. There Charles remained five years, long enough to make Bender the name of one of the maddest chapters of his madcap career. No sooner at Bender than his one aim in life came to be to drag Turkey into a war with Peter. After two years of importunate pleading with the sultan he actually accomplished his purpose. The tsar, who thereupon impetuously carried the struggle into Turkish territory, maneuvered so unhappily that his army was completely encircled. He would have been obliged to surrender unconditionally, had he not been spared this disgrace by the Ottoman commander-in-chief, the grand vizier, who, in return for Azov on the Black sea and a munificent personal bribe, allowed the Russian army to escape.

Charles pushes the sultan into war with Peter, 1711

The disappointed Charles raved like a maniac on seeing his foe elude his grasp. When the slothful sultan, disgusted with the meddling stranger within his gates, at last requested him to leave the country, Charles obstinately refused to budge. It took a regular siege to bring him to understand that his long entertainment in Turkey was at an end. As the Turkish force pressed in on him, he fought with berserker fury against the besiegers until he fell senseless amidst the ruins of his burning house. After wasting five years in the sultan's dominions he at last consented to turn his face homeward (1714).

Charles obliged to leave Turkey, 1714

Charles came back too late to stem the ebb of Swedish power. During his long absence the surrounding states had helped themselves to whatever territories they coveted. Although he met his foes with his accustomed valor, his country was exhausted and his people alienated. In 1718, while conducting the siege of a town in Norway, he was shot when he exposed himself unduly in reconnoitering the position of the enemy.

Death of Charles, 1718

Charles was succeeded by his sister, Ulrica Eleanora. Before the Swedish nobles permitted her to mount the throne, they obliged her to agree to a serious limitation of the royal prerogative. Then they induced the submissive government to end the war by ceding the territories which the victorious neighbors demanded. The north German states of Hanover and Prussia acquired most of the Swedish conquests in Germany, Hanover getting Bremen and Verden, Prussia most of Pomerania. Augustus the Strong, in spite of the abdication wrung from him by Charles XII, was recognized as king of Poland. But Russian Peter, who had contributed most to the defeat of Charles, received by the Treaty of Nystad (1721) the lion's share of the booty. He acquired from the foe Carelia,

Sweden purchases peace at a heavy price

Ingria (Ingermanland), Estonia, and Livonia, in fact, all the Swedish possessions of the eastern Baltic except Finland.

As he neared the end of his life, Peter had reason to congratulate himself. But he could not be sure of the future. Would Russia, after he was gone, persist in the policy of Europeanization? His son and heir, Alexis, refused to accept his father's guidance in this all-important matter and leagued himself with the forces of reaction among the clergy and nobility. For many years the tsar did his best to win his successor over to his views. When his efforts proved without avail, he resolved for the sake of the cause he represented to get rid of his son. The resolution we may praise, the method was revolting. The young prince died (1718) under the blows of the knout administered, we have reason to believe, under the eye of the implacable parent.

Peter destroys his son to hold Russia to his policy

CATHERINE II (1762-1796)

Peter died in 1725. Exactly as he had foreseen, the issue, which on his death came to the front and long dominated the situation, was whether Russia would persist on the trail which Peter had blazed. The crown passed to Peter's second wife, a former Lithuanian serf, who ruled for two years as Tsarina Catherine I. Almost to the close of the century the scepter was tossed capriciously about with little or no regard to any recognizable rule of succession and in sole response to the pressure of the faction temporarily dominant at court. It was chiefly women who were elevated to the throne. They need not detain us further than to note that, though they maintained a conspicuously profligate and corrupt rule, they did not abandon Peter's work. The Russia of the period immediately after Peter's death may be thought of as a ship helplessly drifting in the currents set in motion by the tsar-reformer till the accession (1762) of Catherine II put the helm in a firm hand.

Peter's policy survives his death

Tsarina Catherine II, by birth a petty princess of Germany, came to Russia as the wife of the heir-apparent, Peter III. Extraordinarily intelligent and determined, she was also wholly unscrupulous, and shortly after her husband, an ill-educated and unbalanced youth, had ascended the throne (1762), she led a revolution against him, in the course of which he was dethroned and murdered.

Accession by revolution of Catherine II, 1762

Although Catherine II won the scepter by violence, once in possession of it she wielded it not only with remarkable skill but also with single-minded devotion to the policies mapped out by Peter the Great. Herself of western birth, she naturally favored Western civilization. She was greatly influenced by the intellectual movement called the Enlightenment and adopted many of the ideas which the Enlightenment put in circulation. She cultivated and won the friendship of some of the leading repre-

Catherine continues the policy of westernization

sentatives of the movement, among them the famous Frenchmen, Voltaire and Diderot. It must not, however, be supposed that the rationalist emancipation from the bondage of tradition which she championed spread much beyond the immediate circle of her court. It left completely untouched the masses of the Russian people, who continued to dwell in superstitious darkness.

Since Catherine took over also Peter the Great's foreign policy, she pursued the plan of extending the Russian boundary westward into Europe. Owing to Peter's overthrow of Sweden, she faced a problem which, if identical in principle with that of her great predecessor, was different in practical detail. With Sweden removed from the scene, Catherine's neighbors toward the west, the only ones with whom she had seriously to reckon, were Poland and the Ottoman empire.

Although Poland and the Ottoman empire were, territorially, imposing states, neither of them was likely to offer a successful opposition to a persistent Russian drive. Nonetheless, a difference is to be noted between them. Poland, reduced to what has been expressively called a legalized anarchy, was as open to Russian attack as a flock of sheep to a predatory wolf. The Ottoman empire (Turkey), on the other hand, although brought by internal corruption to a lamentable decay, still had the appearance and, to a certain extent, the resources of a dangerous foe.

Taking up Poland first, we have already noted that at the time of the Northern War it had become so negligible a power that Charles XII of Sweden was enabled to occupy it for a number of years with a mere handful of troops and to impose on it a king of his own choosing. The political misery of Poland was the result of a historic process, in the course of which the nobles had usurped the power of the king and reduced the national parliament, the diet, to impotence. The slow paralysis imposed on the central government brought it about that by the eighteenth century king and diet, although still existent, had become a mockery. To prove the assertion it will suffice to recall the famous parliamentary provision called the *liberum veto*. This conferred on every member of the diet, that is, on every noble, for only nobles were eligible to attend the diet, the right to forbid by his single veto the adoption of a resolution.

By *liberum veto* one man could at his pleasure throw a wrench into the machinery of government. Under these circumstances Poland was necessarily the victim of nobiliary factions, which in their strange infatuation did not hesitate to call upon the foreigner for aid. It is therefore undoubtedly true that Poland has chiefly herself to thank for the ruin that overtook her in the days of Catherine. But that does not, of course, free from responsibility Catherine as well as the rulers of Prussia and Austria, who threw themselves on the Polish quarry and rent it asunder.

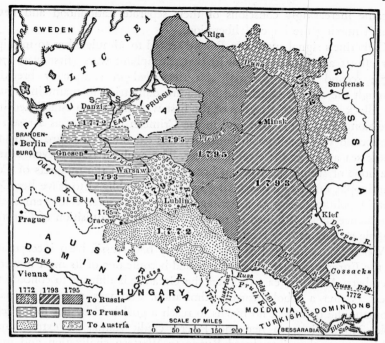

The Three Partitions of Poland of 1772, 1793, and 1795

The complicated political and diplomatic situation leading up to the partition of Poland cannot be treated here. If we remember that Poland had by its nobles been reduced to helplessness and that its neighbors, Russia, Austria, and Prussia, having recently undergone a monarchical reorganization, were steadily waxing in strength, we shall agree that it was a foregone conclusion that, sooner or later, the decadent Polish organism would be overwhelmed. After extended negotiations among Berlin, St. Petersburg, and Vienna, a treaty disposing of certain Polish territories was signed in the year 1772. The partition of that year—called the First Partition—did not wipe Poland off the map; it merely handed over convenient sections to the leagued neighbors. The land east of the Dwina and the upper Dnieper (White Russia) went to Russia, Galicia to Austria, and the province of West Prussia to Prussia.

The First Partition of Poland (1772)

With partition admitted in principle, the logic inherent in events pushed the three powers to a Second and a Third Partition (in 1793 and 1795 respectively), by which the fate of Poland was sealed. Poland ceased to exist as a political entity when its last army, gallantly led by the fiery Kosciusko, went down before the Russians. The Poles themselves, however, by no means disappeared. Apportioned among their enemies, they

The Second (1793) and Third (1795) Partitions

became increasingly conscious of their separate nationhood and never ceased nursing the hope of liberation.

Catherine's signal success in Poland served to stimulate her to multiply her efforts against the Turks. In two triumphant wars (first war, 1768-1774; second war, 1787-1792) she succeeded in completely breaking through the cordon which the Mohammedans tried to maintain around the Black sea. In consequence of the first war the tsarina established herself along the sea of Azov and in the Crimean peninsula; as a result of the second war the Russian boundary was extended westward along the Black sea as far as the river Dniester. The exultant tsarina even nursed the hope of seeing the Russian banners float from the minarets of Constantinople, but, death overtaking her, she was obliged to leave her Constantinopolitan dream as a heritage to her successors. With remarkable persistence they continued to make plans for the acquisition of Constantinople as long as they reigned over Russia.

When Catherine died in 1796, not only had Russia been incorporated in the European state system, but it had become one of its most powerful members. As in the case of Peter the Great, it is difficult to concede the great tsarina a whole-hearted admiration. She was a grossly sensual woman; she balked at no means to reach a goal held by her to be desirable. Nonetheless, to her and Peter's credit stands an extraordinary achievement: they introduced Russia to Western civilization and made it a great European power.

By two wars Catherine establishes Russia on the Black sea

Russia the handiwork of Peter and Catherine

17 GERMAN AFFAIRS: THE RISE OF PRUS-SIA AND THE REBIRTH OF AUSTRIA

THE RISE OF PRUSSIA

THE HOUSE OF HOHENZOLLERN

Frederick William (of Brandenburg), the Great Elector, 1640-88
|
Frederick III (of Brandenburg), 1688-1713
(Frederick I, King of Prussia, 1701-13)
|
Frederick William I, 1713-40
|

Frederick II, the Great, 1740-86	Augustus William
	Frederick William II, 1786-97

PRUSSIA IS A German state created in the Modern Period from inconsiderable beginnings reaching far back into the Middle Ages. The cradle of Prussia is the *mark* or march of Brandenburg, founded in the tenth century, at a time when Germany, which was itself just beginning to take shape as a distinct political entity, was confined in the main between the rivers Meuse and Elbe, and was constantly threatened on the exposed Elbe frontier by the incursions of loosely organized tribes of Slavs. The mark of Brandenburg was created as a German outpost against the hostile raiders. Besides being a different people, the raiders bore in the eyes of the recently Christianized Germans the added stigma of blind and stubborn heathens.

The head of the frontier post, an appointee and servant of the emperor, was an official of broad powers, whose title, *markgraf* or margrave, signified ruler of the mark. Standing at first on the defensive, the margrave presently carried the struggle across the Elbe into enemy territory and by gradual steps took possession of all the land between the Elbe and the Oder, ultimately penetrating even beyond that river toward the Vistula. The lowland character of the north-German plain, entailing the absence of serious natural barriers, gave from the first a powerful impetus to the eastward expansion of the mark. One result of this development was that the margrave, looming larger and larger in the affairs of Germany, was recognized as one of its foremost princes, and was in the fourteenth

The mark of Brandenburg founded in the tenth century

Slow eastward expansion of the mark

century promoted, with six other leading feudal magnates, to the office and title of elector.

The Hohen-zollerns in Branden-burg

The growth of the mark of Brandenburg did not proceed consistently on an upward-moving line. There were grave setbacks, in consequence of which some of the territory gained was again lost; and the periodic extinction of the ruling house was regularly followed by a political confusion which threatened to submerge the whole youthful organism. The fourteenth century was a particularly distressing period when, with the succession to the margraviate in dispute between rival candidates, the arms-bearing knights, among whom the land was distributed, seized the opportunity to enrich themselves at the expense of burghers and peasants. From this anarchical state of affairs the mark of Brandenburg was saved when, in the year 1415, the Emperor Sigismund conferred it on Frederick of Hohenzollern, a south-German nobleman of the Nuernberg area, to whom he was under political obligations.

Importance for Germany of the house of Hohen-zollern

The new margrave and elector proved to be the founder of a dynasty which reigned uninterruptedly in Brandenburg for five hundred years. Under its later representatives it rose to distinction by acquiring the kingship of Prussia and, ultimately, the imperial dignity in a reborn Germany. In fact, it is the expansion of the house of Hohenzollern from its territorial base of Brandenburg, which may be said to constitute the central thread of Modern German History.

The early Hohen-zollerns strengthen the Bran-denburg foundations

The first ruler of the new line, Frederick, gave himself energetically to the difficult situation before him. He overawed the knights by battering down their castles with that recent invention, the cannon; and he made the highways safe for commerce. His son and successor, Frederick II, brought the recalcitrant towns to heel, particularly Berlin, in which town he established his residence. The successors of the first two Fredericks slowly extended the newly gained authority.

Branden-burg passes into the Protestant camp (1539)

In that period of storm and stress, the Reformation, the Elector Joachim II passed into the Lutheran camp. The event occurred in 1539, shortly after his accession. But as Joachim wished to maintain a middle position between Catholics and Protestants, he did not challenge the Protestant leadership which his fellow elector of Saxony had assumed by his early identification with the cause of Martin Luther.

Two lucky territorial accretions (1609, 1618)

Playing a mediocre role throughout the sixteenth century, the Brandenburg electors did not, till the seventeenth century, rise into general view. Even so, the decisive impulse proceeded less from the initiative of any particular ruler than from the accident of two lucky legacies. The elector who stood at the head of the state on the eve of the Thirty Years' War bore the name, John Sigismund, and reigned from 1608 to 1619. When in 1609 the last duke of Cleves and Juliers (Jülich) passed away, John Sigismund claimed this Rhenish territory on the ground of kinship and,

The Growth of Prussia to the Close (1786) of the Reign of Frederick the Great

ultimately (1614) got possession of about half of it, consisting chiefly of the duchy of Cleves. A little later (1618), on the demise of another relative, the duke of Prussia, he succeeded to the duchy of that name. Thus by two happy strokes occurring almost simultaneously, the elector of Brandenburg found himself endowed with valuable lands in the west of Germany on the lower Rhine, and with a promising strip of Baltic shoreland beyond the Vistula.

It should not fail to be recorded that this same John Sigismund who inherited Cleves and Prussia recognized the necessity of a more aggressive attitude than had characterized his immediate Lutheran predecessors. He therefore passed over from Lutheranism to Calvinism; and it cannot be doubted that this fighting faith figured in the more positive policy of the Hohenzollern rulers after this time.

The Hohenzollern dynasty turns Calvinist

Before taking up the story of what happened to the enlarged Hohenzollern territories, it will be necessary to have a look at the inheritance of 1618, the duchy of Prussia. In the Middle Ages, the name Prussia was applied to the Baltic coastal area lying east of the mouth of the Vistula and inhabited by a heathen people called Prussians, usually classified as Letto-Lithuanians. In the thirteenth century the Teutonic Knights, one of those monkish-military orders which owed their origin to the prevalent crusading spirit, undertook to serve the cause of religion and the church by conquering Prussia and converting its inhabitants to Christianity. The enterprise was successful. Either the Prussians accepted the Cross or were wiped out in bloody encounters and replaced by German colonists.

Prussia a thirteenth century creation of the Teutonic Knights

The Grand Master of the Knights, as head of the Teutonic order, became a great potentate ruling over a large area on either side of the Vistula river. A hundred years later his glory began to fade. The state

The Teutonic Knights subjected to Poland (1466)

carved out by the Teutonic Knights bordered on Poland; frequent wars followed with that powerful kingdom; and at last the Knights, crushingly defeated, were obliged to accept an ignominious peace (Treaty of Thorn, 1466). By its terms the king of Poland divided the Teutonic territory into two parts, East Prussia and West Prussia. While keeping West Prussia for himself, he returned East Prussia to the Knights on the understanding that they were to hold it as a fief of the Polish crown.

Prussia a secular duchy

Thenceforth completely overshadowed by Poland, the diminished and dependent state of the Knights led a precarious existence. Plainly the changed times were no longer favorable to medieval military orders. In the days of Luther the then Grand Master, one Albert, a member of the younger, the Franconian, branch of the house of Hohenzollern, became convinced that the order had outlived its usefulness. He joined the Protestant ranks, dissolved the institution of which he was the head, and with the consent of his overlord, the king of Poland, converted East Prussia into a secular duchy with himself as hereditary duke (1525).

Prussia falls to Brandenburg

A hundred years later (1618), on the failure of Albert's direct heirs, the duchy fell, as we have seen, to the Hohenzollern relatives of Brandenburg. A valuable acquisition indeed, but coming to them on the traditional terms: they held it as a fief of the Polish crown.

Brandenburg, a victim of the Thirty Years' War

No sooner had the house of Hohenzollern experienced this fortunate increase than the Thirty Years' War broke out in Germany. The waxing might of the ruler established at Berlin, at the center of the broad north-German plain, might, under favorable circumstances, have assured him a considerable role in the struggle. But the reigning elector, George William (1619-1640), was a timid man; and with his lands situated between the leading combatants, Sweden and Austria, he lived to see them invaded and ruined by both sides, by Protestants and Catholics, by friend and foe. On his death amidst unutterable confusion, he was succeeded by his twenty-year-old son, Frederick William.

Frederick William, the Great Elector, 1640-88

It is because Elector Frederick William, who ruled for nearly half a century (1640-1688), is the real founder of the state of Brandenburg-Prussia that he has been acclaimed as the Great Elector. Without question he is one of the constructive statesmen of the seventeenth century, not unworthy to be bracketed with Richelieu, Cromwell, and William III of Orange.

The Great Elector wins consideration in the Peace of Westphalia (1648)

In the face of the hopeless disorder engendered by the Thirty Years' War, Frederick William could not at once show his mettle. So far as circumstances permitted, he tried on his accession to withdraw from a struggle of world dimensions in which he was no more than a helpless pawn; and to lend weight to his policy of neutrality, he organized from his meager resources a small but effective army. The result was that when the negotiations which ended in the Peace of Westphalia (1648) began, he could insist on a measure of attention being given to his demands. These were by no means modest and led to his receiving as his share of the general spoils four secularized German bishoprics (Halberstadt, Cammin, Minden, and Magdeburg) as well as the eastern section of the duchy of Pomerania on the Baltic.

Frederick William had, by virtue of an ancient agreement between his ancestors and the Pomeranian ducal house, a legally valid claim to all of Pomerania. However, in the course of the Thirty Years' War, victorious Sweden had gained a firm footing in Pomerania and insisted on keeping the western section of the Baltic duchy in its hand as a means of German control. The Brandenburg claim was therefore only partially allowed.

Frederick William and the duchy of Pomerania

The breathing space granted to exhausted Germany by the Peace of Westphalia found Frederick William in a relatively favorable position. He was at the head of a rather extensive territory distributed in three separate groups across the northern plain of Germany, the central unit of Brandenburg-Pomerania being flanked on the east by the duchy of Prussia and on the west by scattered Rhenish lands, of which Cleves was the most important. That the three groups were unconnected with one another constituted, of course, a serious weakness, especially from a military and economic angle. On the other hand, the lack of contiguity was sure to prove a constant stimulus to remedy the evil by filling in the territorial gaps.

Three separate territorial groups under Frederick William

On turning to the Great Elector's powers under the form of government inherited by him we find that they were strictly limited. Brandenburg, Prussia, and Cleves were three distinct states, each provided with its own diet. Each diet, made up of representatives of the nobility and the towns (with the nobility, however, the dominant element), voted taxes and controlled the spending of them. Resolved to maintain a standing army, Frederick William encountered such stubborn resistance on the part of all his diets to his demand for the necessary revenue that he concluded he would have to break their power as the unavoidable preliminary to the creation of a self-sustaining state.

Frederick William in conflict with his diets over the creation of a standing army

France had recently undergone a reorganization in the interest of centralization with the result that the sovereign had come into unchallenged possession of a royal standing army and a royal civil service. Purposing to replace, as France had done, the feudal with an absolute state, Frederick William so successfully undermined the power of his several diets that he ended by bringing the control of taxes and administration completely into his own hands.

Frederick William undermines the diets and creates an absolute state

When this had been accomplished, the Great Elector undertook the work of fusing his three originally distinct territories into a single unit boasting a common army and a common civil service. We may say sum-

The three territories merged administratively

marily that he created a state in northern Germany which achieved an accommodation to modern conditions. In consequence he was able to initiate and carry through both a domestic and a foreign policy which won for him the respectful consideration of his contemporaries.

Measures of domestic reconstruction

Owing, in part to the example of his western neighbors, the Dutch, in part to that of the great French minister, Colbert, Frederick William resolved to revive the economic life of his country, enfeebled almost to the point of extinction by the devastating Thirty Years' War. He encouraged industry and agriculture, built roads and canals to facilitate communication, and called colonists from near and far in order to bring the often immense stretches of abandoned lands again under the plow.

Welcome extended to the Huguenots (1685)

The elector's most notable single achievement in his role of economic legislator is associated with the Huguenots. When, by reason of Louis XIV's bigotry, the Edict of Nantes was revoked (1685) and the Huguenots began to abandon their native land, Frederick William by public proclamation invited the refugees to take shelter with him. Some thousands, largely skilled craftsmen, responded to the call. Settled on favorable terms in the towns of Brandenburg-Prussia, by their industry and intelligence they communicated a powerful stimulus of mind and hand to backward northern Germany.

The Great Elector's chief concern is Sweden

Although it might be contended that the Great Elector won his most lasting laurels in the domestic field, we may not overlook that he also raised his state to a higher level among his European neighbors. From a purely military angle, his state, distributed geographically in three separate sections over the north-German plain, was so open to attack that he was bound to seek to strengthen it by additional territory. As matters stood following the Peace of Westphalia, danger threatened chiefly from Sweden. Firmly planted in western Pomerania, the Scandinavian kingdom threw a shadow all the way to Berlin. This situation would of itself have sufficed to arouse resentment, even if there had not been the additional reason that Frederick William considered western Pomerania to be by an indisputable claim his own.

The ring of Baltic powers hostile to Sweden

Luckily for the Great Elector Sweden had other enemies, far more formidable than himself—Denmark, Russia, Poland, in fact the whole ring of the Baltic powers. The paramount position which Sweden had won at their expense was hateful to them and they were ready to seize upon the least occasion for lowering her pride.

The Great Elector wins the sovereignty of East Prussia, 1660

In 1655 war broke out between Sweden and Poland over many issues but, chiefly, owing to Sweden's desire to strengthen its hold on the southern Baltic coast. During this war Frederick William, whose territories lay between the hostile states, was alternately coaxed and bullied by both of his more powerful neighbors to oblige him to take sides. In these difficult circumstances he steered his course between the combatants with such dexterity that he came out of the war with profit and prestige. In the general peace which concluded the war (Peace of Oliva, 1660), Frederick William received from the king of Poland the suzerainty of East Prussia. Although the elector gained no territory on this occasion, he henceforth possessed East Prussia in full sovereignty. This success would, of course, have been impossible without that standing army which was the starting-point and remained the core of his policy.

More than a decade later an opportunity presented itself, or seemed to present itself, to drive Sweden out of Pomerania. It came by way of the Dutch War inaugurated in 1672 by Louis XIV of France. Frederick William, followed by the emperor and other German states, rose in defense of the threatened Dutch republic, thus making the war general. Thereupon the angered Louis persuaded the Swedes, who were bound to him by treaty, to invade Brandenburg. This unexpected move obliged the elector, who was operating on the Rhine with the contingents of the other German states, to hurry home. Approaching by forced marches and with great stealth, he fell in June, 1675, upon the Swedish army at Fehrbellin and beat it signally.

Sweden, as ally of Louis XIV, invades (1675) Brandenburg

Fehrbellin brilliantly opens the independent military annals of the new state. What followed showed that the victory was not just a lucky stroke. Pursuing the Swedes into Pomerania, the elector actually conquered the province, including the important harbor city, Stettin, at the mouth of the Oder. To his deep chagrin, however, he got no good from his victory, for when Louis XIV closed the Dutch War by the Treaty of Nimwegen (1678), he stood faithfully by his ally, Sweden, and compelled the reluctant elector to disgorge all but a tiny border strip of his Swedish conquest. Though Sweden continued to be a threat to Brandenburg, Frederick William was the first to disclose to the world that Sweden was not invincible.

The elector, after conquering Pomerania, is obliged to give it back to Sweden

Finding the path blocked toward Pomerania, Frederick William tried to advance his interests in the direction of Silesia, where his house had claims to certain districts, to wit, to the four duchies of Liegnitz, Brieg, Wohlau, and Jägerndorf. Since the province of Silesia was in the actual possession of the house of Hapsburg, and since its head, the Emperor Leopold I, refused to admit the validity of the Hohenzollern claims, Frederick William made no headway with them. At last, in 1686, under pressure of the deepening menace to Germany of the designs of Louis XIV, he resolved, drawing close to the emperor, to smooth out all their difficulties. He therefore surrendered, in return for the small district of Schwiebus in Silesia, all his presumptive rights in that province.

The elector adjusts (1686) his Silesian claims with the house of Hapsburg

But the emperor played a double game. While negotiating this arrangement with the elector, he secretly bribed the elector's son, who was not on good terms with his father, to promise to give back Schwiebus on his

accession. Two years later Frederick William died (1688). Although his
son and successor, Frederick, lived up to the bargain, he could and did
maintain with some show of reason that the return of the purchase price
restored the original claims. This Silesian incident is of importance only
because some fifty years later it issued like a ghost from the grave and
proved a terrible boomerang for the Emperor Leopold's successor.

By the emperor's double-dealing the adjustment is invalidated

The Elector Frederick III (1688-1713) presents a sharp contrast to his
imposing, capable father. Physically weak and deformed, he was disinclined to exert himself either in the field or the council-chamber. Nevertheless he achieved a certain luster by winning the title king. For almost
ten years he solicited humbly for this vainglorious distinction at the court
of the Emperor Leopold at Vienna. He appealed to the emperor in the
belief that nothing short of the imperial authority could give the coveted
title validity. Because the Emperor Leopold was disinclined to advance
the fortunes of a rival German house, he at first refused the request. He
would have continued to refuse it, if, around 1700, a new war with
Louis XIV had not loomed, in which Leopold's stake was nothing less
than the vast Spanish heritage. In return for the promise by Frederick of
support in the inevitable war with the French king, the emperor at last
permitted the elector to indulge his vanity.

The Elector Frederick III wishes to acquire the title king

Accordingly, on January 18, 1701, Frederick crowned himself king at
Königsberg, the capital of East Prussia. He reigned henceforth as King
Frederick I in Prussia.[1] The title king in Prussia was given the preference over that of king of Brandenburg for the reason that Brandenburg,
being a fief of the Empire, had an inferior legal status to Prussia, which
since 1660 had been an independent state held in full sovereignty by the
Hohenzollerns. Increasingly applied to the unified Hohenzollern dominions, the designation Prussia in a surprisingly short time drove from
usage the older name of Brandenburg.

Frederick crowned king of Prussia, 1701

Frederick's son and successor, King Frederick William I (1713-1740),
represents a curious, partial reversion to the Great Elector. He had his
grandfather's common sense and love of work but conspicuously lacked
his grandfather's mental acumen, personal dignity, and mastery of European politics. His energy was all but exclusively directed to the army and
the administration, the two main pillars of the rising state. By exercising
the utmost thrift he succeeded in raising his standing army to some
80,000 men, thus putting little Prussia in military matters in a class with
the great states of Europe. And what troops they were! An iron discipline
molded them into a precise military machine, to which a corps of officers,
trained in special military schools, gave a devoted service. It is this king

King Frederick William I (1713-1740) perfects the army

[1] The first form of the title was as here, king *in* Prussia, in order to forestall any criticism
from Poland, which, possessing West Prussia, might have protested against the title king
of Prussia, as implying the sovereignty over all Prussia. Nevertheless, the simpler form,
king of Prussia, came almost at once into general use.

who may be regarded as the father of what came to be called Prussian militarism.

Frederick William I gave at least equal attention to the strengthening of the administrative system created by the Great Elector. The various departments of government, especially the taxes, were fused under a unifying ordinance and the individual officials held to the strictest accounting. Under the king's sleepless supervision his civil service reached as high a level of competence as his army.

Frederick William perfects the civil service

The only foreign action of importance in which this tough, workaday ruler engaged befell early in his reign. On his accession (1713) the War of the Spanish Succession was coming to an end, while the so-called Northern War, waged against Charles XII of Sweden, had entered on its last phase. Defeated at Poltava (1709) by Peter the Great, the wounded Swedish lion had sought cover in Turkey; and during his long absence from the scene of action his neighbors had proceeded to appropriate his lands. Not to be left out in the cold, Frederick William mobilized his army in his turn against Sweden and occupied Swedish Pomerania.

Following Sweden's defeat by Russia, Frederick William occupies Pomerania

When Charles XII at last abandoned Turkey and hurried home, he made a gallant but hopeless effort against his many enemies. On his death in 1718 the Swedish government could no longer blind itself to the writing on the wall. It began negotiations with its neighbors, above all, with sweepingly victorious Russia, in which it acknowledged defeat. The negotiations with Prussia ended in a treaty (1720), which gave Frederick William I the bulk of western Pomerania, including the mouth of the river Oder and the invaluable seaport of Stettin. The heart of the Prussian state was now connected by the course of the Oder with the Baltic sea. Although Sweden retained a slight foothold on the Pomeranian coast, its power had declined so greatly that it ceased to be a peril for its Prussian neighbor.

Frederick William acquires (1720) the bulk of Swedish Pomerania

This sturdy king, who has left such solid memorials behind, amused the European gossips in his day by reason of some of the strangest eccentricities which have ever characterized a human being. His conception of his office was a curious compound of Biblical patriarch and modern drill-sergeant. He had his eye upon everybody and everything. If he suspected a man of being wealthy, he would compel him to build a fine residence to improve the looks of the capital. He had a particular abhorrence of idleness. The very apple-women, while waiting in their booths for customers, were ordered to busy themselves with knitting, while the police were empowered to pick up homeless vagrants and impress them into the army. But his wildest eccentricity was his craze for tall soldiers. At Potsdam, his residence some miles west of Berlin, he organized a giant regiment, for which he gathered recruits from all parts of the world. He coddled his giants like a sentimental father, and was so completely carried

King Frederick William's eccentricities

away by his hobby that he, who was thrifty to the point of avarice, offered enormous prices in all markets for tall men. Nor did he scruple to capture them by force when they refused to enlist.

The king's conflict with the crown prince While these queer doings of the sovereign greatly entertained his neighbors, on at last one occasion the comedy ended in tragedy. The king's son and heir, Frederick, known afterward as the Great, was a self-willed youth who, drawn more to books and music than to soldiering, grew up in all respects the very opposite of his bluff, practical father. Parent and son conceived a strong antipathy for each other; and when the irate father resorted to corporal punishment the proud prince tried to escape to France. Frederick William almost lost his mind from rage. He threw his son into prison, executed an accomplice of the prince on the charge of treason, and spoke wildly for a time of executing his son too. When he at last relented, it was on the promise of the son to submit to a training of unexampled rigor in the civil and military branches of the government.

Accession (1740) and character of Frederick II, called the Great As a result, when, on the death (1740) of his Spartan father, the prince at the age of twenty-eight mounted the throne as Frederick II, he knew every branch of the Prussian service like a thumbed book. Owing to his devotion to art and literature as well as to the refinements of a cultivated society, his intimates imagined that he would abruptly terminate the severe governmental system of his father. They were mistaken. Not only did he jealously maintain and consolidate the inherited organization, but he showed almost at once that beneath a pleasing exterior he nursed as consuming an ambition as any autocrat of history. A crisis in Austria coming to a head some few weeks after his accession furnished him with an opportunity to show his true colors.

DECLINE AND REBIRTH OF AUSTRIA

The rise of Austria under the house of Hapsburg The name Austria, or East Mark, adhered originally to the German territory along the Danube between approximately Passau and Vienna. By absorption of the neighboring Alpine provinces, such as Styria, Carinthia, and the Tyrol, the duke of Austria became in the course of the Middle Ages one of the most influential princes of Germany. In the last quarter of the thirteenth century a new dynasty, the house of Hapsburg, became the ruling family of this enlarged Austrian state and with stubborn ambition and almost unvarying success undertook to promote its fortunes. We have seen that by the time of Emperor Maximilian and his grandson, Charles V, Austria had become so easily the leading German state that the imperial office, although strictly speaking elective, had become virtually hereditary in the Hapsburg line. We have also seen that the imperial office, if a still much coveted honor, conferred little or

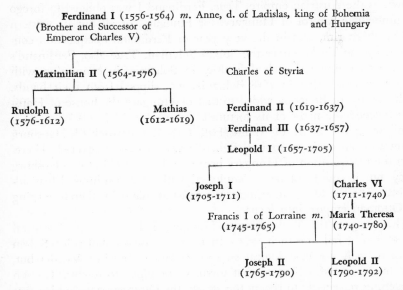

THE HOUSE OF HAPSBURG (German Branch)

Ferdinand I (1556-1564) *m.* Anne, d. of Ladislas, king of Bohemia
(Brother and Successor of   and Hungary
Emperor Charles V)

Maximilian II (1564-1576)   Charles of Styria

Rudolph II   Mathias   Ferdinand II (1619-1637)
(1576-1612)   (1612-1619)
                                         Ferdinand III (1637-1657)

                                         Leopold I (1657-1705)

        Joseph I   Charles VI
      (1705-1711)   (1711-1740)

        Francis I of Lorraine *m.* Maria Theresa
              (1745-1765)   (1740-1780)

              Joseph II   Leopold II
            (1765-1790)   (1790-1792)

no real power on its holder. Such power as an emperor of the house of
Hapsburg possessed he owed to his hereditary Austrian lands together
with the other territories which he or his predecessors had acquired.

The reader will recall that the Emperor Charles V (1519-1556) completely overshadowed Europe in his day because, in addition to Austria, **The Aus-**
he commanded the resources of the Netherlands, Italy, and Spain. He **trian branch**
of the house
will further recall that, on the abdication of Charles V, his vast posses- **of Hapsburg**
sions were divided between his brother Ferdinand, who acquired the **endowed**
Austrian territories, and his son Philip, who received the rest. With Fer- **with the**
imperial
dinand, therefore, the younger or German branch of the Hapsburgs **office**
began an independent career; and in evidence that, in spite of the divi- **(1556)**
sion of 1556, the family was still the foremost dynasty of Germany, Ferdinand was invited to succeed his brother Charles upon the German
throne. Since for the next two hundred years Ferdinand's heirs regularly
won the imperial election, the house of Hapsburg came not unreasonably
to look upon the headship of Germany as its prescriptive right.

At this point we are obliged expressly to take note that from the time
of Emperor Ferdinand I the power of his branch of the Hapsburg dy- **The house**
nasty rested on more than its original Austrian foundation. For, in the **of Hapsburg**
acquires
year 1526, partly by inheritance and partly by election, this same Ferdi- **(1526)**
nand became head of the two large neighboring kingdoms of Bohemia **Bohemia and**
and Hungary. Advanced thus to the sovereignty of three large groups of **Hungary**
territory—Austria, Bohemia, Hungary—occupying the basin of the mid-

dle Danube, he may be regarded as the founder of what came later to be known as the Austrian empire. True, Ferdinand I was obliged to forego the immediate control of Hungary, for Hungary, or all but its western and northern rim, was in the very year of Ferdinand's acquisition conquered by the Turks under the Sultan Solyman. True also, Ferdinand's successors encountered such difficulties in Bohemia, in connection with the Reformation, that in 1618 Bohemia, too, slipped from their hands. With the loss of Bohemia added to that of Hungary the house of Hapsburg touched the nadir of its fortunes.

Loss of Hungary and Bohemia followed by recovery

Following the battle of White Hill (1620), the troubled Hapsburg fortunes began again to mount. Bohemia was at once recovered. Thereupon the reacquisition of Hungary became a leading object of Hapsburg policy, but it could not be accomplished without a crushing defeat administered to the Ottoman empire. We must at this point therefore bring the Ottoman empire into focus.

Zenith and decline of the Ottoman empire

When in 1526 the Turks overran Hungary, it looked as if all central Europe might fall into their grasp. In 1529 the all-powerful ruler, Sultan Solyman, took the next logical step by advancing against Vienna but, after an unsuccessful siege of that town, was obliged to retreat. Though threatening repeatedly to renew the attack, the Ottoman state, which was a characteristic oriental despotism, was before long overtaken by internal difficulties and thereby deprived of its offensive vigor. Almost overnight the once warlike sultans lost their martial character and became content to pass their days in easy self-indulgence amidst the demoralizing pleasures of the harem. Inevitably, in these circumstances the army and administration became cankered with corruption. The march on Vienna of 1529 remained therefore the high-water mark of the Turkish inundation of the continent.

Defeat of the Turks before Vienna in 1683

In 1683, owing to a purely temporary revival effected by a spirited family of grand viziers, the Ottoman empire resumed its invasion of Europe by the Danube route and conducted a second siege of the Austrian capital. The stubborn resistance of the Viennese garrison, seconded by a rescuing movement led by the gallant king of Poland, John Sobieski, not only rendered the second siege as futile as the first but converted it into an utter rout of the Mohammedans.

Further defeats of the Turks and liberation (1718) of Hungary

From this crushing defeat administered to the Turks in the field Austria took courage and boldly resolved to turn the tables on them by assuming the offensive. To her great good fortune heaven presented her at this decisive moment with a gifted general in the person of Prince Eugene of Savoy. We have already encountered him in connection with the wars waged by Europe against the aggressions of Louis XIV. Great as were his services to Austria on the western scene, they were completely overshadowed by his achievements in the Danubian area. In two wars (first war, 1683-1698; second war, 1715-1718) the Austrians, under the magnetic prince, administered such a beating to the Turks that they drove them completely out of Hungary (Treaty of Passarowitz, 1718).

The first Austrian sovereign to resume the rule of Hungary in its full extent was Emperor Charles VI (1711-1740). In Charles's time the leading state of Europe was France. In the eyes of its neighbors France owed its ascendancy to its recent centralization of authority, which the envious rivals undertook to imitate. We have already examined the effect of the French example on the rising German state of Prussia. By the labors of the Great Elector and his successors the Hohenzollern dominion had been converted, allowing for the difference in size, into quite as effective an absolutism as its French prototype. Under the stress of his wars with Louis XIV and the Ottoman sultans the Austrian ruler, too, had felt the need of unifying his many separate territories, and during the brilliant campaigns conducted by Prince Eugene on the Rhine and on the Danube, had at length gone so far as to create a central Austrian army supported by the contributions of all the diverse Hapsburg territories.

The Hapsburg ruler attacks the problem of centralization

This was an auspicious beginning toward administrative unification. But it did not alter the fact that the three main constituent groups, Austria, Bohemia, and Hungary, remained stubbornly distinct, each with its own laws, courts, and finances, and each provided with a vigorous champion of a separatist tradition in a feudal diet or parliament. If Charles VI, in distinction from the Hohenzollern ruler, the Great Elector, made no headway in breaking down the diet barriers, it was due to several circumstances. In the first place his diets represented separate, hostile nationalities and not just privileged bodies within the same nationality as in the Brandenburg-Prussian case; further, he faced, especially toward the end of his reign, the grave problems of succession, and to bring these to a feasible solution, he could not dispense with the concurrence of the ancient assemblies.

The stubborn distinctness of Austria, Bohemia, and Hungary

The problem of succession arose when Charles, having reached his middle years, was obliged to reckon with the fact that he, the last male of his line, would have no male heir. It was the identical problem which the older, the Spanish branch of the Hapsburgs, had faced in the days of Charles II, and which, remaining unsolved in this ruler's lifetime, precipitated the long agony called the War of the Spanish Succession (1702-1713). To forestall a similar calamity Charles determined to change the succession, limited hitherto to males, by having the older of his two daughters acknowledged as his sole and universal heir. In this sense he drew up a solemn ordinance, which received the name of the Pragmatic Sanction. To make sure that the Pragmatic Sanction would be honored after his death, he applied first to the diets of his many territories for

Charles VI regulates the succession by the Pragmatic Sanction

their acceptance of it; and then, to make assurance doubly sure, he knocked at the doors of all the European cabinets to get them likewise to guarantee his regulation of the succession. At often heavy sacrifices he finally secured the endorsement of all the leading states and, reasonably comforted, in October, 1740, laid himself down to die.

Immediately, in accordance with the terms of the Pragmatic Sanction, Charles's daughter, the Archduchess Maria Theresa, assumed the rule of all the Hapsburg lands. It was of course well known that practically all the neighbors coveted some part of the Austrian possessions, many of them on the basis of claims of blood which the Pragmatic Sanction had nullified, others on the ground of legal documents which had often for generations been in debate. Among these latter was the Prussian claim to the four duchies of Silesia. While every claimant was waiting in breathless suspense to see what the other claimants would do, the young sovereign of Prussia, Frederick II, stepped boldly forth and took the bull by the horns. He marched an army into Silesia to secure his claim by force.

It was beyond challenge an act of brutal, undisguised aggression. Immediately, as at a signal, every state of Europe ill disposed toward Austria followed suit, and, regardless of whether it had a claim or not, set its army in motion against the Hapsburg territories. Conspicuous among these adversaries were the two German states, Bavaria and Saxony, and the two Bourbon powers, France and Spain. These four together with Prussia formed a great anti-Austrian alliance which planned to strip Maria Theresa of the bulk of her inheritance. Thus did the Pragmatic Sanction, in spite of the abundant signatures attached to it, prove abortive. The lifelong bogey of Charles VI, to lay which he had made so many sacrifices, the War of the Austrian Succession, had become a reality.

Succession (1740) of Maria Theresa and invasion of Silesia by Frederick II of Prussia

The invasion followed by outbreak of the War of the Austrian Succession

THE AUSTRO-PRUSSIAN RIVALRY

It might have gone hard with Maria Theresa if she had not found splendid resources of heart and mind in herself, and if she had not succeeded in arousing a spirit of loyal devotion among her various peoples. Her enemies were descending upon her in two main directions, the French and their Bavarian ally from the west, by way of the Danube, and Frederick of Prussia from the north. Unprepared as she was, her raw levies gave way, at first, at every point. On April 10, 1741, at Mollwitz, Frederick won a victory over the Austrians which clinched his hold on the disputed province of Silesia.

In the same year the French, Saxons, and Bavarians occupied Bohemia. So complete, for the time being, was the dominion of the anti-Austrian alliance that when, in January, 1742, the imperial election took place, the combined enemies of Austria were able to raise their candidate, the

Frederick defeats (1741) the Austrians, thereby driving them out of Silesia

The French in Bohemia; election as emperor of the elector of Bavaria

Elector Charles of Bavaria, to the imperial throne. The elector assumed his new dignity with the title of Emperor Charles VII (1742-1745). For the first time in three hundred years the crown of the empire rested upon another than a Hapsburg head.

At this point Maria Theresa's fortunes rose again. Her own magnetic enthusiasm did wonders in injecting new life into her weak and battered forces. Not only was the army of the coalition driven out of Bohemia, but Bavaria, the land of the enemy, was invaded and occupied. The Prussians, who had likewise entered Bohemia in order to co-operate with their allies, saved themselves from imminent disaster by a victory at Czaslau (May, 1742). Thereupon Maria Theresa, who saw that she could not meet so many enemies at one and the same time, declared her willingness to come to terms with her most dangerous foe. In 1742 she signed with Frederick the Peace of Breslau, by which she made over to him practically the whole province of Silesia. What is known in German history as the First Silesian War had come to an end. Maria Theresa makes peace with Frederick by the cession of Silesia (1742)

Maria Theresa now prosecuted the war against her other enemies with increased vigor. England and Holland, in order to redress the European balance, joined her, and with each new campaign the scales inclined more visibly in her favor. When the puppet emperor, Charles VII, had lost every foot of land he owned and the Austrian armies had penetrated triumphantly as far west as, and finally beyond, the Rhine, Maria Theresa could feel with elation that she was successfully bringing all Germany under her heel. Maria Theresa's success against the other allies

Aware that in that case he could not possibly hold his new conquest, Frederick was moved to strike a second blow. In 1744 he began the Second Silesian War, in which his calculations were completely successful. He first relieved the French and the Bavarians by drawing the Austrians upon himself, and then he defeated the enemy signally at the battle of Hohenfriedberg (1745). On Christmas Day, 1745, Maria Theresa bought her second peace of Frederick by a renewed cession of Silesia. Frederick II re-enters the war and acquires Silesia a second time (1745)

On Frederick's retirement the war, which, once ignited, could not be easily extinguished, was waged chiefly in Italy and the Austrian Netherlands. In the Netherlands the French won a number of brilliant victories which actually put them in possession of this territory coveted by them for so long a time; but discouraged by the successes of Maria Theresa in Italy and of the English at sea, they agreed at last to treat. In 1748 the Peace of Aachen (Aix-la-Chapelle) ended the War of the Austrian Succession essentially on the basis of mutual restitutions. The, after all, outstanding feature of the peace was the recognition of Maria Theresa as the sole heir of her father. The Peace of Aachen (1748) a vindication of Maria Theresa

Already three years before this consummation the general German situation had again assumed its accustomed form. The Bavarian emperor,

Maria
Theresa's
husband
becomes
Emperor
Francis I,
1745

Charles VII, having died (1745) after being ignominiously chased from all his lands by the Austrian army, the electoral college offered the crown to Francis of Lorraine, Maria Theresa's husband. Therewith the house of Hapsburg, or, as we should now call it, Hapsburg-Lorraine, was back in the German saddle. If the house had, with the exception of certain slight cessions in Italy and the one substantial sacrifice of Silesia, emerged triumphantly from its terrible ordeal, it owed its success almost exclusively to the undaunted courage of the fair and spirited sovereign at its head.

Prussia
a great
power

When Frederick retired from the Second Silesian War, he was accepted into the select company of the great powers of Europe. He did not owe this improved status to the size of his monarchy, which, in spite of the Silesian acquisition, boasted only a modest circumference; he owed it to the efficient army and sound finances inherited from his father and to the audacity and genius contributed by himself.

Frederick's
internal
labors

Alert and intelligent, Frederick was fully aware that only at the cost of unremitting labor could he hope to maintain himself at his perilous elevation. The ten years of peace that followed the Second Silesian War serve to illustrate the economic activities with which he followed up his military success. In the main he may be said to have pursued the course mapped out by his predecessors, merely instilling a fresh energy and enthusiasm into their measures. He reclaimed several considerable stretches of swamp land and settled colonists on the fertile acres thus won; he also improved the highways and constructed canals as avenues of communication particularly suited to the north-German lowlands.

Frederick's
mercantilism
illustrated by
his resolve to
develop the
manufacture
of textiles

Frederick's chief interest, however, was to develop the manufacture of woolen and linen textiles. He thereby enriched the as yet largely agricultural society over which he ruled and liberated it at the same time to a certain extent from its dependence on foreign production. This policy of having the economic life of the country unfold under the strict direction of the government was neither his invention nor that of his predecessors, from whom he took it over. It accorded with the practice of all the governments of the period and was at a later time given the name of mercantilism. It is therefore correct to characterize Frederick as a mercantilist and to declare, while denying him any economic originality, that he practiced his faith with vigor and an undoubted measure of success.

Frederick
an "en-
lightened"
monarch

Frederick reacted with equal vigor to the intellectual influences of his day, summarized under the name of *Aufklärung* or Enlightenment. Championed by advanced thinkers all over Europe, the movement of Enlightenment aimed at overhauling the whole body of the inherited social, legal, and political institutions to the end of bringing them into better accord with the criteria formulated by reason and science since the time of Galileo and Descartes. As the reform of institutions would enable them to render better service to all classes of society, particularly to the poor and the oppressed, there was also a distinct humanitarian element present in the movement of Enlightenment.

Frederick II took great pride in aligning himself with the humanitarians and enlighteners. Among his first acts on mounting the throne was the proclamation of the broadest religious toleration accorded up to that time by any European state. Immediately after, he went on record as the first ruler to abolish torture in criminal cases. He followed this measure up with a sweeping reform of the civil courts in the interest of economy, simplicity, and order. *Specific enlightened measures of Frederick*

By these and similar acts Frederick was, in part at least, responsible for giving the rather stark absolutism of the seventeenth century that peculiar turn, by virtue of which it presents itself to view in the eighteenth century as "benevolent despotism." We make no mistake if we consider benevolent despotism, mercantilism, and enlightenment as three correlated aspects of eighteenth century government and society. *Absolutism assumes the guise of "benevolent despotism"*

It is the benevolent and reforming bent of Frederick which explains his close association with so many French literary men and notably with the prince of them all, Voltaire. He long cherished the plan of making his capital, Berlin, the center from which the new intellectual light was to radiate over the world. To this end he gathered around himself men of many nationalities, but particularly Frenchmen, because in his time that nation furnished the leading spokesmen of the movement of Enlightenment. For a while Voltaire condescended to give up France in order to join the circle about Frederick. But the gushing friendship between the king and the poet-philosopher did not last and, when the bubble burst, Voltaire vanished from Berlin in a mist of scandal. *Frederick's court a literary and intellectual center*

Thanks to an artistic inclination which marked him from his youth and which the cares of office did not succeed in suffocating, Frederick aspired to become in his own person a poet and historian. In his hours of leisure he produced a considerable body of literary work in the French language, but it cannot truthfully be said that it was of any great importance in itself or that it has added appreciably to his reputation. *Frederick a writer of poetry and history*

Following the peace of 1748 the political situation in Germany remained unusually tense because the high-spirited Empress Maria Theresa refused to forget the violence of which she had been the victim. She hoped to get back Silesia and for years carefully laid her plans. As early as 1746 she entered upon a close alliance with the Tsarina Elizabeth, which the two women consciously aimed at Frederick. Next, the man whom she raised to the post of chancellor, Kaunitz, a most skillful player of the diplomatic game, planned the bold step of an alliance with France. In the eighteenth century an alliance between Hapsburg and Bourbon, the century-old enemies, was generally held to be out of the *Maria Theresa lays diplomatic plans to get back Silesia* question. However, since the Silesian wars, Austria had come to regard not France but Prussia as its leading enemy, and Maria Theresa and Kaunitz were very anxious to have France understand that thenceforth they had no further quarrel with it.

The diplomatic revolution of 1756; Austria and France allied against Great Britain and Prussia The Austrian plan of shifting from enmity to friendship with France was greatly aided by the circumstance that England and France were at this time making ready to contest the empire of the seas—a situation which will be treated in the next chapter. Both were therefore on the lookout for allies; and as Prussia, after holding back a long time, was induced at last to sign a convention with England, France, in order not to be isolated, accepted the proffered hand of Prussia's rival, Austria. By the spring of 1756 this diplomatic revolution, as the contemporaries called it, was an accomplished fact. The two leading political issues of the day, the rivalry between England and France, involving the supremacy of the seas, and between Prussia and Austria, touching the control of Germany, were about to be fought out in the great Seven Years' War (1756-1763); and in this conflict Great Britain and Prussia were to consolidate their claims and interests against the claims and interests of France and Austria. The remaining great power of Europe, Russia, instead of remaining neutral in a dispute which did not directly touch it, sided with the cabinets of Versailles and Vienna.

The outbreak of war (May, 1756) between Britain and France draws in the other powers War was formally declared between England and France in May, 1756. At once the storm broke in America, India, and on all the seas. For a moment Frederick entertained the hope of banishing the Anglo-French conflict from the continent of Europe, more particularly from Germany. It was in fact in the hope of this result that he had bound himself in what was originally no more than a neutrality convention to the English cabinet. If on this occasion he deluded himself, it was because Maria Theresa held all the diplomatic trumps and was set upon war as the consummation of her dreams. For not only had she bound France and Russia to her cause, but two smaller powers, Saxony and Sweden, were from the first as good as sure to take her side. With all these allies she might hope to draw a ring around Prussia, which, gradually tightened, would choke to death that hated, upstart power.

Frederick invades Saxony, August, 1756 In this tremendous crisis Frederick's one chance was to move quickly. Therefore, before the coalition had perfected its plans against him, he took the offensive and by a lightning stroke occupied hostile Saxony and invaded Bohemia (August, 1756). Thenceforth he could at least utilize Saxony as a bulwark against Austria.

The successful campaign of 1757 When the campaign of 1757 began, his enemies, having at length completed their preparations, descended upon him from all points of the compass. There is no need of going into the details of this or of any of the subsequent campaigns. Although greatly outnumbered by his enemies moving in on him from the east, north, west, and south, he made the most of his one considerable military advantage of operating on interior lines. Aware of their superior numbers, his enemies would have preferred slowly to close in on and smother him without risking an encounter in the field. It was his game to wreck their plan and he succeeded. At Rossbach, west of Leipzig, he fell suddenly (November 5, 1757) with 22,000 men on a French army, which with its German auxiliaries outnumbered him two to one, and scattered it to the winds. A month later, at Leuthen, in Silesia, he signally defeated, with 34,000 men, more than twice as many Austrians under Marshal Daun, and drove them pell-mell over the passes of the Giant mountains back into their own dominions. At the news of these strokes the Swedes and the Russians, who had been slowly driving into Prussian territory from the north and east, lost heart and withdrew to their own soil. At Christmas, 1757, Frederick was lord of an undiminished kingdom.

In no succeeding campaign was Frederick threatened by such overwhelming forces as in 1757. By the next year his ally, England, had fitted out an army, largely of German mercenaries, which, under Ferdinand of Brunswick, operated against the French upon the Rhine, and so protected Frederick on his western flank. As the Swedish attack, through the incapacity of the decadent government, displayed no energy, Frederick was permitted to make light of his Scandinavian enemy and give all his attention to Austria and Russia. No doubt, even so, the odds against him were enormous. Prussia was a small, barren country of 5,000,000 inhabitants, and in men and resources Austria and Russia together outstripped her many times; but at the head of Prussia stood a military genius with a spirit that neither bent nor broke and that fact sufficed for a while to maintain an equilibrium. After 1757 Frederick's active enemies limited to Austria and Russia

It was Frederick's* policy in the campaigns after 1757 to meet the Austrians and Russians separately in order to keep them from overwhelming him with their combined forces. In 1758 he succeeded in beating the Russians at Zorndorf and driving them back; but in 1759 they beat him in a battle of unexampled carnage at Kunersdorf, which apparently opened the road to Berlin. For a moment now Frederick himself despaired, but somehow managed to raise another force and save the heart of his dominions. The end of the campaign found him not very much worse off than the beginning. Gradual enfeeblement of Prussia in the campaigns of 1758 and 1759

Frederick was evidently getting feeble. The terrible strain continued through years was beginning to tell; and when shortly after the accession (1760) of King George III, the English government resolved to come to terms with France and to desert Prussia, Frederick was pushed to the edge of the abyss. Frederick deserted by England

From what to human eyes looked like unavoidable disaster the king
of Prussia was saved by a mere accident. On January 5, 1762, Frederick's
implacable enemy, the Tsarina Elizabeth, died. As Russia had no direct
interest in the war and had engaged in it only because the tsarina had a
personal dislike for Frederick, there was no reason why her successor,
Peter III, who was an ardent admirer of the Prussian king, should not
come to terms with him. Tsar Peter in his enthusiasm even insisted on
allying himself with his country's late enemy. But little came of this plan,
as he was overthrown and murdered in July, 1762. His wife, Catherine
II, who succeeded Peter, refused to engage further in the war on either
side. Nonetheless, she put Frederick under a heavy debt of gratitude by
ratifying the peace which Peter had concluded.

Frederick saved by the death (1762) of the tsarina, followed by peace with Russia

This same year England and France came to an understanding (Pre-
liminaries of Fontainebleau, 1762) and hostilities between them were at
once suspended at all points. Therewith, of the great powers, only
Austria and Prussia remained under arms. As Austria could not hope to
do unaided what she had failed to do with half of Europe at her side,
Maria Theresa, although with heavy heart, resolved to come to terms.
In the Peace of Hubertsburg (February, 1763) the cession of Silesia to
Frederick received a third and final confirmation.

Peace of Huberts-burg, 1763

From the Peace of Hubertsburg Frederick had still twenty-three years
before him, which, a practically unbroken stretch of peace, he devoted
to the continuation of those internal labors which we have already enumerated. By promoting the welfare of his people according to the
"benevolent" outlook of his age he became the most representative sovereign of Europe.

Frederick's last years a period of peace

Among the political events of this closing period of Frederick's life
only those having to do with Poland and Austria call for special comment. His relation to Poland has already been mentioned in connection
with the Tsarina Catherine's successful extension of her power westward. It is highly probable that the First Partition (1772) was carried out
chiefly at the suggestion of Frederick, who by this arrangement secured
a share in a dominion already earmarked by the tsarina as her exclusive
possession. All three of Poland's neighbors, Russia, Austria, and Prussia,
took part in the partition. Although Prussia got the smallest slice, it was
perhaps the most valuable since it consisted of the province of West
Prussia, by which the detached territory of East Prussia was at last joined
to the Brandenburg nucleus.

Frederick's share in the Partition of Poland (1772) is West Prussia

Although the Empress Maria Theresa did not succeed in her purpose
of regaining Silesia, she played so large a part in the affairs of Europe in
her day that she greatly added to the prestige of her empire. However,
permanently to secure it against rapacious neighbors, she would, as she
came clearly to recognize, have to make it over in accordance with the

current program of centralization. Her very first measures in pursuit of this end aroused such opposition in her two kingdoms of Bohemia and Hungary that, seized with discouragement, she practically gave up the plan. It was only when her son, Joseph, became emperor (1765) in succession to his father, Francis I, and at the same time became co-regent with his mother of the Austrian state that the work of internal consolidation was seriously taken in hand.

Maria Theresa's domestic policy aims cautiously at centralization

The advent of Joseph II marks an all but incredible event: modernity caught up with the Hapsburgs! He was Enlightenment personified and approved of no part of the Austrian inheritance that did not square with the norms of reason and utility. If he had had his way at his accession he would at once and without hesitation have inaugurated a furious reform movement. However, so long as his mother lived, she effectively applied the brakes, for the last word rested, after all, with her. Therefore, between 1765 and 1780, during which time Joseph reigned in association with his mother, he did not get very much done in which he took pleasure. On the great empress's death in 1780, Joseph ruled alone till his own death in 1790. During those ten years he was his own master and enacted as revolutionary a body of statutes as have ever issued from a royal reformer.

Emperor Joseph II (1780-90), a typical "enlightened" monarch

The reforms of Joseph were devised not only to unify and centralize the many Hapsburg dominions but also to destroy the privileges of the clergy and nobility. An unusually informed and kindly man, Joseph showed in his measures much more good will than tact and foresight, for his territories, made up of so many unrelated provinces and distinct peoples, were bound to demur against his ruthless wiping out of their traditional customs and historic rights. The most outraged among them, like the Austrian Netherlands (Belgium) and Hungary, even rose, toward the close of his reign, in rebellion against him.

The furious reforms of Joseph II

Joseph was a dying man when this situation developed, and as there was no other way of terminating the civil war he had stirred up, he undertook to revoke practically the whole mass of his reform edicts. That Joseph II should have tried to carry out a political reorganization along lines partially traced for him by France, Prussia, and Russia is wholly comprehensible. That he failed proved that the Hapsburg dominions were different in that they were composed of so many heterogeneous elements that it was a forlorn hope to recast them in a single uniform mold.

Why Joseph failed

So eager and far-ranging a spirit as Emperor Joseph was sure to favor an active foreign policy. This first appeared when, in 1772, the Partition of Poland was under discussion among the cabinets of St. Petersburg, Berlin, and Vienna. His mother was firmly set against partition as in conflict with her conscience, but, overriding her for once, he joined with

Joseph shares in the First Partition of Poland

Russia and Prussia and secured the province of Galicia as the Austrian share.

His next project was to acquire the better part of Bavaria from the reigning elector by a mixture of persuasion and force. As soon as, early in the year 1778, the arrangement became known, Frederick of Prussia protested and, to make his objection effective, mobilized his army along the Austrian border. For several months war hung suspended over Germany. It was not Joseph but his mother who yielded. An old woman who had had her fill of war, she came to an agreement behind Joseph's back whereby the Bavarian project was abandoned.

War threat-
ened with
Prussia over
Bavaria,
1778

When, following his mother's death in 1780, Joseph was free to pursue his own adventurous course, he directed his attention to the vast moribund Ottoman empire. As there reigned at that time in Russia Catherine II, an equally enterprising spirit and equally set on profiting from the decline of the once powerful Mohammedan state, it is not surprising that the two rulers became allies. The contemplated common war against the Turks broke out in 1787. The Austrian campaign was greatly hampered by the revolutionary outbreak in Hungary against Joseph's domestic reforms. The emperor returned from the campaign of 1789, which took an unfortunate turn and in which he contracted a mortal disease, a dying man. In order to ease the confused situation for his successor, he resolved to pacify his disaffected subjects by the painful act already mentioned: he annulled his reform edicts and died (1790) an utterly defeated man.

War against
Turkey in
conjunction
with Russia

Joseph's sleepless competitor and rival, Frederick II, called the Great, had preceded him in death. When he departed this scene in 1786, he left behind a Prussia which had grown powerful and famous, but a German empire which was still the same broken reed as during the four or five preceding centuries. It was something, nay, much that within Germany there was now a strong and vital organism, for it inevitably communicated a measure of vigor to the whole dead mass. Undoubtedly even the awakening of Austria under Maria Theresa and her son was to no small extent the result of the Prussian example.

Prussia a
dynamic
influence in
Germany

If from now on Austria and Prussia faced each other as rivals and enemies, it was not only because of the bitter Silesian memory but, even in larger measure, because each coveted the headship of a revitalized Germany. Of the hollow official Germany of the eighteenth century the headship rested of course with Austria and its ruler, the elected emperor. However, for practical purposes Prussia from the time of Frederick was quite as strong as Austria and, in substantial equilibrium as the two states were, each watched the other's every move, since each hoped to outstrip the other and oblige the smaller German states to accept its

The future
of Germany
turns about
the rivalry
of Prussia
and Austria

leadership. For, that the structure called the Holy Roman Empire would cumber the earth much longer was highly improbable. We may admit that, when three years before the outbreak of the French Revolution Frederick passed away, the future of the German people was as dubious as ever. But so much at least was clear: it hung on the outcome of the rivalry between Austria and Prussia.

18   GREAT BRITAIN AND FRANCE IN THE EIGHTEENTH CENTURY

GREAT BRITAIN

Significance of the "Glorious Revolution"

WE HAVE SEEN that the Revolution of 1688 had secured the victory in the long civil struggle in England to Protestantism and the parliament. It was without doubt a triumph for the English people, but it was not in any present-day sense a democratic triumph. If henceforth the parliament was the decisive factor in the government, let us not fail to observe that, composed of an hereditary House of Lords and a House of Commons elected by various groups of freeholders, the parliament was exclusively representative of the propertied classes. Therefore, while the Revolution displaced the royal with a parliamentary regime, its socio-economic significance lies in its vesting political control in the landed gentry and the great merchants of the towns. For almost a century and a half, until the Reform Bill of 1832, England was governed by an unusually successful combination of an aristocracy of birth and an oligarchy of wealth.

William III and Mary (1689-1694); *William III (alone)* (1694-1702)

With the accession of William III England adopts an anti-French policy

The sovereign of the Revolution, William III, soon learned that he was not to have his throne without fighting for it. The deposed James had sought refuge with Louis XIV, and the decision of the French king to espouse the cause of James naturally threw England on the side opposed to Louis. With this side, consisting of the emperor, the Dutch, and Spain, Louis had at that precise moment begun the war known as the War of the Palatinate or of the League of Augsburg (1688-1697).

William acts in conformity with the interests of both Dutch and English

The War of the Palatinate marks a turning-point in the fortunes of the French king. Thus far his policy of continental aggression had met with success to no small extent because the England of the restored Stuarts had, when not actively aiding him, remained neutral. With the advent of William, England frankly aligned itself with the continental enemies of all-powerful France. In fact it was to achieve this very purpose that William, who was a Dutchman before he was transformed into an Eng-

340

lishman and who had made it his lifework to defend the liberty of his native land against Louis XIV, had launched the invasion of 1688. But though prompted in the first place by the desire to help the Dutch, William certainly served also the interests of his new kingdom, since in arraying England against France he committed it to that maritime and colonial policy by virtue of which it rose in the following century to a position of overshadowing greatness.

The War of the Palatinate has been dealt with in connection with Louis XIV, except for the phase belonging exclusively to England. Its story carries us to the English dependency, Ireland. In March, 1689, James II effected a landing in Ireland with French aid. Immediately the Irish, strongly Catholic and vehemently anti-English in sentiment, gathered around the deposed monarch. Even before his coming the ancient hatred between Celt and Saxon had once more flamed up in war. The Protestant colonists had been driven from their homes and for a time it looked as if the island might again revert to its original owners. However, a year after James's arrival, in July, 1690, William, who had come to the rescue of the Protestants, defeated James at the Battle of the Boyne. Thoroughly discouraged, James abandoned his supporters and slipped back to France. The measures by which the victorious English now took vengeance on the Irish broke the back of Irish resistance for a hundred years.

William in Ireland; Battle of the Boyne, 1690

Before speaking of these measures it will be necessary to pass the relations of Ireland and England in swift review. When James I mounted the throne in 1603, Ireland had been a dependency of the English crown for nearly five hundred years. For most of that time the English rule had been largely nominal since the representative of the king in Ireland generally controlled no more than the district around Dublin, known as the English Pale. The heart of the island was held by the native Irish, who, divided into tribes and governed by chiefs in accordance with ancient custom, retained a substantial independence. If the Irish could have replaced the inter-tribal warfare which was usual among them with some form of national organization, they might have rid themselves entirely of their conquerors.

For several centuries the English had only a feeble hold on Ireland

Not till the time of Henry VIII did the English take the task of subduing Ireland seriously in hand, and not till the close of Elizabeth's reign was the work completed. On James I's finding himself in possession of a conquered land, he adopted a policy fraught with the gravest consequences. As the likeliest means of securing the continued submission of the island, James resolved to confiscate the northern province of Ulster and colonize it with English and Scotch settlers. The replacing of the inhabitants of Ulster in 1610 with Protestant colonists from the larger

Ireland conquered by Elizabeth; colonization policy adopted by James I island created a situation which is the chief factor down to our day in the complicated Irish problem.

When the English civil war broke out, temporarily annihilating the power of the government, the Irish fell (1641) upon the colonists of Ulster and repossessed themselves of the land. The English revenge for this outrage was adjourned till 1649 when Cromwell, representing the might of the restored nation, undertook to reduce Ireland again to obedience. At the head of a Puritan army he relentlessly beat the Irish into submission.

The rebellion of 1641 and its suppression (1649) by Cromwell

In this connection it should be noted that the Reformation had added fresh fuel to the ancient quarrel of the two peoples. On establishing their national or Anglican church the English had imposed it also, under the misleading name of the Irish church, on their dependency. Nonetheless, the Irish adhered to the church of their choice, the church of Rome. This signified that in the eyes of Cromwell's Puritan army the Irish were not only rebels but also enemies of the Lord, whom to break with the sword was a good deed.

The Anglican church imposed on the Catholic Irish

When the army had completed its savage work, the government of the Commonwealth resumed on an even more extensive scale James's policy of land seizure and Anglo-Scotch colonization; and when, in 1690, William III crushed another insurrection, the Irish were punished with a final and sweeping act of confiscation. Totally dispossessed of their lands and persecuted for their religion, the conquered people might be thought to have been reduced to the last depth of degradation.

England's successive seizures of the land

There was, however, still another evil in store for them in the following century. By prohibiting the importation into England of Irish cattle and Irish textiles, the leading export articles of the smaller island, the English government produced an economic crisis which involved the recent Anglo-Scotch settlers in a common misery with the natives. The exhausted country meekly suffered the new injury.

England's protective policy ruins Irish industries

We have already noted that William's drawing England into the coalition against France enabled him to bring the War of the Palatinate to a close without conceding any fresh gains to France. He spent the following years negotiating with Louis a feasible division of the expected Spanish heritage. But when, in the year 1700, the king of Spain died, leaving a will in favor of the house of Bourbon, Louis XIV disavowed the negotiations with William by sending his grandson, Philip, to Madrid to assume the rule of the undivided Spanish dominions.

A Bourbon prince mounts the Spanish throne (1700)

Out of this daring act grew the War of the Spanish Succession, for which the great opponent of Louis XIV had hardly prepared by a renewal of the continental coalition, when he died (1702). Since William's wife, Mary, had died some years before (1694) without issue, the crown now passed to Mary's younger sister Anne. As it was foreseen even in William's lifetime that Anne, too, would leave no offspring, a special statute had been passed, called the Act of Settlement (1701), for regulating the succession. Supplementing the Protestant provision already incorporated in the Bill of Rights, the Act of Settlement passed over the head of several Catholic claimants and established the succession, on the demise of Anne, in the Electress Sophia of Hanover, granddaughter of James I, and her heirs after her.[1] *The Act of Settlement (1701) regulates the English succession*

We have repeatedly insisted that the Revolution of 1688 and the Bill of Rights of the following year consecrated the victory of the parliament in its long struggle with the king. In the course of the next two or three generations the parliament confirmed its ascendancy by completing the constitutional edifice on its own plan. Without interruption but without haste, act followed act, each enlarging somewhat farther the sphere of the parliament at the expense of the crown until the power came to be vested in every essential particular in the representatives of the people and the monarch was reduced to an ornamental figurehead. Let us recount the contributions toward this result made in the reign of William. *Gradual development of the parliamentary system*

First to be considered is the matter of supplies. The parliaments of the past had been in the habit of voting certain revenues for the king's lifetime, thereby securing to the sovereign a relative independence and enabling him, under favorable circumstances, not to call the parliament at all. William's parliaments now fell into the habit of *annual* grants. The practice greatly enhanced parliamentary influence, since the king, merely to keep the administration going, was obliged to summon the parliament every year. The annual grant obliged the sovereign to present for acceptance an annual budget of expenditures, every item of which fell under the lynx-eyed scrutiny of the victorious institution. Annual budget and annual parliament represent a correlated development which secured the minute control of the purse, and therewith ultimately of the government itself, to the parliament. *Reduction of the royal power by annual grants and annual parliaments*

Hardly less important was the Mutiny Act. By this statute military courts for the punishment of mutiny and other acts of military insubordination were authorized for one year only. While by this device the discipline, without which an army cannot exist, was maintained, the army itself was kept strictly under parliamentary control. Finally, let us note the refusal (1695) of parliament to renew the act subjecting printed matter to official censorship. Henceforth England enjoyed a relatively free and unfettered press, giving public opinion considerable scope in shaping government policy. *The parliament strengthened by the Mutiny Act; and by the freedom of the press*

[1] See genealogical table on p. 261.

Queen Anne (1702-1714)

The event of the reign of Queen Anne (1702-1714) overshadowing all
others was the War of the Spanish Succession. It has been treated elsewhere with due regard to the fact that England won in this conflict a
leading position among the powers of Europe. The applause attending
Marlborough's march of victory from Blenheim to Malplaquet was not
participated in by all his countrymen. Marlborough depended for support
on the Whigs, who in the early part of the war dominated the parliament
and increasingly brought their leading men into the ministry. The queen,
a narrow-minded woman passionately devoted to the national church,
personally inclined to the Tories but was dissuaded from supporting
them by her friend, the duchess of Marlborough, who had gained a complete ascendancy over her.

The War of the Spanish Succession supported by the Whigs

When the war continued interminably, bringing heavy taxation and an
ever-increasing national debt, public sentiment rallied behind the Tory
opposition and encouraged the queen to cast off the Whig yoke. The
Tories were unwittingly assisted by the tempestuous duchess of Marlborough, who carried her meddling with the queen's business to such a
point that the offended Anne at last forbade her the court. Abetted by
backstairs influences, always rife where a weak ruler holds the scepter,
the queen became more and more disgusted with the Whigs and in
1710 peremptorily dismissed them from office.

Queen Anne puts the Tories in office, 1710

There followed a ministry of Tories led by Oxford and Bolingbroke,
who dared cashier the mighty Marlborough himself and open negotiations with France. They terminated in the Peace of Utrecht (1713). Although the treaty was concluded somewhat precipitately and without
proper regard for Great Britain's allies, the main advantages gained by
the Whig conduct of the war even their Tory adversaries refused to surrender. Great Britain acquired from France, Newfoundland, Nova
Scotia, and the Hudson Bay territory; from Spain, Gibraltar and the
island of Minorca, which secured to her the control of the western
Mediterranean. She also received from Spain by an arrangement called
the *Asiento* the right to supply Spanish America with Negro slaves and
to send one trading ship each year to a specified Spanish colonial port.
The Asiento is peculiarly interesting in showing that the wars among
the European powers were coming more and more openly to be trade
wars.

Great Britain's immense gains at the Peace of Utrecht, 1713

While the war was at its height an event of great significance occurred
in the union of England and Scotland. Although the two kingdoms had
possessed a common sovereign ever since the accession in 1603 of the Scottish sovereign, James, to the English throne, from fear of its more power-

ful neighbor the smaller state had for over a century jealously guarded its independence. In 1707 the ghost of ancient rivalry and war was laid forever by a measure, in which the Scottish parliament voted its own extinction and accepted representation in the Lords and Commons seated at Westminster. To mark the fusion of the two countries in one they adopted as their official common designation the name Great Britain.

Union of England and Scotland, 1707

George I (1714-1727) (House of Hanover)

In the year 1714 Anne died, and the crown fell to the German house of Hanover, whose family name was Guelph. Since the Electress Sophia, who had been designated by the Act of Settlement as the eventual heir, had preceded Anne in death, her son, George I, now ascended the throne. Some great stroke on the part of the Pretender, the son of James II, was expected, but when it fell (1715) it turned out to be harmless. The man who claimed to be James III was a soft and unenterprising individual who, having effected a landing in Scotland, was quickly discouraged by the situation confronting him and turned back to France.

Accession of George I of the house of Hanover, 1714

George I (1714-1727), who owed his elevation to the Whigs, naturally chose his first advisers from that party. As the Tories were more or less compromised by their wavering support of the Stuart claim, George, a sluggish individual, who never felt at home in England and never bothered even to learn the English language, clung to the Whigs for the rest of his life. He thus laid the foundations of that long era of Whig control which puts its stamp upon English history for the next fifty years.

George I leans upon the Whigs

The prolonged rule of a single party helped parliament to take another and practically its final step toward acquiring complete control of the state: with George I is associated the establishment of cabinet government. We have already seen that as far back as the reign of Charles II the parliament fell into two groups or parties, each pledged to a certain course of action. As matters stood at that time, though the majority of the Commons might be Whig, the king, still enjoying a considerable prerogative, was free to choose his advisers from among the Tories. Sooner or later it was bound to appear that such a division of power, with the executive pulling in one direction and the legislature in another, was harmful to the public interest, and that to obtain the best results the ministers and the Commons would have to be in essential accord. Under the prevailing drift of English constitutional development there was no other conceivable way of bringing this about than for the king to select his ministers from among the majority party. This George I agreed to do, thereby inaugurating a practice to which continued usage gave the equivalent of statutory sanction. With cabinet and party rule added to the older features of parliamentary practice the English con-

The emergence of cabinet government

stitution may be said to have reached the form which has distinguished it down to our own time.

The Whig ascendancy is inseparably connected with the name of Sir **Sir Robert** Robert Walpole. It was during his tenure of office of more than twenty **Walpole's** years (1721-1742) that party and cabinet government were definitely and **policy of** finally established. Walpole was a coarse, vigorous, and practical-minded **peace** realist. The chief item of his policy was the maintenance of peace, in order first, to secure the Hanoverian succession, and second, to enable the commercial interests to make the most of their unrivaled opportunities beyond the seas. Himself a country squire, he belonged to a social order which was overwhelmingly Tory and sharply antagonistic to the great merchants, with whom, organized under the Whig banner, they disputed the control of parliament. It is a tribute to Walpole's breadth of view that, though a member of the landlord class and far from neglectful of its interests, he recognized the importance of the merchant element and tried in every way to promote its welfare.

Like every great ruler and statesman of his age, Walpole in his eco- **Walpole's** nomic thinking and planning was a mercantilist. Persuaded that it was **mercantilist** the duty of the state to manipulate the processes of production and distri- **policy** bution in the supposed interest of the nation, he promoted colonial **favors the** development, favored the importation of raw products and the exporta- **middle class** tion of manufactured goods, and by countless devices attempted to achieve that *summum bonum* of mercantilist thought, a favorable balance of trade. If his measures were far from being an unmixed blessing, they probably stimulated enterprise along some lines of colonial trade and led to the establishment of a number of favored, that is protected, indus- tries. In any case his policy won the applause and, incidentally, the votes of the traders and industrialists.

But let no one imagine that in his devotion to the trading interests **Favors** Walpole neglected the landlords to whom he himself belonged. The **extended to** solid legislation of earlier days in their favor had culminated in the pay- **the landlord** ment to them of bounties for the export of wheat. These bounties he **class** not only refrained from touching, he even increased them from time to time. With such benefits he attracted at least a part of the country squires, normally Tories, into the Whig camp and was enabled to give the parliament that Whig complexion which it retained for so many years.

While Walpole's economic measures do not differ in any essential re- **Political** spect from those practiced in other countries in that age, it cannot fail **implications** to strike our attention that in its immediate implications his legislation **of Walpole's** appears as a bribe offered to the two classes alone represented in parlia- **legislation** ment and therefore ruling the elections. If, in addition, we see him em- ploying a vast patronage to help him maintain in the Commons the majority he needed to continue in office, we are prepared for the fact that corruption became a very characteristic feature of his system. His cynical attitude toward members and mankind in general found expression in his oft-quoted remark: "Every man has his price."

Resolved to maintain peace, Walpole followed a mercantilist policy, in part at least, on the theory that a nation devoted to commerce necessarily abhors war. It was an illusion disproved innumerable times before and since. Among the advantages obtained for England by the Treaty of Utrecht was, as we have learned, the Asiento with its right of sending one ship each year to trade with the Spanish colonies. It was a slight wedge, which the reckless enterprise of the English traders attempted to convert into a broad breach in order to flood the South American markets with English goods. *English trade aggression produces friction with Spain*

When the Spaniards defended themselves by apprehending traders caught in the act of smuggling, the English mercantile interests raised a resounding clamor. In 1738 a smuggler by the name of Jenkins was paraded through London with a shriveled ear wrapped in cotton-wool, which he declared he had lost seven years before through the savage assault of a Spanish coast guard. Jenkins's miraculously preserved aural appendage proved to be more than an anatomical curio, for it tipped the scales against peace. Pushed by merchant appetite for gain and against his better judgment, Walpole began (1739) a war with Spain. It aimed at greater trading rights (and profits) in Spanish waters and, in view of its origin, is humorously designated as the War of Jenkins's Ear. *War of Jenkins's Ear, 1739*

George II (1727-1760)

Meanwhile George I had been succeeded by his son, George II (1727-1760). He resembled his father in at least the one important particular that he acquiesced in the new party and cabinet development. The British war with Spain had hardly begun when the continental powers, on the heels of the death (1740) of the Emperor Charles VI, became involved in a struggle over the Austrian succession. As England took alarm when France committed itself to a partition of Austria, the government was gradually moved to throw in its lot with Charles's heir, Maria Theresa. Completely out of sympathy with these martial developments, Walpole was at length (1742) forced out of office in favor of men more eager than he to challenge the continental supremacy of France. *England drawn into the War of the Austrian Succession, 1740-1748*

Having already dealt with the War of the Austrian Succession, we need not linger over it at this point. Its importance lies in the fact that it ended in a peace (1748), in which the French acknowledged the defeat of their anti-Austrian project and recognized Maria Theresa as heir to the dominions of her father with the one substantial exception of Silesia, *The peace of 1748 leaves the colonial issue undecided*

which went to Frederick of Prussia. In other respects the conflict was without fruit, the treaty being based on the principle of the mutual restoration of conquests. This meant that the colonial issue, which was rapidly becoming paramount with Great Britain and France, was adjourned for settlement to a later day.

A memorable incident of the War of the Austrian Succession was the attempt of Charles Edward Stuart, son of the Pretender, and known as the Young Pretender, to win back his lost realm. That he was not lacking in the spirited audacity which has often gained a crown is indicated by the fact that, without help from France and with a following of only seven men, he secretly landed on the Scottish Highland coast. The time, July, 1745, was well chosen since the British troops were fighting on the continent in behalf of Maria Theresa. The Highlanders were in this period still divided into clans, at the head of which stood hereditary chiefs. As Celts, with a language and a culture of their own, they were by no means friendly either to the Germanic Lowlanders of Scotland or to the English. Moreover, practically self-governed, they were subjected to King George II in hardly anything more than in name.

Prince Charles Stuart attempts to regain his crown, 1745

That Bonny Prince Charlie, as the Young Pretender was fondly called, had thrown himself upon their mercy, stirred the imagination of the Scottish Highlanders and kindled their hearts to wild enthusiasm. Flocking around him in crowds, they advanced from point to point until by an irresistible rush they captured Edinburgh. For a moment London itself was apprehensive of capture. But when the British troops had been brought home from the continent, it was soon found that the wild courage of primitive clans was of no avail against the discipline of a trained army. On Culloden Moor (April, 1746), the Highlanders were defeated with fearful slaughter by the king's second son, the duke of Cumberland. Prince Charlie, after many romantic adventures, made good his escape; but apparently broken by his one capital failure, he lived ever afterward in indolence abroad (d. 1788). His defeat marks the last Stuart attempt to recover the throne.

Defeat of Prince Charles

FRANCE: THE ANGLO-FRENCH ISSUE

If we now turn to France to treat its eighteenth century development in the same chapter with that of Great Britain, a sufficient reason for this association is that for both powers the eighteenth century signified the climax of the colonial and maritime movement inaugurated almost two hundred years before. That movement must now be brought up to date.

Review of European colonial expansion

We are aware that the leadership of Portugal and Spain in the Age of Discovery made them the earliest and most vigorous colonial powers. They could not keep up the pace and gradually exhibited symptoms of decline. Even so, their vast colonial holdings were in the eighteenth century still substantially intact. Portugal exercised authority over the immense territory of Brazil, while Spain ruled over the rest of South America, the whole of Central America together with Mexico, most of the West Indies, and commanded an important key position in the waters of the orient by her possession of the Philippine Islands. The colonial areas held by Portugal and Spain

In spite of the resistance offered by Portugal and Spain, the three northern states of France, England, and the Dutch republic gradually set up colonial claims of their own. In the seventeenth century, the period of the true greatness of the Dutch, the little nation made a bid for colonies and sea power by which it forged far ahead of its immediate competitors. In the following century the Dutch initiative declined, and in the end the republic remained content with its very profitable holdings in the island archipelago of the East Indies, administratively centered on Java. Main Dutch colonial position is the East Indies

Very probably the partial eclipse of the Dutch was not owing so much to their own diminishing energy as to the concentrated power England and France were able to bring to bear upon the colonial problem as soon as, a little past the middle of the seventeenth century, they had overcome the paralysis laid upon them by their respective civil wars. There followed for each a very rapid development. The English completed the appropriation of the long Atlantic coast line between Maine and Florida, while the French established themselves at the mouths of the two great rivers, the St. Lawrence and the Mississippi. By pushing inland by these two river routes they planned to bring the vast territory wedged between these two lines of penetration under their control. North American claims staked off by England and France in the seventeenth and eighteenth centuries

Before the opening of the eighteenth century France and England had begun to clash over their American colonial claims. The result was that the rivalry, in which they had already become engaged in Europe in consequence of the ascendancy achieved by Louis XIV, was intensified by the constantly mounting importance of the colonial issue. The climax of the Franco-British conflict in Louis XIV's time came with the War of the Spanish Succession (1702-1713). The English effort was by far the greatest single factor in the defeat of Louis; and although Louis was able to negotiate a not dishonorable peace in Europe, he had to make important colonial concessions to the victorious English. We have already learned that these embraced the surrender of Newfoundland and Nova Scotia, signifying an important strengthening of the English grip on the Atlantic coast. First colonial success won (1713) by England over France

In the decades following this first British success both Great Britain and France multiplied their efforts to achieve the leading position on the North American continent. The most effective means to reach this goal was undoubtedly colonization. In this activity the British completely out-

stripped their rivals, for they succeeded in settling many more of their
people along the narrow strip of the Atlantic seaboard than the French
managed to plant over the almost immeasurable basins of the Mississippi
and St. Lawrence. Furthermore, with this rapidly growing body of colonists the British developed a reciprocally profitable trade. It would not
be extravagant to declare that, regardless of what the two home governments might see fit to do or not to do, the advantage in the Franco-
British colonial struggle was almost certain in the long run to rest with
the larger and more active colonial population.

Advantage accruing to the British from a more active policy of colonization

Be that as it may, the two home governments, far from neglecting
American developments, kept an interested eye on them, although they
failed to appreciate the vast potentialities of the as yet embryonic colonial
world. It would have taken a prophet to do that, and the men who sat in
the foreign offices at London and Paris were only average human beings.
If their mortal state did not enable them to penetrate the veil of the
future, it sufficed to give them the conviction of an impending struggle
for power, which, come what may, each group was resolved to win.

Great Britain and France ready to settle the issue by war

In measure as the situation in North America became critical, a parallel
situation developed at the opposite end of the world, in the great Asiatic
peninsula of India. Beginning with Portugal, all the nations of Europe
in turn had, by means of chartered trading companies and commercial
outposts, attempted to establish profitable economic relations with the
teeming masses of that vast land. Not long before the middle of the
eighteenth century it occurred to a daring and imaginative Frenchman,
Dupleix by name, to supplement the commercial penetration already
effected by systematic political control. Since the country was divided
among almost innumerable independent and semi-independent princes,
Dupleix calculated that he could advance the French interest by using
one prince against the other. On next creating an army of native troops
officered by Frenchmen, he put himself in possession of a force with
which he was able successfully to overcome opposition and to acquire
indirect control over a steadily increasing Indian area.

Commercial rivalry in India given (around 1750) a political turn by Dupleix, a Frenchman

The success of Dupleix alarmed the British East India Company, which
foresaw that the carrying-out of the French program would end by
crowding it from the Indian markets. In the nick of time a young company employee, Robert Clive by name, took the matter in hand and, by
copying the political and military measures of Dupleix, succeeded in becoming a rival Indian power. Toward the middle of the eighteenth century the two opposed systems headed respectively by Dupleix and Clive
had begun violently to clash. Therefore at precisely the same moment
the colonial ambitions of Great Britain and France pointed to an irrepressible conflict in the eastern as well as in the western hemisphere.

Clive sustains the British interest by copying the system of Dupleix

Louis XV (1715-1774)

It was a grave misfortune for France that it faced colonial issues of such capital importance for the present and future of the nation under perhaps the most feeble and dissolute monarch of its long history. Louis XV was but five years old when, in 1715, he succeeded his great-grand-father, Louis XIV. Under this vigorous monarch France had won a position of political and cultural primacy in Europe; but as Louis had over-strained the bow, he had met with a setback at the end of his life and had left behind him an exhausted country. Its most pressing need was economic and financial recovery under intelligent, statesmanlike direction.

Accession (1715) to the throne of France by Louis XV at a moment of national exhaustion

As the boy-king was a minor and as, even after he had been declared of age, he was for some time too immature to assume authority, he can hardly be blamed for the failure of France in the first part of his reign to achieve a return to good government and material prosperity. For the first eight years after his accession his relative, the duke of Orléans, acted as regent. After that the power, but not under the title of regent, was exercised by the aged Cardinal Fleury. He effected some minor reforms but, like the Regent Orléans before him, left the finances in their by now traditional disorder.

Authority exercised by the Regent Orléans and Cardinal Fleury

On the death of Fleury (1743) Louis XV, in frank imitation of his great predecessor, declared that he would henceforth be his own master. He did not mean what he said, for he lacked the native intelligence and moral self-discipline conscientiously to attend to the business of a great state. He permitted the power to slip into the hands of favorites and mis-tresses, who plundered the treasury at will and dictated both the domestic and foreign policy, to which Louis then lent the authority of his name. Averse to work of any kind and insatiably frivolous, he took nothing seri-ously save the pursuit of pleasure.

Authority exercised by favorites and mistresses

Admittedly this butterfly sovereign was confronted with a very difficult situation. Louis XIV had established the seat of the government at Ver-sailles, where he had surrounded himself first, with a splendid court and next, with a royal city to serve his and the courtiers' convenience. In order to enhance the magnificence of Versailles "the grand monarch" had not rested till he had drawn thither a large part of the nobility of France to serve as foil to his magnificence.

The artifi-ciality of Versailles

While the nobles no longer exercised the direct political power which had been theirs before the advent of absolutism, they had had so much indirect power bestowed on them that, at least after the death of Louis XIV and under the spineless Louis XV, they virtually controlled the gov-ernment. This has been frequently overlooked by historians hypnotized by the fact that, officially, France was ruled by an absolute, divine right

Louis XV at Versailles under the influence of the nobles

monarch. But when a Louis XV is the absolute monarch, he is satisfied to reflect his environment; and the nobles were the only people Louis habitually met. They poured their complaints into his ear; they overwhelmed him with their views and wishes; they raised an impenetrable hedge between him and his people. In France, as in England, the merchant class was constantly growing in numbers and wealth. To the misfortune of this class and of all France as well, the merchants had no access to a monarch cloistered at Versailles, while under the ruling absolute system they had no constitutional means at their disposal for bringing pressure to bear on the monarch's ministers.

Privileges of the nobles enumerated

When the development of French absolutism had extinguished the political power of the nobles, they remained firmly possessed of a notable body of special privileges. Not only were they exempted from the payment of the property tax, the taille, but the great posts in the diplomatic service and the highest ecclesiastical offices, such as bishoprics and abbacies, were reserved to them. Most important of all, they alone furnished the officers of the royal forces. Their influence at court was uninterruptedly enlisted to keep these unwholesome privileges intact. Finally, since the nobles had always been a military caste and since their advancement both in honor and emoluments depended on war, they regularly threw their weight into the scales in favor of a decision by the sword of every public issue that arose.

The nobles as instigators of war

This attitude of the nobles is well illustrated by two wars in which Louis XV became engaged before the middle of the century. They were both conflicts with the house of Hapsburg, the traditional enemy of the French reigning house of Bourbon. It might be argued that since Bourbon (France) and Hapsburg (Austria) disputed between them the primacy of the continent, they were bound to clash whenever a continental issue was raised on which they did not agree. Admitting the always imminent threat of war, we yet have no difficulty in persuading ourselves that France plunged first, into the War of the Polish Succession (1733-1735), and second, into the War of the Austrian Succession (1740-1748) largely because the nobles raised such a clamor at Versailles in favor of war that the ever irresolute king feebly acceded to their wishes.

War of the Polish Succession (1733-35) brings France the province of Lorraine

From the War of the Polish Succession, which, in spite of its name, was a war with the house of Hapsburg and Germany, France reaped a benefit in the cession by Germany of the duchy of Lorraine. This was a territory which, except for its eastern rim, was inhabited by people of French speech. Its absorption by France was therefore a step in the national unification of the country. It was also another milestone in the extension toward the Rhine of the French eastern boundary begun in the days of Richelieu.

In the War of the Austrian Succession, fought to partition Austria, France was successfully balked by the high courage of the heir to the Austrian territories, Maria Theresa. It would be impossible to indicate the slightest benefit accruing to France from the spendthrift investment in men and resources represented by this war.

War of the Austrian Succession, 1740-48

The worst feature of the influence of the nobles over the foreign policy of France remains to be mentioned. The historical evolution of the country had brought it about that, besides being a continental power clashing with Austria, France was also a colonial and maritime power clashing with Great Britain. For this second rivalry the nobles, as a landed gentry, lacked an immediate understanding. Besides, they had played an inferior role in French colonial expansion, which was the work primarily of the middle classes or bourgeoisie. The merchants had been ably seconded in their colonial efforts by the French civil service, which, since the days of Richelieu, had been intrusted to the middle classes (the third estate) and which maintained a high standard of intelligence and devotion to duty. It had long been clear that the civil administration by middle class servants constituted the real strength of the absolute system. Undeniably, in the eighteenth century the administration suffered disorganization through the corruption and favoritism attending so nerveless a regime as that of Louis XV. Nonetheless, it remained strong enough to make itself felt in an issue of national importance. And we are fully aware that, by the middle of the century, such an issue had come to the front in North America and India.

Colonial expansion the work of the bourgeoisie and the civil administration

With heavy clouds gathering visibly over the French interests in North America and India even the nobles could not fail to give attention to the colonial problem. As they were in their own view the first line of their country's defense, they turned with their usual eagerness to war as the solution of the impending conflict. But they viewed the situation with a fatal bias. Having in the past fought Great Britain on land and in Europe, they fancied they might settle the pending colonial issue in the same manner. At the very least, according to their idea, the government ought to make its main effort on the European continent and to treat the colonial area as a purely secondary theater. This signified, in effect, developing the army at the expense of the navy. Great Britain took the exactly opposite course. The British viewpoint was that a fight over transoceanic lands would be decided by sea power. Let the navy gain control of the waterways and the colonies would fall like ripe fruit into the lap of the victors.

The bias of the nobles for military rather than for naval power

It was the preference of the dominant court party for a war on land rather than on sea that explains the search made by France for a continental ally when it became apparent that the struggle with Great Britain could no longer be adjourned. Traditionally opposed to Austria, France made overtures first to Austria's rival, to recently risen Prussia. But when Prussia, in the hope of remaining neutral in a colonial struggle that did not concern it, signed a convention with Great Britain looking toward neutrality, the court party at Versailles did not hesitate to reverse itself and to enter into an alliance with Austria. This naturally swung Prussia and Great Britain into a formal alliance.

The diplo-matic revo-lution of 1756

THE SEVEN YEARS' WAR (1756-1763)

The war between France and Great Britain broke out in May, 1756. A few months later Prussia and Austria followed suit. The complex struggle is known in Europe as the Seven Years' War (1756-1763), in America as the French and Indian War. While involving the issue of Silesia recently raised between Austria and Prussia, it turned in the main about the epochal question whether North America and India were to be the colonial prizes of France or Great Britain.

Two leading issues in-volved in the Seven Years' War 1756-63

With the French people aware of the gravity of the issue, France made a notable effort in behalf of victory both on land and sea. However, all its efforts were to a large extent nullified by the circumstance that the individual in whose hand the threads of war and policy came together was the absolute, divine right monarch and that this monarch happened to be the despicable Louis XV. As Louis was morally too slack to impose his will on his ministers, generals, and admirals, the situation got out of hand, subordinates gave conflicting orders, and corruption showed its face openly and without shame. It characterizes the intolerable condition at the court that, in so far as a central control might be said to have existed at all, it was exercised by the king's official mistress, Madame de Pompadour. Though possessed of a certain grace of mind and person, she was not even remotely endowed with the intelligence and character to direct the vast war machine with which France was attempting to sus-tain its honor and protect its interests.

French mismanage-ment of the war charge-able to the king and court

The Seven Years' War revealed to the French people that they were the victims of a system which had developed almost countless evils in govern-ment, administration, finance, taxation, and economic practices. We shall learn more of these evils when we treat of the Revolution of 1789, to which they unescapably led. At this point, with the war as our object les-son, we may declare without hesitation that the two most crushing evils were an absolutism that did not function and a privileged nobility which lived parasitically on the unprivileged mass of the French people.

The two main French evils

By the middle of the century a change had come over the French people, for although exploited not only by the nobles but also by the other privileged order, the clergy, they were no longer an inert mass. One element of the population in particular, the townsmen or bour geoisie, had become tremendously dynamic. It was the townsmen who had built up the commerce and industry of France and who had created a stake of considerable value to themselves in the transoceanic colonies. It was they, too, who had developed a body of critics and writers identified with the current intellectual movement, the so-called Enlightenment. Indeed it was largely bourgeois Frenchmen whom the rest of Europe honored as the leaders of the general enlightened attack. Rise of the French bourgeoisie to economic and intellectual dominance

Guided by the norms of reason and utility, the champions of Enlightenment had from the first days of the reign of Louis XV been engaged in subjecting the French and the general European institutional inheritance to a critical scrutiny. Under the leadership of the incomparable satirist and propagandist, Voltaire, they had, even before the Seven Years' War began, succeeded in alienating a large part of the bourgeoisie from the existing social and political system. The Seven Years' War completed the conversion of the bourgeoisie to the cause of reform. For, visibly and palpably, the crushing defeat of France was the result of the system, of which the main features were an absolute king and two irresponsible privileged classes. Not till the indignant townsmen had swept king, nobility, clergy, and the innumerable associated evils from their path would they cease from an agitation, the aim of which, in last analysis, was to preserve themselves and their country. The bourgeois attack led by Voltaire and motivated by self-preservation

At the outbreak of the Seven Years' War the British effort was even more flagrantly unco-ordinated than that of the French. The parliamentary system, considered in itself, was no surer guarantee of governmental efficiency than absolutism. Nor had it, for that matter, been set up on the ground of its efficiency. However, to the good fortune of Great Britain it happened that out of the give-and-take of the parliamentary game there emerged that human rarity, a leader. Not only did he, during his possession of power, co-ordinate the British campaigns on land and sea, but he also set an example of such high spirit that the whole nation gathered in a solid mass behind him. It was not till toward the close of the second year of the war (1757) that William Pitt became secretary of state. In that capacity he so completely dominated the ruling Whig cabinet that he may be said to have constituted for the four years his power lasted the one-man government of his country. The success of Great Britain owing to a leader, William Pitt

In Pitt's mind there was no doubt at all that the war between France and England revolved about sea power and colonies, and he reserved his best effort for this main theater of the conflict. But he did not neglect the secondary continental theater. He supported the British ally, Frederick of Prussia, with a substantial annual subsidy, and, in addition, he organized an army, largely of German mercenaries, which defended Hanover, the homeland of King George II, against French attack. In this manner he encouraged the French to exhaust their strength in military enterprises For Pitt there was a primary and a secondary theater of war far from the colonial scene. With these purely defensive tactics in Europe, Pitt coupled a vigorous offensive in the areas alone decisive for British destiny.

By making sea power his first and central consideration Pitt brought the British navy to such strength that it could carry through a blockade of the French coasts. Consequently the French were unable to send the needed supplies and reinforcements to their armies fighting in North America and India. In 1759, in two attempts to break the blockade, the French fleet was defeated at Quiberon Bay and Lagos. Following these actions, the British blockade was about one hundred per cent effective and may fairly be considered to have been the decisive factor in the war. Cut off from the mother country, the French colonial forces found their resistance enfeebled and finally paralyzed. A strong offensive campaign on the disputed colonial soil was the complementary action by which Pitt resolved to clinch the advantage gained by his command of the sea.

Blockade of the French coasts the decisive feature of Pitt's strategy

Fully to grasp the campaign of the British on American soil we have to go some years back of Pitt's assumption of power. Since the French claimed the St. Lawrence and Mississippi river basins to the fullest possible extent, they of course regarded the headwaters of the Ohio as lying within their sphere. Accordingly, they had built a fort at the point where the Monongahela and Allegheny unite to form the Ohio. As the British refused to admit the French claim, they had in 1755, while still officially at peace with France, dispatched a force under General Braddock to destroy the French stronghold. Refusing to follow the advice of a young Virginian officer, George Washington, who twenty years later leaped into fame in a conflict of another sort, Braddock was badly beaten by the Indian allies of the French and himself killed.

The French hold the headwaters of the Ohio and defeat General Braddock (1755)

This was a discouraging curtain-raiser for the war that followed. The energy of Pitt, on his assumption of power, soon squared the account. In 1758 a better-planned expedition than Braddock's captured the French fort. Rebaptized Pittsburgh, it still proclaims to the living generation the great minister's share in destroying the French empire in America.

The captured French fort renamed Pittsburgh (1758)

As the main French position in America was not in the Mississippi but in the St. Lawrence basin, British success would not be assured till the long line of French posts guarding the St. Lawrence and its tributaries had been reduced. The process, successfully begun in the same year that saw the founding of Pittsburgh, led in the following year (1759) to a well-concerted attack on the main French position at Quebec. It was intrusted to an eager young man thirsting for military glory, General Wolfe. By scaling in the night of September 12, 1759, the precipitous cliffs above Quebec, he was able on the following morning to bring his army into action against the forces of the French governor, Montcalm, on the Plains of Abraham beyond Quebec's western gate. In the course

General Wolfe captures Quebec (1759); death of himself and the French commander

of the battle both of the heroic commanders were killed, but the British held the field and Quebec surrendered. On the capture of Montreal in the following year the whole of Canada passed into British hands.

In India the British victory was no less decisive. With very little support from home the military and diplomatic genius of Robert Clive succeeded in breaking up every attempt of the French to build their power on a group of dependent Indian princes. With an uncanny talent for choosing the right moment for action, Clive regularly scattered the French and their Indian friends just as their fortunes seemed once more to be mounting. His victory at Plassey in 1757 was followed three years later by an equally important British triumph at Wandewash. When, in 1761, the main French stronghold of Pondichéry was captured, the British mastery of the situation was complete.

Clive destroys the French power in India (1757-61)

Confronted with an unparalleled disaster, the French managed to adjourn its formal acknowledgment by persuading Spain to come to their rescue. Under a ruler of the house of Bourbon since the extinction (1700) of the Spanish branch of the Hapsburgs, Bourbon Spain had usually cooperated with Bourbon France in the decades preceding the outbreak of the Seven Years' War under an agreement called the Family Compact. In 1761 the Family Compact was renewed in a particularly binding form. However, it was not merely dynastic concern that prompted the Spanish Bourbons to rush to the aid of the older branch as the war was nearing its close. The overwhelming success of the British against the French colonial empire had filled the Madrid government with alarm for its own possessions and moved it to act with France rather than wait to be attacked at British convenience.

Bourbon Spain comes to the rescue of Bourbon France, 1761

George III (1760-1820)

The Family Compact of 1761 was still undivulged when Pitt got wind of it through his spies. With his accustomed promptness he proposed to throw himself on the Spaniards before they were ready. He encountered unexpected opposition, which emanated in the main from his own sovereign, King George III. At the age of twenty-two George had succeeded to the throne on the death (October, 1760) of his grandfather, George II. He had been brought up in a Tory environment and filled with aversion for the Whigs, under whose long control of parliament the king's prerogative had been reduced to a shadow. "Be a king, George," was the admonition given him from his boyhood by his ambitious mother. So he went cautiously to work to revive the royal power and, as a preliminary measure, established contact with the Tories by introducing one of their members, Lord Bute, into the Whig ministry.

Accession of George III, 1760

On entering the cabinet Bute headed a group, which, with the open connivance of the king, demanded an early peace. A large part of the country was undoubtedly with the king and Bute, since the usual disgust with a war that was lasting too long and was exhausting the country had put in an appearance. It was at this precise moment that the fiery Pitt proposed to widen the conflict by striking at Spain without first waiting for a declaration of war. As Bute swung the cabinet to his side, Pitt was defeated and obliged to resign (1761). That Pitt's position in regard to Spain was well taken had to be admitted by Bute himself a few months later when, in January, 1762, he was forced to meet the now open preparations of Spain with war.

Pitt forced from office (1761) on the Spanish issue

The last-minute intervention of Spain in the Franco-British colonial conflict completely failed of its purpose. Overflowing with confidence and provided with an irresistible war machine, the British swept on to new triumphs by capturing Havana and Manila, the former the leading stronghold of the Spaniards in the western, the other their leading stronghold in the eastern hemisphere. As, in spite of these successes, Bute, supported by the king, did not for a moment desist from his efforts to end the war, he succeeded before the close of the year in reaching an accommodation with both Bourbon powers. Without any doubt Pitt, in Bute's place, would have exacted much more crushing terms. Even with Bute in control, it cannot be denied that by the definitive Peace of Paris, signed on February 10, 1763, Great Britain gained every essential point for which she had fought the war.

Defeat of Spain and Peace of Paris, 1763

In the Treaty of Paris the Spanish Bourbons escaped without paying any important penalty, for Havana and Manila were restored to them. The French Bourbons, however, were obliged to surrender Canada together with all the Mississippi valley area lying east of that river. As for India, while Pondichéry and a few other commercial settlements were restored to France, she was forbidden the development of military power. With Great Britain's mastery of the peninsula put beyond challenge, she was able to expand her Indian rule at her own pace and convenience.

Great Britain master of North America and India

With a vastly enlarged empire in their hands the British were obliged to undertake its organization. The problem, one of the most difficult ever to confront a people, was destined to be a main concern of Great Britain for many decades to come. It is hardly a cause for surprise that the very first attempt at empire organization led to disaster.

Britain's empire problem

REVOLT OF THE AMERICAN COLONIES

Far and away the most valuable of the British dependencies were the colonies of the Atlantic seaboard, inhabited at the time of the Peace of Paris by approximately one and a half million people of European stock and united to the mother country by a common culture. The American colonies enjoyed an unusual measure of self-government. In the recent war they had exerted themselves in behalf of Great Britain, but they made no regular, stipulated contribution to imperial defense. It is not strange that when, on the establishment of peace, the money had to be found to meet the enlarged imperial armament that would have henceforth to be maintained, it should have occurred to the British parliament to draw, to a certain extent, on the American colonists. *The British resolve to tax the American colonies in behalf of imperial defense*

It is equally understandable that the colonists, accustomed to their frontier freedom, should have resented the attempt of the parliament, a body in which they were not represented, to subject them to taxation. In the year 1765 the parliament by means of the Stamp Act imposed a stamp tax on the American colonies. It aroused so much wrath and resistance that it could not be collected, and had, perforce, to be withdrawn. However, as the parliament seized the occasion to assert its theoretic right to tax the colonies, the issue did not die; and with friction growing apace there were frequent outbreaks of mob violence. The British ministry, dominated by an obstinate king, finally resorted to military force. To this measure, signifying war in their eyes, the indignant Americans answered with the resolution to revolt (Declaration of Independence, July 4, 1776). *Resistance of the colonists crowned by Declaration of Independence, 1776*

Vastly important as the ensuing struggle is, its details have no place here. From the point of view of the long colonial duel between Great Britain and France, to which this chapter has been mainly devoted, the decisive event of the War of American Independence was the appeal of the Americans to France for aid. With the French finances in complete disarray, it would have been wise not to listen to the overtures for an alliance made by Benjamin Franklin, the agent whom the rebellious colonists dispatched to Paris. But the French desire to revenge the defeat suffered in the Seven Years' War overcame every other consideration. In 1778 the French joined the rebels and declared war on Great Britain. *France comes to the aid of the Americans, 1778*

It is highly probable that without the aid of France the Americans would not have been able to hold out against the British, who strained every sinew to retain the mastery over their colonies. Small, cumulative successes of the French and Americans led at last to the surrender at Yorktown (1781) of the British army under Cornwallis. It was the supreme event of the war and brought honor, above all, to the great American leader, General George Washington. The discouraged British thereupon opened negotiations, which terminated in another Peace of Paris signed in 1783, exactly twenty years after the earlier Peace of Paris. *The victory of the colonies recorded in the Second Peace of Paris, 1783*

France herself had not been sufficiently successful to gain anything of moment from the new settlement. The colonial balance between her and Great Britain as arranged at the close of the Seven Years' War remained therefore undisturbed. The only really memorable feature of the Second *Main fruit of the Peace of Paris is the independence of the American colonies*

Peace of Paris was the recognition of the independence of the revolted British colonies under the name of the United States of America. A new nation, as yet of modest strength but of incalculable potentialities, had stepped out upon the world stage.

The American revolution produced an interesting repercussion in Ireland. The Protestant colonists in Ireland demanded that the parliament, by which they shared in the rule of the country and from which the Catholic Irish (and that means the native population) were excluded, should be given the right to enact laws without interference from London. Badly shaken by the successful American rebellion, the British government in 1782 gave way. Ten years later the right to vote for members of the Irish parliament (but not the right to sit in it) was extended to Catholics on the same terms as to Protestants. Plainly the two faiths were at last beginning to draw together.

The Irish gain (1782) legislative independence

The larger measure of freedom did not however pacify the island. The continued disturbances induced the British government to consider the advisability of fusing the Irish parliament with the parliament at Westminster. A successful precedent of this kind had been established by the fusion of the English and Scottish parliaments a hundred years before. The plan was carried out in the Act of Union of the year 1800. In exchange for the surrender of their own parliament the Protestant Irish were given representation, along with Englishmen and Scots, in the parliament at London. A consequence of the fusion was that thenceforward the government designated itself officially as the "United Kingdom of Great Britain and Ireland."

The Act of Union (1800); the Irish parliament merged with the British parliament

19 LEADING CULTURAL TRENDS BETWEEN 1648 AND 1789

THE NATURAL SCIENCES

IN TREATING THE outstanding cultural trends of
the period whose political history has been reviewed in the immediately
preceding chapters, we shall begin with the natural sciences. Already in
the period of the Reformation and Counter-Reformation science had, as
we have seen, acquired a new dignity, chiefly through the physico-
astronomical work of Copernicus, Kepler, and Galileo. In the following
period science became so completely dominant among the whole body of
the European intelligentsia that it successfully crowded theology from
the ruling position it had hitherto occupied and inaugurated what, looking at Europe from a purely intellectual viewpoint, we may fairly call
an age of science. *Science replaces theology as the ruling intellectua' interest*

The most illustrious scientific name of the period is that of Isaac Newton (1642-1727). Newton had a mind of vast capacity and made important contributions in almost innumerable scientific fields. In mathematics
he supplied the invaluable invention of the calculus. In optics he originated the spectrum, thus showing that the colors of the rainbow are due
to the decomposition of white light. But so outstanding and indeed revolutionary was his discovery in the field of physics that we are justified in
concentrating attention on this particular achievement. *The titanic figure of Isaac Newton*

In 1687 Newton published a work, the *Principia Mathematica,* which
set the crown on the physical and mathematical labors of his predecessors. In this work Newton proclaimed the universal law of gravitation,
according to the formula that "every particle of matter in the universe
attracts every other particle of matter with a force varying inversely as
the square of the distance between them and directly proportional to the
product of their masses." The simplicity coupled with the completeness
of the law of gravitation overwhelmed the contemporary mind as it continues to overwhelm ours. Here was the explanation of why the planets
revolved majestically in their orbits about the sun as well as why ultimately the feather tossed into the air and the ball propelled from the
cannon's mouth always return to the earth. *Newton discovers the law of universal gravitation*

Newton's law of gravitation projected a universe operating according
to inalterable principles. To thinking man existent within a vast natural

framework regulated by eternal decrees it communicated an exhilarating
Rapid ex- sense of grandeur. Committed with ever waxing success to the task of
tension of extending the boundaries of knowledge, science won a steadily increasing
the range of body of devotees. Not only did they set about enthusiastically to accumu-
science late fresh information in the fields already staked off, but by penetrating
into virgin territory they took the first step toward the creation of many
new scientific specialties.

Before the eighteenth century was far on its way the passion for knowl-
Science be- edge of the world of nature in which the life of man is set had become
comes the so general that literary popularizers undertook to purvey the new discov-
religion of eries to the general public. It was in this manner that, at least for an
the intel- upper stratum of Europeans, science became a veritable religious faith
lectuals which gradually superseded the faith embodied in the various Christian
churches. But before we take up the consequences for Western civilization of this supersession of religion, we shall have to indicate specifically
some of the more important scientific advances of the age.

It was the impetus communicated in the Renaissance to astronomy,
Uninter- physics, and mathematics that secured to these related studies the scien-
rupted ad- tific ascendancy that plucked its ripest fruit in Newton's law of universal
vance in gravitation. But while the Englishman far outshone his scientific con-
the physico- temporaries, we are not to suppose that these lesser figures gave off
astronomical no light. There was, for instance, the Dutchman, Christian Huygens
field (d. 1695). He invented the pendulum clock and made valuable contributions to such fields as mechanics and optics; and among several distinguished astronomers the Englishman, Edmund Halley (d. 1742), deserves to be mentioned for his charting of the orbit of a comet which
he observed in 1682 and whose return in 1759 he correctly predicted.
Very properly it has ever since been called Halley's comet.

It is undeniable that Newton marked the apex of the great era of
Descriptive theoretical formulation inaugurated by Copernicus. Science after Newton
character seemed to pause momentarily for breath, for, while intensifying its ob-
of post- servational and laboratory methods, it contented itself in the main
Newtonian with the more modest task of describing and classifying the vast body
science of data which had been, and were being, accumulated in the ever multiplying departments of knowledge.

The prevailing tendency toward order and organization may be illus-
Mineralogy trated by the work done in mineralogy, botany, and zoology. In mineralogy the first organizing step was the classification of fossils; there followed in due course the classification of minerals and rocks. With fossils, minerals, and rocks at the disposal of the naturalist, he was in
possession of the raw materials for the formulation of a scientific geology. Yet, though the eighteenth century was on the road to this goal, it

was not till the nineteenth century that a genuine science of geology saw the light.

Turning to botany, we learn that the outstanding work in the classification of plants was done by the Swede, Linné, the latinized form of whose name is Linnaeus (d. 1778). So comprehensive and brilliant were his labors that the system he invented was not superseded for several generations. As for zoology, its most remarkable representative was the Frenchman, Buffon (d. 1788). But Buffon was much more than a zoologist. His interest ran to all the sciences and moved him to set forth the stage at which they had arrived in his day in what we may call a scientific encyclopedia. This, published in many volumes as a *Natural History,* is both descriptive and classificatory. In this connection it is interesting to note that the circumspect and cautious Buffon was inclined to deprecate premature classification as an attempt to confine nature within the too narrow limits of a man-made system. *Botany, zoology*

It would now have been normal for chemistry to come to the front, and the Englishman, Robert Boyle (d. 1691), made this very contention before the seventeenth century came to a close. Science had thus far concerned itself with matter in motion; the next logical forward step was to turn to the composition of matter. Nonetheless, chemistry long failed to advance owing to the fact that its devotees took up the problem of combustion and got themselves inextricably entangled in an erroneous theory. Gradually, however, it was made clear that combustion was a question of gases, and this led to the isolation of gases, first, of hydrogen, next, of oxygen. Whereupon the Englishman, Henry Cavendish (d. 1810), demonstrated that water was composed of hydrogen and oxygen, air of oxygen and nitrogen. At this point enters the greatest chemist of the age, the Frenchman, Lavoisier (d. 1794). He for the first time correctly explained the process of combustion and actually separated water into its two components. Finally, he propounded the epoch-making theory that, although matter may alter its state, its mass remains always the same. *Early chemistry culminates in Lavoisier*

INSTRUMENTS AND MACHINES

Since science is so largely a matter of accurate weighing and measuring, there went from the first, hand in hand with its theoretical development, the invention of instruments and machines. We have noted the construction of the telescope and microscope in Galileo's day. Shortly after, the barometer came into use, the product of the combined researches of the Italian, Torricelli (d. 1647), and the Frenchman, Pascal (d. 1662). All three instruments, very crude at first, were by steady improvement made increasingly serviceable. To the growing laboratory equipment a German, Fahrenheit (d. 1736), contributed a greatly im- *Precision instruments* proved mercury thermometer still in use in English-speaking countries.

Interesting inventions: pendulum clock, air pump, steam engine

At the same time interesting machines saw the light, some of which showed possibilities of becoming socially useful by multiple commercial reproduction. We have already mentioned the pendulum clock of Huygens. By experimenting with the force acquired by air through compression, Otto von Guericke (d. 1686), a German, invented the air pump. Observation of the expansion of gases, especially of steam, led a Frenchman, Papin by name, to construct, around 1700, the earliest steam engine, an extremely crude affair. The idea was taken up in England, where Thomas Newcomen constructed (1712) a steam engine to pump water out of coal mines. Though a clumsy instrument, it did the particular work for which it was intended and must be accounted the first commercially successful steam engine. It was not till the Industrial Revolution was well on its way that the improvements were devised which made Newcomen's engine more generally serviceable.

The universal steam engine invented by Watt

The Industrial Revolution will be treated in a later chapter. Suffice it at this point to say that it originated in England in connection with the constantly increasing demand on the markets of the world for woolen and, above all, cotton goods. This demand led to the invention of machinery for spinning yarn to take the place of the slower labor of human hands; and this invention was followed by the invention of machinery for weaving cloth. The very gradual transformation from hand-made yarn and cloth to the machine-made article continued through the second half of the eighteenth century till, in order effectively to operate the new machinery, the solution of the problem presented by the steam engine had imperatively to be found. The man who solved it was a Scotsman, James Watt, who in 1769 took out a patent for a workable engine. It required six more years before Watt installed his first steam engine, to which he, and after him others, constantly added important improvements. It was not till 1800 that the rapid extension of steam engines began even in England; and it was not till a few more decades had passed that they began their triumphal march over the continent and through the world.

PHILOSOPHY

Descartes bases modern philosophy on reason and science

In turning, next, to philosophy let us begin by recalling that in the Middle Ages philosophy was closely allied with theology, and that in the seventeenth century Descartes inaugurated modern philosophy by deserting the alliance with theology in favor of an alliance with mathematics and the natural sciences. Descartes had ended by making reason supreme and by inviting the rejection of every so-called truth that could not be proved. Spinoza, we learned, though propounding a pantheistic version of the universe, was as strict a rationalist as Descartes.

Descartes was thus the fountain-head of a stream of purely rationalist philosophy which held undisputed rule till the appearance of John Locke. Locke appealed to the senses and thereby discredited the ground-and-lofty tumbling inseparable from a too exclusive reliance on reason. He proved so congenial to the particular outlook of the eighteenth century, the century identified, as we shall presently see, with the Enlightenment, that we shall have to give him our close attention.

Descartes challenged by Locke

But before taking up Locke we must concede a word to the German philosopher, Leibnitz (1646-1716). He was a great, a very great mathematician, who independently of Newton invented the calculus; but he was also a believer in God, a Christian. While his mathematical genius persuaded him to rely on reason as the likeliest tool of knowledge, his faith pointed him so strongly to spirit that he ended by seeing in spirit the only reality. His spiritual world in final analysis is made up of atoms, which he called monads. There are many varieties of monads, each in motion and therefore each a force acting according to its particular law. All the monads together reflect the divine harmony of the Creator. Stemming from the belief in a universe so happily constituted was the optimistic conclusion that we live in the best of possible worlds.

Leibnitz asserts the exclusive reality of spirit

John Locke (1632-1704), an Englishman, was mentally the product of Newtonian science and the English political revolution, which substituted the authority of the parliament for that of the king. He became the champion of both these developments and therewith the most representative thinker of his day. Concerned at this point only with his philosophy, we may begin by asserting his common-sense viewpoint, which derived from his practical, earth-bound nature. It was this common sense of his which prompted him, while turning his back on the airy metaphysical systems constructed by the rationalists, to ask himself, and to attempt to answer, the relatively simple question of how we come into possession of knowledge.

Locke and common sense

His views on this head were expounded in his *Essay Concerning Human Understanding* (1690). Therein he discarded innate ideas, that is, the commonly held view that we are born with a stock of ideas, such as God and immortality, in favor of the view that our minds at birth are blanks and cumulatively gather impressions through the senses. This sense material is then molded by certain operations native to the mind, such as reflection, memory, and judgment. While Locke thus predicates reason as a natural, inborn faculty and is therefore in this limited sense a rationalist, he insists on sensations and experience as the primary source of knowledge. On account of this emphasis Locke is called a sensualist or, with equal justification, an empiricist.

Locke refers knowledge to the senses and experience

It was Lockian empiricism rather than the rationalism of Descartes that came to dominate the thinking of the eighteenth century. There was no lack of critics of Locke, for rationalism defiantly held its ground. The vigorous polemics between rationalists and empiricists very properly engage the attention of every historian of philosophy. As, however, the main stream of eighteenth century philosophic thought has its source in Locke, we are justified in conceding the primacy of his empiricism. The Lockian stream has two outstanding tributaries, Hume and Kant.

Locke outlines the main line of eighteenth century philosophy

The Scotsman, David Hume (1711-1776), started from the sensualist position of Locke but challenged the ability of the mind to build up from sensations an edifice of valid knowledge. As our minds are, according to Hume, insufficiently equipped for this work, it follows that we live forever in a world of mere probabilities. Hume's was a skepticism so sweeping that not only philosophy but natural science, on which it rested, became enveloped in a cloud of doubt. The only true and valid science according to him is mathematics. The fullest expression of this negation or pessimism of Hume's is to be found in his *Treatise of Human Nature*.

Hume the skeptic

From this threatened termination in futility, both philosophy and natural science were rescued by the German thinker, Immanuel Kant (1724-1804). What Kant did in a number of critical works, of which the *Critique of Pure Reason* is the most important, was to disentangle science (physics) from philosophy (metaphysics) and to confer on each a definite function and technique. To science he assigned the world of appearances, the so-called phenomenal world. This world it is the business of science to describe by means of general propositions or laws. Science does not and must not concern itself with the unseen reality behind appearances, the so-called noumenal world, which is the proper realm of philosophy.

Kant the reconciler

The separation of science and philosophy into distinct, airtight compartments was a somewhat specious procedure which is not agreeable to present-day thinking. Nonetheless, at the time he wrote Kant rendered a considerable service, for he restored to philosophy its self-respect and at the same time liberated the natural sciences from theological and philosophical tutelage, thereby sending them forward with redoubled assurance on their mission of the increase of knowledge.

Subsequent challenge of Kant's position

THE ENLIGHTENMENT

The scientists and philosophers who, no longer in awe of theology, thought in terms of reason, nature, and law, proudly looked on themselves as bringers of light; and in measure as they drew a following to their standards they gave vigor to a broad cultural movement of revolutionary import which has received the name of the Enlightenment. No sooner had it come into existence than its spread was promoted by innumerable agencies. The most distinguished of these were the scientific academies instituted, usually under government auspices, for the exchange of views among the learned and for the publication of their researches. It will serve to indicate their early appearance on the scene to note that the famous Royal Academy of England was chartered in 1662, the equivalent French Academy in 1666. The Enlightenment promoted by scientific academies

Comparable institutions which now for the first time came to the front in numbers were public libraries, scientifically equipped observatories, and museums for the housing of mineral, botanical, and other similar collections. Together they constituted an indispensable apparatus for the prosecution of their investigations by the specialists; but as they were usually made available also to the public, they served to propagate the new outlook. Finally, there were the journals and newspapers, which, so familiar to the present age as purveyors of every variety of information in easily digested form, were started on their amazing career in this first age of the diffusion of knowledge. Other promoting agencies

What the spokesmen of the Enlightenment proposed to do was to examine the inherited political, juridical, economic, and ecclesiastical institutions in the light of reason and utility. As this was a very large order, it was usual for them to specialize, and while one critic concentrated on the irrational character of the state, another treated of the similar defects of the church, and still others threw themselves on the evil aspects of the law, the courts, the administration, taxation, production, and the general social order. But there was one man possessed of so deep-delving and wide-ranging a spirit that he became the universal critic and thereby the acknowledged captain of the movement. That man was Voltaire. He was a fighter, as were all the members of his band. But neither he nor they were scientists, at least not in a strictly professional sense. They were popularizers of science and of the social consequences that flowed from the application of science to life. This made them reformers or, better yet, humanitarians resolved with reason as their guide to improve the low condition of the human race. The objectives of the Enlightenment

Voltaire (1694-1778) was a Frenchman who began life with the purely literary ambition of winning fame as the author of important epics and dramas. At about the age of thirty, and largely because of his arbitrary arrest and detention in the fortress-prison of the Bastille, a moral change came over him which made him another man. He immersed himself in the science of Newton and the philosophy of Locke; he examined the state of contemporary society and was horrified by the tyranny, cruelty, and absurdity he encountered at every turn; he delved into history to learn whether man in other times and in other places had enjoyed a happier Voltaire turns from literature to social criticism lot. From these studies he emerged as the passionate reformer as which he figures in history and as which he shall here be treated. But before viewing him in this light let us at least take note that his historical studies were so original and fertile that he lifted history out of the dynastic and chronological rut along which it had been laboriously jogging for ages and gave it a new lease of life by directing it to the social and cultural realities. It is this turn toward the essentials of history that is exemplified in his *Age of Louis XIV*. By this and a number of similarly inspired works he takes rank among the great historical innovators.

The immense body of Voltaire's writings

Never has a great cause commanded a livelier intelligence and a busier pen than Voltaire's. His production was immense to the point of incredibility. He poured out an endless stream of pamphlets, satires, essays, tales, letters (ten thousand alone of these!), and topped all this activity with an encyclopedic *Philosophical Dictionary*. The target of his pointed arrows was always the same: the crimes of tyranny, injustice, intolerance, and superstition. But his target of targets was the Catholic church. In his eyes this institution was a jumble of irrational beliefs presided over by a hierarchy dedicated to the single purpose of holding human thought in perpetual bondage. He threw himself on it to the battle cry: *Ecrasez l'infâme* (crush the infamous one). And the church of course fought back with all the vigor it commanded. However, times had changed, for by the eighteenth century the church was no longer strong enough to snuff him out or even to reduce him for more than brief spells to silence.

Popularity and diffusion of works

Thus ever mobilized and in the field, he did not conduct his wars with artillery or musket-fire but with the rapier-like tools of his wit and mockery. Never since writing was invented has there been an author who commanded a more coruscating style and a greater clarity of expression. It was these traits that enabled his works to wing their way like birds over France and across Europe. That is another reason for his unchallenged supremacy: he was read with avidity and delight all the way from Madrid to St. Petersburg.

Voltaire's "Candide"

Since to get the true flavor of a dish it must be tasted, the only effective way to savor Voltaire is to read one of his books. None will perform this service better than his sparkling *Candide*. In this tale a youth named Candide moves through the world amidst innumerable adventures. They constitute the story's framework. But more important than the adventures is their implication that man lives his life amidst an endless succession of cruelties, vices, obscenities, and follies. While these are largely due to inherited and outworn habits and institutions which reflection might correct, they are also due to the inescapable limitations of our mortal state. Let the distinction be carefully noted. It shows that Voltaire, while a heated reformer, possessed also the serene judgment of the true philosopher.

Although the Enlightenment was a movement as wide as Western civilization, its outstanding champions were for the most part French- men. Some of them were hardly inferior in talent and influence to Vol- taire. To this distinguished group belongs Denis Diderot (1713-1784). While Diderot's writings do not flash like those of his Olympian com- patriot, they often carry a more weighty cargo, perhaps because Diderot held a different faith from Voltaire in that he earnestly believed, as ancient Socrates had done before him, that knowledge of itself will correct morals and promote happiness. This conviction explains why he became the editor of the famous Encyclopedia (*La Grande Encyclopédie*) pub- lished between 1751 and 1772 in seventeen volumes of text and eleven volumes of plates. Repeatedly in the long process of its publication it was threatened with suppression by an alarmed government, but Diderot unflinchingly saw his enterprise through to the end. As the broadest and most reliable systematization of contemporary knowledge that had yet appeared his encyclopedia achieved an immense vogue. It is to the edi- tor's credit that his work was not, as some zealots of the Enlightenment urged him to make it, a single immense pamphlet in the interest of re- form. While some biased and subjective articles were slipped into the mass, in the main the specialists, under Diderot's express direction, han- dled the matter assigned to them in the objective spirit proper to an honest work of general information.

Diderot and his Encyclo- pedia

RELIGIOUS ADJUSTMENTS CAUSED BY THE ENLIGHTENMENT

A movement like the Enlightenment, directed more vigorously against theological dogma and the churches founded thereon than against any other single inheritance from the past, was bound to produce impor- tant changes in the religious attitude of men. Some of these had the character of radical novelties, others of mere revisions of existing sys- tems. Giving precedence to the first group, we shall begin by having a look at the Enlightenment's most characteristic religious offspring, deism.

Rise of nev. religious attitudes

Deism originated in England under the influence of the world picture sketched by Newton's law of universal gravitation and Locke's philo- sophic common sense. For both of these thinkers reason ruled the uni- verse and was man's highest distinction. Their followers, as often hap- pens, went farther than the masters. From the universal diffusion of reason they deduced with cold mathematical precision a Supreme Rea- soner and from the universal operation of law a Supreme Lawgiver. Worship of such a Being required neither dogma nor an organized church; it was at bottom no more than the spontaneous expression of a

Deism: its English origin

natural piety and might more appropriately be conducted in a wooded clearing under the open sky than in a walled church built by human hands.

To this novelty of religious thought which, stripped of unessential trappings, was reduced to the single concept, God, its propagators gave the name of deism. By the first half of the eighteenth century a considerable section of the English upper classes had either become avowed deists or were deistically tinctured. Among its many spokesmen the most popular and eloquent was the poet, Alexander Pope, and among his most quoted lines were these:

Deism wins the English upper classes

> "Know then thyself, presume not God to scan;
> The proper study of mankind is Man."

The infiltration into society of deistic thought meant a weakening of the Christian churches, especially of the Anglican church, citadel of the English ruling classes. Even Anglican bishops at times publicly avowed their deistic leanings without offending either their fellow bishops or their parishioners. It is this partial assimilation of deism by Christianity that explains why deism never became militant in England. A faith that is not opposed is either absorbed or dies.

However, on leaping the channel to the continent deism became a fighting issue, first, because it encountered in the churches of the continent and, above all, in the Catholic church a vigorous foe; and second, because it found in Voltaire and his associates a body of uncompromising champions. We have already noted Voltaire's ferocious onslaught on the church of Rome. If he did not attack the churches that swore by Luther and Calvin with equal venom, it was only because they were in his eyes less powerful. In principle they were just as offensive and he as heartily hoped to rob them of their sting. Gradually the Christian lukewarmness that characterized the English upper classes came to dominate the corresponding classes on the continent. They did not turn atheist or even agnostic, except in rare instances. They were satisfied to declare themselves deists, that is, they acknowledged an infinitely remote, abstract God who ceased to arouse any religious emotion and satisfied the demands of reason by being identified as the First Cause.

Deism wins the upper classes of the continent

Unthinkable without the spread of deistic thought are the Free Masons. The first group, organized as a lodge, appeared at London in 1717. Its membership was drawn, in the main, from the common townsmen and was held together by being sworn to the pursuit of useful and humanitarian ends. By the lodge's adoption of secret vows, special costumes, and elaborate ceremonies it met the need for organization coupled with display that has always been potent among men. In the light of its emphasis on duties owed rather to man than to God it as-

Rise and spread of Free Masonry

sumed something of the character of an activated deism. It must have met a very general social-religious hunger, for in the course of a few generations sister lodges had sprung up all over Europe and had even spread across the Atlantic to the English colonies.

It was clear from the first that the established churches, especially of the Protestant denomination, could not remain unaffected by the impact of the Enlightenment and its deistic program. Protestantism had come into existence as an inner experience and owed such vitality as it possessed to the currents of feeling that never ceased flowing from man to God. The contemporary rationalist outlook threatened to dry up this stream and to reduce the churches themselves to hollow forms. The only way to save them from that fate was to set the stagnant stream of religious feeling again in motion. To this end there arose, usually within the churches themselves, an anti-rational movement. In Germany it was called Pietism, in England Methodism. *The Protestant churches refuse to succumb to rationalism without a struggle*

German Pietism, as less important, may be treated first. One leader, Francke (d. 1727), turning fiercely against the lax morals of the day, clamored for a return to a strict puritanical code; another leader, Spener (d. 1705), pleaded for the rebuilding of the mystical ladder that mounted from man to God. More important than these was Count Zinzendorf (d. 1760), who revived the ancient evangelical sect of the Moravians. Once more as of yore they practiced a humble piety which among their more spiritual members was transformed into an ecstatic mysticism. Apart from the partial infiltration of Pietism among the clergy and congregations of the established Protestant churches, it failed to produce any lasting results. *German Pietism*

English Methodism tells a different story. It was founded by John Wesley (1703-1791) with the important help of his brother Charles and of an inspired preacher, George Whitefield by name. Brought up in the Anglican church, Wesley, a man born with a warm sense of the nearness of God, was horrified by the petrified state into which the national establishment had fallen under rational and deistic influences. When first seized by spontaneous Christian fervor, he entertained the hope of winning the church of his birth back to its emotional origins; and it was only when the ecclesiastical rulers angrily rejected and persecuted him as a disturber of their slumbers that he began to organize his own separate congregations. His appeal was to the masses, the unfed sheep of the Lord, and the manner in which they were roused by his preaching and that of Whitefield remains one of the most astonishing chapters in the history of revivalism. *John Wesley founds the Methodist church*

Denied the use of the churches, the Wesleyan revivalists assembled their followers first in the open fields but gradually in chapels erected at their own expense by the rapidly growing congregations. These were then organized as a separate Methodist church, a name derived from a special "method" in private devotions advocated by the founder. Intellectually, Methodism was a throwback to long outmoded and anti-humanitarian doctrines, such as the total depravity of human nature and a blood-wreaking version of the atonement of Christ. Its strength lay in the stirring emotionalism by which it drew the religion-starved common people into its fold. It was early carried by missionaries to the English colonies of North America, where, besides setting up its own Methodist organization, it sent a powerful revivalist current through all its older Protestant relatives.

Its throwback to outmoded doctrines does not impair its vitality

In making the round of the established churches to view the effect on them of the Enlightenment, we cannot omit the mightiest and most venerable of them all, the Roman Catholic church. Faced with the cold rationalism of the eighteenth century, the pope and bishops never ceased denouncing it. One of its most evil fruits in their eyes was that it tended to strengthen the state at the expense of the church; and that the state, even when it was Catholic, was inspired with a new boldness toward its rival was evidenced by the case of the Jesuits. The famous order had proved itself the most vigorous prop of tottering Catholicism during the Counter-Reformation. Made proud and arrogant by its success, it aroused the hostility of the leading Catholic governments by backstairs influences which resembled a system of secret political control. Somewhat past the middle of the century the outraged kings of France, Portugal, and Spain, all three of them faithful sons of Rome, combined to bring pressure to bear on the pope for the removal of the hated meddlers. Unable in the long run to resist, Pope Clement XIV in 1773 published the bull that dissolved the order. But it did not remain dissolved. In 1814, on the heels of the general reaction consequent on the failure of the French Revolution, a later pope brought the Jesuits back to life.

Suppression of the Jesuits, 1773

THE SOCIAL SCIENCES

In measure as God, reinterpreted by science and philosophy, withdrew to an ever greater distance, his creature, man, loomed ever larger on the human scene and became the object of a steadily increasing interest. It was inevitable, too, that after Newton had converted the universe into a machine, man should be visualized as dwelling within the vast embracing frame of natural law. The studies having to do with man, the social studies, were therefore greatly stimulated, very often with the intention of finding the laws under which he acted as he did. For, if the whole universe operated under laws, it was inescapable that man, an inseparable element of the universal machine, was similarly subject to prescriptive rules. Social investigations of one kind or another were as old as the

The natural sciences call the social sciences to life

THE PALACE AT VERSAILLES. An unusual view of the palace erected by Louis XIV in the Italian Renaissance tradition.

THE HALL OF MIRRORS OF THE PALACE. The splendid setting in which Louis held court. (Alinari)

LOUIS XIV OF FRANCE.
After a contemporary engraving by Robert Nanteuil. (Bettmann Collection)

FREDERICK THE GREAT OF PRUSSIA. After a contemporary drawing. (Culver Service)

IMMANUEL KANT. (*top left*)
From a contemporary engraving. (Bettmann Collection)

JOHN LOCKE. (*top right*)
Engraving after a portrait by the painter, Godfrey Kneller. (Bettmann Collection)

SIR ISAAC NEWTON. After an old engraving. (Bettmann Collection)

VOLTAIRE. By the French sculptor, Houdon (d. 1828). (Courtesy of Chicago Art Institute)

Greeks. Under the new dispensation it was hoped to convert what had hitherto been offered as casual human studies into exact social sciences.

Political Science

The greatest writer on government toward the middle of the seventeenth century was the Englishman, Hobbes (d. 1679). He lived through the struggle between king and parliament and in a work called *The Leviathan* propounded a theory of government which is a passionate defense of royal absolutism. When in 1688 parliament finally triumphed over the king, it became necessary to find an apologist of the successful revolution capable of refuting Hobbes.

Hobbes' theory of governmen[t]

It was John Locke, the philosopher, who came forward in this role. In his two *Treatises on Government* (1690) he propounded what has received the name of the contract theory of government. Characteristically for an upholder of natural laws, Locke declared that men possess "natural rights," such as life, liberty, and property; that it is for the safeguarding of these rights that men create governments; and that, in case a government fails to meet its task of sustaining these rights, the people are justified in overthrowing it. By these propositions Locke unambiguously tied up with his contract theory the doctrine of the sovereignty of the people.

Locke propounds the contract theory of governmen[t]

The political doctrine propounded by Locke became an essential part of the general faith of the Enlightenment. However, it had a weakness. This lay in its being a dialectic development from an asserted dogma of "natural rights," behind which lay no other authority than human reason. An entirely different approach to the problem of government would be to interrogate history. The search of the pages of history for data on government would signify a resort to an inductive in place of a deductive method. It would impose, as a preliminary undertaking, a description and classification of governments as they have come and gone through all the ages of man.

The rationa[l] versus the historical approach to the problem of government

The historical, as distinct from the deductive path, was taken by the Frenchman, Montesquieu (1689-1755), who thus became the founder of political science in a modern sense. In his *Esprit des Lois* ("Spirit of the Laws") Montesquieu rejected the "natural rights" and the "social contract" of Locke. He declared that there was no one perfect government suitable for all peoples; and by an analysis of the governments of the past and present he showed that political institutions, in order to be successful, must be adapted to the physical situation and mental peculiarities of the people they are intended to serve.

Montesquie[u] makes the historical approach

Because it did not offer the simple solutions of a rationalizing method

Rousseau follows Locke, not Montesquieu

Montesquieu's work did not have as much influence in the rationalist eighteenth century as that of Locke. And Locke himself, for the continent at least, was largely superseded by Rousseau, who propounded a theory of government so purely rationalistic that it exhibits no connection at any point with the experience of history.

Rousseau exalts the emotions

Jean Jacques Rousseau (1712-1778), a French Swiss of the city of Geneva, was a highly gifted, erratic, and fundamentally unbalanced individual. He hated restraint of any kind and found the greatest happiness of which he was capable in the free indulgence of his emotions. He was enamored of sunsets, moonlight, rolling prairies, and impenetrable forests, and recorded his delight in them in glowing descriptions.

Rousseau augurs the coming of a new, the Romantic Age

The material universe, which the scientists, his contemporaries, were engaged in reducing to mechanical laws, Rousseau saw as an animated, dynamic whole which he passionately worshiped. Although born into the Age of the Enlightenment, he did not hesitate to challenge its faith in the human intellect as the certain guide and liberator of mankind. In the place of intellect he proclaimed the inalienable right of feeling. By virtue of this change of emphasis he became the father, or at least one of the fathers, of the Romantic Age which, destined to replace the Age of the Enlightenment, won a position at its side even during Rousseau's lifetime.

Rousseau, the anarchist, resolves to write on government

At this point we are not concerned with the romantic Rousseau, but with Rousseau, the political philosopher. If logic ruled the lives of men, Rousseau would never have written on politics, since he disbelieved in government of any kind and was a theoretic and practicing anarchist. Still, he was living in an age of political speculation and, possessed of deep faith in his power to deal with every human problem, he saw no reason why he should not write on an issue which, like government, attracted universal attention.

Rousseau's "Social Contract"

As might be expected under the circumstances, Rousseau's famous *Social Contract* (1761) was rationalization pure and simple. He took over Locke's main propositions of contract, right of revolution, sovereignty of the people. But he improved on Locke by an all-important addition, more explicitly treated, it is true, in other writings of his than in the *Social Contract*. Locke had predicated a primitive man who needed for his own protection to be brought under the restraint of law. Rousseau converted Locke's lowly and helpless primitive into a virtuous and noble savage, whom the advance of civilization had progressively degraded from his original free condition.

Consequently the very opening sentence of the *Social Contract* is a call to revolution. It reads: "Man is born free and everywhere he is in chains." It follows that it is necessary for man to throw off these chains in order to inaugurate a free society, which would, of course, be a democracy of equals. Locke had propounded a doctrine of revolution suited to the interests and moderate temper of the English middle classes. The much more sweepingly revolutionary teaching of Rousseau was addressed not to the middle classes but to the disinherited and disfranchised masses. It became the inspiration of the masses in the French Revolution and has remained one of their foremost gospels down to our day.

The "Social Contract" advocates an equalitarian democracy

Political Economy

We have learned in an earlier chapter that the economic theory and practice of the sixteenth and seventeenth centuries were summarized under the name of mercantilism. Mercantilism invited governments to maintain a favorable balance of trade in order to have at their disposal for use in an emergency like war a ready supply of bullion (gold and silver); it prompted them to promote exports and hinder imports; it encouraged ocean-borne commerce carried exclusively in native bottoms. Mercantilist governments regulated and controlled the various processes of production and exchange on the theory that this interference was socially necessary and economically advantageous.

Theory and practice of mercantilism

This program the eighteenth century, so generally critical of the practices of the past, was bound to challenge. The first group of systematic critics appeared in France. They were called physiocrats, owing to their faith that the single source of all wealth was nature (*physis* in Greek). They therefore made much of agriculture, forestry, and mining. Manufacture, which merely converted the raw products of nature into articles of use, was, in their eyes, an activity of a secondary order.

The physiocrats attack mercantilism

The real importance of the physiocrats lay in their insistence that production and distribution are most advantageously conducted when not interfered with by government. They coined the slogan *laissez faire* (hands off!) and agitated in favor of a complete abandonment of government supervision in order that nature and the enterprising individual facing the resources of nature might co-operate to produce wealth in the greatest possible amount.

The physiocrats coin the slogan, laissez faire

What the French physiocrats hesitantly suggested and confusedly set forth, the Scotsman, Adam Smith (d. 1790), brought to a clear and systematic formulation. In his famous *Wealth of Nations,* published in 1776, he advocated with cogent arguments the removal of all restrictions laid on trade by governments. He thus identified himself with the laissez faire of the physiocrats or, as it came after Smith's time to be called, free trade.

Adam Smith formulates the doctrine of free trade

In his general theory of wealth, however, Adam Smith deserted the physiocrats. Living in France, a country still overwhelmingly agricultural, they had declared the basic factor in the production of wealth to be nature, i.e., land. Adam Smith, citizen of a state that was growing **Adam Smith** wealthy through trade and industry, in contradiction of the physiocrats, **for the** stressed human labor as the basic factor. It followed from this position **greatest** that he demanded the greatest possible measure of freedom for the **possible** **freedom** individual producer. A society of untrammeled individuals would re- **for the** quire no regulative principle other than their enlightened self-interest **individual** and, with state interference withdrawn, would soon produce wealth on a scale undreamed of in the period of economic bondage.

It would be excessive to claim that government (political science) **The** and economics (political economy) achieved the status of "sciences" by **eighteenth** virtue of the developments just sketched. It is very doubtful that they **century ad-** have even in our time reached that status. However, it is fair to say that **vance of** **the social** in the eighteenth century the study of government and economics un- **sciences** derwent a significant renovation by the at least partial adoption of a **summarized** method wherein the older deductive processes were subjected to modifi- cation and correction by reference to inductive data.

THE NATIONAL LITERATURES

Since France and England were so indisputably in the European van in the period treated in this chapter, we shall direct our attention to the literature of these two countries. At the close, however, we shall add a brief word on German literature which, in the second half of the eighteenth century, awakened from a long winter sleep.

France

To begin with France, we have in the chapter dealing with its cul- **Brief** tural ascendancy in the days of Louis XIV (p. 303) spoken of the rich **summer of** harvest reaped in both poetry and prose. However, it was the French **the French** **theater** theater, enriched by the tragedies of Corneille and Racine and the comedies of Molière, that was regarded by contemporaries and is still regarded as the special glory of the reign. But though the theater flour- ished, it also died in Louis's time. Great poetry is fed from the un- fathomed well-springs of emotion, and when these were abandoned in favor of the precise demonstrations of reason, poetry became desiccated. Let Voltaire be summoned to the bar to confirm the statement. His great ambition in youth was to win renown as the continuator of the lofty style of Racine. Even after youth had passed he never quite ceased to indulge his early passion for poetic drama. But, able products of a lively intelligence, they were not nourished from the heart and their mimicked emotion falls upon the ear as hollow declamation.

However, it was not only the onrush of rationalism that took the life out of French poetry. The French upper classes had ever since the Renaissance been inspired by ancient literature and were impressed with the strict rules to which it submitted and with the so-called unities of time, place, and action to which, by the supposed dictum of Aristotle, the drama had been obliged to conform. With classical regulation accepted in principle there arose a legislator, Boileau by name, who codified the current practices. His *Art of Poetry* appeared in 1674. It enjoyed an unshaken authority for over a hundred years and explains why the French poetry of the eighteenth century, strait-jacketed, correct, and classical, leaves the pulse unquickened. The poetic
vein runs
dry

The fame of French literature in the Enlightenment springs from its prose. We have already celebrated the finesse, sprightliness, speed, and grace it acquired through the magic of Voltaire's touch. But a score of other writers, most of them contributors to Diderot's Encyclopedia, helped to make it the unequaled instrument it became. Engaged in the main in popularizing the Enlightenment, they employed in this service the essay, the tale, the satire, the comedy, in short, every prose form familiar to the age. The
ascendancy
of French
prose

The first really important novel was written by the unwearied opponent of the ruling rational cult, Jean Jacques Rousseau. It was called *La Nouvelle Héloise* (1761) and unfolded an ordinary story of seduction in terms of such extravagant emotion that it swept the public off its feet. We may call Rousseau's novel the curtain-raiser of a new, the Romantic Age, and agree that it pointed to the decline and early end of its predecessor, the Enlightenment. Rousseau
inaugurates
the Ro-
mantic Age

England

John Milton sang the swan song of Puritanism, *Paradise Lost* (1667), after the cause with which he had been identified had definitely and finally perished. But, never to be forgotten, this great epic, although hung on a Puritan frame and charged with a Puritan purpose, was penetrated with a power of speech and feeling that derived from the age of Elizabeth. This same inheritance persisted in an enfeebled form in John Dryden (d. 1700) and then disappeared under the deistic and rationalist flood that came in with the eighteenth century. In his prose Dryden so effectively accommodated his style to the current demands of simplicity and clarity that he may not improperly be regarded as the founder of the great prose school that came to the front in the next generation. Its leading representatives were the essayists, Addison (d. 1719) and Steele (d. 1729); but they were far outstripped by Swift (d. 1745), the famous deistically-influenced dean of St. Patrick's in Dublin. In such Milton
followed by
an age of
prose works as the satirical *Tale of a Tub* and the bitter but unfailingly amusing *Gulliver's Travels* he cleared the way for the English novel. At about the same time Daniel Defoe (d. 1731) composed in *Robinson Crusoe* a story of adventure that has retained its popularity through all the succeeding generations and takes rank with the best work in this kind of the bitter dean of St. Patrick's.

Emergence
of the
novel From these beginnings the novel took the development that gradually gave it the elastic form and immense vogue that have ever since been its characteristic marks. The men who chiefly shaped it and enlarged its scope were Samuel Richardson (d. 1761) and Henry Fielding (d. 1754). They added to its original core, adventure, the enlivening elements of character and social background. While Richardson, in such a novel as *Pamela,* drips with the sentiment that was becoming fashionable, he tries to give his people their proper and distinct outline. In his *Tom Jones* Fielding presents the vigorous and essentially healthy folk of the English countryside and brushes in their background with the liveliest colors.

The
supreme
poet of the
rationalist
age is Pope The representative poet of the period was Alexander Pope (d. 1744), deist and rationalist. These qualities help explain his sagacious common sense. If we add that he wielded a pen as precise and graceful as Voltaire's, we are prepared to understand how it came about that in his works, and especially in his *Essay on Man,* he was able to set forth his reflections on life with such a flavor of wit and such epigrammatic brevity that they still live on every tongue.

Germany

Lessing a
characteristic
figure of the
Enlighten-
ment The havoc wrought by the Thirty Years' War almost extinguished not only German literature but German civilization itself. Not till the eighteenth century did literature show signs of returned life, and even then a really great figure did not appear till half the century had run its course. This was Lessing (d. 1781), who, while a characteristic product of the Enlightenment, possessed a much broader historical outlook than was usual among contented rationalists. In his drama, *Nathan the Wise,* he made the most effective, because both the most reasonable and the most historical, plea for religious toleration presented in that age.

The
early years
of Goethe
and Schiller With the economic and political life of Germany again on its way to recovery the national sentiment re-awakened and sent its impulses through a host of youthful writers. That does not mean that they threw themselves exclusively on national themes. Their divided interests may be seen in the early work of two of them destined in their ripe years, which belong to the period of the French Revolution and are not here considered, to achieve an abiding reputation. The two outstanding youths were Goethe

(d. 1832) and Schiller (d. 1805). While Goethe's first drama, *Götz von Berlichingen,* harked back to the days of German knighthood and was therefore both national and historical, his next work, *The Sorrows of Werther,* was a novel in the sentimental vein of Rousseau. Schiller, a revolutionary spirit, in his first play, *The Robbers,* and in those that immediately succeeded it, regularly presented a conflict that turned about freedom from oppression, either political or social.

THE FINE ARTS

Italy

We have learned that in Italy during the centuries thus far covered by this book the Fine Arts passed through stages labeled respectively Early Renaissance, High Renaissance, and Baroque. It is not possible to assign precise dates to these periods, least of all to the Baroque. In Chapter 13 we noted that in some respects the Baroque Age may be said to have set in with the death of Michelangelo, that is, before the close of the sixteenth century. In a sketch of the history of St. Peter's at Rome (p. 242) it was shown that by the early seventeenth century the new mode was already strong enough to force the abandonment of the original ground plan in the shape of a Greek cross for one shaped as a Latin cross. This error led to another, which was to provide the east end of the Latin cross with a façade so high that it smothered the master-feature, the cupola. We also took note that the full baroque character of the Square of St. Peter with its obelisk, fountains, and double colonnade successfully brings home that the baroque pretentiousness occasionally culminated in a stage-set of overwhelming effectiveness.

Baroque the last phase of the Renaissance

The word "baroque" comes from the Portuguese and signifies an irregularly shaped pearl. And indeed it is the irregularity and contortion imposed on the definite outline and careful proportions of the High Renaissance that are the most striking features of the baroque style. Its domination dates from the Counter-Reformation which, while it gave birth to an uncontrolled Catholic emotionalism, cultivated at the same time an unexampled ecclesiastical pomp. That meant two exaggerations, an inner and an outer, and together they estranged the Italians from the moderation and balance stemming from classicism. Instead of classical stability, they now craved instability; instead of an edifice or statue or painting of clearly indicated structural parts, they demanded that the structural essentials be hidden under an agitated investiture. St. Peter's at Rome, which, after all, belongs in the main to the High Renaissance, fails to conform, except in some of its late additions, to baroque concepts and feeling. The Square in front of St. Peter's belongs

Stylistic ingredients of baroque

much more truly to that manner. But for an example of baroque in its uninhibited transformation of ordered mass into restless movement it is necessary to turn to such a church as Santa Maria della Salute at the entrance to the Grand Canal at Venice. Sculpture and painting tell the same story as architecture. Exactly like it they resolve the simple structural line into a complicated whirl of curves and rhythms.

France

While baroque made its way to Spain, the temper of the third great Latin country, France, proved too sane and disciplined to do more than give it a distant nod of recognition. Having long looked to Italy for artistic direction, France under Louis XIV continued to do so but contented itself on the whole with the models of an earlier period. These, as under the predecessors of the Grand Monarch, it then reshaped in accordance with the national genius.

The leading monumental structure of Louis's reign was the palace at Versailles pictured opp. p. 372. In the foreground may be seen a single-story summer house called the *orangerie*. Beyond its low roof the palace becomes visible to about two-thirds of its extent. Its immense scale expresses the greatness of the sovereign as whose residence it serves; but, with all its magnificence, it is without a touch of the violent contortionism of the baroque. Its definite lines and harmonious proportions proclaim it an essentially sober Renaissance product. Even the Hall of Mirrors (opp. p. 372), in spite of its extremely rich decorations, does not offend that regularity which was the very essence of Louis's soul. It is this moderation that explains why the neighbors of France, likewise out of sympathy with the extravagances of the baroque, deserted Italian for French artistic leadership in Louis's time.

However, under Louis XV the sobriety favored by his predecessor yielded to the graceful, if fatal frivolity that conquered court and aristocracy and sped them on the dance that ended at the steps of the guillotine. The new temper expressed itself in the light-footed movement of the rococo. Rococo is less an architectural style than a system of decoration which molded all articles of household use and of exterior and interior ornamentation to a perfect accord with its carefree spirit. But observe: while rococo, like baroque, runs to curves, it stays within bounds and is wholly lacking in the obsessed frenzy of the baroque. So rococo, while Louis XV reigned, became the rage. Then, on the accession of Louis XVI, there was the normal reaction against its too transparent insincerities, and a balanced and reticent classicism again began to assert itself. Witness thereof is the Pantheon, erected at Paris in 1780 in the

Marginal notes:

France rejects baroque

Versailles an essentially sober work of the Renaissance

The reign of rococo under Louis XV

WINTER LANDSCAPE. By the Flemish painter, Peter Breughel (d. 1569). An excellent example of the closeness to nature of the art of the Netherlands.

CANVASSING FOR VOTES. From an old print by the pictorial English satirist, Hogarth (d. 1764). (Culver Service)

OEDIPUS AND THE SPHINX. By the French painter, Ingres (d. 1867). It shows
the persistence of classical theme and style into the early nineteenth century.

purest classical style. With the Pantheon, French taste proclaimed its abiding attachment to moderation, poise, and good taste.

French painting responded to the same inspiration as architecture. In Poussin (d. 1665), one of the greatest landscape painters of all time, we have a masterful organization of nature in recessive planes. Poussin belongs to the dignified seventeenth century as decisively as Watteau (d. 1721) belongs to the frivolous eighteenth. Followed by a whole school of court painters working in the same light vein, he has left us an unforgettable portrait of French high society before it was buried under the hot lava of the Revolution.

French painting: Poussin and Watteau

Survival of Burgher Realism

It was the burgher society of the Dutch republic that alone among European groups produced an art which, avoiding classical myth and Christian allegory, was content to reflect the simple scenes of street and home. Dutch painting flourished in the seventeenth century. When in the early eighteenth century its energy evaporated, it looked as if, artistically speaking, the middle classes throughout Europe had given up the ghost. But that was not quite the case. Beneath the unbroken aristocratic surface, middle-class expression occasionally asserted itself. Such an expression is represented by the Englishman, Hogarth (d. 1764). He was undoubtedly stirred by the spirit of Dutch painting, although the satire in which he excelled is native to himself. Opposite p. 380 will be found a scene, *Canvassing for Votes,* which amusingly exposes the corruption practiced in connection with parliamentary elections. But neither for this piece nor for Hogarth's satiric presentations of the ruling classes in serial form, called *Rake's Progress* and *Harlot's Progress,* can it be claimed that they are great pictorial art. Nor was the realistic middle-class note he sounded sustained, for Hogarth had no followers. He was still alive when a portrait school, of which Sir Joshua Reynolds (d. 1792) and Thomas Gainsborough (d. 1788) were the leaders, came to the front and completely occupied the scene. Skillful manipulators of color, they gained an immense popularity by unfailingly giving to the faces and figures of their subjects the elegance and dignity with which, as members of a ruling group, they had presumably been endowed at birth.

Hogarth and the English portrait painters

Another sporadic upholder of realism turned up in France in the person of Chardin (d. 1779). Like Hogarth, Chardin took his cue from the Dutch and tossed his humble scenes from daily life right into the face of the hackneyed and insubstantial allegories of the popular court painters. Not, however, till the appearance of the Spanish painter, Goya (1746-1828), and not effectively till after the French Revolution, did burgher realism speak out with a voice that could not be ignored. It

French Chardin and Spanish Goya

was Goya, passionate hater of the court, the church, and the nobles, who cleared the path for the great, non-aristocratic art of the nineteenth century.

MUSIC

The Enlightenment was completely dominated by Italian music and, more particularly, by that invention of the Italian Renaissance, the opera. Hundreds and thousands of operas were written by Italian composers and performed all over Europe by Italian musicians and singers.

Almost all the instruments now in use were already known in the seventeenth and eighteenth centuries. They were generally of excellent quality, particularly the string instruments. It was in the eighteenth century that the Amati and Stradivarius families of Cremona in northern Italy manufactured violins which for perfection of tone have never been surpassed and which accordingly command fabulous prices in our time. However, the instrument preferred in that age to all others was the human voice. The Italian opera rested almost exclusively on the *bel canto*, the solo performance of the expert singer.

In the eighteenth century in Germany there took place a development which opened an entirely new avenue for music. Its inaugurator was Johann Sebastian Bach (1685-1750), perhaps the greatest musical genius that ever lived. While not neglecting the voice, Bach relied chiefly on the organ and on instrumental music to communicate his profound and richly varied message of religious and secular thought. It was Bach's work with organ and orchestra that has been a leading source of musical inspiration to our own day. Experts never weary of expatiating on his technical resources, on his marvelous polyphony and his intricate, mathematically perfect counterpoint.

In the generation after Bach, Gluck (d. 1787) took over the opera as developed by the Italians and gave it a new lease of life by associating the voice with an appropriate orchestration. At about the same time Haydn (d. 1809) invented the symphony as a means for giving expression by a group of associated musical movements to the wide range of the human emotions. The new form greatly stimulated the development of the orchestra. It rapidly became the magnificent, many-voiced instrument we know today, and the symphony, which prompted its perfection, achieved the honor of being generally regarded as the noblest form available for the musical artist.

By Mozart (d. 1791), whose flowing melody and spontaneous grace have never been surpassed, both the opera, derived from Gluck, and the symphony, derived from Haydn, were brought to the highest perfection they were destined to reach in the eighteenth century.

By their refinement, elegance, and technical discipline Gluck, Haydn,

---

Vogue of Italian opera

The favored instrument of the Italians the human voice

Germany develops instrumental music: Bach

The respective contributions of Gluck and Haydn

The perfection of Mozart

and Mozart fitted harmoniously into the aristocratic atmosphere of the eighteenth century. On their setting, the star of Beethoven (1770-1827) arose to preside over a new century and a new world of feeling. By his devotion to significant and tested form, Beethoven affirmed his attachment to the classicism of the eighteenth century; by giving, on the other hand, a novel freedom of expression to his far-ranging emotions he proved that he was a son of the new, the Romantic Age.

Beethoven, classicist and romanticist

ADVANCE OF WESTERN CIVILIZATION

Considered in connection with the political data of the period with which we are dealing, the cultural trends reviewed in this chapter declare the steady advance of the middle classes. It would not have been an over-bold prophecy to affirm, on the strength of the eighteenth century developments just traced, that the following, the nineteenth, century would belong to them. And it was already clear as day that the middle classes of the coming century would rule a civilization of a much vaster geographical range than had the privileged upper classes which they were engaged in displacing.

The middle classes to the front

Let us glance back briefly at the conquering march of Western civilization. On discussing, at the very beginning of our book, the origin of this civilization, we pointed out that its roots were set in a limited area identical with the domination of the Roman Catholic church in the Middle Ages; that within this area it had everywhere essentially the same characteristics; and that, beginning with the bond of a common religion, the peoples of western Europe had, without exception, been shaped by the same outstanding experiences.

Original narrow confines of Western civilization

The last-mentioned statement does not mean that novel attitudes and significant changes manifested themselves evenly throughout the occident and always at exactly the same time. They usually originated in a limited group, radiating thence till they had been disseminated among the others and become the property of all. The Renaissance, an Italian movement, is a case in point. So is the Reformation, incubated in Germany. As for the cultural contributions of the seventeenth and eighteenth centuries which we have just reviewed, they originated chiefly in England and France, where the middle classes were most alert and a specific middle-class mentality first took shape. However, because western Europe was a cultural unit, the new ideas gradually but regularly filtered through the whole area.

Rapid dissemination of new movements throughout the western area

If, in the light of the past, it was reasonably clear that the occident would, though perhaps with uneasy fluctuations, continue to behave as a unit, it now for the first time became apparent that such was the vigor of its civilization that it would crowd upon the domain of rival civiliza-

tions and gradually supplant them. That the very primitive culture of
the American Indians would go down before European culture had been
demonstrated from the first moment of contact following the discoveries.
By the eighteenth century both South and North America, at least in
so far as they had been brought under colonial rule, already represented
a material as well as a spiritual extension of Europe.

It was far more expressive of the strength of Europe that even relatively advanced civilizations could not resist the European onslaught.
In the days of Peter the Great, Russia surrendered to it bag and baggage; and though the great Slav empire long remained in what we may
call the apprentice class, its acceptance of western methods and objectives
gave it an irresistible drive and prepared the way for the Europeanization of all those areas of Asia over which it had extended its sway.

When the English at last ejected the French from India and systematically attacked the problem of governing their vast new dependency,
another civilization, one of the oldest and most subtle the world has
known, registered the impact of a more vital movement and slowly
retreated before it. In short, if Europe in the sixteenth century, with the
Voyages of Discovery, inaugurated a period of physical expansion, by
the close of the eighteenth century this expansion had led not only to the
economic exploitation of large subject-areas throughout the world but
also to the mental conquest of numerous peoples endowed often with
a by no means negligible civilization of their own.

It is not too much to say that a civilization of a very definite character and hatched in a circumscribed section of Europe was, in the
eighteenth century, reaching out to take possession of every continent.
If it imposed itself often by war and related violent means, it just as
often was taken over voluntarily on the strength of its indubitable superiority. In either case it was busy making the world over in its image.
In the difficult adjustments necessitated by these far-reaching developments lay the assurance of tremendous and prolonged disturbances in
the time to come, but also the promise, no more than the shadow of a
hope perhaps, of the ultimate drawing together of all the peoples of the
earth on the basis of a common body of ideas and institutions.

Spread of Western civilization to the Americas

Spread of Western civilization to Russia

Western civilization penetrates India

The fore-shadowed spread of Western civilization over the whole earth

Section IV

Revolution and Democracy

FROM THE FRENCH REVOLUTION
TO WORLD WAR I (1914)

20

THE FRENCH REVOLUTION (1789-1799)

THE ANCIENT REGIME

ON APPROACHING THE great movement of the French Revolution, we are obliged to return once more to the long reign of Louis XV (1715-1774). Under him the kingdom of France, which his predecessor had made supreme in Europe, suffered a political decline which touched bottom in the Seven Years' War (1756-1763). The loss of European position and prestige was paralleled by a domestic disintegration, for which the government was no less responsible than for the calamitous defeat at the hands of the British. We are aware of the frivolous king's pursuit of pleasure as the chief end of life and of the share in his misrule of the court and the nobles.

Decline of France under the incompetent Louis XV

King and nobles are not, however, the whole story of the declining French vigor. While it is undeniable, as a modern French historian has put it, that Louis XV "gangrened" the monarchy, it is also true that the French state and society were encased in strangling customs and institutions handed down from the past. Without some knowledge of them the plight of the nation will always remain an enigma. The inherited institutions have been summed up as the ancient regime and require setting forth at this point even at the expense of some repetition.

The decline due in part to the ancient regime

In making the crown absolute Richelieu and Louis XIV had been effective without being thoroughgoing. They had destroyed the direct political power of the nobles; they had asserted the royal right of taxation; and they had established a royal army and a royal administration. But they did not touch the social system, which in all its essential features went back to the Middle Ages. If we now undertake to describe it, we shall have France particularly in view; but it should be understood that the French social system so closely resembled that of the whole continent that our description may be regarded as valid in every essential respect for all western Europe, with the exception of England. While England, too, was a class society culminating in a ruling aristocracy, there was not the same gulf between classes as on the continent because all Englishmen alike had been brought under a common law.

Survival of the medieval social system in France and throughout the continent

In its social structure France still legally consisted, as had been the
The two case for centuries past, of three classes or estates. The first and second
privileged estate respectively were the clergy and nobility. They were alike dis-
estates tinguished by titles, honors, properties, and privileges.

The clergy possessed innumerable holdings of land, constituting per-
The first haps one-fifth of the extent of the kingdom, for which they did not pay
estate: the any taxes. In addition, they levied for the benefit of themselves a tax,
clergy called the tithe, on their landed parishioners. Of the revenues from these
two sources, that is, from rents and tithes, a wholly disproportionate
amount was appropriated by the great prelates, the bishops and abbots.
These prelates were almost uniformly younger sons of the great noble
families. They lived in scandalous luxury, while the mass of the priesthood, honorable men for the most part wearing themselves out in the
service of their parishioners, received a pittance hardly sufficient to keep
soul and body together.

The second estate, the nobles, possessed, like the clergy, approximately
The second one-fifth of the soil of France, for which they did not pay the direct
estate: the land tax, called the taille. While they were liable to the other direct
nobles taxes and to the innumerable indirect taxes, they managed in many instances, by reason of their influence with the royal officials, to escape
paying them. Their most precious privilege in their own eyes was their
monopoly of the officer positions in the army and navy and of the higher
diplomatic and ecclesiastical posts. Of extraordinary importance, as we
have had frequent occasion to note, was their unofficial domination of
the court, by which they wheedled grants of money and pensions out of
the king and often decisively influenced his policy.

Beneath these two privileged groups, numbering each about 130,000
The third souls, was the unprivileged mass of the nation, called the third estate
estate com- and numbering some twenty-five million. The third estate fell into two
posed of main classes: the agriculturists or peasants and the townsmen or
peasants and bourgeoisie.
townsmen

The peasants constituted the vast majority of the French people, since
The France, like the rest of Europe, was still overwhelmingly agricultural.
peasants While the peasants elsewhere on the continent were serfs, this, with
subjected to unimportant exceptions, was no longer the case in France. However,
cruel exploi- their improved legal status did not save them from extreme exploitation.
tation They paid many, often very vexatious, customary dues to the noble owner
of the land; they contributed the tithe to the church; and they owed a
long list of direct and indirect taxes to the king. If the calculation of a
close student of this period that the exactions from these three sources
absorbed four-fifths of the income of the peasant cannot be established
with mathematical certainty, we may be sure that in any case he was
inhumanly burdened.

Two peculiarly irritating obligations of the peasants need to be selected from the mass of their burdens because they throw light on the continued serflike status of the tillers of the soil, in spite of their being technically no longer serfs. The nobles alone enjoyed the right of the chase; and in order that game of every kind might be plentiful, the peasants were forbidden to molest it in any way even if it consumed the slender product of their fields. The other particularly annoying obligation was to the government. It was called the *corvée* and consisted of devoting each year, without compensation, a number of days' labor to the maintenance of the public highways. The peasants burdened by the chase and the corvée

While the townsmen were a considerably smaller part of the third estate than the peasants, they had for generations been increasing in numbers, wealth, and importance. This expansion was the automatic consequence of the growth of commerce and industry since the Renaissance. Moreover, as with the seventeenth century an unexampled opportunity had begun to beckon from beyond the seas, the bourgeoisie of France, like that of all the other enterprising nations of Europe, had recently increased at a greatly accelerated pace. It may be thought of as comprising not only merchants, bankers, capitalists, shipowners, and shopkeepers, but also the professional classes of lawyers, physicians, and teachers. In fact, the bourgeoisie embraced the very groups, which, as the most dynamic elements of society, had become conscious of their new importance and at the same time intensely jealous of the honors and privileges by which the two upper orders had been set apart from the rest of the nation. The townsmen or bourgeoisie

On account of their steadily increasing material interests at home and abroad the townsmen felt the need of influencing the government in their own behalf. Unfortunately there existed no constitutional apparatus enabling them to do so. Under the circumstances they looked with waxing discontent on an all-powerful sovereign, who, surrounded by an impenetrable hedge of courtiers, dwelt haughtily aloof from his people in the artificial paradise of Versailles. The bourgeoisie becomes politically disaffected

The criticism directed at the government on the ground of political ineptitude and failure served to swell the stream of socio-economic criticism which had set in with the very beginning of the eighteenth century and which concerned itself with every institution and every intellectual position inherited from the past. The whole European intelligentsia participated in this movement, the so-called Enlightenment. Having treated the Enlightenment with some fullness in the previous chapter, we may content ourselves at this point with repeating that, although the movement originated in England, not only did Frenchmen become its greatest propagandists, but the French champions sprang preponderantly from The Enlightenment a bourgeois movement the bourgeoisie. They sprang, therefore, from the very class with which we have just become acquainted as the most vital element of the third estate.

Upper class share in the Enlightenment

Let us in fairness concede that the Enlightenment drew many valiant recruits, such as Montesquieu and the elder Mirabeau, from the upper orders. That fact proves no more than that the privileged classes themselves were not immune to the current spirit of criticism and that, for the sake of reform, a liberal group among them was fully prepared to identify itself with the leading reforming agency, the bourgeoisie.

A mental revolution slowly under way during the eighteenth century

The total picture presented by France in the eighteenth century cannot be called other than extraordinary. A decrepit government was slowly going to pieces amidst manifestations of incurable disease, while a vigorous bourgeoisie occupied itself with the task of projecting a new system of both government and society. Considered in its totality, the bourgeois program called for as thorough a refashioning as mankind has ever conceived. A little past the middle of the eighteenth century the mental revolution, necessary forerunner of the actual revolution, had already taken possession of the major section of French society. A feeling of growing insecurity at times troubled even the small intelligence of dissolute old Louis XV. He would then relieve his mind with the cynical remark: "Things will hold together till my death." To which his mistress and confidante, Madame de Pompadour, would cheerily respond: "After us the deluge."

ATTEMPTED REFORM UNDER LOUIS XVI

Louis XVI and Queen Marie Antoinette

When Louis XV died in 1774, he was succeeded by his grandson, Louis XVI. The new sovereign, not quite twenty years old, was a shy, awkward man, prone to corpulence and irresolution. To confirm the alliance with Austria, he had been married to Marie Antoinette, daughter of the famous Empress Maria Theresa and a woman—or rather a girl, for she was only eighteen—of unusual vivacity and charm. Had she possessed the political intelligence of her mother, she might have been of considerable help to the dull and bewildered young man who was her husband. But as she lacked the seriousness necessary to wrestle successfully with the problems of government, such influence as she exercised was prompted by nothing better than personal bias and was usually harmful to the public interest.

Louis XVI resolves to introduce reforms

Mixed into Louis's average endowments was a measure of good will, also average, which he was sincerely resolved to exercise in behalf of his people. The ever increasing clamor of enlightened opinion had at last penetrated the secluded precincts of Versailles and made the young king hesitantly desirous to play the part of "benevolent despot" in the manner that had recently become fashionable among his European fellow rulers.

Besides, the finances were in atrocious confusion, and the finances were and still are the most revealing touchstone of every government's solidity. Something had immediately to be done about them, if the services of the state were not to break down and government cease to function. The situation exhibited the following outstanding items: a large debt inherited from the past, an obstinate annual deficit, and an irritated public unwilling to bear additional taxation.

The problem of the royal finances

Louis XVI began his reign with a burst of vigor by dismissing the whole body of discredited ministers inherited from his grandfather. Thereupon he committed the problem of the finances to Turgot, whom he made controller general. The young king could not have made a better choice, for Turgot was not only a leading figure of the economic school of the physiocrats, but a practical administrator as well. He had served for over a decade as intendant of Limoges, where he had successfully introduced a number of important reforms.

Louis calls Turgot to office

Turgot took at once a broad, statesmanlike view of the situation and, instead of losing himself in financial details, developed a program of general national renewal. What France needed, according to him, was to cancel the privileges enjoyed by the feudal orders in the matter of taxation, to put an end to the control of industry by the monopolistic gilds, and to reduce and perhaps, finally, to abandon entirely the minute regulation of commerce and industry as exemplified by the ruling mercantilist practices.

The sweeping reform plan of Turgot

It was a program which aimed at lifting from the country the deadweight of tradition and at fusing the three estates into a single national unit by freedom of trade and equal taxation. Had Turgot been able to impose his policy, it might very well have proved the entering wedge of a movement of reform calculated to modernize France without the violence of a revolution.

Turgot aimed to reform France without revolution

But the program failed. Inaugurated in 1774, it scored a number of successes, such as the establishment of free trade in grain within the kingdom, the abolition of the corvée, and the destruction of the gilds, whereby the various handicrafts were opened to whoever was minded to exercise them. After two years, with his work only just begun, Turgot was dismissed (1776).

The fall of Turgot (1776)

The reason is not far to seek. As soon as the controller general, instead of indulging in the usual window-dressing of ministers of finance, laid the ax to the French upas-tree and attacked the parasitical system of privileges, all the groups which had an interest in the maintenance of abuses combined against him. Clergy, nobles, gild-masters, and the horde of speculators who profited from the different level in the price of grain

Turgot a victim of the privileged profiteers

in the various provinces were equally aroused, as they were also unanimously delighted to have their opposition voiced in the parlement of Paris.

Opposition to Turgot of the parlement and the privileged

The parlement of Paris, like the twelve other parlements established in the provinces, was an integral feature of the privileged regime, since it consisted of a supreme judiciary which was irremovable and hereditary. Enjoying by custom the right of refusing to register the king's edicts, the parlement was moved to throw itself across Turgot's path. At first Louis broke down its resistance, also in accordance with custom, by his command to register the edict. This command had to be communicated in a formal session of parlement, called *lit de justice*.

Louis yields to the pressure of the defenders of privilege

If Louis had maintained his resolute stand, it might well be that he would have worn down the defenders of privilege within and without the parlement. But Louis was weak and, to make matters worse, he lived his life in the exclusive company of high-born gentlemen and ladies who daily poured their disgust with Turgot's revolutionary measures into his ears. Tired of viewing their sour faces, he at last yielded to the pressure of the courtiers and sent the great statesman away. Thereupon frenzied jubilation on the part of the privileged groups, withdrawal of Turgot's edicts, and a prompt return to the old abuses!

The ministry of Necker, 1776-1781

As there was no escape from the pressing financial problem, Louis now handed it over for solution to Necker, a native of Geneva. As a young man Necker had come to Paris, where he had made his fortune as a banker. On accepting office he scored the minor success of somewhat clarifying the muddled finances. However, such small economies as he doubtless effected were completely sacrificed when the government resolved (1778) to make an alliance with the rebellious American colonists in order once more to try conclusions with Great Britain over the issue of colonies and sea power. The enormous war expenditures could be met only by loans, the heavy interest on which embarrassed the treasury more than ever. Thereupon the harried Necker fell back on the radical program of Turgot with the result that the privileged intriguers met the challenge, promptly took up arms against him, and in 1781 persuaded the king to dismiss him.

The nation demands the Estates General

It was now clear that the clergy, the nobles, the court, and the parlement of Paris constituted a cabal which would continue indefinitely to paralyze the feeble volition of the sovereign and keep things as they were. Reform from above was therefore a chimera and the only sure way to remove the accumulated refuse of the ages was for the nation itself to take the work in hand. Swiftly mounting to a revolutionary pitch, the reform sentiment focused at last on the demand for the Estates General.

The Estates General were the old feudal assembly which, having met for the last time in 1614, had perished from disuse. To the ill-informed and romantically minded generation living under the scepter of Louis XVI the Estates General looked like a body genuinely representative of the nation. First here, then there, a cry was raised for the Estates General until the cry at last rose hoarsely as from a single throat. Mistaken view as to the Estates General

Meanwhile the helpless king charged one man after another with the task of rescuing the hopelessly embogged finances. New loans could no longer be floated because the credit of the state was ruined, while fresh taxes could not be levied because the authority of the king had declined to such a point that, whenever the parlement of Paris saw fit to refuse to register a new tax edict, he was no longer able to impose his will on the recalcitrant members. The financial paralysis

By the summer of 1788 the government was completely paralyzed. There was no longer either authority or obedience in the country and the only means of avoiding immediate bankruptcy—the forerunner of a general collapse—was to surrender to the popular will. Louis made his submission in characteristic listless despair. Since Turgot had died some years before, and since Necker was generally held to be the leading reformer after Turgot, the king recalled Necker to office and at the same time issued a call for the Estates General for May, 1789. The king yields to the popular will (1788)

Not till numerous antiquarians had grubbed diligently among ancient records and parchments did the public learn how the long-forgotten Estates General had been constituted. The representatives of the clergy (the first estate), the nobles (the second estate), and the commoners (the third estate) had met in three separate houses and with the decision rendered by houses the privileged orders had always been able to out-vote the representatives of the people by two to one. The Estates General historically constituted as three separate houses

When the public gravely demurred at this situation, Necker took the half-step of decreeing that the third estate was to be given the right to send twice as many delegates to Versailles as either of the other orders, that is, that the commoners should have approximately six hundred delegates, with the same number divided equally between nobles and clergy. On the one really crucial point as to whether the assembly should be constituted in three separate houses, as tradition required, or merged in a single house, as public opinion insisted, the minister refused to announce a decision. However, only in case the Estates General sat as a single house and voted, as the phrase ran, by head and not by order, would the commoners derive any advantage from their double representation. Necker concedes double representation to the third estate

In the spring of 1789 France was stirred by the wholly unfamiliar phenomenon of a general election. In each bailiwick the electors met in three assemblies according to their legal status, and after drawing up a list of grievances in three separate documents called *cahiers de doléances,* elected their respective delegates to the Estates General. On May 5, 1789, Opening (May 5, 1789) of the Estates General

Louis XVI opened the session at Versailles with a few words of welcome and Necker followed with an optimistically tinctured exposition of the financial situation. Neither Louis nor Necker developed a program or offered as much as a trace of leadership.

The third estate balks

The following day the long-agitated question as to how the Estates General were to be constituted surged irresistibly to the front. The two privileged orders at once organized as separate houses, but the third estate resolutely refused to organize except in a single house embracing all three estates.

The Estates General become the National Assembly (June 17)

The result was a complete deadlock which lasted over a month. Then, sustained by an aroused public opinion, the commoners resolved to go ahead on their own plan. On June 17, after once more summoning the other two estates to join them, the commoners boldly organized themselves, not as a separate estate, but as the National Assembly with or without their colleagues of the clergy and nobility. It was a revolutionary act destructive alike of the old constitution and the inherited authority of the king.

The commoners defy the king by the oath of the tennis court (June 20)

Spurred on by the courtiers and, more particularly, by his two younger brothers, the count of Provence and the count of Artois, to defend his rights, Louis now closed, with troops, the hall where the third estate met. To this challenge the undaunted commoners responded by meeting in a near-by enclosure used as a tennis court and taking a solemn vow to continue their sessions until they had given their country a new constitution (June 20). A more frank avowal of their revolutionary purpose was impossible. The king met their defiance by announcing to a formal session of all three estates his inalterable resolution of maintaining the assembly in its ancient tri-cameral form.

The threatened war avoided by the king's submission

So radical a disagreement between king and commoners signified war, unless one side should give way. It was the king who yielded. On June 27 he announced a new inalterable decision in the form of an order to the two privileged estates to join the commoners and complete the happy French family. On that June day the monarchy, manifestly a broken reed, saw its authority slip into the hands of the National Assembly, which in effect took over the government.

THE NATIONAL ASSEMBLY (1789-1791)

Preponderance of the commoners and their noble and clerical sympathizers

In spite of the fact that the National Assembly embraced a large group of clerical and noble irreconcilables, it constituted a fairly homogeneous body respecting the great central matter of the renovation of France. The renovation was desired by many liberal nobles and an even larger body of liberal clergymen who voluntarily added their strength to that of the third estate. Within the clergy, in spite of its being legally a single estate, there existed two distinct social strata, for the great prelates (bishops and abbots) were men of noble birth, whereas the parish priests belonged by social derivation to either the bourgeoisie or the peasantry. With a sizable percentage of the nobles and an actual majority of the clergy siding with the third estate, the reformers enjoyed an indisputable numerical preponderance.

In consequence of its victory over the king the National Assembly began its labors in an atmosphere of extraordinary exultation. Not for themselves, however, were the legislators glad, but for the great cause which they believed they had been called upon to serve. Valuable for the work in hand as such high-minded enthusiasm was likely to prove, the advantage it conferred was canceled by a grave absence of practical experience. Almost to a man the members lacked training in the affairs of government. They were therefore prone to treat all questions from either a theoretical or an emotional angle and to formulate decrees, beautiful in the abstract but hopelessly out of relation to the concrete facts. *Excessive enthusiasm and theoretical bias of the Assembly*

When the Assembly was first constituted, political parties had not yet put in an appearance. But gradually associations, in the nature of parties, began to form about individuals who championed certain measures and showed conspicuous vigor in defending them. *No parties in the Assembly*

Among these outstanding individuals was the Marquis de Lafayette. He had won a great name for himself by the magnanimous offer of his sword, when a young man, to the cause of freedom in America. Though a nobleman by birth, he sympathized with the people, rallied the liberal wing of the nobles about himself, and was accepted by a large and devoted section of the bourgeoisie as its spokesman. No man during the early months of the Revolution had a greater following within and without the Assembly. *Lafayette, the liberal nobleman*

The best representative of the current dogmatic and philosophical spirit was the Abbé Sieyès. In his view government was a clever mechanism, requiring for its successful construction nothing more than a intelligent engineer and planner. When one of his constitutions failed, he was always ready, like a conjurer at a circus, to draw another out of his hat. *Sieyès, the political scientist*

At first not greatly noticed but destined in the end to rise to great influence was the lawyer Robespierre. Sharing with a handful of other members extreme democratic sentiments, for which he was indebted to the radical thinker, Rousseau, whom he worshiped, he never spoke without parading what, at least to his opponents, had the ring of a rhetorical patriotism and a priggish virtue. *Robespierre, the democrat*

The member who without doubt towered head and shoulders above the rest of the Assembly was Count Mirabeau. Mirabeau was a born

Mirabeau, the constitu- tionalist and statesman

statesman, perhaps the only man in the whole Assembly who instinctively knew that a government could not be fashioned at will by a congress of philosophers, but that, to become truly effective, it must be the expression of the moral, economic, and historical forces ruling the nation. He wished, therefore, while preserving the monarchy, to *nationalize* it by injecting into its enfeebled arteries the fresh blood of the commoners. If he had had his way he would have abolished all privileges in order to create a unified people; and he would have given the king a considerable measure of authority on condition that he exercise it in co-operation with a legislature elected by the people.

Reasons for Mirabeau's weakness in the Assembly

Unfortunately Mirabeau never succeeded in acquiring a guiding influence. To begin with, he was a noble and therefore subject to suspicion on the score of birth. To make matters worse, his early life had been a succession of scandals, which had filled the public prints for more than a decade and caused the respectable middle classes to look down on him as a moral outcast.

Calamitous influence of the masses

In strict accord with the oath of the tennis court of June 20, the National Assembly considered its main function to be the making of a new constitution. It was of the highest importance that this work should be done with the greatest possible deliberation and free from extraneous interference. But, owing to the excitement permeating the whole population, the Assembly soon fell under the domination of the street. The growth of the influence of the lower elements, who, while desiring reform, created anarchy, is the most striking concomitant of the great events of 1789. If we understand this fact, we have the key to the extraordinarily rapid descent of French society to a condition not far removed from dissolution.

The growing disturbances throughout France are unchecked

For this degeneration the king and the Assembly were both responsible, as well by reason of what they did not do as by what they did. It goes without saying that the sudden failure of absolutism in 1789 demoralized the existing government services and threw France into confusion. Parisian and provincial mobs frequently fell upon and murdered the royal officials, while the excited peasants everywhere burned and plundered the castles of the nobles. In view of these excesses it would have behooved the king and National Assembly to co-operate to maintain order. But co-operate they would not, because the king, who was under the domination of a reactionary court, looked askance at the triumphant Assembly, and because the Assembly in its turn feared the designs of the court and the king. Mutual suspicion made harmony impossible and played into the hands of the agitators and extremists.

Early in July the court party, of which for the moment the most active member was the king's brother, the count of Artois, fully justified

COUNT MIRABEAU. After a contemporary engraving. (Bettmann Collection)

THE MARQUIS DE LA-FAYETTE. After a contemporary engraving. (Bettmann Collection)

ROBESPIERRE. From a contemporary bronze medal in the Bibliothèque National, Paris. (Bettmann Collection)

GENERAL BONAPARTE. By the French painter, Isabey. Napoleon as First Consul shortly before he became emperor. (Alinari)

the suspicious attitude of the Assembly. The courtiers persuaded the king, who as usual was not hard to persuade (though hard to keep persuaded), to re-establish his authority by means of troops. Soldiers were accordingly concentrated around Paris to overawe the citizens, as the necessary step preliminary to dismissing the ministers, such as Necker, who was popular with the people, and to dissolving the Assembly.

The July plot to dissolve the Assembly by an armed force

At the sight of the soldiers a tremendous excitement took hold of the Parisians; and although, to calm them, the troops were again withdrawn, vast crowds, seizing what weapons came to hand, gathered in the streets. Savagely resolved to teach the court a lesson, the people threw themselves (July 14) on the Bastille, a royal fortress of ancient date and formidable proportions in the eastern section of the capital. After a brief and bloody encounter the small garrison of invalid soldiers, who held the gloomy stronghold, surrendered to the multitude. They were butchered almost to a man, nor were the people satisfied till they had taken in hand the task of leveling the hated fortress with the ground.

The fall of the Bastille, July 14, 1789

Like the famous shot fired at Lexington in 1775, the fall of the Bastille was heard around the world. Everywhere excited opinion interpreted it as signifying the end of tyranny and the dawn of a new era of brotherly love. We must in this connection remember that the Bastille, originally a fortress built to overawe the capital, had in recent generations, although hardly any longer in Louis XVI's time, served as a prison for such Frenchmen as had aroused the displeasure of the government. Arrested on the private order of the sovereign by what was called a *lettre de cachet* (letter with the royal seal), the critics disappeared behind the solid masonry of the Bastille to be held in confinement without trial, subject to the king's pleasure. Therefore, while in plain fact it was the Bastille that fell, in the imagination of the people there fell rather the thing the Bastille symbolized, that is, the absolute system with its principle of government by royal caprice.

The fall of the Bastille symbolic of the fall of absolutism

Seized with exultation, innumerable prophets now made their appearance who forecast a whole new order of existence, when men would live together in peace and plenty under the triple blessing of liberty, equality, and fraternity. As outbreaks of a frenzied excitement, revolutions regularly give birth to similar Utopian dreams. While in the end the dreams are never realized, their presence in the minds of men must not be overlooked, as they are an enormously important factor in the general movement of events.

Expected coming of an era of liberty, equality, and fraternity

The most immediate consequence of the Bastille uprising was that the plan of the aristocrats to turn back the revolutionary tide by force had to be abandoned. Plainly the court party was beaten, and its most violent members, with the count of Artois at their head, showed their disgust by leaving the soil of France, become uncongenial to their para-

The emigration of the irreconcil-able nobles begins

sitic kind. In this way began the so-called emigration, which, continuing in the following years, soon collected in every country of Europe, but chiefly in Germany along the Rhine, many thousand members of the old privileged orders. While most of these *émigrés* were nobles, there was among them a not inconsiderable representation from the clergy. Safe from molestation on foreign soil, the exiles were free to spin plots by which they hoped in time to be restored to the fleshpots of "the good old days."

Louis XVI temporarily reconciled with his people

To recover a little of his greatly impaired popularity Louis now paid (July 17) a formal visit to Paris, during which he put the seal of his approval on everything the people had seen fit to do in the recent emergency. He was received with transports of joy, for his subjects had not yet plucked the traditional loyalty to the ancient ruling family from their hearts.

Self-help of the bourgeoisie: they create a municipal government and a National Guard

Louis's most important official act during his visit to Paris was to accept the two improvisations by which the bourgeoisie had attempted to bring the disturbed capital back to some sort of order. With every man's goods at the mercy of his neighbor, the alarmed property owners had set up, first, a new municipal government, and second, a militia or National Guard pledged to maintain the public peace. Nuclei of order in a dissolving society, these two Parisian institutions were at once imitated throughout France and contributed not a little to keep the country from going completely to pieces.

Lafayette head of the National Guard and effective master of France

It testified to the great popularity of Lafayette that he was elected head of the Parisian National Guard. And when the militia of the capital was affiliated with that of all the provincial towns, Lafayette was promoted to the post of commander-in-chief of the whole organization. His headship of so considerable a force vastly swelled his political importance, more particularly as the regular army, owing to the desertion of its noble officers and the impact of revolutionary sentiment on the rank and file, had to a large extent dissolved. By the summer of 1789 not only had Lafayette become the most powerful man in the country but on him much more than on the all but paralyzed government depended the maintenance of internal order.

Rumors circulated of a new court plot

The test of Lafayette's ability and willingness to preserve the domestic peace did not have long to wait. In October the rumor of another plot on the part of the remnant of the court party ran through Paris. Excited men and women told one another that at a banquet of officers, held at Versailles, the new national cockade of red, blue, and white, the passionately adored emblem of the Revolution, had been trampled under foot and the health of the king and queen drunk amid scenes of wild enthusiasm.

What really happened was an act of homage, without doubt unnecessarily demonstrative, on the part of the officers toward their sovereign. However, suspicion of the king and court had by this time sunk so deeply into the hearts of the Parisians that any invention, no matter how exaggerated, was sure to be believed. Further to blow upon the flames of distrust, demagogues circulated the news that the king was the cause of the famine in the city and that he and the court intercepted the grain-carts outside of Paris in order to reduce the capital to starvation.

The king the object of an incurable suspicion

These charges and alarms served to precipitate a fresh popular explosion. On the morning of October 5, 10,000 women, many of them frenzied by starvation, set out for Versailles to fetch the king to Paris. As they straggled over the muddy roads in a steady downpour of rain all the male riffraff of the suburbs joined them. In the face of this tremendous danger Lafayette, appointed guardian of the civil order, did nothing. Possibly he remained inactive in order to let the king, in whom he had no confidence, feel once more the power of the people. Only when his own Parisian militia refused to wait longer, did he consent to conduct it to Versailles. When he arrived there in the night, some hours after the Paris rabble, he found everything in the greatest confusion. By his timely intercession he did, however, save the lives of the royal family and could with some justification pose as the preserver of the monarchy.

The march of the women on Versailles (October 5) and the part played by Lafayette

If the invaders were prevented from committing the worst excesses, they nevertheless insisted on the demand that the royal family should transfer its residence to Paris. What could Louis do but give his consent? On October 6 the riotous victors, indulging in triumphant song and dance along the road, escorted to the palace of the Tuileries "the baker, the baker's wife, and the baker's little boy," from whose presence in their midst they promised themselves the end of scarcity. The National Assembly, of course, followed the king and was quartered in the riding-school near the palace. Paris had become again, in fact as well as in name, the capital of France.

The royal family brought to Paris on October 6

The October events undermined the last remnant of authority enjoyed by the monarchy, and for this result, whether he planned it or not, Lafayette can hardly escape responsibility. The king at the Tuileries was now practically Lafayette's prisoner, if that was what Lafayette wanted; but Lafayette himself, even though it took him some months to find it out, was henceforth the prisoner of the Parisian populace. The excited populace in its turn was the victim of the innumerable demagogues, who, either from mistaken zeal or for their personal advantage, desired to keep the national temperature at fever heat.

The fevered temperature of Paris

What greatly contributed to the influence of the radical elements was that the year 1789 marked an unparalleled agitation of public opinion. A leading symptom of this general excitement was the innumerable quan-

Pamphlets, newspapers, and clubs

tity of pamphlets and newspapers which reported the events of the day and which not infrequently assumed the form of fanatical exhortations against the existing institutions. Still another witness of the disturbed state of opinion was the formation of clubs. Clubs for consultation and debate became the great demand of the hour. They arose spontaneously in all quarters, in fact, every coffee-house took on, through the irrepressible enthusiasm of its frequenters, the character of a political association.

The club of the Cordeliers: Danton and Marat

Two clubs in particular, the Cordeliers and the Jacobins, were destined to play an important role. The Cordeliers recruited their members from among the Paris extremists. They boasted Danton as their leader, a still unestablished, pushing young barrister in whom there burned a submerged volcanic fire. Another radical who frequented the Cordeliers was Marat. Whether Marat expressed himself by spoken or by printed word, his every utterance was a shrill call to insurrection and violence.

The club of the Jacobins, at first moderate, afterwards radical

In sharp distinction from the Cordeliers, the Jacobins recruited their ranks from the upper levels of the bourgeoisie. They formed a point of concentration for the moderate and educated elements and rapidly spread in numerous branches or so-called daughter societies over the length and breadth of France. Before long, however, the Jacobins, too, succumbed to the extreme revolutionary tendencies which had become the very breath of the country's nostrils. Lafayette, Sieyès, and Mirabeau, originally dominant in their councils, were gradually displaced by men like Robespierre, who skillfully used the club as a means of drawing the radical opinion of the country into a single, irresistible mass.

The National Assembly and the issue of privileges

Against this agitated background of opinion was projected the new governing body, the National Assembly. To its self-appointed task, the making of a constitution, the breakdown of the monarchy obliged it to add the actual rule of the country. Consequently an early pressing matter that came up for settlement was the question of the privileges and monopolies inherited from the past. So far had opinion progressed since the time of Turgot that it now took but a single session to dispose of an issue, the mere broaching of which in Turgot's day had brought about his downfall.

The end of privileges decreed on August 4

In a session of the National Assembly held on August 4, 1789, the liberal nobles renounced voluntarily their rights of the chase, manorial justice, and a vast variety of petty feudal dues. The liberal clerics followed suit by giving up their claim to the ecclesiastical levy called the tithe. Naturally the members of the third estate could not let themselves be outdone by the other two orders and magnanimously laid the trade monopolies conferred by the gild charters on the altar of the fatherland. When the various renunciations of an intoxicated session had been swept into a summary decree it was seen that the whole feudal edifice had been swept away and the road cleared for complete legal equality.

Examined from whatever angle one chooses, August 4 will always be remembered as one of the great days of the Revolution.

Another question inherited from the old regime was the problem of the finances. To save the country from imminent bankruptcy had been, it will be recalled, the immediate cause for summoning the Estates General. An inevitable consequence of the confusion attending the overthrow of the absolute system was that the treasury was reduced to the last extreme of destitution. People very generally ceased to pay taxes, while the turbulent condition of the country, besides making the provisioning of Paris uncertain, precipitated an industrial crisis which caused wide unemployment. Confronted with a totally depleted money chest, the National Assembly was moved to save the situation by an extreme measure. On November 2, 1789, it voted to confiscate the vast property of the clergy, valued conservatively at several hundred million dollars. With this mass of land and houses as security it presently authorized the issue of paper money, called *assignats,* and with this device enabled the harassed government to meet, at least for the time being, its most pressing expenses.

Confiscation of church property adopted as a financial measure

The assignats were a safe financial device on one condition: they must not be multiplied indefinitely, thereby undermining the confidence of the holders in the ability of the government to redeem them. Indefinite multiplication was, however, the very practice adopted. Though the National Assembly exhibited a certain caution, it nonetheless authorized paper money in sufficient quantities to cause its value to drop with each month farther and farther below par. Presently, since bad money always drives out good money, the standard gold and silver coins either were exported or disappeared in the stockings of the peasants, while the steadily declining assignats came more and more into exclusive use. At the close of the Assembly in 1791 the paper inflation was already well under way. When the legislatures which followed found no other solution of the country's financial needs than the running of the printing presses, it became certain that the flood of assignats would terminate in a colossal bankruptcy. We shall hear more of this matter hereafter. At this point it suffices to say that the assignats constitute one of the sorriest chapters of the French Revolution.

Rapid sketch of the disastrous policy of the assignats

When the Assembly confiscated the property of the church it felt obliged to assume the payment of salaries to the clergy. Therewith the clergy fell into a dependence on the state which was made sweeping and complete a year later (July, 1790) by the Civil Constitution of the Clergy. By this measure the French Catholic church was, in effect, transformed into a national church which retained no more than a nominal connection with the universal papacy.

The Civil Constitution of the Clergy (1790)

The reigning pope, Pius VI, met the challenge of this transformation

by declaring the new national church to be heretical and by excommunicating all clergymen who, by taking the special oath of loyalty prescribed
by the Assembly, accepted appointment under the law. The Assembly
was deeply chagrined when an overwhelming majority of the French
clergy chose to render obedience to the pope rather than to the state. Such
recalcitrants were ejected from their livings and, in measure as the
exasperation against them grew, were smitten with heavy penalties. The
resulting schism in the church added a grave religious disturbance to the
many other disturbances with which the country was already afflicted.

The resultant religious schism

Since the National Assembly enthusiastically accepted the task of
sweeping away every trace of the hated ancient regime, it passed a long
succession of enactments, of which the above-noted extinction of privileges and the nationalization of the church are shining examples. At
least one more of these reconstructions must imperatively be noted. It
belongs to the field of administration. Under the ancient regime there
was a superficial administrative uniformity, owing to the dominance of
the royal officials called intendants. The territory of an intendant was
called an intendancy, but at the side of these relatively recent administrative units all the older units imposed by earlier systems, such as provinces, governments, and bailiwicks, had remained undisturbed.

Adminis-
trative chaos
of the old
regime

All this intolerable administrative hodgepodge the Assembly swept
with a single angry gesture into the abyss, replacing it with a system of
admirable simplicity and logic. France was divided into eighty-three departments, approximately of the same area and population and named
after some natural feature, such as a river or a mountain. A department,
comparable to an American county, was subdivided into districts and
communes.

The new ad-
ministrative
unit: the
department

It is noteworthy that this framework has survived to the present day.
Owing to the strong sentiment against centralization prevailing in 1789,
it was provided that the many local government posts were to be no
longer appointive but elective. It is equally noteworthy that the elective
feature of the sweeping administrative reorganization has not stood the
test of time.

All local
officials to
be elective

In view of the abundance of immediately pressing problems with
which the Assembly was obliged to wrestle, we need feel no surprise
that it took two full years to complete its main undertaking, which, we
must always remember, was a new constitution. No sooner had the Assembly been organized than it attacked the problem by drafting for its
guidance a set of general principles. They took the form of a "Declaration of the Rights of Man and of the Citizen" and are roughly comparable to the English Bill of Rights of 1689 and to the first ten Amendments of the Constitution of the United States. The Declaration affirmed
that "men are born and remain free and equal in rights" and that among

"Declaration
of the Rights
of Man"
prefixed to
the con-
stitution

these rights are religious toleration, freedom of speech, and freedom of the press. In sharp reaction to the divine right theory of the old monarchy, the Declaration vested sovereignty in the people, to whom officials of every level of authority were held to be responsible.

Elaborated on this general pattern, the constitution was carefully debated through many months until in the spring of 1791 it was nearing completion. Not only did it set up, in place of the absolute monarchy of the past, a limited monarchy, but so deep-seated was the bias of the legislators against a vigorous central authority that they made the royal executive preposterously weak. The plan of the constitution-makers was to distribute political power as widely as possible among an innumerable body of officials elected by the people and wholly independent of the king. The Constitution of 1791: the weak executive

The constitution created a legislature, which, on the strength of the view widely current in the eighteenth century that executive, legislature, and judiciary must remain strictly separated, was authorized to concern itself only with the making of laws. The legislature, called Legislative Assembly, consisted of a single house elected for a term of two years by the active citizens of the kingdom. Only active citizens exercised the franchise. They qualified as active by the payment of a small direct tax, thereby proving that they were owners of property. The Constitution of 1791: the legislature of a single house

The limitation of the vote to property-owners was a clear indication that the National Assembly was dominated by the bourgeoisie who, in spite of their theoretical enthusiasm for democracy, were ineradicably suspicious of the propertyless masses. These masses figured in the constitution as passive citizens. In view of the thorough democratization of opinion effected since the calling of the Estates General the degradation of the vast majority of Frenchmen to political passivity was a very dangerous measure of the dominant middle class. Division of Frenchmen into active and passive citizens defines the constitution as bourgeois

Throughout the animated discussions on the constitution, Mirabeau fought hard to secure to the king that measure of power which an executive requires in order to function effectively. But he was unappreciated by his colleagues and distrusted by Louis, and in all important matters met defeat. Broken by disappointment and reckless personal excesses he died (April, 1791), prophesying in his last days, with marvelous accuracy, all the ulterior stages of the Revolution. Death of Mirabeau, April, 1791

It is unlikely that the dull king regretted the passing of Mirabeau, although he lost in him his most valuable supporter. Ever since Louis had been dragged from Versailles by force he had been a virtual prisoner in the Tuileries and had lost all influence on the shaping of events. The constitution, which at the time of Mirabeau's death was nearing completion, he regarded with the greatest distaste. It would not be long now before he would be obliged to accept it and, stubbornly averse to Louis's aversion for the constitution the purely decorative role the document assigned to him, he resolved to escape with his family from France.

The flight of the king and royal family was arranged with the greatest secrecy for the night of June 20, 1791. But too confident of his disguise as a valet, Louis exposed himself needlessly at a post-station not far from the eastern border. He was recognized by a suspicious young radical, who galloped through the night to give the alarm at the next change of horses. At the little town of Varennes the bells sounded the tocsin, and the excited people, summoned from their beds, refused to permit the royal carriage to proceed. With safety almost in view the flight came to an end. The fugitives were brought back to Paris, where once again they had the key turned on them in their palatial prison.

The flight of the royal family ends at Varennes (June, 1791)

The flight of the king divided opinion in Paris sharply. It gave the constitutional monarchists, who had a clear majority in the Assembly, their first inkling that they had gone too far in weakening the executive. A monarch was necessary to their governmental fabric, and here was their chosen representative embracing the intended honor by running away from it. Consequently they began to exhibit for the captive and discredited Louis a consideration which they had refused him in his happier days. Many popular leaders, on the other hand, with Danton and Robespierre at their head and with the support of the radical Cordelier and Jacobin clubs, regarded the flight as an abdication and a welcome pretext for proclaiming a republic. For the first time therefore since the beginning of the Revolution monarchists and republicans stepped into the open, divided by a clear-cut issue.

Opinion sharply divided between monarchists and republicans

In July, 1791, an open conflict broke out between the two factions. As the monarchists were still a majority not only in the Assembly but also in the nation, and as they had Lafayette and the National Guard on their side, the victory inclined to them. Thereupon the Assembly, on hearing from the king the very dubious statement that he had never meant to leave the soil of France, solemnly welcomed him back to office; and Louis, in return, to mark his reconciliation with his subjects, accepted and swore to observe the constitution. On September 30, 1791, the Assembly, having completed, however imperfectly, a remarkable work of national renovation, retired from the scene.

The Assembly reinstates the king and closes the session, September 30, 1791

THE LEGISLATIVE ASSEMBLY (OCTOBER 1, 1791-SEPTEMBER 21, 1792)

The first Legislative Assembly, elected on the basis of the new constitution, met the day after the National Assembly adjourned. By a self-denying ordinance, characteristic of the mistaken magnanimity which pervaded the National Assembly, that body had voted the exclusion of its members from the succeeding legislature. The seven hundred and forty-five new legislators were, therefore, all men without experience. That alone constituted a grave danger. It was greatly increased by the fact that most of them were young enthusiasts, who owed their political fortune to the oratorical vigor displayed by them in their local Jacobin club.

Inexperience of the new body of legislators

The radical disposition of the Assembly became apparent as soon as the members fell into party groups. Only a minority, called the Feuillants, undertook to support the constitution. Opposed to them were the Girondists,[1] who frankly favored the establishment of a republic. The majority of the legislators, undecided between monarchy and republic, gradually fell under the spell of Girondist oratory.

The Assembly dominated by the republican Girondists

In the circumstances the Assembly from the very first day strove more or less consciously to put an end to the monarchy. The stages by which it accomplished its purpose need not be here considered. As the supreme blow against the king was delivered when he was forced to declare war against Austria, we may, except for this declaration, which marks a milestone in the Revolution, dismiss the Legislative Assembly from consideration.

Hostility of the Assembly to king and monarchy

The declaration of war against Austria resulted first, from the rising indignation in France over the émigrés, who had gathered in armed bands along the Rhine, and second, from the increasing fear and hatred of monarchical Europe for the Revolution. Frenchmen generally supposed that Emperor Leopold II, brother of Queen Marie Antoinette, was planning a war to punish them for their opinions. While this was far from Leopold's intention, it is true that in August, 1791, he held a conference with the king of Prussia and together with him issued a document which threatened an eventual interference in French affairs (Declaration of Pillnitz).

Austria and Prussia issue the Declaration of Pillnitz, 1791

Ceaselessly ringing the changes on the armed émigrés along the Rhine and the impudent brother of the French queen, held to be, like her, the relentless enemy of the Revolution, the Girondist orators gradually worked up a sentiment for war. They were sincere republican enthusiasts who had brought themselves to the belief that only by means of war would the republic triumph in France and ultimately throughout Europe. Obliging the minister of foreign affairs to make bolder and bolder demands on Leopold, which of course provoked the Austrian ruler to increasingly vigorous replies, they at last ended discussion by launching on April 20, 1792, a declaration of war against the Hapsburg monarchy.

The Girondists declare war on Austria, April, 1792

[1] The Girondists owed their name to the circumstance that many of the leaders hailed from the department of Gironde (Bordeaux).

Unfortunately, Leopold, who was a moderate and rarely capable man,

died a month before war was declared, and it was his dull-witted son, Francis II, who was called to battle with the Revolution. However, the farsighted Leopold had not died without making provision for an eventual war with France. In February, 1792, alarmed by the hostile attitude of the French Assembly, he had persuaded the king of Prussia to league himself with him in a close alliance. The declaration of April 20, therefore, though directed only at Austria, brought Prussia also into the field. Thus began a war which was destined to extend its dominion until it had involved all Europe and carried the French revolutionary ideas around the world.

It is probable that the republican Girondists, who were, at least in

large part, responsible for the war, expected an easy victory. They saw in a vision the thrones of the tyrants crumbling at the irresistible onset of the new democracy and themselves hailed everywhere as the liberators of the human race. The first engagement brought a sharp disappointment. It occurred in the Austrian Netherlands (Belgium), which the French undertook to invade. But the French army, which had been completely undermined in its discipline by the radical propaganda, had no sooner established contact with the Austrians than it scampered away without risking a battle.

Thereupon the Austrians and Prussians prepared an offensive in their

turn and with the coming of summer undertook the invasion of France. At this unexpected turn wrath and terror filled the republicans in Paris. Charging the government with treason, their orators denounced the king as the author of the national calamities. In August the allies crossed the border and proceeded on their march to the capital.

Excitement rose ever to new heights, and when the duke of Bruns-

wick, the allied commander-in-chief, threatened, in a ringing proclamation, to wreak an unexampled vengeance on Paris if but a hair of the king's head were injured, the seething passion burst in a wave of uncontrollable fury. In the early morning of August 10 the people, mobilized for action by their leaders, marched against the Tuileries to overthrow the man whom the radicals of the press and clubs represented as in league with foreign despots against the common mother, France.

When, shortly after midnight, the bells from the steeples rang out the

preconcerted summons over the city, the king and his family knew that the supreme struggle was at hand. Dispersed through the palace in small groups, the beleaguered residents passed the hours between darkness and dawn discussing the chances of the coming day. Of all the soldiers of the king the Royal Guard of Swiss mercenaries could alone be counted on. That fact tells more eloquently than a flood of description the pass to which the ancient monarchy of France had come.

Even so, had Louis XVI now resolved to conquer or die at the head of this faithful regiment, he might have rallied the moderates and constitutionalists, still without any question a majority, around the throne. But a decision of this heroic sort was not to be expected from Louis. He could be patient, tolerant of ideas beyond his grasp, and even generous to his enemies, but he could not form a manful resolution. At eight o'clock in the morning, seeing that the densely massed people were about to storm the palace, he abandoned it to seek shelter with the Legislative Assembly. *The king abandons the Tuileries*

The Swiss Guards, deserted by their leader, made a brave stand. Only on the king's express order did they give up the Tuileries and attempt to effect a retreat to their barracks. But outside the palace walls the odds were no longer in their favor, and the enraged populace, falling upon them, butchered most of them in the streets. *Slaughter of the Swiss Guards*

Meanwhile the Legislative Assembly was engaged in putting its official seal on the popular verdict. In the presence of Louis and the royal family the members voted the suspension of the king from office. At the same time they ordered the election of a National Convention to draw up a new constitution. The present Assembly agreed to hold over till September, when the new body was expected to meet and take up the reins. *Effective end of the monarchy and of the constitution*

The suspension of the king left the government nominally in the hands of the Legislative Assembly and a committee of ministers appointed by that body. But as the capital was in the hands of radical leaders supported by the excited people and nobody paid any attention to the authorities, the real power fell into the hands of the men who had been most active in striking down the king. In preparation of their success at the Tuileries they had, in the early morning hours of August 10, overthrown the municipal government of Paris and now lay intrenched in the city hall or *hôtel de ville*. *The power is usurped by the radical leaders*

Fanatically determined men, like Robespierre and Marat, headed the victorious extremists. But rising head and shoulders above them all was Danton, who, endowed with titanic energy, dominated the situation. In fact it is no exaggeration to say that Danton was the self-appointed dictator of the country during the interlude from August 10, the day of the overthrow of the monarchy, to September 21, the day of the meeting of the National Convention. *The dictatorship of Danton*

As Danton saw the situation the foremost need of the country was to beat back the invasion. He therefore became the spokesman and engineer of national defense. He strove to infuse into the hearts of the citizens an indomitable courage. "What do we require in order to conquer?" he shouted at his hearers. And the ringing answer fell: "To dare, and dare, and dare again!" The fatherland was declared in danger; all occupations ceased except those which provided for the necessities of life and the *Danton organizes the French defense* manufacture of weapons; the whole adult male population was drafted for military service. The clear purpose informing this frenzied enthusiasm was to create an army capable of saving France.

On turning to the invasion, which had been the compelling cause behind the recent tremendous events in the capital, we must imagine it proceeding in the deliberate manner of an eighteenth century campaign. The French armies, hurriedly reconstituted as a republican force by Danton and his helpers, were for some weeks incapable of offering any effective resistance. However, on September 20, at Valmy in the Argonne forest, the republican general, Dumouriez, threw himself across the path of the Prussian army under the duke of Brunswick and brought it to a halt. Inordinately discouraged by the check administered to him, Brunswick ordered a retreat which became almost a rout. In a few weeks not a Prussian or Austrian soldier was left upon French soil.

The invasion checked at Valmy, September 20, 1792

Just before this remarkable success had been achieved by raw and untrained troops a series of frightful crimes committed in Paris had shocked the sensibilities of an attentive world. To understand how they could have occurred we must keep before us the general French situation. With two foreign powers encamped on the soil of France, the unreliable monarchical government had been overthrown by a relatively small band of resolute republicans. For this band, with Danton at its head, the pressing work was to organize the defense of France. Since these men could not let themselves be disturbed in their preparations by monarchist uprisings at home, they resolved to cow their opponents by terror.

The situation leading up to the September massacres

As a first step to the spread of terror through Paris thousands of citizens, suspected of being devoted to the king, were put under arrest. The next step, taken in the early days of September, was to relieve the pressure on the over-crowded prisons by a massacre of the inmates. It may be that the massacre was not deliberately planned. Excesses in time of extreme agitation seem somehow to occur without individual responsibility. Be that as it may, an armed band of assassins went the round of the places of detention and did not terminate its bloody work until it had dispatched some fifteen hundred helpless victims. Not a hand was raised to stop the hideous proceedings. Paris, to all appearance, looked on stupefied.

The September massacres

THE NATIONAL CONVENTION (SEPTEMBER 21, 1792- OCTOBER 26, 1795)

The short interlude of government by an irresponsible radical faction came to an end when the National Convention met (September 21) and assumed control. Its very first measure was to declare the monarchy

Monarchy abolished

abolished. By a happy coincidence the victory of Valmy, which had occurred on the previous day, freed France from all immediate danger from without. The Convention began its career in an atmosphere of republican exultation.

In view of the extremely fluid political situation the composition of the new governing body was a matter of great importance. The Convention was made up of nearly eight hundred members, who, because the monarchists either from terror or indolence had absented themselves from the polls, were solidly republican. But attachment to the same fundamental principle did not hinder the rise of important differences of opinion. The outstanding republican group were the Girondists, to whom the overthrow of the monarchy had been largely due. Its most active competitor was the Mountain,[2] composed of individuals like Danton, Robespierre, and Marat, who inclined to extreme views and who had shown their moral fiber in the recent extraordinary events.
The Convention divided between two minority parties, Gironde and Mountain

Given more to action than to words, the men of the Mountain desired that the war should be made the sole concern of the government until it had been concluded by a victorious peace. The Girondists, too, were for the war. But, high-minded idealists revolving utopian plans, they detested the violence of the radicals and were revolted by that extreme example of violent radicalism, the September massacres.
The issue between the two parties

Between these two groups, and permanently attached to neither, was the great bulk of the deputies, designated as the Plain. Whoever, Girondists or Mountainists, could sway the Plain, would command a majority and thus rule France.
Majority called the Plain

The sessions were no sooner opened than the Girondists demanded an investigation of the September massacres. The action was planned to inculpate the leaders of the Mountain, who, in order to direct attention away from themselves, urged as a counter-measure the immediate trial of the king. Ever since August 10 Louis and his family had been closely confined in prison. In December the deposed monarch was summoned before the Convention, constituted for this occasion as a court of justice. The Girondists, amiable dreamers for the most part, would have spared his life, but the Mountainists, backed by the threats of the Parisian mob, carried the Plain with them. By a very small majority the former Louis XVI, degraded to the rank of citizen Louis Capet, was condemned to death. On January 21, 1793, he was beheaded by the newly invented machine called the guillotine.[3]
Trial and death (January 21 1793) of Louis XVI

[2] So called from the fact that the members took their seats upon the highest tiers of benches.

[3] The guillotine, named for its inventor, a certain Dr. Guillotin, consisted of two upright posts, between which a heavy knife rose and fell. On the victim's having been strapped to a board which was shoved between the posts, the knife was released and instantly severed the head from the body.

The execution of the king raised a storm of indignation throughout monarchical Europe, and a great coalition, which every state of importance joined, sprang to life to build a dam against the raging torrent of the Revolution. Thus did the war with Austria and Prussia in less than the course of a year assume European dimensions.

Europe leagued against France

The members of the coalition planned—in so far as a loose association of states may ever be said to have a plan—to attack France from every side and bring down the colors of the republic in one rapid campaign. The English were to sweep down upon the French coast, the Spaniards to cross the Pyrenees and attack from the south, the Piedmontese to pour over the Italian Alps, and the Austrians and Prussians to operate along the eastern border from the direction of Belgium and the Rhine.

Projected campaign of the coalition

In these circumstances the question of the defense of the French soil became again, as it had been in the summer of 1792, the supreme question of the hour. It was plain that in order to meet her enemies, who were advancing from every point of the compass, France would have to be united and display a superhuman energy.

The question of national defense again to the fore

The new crisis quickly developed the animosities between Gironde and Mountain into implacable hatred. While one party was without question as patriotic as the other, the immediate issue was not love of country but the most practical means for meeting the threatening invasions. Like the idealist philosophers they were, the Girondists insisted on pressing their scruples about the September massacres and on rejecting every war measure which implied an encroachment on the new-won liberties of the individual. Since the situation would not wait on either long-drawn-out debate or moral scruple, the leaders of the Mountain resolved to rid themselves of their rivals. Insurgent bands were set in motion to invade the Convention and howl at its bar for the heads of the Girondist leaders. On June 2, 1793, the Convention finally yielded to mob pressure and excluded from its midst and put under arrest thirty-one outstanding Girondists, among them the brilliant orators Vergniaud, Isnard, and Brissot.

Overthrow of the Girondists June, 1793

The fall of the Girondists meant the removal of the last check upon the fierce determination of the Mountain. The power lay in its hands to use as it would; and the immediate end of power, the Mountain had from the first maintained, was the salvation of France from her enemies. To accomplish that great purpose the party now deliberately returned to the successful system of the summer of 1792, the system of terror. This new phase of the Revolution, famous as the Reign of Terror —it could appropriately be called the Long Reign of Terror, in order to distinguish it from the Short Reign of Terror of August and September, 1792—began on June 2, 1793, with the expulsion from the Con-

The Mountain institutes the Reign of Terror

vention of the moderate republican element, represented by the Girondists.

The Short Reign of Terror of the summer of 1792 had been marked by two conspicuous features: first, an energetic conduct of the war under the leadership of Danton, and second, a bloody repression of the monarchical opposition. The Long Reign of Terror reproduced these elements but developed them into a system. The one indispensable requisite for an energetic pursuit of war is a strong executive. The Mountain, therefore, created a committee, finally, of twelve members, called the Committee of Public Safety, which it endowed with almost unlimited powers. While it is true that the Committee of Public Safety was established some weeks before the Girondists fell, the fact that it did not acquire its dominant position until the summer of 1793 proves how intimately it was associated with the seizure of power by the Mountain.

The Terror establishes a strong executive, called the Committee of Public Safety

Of the famous Committee of Public Safety the most conspicuous figure was Robespierre. For this reason the whole period of the Terror is sometimes identified with his name. But Robespierre, if most in view, was by no means the most active of the Committee members in the affairs of government. He was indeed the hero of the Parisian proletariat and of the Jacobins and swayed the Convention by his oratory, but the man who chiefly provided for the defense of France was Carnot, vigorously seconded by such capable administrators as Prieur and Lindet.

Robespierre the popular figurehead of the Committee of Public Safety

During the prolonged internal convulsions Carnot, Prieur, and Lindet kept as far as possible aloof from politics and quietly and unostentatiously attended to business. It was they, and more particularly always the great organizing genius, Carnot, who equipped the vast popular armies, who appointed the officers and commanding generals, and who mapped out the campaigns. If France was able to confront the forces of the coalition with armies of a hitherto unheard-of size, which finally came close to 1,000,000 men, that was, of course, the work of the Convention, which proclaimed for the first time the basic principle of modern European militarism, universal military service. But the efficient use of this military raw material must be ascribed primarily to Carnot, to whom a grateful people accorded in after years the honorary designation of Organizer of Victory.

The war work of Carnot

At this point we are prompted to inquire into the position, under the Terror, of Danton, the man who had so completely dominated the situation during the invasion of the previous year. It accords well with all we know of his character that it was he who had been chiefly responsible for the creation of the Committee of Public Safety. He had therefore been originally elected a member; but in the summer of 1793 he was somewhat mysteriously dropped from its roll. Possibly he failed of re-

Elimination of Danton from the Committee

appointment through an intrigue of his rival, Robespierre. Although thus crowded out of executive authority, he remained a powerful figure with a strong following in and outside the Convention.

The machinery of the Terror: the Law of the Suspects

With the conduct of the war provided for through a powerful executive, it remained to systematize the repression of the anti-revolutionary elements. The machinery of the Terror, as this systematization may be called, presented on its completion three leading features. First, there was the Law of the Suspects. By this sweeping measure police officials were authorized to arrest any person in any station of life denounced to them as "suspect," a term that could be stretched to mean almost anything. It was afterward said by a wit that all France went about in those days conjugating the verbal expression, "I am suspect," through all its moods and tenses. In consequence, the prisons were crowded from cellar to garret with thousands of victims.

The machinery of the Terror: the Revolutionary Tribunal

To empty the prisons was the function of the second element of the terrorist machinery, called the Revolutionary Tribunal. This was a special court of justice created for the purpose of trying the suspects without the delays incident to the ordinary courts. However, even the Revolutionary Tribunal at first provided many of the usual safeguards for an accused person. With the passing of time they were progressively eliminated until merely to be brought to trial was tantamount to condemnation.

The machinery of the Terror: the guillotine

On sentence of death being pronounced by the judge there remained for the victim the third and last step in the process of the Terror: he was carted to an open square, called the Square of the Revolution, and amid staring and hooting mobs, who congregated to the spectacle every day as to a feast, his head fell under the stroke of the guillotine.

Murder of Marat and execution of Charlotte Corday

Before the Terror had well begun, one of its most active agents, Marat, fell victim to that violence which he had so sedulously preached. Marat, self-styled "Friend of the People," was the mouthpiece of the most degraded and lawless elements of Paris. He had lately developed a thirst for blood that can be accounted for only on the ground of disease. When the Girondists were hunted from the Convention, they enlisted the sympathy of many like-minded idealists of the provinces. Such a one was Charlotte Corday. In her simplicity she regarded Marat as the leading instigator of the Terror. Making her way from her home in Normandy to Paris, she gained admittance to Marat's house and stabbed him in his bath (July 13, 1793). Promptly haled before the Revolutionary Tribunal, she was hurried thence to the guillotine.

Execution of Marie Antoinette

The dramatic incidents associated with so many illustrious victims of the Terror can receive only brief mention here. In October the imprisoned queen, Marie Antoinette, was summoned before the Revolutionary Tribunal. She faced the court with a new dignity, fruit of her recent sorrows, and on receiving her death verdict mounted the scaffold with no less courage than had been displayed by her royal consort.[4]

A few days after the death of Marie Antoinette, twenty-one Girondists, representing the total number at that moment in the hands of the victorious Mountain, traveled the same road. They were followed by the duke of Orléans and Madame Roland, each intensely hostile to the other but charged alike with complicity in the Girondist plots. The duke of Orléans, head of the secondary branch of the house of Bourbon, was an ambitious intriguer, who had from his early manhood nursed a sullen resentment against Louis XVI. To save his life after the overthrow of the monarchy he had joined the Jacobin club and, dropping his hereditary titles, invited eternal ridicule by reintroducing himself to the world as Citizen Equality (Egalité). When in 1792 he was elected as a new-hatched democrat to the Convention, he committed his final act of infamy by voting for the death of the king. *(margin: Execution of the Girondists and the duke of Orléans)*

The very antipodes of the contemptible Orléans was Madame Roland.[5] Her honest enthusiasm for a regenerated public life had a literary origin and naturally attracted her to the fiery and eloquent Girondists. For a time her house had been their meeting place, and she herself, with the emotional extravagance of the period, had been worshiped as the muse, the Egeria, of the republican philosophers. On mounting the steps of the guillotine, she paused to contemplate a statue of Liberty which had been erected near by. Her last words were addressed to the impassive goddess. "Liberty," she said, "what crimes are committed in thy name!" *(margin: Death of Madame Roland)*

It must not be supposed that the Terror was limited to Paris or was directed only against prominent individuals. By means of Deputies on Mission, that is, members of the Convention clothed with the powers of the Committee of Public Safety, and of so-called revolutionary committees set up in every community, the Terror was carried into the provinces on the ground that all France would have to be inspired with the same uncompromising sentiments if the war was to be won. *(margin: Deputies on Mission sent as agents of the Terror to the provinces)*

The French departments, inhabited to a large extent by citizens of small means and moderate opinions, from the first showed signs of restlessness under the violences of the Terror. No sooner had the Gironde, a provincial party, fallen victim to the Mountain, identified with Paris, than the situation became strained and led to the raising here and there of the standard of revolt. Thus the great city of Lyons cast off the *(margin: Revolt in the provinces: Lyons and Toulon)*

---

[4] Marie Antoinette left two children, a princess of fifteen years and the dauphin, Louis, aged eight. The princess was released in 1795, but before that mercy could be extended to the boy, he had died under the inhuman treatment of his jailers. The dauphin is reckoned by legitimists as Louis XVII.

[5] Madame Roland owed her influence in part to her husband, who was a prominent Girondist and had been a minister during the last months of the reign of Louis XVI. Roland made his escape from Paris when the Girondists were proscribed. He committed suicide on hearing of the death of his wife.

authority of the Convention, while the important naval station, Toulon, went a step farther and actually surrendered to the foreign enemy, the English.

Here was matter for thought, but it was as nothing compared with the great rising in the west. The peasants of the region called *La Vendée* armed themselves under the leadership of their priests and nobles to resist the government. The peasants had been first aroused against the Revolution by the attempt to impose on them the new national church, which the pope had condemned as schismatic. When the Convention now (1793) conscripted them for war under the universal service act, they could no longer be restrained and raised the banner of revolt over a wide area.

Peasant revolt in La Vendée

This difficult situation the Convention, or rather its executive agent, the Committee of Public Safety, met with unflinching resolution. It sent an army against Lyons, and in October, 1793, after a brave resistance, the city was taken. Thereupon the Convention resolved to inflict an unexampled punishment, happily only partially carried out: it ordered the destruction of the city and the erection on the ruins of a pillar with the laconic inscription, "Lyons waged war with liberty; Lyons is no more."

The Convention crushes the revolt of Lyons

In December, 1793, a French army regained Toulon, chiefly through the skill of a young artillery officer, Napoleon Bonaparte; and, in the same month, another army defeated the insurgents of the Vendée.

Toulon recaptured

Since a dangerous discontent continued to smolder among the peasants of the west, the Committee of Public Safety was moved to dispatch thither as Deputy on Mission one Carrier, armed with full powers to stamp out the embers. The vengeance wreaked by this madman on the hostile priests and peasants makes the excesses of the Revolutionary Tribunal at Paris look like nursery pastimes. Dissatisfied with the slow process of the guillotine, Carrier invented new methods of wholesale execution. The most ingenious, the *noyade* (drowning), consisted in loading an old vessel with one hundred, two hundred, and even eight hundred victims—men, women, and children—floating it down the Loire, and then scuttling it as it approached the sea. By such means the Terror penetrated to every corner of the land and held all France in obedience to the central government.

The Terror in the west under Carrier

By its very nature, however, the Terror was a purely temporary device. Sooner or later there was bound to occur a division among its supporters; and when division came, the revolutionists were sure to rage against each other as they had once raged in common against the aristocrats and moderates. The great statesman, Mirabeau, had foreseen that development. In a moment of prophetic insight he had declared that the Revolution, like the god, Saturn, would end by devouring its own offspring.

Disruption of the Terror inevitable

Ominous signs of the disintegration of the Mountain, the party of the

Terror, began to appear in the autumn of 1793. The most radical wing, which owed its strength to its hold on the government of the city of Paris and which followed the lead of one Hébert, had turned its particular animosity against the Catholic faith. To replace this ancient cult, denounced as aristocratic and superstitious, the Hébertists, who were atheists, first invented the religion of Reason, and then forced its acceptance upon the city of Paris by a decree which closed all places of Catholic worship.

The radical Hébertists make war on Christianity

Although this reckless measure was soon withdrawn and religious toleration, identified with the Revolution, was reasserted in principle, the more temperate Robespierre took alarm. He was further annoyed with the Hébertists because they became infected with communistic ideas and dared launch an attack on that bourgeois holy of holies, the institution of private property. Disinclined to such extravagances, Robespierre, who, though a republican of the thoroughgoing persuasion of Rousseau, was a typical middle-class lawyer, denounced Hébert and his ilk before the Jacobins. In March, 1794, he abruptly sent them via the Revolutionary Tribunal to the guillotine.

Robespierre suppresses the Hébertists, March, 1794

The overthrow of Hébert was followed by that of Danton, who, falling, carried his friends and satellites down with him. A man of imposing physical and mental stature, Danton had, as we have seen, played a decisive part on more than one occasion. By the spring of 1794 he had ceased to believe in the further necessity of the terrorist system and dared to raise his voice in behalf of mercy. Mercy, to Robespierre and his young follower on the governing committee, the arch-fanatic Saint-Just, was nothing less than treason, and in sudden alarm at Danton's "moderation" they hurried him and his friends to the guillotine (April 5, 1794). Thus Robespierre completely dominated the situation. No wonder that it was now whispered about that he was planning to make himself dictator.

Suppression of Danton and the moderates, April, 1794

Between Robespierre and a dictatorship there stood, in the spring of 1794, only one thing—his own political incapacity. That he had the Jacobins, the municipality of Paris, the Convention, and the Committee of Public Safety in his hands was proved by their servile obedience to his slightest nod. On May 7 he had the satisfaction of wresting from the Convention a decree dictated by his attachment to the deistic faith he shared with his idol, Rousseau. By that decree the Convention solemnly affirmed that the French people acknowledged a Supreme Being and the immortality of the soul. It sufficiently characterizes the intellectual pedantry of Robespierre that he never in his life took anything so seriously as this excursion into theology by a legislative assembly and that he had no inkling of the absurdity of the public festival of June 8,

Robespierre imposes his own deistic faith on the Convention

1794, at which he presided as high priest and proclaimed the gospel of the Supreme Being to the heathen.

Two days after the festival Robespierre revealed the spirit of fanaticism which animated his religious leadership. In order to facilitate the condemnations of the suspect, the Revolutionary Tribunal was quadrupled by the law of June 10 and its procedure stripped of the last vestiges of legal form. Then only did the executions in Paris begin in a really wholesale manner. During the six weeks before the adoption of the new measure, the number of the guillotined in Paris came to 577; during the first six weeks after its adoption, the victims reached the frightful figure of 1,356. No record of devotion to the Revolution, no service rendered on the battlefield, offered a guarantee against arrest and death.

The Terror at its height, June-July, 1794

At last the Terror invaded the Convention itself. Paralyzed by fear, that body submitted for a time to the desperate situation. But when the uncertainty connected with living perpetually under a threat of death became intolerable, the opponents of Robespierre, men of his own party, the Mountain, banded together in order to crush him.

The Convention turns against Robespierre

It characterizes Robespierre's philosophic aloofness from the blood and grime of the Terror that he did not directly participate in the slaughter of these last weeks. He had a personal elegance and moral fastidiousness which distinguished him favorably from many of his associates in the governing clique, low profligates such as Billaud, Collot, and Fouché, who covered themselves with every infamy. With his immense following among the common people Robespierre could probably have overcome his enemies. Instead of organizing resistance, he wrapped himself in an offended silence. On Thermidor 9 (July 27) [6] he and his immediate followers were condemned by the Convention and executed the next day.

Conspiracy against and overthrow of Robespierre, July, 1794

The fall of Robespierre put an end to the Terror, not because Robespierre was the Terror, but because the system had, after a year of wild extravagance, become so thoroughly discredited, even among its own supporters, that the Convention saw itself obliged to return to principles of moderation and legality. The Thermidorians, as the victors were called, had in large part been the vilest instruments of the Terror and

The reaction under the victorious Thermidorians

---

[6] The Convention, guided by its hatred of the royalist past, introduced a new system of time reckoning. Since the birth of the republic was regarded as more important than the birth of Christ, September 21, 1792, the day when monarchy was formally abolished, was voted the beginning of a new era. In an effort to detach the people from Catholicism the Christian calendar was scrapped and a common sense, republican calendar devised. Its chief features were a week of ten days and a year of twelve months of thirty days each. The months were given such poetic designations as Nivose (Snow month), Pluviose (Rain month), Thermidor (Heat month), etc.

It is worthy of notice that the Convention, a body of men unhampered by tradition, discussed many rational reforms and carried some of them into effect. One change has invited wide imitation: the many conflicting systems of weights and measures in use in France were supplanted by the uniform metrical system.

had dipped their hands into every kind of crime. In now applying the brakes, they did no more than bow to the force of circumstances. Supported by the Plain, the men of the middle ground in the Convention, they studiously heaped all the blame for the past year on the dead Robespierre and hypocritically assumed the character of lifelong lovers of law and order.

Slowly the frightened bourgeoisie recovered its courage and rallied to the support of the Thermidorian moderates. Therein lay the real significance of the new revolutionary phase. With the bourgeoisie, the property-owning element, once more in the ascendancy, the radical Parisian proletariat, identified with the defeated Mountain, was brought under control. Consequently the Thermidorians could by a succession of acts completely liquidate the late system. The municipality of Paris, the citadel of the radicals, was dissolved, the Revolutionary Tribunal discontinued, the guillotine dismantled, the powers of the Committee of Public Safety restricted; and, to make victory sure, the Jacobin club, the nursery of radicalism, was closed. During the next year—the last of its long lease of power—the Convention ruled France in substantial accord with the opinions of the bourgeoisie, the chief makers and beneficiaries of the Revolution.

Liquidation of the Terror by the Convention

If the Terror fell, its overthrow resulted not only from the domestic opposition it aroused but also from the fact that it had accomplished its end. Its cause, as well as its excuse, was the danger of France. And regardless of the excesses it committed, it had successfully mobilized the country against a tremendous coalition.

The Terror saved France

On this defense the reader must now bestow a rapid glance. In the campaign of 1793, during which the Committee of Public Safety was engaged in creating its republican armies on the basis of the law of universal military service, the French had been obliged to give way at certain points. By 1794, however, the military groundwork, largely owing to Carnot's organizing talents, had been laid and the republican armies, numerous, well-equipped, and commanded by young men of ardent spirit, were enabled to carry the war into the territory of the enemy. Thus the tables were turned and monarchical Europe, instead of invading republican France, found itself invaded.

On the creation of its new army France takes (1794) the offensive

In the course of this year (1794) an army under Jourdan conquered Belgium. Shortly after, Pichegru occupied Holland. Belgium, which ever since the Treaty of Utrecht (1713) had been a dominion of Austria, was promptly annexed to France. Holland, left nominally independent, was constituted as a republic and subjected to French influence.

Conquest (1794) of Belgium; subjection of Holland

It was a great help to the republic in winning its victories in Belgium and Holland that its two leading continental enemies, Austria and

Prussia, had fallen to quarreling and had ceased to co-operate. The ani-

France helped by the quarrel between Austria and Prussia over Poland

mosity between them was caused by the revival of an issue already some twenty years old, the partition of Poland. As Russia was about to appropriate what had been left of Poland after the First Partition of 1772, the attention of Prussia and Austria was diverted from the west, and each intrigued against the other at St. Petersburg in order to increase its own and diminish its rival's share in the Polish spoils.

Prussia deserts the coalition and signs the Treaty of Basel (1795)

Largely in consequence of the violent disagreement between Austria and Prussia over Poland, the French armies were able to occupy all western Germany up to the Rhine. At this point the reigning sovereign of Prussia, Frederick William II, a man of huge bulk but puny understanding, resolved to come to terms with revolutionary France in order to be free to bring his undivided strength to bear on the Polish problem. He opened separate negotiations with France, which, since the overthrow of Robespierre, had passed under moderate control, and in April, 1795, concluded peace at the city of Basel.

The peace with Prussia followed by peace with Spain

By the Treaty of Basel the king of Prussia agreed to give France a free hand on the left bank of the Rhine. As a few months later Spain also abandoned the coalition and made peace with France, the republic was manifestly emerging as victor from the great struggle. However, fighting was by no means over, since Great Britain, Austria, and Sardinia (Piedmont) showed no inclination as yet for an accommodation.

The Convention completes a republican constitution (1795)

Greatly strengthened by its military triumphs, the Convention at last took up the task for which it had been originally summoned, and in the course of the year 1795 gave the country a new constitution. When the document was ready, the deputies, fearful that a free election might bring the royalists back to power, resolved to provide for the continuation of the republican regime. Accordingly they passed a law by which they virtually perpetuated themselves through a provision declaring that two-thirds of the new legislature must be composed of men who had sat in the Convention.

Uprising of the monarchists against the Convention

Over this high-handed measure the monarchists, who, favored by the powerful reaction against the Terror, had become both numerous and bold, waxed so exceeding wroth that in October they organized an armed rebellion and swept down on the Convention in order to force it to rescind the objectionable law. After a long succession of riots instituted by radicals, France now witnessed the strange phenomenon of an uprising of conservatives. Nothing could have shown more convincingly the recent sharp turn-about of opinion.

The Convention was sufficiently in earnest about its republicanism to resolve to defend itself. It intrusted the task to a deputy by the name of Barras, a prominent Thermidorian. Barras, who was no soldier, committed the undertaking to a young officer and acquaintance of his,

Napoleon Bonaparte. Having already creditably distinguished himself in connection with the recapture of Toulon in 1793, Bonaparte wanted nothing better than this new opportunity. When the insurgents marched against the Convention on October 5, 1795, he received them with such a volley of grapeshot that they fled precipitately, leaving hundreds of their comrades dead upon the pavement.

Napoleon Bonaparte defends the Convention, October, 1795

The Convention could now finish its remaining business in complete security. On October 26, 1795, its stormy, cowardly, and yet, in many respects, highly creditable career, came to an end, and the new constitution went immediately into effect. It is called the Constitution of the Year III from the year of the republican calendar in which it was completed.

End of the Convention, October 26, 1795

The main provisions of the new constitution mark a return from the loose liberal notions of the constitution of 1791 to a more compact executive. Nevertheless, the tyranny of the old regime was still too near for the objections against a too-powerful executive to have vanished entirely. Therefore a compromise was found in a multiple executive of five members, called the Directory, to be elected by the legislature. The legislature was composed of a lower house, called the Council of Five Hundred, and a senate of two hundred and fifty, called the Council of Ancients. The bicameral feature, too, represented a departure from the constitution of 1791, whose single legislative chamber had proved a failure. Evidence that the constitution was essentially a bourgeois document was supplied by the fact that the election for the legislative Councils was indirect and that the right to vote depended on the possession of property.

The Constitution of the Year III described

THE DIRECTORY (1795-1799)

The Directory wished to signalize its accession to power by terminating the war with a brilliant victory over the remaining members of the coalition, Great Britain, Sardinia, and Austria. But an attack upon Great Britain was, because of the insufficiency of French naval power, out of the question. Austria and Sardinia were more vulnerable, and against them the Directory now resolved to strike with the combined armies of France. In accordance with this intention, the Organizer of Victory, Carnot, who had been elected a Director, worked out a plan by which the Austrians were to be attacked simultaneously in Germany and Italy and forced back upon Vienna.

The Directory plans a concentrated attack on Austria and Sardinia

Two splendid armies under Jourdan and Moreau were assigned to the German task, which was regarded as by far the more important, while the Italian campaign, undertaken largely to divert the attention of the Austrians from Germany, was intrusted to a poorly equipped army of 30,000 men, which, through the influence of Director Barras and in

Austria to be attacked in Germany and Italy

reward for services rendered in connection with the October insurrection, was put under the command of General Bonaparte. But the unexpected happened. By the force of his genius Bonaparte upset completely the calculations of the Directory and gave the Italian campaign such importance that he, and not Jourdan or Moreau, decided the war.

Bonaparte's task was to beat, with his army, an army of Austrians who, together with their Piedmontese allies, considerably outnumbered him. Resolved to meet his two enemies separately, he managed by a swift and secret movement to wedge his way between them, and by forcing the Piedmontese away from the Austrians toward Turin to hold them at his mercy. As a result the king of Sardinia-Piedmont sued for peace and retired from the war (April, 1796).

Bonaparte's campaign: he obliges Sardinia to surrender, April, 1796

Demoralized by these successes of the French, the Austrians fell back toward Milan. But Bonaparte, who broke every rule of the old deliberate strategy and moved with the stealth and swiftness of a beast of prey, outflanked them and, before May was over, had by a series of engagements driven them out of Lombardy. In acute alarm the pope and the other small sovereign princes of Italy now hastened to buy peace of France by the cession of territory and of priceless works of art, while the Austrians, for their part, tried again and again to recover their lost Lombard province. At Arcola (November, 1796) and then at Rivoli (January, 1797), Bonaparte, by his astonishing alertness, beat signally the forces sent against him, and, as a result, captured the main Austrian stronghold of Mantua (February, 1797). A few weeks later he entered the Tyrol and threatened to march on Vienna.

Bonaparte's campaign: he drives the Austrians out of Italy

Meantime, the Archduke Charles, commander of the Austrian forces in Germany, had beaten Jourdan and Moreau in the campaign of 1796; but when fresh French armies crossed the Rhine early in 1797, the emperor decided to sue for peace. As the most immediate pressure came from Bonaparte, he opened negotiations with him. They terminated in the Peace of Campo Formio (October, 1797). By this treaty Austria ceded her Belgian provinces as well as Lombardy, recognized northern Italy as a sphere of French influence, and accepted for herself the principle of the Rhine boundary, the actual cession to be arranged later by a treaty with the Holy Roman Empire. In return for these concessions Austria received at Bonaparte's hands the ancient republic of Venice, which the young general had just seized with more than a soldier's usual absence of scruple.

The Peace of Campo Formio, October, 1797

In spite of Austria's continued foothold in Italy through its acquisition of the Venetian republic, the Peace of Campo Formio substantially delivered the peninsula into the hands of the French. They converted ceded Lombardy into the Cisalpine republic and the former city-state of Genoa into the Ligurian republic. Both of these states were modeled on the

Two Italian republics established as clients of France

French republic and were subjected to control from Paris. They became, like Holland before them, timid clients of the triumphant Directory.

When Napoleon returned to France he was greeted as the national hero, who, out of the bramble war, had plucked the jewel peace. And what a peace it was! Not only did it establish France firmly in northern Italy, but, more impressive still, it gave her, in so far as the consent of Prussia and Austria could effect that transfer, the whole left bank of the Rhine. It could not be denied, however, that by these acquisitions the republic had reverted to the war-aims of the former Bourbon monarchy and had turned its back on the eloquent declarations against conquest with which it had begun the struggle with Europe back in 1792. In the exhilaration of victory the early idealistic professions were conveniently forgotten and the victorious general welcomed home with all but divine honors. General Bonaparte the hero of triumphant France

That Napoleon Bonaparte should become the foremost man of France before he had reached the age of thirty would never have been prophesied by the friends of his youth. He was born at Ajaccio, on the island of Corsica, in 1769, of an impoverished family which claimed the honors of nobility. The inhabitants of Corsica, Italians by language and customs, had for many generations been subjected to Genoa. Toward the middle of the eighteenth century they roused themselves to win their freedom by a determined effort. When the Genoese discovered that they could not stamp out the insurrection, they ceded (1768) Corsica to Louis XV, king of France. At the time of Napoleon's birth, therefore, the French were engaged in establishing their rule over an alien people who resisted them heroically but without success. Birth of Napoleon (1769) on the Italian island of Corsica

In the midst of the patriotic indignation caused by his country's overthrow young Bonaparte grew up. When he was ten years old, his father took him to France to enter him as a cadet in the royal military school at Brienne. On graduation he was commissioned a lieutenant of artillery. It was while he was serving in this capacity among a people whom he still detested as the oppressors of his native island that the French Revolution broke out. The collapse of authority in France persuaded him to return to Corsica to spur his countrymen to shake off the French yoke. Only when the attempt failed did he in 1793 return to the mainland. In the general confusion of that terrible year his treason, for that was what his attempt to free Corsica came to, was overlooked, and he was able to play a notable part in the recapture of the great port of Toulon from the English. Two years later (1795) he defended the Convention against a rebellious attack and, rewarded with the command of the army of Italy, dictated the Peace of Campo Formio, thereby becoming the dominant figure in French public life. How Corsican Bonaparte became the leading French general

In 1797, after two years of existence, the Directory had reason to con-

gratulate itself. Belgium, Holland, Italy, and the Rhine boundary sounded
a roll call of brilliant achievements and assured France a dominant position on the continent. Unfortunately, with the country still agitated with
the divisions and crises of the preceding years, the domestic situation
continued to be a source of unrelieved alarm. Representative in the main
of the middle classes, the Directory attempted to steer a middle course,
thereby inviting the hostility of the two extreme parties, the democratic
radicals and the royalists. Only by recourse to violence and illegality did
it survive the repeated attack of these two groups.

Domestic difficulties of the Directory

A special cause of continued concern was religion. The new national
church based on the Civil Constitution of the Clergy of 1790 was not
rooted in the love of the people and had in the course of the Terror declined to insignificance. In so far as the French people were attached to
religion at all, they were devoted to the orthodox Catholic church,
which the state regarded as its enemy and subjected to harsh persecution.
As the Directory, more from necessity than choice, enforced the repressive laws against the orthodox clergy, the always latent and sometimes
active turmoil over religion never ceased.

The religious muddle caused by the Civil Constitution of the Clergy

An even graver difficulty sprang from the chaotic national finances.
We have seen that in its very first year the Revolution resorted to paper
money, called assignats, as a way out of the financial confusion inherited
from the old regime. Ever since that time the government printing
presses had served as the leading source of French revenue. With each
new billion of currency issued the value of the paper franc disastrously
declined. By 1797 it took about a basketful of assignats to buy a basketful
of vegetables. As therewith the assignats, which, we must remember,
were government obligations, had lost their usefulness, the Directory
rid itself of them by a simple act of repudiation. This was of course
bankruptcy; and when the Directory now issued a new paper money, the
people refused to put any faith in it. The currency muddle not only embarrassed the government but paralyzed the whole economic life of the
country.

The financial muddle caused by the assignats

After Campo Formio only Great Britain remained at war with France.
During the long struggle Great Britain had been as uniformly successful
at sea as the republic had been successful on land. As neither side was as
yet ready to negotiate a peace, the Directory resolved to strike its stubborn antagonist a blow by the occupation of Egypt. Apparently the plan
originated with General Bonaparte, whose prestige after the brilliant
Italian campaign was such that his slightest wish carried the weight of
a command.

The war with Great Britain: Bonaparte proposes to occupy Egypt

Egypt did not belong to Great Britain. Nominally a province of the
Ottoman empire, it was in reality ruled by a military order of landlords,

called Mamelukes. Bonaparte, essentially hardheaded, had an imagination which occasionally ran away with him. It was his idea to threaten
Great Britain's connection with India by occupying Egypt and by this
indirect pressure to bring her to her knees.

With great secrecy a fleet was prepared at Toulon together with transports sufficient to carry 25,000 men. With Bonaparte in command the
expedition put out to sea in May, 1798, and successfully eluded the British
fleet under Nelson, who lay in wait for the French. Hardly, however,
had Bonaparte landed his army near Alexandria, than the eagerly pursuing Nelson hove in sight and without a moment's delay attacked the
French fleet lying at anchor in Abukir Bay. On August 1, in the course
of a few hours, he shot it into wreckage. Thus cut off from Europe,
Bonaparte and his army found themselves shut up in Egypt as in a
prison.

In this way the Egyptian campaign was lost before it had fairly begun.
Bonaparte could blind his soldiers to the fact but he hardly blinded
himself. Of course he did what he could to retrieve the disaster to his
fleet by his successes on land. By his victory over the Mamelukes in the
battle of the Pyramids, he made himself master of the country. In the
following year he marched his men across the Isthmus of Suez into
Syria. The seaport of Acre, which he besieged in the hope of establishing
communication with France, repulsed his attack, while the plague decimated his brave troops.

Sick at heart over his failure, Bonaparte returned to Egypt and, despairing of a change in his fortunes, resolved to desert his army. With
the good fortune that had regularly attended him so far, he contrived in
a small ship to elude the watchful British. On October 9, 1799, he landed
on the coast of France. Though the army he had deserted was irretrievably lost,[7] that fact was forgotten amid the rejoicings over the return of
the national hero.

The enthusiastic welcome of France, which turned Bonaparte's journey
northward to Paris into a triumphal procession, was owing largely to
the new dangers to which the country had been exposed during his absence. Bonaparte was hardly known to have been shut up in Egypt when
a new coalition was formed against the hated republic. Encouraged by
a lavish offer of subsidies, Austria and Russia agreed to join Great Britain
in a supreme effort to break the French grip on the continent. In the
campaign of 1799 the Austrians and the Russians gained such a succession of victories that they drove the French out of both Italy and Germany. It was while the country was under the depressing effect of this
change of fortune that Bonaparte unexpectedly reappeared in Europe.

[7] The army surrendered to the English in 1801.

The Directory completely discredited

No wonder that the hopes of the nation gathered around the dashing Corsican. What other general had exhibited such genius as Bonaparte, had won such glory for himself and France? If we recall the religious and financial embarrassments of the country and the continued uncertainty of all social relations, we can understand that the Directory's defeat in the campaign of 1799 attended by the loss of both Germany and Italy was held to be the last straw. Refusing to believe any longer in this government, public opinion turned spontaneously to Bonaparte as to a savior.

The coup d'état of November, 1799

The general was no sooner apprised of this state of the French mind than he resolved to act. With the aid of some of the Directors themselves, who no longer believed in their own system, Bonaparte hatched a conspiracy to overthrow the government. The only resistance of note was offered by the Chamber of Five Hundred and was overcome by the use of troops. The ease with which the *coup d'état* of November 9-10, 1799 (18-19 Brumaire), was executed enforces the contention that the Directory had not succeeded in establishing itself in the hearts of the people.

21 NAPOLEON BONAPARTE AND THE FRENCH EMPIRE (1799-1815)

THE CONSULATE

THE OVERTHROW OF the republican government of France by a successful and admired general delivered the country into his hands. If Napoleon Bonaparte did not immediately establish a dictatorship, it was because he was wise enough to recognize that there was still a strong democratic sentiment abroad in the land, and that it would be well for him to ease his way into complete control through a system intermediary between republic and autocracy.

In accordance with this plan Bonaparte and his fellow-conspirators of Brumaire elaborated a constitution which culminated in an executive called the First Consul. This office Bonaparte assigned to himself. There were also a Second and a Third Consul, but as they were given no power to speak of, we may disregard them. The constitution, called the Constitution of the Year VIII, since the republican calendar was still in use, attributed so much power to the First Consul that he completely dominated the government.

To preserve democratic appearances three bodies were established which were intrusted with legislation: a senate, a tribunate, and an assembly. But as the senate was appointed by the consuls, the tribunate debated but did not vote, and the assembly voted without debating, it is clear that the three legislative bodies enjoyed no authority. Furthermore, only property holders voted, and by their vote they did no more than draw up lists from which the consuls selected the legislators. The legislators were therefore a handpicked group. In short, the constitution was a screen set up to hide from view the one-man rule of General Bonaparte.

With the government resting safely in his hands, the First Consul was free to give his attention to the war. Very opportunely for him, Russia retired from the struggle at the close of the campaign of 1799, being disgusted with Austria and unwilling further to co-operate with her. As the enemies of France were thus reduced to Great Britain and Austria, the general military situation assumed a striking resemblance to that of 1796.

Bonaparte resolved to meet the situation by a plan analogous to that employed on the earlier occasion. Neglecting England as inaccessible and

Bonaparte in complete political control

Bonaparte as First Consul dominates the government

Other features of the Constitution of the Year VIII

The Second Coalition weakened (1799) by withdrawal of Russia

concentrating his attention on Austria, he sent Moreau into Germany,

while he himself undertook again to meet Austria in Italy. By a strenuous and picturesque march in the early spring over the Great St. Bernard
Pass he was enabled to strike across the Austrian line of retreat and force
the enemy to make a stand. At the battle of Marengo (June 14, 1800)
he crushed the Austrians and recovered all Italy at a stroke.

Again Francis II had to admit the invincibility of French arms. In the

Peace of Lunéville (1801) he reconfirmed all the cessions made at Campo
Formio. As the Holy Roman Empire became a party to the treaty, the
cession of the left bank of the Rhine was on this occasion made definitive.
It is this feature of the Rhine boundary which high-lights the Peace of
Lunéville. As the treaty, in addition, redelivered Italy into Bonaparte's
hands, he straightway re-established the Cisalpine and Ligurian republics
in their old dependence upon France.

Again, as in 1798, the only European state which held out against

France was Great Britain. How reduce the great sea power to submission? The French naval resources were as inadequate as ever for a direct
attack; and as for striking at the British communications, the unhappy
memory of Egypt quickly disposed of the idea. In these circumstances
Bonaparte opened (1801) negotiations with the British government, and
in March, 1802, concluded, substantially on the basis of mutual restitutions, the Peace of Amiens.

After ten years of continuous warfare France was at peace with the

world. It was an auspicious moment for the prosecution of that work of
internal reconstruction, which, after the long revolutionary storms, had
become a crying need and which, in point of fact, the First Consul had
firmly in mind from the day of his accession to power. A soldier by instinct and training, Bonaparte had a spontaneous faith in the principle
of order. With the swift intelligence and inexhaustible energy that were
among his leading characteristics, he achieved a quick and remarkably
thorough mastery over the problems of government, of which he had
thus far had no experience.

In the following paragraphs we shall summarize the institutions with

which Bonaparte endowed France in the course of the next few years.
They were all directed at the creation of an orderly society, wherein
every citizen could go about his daily business in complete security.
Moreover, this orderly society was to embody the main achievements of
the Revolution, such as the abolition of privilege and complete equality
before the law. Although Bonaparte rejected the radical excesses of the
Revolution, he completely identified himself with its most conspicuous
benefits. To remove all doubt concerning his purpose he announced in a
public proclamation that he regarded his task to be to "close" the Revolution and to "consolidate" its results.

The most immediate concern of the First Consul was to restore economic activity in order to bring back some measure of material prosperity. In this endeavor the repudiation by the Directory of the worthless assignats proved a help by making possible the return to a sound money basis through the resumption of specie payments. With a stable coinage again in use business regained confidence and commerce and industry awakened from their long depression. A central bank, called the Bank of France, contributed to this end. So did the government's adoption of an active policy of public works. In the course of the following years marshes were drained, harbors improved, and the country provided with a better system of communications by numerous new canals and highways.

The rapid business recovery

An equally pressing matter was a stable administration. The National Assembly had launched (1791) a new administrative system based on the division of France into departments. In an excess of democratic zeal it had completely decentralized the government by making every local office elective. Under the Terror, and afterward under the Directory, a return had been inaugurated to appointed officials, and this trend was, under the First Consul, carried to its logical conclusion.

Administrative weakness corrected

Every department received an official head, called prefect, who owed his appointment to the First Consul and held office subject to that ruler's pleasure. By means of the prefects the whole country was bound together by threads that met in a single hand. With his sense of military precision Bonaparte so perfected his system that no monarch by divine right has ever to an equal degree made his will felt through the length and breadth of his dominion. In exchange for democracy, the will-o'-the-wisp pursued through blood and fire for ten agitated years, France was endowed with an administration completely under the control of the central government. It is an interesting circumstance that, in spite of the many subsequent revolutions experienced by France, the Napoleonic centralization continued unchanged into the twentieth century.

Bonaparte imposes a strongly centralized administration

By attempting to set up a French national church the National Assembly had, as we are aware, produced a religious schism which had greatly contributed to the revolutionary confusion. The new church had proved an unqualified failure because both clergy and people preferred the old church and clung to it in spite of persecution. As a child of the deistic eighteenth century Bonaparte had no positive religious views and held to the loose opinions characteristic of the intelligentsia of his time. However, with his firm grasp of realities, he had no difficulty in convincing himself that Catholicism was a living force and that it would strengthen him and his regime to enlist it on his side. No sooner therefore had he acceded to the government than he opened

Abandoning the French national church, Bonaparte negotiates with Rome

negotiations with the pope with a view to a settlement of the religious schism.

The result was a treaty of peace, called the Concordat (1801). By its terms the church resigned its claim to its confiscated property and the state undertook the maintenance, on a liberal basis, of the priests and bishops. While the state assumed the right of nominating the leading clerical officials, the bishops, their appointment had to be ratified by the pope before they could exercise their functions. Although the experiment of a national church was repudiated and the Catholic church restored, the restored church was without any question reduced to a much greater dependence on the state than had formerly been the case.

The Concordat of 1801 ends the religious schism

Occupied with these important labors, Bonaparte also found time to promote the reorganization of French law. The legal confusion reigning in France before the Revolution is indescribable, for statutory law, Roman law, and numerous local customary systems contended with each other in the liveliest fashion for ascendancy. True, the Revolution had swept this monstrous legal jungle out of existence. However, while declaring for a new system to be constructed on simple and rational principles, it had not got beyond the preparatory labors.

Destruction by the Revolution of the inherited systems of law

Bonaparte at once set a commission of legal experts to work to bring the new system to completion. A Herculean task, it was not ready till 1804, when it was presented to the public as the Civil Code, called afterward, in honor of the driving power behind its preparation, the Napoleonic Code. No legal clarification of commensurate scope had been undertaken in Europe since, in the sixth century, the Roman law had been codified under the direction of the Emperor Justinian. Justinian's famous code was made the basis of the Napoleonic Code, but numerous and important modifications were introduced, dictated by the novel equalitarian and humanitarian principles spread abroad by the Revolution.

Completion and publication of the Napoleonic Code

Bonaparte also planned a national educational system in three main stages: primary, secondary, and university. He succeeded in realizing his program on only the secondary and university levels. Primary education, owing to its cost as well as to the pressure of events, never emerged beyond the stage of a project. It hardly requires express mention that the spirit breathed into the revamped education gave support to the autocratic system identified with the First Consul.

Bonaparte projects a system of education

In no review of the consolidation of the changes brought about by the Revolution may the French peasantry be overlooked. On the confiscation of the landed property of the clergy and nobility the peasants acquired the farms, on which they were settled, as freeholds. Since they were still enjoying their improved position when Bonaparte came to power, they cannot be said to have owed any thanks to him. However,

Bonaparte confirms their farms to the peasants

when by "closing" the Revolution he declared that property rights acquired through the confiscation of the estates of the former privileged classes should remain forever inalienable, he made the peasants his enthusiastic supporters. It is interesting to note that they afterward stood by him through good and evil days alike. It is even more interesting, and historically more important, that these numerous small freeholders have proved the most conservative and stabilizing element of French society down to our day.

By these achievements Bonaparte proved that he could employ his flexible genius in the labors of peace with the same effectiveness he had shown in purely military matters. When, after the Treaties of Lunéville and Amiens, France was again, after ten years, at peace with the world, Bonaparte, the uncrowned ruler of France, may be said to have stood at the parting of the ways. Either he might continue the domestic upbuilding of France or he might return to the policy of conquest inherited from the Revolution. At least we are tempted to credit him with this choice, although it is just as likely that he was under pressure by an assortment of circumstances over which he had little or no control.

Bonaparte at the parting of the ways

Let us examine the iron-clad facts of the general European situation. The revolutionary wars had enabled France to absorb Belgium and carry her eastern boundary to the Rhine. In addition, she had surrounded herself with a ring of small client states: the Batavian republic (Holland), the Cisalpine and Ligurian republics (northern Italy), and the Helvetic republic (Switzerland). This signified a domination of the continent which exposed every remaining independent state to the threat of subjection.

French domination of the continent

The consequent uncertainty and alarm were, by the policy of Great Britain, made explosively dangerous. Great Britain in its own ocean realm had proved itself as unqualifiedly superior to France as France had proved its superiority on land over its continental rivals. While the two powers had come to terms at Amiens, the bickerings over the execution of the treaty continued uninterruptedly, making it perfectly clear that neither believed in the other's sincerity.

Impermanence of Franco-British peace

As a matter of fact the peace did not last much more than a year. Already by 1803 the two powers had reopened hostilities. From that moment the continental states became increasingly restless, especially as British diplomacy never ceased to agitate at Vienna, Berlin, and St. Petersburg to the end of persuading these governments to join in a new coalition against the common enemy.

Renewal (1803) of the Franco-British war

If to these factors, fairly beyond the control of Bonaparte, we add his unbounded passion for power, we touch upon the single feature in the situation for which we may insist on his accepting responsibility.

He was, after all, a soldier, whose profession was war; and he had, besides, an imagination that delighted in picturing himself as a conqueror
of the dimensions and fame of a Julius Caesar and an Alexander the
Great. The fortunes of Bonaparte unfolded, therefore, under the double
pressure of the European dis-equilibrium created by the Revolution and
his vast personal projects.

The vaulting ambition of Bonaparte

THE EMPIRE

From the day of his seizure of the government Bonaparte was resolved to make his position permanent. He took the first step in this
direction when, in 1802, he had himself made First Consul for life. Two
years later (May, 1804) he dropped the last veil of republican pretense
by assuming the title Emperor Napoleon I. The final step in this process
of self-aggrandizement was taken, when, on December 2 of the same
year, in the presence of the highest Catholic dignitary, Pope Pius VII,
and standing erect before the high altar of the cathedral church of Paris,
he placed the imperial crown first on his own head and then on the head
of his wife, Josephine.

The First Consul becomes (1804) Emperor Napoleon I

So innocuous was the Constitution of the Year VIII that it was permitted to continue in force even after the republic had been formally
replaced by the empire. However, certain republican landmarks and
symbols began inevitably to disappear. Among the first to go was the
republican calendar. France, again become Catholic, reverted to the
ancient Christian manner of reckoning time. Furthermore, since there
was now again a monarch, there had inevitably to be called into existence a court, an etiquette, and a nobility. While the emperor succeeded in persuading some few members of the ancient nobility to accept
the new regime and take service under him, he was in the main obliged,
in order to have a nobility at all, to distribute nobiliary titles among his
leading military and civil collaborators. They constituted, in distinction
from the old royal, the new imperial nobility.

Republican landmarks disappear

On France itself becoming a monarchy, the subject-republics that lined
the borders could not possibly be permitted to continue. At a nod from
the new-hatched emperor the Batavian republic became the kingdom of
Holland and accepted Louis Bonaparte, a younger brother of Napoleon,
as its king. In like manner the Cisalpine republic became the kingdom
of Italy and, on prompting from Paris, invited Napoleon himself to
assume the kingship. In May, 1805, he crossed the Alps and crowned
himself king at Milan. As for the Ligurian republic (Genoa), it was,
like Piedmont some years before, directly incorporated in France.

The client states adjusted to the imperial system

Long before this imperial transformation was complete, indeed before
it had much more than begun, the irrepressible conflict between Great

Britain and France had, as already noted, been resumed (1803). Emperor Napoleon prepared a great armament on the coast at Boulogne and talked and acted as if he intended to invade England. But since Britain continued as before to rule the sea and Britain's most daring admiral, Nelson, lay in watch for the French in the English channel, Napoleon's project cannot be called other than chimerical. No one can have known it better than himself. We may therefore doubt that he ever seriously entertained the invasion idea with which he tried to frighten his British foe. In any case in the summer of 1805 he suddenly ended the Boulogne activities.

On the renewal of war with Great Britain Napoleon prepares a great armament at Boulogne

Napoleon abandoned the camp at Boulogne because Great Britain had succeeded in playing upon the alarms of Austria and Russia until they agreed to join her in a new coalition. No sooner did Napoleon get wind of this state of affairs than, dropping the impractical British project, he attacked the immediately pressing problem of defeating the enemies he could actually reach.

The Third Coalition (1805)

The military genius of Napoleon presently celebrated new triumphs. At Ulm he surrounded and captured an Austrian army of 50,000 men; and on December 2, 1805, he followed up this advantage by administering a crushing defeat to the combined Austrians and Russians at Austerlitz in Moravia.

Victory of Austerlitz, 1805

With his capital, Vienna, and much of his territory occupied by the enemy, Emperor Francis II was obliged once more to bow down before the invincible Corsican and sign the Peace of Pressburg (December 26, 1805). By this document he gave up his recent Venetian acquisition to Napoleon's kingdom of Italy and the Tyrol to Bavaria. This southGerman state had, during the recent campaign, acted as Napoleon's ally.

Austria signs the Peace of Pressburg, 1805

These provisions introduce us to a characteristic feature of Napoleon's policy of conquest. He did not plan to incorporate all the provinces which he might conquer directly with France but rather from France as a self-enlarging center to rule over a ring of dependent territories governed by princes under his control. More particularly in regard to Germany, his policy was to reduce the influence of the two great powers, Austria and Prussia, by so strengthening certain smaller states that they would be brought to an approximate level with Austria and Prussia. Therefore Wurtemberg, like Bavaria, was endowed with additional territory at this time and both these states were raised to the rank of kingdoms.

Napoleon's German policy

Napoleon now pondered a more sweeping plan by which he might bring all Germany, except Austria and Prussia, under his direct control. Following the Treaty of Lunéville (1801), the complicated political map of Germany had been greatly simplified by a measure of the Reichstag

whereby numerous small states, mainly bishoprics and free cities, had lost
their independence. They were distributed among the larger states to
compensate them for losses sustained by the surrender to France of
the German lands on the left bank of the Rhine. Napoleon gave his
blessing to the movement; in fact, without his all-powerful consent it
could not have been inaugurated, much less carried through. Instead
of some three hundred German states, there were, after this sweeping
compensatory operation had been completed, only a hundred states left.
The healthy process of reduction, once inaugurated, continued through
the following years.

In effective control of Germany after the renewed defeat of Austria in
1805, the emperor resolved to bring the states that had survived the
recent territorial adjustments (always excepting Austria and Prussia) into
a combination under his presidency. The result was the creation in
July, 1806, of a German union called the Confederation of the Rhine,
of which Napoleon became the informal ruler under the title of Protector. As the members of the Confederation, in effect, seceded from
the Holy Roman Empire, that ancient relic came at last to the end of
its days. The Hapsburg emperor, Francis II, performed the final rites
over the remains when, a few weeks later, he resigned the crown which
his ancestors had worn for so many centuries.

Unwilling to employ a lesser title than the one to which he was accustomed, Francis had, even before the Confederation of the Rhine was
formed, converted his personal dominions, of which Austria was the
core, into an empire. Consequently, on taking the novel title, emperor
of Austria, he was privileged to feel that by his loss of the older title he
had not suffered any diminution of dignity.

In examining Napoleon's reorganization of Germany we should not
fail to note that, exactly as in the earlier case of Italy, he brought to Germany many of the outstanding benefits of the Revolution. In all the
regions to which he had thus far or to which he afterward penetrated
serfdom and feudalism were abolished and the law made equal for all
classes of citizens. In spite of his restoration of monarchy, Napoleon
always thought of himself as "the son of the Revolution." In the eyes of
the humbler subjects of the states brought under his influence he was
an unqualified benefactor. The favor with which he was everywhere
regarded by the common people was without any question a factor in
the success he had thus far won; and his popularity as leveler of the
feudal system continued to smooth the path for him till, owing to developments to be taken up in due time, he lost his precious halo of liberator.

The only German state which so far had not yet felt the might of
Napoleon's arms was Prussia. As early as 1795 (Treaty of Basel) Prussia
had retired from the revolutionary wars; and although constantly im-

Marginal notes:

Simplifica-
tion of the
German
map after
Lunéville
(1801)

Confedera-
tion of the
Rhine; end
of the Holy
Roman
Empire
(1806)

Francis
assumes the
novel title
emperor of
Austria

Napoleon,
"the son of
the Revolu-
tion," plays
the role of
liberator

portuned by the other powers to join in their efforts to lower the pride of France, it had steadily refused to do so. King Frederick William II (1786-1797) and his successor, Frederick William III (1797-1840), stubbornly clung to neutrality in the pusillanimous persuasion that it was the safest course to pursue. Of the bold initiative, which had been a leading trait of the great Frederick, not so much as a trace had descended to his muddle-headed successors. The result was that when, following the formation of the Confederation of the Rhine, Frederick William III discovered that Napoleon was securely camped on his doorstep, he and his advisers were seized with a sudden panic. Charges and countercharges exchanged between Berlin and Paris produced a growing irritation. In the autumn of 1806 it led to a state of war.

Prussia: its long neutrality ends in the war of 1806

The Prussian army represented the highest development reached by the military science and art of the eighteenth century. Never more convincingly than in the campaign of 1806 was the proof given that with the French Revolution and the fiery nationalism it engendered a new military age had dawned on Europe. The Prussian soldiers were a docile, well-drilled body of mercenaries; the French soldiers were a national army animated with revolutionary and patriotic sentiments. The Prussian officers believed in the slow, methodical procedures of a warfare preponderantly defensive; the French officers put their faith in a swift and decisive offense.

The old and the new warfare compared

Of the new methods of warfare the most brilliant exponent was the emperor himself. Having already tested them in numerous campaigns, he now displayed them in a particularly masterful manner against Prussia. The core of the new system was to be better prepared than the enemy, to march more rapidly than he, and finally, to strike him without delay and with concentrated energy at the weakest spot of his battle line.

Napoleon, leading exponent of the new warfare

The battles of Jena and Auerstädt, fought on the same day (October 14, 1806), decided the issue. By these two battles the Prussian army was so crushingly defeated that the whole state was threatened with collapse. With the remnant of his troops King Frederick William III fled to the easternmost province of his dominion in order to establish contact with Alexander of Russia, with whom he had formed an alliance and who was coming to his aid.

Defeat of Prussia, October, 1806

Napoleon entered Berlin without encountering further opposition. As the unbeaten Russians were still in the field, he promptly moved his army eastward in search of them. A cruel winter campaign in eastern Prussia proved indecisive. When spring came, Napoleon met the Russians, together with what was still left of the Prussian army, at Friedland and decisively defeated them (June, 1807).

Defeat of Russia at Friedland, June, 1807

There now came a dramatic turn. Convinced that it was imprudent to

Napoleon and Alexander open negotiations for peace penetrate farther to the east at that time, Napoleon arranged to meet Alexander on a raft moored in the river Niemen and in this picturesque setting made such favorable overtures of peace to the tsar that they were quickly accepted. In a succession of private interviews the two rulers discussed not only the immediate quarrel between them but the innumerable problems of Europe as well. Alexander was a mercurial young man, easily elated and easily discouraged. He had absorbed some of the current liberal ideas and was by nature a consummate intriguer. While he was doubtless swept along by the firmer character and more penetrating intelligence of Napoleon, we need not believe that he fell so blindly under the Corsican's spell as to forget his own interest. In fact it might be plausibly contended that when the imperial deliberations crystallized in the form of a treaty, the document gave quite as much to Alexander as it gave to Napoleon.

The Tilsit peace and alliance of 1807 The treaty, signed in July, 1807, at the Prussian city of Tilsit, was a complete turn-about, since it transformed the late enemies into allies. In exchange for a free hand against his two neighbors, Sweden and Turkey, Alexander agreed to join Napoleon in his war against Great Britain. In the romantic language to which both the signatories were on occasion prone, they entered a partnership to rule Europe between them, one as emperor of the west, the other as emperor of the east.

The Treaty of Tilsit completely crushes Prussia At the same time there was drawn up at Tilsit a treaty with the other state with which Napoleon was at war, with Prussia; and this treaty breathed everything save friendship and alliance. The fact was that the emperor had defeated Prussia so completely that he could do with it very much as he pleased. Accordingly, he reduced Prussia to half its former size by depriving it of its recent Polish gains as well as of all its scattered territories west of the river Elbe; he levied an indemnity much larger than the war-drained country was able to pay in many years; he maintained in the reduced Prussian state a French army of occupation at Prussian expense; and he restricted the Prussian army to 42,000 men. By these stipulations Prussia was stricken from the list of the great powers and became, in effect, a French dependency.

THE EMPIRE AT ITS ZENITH

Napoleon's power at its zenith (1807) The Peace of Tilsit carried Napoleon to the zenith of his career. True, he continued for five years after 1807 to absorb new territories, but increased dominion did not, after Tilsit, signify increased strength. It will therefore be profitable, with the map before us, to review Napoleon's situation in the months following his alliance with Alexander. He ruled directly and as autocrat an enlarged France, which overflowed into Germany and Italy. This central nucleus he had surrounded with a long list of dependencies, in which subject-princes exercised power under his direction.

Many of these subject-princes were members of his own family raised to the princely dignity in the belief that they would prove more loyal than strangers. Thus his brother Louis had been made king of Holland, his brother Joseph king of Naples, his brother Jerome king of Westphalia. Westphalia was created after Tilsit out of territories in western Germany taken from Prussia and a number of other German states. As a sister, who had married the brilliant cavalry general, Murat, insisted on not being overlooked in the exaltation of her family, her imperial brother provided for her and Murat another west-German dominion, the grand duchy of Berg. Both Berg and Westphalia were incorporated in the Confederation of the Rhine. Of this Confederation Napoleon was president under the title, Protector, and by its means he held Germany in the hollow of his hand.

Napoleon establishes his relatives on European thrones

We are not yet at the end. Napoleon himself was king of Italy. However, as he could not be present simultaneously at Paris and Milan, he ruled in the latter capital through a viceroy, his stepson, Eugène Beauharnais, son of the Empress Josephine by her first marriage. The Swiss Confederation being too important to be overlooked, Napoleon had drawn it into his system by reserving to himself a general supervision of its affairs under the title Mediator. On depriving Prussia of her Polish spoils, he had assembled them in the duchy of Warsaw. Over this he exercised control by imposing on it as ruler a dependable German prince, the king of Saxony.

The review of Napoleon's power continued

If we now add that by a succession of unparalleled victories Napoleon had broken the might of Austria and Prussia and had brought Russia to his side as an ally, we shall agree that he had climbed to a higher eminence than any European conqueror since the far days of Charlemagne. The only cloud still obscuring his horizon was the war with Great Britain. Having, however, just acquired Alexander as an ally, he might feel that he could look with unshaken confidence into the future.

The enduring menace of Great Britain

Nonetheless, the confidence of Napoleon in his future, or, according to a mystic phrase frequently on his lips, in his star, was mistaken. The war with Great Britain and the vast embroilments resulting therefrom led in the course of a few years to his ruin. Henceforth it is the story of Napoleon's decline and fall that will engage our attention. By way of introduction we shall return to his struggle with the mistress of the seas and carry the tale through the years just reviewed and signalized by the glamorous names of Austerlitz, Jena, and Friedland.

Great Britain proves a stone of stumbling

We have followed the resumption of the war between France and Great Britain in 1803 to the abandonment by Napoleon of the armament

assembled by him at Boulogne. In the desperate hope of covering up his
Boulogne failure by a naval victory, he ordered his admiral, lying with his
fleet in the harbor of Cadiz, to attack without further delay the blockad-
ing English fleet under Nelson. As Spain had become Napoleon's ally and
had accommodatingly placed its navy at the French admiral's disposal,
Napoleon was perhaps justified in entertaining a modest hope of victory.
It was completely dashed by the battle of Trafalgar, which took place on
October 21, 1805. The British fleet practically blew the united Franco-
Spanish fleet off the face of the waters. While the intrepid Nelson himself was killed, his death did not alter the fact that British supremacy
on the high seas had been established more authoritatively than ever.

The British victory of Trafalgar, 1805

Unable henceforth to injure Great Britain by direct attack, Napoleon
resolved to bring her to submission by the indirect method of destroying her commerce and sapping her wealth. In this new warfare he fired
the opening gun, when in November, 1806, he issued from Berlin a
decree by which he ordered the seizure of all British goods in his own
and allied territories and excluded from his own and allied ports all
British ships. His calculation was that the continent itself, and chiefly
his own France, would produce the manufactures hitherto furnished by
Great Britain, and that the needed supplies of non-European articles,
such as sugar and coffee, would be delivered by the vessels of neutral
powers, primarily by the United States.

Napoleon resorts to economic war: the Berlin Decree of 1806

To destroy this latter hope the British answered the Berlin Decree
with an Order in Council whereby, under penalty of seizure, they forbade neutral ships to visit ports from which the British were excluded,
unless they had first put in at British ports to take on a consignment of
British goods. To this measure Napoleon's counterblast was to declare
every neutral vessel which obeyed the British order subject to confiscation. Plainly each side refused to recognize such a thing as neutrality
and insisted that a trading outsider must do its particular bidding.

Measures and counter-measures of France and Great Britain

On defeating Austria and Prussia in 1805 and 1806 respectively, Napoleon obliged them, too, to follow his lead and close their ports to British
goods and ships. At Tilsit, in 1807, he also persuaded Russia to fall in
line. Indeed, Alexander went so far as to agree to join Napoleon in
forcing the closure of ports to British goods and ships on every state
of Europe. No neutrals were to be tolerated on any pretext whatever,
and the continent was to be flung into the Franco-British struggle as an
economic whole. It is for this reason that Napoleon's economic policy
goes usually under the name of the Continental System.

The Continental System at-tempts to unify the continent against Britain

With the two emperors standing together to enforce the Continental
System every European state submitted with a single exception. The
exception was little Portugal, far to the west on the Atlantic coast. Economically dependent on Great Britain, the government of Portugal

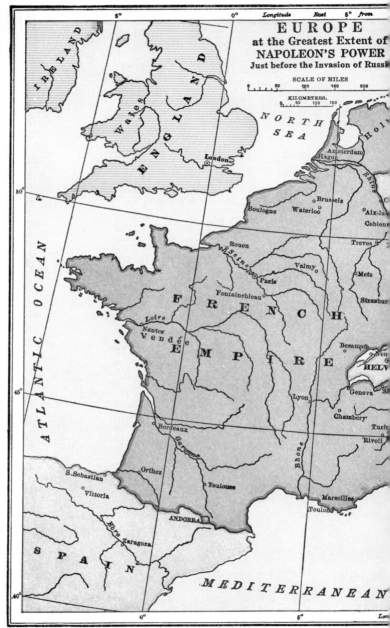

EUROPE
at the Greatest Extent of
NAPOLEON'S POWER
Just before the Invasion of Russi

SCALE OF MILES

KILOMETERS.

Note to the Student: The Rhine boundary, the ancient goal of Fren
ambition, was reasonably assured before Napoleon came to pow
Observe how his policy led to 1) untenable conquests and 2) insecu
dependencies. *Conquests:* Holland, German Coast (Hamburg, Breme

Lübeck), Western Italy (Piedmont, Tuscany, Papal States), Illyrian
Provinces. *Dependencies:* Confederation of the Rhine, Duchy of War-
saw, Helvetic Republic, Kingdom of Italy (Eugene Beauharnais),
Naples (Joseph Bonaparte, Murat), Spain (Joseph).

plucked up courage to reject the imperial command to close its ports to British goods. Thereupon Napoleon sent an army over the Pyrenees and across Spain, which forced the Portuguese royal family to seek sanctuary in Brazil, and occupied the country (November, 1807). It was, at least superficially, another triumph for the emperor. He had hermetically sealed, or seemed to have sealed, the continent from St. Petersburg to Lisbon, from Naples to Antwerp and Hamburg, to the products and ships of the hated "nation of shop-keepers." *Portugal alone resists Napoleon and is occupied, 1807*

With success apparently in sight, difficulties and ever new difficulties rose in Napoleon's path, which checked and finally overwhelmed him. There was the usual complicated nexus of circumstances. The cessation of trade with England brought ruin to the continental middle classes and poverty and suffering to the workers. Then there were the continuous wars for which the dependent states had regularly to supply a stipulated quota of conscripts. As a result the popularity which the emperor had originally enjoyed as the bringer of the revolutionary benefits was gradually replaced by a sullen irritation. The new state of mind was sedulously fanned to flame by the unreconciled patriots to be found in every country which had been obliged to assume the Napoleonic yoke. These men were cut to the quick by the disgrace of their country's subjection and pictured Napoleon as a cruel tyrant and heartless conqueror against whom the nation must needs assert itself or perish. *Economic misery and wars make Napoleon an object of hatred*

The growing popular unrest was bound to reach the defeated governments, which were only too pleased to learn of the spread of national sentiments, giving them hope of regaining their lost independence. They were therefore quick to enter into secret correspondence with Britain, which for its part never ceased to lure them with promises of financial assistance. They also made such military preparations as they dared with a view to an early resumption of the war with their hated overlord. Such were the uneasy elements of the general situation in the years following the enforcement of the Continental System. Nothing short of a review of the actual events, however, will enable us to comprehend the overwhelming Napoleonic catastrophe. *The rise of nationalism causes the defeated government secretly to prepare for liberation*

THE ROAD TO RUIN: SPAIN

The occupation of Portugal unescapably carried with it the occupation of Spain, through which country alone Portugal could be reached. From the beginning of the revolutionary wars Spain had played a wretched part, largely because of the despicable character of its Bourbon king, Charles IV, and the rank corruption of his court. Although Charles, on the execution of his Bourbon relative, Louis XVI, had joined the great anti-French coalition, he had never more than halfheartedly *Spain, hitherto the ally of Napoleon*

exerted himself and in 1795 had withdrawn from the war entirely. On the rise of Napoleon, he had actually entered into an alliance with France and, joining his fleet with that of Napoleon, had been punished by the British for his subservience by having his ships shot to wreckage at Trafalgar (1805).

Napoleon
acquires
title to
Spain by
the trick of
Bayonne,
1808
In return for these good offices Napoleon now planned to seize the country of his ally for the reason, defensible on military but hardly on any conceivable moral grounds, that he could not securely occupy Portugal without being completely sure of Spain. Taking advantage of a quarrel between Charles IV and his son and heir, Ferdinand—two clowns as contemptible each in his own way as any that have ever masqueraded in royal mantle—he invited the pair to the French town of Bayonne, just across the Spanish border, in order to lay their quarrel before him for adjudication. There the trap closed on them and the two zanies were forced to resign their rights to the Spanish crown to the wily arbiter (May, 1808).

The most capable of the brothers of Napoleon was probably his older brother, Joseph. In 1806 Joseph had been made king of Naples. In characteristically arbitrary fashion the emperor now promoted Joseph to the throne of Spain and transferred his brother-in-law, Murat, from Berg in Germany to the vacated Neapolitan throne.

Hardly had Joseph arrived at his capital, Madrid, when the Spanish people rose in spontaneous insurrection against him and the French army of occupation. By disposing of them as if they were a nation on the auction block, Napoleon had so deeply wounded their pride that they were prepared to stake life and happiness against the usurper. The emperor therefore faced a phenomenon entirely new in his experience—a national uprising. Thus far in his victorious career he had dealt with petrified absolute governments completely out of touch with their subjects. On the destruction of their armies in battle these governments had promptly acknowledged defeat and sued for peace. It would have accorded with the rules of the political game as the emperor knew it, if on the abdication of the Bourbon line and the establishment in its place of Joseph Bonaparte, the Spanish people had joyfully acclaimed their new sovereign.

Napoleon was surprised and angered by the resistance of the Spanish people. Resorting to the only means of overcoming opposition with which he was familiar, he poured a large army into Spain and challenged the Spaniards to settle the issue once and for all in the field. But the Spaniards neither would nor could accommodate him. Their own government having disappeared, they had no regular army; and obliged to organize and arm themselves as best they could, they assembled in small bands which conducted an annoying guerrilla warfare. Under daring leaders, who knew every foot of the difficult Spanish terrain, these bands would ambuscade a French detachment or rear-guard and would be off to the hills before the main army could be brought into action.

The very first summer of this kind of fighting showed that a way had been found of checkmating the great war-lord. As Napoleon clung stubbornly to his plan of keeping Spain in control, there now began a draining of his resources into Spain which was bound in the long run to prove exhausting. To make the situation worse, Great Britain was quick to take advantage of the peninsular disturbances. A British army under Arthur Wellesley, better known under his later title of duke of Wellington, landed in Portugal and succeeded in driving the French out. *Britain sends an army to Portugal*

As their next step the British began helping the insurgent Spaniards by supplying them with money and arms. Only once, in the winter of 1808-9, did Napoleon himself come to Spain to attempt to set matters right. He succeeded in driving the British to their ships and the Spaniards to their hills. No sooner, however, had he gone back to France than the guerrillas left their retreats and the British effected a new landing. The Spanish war went on and on. *The British come to the aid of the Spaniards*

In short, Napoleon learned through the Spanish instance that a people determined to live free cannot be conquered. In 1809 General Wellesley was given supreme command of the British forces in the peninsula, and from Portugal as his base, undertook to force his way by cautious stages to Madrid. Naturally the news of the French reverses in Spain was eagerly circulated among the peoples of central Europe, particularly among the Germans. It stimulated their new-born nationalism and spread the conviction that if they would but imitate the Spaniards, they too would get rid of the tyrant and the manifold woes connected with his rule. *Spanish nationalism stimulates nationalism everywhere*

THE ROAD TO RUIN: AUSTRIA

Sensing the mounting tide of German popular feeling, Austria was moved in 1809 to utilize it in a new effort to throw off the Napoleonic hegemony. The attempt was premature. Prussia could not help, for Prussia was occupied by French troops, while the princes of the Confederation of the Rhine were so deeply pledged to Napoleon that they would permit no national propaganda in their territory. In consequence only isolated groups of Germans rose here and there in response to the Austrian call to arms. *Austria's attempt (1809) to arouse a German insurrection fails*

In these circumstances Napoleon was free to apply to Austria the swift and concentrated tactics in which he excelled. However, that his enemies were no longer the military martinets they had been, but had profited from the French lesson, was proved by the obstinate and at times even

successful resistance offered by the Austrian army. Nonetheless, by a
Renewed battle fought just outside of Vienna, at Wagram, Napoleon laid Austria
defeat of a fourth time at his feet (July, 1809). In the subsequent treaty (Peace of
Austria at Vienna) Austria had to cede much territory to the victor. Very probably
Wagram she would have received even harsher treatment than she did, if certain
developments occurring at this juncture had not obliged Napoleon to
provide for a change of system.

In the two years that had elapsed since Tilsit, Tsar Alexander had
Rift in the gradually drifted away from his alliance with Napoleon. While there
Tilsit alli- were many reasons for discontent on his part, the leading reason was
ance caused without question that source of general European complaint, the Conti-
by the nental System. Russia, a purely agricultural country, had been in the
Continental habit of exchanging its surplus grain for British manufactures. On the
System closing of its ports an economic crisis followed which induced Alexander secretly to admit the forbidden goods. To Napoleon's impatient
outcry he answered with evasions. Recognizing that the Tilsit alliance
was going to pieces and that Alexander might have to be kept in line
by coercion, Napoleon saw the necessity of getting support for an eventual war against Russia from beaten Austria. Hence the relative leniency
of the peace concluding the war of 1809.

There was also a personal reason for treating Austria indulgently.
The Having no children by the Empress Josephine, Napoleon had for some
Austrian years been considering divorce. He now made up his mind that the young
marriage archduchess, daughter of Emperor Francis, would be a desirable bride
(1810) both in herself and because of the resulting association of the upstart
followed by house of Bonaparte with the ancient Hapsburg family. Accordingly, the
the birth of divorce from Josephine was pronounced and, immediately after, the mar-
an heir riage to Marie Louise was celebrated with great pomp. In the following
year (1811) the young empress gave birth to a son, on whom the father
bestowed the high-sounding title of king of Rome. Boasting at last a
direct heir, he might flatter himself that his dynasty had been greatly
strengthened.

In these years the edifice of the emperor's power reached its greatest
Continued outward magnificence. But ominous cracks kept appearing, indicative
extension of of imperfect foundations. It was always the same story: Europe could
the empire: not support the hardships of the Continental System. In 1810 the em-
absorption peror ended a long quarrel with Pope Pius VII over the secret admis-
of the papal sion to his state of English goods by carrying the Holy Father, a pris-
dominion oner, to Fontainebleau (near Paris) and by incorporating his territory in
the ever expanding French empire.

For the same misdemeanor Napoleon deposed his own brother Louis
and annexed the kingdom of Holland to France. To enable his anti-
British orders to be carried out by his own trusty officials, he followed

up the occupation of the Dutch coast with the seizure of the North
sea coast of Germany with the two great ports of Bremen and Hamburg.
Every such acquisition added to the bulk but not to the strength of the
empire.

Absorption
of Holland
and the
German
coast

THE ROAD TO RUIN: RUSSIA

In the course of the year 1811 the rupture between Napoleon and
Alexander became complete; and in the spring of 1812, in order to punish
the tsar for his rejection of the Continental System, Napoleon set in
motion toward Russia the greatest armament Europe had ever seen. Its
composition reflected the cosmopolitan character of the empire. Of the
total host of 600,000 men less than half were French. Germans, Italians,
Poles, Dutch, and Danes, drawn from the French subject-states, made up
the bulk of Napoleon's army.

The
invasion
of Russia,
1812

At first all went well, except for the fact that the Russians refused to
make a stand. Their policy was to retreat before the invader, thus drawing him deeper and deeper into the interminable Russian plain and farther and farther from his supplies. Not till just before Moscow did the
Russians offer battle. On being defeated in the bloody battle of Borodino
they fell back to and beyond Moscow, permitting their ancient capital
to be occupied (September 15) by the French army.

Napoleon
reaches
Moscow

Here an immense surprise awaited Napoleon. In his view the Russians
would hurry to ask for peace as soon as Moscow had fallen. Instead,
the residents not only evacuated their city but deliberately set it on fire
in order to make it untenable for the enemy. As Napoleon entered the
gates, Moscow burst into flames about him and his advancing host.
Only the old fortified core, the Kremlin, did he succeed in saving from
destruction. When the fire had burned itself out, the conqueror sat in
the Kremlin surrounded by wreckage and desolation. The ominous
meaning of the destruction of Moscow was that in Russia, as in Spain,
national feeling had been aroused to a pitch akin to fanaticism.

Moscow
destroyed
by fire

Unable to divest himself of the hope that Tsar Alexander would offer
to make peace, Napoleon lingered among the blackened ruins of Moscow for over a month. It was a fatal delay. For when the emperor at
last ordered the inevitable retreat, he and his army were overtaken by
the fierce Russian winter. The roads were soon churned to liquid mud,
rain alternated with snow and ice, the horses that drew the cannon and
the baggage perished, diseases multiplied, food failed. To all these
miseries were added the incessant raids of the swift-moving Cossacks,
who harried the outposts and killed the stragglers. Napoleon directed his
demoralized army during the early stages of the retreat. Then, aware that
he was needed at home, he set out for Paris. Late in December, a few
thousand starved, broken, and half-crazed men, the miserable remnant

The
disastrous
retreat from
Russia

of what had been proudly called the Grand Army, tottered across the Russian boundary into the comparative safety of a German area held by French reserves.

While the loss of his army was in itself a most serious setback for Napoleon, it would become a downright catastrophe should it encourage Germany, long throbbing with suppressed rebellion, to rise in revolt and create fresh complications at a juncture when the emperor needed all his vigor to repair the supreme disaster of his career. As alive to the situation as Napoleon, the German patriots were persuaded that it was now or never for their oppressed country. Their aim was, of course, a general national rising. But they did not fail to see that its success would be best assured if it could be organized around Prussia as a nucleus.

During the six years that had elapsed since her crushing defeat by Napoleon, Prussia had experienced a remarkable renewal. Many of her leading men had been brought around to the view that the overthrow of 1806 was the fruit of her backward social and political condition, and that to rise again in the world Prussia would have to adopt the main reforms of the French Revolution.

Temporarily silenced by his disasters, the pedantic and conservative king hesitatingly yielded to the importunities of his advisers. First under Stein, and when Stein was dismissed at the instance of Napoleon, under Hardenberg, Prussia was by royal decree relieved of the main evils of feudalism. Serfdom was abolished and the peasants made freeholders. This was done by the surrender of a fraction of their farms to their former lords as compensation for the feudal services from which they were relieved. Furthermore, the rigid caste system was destroyed and all occupations and professions declared to be open alike to nobles, middle class, and peasants.

At the same time the army was reorganized on the basis of the French revolutionary principle of universal compulsory service. The obligation assumed in the Peace of Tilsit to limit the Prussian army to 42,000 men was a serious drawback. It was cleverly evaded by replacing each body of 42,000 men by another body of the same size as soon as its predecessor had acquired the requisite military training. In this way Prussia surprised Napoleon, when the call to arms came, by being able to mobilize several hundred thousand men.

When the people of Prussia, inspirited and unified by these reforms, got news of the destruction of Napoleon's army on the snow-swept plains of Russia, they openly and exultantly expressed their glee. No debate, no delay on the part of the timid king was suffered. Swept helplessly along by the mounting tide of enthusiasm, Frederick William III was obliged to sign a treaty of alliance with Russia and to declare war against France (March, 1813).

The threatening German revolt

The renewal of Prussia

Abolition of serfdom and abandonment of the caste system

The Prussian army reorganized on a national basis

Prussia declares war, March, 1813

The disastrous campaign of 1812 would have reduced any other man than Napoleon to complete exhaustion. He faced the new situation as undaunted as ever. By gigantic efforts he succeeded in mustering a new army, and in the spring of 1813 hurried to Germany resolved to crush the Russian and Prussian forces. Only by gaining a swift success over these enemies already in the field could he keep Austria and the subject-states of the Confederation of the Rhine from declaring against him. *Napoleon resolves to hold Germany*

At Lützen (May 2) and at Bautzen (May 20) Napoleon maintained his ancient reputation by driving the united Prusso-Russian forces from the field. But clearly the day of the Jenas and Friedlands was over. Not only did the French capture no cannon or men, but the losers fell back in good order on Silesia. Napoleon had to confess that his victories had been paid for by such heavy losses that to win at this rate was certain ruin. On June 4 he agreed to an armistice in order to reorganize his troops and to take stock of the political situation. *The campaign of 1813: the first half*

Both parties now became aware that the German issue hinged upon Austria and that the side which she might join would have a decisive preponderance. In these circumstances, Prince Metternich, the intelligent and crafty chancellor of the Austrian empire, undertook to play the role of mediator. He drew up a general peace plan, which Napoleon indignantly rejected because it trimmed his power more than he was prepared to admit. As a result Austria threw in her lot with Russia and Prussia. The event signified an anti-Napoleonic coalition, in which for the first time all three continental powers were aligned, with Great Britain, in a united effort to beat down the hitherto invincible Corsican. *The summer armistice: Austria enters the war*

When toward the end of August the truce of June 4 expired, there took place a concerted forward movement on the part of the allies. Prussians, Russians, and Austrians drove from different directions on the French, who had concentrated their forces in Saxony with a view to holding the line of the river Elbe. Having fewer men at his disposal than the enemy, Napoleon was gradually reduced to the defensive, outmaneuvered, and finally, in a savage battle at Leipzig lasting three days (October 16-18), completely crushed. With the remnants of his army he made his way westward across the Rhine. *The campaign of 1813: the second half culminates in the battle of Leipzig*

If the emperor could have imagined a future for himself on the French throne in the role of a defeated conqueror, he might have ended the war after the rout at Leipzig. For, still afraid of his rare genius, the allies offered him a remarkably favorable peace, which included the Rhine boundary. When he rejected the offer, they were obliged to invade France to bring him to terms. His defensive campaign, conducted in the winter of 1813-14 with slender forces, was, from a military standpoint, one of his most brilliant achievements. However, he was hopelessly out- *The allies invade France and enter Paris, March, 1814* numbered and could not prevent the allies from entering Paris on March 31, 1814.

Napoleon's hopeless situation As Napoleon looked about him he could no longer deceive himself. He saw the north and east of France in possession of the victors of Leipzig, while the south was being rapidly taken over by the British under the duke of Wellington. Having driven the French out of Spain in 1813 by the battle of Vittoria, Wellington had pressed after them through the passes of the Pyrenees onto French soil.

Abdication of Napoleon; restoration of Louis XVIII Unable to offer further resistance, Napoleon on April 6, 1814, at the castle of Fontainebleau, abdicated his throne. The victors sent him to the small island of Elba (off the coast of Tuscany), of which they gave him the full sovereignty. Then they took up the question of the government to be given to defeated France. Only after considerable debate they agreed, in a treaty signed at Paris, to the accession to the throne of Louis XVIII, brother of the king who had been guillotined in 1793. It was further stipulated that Louis should accept the chief social and political reforms of the Revolution, and that he should be put in possession of a France endowed with the boundaries it had possessed at the outbreak of the revolutionary wars.

The Congress of Vienna, 1814-1815 These preliminaries arranged, the victors agreed to meet again in the autumn at Vienna to discuss the innumerable remaining problems of European reconstruction. Vienna was chosen as the seat of the congress in compliment to the Austrian Chancellor Metternich, who had come to be recognized as Napoleon's most uncompromising opponent. Of course the leading representatives of the European states, great and small, attended the meeting. Prominent among them were the fluid and impressionable Tsar Alexander, the grave duke of Wellington, the ardent Stein, who together with Hardenberg had presided over the renewal of Prussia, and the subtle, insinuating Talleyrand, who came as the representative of Louis XVIII to look after the interests of France.

THE RETURN FROM ELBA AND THE HUNDRED DAYS

Napoleon escapes from Elba, 1815 The Congress had not yet completed its labors, when it was thrown into confusion by a startling event. After only ten months of residence on Elba, Napoleon made his escape from the island and on March 1, 1815, landed on the coast of France.

Napoleon's calculation The resolution formed by Napoleon once more to try conclusions with united Europe was the resolution of despair. Without doubt it was folly on the part of the allies to have expected that a man like him, with a burning craving for activity, would ever content himself with the tiny island-realm of Elba. It was even greater folly on the part of Napoleon to fancy that he could thwart the will of united Europe. A gambler by nature, he waited till he heard of a rift among the powers in session at Vienna. The rift signified a chance and he plunged into the adventure.

On landing on the French coast Napoleon unfolded the imperial banner and was heartened by seeing his former soldiers rally to it by the scores and hundreds. Marshal Ney, who was sent out by Louis XVIII, the restored Bourbon king, to take Napoleon captive, broke into tears at sight of his old leader and folded him in his arms. There was no resisting Napoleon's magnetic personality. The familiar *"Vive l'empereur!"* rang through France till the lukewarm partisans of the Bourbon dynasty fell away from it with feverish alacrity. As once before, Louis fled across the border, while, hailed by soldiers and peasants but hardly by the bourgeoisie, whom his perpetual wars and despotic government had estranged, Napoleon again entered Paris. Napoleon's triumphal march to Paris

The Hundred Days, as Napoleon's restoration is called, form a mere after-play to the great drama which began with the coronation at Notre Dame, reached its climax at Tilsit, and had the curtain rung down on it at Fontainebleau. Napoleon's empire was a thing of the past and could not be revived against united Europe. And that Europe *was* united was proved by the action taken at Vienna by the members of the coalition within a few hours after they had received the news of Napoleon's return: unhesitatingly they renewed the war and prepared for a fresh invasion of France. The reign of a Hundred Days

The issue was decided with spectacular suddenness in Belgium. There Wellington stood at the head of a composite Anglo-Dutch-Hanoverian army, and thither marched to his assistance from the lower Rhine, where he had been in winter quarters, Marshal Blücher with his Prussians. These enemies, because they were closest at hand, Napoleon resolved to meet first. With his usual swiftness he fell upon and defeated Blücher on June 16 at Ligny, before this general could unite with the forces under Wellington. Leaving Marshal Grouchy with 30,000 men to pursue the Prussians, Napoleon next turned, on June 18, against his remaining adversary. Napoleon seeks the enemy in Belgium; battle of Ligny

Wellington, who had taken a strong defensive position near Waterloo, resolutely awaited the French attack. All afternoon Napoleon hurled his infantry and cavalry against the "iron duke's" positions without dislodging his tough opponent. When in the late afternoon the Prussians unexpectedly made their appearance on his right, he was caught between two fires. Blücher had evaded his French pursuer and by a forced march had reached the battlefield. Before the lingering June sun went down, Napoleon's army had been annihilated. Battle of Waterloo, June 18, 1815

Precipitately the emperor fled to Paris and there abdicated a second time. Deserted by all in his misfortunes, he planned to escape to America; but finding the coast guarded by English cruisers, he was obliged to take

refuge on the British ship *Bellerophon*. He was carried first to England,
and thence, in accordance with the verdict of his victorious enemies, to
the remote and rocky mid-Atlantic island of St. Helena. There, six years
later (1821), he died, a lonely and embittered exile.

Napoleon banished to St. Helena

At Paris, meanwhile, the allies once more restored Louis XVIII to his
ancestral throne by virtue of a new instrument called the Second Treaty
of Paris. It granted the defeated power a somewhat less generous peace
than the treaty of the previous year. France was obliged to pay for her
renewed acceptance of Napoleon by having imposed on her a few border
rectifications, a money indemnity of 700,000,000 francs, and the restoration of the immense art treasures which Napoleon had systematically
pilfered from the countries he had defeated.

Second restoration of Louis XVIII

With Napoleon's downfall one of those reactions took place characteristic of the eternal seesaw of human attitudes and emotions. Not only
was his militarism discredited but no less so were the revolutionary principles in which he had had his origin and with which he, "the son of the
Revolution," had been identified to the end. The victory over him was
therefore widely interpreted as a victory of the system which the Revolution had attacked and which had as its leading elements the monarch
by divine right and the two privileged orders of the clergy and nobility.
It followed that this system experienced a revival, but, as we shall see in
later chapters, the revival was incomplete and, above all, temporary.

Napoleon's fall followed by political reaction

A return to the political and social system of the eighteenth century
of more than brief duration was impossible for many reasons fairly re-
ducible to one. That reason was that the French Revolution signified the
coming-of-age of the French middle class and, owing to the contemporary expansion of trade and industry, of the middle classes throughout
Europe. As spokesman of these classes the French bourgeoisie had not
only voiced but actually realized a set of social-political propositions expressive of the development reached by Europe at that time. While it is
undoubtedly true that these propositions did not shine so brightly immediately after 1815 as in the two preceding decades, they were obscured,
not extinguished. They could not be more than obscured, since with the
dawning nineteenth century the middle classes entered on so amazing a
development that the century may very properly be called their century.
In this, their century, they successfully instituted throughout the western
world a politico-social system exactly adjusted to their needs and outlook.

The reaction bound to be ephemeral

The nineteenth century program of the middle classes will, in the
following chapters, become familiar to us under the name of liberalism.
At this point it is important to observe that all the leading features of
this liberalism had been brought to the front by the French Revolution.
In now ringing down the curtain on the revolutionary era we may profit-

Nineteenth century liberalism derives from the French Revolution

ably recall these features, in the first place because they will summarize for us the significance of the period just concluded, and further, because, although enfeebled after 1815, they were so far from dying that they became the core of the middle-class program of the new century.

The five main social-political propositions promulgated by the French Revolution were the following:

1. The absolute or divine-right monarchy must give place to a limited monarchy exercising the precise powers conferred by a written constitution. **1. Limited monarchy**

2. To remind the monarch (or the president of the republic which might replace the monarchy) that he holds office to the end of serving not himself but the people he rules, he must agree that his power derives from them. **2. Sovereignty of the people**

3. In order that the law may become equal for the whole citizen body, privileges must be abolished and the privileged, that is, the nobles and clergy, be reduced to a legal level with the commoners. **3. Equality before the law**

4. Cancellation of the monopoly rights of any particular religion must be coupled with toleration of all reasonable faiths and cults. **4. Religious toleration**

5. The nationalism spread by the French Revolution throughout Europe must be recognized as a legitimate force. Not until, by the French Revolution, all classes had been fused into a single legal class of equal citizens did the nation in a modern sense come into existence. The newborn French nation became for Frenchmen the object of an enthusiasm suggestive of religious worship. From this flaming nationalism of the French was kindled the nationalist fervor of all the other peoples of Europe. Nationalism, born in the revolutionary period, ranks as one of its most important creations. **5. Nationalism**

THE CONSERVATIVE REACTION AND THE REVOLUTIONS THAT UNDER-MINED IT (1815-1830)

THE CONGRESS OF VIENNA

THE CONGRESS OF VIENNA, which met to arrange the affairs of Europe after the overthrow of Napoleon, assembled its innumerable decisions, before adjourning, into a Final Act. Taken in connection with the Peace of Paris, which restored Louis XVIII to the throne of France, this document traces the political geography of reconstructed Europe. It also reveals the principles underlying the decisions of the victor powers which wrote the treaty. While it is correct to describe them sweepingly as conservative and reactionary, it is indispensable to subject them to a detailed examination.

The Final Act of the Congress of Vienna

The man recognized by the members of the Congress as the leading conservative figure was Prince Metternich, the Austrian chancellor. He was filled with particular horror at the brusque manner in which the Revolution had shifted the boundaries of the European states and had made and unmade dynasties. He was for returning as far as possible to the situation and map of 1789 by the application of the principle of "legitimacy."

The Congress guided by "legitimacy"

Legitimacy was the invention of Metternich's very cunning rival, the Frenchman, Talleyrand. This one-time bishop had left France at the coming of the Terror, had been accepted into favor by the Directory, and for a time had served Napoleon as his foreign minister. Slippery as an eel, he had in 1814 made himself acceptable to Louis XVIII and been sent by him as his representative to Vienna. It was Metternich, however, whose adoption of legitimacy made it a basic idea of the reconstruction effected at Vienna. It signified that the numerous rulers whom the Revolution had driven from their thrones were considered to have a theoretic claim to restoration to their states within the prerevolutionary boundaries.

Legitimacy signifies the restoration of the pre-revolutionary dynasties

In actual practice, however, legitimacy was modified by two other considerations. The first of these was territorial compensation. This was the polite name given the traditional land hunger of the great powers. Having issued as victors from the struggle, they were resolved to strengthen themselves to the best of their ability by additions of territory, and they succeeded in doing so, often in direct contravention of the much-lauded legitimacy and of course also of nationalism, which as a revolutionary principle was regarded with frank aversion by the triumphant reactionaries.

Legitimacy modified: (1) by territorial compensation

The other consideration that entered into the Viennese arrangements and caused an uneven application of the principle of legitimacy was hostility to France. As France had proved to be the strongest power of Europe and, through its strength, the disturber of European peace, the victors argued that the states established along its border would have to be buttressed in order to enable them to offer better resistance to a future French thrust than had been the case in the past. Legitimacy, territorial compensation for the victors, and hostility to France are the three considerations, out of the interaction of which grew the rearrangements of Europe sanctioned at Vienna.

Legitimacy modified: (2) by hostility to France

Beginning our review of the Viennese reconstruction with Italy, we note that its restoration to the conditions prevailing before the Revolution was largely carried through. Such ousted rulers as the pope, the king of Naples, and the grand duke of Tuscany were again seated on their thrones. But there were two notable exceptions to the general rule: the republics of Genoa and Venice were not revived. In order to strengthen the kingdom of Sardinia against France, Genoa was annexed to that state; in order to compensate Austria for the loss of Belgium (Austrian Netherlands), Venice, together with the Adriatic coastal area of Dalmatia, was attached to the Danubian empire.

Pre-war Italy restored with two exceptions

On the northeastern border of France lay Belgium and the Dutch republic. Both of them had been conquered and incorporated in France in the course of the Revolution. To erect an effective bulwark against France at this danger point the two territories were consolidated and placed under the rule of the house of Orange, the "legitimate" dynasty of the Dutch state. The new creation received the name of the kingdom of the Netherlands.

Belgium and the Dutch republic merged

Great Britain, the most stubborn and successful of the enemies of the Revolution, was rewarded with valuable colonial areas and with naval outposts captured from France and, more particularly, from the Dutch, who, in punishment for having been incorporated in France, were regarded as legitimate prey. The most important of the British acquisitions were South Africa (the Cape), the island of Ceylon, the island of Malta (in the middle Mediterranean), and the North sea island of Helgoland.

Colonial acquisitions of Great Britain

The Swiss Confederation, which Napoleon had brought within his system, was restored to independence. The case of Sweden was complicated by its loss of Finland in 1809 to Russia. Owing to its having joined against Napoleon in 1813, some compensation for the loss of Finland was felt to be due; it was given Norway, which was taken from Denmark. As Denmark had stood by Napoleon through thick and thin, it seemed appropriate to let it feel the wrath of the victors.

Switzerland, Sweden, Denmark

The region that gave the Congress the greatest difficulty was central Europe, embracing the two grave problems of Poland and Germany. In fact such violent differences of opinion regarding the Polish and German problems arose among the four victor powers, Russia, Prussia, Austria, and Great Britain, that for a while it looked as if the contenders might bring the issue to the decision of the sword. In the end an accommodation was reached which represented a very involved series of compromises.

Compromise reached over Poland and Germany

Napoleon's creation, the grand duchy of Warsaw, had been occupied by Tsar Alexander on its evacuation in 1812 by the French, and Alexander was firmly resolved not again to give it up. The final settlement arranged that Alexander should surrender the western province of the grand duchy, called Posen, to Prussia and constitute the remainder as the kingdom of Poland with himself as king. Thus was the Polish state reconstituted, though within restricted boundaries and with a foreigner, the Russian tsar, as sovereign.

A Polish kingdom created with Alexander as king

The strict application to Germany of the principle of legitimacy would have meant the re-establishment of the Holy Roman Empire with its approximately three hundred sovereign states. In the course of the revolutionary wars they had been steadily reduced by a process of fusion till in 1815 there were only thirty-eight states left. They were divisible, on the score of size, into three groups: a group of two great powers, Austria and Prussia; a group of five middle-sized states, Bavaria, Wurtemberg, Baden, Saxony, and Hanover; and a final group of petty principalities, like Weimar and Hesse, together with the three city-republics of Hamburg, Bremen, and Lübeck. As everybody recognized the impossibility of unscrambling these thirty-eight states into the original three hundred component parts, the idea of bringing the Holy Roman Empire back to life was not even suggested.

Germany composed in 1815 of thirty-eight states

However, some kind of association among the German states to replace the vanished Holy Roman Empire was considered desirable. The newborn German nationalism raised its voice in behalf of an effective federal union, but it could not make itself heard among German state governments intent each one on preserving its cherished sovereignty. The result was that the thirty-eight states agreed to effect a loose association of sovereign units, to which they gave the name of the German *Bund* (Confederation).

Creation of a loose German Confederation, the "Bund"

It remains to consider the reconstruction of Prussia. During the final struggle with Napoleon its allies had promised to restore it approximately within its pre-war boundaries. However, Prussia created a difficulty for itself when it relinquished its claim to the major part of the grand duchy of Warsaw (created by Napoleon from Prussian spoils) to Tsar Alexander. To compensate Prussia for its Polish losses the tsar promised his friend, the Prussian king, an equivalent territory of a strictly German character. After much haggling this German equivalent was found. Prussia received one-half of the state of Saxony and considerable territory on the left bank of the Rhine. This latter territory it organized as the Rhine province. While the cutting in half of Saxony in order to indemnify a great power was a clear infringement by the Congress of its own norm of legitimacy, the entrenching of Prussia strongly on the Rhine was in full accord with the rival norm of building a bulwark against France.

Prussia compensated with German territory for its former Polish territory

As is well known, the building of a national German state in the course of the nineteenth century to replace the feeble Bund took place under the leadership of Prussia. More than any other single factor the responsibility put on this state in 1815 to maintain a watch on the Rhine against France promoted Prussia to this leadership.

Prussia wins the leadership of Germany

THE NOMINAL HOLY ALLIANCE; THE EFFECTIVE
QUADRUPLE ALLIANCE

So powerful and universal was the political reaction among the governing circles of Europe that it drew much of literature, art, and philosophy into its service and made them the propaganda agencies of the conservative cause. Many people, even one-time skeptics, again became devoutly Christian; many others were mystically exalted by the revulsion which had come over the world and which had caused Europeans almost as of one accord to face backward.

The conservative reaction is general

Among the mystic group was no less a personage than Tsar Alexander. Throughout his life he proved himself a weather-vane responsive to all the changing winds of opinion. On the fall of Napoleon he submitted a document to his European fellow-rulers which he requested them to sign and by the terms of which they pledged themselves to govern their states in accordance with the brotherly sentiments so eloquently sounded in the New Testament. As the document, a mass of well-meaning platitudes, failed to commit the rulers of Europe to anything politically tangible or practical, all but two, in compliment to Alexander, signed it. One of the two was George III of Great Britain, who, owing to insanity, had been replaced by a regent; the other was the sultan of Turkey, who, as a Mohammedan, was spared the humiliation of attaching his name to a document reeking with Christian moralisms. This harmless communication, not unfairly characterized by the

Alexander creates a Holy Alliance among European sovereigns

cynical Metternich as verbiage, has received the name of the Holy Alliance.

The effective Quadruple Alliance of the victors

When the Holy Alliance became known among the European middle classes, who, although temporarily under a cloud, maintained a sullen opposition to the ruling conservatism, they signalized it as a league among the freshly dominant sovereigns to maintain the system set up at Vienna. That was not exactly the case, since, as we have seen, it carried no positive obligation whatsoever. However, a secret treaty among the four victor powers to maintain their system by co-operative action had received their signatures and was regarded by them as the solid guarantee of their triumph. The secret agreement bore the name of the Quadruple Alliance.

It is confused with the Holy Alliance

When, in 1818, the restored Louis XVIII was held to have proved his staunchly conservative character, defeated France was admitted to the Quadruple Alliance, thus making it a Quintuple Alliance. The liberal opponents of triumphant conservatism not unnaturally confused the two documents and spoke angrily of the Holy Alliance as the enemy when the really effective enemy was the Quintuple Alliance. The mistake is not particularly important. It obliges us, however, in studying the period, to keep constantly in mind that when liberal orators and newspapers denounced the much publicized Holy Alliance, they were really directing their shafts at the secret Quintuple Alliance of which they had very imperfect knowledge.

The Quintuple Alliance a League of Nations?

The Quintuple Alliance, embracing the five great powers, made an interesting attempt to give itself something of a permanent organization. The member states agreed to meet from time to time in congress to consider the state of Europe. Because of that circumstance, the Quintuple Alliance has in our own day been looked upon in some quarters as a forerunner of the League of Nations established a hundred years later. While this suggestion may not be scornfully dismissed, we should remember that the Quintuple Alliance never had any other object in mind than to maintain at all costs and, if necessary, by force, the arch-conservative system of Vienna.

The Quintuple Alliance a means to suppress revolution

This immutability, desired by all, was passionately championed by the acknowledged leader of conservative Europe, Prince Metternich. He sponsored not only recurrent congresses but also military intervention by the powers to the express end of crushing revolutionary agitation wherever and whenever it might again show its head. By congresses and military intervention Europe was, according to Metternich's plan, to remain a united conservative family free from the taint of revolution.

While the opponents of this system were overawed by it during the years immediately following its establishment, it was not at all likely that they would submit to its program of stark reaction for an indefinite

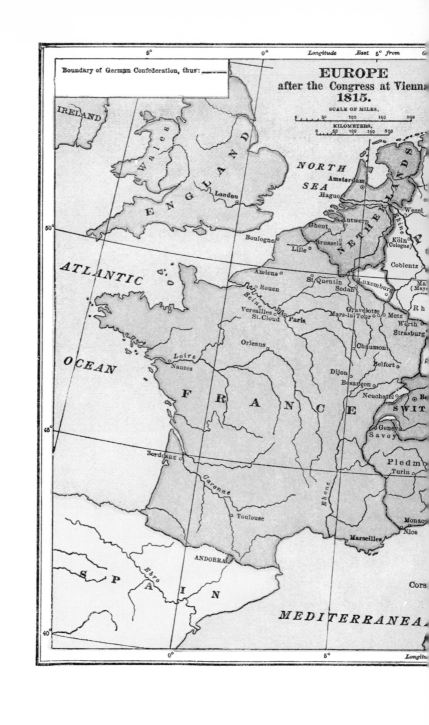

EUROPE
after the Congress at Vienna
1815.

NOTE TO THE STUDENT:
Note the following important
arrangements effected by the
Congress of Vienna: 1) Italy.
Lombardy and Venice are
Austrian outposts. The rest
of Italy is parceled out among
many rulers. 2) The German
Confederation does not include
all of Prussia and Austria. Its
eastern boundary is identical
with that of the former Holy
Roman Empire. 3) The kingdom of the Netherlands includes Belgium and Holland.

From Ferdinand Schevill, *A History of Europe,* Harcourt, Brace and Company, Inc.

time. We have repeatedly pointed out that the opponents of conservatism were in the main the middle classes, who had triumphed temporarily in the Revolution and who remained attached to a program which had given them definite benefits. Under the rough trampling of an unrestrained conservatism, the defeated system, from 1815 on generally labeled liberalism, experienced a gradual revival and before long undertook to join battle with its foe all along the line. From this struggle of a resuscitated liberalism with its overconfident and arrogant rival, European history takes its special color from 1815 to 1848 and, in many respects, even down to 1870.

Liberalism gradually resumes the battle with conservatism

REVOLUTION: SPAIN AND NAPLES

The first serious test of the policy of immobility, to which the ruling states had committed themselves, came when a number of Mediterranean countries were swept by revolution. The beginning was made by Spain. On the fall of Napoleon, Spain had experienced the typical legitimist reaction, for the representative of the deposed Bourbon dynasty, Ferdinand VII, was restored to the throne. As the Spaniards in the course of their remarkable resistance to Napoleon had drawn up a constitution for themselves, called the Constitution of 1812, Ferdinand, to make sure, on re-entering Madrid, that he would be accepted by his people, bound himself with an oath to observe it.

Spain under the restored Bourbon, Ferdinand VII

No sooner, however, was Ferdinand securely established in his capital than he repudiated his oath, assumed the character of an absolute monarch, and cruelly persecuted the patriotic defenders of the constitution. At the same time he made the clergy and nobility, whom he restored to all their privileges, the honored pillars of the throne. He even went so far as to re-establish the Inquisition, which the leaders of the rising against Napoleon had shelved as an outmoded instrument of religious uniformity.

The violent reaction inspired by Ferdinand VII

Before long, evidence of disaffection accumulated at many points but with particular frequency in the army. This was primarily owing to the fact that King Ferdinand was engaged in transporting the army across the Atlantic to South America in order again to reduce to obedience the revolted Spanish colonies. The colonies had revolted in the first instance against the alien ruler, Joseph Bonaparte, imposed on Spain by his imperial brother. Having tasted the delights of independence, they now refused to accept the restored Bourbon.

Ferdinand undertakes to bring the Spanish colonies again to heel

Among the Spanish soldiers about to be sent thousands of miles across the ocean there developed a passionate aversion to the expedition. Suddenly, in January, 1820, some companies about to be embarked at Cadiz mutinied and proclaimed the Constitution of 1812. Instantly soldiers in neighboring garrisons took up the constitutional cry. When the news

The successful Spanish revolution of 1820

reached Madrid, soldiers and citizens joined forces and refused to end their demonstrations till the frightened and cringing king had agreed to rule under the Constitution of 1812 and to renew his oath to it.

The success-
ful Neapoli-
tan revolu-
tion of 1820

The successful Spanish revolution caused it to be imitated in the kingdom of Naples. Here, too, legitimacy had triumphed in 1815 and had brought the restoration of the Neapolitan branch of the house of Bourbon, of which the representative was a sovereign bearing the same patronymic as his Spanish relative. Not only in name but in faithlessness and moral turpitude as well, Ferdinand of Naples was indistinguishable from his cousin of Madrid. Consequently he was equally unpopular with his subjects, who, on receipt of the news of the Spanish insurrection, promptly rose against the despicable monarch. Yielding to the general clamor, King Ferdinand of Naples agreed to convert his state into a limited monarchy on the Spanish model.

The
successful
Portuguese
revolution
of 1820

Next, the revolutionary infection spread to Portugal. The Portuguese royal family had fled to the Portuguese colony, Brazil, on the invasion in 1807 of Portugal by Napoleon. It had found life across the Atlantic so agreeable that it was slow to effect a return. Consequently the Portuguese government was conducted by a regency. Raising the banner of revolt against the regency, a liberal uprising obliged it to adopt a constitutional system.

The Con-
gress of
Troppau,
1820

Against these revolutionary movements the indignant Metternich at once resolved to mobilize his machinery of congresses and intervention. His surprise was great when he discovered that the harmony or, in diplomatic language, the "concert" hitherto existing among the five leagued powers had suffered a breach. On summoning (1820) a congress at the Austrian town of Troppau to consider the Neapolitan revolution, which, being closest to Austria, was in his mind the most threatening of the insurrectionary movements, he learned that his proposal to intervene in Naples did not have the support of France and Great Britain. He did, however, prevail on the more deeply conservative Russia and Prussia to join him in accepting Neapolitan intervention "in principle." Before taking further action it was agreed to give King Ferdinand of Naples an opportunity to be heard.

The Con-
gress of Lai-
bach, 1821

To serve the convenience of the Neapolitan monarch the congress adjourned to Laibach, an Austrian town on the Italian border. Here the hypocritical and vindictive Ferdinand denounced his late liberal acts as wrung from him by force and pleaded to be rescued from his people. The upshot was that Austria accepted a mandate from Russia and Prussia (France and Great Britain abstaining) to restore "order" in the south-Italian state.

The victorious Neapolitan liberals had not been able to create a strong and coherent government. For one thing they lacked experience. It was perhaps even more unfortunate that they had a falling out with the island of Sicily, which was refused the home rule it demanded as the price of co-operation. On the approach of the Austrian army sent against Naples by Metternich the Neapolitan soldiers took to their heels, the liberal government collapsed, and King Ferdinand was restored as absolute king.

Austria suppresses the Neapolitan revolution, 1821

When certain patriotic elements in the Italian north, more especially in Piedmont, tried to create a diversion in the rear of the Austrian forces, Austria marched an army also into Piedmont to suppress the agitation. In this manner did Metternich in 1821 put out the revolutionary fires and make Italy safe for conservatism.

Metternich makes Italy safe for conservatism

With this success the attention of the three eastern courts swung to Spain. They burned with eagerness to suppress also the liberal movement in Spain but recognized that they could not be successful in that distant peninsula without the co-operation of France. They were therefore greatly rejoiced when the government of Louis XVIII experienced a change of heart. At a congress held at Verona (1822) not only did France accept the principle of intervention, but it also agreed forcibly to overthrow the Spanish revolution in the name of conservative Europe. Nonetheless, the rift which had appeared in the concert of the powers was not entirely mended since Great Britain refused to subscribe to the French action.

The Congress of Verona votes to suppress the Spanish revolution

The downfall of Spanish liberalism before the advancing forces of France was as swift and ignominious as that of Naples and for substantially the same reasons. The liberals in both of these countries were a small minority because the bourgeoisie, from which class the liberals in the main sprang, was a relatively unimportant group. The vast majority of the population of both Naples and Spain consisted of illiterate peasants attached to their ancient customs, above all, to the Catholic religion, and completely lacking in understanding of, and sympathy for, the liberal cause. The consequence of the French intervention was the restoration of Ferdinand VII as absolute monarch and his ferocious persecution of his defeated liberal opponents. While celebrating orgies of vindictiveness, he took occasion to point out to the four sponsoring powers that their work would not be complete unless they extended their services to the revolted Spanish colonies and brought them too once more under his scepter.

France restores Ferdinand VII as absolute monarch, 1823

Metternich and the powers associated with him took the Spanish proposal under advisement. Their principles made them willing and even eager to punish the colonial revolutionists, but they did not fail to recognize that they were confronted with insurmountable difficulties. Great Britain had detached itself from the concert of Europe and Great Britain completely dominated the ocean routes with her navy. At this very time too (1822), the British foreign minister, Lord Castlereagh, who had

Metternich takes up the question of the revolted Spanish colonies always sought, in spite of differences, to maintain friendly relations with Metternich, was succeeded by the much less amenable Canning; and Canning intimated in no uncertain terms that he was not in favor of an European action directed against Spanish colonial independence.

Canning was induced to take the stand he did by important considera-

Great Britain favors the Spanish colonies

tions of British trade. With the breakdown of the authority of the home government the trade monopoly maintained in its colonies by Spain had also broken down, and the enterprising British merchants had succeeded in getting the profitable South and Central American markets into their hands. Great Britain therefore favored the independence of the colonies, since it was only too clear that if the authority of the mother-country should be restored, the former Spanish trade monopoly would be re-established as a matter of course.

As Canning did not wish singlehanded to oppose the consolidated

The United States of America enters the lists against conservative Europe

continental powers, he was greatly cheered to find that another state favored Spanish colonial independence as much as himself. That was the United States of America. The United States was not prompted by con-siderations of trade, for it had no trade with South America. It was pushed to take the position it did by the desire for national security and, to a certain extent also by a natural sympathy for republics which owed their existence to a declaration of independence against an oppressive mother-country. In the year 1822 the government at Washington formally recognized the independence of the Spanish colonies. That in itself was a bold, a decisive step. Then in December, 1823, it took the much bolder step of warning the European reactionaries off the premises by a decla-ration containing the statement that it would look upon intervention in South America "as the manifestation of an unfriendly disposition toward the United States."

This famous declaration was issued by President James Monroe and

The Monroe Doctrine a contribu-tory factor in blocking intervention

has since figured in American history, not without important extensions of its original meaning, as the Monroe Doctrine. In thus challenging Metternich and his associates President Monroe had the support of Can-ning and the British government. The co-ordinated action of these two states put an end to all further talk on the part of the European cham-pions of absolutism to interfere in the affairs of the western continent. When Canning now followed the lead of the United States and formally recognized the independence of the newly established South American republics, the incident could be considered as closed.

In the South American issue the leagued reactionaries of Europe may

Portugal goes con-servative without in-tervention

be said to have received their first serious check. As they also failed to punish Portugal, they were plainly no longer all-powerful even on the European continent. True, the Portuguese liberals did not long maintain their ascendancy, for they succumbed to a national conservative rising.

However, Portugal became conservative by its own action and not because of an army of occupation dispatched by an European congress.

REVOLUTION: GREECE

From the foregoing it is clear that the reactionary program, to which all the powers had at first subscribed, was not long maintained, owing to the early defection of Great Britain. There now occurred a revolution in Greece, which aroused so many sympathies not only in liberal but also in conservative circles that the idea of congresses and intervention in the interest of political immobility suffered complete shipwreck. It was while the Congress of Laibach was in session (1821) that the startling news reached its members that revolt had lifted its head also in southeastern Europe and that the Greek people, who had been subjected for approximately four centuries to the sultan of Turkey, had risen to win independence.

The Greek revolution begins in 1821

The Greek revolution obliges us to glance at the Balkan peninsula. When the peninsula was overrun in the fifteenth century by the Ottoman Turks, it was inhabited by a number of Christian peoples. The Greeks dwelt in the main in the southern tip of the peninsula and on the islands of the Aegean sea. North of the Greeks lived the Albanians (along the Adriatic sea) and two related Slav groups, the Serbs and the Bulgars. The region north of the Danube river was the home of the Rumans or Rumanians, who spoke a Latin dialect and claimed to be descendants of ancient Roman colonists. All these peoples had been granted a measure of religious toleration by their Ottoman conquerors, but, deprived of arms and economically exploited without redress or mercy, they had become hewers of wood and drawers of water—essentially nations of Christian serfs.

Condition of the Christian peoples of the Balkan peninsula

The invading Turks never amounted to more than a thin layer of privileged rulers imposed on the mass of the ruled. They owed their authority to the fact that they had entered the peninsula as an invincible warrior band and had consistently clung to that role. Never did they even attempt to plant the land with their own people. In these circumstances the continuation of their rule depended on the maintenance of the army on its original efficiency level. By the eighteenth century, however, the army, of which the famous Janissaries were the core, had been overtaken by an appalling disorder and, instead of proving, as had once been the case, its superiority over the European armies it encountered, it was now regularly beaten by them. As a result, by the opening of the nineteenth century a good deal of Ottoman territory in the Danubian basin (Hungary) had been conquered by the advancing Austrians, and a good

The decline of the Ottoman army invites the encroachments of Austria and Russia

deal more territory in the Black sea area had fallen before the still more vigorous drive of the Russians.

The chief cause of this military decay was the sultan, who, as head of the army, was also the autocratic sovereign of the empire. In the early days the sultans had lived and campaigned with the army and were personally responsible for its equipment and discipline. After some centuries of success their moral fiber had weakened. The sultans of the eighteenth century no longer went on campaign; they were content to loiter among the soft delights of their palace and gardens at Constantinople; and they became the voluntary prisoners of that characteristic institution of the polygamous near east, the harem. The failure of authority at the top caused indiscipline to spread like a canker throughout the ranks of the army.

Fatal decline in the character of the autocratic sultans

By the beginning of the nineteenth century Europe was facing, as one of its gravest problems, the dissolution and consequent probable partition of the Ottoman empire among the contentious great powers. The only conceivable check to the visible decay would be an internal reform beginning with the sultan himself. Almost miraculously such a sultan at last appeared in the person of Mahmud II (1808-39).

Europe faces the problem of partition

It was too late. For, in addition to the onslaught of the European powers which had already been proceeding for a hundred years and which, once begun, could not be stopped, the Christian subject peoples now entered the game. They were heartened by the decay of the Ottoman state and encouraged, one after the other, to strike a blow for freedom.

Ottoman decay encourages revolt

Not many years following the Congress of Vienna signs of an approaching rising appeared among the Greeks. They had been recently experiencing a national revival, largely through the influence of the French Revolution. They had turned with enthusiasm to the great past of their people; representative Greeks had engaged in travel and study in western Europe and communicated the stirring message of Western civilization to their countrymen; and Greek merchants, taking advantage of the long revolutionary wars which had driven French commerce from the Mediterranean, had brought a measure of prosperity to some of the Greek coastal areas beyond anything known for centuries.

The Greek national revival

The plan of the Greek leaders, who had with great secrecy spun the threads of the conspiracy leading to the outbreak of 1821, was to raise the whole peninsula with its several Christian peoples against the alien Moslem masters. This proved impossible, first, because national sentiment was as yet less awakened among the other Balkan groups than among the Greeks, and second, because the other groups refused to accept the leadership of the Greeks. There had always been an intense rivalry and even hatred among the various Christian peoples of the peninsula because of bitter memories reaching back to the Middle Ages. No

The Greeks fail to arouse the other Christian peoples

sooner had the process of liberation from the Turkish yoke begun than the ancient rivalry came again to life, contributing, as we shall have only too frequent occasion to see, an added element of mischief to an already amply unfortunate situation.

On the failure of the Greek leaders to win the support of the other subject peoples, they conducted the rising by and for themselves. By a sudden and well-concerted assault they succeeded in clearing almost all of the Morea (the ancient Peloponnesus) and central Greece of the Ottoman enemy. Deeply alarmed, Mahmud II, the first active sultan after a long succession of do-nothing rulers, made a formidable effort to recover the lost territory. His forces penetrated (1822) into the revolted districts but failed to break the resistance of the Greeks. *Early successes of the Greeks followed by a deadlock*

Lacking an organized army, the Greeks wisely resorted to harassing guerrilla tactics. In their exasperation the Turks committed abominable atrocities, to which the Greeks did not hesitate to respond in kind. The butchery practiced by both sides staggers the mind and becomes intelligible only by remembering that the animosity, usual between master and risen slave, was in this instance magnified by the religious hostility between them. *Mutual butchery of Greeks and Turks*

In the year 1824 Sultan Mahmud, at the end of his resources, invited the help of Mehemet Ali, pasha of Egypt. Technically Mehemet Ali was the sultan's vassal; in reality he was an independent sovereign. An energetic and intelligent man, he had attempted to reform his Egyptian state according to the western pattern and had become the master of an efficient army and a seaworthy fleet. *The sultan gets the aid of Mehemet Ali*

Not till he had struck a most advantageous bargain with the sultan did the wily Egyptian go into action. Thereupon he sent his son Ibrahim against the Greeks in their main stronghold of the Morea. By 1826 the Egyptian forces had achieved such startling successes that to the casual view the Greek cause seemed doomed. At this point, in the very nick of time, certain European powers injected themselves into the situation and dramatically changed the complexion of affairs. *The Egyptians stamp out the Greek revolt*

If we now return to the concert of Europe, resting on the Quintuple Alliance, we may assure ourselves that, in so far as it was directed by and dependent on Prince Metternich, it was not likely to take action in favor of the sultan's rebellious subjects, even though these subjects were Christians and the sultan a Mohammedan. On the other hand, liberal and, to a certain extent, even conservative groups of people throughout Europe would follow the Greek rising with a cordial sympathy. Indeed so active was the sympathy that innumerable volunteers, most famous among them the illustrious English poet, Lord Byron,[1] put their swords at the service of the Greeks. While their assistance was gratefully received by the in- *Wide sympathy for the Greeks*

[1] Byron died of fever, a martyr to the Greek cause, in 1824 at Missolonghi.

surgents, it did not suffice to hinder the uninterrupted successes in the field of Egyptian Ibrahim.

Intervention considered by Great Britain, followed by Russia

The first power to consider intervention in behalf of the struggling Greeks was Great Britain. Reluctant to go ahead singlehanded, the British government was greatly cheered when, at the height of Ibrahim's success, it was informed that the Russian government was also weighing the problem of Greek aid. The news represented an amazing change of front. The once liberal and always unaccountable Tsar Alexander I had become a conservative, as rabid, if anything, as Metternich, with a violent distaste for rebellion in any form. However, Alexander died in 1825. In default of a direct heir, he was succeeded by his brother Nicholas I. While Nicholas was as fanatical a reactionary as his brother or Metternich, he was also a Russian nationalist. As such, he regarded the sultan as his implacable enemy and could not support the thought of his re-establishing his shaken power by the subjugation of the Greeks.

Intervention of Great Britain, Russia and France

The upshot of diplomatic exchanges was a treaty (1827) between London and St. Petersburg, to which presently France also became a party. It pledged the three signatories to bring the Greek war to a close on the basis of a modest measure of self-government secured to the rebels. Here was a novel intervention indeed! When we note that it was to be exercised not against, but in favor of, revolutionists, we can come to no other conclusion than that the Metternichian system had gone to pieces.

The allies win the battle of Navarino (1827)

As soon as the three powers had reached their agreement they ordered their fleets to proceed to the bay of Navarino, Ibrahim's base in the Morea. They came to announce the end of warfare; and when Ibrahim, outraged at the interference, failed to comply promptly with the request to suspend hostilities, a battle ensued in which the combined Turco-Egyptian fleet was shot to driftwood (October 20, 1827) by the European allies.

The Russo-Turkish war of 1828-29 carries the Russians to Adrianople

The roar of the guns at Navarino announced to the world the birth of a new Christian state. But the sultan was not yet ready to concede the point. Profoundly irritated, he opened a heated correspondence with his chief enemy, the tsar, which Nicholas shrewdly utilized to issue a declaration of war. Thus the Greek rebellion culminated in another Turco-Russian conflict, in which the Russians more signally than on any earlier occasion exhibited their superiority. Their forces crossed successively the Danube river and the Balkan mountains and in 1829 reached Adrianople, only a few days' march from the Turkish capital.

The Peace of Adrianople (1829) concedes to Russia a Balkan hegemony

At this point the sultan's resistance collapsed. In the Peace of Adrianople (1829) he accepted all the Russian demands. Not only did he concede to the three powers the right to settle the affairs of Greece as they saw fit, but he renewed and enlarged certain former promises he had made of home rule to Serbia and to the two Rumanian provinces, Wallachia and Moldavia. In addition he acknowledged the tsar as the guarantor of these concessions. The effect of the Treaty of Adrianople was nothing less than to make the tsar co-sovereign with the sultan over considerable parts of his Balkan dominions.

After prolonged discussions touching the settlement of Greece the three powers agreed at length on these points: (1) that Greece was to be not merely autonomous under the sultan but an entirely independent kingdom; (2) that its northern boundary against the Ottoman empire was to be rather ungenerously drawn from Arta to Volo, thus leaving large numbers of Greeks outside the kingdom; and (3) that the crown of the kingdom was to be given to a young Bavarian prince, Otto by name.

The powers establish an independent Greek kingdom

It was not till 1832 that these conclusions were finally arrived at. The long delay was owing to the fact that shortly after the Peace of Adrianople Europe was shaken by a new revolution in the old center of disturbance, France.

The Greek settlement delayed till 1832

REVOLUTION: FRANCE

The restoration of the Bourbons in 1814, and again in 1815, was the work not of the French people but of the victorious allies, for the old royal family was as good as forgotten in France and aroused no popular enthusiasm. Its position, therefore, was precarious and its success would depend on the wisdom and temperance of the new king. Louis XVIII, the most moderate and intelligent member of his family, made a not unpromising beginning. He issued a constitution (*la charte constitutionelle*), which recognized the institutions of Napoleon—his administrative and legal systems, his church, his army, and even his nobility—and conceded to the people a share in legislation by two houses, an appointed Chamber of Peers and an elected Chamber of Deputies.

Louis XVIII grants a constitution

The constitution bore a certain resemblance to that of England, except that the ultimate control remained with the king, since the ministers were responsible to him and not to the chambers. It made its strongest bid for popular support by its declaration that those objects of eighteenth-century criticism, the feudal privileges and the absolute monarchy, had departed never to return.

The constitution a not illiberal document

Having wisely inaugurated a policy of conciliation, the king turned his thought to the task of creating confidence and allaying suspicion. This was difficult in view of the fact that he was surrounded at court by the noble émigrés, who had returned to France on the fall of Napoleon and fatuously imagined they had brought the old times back with them in their traveling-kits. At their head was the count of Artois, the king's fanatic younger brother and eventual heir, who in twenty-five years of exile had learned nothing and forgotten nothing.

The reactionary nobles headed by the count of Artois

Artois and his friends thought chiefly of revenge and repression. More

royal than the king and commonly called ultra-royalists, they did not propose, at least for the time being, to overthrow the constitution. They
aimed rather to bring the press under control by a severe censorship and
by devious election devices to secure a majority in the lower house. This
was not particularly difficult since, the franchise being dependent on a
high property qualification, only about 100,000 citizens were entitled to
vote. On account of this limitation of the suffrage, the monarchy rested
in last analysis on a thin, upper stratum of the well-to-do.

Louis XVIII, with laudable common sense, at first resisted the clamor
of the ultras and leaned upon the constitutionalists. However, he was too
weak a man to maintain his position in the face of continued pressure.
The assassination in 1820 of his nephew and ultimate heir, the duke of
Berry, shook him profoundly. Although the murder was the deed of a
fanatic, who had acted on his own initiative, the courtiers insisted clamorously that the real responsibility rested with the liberal ministry. Louis
therefore replaced it with a ministry of ultras.

Full triumph
of reaction
on the
accession
(1824) of
Charles X
Thus at last the conservatives had won. Controlling the king, the
ministry, and the chambers, they muzzled the press, passed restrictive
electoral laws, and identified France with the policy of Metternich by
accepting, in 1822, the mandate to suppress the Spanish revolution. With
the ultras floating on the tide of power Louis XVIII died (1824). He was
succeeded by the count of Artois, under the title Charles X. The succession of this leader of the émigrés added the finishing touch to the triumph of the forces of reaction.

Events now rapidly traveled toward the inevitable climax. By passing
an act which distributed one billion francs among the ancient nobility as
an indemnity for their estates confiscated during the Revolution and by
other measures of like tenor, the government deeply offended the bourgeoisie, who made up the bulk of the voters and, as men of property,
had to pay the taxes to meet the indemnity. In the elections of the
year 1827 the government suffered a signal defeat. Though Charles X
now changed his ministers, he clung with such stubborn infatuation to
his reactionary policy that the Chamber of Deputies opposed him with
constantly increasing firmness.

With the courage of the self-righteous, Charles X at last resolved to
break the resistance of his legislature by an illegal act, a so-called *coup
d'état.* On July 26, 1830, he issued four ordinances by which, in the hope
of getting a more docile chamber, he arbitrarily changed the laws governing the elections and the press.

The four ordinances sounded a challenge which was immediately taken
up by bands of republican workmen and students. Parading the streets
with loud cheers for the constitution, they presently raised the ominous
cry, "Down with the Bourbons!" The king himself was at his palace of

St. Cloud, just outside the capital, and the few thousand troops he had in Paris were not adequate to keep the insurgents in hand. Occasional conflicts led to a pitched battle, in which the soldiers, outnumbered and fighting without enthusiasm, yielded ground until their commander ordered them to evacuate the capital. On the night of July 29, after three days of street fighting, the victorious people rested from their bloody and triumphant work.

The successful revolution of July, 1830

In spite of Charles's misrule, there still existed in France a large body of monarchists of a liberal trend. These men now stepped forward to prevent a radical victory. In contrast to the republican workmen, who had done the street fighting, the monarchists belonged to the bourgeoisie. In their opinion the need of France was not the republic demanded by the street fighters, but a constitutional monarchy, genuine and trustworthy. They also knew precisely the monarch the situation called for: Louis Philippe, duke of Orléans.

The middle class turns to Louis Philippe

The duke was head of the younger branch of the house of Bourbon and had a revolutionary record. He had even served for a time (1792-1793) as a volunteer in the republican army. This, and the fact that his father was the unsavory Egalité of Jacobin fame, had dug an unbridgeable chasm between him and the older branch of his house. In spite of this quarrel, he was of the blood royal, and this fact joined with his revolutionary role made him the logical candidate of the moderates. At their summons he left his country estate for Paris and with the help of the aged Lafayette conciliated the workers, thus becoming practically the unanimous choice of the nation.

Louis Philippe head of the younger Bourbon line

The first concern of the revolutionary government was the inevitable struggle with Charles X. But the frightened king agreeably disappointed expectations. In a fit of despondency he resigned in favor of his little grandson, son of the murdered duke of Berry, and fled to England. The Chamber of Deputies chose to take no further note of his acts and on August 7 proceeded to proclaim Louis Philippe king of the French.

Louis Philippe made king

The substitution of the younger for the older branch of the house of Bourbon, which at first blush seems to measure the whole achievement of the so-called July revolution, does not fully express the change which came over France in 1830. In the first place, although the old constitution remained in force, it was liberalized somewhat by a slight revision, more particularly by a measure which sufficiently lowered the property qualification for the franchise to bring about a doubling of the number of electors. It is even more noteworthy that the accession of Louis Philippe involved a fundamental theoretical change. Charles X, the embodiment of legitimacy, had been identified with the émigrés and the church, and had ruled by the grace of God. To indicate that Louis Philippe ruled by grace of the people, his title was changed from king of

Small but definite results of the revolution

France to king of the French. In the eyes of orthodox royalists he was therefore twice illegitimate and detestable.

The surest supporters of Louis Philippe's throne were the property-owning middle classes. For this reason the July monarchy is often called the reign of the bourgeoisie and Louis Philippe himself the king of the middle class (*roi-bourgeois*). Caricatures habitually represented him as a thickset, comfortable grocer, providently going about with a huge umbrella. The final evidence of the revolutionary basis of the July monarchy was the replacement of the lily banner of the Bourbons with the famous tricolor (three vertical stripes of blue, white, and red) of the Revolution.

Louis Philippe identified with the bourgeoisie

The report of the revolution in Paris spread swiftly abroad, everywhere rejoicing the liberals and alarming the conservatives. Since the work of the reaction had been so easily undone in France, there was good reason to think that the national and liberal sentiment, offended by the Congress of Vienna and outraged by the police-control of Metternich and the tsar, might assert itself with success in other regions of Europe. France, since the Revolution of 1789 the acknowledged leader of progressive opinion, had given a signal to which her imitators and admirers everywhere enthusiastically responded.

The revolution encourages imitation

REVOLUTION: BELGIUM

The first people to be seized with the French infection were the Belgians. It will be remembered that by the Congress of Vienna the old Austrian Netherlands had been annexed to Holland in order to create a strong buffer state on the French border. But the union was unhappy. The Belgians felt that they were not admitted to equality by the Dutch, who reserved the most important offices to themselves, while the fact that one people was Protestant and the other Catholic caused considerable, more or less open, friction.

Causes of Belgian discontent with the arrangement of 1815

There was, furthermore, the important, if somewhat hidden issue of nationality. While one-half of the Belgians were Flemings, and, as a Germanic people, closely related to the Dutch, the other half were Walloons, that is, Celts who used the French language. Finally, the Belgians, whether Flemings or Walloons, were imbued with French civilization and looked rather toward Paris for light and guidance than toward The Hague.

Other differences between the partners

In August, 1830, a revolt, begun in Brussels, the capital of Belgium, spread so rapidly over the face of the land that the Dutch army had to abandon the country, excepting a few fortresses. King William, who had at first treated the Belgian separatist movement with contempt, now offered concessions. They were not acceptable. Nothing short of complete

The Belgian revolt (August, 1830)

independence would satisfy the revolutionists. Since the Dutch king resisted this demand, war seemed to be unavoidable.

When a conference of the powers met at London to deliberate on the issue, it was once again seen that the Metternichian system had lost its vitality, for the conference actually decided to yield to the will of the Belgian people and sever them from the Dutch. The truculent Dutch king was cowed into acquiescence and, not without many difficulties and delays, a Belgian popular assembly declared Belgium a constitutional monarchy and elected a small German prince, Leopold of Saxe-Coburg, king. The boundary of the new state caused a prolonged dispute with the offended king of the Netherlands. This matter, too, was at last disposed of, and Belgium, a new kingdom under a new dynasty, was added to the fraternity of nations.

Belgium wins independence under a king of its own

REVOLUTION: ITALY AND GERMANY

In central Europe, in Italy and Germany, the revolution was not received with as much enthusiasm as might be expected, when we consider that in these countries the liberal groups had been balked of their dearest hopes by the treaties of 1815. In Italy there was no outbreak outside the papal states, where the government, exclusively in the hands of the pope and his clergy, was comparable in its conservative and unprogressive temper with that of Turkey.

The revolution of 1830 in Italy

Of course the pope called in the Austrians, who quickly extinguished the revolutionary fire. The fact was that Italy, in consequence of the defeat of its liberal hopes in 1821 and of its recent experience of Austrian omnipotence, was not yet prepared for another uprising. The total result of the year 1830 for the peninsula was an increased sense of enslavement to Austria and an increased hatred of the oppressor.

Austria comes to the aid of the pope

In Germany political activity had been reduced to very meager proportions between 1815 and 1830. The Bund, precisely as its conservative projectors had planned, was treated as practically nonexistent by the thirty-eight member states and soon became a general laughingstock. The only occasion on which it showed signs of life was when, at the instance of Metternich, it adopted severe police measures to bridle the expression of liberal opinion in the German press and universities and to hunt the sporadic German democrats to their holes. These repressive activities were incorporated in the so-called Carlsbad decrees of 1819. Originating with the Austrian chancellor, they were made effective for all Germany by action of the Bund. They register the high-water mark of the triumphant reaction.

Metternich imposes (1819) the Carlsbad decrees on Germany through the Bund

In the middle-sized states of south Germany—Bavaria, Wurtemberg, Baden—constitutions had been granted by the rulers after 1815. In these

three states all that Germany could show in the nature of popular political activity during the period from 1815 to 1830 took refuge. The two
great states, Austria and Prussia, and almost all of the small north German states, were, in respect of popular participation in politics, as dead
as extinct volcanoes. Throughout this area absolutism flourished unchecked.

Absolute governments the rule in Germany

In Austria the reaction presented to view no single redeeming feature;
Metternich's hand seemed to have paralyzed the popular energies. In
Prussia the case was somewhat different. The king had indeed not ful-
filled his promise to his people, given at the height of the struggle with
Napoleon, to create a representative government, but he offered some
compensation for this breach of faith by a high-grade administration and
a progressive economic policy.

The case of Prussia

A really notable achievement along economic lines brought about at
this time by Prussia was the German Customs Union, called *Zollverein*.
Inaugurated by Berlin in 1818 and brought to completion after patient
efforts continued through a generation, the Zollverein gathered around
Prussia, under a uniform tariff system, all the German states except
Austria. The reader will at once see that by unifying Germany economically the Zollverein promoted prosperity by providing trade and industry
with a market of national scope. This strengthened the middle classes
and, in addition, pointedly showed the way to a possible future political
unification to replace the mock confederation of the Bund.

Prussia creates the German Zollverein

Such was the general German situation, modified by the circumstance
that in 1830 the Zollverein was still in an early, experimental stage, when
the news of the revolution in Paris traveled across the Rhine. If a movement of revolutionary change were to be really effective in the German
area, it would have to be initiated in the great states, Austria and Prussia.
As the people in these two states failed to stir, such outbreaks as occurred
never acquired more than a local character. In some of the absolute states
of north Germany—Hesse-Cassel, Brunswick, Saxony, Hanover—there
were risings which were quickly quelled by the grant of a restricted form
of representative government. Phlegmatic Germany, unused to the exercise of political rights, had not acquired the revolutionary habit. The net
result of the action of 1830 came to this: the establishment of a limited
form of constitutionalism in some of the lesser states.

The in-significant revolution of 1830 in Germany

It deserves notice not only that the German movement of 1830 was
limited to a few local disturbances, but also that it was exclusively concerned with constitutional aims. No cry was raised for a more effective
national organization, and no hand was lifted against the feeble and
despised Bund. In the light of the relatively unimportant happenings of
1830 we are forced to the conclusion that while the liberal movement in
Germany was more developed than the national movement, both alike,

The German movement of 1830 has a liberal, not a national character

hardly yet out of their swaddling clothes, awaited the development of a more powerful middle class propelled by an organized political opinion.

REVOLUTION: POLAND

If the year 1830 saw hardly more than storm-signals in Germany, it witnessed a fierce tempest beyond the eastern boundary of Germany, in Poland. We have seen that at the Congress of Vienna the Tsar Alexander, to whom had been assigned Napoleon's creation, the grand duchy of Warsaw, converted it into the kingdom of Poland with himself as king. At the same time he gave it a constitution, by which it became a political entity with a Polish administration and army and with a Polish diet enjoying a consultative voice in internal affairs.

Alexander creates (1815) the kingdom of Poland

That Alexander's constitution represented an act of unusual liberality on his part and for the period cannot be denied. But it did not satisfy the nationally inflamed Poles. They chafed under the remaining restrictions on their independence, as they nostalgically recalled the time when the parts were reversed, and they, and not the Russians and their tsar, dominated eastern Europe.

Dissatisfaction of the Poles

The discontent was kept under control as long as Alexander, giver of the constitution, lived. No sooner, however, had Nicholas I succeeded his brother (1825) than the evidences of friction multiplied. To the accumulated discontent the excitement spread through Europe by the July revolution in France applied the torch, and in November, 1830, the capital, Warsaw, rose in insurrection. The country at once took the cue from the metropolis; the few Russian troops in Poland withdrew with all possible speed; and not without surprise at the ease of the achievement, the Poles discovered that they were free under a revolutionary government.

The Poles rise in revolt, November 1830

Plainly the success of the movement would depend on united, vigorous, and intelligent action. But that combination was hard to achieve, owing to the political inexperience of the Polish leaders and to the lamentable social divisions inherited from the past. For one thing the great nobles, who as owners of vast estates were the most powerful group in the country, did not see eye to eye with the democratic element in the city of Warsaw, which was largely responsible for the revolution. More important still, the bulk of the nation were agricultural laborers in a condition little above that of brutes. Serfs for centuries, they had indeed been liberated by Napoleon (1807). But as nothing had been done to convert them into peasant-proprietors, they lived from hand to mouth and were, at least in a material sense, no better off than before their formal liberation.

Internal difficulties of the Polish revolutionary government

In spite of these handicaps, the revolutionary government succeeded in creating a spirited national army. With next to no training and with

Tsar Nicholas crushes (1831) the Polish revolution

a very deficient equipment it sustained a most honorable combat, when, in the spring of 1831, Tsar Nicholas launched his Russian legions against it. However, valor alone could not prevail. At Ostrolenka (May, 1831) the Russians overwhelmed the Poles with their numbers, and a few months later (September) entered Warsaw in triumph. Thus the seal of fate seemed to have been set upon the death sentence pronounced by the partitions of the previous century.

Nicholas I abrogates the Polish constitution

When the Russian autocrat again took hold, it was with the grim resolve to make every possible provision against another Polish revolution. Nicholas I firmly believed that he had been trifled with because he and his predecessor had proved themselves too generous. He would not err in that way any more. He began by abrogating Alexander's constitution, not without calling attention to the fact that the Poles had preceded him in abrogating it by rising in revolution.

The systematic repression of the Poles

Then Nicholas merged the ex-kingdom with Russia as a Russian province and carried through a succession of measures which aimed to break the rebellious spirit of the Poles. The first measure was to saddle a Russian army of occupation on the Poles. It was followed by making Russian the official language of the country and putting the native press under strict supervision. Finally, most of the Polish educational institutions were closed. Poland fell into a deep eclipse. And yet, bound and gagged as they were, the Poles silently and tenaciously clung to their precious national memories.

Results of the revolution of 1830

Reviewing the revolution of 1830 throughout Europe, we may assert that though its fruits, outside of France and Belgium, were small, a new era was plainly struggling into being. Liberalism, as yet indubitably monarchical but affirming the right of every people to share in the political direction of the state, had called general attention to itself and could never again be treated as a negligible political force. Nationalism, too, closely allied with liberalism, had asserted itself, successfully in Belgium, unsuccessfully in Poland. Through the revolutions of 1830 the reactionary system of 1815, already weakened by the uprisings of the twenties, received its final blow; and although Metternich and other arch-conservatives might hope to revive it and actually never ceased trying to do so, their effort was foredoomed to failure because a new day had dawned over Europe.

23 THE REIGN OF LOUIS PHILIPPE (1830-1848) AND THE REVOLUTIONS THAT FOLLOWED HIS OVERTHROW IN 1848

THE REIGN OF LOUIS PHILIPPE

WE HAVE SEEN that Louis Philippe, who became king of the French in consequence of the July revolution, owed his throne to the favor and power of the bourgeoisie. Called king of the bourgeoisie, the jocosely intended phrase actually and precisely defined his political status and, to a certain extent also, his personality. Abandoning the traditional pomp of royalty, he exhibited an easy fellowship with men of all classes, lived simply in the midst of his numerous family, and, like his bourgeois subjects generally, was shrewd, thrifty, and obstinate.

King Louis Philippe identified with the middle class

The July monarchy never enjoyed a day of complete and unquestioned security. In the legitimists and the republicans it had from the start two uncompromising political opponents. The legitimists, devoted to the older Bourbon branch, worked at all times against Louis Philippe, but, apart from a single outbreak in the old royalist center of the west, the Vendée, they were content to bide their time. In the Vendée, the duchess of Berry, mother of the young Bourbon claimant, whom legitimists called Henry V, picturesquely headed a movement (1832) which, though giving some trouble to the government, by its failure to arouse the masses proved that legitimism was completely lacking in popular support.

The opponents of the July monarchy: (1) the legitimists

Far more serious was the enmity of the republicans. The leaders were stubborn enthusiasts, often of the middle class, who drew their inspiration from the doctrines of the Revolution. The rank and file of the party was recruited from the workingmen of Paris, Lyons, and other industrial centers. Prepared to take risks for the cause in which they believed, the republicans appealed in 1832, and again in 1834, to arms only to invite suppression at the hands of the government.

The opponents of the July monarchy: (2) the republicans

After the rising of 1834 Louis Philippe's government passed a series of repressive acts (the September laws, 1835). By special courts for the trial of offenses against the security of the state these acts made republicanism a felony, and by an extraordinarily severe censorship of the press they drove all republican agitation underground.

The government enacts repressive legislation

469

Far more important than all the surface agitations of politics and
indeed largely explanatory of them was a social and economic upheaval
inaugurated in Louis Philippe's reign. The upheaval has received the
name of Industrial Revolution. As it will later be given a systematic
treatment, it will here suffice to indicate some of its leading aspects. We
have already noted that the Industrial Revolution was an offspring of
science and that its powerful emblem was the machine. Louis Philippe's
reign saw the dawn in France of the machine age. It signified, in the
French as in every other case, the familiar changes associated with factories and slums and the innumerable problems born of the conflict between capital and labor.

The most immediate effect of the Industrial Revolution was to
strengthen the position of the middle classes since, as the groups endowed
with capital, they became the powerful masters of the machines. But the
workingmen, too, were strengthened, though at first only in numbers.
Since the law forbade them to form trade unions for the purpose of protecting their economic interests, and since, after 1835, it also prohibited
their agitating politically through a republican organization, they were
wholly at the mercy of their employers.

Greatly exasperated by their bondage, the workingmen inclined a willing ear to a new type of agitator, who taught that as long as the bourgeoisie owned the means of production the existing injustice would inevitably continue. The only effective cure, according to this radical teaching, was for the working people to overthrow the regime of private capital and to possess themselves of the machines and factories.

A French journalist, Louis Blanc, was the first to preach in clear terms
this doctrine, in which we recognize a type of thinking afterwards called
socialism. The most striking feature of Blanc's program was the proposal
that an associated group of workmen should apply to the state for a loan
of capital in order to undertake the co-operative management of a factory under the name of a national workshop.

While Blanc and his followers were sincere republicans, their position,
envisaging a radical economic upheaval, went far beyond the purely
political demands of traditional republicanism. This difference of purpose between republicans and socialists should be carefully noted, as
under Louis Philippe a deceptive impression of republican and socialist
unity was created because both parties stood shoulder to shoulder against
the government.

Though the socialist development had great potentialities, we must
not credit it with an important role in the official political life of France
in the reign of Louis Philippe. Under the constitution politics was the
exclusive preserve of the middle class and, apart from occasional flurries

---

The Industrial Revolution comes to France

Effect of the Industrial Revolution

The workers develop a radical outlook

Louis Blanc and the rise of socialism

Divergent aims of republicans and socialists

Politics the preserve of the bourgeoisie

caused by legitimists and republicans, only the bourgeoisie and their affairs held the public stage.

Had this middle group remained united, it might have continued its rule almost indefinitely. But it fell apart over an issue as irrepressible as life itself. The question of bourgeois control of the state came to a head in the Chamber of Deputies, where one political party took the usual conservative position that the existing system was so entirely satisfactory that it required no change at all, while a minority party scouted this immobility and advocated a moderate program of reform.

The bourgeoisie: conservatives and progressives

What the liberal minority particularly urged was the lowering of the franchise requirement with a view to enlarging the body of the electors. It was a famous historian of the French Revolution, Thiers by name, who assumed the leadership of this minority. The equally famous historian of civilization, Guizot, served as the head of the conservatives. This facing each other as leaders of the major political parties of their time of two eminent historians deserves to be noted as a unique political instance. The king himself leaned strongly toward the conservatives, indeed he had so consistently leaned toward them from the first day of his reign that with unimportant intermissions they may be said to have held the power so long as the Orléanist rule lasted.

The conservatives, supported by the king, control the government

In 1840 the king put Guizot in charge of the government, and Guizot steadily maintained himself in office with the support of a majority among the deputies. To be sure, he employed highly questionable means to hold his followers together since he rewarded party fidelity with distributions from the vast patronage at his disposal. Although, with a majority in the Chamber of Deputies backing him up, Guizot's rule was constitutionally impeccable, it was profoundly corrupt. This situation led the minority under Thiers to insist with greater and greater vehemence that the way to break the iron ring of the conservatives was so to enlarge the electorate as to make bribery by a system of individually distributed favors impracticable.

The minority under Thiers demands an enlarged electorate

The method which Thiers chose to carry his agitation for electoral reform among the people was a series of banquets, at which the immobility and corruption of the government were denounced by fiery speakers. During the year 1847 these propagandist banquets were in progress throughout the country. On February 22, 1848, a banquet was planned for the city of Paris, and, to lend the occasion as popular a character as possible, it was to be inaugurated with a public procession.

The reform agitation conducted by public banquets

THE REVOLUTION OF FEBRUARY, 1848

Scenting danger, the government prudently forbade the meeting. Crowds gathered nevertheless and demonstrated noisily to show their

displeasure with this interference from above. The next day the rioters
resumed their activity. They called so insistently for reform that the king
yielded and dismissed the unpopular Guizot. This met the wishes of
Thiers, who hoped to step into Guizot's shoes; but the passion of the
populace having been aroused, the agitation mounted steadily like a flood
until, on February 24, it burst all bounds.

The morning of that day began with an assault upon the district of the
Tuileries by the republican masses. They exhibited such savage determination that the aged and timid king abdicated the throne in favor of his
little grandson. While the sovereign with his queen sought safety in
flight, his daughter-in-law, the spirited duchess of Orléans, led her young
son, the count of Paris, to the Chamber of Deputies and had him proclaimed king.

The action failed to save the Orléanist dynasty. The republican masses
invaded the hall, dispersed the deputies, and set up a Provisional Government. Owing to the fact that the socialists had helped in the street
fighting and were in possession of certain strategic buildings, some of
their leaders, including Louis Blanc, were absorbed into the improvised
ministry. Momentarily united, republicans and socialists began their rule
by triumphantly announcing to the world that France was henceforth a
republic. It carries the historic label of the Second Republic.

The harmony between the two groups lasted long enough for the
Provisional Government to proclaim universal male suffrage and complete freedom of the press. As soon, however, as the socialist minority
insisted that the political revolution was merely a curtain-raiser to a
sweeping economic revolution, the harmony was threatened. To keep the
socialists in the government the republicans were obliged to offer them
two concessions. One was purely theoretical, for it proclaimed every
man's "right to work"; the other, more practical, was the acceptance of
Louis Blanc's socialist remedy of the national workshops.

The two commitments represented the limit of the concessions which
the republican ministers were prepared to make to their socialist colleagues. And even these were quickly jeopardized. For when, early in
May, the National Assembly, elected to give France a new constitution,
met in the capital and took over the powers hitherto exercised by the Provisional Government, it was at once seen that the National Assembly
would not tolerate even the mildest socialist experiments.

What had happened was that the French people, called to the polls to
choose between republicans and socialists, had shown their horror of the
unfamiliar tenets of the new school of thought by returning an overwhelming republican majority. Alarmed at this situation, the socialists
rose in rebellion (May 15), on the suppression of which the angered republicans revenged themselves by abolishing the national workshops.

The
canceled
banquet of
February
22, 1848

Abdication
of Louis
Philippe

Republicans
and social-
ists unite to
proclaim the
republic

Two conces-
sions made
to the social-
ists to bind
them to the
republicans

The
National
Assembly
in power

The
National
Assembly
is anti-
socialist

On being threatened with the loss of the one substantial advantage accruing to them from the recent revolution the socialists made a second attempt to overthrow the National Assembly. They were not crushed till after four days of the bloodiest fighting Paris had thus far ever seen (June 23-26, 1848). Several thousand men were killed defending the barricades they had erected, and other thousands, captured by the victorious soldiers, were either shot without more ado or sent into exile. In consequence of its disastrous defeat the socialist party was eliminated for many a day from the political situation.

The second rising of the socialists and its bloody suppression

A great deal of interest has always attached to the national workshops because they represent the first experiment with a frank socialist label made by the government of any European state. But the interest is spurious since the national workshops, as actually instituted, were socialist only in name. Accepted by the republicans against their conviction and under street pressure, the national workshops plan was intrusted to an anti-socialist management for the express purpose of sabotaging it.

The national workshops experiment reviewed

Instead of specially trained and reliable workmen being joined in a co-operative enterprise supported by capital advanced from state funds— the program of Louis Blanc—the republican enemies charged with the execution of the plan indiscriminately sent off all men who registered at the bureau of labor to work with pick and shovel at the fortifications of Paris. This was a not unfamiliar method in France and elsewhere of meeting the unemployment situation. It may be defended on the additional ground that the public disturbances had closed the factories and thrown out of work thousands of men who had to be provided with subsistence with a minimum of delay.

Deliberate falsification of Louis Blanc's proposal by its republican enemies

As the unemployed grew from week to week, their number threatened to become fantastic and the expense unbearable. That the anti-socialist majority of the Assembly had no stomach for this type of poor relief is intelligible since its cost would have to be met by fresh and unpopular taxes; and that this majority finally resolved to end the drainage of the public purse by suppressing an extremely haphazard system of unemployment relief, falsely called national workshops, is also intelligible. But when the socialists then and afterward contended that their scheme had never been tested, they were undoubtedly supported by the facts. In short, so far as the experiment of 1848 is concerned, no light whatever was shed on the workableness of the national workshops proposal.

The failure of the falsified experiment proves nothing

ELECTION OF LOUIS NAPOLEON TO THE PRESIDENCY OF THE SECOND REPUBLIC

A safe inference from the savage struggle of the spring of 1848 was that France, although a republic, was not ready to indulge in hazardous economic experiments. With the socialists eliminated from the situation the republican majority of the Assembly proceeded to fulfill its mission of giving France a constitution. Insisting on the democratic principle that "all public powers emanate from the people," it drew up a document which vested the legislative power in a single assembly of 750 members elected by universal male suffrage. The executive power was conferred on a president elected for four years. As to the manner of the president's election, it was agreed after long debate that he was to be chosen directly by the people.

The Constitution of 1848

In order to put the new constitution in force the presidential election was ordered for December 10, 1848. To the surprise of all observers unacquainted with the heart of the French people their choice fell, not upon General Cavaignac, the candidate of the republicans and the hero of the recent battles against the socialists, but upon Prince Louis Napoleon.

Louis Napoleon elected president

That this prince should ever be called to the head of the nation by popular vote could hardly have suggested itself to the most prophetic spirit. He was the son of Napoleon's brother Louis, king of Holland, and of Hortense Beauharnais, the sparkling and intelligent daughter of Empress Josephine by her first marriage. After the death (1832) at Vienna of Napoleon's only son, who figures in Bonapartist tradition as Napoleon II, Louis Napoleon (born 1808) was regarded as the head of his house. As such he felt it his duty to conspire for his restoration and made two attempts, in ludicrous imitation of Napoleon's return from Elba, which were greeted by Europe with bursts of Homeric laughter.

Louis Napoleon obsessed with the idea of restoration

In 1836 Louis Napoleon suddenly appeared in Strasburg, but in spite of his uncle's hat, sword, and boots, donned for the occasion, was only stared at by the amused populace and promptly marched off to prison. King Louis Philippe felt so secure that he freed the theatrical hero without more ado.

His appearance (1836) at Strasburg

Undaunted, the young man in 1840 made another attempt to rouse France by crossing from England to Boulogne. Unfortunately the boat conveying him and a few helpmates capsized and, wet and dripping, he was fished out of the channel by the ubiquitous police. Punished for this second escapade with imprisonment for life, he effected his escape after a number of years and again took up his residence in England.

The attempt (1840) of Boulogne

On the proclamation of the republic Louis Napoleon became a candidate for the National Assembly and easily won a seat in that body. Plainly he was outliving the ridicule he had aroused and by manifesting a measure of liberal thinking and, above all, by clever trading on the magic name of Napoleon was rallying about him all those classes, especially the peasants, who clung to the traditions of the empire.

Elected to the National Assembly

When, some months later, his compatriots elected him president, rather than of him they were thinking of the dead warrior whose brilliant vic tories his name recalled. Undeniably, however, the election to the presidency of a prince, who had never let an opportunity pass to declare himself heir to the French throne, indicated that republicanism as a principle was not yet deeply anchored in the national conscience. In these circumstances it might well be that the Second Republic would not enjoy a long life.

Significance of Louis Napoleon's election to the presidency

REVOLUTION AT VIENNA SETS OFF REVOLUTIONS THROUGHOUT CENTRAL EUROPE

If the revolution of 1830 produced no great stir in Central Europe, it was, as we have seen, because the liberal and national sentiments had not yet become powerful and, more fundamentally still, because the middle classes, the historic carriers of these sentiments, were insufficiently developed to make successful headway against the conservative interests in control of the government. Hence in the period after 1830 the reaction remained in the saddle throughout Germany, Austria, and Italy. Nevertheless the areas of popular unrest began to multiply, while the growing well-being and self-assertion of the business and professional groups were an unmistakable indication that the days of an unshaken conservatism were numbered.

Growth of unrest in Central Europe after 1830

To people in the hopeful state of mind of the Central European liberals the February revolution at Paris came as a trumpet call to action. Owing to the fact that Austria was the dominant power and had a foothold in both Italy and Germany, it was clear that, should revolution break out in Vienna and overthrow the Austrian government at its center, revolution in Italy and Germany would follow as a matter of course. And precisely this is what happened. On March 13, 1848, the people of Vienna rose and drove from office and out of the city the aging Prince Metternich, who for almost half a century had guided the fortunes of the Austrian empire and for part of that time those of Europe itself.

Risings throughout Central Europe in 1848

With Metternich's ignominious flight the whole Vienna government collapsed without more ado. Absolutism was renounced, and the feeble-minded Emperor Ferdinand, frightened by the tumult in the streets, speedily promised a constitution, a parliament, freedom of the press, and whatever else the rioters exacted. With the suddenness of melodrama a new era seemed to have dawned upon the petrified realm of the Hapsburgs.

The emperor of Austria bows to the revolution

No sooner had the revolution at Vienna become known in Germany than Berlin followed suit and was followed in its turn by the capitals of all the smaller German states. Everywhere the uprising took the form of a demand for both a liberal constitution and a tighter national union to replace the ineffective Bund. But as it will make for a better understand-

Revolution in Germany; its story deferred

ing if we will first follow through from beginning to end the tremendous happenings within the Austrian empire, we shall defer discussion of the German commotions to a later point in this chapter.

The complex nationality situation in the Austrian empire

The Austrian empire as re-established at the Congress of Vienna was as strange a patchwork of provinces and peoples as has ever been pieced together by fortune and policy. The original duchy of Austria along the upper Danube, together with the Alpine dependencies of Styria, Carinthia, and the Tyrol was inhabited by Germans. Hungary, along the middle Danube, was inhabited by Hungarians (Magyars) closely enveloped on the north and south by Slavs. Of Slavs there were seven distinct groups, Czechs, Slovaks, Poles, Ruthenians, constituting a continuous northern belt, with Slovenes, Croatians, and Serbs strung along in an unbroken southern belt. (See Austrian Nationality Map, opp. p. 580.) Finally, in Lombardy and Venetia, the latter incorporated in 1815, lived Italians. The expectation that these many diverse peoples could be persuaded to live together as brothers in a common household did not fail of a measure of fulfillment as long as the emperor at Vienna exercised an unimpaired absolute power and the national sentiment of the different groups had not yet been awakened.

Uprising of the component nationalities of Austria

However, as soon as the revolution at Vienna had overthrown the emperor's power at the focal point, the nationalist passion of the various peoples was fanned into flame and the whole Hapsburg structure threatened to fly apart with violent centrifugal action. In the course of a few weeks the Italians at Milan and Venice, the respective capitals of Lombardy and Venetia, drove out the Austrian garrisons and declared for independence; the Hungarians, ignoring Vienna, set up their own government at Budapest; and while the Slavs remained relatively quiescent, some of them, notably the Czechs of Bohemia, inaugurated a program looking, if not toward complete sovereignty, at least toward a measure of home rule. To the casual observer the proud Austrian empire seemed to have reached its end. Let us follow these uprisings in their leading centers.

THE ITALIAN UPRISING

The Italians of Lombardy and Venetia appeal to all Italy for help

In Italy the fall of Metternich was no sooner reported than the people of Lombardy and Venetia, long restive under his lash, rose, fell upon the troops, and declared for independence. The Austrian army, yielding to the sudden pressure, retired in good order under its general, Radetzky, to a chain of impregnable fortifications prepared for just such an emergency at the foot of the Alps and known as the Quadrilateral. A Provisional Government set up at Milan appealed to all Italy for help and especially to Charles Albert, king of Sardinia-Piedmont, the most powerful of the independent Italian princes and the only one imbued with any genuine sentiment for the national cause.

Since for the moment the national movement was irresistible, the other Italian rulers, such as the king of the Two Sicilies, the grand duke of Tuscany, and the pope, who traditionally served only their local interests, made a gesture of acquiescence toward the national struggle and agreed to send contingents to fight side by side with their northern fellow countrymen for the liberation of the peninsula from the Austrian yoke. It was Italy's first great national war, its purpose the expulsion of the foreigner.

The other Italian states agree at first to help

In this enterprise, originating in the spontaneous action of the people, there was a military weakness which no enthusiasm could overcome. Among the motley and undisciplined Italian contingents the Sardinian army was the single efficient body and its numbers were too small to resist the Austrian legions. When on July 25 the decisive clash came at Custozza, within the Quadrilateral, whither the king of Sardinia had led his army in order to dislodge the Austrians, the veteran General Radetzky inflicted a crushing defeat on the Italians. As a result Radetzky reoccupied Lombardy and obliged Charles Albert to sue for a truce. When at the expiration of the truce the war was renewed, the Austrians won another great victory at Novara (March, 1849), and the struggle was over.

Austria crushingly defeats the Italians

Sick at heart, the defeated Charles Albert abdicated, and his son and successor, Victor Emmanuel, made haste to sign a treaty with Austria by which, in return for abandoning the national cause, he received back his undiminished realm.

The peace

The treaty left the Austrians free to deal with their two revolted provinces of Lombardy and Venetia. Milan, the capital of Lombardy, being, as a result of Custozza, already in their hands, the Austrians now laid siege to Venice and, after a courageous defense, the city capitulated (August, 1849).

Lombardy and Venetia reconquered

Though the struggle in the north against Austria marks the climax in the drama of the Italian revolution, the rest of the peninsula shared in varying degree in the aspirations and delusions of that year of turmoil. The attitude of the pope, the grand duke of Tuscany, the king of the Two Sicilies, and the other smaller princes has already been indicated. Thoroughly intimidated for the time being by the sweep of the revolution, they yielded to every liberal and national demand urged by the insurgent leaders.

The revolution at first successful in the rest of Italy

However, as soon as the national cause had suffered defeat, the local rulers recovered their courage, dismissed their liberal advisers, and reverted to the beloved system of absolutism. The king of the Two Sicilies was the first to cast aside his liberal mask. A despot without a scruple or,

Triumph of reaction at Naples

rather, a sovereign in vaudeville trappings, he overthrew the constitutional system, first in Naples and afterward in Sicily. Thereupon a reaction worse than that imposed by the Austrians in Lombardy, because its
author was more despicable, fastened upon the fair provinces of the south.

THE ROMAN EPISODE

The revolution at Rome

Far more memorable than at Naples were the revolutionary occurrences in the State of the Church, of which Pope Pius IX was sovereign.
In fact the course which the revolution took at Rome throws so much
light on certain crucial Italian problems that we must examine it somewhat more fully.

Pius IX at first participates in the national movement

Pius IX, elected to the papacy in 1846, was a kind and affable man,
with a reputation for liberalism which he owed to nothing more convincing than an occasional good-natured word and deed. However, as a
born Italian, he did in a measure sympathize with the Italian national
movement; and when Lombardy revolted against Austria, he gave evidence of his approval by sending a papal contingent to the rebels' aid.

Pope Pius withdraws from the war

When, some months later, the pope became aware of the consequences
of this step, he called a halt. To send troops against Austria meant a
declaration of war against that power and the adoption of a partisan
policy inconsistent with his position as head of the universal church. He
found himself in a dilemma, the inevitable consequence of his dual character; for as pope and successor of the Prince of Peace he had spiritual
obligations toward the whole Catholic world, while as secular lord of an
Italian territory he had temporal obligations, the imperative one at the
moment being to join with the rest of the nation against the foreign
oppressor. Obliged to choose between his obligations to Catholicism and
those to his temporal state, he naturally preferred the greater to the lesser
and, to the relief of Austria but to the immense indignation of his Roman
subjects, withdrew from the Austrian war.

The Romans set up a republic

The incident proved that a pope who wished to play a consistent international role could never follow exclusive national ends. But the Romans,
who were not reflective historians but passionate Italians, showed their
disgust with their sovereign by rising in revolution. A strong republican
faction inveighed against Pius as a traitor to Italy; and when, alarmed
at the situation, he sought refuge (November 24, 1848) with his friend,
the like-minded king of Naples, the revolutionists took affairs into their
own hands and converted the papal dominion into a republic.

Joseph Mazzini

The leading spirit of the revolutionary government of Rome was Joseph Mazzini. A Genoese by birth, he was a high-minded, lifelong
prophet of Italian unity and a tireless conspirator against the selfish
reigning houses of his divided country.

The Roman republic never had more than a fighting chance to survive. Catholics the world over were horrified at the dispossession of the Holy Father, and several Catholic governments pondered measures looking to his restoration. Louis Napoleon, recently elected president of the French republic, was especially delighted at the opportunity offered to curry favor with the Catholic clergy and peasantry of France; and intent only on his own advantage and heedless of the fact that he was pitting one youthful republic against another, he sent an army to Rome to sweep Mazzini and his followers out of the city.

Louis Napoleon sends an army to restore the pope

General Garibaldi, who had been created commander-in-chief of the Roman forces, offered a gallant but unavailing resistance. In July, 1849, the French entered the conquered city. And when now, on the invitation of his French rescuers, the disillusioned pope returned to his capital, he was cured of such slight predilection for reform as he may once have felt and re-established the traditional autocratic system with all its time-worn abuses.

Defeat (1849) of the Roman republic

Thus with a harvest of disappointments the Italian revolutionary action of 1848-1849 came to a close. Affairs relapsed to their former state; the brave effort had been in vain. However, one memory, which was also a hope, shone out like a star in a darkened sky. The Italians had found in the king of Sardinia a sovereign dedicated to their cause and they recognized in his army the means of resuming the war at some future day. True, Charles Albert had been defeated; but not only had he stood by Italy till his overthrow, but his successor, Victor Emmanuel, showed an even more resolute spirit.

The house of Savoy the Star Shining in Darkness

Unmoved by either Austrian threats or bribes, King Victor Emmanuel refused to give up his interest in Italy or to join the ranks of the reactionaries by withdrawing the constitution granted to his country in 1848. Such sturdy attachment to the liberal-national program roused a love and admiration which drew the eyes of the Italians of north and south alike toward Piedmont and the house of Savoy.

King Victor Emmanuel stands by the national program

THE IMPERIAL ARMY SAVES THE EMPIRE

While the Austrian army under Radetzky was occupied in the manner we have seen with extinguishing the rebellious fires in Italy, other army units were obliged to attend to rebellions in other areas of the empire's extensive dominions. Let us pause for a moment to recapitulate. The revolution had its beginning with a rising of the Germans at Vienna. It was promptly followed by upheavals among the Italians, Hungarians, Czechs, and a number of smaller groups we can afford to disregard. The Vienna rising had completely disorganized the government at its center and, owing to the fact that the emperor was a half-wit and his ministers men

Solid discipline of the Austrian army

of weak resolution, the chaos steadily deepened rather than improved. It is more than likely that Austria would have fallen permanently apart, had it not been for the one solid institution inherited from the past—the imperial army. Its ancient traditions and effective discipline held it together, and, in spite of the confusion at Vienna, it operated with dispatch and resolution.

The Austrian army versus the revolution

In Italy, as we have just seen, the army furnished incontrovertible evidence of its strength. Elated by the Italian victory, the Austrian generals in command in the other rebellious areas became desirous of applying Radetzky's remedy of the sword to the situation under their eyes. In their view an unruly multitude imposing its will by street demonstrations will always be found incapable of standing up against trained soldiers under professional command.

The army victorious at Prague and Vienna

When, in June, 1848, General Windisch-Grätz, commanding at Prague in Bohemia, came to grips with the insurrection of the Czechs, he snuffed it out without much trouble. His next step was to attack the revolution of the Germans in Vienna. Arriving in October before the city, he encountered a resistance which snapped like a wooden sword when his troops stormed the gates and forced their way into the town.

The Hungarian revolt alone remains

In this way by late autumn of 1848 the Czech and German revolutions had once more been brought under control. As at that time the Italian cause was already declining to its setting, only the Hungarian revolt remained to be dealt with. With that movement out of the way Austria would be her accustomed self again.

THE HUNGARIAN UPRISING

Hungary under the Hapsburgs

It was in the sixteenth century, in the time of Ferdinand I, that the crown of Hungary had passed into the possession of the house of Hapsburg. The kingdom of the Magyars had an ancient constitution which conceded considerable power to a characteristically feudal parliament of noble landholders. Although the Hapsburg sovereigns, aiming at the unification of all the territories under their rule, had frequently set the Hungarian constitution at naught, they had never succeeded in entirely abrogating it.

Virtual independence of Hungary

The Magyars for their part clung stubbornly to their political inheritance; and when the Viennese absolutism collapsed abruptly through the impact of the revolution of March, 1848, they gained at a stroke all that they had been demanding. As a result Hungary to all intents and purposes seceded from the Austrian empire, although it continued to recognize the Hapsburg sovereign as its king.

With the insurrectionary fires extinguished in Italy, Bohemia, and at

Vienna, the baffled central government again plucked up courage and ceased to cringe before the Magyars. Disputes over questions of competence between the revolutionary parliament at Budapest and the Hapsburg sovereign at Vienna led to a state of war, and in December, 1848, an Austrian army was dispatched against the Hungarian capital. *The Austrian army invades Hungary*

The struggle which followed is a splendid tribute to the lofty spirit of the Hungarians. Ever since the revolution had begun, the movement had been under the powerful guidance of Louis Kossuth, who, at the approach of the supreme crisis, assumed the dictatorship of the country. Kossuth put the army under the command of a very capable native general, Görgei by name, who by the adoption of a bold strategy succeeded in driving the Austrian army back upon Vienna. *Hungary under the dictatorship of Louis Kossuth*

Elated by this success, Kossuth, a convinced republican, issued a decree declaring the deposition of the house of Hapsburg. The measure was of doubtful wisdom, for not only did it divide the Hungarians, many of whom, perhaps a majority, were royalists, but it reduced the Viennese court to desperation. *Hungary proclaimed a republic*

In this state of mind the Viennese government accepted the proffered help of Tsar Nicholas. The Russian autocrat, long waiting for an opportunity to ride into the lists as the plumed champion of the cause of monarchy, promptly sent an army across the Carpathians which took the Hungarians in the flank. Caught between two fires, the insurgents gave a good accounting of themselves; but by August, 1849, their forces had been overwhelmed and, with Kossuth, Görgei, and the other leaders either captured or driven into exile, the movement for Hungarian independence came to a tragic close. *The Hungarian revolt crushed (August, 1849)*

Thus by the action of the army Austria had overcome the revolutionary crisis. But to give the army's successes in the field even the appearance of durability the torn and feeble government at Vienna would have to be reorganized in the traditional manner. This work, thoroughly congenial to his iron-willed conviction that Austria could not possibly function except as an absolutism, was assigned to Prince Felix Schwarzenberg. Made prime minister in the late autumn of 1848, his first step was to persuade the imbecile Emperor Ferdinand to abdicate (December 2) in favor of his alert eighteen-year-old nephew, Francis Joseph. It was not so easy to get rid of what the revolutionists regarded as their most promising achievement. This was a parliament of all the peoples of the monarchy summoned to the capital to elaborate a general Austrian constitution. Through all the months of turmoil just reviewed the members had clung single-mindedly to their labors with the result that on March 1, 1849, they added the final touch to a very democratic document. In reward for their exertions Schwarzenberg promptly sent them about their business *Absolutism re-established at Vienna*

and tore up their constitution. A few months later, the Hungarian revolution had been smothered and an unchallenged absolutism again sat
enthroned at Vienna.

THE GERMAN REVOLUTION

On turning now to the German revolution, which was running its own
particular course all the while Austria traversed the many crises we
have recorded, let us note once more that it set in promptly on the heels
of the March uprising at Vienna, and that it reached every German
state, large or small. Wherever it raised its head it was animated first,
by the liberal purpose of endowing each German state-unit with a democratically inspired constitution, and second, by the national purpose of
replacing the incapable Bund with a genuine and effective federation. We
shall therefore have to keep the two distinct but related movements constantly before us. And since it is impossible, and also needless, to follow
the liberal (or constitutional) action at each one of the many German
capitals, we shall content ourselves to follow it at Berlin, the capital of
Prussia. This is fully justified by the circumstance that Prussia overshadowed the other German states and that, consequently, the fortunes
of constitutionalism in Prussia were pretty much bound to determine its
fortunes everywhere else. The national aspirations, on the other hand,
were centered, by developments of which we shall presently hear, at
Frankfort-on-the-Main. Because this ancient town had served as the
meeting place of the electors of the defunct Holy Roman Empire, there
lingered about it something of the aura of a former capital of the German nation. Berlin and Frankfort-on-the-Main will figure as the focal
points of our story and our attention will be kept swinging pendulum-
wise from one to the other.

Our two
centers of
attention
will be
Berlin and
Frankfort

We begin with Berlin and take as our starting-point the revolution
that broke out there on March 18, five days after the example set by
Vienna. In view of the failure of the Prussian people to respond to the
revolution of 1830 this action of theirs may seem surprising. But the last
decade had seen some not unimportant changes. The old king, Frederick
William III, who had endeared himself to his people because of his
connection with the War of Liberation against Napoleon, had died in
1840. His successor was his son, Frederick William IV, and the new
generation he faced let it be known in no uncertain tones that, while it
approved of the efficient administration maintained by the state, it did
not intend to let itself be excluded any longer from a share in legislation.

The new
king,
Frederick
William IV,
faces an
altered
situation

In spite of his firm belief in divine right, the new king had, as early
as 1847, yielded so far to public opinion as to summon to Berlin the
representatives of the several provincial estates. The assembly, called the

United Diet, at once assumed the airs of a Prussian national parliament; and although it did not accomplish anything, the fact that the king had been obliged to call it together proves that the revolution of 1848 had been preceded by the birth of a new public spirit. The Prussian United Diet of 1847

As a result of the March days, which did not pass without the spilling of blood, the intimidated king surrendered completely to the people. Not only did he, by withdrawing his troops from the city, hand Berlin over to the insurgents, but he promised to call an elected parliament and, in addition, to promote to the best of his ability the cause of German unity. The king yields to the March revolution

Owing to a like action in the lesser capitals, all Germany was in the course of a single week pledged to the constitutional system. But there was to the uprising that other aspect already pointed out: it was animated by a fiery nationalism, and the middle-class leaders of the revolt were aware they must strike while the iron was hot if they were to realize their aspirations. The revolution is liberal and nationalist

Consequently, before the month of March had gone these leaders came together informally and decided of their own usurped authority to issue a call for a general German parliament. Its members were to be elected by universal male suffrage and its purpose was indicated in precise terms as the creation of a genuine federal government. To this invitation of their liberal leaders the German people responded with an extraordinary and apparently united enthusiasm. The revolutionists summon a national parliament

When the German parliament, elected on these terms, assembled in May, 1848, at Frankfort-on-the-Main, it was found to be by every moral and intellectual standard a very distinguished body of men. But all the learning and high principles of the members did not serve to cancel one fatal defect inherent in their position: so long as they had at their disposal neither an administration nor an army, that is, so long as they possessed none of the realities of power, their status hardly differed from that of a debating society. A German parliament assembles at Frankfort in May

In the early days of the revolutionary triumph the weakness of the German parliament was offset by the irresistible public opinion behind it. But should opinion sag, as it has an invariable way of doing, and should the state governments, panic-stricken by the first shock communicated to them by the revolution, recover breath and courage—what then? Let us recall that the Bund of 1815 had been expressly established to guarantee the sovereignty of the thirty-eight member states. It was certain that these states would not lightly yield their dearest possession. Austria and Prussia, in particular, proud of their position as great powers, could hardly be expected without some show of resistance to recognize as their superior the democratic and revolutionary body sitting The sovereignty assumed by the German parliament certain to be challenged at Frankfort. Sooner or later Austria or Prussia or both together would follow an independent policy, and the clash would be at hand, testing the question whether ultimate control rested with the revolutionary German parliament or with the individual states.

The clash came over the Schleswig-Holstein question. This, one of the most confused of the minor issues of nineteenth century history, haunted the European chancelleries like a nightmare for more than a generation. But, leaving to one side its many legal complications, it becomes simplicity itself the moment we view it from a national angle. The united duchies of Schleswig and Holstein occupied the southern half of the peninsula of Jutland and were inhabited, except for the northern rim of Schleswig, which was Danish, by a German population. By an accident of inheritance the king of Denmark was also duke of Schleswig and Holstein; but the two duchies were in no sense a part of Denmark and lived under their own legal and administrative system. This independence of Denmark the two duchies, because they were preponderantly German, were firmly resolved to preserve.

The Schleswig-Holstein question

Toward the middle of the century an issue dawned which put the Germans sharply on their guard. The royal house of Denmark, about to die out in the male line, was faced by a constitutional difficulty. By the law of Denmark the crown would descend to a female line, while by the Schleswig-Holstein law, at least as interpreted by the German population, the crown of the united duchies would pass to the nearest male relative.

Denmark and the duchies face separation

There was therefore the prospect of an early divorce between Denmark and the duchies which rejoiced the Germans as much as it grieved the Danes. In 1846 the king of Denmark took the grave step of issuing a public declaration to the effect that, come what might, he would see to it that the union between Denmark and the duchies should be maintained.

The king of Denmark for union at all costs

This royal declaration the German population regarded as a breach of law and custom. They were thrown into a revolutionary mood and, taking advantage of the general agitation of 1848, they rose in revolt, proclaimed Schleswig-Holstein independent of Denmark, and appealed to the German parliament sitting at Frankfort for support.

The Schleswig-Holstein revolt

The German parliament at once responded with encouraging words. However, when it came to deeds, it found itself hampered by the fact that it had neither an army nor money at its disposal. In consequence it was obliged to appeal to Prussia, which bordered on the duchies, to go to the aid of the rebels. Entering Schleswig-Holstein, the Prussians drove out the Danes, but the latter retaliated by seizing the Prussian merchant vessels in the Baltic.

The German parliament appeals to Prussia

This fact, coupled with the strong intercession, in behalf of Denmark, of Russia and Great Britain, induced King Frederick William, who had only with reluctance obeyed the German parliament, to sign a truce with Denmark (August 26). By its terms he practically redelivered the duchies into the hands of the Danes.

Informed of this action, the legislators at Frankfort branded Frederick William a traitor and declared the truce he had concluded null and void. On sober second thought, however, they recognized that without an army of their own they could not coerce Prussia and, reversing themselves, regretfully endorsed all that Prussia had done.

The incident was highly instructive as to the distribution of power between Prussia and the German parliament. Greatly humiliated, the members turned to the constitutional labors for which they had been summoned, resolved to bring them to a conclusion before the revolutionary tide which had swept them to power had completely ebbed.

The successful assertion of his independence against the Frankfort assembly greatly encouraged Frederick William IV and the only temporarily subdued conservative elements of his kingdom. He was further emboldened to resume his traditional role by the autocratic recovery under way in neighboring Austria. When in October, 1848, General Windischgrätz forced his way into Vienna with troops, Frederick William made the inevitable deductions. The earliest concessions imposed on him by the insurgents had been that Berlin should be cleared of troops and a parliament be summoned to provide Prussia with a constitution. This parliament, having been duly elected and organized, was through the summer months getting along with a constitution of, in the king's eyes, an excessively democratic character. He would have none of it, and on December 5 proceeded to act. He declared the parliament dissolved and at the same time, to overawe the opposition, sent his troops back into Berlin.

With these successes to his credit, the king might now have returned to the old absolutism without more ado. Deterred by certain moral scruples, he resolved to offer his subjects a constitution of his own making. It was a document which fell far short of the liberal demands. In its final form (adopted in 1850) it left to the royal executive the appointment of the ministers, who therefore acted as agents not of the representatives of the people but of the king.

In the matter of the franchise the so-called three-class system was adopted. By this system the men of voting age were divided into three classes in accordance with the amount of taxes paid by them. The first class, therefore, contained only comparatively few wealthy men who paid the first third of the taxes; the second class was considerably larger; and the third included the overwhelming majority of the voters. As each class received equal representation in the electoral college, the first two classes by uniting could always out-vote the third class. It was a plan to secure control to the propertied interests.

Prussia no longer absolute

Nevertheless, a Prussian legislature, which made the laws and voted the taxes, secured to the Prussian people henceforth a definite, if limited, share in the government. It also furnished evidence that in Prussia almost alone in Central Europe the revolution had not been entirely in vain.

Again the German parliament

With the strong winds of reaction blowing over Germany, the German parliament at Frankfort could not escape their chill. Granted that its failure to impose its will on Prussia in the Schleswig-Holstein matter had exposed its weakness to Germany as well as to its own membership, nonetheless, and in despite of this unhappy circumstance, it resolved to go through with its appointed task and unite the German fatherland within the framework of an effective federation.

The German parliament and Austria

On proceeding with its strictly constitutional labors the parliament was not long in discovering that the greatest barrier in its path was Austria. The delegates from the German areas of Austria demanded the inclusion of these areas in the prospective federation and the parliament was entirely willing to accommodate them. But the government at Vienna would have none of this partitioning of the empire and insisted on the incorporation in Germany of the undivided monarchy. This in its turn the parliament, engaged in building a German national state, firmly rejected. The upshot was that the assembly voted the exclusion of the Hapsburg monarchy in its entirety from the proposed union.

The parliament offers the crown to the king of Prussia

The elimination of the Hapsburg empire settled almost automatically the related difficulty of the headship of the new Germany. Not without heated discussion, it was decided that the chief executive should be a hereditary emperor and that the post should be offered to the king of Prussia. In April, 1849, a deputation from the parliament journeyed to Berlin to offer the crown of united Germany to Frederick William IV.

The king of Prussia rejects the German crown

His answer was a refusal. Frederick William was too deeply persuaded of the divine right of sovereigns to have any sympathy for a popular and democratic honor; he was convinced that the constitution was in many features unworkable; and—he was afraid of Austria. Under the energetic Schwarzenberg, Austria was at that moment effecting a phenomenal recovery and notified Berlin in no uncertain language that the acceptance of the imperial office by a Hohenzollern would be deeply resented. The Viennese view was that if the German crown was to be revived, it must revert to the house of Hapsburg, which had worn it for so many centuries. Frederick William was a weak, well-meaning man of mystical, confused ideas, and, like all waverers, always ended by yielding to resolute pressure.

The committee of the parliament returned to Frankfort to report its failure. Thereupon the German parliament sadly acknowledged its inability to go on with its work and, not without a flurry of revolt, retired from the scene.

The parliament dissolves

Frederick William IV, who, in spite of his refusal of the German crown, felt that he was pledged to do something for the national cause, now made an attempt to persuade the German governments to negotiate among themselves about the basis of a new union. His thought was that since the people, acting through their representatives at Frankfort, had failed to solve the German problem, it behooved the sovereign princes to try their hand at it.

The king of Prussia presents a German plan of his own

Against this plan, too, because, exactly like that of the Frankfort parliament, it excluded the Austrian empire, the Austrian government threw the weight of its influence. Finally, Vienna came to the front with its own German plan. It proved to be nothing other than the discarded Bund of 1815. Of this hollow confederation the great attraction was that it left Austria in Germany; that it did not impair the sovereignty of the member states; and that it reduced the king of Prussia to the level of the other German princes.

Austria's counter-proposal

Although in the spring of 1848 the Bund had fallen like a house of cards before the first revolutionary gust, Austria once more actually set it up at its former seat, at Frankfort. This done, it issued an invitation to all the former members to enter and complete the happy German family. With their eyes directed, now as always, to their precious sovereignty, the German princes to a man deserted Frederick William's proposed union under Prussia and gathered under the Austrian standard. Almost before he knew it, the Prussian king found himself alone like an actor on a deserted stage. When Austria, aware that she was dealing with a timid man, now haughtily ordered him to give up every idea of a closer union and himself join the Bund, he yielded without risking an open breach (Treaty of Olmütz, November, 1850). The old Bund—this was the ridiculous mouse that issued from the tremendous two years' labor of the nation for a better union.

Austria re-establishes the old Bund (1850)

In this general collapse of German hopes and illusions the Schleswig-Holsteiners, who had rebelled against their sovereign, the king of Denmark, could not escape disaster. Abandoned by Prussia in August, 1848, they several times renewed the fray with their own resources, only to be definitely crushed by Denmark in 1850.

The Schleswig-Holstein revolt crushed

A conference of the powers came together in London to consider the case of Schleswig-Holstein and decided the succession question contrary to the wishes of the German population. It was agreed (Protocol of 1852) that the personal union between Denmark and the duchies should be maintained and that, on the extinction of the reigning line, Prince Christian of Glücksburg should succeed to both inheritances. Although the people of Schleswig-Holstein protested against the decision, they yielded for the time being in the expectation of finding a future occasion to assert their rights.

With the German parliament departed from the scene, the duchies of Schleswig and Holstein redelivered to the Danes, the Bund set up again at Frankfort, and Austria restored under an absolute sovereign, the Metternichian system with all its attendant miseries and abuses had been given a new lease of life. National and liberal circles were filled with despair. But as no evil is without some grain of good, the recent crisis had shown two things: it had proved that the greatest enemy to German unity was the Austrian court, and that a German union, if it ever came about, would have to be effected under Prussian leadership.

Prussia's prestige, it is true, was, after her many failures, lamentably low. But something remained: it was not forgotten that the national hopes had for a short time turned enthusiastically to her; and by her adoption of a constitution, however short of liberal expectations, she had begun to divorce herself from eighteenth century forms in order to plant her feet in the present.

24 GREAT BRITAIN FROM 1815 TO THE SECOND REFORM BILL (1867)

RULERS OF GREAT BRITAIN

George III (1760-1820)

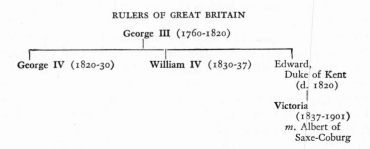

George IV (1820-30)   William IV (1830-37)   Edward,
Duke of Kent
(d. 1820)

Victoria
(1837-1901)
m. Albert of
Saxe-Coburg

THE BRITISH PARLIAMENTARY SYSTEM IN 1815

THE GREAT BRITAIN which was victorious over Napoleon and which with its three continental allies undertook in 1815 to reshape Europe was animated by the resentment against the French Revolution common to all the victor powers. This national state of mind found political expression in the domination of the Tory party and in the determination of the party to uphold without change the whole body of inherited institutions. At the core of these institutions was the parliamentary system which, the product of the revolution of 1688, had transferred the political control from the king to the House of Commons and, more immediately, to the ministry (cabinet) representing the majority party in the Commons.

The Tory party resolves to uphold the inherited institutions

Owing to its astonishing success since its creation this British governmental system enjoyed an enormous prestige not only at home but also among the liberal groups of the continent. And yet it was not really liberal, or rather it was liberal only in comparison with the absolutism prevailing elsewhere. Closely considered, it was a system conferring political rights exclusively on property owners and, more particularly, on large owners of landed property. Conclusive evidence on this head is supplied by the composition of the two houses of parliament. While it goes without saying that the Lords, a house of feudal, i.e., agrarian, origin and character, consisted (aside from the bishops of the Anglican church, the so-called lords spiritual) of great landholders, it is less self-

The British parliamentary system built on property

489

evident, but nonetheless true, that the landed interest dominated also the House of Commons.

The situation in the Commons becomes clear only by an examination

of its composition and of the prevailing system of election. There were three classes of constituencies: the counties elected 186 members, the boroughs 467, and the universities five, making a total membership of 658. Neglecting the university members because numerically unimportant, we may begin with the county members and note that the county franchise was enjoyed by holders of farm land worth an annual rental of forty shillings.

It was the boroughs with their 467 members that chiefly invited the

criticism of reformers. By boroughs should be understood what in America are colloquially called towns and cities. As each borough had its own franchise law, the number of voters might be few in one borough and relatively large in another, but always there was a property qualification and the general statement stands that the borough members, as a whole, were appointed by no more than a handful of electors.

There were other evils. Since the list of boroughs having the right of

representation had been drawn up in the reign of Charles II and had never since been revised, it happened that not a few of them had by the vicissitudes of history dwindled to petty villages. Of such reduced boroughs the largest neighboring landowner had usually acquired control and sent up to Westminster some relative or dependent responsible to no one but to the patron who appointed him. Such a borough was picturesquely described as a "pocket" borough. Since many other boroughs were small and had so restricted a franchise that the few voters could either be bought or cleverly influenced by socially eminent lords or economically powerful millionaires, it followed that the taunt was justified which lumped such diminutive boroughs with the pocket boroughs as "rotten."

While pocket and rotten boroughs sufficiently tell the prevailing tale

of inequality and corruption, it should be further noted that the south and east of England were favored at the expense of the north and west. This resulted from the system having been shaped in the seventeenth century, when the south and east overshadowed the other sections in point of wealth and population. But since the middle of the eighteenth century the Industrial Revolution had produced a startling change. It had brought into existence new towns such as Manchester, Birmingham, and Sheffield in the coal and iron districts of the English north. Themselves totally unrepresented in parliament, they had to submit to seeing numerous microscopic boroughs of the south admitted to an honor to which they aspired in vain.

In sum, the House of Commons did not reflect the British social structure. According to an eminent authority over two-thirds of the total membership were not so much elected as appointed in one way or another by a limited body of patrons. In the circumstances, though called the Commons, the lower house belied its name since it represented not the commoners, but a tight little oligarchy of landlords and merchants.

The inequality evil summarized

This system was remarkably expressive of the period in which it arose, for at the end of the seventeenth century the landed aristocracy and the great merchants undoubtedly were the most vital elements of English society. But since the middle of the eighteenth century a change had been going on, owing to the revolution connected with machines and factories. A new industrial society had come to the front, the leaders of which with their wealth and energy were sure to insist on more adequate representation.

The system reflected an earlier society

It is highly probable that the new industrial society would have been heard from before the eighteenth century came to a close if the French Revolution had not broken out and, by involving Great Britain in war, produced the usual war-time tightening of the reins of government. When, in 1815, the victory fell to Great Britain and its allies, the spirit of reaction triumphed throughout Europe. The victory over Napoleon, won under Tory guidance, so heightened the prestige of the conservatives at home that they were able to extol the inherited system as well-nigh perfect. One enthusiastic lord declared it to be "the best that ever was since the creation of the world and it is not possible to make it better." It was but natural for such a government to identify itself, in its foreign policy, with the Holy Alliance and, in the domestic field, to set its face grimly against change.

British conservatism strengthened by the French Revolution

FROM TIMID TORY REFORMS TO THE BOLD WHIG REFORM OF PARLIAMENT (1832)

In spite of Tory prejudice and stubbornness, a few years of peace sufficed to blow into flame the justified discontent of the rapidly multiplying middle classes. Most of them, as men of means, possessed a natural caution and asked for nothing more than for political recognition of their type of property (machines, factories, capital). But some of their allies—journalists, pamphleteers, and social students, in short, the important group of intellectuals—went farther and, taking their cue from the French Revolution, advocated such far-reaching demands as universal suffrage and a secret ballot. These men called themselves "radicals" and aroused such fierce indignation among the governing Tories that their agitation was at last (1819) suppressed by special acts, which struck at the traditional liberty of Englishmen by severely limiting the

The Tories encounter both a moderate and a radical opposition freedom of the press and of assembly. This was the high point of the reaction.

Nonetheless, the critics, moderates and radicals together, gradually won

A group of Young Tories in favor of concessions

over a constantly increasing body of public opinion. Consequently, even among the Tories a younger and more elastic group came to see the advisability of offering concessions. In 1822, with the advent of Canning to the foreign office, this group succeeded in persuading the party to inaugurate a modest era of reform.

As has been noted in another connection, the first act of Canning

A first modification (1823) of the severe tariff system

on his assumption of the reins of foreign policy was to dissociate himself from the Holy Alliance by supporting revolution in the Spanish colonies. But we are more interested at this juncture in the domestic program of him and his colleagues. It was as much of an innovation as his foreign policy, for it broke with the inherited economic system by simplifying the customs tariff. The duties on many articles of import were reduced, while a few duties were actually abolished. More particularly the duty on corn, with which word the English designate all cereal grains, instead of being kept at the established prohibitory figure, was sufficiently lowered to permit a limited importation (1823). All this was not free trade—far from it; but it was a breach with the traditional exaggerated system of protection. In final analysis it was a concession by the ruling landlord group to the new manufacturing and commercial interests which needed open avenues of trade and cheaper foreign food.

Before long, another concession to liberal opinion was recorded in the

The Dissenters relieved of civil disabilities (1828)

cancellation of the civil disabilities resting on the descendants of the Puritans, designated by law as Dissenters. Enjoying since 1689 freedom of worship, the Dissenters had gradually, by a process of connivance, been admitted to public office, although the so-called Test Acts of Charles II's reign formally excluded them. As there was no use in clinging to laws which had become ineffective, the Test Acts were in 1828 abolished, thus making the Dissenters at last full-fledged citizens, enjoying all the political rights of Anglicans.

While the cancellation of these Acts redounded also to the benefit

The Catholics restored to full civil rights (1829)

of Catholics, certain special laws excluded the Catholics from both houses of parliament. The Old Tories, led by their famous man of iron, the duke of Wellington, were very reluctant to admit the Catholics into the national legislature. But Catholic Ireland was prepared to rise in rebellion over the issue, and Wellington, in order to avoid civil war, in 1829 permitted the Catholic Emancipation Bill to become a law. Thus at last vanished the religious intolerance which the Reformation had driven so deeply into the English and Scottish law and conscience.

With the door slowly swinging open to reform, it was impossible to avoid the reform of that institution, the parliament, against which criticism aimed its sharpest shafts. As the Tories stubbornly resisted the growing agitation, they were, on the strength of a Whig victory at the polls, replaced in 1831 by a Whig ministry. In the following year a Reform bill was put through the Commons by the Whig leader, Earl Grey. When the stubborn Tory majority of the House of Lords refused to accept it, Earl Grey persuaded the reluctant King William IV to threaten, in case of continued resistance, to nominate enough new peers to assure the passage of the bill. The threat sufficed and the bill was grudgingly passed. In June, 1832, it became the law of the land. *Passing of the Reform Bill of 1832*

Far from being a radical measure, the Reform Bill was nothing other than a patchwork concession to the new manufacturing elements. It did, however, destroy the worst abuses of the old system by abolishing the rotten boroughs and by creating a more uniform franchise. At the same time it admitted the new towns of the industrial north to representation. Its two main provisions were: (1) *A redistribution of seats.* Seats to the number of 143 were taken from the rotten boroughs and redistributed in such a way as to put an end to the most glaring cases of unequal representation. (2) *A more uniform electoral franchise.* In the counties the franchise was given to all holders of land worth £10 a year; also to all tenants-at-will (a peculiar English legal category) of lands worth £50 a year. In the boroughs all occupants of *houses* (whether as owners or tenants) were given the vote, provided the house was worth £10 a year. *The Reform Bill described*

By this reform the total number of voters was approximately doubled. The increase fell, in the counties, to the farmers and tenants, in the boroughs to the middle classes. These last were the particular beneficiaries of the act since by reason of the steady expansion of manufactures after 1832 their numbers increased rapidly, enabling them to make their power felt more effectively with each new election. It would be a grave error to say that by the Reform Bill of 1832 the middle classes achieved a position of control; but it may be safely declared that, from 1832 on, the middle classes, representing developing industry, shared the power with the older aristocratic interests founded on land tenure. *Triumph of the middle classes foreshadowed by the Reform Bill*

GRADUAL SPREAD OF LIBERALISM CULMINATES IN THE SECOND REFORM BILL (1867)

The next generation witnessed a development based on the above-described situation. To prepare for it as well as possible the Whigs, who had put through the parliamentary reform and looked to middle-class support, reorganized themselves as the Liberal party. Before long, the Tories, aware that a new day had dawned and desirous of casting off the opprobrium that had come to be attached to the Tory label, presented *Whigs and Tories renamed Liberals and Conservatives* themselves to the public under the name of Conservatives. Henceforth the parliamentary battle was waged between these two heirs of the Whigs and the Tories.

That battle, even when the Conservatives were in power, exhibited the steadily growing ascendancy of reformed and liberal opinion. In order to gain the favor of the widened electorate the former Tories were themselves obliged to become the advocates of change; and conservatism came to signify hardly anything more than a more deliberate variety of liberalism. It is therefore less important to follow the succession of ministries after 1832 with their constantly shifting roster of names than it is to record important parliamentary acts and outstanding public developments indicative of the continuing movement of reform. Of the former category the abolition of Negro slavery throughout the British empire (1833) must certainly have mention. Nor may the Municipal Corporations Act of 1835 be omitted. This act was an inescapable corollary to the Reform Act, since it enabled the middle-class townsmen just admitted to the parliamentary franchise to elect and control the government of the country's industrial centers.

Plan to focus attention not on successive ministries but parliamentary acts and public events

Touching the more basic matter of the continued reform of parliament both Liberals and Conservatives took a negative position. The system, as recently corrected, was in their view as perfect as human ingenuity could make it. Unless we reflect that we are dealing with privileged groups of the population such unctuous self-satisfaction must fill us with amazement. However, to a body of writers and agitators whom contemporary opinion labeled "radicals," the narrow franchise was an unendurable scandal and they resolved to end it by drawing the lowly industrial workers on to the political scene. Since no one knew better than these slaves of the machines that the boasted Reform Bill had brought them no benefit, they willingly gathered in great mass meetings to hear the enumeration of their wrongs by their ready-tongued champions.

Radicals agitate for a widened electorate

The agitation gradually crystallized in a program laid down in a People's Charter of six such sweeping demands that they intensified to frenzy the aversion the property holders already felt toward the further enlargement of the vote. It is worth enumerating them, since they sketch a program of so advanced a democratic order that some of them still in our day await fulfillment. The demands were: (1) universal manhood suffrage; (2) annual parliamentary elections; (3) equal electoral districts; (4) the protected (secret) ballot; (5) no property qualifications for members of parliament; (6) payment of salaries to members of parliament.

Agitation comes to a head in the People's Charter

The chartist agitation lasted some ten years with many ups and downs, since the undisciplined workers deserted their upper-class organizers with much the same alacrity and ease that they gathered about them.

The movement rose to a climax in a last great effort in 1848. The Paris revolution of that year suggested to the radical manipulators to try to intimidate parliament by the presentation of a monster petition in favor of reform. When the government prepared to defend itself with troops under the now very old but still very authoritative duke of Wellington, the chartist demonstration fizzled miserably and went out.

Climax and end of chartism (1848)

It was never revived. Its weakness lay in its being the program of a radical intelligentsia and that it called for more political responsibility than the backward workers themselves wanted or even understood. Most workingmen leaders familiar with their class and its most pressing needs had therefore kept aloof from the movement. They saw that economic advancement at the moment was more important than political advancement and that the measure most immediately conducive to the betterment of the worker's lot was the expansion of trade-unionism. The British government of the past with its aristocratic and landlord complexion had always been sternly opposed to association among workers for the improvement of their status and as late as the year 1800 had passed a statute forbidding all such combinations under penalty of imprisonment. However, in 1825 the Tories, who were at the time in power and who had come to feel a certain sympathy for the workers for no better reason than that they were exploited by industrialists, owners of a form of wealth the landed Tories affected to despise, passed a bill somewhat cautiously legalizing trade-unions. Nonetheless, the act was understood to declare that combinations might be formed to press by peaceful means for the increase of wages and the shortening of the hours of work.

First cautious authorization of trade unions (1825)

The statute of 1825 was the starting-point of the vast movement of trade-unionism that marked the course of the nineteenth century. But it did not get under way with any great speed. The workers in the main were, physically, a starved and enfeebled and, morally, a groveling lot and had patiently to be brought to a higher level and braced to stand together in their own defense. Besides, chartism for a while constituted a distraction by sending many workers off on a false trail. Naturally, it was the more skilled and hence the better paid and more self-reliant workers who first took advantage of the right to organize. Then, in the course of the forties and fifties the less skilled took heart and, with collective bargaining employed as a legal weapon, succeeded without resort to violence in effecting a measurable, if often no more than inchwise, improvement of their condition. From around the middle of the century dates the federation of local unions into unions of national extent. It was followed by the formation of permanent trades councils in the leading industrial centers. When in 1864 there was held at London the first national trades union congress, which

The extraordinary advance of trade-unionism between 1825 and 1867

constituted a kind of labor parliament, trade-unionism may be said to have passed its period of growing pains and to have come of age.

Side by side with the trade-union movement went on the co-operative movement. It emanated originally from upper-class individuals of a humane and charitable disposition but did not get fairly started till the workingmen themselves took it in hand. The first thoroughly successful co-operative was established at Rochdale in 1844 and led to innumerable imitations. By buying foodstuffs and other needful supplies at wholesale and retailing them direct to their members without charging the usual middleman's profit, the co-operatives materially reduced the worker's cost of living; and when, gathering strength, the local co-operatives now proceeded to affiliate in societies of national scope, not only was the worker's cost of living still further cheapened but there was aroused in him a new pride and self-respect over his feeling himself a cog in a vast machine instituted and operated by men of his own kind throughout the land.

The humanitarians, who hardly did more than applaud the co-operative movement from the sidelines, played a more decisive role in another working-class interest. While not a particularly numerous, they were an exceedingly influential group, as they dominated the press, literature, and the arts. And what gripped their minds and hearts and forced them to strip for action was the sufferings of the factory and mine workers and the horrors of their exploitation. It will suffice to name Elizabeth Barrett Browning, the poet, and Charles Dickens, the novelist, to bring to mind that many of the leading literary figures of the day were passionately enlisted in behalf of the victims of the Industrial Revolution. By arousing public opinion over some particularly flagrant condition among the herded workers of a factory town or mining village they obliged parliament to reconsider its settled unconcern over the relations between employer and employed. The ruling classes, and particularly the industrial middle class, had adopted this attitude, familiar as laissez faire, because it accorded with their private interest; but the public defense of their position ran to the effect that intervention by the state interfered with correct economic procedure because it impaired the freedom of employer and worker to come to a mutually satisfactory agreement. While the employer argument conjured up the picture of two equals engaging in an amicable parley before coming to terms, the reality was far otherwise. The hungry, uneducated, and, in the early days, unorganized worker was absolutely at the mercy of the factory owner, who controlled all avenues to work and could dictate the most grinding conditions before he would permit the starved applicant to lay a hand to the wheel.

Under powerful pressure from the humanitarian elements parliament

The co-operative movement among the workers

Humanitarian sentiment mobilized in behalf of the workers

reluctantly and very gradually broke with its laissez faire attitude and adopted measures protective of the abused workers. The first important step on the new road was the Factory Act of 1833, and a more moderate check on the "freedom of contract" extolled by the employers as the highest economic wisdom can hardly be conceived. The law applied solely to textile mills and forbade the employment of children under nine years of age. For children between nine and thirteen and for young persons between thirteen and eighteen years it fixed a working day of nine and twelve hours respectively. As nothing was said about grown men and women, their working day might continue to run to fourteen or fifteen hours, a figure by no means unusual.

The modest beginning of Labor Legislation: the Factory Act of 1833

Worse than in the cotton mills were the labor conditions in the coal mines. The scandal cried to heaven and the humanitarian writers saw to it that it reverberated over the earth. They forced an official investigation on parliament which laid bare to the view of the nation a system exhibiting all the horrors of human slavery. The result was the Mines Act (1842), which again observed the greatest caution in laying restrictions on the captains of industry. In fact it did no more than forbid the employment in underground work of women of any age and of boys under ten years. But the ball had started to roll and could not be stopped. Every few years parliament let itself be coerced into issuing a new measure of protection, each new act more sweeping than its predecessors. In 1847 was passed the Ten Hours Bill which, though not quite so generous as the title indicated, did, however, establish a maximum working day of ten hours for all women and for "young persons" (males) under eighteen. Between 1861 and 1867 came a succession of acts by which the restrictions the earlier acts had put on the textile industries were made applicable to bleaching and dyeing establishments, bakeries, potteries, and practically to all industries whatsoever.

The Mines Act of 1842 followed by other ameliorative acts

Meanwhile the employer class, which had had the labor legislation rammed down its unwilling throat, had been compensated with a great concession, the repeal of the Corn Laws. It will be remembered that even the Tory proponents of these laws had in 1823 been induced somewhat to mitigate their severity. Presently the employers and their middle-class supporters became persuaded that what the country needed was not mitigation but outright abolition. In 1838 was formed the Anti-Corn-Law league. It grew rapidly under the executive genius of Richard Cobden and the emotional oratory of John Bright, its two leading sponsors. Abolition would mean cheaper food for the masses and, consequently, lower production costs for the manufacturers. Cobden and Bright were both well-to-do factory owners and instinctively hostile to the great profiteering landlords. With every year they gained new adherents but might not have triumphed as soon as they did, had it not been

Agitation of Cobden and Bright and repeal of the Corn Laws (1846)

for a terrible famine that visited Ireland in 1845. Owing to the almost total failure of the potato crop, over a million people died of starvation and incidental diseases. The lesson was not lost on even the Conservative party, which happened to be in power at the time under the ministry of Sir Robert Peel. A personal element figured in Peel's decision: he was not a rich landlord, like most of his party, but a rich factory owner. Against the majority of his party affiliates and with the enthusiastic support of most Liberals he put through the repeal of the Corn Laws (1846).

As soon as the protection of the leading foodstuffs had been abandoned there was no object in clinging to any feature whatever of the traditional system of customs duties. In addition to cereal grains, the existing laws protected all articles of home manufacture. With its advantage of an earlier start and its abundant supplies of coal and iron, Britain had so completely outstripped the other countries of the world in machine production that, besides completely dominating its own market, it had been able to invade those of all its neighbors. Since Britain had nothing to lose and everything to gain from an intense exchange of goods, parliament gradually swept away the import duties on hundreds of articles. By 1860 there was only a handful of dutiable articles left. Of these tea, wine, and tobacco were the most important; and even this list was maintained, not with a view to protection, for Britain grew none of these articles, but solely for revenue purposes. By these measures Great Britain had, as a result of manufacturing and middle-class pressure, thrown the ancient protectionist theories overboard and committed itself to the widely discussed but never yet tried experiment of free trade.

Adoption of Free Trade as a national policy

By the early sixties the combined effect of co-operatives, social legislation, free trade, and, above all, of the powerful growth of trade-unionism had greatly altered the national picture. Workers in general and organized labor in particular had achieved a new dignity and could no longer be denied political recognition. This was so plainly self-evident that both the Liberal and Conservative parties, headed respectively at the time by Gladstone and Disraeli, entered into rivalry with each other for the honor of enfranchising the large body of their countrymen who could no longer be ignored. After much complicated parliamentary jockeying it was the Conservatives under Disraeli who in 1867 carried the Second Parliamentary Reform Bill.

By 1867 a Second Reform Bill had become inevitable

Far from radical, the new Reform Bill was a moderate measure that followed along the lines of its moderate predecessor of 1832. It transferred 58 seats in the House of Commons from smaller to more populous boroughs. It also added twelve new seats, thereby increasing the total membership to 670. Above all—and here lies the kernel of the

The Second Reform Bill described

measure—it widened the suffrage. In case of the counties it cut the property qualification in half, while in the boroughs it enfranchised all *householders,* regardless of the rental value of the house, as well as all *lodgers in tenements,* whose lodgings were worth £10 a year. As the organized laborers could meet these conditions, it followed that the reform enfranchised substantially all trade-union members.

THE BRITISH EMPIRE

When Great Britain lost its North American colonies, prophets made themselves heard to the effect that its empire aspirations had been dealt a mortal blow. They were wrong. Even after surrendering the middle Atlantic seaboard there were left the two gains of the Seven Years' War with France, Canada and India, both of them regions of immense potentiality. Then there was the vast island-continent of Australia, won for his homeland by the explorer, Captain James Cook, in the second half of the eighteenth century. True, it was at the time of its discovery held to be a desert incapable of supporting human life, but closer examination had exploded that over-hasty judgment. If we now add Dutch South Africa, won by the Vienna settlement of 1815, it will have to be granted that Great Britain entered on the nineteenth century not only as the most far-flung colonial empire of the world but also as the empire with the greatest opportunity of a truly imperial development.

The main colonial areas of Great Britain in 1815

Immediately on the close of the Napoleonic wars a considerable British emigration set in to the vast, sparsely settled lands of Canada, Australia, and Cape Colony, under which name South Africa entered the British family. It was stimulated by an economic crisis that had gripped the island-kingdom and that was the familiar aftermath of war. Strengthened by these newcomers, the already planted colonists were organized in separate colonies or provinces, each with a limited measure of self-government. Supreme over each province was a governor appointed nominally by the king but actually by the ministry. He could veto at his pleasure any act of the local legislature. This made for unceasing friction, and in British North America led in 1837 to a revolt.

The authoritative form of colonial government

CANADA: HOME RULE FOLLOWED BY FEDERATION

The situation in British North America was at the time as follows: there were four maritime provinces, Newfoundland, Nova Scotia, New Brunswick, and Prince Edward Island, all preponderantly settled from Great Britain; along the St. Lawrence lay the province of Lower Canada, overwhelmingly French in population; and north of Lake Ontario the largely English-speaking province of Upper Canada. Although the revolt

The Canadian rebellion of 1837 and Lord Durham's report

of 1837 was easily suppressed, the British government, directed by a Liberal ministry, was sufficiently alarmed to send out as High Commissioner the extreme Liberal, Lord Durham, to investigate the situation and submit a report on it. The report was a liberal masterpiece, for it recommended first, that the existing self-government be expanded to a genuine parliamentary regime, with the governor sent from Britain playing the same purely ornamental role as did the king at home; and second, that Upper and Lower Canada should be united and that eventually the other provinces should be joined with them in a comprehensive federation.

The British parliament did not move as fast as its admirable agent. However, in 1840 it authorized the union of Upper and Lower Canada and in 1849 granted them the desired self-government. Since the favor extended to the two Canadas could not be denied the maritime provinces, they, too, were made self-governing. And when in 1859 British Columbia on the west coast, having through immigration acquired a sufficient population, asked to be raised to the self-governing level of the other provinces, its wish was promptly satisfied. The sharp-sighted Lord Durham had foreseen a future movement in favor of federation, and on its now getting under way, it led irresistibly to an experimental inter-colonial convention. Held in 1864 at Quebec, it adopted a series of constructive resolutions. These, after due consideration by the British parliament, led in their turn to the adoption (1867) of the British North America Act. It provided for a close federation of the two Canadas, Nova Scotia, and New Brunswick, to be called the Dominion of Canada. The union was to have a federal parliament of two houses, a Senate and a House of Commons, and its executive organ was to be a ministry responsible to parliament. The British government would be represented by an official called the governor general. He was to serve as a reminder of the home-tie but be substantially no better than a figurehead. The other provinces were given the privilege of joining at their pleasure which, with the exception of Newfoundland, they did after a short delay.

The Canadian solution of the very grave question as to what form the relation of mother-country and colony was to take was memorable and momentous. It left the distant colonists free to organize their lives without interference from an absentee ruler, and at the same time it safeguarded the deep-rooted cultural and sentimental ties between the adventuring settlers and their unforgotten land of origin. When, in measure as their settlement proceeded, the Australian colonies were granted self-government after the Canadian pattern, it was clear that, ultimately, federation was in the cards also for them. But that is a story belonging to a later chapter, as is also the story of the parallel movement among the colonies of South Africa. Our last word on the emergence of the Dominion of Canada in 1867 may well be that it foreshadowed that amazing multiplication of a nuclear Great Britain brought about in the twentieth century under the name of the British Commonwealth of Nations.

INDIA: ITS HISTORY UNDER BRITAIN TO 1857

The remaining great area under British control, India, constituted a case by itself, for here, in distinction from the men and women largely of British origin to be found in Canada, Australia, and South Africa, the government faced several hundred million Asiatics distributed over an immense peninsula so sharply cut off from the rest of Asia by the high and almost insurmountable barrier of the Himalaya mountains as to constitute in effect a separate continent. Far from being a unified body, the inhabitants of India fell into forty or fifty different peoples employing more than a hundred different languages. The leading influence making for union among them was the Hindu religion, to which the major portion of the population adhered. However, the Mohammedan religion commanded a considerable body of votaries, though less than half the number following Hinduism. It was a grave misfortune that Hindus and Mohammedans were stirred with spontaneous, unreflecting animosity toward each other and that consequently religion, the most important factor making for unity, was also a leading cause of India's incurable division.

India: land and people

There were other evils besides the spiritual rift between Hindus and Mohammedans, such as over-population, recurrent famines, and a rigid caste system that raised insuperable barriers among social groups. All these handicaps, which had come into existence long before the British entered the country, had converted it into as disturbed and anarchic a region as might be found anywhere under the sun. Having come originally for no other purpose than trade, the British were chiefly interested in imposing the internal peace that a flourishing trade requires and tended to regard the age-old ills of the country as none of their concern.

The age-old ills of India

The reader will recall that the penetration of India was effected, beginning in the seventeenth century, by a group of merchants associated under government protection in the East India Company. In the eighteenth century the East India Company had, with the help of the government, defeated the rival French India Company supported by the French government. Thereupon it took into its hands the administration of the various sections of the country acquired in the course of the conflict. Committed to a policy of unceasing trade expansion, the Company under ambitious governors steadily enlarged the territory under

The East India Company brings all India with its borderlands under its control

its control. Either the native princes, whose number was legion, were dispossessed and their lands annexed by force or they were brought by judicious threats into a relation of acknowledged vassalage. The abundant successes achieved by this policy in the second half of the eighteenth century were supplemented by still greater successes gathered in the course of the nineteenth century. At the same time military expeditions were sent east and west across the border of India and a wide belt of territory acquired to serve as a protective wall around the conquered land.

Growing irritation of the native population
It need hardly be said that these measures of systematic subjection and exploitation were not relished by the native population. The worst injury of all they felt to be the interference with their peculiar customs and ways of living constituting, in their sum, their distinctive civilization. With this Indian civilization the Western civilization with which the British were identified clashed violently at innumerable points. By the middle of the nineteenth century the native irritation and unrest had become so serious that any, no matter how slight, untoward incident might suffice to produce a rebellious outbreak.

The Sepoy mutiny of 1857
The East India Company maintained the peace of the land and conducted its numerous border wars with largely hireling native troops trained and led by British-born officers. These native troops were called Sepoys, and in 1857 large bodies of them stationed through northern India mutinied. The occasion may seem unbelievably trivial to inhabitants of the west but was not so to the Sepoys because of their peculiar religious beliefs and taboos. It happened, from thoughtlessness, it may be supposed, that the Sepoys had had cartridges served out to them greased with the fat of cows and pigs. This in their eyes was a deliberate insult, since the cow was a sacred animal to the Hindus, while to the Moslems pork was so offensive that they might not even touch it. Regiment after regiment rose in rebellion over the cartridge incident, murdered its British officers, and, joined by excited civil elements, committed horrible atrocities against the British traders settled among them. With the greatest promptness, because so much was at stake, the government at London prepared to suppress the mutiny and punish its authors. A campaign conducted with superior numbers and equipment quickly scattered the mutineers and wreaked a revenge on them that outdid in ferocity the worst misdeeds of the insurgents. By 1858 the struggle was over, peace again reigned in the land, and the British parliament sat down to give the whole complex Indian situation a thorough going over.

The upshot was the Better Government of India Act. First of all, it deprived the East India Company of its political power; and as, under the influence of the free-trade movement, its commercial monopoly had already been canceled a generation before, it now lost every reason for existence and quietly dissolved. In its place political authority was vested in a cabinet minister called Secretary of State for India, while the actual administration of the immense possession was intrusted to a viceroy, appointed by the crown, who ruled at Calcutta with the support of an administrative council. The native Indians continued as before to be excluded from any share in the government of their country. All that the new set-up in essence came to was that the East India Company had been succeeded as ruler of India by the presumably more efficient central government. Something would sooner or later have to be done about consulting the voiceless masses concerning their affairs; but how that was to be brought about and when was a question left for a later period to decide.

The British government assumes control

THE INDUSTRIAL REVOLUTION

ORIGIN AND SPREAD OF MECHANIZATION

Rise of the English middle classes

IT HAS BEEN repeatedly emphasized in the course of this book that a leading consequence of the modern politico-social development had been to give an increasing importance to the middle classes, and that up to the time of the French Revolution it was the middle classes of Holland and England which had reaped the greatest benefits from an altered world. Among them the abandonment of older attitudes and customs and the experimentation with new ways had gone farther than among any other broadly corresponding groups. It is therefore not surprising that it was, in the main, under pressure from the English middle classes that the stiffnecked monarchy of the Stuarts had been replaced by the parliamentary regime.

The gild system replaced by the domestic system

It was also in England that the medieval gild system, which minutely regulated the production and sale of goods, first gave way. By the eighteenth century, when the gilds still exercised an unbroken domination over the industry of countries like France and Germany, they had as good as vanished altogether from English soil. In their place had appeared, above all in the flourishing textile industry, a free contract arrangement, in accordance with which a small number of wholesalers advanced the raw material (wool, cotton) to individual workers, who converted it into the finished fabric in their homes and on its redelivery to the wholesaler effected a financial settlement. Under this system, commonly called the domestic system, the workers laboring in their homes still had the appearance of independent producers. It is evident, however, that they had become dependent on a well-to-do man or group of men who had advanced the raw material and who determined the price to be paid the worker for the finished article.

The gild system opposed to change

Such a system attached a wholly novel importance to personal initiative and stimulated the spirit of invention. In any case it was again in England, after gild obstructionism had become a thing of the past, that men first perfected devices which greatly improved the ancient processes of the textile industry. It would be easy to prove that so long as the gild system, whether in England or elsewhere, exercised its conservative sway, the manufacturing processes would follow the same familiar groove for centuries.

But there is something besides the decay of the gild system and the birth of inventions that accounts for the transformation of the English industrial scene. That something, as fundamental as either, is known to trade as the market. The enterprising men whose purpose it was to dispose of goods in quantity lots originally made their plans with an eye to the national, that is, the English market. Before long they took in the neighboring continental markets, and on the growth of the American colonies, where they enjoyed a trade monopoly, they gave these dependencies a very particular attention. The market outlook was therefore constantly widening and became a powerful stimulus to the production of more goods, chiefly textiles. In all the above-listed areas, moreover, the population was on the increase, which meant, always keeping the textile industry in mind, more bodies to clothe. Now add that the standard of living was rising and we face an increased consumption of the individual buyer. The only way to meet this expanding demand for goods was either to employ more workers or, if workers were not indefinitely available, to improve their tools. Not till this market pressure obliged human ingenuity to exert itself did inventions make their appearance.

Market pressure as a factor prompting invention

The two main devices of the textile industry were the spinning wheel for making yarn or thread and the loom for making cloth. The spinning wheel and loom of the early eighteenth century were still essentially what they had been since the Middle Ages and almost, we may add, from time immemorial. In 1753 a certain John Kay patented a "flying shuttle" which speeded up the carrying of the weft across the warp and easily doubled the amount of cloth one man could produce in a working day. It came only slowly into general use, as workers, being conservative by nature, preferred the traditional practice. The statement holds for all subsequent inventions and explains the rather deliberate pace of industrial advance. Around 1767 James Hargreaves made a frame with eight spindles, wherewith one worker by turning a wheel could spin eight threads where by the same expenditure of effort but one thread had been spun before. In honor of his wife Hargreaves called his invention the "spinning jenny." Invention was now launched on its way and hardly a year passed without some improvement being added to the already achieved spinning and weaving novelties. Thus Samuel Crompton in 1779 devised a "spinning mule" and Edward Cartwright followed in 1785 with a "power" loom, called so because the motive power for his loom was supplied no longer by men but by horses. We get some idea of the imperfect and experimental character of these early inventions when we learn that it took several decades of continued testing and adjusting

Early spinning and weaving improvements

before Cartwright's power loom was sufficiently established to invite general adoption.

Other inventions come to the aid of the textile industry

Inventions and discoveries in other fields came to the aid of the textile industry. Chemicals were made available for more rapid bleaching; they were followed by a series of new chemical dyes. A large percentage of the cotton output was in the form of printed calicos, and in 1785 a cylindrical machine was invented by Thomas Bell that greatly speeded up calico printing. No less important was the labor-saving device elaborated by an American, Eli Whitney. In 1792 he built the "cotton gin," which separated the cotton seeds from the raw cotton and did the work of innumerable plantation "hands." The invention, coupled with the growing demand for cotton by the English market, transformed the southern belt of the United States into the world's greatest cotton-raising area with the double result of making the exporting planters rich beyond their dreams and of clamping the yoke of slavery on their Negro plantation workers apparently to the end of time.

Development of the mining industry

To the textile expansion the simultaneous development of the mining industry made an invaluable contribution. Indeed, without it the textile development would not have got very far. England possessed abundant supplies of coal and iron but before the eighteenth century there was not much demand for either. The common fuel of the past as far back as the dawn of history had been wood, and its recent reckless consumption was visibly destroying the English forests. In addition to a hundred other uses, wood was also, through its conversion to charcoal, employed for smelting iron ore. As wood became more scarce and consequently more expensive, it occurred to smelters to substitute the cheap and easily obtainable coal for wood and, after some failures, a method was discovered for converting coal to the more efficient coke. A furnace charged with coke and iron ore and with a water-driven bellows to blow air into the charge was found just as serviceable for producing iron and decidedly more economical than the old charcoal furnace. As an index of development we may note that the output of smelted iron, called "pig iron," increased from 10,000 tons in 1700 to 50,000 tons in 1770. However, the "pig iron" contained many impurities which weakened it and impaired its usefulness. It was therefore another forward stride when Henry Cort in 1784 developed certain "processes" by which iron acquired a greater purity and toughness. It was thus put on its way to becoming high-grade steel.

Now only was it possible to build an efficient steam engine. New-comen's engine, constructed as early as 1712, had proved serviceable in the coal industry, where it was used to pump water out of mines; but its inadequacies were so numerous that engineers despaired for a long time of improving it. To this unhappy defeatism James Watt (1736-

1819), a Scotsman, put an end. In 1769 he patented a workable steam engine which he continued in the following years steadily to improve. Not, however, till around 1800 had the steam engine acquired the safety and efficiency that made possible its general adoption as the motive power for the new spinning and weaving machinery. An unavoidable consequence was that this constantly enlarged machinery, hitherto constructed of wood, had also, like the steam engine, to be made of iron. In sum, by 1800 unmistakable signs pointed to the coming of what was then appropriately called the coal-and-iron age.

Watt invents an engine which can drive the new textile inventions

Without cheap and abundant coal and iron the next industry to be developed, the transportation industry, would have made no headway. The newly risen large-scale manufacturers naturally clamored for better means of getting the raw cotton to the mills and the finished product to the market. This signified, in the first instance, hard-surfaced roads and, wherever practicable, easy water communication by a network of canals. In the early decades of the nineteenth century a notable development of these two simple travel facilities took place. A special problem was posed by the need of transporting such heavy commodities as coal and iron, and presently the thoughts of some mine owners turned to Watt's steam engine as a desirable replacement of horses for drawing coal cars. Experimentation went on apace but was not even partially effective till 1825, when George Stephenson built a locomotive that hauled a number of coal cars over iron rails for the short distance between a mine in Durham and the port of Stockton. Because it proved too expensive, this railroad was again abandoned; and it was not till 1830 that Stephenson's son, Robert Stephenson, designed a really successful locomotive, called the *Rocket,* which ran between the cotton center of Manchester and the port of Liverpool. There followed at once the building of other short stretches of railroad till between 1840 and 1850 railroad building became a mania and in a few years covered England with a close network of thousands of miles of track.

The steam engine made available for transportation purposes

Even before the successful application of the steam engine to transport by land it had been applied to travel by water. After viewing attempts along this line made in England, Robert Fulton (1765-1815), an American, returned to his homeland and constructed a paddle-wheel steamer, the *Clermont,* which in 1807 began to ply between New York and Albany. Steamers now rapidly took over the river traffic in both America and Europe, but for a long time ocean-shipping was beyond their reach and remained the province of amazingly improved sailing vessels. Not till ocean steamers were given iron hulls to increase their cargo space and the paddle wheel was supplanted by the propeller, and that was not till past the half-century, did they prove a financially profitable

The first river steamer (1807) not followed at once by ocean steamers

venture. Their long up-hill struggle is evidenced by the fact that it was not till 1870 that the world's ocean-steamer tonnage began to catch up with its sailing tonnage and not till about 1900 that sailing tonnage became definitely a minor factor in world shipping.

Improved communications: telegraph and telephone

Transportation is a subdivision of a vaster field, communication, and communication was greatly advanced by the contemporary development of electricity. For a long time the advances in electricity were exclusively in the department of theory. The first important practical application of the new knowledge that had been garnered made its appearance in 1837, when Charles Wheatley in England and Samuel Morse in America simultaneously patented an electric telegraph. With unbelievable speed wires began to be stretched along telegraph poles till these carefully aligned rows of stripped tree-trunks became a conspicuous, if not a beautifying, feature of the European and American landscape. In 1851 a cable carrying a telegraph wire was strung between the French and English coasts, and in 1866 a similar and more powerful cable was laid across the Atlantic ocean, establishing instantaneous communication between Great Britain and the United States. Some four decades later Alexander Graham Bell invented the telephone (1876), which promptly achieved universal use.

The Industrial Revolution passes to the continent and the United States

The period between 1770 and 1830 is usually designated as the pioneering stage of the Industrial Revolution and was, in the main, limited to Great Britain. It was followed by a main stage extending from 1830 to 1870 and, with subsequent fortifying developments, down to our own time. Two outstanding phenomena of the main stage deserve special attention: first, the uninterrupted transformation of innumerable hand industries into machine industries; and second, the spread of the whole industrial movement to the European continent and the United States. As the process of mechanical transformation has received a fair measure of attention in treating the textile and mining industries, we can leave the later transformation of the printing, milling, lumbering, and scores of other industries to the imagination and concentrate on the spread of the Industrial Revolution to England's neighbors.

The early industrialization of Belgium

No European country even attempted to follow in England's footsteps till the peace that attended the overthrow of Napoleon. Almost at once Belgium undertook a movement of mechanization with the indirect help of English capital and the direct help of English engineers. However, not till after 1830 did the movement gain momentum. It was then so sharply speeded up that by 1870 Belgium had become the most densely populated country of Europe and, making allowance for the difference in size, as intensively industrialized as its British exemplar.

In France industrialization proceeded more slowly and never at any time remotely achieved the Belgian thoroughness. France had always been distinguished by an active, thrifty peasantry, and this numerous class saw to it that the country did not abandon its vigorous agricultural tradition. Nonetheless, the Industrial Revolution gradually got a foothold, showing results, first of all, in mining and metallurgy. With the reign of Louis Philippe (1830-1848) the bourgeoisie came into political control and turned with enthusiasm both to machine industry and railroad construction. As the French had long specialized in luxury articles produced by hand, power-driven machinery was slow to establish itself in the textile industry. However, here too it gained ground, especially on Louis Philippe's being followed by Napoleon III, who was just as friendly to the bourgeoisie and far more sympathetic with its material ambitions. Since the riches of France in coal and iron lay in the north and east it was on these areas that the Industrial Revolution took particular hold. *Industrializing of France slower and less complete*

Germany, composed after 1815 of thirty-eight sovereign states, was even slower than France to take up the Industrial Revolution. The establishment in the thirties of the *Zollverein,* whereby almost all the German states became a single economic unit, stimulated business enterprise and marked the earliest stage of industrialization. Promise of a possible future development lay in the possession by the various states of very considerable resources of coal and iron, but the promise remained unfulfilled till the political unification achieved in 1870. However, railroad building got an early start under state direction and proved an incentive to increased production. In any case rapid, and finally even precipitate, industrialization did not set in till the unification date. In such other continental countries as Italy and Austria-Hungary industrialization came even later than in Germany and never acquired a comparable energy. Farther east, in backward Russia, mechanization delayed its appearance till the very end of the nineteenth century. *The case of Germany and the other large European states*

In the United States of America the Industrial Revolution acquired a modest foothold in the eastern seaboard states in the early decades of the nineteenth century and, by the time of the Civil War, was so well established that it was largely owing to their industrial superiority that the northern states were able to crush the agricultural southern Confederacy. No sooner had the Civil War ended than mechanization went forward with giant strides and has continued to do so to our own time. An energetic population took advantage of the country's unrivaled resources in coal, iron, copper, zinc, and practically every desirable raw material, and long before 1900 had carried the United States abreast of the world's industrial leaders with every prospect of ultimately heading the procession. *The intensive industrialization of the United States*

LEADING SOCIAL AND ECONOMIC CONSEQUENCES OF THE INDUSTRIAL REVOLUTION

In turning now to the leading social and economic consequences of the Industrial Revolution let us be clear in our mind that it is rarely possible to distinguish between them, as every economic change develops a social by-product and vice versa. We shall start with four of the more immediately apparent consequences and close with two that are more complicated and deep-delving.

1. Increase of Wealth as Measured by Articles of Use. By its method of mass production the Industrial Revolution enormously increased possessions, especially of articles of use. Not only were clothes, shoes, hats, china, carpets, chairs, and other personal and household goods thrown on the market in hitherto unheard-of quantities but, produced by machines at a lower cost, they could be sold at a lower price. The lower price in its turn stimulated consumption and attracted an increasing number of buyers. British statistics show that the value of cotton manufactures rose from $1,000,000 in 1760 to $600,000,000 in 1910. If we assume that half of each total was exported and allow for a greatly increased population, we still have an increased individual consumption of cotton goods in Britain of something like two hundred per cent. A similar if not so large an increase may be assumed for many articles besides cotton goods. However, it must not be overlooked that the distribution was very uneven: it hardly, if at all, benefited the mass of the poor.

2. The Manufacturing Towns Are Located near the Coal and Iron Beds. The new means of transportation, railways and steamboats, made it possible to tap supplies of raw products which in the days of the horse-drawn vehicle and the sailing vessel were inaccessible. Nonetheless, because long hauls increase production costs and it is cheaper to transport finished goods than the much bulkier raw products, manufacturing centers have as a rule arisen in close proximity to coal and iron deposits. The accompanying map, which locates the main coal and iron areas of Europe, brings out most interestingly their relationship to the main industrial regions.

3. The Search for Markets Culminates in Imperialism. In measure as goods were multiplied beyond the power of the European people to absorb them, it became necessary to find American, African, and Asiatic markets on which to unload the surplus. In this way it happened that somewhat past the middle of the nineteenth century the European states entered on a new and more intensive phase of colonial expansion. This, toward the end of the century, became a savage competitive scramble

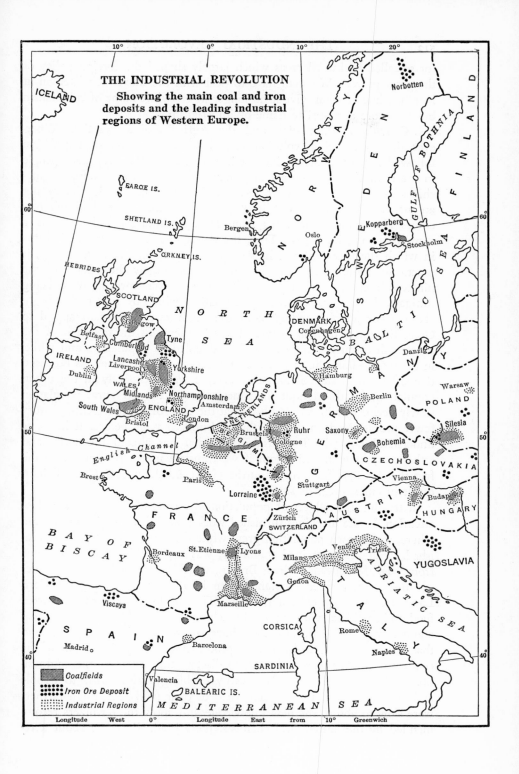

THE INDUSTRIAL REVOLUTION
Showing the main coal and iron deposits and the leading industrial regions of Western Europe.

ICELAND

FAROE IS.

SHETLAND IS.

ORKNEY IS.

HEBRIDES

SCOTLAND

Glasgow

Belfast

Cumberland

IRELAND

Lancashire
Liverpool

Dublin

Tyne

Yorkshire

WALES

Midlands

Northamptonshire

South Wales

ENGLAND

Bristol

London

Amsterdam

English Channel

Brest

Paris

Lorraine

FRANCE

BAY OF BISCAY

Bordeaux

St.Etienne

Lyons

Viscaya

Marseille

Madrid

Barcelona

Valencia

SPAIN

CORSICA

SARDINIA

BALEARIC IS.

MEDITERRANEAN SEA

NORWAY

Bergen

Oslo

NORTH SEA

DENMARK
Copenhagen

SWEDEN

Kopparberg

Stockholm

BALTIC SEA

GULF OF BOTHNIA

FINLAND

Norbotten

POLAND

Warsaw

Danzig

Hamburg

Berlin

GERMANY

NETHERLANDS

BELGIUM

Brussels

Ruhr

Cologne

Saxony

Silesia

Bohemia

CZECHOSLOVAKIA

Stuttgart

Zürich

SWITZERLAND

Vienna

AUSTRIA

Budapest

HUNGARY

Milan

Venice

Trieste

Genoa

ITALY

Rome

Naples

ADRIATIC SEA

YUGOSLAVIA

Coalfields

Iron Ore Deposit

Industrial Regions

Longitude   West   0°   Longitude   East   from   10°   Greenwich

for so-called backward areas which largely shaped the foreign policy of the great powers. We shall have to deal with the movement later on at length, when we shall give it no longer its erstwhile name of colonialism but the more appropriate name of imperialism.

4. Growth of Population and the Agricultural Revolution. Wherever the Industrial Revolution took hold, an increase of population followed for a number of inter-acting reasons. In the first place people in great numbers abandoned the country for the towns, where the machines needing workers were located. This of itself would signify not an increase but merely a shift of population. But the call of the machines also drew immigrants from foreign countries and acted as a stimulus to the birth rate. True, the death rate in the wretched slums in which the workers were herded was so high that, at least at first, it practically nullified the increased birth rate. But by the middle of the nineteenth century the evils resulting from overcrowding were being mitigated by progressive sanitary regulation, which by 1900 had brought about a considerable reduction of the death rate. We again appeal to Great Britain as offering a typical development. In the first half of the nineteenth century Britain more than doubled its population, and while, in the second half, the rate of increase slackened, still there was no cessation of growth. But observe: the increase was exclusively in the urban population, for throughout the nineteenth century the rural population slowly declined, with the result that at the close of the nineteenth century fewer people lived on the soil than a hundred years before. It helps us understand how the Industrial Revolution has altered the social and esthetic aspect of the kingdom if we translate into a mental image the fact that by 1900 fully three-fourths of the inhabitants of Great Britain dwelt in cities, great or small.

In treating the subject of population, the issue of food calls for close attention. While machines furnished work they did not feed mouths, and where, if the town population grew while the country population diminished, or at best remained stationary, was the additional food to come from? To this question Great Britain, which we are using for purposes of illustration, defined its stand when in 1846 by abolishing the Corn Laws it ceased to protect agriculture. That meant resorting to imported food, to be paid for with exported machine products. However, there was another way which Britain could have followed, and partially did, and that was to make agriculture more productive. For, by the middle of the century chemistry was beginning to disclose the secrets of the composition and enrichment of soils, thereby enabling agriculturists to double and even quadruple the per acre yield of their fields. Although farmers were slow to absorb the new knowledge and apply the fertilizers recommended by the agricultural chemists, there gradually came about a reformed agriculture in all the more advanced countries of the world which, in effect, paralleled the Industrial Revolution with an Agricultural Revolution. Its importance can hardly be exaggerated, for, without the tremendous increase of food production which the Agricultural Revolution made possible, the increase of population stimulated by the Industrial Revolution would have been halted at an early stage.

5. **Industrial Capitalism.** Capital and capitalism have from the start figured in this book. We have tried to make clear that capital has been present in society from the earliest times when it signified so simple a thing as "savings" (p. 253). And that is what capital signifies, fundamentally, to this day. When, in the Renaissance, individual savings began to be assembled by merchant companies or banks for the purpose of undertaking risky, distant enterprises, we encounter what we may call organized or company capitalism and with the progressive enlargement of trade in the seventeenth and eighteenth centuries this company capitalism was progressively intensified. With the arrival of the Industrial Revolution we get a further and greatly magnified intensification, in the course of which capitalism took such a firm hold on every economic activity that it brought all society within the range of its influence. We may define the new phase as Industrial Capitalism and justify the term by showing how it originated and operates.

As soon as the decision was made in favor of machines, capitalism at once waxed in stature, because money had to be found first, for the machines, which were expensive, and second, for the factories in which they were to be housed. Nor was that all, since funds had also to be made available for wages to be paid out before there was any return from the sale of goods. Therewith we come face to face with the investment system, which goes back at least to the Renaissance phase of capitalism and, like it, has since become progressively intensified. By means of the investment system industry and commerce draw the capital they require to function not only from the opulent few but also from members of such professions as law and medicine, from clerks and other members of the so-called white collar class, and even from the better-paid workers. All these groups command savings, possibly small, certainly not large in amount, from which they desire a return either in the form of interest on bonds or dividends on certificates of ownership called shares.

Nonetheless, the relatively broad role of the general public in the latest phase of capitalism must not induce us to close our eyes to the fact that the control of the invested sums that keep the wheels of industry and commerce turning was taken over by a picked body of bankers and managers in immediate charge of the various business undertakings. Here is perhaps the most characteristic feature of the Age of Industrial

Capitalism: the money supplied by the many was employed by the few often enough to advance their own selfish interest and with little or no regard for the many small and widely scattered shareholders, constituting the body of legal owners.

6. Depressed Status of the Industrial Workers. In broaching the status of the industrial workers we raise an issue which, from a strictly human angle, is the most important development of the Industrial Revolution. We have touched on the matter before but must now be more explicit. On being drawn from their homes, where they had labored in at least a kind of semi-independence at spinning wheel and loom, the migrants settled in such accommodations as they could find close to the factories that housed the machines. At once they learned that they were at the mercy of the employers, who owned the only available means of livelihood and presented the applicants for work with the alternative of working at the offered terms or starving. They were unknown to one another, they lacked even the rudiments of an education, and their repressed rural life had not taught them to exercise a bold initiative. Should they, however, be prompted by their misery to combine in the hope of improving their situation, they encountered statutory legislation of ancient date which forbade them to form associations with a view to increasing their wages or reducing their hours of labor. The British parliament had renewed such a prohibitive statute as late as the year 1800, when the Industrial Revolution was already well on its way. At the time the measure was voted the wages of textile workers were literally starvation wages and the working day was commonly reckoned at from twelve to fourteen hours!

Besides low wages and long hours of work there was the further evil of periodic unemployment. Again and again unemployment descended like a bludgeon, sometimes owing to the ever-recurring industrial crises, sometimes to the employer's discovering that men could be dispensed with because women and children were able and willing to perform the same work at a reduced wage. The attendant social degradation completes the picture. The towns, springing up like mushrooms around the factories, exhibited a disorder indicative of the complete absence of anything remotely resembling a plan on the part of the town authorities. The workers and their families were herded in cheap tenements constituting a slum, with disgustingly filthy streets and the scantiest supply of such hygienic necessities as light, heat, and water. Of course disease became rampant, periodically assuming an epidemic form and mowing down its victims by the hundreds. Even in the most favorable years the death rate of the slum was high; among infants and children, more particularly, owing to the lack of milk, soap, and fresh air, it was so excessive as to reach the proportions of a national calamity.

Since the middle classes had launched the Industrial Revolution and were intensely proud of their achievement, we may fairly charge them with the resulting degradation of the workers. It behooves us therefore to turn our attention to the middle classes and examine their regime and philosophy or, to give it a less pretentious name, their politico-economic outlook.

THE POLITICO-ECONOMIC OUTLOOK OF THE (CHIEFLY BRITISH) MIDDLE CLASSES

Since the "Glorious Revolution" of 1688 was mainly a product of the British middle classes, it was already possible at that time to speak of their program, especially as it received a much heralded exposition at the hands of their most authoritative spokesman, John Locke. Nonetheless, it was not till, in the course of the Revolution of 1789, the French bourgeoisie proclaimed a practically identical program that it was adopted by the middle classes throughout the continent. And so firm a hold did it take on them that even the autocracy of Napoleon and the general reaction that followed his overthrow did not cause it to disappear. Under the name of liberalism it became the openly or secretly avowed faith of the temporarily depressed burgher elements. At the close of our story of Napoleon (Chapter 21) we took note of its persistence and enumerated its articles of faith under five heads: limited monarchy (or constitutionalism), sovereignty of the people, equality of all before the law, religious toleration, and nationalism.

The substance of liberalism

Around this program of liberalism, essentially political in import, the domestic development of every country of the continent revolved during the first half of the nineteenth century. The development of Great Britain during the same period also revolved around it, except that in Britain it took on a somewhat altered aspect, owing to the incorporation of an article from the economic field. To grasp how this came about we must recall the eighteenth century preachment of laissez faire by the French physiocrats and its free-trade equivalent, advocated by Adam Smith. Laissez faire and free trade were counter-proposals to the existing practice of mercantilism, on the strength of which governments, in the supposed interest of their peoples, undertook narrowly to regulate their economic life and arbitrarily to manipulate the processes of production and distribution.

British liberalism carries an economic rider

Stimulated by the teaching of Adam Smith and much more by the picture under their eyes of the extraordinary expansion of British industry, observers of a scholarly bent undertook to examine the contemporary economic phenomena in the objective manner of the natural scientists to the end of discovering their "laws." Before long they had formu-

Rise of the "classical" school of political economy

lated a body of such "laws" or, it is more prudent to say, economic doctrines, which to themselves and their generation seemed so irrefutable
that they were acclaimed as "classical" and their propounders as the first
or "classical" school of the new science of political economy.

Among the shining lights of the school we may select Thomas Malthus
(d. 1834). Malthus held that since population tends to increase faster
than the food supply, it can be checked (for checked it must be) either
by famine, war, and pestilence or by abstention from procreation by
individuals incapable of supporting a family. He presented this abhorrent
alternative as a law of nature on a par with the succession of the sea-
sons and the daily revolution of the earth around its axis, and concluded
that, if the factory workers did not observe it and together with their
families died of starvation, they had only themselves to blame. Another
"classical" economist was David Ricardo (d. 1823). He, too, held that
every national economy operated under immutable laws, some of which
he, a latter-day Newton, had the happiness of discovering and formulating. Among them was what he called "the iron law of wages." By the
operation of this law, he declared, it was forever impossible for workingmen to earn anything more than what was necessary for bare subsistence.

From these samples of their pronouncements it is clear that the "classical" economists were conscious or unconscious mouthpieces of the rising industrialists and that they advocated with pseudo-scientific detachment every variety of freedom beneficial to their clients: free trade, free
contract (meaning the right of the employer to "hire and fire" workingmen at his pleasure and without redress on their part), freedom of
competition, and, of course, freedom from interference on the part of the
government, moved to intervene in behalf of the workers on the erroneous
theory that their hard lot was due to their masters when, in point of fact,
it derived from immutable "natural laws." For at least the extreme champions of the "classical" ideology the state was to become an institution
of such exemplary modesty that it habitually kept out of sight. Should
it step forth into the light of day, it was to do so reluctantly in the role
of a policeman called to maintain order and arrest disturbers of the peace.
Generally speaking, the state was to entrust the economic field, that is,
the whole vast area concerned with the struggle for a livelihood, to the
middle classes, endowed, morally, with courage and initiative, and, materially, with the indispensable machines and factories.

Into the generally current political liberalism of the first half of the
nineteenth century the British liberals, and to a less extent their compeers on the continent, imported the above-enumerated economic freedoms, and they held their place in the party program till far into the
century's second half. They then began to drop out of view, to be at last

completely abandoned. The turn-about, involving a considerable re-definition of liberalism, will be made clear at the close of this chapter. At this point it suffices to caution the student against the loose use not only of the word "liberalism" but also of the even less determinate word "liberal." They are both weasel words, as are also, though to less degree, such words as capitalism, socialism, and individualism. Abstractions, alas, are hard to hold to a definite content. However, since the just cited abstractions represent operating historical forces, they will have to continue to be employed in historical exposition, with sleepless attention, let us hope, to their fluctuating meaning. And once more and, finally, let us be clear that the liberalism of the early nineteenth century was the characteristic faith of the middle classes and that a central feature of that faith, especially in Great Britain, was that the masters of enterprise or, as we in America collectively call them, the business men, should be left free to conduct their affairs with no interference on the part of the government, acting in the supposed interest of the general public or of an oppressed section thereof.

Liberalism casts off its "classical" doctrine but not till late in the nineteenth century

ATTACK ON THE MIDDLE-CLASS PROGRAM CULMINATES IN MARXIAN SOCIALISM

From the very beginning of the Industrial Revolution the advancing middle classes encountered criticism and opposition which, scattered and unsystematic at first, steadily gained in power till, long before the close of the nineteenth century, it put the middle classes completely on the defensive. As long as the workers themselves were insufficiently organized, they offered no better than a feeble resistance to the masters of the machines; the prophecy might have been ventured even in those early days that until the workers opened battle in their own behalf their depressed condition would not be effectively remedied. And so, in fact, it fell out; and since working-class organization was slow to get under way, it did not develop genuine fighting strength till the second half of the nineteenth century. If we turn for evidence to Great Britain, where worker initiative was first to appear, we have already noted in our British chapter (p. 495) that it was not till 1825 that parliament gave a somewhat ambiguous permission to workers to combine for the purpose of increasing wages and reducing the hours of work, and that it was not till almost half a century later (1867) that parliament went the length of politically enfranchising the trade-union membership. As the continent lagged far behind Britain, we are on safe ground when we contend that the movement of worker self-help was ineffective during the early decades of the nineteenth century.

Worker opposition slow to take shape

The first efforts in behalf of the workers were made by individuals moved to compassion by the misery and suffering that met their eyes. They belonged either to the middle classes or to the nobility and, in their attempt to mitigate some of the most crying evils of the factory towns, they created associations for giving medical aid, improving the housing conditions, distributing milk among babies, and other similar relief purposes. Activities of this nature come under the head of philanthropy. While conceding that philanthropy alleviates suffering and honors those who sincerely practice it, we cannot but agree that it only scratches the surface and does not represent a serious attack on the rooted evils of industrialism.

Philanthropy comes to the aid of the workers

Philanthropy is an offspring of the larger humanitarian movement which was a feature of eighteenth century liberalism and which, in spite of the rise of the harsh "classical" economy, refused to die in the nineteenth century. That it persisted here and there even among successful factory owners is evidenced by the case of Robert Owen (1771-1858). He indulged in generous-hearted social work among his own employees at his large cotton mill in Scotland and became the advocate of a plan of profit-sharing between owner and workers. At his own expense he started a number of enterprises of this sort, one of them at New Harmony, Indiana, but they lacked a sound foundation and failed. In France similar projects were set forth by Saint Simon (d. 1825) and Fourier (d. 1837). Saint Simon advocated a co-operative state directed by scientists and engineers, and Fourier sponsored the organization of society into co-operative groups, which he called phalanxes. While both agreed that the system of capitalist control would have to be abandoned if ever the workers were to have their due, they built up nothing that outlived their own day.

Humanitarians devise plans to help the workers

It has become customary to label Owen, Saint Simon, Fourier, and others of their generation who projected similar plans as Utopian socialists on the ground that their proposals got nowhere because they were not rooted in the realities of the economic situation. The Frenchman, Louis Blanc (1811-1882), carries the same label, owing to the fact that his much-mooted cure of worker oppression, "national workshops" to be financed by the state, still had a richly visionary character. Utopian or not, these men should certainly be regarded as socialists since, one and all, they were opposed to the individualism implicit in middle-class liberalism and hoped to replace it with some form of co-operation or collectivism. For an unqualified individualism is what the many freedoms making up the liberal faith came to. This individualism proclaimed as its economc ideal the untrammeled man who practiced an enlightened selfishness and who, in his pursuit of wealth and happiness, was not to be hampered by government action. It was specifically against this outlook

The so-called Utopians, as anti-individualists, define themselves as socialists

that the early company of philanthropists, humanitarians, and Utopians in varying degree reacted. They thus gave birth to an anti-individualist movement for which the most appropriate name is socialism and which was destined to grow until the time came when it was able to do battle with triumphant individualism on equal terms.

The man who did more than anyone else to make socialism a power among workers and in the world at large was Karl Marx. His variety of socialism is usually set off from that of his Utopian predecessors by being called "scientific"; and scientific it may be called if we agree that a close study and analysis of the facts involved in the conflict between capital and labor are the substance of science. Karl Marx (1818-1883) was a German Jew, a native of Rhenish Prussia, who, after studying philosophy and winning the doctor's degree at the University of Jena, published a liberal newspaper until it was suppressed by the Prussian police. He then lived as an exile in France and Belgium till the revolution of 1848 enabled him to return to Germany and re-establish his original newspaper. In the same year there returned to Germany a man with whom Marx had become joined in a friendship that was to be broken only by death, Friedrich Engels. Like Marx a native of Rhenish Prussia, Engels had as a young man been sent to England by his father, a prosperous cotton-spinner, to take charge of a branch factory near Manchester. There the degradation of the workers had so profoundly disturbed him that he had enlisted in their cause with all his heart and mind. When the revolution of 1848 sounded its tocsin, he hurried back to Germany to join forces with Marx in the movement of liberation.

Karl Marx and Friedrich Engels

On the failure of the revolution the friends were obliged to flee. But their efforts had not been wholly in vain, for at the height of the insurrection they had issued a pamphlet, the *Communist Manifesto*, which became the fundamental charter of socialism. There was still, as has already been observed, a certain fluctuation in the terminology employed in connection with the economic struggle of the day, and therefore it is not strange that what Marx and Engels issued as a *Communist Manifesto* was by themselves afterward declared to be a socialist manifesto. On taking refuge, this time in England in the vicinity of Engels, Marx continued his economic studies and in 1867 put out the first volume of a complex work, called *Capital*, wherein he showed in detail the various ways in which the capitalists exploited the workers. The last two volumes were not published till after Marx's death, under the editorship of the devoted and ever self-effacing co-author of the *Manifesto* and doubtless also with important, unindicated contributions from his pen.

The fundamental socialist writings: the "Communist Manifesto" and "Capital"

As set forth by the above-mentioned works and numerous special articles as well, Marxian socialism is not only an economic theory but also a way of life. In opposition to current middle-class views, with their

Marxian socialism stresses equality and co-operation

emphasis on freedom and individualism, it stressed equality and the good of the working masses to be achieved by co-operative action. The equality which is its goal will be attained when the many take over from the few the machines, the railways, the mines, in sum, the total characteristic means of modern production. The transfer need not be accomplished by violence and bloodshed. It may, indeed it must, result from the continuing action of historical forces, which operate like laws of nature and from which there is no escape.

The two major Marxian concepts: economic determinism and class conflict

And therewith we come upon Marx's philosophy of history, usually described as "economic determinism." The expression signifies that, according to Marx, the material and economic conditions prevailing in a particular society at a particular time exclusively determine the character of its civilization, including its religion, its morals, and its art. If, this much conceded, we reflect that no society and no civilization are ever at a standstill but eternally in process of change, it follows that the class in possession of power is always threatened by a repressed but rising class aspiring to replace it. This is the famous doctrine of "class conflict," which Marx illustrated from the history of Europe in something after the following fashion: When in the age of feudalism the land-holders ruled society, they found themselves gradually challenged by the urban middle classes, which by the nineteenth century had succeeded in pushing the feudal masters from the seats of power; but by reason of the ever operative class struggle the middle classes were now in their turn challenged by the workers, a new class which the middle classes with their factory system had themselves called into being. As the mass of the workers is constantly growing, they will presently so overwhelmingly outnumber their masters that it will be an easy (and probably bloodless) task to dispossess them and vest the title to the appropriated means of production in the commonalty. This triumph will give us the final, the socialist, society and civilization.

The Marxian tactics

Now, while the socialist order is bound to be brought about by the operation of relentless historical forces, the workers can hasten the day by becoming class-conscious. This requires their absorption of the Marxian faith coupled with their unalterable determination to rebuild society in accordance with the Marxian program. To this end they must stand shoulder to shoulder like an army marching to conquest. As a class name for this army Marx proposed the word proletariat (meaning the unpropertied, the disinherited), and with the purpose of winning them to united action supplied them with an electrifying slogan: "Proletarians of all countries, unite! You have nothing to lose but your chains!"

By 1864 the Marxian cause had made enough converts throughout Europe for Marx to attempt to give them an organization. He founded the International Workingmen's association, afterward called the First

International. It remained feeble, was riven by internal division, and in the early seventies decreed its own dissolution. Luckily for the perpetuation of the movement, a strong workingmen's party came into existence in Germany in 1875 which under the able leadership of Wilhelm Liebknecht and August Bebel prospered extraordinarily. It called itself the Social Democratic party of Germany and urged the formation of similar parties by the workingmen of all the neighboring countries. The short-lived First International

The creation of national Social Democratic parties followed so rapidly that within a decade or two they were to be found practically everywhere. In each instance they commanded a growing following of workers (usually with a sprinkling of intellectuals), conducted newspapers, elected representatives to parliament, and set up a very active propaganda apparatus. Thus encouraged, in 1889 they dispatched delegates to Paris, where they created an international federation of Social Democratic parties, the so-called Second International. It maintained a permanent central office and held rousing periodic congresses until overtaken by the calamity of World War I. This released such a savage outburst of nationalist passions that the pacifist international union of the Social Democratic parties fell to pieces. The national Social Democratic parties found (1889) the Second International

Toward the end of the nineteenth century, insofar as the workers engaged in politics at all, they had in their vast majority in Europe, though not in the United States, entered the Social Democratic ranks. But there were champions of programs and panaceas other than that of Marx, and some of these succeeded in gaining enough adherents to figure as rivals of his particular program. In the course of his slow uphill climb Marx had come to grips with a Frenchman by the name of Proudhon, who preached a violent anarchism; and when, later, the Russian, Michael Bakunin (d. 1876), took over the Proudhon doctrine, Marx quarreled sharply with him and had him, as a wolf in sheep's clothing, tossed out of the First International. Nevertheless anarchism continued its existence even after the demise of its chief promoter, Bakunin, and by its teaching of violence, coupled with its rejection of every form of government ever practiced among men, had no difficulty in winning over a restless handful of workers to whom the Marxian pacifism was temperamentally distasteful. Bakunin's anarchism commands a measure of worker support

This situation explains the rise just before the new century of the movement of syndicalism, which claimed to be neither anarchism nor socialism and hovered between them. Its outstanding prophet was a French engineer, Georges Sorel (d. 1922), who declared that he followed Marx rather than Bakunin but who nonetheless made violence the heart of his doctrine. Without violence or, as he called it, direct action, the proletarian victory to which he subscribed with Marx would never come The syndicalism of Sorel about. Sorel won a considerable following in France, Italy, and Russia, in which countries a growing impatience had by 1900 begun to make itself felt over the participation of the various Social Democratic parties in the parliamentary game and with the sordid jockeying for political office that inevitably followed.

A final evidence of the waxing power of economically and politically organized labor was the alarm it threw into the middle and upper classes and the consequent gradual change effected in their economic and moral attitude. In order to conciliate the workers, the ruling classes, or at least many individuals among them, began a retreat from the extreme individualism of their immediate past, openly acknowledged the wrong done the workers by industrial exploitation, and, instead of opposing, switched about and earnestly favored government interference in the workers' behalf. This is the neo-liberalism mentioned earlier in this chapter. As it was not shared by the whole body of liberals, we encounter for a time two liberal groups, each claiming to represent the true liberal faith but sharply divided on the issue whether legislation in behalf of workingmen was or was not good liberalism. We may anticipate the outcome, which wavered long in the balance, by noting that the champions of interference so conclusively took possession of the field that before long, but not till the new century, they proclaimed themselves as the only hall-marked spokesmen of liberalism and denounced their former unreconstructed associates as practically indistinguishable from stiff-necked tories.

Let us be in no doubt that the conversion of the middle classes to protective worker-legislation was solely due to the growing power of the workers, manifested first, by their organization in trade-unions and second, by their participation in politics through vigorous labor parties. While these class-conscious activities released a storm of hate among the more obdurate members of the middle classes, the more sensible majority among them inclined to counsels of moderation. They exhibited their change of heart by gradually pouring out a veritable flood of legislation regulating wages and hours of work, improving the hygienic conditions in the factories and towns, restricting or forbidding outright the labor of women and children, and appointing government inspectors to enforce the ameliorative measures. At last they went the length of actually insuring workers against some of the worst evils of their lot. These evils, once considered irremediable by the "classical" economists, were sickness, accidental injuries, invalidism through old age, and unemployment. The passing from protective legislation, usually called Social Legislation, to Insurance Legislation marks an important milestone in the expanding provision made by governments for the better life and greater security of what in all industrial countries was fast becoming or already had be-

The organized power of the workers moves the middle classes to favor Social Legislation

Social Legislation culminates in Insurance Legislation

come the major part of the population. The first experiment with Insurance Legislation was made in Germany in the eighties. We shall leave its details together with the whole subject of German labor legislation to our German chapter; as regards British Social Legislation culminating in Insurance Legislation the reader is referred to our two British chapters, 24 and 29.

26 THE RISE OF NAPOLEON III AND THE UNIFICATION OF ITALY

HOW THE PRINCE-PRESIDENT BECAME EMPEROR NAPOLEON III

The monarchists in control of the Legislative Assembly

THE INDICATION FURNISHED by the choice of Louis Napoleon as president that France did not really want the Second Republic was converted into positive proof by the elections of May, 1849, to the Legislative Assembly. To this first parliament under the new constitution the country returned an immense monarchical majority. The only reason the Second Republic was not immediately overthrown was that the monarchists were divided into three groups: legitimists, favoring the older Bourbon line; Orléanists, devoted to the family of Louis Philippe; and a rising Bonapartist faction, supporting the president. While doing his best to strengthen his personal supporters, Louis Napoleon, who desired, above all, to weaken the republic, encouraged a combination of all the monarchists to reduce the popular rights secured by the recent revolution.

Anti-republican enactments of the Legislative Assembly

To such action the Legislative Assembly hardly needed to be encouraged. Yielding to its strong conservative bias, it limited the freedom of the press and forbade political meetings. In 1850 it capped its anti-republican enactments by a bill which put an end to universal male suffrage, unquestionably the most important popular achievement of the recent revolution. By making the suffrage dependent on certain residence and tax requirements, the bill practically deprived the whole body of the workingmen of the franchise.

The president destroys the Roman republic (1849)

Evidence of the prince-president's close attachment to the conservatives (monarchists and clericals) was at the same time furnished by the military expedition sent in the spring of 1849 against the Roman republic. While the responsibility for this action, of which mention has already been made, falls upon Napoleon, he could not have carried it through without the support of the powerful Catholic sentiment in the Assembly and among the French peasantry. To this Catholic sentiment Louis Napoleon catered from his first appearance on the French scene and continued to do so till the end of his reign.

More than a year passed before the monarchical majority of the Assembly perceived that the president was indeed playing their game, not however for their sake but for his own. In view of his past exploits they looked upon him as a rather comic figure, kicked upstairs by capricious Fortune and not sufficiently intelligent to prove an enterprising executive. Under cover of the Assembly's contempt he was therefore able to pursue unmolested his program of imperial restoration. *The Assembly underestimates the president*

As the Industrial Revolution had come to the country and with it an era of railroad building, the president was constantly invited to all parts of France to assist at the formal opening of some new section. He was a clever politician and eager to show the people that he was identified with the interests they had at heart. On his appearance among them he never failed to make a speech. Beginning with railroads and the blessings of industrialism, he rose rapidly to a vision of the past glories of France under his great uncle. With the last sentence he had the crowd shouting, *"Vive Napoléon!"* while a few, perhaps specially planted, individuals so far forgot their republican manners as to burst into *"Vive l'empéreur!"* In this way he built up a powerful personal following. When the Assembly, at last enlightened regarding his fixed purpose, drew away from him, it discovered that the conservative elements of the country, consisting of clericals, peasants, wealthy land-owners, industrialists, and even shop-keepers fearful of the new socialist doctrines, had rallied to the president, while the liberal elements, weakened but not negligible, declined to back the Assembly because offended by its anti-popular legislation. *How Louis Napoleon built up a personal following*

In 1851 Napoleon, rendered confident by the large personal following he had brought together, let fall the last veil from his plans. The constitution had fixed the presidential term at four years, without the right to re-election. Since by the operation of this article Louis Napoleon would have become a private citizen once more in 1852, his ambition led him to resort to a coup d'état, that is, an illegal use of force. Alleging that the recent disfranchisement of the workers by the Assembly was a wrong that needed to be righted, he demanded that the legislature repeal its act. When the deputies refused, Louis Napoleon made their action his excuse for destroying the republic. *The president resolves (1851) to destroy the republic*

The coup d'état was set for December 2, 1851. A preparatory step, taken during the preceding months, had been to win over the leaders of the army and to fill the civilian key-positions with his followers. With these arrangements made, the success of the conspirators was assured. While the troops occupied Paris, closed the hall of the deputies, and put the president's leading opponents under lock and key, the president himself announced by placard the return to the system of the great Corsican as embodied in the Constitution of the Year VIII. The country, called upon to express its opinion upon these proceedings by plebiscite, indorsed the coup d'état by an overwhelming majority. *The coup d'état of December 2, 1851*

Louis Napoleon erected his government on a granted constitution, which he provided with a false façade of liberalism by means of a legislature elected by universal suffrage. But since the legislature, called Chamber of Deputies, could not propose laws nor even amend those submitted to it for approval by the emperor's hand-picked Council of State, it cannot be said to have exercised any substantial power. Control was concentrated in the sole hand of the chief executive. In these circumstances there was nothing left to make the triumph of absolutism complete but to gather its last fruits. Exactly a year after the coup d'état the president assumed the title of Emperor Napoleon III. Thus was the Second Republic followed by the Second Empire.

The president proclaims himself Emperor Napoleon III

NAPOLEON'S DOMESTIC POLICY

Emperor Napoleon's contemporaries were inclined to look on him as a political enigma. True, he often said and did contradictory things, but no more so than other politicians before or since obliged to win popular favor in order to keep afloat. The, after all, outstanding elements of his character are so clearly apparent as to be undebatable. His being the heir of the Napoleonic tradition filled him with an animating fire which a much-remarked, inborn dreaminess banked down occasionally but never smothered. It was this heirship that gave him the same faith in himself as a marked figure, a man of destiny, that had possessed his worshiped uncle and exemplar. That he would ultimately reach the throne had been axiomatic with him from his early boyhood. But as he was not, like the founder of his house, a military man, his tactics to achieve his goal were adjusted to his civil status and were dictated by a far above-the-average political sagacity.

Character of Napoleon III

In Napoleon's view of the French people a government that hoped to survive would have to take account of the fact that France, in spite of a numerous, free-thinking bourgeois element, was a deeply Catholic country and that what the substantial property-owning groups in town and village primarily asked of their government was order and security. While shaping his policy to meet the wishes of this weighty portion of the population, thereby giving it a prevailingly conservative complexion, he did not overlook the interests of any other group with the hope, in the end, of lining up the whole people behind him. He was free to indulge this hope for, in spite of his imperial obsession, he was not a petrified traditionalist but essentially a modern man. With all his heart he identified himself with the great transforming movement of the age, the Industrial Revolution, and was resolved to shower France with its manifold blessings.

The main elements of his program

Already under the previous government the Industrial Revolution had begun its inroads on French society. But, instead of the rather somnolent approval bestowed on it by the unenterprising Louis Philippe, it was backed with unrelaxed vigor by the new ruler, whose not unjustified boast was that he knew his time and marched abreast of it. He interested himself at once in the mechanization of industry and to help it along encouraged the formation of a bank, the *Crédit Mobilier,* the object of which was to provide capital for industrial promotion. But, particularly attentive to the solidly Catholic peasantry, Napoleon did not let the fact escape him that there was going on in his day not only an Industrial but also, owing to the wonders revealed by chemistry, an Agricultural Revolution, and by a national mortgage bank, the *Crédit Foncier,* he made capital available also for agricultural expansion. In order fully to do their work both revolutions required improved communications. Therefore the emperor lent himself with equal zest to the extension of the telegraph and railway facilities. The following figures tell an interesting tale: While at his accession to power there were only 2,216 miles of railway lines, by 1869 the French network had reached 14,230 miles. And between the same two dates the output of industrial goods and agricultural products had increased at a lower but still extremely impressive rate. Inevitably the development was attended by the wildest speculation, and "boom" years alternated with depressions in the manner characteristic of the capitalist system from the first; but there is no denying that the country, and especially the middle classes, were sustained by an elated feeling of material well-being and prosperity.

He promotes both the Industrial and the Agricultural Revolution

Nor did the emperor forget the underprivileged and often starving masses. Great public works, such as highways, canals, and harbors, were undertaken which gave employment to thousands. There were also established savings banks, convalescent homes, orphan asylums, and similar institutions calculated to take some of their worst burdens off the backs of the poor. No better evidence as to whether contemporary governments were favorable or not to the lower orders is available than their attitude toward organized labor. In Great Britain, for instance, trade-unions continued to be regarded suspiciously till past the middle of the century. It was therefore a notable concession when a French law of 1864 legalized trade-unions and recognized the workers' right to strike in order to raise wages and lower hours of work. Thereupon, encouraged by their improved economic status, the workers again awakened politically; and their renewed activity on this level helps explain the livelier tempo of domestic politics which marks the second decade of Napoleon's rule and of which we shall hear in the next chapter.

The workers are not overlooked by Napoleon

No account of the public works promoted by the emperor is complete that does not mention the transformation of Paris. It is a tribute to his

The transformation of Paris

modernism that he recognized that the growth of population and the intensified circulation of men and goods consequent to the new means of communication required a demolition of the dingy, crowded quarters and the straightening of the crooked streets of ancient Paris. At Napoleon's orders an energetic administrator or, as we would now say, city-planner, Baron Haussmann by name, worked out their replacement with a system of broad boulevards and spacious parks whereby Paris took on an appearance of metropolitan magnificence which gave it that pre-eminence among the world's capitals it has retained to this day.

Role of the Empress Eugénie

To speak of the resplendent capital is to recall the glittering entertainments which became an outstanding feature of the court conducted at the palace of the Tuileries. They would not have been possible without the Empress Eugénie, a Spanish countess whom Napoleon married in 1853. Her youth, vivacity, and beauty admirably fitted her to play the part of presiding genius over a household conducted on an imperial scale.

THE CRIMEAN WAR

The emperor yields to the lure of military glory

When we come to the field of foreign policy, we are made aware that the temporizing, modern politician in Napoleon and the impersonator of a masterful military tradition did not always live harmoniously together. Carrying the name he did, he was driven to reaffirm the primacy of France in Europe by an active foreign policy culminating when necessary in war. He had conned the writings of his famous uncle as though they were a book of holy prophecies and had not overlooked the passage wherein that master of warfare had declared that what the French people desired above all things was miltary glory. To this lure the nephew hesitantly yielded from the start of his reign. Thereupon, tricked by initial successes, he proceeded on his dangerous way till in the end he was overtaken by the same fate that destroyed his great namesake.

The plan of Tsar Nicholas to partition Turkey rejected by Great Britain

Napoleon III had hardly seated himself on the throne when a brilliant opportunity presented itself for fishing in the ever troubled waters of the near east. The alarming feebleness shown by the Ottoman empire in the Greek War of Liberation persisted during the succeeding decades. It prompted Tsar Nicholas of Russia confidently to expect the early dissolution of the rival state. He referred cheerfully to the sultan as "the sick man," and became convinced that Russia and Great Britain, as the likeliest heirs, should anticipate the sick man's demise by coming to an agreement on the division of the heritage. But as every probable scheme of division would place Russia in possession of Constantinople, Great Britain hesitated. It pleased her that so strategic a point as the great city on the Bosporus should be in the hands of the feeble sultan, incapable of threatening her at sea. The thought of the powerful tsar in the sultan's place was intolerable. Great Britain broke off the conversations with a firm rejection of the tempter.

In April, 1853, Tsar Nicholas's disappointment discharged itself in an act of aggression against Turkey. He made the demand on the sultan that he, the tsar, be conceded a special position within the Ottoman empire by the sultan's acknowledgment of him as the protector of all Christians of Greek Orthodox persuasion within the Ottoman realm. As the acceptance of this demand would have made Nicholas co-sovereign with the sultan in the Turkish dominions, the British ambassador at Constantinople urged the Ottoman government to refuse. The answer of the Russians to this rebuff was to occupy Moldavia and Wallachia (the Danubian principalities) in order to enforce their claim. In the end, after much diplomatic sparring, in which all the powers took a hand, another war broke out between the tsar and the sultan. *Tsar Nicholas follows up a demand on the sultan with an act of war*

On this occasion the Ottoman government was not left, as in 1828-1829, to face the Russians without an ally. Great Britain, having prompted the sultan to resistance, was in honor bound to help him and was of course vastly pleased when Napoleon III ranged himself on the British side. The emperor was chiefly prompted to this action by the opening it afforded of playing a flashing role on the world stage. But like the politician he was, he hid his plan under a pretext. The sultan had granted certain privileges of worship at the Holy Places of Palestine to groups of both Latin Catholic and Greek Orthodox monks. In their rancorous dislike of each other they often quarreled and then appealed their case to their respective champions, France and Russia. When on the most recent of these occasions Napoleon undertook to plead the cause of his clients with the court of St. Petersburg, he met with a curt rebuff. This enabled him to allege to the French people that in joining in a war against Russia he was protecting Catholic interests, when in reality he was only making war for the sake of glory. *Great Britain and France come to the aid of the Ottoman empire*

In March, 1854, Great Britain and France signed a treaty of alliance with the Ottoman empire and followed it up with a declaration of war on Russia. In this way what had threatened at first to be merely another in the long succession of Turco-Russian conflicts became an European war, the first on a continental scale since the overthrow of Napoleon I.

The first important move of the campaign of 1854 was that the Russians retired from the Danubian principalities into their own territory and stood on the defensive. The allies therefore were obliged to agree at what point to attack the Russian colossus and finally hit upon the fortress of Sebastopol in the Crimea (hence the name Crimean War). The conflict practically reduced itself to the siege of this great stronghold, which the Russians defended skillfully and vigorously for a whole year. *The war (1854-56) concentrated in the Crimea*

The Treaty of Paris (1856) strengthens the sultan at the expense of the tsar

The fall of Sebastopol in September, 1855, discouraged the Russians greatly. Tsar Nicholas, whose pretensions had caused the war, had died during the siege and was succeeded by his more moderate and conciliatory son, Alexander II. Alexander was only too glad to suggest negotiations. They led to a general European congress at Paris and to the signing in March, 1856, of a peace. As the Ottoman empire had been the ally of France and Great Britain, the treaty recorded, even though the fighting had been done by the two western powers, a victory of the sultan over the tsar. Consequently the tsar was obliged to renounce not only his plan of a protectorate over the Greek Christians but also certain special rights secured by earlier treaties with regard to such territories as Serbia and the Danubian principalities (Rumania), which under earlier Russian pressure had secured a certain measure of self-government. In fact Russia was put on an exact level with all the other powers in regard to the Ottoman empire, the independence and territorial integrity of which were solemnly guaranteed.

Some anti-Russian provisions of the treaty

As for the Christian subjects of the sultan, who were chiefly, it must always be remembered, of the Greek Orthodox faith, the treaty affirmed that their proper and natural protector was their Mohammedan sovereign and he alone. To discourage Russia from renewing her attacks on Turkish territory, the conferees wrote a provision into the treaty neutralizing the Black sea and obliging Russia to promise to maintain neither a naval base nor warships on Black sea waters. Doubtless these arrangements dealt Russia a heavy blow. Whether they would have a long life was another question, since they were based on the absurd assumption that the disintegration of the Ottoman empire, which had been going on for several centuries, could be stopped at the command of interested diplomats. Was it possible, in the nature of things, to decree either the cessation of Turkish decay or the arrest of Russian growth?

Napoleon's increased prestige as a result of the war

The Crimean War, signalized by the spectacular capture of Sebastopol chiefly through the action of French troops and brought to a close at Paris under the eyes of Napoleon, greatly enhanced the emperor's prestige, though, as already remarked, it would be hard to say what advantage it gave to France. Napoleon III's foreign policy was personal, not national. That is the conclusion which his whole reign confirms, more particularly by reason of the measures he now took regarding Italy.

NAPOLEON III AND THE UNIFICATION OF ITALY

As the actions we have scanned must by now have convinced us, Napoleon, in spite of his name, was less a soldier than a clever politician endowed with a consuming ambition and certain liberal ideas derived from the age in which he lived. We have seen that he backed the Industrial Revolution. At the same time he was so persuaded of the power of nationalism that, wisely, as the event proved, he looked upon a thoroughgoing nationalist reorganization of Europe as an inevitable future development.

It was characteristic of the softer or liberal side of Napoleon's nature that he was occasionally willing to risk something in behalf of a cause which stirred his soul. The spectacle of Italy in chains had excited his sympathy when, as a young exile from France, he had found refuge on Italian soil. It was even popularly held that he had in his early manhood belonged to an Italian revolutionary society, the famous *Carbonari*. His youthful memories now led him to play with the thought of the liberation of the peninsula from Austrian rule. It was a generous impulse, without doubt, but rooted in his personal predilections, not in the necessities of the French state of which he was the official guardian.

Ever since the failure of the rising of 1848-1849 Italy had been under the heel of Austria, re-established once more in the revolted provinces of Lombardy and Venetia and obsequiously wooed by the petty rulers of her numerous states. But there was one exception to this degradation. The young king of Sardinia-Piedmont, Victor Emmanuel II, maintained a dignified aloofness and, even in the face of repeated Austrian threats, upheld the charter that had been granted his people during the late conflict and ruled them as a constitutional monarch. What wonder that he shone like a beacon of hope over enslaved Italy and drew to himself and to his state the eyes of the patriots from every section of the peninsula? In the year 1850 he appointed Count Camillo di Cavour his minister of agriculture and in 1852 promoted him to the premiership. Therewith he put at the helm the man who was to reopen the Italian question and solve it in the only way that it could be solved, that is, by the ejection from the peninsula of Austria.

Cavour, a Piedmontese of ancient lineage, had in early youth absorbed the liberal and national views that were beginning to be diffused throughout central Europe. He was attracted by the economic, social, and political problems presented by backward Italy and, more particularly, by his own Piedmont, and gave himself a thorough education in these fields by a course of systematic reading fortified by travel, especially in France and England, the two most advanced societies of Europe.

It was in this formative period that Cavour became persuaded that of the many projects bruited among Italians for their unification the only practicable one hinged on the solid unit of Sardinia-Piedmont. The notion of a federation of the corrupt and reactionary tyrannies that held sway on either side of the Apennines with, possibly, the pope as president struck him as a bad dream. Nonetheless, it had many adherents, as was also the case with the project championed by the famous patriot and life-long conspirator, Giuseppe Mazzini, of a general rising of the common man terminating in an equalitarian republic. In Cavour's view, given the corrupt nature of man, Mazzini's project was not so much a bad as too good a dream and completely outside the range of practical politics. Now Cavour, too, was an idealist but one who believed, while looking toward the sky, in never losing contact with the earth. He was therefore firmly convinced that Sardinia-Piedmont, as the only truly Italian state in existence, would, small and weak as it was, have to shoulder the responsibility of assembling the scattered bits of Italy into an effective unit.

Cavour's liberal domestic policy

Cavour's earliest effort as minister of state was to commit conservative Piedmont to a modern liberal transformation. Since it had no industry to speak of and no capital, he could not introduce the Industrial Revolution. In lieu thereof its considerable agriculture could be intensified by the new chemical knowledge touching soils and crops. Even before being called to public office he had helped found an Agricultural Society and this, spread in numerous branches through the land, prompted a notably increased production of foodstuffs. Having become minister, he negotiated treaties of commerce with neighboring states to stimulate the exchange of goods, and with the same design he promoted the extension of the highway and railroad system. The country's largest landlord was the Catholic church. Cavour confiscated over half of its six hundred monasteries and put a stop to further enrichment of the church by forbidding it to acquire property without the consent of the government.

His foreign policy aims at close association with France

Nonetheless, domestic affairs were only a minor feature of Cavour's activities, since his major concern was always with Austria and its hateful mastery of the peninsula. He knew Austria could not be driven out other than by war, and he knew that Sardinia-Piedmont could not successfully conduct such an enterprise with its own limited resources. It would have to find an ally among the great powers, with France in all probability alone available for the role. France had through all the generations of the past contested Austria's hegemony in Italy and, besides, at this precise juncture was ruled by a sovereign with an unconcealed sympathy for the oppressed Italian people.

The Plombières agreement (1858)

With remarkable dexterity Cavour manipulated the complicated elements of the general European situation. In order to curry favor with both Great Britain and France he took their side in the Crimean War and caused idle gossips throughout Europe to burst into uncontrolled laughter when he dispatched a Piedmontese expeditionary corps to Sebastopol to fight against Russia, with which he had neither contact nor conflict. However, he laid Great Britain and, more particularly, France under obligation to Sardinia-Piedmont and, having gained a direct approach to Napoleon, was able to lure him with the prospect of a greater than the

Crimean glory to be won nearer home. In July, 1858, Napoleon agreed to meet Cavour with conspiratorial secrecy at Plombières. There the two hatched out an agreement to make war on Austria and drive her from the peninsula. The provinces of Lombardy and Venetia together with the Romagna were to become the prize of Sardinia-Piedmont, but the other Italian provinces were to stay, in the main, as they were. The reward of France would be the cession to her by Victor Emmanuel of Savoy and Nice.

The war, begun in April, 1859, was not long drawn out. By two victories, at Magenta and at Solferino, the allies—France and Sardinia— drove the Austrians out of Lombardy, back upon a prepared area of defense called the Quadrilateral. Italy was ablaze with bonfires, and with tumultuous enthusiasm hailed Napoleon as its liberator wherever he appeared. *The war of liberation of 1859*

But much remained to be done. The immediate military objective of the allies was now the Quadrilateral, made up of the four great fortresses of Verona, Peschiera, Legnago, and Mantua, and one of the strongest defense positions in Europe. Until the Quadrilateral had been taken, the Austrians remained securely ensconced in the peninsula. Just as everybody was expecting a fresh advance against the Austrians, the telegraph flashed the news of a dramatic change: Napoleon, without inviting Victor Emmanuel to attend him, had met the Emperor Francis Joseph of Austria in private conference at Villafranca and arranged a peace (July 11). *Napoleon concludes peace at Villafranca*

By the terms of the Peace of Villafranca Austria agreed to give up Lombardy, but was permitted to retain Venetia and therewith a powerful foothold in the peninsula. Disgusted with what he stigmatized as Napoleon's perfidy, Cavour resigned from office, luckily only temporarily. His less excited sovereign, King Victor Emmanuel II, regretfully accepted the Villafranca arrangements because, even though they did not bring everything that had been bargained for, they conferred invaluable benefits on his state. *Villafranca a keen disappointment to Cavour*

The considerations which moved Napoleon to his sudden turn-about were many. He was not a masterful character and easily fell victim to his fears. One of these concerned the military problem of breaking through the Quadrilateral. So strong was this position that not improbably the French might bleed themselves to death before it. The second fear concerned Prussia, which, alarmed lest it be attacked after Austria was finished, prepared to mobilize on the Rhine, thereby threatening Napoleon's flank. Finally, he was filled with consternation by the wild nationalist tempest sweeping over Italy all the way from the Alps to the straits of Messina. *Napoleon's reasons for making peace*

Napoleon had not reckoned with such extravagant excitement. It might at any moment sweep the reactionary, anti-national rulers, including Pope Pius IX, off their thrones. But the emperor had committed himself to the pope as far back as 1849, when he had, for the pope's benefit, destroyed the Roman republic of Mazzini. He had made the commitment in order to win over the French clergy and peasantry, whose support he then needed and still needed no whit less than before. The mounting tide of Italian nationalism must under no circumstances be permitted to wash over Rome and the pope. Of the many considerations that prompted Napoleon to negotiate his precipitate peace, this of the runaway Italian situation was probably the most pressing. So anxious was he to wash his hands of the whole troublesome business that no sooner was the treaty signed than he handed over Lombardy, representing less than one-half of the stipulated terms, to Victor Emmanuel, renounced his own agreed reward of Savoy and Nice, and hurried home in the hope that, the war over, the Italian turmoil would die down.

To this turmoil we must now give our attention. Its examination will familiarize us with the piecemeal method by which the Italian territories were added to the Sardinian core. Elated by the war against Austria, the enemy of all true Italians, Tuscany, Modena, Parma, and the Romagna (the northern section of the Papal States), making up together north-central Italy, rose in the summer of 1859 against their princes and, driving them from their dominions, declared for annexation to Sardinia. Victor Emmanuel, pleased though he was, dared not accept these territories without the consent of the all-powerful Napoleon. Feverish negotiations followed. They ended in March, 1860, in a new agreement by which Napoleon permitted the annexation of the above-listed territories in return for the revived surrender to France of Savoy and Nice.

The arrangement was like any other political deal, except for the novel provision that it was to be preceded by a popular referendum. In both Nice and Savoy the French language was in common use, and a majority voted for annexation. The surrender of Alpine Savoy particularly wounded Victor Emmanuel, for it was the original home of his dynasty. But as Savoy, with even Nice thrown in, was manifestly worth less than the north-central states, Cavour, who had returned to office, persuaded Victor Emmanuel to yield.

The acquisition of Lombardy and the north-central states represents the first and second steps in the process of Italian unification. The third step was the capture in the summer of 1860 of the kingdom of the Two Sicilies. This was accomplished by a buccaneering expedition led by Italy's famous soldier of fortune, Giuseppe Garibaldi. Secretly encouraged by Cavour, Garibaldi gathered, at the port of Genoa, one thousand volunteers, called from their conspicuous attire his thousand Red Shirts,

---

Marginal notes:

The outstanding reason was the inflammatory Italian situation

After acquiring (1859) Lombardy, Sardinia acquires (1860) the north-central states

Napoleon acquires Savoy and Nice

Garibaldi conquers (1860) Sicily and Naples

and in May suddenly set sail for Sicily. He had only to show himself
for the Sicilians to toss their hats into the air and abandon the hated
Bourbon king. Sicily conquered, Garibaldi crossed the straits to the
mainland, and again proof was furnished that the imported, Spanish-
minded Bourbon dynasty had never taken root among the people. The

THE UNIFICATION OF ITALY

victory fell again to Garibaldi and, acclaimed as a savior, the conqueror
in September entered the unresisting city of Naples.

Being, like the famous conspirator, Mazzini, a convinced republican,
Garibaldi now took up the plan of organizing his conquest as a separate democratic state. The project alarmed and outraged Cavour, who
regarded it as a crushing defeat of his unitary policy. He therefore
persuaded his king to march Piedmontese troops into the southern kingdom in order to dispute Garibaldi's possession. In the face of this opposition and on the still more impressive ground that the southern Italians manifestly desired annexation to Sardinia, Garibaldi yielded his
position and generously surrendered his conquest into the hands of King

Garibaldi avoids a threatened conflict by handing over his conquest to Victor Emmanuel

Victor Emmanuel. A plebiscite taken (November, 1860) in Sicily and Naples gave a staggering majority for absorption into the northern kingdom. With the capture and exile of the Bourbon king, Francis II, who made a last stand at the fortress of Gaeta, the Neapolitan incident was brought to a happy close.

Annexation (November, 1860) of the bulk of the Papal States

Meanwhile another issue had arisen and become pressing. On sending Piedmontese troops into Naples, Cavour had been obliged to march them through the eastern section of the Papal States. The traverse had made the statesman aware that these territories (Ancona, Umbria), too, passionately desired annexation to Sardinia. The weak forces of the pope were easily driven off and, again encouraged by a favorable plebiscite, Cavour carried through the annexation of these papal territories (November, 1860).

Garibaldi halted by Cavour

With these successes won, the tempestuous Garibaldi attempted to wring from the king permission to lead an expedition against the city of Rome in order to wrest it from the pope and make it the seat of the national government. But as Rome was held by French troops and the attempt to capture the capital of the pope would have meant a war with France, Cavour interposed a firm veto.

Cavour brings the movement of unification to a temporary stop

Cavour was the kind of statesman who knew exactly when to go forward and when to retreat. He fully agreed with Garibaldi and the impulsive patriots that Italy would remain a torso until Rome and Venice, too, had been joined to the Italian trunk, but he took a realist's view of the world and reckoned with conditions as he found them. Just as to drive upon Rome would precipitate a war with France, so to descend upon Venetia would cause a war with Austria. For neither of these conflicts was Italy at the moment, according to Cavour, prepared. He therefore resolved to bide his time, convinced that sooner or later incidents would turn up which would play into his country's hands and enable it to complete the work of unification so happily begun. It was folly to overlook that for the moment all further advance was blocked.

Sardinia transformed into the kingdom of Italy, 1861

In view of these paralyzing elements of the general situation, Cavour resolved to inaugurate a period of domestic consolidation. In consequence of the rapid march of events since 1859 he had upon his hands a kingdom of Sardinia plus a mass of annexations several times Sardinia's size. In February, 1861, he summoned to Turin, the Sardinian capital, elected representatives from all the recent acquisitions. They enthusiastically proclaimed the transformation of Sardinia into the kingdom of Italy.

Italian problems

It was a proud and uplifting moment in the history of a reborn people. There was much and by no means easy work ahead. An administration, an army and navy, a modern economic system, had to be evolved, not to mention the necessity of finding an accommodation with the pope, who, outraged by his spoliation, had excommunicated the king, Cavour, his own rebellious subjects, in fact, any and everybody conspicuously connected with the movement of Italian unification.

The important work of domestic regeneration had hardly begun when the great Cavour, worn out by his labors, died (June, 1861), and the cloak of the inspired statesman fell upon the shoulders of well-meaning but humdrum politicians. Twice, following the death of Cavour, the impatient Garibaldi took the bit between his teeth and charged upon Rome, resolved to repeat his buccaneering exploit of 1860. Both attempts were failures because the government of King Victor Emmanuel, true, in spite of temptation, to Cavour's counsels, refused to follow a lead certain to precipitate a war with France.

Death of Cavour (1861) followed by no change of policy

Exactly as the great leader had prophesied, fortune before long successively produced the two opportunities which enabled Italy to realize her hopes with regard to Venetia and Rome without exposing herself to excessive risks. The first opportunity occurred in 1866. In that year there broke out the long-threatening war in Germany between Austria and Prussia, of which we shall read in the next chapter. Prussia naturally appealed to Italy for help, and the two powers, on both of which Austria rested like an incubus, made an alliance. Austria was obliged to face two enemies at once and, although victorious over Italy, defeating her army at Custozza (June 24) and her navy at Lissa in the Adriatic (July 20), was so conclusively crushed by Prussia at Königgrätz (Sadowa) that she had to come to terms with her foe.

Italy allied in 1866 with victorious Prussia against Austria

In the hope of winning French favor, the emperor of Austria had, on receipt of the news of his decisive defeat, handed over Venetia, the province for which the Italians were fighting, as a gift to Napoleon III. On the formal conclusion of peace the French emperor passed on his gift to King Victor Emmanuel. He could not do otherwise, since Prussia, on making peace with Austria, carried out the obligation it had assumed toward its ally by insisting on the transfer of Venetia to Italy. It was promptly incorporated in the Italian mass and toward the close of the year the old republic of St. Mark gave Victor Emmanuel a rousing welcome in its midst.

Italy acquires Venetia

The Patrimony of St. Peter (Rome and its immediate environment) now alone remained outside the reconstituted nation. If the question had been submitted to the Romans whether they wished to be governed by the pope or by the king, there can be no doubt for whom they would have declared. But French troops continued to hold the city for the pope, and Napoleon made it plain that, much as he had done for Italian unity, his complaisance stopped at the walls of the Eternal City. To wrest Rome from the pope would have precipitated a French war.

Rome held for the pope by French troops

The upshot was that the Italian government resolved to adjourn the issue; and when, in 1870, a war broke out between France and Prussia,

its patience was fully rewarded. Obliged to mobilize his full strength against the Germans, Napoleon III withdrew his garrison from Rome and, shortly after, was rendered wholly impotent by his defeat and capture at Sedan. There was now no one to hinder the march on Rome. In September, 1870, the Italian army entered the city amid the plaudits of the citizens. Although Pope Pius IX poured renewed anathemas on his despoilers, he was not disturbed in his vast official residence, the Vatican palace, from which he continued to rule the Catholic world. In this manner Rome, while remaining the central seat of Catholic Christianity, became also the capital of the newborn Italian state.

27 THE UNIFICATION OF GERMANY AND THE FALL OF NAPOLEON III

THE ARMY REFORM BILL

ALTHOUGH, FOLLOWING THE failure of the German revolution of 1848, Prussia remained a constitutional state, this success offered only a slight consolation to the dejected liberals, for a dark reaction spread its shadows over the country. The erratic king, Frederick William IV, once more openly expounded his views of divine right and, leaning on the landowners (Junkers), the army officers, and the Lutheran clergy, reduced the action of the Prussian parliament to the smallest possible scope. The press was muzzled and political meetings were forbidden. As, in addition to the loss of credit resulting from this domestic situation, Prussia suffered an impairment of prestige for having at the dictation of Austria (1850) re-entered the obsolete Bund, her influence among the liberal and nationalist elements of German society temporarily disappeared.

Prussia in the shadow of a political reaction

In the year 1858 there occurred a change, slight in itself but destined to become significant. In that year, owing to the appearance of symptoms of insanity, the romantic and reactionary Frederick William IV was replaced by his brother William, first as regent and, on the demise of the patient in 1861, as king.

Accession of William I

The advent of William I was hailed as the dawn of a new era and attended by a revival of hope among the liberal elements. Endowed, in sharp contrast to his temperamental brother, with a matter-of-fact mind and having, besides, through long association, a deep professional interest in the army, the new ruler inaugurated at once what seemed to him an urgent military reform. The Prussian army, a creation of the Napoleonic wars, was based on a law of 1814 which prescribed universal military training in the form of three years' service with the colors and two years in the reserve. At the time this system was adopted some 40,000 recruits reported annually for training and the total standing army was slightly in excess of 120,000 men. Since then the population of Prussia had increased by more than fifty per cent. But as only 40,000 recruits could be accommodated annually on the basis of the existing financial arrangements, the principle of universal compulsory training had in practice been abandoned.

William resolves to reform the army

The
Prussian
parliament
provisionally
passes the
Army Bill

The new sovereign determined to make military training once more general, not only, of course, because of his devotion to the principle but also, and chiefly, because its strict enforcement would provide a larger army and secure for Prussia a greater degree of consideration in the councils of Europe. At the same time he wished to introduce a few minor changes, such as the extension of the service in the reserve from two to four years, which recommended itself to him as providing a further increase in the army, welcome in the event of war when the reserve would be called to the colors. He had an Army Reform Bill presented to the parliament (*Landtag*) which actually voted the recommended changes in a provisional form.

Then a hitch occurred. The liberals had acquired a majority in the lower house and, desiring to reduce military expenditure, demanded certain concessions, above all, the reduction of the service with the colors from three to two years. This attempt to interfere in the organization of the army, which he looked upon as a branch of the government pertaining to himself alone, deeply angered the king. On the strength of the provisional grant of the necessary sums William had already begun the re-organization of the army. He now persisted in finishing the work, while his liberal opponents with ever waxing shrillness denounced the unconstitutionality of his action.

In this way it came about that, beginning with the year 1861, Prussia entered upon a lively struggle between executive and legislature. While it turned immediately about the Army Reform Bill, it involved also the question of the constitution, since the king insisted on giving permanent character to a measure only provisionally authorized by the parliament, thereby engaging in unauthorized expenditures.

When, on dissolving parliament and calling, in 1862, for new elections, an even larger liberal majority confronted William in the new house, he was so dejected and at the same time so committed to his policy that he resolved to resign. However, his minister of war, von Roon, persuaded him to make a last attempt to get the Army Bill adopted under the direction of a new prime minister. For this post Roon recommended a certain Otto von Bismarck, and in October, 1862, Bismarck accepted the king's appointment. A Brandenburg squire of ancient family, Bismarck was born in 1815 but did not make his public début till the revolutionary commotions of 1848 drew him from his country retirement. He promptly signalized himself as an arch-conservative, a fearless defender of the undiminished royal prerogative. On the strength of his militant royalism he was, when the revolution had been crushed, advanced to the diplomatic service and given the post of Prussian representative in the reconstituted Bund at Frankfort-on-the-Main.

At Frankfort, where he remained eight years (1851-1859), Bismarck

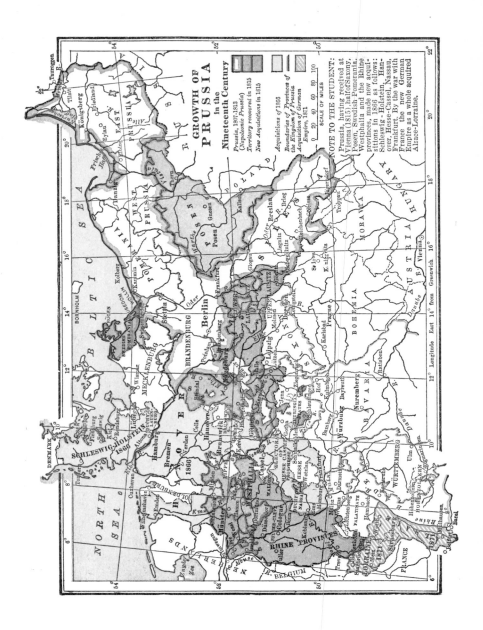

GROWTH OF
PRUSSIA
In the
Nineteenth Century

Prussia, 1807-1813
(Napoleonic Prussia)
Territory recovered in 1815
New Acquisitions in 1815

Acquisitions of 1866
Boundaries of Provinces of
the Kingdom of Prussia
Acquisition of German
Empire, 1871

SCALE OF MILES
0   20   40   60   80   100

NOTE TO THE STUDENT:
Prussia, having received at Vienna (1815), half of Saxony, Posen, Swedish Pomerania, Westphalia and the Rhine provinces, made new acquisitions in 1866 as follows: Schleswig - Holstein, Hanover, Hesse-Cassel, Nassau, Frankfurt. By the war with France the new German Empire as a whole acquired Alsace-Lorraine.

was afforded an incomparable opportunity for meeting the representative men of all the German states and for penetrating to the very core of the complicated issues revolving around the problem of German unification. Above all, he learned that the multi-national Austrian empire made a genuine German unification impossible and he became that country's vigorous and outspoken enemy. In 1859 Bismarck was sent as ambassador to the court of St. Petersburg and, after two years, to Napoleon's court at Paris. To the schooling in German affairs acquired at Frankfort he thereby added a magnificent mastery of the general European situation and, on giving up in 1862 the Paris appointment for the Prussian prime ministership, he was already in possession of a program which, if necessarily indefinite as to details, was absolutely clear as to its main purpose. This was to achieve German unity under the leadership of Prussia to be secured by the elimination of Austria from German affairs. In the pursuit of this goal the unhappy makeshift, the Bund, really an invention of Austria for Austrian ends, would have to attend Austria into the discard. Tremendous proposals, these, with incalculable risks, with which to wrestle was not to be thought of without powerful army backing. Bismarck did not have to be a devoted subject of his king to support the disputed Army Bill. The enlarged, efficient army was the solid pillar of his Prusso-German program, and he was prepared to defend it against the recalcitrant Prussian parliament with all the fighting zest at his command.

As soon as the new prime minister with his long conservative record and his provocative self-assurance presented himself before the house, a tremendous storm broke loose. He refused to consider even for a moment a retreat in the matter of the Army Bill and with apparent tranquillity faced the prospect of a civil war, which seemed not so very remote in view of the uncompromising position of the two opponents. Before that pass was reached, however, events occurred which drew public attention elsewhere. They enabled Bismarck by a series of brilliant successes in the field of German politics to effect a complete reconciliation between the sovereign and his offended parliament and people.

THE DANISH WAR FOLLOWED BY THE AUSTRIAN WAR

In the year 1863 took place the long-expected death of Frederick VII of Denmark, the last male of his line. By the verdict of the powers, known as the Protocol of London (1852), he was succeeded at Copenhagen by his relative, Christian IX. But the duchies of Schleswig and Holstein, which had never accepted the Protocol, immediately proclaimed the duke of Augustenberg, who, according to their view, was the rightful successor so far as the two duchies were concerned.

At bottom the action of the duchies was due much less to legal than to nationalist considerations. They wished, as Germans, to break the ties that bound them to Denmark, and they counted confidently on the support of this program by German public opinion. They were not mistaken. Even the Bund, sluggish by nature and not inclined to enterprise, was sufficiently stirred to plan an intervention in their behalf. But before the measure had been fairly launched, this feeble organization was rudely pushed aside from an unexpected quarter.

Convinced that the Bund was unable to meet the crisis but that Prussia could, Bismarck persuaded Austria to join him in settling the issue in a manner conformable to genuine national requirements. Luckily for the Prussian minister, King Christian IX played into his hands. Immediately on his accession the king signed a bill incorporating Schleswig, the northernmost of the two duchies, with Denmark. This was a clear breach of the London Protocol, which recognized Christian IX as the successor of Frederick VII on the understanding that he would respect the historical union of the two duchies.

The counterstroke of allied Prussia and Austria was to send an ultimatum to Copenhagen, demanding that the unwarranted incorporation of Schleswig with Denmark be withdrawn without delay. When Christian, under pressure from the Danish nationalists, refused to yield, Berlin and Vienna declared war. In January, 1864, Prussian and Austrian troops entered the duchies side by side. In a swift campaign they brought Denmark to her knees. By a peace signed in August Christian IX ceded Schleswig and Holstein to the victors.

The question now was how to divide the spoils. Bismarck faced it with level gaze, plainly regarding it as the door through which to enter on the larger question of German unity. As we have seen, he believed that the preliminary to an effective reorganization of Germany was the exclusion from Germany of Austria; and since he knew that Austria would never depart voluntarily, he was prepared at need to resort to war to drive her out. Consequently the negotiations over the settlement of the Schleswig-Holstein matter were interminably spun out. It took Bismarck two years to persuade King William that any settlement of the issue that Austria might propose was unacceptable. Then only did William agree to refer the issue to the field.

As soon as war with Austria became reasonably certain, Bismarck established contact with that other enemy of Austria, the young kingdom of Italy. In April, 1866, he signed an alliance with Italy which, in the event of victory, promised Venetia to King Victor Emmanuel. Since the rulers of the other German states feared, and with reason, that a renovated Germany under Prussian guidance would impair their sovereignty, most of them, and more particularly the rulers of the larger states, such as Bavaria, Wurtemberg, Baden, Saxony, and Hanover, sided with Austria.

With these arrangements made, in June, 1866, Austria and Prussia, the two apparently well-matched combatants, took the field. While the ostensible issue between them was the division of the Schleswig-Holstein booty, by a declaration which Bismarck had the Prussian representative read to the Bund at Frankfort, he had made it clear to all concerned that the real issue was the reorganization of Germany on a different and more solid basis than the impotent Bund. *The real issue: the reorganization of Germany*

Although a part of the Prussian army had to be detached against the German allies of Austria, the Austrians, too, were hindered from concentrating in a single mass by the obligation of sending an army to Venetia to defend that province against the Italians. Weakened only by these subtractions the Austrians and Prussians, assembled in two great armies, made ready to meet each other in Bohemia. *The main theater of war is Bohemia*

Proof was now given that the reform of the Prussian army had been a timely measure. The Prussians were more quickly mobilized than the Austrians and showed themselves to be much better armed and disciplined. By the admirable arrangements of the great strategist, Moltke, three Prussian columns were made to converge on the Austrian army, assembled in and about the fortress of Königgrätz in Bohemia. They caught their opponents at Sadowa as in a vise and crushed them utterly (July 3). The war had hardly begun when it was over. Hence its common name of the Seven Weeks' War. It was of little consequence that the Austrians in Italy defeated the Italians at Custozza, or that the Prussians completed their triumph by defeating the forces of Austria's German allies. Incapable of continuing the struggle, Austria was obliged to open negotiations. A truce in July was followed in August, 1866, by the definitive Peace of Prague. *The decisive battle of Königgrätz (Sadowa), July 3, 1866*

By the Peace of Prague, Austria agreed to cede her rights to Schleswig-Holstein to Prussia, to accept the dissolution of the Bund, to withdraw from German affairs, and to leave Prussia free to form a confederation of the states of northern Germany, that is, those states lying north of the river Main. The four south-German states (Bavaria, Wurtemberg, Baden, and Hesse) were accorded the right to form a federation of their own. Even though, in addition to her claim to Schleswig-Holstein, Austria gave up Venetia to Italy as stipulated in the Prusso-Italian alliance, in view of the immensity of her disaster her territorial losses were relatively unimportant. If, further, we take into account the relatively small indemnity Austria was required to pay, we shall have to admit that she received unusually lenient treatment. For this treatment there *Concessions imposed on Austria by the Treaty of Prague, 1866* was a reason: Bismarck was a provident statesman and foresaw the advantage of not having a permanently embittered neighbor to the south of the new Germany he was calling to life.

Bismarck incorporates a number of hostile north-German states in Prussia

As soon as these arrangements were assured, Bismarck approached the German allies of Austria. He divided them into two groups, of the north and south respectively. With the four southern states of Bavaria, Wurtemberg, Baden, and Hesse he made peace on easy terms because, hoping to add them at some future date to the Germany he was shaping, he was anxious not to offend them irreconcilably. A very different lot awaited the hostile northern states of Hanover, Nassau, and Hesse-Cassel. As they thrust a disconcerting wedge between the mass of Prussia around Berlin and her possessions on the Rhine, he incorporated them with the monarchy of the Hohenzollerns.

Formation (1867) and Constitution of the North German Confederation

The immediate task awaiting Bismarck after the war was to create the North German Confederation authorized by the Peace of Prague. In the stress of civil war the old Bund had gone to its reward, with no greater outburst of sorrow than had attended, exactly sixty years before, the demise of the equally futile Holy Roman Empire. For the first time since the Middle Ages Germany was to be represented by a politically effective entity. The twenty-two states which made up the North German Confederation accepted the king of Prussia as chief executive under the title of president, while the legislative power was intrusted to a Federal Council, or *Bundesrat,* representing the participating governments, and a parliament, or *Reichstag,* representing the people and elected by universal male suffrage.

The king of Prussia the dominant element in the constitution

Although the twenty-two member states preserved a broad measure of autonomy, they lost their leading sovereign rights, which were taken over by the new federal institutions, the Bundesrat, the Reichstag, and, above all, the king of Prussia in his capacity of president. While the constitution, drafted by Bismarck, made in the elected Reichstag a considerable concession to liberal opinion, the document was so framed that the head of the new state, that is, the king of Prussia, exercised effective control.

The south-German states fail to form a confederation of their own

The south-German states, free, by the terms of the Treaty of Prague, to form a confederation of their own, failed to do so. Dangerously isolated, they played for a time the role of wandering comets of the German system. Then, on the coming to a head, four years later, of a slow-maturing crisis with France, they were drawn by an irresistible outburst of nationalist fervor into the North German Confederation.

The fatal Franco-Prussian crisis of 1870 had its earliest, barely noticeable roots in the Danish War of 1864. This war brought an advantage to Prussia without an equivalent advantage to the Second Empire. Largely owing to the fact that the principle of nationalism was involved, to which Napoleon had a sincere attachment, he failed to intervene. He could not remain equally indifferent over the far more considerable advantages gained by Prussia through her war with Austria. He therefore threatened to step between the two German powers as arbiter; but the Prussian victory was so speedily won that Bismarck came to terms with Austria in the Treaty of Prague before Napoleon could force his way into the negotiations. In the summer before this war broke out, in 1865, Bismarck had paid a visit to the emperor to sound him out on the coming German developments and, when the talk swung round to French compensations in return for possible Prussian gains, had made some vague, strictly oral offers. On Napoleon's bringing them up after the victory of Königgrätz he met with evasion. Vainly in the subsequent months and years did he appeal to Bismarck to give his consent to French annexation first, of the Bavarian Palatinate, next of Belgium, and, finally, of the small border state of Luxemburg. Great was his vexation over the diplomatic fiascos he suffered in connection with his successive proposals, and inevitably his personal vexation carried over to the French people. They saw with understandable alarm the looming of a strong, united Germany beyond the Rhine, where for ages there had been nothing more formidable than a heterogeneous assortment of bickering fragments.

Napoleon unable to squeeze any "compensation" out of Bismarck

THE DECLINE OF NAPOLEON III

We left Napoleon III at the conclusion (1859) of the Italian War, in which he touched the meridian of his fortunes. The decline that followed was gradual and is equally traceable in the foreign and domestic fields. If we take the foreign field first, we notice that he still scored occasional but diminishing successes. At the Congress of Paris (1856), which closed the Crimean War, his devotion to the principle of nationalism had prompted him to play the role of the champion of the Rumanian people who inhabited the Turkish provinces called respectively Moldavia and Wallachia. Not only was it Napoleon who, through the Congress of Paris, secured for the two provinces a broad self-government under the sultan, but again it was he who followed up that first advantage by supporting every effort made by the provinces to be joined together under a single prince, thereby creating a united Rumania. After diplomatic sparring covering many years a state of Rumania ruled by Prince Alexander Cuza was at long last (1862) established with full recognition by the powers. No less than the Italians, the Rumanians owe an unrepaid and unrepayable debt to the sovereign who helped them to achieve their nationhood.

Napoleon forwards the cause of Rumanian nationalism, 1856-62

When, in 1863, the Poles revolted against Tsar Alexander II, Napoleon was once again moved to interfere in behalf of an oppressed na-

Failure of
Napoleon's
intervention
in behalf of
Poland

tionality. However, as he was not prepared to go to the length of war with Russia and, even had he wished to do so, could not have conducted a successful campaign against so distant an empire, he had to content himself with dispatching a weak protest to St. Petersburg over reported Russian "atrocities." Its only effect was to dig an impassable chasm between the two rulers. We may book Napoleon's Polish failure as a set-off to his Rumanian success.

A far more resounding failure followed. It carries the name of Mexico.

By 1815
France
had been
stripped of
her original
colonial
empire

In these same years, the early sixties, Napoleon turned his gaze to trans-Atlantic Mexico with a view to bringing it under his control. But before we can intelligently follow him into this unhappy venture, we must consider his total colonial policy. We are aware how in the course of her eighteenth century struggle with Great Britain France had lost most of her original colonial empire. Napoleon I practically surrendered the remainder when, in 1803, he sold the vast region called Louisiana, embracing the fertile valley west of the Mississippi, to the United States. On emerging from the Vienna settlement of 1815 France had, apart from a few islands in the West Indies and a number of insignificant outposts on the African and South American coast, nothing to boast by way of an overseas empire.

Just before the overthrow in 1830 of the restored Bourbon ruler,

Napoleon
creates a
new French
colonial
empire

Charles X, this king had turned his attention to Algeria, directly to the south of France across the blue waters of the Mediterranean. In following up this lead his successor, the Orléanist monarch, Louis Philippe, had become involved in a troublesome war with the native Arabs from which, not long before his own dethronement, he had emerged as victor. So far was Louis Philippe's successor, Napoleon III, from repudiating the Algerian policy of his Bourbon predecessors that he vigorously crushed the many new uprisings attempted by the spirited Mohammedans and, in the hope of making his victory stick, set up a vigorous civil administration in the conquered province. A little later (1858-1863) he succeeded in planting the French flag over Cochin-China and Cambodia, extensive areas of southeastern Asia, which at a later time were consolidated under the name of Indo-China. With this advance the Second Empire had impressively established itself in Asia as well as in Africa. Then the thought came to Napoleon to cross the Atlantic, to Mexico, where one of those opportunities beckoned which seem as though made to order for an ambitious imperialist.

Since its liberation from the Spanish yoke in the early twenties of the nineteenth century Mexico had been a republic afflicted with interminable troubles. By suffering defeat in a war (1846-1848) with its powerful neighbor to the north, the United States, it had lost the huge territory north of the Rio Grande all the way to the Pacific coast. Even worse than this devastating amputation, Mexico had at no time enjoyed any respite from internal disorders. In 1860 the Liberal party, headed by a full-blooded Indian, Benito Juarez, triumphed decisively over the Conservatives, identified with the great landholders and the Catholic clergy. Juarez promptly carried through an anti-clerical program which culminated in the confiscation of all ecclesiastical property (except churches) and in the suppression of the religious orders. When on the heels of this radical legislation the energetic reformer found himself facing a totally depleted treasury, he took the unavoidable step of suspending the interest payment on Mexico's foreign debt. Thereupon Great Britain, Spain, and France, stirred to action by the indignant outcry of the bankers who had floated the Mexican loans, carried out a joint intervention, in the course of which they occupied Vera Cruz till a settlement was achieved. Great Britain and Spain thereupon withdrew. But the French forces lingered on and, reinforced by the arrival of fresh troops, levied war on President Juarez to the end of bringing Mexico under French control. When Juarez had been driven out of Mexico City into the mountains (1863), Napoleon invited Archduke Maximilian, younger brother of Emperor Francis Joseph of Austria, to become emperor of Mexico. On the surface this looked as though he were disposing of his conquest for the benefit of the rival house of Hapsburg, but the reality underneath the surface was very different. Since poor Maximilian was no better than Napoleon's man of straw, such power as he possessed in Mexico rested solely on French bayonets. Consequently he could undertake nothing without Napoleon's consent and, holding power as the puppet of his sponsor, ended as his victim.

How it happened that Napoleon's ambition turned to Mexico

The end of this ill-considered chapter of slapdash imperialism came when the government of the United States brought the long Civil War (1861-1865) to a triumphant conclusion. Napoleon's Mexican adventure represented an extravagantly bold breach of the Monroe Doctrine, become since its proclamation in 1823 the chief directive of the foreign policy of the youthful American republic. The conquest by Napoleon of the state neighboring the United States immediately to the south would never have got beyond the stage of project, had not the Washington government been paralyzed for four years by its internal disorders. The moment these had been overcome, France was informed in firm tones that its occupation of Mexico would have to cease. Napoleon shuffled a bit, fearing the blow to his political prestige, but did not dare refuse. In the spring of 1867 the French troops effected their withdrawal. At once President Juarez rushed down from his mountain retreat, recovered the land of which he was the chief magistrate and, on capturing

Disastrous end of the Mexican venture, 1867

Emperor Maximilian, promptly sent him before a firing squad (June, 1867).

The domestic repercussion of Napoleon's foreign failure

Nor is the humiliation suffered at the hands of the United States and the Mexican patriots the whole story of the Mexican disaster. While Napoleon's failure to intervene in the Austro-Prussian War of 1866 was owing, in the main, to the swiftness of the Prussian victory, the absence of the best French troops in faraway Mexico was a powerful contributory factor. Fatally weakened in military might, Napoleon did not dare to project himself other than cautiously into the German conflict. The domestic consequences of the repeated defeats and setbacks suffered in the foreign field were prompt to put in an appearance. In fact, as early as the victorious Italian campaign of 1859 the French public had begun to show signs of restlessness. Some groups criticized Napoleon's conduct of the war. Even larger groups took issue with its outcome. The emperor felt his credit slipping and, in the hope of re-establishing it, resolved to appease his critics by loosening the tight shackles of the Legislative Assembly. He conceded this body a somewhat enlarged measure of freedom of discussion and the right to have its debates communicated in full to the public.

The Absolute Empire is replaced (1870) by the Liberal Empire

However, it was not till the Mexican misadventure and his failure to take a hand in the German crisis of 1866 that Napoleon's foreign policy met with, not debatable setbacks, but crushing fiascos. So greatly did they encourage the opposition that the emperor, with the greatest reluctance, made ever fresh concessions to his ever more clamorous critics. In 1868 a liberal press law was followed by a measure conceding to the French people a limited right of public meeting. Therewith the remaining absolutist barriers could no longer be maintained, and in 1869-1870 the whole autocratic constitution was scrapped for a new constitution with free elections, political parties, a ministry responsible to the Legislative Assembly, and all the other features of a genuine parliamentary regime. The Absolute Empire had been transformed into the Liberal Empire! A plebiscite, held on May 8, 1870, endorsed the change by a huge, five-to-one majority. To superficial appearances the Second Empire had renewed itself by a restorative dip into the fountain of youth. In plain fact it was nearing its end, for, counting from the rosy promise of that May referendum, it had only four more months to live.

THE FRANCO-GERMAN WAR OF 1870-1871

The Second Empire fell over the issue of German unification and the exasperation that had arisen in court circles and among the French public in general in consequence of the successive diplomatic rebuffs suffered at the hands of a Prussia visibly expanding into a greater Germany. A dangerous frame of mind had taken possession of a large section of the French government and people, to which an equally large section of the Prussian government and German people had responded in provocative kind. In the circumstances the prevailing mutual suspicion and excitement needed only to be fanned to flame by a relatively unimportant incident to lead to a state of war. This incident takes us to Spain. French exasperation over Prussian successes

In the year 1868 a revolution occurred in Spain which drove the Bourbon sovereign, Queen Isabella II, out of the country. Immediately the Spanish generals at the head of the revolt began to scout Europe for a sovereign to take Isabella's place and, among other possible candidates, turned their attention to Leopold of Hohenzollern-Sigmaringen, a minor member of the Prussian reigning house. After much hesitation Prince Leopold in June, 1870, signified his willingness to accept the Spanish crown, subject to election by the Spanish cortes. At once so frenzied a protest made itself heard on the part of the French government and press that on July 12 the prince again withdrew his candidature. A Prussian prince announces and withdraws his candidature to the Spanish throne (June, 1870)

This should have settled the issue. But the strong war party at Paris, headed by the foreign minister, the duke of Gramont, was set on getting even for past rebuffs by publicly humiliating Prussia and refused to let the issue drop. Hardly had Gramont heard of Leopold's withdrawal when he wired the French ambassador, Benedetti, to seek out King William at once and demand a letter from him wherein the king apologized for the recent candidature of his relative and promised never in the future to let it be renewed. Since the king had gone to the little town of Ems to take the waters, the ambassador on July 13 tracked him to this resort and asked for an interview. Scenting at once an act of diplomatic blackmail, William firmly rejected the French demands. Then he telegraphed a detailed account of the incident to Bismarck at Berlin. Gramont re-opens the issue and is rebuffed

Bismarck, convinced that the rejection by the prince of the Spanish candidature was a sufficient concession to French feeling and ready to go to war over a matter in which France had put itself in the wrong, gave to the press for general publication an offensively concise version of the Ems dispatch. Though his "editing" can hardly be called a falsification, as has been often charged, it was a conscious act of provocation intended as a resounding counterblast to Gramont's impertinent demand. The effect in Paris of the Ems message was electric. Press and public declared that French honor had been sullied, and the government, carried off its feet, decided for war, which the Chamber of Deputies formally voted on July 19. The "edited" Ems dispatch provokes France to declare war (June 19)

The advantages in the struggle which now ensued were, from the be-

ginning, with Prussia. The first success was achieved in connection with
the south-German states. Napoleon was hoping that they would, out of
aversion for Prussia, with which they had been recently at war, side
with him. But the far-seeing Bismarck had provided for just such an
emergency. Immediately after the war of 1866 he had apprised the
south-German governments of Napoleon's demand for Rhenish territory and had so shocked them with this revelation that they signed
offensive and defensive treaties which obliged them to fight shoulder to
shoulder with Prussia in the event of a French war. Even without
these alliances, however, the south-German governments could hardly
have remained neutral, for the people of southern Germany were aroused
to explosive enthusiasm and insisted on regarding the cause of northern
Germany as their own.

From a purely military point of view, too, the preliminary advantages
were all with the German side. The North German Confederation and
its south-German allies were ready sooner and mustered a larger and
better-organized army than Napoleon. In consequence, the famous General Moltke, who acted as chief-of-staff of the German forces, could assume the offensive and carry the war into France.

The Germans found the French drawn up in two main bodies, one in
Alsace under General MacMahon, the other in Lorraine under Emperor
Napoleon himself. A simultaneous attack on these concentrations on
August 6 was crowned with a double victory, obliging MacMahon to
abandon Alsace and Napoleon to fall back on the great fortress of Metz
on the Mosel. The combined German armies thereupon directed their
attack on the French forces covering Metz, and by three bloody battles,
culminating in the battle of Gravelotte (August 18), succeeded in blocking the westward retreat of the French and bottling up the chief French
army in the leading fortress of the eastern frontier.

Just before the situation around Metz had become acute, Napoleon
made his escape to the army of MacMahon, which he now tried to bring
up, as fast as possible, to the relief of Metz. But he was ruinously defeated at Sedan and obliged to surrender with all his troops (September
2). After a moving interview with King William, the fallen emperor
was sent to Germany as a prisoner of war.

Thus far the campaign had been managed with extraordinary skill
and dispatch on the part of General Moltke. The war had hardly lasted
a month, and already Napoleon, at the head of one French army, had
been captured, while a second French army, commanded by Bazaine,
had been locked up in Metz. Apparently, it remained only to march
upon Paris and dictate terms of peace. Accordingly, a German army of
200,000 men proceeded westward, and toward the end of September
undertook the investment of the French capital.

The south-German states align themselves with Prussia

The mili-tary advan-tages from the start with the Germans

The German victories (August) before the fortress of Metz

Surrender of Napoleon at Sedan, September 2

The war reduced to the siege of 1) Metz and 2) Paris

Meanwhile important developments had occurred in that capital. The calamity of Sedan had hardly become known when Paris rose in indignation against the luckless imperial government. The Empress Eugénie, whom Napoleon had left behind as regent, fled in dismay and, amid scenes of wild disorder, France was declared a republic (September 4). At the same time a number of men, the most prominent of whom was Gambetta, set up, for the purpose of effectively prosecuting the war, the provisional Government of National Defense.

Overthrow of the empire; proclamation of the republic (September 4)

The sieges of Metz and Paris mark the last stage of the war. If the Germans entertained the hope of settling matters in a few weeks, they were greatly mistaken. Gambetta, supported by the aroused patriotism of the country, made a most active and honorable resistance. But his raw levies were no match, in the long run, for the disciplined soldiers of the enemy. The surrender of Bazaine at Metz, on October 27, withdrew from the war the last veteran army which France boasted. Undismayed, the Parisians held out, until, forced by hunger, at last they, too, on January 28, 1871, agreed to capitulate.

Capitulations of Metz and Paris lead to peace negotiations

The war was over. In a preliminary treaty signed in February at Versailles and made definitive at Frankfort in May, 1871, France had to buy peace from Germany by paying an indemnity of one billion dollars and by ceding to the victor Alsace and the eastern section of Lorraine. In March the Germans began their homeward journey.

Peace of Frankfort (May, 1871)

It was not the old divided fatherland to which the soldiers returned. The great victories won by the united efforts of north and south had aroused a boundless enthusiasm. In all circles the feeling prevailed that the present happy military union must take a permanent civil form; and, yielding to this sentiment, the south-German governments signed agreements with Prussia by which they entered the North German Confederation. At the same time it was stipulated that the completed union was to be called the German empire, and that its head, the king of Prussia, should take the title German emperor.

Creation of a united Germany

On January 18, 1871, the completion of these arrangements was announced to the world by the ceremonial proclamation of William I as German emperor. Because the war was still going on, the event took place in the Hall of Mirrors, the vast assembly room in Louis XIV's sumptuous palace at Versailles. Bismarck, the architect of Germany, was raised to the rank of prince. He took the post of chancellor, thereby becoming the head of the national administration.

Proclamation of King William as German emperor (Jan. 18, 1871)

The peace which France signed with Germany at Frankfort was authorized by a National Assembly elected by the people and convened at Bordeaux. It assigned the executive authority, provisionally, to Thiers, a former Orléanist and a man of moderate views. Being largely composed of monarchists, for the country was still prevailingly conserva-

The peace with Germany authorized by the National Assembly

tive, the National Assembly inevitably aroused suspicion among republicans and radicals as to its ultimate intentions. In March, as soon as peace was assured, the Assembly left Bordeaux and moved to Versailles in order to be nearer to the ancient heart of the country, to Paris.

The Paris radicals set up the Commune (March, 1871) Thoroughly persuaded that the Assembly's next step would be the establishment of a reactionary regime, the extreme radicals, a mixed group of socialists, republicans, and anarchists, resolved to anticipate their opponents by rising in revolution. Taking possession of Paris, they set up a government which they called the Commune. "Commune" in French usage means the town or city considered as a political entity, and has nothing in common with what in English is designated as communism. Made up of many diverse elements, the Commune had no particular program apart from the setting up of radical Paris as a political unit in as complete independence as possible of the conservative National Assembly and its executive agent, Thiers.

The National Assembly crushes the Commune There followed a bitter civil war which lasted two months (March-May, 1871). It took the form of a siege of Paris by the national government at Versailles—the second siege sustained by the unfortunate city within a year! The issue was decided by the larger forces and supplies of the national government. In May the insurgents made their last stand in the heart of the capital. When resistance became hopeless, a few desperadoes set fire to Paris and succeeded in destroying the palace of the Tuileries, the City Hall (*Hotel de Ville*), and a few other historical structures. The exasperated victors knew no mercy. Thousands of men connected or suspected of connection with the insurrection and representing every shade of radical opinion were shot without trial; thousands more were transported to the colonies or condemned to imprisonment with hard labor.

The problem before the National Assembly The National Assembly became the unchallenged government of France. With what kind of constitution would it endow the country? The year that gave to Germany, which for centuries had been a political laughingstock, a strong government, brought to France, which, during these same centuries, had been the synonym of political strength, a troubled and harassed government faced with the necessity of reconstructing the country from the foundations.

28 ITALY, FRANCE, GERMANY, AND AUSTRIA-HUNGARY TO THE OUTBREAK OF WORLD WAR I

ITALY FROM 1870 TO 1914

THE HOUSE OF SAVOY

Victor Emmanuel II (1861-78)

|

Humbert I (1878-1900)

|

Victor Emmanuel III (1900-43)

THE KINGDOM OF Italy, whose history we have followed to the capture of Rome in 1870, was based on a constitution which established a parliamentary form of government. The upper house, the Senate, was a body of notables appointed by the king and possessed of little power, while the lower house, called the Chamber of Deputies, controlled the cabinet or ministry, which ruled the country. It was in effect the English system.

Italy a constitutional monarchy

In spite of the fact that the new state had been precipitately formed by joining together territories dissociated for centuries, it was given a centralized administration by means of officials called prefects. The prefects were appointed by the cabinet and represented the government in their respective territories. Thus centralized, the new Italy was, administratively, modeled less on an English than on a French plan.

Italy centralized administratively

Such close outward unification did not put an end to the many inner cleavages inherited from the past. Lombardy continued to look with suspicion on Piedmont; Tuscany had little or no sympathy for the problems of Sicily; and so on through the whole list of the former political divisions. Consequently, when the deputies came up to the capital at Rome, they did not hesitate to use their best efforts to procure advantages for their immediate constituents without regard to the interest of the nation as a whole. In short, with political unity achieved, the no less important moral and cultural unity remained still to be won. People had for so many centuries been Lombards, Neapolitans, and Romans that it was only natural that they could not at once divest themselves of their past and feel and act as Italians.

Persistence of the inherited provincial divisions

Of the many inherited differences the most disturbing one was rooted

North and
south have
a different
social and
economic
structure

in history and dug a veritable chasm right across the middle of the peninsula at about the latitude of Rome. Owing to conditions reaching far back into the past, the Italian north was socially and economically a very different world from the Italian south. Beginning with the Middle Ages the north had developed numerous and prosperous cities with an appropriate urban culture, whereas the south had remained substantially feudal and agrarian. This distinction still obtained when the new kingdom was founded and, in spite of every effort on the part of the new government to eradicate it, continued stubbornly to persist.

In the south the chief wealth was land. It was held in large estates

The differ-
ent land sys-
tems in the
south and
north

by the descendants of the feudal barons, who cultivated it not by peasants working each one his own inherited holding but by gangs of laborers constituting an agricultural proletariat. In the north, on the other hand, the land was held to a very large extent by a free peasantry, which had, perforce, a very different outlook on life from the serflike children of the soil to be found south of the capital.

Still more important in differentiating the two areas was the circum-

stance that the dominating economic factor in the north was not the land but the town. True, the once flourishing towns of the valleys of the Po and Arno had in the post-Renaissance period fallen into considerable decline. But they had never ceased to cherish their great traditions, and with the expansion of commerce and industry which characterized the nineteenth century, they courageously girded their loins to renew the race with their urban competitors of France, Germany, and England.

In this resolution the towns were badly handicapped by the poverty of

Italy in natural resources. The peninsula has no coal and little iron, that is, it is deficient in the raw materials which constitute the basis of modern machine industry. Italy was obliged to import these articles from England and Germany, thus making them unduly expensive. Fortunately a substitute for coal was gradually secured through the development of electricity from the ample streams flowing from the Alps and the Apennines. The Italians proudly refer to the upland snows which feed their rivers as "white coal." From its increasing transformation into motive power they confidently expected a progressively intensified industrialization.

While the Italians, on the whole, made notable headway in developing

While the
north be-
came indus-
trialized, the
south
suffered
an agricul-
tural crisis

a machine industry, the movement, for the reasons indicated, was limited to the north. While this region exhibited the familiar phenomena of multiplying factories and banks, of organized workers leaning toward socialism, and of an influential popular press, the south showed few or none of these signs of the times. Moreover, its one source of livelihood, agriculture, was visited by the crisis which overtook European agriculture in general after the abundant American foodstuffs began to find their way across the Atlantic. They tended to drive the Italian products, above all, Italian citrus fruits, from the European market. There resulted a deplorable distress among the Italian farm hands accompanied by a savage revolutionary unrest.

It would be unfair not to admit that the Italian government recognized from the start that the bridging of the chasm between north and south was one of its main concerns. The two sections were to be assimilated by the raising of the backward medieval area to the moral, cultural, and economic level of the more advanced region. The available means to this end were, on the one hand, public schools, on the other hand, improved communications by highways and railroads. Unfortunately the limited revenues of the state obliged the government to move slowly in applying these time-tested remedies.

The government attempts to raise the south to a higher level

One of the worst heritages of the tyrannical and at the same time feeble Bourbon government of Naples was the curse of brigandage which rested on the country. It required veritable military expeditions before the organized robber bands, who hid out in the Apennine mountains, were mopped up. An even worse affliction were the secret criminal societies, the *camorra* in Naples and the *mafia* in Sicily. For generations past they had terrorized and plundered their helpless fellow citizens. Cautiously the government declared war on them, cautiously because, in the face of their great power, the government itself was none too strong. While it forced these predatory elements somewhat to draw in their horns, such was the immense subterranean power they commanded that the twentieth century found them discredited perhaps, but still throwing their evil shadow across the southern scene.

The government fights brigandage and secret criminal societies

The most effective tool for raising the level of any people long sunk in ignorance and misery is by universal consent the public school. The educational situation even in the relatively advanced north was not encouraging at the time of the founding of the kingdom. Illiteracy was general, proceeding from bad to worse in measure as the inquirer penetrated deeper into the Italian boot. Owing to the poverty of the population and the consequent lack of public funds, the establishment of a general system of elementary education was not even attempted till 1877. A bill, passed in that year, making education free and compulsory for all children indicated good intentions but failed to become immediately effective because there was not enough money on hand to build schools on a liberal scale and to prepare qualified teachers.

The nation-wide elementary school not created till 1877

In the course of the following decades a slow but indisputable improvement took place so that by the beginning of the twentieth century schools had greatly multiplied and illiteracy been much reduced. Just before World War I illiteracy in the northern provinces had been

The greatly reduced illiteracy of both north and south

cut down to twenty-five per cent of the population; in the south, something more than fifty per cent of the people had at that time not yet learned to read and write.

Another problem of the new state arose from the heavy taxation required in order to meet expenditures. Again let us take note that Italy, although one of the most beautiful countries in the world, is poor even in those agricultural resources which are its mainstay. On beginning its existence as a united kingdom, it was obliged not only to set up an expensive administration and create ports, railroads, highways, and specialized institutions for every variety of professional training, but also, since it craved to be a great power, to create an army and a navy. In consequence there was an annual deficit, which produced a steadily mounting national debt together with a ceaseless tightening of the tax-screw. It is doubtful if any people of Europe was more severely and ingeniously taxed than the Italians. While it would not seem to be a record to be particularly proud of, in proportion to their population and national income, the Italians achieved a dizzier height of national indebtedness than such rich neighbors as France and England.

Italy burdened with heavy taxes and a vast public debt

At the turn of the century there was an improvement. The annual deficit was overcome; the budget was balanced; and the taxes, though remaining a cruel load, at least no longer tended to increase. In short, Italy was by way of overcoming its financial difficulties, largely on account of an indubitable improvement in its general economic situation.

Improved Italian finances by 1900

The economic advance by that date was evidenced by increasing manufactures, especially of silk and cotton fabrics, and the consistent upward trend of Italy's foreign trade. In the urban north such industrial centers as Milan and Turin expanded rapidly. Their large bodies of workers formed trade-unions, agitated for better hours and wages by means of strikes, and wrung concessions from the parliament, which took the familiar form of labor legislation. In short, by 1900 Italy was going the road already traveled by the countries which had led the way in modern development. Though continuing to lag behind its wealthier neighbors, it could take legitimate pride in having mastered many of the difficulties with which it had been obliged to wrestle.

All the phenomena of a modern industrial society apparent by 1900

One of the difficulties Italy failed to master sprang from overpopulation and its attendant phenomenon, emigration. Having one of the highest birth rates in the world, Italy experienced a steady growth in numbers. Expanding industry was not able to absorb all of the human increase, especially as the south did not become industrialized. To make the situation worse, agriculture, the only important occupation of the region south of Rome, entered in the eighties on the crisis already mentioned. While it was in part produced by the flood of cheap foodstuffs

Overpopulation and emigration

and citrus fruits from America, another and local factor entered into the situation. Some of the landlords, turning to the newer capitalist methods of production, introduced machinery and consequently employed fewer men. What could the increasing army of the unemployed do but emigrate? Unskilled field-workers, they had nothing to offer but their hands, their common labor, which turned out to be the very article in demand in countries experiencing a more intensive industrial transformation than Italy.

In the decade and a half before World War I a half million Italians were, on the average, annually abandoning their native land. They flowed in rivulets into every industrial country of Europe, but in broad streams into such new regions as the United States of America and the Argentine. The vast preponderance came from the backward south, thus making it quite clear that the lack of industry in this region, plus the agrarian crisis, furnished the explanation of the exodus.

Emigration directed chiefly to the United States and the Argentine

Emigration proved to be a social safety-valve and was welcomed as such by many intelligent Italians. But projecting our thought into the future, let us ask what is likely to happen when the countries to which the Italian overflow has been chiefly directed undertake to check it by restrictive legislation? Italy will be threatened with explosion! Against this disaster a wise government will have to make provision not by attacking emigration, which is no more than a symptom of economic disequilibrium, but by curbing overpopulation through inculcating birth-control. It cannot be held other than doubtful that the Italian government, set over a Catholic people, will ever advocate a measure of relief which the Catholic church has denounced in the most unqualified language.

Without emigration Italy is threatened with explosion

Like all modern states which have committed themselves to machine production and popular education, Italy became increasingly democratic. On the founding of the kingdom, tax-paying and educational qualifications limited the franchise to a small number of well-to-do citizens. Then, in 1882, a law was passed by parliament which first, reduced the property qualification and, next, in order to stimulate education, offered the vote to all males who could read and write. The masses refused to be satisfied with this reform. Their continued agitation at length produced the measure of 1912, which practically established universal male suffrage.

Gradual democratization of the franchise

The Problem of the Papacy

Another grave issue was the relation of the new kingdom to the pope. In consequence of the unification movement the Holy Father had gradually lost his territories and in 1870 was obliged to give up Rome itself to the victor. Although he appealed to Catholics throughout the world for help and received abundant material and spiritual evidences of their sympathy, no existing government was willing to come actively to his support. He was in his own eyes a prisoner of the Italian state; and in order to give this theory an appearance of reality he refused ever to leave the Vatican compound, consisting of the Vatican palace, the palace grounds, and St. Peter's church.

The pope regarded himself as a prisoner of the Italian state

To counteract papal propaganda and meet, if possible, justifiable Catholic expectations, the Italian parliament passed in 1871 the so-called Law of Papal Guarantees. Thereby the kingdom pledged itself to look upon the pope as a sovereign on a par with the Italian monarch; to permit him to use the Italian post, telegraph, and railways free of all interference from the state; to suffer him to send and receive ambassadors without the exercise of any supervision. In brief, the law conceded to the pope all the rights traditionally associated with sovereignty. Two notable additional features of the arrangement were first, that the pope was to receive over half a million dollars annually from the national treasury as an indemnity for his losses; and second, that his two great palaces in Rome, the Vatican and the Lateran, were to be extraterritorial, that is, that they were to be regarded as legally outside of Italy and hence not subject to Italian authority.

Italy tries to placate Catholic opinion by the Law of Papal Guarantees (1871)

This law, passed by the parliament, bound Italy but it did not bind the pope. Pius IX rejected it with every show of scorn on the ground that his acceptance would be construed as a blanket pardon issued to the Italian state for its many usurpations. His successors throughout the period under review took the same stand. It is true, however, that since king and pope dwelt side by side in the same community, they did, even in the days of unbending Pius IX, work out by undercover negotiations a sort of *modus vivendi*. To this minimum agreement the successors of Pius IX were willing to adhere. For a broad reconciliation on any basis the state might see fit to offer, the popes were in the period here considered not prepared. Therefore the latent war between papal and royal Rome, between church and state, continued unabated.

Latent war between pope and king, church and state

Foreign Policy: Nationalism and Imperialism

The foreign policy of Italy, like the foreign policy of all the European states after 1870, was inspired by the related forces of nationalism and imperialism. Nationalism concerned itself more particularly with winning for Italy the various near-by areas inhabited by Italians but belonging to other states. The most hotly coveted of these areas lay in Austria-Hungary and comprised the Trentino, that is, the region around the Alpine city of Trent, and the important Adriatic port of Trieste, together

Italian nationalism (irredentism) aims to acquire certain Austrian territories with the surrounding territory. The Trentino and Trieste were regarded as the enslaved children of a common mother, as unredeemed Italy (*Italia irredenta*); and nationalism in its most ardent form assumed the name of irredentism.

In so far as the Italians took a wider view of national expansion, they embraced within their survey the whole Mediterranean basin and its dependent regions. Capitalists, company promoters, and manufacturers largely made up this category of patriots. Desiring, like their kind throughout Europe, new markets and colonies, they may very properly be classified as imperialists. *Italian imperialism aims at the Mediterranean*

The government was constantly pressed by both irredentists and imperialists to take action in the foreign field in accordance with the particular objective of each group. For a long time the government maintained a hesitating attitude. If it yielded to the irredentists, it would have to reckon on a war with Austria; if it let itself be swayed by the imperialists, there was the prospect of a clash with Great Britain and France, which between them ruled the Mediterranean. *The seesaw between nationalism and imperialism*

No decisive step was taken till 1881. In that year France, already in possession of Algeria, suddenly pounced on Tunis, the territory adjoining Algeria to the east. This carried her colonial empire to within a short sea passage of the island of Sicily; and Italy, which had long looked wishfully toward Tunis but had been afraid to act, resented this encroachment. *The French seizure of Tunis (1881)*

So general was the wrath against France that the government took the significant step of seeking the support of Germany, the powerful rival of France. Negotiations with Berlin culminated in Italy's joining the existing partnership of Germany and Austria, thus constituting the league of the three central European states known as the Triple alliance (1882). *Creation (1882) of the Triple alliance*

The consequences of this commitment are easy to grasp; the irredentist (nationalist) movement was discouraged by the government as offensive to Italy's new ally, Austria, while the imperialist movement received official sanction. Fortified by the Triple alliance, the government resolved actively to enter the field of African politics. Unfortunately Great Britain and France had already picked up all the really valuable African areas, such as Egypt, Algeria, and Tunis, leaving for the younger power no more than the poor crumbs from their full board. *Italy decides on an imperialist course*

Nonetheless, the government was minded to go ahead, and fixed its attention on the African region to the southwest of the Red sea. Having acquired a foothold on that sea and on the neighboring Indian ocean by means of the two colonies, called respectively Eritrea and Somaliland, it was induced to regard these relatively worthless possessions as a convenient base to seize the economically valuable kingdom of Abyssinia (Ethiopia), which lay between them. *A foothold gained on the Red sea and the Indian ocean*

To this plan the Abyssinians, a hardy and warlike people, offered a valiant resistance. In 1896, at Adowa, they practically annihilated the Italian army which had been sent against them. Thus ended the first great imperialist enterprise of the young kingdom. The independence of Abyssinia had to be formally acknowledged by the defeated aggressor.

The attempt (1896) to conquer Abyssinia

Somewhat sobered, the country refused for a while to sanction further colonial ventures. Without abandoning the Triple alliance the government was moved to re-establish good relations with France. In 1902 it signed a secret agreement pledging itself not to take part in a war of aggression against the Third Republic. In return for this assurance France agreed to interpose no difficulties, if Italy should at some future time see fit to occupy the north-African territory of Tripoli. It goes without saying that the Franco-Italian understanding of 1902 enfeebled the structure of the Triple alliance. Nonetheless, Italy clung to this association to the very eve of World War I, thereby illustrating the shifty practices, which, under the increasing imperialist competition of the period, characterized not only her but, in varying measure, every other European power.

The secret agreement (1902) with France

Although the Roman government was now assured that France would not interpose her veto in case Tripoli were seized, it did not act at once. The chief reason for the postponement was that Tripoli belonged to Turkey, which was certain to resent its occupation. But as delay did not remove this difficulty, Italy in 1911 at last brought her courage to the sticking-point, swooped down on the Tripolitan desert, and provoked, as she had feared would be the case, a war with the Ottoman empire. However, the war was not seriously waged by the Ottoman empire, which, before many months had passed, recognized that it must, in its feebleness, come to terms with the aggressor. In 1912 Tripoli, rebaptized Libya by its conquerors, became an Italian colony.

Seizure (1911) of Tripoli, rebaptized Libya

Unfortunately, except for a narrow strip along the shore, Libya is a trackless sand-waste incapable of being made fruitful or of absorbing any considerable body of colonists. Nonetheless, the Tripoli venture was enthusiastically endorsed by the Italian people. In the circumstances it is not surprising that the government should have argued that, since the citizens applauded the acquisition by war of a useless desert, they would certainly approve the winning by the same means of the small but populous unredeemed areas close at hand. This signified the turning to irredentism and against Austria. The movement was systematically fanned into flame by its nationalist supporters and largely determined the attitude of both the government and the people of Italy at the outbreak of World War I.

The victory of 1912 popularizes the idea of conquest by war

FRANCE FROM 1870 TO 1914

How the National Assembly Reluctantly Adopted a Republican Constitution

On the defeat of France by Germany in 1870-1871 the government passed into the hands of the National Assembly. It was this body which made peace with the victor. At the same time it was obliged to put down the savage insurrection of the Paris radicals familiar under the name of the Commune. Thereafter it was free to give its attention to the major concern for which it was summoned—to provide the country with a definitive government. Perhaps because the elections to the Assembly had occurred during the distractions of the war, perhaps because the sentiment of the country was not yet friendly to republicanism, about 500 out of the 700 deputies elected were monarchists.

The National Assembly (1871) has a monarchical majority

Nothing, therefore, would have been easier than to abolish the Third Republic, provisionally proclaimed on September 4, 1870, if only the monarchists could have agreed on a monarch. It was here that a hitch occurred, exactly as in the earlier instance of 1849. A large body of Orléanists desired to restore the grandson of Louis Philippe, deposed in 1848; a smaller body of Legitimists held out for the grandson of Charles X, deposed in 1830; and a handful of deputies were found audacious enough to champion the young fifteen-year-old son of Napoleon III, deposed in 1870.

Three monarchical candidates

Under the circumstances the monarchists so successfully frustrated themselves that they lost their cause. Only once, in 1873, did a ray of hope illumine their sky. In that year the Orléanists and Legitimists, who between them commanded a majority of the votes, came to terms. They agreed that the Legitimist chief, the count of Chambord, should be made king on the understanding, made possible by the fact that he had no children, that he would accept as his successor his Orléanist cousin, the count of Paris. So far, so good. But the count of Chambord was a rock-ribbed Bourbon; and when he now declared that he would rule under no other flag than under the lily banner of his ancestors, the restoration project foundered on the objection of the Orléanists. As far back as 1830 the Orléanists had accepted the revolutionary tri-color (red, blue, and white). They were stoutly convinced that the country would never renounce the newer symbol.

How the monarchist plot of 1873 suffered shipwreck

With the greatest reluctance the Assembly, balked of its hope to establish a monarchy, familiarized itself with the idea of a republic. The former Orléanist, Thiers, who had provisionally been made president, indicated the gradual swing away from monarchy when he coined the phrase: "The republic divides us least." However, when he undertook

Thiers
deposed
(1873) as
executive
in favor
of Marshal
MacMahon

to act on his conviction and leaned somewhat too openly toward a re-public, the monarchical majority punished him with deposition from his post (1873) and elevated a general and an avowed monarchist, Marshal MacMahon, to the presidency. However, as a king acceptable to the majority could not be found, and as the Assembly, called to give France a permanent government, could not go on sitting forever, in the period 1873-1875 a constitution was at last drawn up.

Although the new constitution avoided the use of the word republic,

it nonetheless, in effect, established that form of government. The execu-tive was vested in a president elected for a term of seven years by the two houses of the legislature meeting in common session. The two houses were called the Senate and Chamber of Deputies respectively. While the senators were elected by local departmental bodies, the deputies, thought of as the immediate agents of the nation, were elected on the basis of uni-versal manhood suffrage.

As the French ministry, which rules the country, must command a

majority in the Chamber of Deputies, this body is plainly the kernel of the system. Its predominance so strikingly parallels that of the British House of Commons that the French republic and the British monarchy may be said to work in the same way. Each has the parliamentary system and the French president, like the British king, is to a large extent a purely ornamental official. An important difference in the working of the two systems results from the many parties in the Chamber of Deputies. Since no single party ever commands a majority, the ministry rests on a combination of parties, called in French parliamentary usage a *bloc*.

When, on the disappearance of the National Assembly (1875), fresh

elections were held, the republicans won a majority of the seats in the Chamber of Deputies. The proof was thus given that the country was being converted to republican ideas. Of course the monarchists did not give up the fight, but their continued divisions made them impotent and lost them the favor of the voters. In the elections of 1879 the upper house, too, was carried by the republicans. Thereupon the monarchist President MacMahon saw that the game was lost and resigned. He was replaced by Grévy, a thoroughgoing republican. Thus, after a decade of uncertainty, France had become endowed with a constitution, a legislature, and an executive alike of republican persuasion. More and more firmly with each succeeding decade the republic became established in the hearts and minds of the citizen body. Before the passing of another decade the mon-archists had dwindled to a negligible faction.

The Bourgeois Character of the Third Republic

In the light of its history since 1879 the republic may be described as parliamentary, nationalist, anti-clerical, and capitalist. That means that the bourgeoisie has been in the saddle and that it has been able to pass the laws and impose the policies which accorded with its outlook and interests. Of course the bourgeoisie encountered opposition, on the one hand, from the monarchists and their close allies, the clericals, on the other hand and in steadily increasing measure, from the workingmen, represented by the socialists. *The republic identified with the bourgeoisie*

The bourgeois republicans in the Chamber of Deputies thus constituted a central mass flanked by radical extremes. They have not failed, when hard pressed, to make concessions both to the Right and to the Left, more particularly to the Left in the form of that Social or Labor Legislation with which every modern country has been obliged to protect its industrial population against the extreme exploitation of the capitalists. The French labor code followed the same lines but did not go so far as the comparable codes of Great Britain and Germany. Despite these legislative favors extended to the Left, the history of the Third Republic during the period here considered presents itself to view as the record of an unusually capable, energetic, and successful bourgeoisie. *The republicans obliged to concede Labor Legislation to the parties of the Left*

An examination of the administrative system of the republic will bear out this contention. The centralization imposed on France by the first Napoleon and symbolized by the prefect, who is appointed by and remains responsible to the national government, so exactly suited the unitarian sympathies of the bourgeoisie that no attempt was made to alter it. It was the middle classes, let us always remember, who first raised the cry: France one and indivisible! A slight concession to local self-government may be seen in the fact that with the prefect, head of the administrative unit called department, was associated a general council of the department elected by manhood suffrage. However, as the central government reserved to itself the right to veto any act of the general council, the omnipotence of the ministry and of its agent, the prefect, cannot be said to have been impaired. *The republic strongly centralized by means of prefects*

Among the earliest measures of the republic was the complete reorganization of the army, as was only natural after the military chaos precipitated by the German victory. It was natural, too, to imitate the system of the victors by adopting the principle of universal, compulsory military service. This signified that every Frenchman, unless excused on account of infirmity, received the training of a soldier and, well into his middle period, was liable to service in time of war. Strongly and even excessively patriotic in accordance with French middle-class tradition, *The republic develops a strong army and navy*

the republican government spared no expenditures on either the army or navy and by tireless efforts attempted to carry both these services to the highest possible level of efficiency.

Reasons for the anti-clericalism developed by the bourgeoisie

More than by any other group of measures has the internal history of the Third Republic been colored by its open and determined anti-clericalism. There are many reasons why the Catholic church drew the fire of the republicans. Ever since the eighteenth century the French middle class had been critical of the church and been attached more or less enthusiastically to a skeptical, Voltairean philosophy. This of itself might not have led to action if, in the decade from 1870 to 1880, when the republic was obliged to fight for its life, the church had not so hotly supported the cause of monarchy.

The republic creates a system of lay schools in the face of Catholic opposition

No sooner did the republican majority come into secure possession of the government than it showed its hand by launching a campaign for a public school system to be maintained by the state. This was an attack on the church for two reasons: first, because the church had always insisted, as a matter of principle, that the education of the young was its own proper function; second, because in so far as there already existed a general primary school system in France it was under ecclesiastical direction. To be sure, the relatively large number of French illiterates proved that the church had not taken its educational task very seriously.

The lay schools launched in 1881

Beginning with 1881, the republican majority enacted a number of educational laws which gradually gave France an excellent new system of public schools. In these schools instruction was given free of charge by teachers who were not priests but laymen specially trained in normal schools maintained for this purpose by the state.

The church schools in competition with the state schools

The inauguration of a rival, state-controlled system of education moved the church to make a belated effort to extend and render proficient its own hitherto neglected system. Unless it undertook to compete with the state, it was threatened with loss of its hold on the youth of the nation. Church schools therefore multiplied rapidly and in them, in contrast with the lay teachers of the state schools, instruction was given by special teaching orders of Catholic brothers and sisters. Thus France, which had hitherto conspicuously lacked primary schools, suddenly had too many, that is, it had two rival systems competing with each other for the favor of the public.

The state resolves to destroy the ecclesiastical schools by the Law of Associations (1901)

Not only did this competition frequently assume a bitter form, but the ecclesiastical schools were too often successful, owing to the decisive influence exercised by the parish clergy over the minds of the peasants. Against the orders of the village priests these simple folk did not dare send their children to the state schools, even though in these publicly maintained institutions there was no tuition to pay. At last the state resolved to end the conflict and set up an educational monopoly by closing the ecclesiastical schools. Instead, however, of striking a direct blow at them, it passed (1901) the Law of Associations, which forbade a member of any unauthorized order (or association) to give instruction in a French school.

As the ecclesiastical schools were staffed by orders (both brothers and sisters) which had never received formal authorization from the state, the teachers were automatically eliminated and most of the institutions obliged to close their doors. In this manner the issue was decided in favor of the system of lay schools maintained by public taxation. Its merit is attested by the steady fall of the French illiteracy figure. By 1912 only four per cent of the annual quota of army recruits could no longer read and write. The state schools, become supreme, render good service

Warming to the combat, the anti-clerical majority in the Chamber of Deputies now resolved to attack the church in its last stronghold, the Concordat of 1801 (p. 428). By this arrangement state and church were closely tied up together, the most conspicuous single bond between them being the obligation assumed by the state to pay the salaries of the clergy. To put an end once and for all to the principle of inter-dependence and in order to set each of the former partners on his own feet, the legislature enacted in 1905 the Law of Separation between church and state. The republicans resolve to cancel the Concordat of 1801

By the terms of the Law of Separation the Concordat of 1801 was abrogated; the state ceased to pay the salaries of priests and bishops; and the famous seizure of ecclesiastical property of the year 1789 was duplicated by the appropriation of the very extensive property which had been acquired by the church since that time. However, the government did not want public worship to cease. While anti-clerical, it was not anti-Christian. The bill therefore provided that the appropriated churches were to be made over to associations of Catholic laymen, who, on pledging to the state submission to its laws, might hand them over to the clergy for religious services. Leading features of the Law of Separation (1905)

From this feature of the law it is plain that its success depended on the willingness of the worshipers to form lay associations. In many cases they were disposed to do so, even though tradition was against the practice, for the rule in the Catholic church had been for centuries that not the laity, but the clergy, must administer ecclesiastical property. However, before any headway had been made with the formation of lay associations the pope took a hand in the affair. This was Pius X, who, in a public declaration, condemned the Law of Separation *in toto* as an infringement of the rights of the church and ordered the Catholic laity to withhold the demanded co-operation. Pope Pius X rejects the Law of Separation

A complete deadlock ensued. For a period it seemed likely that the police would close the churches and bring public worship to an end throughout the country. In order not to offer this extreme offense to

Catholic sentiment the parliament gave way and canceled the requirement touching the formation of lay associations. By an act of 1907 the
parish priests were permitted to take over the churches on signing an
agreement with the mayors of the towns, acting in behalf of the government. On this basis public worship has been maintained without interruption ever since.

*The parlia-
ment yields
(1907) in
the matter
of lay asso-
ciations*

It was the ill luck of the Third Republic that, established only after
overcoming many resistances, it developed a fighting spirit and, as the
struggle with the church indicates, was tempted to push its policies to the
limit. If an excuse were needed for this attitude, it might be found in the
bitter animosity and subterranean plotting of its main enemies, the royalists and clericals, usually fused into a single mass. On two occasions at
least they precipitated a crisis which all but overthrew the republic.

*The fighting
spirit of the
republic*

The Boulanger and Dreyfus Incidents

The first crisis carries the label Boulanger. Boulanger was a general
who, toward the end of the eighties, resolved to take advantage of the
fact that the majority of the army officers held monarchical and clerical
sentiments. He aroused their enthusiasm by promising to lead them in
a war of revenge against Germany; and he proved himself a skillful
rabble-rouser by riding down the avenue on a prancing black war-horse
and proposing, with a lively gesture in the direction of the Chamber of
Deputies, to throw the rascals out. As there were some indubitable rascals
in the seats of authority this was a popular rallying-cry. Grave financial
scandals had recently broken in connection with the Legion of Honor
and a French Panama Canal project, which caused the confidence in the
republican regime to be shaken. Luckily for the republic the theatrical
general turned out to be a man of putty. When his plot had ripened to
the point which required him to step out into the open, his courage
failed him and he fled ignominiously to Belgium (1889) where, two
years later, he committed suicide. He had probably never been very
dangerous in himself. The peril to the republic lay in the men, monarchists and clericals, who hid behind him.

*The plot
of General
Boulanger
ends in
failure
(1889)*

In sharp contrast to General Boulanger, Dreyfus was not the agent
of a clerico-royalist cabal but its victim. A republican and a Jew, he had
entered the army and risen to the rank of captain. His religious faith
and political connections made him distasteful to his Catholic and monarchical fellow officers and induced a number of them to plot his ruin.
They forged documents, which pretended to prove that he had sold valuable military secrets to Germany. Arrested and convicted by court-martial,
he was deprived of his epaulets and sword in a colorful public ceremony

*Captain
Dreyfus
convicted
of treason
by forged
documents
(1894)*

and then committed to prison on desolate Devil's Island, off the coast of South America.

The sentence befell in 1894 and met with universal approval as bringing a traitor to his just reward. However, after a few years facts came to light which pointed to the innocence of Dreyfus; and a movement for a re-trial developed which became irresistible when the famous novelist, Emile Zola, seconded by the equally famous Anatole France, put themselves at its head. Meanwhile, the whole body of monarchists and clericals had fatuously identified themselves with the original, small group of plotters and moved heaven and earth to keep the case from being reopened. In 1899 it was reopened and in a new court-martial Dreyfus's earlier life sentence was reduced to ten years. Thereupon President Loubet pardoned him, but his partisans did not rest till in 1906 the Supreme Court completely exonerated the martyred officer and he was restored to his due rank in the army. *The Dreyfus case reopened and Dreyfus vindicated*

Particularly revolting to Frenchmen was the revelation afforded by the long-drawn-out Dreyfus agitation that the army was honeycombed with anti-republican sentiments. Resolved that this condition should not continue, the government dismissed the worst reactionaries from the service and took measures to train an officer body devoted to the democratic regime. The Dreyfus case was a trial of strength between the republic and its reactionary enemies and the republic had won. *The army cleansed of its anti-republican elements*

Colonial Expansion

A characteristic interest of the dominant French bourgeoisie was to promote material prosperity in every possible way. Attentive to the counsels of bankers and capitalists, the parliament strongly supported public works, such as highways, railroads, canals, and harbors. Above all, it threw itself enthusiastically into colonial expansion. In the previous chapter we learned how, under Napoleon III, France had again come forward as a colonial power with its main footholds in Algeria (Africa) and in Indo-China (Asia). As soon as the Third Republic had become firmly established, it entered on a vigorous policy of expansion from these two centers. *The bourgeois republic backs the colonial movement*

The Indo-China center was by a succession of military expeditions so enlarged and strengthened that it made France a power in Asiatic waters second only to Great Britain. The main effort, however, of the republican empire-builders was directed to northwestern Africa. In 1881 Tunis was seized from under the very nose of Italy. Presently the French began a systematic penetration southward from Algeria and Tunis into the Sahara desert and by feeling their way inland at the same time from Senegal, *All of northwestern Africa comes into French possession* the Ivory Coast, and the Congo river system, got into their possession practically the whole northwestern mass of the black continent.

The outstanding importance of Algeria and Tunis

The different parts of this vast area are of very unequal value. Its core, the Sahara desert, is for the present a complete liability. The colonies on the coast of the gulf of Guinea are in a higher category, as they afford a limited opportunity for trade in such tropical products as cocoa, palm-oil, rubber, and mahogany. Concerning the value of Algeria and Tunis, however, there can be no dispute. They are not unsuited for settlement by whites and under stimulation from French capital have become increasingly productive in dates, figs, and citrus fruits. The immense potentiality of these two Mediterranean regions is proved by the fact that their trade with the homeland has, in recent decades, risen by leaps and bounds.

The republic plans and achieves (1912) the conquest of Morocco

Considered as a whole, the value of the French African empire must, from a middle-class viewpoint, be regarded as very great. In order to round it out, the government formed, in the first decade of the twentieth century, the project of acquiring the independent sultanate of Morocco to the west of Algeria. As Morocco was coveted also by other powers, a difficult and strained situation was created which more than once threatened to plunge Europe into war. We shall examine the Morocco incident when we review the pre-war diplomacy of Europe as a whole. It will suffice at this juncture if we record the success of the French Moroccan plans. They culminated in 1912 in the incorporation of all but a northern Moroccan belt—which went to Spain—in the African empire of the republic.

Foreign Policy: Dual Alliance and Triple Entente

Leading event in French foreign policy the alliance (1890) with Russia

The foreign policy of France between 1870 and 1914 was determined first, by her historic position in Europe, and second, by her colonial ambitions. As her traditional primacy on the continent had been overthrown by the victory over her of Germany, her wounded pride filled her with an unwavering antagonism toward her eastern neighbor. The patriot mass of Frenchmen craved and looked forward to "revenge." In 1890 France entered into friendly relations with Russia, which ripened into a Dual alliance and gave the republic an improved standing as against Germany, fortified since 1882 by the Triple alliance.

The Franco-British colonial agreement of 1904; the Triple entente

In the pursuit of her colonial ambitions France followed an elastic policy of entering into negotiations with the other colonial powers, according to the necessities of the moment. This bargaining culminated in 1904 in a sweeping colonial agreement with Great Britain. The crux of this agreement was that, in return for surrendering its claims in Egypt to Great Britain, the republic received British support for its Moroccan program. Great Britain, thus brought into intimate association with

France, undertook to cultivate closer ties with France's ally, Russia, and from the spinning of these various threads there sprang, around 1908, the so-called Triple entente.

This diplomatic development, the detailed story of which is reserved to a later chapter, is briefly mentioned here to bring out the fact that France, like all the other powers, was moved in her foreign policy by two master influences, distinct and yet related. These were nationalism and imperialism. Nationalism prompted her, more particularly, to set about restoring her position in Europe as against Germany; imperialism, with its search for markets and colonies, moved her to extend her control over sparsely settled and backward areas with all the energy at her command.

The master forces of French foreign policy: nationalism and imperialism

GERMANY FROM 1871 TO 1914

THE HOUSE OF HOHENZOLLERN

William I (1871-88)
|
Frederick III (1888)
|
William II (1888-1918, deposed)

The German Empire: Predominance of Prussia

The German empire, forged in the fire of three wars fought between 1864 and 1871, rested on the constitution of 1867, together with the modifications adopted on the occasion of the incorporation in the empire of the four south German states (1871). The constitution, which, like the empire, was largely the creation of Bismarck, aimed at combining three factors: (1) the ascendancy of Prussia; (2) the self-government of the twenty-five component states; and (3) the national solidarity of the German people. The aim was essentially sound, as these three factors ruled the situation.

Three elements combined in the German constitution

Accordingly, Bismarck made special provision for each of these factors. To Prussia he secured a dominant position in the upper house, the Bundesrat, and to the king of Prussia the headship of the new state with the title of German emperor; to the component states he guaranteed their semi-sovereignty by leaving them in control of local interests and by giving them representation in the Bundesrat; to the German people he conceded the opportunity to voice their opinion by means of a lower house, the Reichstag, elected by universal manhood suffrage.

Provision made for each of the three dominant elements

We may agree that the architect of German unity desired to establish a balance among the three historical forces with which he was obliged to deal. However, he was himself a Prussian and owed his notable achievement to the power of the Prussian state. We need not be surprised, therefore, that, perhaps as unconsciously as consciously, he tipped

The predominance of Prussia in the German set-up

the balance in favor of Prussia by shaping the constitution in such a way as to make Prussia count for much more than the other two factors.

It might be contended that no other outcome than this was possible, since Prussia was twice as large as all the other German states put together and boasted twice as many inhabitants. In simple truth, what was the new German empire but a somewhat enlarged Prussia? This much established, the social-political consequences must be carefully noted. Prussia had until 1848 been an absolute monarchy and even under the constitution of 1850 the king continued to dominate the administration. Furthermore, Prussia in 1871 was still, in spite of the advance of industry, an agrarian state, wherein the landholders, called Junkers, played the leading role. Hence the predominance of Prussia signified the predominance of conservative influences coupled with a resolute resistance to democratic currents of opinion.

The popular house, the Reichstag, possessed great powers since it voted the taxes and framed all legislation. But it did not control the chancellor and the other federal ministers, who were appointed by the chancellor and acted as his agents. In other words, while Germany had a constitutional government, it did not, like Great Britain, France, and Italy, have a parliamentary one. Liberalism in its many varieties down to extreme radicalism could speak and agitate, but conservatism was in the saddle.

The outstanding event in the domestic history of the new empire between 1871 and 1914 was its rapid and thoroughgoing industrialization. Already by the turn of the century Germany had, in the production of machinery and machine-made goods, overtaken the other countries of Europe with the exception of Great Britain. In the new century it began to press more and more closely on British heels.

Era of Co-operation Between Bismarck and the National Liberal Party

Socially and politically the industrialization of Germany signified the steady advance of the middle classes. Even though the government, itself conservative, favored the conservative landlords, it could not ignore the rising bourgeoisie, especially as it did not fail to see that this urban group produced the increasing wealth by reason of which Germany was winning a larger consideration among the nations. During the period of almost a decade following the creation of the empire, Bismarck worked in close association with the middle classes. They were represented in the Reichstag by the National Liberal party, which in consequence of elections conducted in an atmosphere of national elation ruled that body. The partnership was facilitated by the circumstance that, by unifying

Germany, the great statesman had realized the fondest dream of the middle classes. He thereby became for them a patriotic idol, whom it was customary to regard with almost religious reverence. With such a leader the middle classes were proud to be associated in the abundant legislation that awaited the first parliament of the re-constituted nation.

Accordingly, under Bismarckian inspiration the National Liberal party passed a body of laws which deserve to be sketched because they gave the new German state an efficient, modern character. The divergent coinage systems of divided Germany were replaced by a single system of which the unit was the *mark* (worth about 24 cents). A central national bank, called the *Reichsbank,* was set up to give stability to the national finances. The many crazy systems of weights and measures were replaced by the metric system, invented in France during the great Revolution and afterward adopted, on account of its convenience, by numerous other countries. *(Unifying German legislation)*

Owing to the prestige enjoyed by the Prussian army system after the victories of 1864, 1866, and 1870, it was extended to the south-German states. Theoretically the middle classes, as Liberals, were opposed to a powerful standing army. But like the rest of the world they kowtowed to success and could, besides, salve their conscience by means of the central feature of the army system. This was universal compulsory service, which, as falling on all alike, had a democratic flavor. *(Prussian universal military service imposed on all the German states)*

One of the most constructive measures of this period of reorganization was the remodeling of the system of national justice. The law courts were endowed with a simplified and uniform procedure and the whole legal edifice crowned with a Supreme Court of the empire located at Leipzig. At the same time commissions of jurists were empowered to prepare new and modernized codes of both criminal and civil law. These codifications, reminiscent of Justinian and Napoleon I, required careful and prolonged study. In due time, however, the new codes were presented to the Reichstag and, after a searching revision, were made the basis of an improved and uniform system of national justice. *(Simplification of the courts; codification of the law)*

A quarrel with the Catholic church belongs to this period of harmonious co-operation between the middle classes and him whom they admiringly called the Iron Chancellor. Although the quarrel was not of bourgeois origin, burgherdom in Germany, especially Protestant burgherdom, was unfriendly to ecclesiastical pretensions and ready and eager to reduce them. The conflict began over the new claims put forth by the papacy in connection with the Declaration of Infallibility in 1870. Believing firmly in the omnipotence of the state, Bismarck had long held that the Catholic church exercised too much power in the Catholic sections of Germany. Moreover, he suspected that papal infallibility was the first gun *(Inauguration of a conflict with the Catholic church)* fired in a Catholic campaign for even greater freedom of the church from state supervision.

Sharp exchanges between the two rival authorities led Bismarck to take drastic action. In the period 1872-1875 anti-Catholic laws were passed which aimed to bring the Catholic clergy more completely under the control of the state than had been the case in the past. To this end civil marriage was made obligatory, the ecclesiastical ceremony becoming purely optional; priests were required to obtain their education no longer in ecclesiastical seminaries but in the schools of the state; and the Jesuits, as the uncompromising supporters of the pope, were driven from the empire.

Laws passed to bring the Catholic clergy more completely under state control

The country was soon in an uproar, as the clergy resisted the new laws and invited its Catholic following, which constituted over one-third of the total German population, to support its ecclesiastical superiors. The Catholics complained that they were the victims of religious persecution, while the Protestant middle classes, which stood behind Bismarck, declared somewhat grandiloquently that theirs was a *Kulturkampf,* that is, a struggle for civilization. The word Kulturkampf supplied the label under which the conflict passed into history.

The conflict called Kulturkampf by its middle-class supporters

After a few years the chancellor, who had the elastic mind of a creative statesman, recognized that he could not coerce the church and that he must beat a retreat. The only way to placate his adversaries was to withdraw the obnoxious legislation. Act on act was therefore canceled in gradual stages until, ten years after the Kulturkampf had begun, practically nothing remained of the anti-Catholic laws save obligatory civil marriage.

Unable to coerce the church, Bismarck gives up the conflict

Indisputably the Catholic church emerged from the struggle with that added prestige which victory regularly confers. An event of the greatest importance attending the Kulturkampf must not be overlooked. For greater effectiveness the clergy had organized the laity into a political party, ready and able to defend the Catholic cause in the Reichstag. This party took the name of the Center party and thenceforth contended for power with the older parties of the Conservatives and the National Liberals. To these three parties was added, at about the time of the birth of the Center party, the party of the workers, the Social Democratic party. It was among these four parties, together with minor dissident groups which we may disregard, that the battle for political power in Germany was waged through the period here under consideration.

Birth of the Center party; its rivals are the Conservatives, Liberals, and Social Democrats

Bismarck and the National Liberals Part Company

Toward the end of the seventies Bismarck, whose massive figure overshadowed every phase of German life, came out for two measures which only a section of his chief supporters, the National Liberals, would accept. They split into two separate liberal factions, one supporting Bismarck's new course and retaining the National Liberal label, the other calling itself Progressive and passing over to the opposition. Of course liberalism, thus divided, lost much of its earlier importance. The two measures which Bismarck was resolved to convert into laws represented incisive innovations. The first involved the issue of free trade versus protection; the second witnessed the chancellor's alarm over the spread of socialism. It was this alarm that was probably the chief reason for Bismarck's ending the Kulturkampf. He could not fail to see that in a struggle with anti-religious socialism he would nowhere find a firmer supporter than in the Catholic church.

Bismarck favors two measures which split his liberal following in two

In tariff matters Germany had, ever since the creation of the Zollverein, been governed by a regime of low duties levied on foreign goods. It was a policy, if not of free trade, at least of trade encouragement. In the seventies the industrialization of Germany was under way but was not yet so effectively carried through as to enable Germany's young industries to compete successfully against its more advanced neighbors. A group of manufacturers demanded protection; and as the landlords, vexed by the importation of cheap, chiefly American and Russian foodstuffs, made the same demand, Bismarck resolved to give up the low schedules hitherto in force and to insure the home market to the German industrial and agricultural interests by increased duties. The new protective tariff was successfully put through the Reichstag in 1879 with the support chiefly of the Conservatives and the Centrists, on whom with occasional help from the reduced National Liberals he continued to lean for the remainder of his term in office.

Germany adopts (1879) a protective policy

Before we consider the chancellor's socialist legislation let us agree that the Industrial Revolution, which increased the power and the numbers of the bourgeoisie, increased the numbers and at least the potential power of the workingmen in the same proportion. From the first appearance of machines radical writers and thinkers had attempted to win the new class of wage-earners to their ideas. No startling headway was made till by a fusion in 1875 of two distinct socialist groups, a united Social Democratic party saw the light. At once the workers began to give this party their allegiance, with the result that the socialist representation in the Reichstag rapidly increased.

The Social Democratic party attracts the workers and steadily increases its representation in the Reichstag

This phenomenon greatly alarmed Bismarck, for socialism was a revolutionary doctrine which aimed to replace the existing state of the propertied classes with a socialist state governed by, and in the interest of, the unpropertied workers. How meet the dangerous situation? Bismarck resolved on both repression and persuasion. On the one hand, he would have the Reichstag pass an anti-socialist law forbidding socialist agitation whether conducted by means of newspapers, books, or public meetings; on the other hand, he would promulgate an elaborate labor code, which would protect the workingmen against some of the worst evils of their lot. By his labor code he hoped to persuade the workers that the existing state, far from being ill-disposed to them, was deeply concerned for their welfare and could actually bring about the improvement which socialism merely projected as a distant dream.

Bismarck resolves on conversion of the workers by (1) repression and (2) persuasion

The repressive anti-socialist law, passed in 1878, proved a complete failure. Socialist agitation, denied the right of public utterance, went underground and won the added attraction which results from martyrdom. It was the Kulturkampf over again with a different cast of characters. And since socialism flourished in spite of repression, the government, exactly as in the case of the Kulturkampf, came to see the futility of its measure. In 1890 the law was permitted to lapse. By that time, however, Bismarck, the father of the law, was no longer in office.

On proving a failure the anti-socialist law is permitted to lapse (1890)

Much more important was the other, the persuasive feature of Bismarck's socialist legislation. In its entirety it constitutes an immense, ameliorative labor code. A part of it dealt protectively with the work of women and children and provided more humane conditions in factories; that is, it followed a line already taken by such older industrial countries as Great Britain. Another part, far more original, in fact representing one of the most important contributions made to Social Legislation in this period, took up workingmen's insurance. Three types of insurance were put into effect by successive measures passed between 1883 and 1889: (1) insurance against accident; (2) insurance against sickness; (3) insurance against invalidism and old age. As the workingmen were required to make contributory payments to the funds established in connection with types two and three, they were invited to share the control of these funds with the employers. The responsibilities of management imposed, in connection with these large and growing funds, on both employers and employees exercised a beneficent influence on the whole economic situation.

Bismarck's labor code includes Insurance Legislation

Without doubt the German Insurance Legislation did much toward developing in Germany one of the most vigorous bodies of workingmen to be found in the world. But let us make no mistake about one thing: though the wage-earners gladly profited from the insurance enactments, they did not show the least inclination to give up their antagonism to the capitalist state and society or to abandon the Social Democratic party.

The workers not weaned from socialism

Accession and Reign of Emperor William II

In 1888 William I, the first ruler of reunited Germany, died at the more than patriarchal age of ninety-one years. As his son, Frederick, who was already dwelling in the shadow of death at the time of his accession, reigned only three months, the scepter passed to Frederick's oldest son, William. Emperor William II (1888-1918) was an intelligent, active, and nervously unbalanced individual afflicted with an excessive self-esteem. The German system, which conceded an all but autocratic fullness of power to the sovereign, suited him exactly, except for the circumstance that under his modest, self-effacing grandfather the functions of the sovereign had, in effect, been taken over by the chancellor, by Bismarck.

Accession (1888) and character of William II

The young and restive William chafed under this inherited tutelage. Suddenly, two years after his accession, he dismissed (1890) the too-masterful Bismarck from office. Thenceforward he planned to be himself the director of German policy. By appointing more subservient and less authoritative men to the chancellorship he maintained a personal ascendancy that was but rarely challenged. The period after 1890 was for Germany as distinctly the age of William II as the period before 1890 had been the age of Bismarck.

Dismissal (1890) of Bismarck and assumption of power by William II

The extraordinary activity of William, which manifested itself, among other ways, in voyages over Europe coupled with theatrical displays and bursts of emotional oratory, soon gave German foreign policy a hasty, hectic character which caused it to be looked upon with suspicion. This was regrettable, since William was a man of peace at heart who, in spite of provocative explosions, desired to cultivate good relations with his neighbors. In short, by lack of a dignified self-control, he proved himself the most inept diplomat of his time. We shall follow the German foreign policy within the whole frame of European relationships in a later chapter (Chapter 34).

William's instability reflected in German foreign policy

At this point it is more important to define the imprint which William gave to domestic developments in Germany. It was characteristic of his mental vivacity that he interested himself in every movement within the whole range of German life, in the great basic activities of agriculture, industry, and commerce as well as in religion, science, and art. And it indicated his excessive self-esteem that he considered himself capable of advancing one and all of these interests by his personal contribution. If much of his multitudinous activity was too superficial to have any value, it is possible that his close attention to the material development of his country somewhat accelerated its advance along the road it was already traveling. In any case industry developed during his reign at a constantly increasing speed; and commerce and agriculture—the latter only because of the protection it enjoyed through a high tariff on imports—did not lag far behind.

Material prosperity advanced by William

It was an era of remarkable prosperity measured by the index of statistics. The tonnage of the German merchant marine rose rapidly until it was exceeded only by that of Great Britain. The amount, variety, and value of manufactured articles increased each year. So also did the country's foreign trade, the outstanding feature of this trade being the steadily swelling mass of machinery and machine products flowing beyond the German boundaries. It is noteworthy that Germany developed certain specialties, for which, owing to their excellence, there arose a general demand. Among these figured electrical appliances and a large variety of chemical products, especially dyes; also precision instruments such as microscopes, field glasses, and the like, depending on careful lens-grinding. The movement of population was in tune with these impressive advances. Between 1870 and 1914 the population grew from forty-one millions to over sixty millions, and most of this increase belongs to the period after 1890, that is, to the era of William.

Statistical items illustrating German prosperity

In order to put through his economic program William, or his chancellors acting for him, had to command a majority in the Reichstag. He sought support where he could find it, but on the whole, like Bismarck in his last period, leaned on the Conservatives, the Catholic Center, and that section of the Liberals identified with "big business." Since his policy boosted the interests of all these groups, he was in a position to ask for a return favor and accordingly pressed for the enlargement of the already powerful army and the strengthening of a service which Germany had thus far neglected, the navy. This close attention to national defense was a feature of the contemporary policy of all the powers and need not be interpreted in the case of any of them as an obstinate will to war. It did, however, signify that they, one and all, nursed plans of colonial expansion, for which they thought it well to provide the backing of a formidable armament.

William champions the enlargement of the forces of national defense

Overseas expansion is the key to William's persistent agitation for a navy. Resolved to push Germany into the colonial race, he was obliged to provide the country with sea power. Sea power had not been a part of the national program in the age of Bismarck. By means of a tireless personal propaganda the emperor succeeded in arousing the interest of both people and Reichstag in his plans. In 1898 a naval bill was passed by which the first step was taken toward the creation of an effective fleet.

Germany acquires a formidable navy

By supplementary bills in the following years new naval units were added till, in the course of another decade, the German navy had overtaken the navies of all the countries of Europe with the single exception of Great Britain. By an immense naval expansion of its own the island-kingdom maintained its traditional ascendancy, not, however, without displaying increasing signs of annoyance and wrath at its impertinent competitor.

Great Britain resents the German navy

For his economic as well as for his national defense policy William depended, as we have seen, on those Reichstag parties which drew their strength from the possessing classes. By caressing them he mortally offended the workingmen organized in the Social Democratic party. Throughout his reign there was open war between him and the Social Democrats with the immediate advantage resting with the emperor, who from his loftier platform hurled the thunders of his wrath at the lowly heads of his adversaries. Not that he was ill-disposed to workingmen as such. He gave unstinted support to the Labor Legislation inaugurated by Bismarck; and it was probably due to his personal intervention that Bismarck's anti-socialist law was permitted to lapse after the chancellor's dismissal in 1890. Sharp antagonism between the emperor and the Social Democrats

By making it clear that the chasm between himself and his revolutionary antagonists was unbridgable, the emperor engaged them in a desperate struggle. However, in spite of all he could do, the Social Democratic party continued steadily and ominously to grow. In the elections of 1912 it came dangerously near to polling as many votes as Conservatives and Liberals combined and returned a membership which made it the largest single party in the Reichstag. This separation of Germany into two irreconcilable groups of monarchists, who supported the existing order, and socialists, whose goal was a republic, did not augur well for the future. Steady growth of the Social Democratic party in the reign of William

William's Colonial and Imperialist Policy

A country which, like Germany after 1871, was politically powerful and economically dominated by the Industrial Revolution, was bound to seek colonies and engage in the imperialist game. The cautious Bismarck at first discouraged the merchants who looked beyond the seas for markets and territory; but when, in the eighties, he saw an opportunity to go ahead without encountering too much opposition from the older countries already in the field, he assumed for Germany the protection of certain areas in the only still available continent, in Africa. Bismarck's colonial policy

The policy thus inaugurated, William II, throwing Bismarck's caution to the winds, continued to pursue with characteristic zeal until by 1914 his country had amassed a considerable colonial empire. To be sure, owing to Germany's late appearance on the scene, her extra-European possessions could not remotely compare either in extent or value with those of such older powers as Great Britain and France. However, they sufficed to make her a factor in the colonial race. A fair-sized colonial empire amassed under William II

The bulk of the colonies acquired by Germany lay in Africa in three groups: Togo and Kamerun on the coast of the gulf of Guinea; German Southwest Africa; and German East Africa. Smaller, but not negligible, were the German holdings in the Pacific ocean. They consisted chiefly of scattered island groups like the Marshall chain and the Carolines. In The German colonies enumerated

the country's own eyes the chief jewel of its eastern possessions was the flourishing colony of Kiaochow in the Chinese province of Shantung.

William II commits Germany to imperialism or world politics

Taken together with her strong army and navy and her expanding commerce and industry, her colonies had the effect of pushing Germany into the imperialist game. Although we shall study German imperialism in connection with all the other imperialisms at a later time, we must insist, even at the risk of repetition, that it did not fully dominate German foreign policy till the reign of William II. Under Bismarck, a statesman rooted in the realities immediately surrounding him, foreign policy had been determined almost exclusively with reference to the herditary enmity with France.

German imperialism encounters the "encirclement" of the Triple entente

When the restless William II persuaded himself to disregard the enmity with France and, pursuing imperialist designs, plunged into world politics, he blazed a path which became decisive for German destiny. By reaching beyond Europe William antagonized Russia and Great Britain and drove them into the arms of France. In the end the three arranged a Triple entente which hemmed Germany in by drawing an iron ring around her. This was the precarious situation in which Germany found herself at the outbreak of World War I.

AUSTRIA-HUNGARY FROM 1867 TO 1914

The Compromise of 1867

The problem before Austria: centralization or federalism

Between 1859 and 1866 the Austrian empire suffered a series of defeats which drove it out of Italy and Germany and caused it to rock uneasily on its foundations. The emperor, Francis Joseph I (1848-1916), was still a young man at the time of these misfortunes and flexible enough to reach the conviction that the traditional absolutism would have to be given up. But with what was it to be replaced? There were two main schools of thought among his advisers: the first school held that the unity of the empire should be maintained at all costs and be visibly symbolized by a central parliament at the capital, Vienna; the other school contended that the empire should be decentralized by being broken into its component provinces and nationalities. While both solutions accepted the idea of popular representation, the first aimed at centralization, the second at federalism.

Adoption of the Compromise (1867) by which the Austrian empire is split in two

In the end neither of these proposals, neither centralization nor federalism, triumphed, but a third program, proposed and championed by Hungarian leaders and conferring on Hungary a privileged position. It is known as the Compromise (*Ausgleich*) of 1867 and created what is usually and properly called the dual system, since it divided the Hapsburg territories into two sections, Austria and Hungary. As defined in the Compromise, Hungary embraced the eastern half of the monarchy, that is, Hungary proper, together with its historical dependencies, Croatia, Slavonia, and Transylvania; Austria embraced the remaining, the western, provinces, seventeen in number.

It was agreed in the Compromise that each half of the Hapsburg dominion was to have its own constitution, parliament, and administration and become, in effect, a separate state. However, as the two halves would continue to have the same executive, called emperor in Austria and king in Hungary, they would necessarily have an important common bond and might aspire, though distinct administratively, to figure as a unit in the European system. To this end it was provided that the departments of foreign affairs, war (including both army and navy), and the finances necessary to support these services, were to pertain to both sections together and that they were to be presided over, not by Austrian or Hungarian, but by Austro-Hungarian ministers. As such ministers could not be made responsible to either the Austrian or the Hungarian parliament, it was arranged that they should appear periodically before the so-called *Delegations*. These were made up of a body of one hundred and twenty delegates, sixty from each of the two parliaments, and these delegates had the function of approving the budget drawn up for the common services.

Constitutional arrangements by which Austria and Hungary remained a unit

Let us admit that the machinery of the Compromise of 1867 was far from simple. However, the central idea was clear enough. It was that, while the old Hapsburg monarchy, because it had fallen on evil days, was to be broken into two halves, it was still, in respect of certain specified interests, to remain one in order that it might continue to count with its traditional weight at the council board of Europe. In point of fact, under the new name of Austria-Hungary the Hapsburg monarchy, in spite of its bifurcation, continued to figure as a great power.

Austria remains a great power under a new label

Turning now to examine the new creation, not from the constitutional but from the nationalist viewpoint, we immediately make a discovery of the greatest importance for our grasp of its stormy history. Practically from its birth, and certainly from its acquisition in 1526 of Bohemia and Hungary, the Hapsburg monarchy had presented itself to view as an accumulation of many nationalities. This fundamental truth was ignored in 1867 when the two strongest groups, the Germans and the Magyars (by which name the Hungarians called themselves), undertook to divide the government between them. It was a hazardous undertaking since, although each dominated historically in its particular section, it fell short of constituting therein a majority of the population.

The Compromise establishes the ascendancy of the Germans and Hungarians

For the time being the difficulty was met by limiting the franchise in such a way that the rival groups, which were mostly a repressed and backward peasantry, were accorded an inadequate representation in the parliament. Naturally these nationalities, Czechs, Poles, South Slavs and Rumanians, entered a protest against the discrimination of which they were the victims. However, since both constitutions, the Austrian as well as the Hungarian, were improvements on what had gone before, and since the less favored nationalities received some representation, though not in proportion to their numbers, they ended by accepting the new arrangements and sent deputies to the two parliaments, which met respectively at Vienna and Budapest.

The other nationalities accept the dual system under protest

On taking their seats in either one or the other of the two parliaments, the representatives of the minority groups showed themselves animated by a single purpose. It was to replace the reigning dual system with a loose federal organization. By this organization the predominance of the Germans and Magyars was to be terminated in favor of a system giving each racial group parliamentary representation proportionate to its numbers as well as a fuller control of its local affairs.

The minority groups desire a federal system

We have seen that ever since the awakening of its slumbering nationalities under the impact of the democratic tidal wave of 1848, the polyglot Hapsburg monarchy had been riven with racial strife. For the reasons just given, that strife, far from being abated by the settlement of 1867, became more acrid than ever. It may without exaggeration be declared to constitute the substance of Austro-Hungarian domestic history throughout the period here under review.

The interracial strife

While the racial issue dominated both halves of the monarchy, it ran in each a distinct and particular course. In Austria the dominant Germans were confronted by Czechs, Poles, Ruthenians, Slovenes, and Italians; in Hungary the centrally located Hungarians were completely surrounded by a hostile fringe of Slovaks on the north, Rumanians on the east, Serbs and Croatians on the south. Only a close study of the accompanying map can clarify the extraordinary confusion. Figures, too, will help in giving an idea of the distribution of strength among the warring groups. By the census of 1910 Austria-Hungary had 51,000,000 inhabitants distributed (in round numbers) as follows: 12,000,000 Germans, 10,000,000 Magyars, 8,500,000 Czechs (and Slovaks, who, as closely related to the Czechs, are lumped with them), 5,000,000 Poles, 5,000,000 Serbs and Croatians, 4,000,000 Ruthenians (called also Ukrainians), 3,200,000 Rumanians, 1,400,000 Slovenes, 750,000 Italians.

The nationality problem brought home by means of figures

The racial conflict was carried into the smallest concerns of everyday life and became the poisoned meat and bitter drink of these distracted peoples. Constitutionally, however, the struggle revolved around the issue mentioned, which was the privileged political position of the Germans and Hungarians. What the opposition nationalities specifically demanded was universal male suffrage in order to replace the existing limited fran-

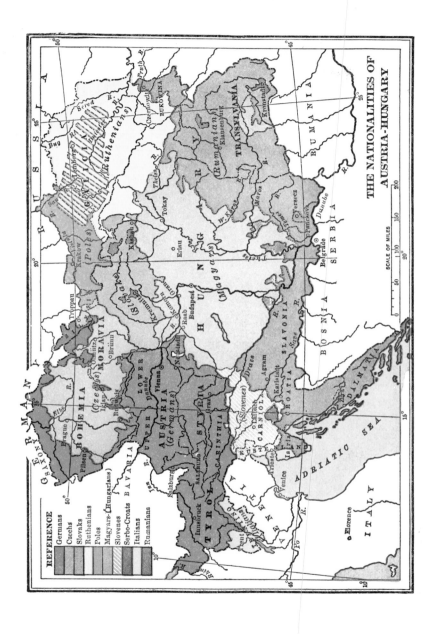

THE NATIONALITIES OF
AUSTRIA-HUNGARY

REFERENCE
Germans
Czechs
Slovaks
Ruthenians
Poles
Magyars (Hungarians)
Slovenes
Serbo-Croats
Italians
Rumanians

SCALE OF MILES
50   100   150   200

chise with a system which would automatically terminate the ascendancy of the Germans and Hungarians, since each was a minority in its own section. So ferocious were the words exchanged on the floors of the two parliaments, as well as in the press and public meetings, that foreign observers frequently expressed surprise that Austria-Hungary did not dissolve under their very eyes. However, as long as the leaders could talk and agitate, they considered an accommodation to be not impossible and preferred to suffer the current evils rather than risk the awful hazards of a revolution.

Constitutionally the struggle in both Austria and Hungary hinges on the demand for universal suffrage

Let us now follow first, the history of Austria and Hungary considered as separate entities; and second, the history of Austria-Hungary, under which name the ancient monarchy continued to do business as a great power.

The Separate Story of Austria

Under the constitution with which Austria was endowed after the Ausgleich, the parliament was made up of a House of Lords of partly hereditary and partly appointed members and a much more important House of Representatives elected, as already noted, on the basis of a limited franchise. During approximately the first decade of the new regime the German Liberals, who drew their strength from the middle classes, were in control. They passed laws expressive of their outlook and by means of them effectively modernized many of the institutions of the backward state. Complete religious toleration was decreed; a public school system was established with the feature of compulsory attendance for both boys and girls; justice was reformed by a codification of the laws; and the courts themselves were brought closer to the people by the requirement, in certain instances, of trial by jury. Since the army after its defeat by Prussia needed to be reorganized, it was rebuilt on the principle of universal military service, by which feature the Prussian success was supposed to have been obtained.

Austria is transformed by liberal legislation

Encouraged by the many legislative evidences that their day had at last dawned, the middle classes developed a considerable economic initiative and set about appropriating for Austria the advantages of the most characteristic movement of the age, the Industrial Revolution. In some of the Austrian provinces, chiefly in Bohemia and Moravia, there were rich deposits of those raw products, coal and iron, which form the necessary basis of an industrial transformation. Mined in ever increasing quantities, they served to operate great factories and gradually called to life all the familiar phenomena of mass production.

The Industrial Revolution comes to Austria

The wealth of the middle classes grew; the population of the factory towns showed a rapid increase; the workingmen, at first helpless and exploited, undertook to improve their condition by means of strikes, on the one hand, and by the formation of unions, on the other. In short, renovated Austria somewhat belatedly followed in the footsteps of Great Britain, France, and Germany, and between 1867 and 1914 brought itself economically and socially fairly abreast of them.

Appearance of all the familiar industrial phenomena

But the consequences of the economic revolution were fatal to the very group which chiefly championed the movement. The Germans were the shopkeepers, traders, bankers, and capitalists who overwhelmingly constituted the Austrian middle classes. What they gained by the advent of industrialism in respect to wealth and social consideration, the various Slav groups, such as the Czechs, Poles, and Slovenes, gained in numbers by supplying the factory workers. An unexpected effect of the Industrial Revolution was, therefore, that it intensified the national strife, since the workers, on invading the towns and organizing themselves in trade-unions, could put an energy into their demand for equal political treatment of which they were incapable so long as they had been a docile, widely scattered peasantry.

The Industrial Revolution strengthens the workers, who are preponderantly Slavs

Under the circumstances the agitation for an enlarged suffrage became irresistible. Already before the close of the seventies the German Liberals lost the control of parliament; and when, in the subsequent decades, the franchise requirements were lowered by successive stages and new classes of voters were admitted to the polls, the German Liberals became a steadily decreasing minority. Finally, in 1907 the opposition groups reached the goal which they had set themselves from the start. In that year the Austrian parliament passed a measure establishing universal manhood suffrage.

Universal manhood suffrage is established (1907)

It should not escape our attention, however, that long before 1907 the various Slav groups had combined to form a parliamentary majority. Acquiring thereby control of the ministry and government, they had, by appropriate legislative measures, obtained complete parity with the Germans in the matter of schools, courts, and public administration. Like all rising nationalities, the Slav peoples were particularly sensitive in the matter of language and demanded, and largely succeeded in winning, the same official consideration for their various tongues as for the more universal German.

Slav parity in schools, courts, and administration

The decline of German and the advance of Slav influence hardly, if at all, alleviated the nationalist strife. This was in part due to the fact that the Slavs themselves were mutually antagonistic. The Czechs could not be counted on to co-operate with the Poles, and the landowning Poles were hated by the peasant Ruthenians of eastern Galicia as heartless feudal oppressors. With a dozen nationalist parties contending for mastery the Austrian parliament often resembled a madhouse and legislation came to a standstill. But not even extreme national zealots suggested

Austria, undermined by nationalist strife, held together by tradition

dissolution—not yet. The economic ties which the recent industrialization had made more numerous and vital could not be cut without grave injury; and, more important still, there was the old tradition of a common destiny personified by the emperor, Francis Joseph. Judicially minded Austrians of whatever nationality usually admitted that their crazy commonwealth was likely to hold together at least as long as he lived.

The Separate Story of Hungary

Hungary too, like Austria, was, after 1867, governed by a parliament of two houses, a House of Magnates and a Chamber of Deputies. The lower house was elected on the basis of a franchise so narrow and so subject to government manipulation that the overwhelming majority of the deputies were regularly of Hungarian nationality.

The Hungarians in the ascendancy

If we compare the history of the two Hapsburg sections for the period in question, we are struck by both a resemblance and a difference. On the one hand, in Hungary as in Austria there was uninterrupted nationalist strife; on the other hand, in sharp contrast to what happened to the Germans, the Magyars successfully maintained their ascendancy in the political and administrative fields.

The Hungarians maintain their ascendancy

There were two good reasons for the Magyar success: first, the Magyars formed a solid central block in the rich valley of the middle Danube. Around them in a circle lay the smaller bodies of the Slovaks, Ruthenians, Rumanians, and Serbo-Croatians. Not only were these groups out of physical contact with one another, but they were spiritually divided, since they spoke different languages and were ruled by antagonistic traditions.

Two reasons for Hungarian ascendancy: (1) geography

A second reason for continued Magyar ascendancy was that the Magyars were a landlord group, while the Slavs and Rumanians were backward, unorganized peasants. If the Industrial Revolution, which is the nursing-mother of both nationalism and democracy, had come to Hungary, Magyar control would have been threatened. Some factories were, indeed, built, but not enough of them to disturb the economic and political balance. Unattacked by the forces of change, Hungary remained an agricultural state, essentially feudal in structure and passionately Magyar in spirit and organization.

The Hungarians (2) a dominant landlord group

The failure of Hungary to be industrialized must not be interpreted as meaning that wealth did not increase. The soil of the Danubian basin is unusually fertile, indeed one of the richest in the world, and the Hungarian landlords, possessing capital and won over to modern scientific methods, succeeded in doubling and trebling the value of their crops and herds.

The wealth of Hungary rests on agriculture

The political
struggle in
Hungary
centers about
the unequal
franchise

Politically, and ultimately socially, the hegemony of the Magyars depended on their successful defense of the unequal franchise. Little as it conceded to the racial minorities in principle, it was in addition so unscrupulously manipulated by the ruling caste that non-Hungarians were hardly represented at all in the parliament at Budapest. That did not, of course, hinder the injured groups from finding leaders who agitated in their behalf. When these leaders did not raise their voice for universal suffrage, they demanded at the very least an improved franchise for their constituents.

The Hungarian political
cal system
unchanged
between
1867 and
1914

As every suggestion of reform was violently resisted by the beneficiaries of privilege, it happened that, when World War I broke out in 1914, the Hungarian political situation was still essentially unchanged from what it had been in 1867. There was, however, this notable moral difference: The struggle for national rights and a better representation on the part of the subject peoples had become so embittered that it did not seem credible that Magyar ascendancy could be maintained much longer.

The Story of Austria-Hungary

Austria-
Hungary
does not
seek trans-
oceanic
colonies

If we turn now from Austria and Hungary to Austria-Hungary, we are in effect confronted with the foreign department of the dual partners, for toward the outside world they had agreed to act as one under their common sovereign, the emperor-king Francis Joseph. It must be self-evident that a state of such little inner coherence as the Hapsburg monarchy could not possibly play as decisive a role in Europe as the nationally compact powers round about it. The enormous national energy which prompted the governments of Great Britain, France, Italy, and Germany to seek markets and colonies beyond the seas and face the hazards of an imperialist policy was inoperative in the case of distracted Austria-Hungary. We need not wonder, therefore, that it kept entirely out of the feverish colonial competition.

The security
of the Haps-
burg mon-
archy threat-
ened by the
push of
Russia into
the Balkan
peninsula

So greatly was Austria-Hungary paralyzed by the domestic chaos that it clung, in the main, to the purely conservative policy of maintaining itself in its existing strength. As Francis Joseph and his advisers saw the situation after 1867 their state was threatened chiefly on its southeastern border in the direction of the Balkan peninsula. Its insecurity on this side did not come from the small Balkan states or the decaying Ottoman empire. It came from powerful Russia, which, for more than a hundred years, had been engaged in extending its influence over this area. Should Russia gain a privileged position in the capitals of the young and feeble Balkan states, or should it succeed in appropriating the lands of the Sick Man of Europe, on which for some decades it had fixed an almost hypnotized gaze, the very existence of Austria-Hungary would be jeopardized. Therefore, throughout the period from 1867 to 1914 the leading element in the Austro-Hungarian foreign policy was fear of Russia.

Naturally, this fear became dormant whenever Russia for one reason or another turned away from Balkan affairs; and it became wakeful and intense as soon as Russia became active in this area. Indeed a Russian forward movement in the Balkans regularly produced an Austro-Hungarian crisis. As we shall learn in greater detail in a later chapter, in the year 1877 Tsar Alexander II returned to the policy of his ancestors and levied war on his old enemy, the sultan. So overwhelming were his victories that it seemed not unlikely that he would bring the whole peninsula under his influence. The prospect caused such alarm at Vienna that the government prepared for war. Luckily Great Britain was equally excited over the Russian designs and by joining with Austria-Hungary effected a diplomatic intervention which obliged Russia to moderate her terms.

A crisis precipitated by the Russian victory over the Ottoman empire in 1877-78

At a Congress of the powers held in 1878 at Berlin to bring the crisis to a settlement there was the usual trading among the participants. In return for the advantages conceded to victorious Russia, Austria-Hungary was compensated with the gift of the two Ottoman provinces, Bosnia and Herzegovina. These adjoined Hungary on the south and were regarded at Vienna as giving the monarchy the greater military security of which it stood in need. To be sure, the two provinces were not handed over to Francis Joseph outright. It was stated in the treaty that Austria-Hungary was to administer them and that meanwhile the titular sovereignty of the sultan of Turkey was to remain intact.

The Congress of Berlin (1878) gives the Hapsburg monarchy Bosnia and Herzegovina

From the moment of the acquisition by the Hapsburg monarchy of Bosnia, the rivalry between it and Russia over southeastern Europe never slumbered. The situation explains why in the following year (1879) Austria-Hungary, in order to strengthen itself against Russia, entered into a close alliance with Germany. This is the union which by the admission of Italy in 1882 became the Triple alliance. As these matters will be treated in our review of European diplomacy, it will suffice if we note at this point by way of general characterization of Austro-Hungarian foreign policy that down to the great catastrophe of 1914 it revolved around the three indicated factors: rivalry with Russia; the occupation of Bosnia and Herzegovina; and the Triple alliance.

The never-slumbering Austro-Russian rivalry over the Balkans

GREAT BRITAIN FROM THE SECOND REFORM BILL (1867) TO THE OUTBREAK OF WORLD WAR I

RULERS OF GREAT BRITAIN

Victoria (1837-1901) *m*. Albert of
     | Saxe-Coburg
Edward VII (1901-10)
     |
George V (1910-36)
     |

Edward VIII (1936)   George VI (1936-)

COMPOSITE PORTRAIT OF GREAT BRITAIN DURING THIS PERIOD

The Workshop of the World

ONLY BY KEEPING before us the characteristic social and economic aspects of Great Britain in the second half of the nineteenth century will the political developments to be treated in this chapter become intelligible. It is indispensable never to forget that in this period the Industrial Revolution was mounting to a climax and that in its irresistible advance it was affecting the living conditions of every man, woman, and child in the kingdom. If already in the first half of the century Britain had been acclaimed as "the Workshop of the World," more than ever did it merit this designation in the century's second half, even though industrialization had meanwhile spread to other countries and was raising up rivals, more particularly Germany and the United States, who boldly pressed on the heels of the leader. However, as no other country surrendered to machine production so unreservedly, Britain easily and visibly retained its workshop eminence.

Trade items indicative of Britain's industrial primacy

Selected data supported by statistics will substantiate the claim. Every year within the limits of our present survey witnessed an increased production of the two basic raw products, coal and iron. The statement is equally true of the long list of articles moving from the factories to the world markets, such as cotton, woolen, and linen goods, pottery, boots and shoes, and of course machines of every conceivable variety. The growth of shipping kept pace with the growth of exports, for industrial supremacy could not have been achieved without a parallel maritime supremacy. London became a port annually loading and unloading a greater mass of merchandise than any other port in the world; and Liverpool was not far behind London. It was only about the time of the Second Reform Bill that sailing vessels began to be sweepingly replaced by steamers with their greater speed and larger carrying capacity. While the tonnage of the British merchant marine in 1867 was somewhat over five million, it had enlarged to nearly twelve million in 1914. The accumulation of capital seeking investment tells the same story. It proceeded so rapidly that after providing the very considerable requirements for industrial development at home, so much remained that it overflowed into the many other countries in need of this indispensable lubricant. It is estimated that on the eve of World War I Britain's external investments aggregated not much short of twenty billion dollars. Consequently a broad stream of annual tribute poured into the tight little island in the form of a return on stocks and bonds.

Look now at the population. It showed a similar increase for the excellent reason that the mounting production of goods enabled a mounting number of people to live. For the machine-made goods, though not themselves edible, were exchangeable for the foodstuffs of every clime. The population increase was frankly staggering. At the beginning of the century (1801) Great Britain had about ten million inhabitants. By 1867 the ten million had swollen to twenty-five million and by 1914 to approximately forty-one million. In the last-named year metropolitan London alone had almost as many inhabitants as all England (which does not mean Britain) possessed a hundred years before. *Growth of population*

However, the song of triumph chanted by these figures was somewhat dampened by the sounds of lamentation issuing from the countryside. Though not at once, within a generation after the adoption of free trade, British agriculture went into a decline which ended in a tailspin. Such countries as the United States, Canada, Australia, and Argentina were able to deliver wheat at Liverpool at a price below the British cost; and when the refrigerator ship was invented, they could do the same with beef and mutton. This swamping of the home market with foreign grain and meat had many consequences, among them a cumulative shrinkage of the acreage put to grain and grass, an accelerated migration from the village to the town, and the steadily deepening distress of the villagers who remained behind. Its agricultural problem became an Old Man of the Sea who settled on Britain's back for keeps. But, strange at first blush, the Old Man did not put an end to the ascendancy of the titled aristocracy. An alert and even enterprising group, they had from an early date invested their surplus funds in industry and, by the time the agricultural depression set in, were no longer, in the mass, dependent on agriculture for their living. It was a further help that the upper middle class, which by its rise to wealth had become sharply differ- *The decline of agriculture* entiated from the bulk of its original social order, was only too ready to bolster its deficient social credit by marrying off its daughters, their youth and beauty baited with magnificent dowries, to impecunious noblemen.

*The prob-
lem of the
poor: 1) on
the land;
2) in the
towns*
But if the aristocrats found a means of evading the consequence of the sharp agricultural decline, the farmers and field-hands did not. Their wretched state was a source of constant tribulation to the government, as was also the no less anxious lot of the swarming factory workers in the towns. It is at this point that we encounter the anomaly that has vexed all industrial countries without exception but none perhaps in the same degree as Great Britain. This land, this Britain, which had become the richest country in the world, lived under an economic system which permitted the teeming profits of industry to be appropriated by a small upper group and which successfully withheld all but a negligible fraction thereof from the lowly servants of the machines, not improperly conceived as their slaves. In spite of measurable improvements in their lot that had been effected in the first half of the nineteenth century and that continued to be effected uninterruptedly in the second half, it remains true that the workers lived, in the main, in squalid, blighted areas in a state of economic insecurity that never gave them respite. While it is proper in taking in the total British picture to note the dignified ease and cultivated luxury of a thin upper crust, it is indispensable to observe that in the smoke-blackened lowlands far below the beneficiaries, who dwelt in the sun upon the heights, there lived the herded masses harried by woes from which there was apparently no escape.

THE ROLE OF THE TWO PARLIAMENTARY PARTIES

*Both parties
in favor of
ameliorative
legislation*
Whenever the country's governing body, the parliament, met, it faced the general situation which has just been outlined. Although it may be assumed that the two political parties contending for control of the nation felt an equal concern for its problems, they adopted a somewhat different attitude toward them, the Conservatives hesitating to promote change, the Liberals cautiously favoring it. However, as they were in competition for public support, exactly as was shown in Chapter 24 to have been the case in the period 1815-1867, in the period here reviewed each in turn sponsored ameliorative legislation. In these circumstances the party struggles in the House of Commons, though constituting exciting drama, are less important than the legislative acts that issued from them. Less important, too, are the party leaders who headed the successive cabinets. Let the reader interested in these foreground happenings resort to the detailed histories, where, as is proper to such works, they are treated at length.

It is therefore submitted that in a compressed work such as this the important legislation of the period has a prior claim; and in now taking it up, it is necessary to recall that the Second Reform Bill was a milestone. It plays this role because in enfranchising a large part of the workers it for the first time brought democracy upon the scene. Waxing stronger with each passing year, democracy won to its cause an ever larger segment of public opinion so that both parties were obliged to make their reckoning with it and competitively promote the measures it demanded. Even the briefest review of the ministries of Benjamin Disraeli (1804-1881) and William Gladstone (1809-1898), respectively the heads of the Conservative and Liberal parties, will prove the contention. Beginning in the sixties, for almost twenty years these two men served alternately as heads of the government. But the measures they passed, and for that matter those passed by their successors after them, compose into a coherent tale of progressive democratization, for which both parties may therefore claim credit.

Both parties under the same democratic pressure

EVIDENCES OF THE GRADUAL DEMOCRATIZATION OF GREAT BRITAIN

In 1871 parliament passed a Trade-Union Act which terminated the continuing uncertainty regarding the right of the unions to exist. They were empowered to hold property and to defend actions at law, and, at least by implication, were secured in that right of collective bargaining which they had long been exercising. In the next year the secret ballot, a democratic demand originally put out by the Chartists, was enacted for parliamentary elections; and in 1875 the Trade-Union Act of 1871 was extended by conceding the workers the right of peaceful picketing. With these encouragements the whole movement entered on a period of accelerated expansion. From 83 major trade-unions in the early seventies the number had by 1890 gone to 490 and by 1906 to 675. And in the thirty intervening years the total trade-union membership had risen from about 200,000 to a little short of 2,000,000. The new consciousness of strength led in 1906, as had been long anticipated, to the formation of a political party of the workers, which took the name of the Labor party. It was only because the workers were themselves of the slow-moving British breed that the Labor party did not at once capture the labor vote. But with the passing of the years this mental hazard tended to disappear with the result that the workers made their way in ever greater numbers into the political party sworn to their cause.

The trade-union movement culminates (1906) in the Labor party

In 1884 the Third Reform Bill was passed, which enfranchised about two million rural workers. This was done by the simple device of con-

ceding the vote in the counties on the same terms as already established
for the boroughs, thus canceling the property qualification which had
hitherto obtained. It was estimated that, following this reform, there
were over 1,800,000 male adults still excluded from the polls. Since, for
the most part, they were unorganized casual laborers, they were not able
to bring pressure to bear on the parliament. It was not till the economic
and moral shake-up caused by World War I that the suffrage was completely democratized by being extended not only to all adult men but
to all adult women as well.

The Third
Reform Bill
(1884)

For measuring democratic advance there is no better yardstick than
the educational facilities extended to the common people. Oligarchic
Britain of the eighteenth and early nineteenth centuries was richly provided with educational institutions adapted to the purpose of a governing class, but showed no concern for the education of the poor. Such
primary education as existed was conducted by the churches, especially
the Anglican church. They took their responsibility so lightly that as
late as 1870 no more than half of the nation's children received even a
rudimentary schooling. It was the disclosure of this disgraceful situation
that moved parliament to take its first important step toward providing
primary education for all. By the Education Act of 1870 secular schools
under local boards, and therefore called board schools, were set up wherever the church schools were inadequate. Twenty years later (1891)
the government provided for the free education for every child whether
in a board or church school. So steadily were the expenditures in support
of the system enlarged that by 1913 local and national government
grants for free popular education had risen to $150,000,000, and every
boy and girl in the kingdom was compelled to attend school until the
fourteenth year.

The win-
ning of
compulsory
free educa-
tion

Turning now to social legislation for evidences of democratization,
let us recall that in their early days both Conservatives and Liberals
were strongly disinclined to intervention by the state in behalf of the
oppressed factory workers; but so crushing was the exploitation of the
workers and so revolting the spectacle of their misery and suffering that
under pressure from an aroused public opinion a number of acts corrective of the worst abuses were gradually passed, beginning with the
timid Factory Act of 1833. Other timid acts followed until even the Liberal party, which drew its main support from the industrial capitalists,
gave up its uncompromising attitude and helped to swell the enactments
of ever greater number and scope aimed at humanizing the wretched
labor conditions. In their sum the ameliorative laws successively reduced
the hours of labor for every category of worker; provided for heat, light,
and fresh air in the factories; instituted protective devices against dangerous machinery; and subjected all factories to rigorous government inspec-

Social
legislation
culminates
in the
sweeping
acts of 1878
and 1901

tion. By 1878 the legislation had grown to such proportions that its parts had to be brought into harmony by merger into a single act. And with protective measures continuing to drop after 1878 from the legislative mill a new and even more elaborate labor code had to be drawn up in 1901.

By the beginning of the twentieth century very few people could still be found in Great Britain prepared to uphold, without considerable subtraction, the old laissez-faire doctrine. Indeed the right and duty of the state to protect its weakest members had gained such general recognition that it was no longer stoutly opposed in any quarter. Outstanding evidence of the new trend was the transformation it produced of the Liberal party. Resting from its early days on middle-class views and interests summarized as liberalism, the Liberal party had championed an untrammeled economic individualism, of which the main items were the right of free contract between employer and employee and freedom from interference by the state in the employer-employee relationship. These particular features of liberalism were now tossed overboard and the Old Liberalism was replaced by the New Liberalism, which made its favorite dish of what it had once abhorred. Interference by the state in behalf of the workers became the very touchstone of the New Liberalism, which did not hesitate to pillory such of its one-time associates as did not subscribe to the new enlightenment and to hold them up to scorn as masked reactionaries. But let us guard against exaggerating the liberal somersault. While reneging on the economic doctrine of laissez faire, the New Liberalism held fast and even deepened its devotion to the original political content of liberalism, involving such items as sovereignty of the people and freedom of the press, assembly, and religion.

Birth of the New Liberalism

This excursion on the New Liberalism (which presently made its appearance in other industrial countries, especially in the United States) was made necessary by the legislation introduced and carried by the Liberal party, which in 1906 was returned to power in a landslide of unheard proportions. In addition to its own overwhelming majority it enjoyed the support of the twenty-nine members of the newly-formed Labor party and of some eighty Irish nationalists and, although weakened by subsequent elections, it continued to hold office up to and into World War I. Its effective, though not actual, leader was the radical Welshman, David Lloyd George, who served in the cabinet as chancellor of the exchequer. In the period 1906-1912 the Liberal ministry under Lloyd George's inspiration enacted a body of laws which, going far beyond the early program of protection, concerned itself with insuring the worker against the worst risks which habitually threatened him. These were sickness, accidents, invalidism through old age, and periodic

The Liberal party enacts (1906-1912) the Insurance Code

unemployment. The many enactments of the indicated period taken together constituted a comprehensive Insurance Code that gave the worker a security beyond anything anywhere yet proposed. True, Germany had the honor of having pioneered in Insurance Legislation some twenty years earlier and the German measures had served as a guide to their British imitators; but if the German code enjoyed priority, the British code went farther by insuring the worker against more hazards, especially against unemployment.

How the Insurance Code operates

Under the British insurance legislation workingmen receive benefits in the form of medical attention, hospitalization, and cash whenever they are incapacitated or thrown out of work from any of the above-specified causes. The funds necessary for this immense social service are created by contributions from three sources, the employers, the employees, and the state. It deserves to be noted that, if under this arrangement the employers and the state may be conceived as divesting themselves of revenue in behalf of a particular social group, the beneficiaries of the system, that is, the workers, are not pauperized. They are obliged to consent to a not inconsiderable deduction from their wages in order to enter into the enjoyment of the insurance legislation.

The Parliament Bill of 1911 curbs the House of Lords

The democratic radicalism of Lloyd George revealed itself even more strikingly in his tax program. In 1906 he drew up a budget, the heavy expenditures of which were to be met by an income tax so steeply graduated that the rich would have to bear a burden with which it had never before occurred to any budget-maker to load them. Passed by the Commons, the budget was indignantly rejected by the Lords, thus initiating a sharp struggle between the two houses. Lloyd George ended it by one of the most drastic constitutional measures taken since the establishment of parliamentary government. By the Parliament Bill of 1911 the Lords were permanently deprived of their power to block legislation desired by the Commons. They were left no more than a suspensive veto, which means that they could hold off legislation sent up to them from the Commons for a two-year period. If within this span a piece of disputed legislation was passed by the Commons in three successive sessions, it automatically became the law of the land.

THE IRISH QUESTION

Main stages of the English subjugation of Ireland

One of the gravest questions confronting Great Britain throughout the nineteenth century up to the eve of World War I was Ireland. In the course of their age-long warfare against the Irish, the English had adopted against them a series of measures of unrivaled severity. They had dispossessed the Irish of their land; they had established their own Anglican church among them, in spite of the fact that the Irish adhered staunchly to Catholicism; they had planted Anglo-Scotch colonists in the province of Ulster; they had imposed on the Irish a purely Protestant local administration; and finally, in 1800, they had destroyed the last remnant of Irish legislative independence by merging the Irish parliament with the British parliament at Westminster.

Not long after the return of peace in 1815 a movement began among the Irish which aimed at removing some of the worst oppressions of which they were the victims. Its leader was Daniel O'Connell. He directed his efforts against the exceptional laws in force against Catholics and was largely instrumental in producing the legislation of 1829, which won for the Catholics full civil rights throughout the realm. On O'Connell's next directing his agitation against the Act of Union of 1800, the government suppressed him and scattered his following by force. Thereupon the Irish continued their anti-English agitation by means of secret societies. Their fanatic members did not scruple to carry on an irregular warfare against the English landlords by maiming cattle, burning farms, and by occasional murders.

The beginning of Irish agitation: O'Connell

By the sixties the anarchic situation on the island had become so intolerable that Gladstone persuaded the Liberal party to attempt to mollify the Irish by removing some of the more conspicuous evils of which they complained. In 1869 he succeeded in putting an act through parliament which disestablished the Anglican church in Ireland, known to the law under the derisive name of the Irish church. Therewith, the hated tithes, which the Catholic peasants had been compelled to pay for the maintenance of a religious establishment scrupulously avoided by them, were abolished. True, the Anglican church was permitted to retain its buildings and a part of its rich endowment, but as it was reduced to the same legal footing as the Catholic church and every other Christian denomination, a loathed supremacy had been replaced by religious equality.

Disestablishment (1869) of the Irish church

This resolute step toward righting Irish wrongs Gladstone immediately followed by another. In 1870 he passed a Land Act, which aimed to give a meager measure of protection to the native tenants of the land against the legal owners. To grasp the situation we must recall that, as a result of the confiscations of the previous centuries, the landlords were not only, generally speaking, Englishmen but, in addition, absentees who managed their estates through hard and unsentimental agents. Because the law had been made by the conquerors, the Irish peasants, who tilled the soil without possessing it, enjoyed not even the most rudimentary security on their farms and could be evicted from them at the pleasure of the owners.

The insecure tenure of the Irish peasants

A more recent evil, overpopulation, made a bad situation worse by inducing the peasants to raise their own rents through bidding reck-

lessly against each other for their tiny, unproductive holdings. Of this
particular affliction, it is true, the terrible famine of 1845, of which mention has been made in connection with the repeal of the Corn Laws,
produced a partial mitigation by inducing the peasants to emigrate in
swarms to hospitable America.

Other evils:
overpopula-
tion, famine,
emigration

What the Land Act of 1870 and a second Gladstonian measure of 1881
tried to do was to curtail the arbitrary power of the landlords and give
the farmers a more secure tenure. Hardly had the Irish gained this much
when they made it plain that nothing short of complete repossession of
the land would satisfy them. In the face of an intensified agitation which
hesitated at no violence, the Conservative ministry of Lord Salisbury
resolved in 1891 on a heroic measure. It brought forward and carried the
Land Purchase Act, which invited the peasants to buy the lands they
occupied out of a fund put at their disposal by the government. Prospective purchasers had to agree to reimburse the government by means of
small annual payments extending over a number of decades. The Land
Purchase Act of 1891, together with supplementary legislation enacted
during the succeeding decade, has gone far toward settling the vexed
land question. Its effect has been to abolish the foreign landlords and to
raise the Irish farmers to the level of self-respecting peasant-proprietors.

The Land
Acts of 1870
and 1881
lead to the
Land Pur-
chase Act
of 1891

Meanwhile the movement for autonomy or Home Rule begun by
O'Connell had never entirely died out. In the eighties it was powerfully
revived under the guidance of a clever politician, Charles Stewart Parnell,
who resolved to employ his following of approximately eighty Irish members to paralyze the business of the House of Commons until Home Rule
was given a hearing. As noise-makers and parliamentary obstructionists
the Parnellites succeeded in hanging up a world record.

Parnell
revives
the Home
Rule issue

In 1885 a brilliant opportunity presented itself to Parnell. As a result
of the elections of that year neither Conservatives nor Liberals commanded a majority in the Commons without Irish help. Accordingly, the
Liberals entered into an agreement with the Irish by virtue of which,
in return for Parnell's support, Gladstone promised to back the Irish
demand. However, Gladstone's Home Rule Bill was defeated in the
Commons by the defection of a hotly nationalist section of his own Liberal party (1886).

Defeat
(1886) of
Gladstone's
Home Rule
Bill

On returning to office in 1892 Gladstone successfully pushed a second
Home Rule Bill through the lower house only to have it defeated in the
upper house, the Lords (September, 1893). Thereupon, for more than a
decade, during which the Conservatives governed the country, the home-
rule issue slumbered. Even after the Liberals had again gained power
(1906), they failed to take action on Home Rule until a decline in the
number of their supporters forced them once more to seek the alliance
of the Irish party.

Defeat
(1893) of
Gladstone's
second
Home Rule
Bill

In the year 1912 a third Home Rule Bill was passed by the Commons. In spite of the opposition of the Lords, the bill, two years later, under the operation of the Parliament Act of 1911, would have become a law, had not the outbreak of World War I by the unanimous action of the Commons caused the issue to be adjourned till the return of peace.

The Third Home Rule Bill of 1912

THE BRITISH EMPIRE

The Dominions

In Chapter 24 we took account of the outstanding development during the period 1815-1867 within the vast areas subjected to Great Britain and constituting the British empire. This development, a brilliant novelty, pertained to the group of North American colonies. After having been first granted provincial self-government, the American colonies were in 1867 authorized to form a self-governing federation called the Dominion of Canada. It proved even more successful than its optimistic well-wishers had forecast. In measure as, in the period after the founding of the Dominion, the vast western expanses of Canada became settled, they were organized into self-governing provinces which, on application, were then absorbed into the Dominion. In this way first, Manitoba and British Columbia (1870-1871) and finally, Alberta and Saskatchewan (1905) were joined with the territory to the east till the Dominion of Canada appeared as a file of sister-provinces standing hand in hand across the continent from the Atlantic to the Pacific ocean.

Again Canada, the model dominion

Although Canada had a considerable French population, it was preponderantly British, and in any case white and European. It was therefore inevitable that the other white and European areas under British control should follow the Canadian pattern. Turning our attention first to Australia, we note that the uninterrupted stream of immigration from Great Britain led, as in Canada, to the formation of a number of provinces under cabinet-appointed governors. Shortly after the middle of the century four of them, New South Wales, Victoria, Tasmania, and South Australia, had already become self-governing under their own constitutions. In the following decades Queensland and West Australia were added to the list. When the separate colonies indicated a desire to federate, they met with hearty encouragement from London. The result of multilateral negotiations was that on January 1, 1901, a new political entity, the Commonwealth of Australia, came into being. Its constitution provides, as in the case of the Dominion of Canada, for parliamentary government with a ruling cabinet responsible to the lower house of a bicameral legislature.

Creation of the Commonwealth of Australia, 1901

It should not be overlooked that the island group of New Zealand, owing to its lying at a distance of 1200 miles from the mainland, refused to join Australia. In the year 1907 New Zealand was raised to the same level as the Commonwealth of Australia by its acknowledgment as a dominion with all the self-governing features pertaining to that status.

The Dominion of New Zealand, 1907

There had thus come to birth three self-governing dominions, Canada, Australia, New Zealand. A fourth, South Africa, was to follow but only after certain obstacles had been cleared from its path. The focal point of British influence in this area was Cape Colony, seized from the Dutch during the Napoleonic wars. The British immigrants arriving in large numbers after 1815 were not welcome to the original Dutch settlers. These, locally called Boers, were farmers scattered over the vast African plains, the so-called veld. An additional circumstance is not to be overlooked: the two white groups, British and Dutch, had established themselves in a country of native Negroes, who at the close of the nineteenth century still outnumbered the combined white groups in the ratio of four to one.

The racial situation in South Africa

In these difficult circumstances the development of Cape Colony proceeded much more deliberately than that of Canada and Australia. Not till rather late in the century were Cape Colony and Natal (a province on the northeastern edge of Cape Colony) conceded even the usual measure of self-government. By that time many of the earlier settlers, the Boers, finding British rule distasteful, had trekked into the open veld to the north of Cape Colony, where they founded the two republics of the Orange Free State and the Transvaal. In 1884 the quiet pastoral existence of these two farmer communities was suddenly threatened by the discovery of gold, for greed of the precious metal drew a horde of adventurers, chiefly British, into the land. Flocking thither in ever greater numbers, they demanded citizenship with the ultimate object of bringing the Boer states under the British flag. When the farmers resisted the demand of the strangers to be received into their midst, a state of friction resulted which finally led to war with the sponsor of the strangers, Great Britain.

The two Boer republics threatened by the discovery of gold

In the prolonged struggle (1899-1902) the Boers defended their independence with the utmost valor. It was without avail in the face of the resources of the greatest empire in the world. When the Boers, at last crushed under the superior weight of arms, acquiesced in the extinction of their republics, Great Britain conceded them honorable terms. After a period of probation it even granted them a measure of self-government.

Defeat of the Boers and grant of self-government

The grant of self-government enabled the Boers to see that they now had identical interests with the neighbor provinces of Cape Colony and Natal. Accordingly, the four provinces entered into conversations and in

1909, with the sanction of the London authorities, agreed to form a South African Union. The constitution guaranteed complete equality to the two white peoples, the Dutch and the British, and to their respective languages. However, it refused citizen rights to the native Negroes who, as we have seen, were many times as numerous. Of several grave problems this of the politically excluded Negroes is by far the gravest confronting the South African Union. A further consequence of its numerical inferiority was that the white population felt the need of a strong federal government. The constitution therefore greatly strengthened the central institutions at the expense of the constitutive provinces. This centralization represents a significant departure from the course followed in the related cases of Canada and Australia.

Formation (1909) of the South African Union

India

The remaining large single area under Great Britain was India. In Chapter 24 we sketched its fortunes through the Sepoy rebellion (1857) and noted that, following its suppression, the rule of the East India Company was replaced by that of the British government. Thenceforth India was the responsibility of a cabinet member entitled Secretary of State for India, and was governed on the ground by a viceroy at Calcutta (after 1912 at Delhi) aided by an administrative council. Since the viceroy's rule was practically an unlimited despotism, the question at once arises: why this outmoded system for India when the self-governing dominion system had happily solved the colonial problem for Canada, Australia, New Zealand, and South Africa? To answer that the dominions were in the main white and British, while the several hundred million Indians were dark-skinned, fails to hit the mark, unless we insist on the mental and moral implications of this color distinction. The more satisfactory answer to the question is that the dominion whites were products of Western civilization and sharers with the mother country of a particular way of thinking and living, whereas the dark-skinned Indians had a civilized past of their own that provided them with an entirely different outlook.

India governed despotically by a viceroy

To make a difficult situation worse, the dark-skinned folk had behind them not one past and one civilization but a number of different pasts and divergent civilizations and were hopelessly divided in numerous other respects. In short, though we speak of the inhabitants of the peninsula as Indians and thus confer on them by our western habits of speech a common nationality, this cement so binding in the west was entirely absent. In point of cold fact India was a hodgepodge of languages, peoples, and even religions, for though Hinduism claimed about 200,000,000 followers and Mohammedanism, 70,000,000, even these two main faiths were split into numerous sects. The beginning of understanding of the

India a world of heterogeneous peoples

Indian situation is to recognize that the word India is a purely geographical expression and does not designate a nation in the western sense.

Now, while this confused and heterogeneous India was a source of perpetual annoyance to its British overlords, they never for a moment thought of easing their minds by casting it adrift. They did not do so because of the almost incalculable advantages they derived from the trade with a consumer block of about 300,000,000 persons and therefore seven and eight times as numerous as themselves. The practice had developed, especially with the coming of the industrial nineteenth century, for the British traders to carry away from India the raw products which this vast and overcrowded land produced at a trivial labor cost and to return them in the more expensive form of manufactured goods. This exchange expanded with every decade until the time came when the loss of it would have produced a collapse of the whole British economy. It was this situation that gradually made India the object of a passionate British attachment and accounts for a statutory enactment tantamount to a declaration that Britain would never of its own free will surrender this treasure house.

The supreme importance of India for the British home economy

This statutory enactment was a parliamentary bill of 1876 and ran to the effect that India, which to the soberly observing eye was nothing but a vast heap of broken fragments, was a united empire and Queen Victoria its sovereign. On the strength of this act she added the title Empress of India to the others of which she was already possessed. At the same time the whole Indian-empire concept, long in process of gestation, experienced a considerable expansion. While of this widened concept India remained the core, this central mass was buttressed by Baluchistan on the west and by Burma on the east. Burma in its turn was extended down the Malay peninsula all the way to its strategical tip at Singapore. With these right- and left-flank additions India was enlarged to comprise all southern Asia and to achieve the crowning merit of commanding at Singapore the approach to important additional lands actually or prospectively British, Australia and the coast of China. More and more the home economy came to be inextricably tied up with this vastly expanded India and, in measure as the interdependence grew, the patriotic emotions of the islanders were excited by it until they were prepared to defend their acquisition as though it were an integral part of themselves, their inseparable Siamese twin.

India, declared an empire (1876), expands in all directions

Meanwhile the sporadic opposition the Indians had manifested from the first took on a more organized and dangerous form. By learning English and studying abroad, chiefly in England and the United States, many Indians had come to absorb western ways, especially that most questionable and disturbing of all, nationalism. Although, in view of the

Rise of Indian nationalism

incurable Indian divisions, nationalism was bound to be a very mixed product, it could and did feed on the common aversion felt for the foreign interloper, and rapidly expanded its following. To appease it the British government hesitantly gave up its autocratic attitude and entered the path of political concessions. As early as 1882 it invited a limited participation of Indians in local government; and in 1909 it went the much greater length of permitting a number of natives (always strictly a minority) to sit in the advisory councils of some of the provinces and even in the central council of the viceroy. None of these favors even remotely satisfied the nationalists, and they continued their agitation until with the outbreak of World War I their movement was rudely quashed, while the head of the government, the authoritative viceroy, put the soldiers and resources of India at the uncontrolled disposal of Great Britain.

The Mediterranean Life Line and Egypt; the Crown Colonies

The enormous importance of India in the eyes of the British governing classes was brought home to the world by the all but hypnotized gaze they fixed on the Mediterranean sea. They called it the British life line, and such indeed it was if there was any justification to the view that a free circulation of the blood from the British heart to the distant Indian dependency was an undebatable prerequisite of empire health and well-being. When Great Britain in the early years of the eighteenth century seized Gibraltar from Spain, it was for the double purpose of threatening France and protecting its trade with Syria and the near east. The trade with India and the far east at that time went around Africa and it was, in its turn, made reasonably secure by the seizure from the Dutch during the wars with Napoleon of Cape Colony.

Creation of the Mediterranean life line

Then, a rather exceptional instance, the British slipped up. They permitted a French company under a famous engineer, Ferdinand de Lesseps, to pierce the isthmus of Suez with a canal. No sooner was it opened for traffic in 1869 than it attracted the Europe-Asia trade and caused the much longer, and therefore much more expensive, route around Africa to be almost abandoned. Putting their heads together, the chagrined British officials worked out a way of making good their indefensible delinquency. In 1875, during the premiership of Benjamin Disraeli, the government bought for the laughably small sum of $20,000,000 the canal shares of the ruler of Egypt, the khedive.

Disraeli buys the khedive's canal shares 1875

The purchased shares signified mastery of the canal, the control of which thus passed into British hands. It is necessary to make some acquaintance with the character and habits of the khedive, whose name was

Rising of the Egyptians against Franco-British financial control

Ismail, to understand how ever he could have been brought to divest himself of his invaluable property. Ismail (1863-1879) was a fantastic spendthrift with delusions of grandeur that suggest he had been brought up on an exclusive diet of the *Arabian Nights*. He sold his canal shares to satisfy the importunate French and British bankers who for years had been his accommodating money-lenders. A few weeks after he had appeased them by tossing Disraeli's gratuity into their yawning maws, he was as badly off as ever, whereupon the usurers refused to be satisfied with anything less than a permanent Franco-British control commission set over the Egyptian treasury. This humiliation the Egyptian people so deeply resented that they rose against Ismail's successor to the cry of Egypt for the Egyptians and, holding him a prisoner in his palace, violently terminated Franco-British control.

Egypt a British dependency, 1882

After inviting France to join it in reducing Egypt by force and receiving a negative reply, the British government went in alone. In 1882 it bombarded Alexandria, occupied Egypt with an army, and restored the deposed khedive on the understanding that he would content himself with playing the role of the obedient vassal. In that year Egypt became a British dependency and still held that status in 1914 when World War I broke out.

Main points of support of (1) the Mediterranean and (2) the African route to India

Gibraltar to the west and the Suez to the east meant the control of the two entrances (or, alternately, exits) of the Mediterranean sea, the British life line. The hold, excellent in itself, was further strengthened by the island of Malta, inhabited by Italians and acquired in the Viennese settlement of 1815, and the island of Cyprus, inhabited by Greeks and acquired from Turkey during the negotiations that led to the Berlin settlement of 1878. After passing the Suez eastward the life line traveled the waters of the Red sea. This required the command of that sea at its southern exit, at Aden. Since the older, the African route to India, though less important than it had once been, was still far from negligible, Britain never ceased strengthening it by means of naval stations, protectorates, and other forms of imperial control. It was in pursuit of this control that Britain planted her flag over Sierra Leone, the Gold Coast, Nigeria, Zanzibar, and British East Africa.

Other scattered possessions governed as crown colonies

Beyond Singapore, at the end of the long tongue of the Malay peninsula, Britain laid claim to numerous island groups extending to Australia and beyond; and on the coast of China it possessed the priceless port of Hong Kong. In this resounding catalogue of empire, the western hemisphere should not be overlooked, for a continuous island chain around the Caribbean sea gave Britain a commanding position in those waters also. Although there was great variation in the form of government imposed on these minor but still important footholds scattered over the seven seas, in the main they rated as crown colonies and were ruled by a governor appointed by and responsible to the London cabinet and advised by some sort of native representation.

BRITISH FOREIGN POLICY DURING THE NINETEENTH CENTURY

To review the foreign policy of Great Britain during the century between the Congress of Vienna and World War I is to become aware that it was determined by the world interests of which the little island had become the guardian. Although the ministries, whether of Conservative or Liberal complexion, were alike prompt to defend these interests against attack, it is undeniable that, for a time at least around the middle of the century, the Conservatives were more eager than the Liberals to take advantage of any opportunity that might offer to pass from the defensive to the offensive and thus add another dependency to the existent colonial mass. On account of their more hesitant attitude toward expansion, the Liberals were sometimes taunted by their opponents as being "Little Englanders." *Conservatives and Liberals equally prompt to defend the empire*

The main support of the British position in the world was the British navy. Not only was it the largest and most powerful navy in the world, it was as a matter of principle always kept at the size of the combined navies of any two conceivable European adversaries. The army, on the other hand, did not engage in the competitive armament race of the continental powers on the theory that Great Britain was not a land but a sea power. Nonetheless, the army was kept strong enough to wage the almost ceaseless border conflicts inseparable from a movement of practically uninterrupted colonial expansion. Rated as wars, these conflicts were generally on the diminished scale of so-called punitive expeditions. In India they were directed against Afghans and Burmese; in the near east, against Arab or Bedouin tribes that interfered with trade; in Africa, against Zulus and Sudanese. In their sum they were such common occurrences that it was a relatively rare event for the famed *pax Britannica* to reign through the whole extent of the far-flung empire. *The never-ending border warfare*

In a quite different category were the wars engaged in with civilized sovereign states. The first of this kind waged by the London government after the settlement of 1815 was leveled at the huge but petrified dominion of China. Over an attempt on the part of China to forbid the importation of opium from India a conflict developed in 1840 wherein the ancient empire, operating with medieval tools of war, went down like a house of cards before the British assault. When peace was made (1842) China was obliged to surrender the island of Hong Kong off the Cantonese coast. Before long, Britain had converted it into a commercial and naval stronghold which dominated the eastern Asiatic waters. *War with China and acquisition of Hong Kong (1842)*

Two con-
flicts with
Russia over
the Ottoman
empire

The war with Russia called the Crimean War (1854-1856) demanded a far greater expenditure of ships, men, and money. It was waged (see Chapter 26) with France as an ally in order to hinder the tsar from bringing the sultan under his rule, and, since it achieved its purpose, may be set down as a British victory. Twenty years later, in 1878, a second war with Russia over the same issue (see Chapter 30) was averted only by Russia's beating a diplomatic retreat just before it was too late, and agreeing to adjudicate its quarrel with Great Britain at a congress to be held at Berlin. The second, bloodless victory over Russia was credited by public opinion to Prime Minister Disraeli, whom accordingly Queen Victoria raised to the peerage as Lord Beaconsfield.

Disraeli,
exponent
of the new
nationalist-
imperialist
fervor

More important however in the long view than the rebuff to Russia in 1878 was the patriotic fervor which in the course of the controversy Disraeli had succeeded in calling into being. The recent unification of Italy and Germany had flooded Europe with a fiery nationalism; at precisely the same moment the Industrial Revolution with its scramble for foreign markets had given birth to a fiercely competitive imperialism. Plainly there was ahead for Europe a period dominated by nationalist and imperialist emotions and Disraeli's historical role may be defined as having brought the onset of this period to the consciousness of the British people. No one before him had succeeded in whipping their nationalist and imperialist passions to so savage a blaze. For weeks during the critical year of 1878 the London music halls rang with a brawling chant running to the words: "We don't want to fight, but by jingo if we do, we've got the ships, we've got the men, we've got the money too." From this crude jingle sprang the crude word "jingoism." It signified the new nationalist-imperialist fervor which an expert government would know how to mobilize henceforth at a moment's notice. If at the termination of a crisis it became a sleeping lion, it could always be fetched up with a bound and a roar at the approach of a new crisis.

Since
nationalism
and imperi-
alism domi-
nate the
people, they
dominate
both parties

From Disraeli's time British foreign policy was with the almost solid support of the British people animated with the spirit of offense and directed to continued expansion. When the Egyptian crisis of 1882 arose, it was Gladstone, rated a "Little Englander," who was prime minister. Yet Gladstone made war on Egypt and incorporated it in the empire. In 1899, when the Boers planted themselves across the path of British expansion, the government of Lord Salisbury, resting on the Conservative party, took up the challenge and reduced the Boers to submission. The point to observe is that, in spite of important differences of opinion between Conservatives and Liberals touching domestic issues, they conducted an identical foreign policy inspired by an identical nationalist-imperialist program. Of this, final and conclusive evidence was afforded by the Liberal ministry of Asquith and Lloyd George, in charge of affairs at the outbreak of World War I. Theirs was a government that by championing Insurance Legislation had enveloped itself in an all but visible humanitarian aura. But when war loomed, these Liberals exploded in a fervor of patriotism and surrendered themselves to their military task with an energy that could not have been outdone by the Conservatives.

30

THE RUSSIAN AND THE OTTOMAN EMPIRES FROM THE CONGRESS OF VIENNA (1815) TO THE OUTBREAK OF WORLD WAR I

The expansive energy of Western civilization

THROUGHOUT THIS BOOK interest has been focused on Western civilization, which has been represented as originating in early medieval times within the territories embraced by the Latin Christian church. In the period of the Renaissance its slowly gathering energy began to burst through these narrow geographic bounds. The movement of expansion thus inaugurated has continued ever since until Western civilization at present dominates the world.

Russia under Peter I enters the circle of Western civilization

In the vast eastern plain of Europe, on which the Russians, a Slav people, dwelt, the expanding civilization of the west celebrated toward the end of the seventeenth century one of its most remarkable victories. It was Tsar Peter the Great who resolved to westernize his land and people and who, in pursuit of this plan, provided himself with an army and an administration on the European pattern. His amazing energy enabled him to impart to the sluggish Russian mass a slow but irresistible movement. In consequence it was able, even in Peter's day, to push the weakening might of Sweden from the Baltic; and, in the days immediately after Peter, it flowed westward into Poland and, in addition, crowded the once irresistible Ottoman empire from the northern shore of the Black sea.

The Ottoman empire confronted with the problem of westernization

When with exceptional frankness the Tsarina Catherine II (1762-1796) indicated that the goal of Russian political endeavor would for her and her descendants be Constantinople and the straits, it became clear that the Ottoman empire was doomed unless it found means of bringing the powerful Russian offensive to a halt. It was equally clear that the most effective way of stopping the Slav power would be for the Ottoman empire to follow the Russian example and, after reforming its army and administration in the European manner, to carry through a sweeping policy of westernization.

THE STORY OF OTTOMAN DECAY TO THE PEACE OF PARIS (1856)

Every diagnosis of the Ottoman malady must begin with distinguishing between the Ottoman empire and the Turks. The Ottoman empire was the vast, racially extremely mixed dominion around the bend of the eastern Mediterranean which the Mongoloid Turks, hailing from the central plateau of Asia, had amassed in several centuries of conquest. Content to exploit, the Turks made no effort to assimilate the peoples whom they had vanquished. In the course of their victorious push they had entered Europe by crossing the Dardanelles. When, in 1453, they at last captured Constantinople, they made the Balkan peninsula the keystone of their empire and Constantinople its capital city. The Turks create the racially mixed Ottoman empire by conquest

For many generations the Turks gave evidence of being endowed with an unusual degree of energy and intelligence. With the seventeenth century a decay set in which gradually undermined their institutions. The army, boasting as its core the once irresistible Janissaries, degenerated into a wretched, undisciplined militia; the administration, intrusted to provincial governors called pashas, became a hotbed of intrigue, jealousy, and graft; and the central authority wielded by the head of the state became a mockery in the hands of sultans who, forgetting the active, manly tradition of their forebears, were content to pass their inert lives in the voluptuous atmosphere of the imperial harem. Decay of the Turkish army and administration

As Asiatics, on the one hand, and as Moslems, on the other, the Turks were so utterly removed from an understanding of the Christian west that they were not prompted to utilize western experience in order to correct the abuses from which they suffered. A like unwillingness to learn from example did not, however, weigh upon the Christian peoples of the Balkan peninsula who, since their conquest in the fifteenth century, had been ground under the heel of the Turks. Toward the close of the eighteenth century two of these depressed groups, the Greeks and the Serbs, exhibited signs of a new courage. Their refreshed spirit drew its strength to a large degree from the conviction that their rulers were no longer the same men as of yore and might be faced in the field with some chance of success. The Greeks and Serbs first to awaken among the conquered Balkan peoples

At the same time certain leaders arose among the Serbs and Greeks who advocated a national renovation to be achieved by assimilating the outlook and methods of western Europe. It was in 1804 that Serb leaders of the Belgrade area started their first revolt against their Turkish masters. Though the rebels were defeated, they rose again and sustained their cause with such stubbornness that by 1817 they had wrested from the sultan a not inconsiderable measure of self-government for a Serb core of relatively small extent. When, in 1821, the Greeks in their turn Success achieved by Serbs and Greeks in the early nineteenth century felt encouraged to rise, they gained even more than the Serbs, for, as we learned in Chapter 22, they won not only autonomy but independence.

In this way a notable breach was made in the Ottoman house by the revolutionary action of two Christian peoples subjected to the Turks. With Serbs and Greeks pointing the way, would not the other oppressed groups, the Rumanians, the Bulgars, and the Albanians, follow? Sooner or later the Balkan nationalist awakening, based on a new self-reliance as well as on the absorption of the western outlook and methods, would reach all the Balkan groups, and the feeble sultan, the Sick Man of Europe, as he was coming to be called, would be confronted with the rebellion of the whole peninsula.

The certain awakening of all the Balkan peoples

A decadent government, an ambitious, forward-pressing Russia, and the awakening Christian nationalities of the Balkan peninsula are the three leading factors in the general nineteenth century situation of the Ottoman empire. But there is a fourth. If the end of the Ottoman state was at hand, it was not likely that the other European powers would leave the field to Russia as sole eventual heir. They would all be sure to insist on getting some portion of the booty. In this way the Ottoman empire became a leading factor in that conflict of rival imperialisms which kept mounting through the nineteenth century until it terminated in the vast conflagration of World War I.

The four factors of the Ottoman problem of the nineteenth century

Already at the time of the Greek revolt of the twenties the enumerated factors were in full operation. The Turks proving themselves too feeble with their own strength to subdue the Greeks, the powers intervened to stop the war, and when they did not go far enough in their demands on the sultan to suit Russia, Tsar Nicholas I made war on Turkey in his own behalf. Winning easily, he imposed on the sultan the Peace of Adrianople (1829), by which he acquired what amounted to a protectorate over Serbia as well as over the two Rumanian provinces, Moldavia and Wallachia.

Again the Russo-Turkish War of 1828-29

Thus did Tsar Nicholas succeed in planting his foot firmly in the Balkan peninsula. At this juncture fate itself came to his aid by raising up against the sultan another and an unexpected enemy. This was Mehemet Ali, pasha of Egypt. We have encountered him in the Greek War of Liberation, wherein he took a part which might have proven decisive, had not the powers interfered and wrecked his fleet at Navarino (1827).

Mehemet Ali, pasha of Egypt, and the Greek War

Mehemet's distinction was that he had copied the west to some extent and had provided himself with an army and a navy on the European model. He was, in consequence, more powerful than his overlord, the sultan. When, following the Navarino disaster, he demanded a reward for his services against the Greeks in the form of southern Syria, he was in a position to enforce his request with threats. From this tense situation there developed in 1831 a war between master and man, in which the

Mehemet Ali rebels against the sultan and defeats him (1833)

pasha was successful. In fact he was so extraordinarily successful that Mehemet's army, commanded by his son Ibrahim, might have taken Constantinople itself if Tsar Nicholas had not interposed his veto (1833).

In consequence of Russian protection asked for and received, the sultan, Mahmud II by name, was reduced to the status of a Russian ward and burned with thoughts of vengeance on his disobedient vassal of Egypt, the cause of his humiliation. In 1839 Sultan Mahmud believed he was strong enough to renew the war with the hated Mehemet. He was again disastrously defeated. As at the very height of the conflict Mahmud died, leaving the scepter to a youthful, untried heir, the Ottoman empire seemed to have become the prize of Mehemet Ali. *Second defeat of the sultan (1839)*

If Tsar Nicholas could, by his sole action in 1839, have "saved" the Ottoman empire from the Egyptian pasha as he had done in 1833, he would beyond a doubt have completed its reduction to a Russian dependency. But this time the other powers were on the alert and insisted on having a hand in "saving" the Ottoman state. The result was that, though only after a terrible crisis in which the specter of a general war loomed over Europe, the powers, in temporary agreement, undertook to regulate the relationship of sultan and pasha. *The concert of Europe "saves" the Ottoman empire*

After a severe chastisement at the hands of European forces, which Mehemet Ali invited by refusing to bow to European dictation, he and his army were obliged to fall back on Egypt. This province was then accorded to him as his hereditary possession, though he was to acknowledge the sultan as his suzerain. So much, but not a jot or tittle more would the powers concede to the pasha in return for his two sweeping victories over his master. This done, Mahmud's young son was enthroned on the Bosporus. The new ruler, Abdul Medjid I, owed his elevation to the action of all the powers, not to Russia alone—that is the leading point to be noted. *The settlement decreed (1841) by the powers*

It should also be noted that in this crisis Tsar Nicholas had acted along with the other powers and had, in apparent agreement with them, restored the Ottoman empire. At bottom, however, he saw the Ottoman problem in a radically different light from his collaborators. Convinced that no amount of tinkering could save the Ottoman empire, he interpreted the informal European protectorate assumed in 1839 as a step preliminary to a peaceful partition of the territory. The other powers, however, and particularly Great Britain, because a partition would inevitably carry Russia to the key position of Constantinople, opposed this deduction with all their might. They wished to employ the protectorate to the end of "reforming" the Ottoman empire in order that it might become strong enough to resist all further Russian encroachment. *Growing misunderstanding between Russia and the other powers*

Such are the elements that account for the Russo-British antagonism which ruled the near east for the rest of the century. Great Britain was set on putting through the policy of reform; and because it upheld at the same time the idea of an Ottoman empire in possession of an unimpaired sovereignty, it gained and held the ear of the sultan and of a small group of reforming Ottoman officials.

Great Britain favors the reform policy

Largely owing to British pressure, the Ottoman empire now actually, if hesitatingly, entered on the path of reform. Already in 1826 Sultan Mahmud had, on his own initiative, got rid of the worthless and ever-mutinous Janissaries. On foundations laid by him there was now built up under his son and successor a new Ottoman army, equipped, disciplined, and organized in the manner of Europe. Undeniably this reformed army became the most important single factor in the renewed lease of life of the Ottoman state. At the same time a partial reshaping of the administration was undertaken with a view to an improved centralized control.

Ottoman reform limited largely to the army

As, however, the corruption of officials persisted and the mass of the Turkish people fiercely opposed the spread of European ideas, the old evils proved ineradicable. Discontent multiplied throughout the state, and repeated risings furnished Tsar Nicholas with all the ammunition he needed to sustain his favorite thesis that Ottoman reform was a delusion and that the only logical course for the powers was to arrange for an early amicable division of the sultan's lands. Aware that, to carry out this policy, he would have to gain the consent, first of all, of Great Britain, the tsar repeatedly approached the British cabinet with partition projects with no other outcome than their polite rejection.

Tsar Nicholas again broaches partition to Great Britain

The upshot was that, disappointed and enraged, Nicholas resolved to proceed alone. In 1853 his ambassador at Constantinople was ordered to present an ultimatum which called for the recognition of the tsar as the protector of all Greek Christians resident on Ottoman soil. This embraced the bulk of the sultan's Balkan subjects. To anyone who could read between the lines the demand signified the substitution of a Russian for the informal European control of Turkey in operation since 1839.

The tsar undertakes (1853) another war against the sultan

It was this ultimatum which led to the Crimean War (1854-1856), which we have already treated. As Russia was defeated, the victors, Great Britain and France, in dictating the Peace of Paris, deprived the great Slav power of all the special advantages within the Ottoman empire accumulated by previous treaties. In other words, they reduced Russia, in respect to the Turkish dominion, to an exact level with all the other powers. In order to give the sultan the greatest possible security against a renewed future aggression on the part of the tsar, the two western powers even went the length of forbidding Russia to maintain a navy on the Black sea. As a final favor to the sultan they canceled the informal protectorate exercised by all the powers at Constantinople since 1839 and

The victors deprive Russia of past advantages won over Turkey

welcomed the Ottoman empire as an equal, sovereign state into the comity of European nations.

Considered in its entirety, the Treaty of Paris of 1856 was one of the most futile attempts ever made by so-called statesmen to change the order of nature. The Ottoman empire was treated as though it were a vigorous going concern, when whoever took the trouble to look at it with half an eye could see that disease persisted and that the oppressed subject peoples were perpetually on the verge of revolt. Russia, on the other hand, was put under disabilities, especially in the banishment of its navy from the Black sea, to which no great power could be expected to submit.

The result was that this particular Russian disability was soon canceled. When, in 1870, the Franco-German War broke out and the attention of Europe was absorbed by the struggle, the tsar seized the opportunity to declare that he would no longer hold himself bound by the Black sea clause. To mark the resumption of his complete independence in the Black sea waters he undertook the construction of a navy and an appropriate naval base. Fifteen years after the capture of Sebastopol, Russia rebuilt that ruined port. It was an act tantamount to the declaration that the Slav empire had resumed its interrupted march on Constantinople.

The Treaty of Paris (1856) proves futile

Russia rebuilds (1870) its naval power in the Black sea

THE WESTERNIZATION OF RUSSIA RESUMED BY ALEXANDER II

While it is true that Russia was opened to Western civilization by the initiative of Tsar Peter I and his successors, and, among them, more particularly by Catherine II, an inevitable consequence of their labors was that, by the beginning of the nineteenth century, a small but growing body of their subjects had come to share their enthusiasm and to look hopefully forward to the remodeling of Russian life and institutions in accordance with European standards. Such early converts belonged exclusively to the upper, traveled circles and may be thought of as advocating in a loose sort of way the program of western liberalism. They were agreed that the serfdom of the peasants, the religious intolerance of the orthodox clergy, and the autocracy of the tsars called for measures of reform, but they were not prepared, for the present at least, to translate their views into action. A circumstance that greatly strengthened their position was that Tsar Alexander I (1801-1825), as a young man, entertained identical opinions. However, following the convulsions that attended the downfall of Napoleon, his innate emotional instability produced a complete turn-about and threw him into the arms of Christian mystics and political conservatives. Not only did he in this second period saddle Europe with the Holy Alliance but he rejected with violence the reform program to which he had once so fervently subscribed.

The question of reform under Alexander I

When Alexander was succeeded by his brother, Nicholas I (1825-1855),
who, an autocrat by nature, had always detested liberalism in all its forms
and works, a group of westernized officers, despairing of reform under
the new sovereign, rose in revolt clamorously demanding a constitution.
Their futile action had no other effect than to cause the tsar to close his
mind more tightly than ever against change. While, therefore, during the
reign of Nicholas there was a fierce resistance to everything faintly savoring of liberalism, it is also true that, invisibly and beneath the surface,
the reform movement waxed steadily stronger till it comprised a rapidly
growing body of adherents scattered through the rare cities of the vast
Russian plain and drawn much less now from the upper aristocratic level
than from the intellectuals and the bourgeoisie.

It should consequently cause no surprise that on the crushing defeat
of the autocracy in the Crimean War the reform groups should have
been inspired with a new courage and have come eagerly forward, declaring by book, pamphlet, and newspaper that the hour had at last struck
for a radical revamping of the inherited institutions. They insisted that
the repression which had characterized the reign of the late Tsar Nicholas must cease, and let it be unmistakably understood that, should the
desired reform not be instituted from above, it would infallibly be
brought about by revolution from below. The new tsar, Alexander II
(1855-1881), was not insensible to the liberal pressure. When we consider,
further, that he was of a humane and kindly disposition and had with
his own eyes witnessed the breakdown of the traditional Russian system
in the late war, we have no difficulty in understanding how it came
about that he turned away from his father's negative policy and inaugurated a program of reform.

Alexander's reform labors, covering some seven or eight years, culminated in three enactments, of which the emancipation of the serfs produced by far the loudest reverberation in the world. Since Russia still
possessed the character of a primitive agricultural society, its peasant-
serfs constituted almost ninety per cent of the population. They were
settled through the country in villages, each of which was in respect to
certain internal concerns a self-governing community called *mir*. It was
the collective mir which made itself responsible to the landlord for the
rental payment for the village land and, in addition, through a meeting
of the family heads periodically redistributed the land among the mir
members. It will be seen at once that the mir was a communistic, equalitarian institution sharply distinguished from the competitive farm units
which result from the regime of private property. The small allotments,
the primitive method of cultivation, the heavy dues exacted not only by
the landlord but also by the state and the church and, finally, the enforced attachment of the peasants to the soil crushed them under bur-

dens that made their lot little better than that of the beasts of the field. Alexander II began by freeing the serfs on the estates belonging to the imperial family; then, after a careful examination by special commissions of the whole complicated problem, he issued in 1861 his famous Emancipation Manifesto, following it up with measures which, while liberating the peasants from the yoke of serfdom, failed to convert them into freeholders.

In virtue of these measures a part of each estate was, against adequate compensation paid by the government to the landlord, surrendered by him to the mir, which remained intact and acquired title to the surrendered acreage in return for the obligation to reimburse the government for its outlay by annual payments spread over a period of forty-nine years. The landlords, as the happy recipients of unexpected government cash, were pleased with the settlement; the peasants, on the contrary, were disappointed from the first and became ever more so with the passage of time. For, except a welcome personal freedom, what did they get out of the emancipation so ecstatically besung by editorial writers all around the globe? They cultivated no larger allotments of land than before and they paid the identical exactions with the unimportant distinction that the payment formerly made to the landlord was now made to the government. Indeed they were often worse off, for, owing to the increase of population and the consequent necessity of providing for more families, the always scanty individual allotment to the mir member showed a disastrous tendency to shrink. A generation passed before the jubilant liberals awakened to their self-deception over the emancipation; the peasants were not deceived for a day. Freed from serfdom to the landlord, such peasants as did not abandon the mir (as they were now at liberty to do) had become, in effect, serfs of the state. So at least, with the usual ingratitude of man, they commonly designated themselves. In the case, however, of their abandoning the mir, two courses were open to them. Either they might direct their footsteps to the vast unoccupied tracts of Siberia or remain behind as casual laborers tramping the roads on the lookout for work. In the latter instance they would with rage and misery in their hearts covetously eye the large and comfortable estates of which their former masters, the nobles, remained possessed even after the considerable subtraction represented by the surrendered mir.

Everything considered, the two other capital reforms of Alexander effected more enduring changes than the emancipation of the serfs. By a series of enactments the inherited, haphazard system of justice was completely overhauled. Drawing on several western systems for guidance, the tsar in 1862 set up civil and criminal courts, constituted at the bottom of the scale by locally elected justices of the peace and moving upward

Success and failure of emancipation

Two other reforms: (1) justice; (2) zemstvos

through district and circuit courts to a supreme court seated at the capital. Equally and possibly even more important was the creation in 1864 of local administrative bodies called *zemstvos*. The thirty-three provinces (officially called "governments") into which Russia was divided were in their turn subdivided into districts. Under the new arrangement each district was endowed with a local assembly or zemstvo, composed of representatives of the nobility, the townsfolk, and the peasantry; and each district zemstvo was authorized to send delegates to the more comprehensive provincial zemstvo. The significance of this invitation to the Russian people to school themselves in the practice of self-government can hardly be exaggerated. True, both district and provincial zemstvos came under the supervision of the Minister of the Interior and were strictly enjoined from discussing issues of national scope. Nonetheless, they were charged with important responsibilities, for they were empowered to levy local taxes and look after such concerns as schools, hospitals, churches, poor relief, and public health. Not long afterward a similarly limited system of self-government was extended to the towns in the form of town councils called *dumas*.

Alexander reverts to reaction

Naturally enough these definitely democratic concessions persuaded the liberals that they would presently be crowned by a decree establishing a national parliament. Their hope was destined to remain unfulfilled. Alexander had already moved farther into the liberal camp than his most intimate advisers considered safe. Hesitantly, but in final count violently, he reverted to the autocracy of his father Nicholas and for the remainder of his life identified himself with the conservatives and their narrow three-fold slogan: Autocracy, Orthodoxy, Nationalism.

The Polish revolt of 1863

Many conjectures have been offered in explanation of Alexander's political about-face. Considering that he was never really a liberal at heart, it might be argued that sooner or later he was bound to beat a retreat from uncongenial territory. But if a particular event may be adduced as applying the final fillip to retreat, it would be the revolt of Poland. Alexander had shown a certain indulgence to the Poles by returning to them some elements of the self-government they had enjoyed prior to their revolt of 1830. But as nothing would satisfy their national pride short of complete independence, they rose again in 1863, not as a united nation this time but in scattered guerilla bands. The well-armed Russians had little difficulty in destroying the rebels and reestablishing the tsar's authority. To the uneasy Alexander the rebellion served warning of what was only too likely to happen when an autocrat relaxes his hold. He would not err in that way any more.

Rise of nihilism

The tsar's relapse into reaction was a vast disappointment to the liberals. But already the young generation was turning from liberalism to newer faiths. Of this change Turgenev in his novel, *Fathers and Sons* has given us the classical expression in the person of the student, Bazorov. This young man no longer believes in the earlier reform programs, regardless of whether they stemmed from a liberal or a romantic root. He has been captured by science, and because everything his elders believed is rank superstition in his eyes, they label him *nihilist* (from the Latin *nihil,* meaning "nothing"). He and his kind represented themselves as following exclusively the dictates of reason. Their vaunted rationalism suggests a certain kinship with eighteenth century Enlightenment. Like the Enlightenment, nihilism in the beginning was a purely intellectual movement concerned with casting off outworn traditions. Again like the Enlightenment, which in the French Revolution was transformed into action, the time came when nihilism turned militant and inspired a generation of relentless fighters against autocracy.

Another faith that attracted the younger intellectuals was anarchy. Its Russian champion, Bakunin, was early obliged to flee from his country, and spent the rest of his life abroad. He tried at one time to ally himself with Marx and Engels but was rejected by them on account of his unbridled revolutionary sentiments. He hated not only the tsarist autocracy but government of every kind. In short, he preached no-government, a blessed condition that man will attain when, together with the state, he divests himself of such other tyrannical restraints as religion and the family. In the generation growing up in the third quarter of the nineteenth century there were to be found considerable bodies of both nihilists and anarchists, and their existence furnished evidence that Russian society was disturbed to its very foundations. *Spread of anarchism*

Of this disturbance the final and conclusive proof was supplied by the terrorists. These were bands of young men (and women, too) who, weary of waiting for the demise of the autocratic regime, resolved to speed that happy day by violence and murder. In effect they levied private war on their enemy, the tsar, through dispatching by dagger, pistol, or bomb such officials as had made themselves particularly offensive. Of course the exasperated government responded by doubling its measures of oppression. Its secret police, operating outside the law and bound by no moral restraints, seized the suspected adherents of the terrorists by the thousands and sent them marching in endless chain-gangs to the ice-bound wildernesses of Siberia. There they lived and died before their time in the equivalent of the inhuman concentration camps of our latter-day dictators. After several attempts on Alexander's life he was at last, on March 13, 1881, killed by a bomb tossed under his carriage as he was driving through the streets of St. Petersburg. *The terrorists*

He was succeeded by his son, Alexander III (1881-1894), a giant of a man and as dour and unsmiling a despot as ever sat on a throne. He increased the arbitrary powers of the secret state-police, destroyed such liberties of the press as still survived, put the teaching staffs of the universities under sharp surveillance, and by these and other methods of extreme repression gave the appearance, at least, of having successfully stifled opposition. There we will leave the domestic situation, while we examine the resumption during the reign of Alexander II of Russia's irrepressible conflict with the Ottoman empire.

The grim reactionary, Alexander III

THE TURCO-RUSSIAN WAR OF 1877-1878 AND THE
CONGRESS OF BERLIN

It was in 1875 that Alexander II's attention again swung to the Balkan peninsula, owing to the fresh rebellion there of a subject people. The Christian Serbs of the provinces of Herzegovina and Bosnia rose against the sultan rather than bear any longer the cruel oppression of his tax collectors. They gained the sympathy and support of the two already liberated Serb states of Serbia and Montenegro, which went the length of declaring war on the sultan, thereby spreading alarm and agitation throughout Europe.

The revolt of Bosnia and Herzegovina produces a new Balkan crisis (1875)

Of course the two pigmies, Serbia and Montenegro, could not long stand up against the Ottoman empire. The powers interfered to save them from punishment but at the same time made their usual concession to European and Christian opinion by ordering the sultan to undertake a general Balkan house-cleaning. When he resisted this pressure, Russia, as on more than one earlier occasion, took the bit between its teeth and in April, 1877, declared war on the recalcitrant monarch.

Russia begins another war against Turkey (April, 1877)

Immediately a vast Muscovite army moved into and across the provinces of Moldavia and Wallachia. Following the Peace of Paris, these two provinces had, with the consent of Europe, been merged under the name of Rumania. In this manner still another state had issued from the fermenting vat of the Balkans, self-governing Rumania following in the footsteps of self-governing Serbia and independent Greece.

The birth of Rumania (1856)

The Russians drove the Ottoman forces, like sheep, before them toward the passes of the Balkan mountains. Had it not been for a remarkable soldier, Osman Pasha by name, the war would have ended for the Turks with a swift, ignominious collapse. Osman saved the honor of the Turkish army. He gathered such forces as he could lay his hands on, threw himself into the fortress of Plevna, and there held the whole Russian army at bay for many months.

The siege of Plevna, the outstanding episode of the war

When, in December, 1877, Plevna, owing to starvation, was obliged to yield, the Russians encountered no further obstacle. They poured in an irresistible stream across the Balkan mountains into the Thracian plain. Early in the new year they camped on the shores of the sea of Marmora

The sultan obliged to sue for peace

in full view of the minarets of Constantinople. Reduced to utter help-lessness, Sultan Abdul Hamid II was obliged humbly to sue for peace.

At this turn an enormous excitement seized upon the chancelleries of Europe, more particularly of Austria and Great Britain. They saw Russia in complete possession of its prey, and in order to bring home to the tsar that they did not intend to let him devour it by himself in total oblivion of his neighbors, they made frantic gestures of displeasure— Austria by mobilizing an army on the Rumanian border, Great Britain by dispatching a fleet to the Dardanelles.

Austria and Britain threaten Russia

It was a critical situation that became positively explosive when Russia in a treaty negotiated at San Stefano (a suburb of Constantinople) at last revealed the terms it was willing to concede to its beaten foe. The main feature of the treaty was the reduction of Turkey-in-Europe to such small dimensions that its Balkan role might be looked on as ended. Ex-cept for a Turkish remnant around Constantinople and except for the already liberated states of Greece, Serbia, Montenegro, and Rumania, the Balkan area was to be constituted as Bulgaria. This Big Bulgaria, organ-ized under Russian tutelage, was the surprise rabbit Russia drew out of the San Stefano hat.

Russia wrests the Treaty of San Stefano from Turkey (March 1878)

To the envious eyes of Austria and Great Britain Big Bulgaria meant just one thing: the control of the Balkan peninsula by Russia. They therefore insisted that the Treaty of San Stefano should be submitted for revision to a congress of the powers. Undoubtedly they would have gone to war, had not the tsar given way. If Alexander II yielded, it was because he was isolated and could not count on any power to give him help against the Anglo-Austrian combination.

Austria and Britain oblige Russia to negotiate

In June, 1878, there took place the Congress of Berlin. It met under the presidency of Prince Bismarck and revised the Treaty of San Stefano according to the wishes of Austria and Great Britain. To be sure, Russia was not deprived of all the fruits of victory. By receiving from Rumania southern Bessarabia she was able to carry her boundary to the northern mouth of the Danube delta. For this loss Rumania was compensated by the Dobruja, taken from Bulgaria. In addition, the tsar was permitted to strengthen his territorial position at the other, the eastern, end of the Black sea by the acquisition of a part of the Armenian borderland.

The Con-gress of Ber-lin (1878) concedes something to Russia

Even for these relatively scanty rewards Austria and Great Britain in-sisted on a full equivalent for themselves. Bosnia and Herzegovina, the Serb provinces where the conflagration had started, were intrusted to Austria "to occupy and administer." The sultan's sovereignty over the ceded lands remained theoretically intact. As for Great Britain, the com-pensation secured by her was the cession by the sultan of the east-Mediterranean island of Cyprus.

"Compensa-tions" se-cured by Austria and Britain

The really memorable feature of the Treaty of Berlin is what the powers did to the Russian plan of a Big Bulgaria. At the bidding of the

The Big Bulgaria of San Stefano broken into three parts

congress Big Bulgaria was broken into three sections. Between the Danube and the Balkan mountains a self-governing *principality of Bulgaria* was set up with no obligation to the sultan save the payment of an annual tribute; south of the Balkans a province, to be called *Eastern Rumelia,* was conceded civil autonomy on the understanding that it was to be occupied by Turkish military forces; and finally, the important province of *Macedonia,* occupying the Vardar valley, was handed back to the sultan in order to enable him to continue to play an effective Balkan role. Though more hesitantly than at Paris twenty-two years before, the powers tried to blow the breath of life into the moribund Ottoman state. Except by attempting to strengthen the Ottoman empire they knew no way to thwart the territorial ambition of Russia.

Nonetheless, the Treaty of Berlin represents an advance in statesmanship over the Paris arrangements. For the first time since confronted

The Congress declares Serbia, Montenegro, and Rumania independent

with the Balkan confusion the powers outlined a constructive plan for the peninsula. The young states, Serbia, Montenegro, and Rumania, which had, largely by their own efforts, broken the Ottoman yoke in the course of the recent decades, were, albeit grudgingly, given small increases of territory. Above all, they were freed of the last vestige of their former bondage to the Ottoman empire and declared free and independent. In the case of the tiny mountain eyrie of Montenegro this international guarantee of liberty was hardly necessary, for the brave mountaineers had as early as the eighteenth century renounced every trace of dependence on the sultan.

While Greece could not be advanced in status, having already been

Greece strengthened by Thessaly

declared independent half a century before, it could be strengthened by a territorial addition. Accordingly, the powers handed over to it the province of Thessaly.

If we add that by establishing the principality of Bulgaria, the powers

The Congress foresees the end of the Ottoman empire

set another Christian people, the Bulgars, on the path of freedom, we are justified in saying that although the congress once again resuscitated the Ottoman empire, it at the same time cautiously envisaged a not too distant future in which the Balkan peninsula would be taken over by the Balkan peoples themselves.

BALKAN DEVELOPMENTS AFTER 1878

Notable progress made by Serbia, Greece, and Rumania

In the period following the Congress of Berlin the young Balkan states in the main justified the confidence placed in them. The rulers of Rumania and Serbia took the title of king to mark their arrival at full sovereign status. Both the new kingdoms, and the older kingdom of Greece as well, engaged with eagerness in the work of spreading through

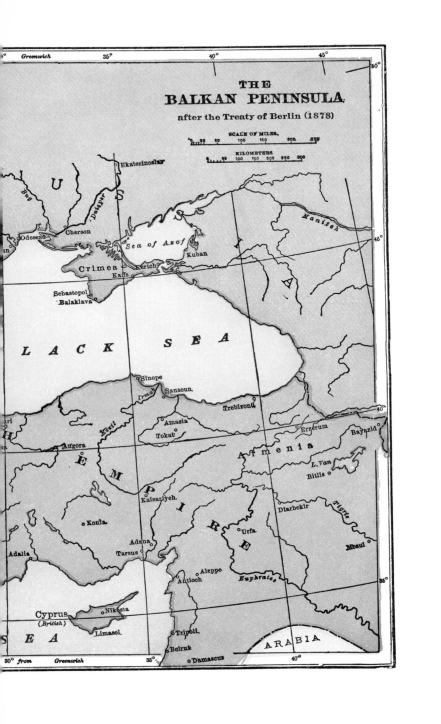

THE
BALKAN PENINSULA
after the Treaty of Berlin (1878)

SCALE OF MILES.

KILOMETERS

Greenwich   35°   40°   45°   50°

U

Ekaterinoslav

Bug

Dnieper

Cherson

Odessa

Sea of Azof

Kuban

Manitsch

Crimea   Kertch

Kaffa

Sebastopol

Balaklava

B L A C K   S E A

46°

45°

Sinope

Irmak   Sansoun

Amasia

Tokat

Trebizond

Erzerum

Bayazid

40°

Armenia

L. Van

Bitlis

Kizil

Angora

E
M
P
I
R
E

Kaisariyeh

Diarbekir

Tigris

Konia

Urfa

Adana

Mosul

Tarsus

Adalia

Aleppo

Antioch

Euphrates

35°

Cyprus
(British)

Nikosia

Limasol

S E A

Tripoli

Beirut

Damascus

ARABIA

30° from   Greenwich   35°   40°

their backward communities the science and education of the west. They also encouraged the construction of highways and railroads and the multiplication of modern financial and industrial enterprises.

More notable perhaps than the progress made by any other Balkan people after 1878 was that made by the Bulgars. True, as the most recent folk to rouse themselves from slumber, they had also the greatest distance to travel. The official status of their principality as defined at Berlin was still far from satisfactory. A Bulgarian assembly, elected to nominate a ruler, called to office a young German prince, Alexander of Battenberg. They called him not in his character of a German, but because he was a nephew of Tsar Alexander II. Unhappily Russia, which had liberated Bulgaria, could not divest itself of the idea of control and kept the young prince in the strictest leading-strings. The Bulgars make Alexander of Battenberg their prince

When Tsar Alexander III (1881-1894) succeeded his father, the situation in Bulgaria became increasingly difficult. The new tsar was a gloomy despot who expected the Bulgars to show their eternal gratitude to his house by obedience to his every wish. As a result the Bulgars developed a resentful hostility toward him. They nursed a strong nationalist fervor and resolved no longer to take orders from their too exacting benefactor. When Prince Alexander, equally anxious to escape Russian tutelage, threw in his lot with his people, they felt strong enough to go ahead politically without further regard for Russia. The Bulgar patriots reject the authority of the tsar

In 1885 the political leaders of Bulgaria entered into a conspiracy with the political leaders of Eastern Rumelia and, before Europe knew what was going on, Eastern Rumelia had been incorporated with Bulgaria. As from the nationalist viewpoint Eastern Rumelia was Bulgar territory, the ultimate union of the two provinces may be considered to have been inevitable. Nonetheless, it ran counter to the Treaty of Berlin and caused an immense disturbance in the foreign offices of all the powers. Eastern Rumelia incorporated in Bulgaria (1885)

Tsar Alexander III was more deeply outraged than anyone else, for he regarded Prince Alexander of Bulgaria as his ward and scouted the idea of Alexander's taking any, even the least, step without previous consultation. Unprepared at the moment to take action himself, he was delighted when Bulgaria's neighbor, Serbia, in a burst of jealousy over the territorial enlargement of Bulgaria, declared war. This treacherous Serb attack Prince Alexander victoriously repulsed. Indeed the Bulgarians would have invaded and punished Serbia, had not Austria intervened in its behalf. The growth of Bulgaria is resented by Serbia, which declares war (1885)

Under Austrian mediation a peace was quickly patched up (1885). However, a novelty had made its appearance in the world of the newly created Balkan states from which sprang a fresh crop of troubles. The five Christian states of recent origin—Greece, Serbia, Montenegro, Rumania, Bulgaria—had a common enemy in Turkey, but they were not The small Balkan states adopt the principle of "compensation"

by any means overburdened with good will toward one another. In case any additional territory was to be taken from the sultan, each state desired the prize for itself; or should an increase be achieved by one state, the others would at the very least expect "compensation" for themselves.

This was the "principle" behind Serbia's frivolous attack on Bulgaria.

Macedonia, a province in which every Balkan nationality stakes out a claim

Now let us, with the aid of the accompanying map, look about in the Balkan peninsula. The most considerable Balkan province still ruled by the sultan after 1878 was Macedonia. For geographical reasons, involving such matters as the tilt of the land and the flow of the rivers, Macedonia was the very heart of the peninsula. And because the Balkan nationalities had all drifted thither at one time or another in the course of the ages, each had some nationals residing there and could on nationalist grounds set up some sort of claim to ownership. Therefore they all peered over into Macedonia as into a Promised Land and, even while the sultan still ruled therein, staked off imaginary future segments for themselves.

Russia's disappointment over recalcitrant Bulgaria, coming as a climax

The kidnapping (1886) of Alexander and his abdication

to her disappointment over the Treaty of Berlin, provoked her government to adopt an extreme measure. It instigated a conspiracy to get rid of Alexander of Battenberg, who had made himself offensive because he had become a Bulgar nationalist when he should have remained a liveried Muscovite butler. Alexander was kidnapped by the conspirators in the depth of night, forced to sign a letter of abdication at the point of a gun, and bundled out of the country. This was in 1886. He might have reoccupied the Bulgar throne, because his people were enthusiastically devoted to him. But in the hope of winning back for Bulgaria the favor of the tsar by his personal disappearance, he voluntarily made his exile permanent.

The gesture was wasted. The angry Bulgar nationalists refused to

Ferdinand succeeds Alexander

truckle to the tsar and offered (1887) the vacant throne not to the candidate of Russia but to a man of their own choosing, Ferdinand of Saxe-Coburg. Prince Ferdinand became the second ruler of Bulgaria. An ambitious man not without understanding, he never ceased trying to patch up the quarrel with his Russian adversary. But only after Alexander III had been followed (1894) by Nicholas II did he succeed. By promising Nicholas to have his son and heir, who would normally have been reared a Catholic like himself, brought up in the Orthodox faith, he was readmitted to favor.

But we are anticipating. On being checkmated in Bulgaria, Alexander

Russia turns its attention to Asia

III turned his back, as it were, on Europe and fronted toward Asia. He had had enough of the Balkan peninsula for the present. His son and successor, Nicholas II (1894-1917), for the first decade of his reign followed the same course. From this shift of attention dates an important chapter in Russian as well as Asiatic history.

THE RUSSIAN ADVANCE INTO ASIA

Asia represented no new interest for Russia. Even before the reign of Peter the Great, Russian fur-traders had begun to penetrate the vast stretches of ice-bound Siberia. As Siberia is but an eastward extension of the Russian plain, the movement presented no particular geographic obstacles. By the early nineteenth century Russia had appropriated the whole of northern Asia, although she did not at that time derive any considerable economic benefits therefrom. The country was sparsely populated and inordinately cold and boasted little to lure the adventurer except the rich pelts of its fur-bearing animals. *The slow Russian advance across Siberia*

Not till the second half of the nineteenth century did it dawn on the governing circles of St. Petersburg that their Siberian dependency possessed mineral and agricultural resources which, under systematic development, would prove of inestimable value. At that time the Russian claims already extended clear across Siberia to the sea of Okhotsk on the Pacific ocean. With the improved prospects in this area it became desirable to reach southward toward warmer waters not blocked with ice through the major part of the year. A southward move necessarily meant a clash with China. Therewith began a new and aggressive phase of Russian expansion in Siberia. *The Russian government awakens to the economic importance of Siberia*

China, the most populous country in the world, was an ancient state with a civilization that represented one of the most remarkable achievements of mankind. In the course of its unfolding the Chinese had developed a sense of superiority to the rest of the world, from which, as manifestly inferior, they had loftily resolved to seal themselves off by closing their ports to foreign trade. When expanding Europe encountered this annoying situation, it raised such a cry of dismay and protest that, in the second half of the eighteenth century, the government at Peking was moved to make a concession: it opened the port of Canton in southern China to western trade and merchants. By the nineteenth century this single opening proved insufficient for the mounting trading fervor of the west, and first Great Britain, followed shortly by France, resorted to force to pry open the invaluable market represented by 400,000,000 prospective customers. Vast and proud as it was, China proved lamentably weak, and in successive treaties with the aggressive powers was obliged to consent to the opening of port after port on its long coast to the commerce of the world. Incidentally, while extending their trade privileges, Great Britain and France did not forget to satisfy their ever active territorial hunger. In 1842 Great Britain acquired the island of Hong Kong, commanding the entrance to Canton, and, shortly after, began to intrude on Burma, while France occupied Cochin China *China forcibly opened up for trade by Great Britain and France*

and from that southern foothold undertook to creep northward up the Chinese coast.

The story of Chinese penetration coupled with the related story of the appropriation or the attempted appropriation of all of Asia by the competitive imperialisms of Europe will be presently resumed. At this point we are solely concerned with the expansion into northern China of Russia and have taken account of the British and French action in southern China merely to bring out that Russia's was not an isolated act, and that the two other most active imperialisms of the west had, around the middle of the nineteenth century, let their attention swing to China as their next most promising victim. Apprised of China's inability to offer resistance by the happenings in the south, Russia in 1858 seized the land north of the Amur river, and two years later added thereto the strip of coastland some seven hundred miles in length beyond the Amur and fronting upper Japan. At the southernmost point of the strip the triumphant Muscovites promptly began the construction of a port, to which they gave the name of Vladivostok.

Russia extends her territory to the Chinese coast and founds Vladivostok

The Pacific coast does not indicate the only direction of Russian expansion in Asia in the nineteenth century. Simultaneously with the Pacific advance military expeditions undertook to push southward into central Asia. In the course of the reigns of the second and third Alexander these expeditions took possession of the immense territory which goes under the name of Turkestan. By the time Nicholas II mounted the throne, Russia-in-Asia had experienced such a tremendous expansion that it embraced twice as much territory as Russia-in-Europe.

Russia expands into central Asia (Turkestan)

In these circumstances it is not surprising that when, in the eighties, Russia found itself effectively stopped in the Balkan peninsula, it should have turned with a sigh of relief toward Asia, where its urge to expand encountered so few obstacles. But here, too, there was a fly in the ointment. In spite of the acquisition of a Pacific coast line reaching as far south as Vladivostok, the line of winter ice had not been passed. During the severest part of the cold season shipping in this newly acquired harbor had regularly to be suspended. What the governing group at St. Petersburg felt it needed was a port of trade open all the year round.

Vladivostok not a solution of the problem of an ice-free port

This ice-free port could only be had from China by penetrating still farther southward. Another consideration entered into the problem. In 1891, in pursuit of its new purpose of Siberian development, Russia had begun the construction of a great trans-Siberian railway. For its eastern terminal the engineers at first had their eye on Vladivostok. But would not a terminal farther south, with waters open all the year, be more satisfactory? In this way the issue of an ice-free port moved the tsar to search the map for a more desirable haven than Vladivostok. He put his finger on Port Arthur. While he was still pondering the problem of how

Russia fixes on ice-free Port Arthur as the best terminal for the Siberian railway

to go about acquiring Port Arthur, a war broke out (1894) between China and Japan.

We have seen that three European powers, Great Britain, France, and Russia, had come to the far east in pursuit of trade and territory. For many decades their course was relatively easy, for they had to deal with a pacifist and disorganized China which gave way to every resolute pressure. But before long they had to deal also with Japan, which turned out to be a very different matter.

The imperialist powers and Japan

RUSSIA AND JAPAN

Like its great neighbor on the mainland, the island-empire of Japan had long ago shut itself off from the rest of the world and become, in effect, a hermit state. The Japanese people, however, had never developed the pacifist tendencies that came to rule their Chinese neighbors. On the contrary, owing to a social system comparable to the feudalism of Europe during the Middle Ages, the Japanese were dominated by a warrior caste, the members of which never ceased to engage in the practice of arms and to mold their spirit by a code akin to that of medieval chivalry. This code, called *bushido,* exalted the military virtues above all others. In consequence the reaction of the Japanese to the trade pressure brought to bear on them by foreigners was very different to that of the Chinese. In 1853 the government of the United States of America, as much concerned with trade as the European powers (though unconcerned as yet with territorial expansion), sent Commodore Perry to Japan with a squadron of four warships. Perry, politely enough, presented his government's request for trade facilities. A more practical people than the Chinese, the Japanese recognized at once that with their outmoded swords and bucklers they were helpless before the mechanized equipment of the Americans, and with an unusual elasticity of spirit, though with rage in their hearts, accommodated themselves to the novel situation. In 1854 they signed a treaty with the United States opening certain ports to American trade; and, shortly after, they extended the same privileges to other trading nations. From this auspicious beginning it was but a step to further concessions by which in the course of a few years all Japan was thrown open to the west.

Japan opened to trade (1853) under a threat of the U. S. navy

Thus promptly did the Japanese yield to unanswerable military pressure. The deeper consequences of that pressure were more gradually revealed. In their sum they represented a resolve on the part of the country to make itself over, to the best of its ability, in the European and American image. In pursuit of this aim the feudal system was, politically speaking, liquidated and their emperor, whom the dominant feudal chiefs had obliged to withdraw to a life of monastic seclusion, was re-

The westernization of Japan

stored to power. Then in a kind of fury the Japanese took over the science, the education, the medicine, the engineering skills, the machines, and the capitalism of the west with at least so much superficial success that by approximately the year 1900 they presented themselves to view as an oriental version of European society. And since Europe was the model constantly before their eyes, they gave particular attention to the creation of an efficient army and navy. Not long before the end of the century they crowned their imitative labors by endowing themselves with a constitution which set up a legislature of two houses, the lower or popular house to be elected by a restricted suffrage. The executive power was vested in their emperor, the *mikado,* who had never ceased to be venerated by his people as the authentic descendant of the sun goddess.

Japan an
imperialist
power

The westernization of Japan carried with it all the social-political consequences with which we are familiar. One of the most important was that passion for trade and markets, which, when it includes the acquisition of territory, is called imperialism. Before long, the Japanese were looking around in the approved imperialist manner for commercial possibilities as well as for areas available for expansion and fixed their attention on Korea, just across the straits on the Asiatic mainland.

The Chinese-
Japanese
War (1894-
95) over
Korea

Korea was a kingdom which China claimed to be subject to its suzerainty. China, therefore, protested against the Japanese attempt to get control of Korea. Over this conflict war broke out in 1894. It was settled in short order by a sweeping Japanese victory. China, an immense, unwieldy bulk unflinchingly attached to ancient tradition, went down before the small island-kingdom of Japan for no other reason than that Japan, with the aid of machinery and guns, had become Europeanized.

The gains
demanded
by Japan

In the peace which Japan dictated at Shimonoseki (1895), not only did she detach Korea from China but also she acquired possession of the Liaotung peninsula. At the southern tip of this peninsula lay Port Arthur, suitable for development as both a commercial and a naval port.

Russia,
France, and
Germany
"protect"
China

Immediately Russia was up in arms. Was not Port Arthur the very point she had secretly fixed on as the logical terminal of the trans-Siberian railway? By persuading France and Germany to join her in protest, she obliged Japan to relinquish her claim to all territory on the Asiatic mainland and to content herself with the miserable reward of the Chinese island of Formosa.

Russia, Ger-
many, and
France pre-
sent their
bills to
China

Then the three western powers, dominant for the moment, paid themselves for the trouble they had taken to "protect" China. Between 1895 and 1898 France forced various concessions which culminated in the seizure of Kwangchow in southern China; in 1897 Germany seized, under the guise of a lease, the bay of Kiaochow in the province of Shantung; and in the following year Russia forced the government at Peking to give her a lease to the Liaotung peninsula together with Port Arthur and to permit her to extend the trans-Siberian railroad to this point all the way across the Chinese province of Manchuria.

If Japan had been deeply chagrined by the loss of the prize seized in successful war, the appropriation of it by Russia filled her with consternation. Unless Russia be halted, the imperialist role on which Japan had set her heart would have to be abandoned. She felt more and more drawn to Great Britain. That great naval power was hardly less disturbed than Japan over the rapid growth of Russian influence in China and Chinese waters. To keep at all costs abreast with the Russians the British, in 1898, matched the appropriation of Port Arthur by occupying the Chinese harbor directly opposite Port Arthur, called Weihaiwei. *The anxious Japanese turn for help to the equally anxious British*

Early in the twentieth century (1902) Great Britain and Japan signed an alliance. By its terms Great Britain pledged itself to come to Japan's assistance if Russia, in the event of a war with Japan, should gain the support of an European power. *Their alliance*

In these circumstances the Japanese felt encouraged to challenge the Russian advance into Asia. They waited till the Muscovites, firmly established at Port Arthur, made ready for their next and particularly dangerous advance, which was to take over Korea. Sharp notes of remonstrance dispatched by the Tokyo government were answered by still sharper notes from St. Petersburg. Then the inevitable happened. In February, 1904, the desperate Japanese threw themselves on the Russian fleet assembled in the waters of Port Arthur and on the Russian armies in Manchuria and in the ensuing war were steadily victorious. By the summer of 1905 the Russians were at the end of their tether; and when President Theodore Roosevelt offered to act as mediator between them and Japan, they gladly accepted the plan. *The war between Russia and Japan 1904-1905*

In September, 1905, a peace was signed at Portsmouth, New Hampshire, by the terms of which Russia transferred her lease of Port Arthur and the Liaotung peninsula to Japan and acknowledged that Korea belonged to the Japanese sphere of influence. The valuable and much-contested Manchuria was to be returned to the civil administration of China. As a result of the war Russia still remained a great Pacific and Asiatic power, though with chastened ambitions. Japan, on the other hand, assumed the leading place in the far east. She had administered a sound beating to her most pressing European rival and might claim admission to the high company of the imperialist powers on a basis of equality. In striking evidence of her increased prestige, in 1910 she deposed the ruler of Korea and incorporated his land with the Japanese empire. *Advantages won by Japan at the Peace of Portsmouth (1905)*

THE RUSSIAN REVOLUTION OF 1905

The industrialization of Russia

While Tsar Alexander III is a synonym for repression in its most savage form, there is associated with his reign a development of another kind which ventured to challenge repression and which, in the long run, overcame it. Slowly under Alexander and more rapidly under his son and successor, Nicholas II (1894-1917), the Industrial Revolution invaded this exclusively agricultural society and altered its complexion. Father and son themselves lent their support to the movement, to no small extent from fear that, unless Russia be equipped with modern armament from its own factories, it would not be able to continue in the frenzied race of the rival imperialisms. Consequently, under direct government inspiration there began the tapping of Russia's immense reserves of raw products, of the coal and iron of the Ukraine, of the oil wells about the Black and Caspian seas. At the same time the insufficient communications were improved by stringing telegraph wires in every direction and by extending the as yet very fragmentary railway system. A trans-Caspian line was laid out, and in 1891 an even more extensive line was planned to span the enormous width of still almost desert Siberia. The need of capital for these ambitious developments was met by inviting the participation of western Europe with promises of an interest return far beyond what the home market offered.

Growth of middle-class liberal and working-class radical parties

Presently all the familiar phenomena of a nation-wide industrial boom put in an appearance. In such large cities as Moscow, St. Petersburg, Kiev, and Odessa factories sprang up like mushrooms after rain and over a hundred sleepy market centers were transformed into small but busy manufacturing towns. The corresponding social changes followed on the heel of these developments. By, say, the year 1900 there had come into existence a sizable middle class of bankers, engineers, lawyers, and merchants, devoted to the freedom of the press, constitutional government, and all the other articles of the western liberal credo; and equally important, if not more so, immense peasant hordes that, answering the call to labor, had become factory operatives, were won to the more radical cures of revolutionary agitators. Let the year 1898 stand as an organizational landmark, for in that year the Russian Social Democratic party saw the light. As radical parties have a habit of doing, it split before long into an extreme and a moderate group. The extreme group which, because it commanded the majority of the delegates to the party convention, called itself *Bolshevik* (meaning majority), favored an uncompromising, anti-bourgeois policy, whereas the minority, called *Menshevik* (meaning minority), were not averse to compromise.

When the war with Japan broke out in 1904 and the telegraph reported an uninterrupted succession of Russia defeats, the invigorated groups of liberal business men and radical workers could no longer be held down. Their multiplied publications poured blame and abuse on the government, which, in the face of its pitiful war record, was obliged to relax its censorship. Now, too, the almost forgotten terrorists again crawled out of their holes. In the summer of 1904 a bomb tossed at von Plehve, minister of the interior and head of the abominable secret police, blew him to bits; a few months later an assassin even reached up into the imperial family and dispatched the grand duke Serge. Already profoundly depressed, Nicholas II lost all hope of silencing the opposition in the face of the sanguinary events that occurred on a January Sunday of 1905. On that day an army of workingmen descended on his palace at St. Petersburg to present a petition demanding reform. When they refused to disperse, the palace guard was ordered to fire and did not cease till it had heaped the square before the imperial residence with bloody corpses. *The outbreak of violence*

It was this agitated domestic situation which largely accounts for the readiness of Nicholas II to bring the war with Japan to a close. However, as, in spite of the Peace of Portsmouth, the public excitement refused to die down, the soft and impressionable ruler suddenly lost heart and in October, 1905, issued a manifesto which was an all but complete surrender to his critics. The manifesto promised to the inhabitants of the empire the fundamental western liberties of conscience, speech, and assembly and, to render them effective, called for the election of a Russian parliament under the name of *duma*. Back in the reforming days of the second Alexander the name had been given to the municipal councils which ranked among his outstanding innovations. The new duma was still to be a council, a council, however, no longer of municipal but of national scope. *The Manifesto of October, 1905*

To the striking surrender of absolutism another factor contributed which must not be overlooked. The immense area of the Russian empire, covering eastern Europe and northern Asia, was settled not by one but by some scores of peoples who had all been brought under the Russian scepter by military might. The Russian people, the so-called Great Russians, were indeed the central nucleus of the state. But along the western border toward Germany, in the Caucasus mountains toward Turkey, and throughout Siberia other groups, great and small and representing every conceivable divergence of blood, speech, and customs, made their home, accommodating themselves as best they could to the fact of their subjection to the Russian tsar. *Russia a conglomerate of many peoples*

Closely scrutinized, Russia was not a consolidated national state but an agglomeration of discordant nationalities somewhat like Austria-Hungary. Along the western border alone there were more than half a dozen distinct peoples: Finns in Finland; Ests, Letts, and Germans in the Baltic provinces; and farther south, Lithuanians, Poles, and Ukrainians, the last-named also called Little Russians. In the nineteenth century these had all been sorely afflicted with the "Russification" policy of the tsarist government. This was a systematic attempt to deprive them of their languages, religions, and whatever other cultural inheritances they cherished with a view to transforming them into hallmarked Great Russians, obedient to the tsar and devoted to the Orthodox religion.

The many nationalities strung along the western border of Russia

In consequence of the Russification policy, these border nationalities nursed a deep grudge against the government; and when the revolution of 1904-1905 broke out, they promptly joined the movement of revolt. Especially the Finns and Poles, among whom the memories of their lost independence were a smoldering fire, exhibited ominous signs of unrest. These stirrings all along the border made a deep impression on the alarmed tsar and undoubtedly were a factor in the surrender signified by the October manifesto.

The border groups join the revolution

Great were the rejoicings through all the cities of the realm at the fall of the absolute regime. But the bonfires were premature. The first duma met in 1906 and, on showing a disposition to give orders to the ministers as though they were the agents not of the tsar but of the duma, was promptly dissolved. A second duma, which came together in 1907, pleased the government as little as its predecessor and met the same fate. The fact is that a reaction had set in. The frightened landlords, clergy, army officers, and administrative officials had organized what they called the *Union of the Russian People,* which undertook to meet and overcome its opponents not so much at the polls as through armed bands of assassins called Black Hundreds. The opponents, hopelessly divided, rapidly lost ground. The liberals distrusted the radicals, and the radicals split up into numerous contentious groups. The division already referred to among the Social Democrats was a case in point. Moreover, the vast majority of the population was still the ignorant and superstitious peasantry, which, as solidly conservative by temperament if not by rational choice, lined up behind the reactionaries. We can spare ourselves the details of the unhappy story of how the revolutionary fervor ebbed away before a rising tide of energy enlisted for the autocratic regime.

The revolution defeated by the return of reaction

Not many years after the issuance of the famous October manifesto his smiling courtiers were able to congratulate the tsar on the recovery of his authority. After repeatedly dissolving the duma until by severely restricting the suffrage he had secured a majority which bowed to his reasserted supremacy, he suffered it to live on as a harmless political appendage. Nonetheless, it was not so harmless as in his consciousness of triumph the tsar was pleased to imagine. Its mere existence sufficed to remind the defeated liberals and socialists that their co-operation had once

The duma remains as a symbol of revolution

put the autocracy on the defensive and to inspire them with the hope that a happy turn of the wheel of time would infallibly supply them with another opportunity to come to grips with the hated system. This was the uneasy domestic situation when the year 1914 came round and plunged Russia and the world with it into war.

THE TURKISH REVOLUTION OF 1908

In treating of the Congress of Berlin we noted that, by acting together, Great Britain and Austria succeeded in saving the Ottoman empire from wreckage at the hands of Russia but that they did not save it from being severely penalized. The congress sanctioned the creation of the principality of Bulgaria, thus effecting the release from Ottoman bondage of still another Christian people. Furthermore, in express articles of the general treaty it drew up it required the sultan to introduce "reforms," meaning an improved administration, into the three disturbed regions of Armenia, Crete, and Macedonia, representing about all the Christian areas still under the sultan's sway. The sultan obliged to swallow these humiliations was Abdul Hamid I (1876-1909). He was, for a sultan, not without a measure of intelligence and energy but, lacking the moral vigor necessary to the ruler of a well-ordered state, he was forced, in order to keep himself afloat, to have recourse to the subterfuges of the weak: to deceit, violence, and fraud. In any case it was by these means that he resolved to evade the responsibilities laid on him by Europe in regard to the three Christian regions still under his sovereignty.

Obligations laid on the sultan in regard to three Chris tian areas

Armenia was the name of a district of northeastern Asia Minor with very uncertain boundaries. The Armenians themselves were an ancient people whose proudest boast was that they had been among the earliest converts to Christianity and that their church, founded by St. Gregory, was the most ancient of all existing Christian churches. Long a "backward" group, like all the other Christians conquered by the Turks, they had recently by their own unaided efforts raised themselves to a higher economic and educational level. It was the improvement due to their own initiative which had persuaded the Congress of Berlin to give them a nod of approval. But it also led to their undoing. For to Sultan Abdul Hamid nothing was more alarming than the prospect of an independent Christian state in the Asiatic heart of his dominions, and he resolved to exorcise the danger by any means that would serve his purpose.

Armenia and the Armenian

In the period 1894-1896 the sultan's agents conducted a series of systematic massacres in distant and inaccessible Armenia to which it is calculated 100,000 men, women, and children fell victim. Many individuals in Europe voiced their horrified protests against the inhuman slaughter, but the governments did nothing. Their mutual jealousies coupled with

The Armenian massacres, 1894-1896

the remoteness of Armenia prevented direct interference, as Abdul Hamid had correctly calculated. The western liberal press hurled excoriating epithets at him, such as "Armenian Butcher" and "Red Sultan," but what alone mattered so far as he was concerned was that, aside from being mildly rebuked by the ambassadors of the powers, he suffered no penalty for his crime. The powers, in effect, dropped the treaty article dealing with Armenia into the well of oblivion.

As for the island of Crete, Abdul Hamid followed the familiar Ottoman pattern of treating the issue dilatorily. After waiting some years for the promised amelioration of their lot, the Cretans, who were passionate Greeks and Christians, rose, as they had done before, against their masters. The rising occurred in 1897 and was attended by a novelty. The free Greeks of the kingdom were so deeply stirred by sympathy for their Cretan brothers that they forced their reluctant sovereign, George I, to declare war on the sultan. In the ensuing conflict the ill-prepared and ill-equipped Greeks were crushingly defeated but suffered no abiding ill effects from their collapse. For in this instance the powers, being close at hand, interfered and, indisposed to seeing Greece once again returned to Turk dependence, effected a settlement. While obliging the Greeks to pay the victors a money indemnity, they took Crete under their wing and endowed it with an exclusively Greek administration. The only wish of the Cretans that remained unfulfilled was their union with the kingdom. Even for this they did not have to wait long, since it was achieved on the trail of the disturbances that overwhelmed the Turks in the form of the Balkan wars of 1912-13. Crete was an instance in which the foxlike twistings and turnings of Abdul Hamid proved of no avail.

How a lost war (1897) freed Crete

It remains to consider Macedonia. We have become acquainted with it as the core of the Balkan peninsula and an area embracing elements of practically every nationality residing on the explosive Balkan soil. Hardly, therefore, had Macedonia been returned to Turkey at Berlin when the various nationalities, but especially the Bulgars, the Greeks, and the Serbs, organized propaganda services among the Macedonians to the end of winning over as many as possible to their respective causes. When the sultan, as legal lord of the land, interfered with these impertinent activities, the propagandists resorted to arms both against the sultan and against each other. They started a civil war which culminated in murder and arson and converted the divided province into a living hell. In 1903 the powers attempted to end the scandal by setting up an international police force intrusted with the task of pacifying the territory. This body had some success in the open country but in the difficult mountain region the rebellious fires could not be extinguished. Then suddenly out of a clear sky there burst an amazing event, the Turkish revolution.

The Macedonian civil war

Innumerable as had been the nineteenth century revolutions of the

Balkan Christians, they were not till 1908 matched by a revolution of the Balkan Turks. The unique event was a clear indication that at long last the Turks themselves had been bitten with the western virus and wanted to exchange their decrepit absolutism for a constitutional monarchy. The movement broke on an astonished Europe without warning but was not so sudden as appeared to the casual observer. Throughout the generation following the Congress of Berlin a growing number of Turks had made contact with western ideas and institutions. Seduced by these novelties, exactly as non-Europeans all over the world were being seduced by them, they had gradually come to the conclusion that, unless the mass of their countrymen were won over to the western outlook, the Ottoman state was doomed. The westernizers gave themselves the party designation of Young Turks; and because the frightened Red Sultan had promptly loosed his Argus-eyed police against them, they had been obliged to make their escape abroad and gather in a number of foreign centers. From there they flooded their country with revolutionary literature smuggled across the border by secret underground channels. As the Turk officer class was the most alert and enlightened element of the Moslem population, the Young Turks drew their strength largely from this source.

The Young Turks prepare for revolution

It was this situation that explains the quick success of the revolt. What happened in July, 1908, was simplicity itself: the officers of certain leading army units stationed in Macedonia wired the sultan that unless he at once declared himself in favor of a constitutional regime, they would renounce their allegiance to him. The army, the sole prop of Abdul Hamid's throne, had thus turned against him. With abject servility the panic-stricken ruler signified his assent to the demand.

The quick success of the army action of July, 1908

A few months later Abdul Hamid tried in his treacherous way to cancel his promise. This time—it was in April, 1909—the army, instead of negotiating, marched on Constantinople and deposed him. By raising to the throne his imbecile brother, Mohammed V, the rebels acquired an unchallenged control of the state.

The sultan forced to abdicate

In execution of their program the Young Turks proclaimed a constitution and summoned a parliament of the empire on the western pattern. They proposed a reform of the law, the administration, and the schools. We do not challenge their sincerity when we point out that to give such sweeping measures a really effective character calls for many years of preparatory study and a still longer period of application. The Young Turks were aptly described by an observer on the ground as "young men in a hurry." Their excuse may have been that they had to hurry because the Ottoman house was falling about their ears.

The precipitate reforms of the Young Turks

There was another difficulty. The Young Turks in absorbing to the best of their ability the western mentality had perforce become nationalists. But, ruling an empire extending from Europe into Asia Minor and around the bend of the Mediterranean, they were under compulsion to be also imperialists, and showed themselves as little inclined as any other imperialist group to divest themselves of non-Turk territory. No sooner had the news of the revolution become known than it caused liberation bonfires to be lighted throughout the empire in the naïve expectation that everybody had now become free. Freedom is a delusive word of many meanings, but for the subject peoples, whether Christian or Mohammedan, it had but a single meaning: freedom from the Turks! The result was that they demanded self-government on so broad a scale that, if granted, the empire would have been broken into fragments. But nothing was farther from the minds of the Young Turk leaders than imperial fragmentation. They insisted that under the new constitution all the residents of the empire, regardless of race or religion, had acquired equal rights but that they had also assumed equal duties, pre-eminent among them being loyal support of the new regime. This position to the non-Turks signified "Ottomanization," that is, reduction to a common Turkish norm, and as soon as this prospect raised its head they met it with sporadic revolt in both Asia and Europe. Within a year or two of the delirious welcome with which the revolution had been greeted, the disillusioned Bulgars, Greeks, and Serbs resumed their Macedonian violences against each other and, of course, with special gusto against their common enemy, the Turks. However, overtopping the renewed disturbances in Macedonia, with a sound like thunder there fell on the ears of the harassed government the news of an Albanian rising.

The Albanians, the oldest of all Balkan peoples, occupied the rugged mountain region to the west of Macedonia along the Adriatic sea. Because they were the most isolated they were also the most backward of the subject groups. Indeed so primitive were they that they had not yet achieved that prerequisite of even the simplest culture, an alphabet and a written language. Just the same they were a hardy, vigorous race; and now that they had, though belatedly, resolved to follow in the footsteps of the Greeks, the Serbs, and the Bulgars, they would not be gainsaid.

When the Young Turks levied war on the insurgent Albanians, they completely failed to subdue them. The struggle dragged on for months and years; and while the government was involved in it up to its neck it was attacked by Italy, which demanded the surrender of the north-African province of Tripoli. Obliged to turn against the Italians, the Young Turks in 1912 reluctantly came to terms with the Albanians. They granted the mountaineers a very favorable peace. Not only were the Albanians conceded a handsome measure of self-government, but the boundaries of the new state were so generously drawn that they included, toward the east, a considerable section of Macedonia. At once a savage

The subject peoples accept the constitution but reject Ottomanization

Revolt of the Albanians

The Turks give the Albanians a part of Macedonia

cry of indignation rose from all the other Balkan groups which for several decades had been laying plans for the taking over of this central and key province. While no agreement had ever been reached among the Bulgars, Serbs, and Greeks as to their respective shares, it had never occurred to them in their wildest dreams to regard the Albanians in the light of rivals. And here in legible print was the Ottoman-Albanian peace treaty which projected upstart Albania far into the Vardar valley! Although vociferous in their protest, the three angered groups knew in their hearts that protest would get them nowhere and that the only effective way of acquiring Macedonia was by an act of war.

With this, we have arrived at the Balkan wars of 1912-1913. They served as curtain-raiser to World War I and cannot be understood except in the context of the general movement of European diplomacy. Nor can the descent of Italy on coastal Tripoli, just referred to, be understood save in the same context. We are therefore under the necessity of dropping the domestic story of the Ottoman state until we have traced the origin of the rival systems of the Triple alliance and the Triple entente and pursued their shifting relationship into the crisis of the Balkan wars and World War I that promptly followed.

Outbreak of the Balkan wars of 1912-1913

31

THE PARTITION OF AFRICA

Preceded by an Analysis of Foreign Policy as Practiced by the Great Powers

THE NATURE OF FOREIGN POLICY

Foreign policy functions through diplomacy and war

MUCH SPACE HAS been given in this book to foreign policy, the instruments of which are diplomacy and war. Many recent historians, who stress civilization more than politics, are inclined to treat the wranglings of diplomats as unimportant or even to overlook them entirely. However, so long as states behave toward one another as free and independent organisms responsible to no one under God, the historian, regardless of the preference he may have for the positive achievements of mankind, will not be able to exempt himself from scrutinizing the foreign policy of states with the greatest care.

Our concern is with the foreign policy of the great powers

In the many centuries covered by this book the European states have regarded themselves as free and independent, that is, as sovereign. Each state has presented itself to view as an organism concerned with the problem of development. Like everything else that lives and grows, it has tried to add to its strength and become as powerful as the circumstances permitted. There is, however, a difference to be noted among the competitive state units. The lesser states, such as Switzerland and Denmark, are so completely overshadowed by a group of stronger neighbors that their scope for development is definitely circumscribed. The biological urge of growth, in its pure and unadulterated form, applies only to the large entities called the great powers.

The great powers attain their ends preferably by peace, if necessary by war

Of each of the great powers it may be said that the only restraint on its expansion is the urge for expansion manifested by the other powers. However, while they are in competition, the competition does not hinder them from acting on the principle that peace is, on the whole, more desirable than war and consequently from treating with one another through the orderly and established channels of diplomacy. Nonetheless they invariably hold war in reserve as a last resort, in their own diplomatic language as an *ultima ratio*. In sum, the conventional attitude of every foreign office may be described as consisting in lavish professions of a deep love of peace coupled with the significant hint that the state, as an unimpaired sovereign body, will defend its essential interests, if necessary, by war.

Since all states alike try to promote their interests, the form of government of a given state has, general opinion to the contrary notwithstanding, very little bearing on its foreign policy. Undoubtedly many people incline to think of the absolute monarchy as prone to war largely because it is absolute. But an oligarchy or a republic may just as readily appeal to arms because, so far as its foreign contacts are concerned, it is no less sensitive and intransigent than a monarchy. A thousand years of European experience show that monarchies, oligarchies, and republics alike have looked upon the pursuit of what they conceive to be their interest as their main reason for existence.

Foreign policy largely independent of the form of government

While the central principle governing the action of every great power in the foreign field has remained the same throughout the Modern Age, its application has varied in response to the ever-changing general situation. When this history opened, in the period of the Renaissance and Reformation, each state sought to extend its power exclusively within the narrow bounds of Europe. Then came the colonial movement with which the Americas and Asia fell within the range of the competitive states. As a result the wars of the seventeenth and eighteenth centuries came to have, in steadily growing measure, a colonial character.

Unchanging in spirit, foreign policy frequently changes its objective

Toward the middle of the nineteenth century the European chancelleries turned a hypnotized attention on the unification movement in Italy and Germany. Its motive force was the sentiment of nationalism. Gaining ground also in multi-national states like Austria-Hungary, Russia, and the Ottoman empire, nationalism threatened to disrupt these vast aggregations and to bring about their reorganization on a strictly nationalist basis. Inevitably a movement with such disturbing implications attracted the alarmed attention of the foreign offices of all the neighboring countries.

The emergence of nationalism

While thus intensely concerned with nationalism in Europe, the foreign office heads did not fail to let their attention be drawn to all the other continents of the globe as soon as steam and electricity had annihilated distance and the system of machine production had increased beyond all expectation the prospect of profits to be derived from remote markets. On their pursuing the advantages which beckoned over the face of the earth they engaged in empire-building or, as it is commonly called, imperialism.

The emergence of imperialism

That gives us, since approximately the middle of the nineteenth century, two main ingredients of foreign policy, nationalism and imperialism. Of the two nationalism has been repeatedly dealt with. It manifested itself in the first place as the firm determination of those national groups which through some accident of history had been broken into fragments (Italy, Germany) or had been brought into subjection to some powerful neighbor (Greece, Serbia, Poland, Ireland) to regain their unity and independence. After the achievement of Italian and German unity the chief field for the display of nationalism was eastern and southeastern Europe.

However, we should not fail to note that no country escaped the impact of nationalism, not even those which, like France and England, had achieved national unity many centuries before. Wherever nationalism had already gained its immediate end of unification, it continued to exist under the name of patriotism; indeed so little differentiated are nationalism and patriotism that they reduce themselves pretty much to the same thing. And now observe: in the nineteenth century nationalism (or patriotism) became a universal energy and, like a wine too freely quaffed, mounted to the heads of all the European peoples.

In every European country could be encountered the phenomenon of the super-patriot (or super-nationalist). In Germany he was called a pan-German, in Russia a pan-Slav, in England a jingo, in France a chauvinist. Under all these labels he exhibited an identical mind. Joining with countrymen of the same disposition, he constituted a band, small perhaps but very noisy, which caused extraordinary mischief by exciting to savage vociferation the corresponding bands in all the neighboring countries. They shook their fists and gritted their teeth at one another across the international boundaries and created a very dangerous condition of general nervous tension.

Here lay a peril for the peace of Europe which was indefinitely multiplied by what we have isolated as the second element of foreign policy in recent generations, imperialism. This was, historically viewed, nothing else than the colonialism of the eighteenth century carried to an explosive intensity by the great nineteenth century movement called the Industrial Revolution. Let us enumerate the more important novelties injected into the situation by the industrial developments. First to consider are the new means of communication—railroads, steamboats, telegraph, and in the most recent period, the automobile, radio, and airplane. Their total effect was to destroy space and to bring all countries within easy reach of one another.

No less effective in bringing peoples and continents together was the enormously increased machine production, for which Europe required non-European consumers. These often backward outsiders could pay for the finished goods delivered to them only with native raw products such as wheat, cattle, fruits, minerals, rubber, palm-oil, spices. As inventions multiplied and articles serving our human convenience were put forth which surpassed even the dreams of visionaries, it was revealed that there was no country which did not desire these devices and which did not possess something of its own to offer in exchange for them. Under the operation of these influences a dense net of traffic was flung around the world from pole to pole.

But Europe did not content itself with just this immediate result of an intensified exchange of goods. The traders who visited a backward people **Imperialism** often ran grave risks in respect both of their persons and their goods **develops into** and naturally appealed to their home government for protection. The **a political** easiest way to give protection was to raise the country's flag over the for- **backward** eign land and by annexing and policing it to replace insecurity with **areas** law and order. In this manner a scramble was presently inaugurated among the European powers for all those backward areas of the earth which had not been appropriated by the earlier colonial struggle.

Imperialism develops into a political scramble for backward areas

The movement may be compared to the gold-rush to California in 1849 or to distant Alaska in the nineties. At any rate, in the course of **By 1900** little more than a generation following the Franco-German War of 1870, **the un-** much of Asia, most of Africa, and all of the Pacific archipelago had been **claimed or** taken over by the grasping European rivals. By the beginning of the **"backward"** twentieth century the backward areas which might be conceived as still **areas are** available for seizure were reduced to Morocco at the northwestern corner **few in** of Africa, China and Persia in Asia, and the Ottoman empire, straddling **number** Europe and Asia at the straits of the Bosporus and the Dardanelles.

On approaching the partition of these still immense lands—think of China and the Ottoman empire!—the powers became more and more **Inability to** exasperated with one another. And before an agreement was in sight, **agree on a** they lost control of their passions and engaged in the vast conflict now **division** generally called World War I.

In Chapter 34 we shall trace the successive diplomatic steps which led to the catastrophe of 1914. Concerned at this point with the nature of **How a** foreign policy, we can most effectively drive our analysis home by a con- **backward** crete example. Let us trace the events that led to the appropriation and **area was** partition of Africa. **appropriated**

THE PARTITION OF AFRICA

The older colonialism had not paid much attention to Africa except as a source for the black slaves required for working the plantations of **Early colo-** North and South America. In this unsavory business the Portuguese, as **nialism had** the first explorers of the African coast, took the lead but soon had to **no interest** reckon with many rivals desirous of cutting in on the huge profits. The **in Africa** English, the French, and the Dutch established themselves alongside of **except as a** the Portuguese on the Guinea coast and all of them together engaged in **source for** an ignoble competition for the trade in human chattels. **slaves**

Then in the first half of the nineteenth century, in response to a growing humanitarian sentiment in the western world, the slave trade was
abolished by one after the other of the conscience-stricken nations. As a
result Africa was again left to itself, indeed so completely to itself that
around 1850 it continued to engage the attention of only two powers:
Great Britain, which during the Napoleonic wars had supplanted the
Dutch at the southern extremity of the continent, in Cape Colony, and
France, which in 1830 had effected a lodgment on the Mediterranean
coast opposite its shores, in Algeria. Portugal, by reason of a series of
ancient trading posts, could set up a claim to large tracts of the African
coast but the claims were not pressed.

Around 1850 only three states have a foothold in Africa

Shortly after the middle of the century the interest of Christian missionaries and scientific explorers was directed toward Africa; and the
wonders which these adventurous souls reported touching the impenetrable jungle with its exotic vegetation and its fabulous animal life, ranging from boa constrictors and elephants to hairy apes and an almost endless variety of human beings not far removed from apes, stimulated the
imagination of the civilized world. Africa loomed before the Europeans
steeped, as they thought of themselves, in the light of knowledge as the
Dark Continent; and rapidly multiplying scientific expeditions undertook
to inventory its rivers and mountains, its fauna and flora, its primitive
peoples following amazing customs and practicing unbelievable religious
rites.

A fresh interest in Africa aroused by missionaries and scientists

Immediately after the missionaries and explorers or even simultaneously with them came the traders with their beads, their trinkets, and
their many kinds of useful manufactured wares. We have learned that
from the start Western civilization has combined restless mental curiosity
with a keen sense of material values and that the two energies, physical
and intellectual, have always functioned in close association. But we have
also learned that in the long run it is the trader that dominates the scene
and shapes it to his purposes. At the time of this new outburst of exploration Europe was, as we are aware, in the throes of a feverish trade competition brought about by the Industrial Revolution. All the powers as of
one accord recognized the possibilities presented by long-neglected Africa
and each made haste to pledge its support to those of its nationals who
undertook to penetrate the continent with their alluring sample-cases and
their ingratiating sales talk.

Africa invaded by competing traders

There followed an unseemly scramble which inescapably led to conflicting territorial claims. To adjust them the powers resorted, in accordance with established custom, to diplomacy; and behind their negotiations appeared, also according to custom though decently veiled from
view, the grim specter of war.

Conflicting territorial claims

In the winter of 1884-1885 an international conference was held at

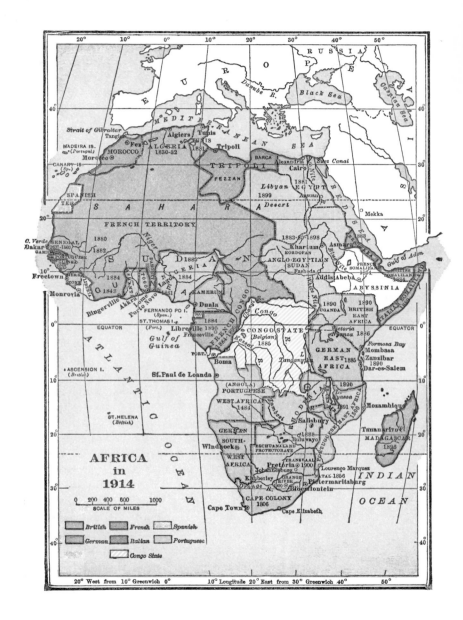

AFRICA
in
1914

SCALE OF MILES
0   200 400 600   1000

British
German
French
Italian
Spanish
Portuguese
Congo State

Berlin for an amicable discussion of the disputes occasioned by the head-over-heels scramble for African territory. One of its most notable acts was to confer the immense basin of the Congo river on Leopold II of Belgium. Leopold, though born a king, was a typical nineteenth century businessman and promoter. In the early eighties he had employed the explorer, Henry Stanley, to stake out a claim for him in the Congo area, a region known to be rich in ivory, palm-oil, and rubber. Stanley had achieved fame when an American newspaper proprietor had sent him to Africa in 1871 to find David Livingstone, who had vanished from sight in its impenetrable south-central jungles. Livingstone (1813-1873), a Scotsman by birth, deserves to be commemorated in even the sketchiest tale of the opening of the Dark Continent, since he represented in their purest form the combined missionary and exploring passions with which its penetration had been inaugurated. Stanley duly found the high-minded Livingstone (who in his own view had never been lost), and then continued his explorations in the pay and interest of profit-seeking Leopold. The curious upshot of this combination of circumstances was that the Berlin conference assigned the vast Congo valley under the name of Congo Free State to Belgian Leopold as his personal estate.

The Berlin conference (1885) gives the Congo Free State to Leopold II of Belgium

However, the most important act of the Berlin conferees was of another sort and sprang from their desire not unnecessarily to come to blows over their conflicting African claims. They therefore agreed that they would respect the claims each one had already staked off and settle the difficult question of the boundary of each claim by amicable negotiation.

The Berlin declaration

Under this ruling it came about that numerous friendly settlements saw the light, of which we will specifically name, for purposes of illustration, the Anglo-German and the Anglo-French treaties of the year 1890. By means of them Great Britain delimited her African claims, on the one hand, as against those of Germany; on the other hand, as against those of France. As Italy presented itself with African claims of its own and the Portuguese revived numerous claims which neglect had permitted to become all but forgotten, Great Britain saw fit to come to terms also with Italy and Portugal. Since what Great Britain saw fit to do was done by all the other powers too, the upshot was that in the course of a few decades following the Berlin conference, a long list of treaties had been drawn up which substantially partitioned Africa among its various European claimants.

Amicable treaties bring about a general partition of Africa

Although the partition of Africa proceeded systematically and, on the whole, amicably, it was enlivened by a number of dangerous crises, some of which even led, as was always possible under the ruling system, to war. The two powers which led the way in the appropriation of African land were Great Britain and France.

The main prizes go to Britain and France

The colonies secured by Germany

Germany, a late-comer at the colonial banquet, was a poor third. However, she secured a foothold on the east coast (German East Africa), on the southwest coast (German Southwest Africa), and on the west coast above the equator in Togoland and Kamerun.

The African objectives of France and Britain

France and Great Britain operated with far more ambitious programs. France concentrated on northwestern Africa with a view to building up a colonial empire extending from its starting-point in Algeria clear across the desert of Sahara to the gulf of Guinea. Great Britain strove to reach northward from Cape Colony toward the equator. Then, establishing herself at the mouth of the Nile, she engaged in a southward drive up that river in the hope that her two African movements might ultimately join hands. This was an even more magnificent project than that of the French and the attempt to realize it produced a succession of very serious convulsions, which we must briefly notice.

Clash of France and Britain over the Sudan (1898)

It was in the year 1882 that Great Britain landed an armed force at the mouth of the Nile in Egypt, in order to protect the sea-route across the isthmus of Suez. Her act involved two consequences: first, the beating down of the resistance of the native Egyptians, and, after some years, the conquest of the immense region of the upper Nile known as the Sudan and regarded as a subject province of Egypt. But the French desire to build up an empire around the Sahara envisaged an eventual foothold in this same upper Nile region; and in 1898 a French military expedition plunged across the jungles of central Africa to raise the French flag over the strategic river town of Fashoda.

France surrenders its claim to Fashoda

Immediately the British marched southward from Khartum and demanded the departure of the French from a town which they considered to lie within their political sphere. The moment the hostile forces faced each other, France went tense and all Europe became anxious. In the end the Paris government drew in its horns and left Great Britain in possession. While war was happily avoided, the incident showed with what heavy risks the imperialist competition was at all times attended.

Conquest and annexation of the two Boer republics (1899-1902)

At the other end of Africa, in Cape Colony, the British advance produced a very serious war when it was resisted by the two Boer republics, the Transvaal and the Orange Free State. The conflict broke out in the year following Fashoda, in 1899, and might easily have drawn France as well as Germany into its vortex if these powers, instinctively hostile to the increase of British territory, had been able to give the Boers effective help. As Great Britain commanded the sea-ways with her superior fleet, France and Germany, as prevailingly land-powers, had to acknowledge their impotence to interpose themselves between the British giant and the two Boer dwarfs. Great Britain annexed the conquered republics (1902) but magnanimously, after a few years, granted them self-governing rights.

Another series of African crises centered around the African activities of France and Italy. In 1881 France suddenly occupied Tunis in order to round off her Algerian holdings. The Italians, who had themselves been long casting a fond eye on Tunis, were outraged and would have gone to war if there had been any likelihood of their measuring swords with their Gallic rivals with some reasonable chance of success.

The seizure by France of Tunis (1881)

In the circumstances the Italians swallowed their wrath and provided against a repetition of the Tunisian surprise by an alliance with Germany and Austria (the Triple alliance of 1882). They did another thing. Determined to extend their relatively worthless African possessions along the Red sea (Eritrea) and the Indian ocean (Somaliland), they levied war in 1895 on the independent kingdom of Abyssinia, only to be badly beaten at Adowa. Here was the case of an European power successfully resisted by a native state, a unique instance of this kind in the history of African conquest. With bitterness in their hearts the Italians were obliged to acknowledge the independence of Abyssinia (also called Ethiopia).

Italy attempts (1895) to seize Abyssinia and is defeated

At the northwestern corner of the continent lay another native state, the empire of Morocco, which at the time that Abyssinia beat off the Italian attack enjoyed, like Abyssinia, a formal independence. However, France had already earmarked Morocco for conquest and in the early years of the new century began a cautious diplomatic action intended to prepare the ground for a successful penetration. We shall presently hear of this Morocco plan in another connection, for it produced a radical shake-up of European diplomatic relations and left a bitterness behind which augured ill for the continuance of the precarious peace among the powers. It will serve every present purpose if we note that France successfully stalked her Moroccan prey and in 1912 added Morocco to her colonial exhibits. She was, however, prudently moved to placate her neighbor, Spain, by the surrender of a strip of Moroccan shore-land directly opposite the Spanish coast.

France acquires Morocco (1912)

In looking back over this compressed story of the partition of Africa we can suggest no better method for grasping its results than a study of the accompanying map. It presents the situation of 1914 and shows the dominant position achieved by Great Britain and France. Great Britain in control of Egypt and the Sudan in the north and of southern Africa (organized since 1909 as the South African Union) was fairly on the way toward their junction in the latitude of the equator, although this had not yet been brought about. France possessed, with a few exceptions, the whole northwest in a solid block. Compared with these vast land masses the African colonies of Germany were unimpressive, especially as they lay dispersed in four distinct units: East Africa, Southwest Africa, Togoland, Kamerun. Italy came, a poor fourth, after Germany. Having in 1912 seized Tripoli from Turkey, it therewith possessed, besides the

The partition of Africa summarized

rather inaccessible Eritrea and Somaliland, a colony on the near-by Mediterranean; but Tripoli was, like the earlier holdings, largely a heat-scorched desert. Spain and Portugal, though declining powers, must not be overlooked. The former had a foothold on the west coast and in northern Morocco, the latter possessed in Angola and Mozambique two tropical regions it did not bother to develop. King Leopold's personal farm, the Congo Free State, was ceded by him to Belgium in 1908 and became the Belgian Congo. Our roll call ends with two dark-skinned states, the highly important Abyssinia (Ethiopia) and the much more deeply tinctured but far less important Liberia, both of which, wonder of wonders, still preserved their independence. They were the only native communities remaining in this enviable class.

32 THE LESSER STATES OF EUROPE FROM THE CONGRESS OF VIENNA (1815) TO THE OUTBREAK OF WORLD WAR I

THE LESSER STATES of Europe are lesser merely in respect to area, population, and power. In their institutions and civilization they are as representative of Europe as the great states which adjoin and overshadow them. From medieval days each one of them has led its own life within the general European frame and has exhibited its own characteristics. That means they have all passed through all the phases of the Modern Age and were agitated and shaped in turn by the Reformation, by absolutism, and, more recently, by democracy, the rise of the middle classes, the Industrial Revolution, and revolutionary socialism. Our brief review can do no more than trace the incidence of the above forces on the several small states and to point out the special developments resulting therefrom.

The small states as representative of European civilization as the great states

SPAIN

Having already dealt with the Spain of the Restoration Period, we have learned that the Bourbon monarch, Ferdinand VII, tried, with the help of the church and the nobility, to re-establish the absolute regime and that he met with opposition on the part of the liberal elements which had come into existence during the struggle with Napoleon. Obliged (1820) to concede a constitution, he was, with the aid of the Holy Alliance, enabled to overthrow his opponents and reassert his power (1823). Perhaps the worst consequence for Spain of his fiercely reactionary attitude was the estrangement of the South American colonies and the successful assertion of their independence.

Ferdinand VII (1815-1833) identified with absolutism

The question which emerged in Ferdinand's day was whether Spain would hold fast to the governmental system of the eighteenth century or whether it would accommodate itself to the newer demands for constitutional government. Political in appearance, the question had profound social and economic implications. In last analysis the victory of the constitutionalists would depend on the concomitant transformation of Spain by education, science, and industrialism.

Political transformation is dependent on social change

Now it is a fact that this social transformation was not carried through

641

or, rather, that it made headway at so snail-like a pace that many decades

passed before the new energies acquired sufficient momentum seriously to threaten the inherited political system. The situation was further, and most unhappily, complicated by a disputed succession. When Ferdinand VII died in 1833, he left the crown to his infant daughter Isabella, thereby setting aside his brother Carlos, who considered himself to be the lawful heir. Civil war followed between Carlists and Christinists, the latter taking their name from the regent-mother, Christina. When the Christinists at last triumphed, they perpetuated the civil disorder by falling into factions among themselves.

The fact that Isabella came of age in 1842 and thenceforward reigned in her own name effected no improvement. The dreary civil struggle dragged on because an equilibrium could not be established between the two contending forces of absolutism and constitutionalism. Promises of reform were not kept; constitutions were issued only to be revoked. At length all parties alike lost patience with the dishonest game and Queen Isabella was obliged to flee abroad before a general rising (1868).

A period of agitated experimentation followed. In reality the power passed into the hands of successive military dictators. During the ascendancy of Generals Serrano and Prim the crown was offered to Leopold of Hohenzollern-Sigmaringen, thereby producing the so-called Spanish Incident which precipitated the Franco-German war of 1870. On Leopold's refusal of the crown, an Italian prince, Amadeo of Savoy, was chosen king and actually reigned two years before he gave up in disgust. Thereupon a republic was staged which cut so unhappy a figure that the disillusioned country at length declared itself ready and eager to return to the Bourbons in the person of the banished Isabella's son.

In 1875 this young Bourbon mounted the throne under the title of Alfonso XII. A youth of good intentions, he issued a constitution which, at least so far as appearances went, established a parliamentary government of the British type. On Alfonso's death in 1885 the crown was transmitted to his posthumous son, Alfonso XIII. For seventeen years the government was carried on very capably by the queen-mother, Maria Christina, who gave her sincere support to the constitutional regime.

When in 1902 King Alfonso XIII took over the reins in person, constitutionalism seemed to be seated firmly in the saddle. The youthful sovereign took his oath of office seriously and by reason of his considerable personal charm won many hearts. But the old difficulties, connected with the administrative corruption and the recurrent army cabals, persisted, while new difficulties arose from the spread in the urban centers of a radical and anarchist opinion so extreme that it did not hesitate to commit murder to the end of stimulating revolt.

Owing to the recurrent crises springing from these complications, the constitution was periodically suspended and the maintenance of public order intrusted to the army. Our judgment can hardly be other than that even in the first decade of the twentieth century Spain was still in the apprentice class among modern nations. She had assumed a modern political dress, but the changes necessary in her social structure and mental outlook, if the political reforms were to be effective, failed to put in an appearance. The backward social structure

It cannot be maintained, however, that Spain in the nineteenth century effected no reforms. Thus, the Inquisition had been abandoned for good before the middle of the century. But the fall of that outmoded institution hardly weakened the hold of the Catholic church on the people. By means of the parish clergy as well as of the numerous orders of brothers and sisters the church continued to dominate the important realm of education. Moreover, the education which, with the financial support of the state, the church extended to the people was so inadequate that at the beginning of the twentieth century illiteracy still stood at over fifty per cent, one of the highest rates to be found in Europe. The unbroken authority of the church illustrated by its control of education

If to the domination of the church we add a feeble bourgeoisie, owing to the backward state of commerce and industry, and the impoverished peasant masses, steeped in ancient superstitions, the failure of Spain to keep abreast of her neighbors becomes intelligible. Other influences might be adduced which help account for the Spanish stagnation. No one familiar with the forces of geography will fail to give due weight to the isolation from the rest of Europe to which peninsular Spain is condemned by the tall barrier of the Pyrenees. Many causes for Spanish backwardness

Nor should the poverty of much of the soil, especially on the arid central plateau, be overlooked. It condemns a large section of the peasantry to a bare subsistence level. On the other hand, Spain is unusually rich in minerals, more particularly in iron, copper, and silver; and the reflection will not be denied that an energetic utilization of these resources would go far toward equalizing the poor returns from agriculture. As nothing is done or at least nothing adequate, we are driven to fall back on the ancient charge of a certain sloth in the national character. A satisfactory analysis of the backwardness of Spain would have to take account of the several indicated, and doubtless of many other, factors. Natural drawbacks and advantages of Spain

To the province of Catalonia with its busy capital, Barcelona, the above-suggested moral and economic strictures do not apply. The Catalans of the Mediterranean coast speak a language closely related to that of the people of southern France. They have never been more than superficially assimilated with the Spaniards and a vigorous section among them has never ceased to ask for the home rule which they enjoyed up to the time of Philip II. By the development of commerce and industry and the introduction of modern scientific and educational methods they have The exceptional case of Catalonia tried to bring themselves into line with the rest of Europe and have chafed impatiently under the restraints put upon them by the backward government at Madrid.

Catalonia at the beginning of the twentieth century presented a very sharp contrast to the rest of Spain. But perhaps because it is a small area and needs Spain as the market for its manufactures, it did not too blindly insist on that provincial autonomy which was nonetheless constantly on its tongue.

Catalonia aims at autonomy

A backward country like Spain, set in the midst of vigorous and grasping neighbors, was not likely to retain the colonies it had assembled in other, happier days. We have already observed how the lusty South and Central American dependencies cast off the Spanish yoke in the time of the detestable Ferdinand VII. In the second half of the nineteenth century Cuba and the Philippine Islands represented the most valuable fragments remaining from what once had been the greatest colonial empire of the world.

Spain's vanishing colonial empire

In these colonial remnants incurable mismanagement created chronic discontent which periodically led to serious uprisings. It took enfeebled Spain ten years to suppress the Cuban rebellion of 1868. In 1894 Cuba rose again; and when a large Spanish army had committed frightful depradations without attaining its goal, the United States of America interfered by taking the side of Cuba.

The rising of Cuba causes the United States to intervene

In 1898 a short war took place in which the powerful young republic signally defeated the decrepit kingdom. When Spain sued for peace, it was forced to acknowledge the independence of Cuba and, in addition, to cede to the victor the island of Puerto Rico and the Philippines. For the latter the United States, by way of compensation, gave the sum of $20,-000,000. The only colonial possessions remaining to Spain after 1898 were the Canary Islands, the Rio de Oro region in western Africa, and a few isolated points along the Moroccan coast.

Defeated Spain gives up (1898) its remaining colonies

In 1904 a prospect opened to Spain which she resolved to make the most of. In that year France and Great Britain arrived at their famous understanding by virtue of which France was accorded a free hand in Morocco. Her aim was to take over as much of Morocco as possible in order to round off her African empire; but she did not fail to see that it would be the part of wisdom to buy the consent of Spain by pressing a handsome bribe into her hand. Accordingly, the northern rim of Morocco, opposite the Spanish coast, was indicated as the reward of Spain whenever the Moroccan booty would be ready for appropriation.

Spain shares in the Franco-British Morocco deal of 1904

When in 1911 the French at length came out into the open and seized the capital city of Fez, they duly invited Spain to possess herself of her allotted portion. It proved an enormously difficult enterprise. The coastal segment, called the Rif, constitutes an area of rugged mountains held by

Spain imperfectly subdues Spanish Morocco

warlike and fanatic Moslem tribes. It required a large army, costing huge sums, to reduce them to obedience, and even then there was never any telling when they would break out again.

PORTUGAL

The history of Portugal in the nineteenth century ran a course strikingly parallel to that of its peninsular neighbor, Spain. There was the same struggle between absolutism and constitutionalism; the same weakness of liberalism, owing to the failure of the country to effect a thoroughgoing social-economic transformation; and when constitutional government was at last victorious, there was the same absence of that fresh national vigor which other countries drew from the plunge into the renovating waters of modern thought and enterprise. *Parallel development of Portugal and Spain*

We are aware that when Napoleon seized Portugal in 1807, King John VI and the royal family sought refuge in the great Portuguese dependency of Brazil, where they chose to remain even after Napoleon's rule had been overthrown. Great Britain, which in the course of its struggle with Napoleon had made Portugal a British military base, continued its control after 1815. The rising of 1820 brought the Liberals into power, who championed a constitutional regime. In order to save his throne John VI, on the urgent invitation of his subjects, returned to his native land, and with an intelligence and adaptability unusual in a legitimate sovereign agreed to accept a limitation of his absolutism. *Even after the restoration of 1815 the royal family continued to reside in Brazil*

Then an unexpected difficulty appeared. When the Brazilians discovered that John had abandoned them for his tiny homeland, they declared themselves independent of Portugal and hailed John's son, Pedro, as their sovereign. In 1826 King John died and Pedro, as his heir, was proclaimed his successor at Lisbon. But as the Brazilians would have none of Pedro on these terms, he was obliged to resign the Portuguese crown in favor of his infant daughter, Maria. In this peaceful way Brazil and Portugal were separated, never to be joined again. *Complete separation between Portugal and Brazil*

Although King John had, on his return to Portugal, agreed to be a constitutional sovereign and his youthful successor, Maria, did the same, powerful reactionary elements within the country resisted this development and plunged the nation into domestic disturbances similar to those which troubled neighboring Spain. Gradually, however, the situation consolidated, and under the reign of Maria's sons and successors (Pedro V, 1853-1861; Luiz I, 1861-1889) the country took on the appearance of having settled down to an orderly evolution in a constitutional sense. *Apparent consolidation of the constitutional monarchy*

The quiet turned out to be deceptive. Under Carlos I (1889-1908) administrative corruption, financial crises, and electoral frauds promoted by the party leaders in their private interest gained the upper hand and

The monarchy overthrown and a republic declared (1910)

involved the country in renewed tumult. In 1908 King Carlos paid the price of failure by meeting death at an assassin's hand. His youthful and inexperienced son, Manoel II, succeeded to a quaking throne and two years later was driven into exile by a republican rising.

The precariously established republic

Since 1910 Portugal has enjoyed the doubtful blessing of being a republic, doubtful because the people experienced no essential change of heart or mind and were as little ready to turn the republic into an active, going concern as they had been in the case of the constitutional monarchy. The corruption of officials and the brazen manipulation of elections continued exactly as before. As in other ill-governed republics the only escape from disorder proved to be dictatorship.

The republic adopts an anti-clerical policy

One departure from earlier practice deserves to be noted. Republican Portugal, perhaps in imitation of republican France, adopted a severely anti-clerical policy. In 1911 the religious orders were expelled and a law passed separating church and state. To resist this movement the strong conservative elements were ready to go far, even to the length of revolution. In short, for many years ahead the republic was sure to be in unstable equilibrium.

Brazil, at first an empire, becomes (1890) a republic

Perhaps Portuguese patriots take some comfort in the thought that the real and greater Portugal is their former colony of Brazil. Become an independent empire in 1822, it has steadily grown in wealth and power by the exploitation of the resources of its immense tropical hinterland. Emperor Pedro I was followed by his son, Pedro II, a prince with an unusually liberal outlook. When he discovered after a reign of over four decades that his subjects preferred a republic, he resigned his crown without a struggle. Since 1890 Brazil has been a republic of federated provinces, each of which is endowed with a large measure of autonomy.

Portugal's two African colonies, Angola and Mozambique

Portugal's colonies, other than Brazil, have remained under its aegis. In area they are not inconsiderable, comprising as they do the extensive territories of Angola on the west coast of Africa and Mozambique on the east coast. Being undeveloped, they are rather a liability to the treasury than an asset, and may, especially if they should suddenly disclose any promising economic resources, be taken over, doubtless to a ringing accompaniment of high-minded sentiments, by some strong power like Great Britain.

The Azores

Her near-by island possessions, the Azores and Madeira, are Portugal's surest, as they were her earliest, acquisitions. Populated with Portuguese, they are not governed as colonies but are directly incorporated with the home country.

The many handicaps of Portugal

Composed of a population eighty per cent of which consists of a peasantry pushed to the margin of starvation, Portugal is socially and economically not a well-balanced country. The impression deepens when we observe that at the time of the proclamation of the republic it had an illiteracy record worse than that of Spain, since seventy per cent of the population could neither read nor write. Because its middle classes have remained feeble, its trade is dominated by an outside power, Great Britain. Great Britain also dominates, and for the last two centuries has dominated, Portuguese foreign policy to such an extent that Portugal may be regarded as to all intents a British dependency.

SWITZERLAND

On dealing with the Swiss Confederation in the Period of the Reformation, we noted that it had grown steadily from small beginnings until it achieved a well-defined position in the system of European states. In the Peace of Westphalia (1648) its independence of the Holy Roman Empire, to which it had originally belonged, was made an article of international law. Swiss independence confirmed, 1648

In spite of these promising beginnings the seventeenth and eighteenth centuries represent a period of stagnation through a convergence of extraordinary forces and conditions, which may be briefly enumerated: (1) The Confederation was a loose union, purely for defense, among thirteen sovereign cantons. (2) There existed a wide diversity of governing principles among the cantons; while some maintained a very democratic system, the majority were ruled by narrow oligarchies. (3) There were regions classified, some as allied, others as subjected districts; in either case they possessed a colonial status and did not enjoy equality with the thirteen constituent cantons. (4) The fierce religious animosities carried into Switzerland by the Reformation continued to smolder in spite of the settlement of Kappel (1531). From all these causes the Confederation fell, in the eighteenth century, into a complete state of coma. Such feeble public life as there was unfolded itself within the provincial limits of each canton. The long stagnation of the Swiss Confederation may be explained on four grounds

When the storms of the French Revolution broke, this whole antiquated system went down in ruin. The French did not scruple to interfere in Switzerland; and first the Directory, and later Napoleon, imposed a better and more compact organization on the country. Swept, owing to resentment against French tyranny, by an unreasoning reactionary sentiment, the Swiss returned in 1815 to the loose union of pre-revolutionary days. That meant that narrow burgher oligarchies once more took over in most of the cantons. The Swiss return in 1815 to their traditional loose union

The burgher oligarchies did not, however, renew their grip on the so-called allied and subjected lands. Having won their independence during the French disturbances, these regions were happily left in possession of their new-won rights. Thus it was a group, not of thirteen but of twenty-two free cantons, which revived the old constitution. After 1815 twenty-two constituent cantons

The Congress of Vienna did Switzerland a good turn by presenting it with a guarantee of perpetual neutrality. By acquiring a neutral status the country was freed from the necessity of entering the perilous game of European power politics.

Perpetual neutrality of Switzerland

A few years of the stuffy reaction which descended on Europe after 1815 sufficed for the suppressed revolutionary sentiments to revive and produce a general ferment. The narrow oligarchies of the cantons were attacked by opposition parties demanding popular rights. At the same time the liberals proceeded to assault the impotent federal government by demanding a more effective centralized system. Results followed in short order. Immediately after the revolutionary disturbances of 1830 had shaken the Metternichian system, the local Swiss oligarchies, as though stunned by the new spirit, gave way with such surprising swiftness that before long the cantonal governments had been generally democratized.

The oligarchies of the cantons yield to democratic reforms

It was now the turn of the feeble federal constitution. As the seven Catholic cantons, inhabited largely by conservative peasants, feared the consequences of a strong union, they resolved to resist federal reform by means of a league, known as the *Sonderbund*. As this was a measure tantamount to secession, the other cantons declared war against the Sonderbund and in a brief campaign won the victory (1847). They crowned it by drawing up (1848) a new constitution, which established an effective union imbued with democratic principles. With slight changes it is still in operation.

War of the Sonderbund followed (1848) by an effective federal constitution

By the constitution of 1848 the supremacy of the federal over the cantonal powers was raised beyond a doubt, but the cantons were not deprived of their local rights. In its dovetailing of central and local powers Switzerland offers a strong resemblance to the political system of the United States. The national legislative power is vested in a *Federal Assembly* of two houses: the *Council of States,* much like the United States Senate, consists of two delegates from each canton, while the *National Council,* comparable to the House of Representatives, is elected by the people on the basis of universal manhood suffrage. In sharp distinction from the United States, however, the national executive is not a single person, but a committee of seven, called the *Federal Council,* and elected by the Federal Assembly. Although one of the seven presides under the title of *President of the Council,* his authority is hardly greater than that of his six colleagues.

The Swiss constitution of 1848 compared with the constitution of the United States

Since the fundamental reforms effected between 1830 and 1848 the Swiss have not ceased to bring the democracy to which they are dedicated to an ever fuller expression. In some of the smaller mountain cantons there had survived from past ages a kind of enlarged town meeting, called *Landesgemeinde,* which dispatched its business directly by electing

The Swiss devoted to the theory and practice of democracy

magistrates and voting laws in an open session. As the larger cantons found it impracticable to conduct business on the town-meeting plan, they were obliged to legislate indirectly through elected representatives.

In an effort to give every citizen the advantage of direct participation in the work of legislation the Swiss devised the measures known as *referendum* and *initiative*. By the referendum, laws passed by the legislature, whether of the individual canton or of the federation, may be submitted for final acceptance or rejection to the vote of the people; by the initiative the right is conceded to a certain number of citizens to propose a measure which, should the people favor it in a special election, must then be converted into law by the legislators. It is probable that the theory of democracy has been more broadly applied and has achieved a more complete success in Switzerland than in any other country of the world.

The Swiss institute the initiative and referendum

Switzerland presents an anomaly in an age in which nationality is usually determined by language since, although speaking three languages, the Swiss constitute a distinct nation. If to the German, French, and Italian groups we add the small body in the valleys of the Grisons who speak a dialect derived from Latin called Romansch, we may even speak of four Swiss language groups. That about 70 per cent of the population speak German, 21 per cent French, and 7 per cent Italian brings out the fact that the Confederation, which began among German peasants and mountaineers, is still preponderantly German. If the language groups do not quarrel, it is because German, French, and Italian enjoy equal recognition as official languages; and further, because each group, treating the others with respect, refrains from attempting to gain an unfair advantage. The fine spirit of good will among the Swiss is the best guarantee of continued domestic harmony.

The Swiss a nation composed of four language groups

The great political advance of Switzerland in the nineteenth century was brought about by the remarkable expansion of the economic and mental life of the whole Swiss community. The country has shared as fully as its resources permitted in the newest phase of Western civilization. Its educational system from the obligatory public school at the bottom to the numerous professional institutions at the top enjoys a merited renown. Illiteracy has practically ceased to exist.

The well-organized educational system of the Swiss

A people so alert and disciplined was sure to draw notable advantages from the Industrial Revolution, in spite of the lack of a seaboard and the absence of coal and iron. Switzerland is, therefore, far from being a negligible manufacturing area. At the same time there has been an impressive advance in dairying and cattle-raising, occupations in which the upland valleys have distinguished themselves from the earliest times. A Swiss specialty, the tourist industry, deserves mention since, while resting on the scenic beauties of the Alps, it bears witness to an intelligence

The various sources of Swiss material prosperity

which neglects no opportunity to draw a return from all the available resources of the country.

The Confederation has refused to rely for safety exclusively on the neutrality guaranteed to it at the Congress of Vienna. It created a small but highly efficient standing army, intended to serve as the nucleus of the considerable national militia which was subject to call in time of war. Of this national militia every male citizen was required to be a member and to report periodically for service in order to gain the necessary training. A firm, self-reliant spirit is characteristic of the Swiss and helps explain their high status among modern nations.

The Swiss create a military system to safeguard their independence

BELGIUM

A child of the revolution of 1830, Belgium is one of the youngest states of Europe. When the great powers found themselves unable to stop the revolt of the Belgians against the Dutch, they made the best of a bad business and not only accepted Belgian independence but tried, as in the case of Switzerland, to protect the new state against attack by guaranteeing its neutrality.

Belgium an offspring of the revolution of 1830

The constitution adopted in 1831 by the liberated Belgian people continued in use throughout the period here treated. It established a hereditary monarchy together with a bicameral parliament, of which the upper house was chosen by rather involved methods, while the lower house was elected directly by the eligible voters. Owing to a relatively high property qualification, the eligible voters were for many decades limited to a small body of well-to-do citizens. Leopold, a German prince of the house of Saxe-Coburg, was elected king and proved an exceptionally intelligent sovereign (1831-1865). He was succeeded by his son, Leopold II (1865-1909), as intelligent as his father and a shrewd and grasping businessman besides. Leopold's successor was his nephew, Albert I (1909-1936).

The constitution described

On attaining independence Belgium engaged in economic activities which brought remarkable results. The country took full advantage of its fortunate geographical situation on the North sea and by means of one of the most elaborate networks of canals and railways in the world has tied up the great port of Antwerp with a hinterland including the populous Meuse (Maas) and Rhine valleys. It has made its rich coal beds the basis of an industrial development which is surpassed only by that of such great nations as Great Britain and Germany. Finally, it has witnessed, on the part of its numerous small landholders, the application of scientific methods to agriculture and kitchen-gardening, whereby the wealth and comfort of the country people have been greatly increased.

The economic development based on natural advantages

Just before World War I little Belgium had reached a population of 7,500,000 and was the most densely settled state of Europe.

The limited suffrage put the government of Belgium after 1831 in the hands of the middle classes, who divided their favor between a Catholic and a Liberal party. Belonging to the same social class and having identical economic interests, Liberals and Catholics differed chiefly as to the control of education. For a brief period the Liberals were sufficiently strong to eliminate clerical influence from the public schools. *The Catholics and Liberals differ on education*

At last, in the eighties, the Catholics so decidedly gained the upper hand that they held power almost uninterruptedly through the remainder of the period here under discussion. Of course they restored religious instruction in the public schools. What is more surprising, yielding to popular clamor, they canceled the property qualifications and established universal manhood suffrage (1893). However, they showed a lingering distrust of the common people by conceding one or two additional votes to citizens of wealth or education (plural voting). *The Catholics restore religious instruction and grant universal suffrage*

Since the Liberals had meanwhile almost completely disappeared as a political factor, their place as an opposition party was taken by the Socialists, who made a point of defending the interests of the growing body of workingmen. In conformity with the views of their brethren throughout Europe, the Belgian Socialists persistently attacked both plural voting and clerical control of the schools. *Rise of an active Socialist party*

Belgium is troubled by a language issue arising from the fact that the population is about evenly divided between a Celtic group, called Walloons, and a Teutonic people, closely related to the Dutch and called Flemings. The Flemings hold the northern part of the country and being, generally speaking, farmers and peasants, are conservative-minded and devoutly Catholic. The Walloons employ the French tongue, are chiefly engaged in industry, and look on Paris rather than Brussels as their intellectual capital. *The population consists of Flemings and Walloons*

Owing to the prestige associated with the French language, this speech has from the founding of the state enjoyed a privileged position in the administration, courts, and schools. Toward the middle of the century the Flemings began to protest against this ascendancy and inaugurated a campaign for equal rights for their own neglected tongue. Partial concessions were made by the government without satisfying the Flemish nationalists. It may be assumed that nothing short of the equal treatment observed in Switzerland will end their agitation. *The struggle to win equality for the Flemish speech*

In 1908 Belgium made a daring plunge into colonialism by taking over the huge African territory of the Congo after it had been developed by the personal enterprise of their king, Leopold II. It was in 1885 that Leopold obtained, from a colonial conference held by the powers at Berlin, recognition of himself as the sovereign in his own name of the

vast tropical jungle called the Congo Free State. Devoting himself to its
development like any other money-making capitalist, he soon succeeded
in drawing truly princely revenues from its great resources of ivory and
rubber. When it was discovered that the abnormal profits were ground
out of the black natives by a cruel system of forced labor, a cry of indignation rang through Europe which obliged Leopold to introduce reforms
and, finally, to transfer the colony to the Belgian state.

Belgium takes over (1908) the Congo Free State as a colony

The Belgian administration of the Congo proved energetic and enlightened to an unusual degree. The wealth of this immense area was
systematically developed with a view to supplying the homeland with
such tropical products as served to stimulate Belgian industry.

Belgium's rule of the Congo

THE KINGDOM OF THE NETHERLANDS

The kingdom of the Netherlands, established in 1815 by the Congress
of Vienna, was dismembered in 1830 by the revolt of its Belgian provinces. Reduced to the area of the former Dutch republic, it has continued
to operate under the official name adopted in 1815. However, in English-
speaking countries it is generally referred to as Holland.

Extent of the king-dom of the Netherlands

The powers at Vienna recognized William I of the historic house of
Orange-Nassau as king of the Netherlands. A typical conservative of his
age, he granted a constitution which left the power substantially in his
own hands as autocrat. Not even the Belgian disaster broke his stubborn
will, and it was not till the reign of his son, William II (1840-1849), that
a new and more liberal fundamental law was adopted. Doubtless the
general ferment of 1848 rather than the sovereign's insight prompted
this act of royal generosity.

The conservative constitution not liberal-ized till 1848

By the constitution of 1848 the power of the king was held in check
by a parliament of two houses. The upper house was composed of members elected by the legislatures of the eleven provinces which compose
the kingdom. The lower house was chosen directly by the voters, a limited body determined on the basis of property. By conceding important
rights of self-government to the eleven constituent provinces, the Dutch
system took on a balanced federal character like that of Switzerland and
the United States.

The constitution of 1848 described

The narrow suffrage invited attack on the part of the Liberals with
the result that successive acts of parliament gradually widened the franchise. William II was succeeded in 1849 by William III, on whose demise
in 1890 his daughter Wilhelmina mounted the throne. A strictly constitutional sovereign, she enjoyed to the full the traditional devotion of her
countrymen to the house of Nassau.

The widened franchise

The inhabitants of the kingdom are a homogeneous group of Germanic origin speaking the Dutch language. Perhaps the domestic ques-

tion which has agitated them more than any other is the place of religion in the educational system. Their Calvinistic faith had been such a factor in their history that large numbers of conservative Protestants felt an aversion for an education divorced from religious instruction. In this they were of one mind with the Catholics, who constitute an important and growing element of the community. However, in Holland as elsewhere, a Liberal party advocated strictly secular schools and in this position the Liberals were supported by a party of more recent origin, the Socialists.

The solution of the educational problem arrived at among these rival groups was a compromise. A public school system without religious instruction was created for those who desired the purely secular school. At its side operated the school systems of the Calvinists and Catholics. All three systems alike were subsidized from the public purse. Since attendance at one or another of these schools was compulsory, illiteracy has been practically abolished.

The economic development of Holland has steadily continued along the lines traced by its remarkable past. It was the full utilization by the people of its seaboard position that had won for the country its seventeenth century eminence. The decline since that epoch has, after all, been relative rather than absolute, for, considering its small size and its population of about 7,000,000, the former republic still maintains a very notable position not only in commerce but also in agriculture. Among its rich lowland meadows a dairy industry developed which matched or excelled that of the upland pastures of the Swiss. Even more important was commerce, which, concentrated in the two seaports of Amsterdam and Rotterdam, threw a bridge from Holland to every country of the world.

The still very considerable remnant of Holland's colonial empire contributed in no small degree to the nation's prosperity. The Dutch possessions consist of Guiana (South America) and a group of tropical East Indian islands, of which Java, Sumatra, and Borneo (in part) are the most important. From this eastern source the Dutch merchants supplied the European markets with spices, coffee, sugar, rubber, and similar tropical products. Owing to the absence of mineral resources Holland did not turn to manufacturing, as did its neighbor Belgium. That, in the light of all the facts, the country has made the best possible use of its natural advantages hardly admits of dispute.

Like Belgium, Holland occupies an advantageous but also dangerous position in close proximity to such great powers as France, Germany, and Great Britain. Switzerland and Belgium, in spite of the neutrality guaranteed to them by the powers, did not fail to provide for their defense by the creation of an army. Evidently they nursed a conviction that their independence rested in last resort not on international promises but on

their own prowess. We need therefore feel no surprise that the kingdom of the Netherlands, which enjoyed no similar international guarantee, was at particular pains to provide against attack. Beginning with 1898 the militia was reorganized with a provision for compulsory military training of the individual citizen. This reform enabled the Dutch to mobilize at need a numerous and by no means negligible army.

As the grand-duchy of Luxemburg, wedged between France, Belgium, and Germany, was in 1815 given as a personal possession to William I, king of the Netherlands, a word concerning it may be inserted at this point. William reigned as grand-duke in Luxemburg, which was not a part of the Netherlands. For geographic and military reasons Luxemburg was in 1815 incorporated in the German Bund and William, in respect to Luxemburg, was a German prince.

When the Bund disappeared as a result of the Austro-Prussian war of 1866, Luxemburg, left high and dry, was coveted by Napoleon III. It would have been surrendered to him for a consideration by its then sovereign, King William III of the Netherlands, if Prussia had not interfered. To adjust the uncertainties which enveloped the status of the grand-duchy, a conference of the powers, held (1867) in London, confirmed William III as grand-duke, and, declaring the little territory to be an independent state, put it under the collective guarantee of the powers.

On William III's death in 1890 he was succeeded in the Netherlands by his daughter Wilhelmina, but in Luxemburg, which did not recognize female succession, by his nearest male relative, Adolphus of Nassau. Thus the personal tie, the only one which had ever existed between Holland and Luxemburg, was snapped. Since 1890 Adolphus and his descendants after him have ruled this Lilliputian state as constitutional princes.

THE SCANDINAVIAN STATES

The three Scandinavian states, Denmark, Sweden, and Norway, have

so much in common that it is proper to group them together. Danes, Swedes, and Norwegians represent branches of the same North-Germanic stock; they speak three distinct, though closely related languages; they adhere alike to the Lutheran faith; they live by agriculture, commerce, seafaring, and fishing, rather than by manufactures, though Sweden's industry is far from negligible; they are intellectually alert and have provided themselves with advanced educational systems; and they have passed in recent years through a similar social and political evolution.

The three Scandinavian countries do not support a large population. On the eve of World War I the inhabitants of Denmark numbered about 3,400,000, those of Sweden about 6,000,000, and those of Norway about 2,700,000. By their enterprise, intelligence, and sturdy qualities the peoples of all three countries have won an eminent position in the modern movement of civilization. Population of Denmark, Sweden, and Norway

Denmark. To punish the king of Denmark for clinging to Napoleon, the victor powers transferred (1814) his dependency, Norway, to Sweden. In 1864 he lost Schleswig and Holstein, which two years later were incorporated in Prussia. By these successive liberations from foreign bodies Denmark was not so much injured as helped, and doubtless owes much of its recent rapid advance to its freedom from nationalist worries. Loss of Norway (1814) and of Schleswig-Holstein

Up to the middle of the nineteenth century the Danish political situation was marked by stagnation with the result that the king's absolutism was hardly challenged. The revolutionary fervor which seized on Europe in 1848 weakened the royal position. Consequently Frederick VII issued a constitution (1849), which, revised in 1866, is still in force. Absolutism yields to constitutionalism

Christian IX, who ruled from 1863 to 1906, tried to stem the democratic trend and, against the wishes of the lower house, insisted on carrying through a policy of military preparedness. He appointed ministers at his pleasure, and when he could not get a majority in the chamber for his budgets, enacted them by royal decree. He thus created a serious situation, which was solved without civil war by the resolute pressure of the farmers, who constitute the bulk of the nation. The unconstitutional practices of Christian IX

The farmers had steadily improved their condition by intensive dairy-farming coupled with an amazingly effective chain of co-operative societies. By these co-operatives great quantities of butter, cheese, and eggs were sold to Great Britain and Germany. By the turn of the century the farmers dominated so completely both the economic and political situation of their country that the king in 1901 was obliged to end the domestic conflict by installing a cabinet representing the majority party in the lower house. The farmers assume (1901) political control

Since the popular victory of 1901 the democratization has proceeded at a steadily accelerating pace. It was championed by the farmers organized as the Liberal party, and afterwards, with even greater ardor, by a growing group of Socialists. The suffrage was enlarged by stages till the vote came to be enjoyed by all adult men and women. At the same time the army was treated as an unnecessary luxury and reduced to a militia basis. The broad democratization since 1901

In conformity with the politico-social outlook of a prosperous community of socialized farmers, Denmark has shown so little taste for colonialism that, instead of reaching out for new colonies, it has disposed of most of those that it had. In 1903 Iceland was granted a measure of home rule which was subsequently (1918) expanded to complete independence. Although the disposal of the three Danish West Indian islands, St. Thomas, St. Croix, and St. John, lies beyond the years em- Denmark surrenders most of its colonies braced by this chapter, it deserves for the sake of completeness to be here recorded. In 1917 the three Danish islands were sold to the United States and renamed the Virgin Islands. Denmark retained a slight hold on Greenland, but the possession of this glacial region was not calculated to arouse any rosy dreams of colonial grandeur.

Sweden. That Sweden had, in the seventeenth century, been a great European power has in more ways than one subtly affected its history down to our own time. It was the Russia of Peter the Great that dragged Sweden from its eminence and absorbed most of the Swedish conquests along the east shore of the Baltic. A century later, in 1809, Tsar Alexander I crowned the work of Peter by capturing Finland from his Scandinavian neighbor. It was at this juncture that Sweden sought to strengthen its hand against Russia by elevating one of Napoleon's marshals, Bernadotte, to the Swedish throne. Once in Sweden Bernadotte, instead of playing Napoleon's game, joined the emperor's enemies, and on Napoleon's overthrow was rewarded for his help by the cession of Norway.

The Frenchman, Marshal Bernadotte, king of Sweden (1809)

Up to this time (1814) Norway had belonged to Denmark. Outraged by this treatment of them as a diplomatic pawn, the Norwegians rose in arms and forced Sweden to recognize their independence under their own separate constitution. Then they elected the king of Sweden as their own king, thus establishing the familiar form of connection between two separate states known as a personal union. Besides the monarch, the two kingdoms had no institution in common other than the diplomatic and consular services. Even this restricted association led to friction, which culminated in 1905 in a complete rupture. We shall treat of it in the following section.

Sweden and Norway have separate constitutions and a common king

Marshal Bernadotte reigned as king under the title of Charles XIV till 1844. He and his descendants have identified themselves so thoroughly with Swedish interests that, though of French origin, the family could not be more popular if it were a native house. Sweden, in distinction from democratic Norway and Denmark, was in the days of Bernadotte an aristocratic society of great landholders lording it over a dependent peasantry. This upper order nursed dreams of Swedish greatness, favored military preparedness to resist further Russian encroachments, and set its face against the contemporary liberal movement. It was of one mind with its French ruler in standing by the old system of government inherited from feudal times.

Aristocratic influences long retain an ascendancy in Swedish public life

However, the modern movement of science and industry gradually strengthened the middle classes, and in 1866 under their influence the medieval diet was replaced by a modern parliament of two chambers. A fairly high property qualification restricted the body of electors and proved the conservative character of the reform. Not till 1909 were con-

Sweden gets a modern constitution (1866) and is democratized (1909)

stitutional amendments carried celebrating the full triumph of democracy by the establishment of universal manhood suffrage.

This political transformation should, as usual, be interpreted in the light of the contemporary social-economic movement. The Swedish natural resources, consisting chiefly of iron, forests, and water-power, have served since 1850 as the basis of an industrial movement which has strengthened both the middle classes and the proletariat. While the land-holding aristocracy is still powerful, it can no longer stand up against a union of the newer orders represented in politics by the Liberal and Socialist parties. Many signs indicate that in the future the struggle for political control will be between these two latter groups as the really decisive factors in present-day Sweden. Conservatism, resting on the power of great landlords, is clearly a lost cause.

Sweden builds up an industry

Norway. We have seen that it was owing solely to the firm resolution shown by Norway in 1814-1815 that the country gained its independence under its own constitution and was joined to Sweden in a purely personal union. Even this loose association proved irksome for a number of reasons. Norway is a coast and mountain land of small farmers, fishermen, sailors, merchants, and Protestant clergymen—in a word, as democratic a society as can be found anywhere in Europe. Even the constitution of 1814, constructed in a period of general reaction, was for its time an unusually democratic document since it vested supreme authority in a parliament (*Storting*) and gave the vote to all taxpayers.

The Norwegian constitution of 1814 a very democratic document

The plentiful energy of the Norwegians was in the nineteenth century poured chiefly into the shipping business. They developed the carrying trade to such a degree that by 1900 their merchant marine had reached a tonnage which ranked it above the merchant marines of even the great powers, with the exception of Great Britain and Germany.

Norway develops a vast carrying trade

The expanding carrying trade produced an increase of national self-esteem, making the domination of Sweden in the consular service, the business of which was to look after shipping, decidedly irritating. Not unnaturally the people raised a clamor for Norwegian consuls. In addition, they made the highly emotional demand for their own Norwegian flag on Norwegian ships instead of the legal flag symbolic of the union with Sweden. When the king, who was Oscar II, refused to yield, the Storting in 1905 dissolved the union by legislative act. The crisis terminated by Oscar wisely bowing to necessity. Norway, free of the last Swedish bonds, thereupon elected (1905) to its throne a Danish prince, who took the title Haakon VII.

Norway dissolves (1905) the union with Sweden

A society which, like that of Norway, was founded on the vigorous self-respect of farmers and sailors, was sure to prove friendly to the democratic doctrines current in our age. From 1870 on they would have been incorporated in the Norwegian political system with a minimum of

delay, had not the conservative-minded Swedish king imposed a halt.
Only slowly was his resistance overcome. In 1884 he was obliged to accept the parliamentary system, that is, he declared himself ready to concede the ministerial posts to representatives of the majority party in the Storting. In 1898 the limited franchise was replaced by universal manhood suffrage. With the Swedish brakes removed by Norway's declaring itself independent, the democratic chariot moved forward at an accelerated pace. In 1907 women received the vote, first with certain limitations, finally (1913) on the same basis as men. Norway claims the honor of being the first sovereign state of Europe to admit women not only to the vote in national elections but also to a seat in parliament.

Stages by which Norway became a thoroughgoing democracy

33 LEADING CULTURAL TRENDS OF THE NINETEENTH CENTURY

IN DEALING IN this chapter with the leading cultural trends of the nineteenth century the reader is warned against assuming that they are or can be precisely located between the years 1800 and 1900. That is not the way with trends since, as mental and spiritual phenomena, they have a fluidity and indeterminateness as to their beginning and end already fully revealed by our treatment of them in the Renaissance (Chapter 3), the Reformation (Chapter 13), and the Eighteenth Century (Chapter 19). The present chapter should therefore be looked upon as a continuation of its cultural forerunners with the fact at the same time kept in mind that a later and concluding chapter (Chapter 45) will deal with the trends more specifically carrying the twentieth century imprint.

THE NATURAL SCIENCES

Turning first to the natural sciences, we shall be better prepared to grasp their nineteenth century phase if we pause to recall the preceding development. In putting out his theory of the ordered movement of the planets around the sun Copernicus stimulated investigation into the whole body of phenomena connected with matter in motion. These researches, conducted by many scholars, among whom Kepler, Galileo, and Newton are the most shining names, culminated in the theory of gravitation and the recognition of an eternally established, majestic universe of law. *Early science concerned with matter in motion*

Hand in hand with these brilliant physico-astronomical discoveries went the development of mathematics. Mathematics reached its eighteenth century culmination with the invention of the calculus by Newton and Leibnitz. It was the calculus that made possible the accurate and complicated measurements demanded by the study of moving objects and it was in mathematical terms that the laws of motion not only of solid bodies but also of such physical phenomena as sound, heat, and light were stated. *Concomitant development of mathematics*

These magnificent achievements of the physicists and mathematicians prompted every other kind of scientist to fresh endeavor. Consequently, important advances were made in the eighteenth century in such subjects as botany, zoology, mineralogy, and ethnology. Far and away the

most promising development, however, occurred in chemistry and is marked by the great name of Lavoisier. Almost at once with Lavoisier's discoveries there was a crowding of investigators into the chemical field. This signified that a new type of curiosity was gaining ground, the curiosity to follow up the study of matter in motion with the study of the composition of matter.

Now, the developments that in the nineteenth century took place in

chemistry and every other natural science followed so thick and fast and were in themselves and in their implications so overwhelming that merely to list them would completely throw off balance a book, which, like this, is mainly a political history in a social and economic setting. Moreover, if the attempt to list them were made unattended by the explanatory comment necessary to give them meaning, the enumeration would read like excerpts plucked at random from an all-time Who's Who in Science. Certainly better in the circumstances than so unprofitable a catalogue is a generalized statement which, after setting forth the intensified pursuit of science in the nineteenth century and indicating the many new sciences that came to birth owing to the greatly increased refinements of research, is content sharply to focus attention on the concept of evolution. For it was this concept that, after a long and bitter struggle, won universal acceptance and served to assemble the huge and disjointed mass of modern knowledge within a common unifying frame.

The first feature to attract attention in the proposed general survey of

nineteenth century science is that it falls into two divisions, experimental or "pure" science and applied science. The former adheres strictly to the intellectual tradition of the two previous centuries, the latter, twin-brother of the Industrial Revolution, concerns itself with the application of the proven knowledge of "pure" science to the invention of serviceable technological devices. The end of "pure" science was and is knowledge, the end of applied science, social utility. That among the intellectual elite the former study enjoys the greater reputation is shown by the academic honors, citations, and medals directed in an uninterrupted stream to its leading votaries. In the eyes of the common man, however, the applied scientists with their proffer of immediate material benefits shine out with greater luster. The point for the historian of science to note is that the age in general was unrestrained in its admiration of both kinds of scientists and that it was their co-ordinated labors that have given us the mechanized world in which we live, with its multiplied goods, its countless easements of human drudgery, and its unceasing speeding up of every form of communication.

It was the brilliant successes of science that drew to it an ever increasing number of enthusiasts and spurred them on to extend and deepen their investigations. Back in Galileo's day a natural scientist looked upon the whole of the as yet undifferentiated world of nature as his province. The tendency, in spite of growing specialization, persisted into the eighteenth century. But with the nineteenth century those classificatory refinements set in that make a fully equippd, present-day university a bewildering assembly of closely circumscribed and yet subtly interrelated scientific specialties. Galileo, returned to life, would gaze at these branchings and sub-branchings of the natural world with undisguised amazement. And yet they developed with unescapable necessity from the impassioned pursuit of the facts of nature to which he and the noble company of his compeers had set the example.

The effects of continued specialization

To grasp the extent of the vast expansion of the natural sciences, let us have a quick glance at the progressive filiation each one experienced, beginning with the oldest science, with physics. Through the intensified labors of nineteenth century physicists their subject burst through its ancient boundaries and staked off new fields of investigation. Such are, to name but a few, thermodynamics, spectroscopy, magnetism, and electricity. Chemistry took the same turn. On concentrating, at the beginning of the century, on the atomic composition of matter, it was able gradually to identify the ninety-two irreducible elements to be found in nature. This great achievement led to a new chemical department, to synthetic chemistry, which concerned itself with making organic substances artificially in the laboratory. Further developments were electrochemistry, bio-chemistry, bacteriology, in each of which chemistry entered into alliance with a neighbor science. More and more sciences began to merge at their borders, thus giving birth to a whole series of novel scientific combinations. And in every scientific field, in the old and the new alike, but in no field more than in chemistry, the discoveries made in the laboratories by the experimental method were promptly exploited industrially. In fact, to applied chemistry are due some of the greatest and most revolutionizing industries of the age. It was applied chemistry that gave us the newest textile dyes, developed cellulose, fructified agriculture with artificial fertilizers, preserved food, refined petroleum, and performed scores of other marvels too numerous to mention.

The new activities of physics and chemistry

Geology repeats the story. It did not become a true science till the publication in 1827 of Charles Lyell's *Principles of Geology*. Therein he declared that still observable geological processes, such as earthquakes, volcanic eruptions, the erosive action of rivers, the rising and sinking of land, continuing through eons of time would suffice to explain how the earth had assumed its present physical appearance. Lyell's work by prompting the intensified study of fossil remains led to a fruitful development of paleontology; and the study of the fossil remains of man

The developments stemming from geology

pushed back the origin of *homo sapiens* thousands of years and put anthropology on a new foundation.

The rise of biology

With so much new knowledge accumulating in all the natural sciences, it seems invidious to say, and yet it can hardly be denied, that the most epoch-making development of the century took place in biology. The very word was not put into currency till the beginning of the century. But that does not mean that the kind of inquiry involved in biology did not till that late date see the light of day. For, concerned with the most pressing of all phenomena, with life itself, it had stimulated speculative interest in every generation. It had even been systematically pursued as far back as the fourth century B.C., when Aristotle and his followers had assembled an imposing body of pertinent data. In a sense all observers since Aristotle of the life-cycle of plants and animals may be thought of as at least rudimentary biologists. But biology, as we understand the term, was not born till 1839, when a German, Theodor Schwann, formulated the theory that all living things originate and grow in small structural units called "cells." The cell pointed to a common denominator of all organic structures and challenged the established concept of the fixity of species. This indeed, even before the discovery of cells, had been challenged by the French zoologist, Lamarck (d. 1829). It was Lamarck who first adduced evidence of the variability of species and suggested the factors that might be conceived to account for the phenomenon.

Wallace and Darwin hit on the theory of evolution at the same time

With the variability concept beginning to displace the fixity concept, with the cell accepted as the substructure of all living forms, with the deepening intuition in all quarters of the kinship of the infinite variety of living forms, the need became ever more pressing for a concept expressive of these unifying intimations. It was met by an Englishman, Charles Darwin (1809-1882). He had begun his career as a naturalist by a five-year voyage on a British surveying vessel, the *Beagle*. More and more intently he was led to ponder the problem of the inter-relation of species until he thought he had found the solution and committed it to paper. In the year 1858 his countryman, Alfred Russel Wallace (1823-1913), sent him a paper which formulated in clear and unambiguous terms what came to be called the theory of evolution. Its substance was that animal and plant species in their innumerable present forms have derived through millennia of slow change from a common original source. The conclusions of Wallace agreed in every particular with the views Darwin had intrusted to his article, which, although written, he had not yet published. Delighted to have his own hypothesis confirmed, he promptly read both papers before a London learned society. The very next year (1859) he published his epoch-making book, *On the Origin of Species*. Therein not only did he formulate the general theory of evolution but on the strength of evidence accumulated through years of patient examination of living and fossil forms, especially of marine life, he set forth Natural Selection as the factor which might be conceived as having brought about the immense variety of existing vegetable and animal species.

While prepared to admit the operation of other forces in the production of new species, Natural Selection was in Darwin's opinion the outstanding one. In his view Natural Selection signified the likelihood of survival on the part of that individual of a given species which is endowed with some minute variation calculated to give it a better chance of life in its environment. Producing offspring in its turn emphasizing the same variation, the first variable individual might, it was suggested, by imperceptible accumulations through many generations become the ancestor of a new type or species. *How Natural Selection might produce a new species*

In this manner was launched the theory of evolution. Embracing all life, evolution makes, of course, no exception of man. Our human kind is of the same essential stuff as the wolf, the rat, the rose, and the jellyfish. If it flatters our vanity to put man on a special pedestal, the only scientific justification for our bias lies in the circumstance that man is manifestly a species making a very late appearance in the endlessly spun out evolutionary process. *Natural Selection as the basis of a sweeping theory of evolution*

There is something beautifully unifying and inclusive about the evolutionary theory. Bred in the hard realm of science and having a solemn scientific air, it yet brings to many people something of the expansive feeling of religion. By all such it is welcomed as a new hope, a credible modern pantheism. We should not fail to note, however, that to the strict scientist it is still what it was to Darwin—a useful hypothesis and nothing more. That means that, admitting the evidence in favor of an evolutionary development of animate nature to be overwhelming, the method by which the development takes place and which Darwin assumed to be Natural Selection is still subject to redefinition. *The theory of evolution not dependent on Natural Selection*

Ever since Darwin argued in favor of Natural Selection, additions to, and modifications of, his theory have been in order. As early as 1866 an Austrian monk, Gregor Mendel by name, contributed important new data touching organic inheritance; and a generation later the Dutchman, de Vries, adduced evidence favoring the view that new species are often produced not by slow stages but suddenly as "sports." *Darwinism modified by Mendel and de Vries*

While the manner in which evolution works is still far from clear, evolution itself may be accepted as certain. Beginning with Darwin's time, it was given an ever-broader application until it at last became the enveloping framework for the whole mass of knowledge constituting the universe of modern man. *Evolution a convenient unifying framework*

THE RELIGIOUS CRISIS

The conflict between evolution and the Christian religion

With the tendency established to universalize the evolutionary concept, the Christian religion in its Roman Catholic as well as in its various Protestant forms could not fail to be profoundly affected. All Christians alike accepted the Bible account of creation, according to which God made the world in six days, gave every species its definite, individual form from the start, and, as a final, special act of grace, fashioned man in his own image. Unquestioning believers therefore violently rejected a theory which shattered the Bible story in every particular and, for good measure, intolerably humiliated man by endowing him with an apelike ancestry. It was no mitigation of the outrage that the ape ancestry lay a few hundred thousand years behind man, the crowning species of the evolutionary ladder.

Protestants compromise with evolution

Following the first instinctive rejection of evolution, some Christians sought an adjustment to its teachings. For Protestants this was much easier than for Catholics, since, while all Protestant churches rested on the foundation of the Bible, they had, beginning with the first Protestant, with Luther, hesitatingly asserted the right of private judgment.

Protestants helped by the exercise of private judgment

The right of private judgment opened an avenue of escape from doctrinal control which the more adventurous Protestants had for generations back taken advantage of to assimilate the data of science and the modern philosophies to which science had given rise. If the official Protestant creeds of the nineteenth century were still largely what they had been from the beginning, Protestants themselves had imperceptibly changed and were, therefore, in part at least, prepared to weigh the evidence for evolution and to come to terms with it.

Protestant scholars humanize the Bible

Protestants were greatly helped in their adjustment to the evolutionary doctrine by the rise among them of Biblical scholarship. At the very time that the biologists were accumulating the data that prepared the way for the evolutionary hypothesis, students of the Bible made the discovery that, far from being a continuous outpouring under divine inspiration, it was the work of many different authors writing each one under special conditions reflected in the text and subjected to revisions by later editors. In short, the Bible, too, was a variable species, an indubitable evolutionary product.

The Protestants increasingly reconciled to Biblical scholarship

This reduction of what had been revered as Holy Writ to a man-made document was violently rejected by the orthodox elements in control of the various churches. To them the disturbing Biblical scholarship had the same diabolical origin as Darwinism. Nonetheless, the new views, supported by evidence that could not be ignored, gradually won over increasing numbers both of the laity and the clergy within the Protestant denominations and, in spite of stubborn resistance on the part of the orthodox, promoted a reconciliation between the ancient faith and the modern discoveries.

By the turn of the century much of the fury which had marked the struggle in its earlier phases had disappeared. Without doubt, important orthodox groups cling to this day to what is to them the security and finality of their divine inheritance. However, if to generalize a complicated situation is not too hazardous, the statement may be ventured that the Protestant churches either have already or are about to adjust themselves both to scientific discovery and to its offspring, Biblical scholarship. Many of their leaders at least are of the opinion that it is only by assimilating the modern outlook that Protestantism will succeed in retaining its hold on its followers. ^{The Protestants increasingly reconciled to the modern outlook}

The quarrel of Catholicism with the evolutionary theory and Biblical criticism was from the first far more uncompromising and the possibility of an adjustment much more remote. Catholicism is based on an absolute, unalterable body of doctrine, and possesses in the church a powerful institution to defend its position. Moreover, this vast organization has at its head a single, authoritative official, the pope. When he speaks, even great states are obliged to take notice, since his views determine the attitude of tens of millions of devoted followers. ^{Catholicism unable to make the Protestant compromise}

Ever since the advent, with Copernicus, of modern science and, with Descartes, of modern rationalism the papacy had found itself out of sympathy with the direction taken by European thought. The French Revolution, with its confiscation of church property and its fanatic persecution of the clergy, did not improve the situation. Quite naturally, Catholicism became violently anti-revolutionary and anti-liberal and identified itself in every country of Europe with political conservatism. ^{Catholicism rejects the modern outlook}

Throughout the first half of the nineteenth century the Catholic clergy regularly stood shoulder to shoulder with the forces of the past, with the nobility and the absolute monarchy. Then came the Italian nationalist movement. It greatly strengthened the church's aversion for every specifically modern development, since the pope became the leading victim of Italian nationalism and was subjected to a long series of acts of spoliation in the name of peninsular unity. ^{Catholicism identified with political conservatism}

To Pius IX, in whose long reign (1846-1878) Italian unification took place, liberalism and nationalism must have seemed to be indistinguishable evils. On the spread, at precisely the same moment, of the evolutionary fervor the pope's cup overflowed and he saw the whole modern movement as a systematic, sinister attack on the Catholic church. Thirsting for the fray, for he was a man of deep convictions, he denounced the age in fiery invectives. They culminated in 1864 in an encyclical, to which he attached a *Syllabus of Errors,* recounting the principal aber- ^{Pope Pius IX issues his "Syllabus of Errors" (1864), sweepingly condemning the modern world}

rations of our times. Free-thinking scientists, advocates of religious toleration, supporters of lay marriage and lay schools, opponents of the
temporal power of the church—such are a few of the human categories
which the pope solemnly condemned. Indeed it would be difficult to discover a single distinctly modern movement of thought or politics which
Pius IX did not declare to be in conflict with historic Catholic Christianity.

The Vatican Council proclaims the dogma of papal infallibility   It is clear that in the eyes of Pius IX the church was fighting for its
life and that it needed to draw its ranks together and put itself without
reservation under his supreme command. This frame of mind explains
his calling an Ecumenical Council of the church. The last previous meeting of such a body had taken place at Trent three hundred years before.
The pope summoned the new council to his palace of the Vatican and,
not without some difficulty, persuaded the assembled prelates to promulgate (1870) the dogma of papal infallibility.

Significance of papal infallibility   The dogma declared that when the pope speaks *ex cathedra,* that is,
when in his official capacity he makes a statement regarding faith or
morals, his word must be accepted as infallible. If, as historians have
frequently pointed out, infallibility has always been attributed to Catholic
dogmas, it is undeniable that the definition of dogma in the past had,
in the main, been reserved to the church Councils. This historical function the Vatican Council of 1870 resigned into the hands of the pope.
Henceforth there was no reason for ever again summoning a Council.
The pope, long absolute in the government of the church, had become
equally absolute in matters of faith and doctrine. With the command
of the forces of Catholicism unified in his hand, he might feel that the
church was in the best possible position to meet the assault of its many
enemies.

Leo XIII comes to terms with modern governments   On the death of Pius IX, Leo XIII (1878-1903) succeeded to the throne
of St. Peter and continued the struggle with the system of modern
thought as well as with the European governments whether under liberal or conservative direction. But soon a difference made itself noticeable. Inclining, in distinction from the downright Pius IX, to the subtle
and elastic diplomatic tradition of the papacy, Leo XIII saw no reason
for quarreling with states merely because their governments did not conform with certain traditional norms. He let it be known that to him the
political form was immaterial; also he took a strong stand against capitalist exploitation of labor and in favor of trade-unions, collective bargaining, and social legislation. His championship of the workers reached its
peak in the famous encyclical of 1891, which made the great stir it did
only because the modern world, and perhaps the papacy itself, had forgotten that Christianity owed its rise to its solicitude for the oppressed

and heavy-laden. By this evangelical policy Leo XIII re-entered the political arena with the organized support of both the Catholic bourgeoisie
and the Catholic workingmen.

PHILOSOPHY: FROM IDEALISM TO POSITIVISM AND MATERIALISM

Because philosophy is one of the best available mirrors of the movement of human thought, this book has attempted to trace the line of *Eighteenth*
philosophic thought from the Middle Ages through the eighteenth cen- *century*
tury. In the last-named century the rationalist philosophies, which *philosophy*
culminates
stemmed from Descartes, disputed the field with the empiricist or sen- *in the*
sualist philosophies, of which the fountainhead was Locke. Toward the *Kantian*
close of the century Kant had attempted to reconcile the two tendencies *compromise*
by distinguishing between a knowable world of sense-perceptions and an
eternally unknowable world of essences. This is called the Kantian dualism. Since in his later years Kant identified the unknowable world with
God, he may be said to have departed from his earlier, strictly rational
position and to have made a compromise with faith.

The Kantian compromise became the point of departure for a stream
of German philosophic thought which rests on the emotions and again, *German*
as in the Middle Ages, appeals for its validity to faith. It is called ideal- *idealistic*
ism but, in the light of its origin in the age of feeling inaugurated by *philosophy*
Rousseau, it might more properly be called romanticism.

We usually think of romanticism as a movement in literature, music,
and art, and such, as we shall presently learn, it in the main was. But it *Romanti-*
was also a sweeping reaction, which set in toward the end of the eight- *cism a*
reaction
eenth century, against the over-sober rationalism of the age. This reaction *against*
was bound to penetrate the realm of philosophy and, as we have seen, it *rationalism*
caused the aging Kant to modify his earlier rationalism.

The successors of Kant did not hesitate to throw off completely the
rationalist chains and develop philosophies based on the emotions, which *German*
the eighteenth century had despised. Our emotions normally play quite *idealism*
asserts the
as large a part in our life as our thoughts and cannot be set aside with- *identity of*
out causing in the end a violent rebound. Fichte and Schelling are the *God and*
German pioneers in the projection of vast absolute systems, wherein the *nature*
Kantian dualism is rejected and the oneness of God and nature made a
basic premise. The idealist (or romantic) movement culminated in Georg
Friedrich Hegel (d. 1831).

While Hegel piled still another absolutism on those of his immediate
predecessors, he cast his absolutism in the evolutionary mold which was *The evo-*
beginning to assert itself as a leading trend of contemporary biology. As *lutionary*
philosophy
a result God and man lost their static character and became endowed *of Hegel*
with the same unfolding and expanding energy as the biologists were

engaged in attributing to the innumerable forms of life. By adopting the dynamic evolutionary concept Hegel brought German idealism into touch with contemporary science. The philosophy of an uninterruptedly expanding creation spread an optimism which strikingly accorded with the prevailing "progressive" temper of the nineteenth century and which explains the vogue enjoyed by Hegel in some sort to this day.

However, even in Germany the optimism of the idealist school did not remain unchallenged. For Schopenhauer (d. 1860) the world was a vast machine operating under immutable law, and the living forms, including man, which it embraced were the helpless victims of a blind Will. He expounded this philosophy in his chief work, *The World as Will and Idea*. There was no kindly Creator, no benevolent Father. There was nothing but a tyrannical First Cause, incomprehensible and unfathomable. The essense of Schopenhauer is a black pessimism.

Schopenhauer and the philosophy of pessimism

The leading German follower of Schopenhauer was Nietzsche (d. 1900). He was a gifted poet, in a strictly professional sense no philosopher at all. His main work, *Thus Spake Zarathustra,* is one of the great monuments of German literature. While accepting man's helplessness in a mechanical universe under eternal law, Nietzsche does not subscribe to Schopenhauer's despair. He preaches courage in the face of the Unknown, extolling courage as the highest attribute of man. To this courage he gave the name of will-to-power, with very unhappy consequences for the age. For, distorted by his followers, it was made the excuse for a ruthless use of force in the political field. For Nietzsche himself the will-to-power was not to be exercised in behalf of the state (which he abominated) but for the higher cultural development of the individual. From its sustained application, so he hoped, there would after many generations evolve a higher type of man to which he gave the name of superman. For this dreamer, who went insane ten years before he died, superman is the light shining in darkness, the only conceivable end justifying the agony of existence.

Nietzsche and the philosophy of the superman

In contrast with Germany, France and England developed philosophies which ignored the transcendental issues as beyond our ken and substantially concerned themselves with systematizing the fresh bodies of knowledge which the age was engaged in accumulating. This French and English tendency to deal with the material facts of life may perhaps be explained by the domination which the machine had acquired in France and England and alone, till past the middle of the century, in these two countries.

Practical direction of philosophy in France and England

The most important French materialist philosopher was Comte (d. 1857). He propounded the view that with the nineteenth century a new age had dawned on mankind which he called scientific. The character-

CHARLES DARWIN. From an engraving by Rajon. (Bettmann Collection)

JOHANN WOLFGANG GOETHE. After a contemporary painting.

LUDWIG VAN BEETHOVEN. After a contemporary painting.

RICHARD WAGNER. After a photograph. (All from Bettmann Collection)

istic feature of the scientific age is that it no longer seeks to unriddle the universe, but is content with discovering and arranging in their proper order innumerable tiny new facts. As Comte was chiefly interested in man and society, he took the position that his proposed social fact-finding would inevitably lead to a social science as reliable and precise as the natural science, which, since the seventeenth century, has given man an increasingly fruitful control of the external world. *Comte plans a social science as fruitful as natural science*

Comte is often called the founder of sociology. The designation may pass, provided it is understood that he meant by sociology not what we in America conceive by that term but the sum of the social studies. These he hoped in due time to raise to the level of authentic sciences. Social science and natural science alone held the promise of "positive," that is, certain and reliable results, declared Comte, and their cultivation, to the strict exclusion of theology and metaphysics, is the essence of Comte's philosophy of positivism. Theology and metaphysics, said Comte, are dead, and their day has passed. *Comte's philosophy called positivism*

The Englishman, Herbert Spencer (1820-1903), celebrated his devotion to science in an enormous work in ten volumes, entitled *Synthetic Philosophy*. His central position is that all matter, organic and inorganic alike, has been evolved by natural processes. He took the theory of evolution as his framework and assuming, like Darwin, a "struggle for existence" and the "survival of the fittest," showed that the human mind, the political organization of society, our systems of ethics and economics are, after the severe testing of innumerable generations, exactly what they ought to be. *Spencer's philosophy of evolutionary materialism*

In distinction from the philosophy of the German idealists, Spencer's is an outspoken materialist philosophy. It brings us a message of optimism and "progress," since, if there has been a slow ascent from the jellyfish to man, we have every right to deduce a future for our kind compared with which the present is hardly better than a state of misery. *Spencer's optimism*

Toward the end of the century the first definitely native philosophy made its appearance in the United States. Rejecting the ancient issues of metaphysics and using the scientific method as its tool, it received the name of pragmatism. But as it did not come to full expression till the twentieth century, we may dismiss it here with a mere mention. *Pragmatism*

THE SOCIAL SCIENCES

Our treatment of eighteenth century trends (Chapter 19) brought out that the study of man and society was by that time not only on its way but in certain areas, such as political economy and political science, had already made notable advances. The nineteenth century tremendously expanded the range and depth of these beginnings. That traditional

metaphysical speculation yielded ground to the material mundane actu-
The alities has just been indicated by the rise of the evolutionary philosophies
nineteenth of Comte and Spencer. Simultaneously, there took place not only an in-
century tensified pursuit of the already established social studies, but new social
advance in studies were initiated in consequence of the discovery and staking-off of
the social new and hitherto neglected realms of human experience. Among these
studies were archaeology, anthropology, ethnology, psychology, and, of course,
sociology, the particular contribution of the earth-directed, positivist
philosophy of Comte. Admitting that one and all of these studies had
attracted the attention of an occasional forerunner and were not sudden
births, the fact remains that they were not systematically attacked till
the nineteenth century and did not till then yield their stirring and
abundant factual harvest.

Since it will not be possible to be other than selective and indicate
The the development in one or another of these fields, let us choose archaeol-
unfolding ogy. If systematic archaeology may be said to have made its bow to the
wonders of world with the excavations conducted in the eighteenth century at Pom-
archaeology peii and Herculaneum, it gained new energy from its successful attack,
beginning around 1800, on Egyptian remains. It will always be a source
of romantic gratification that the chance turning-up of the Rosetta Stone
with its parallel Greek and Egyptian inscriptions enabled the French
scholar, Champollion, to decipher the latter and thereby open up a new
and wonderful world of knowledge. From Egypt, archaeology spread by
natural stages to Greece, Rome, Palestine, and all the other Mediterranean
areas; and, once on its way, it refused to be satisfied till it had reached
out to the heaped evidence of dead or dying civilizations in India and
China, in Mexico and Peru.

The exciting disclosure of the long and fruitful life of man on earth
Archaeology greatly stimulated the related study of anthropology. Instead of man's
tied up with having come into existence a few thousand years ago, in fact precisely,
anthropol- according to official Christian reckoning, in the year 4004 B.C., he was
ogy and proved by skeletal remains discovered in ancient geologic layers to have
ethnology roamed the earth in neolithic and paleolithic times, that is, as far back as
anywhere from 20,000 to 100,000 years. From these remains, often no
more than broken fragments of bone, he could, with the help of other
even more remote finds, be traced back to an apelike ancestor, who
through some hundreds of thousands of years of incredibly slow accretions might be assumed to have at last achieved the authentic human skull
and figure. At this point anthropology, which had become tied up with
archaeology, merged imperceptibly with another neighbor. This was
ethnology, which made its main concern the discovery of the various
races of men together with their wanderings, fusions, habitats, religions,
and cultures.

The related labor of archaeologists, anthropologists, and ethnologists may be described as essentially fact-finding; and the facts, when set forth by accredited scholars, could be and were accepted as true and above dispute. Differences did not arise till it came to the interpretation of the facts and this state of things, it should be observed at once, ran completely counter to Comte's positivist blue-print. According to Comte, fact-finding, divorced from hampering speculative procedure, would of itself lead to certain knowledge, that is, to a social science on an exact par with natural science. It was in the persuasion that this was the case that the devotees of the social *studies* gradually adopted for their pursuits the more high-sounding label of social *sciences;* and so enthusiastically received was their decision that the scientific designation before long covered and to this day continues to cover these studies in all our higher institutions of learning.

Under Comte's influence the social studies are elevated to social sciences

Nonetheless, applied to the social studies, the word science is a misnomer, unless it be agreed that science in reference to the world of nature means one thing and in reference to the world of man another. It cannot possibly mean the same thing in both worlds since natural science rests ultimately on objective, invariable mathematics, whereas social science in last resort rests on nothing more substantial than variable, subjective opinion. In short, the Comtean declaration that fact-finding alone will lead to demonstrably correct conclusions has been proved to be wrong. Therefore our social studies are still studies and not sciences, at least in the sense the word carries in the field of nature. But let not that circumstance be interpreted as the bankruptcy of fact-finding. Fact-finding, pursued with method and passion, has led to enormous accumulations of valid knowledge. Without them the great desideratum, scientifically precise conclusions about man and society, will remain forever unattainable. That they have not, at least up to the present, been attained is due to their manipulation by the evaluating judgment of the individual investigator. The decisive role of this human and unescapably fluctuating factor is revealed by an examination of the course followed by any one of the social studies in the century under review. Let us for purposes of illustration turn to political economy.

Why the social studies are not and probably never can become sciences

In the early nineteenth century there arose in England a school of economists who diligently gathered the facts touching the industrial transformation going on under their eyes and then proceeded, in the manner of the natural scientists, to reduce them to generalizations or "laws." Their work met with such broad acclaim that they were hailed as the "classical" school of political economy and their conclusions accepted as the "scientific" and therefore final word on the subject. However, toward the middle of the century, their work was challenged by a group of continental, chiefly German, economists. These men had no difficulty in

The reign of opinion in economics: the "classical" followed by the "national" school showing that the "classical" doctrine rested ultimately on a number of tacit presuppositions. These, treated as undebatable, self-evident truths, maintained in substance that the central concern of economics was the individual producer, and that to check his freedom of action by the regulatory interference of the state was to cut down production with calamitous consequences for the whole population.

The "classical" school a rationalization of middle-class supremacy

Now these continental economists were the products of nationalism and, as such, shaped their thinking by a set of suppositions running to the effect that the proper concern of economics was not the individual producer but the nation. It is for this reason that they are called the "national" school. They made clear that their "classical" predecessors were the conscious or unconscious spokesmen of the new industrial masters of the middle class, that they had conducted their fact-finding from this strictly partisan angle, and that their ringing conclusions or "laws" were nothing but a reasoned justification of the achieved domination in the economic field of the factory-owner and capitalist.

The "national" school a rationalization of the revived concern for the nation

While the criticism of the "national" school was effective and caused the "classical" school gradually to lose credit, the "national" school, too, was based on presuppositions as human and selective as those of their predecessors. Making the nation their supreme concern, instead of exclusively championing the industrial middle class they took into account also the nation's other constitutive groups, such as the landowners and the workers, and, conducting their fact-finding from this outlook, came to conclusions at considerable variance from those of the "classicists." Rejecting the demand for freedom from government regulation, they took the precisely opposite position and insisted on the right and duty of the state to intervene at every stage of the economic process in the interest of the nation as a whole. It will not escape the alert reader that the "national" school harked back to the mercantilism of the eighteenth century and to what was then and has since been called a policy of protection, whereas the individualist "classicist" school, which had come to birth as a violent reaction to mercantilism, was committed to free trade.

Marxism a rationalization of the prophesied triumph of the workers

Do these two hotly opposed systems look like "science"? A third school that came to the front in the second half of the century strongly denied it and at the same time put forth an economic doctrine for which it claimed the "scientific" character absent from its rivals. I am referring to the Marxists, whose system is expounded in Chapter 25. Suffice it at this point to bring out that Marxism was as definitely based on a debatable human presupposition as its two predecessors. This presupposition was that the concern of economics was not the industrial middle class, as with the "classical" school, nor the nation as with the "national" school, but the ever growing mass of the industrial workers.

By letting their fact-finding be guided by this norm the Marxists had no difficulty in assembling material enabling them to formulate such principles as economic determinism, the class conflict, and surplus value, by means of which they provided their system with its indispensable intellectual underpinning.

In the light of these fundamental and persisting disagreements among economic investigators, whose professional honesty is above challenge, we are permitted to insist that political economy has not yet achieved a "scientific" status. Nor by the same token has any other study concerned with man and society. In the interest of clear thinking it is therefore desirable to reject the claim, first, that fact-finding can of itself produce general propositions of a validity comparable with those of the natural sciences, and second, that the social studies, immensely enriched though they have been by minute and methodical research, have in the nineteenth or, for that matter, in the following twentieth century, truly won for themselves the rating of sciences.

The social studies still shaped by judgment or opinion

INTERNATIONAL RELATIONS

The contradiction, repeatedly treated in this book, between the common culture of Europe and the ferocious rivalry of its component states, was manifested in an exaggerated form in the nineteenth century. We have learned in the course of our long journey that at the beginning of the Modern Period the then existent sovereign states engaged in a struggle for power which did not reach beyond the boundaries of western Europe. Then, when the discoveries had disclosed colonial opportunities in Asia and in the Americas, the struggle was intensified, because the stakes of power had undergone a vast enlargement. The eighteenth century conflict between France and Great Britain, of which the prizes were North America and India, may serve to recall to the reader that the theater of European action at that time was no longer Europe, but all of the seas and most of the continents of our globe.

Intensification of the power struggle among the European states

The impact on this situation of the Industrial Revolution and all that the Industrial Revolution implied by way of multiplied goods and improved communications was bound to be extraordinary. Directing our attention first to communications, we note that the railway, the steamboat, the telegraph, and the telephone had the effect of contracting the earth and making the most distant continent more accessible to Europe than any single European country had been to its immediate neighbors in the days before these epochal inventions.

Nineteenth century communications annihilate distance

All European nations without distinction took immediate advantage of the new resources. Finding almost at once, however, that they were unable to derive full profit from improved communications confined within the narrow national boundaries, they were driven to make arrangements with their neighbors for the co-ordination of the new services. The gradual extension of these arrangements had the striking result of drawing the whole earth into an unbroken system of communications.

The first item of the new and practically directed internationalism to emerge was the Universal Telegraph Union (1875). It was followed by the Universal Postal Union (1878) and this by rapidly multiplying international agreements regarding the steamboat and the railway. By the last quarter of the nineteenth century communication by means of telegraph and post could be effected between even the most distant countries with a speed and a security of which the previous century had not so much as dreamed. At the same time men and goods could make a continuous passage by steamboat and railway around the earth under the guaranteed protection of the government of every country touched upon in the journey.

Thus, from the viewpoint of communications, the world had, in effect, become a co-operative commonwealth. And the spirit of co-operation was strengthened by many other agencies, for instance, by science. A scientific principle or practical invention put out in one country was immediately appropriated by all the others, making possible an even scientific advance all along the line. Welcoming this interdependence, the various groups of scientists founded international societies of physicists, chemists, anthropologists, historians, engineers, and so forth in order to exchange views and to organize the search for knowledge on a world-embracing plan.

As the rival governments of the European states took an active part in promoting the scientific contacts as well as the various communication agreements, it will not do to represent them as consistently hostile to international co-operation. However, when it came to the issue of power as represented by markets and colonial dependencies, they maintained their traditional selfish stand. The Industrial Revolution, which multiplied communications, also enormously multiplied articles of common use. As these machine-made products could be absorbed only in part by the inhabitants of the country which produced them, they had to be disposed of to other countries. This brought about a feverish search for markets, and, as the markets of subjected groups held the promise of better control, the industrialized countries entered on an intensified competition for colonies or, in lieu of colonies, for what came euphemistically to be called spheres of influence.

It was during the last quarter of the nineteenth century that competition among the European powers for markets and colonies entered on its most intensive phase. The word phase is carefully chosen, for in its origin the colonial movement, viewed as a whole, goes back to the Age of Discoveries. It had since its beginning passed through the several phases treated in this book in connection with the colonial expansion of the European states. The nineteenth century phase is, therefore, nothing more than the culminating stage of early colonialism. However, as it has a particular physiognomy, it has quite properly received a particular name. That name is imperialism. In Chapter 31 we showed how by the last quarter of the nineteenth century imperialism had become the main directive factor in the foreign policy of every great European power. The name given to the most recent form of this competition is imperialism

In consequence of their imperialist programs the European powers were moved to increase their armaments both on land and sea. Plainly, without a strong army and navy it was impossible to participate in the imperialist game. Competitive colonialism unescapably imposed competitive armaments. It therefore followed that whenever one power increased its army and navy or adopted a new and more efficient weapon of destruction, all the other powers were impelled to follow a similar course. We thus face this perplexing and contradictory situation: While science and improved communications were engaged in transforming the world into a co-operative commonwealth, imperialism and competitive armaments were having precisely the opposite effect and threatened almost from moment to moment to precipitate a conflict of world dimensions. Not only would such a conflict put an end to the co-operation so vigorously promoted by science and communications, but it might even prove so destructive as to bring down in ruin the whole edifice of Western civilization. Imperialism causes competition in armaments

The competing governments and peoples did not close their eyes to the risks they were running. In some instances the governments engaged in negotiations with each other for the peaceful adjustment of at least their minor political differences. They even took up by exchanges among their respective foreign offices the most immediately dangerous subject of armaments. They did not, however, succeed in reaching any agreements which may be said to have materially improved the situation. Peoples and governments aware of the dangers of imperialism

A hope seemed to dawn on Europe when, in answer to an invitation by Tsar Nicholas II, delegates from most of the countries of the world met (1899) at The Hague, in the Netherlands, to consider means for the preservation of the imperiled peace. The modest result of much discussion was the setting up at The Hague of a permanent court of arbitration, to which governments were urged (but not compelled) to submit their disputes. A second Hague conference held in 1907 got no farther than its predecessor. The two Hague conferences (1899, 1907) achieve little

The most pressing issues inviting the attention of a conference called

Reasons for
the failure
of the two
Hague
conferences
to promote world peace would necessarily be the reduction of armaments and the control of the nationalist-imperialist fury. No headway was made with either of these issues at the two Hague conferences. So long as each European state clung to its traditional sovereignty as its most precious possession, it would reject even the slightest curtailment of its authority in these fields. And so long as this frame of mind prevailed, Europe would remain exposed to the threat of war and to the concomitant threat of the destruction of its boasted civilization.

LITERATURE, THE FINE ARTS, AND MUSIC

The arts of
expression
have a small
but assured
place in this
history
So small has been the space given in this history to literature, the Fine Arts, and music that the thought may have occurred to some readers that these vast subjects might better not have been broached at all. In justification of his course the writer begs to refer to his purpose as stated in the first chapter. He there committed himself to a political history in a social-economic setting. But so definitely is politics (or government) itself a cultural activity that it cannot be entirely divorced from literature, the Fine Arts, and music (in their sum the arts of expression) without imparting a distorted view both of the nature of man and the nature of civilization. This book has therefore from the start pledged itself to call attention to the play of these arts. Our presentation has been and will remain lamentably meager. Nonetheless, an important service will have been rendered if the reader has at least had it brought home to him that man, whom he has chiefly studied in these pages as a political and social being, is also a creature imaginatively endowed and bent on giving expression to his aspirations by every available avenue of art.

Our pur-
pose no
more than
to indicate
ruling
trends
It accords with our limited purpose that in treating the literature and art of the earlier periods we have contented ourselves with indicating and illustrating a few significant trends. We shall pursue the same course in this chapter on the literary and artistic manifestations of the nineteenth century. However, as our procedure eliminates from consideration immense bodies of data which would have to be included in a detailed history of the several arts of expression, it will make for better understanding if we specify some of these deliberate omissions.

Each nation
boasts a
history of its
particular
literature
and art
Since Europe is an aggregate of nations, each with its own language and genius, each has been found by us to have its own literature, music, and art. The statement holds also, of course, for the nineteenth century which, as we know, was an intensely nationalist period. So distinct is the imprint which a particular nation puts on its artistic products that no sensitive spirit will confuse them with the creations of any other nation. It is therefore usual and even necessary to write separate histories

of English, French, Italian, and every other European literature. And the same practice is habitually followed in connection with the music and Fine Arts of the different national groups.

Lack of space, if there were no other reason, would preclude our undertaking the gigantic task of following the literary and artistic developments of each of the European nations. But there is another reason for not doing so, for we are committed by our past practice to the laying down of trends common to the expression of all the nations. In spite of manifest differences of expression traceable to national genius, there are also common trends because of a situation on which we have never ceased to insist. Although Europe is composed of many distinct nations, they have, from the early Middle Ages, moved forward and still continue at this day to move forward on the same broad cultural lines. Their differently flavored poetry, painting, and music have, therefore, a common denominator; and it is their common denominator which makes possible our summarizing procedure of indicating ruling trends. *The several national expressions reveal common trends*

Another striking omission will be esthetic discussion. All periods, but the nineteenth century more fervently than any of its predecessors, asked the question: What is the function of art in a civilized community? As employed in this question the word art designates the total product of the imagination and therefore signifies literature and music as well as painting and sculpture. Is the function of art in this sense to amuse? Is it to instruct? Is it to elevate? Again, is art an attempt to give a culture its highest and noblest expression? Or is it rather a means of escape from an actual world become unendurable into a dream world of order, serenity, and loveliness? While anybody can see at a glance that questions such as these raise issues of immense importance for this field, we shall resolutely leave them to one side as involving matter beyond our immediate plan. *Esthetic discussion not part of our plan*

The nineteenth century trends to which we shall call attention are three: a classical trend, a romantic trend, a realist trend. This is the chronological order in which the three trends appeared, although a certain overlapping, on the one hand, and the reappearance of a trend after disappearance, on the other hand, make it impossible to lay down exact dates. It will give us a foothold on rather uncertain ground if we agree that the romantic trend, which put in an appearance toward the end of the eighteenth century, reached its climax around 1830, and that it then yielded ground to realism, which achieved its greatest vogue around 1880. Classicism was the dominant trend of the seventeenth and eighteenth centuries and, although routed first by romanticism and then by realism, continued to make itself felt and to boast a following throughout the nineteenth century. *The three leading nineteenth century trends: classicism, romanticism, realism*

Before proceeding farther, a working definition of the three trends will

be in place. Classicism in the field of art signifies a conviction in favor
Working of order and form; it also implies submission to law and a severe self-
definitions discipline. Romanticism is a reaction against the order and rationality
of classi- of classicism in favor of a free or at least a freer reign of the emotions.
cism, ro- It wishes to replace the cool objectivity of classicism with subjective
manticism, warmth. Realism is a reaction against both romantic disorder and tra-
realism ditional classic form. It is substantially the modern scientific spirit projected into the world of art. The aim of realism is exact observation of
the inconspicuous details of existence to the end of building up by their
means the true or "real" picture of man and his universe. An alert mind
will have no difficulty in recognizing the political counterparts of these
trends. The political equivalent of classicism is conservatism; of romanticism and realism respectively, it is liberalism and the outspoken materialism of social democracy.

While, with an eye directed more particularly to literature, it is per-
Caution to mitted to speak of the twenties and thirties of the nineteenth century
be used in as "romantic" and of the seventies and eighties as "realist," the state-
applying ment should not be understood to mean that other and contrary influ-
our formula ences did not make themselves felt in the indicated decades. In litera-
of the three ture (and art in general) there are always laggards as well as precursors
trends bent on traveling an individual path. It should also be noted that the
prevalence in literature of a particular trend at a particular time is no
assurance of the dominance of that trend at exactly the same time in,
say, sculpture or music. These statements are here set down as warnings
against letting the artistic picture become oversimplified. We may, in a
preliminary survey such as this, insist on our three trends and on their
successive domination in the nineteenth century, but we must not apply
our formula too rigidly, for, if we do, it will be smashed to bits by the
irrepressible energy which operates in the arts and which is forever
bursting through the bounds set by the ordering intelligence.

With these precautions taken against misunderstanding, we shall fol-
Our theory low the rule of the successive trends in nineteenth century expression
of trends by a process of selection. No other course is open to us, since we have
to be illus- agreed that a presentation of the many separate national manifestations
trated by the of literature, music, and the Fine Arts is out of the question. Our plan,
method of which is purely illustrative, will be to follow the reign of trends in
selection European literature by means of English literature, the reign of trends
in European painting by means of French painting, and the reign of
trends in European music by means of German music. We shall pass
over sculpture entirely and treat architecture at the close as a special
case for reasons to be set forth at that time.

English Literature

In Chapter 19 we learned that the classical theory and practice embodied in the poetry of Dryden and Pope were gradually challenged until, at the very end of the eighteenth century, their vogue was definitely terminated by Wordsworth and Coleridge. The two young rebels objected to the subject matter and verse forms of the classical period and declared in favor of that freedom from restraint which, first preached eloquently by Rousseau, we commonly call romanticism. *Classicism yields to romanticism*

William Wordsworth (1770-1850) is a vastly important figure in the development of the poetic trends of the new century. He advanced the theory that the proper subject matter of poetry was the experience of simple country folk, and its proper style their unaffected vocabulary and syntax. At the same time he was a close observer of nature and embodied its many moods in his verse with a delicacy perhaps never before attained. The substance of Wordsworth's poetic contribution is therefore the exaltation of man and of nature, than which the democratic nineteenth century boasts no more characteristic themes. *The core of Wordsworth's poetic theory*

The leading figures of the next generation of poets were Byron, Shelley, and Keats. If romanticism is identified with rebellion against restraint, all three, and particularly Byron and Shelley, were vigorous romantics. Comparing them with Wordsworth, we become aware that romanticism is a very complex movement and presents a different facet with every separate practitioner. While Wordsworth rebelled against literary bondage, he was politically and socially, at least after the first flush of youth, a stubborn conservative. Lord Byron (1788-1824) and Shelley (1792-1822), on the other hand, found themselves so out of sympathy with the inherited institutions and conservative temper of their native land that they became voluntary exiles. A good part of the poetry of both deals with revolt, Byron's revolt taking the form of poetic epics and dramas of adventure, Shelley's expressing itself in dreams of a coming golden age (Byron: *Childe Harold, Don Juan;* Shelley: *Epipsychidion, To a Skylark*). *The romanticism of Byron and Shelley takes the form of revolt against government and society*

Concerned solely with defining the romantic protest of these poets, we are making no effort to set forth their many and diverse literary qualities. Nor shall we make that attempt with John Keats (1795-1821). We shall content ourselves with noting that by his delicate response to the sensuous overtones of words and by his flight from reality into the land of faëry he represented still another aspect of romanticism, which was the escape from time into eternity by self-intoxication (*Ode to a Nightingale, La Belle Dame Sans Merci*). *The romanticism of Keats is self-intoxication*

The leading contribution made to romantic prose at the beginning of the nineteenth century was the succession of Waverley Novels by Sir Walter Scott (1771-1832). There was nothing distinctly rebellious about Scott either from a political or a literary angle. From his boyhood he was fascinated by the past—above all, by the Middle Ages of his own Scotland; and he brought the past back to life, first in a series of poetic ballads, and afterward in novels of love and adventure that took Britain and all Europe by storm. But if he was not rebellious, he was romantic, and his romanticism consisted in breaking down the disdain which the preceding rationalist age entertained for the "superstition" and "barbarousness" of the earlier epochs and particularly of the Middle Ages. His broad, kindly humanity popularized a sympathetic approach to all peoples who at any time have lived and struggled on our earth.

The Waverley Novels are a romantic excursion into history

Meanwhile the Industrial Revolution was transforming England and bringing pressing social problems to the front; above all, the problems associated with the misery of the exploited workers. Unnoticed by the Wordsworth-Scott generation of writers, they at last forced themselves on the attention of authors and produced a less dream-shot and more realistic literary attitude.

Rise of social problems

Evidence of a more immediate contact with life is supplied by the turn the novel took in the hands of Charles Dickens (1812-1870). While his humanitarian and reformist zeal spring from a well of strong romantic feeling, his delight in character, especially in the aspects of the lower classes, reveals that he is pleased with his fellow men for their own sake and moved to present them realistically, that is, exactly as he finds them (*Oliver Twist, Dombey and Son, David Copperfield*).

Dickens: humanitarian, romanticist, realist

No less humanitarian than Dickens and a much more accurate observer of the effect of the new machine industry on her countrymen was George Eliot (1819-1880), pen name of a woman, Mary Ann Evans. Such novels of hers as *Silas Marner, Adam Bede, The Mill on the Floss,* prove how dangerous the simple labeling of a writer as either romantic or realist may be. It is plain that the work of George Eliot, while painstakingly close to the facts, is steeped in that emotional glow which is the very essence of romance.

George Eliot, the sympathetic, close observer of the small facts of life

A third writer of this period, Thackeray (1811-1863), who dealt with the upper middle class in his novels (*Vanity Fair, Pendennis, The Newcomes*) is a social observer relatively unaffected by romantic attitudes and reformist zeal. His cool intellectualism pushed him into the practice of combining precise observation with satirical reflection. He thus achieved the double eminence of a creative artist and of a satirist related to the manner and outlook of the great Swift.

Thackeray, portraitist and satirist of the middle classes

More directly than from Swift, however, Thackeray stems from another eighteenth century writer—from Fielding, author of that earliest novel based on exact observation of English life, *Tom Jones*. Fielding and his work should serve to admonish us not to take our three basic trends too seriously. For, if the author of *Tom Jones* could write his realist novel at the height of the reign of classicism, we must be prepared to admit that some individuals always manage to escape being captured by dominant trends. The continuous stream of English literary realism

An even more startling instance of this escape is the novelist, Jane Austen (1775-1817), who with unrivaled skill unfolded a realist picture of life among the English gentry at the precise time when the country was passing, bag and baggage, into the romantic camp (*Pride and Prejudice, Sense and Sensibility*). The realist, Jane Austen

The second half of the nineteenth century fell intellectually under the spell of science and the doctrine of evolution, and this state of affairs was reflected in the novels of George Meredith (1828-1909) and Thomas Hardy (1840-1928). Their interpretation of the science to which they both render homage sets them at opposite poles to each other. Meredith is the optimist who believes that evolution points to the increase of human intelligence and that intelligence or "brain" will ultimately save the race (*Diana of the Crossways, The Egoist, Lord Ormont and His Aminta*). For Hardy, on the other hand, man dwelling in a mechanical universe under inalterable law is the utterly helpless victim of blind forces, of which his intelligence serves merely to make him tragically aware (*Tess of the D'Urbervilles, The Return of the Native*). Meredith found his material in the ruling classes; Hardy found his among the country people. Each proved an accurate observer and brilliant psychologist within his chosen social range. The doctrine of evolution and the literary worlds of Meredith and Hardy

The two leading poets of the second half of the century were Alfred Tennyson (1809-1892) and Robert Browning (1812-1889). Tennyson was content, in the main, to dwell in the romantic world fashioned by his immediate predecessors. He lived interchangeably in fairyland and in the Middle Ages (*Idylls of the King, Maud*). Browning was a vigorous individualist with a Renaissance zest for life. Consequently his verse breathes an optimism contrasting sharply with the lilting melancholy of much of Tennyson and of the other dedicated romantics (*Dramatis Personae, The Ring and the Book*). Tennyson and Browning

In the last decade of the century all the earlier literary tendencies seemed for a moment to converge, while a few new and disconcerting fashions came to sensational expression. Among these was a movement of esthetic withdrawal from the rude actualities that propagandized itself under the slogan, Art for art's sake. Perhaps its leading representative was Oscar Wilde (1856-1900). Many people alive at the time interpreted the dominant eclecticism to mean bewilderment and decadence. The last decade a period of eclecticism

Refusing to echo this judgment, let us use the eclectic last decade of the nineteenth century once more to issue a warning against a too literal application of our formula of trends. While the formula is useful, it is

The three trends eternally recurrent

well to remember that in a sense classicism, romanticism, and realism are always with us. This is true for the simple reason that they conform to types of thought and feeling to which men are at all times naturally disposed.

French Painting

Toward the end of the eighteenth century French painting reflected

The rococo style replaced by a sober classicism

the change in French life from the gaiety and frivolity of a carefree court and aristocracy to the seriousness and sobriety of a bourgeoisie preparing to inaugurate a political and social revolution. The result was the replacement of the light, graceful, animated rococo style by a revived, a "pure" classicism of dignified bearing and cool, neutral color.

The leading representative of this neo-classicism was Jacques Louis

David, representative of classicism

David (1748-1825). It is an interesting biographical detail that, although politically David shared in all the emotional extravagance of the extreme democrats, for he was a member of the revolutionary Mountain party, so far as his art is concerned he never departed from a disciplined classical creed and practiced it unchanged under four successive governments.

However, the greatest painter of the neo-classical dispensation, and a

Ingres, the greatest of the classicists

great painter by the standard of any age, was Ingres (1780-1867). Since the classicist faith centered on form, Ingres aimed at good drawing, achieving an excellence in this field which has rarely been equaled. In his opinion and in that of the classicists in general, color was subsidiary to form, and he used it, as can be readily seen in all his work, for no other purpose than to clarify his form.

So firmly established in the realm of painting was the classical sense

Delacroix, champion of romanticism

of restraint that romanticism with its emotional impulses was long held at bay. Bound, however, in the long run to assert itself, it came to triumphant expression in Delacroix (1798-1863). At once, form yielded its ascendancy to color, classical themes were replaced by medieval themes, and remote and exotic subject matter, such as African lion-hunts, came within the purview of the artist. Delacroix took delight in large canvases with many figures in deep perspective, bound into a whole by tumultuous swirls of color (e.g., his "Entrance of the Crusaders into Constantinople"). Such blazing energy naturally drew the young generation within its orbit.

At the side of Delacroix, who was chiefly a figure painter, there sprang

Corot and the romantic landscape painters of the Barbizon school

up a romantic school of landscape painters. This was an inevitable consequence of the nature worship of the romantic period. At the head of the landscape group we may put Corot (1796-1875), who with his attendant band constitutes the Barbizon school (so-called from the village of Barbizon, in the forest of Fontainebleau, where they congregated).

While Corot was a close and accurate student of nature, his romantic feeling prompted him, above all, to set forth the brooding mystery of forest, field, and water. (See "Just before Sunrise," opp. p. 685.) All the members of the Barbizon school may be thought of as having been poets as well as painters; and exactly as in the case of poets, especially of romantic poets, their sentiment not infrequently degenerates into simpering sentimentality.

It was a sign of the healthy condition of painting in France that individual rebels never ceased to rise against whatever manner happened to be in the ascendancy. The history of French painting is largely the story of these rebels, men like Courbet, Daumier, and Manet. Each made his influence felt against the ruling style, whether it was classicism or romanticism. However, as we cannot enter into the work of all, we shall select one of them for consideration, Renoir (1841-1919), than whom no one painter commanded a bolder vision nor won and retained a wider following.

The long and able line of rebel painters

What distinguished Renoir was the determination to see the life of his time as it was with the directness of a democrat and the precision of a scientist. Son of an age over which science and democracy reigned, he felt classicism to be an outmoded pose and romanticism a reprehensible softness. The business of the painter, according to him, was a cool, objective observation of man and nature in order to record them as nearly as possible as they actually were.

Renoir and his realist creed

We may therefore hail Renoir as a modern scientific realist. He took his subjects exactly as he found them, in or out of doors, in sunshine or shadow, and presented them in a composition, which, although always carefully calculated, seemed to the observer to be as casual as life itself. As at the same time he was interested in the problem of light, he adopted the technique that had been invented to render the intensity and vibration of light and which is known as impressionism. (See "Luncheon of the Boating Party," opp. p. 685.)

Renoir, the impressionist

While impressionism may be identified as realism, it is more particularly a technique invented during the ascendancy of realism and employed by most of the realists in the last two decades of the nineteenth century. Impressionism probably resulted from the vogue of science after the middle of the nineteenth century and is not the invention of a single individual. As it happened, the attention of painters had swung to the problem of light, which the science of optics informed them was a fusion of the seven primary colors visible in the spectrum. Accordingly, they developed a method of covering their canvas with innumerable small dabs of primary color placed side by side. These variously tinted dabs were all that appeared to the observer at close range, but if he retired across the room, they took on the shape of tree or house or animal, not

Impressionism a technique for reproducing the intensity and vibration of light over-distinct, it is true, but steeped by way of compensation in a shimmering aura of translucent sunshine.

Monet and the landscape of impressionism

While Renoir was an impressionist figure painter and while many other impressionist figure painters could be named, impressionism will always be associated with landscape, for which it seemed to be particularly adapted. Among the notable impressionists who specialized in landscape, Claude Monet (1840-1926) is probably the most famous. Drawn, like the whole generation of scientific realists, to the problem of light, he became aware that the appearance of objects in nature changes every moment in measure as the light shifts. He would therefore go out at sunrise with a dozen canvases in order to paint the same subject in the altered aspect it presented with each new hour. There resulted twelve sketches, that is to say, twelve fleeting impressions (whence the name of the school) of, say, a field of wheat bathed in light and air. The wheat field was unimportant, the light and air everything. And if Monet painted a railway station or Westminster Abbey, it was the same story. There was no structure or design in his painting, after the manner traditional to the art. There was just an impression communicated in a momentary flash, quick as a dagger thrust.

Triumph and decline of impressionism

By the close of the century the painters in every country of the occident had taken over the method of the French impressionists. Never was there a more sweeping triumph. Then, with the twentieth century a violent reaction against impressionism took place, and painting rediscovered some old and at the same time invented many new ways of expression.

German Music

Beethoven, the fountainhead of nineteenth century music

Nineteenth century German and, for that matter, European music has its source in Beethoven (1770-1827). To the objective classical tradition in which he was reared Beethoven remained steadily devoted, even though he transfused it with the subjective range of feeling he shared with the romanticism of his day. While his always nobly conceived compositions are distributed among all the leading musical forms, such as sonatas, concertos, and masses, he reached his greatest height in his immortal nine orchestral symphonies. In these he measures all the heights and depths of the emotions without ever surrendering that restraint which stamps a work of art as classic.

The triumph of romanticism

The generation of composers after Beethoven so wholeheartedly yielded to the subjective and emotional elements implicit in the romantic movement that they are its unambiguous and hallmarked product. Among them we may name Schubert, Weber, and Schumann.

Haunted by an inexhaustible flow of melody, Schubert (1797-1828) produced a body of romantic songs which won for him a lyric crown no

THE UPRISING. By the French artist, Daumier (d. 1879). A notable expression of the revolutionary undercurrent of the nineteenth century. (Courtesy of Phillips Memorial Gallery)

THE THIRD-CLASS RAILWAY CARRIAGE. By Daumier. In the democratic nineteenth century the common people became a favorite theme of art. (Culver Service)

JUST BEFORE SUNRISE. By the romantic landscape painter, the Frenchman, Corot (d. 1875). (Courtesy of Chicago Art Institute)

LUNCHEON OF THE BOATING PARTY. By the French impressionist painter, Renoir (d. 1919). (Phillips Memorial Gallery)

succeeding song-writer has ever taken from him. The most important single contribution of Weber (1786-1826) was an opera, *Der Freischütz,* for which, following the nationalist trend characteristic of romanticism, he utilized German legend and German musical themes. Both Schubert and Weber have a national flavor not to be found in the more objective and universal music of the eighteenth century.

Schumann (1810-1856) illustrates the perils of romantic art. He is the master of delicate shades of sentiment, but under the stress of feeling his form tends to become brittle and fall to pieces.

Romantic music reached its apogee in Richard Wagner (1813-1883). He directed his extraordinary talents to a form of opera he called the music drama, for which with an unusual endowment of diverse gifts he wrote both libretto and music. His choice for his music dramas (*Lohengrin, Tannhäuser, Die Meistersinger, Der Ring des Niebelungen*) of German subject matter indicates his romantic orientation, which is, however, chiefly and overwhelmingly disclosed by his exaltation of the human passions and his vehement expression of them.

Aspiring to a fullness of utterance not reached by any of his predecessors and, let us add, not desired by them, Wagner became a musical innovator and revolutionary. His innovations are particularly apparent in the orchestra. He greatly enlarged the part assigned to the brasses and wood-winds, thereby achieving a volume of sound and a range of tonal color which, according to their temperament and training, delighted or offended his contemporaries. In the end more listeners were delighted than offended, with the result that, if Wagner's music dramas produced no progeny and constitute a unique performance, the multiplied expressivenessness of his orchestra has been taken over so generally that, on its formal side, music has down to our day been strongly under Wagnerian influence.

The emotional and instrumental excess associated with Wagner was, as already said, not to everyone's taste. But until Brahms (1833-1897) appeared, there was no one to lead an effective reaction against Wagner. Brahms illustrates the point repeatedly made that no one trend will at any time be found in sole command of a given field of art. With his solidly constructed compositions Brahms harks back to Beethoven and, like his great exemplar, he has to his credit a majestic roster of sonatas, concertos, requiems, and four incomparable symphonies. However, a master in his own right, Brahms is not just a classical traditionalist. Whatever was serviceable in the compositions of his day he added to his stock of knowledge, not scorning to learn even from Wagner, his romantic antipode, something of the technique that made the Wagnerian orchestra such a responsive and sonorous instrument. But Brahms had

Schubert, Weber

Schumann

Romantic music culminates in Richard Wagner

The increased volume and range of Wagner's orchestra

Brahms sustains the classical tradition

also a romantic vein, as is most apparent in his *Lieder,* which are unsurpassed unless it be by those of the song-intoxicated Schubert.

Music becomes experimental

Toward the close of the century a protest began to make itself felt against both classical and romantic music. There followed an era of experimentation, during which music took the many different and often confusing paths that mark its latest, its twentieth century phase.

Western Architecture

Continued domination of classical principles of construction

Ever since the revival of classical architecture in the fifteenth and sixteenth centuries, the builder's art throughout Europe had been governed by classical principles. The result was, happily, not a static classicism of a single type. The classical principles were broad enough to permit variety in application and, as we have learned, Italian forms were succeeded by French forms, the heavy monumental baroque by the graceful agitated rococo.

Reasons for the ruling conservation

The vogue of classicism in its several developments continued almost undisturbed throughout the nineteenth century. The explanation of this conservatism, at first blush surprising for a period characterized by revolutionary changes in so many other fields, would seem to be that the classical principles are simple and rational, and that the structures, chiefly of a public character, raised in accordance with these principles, adequately met the need which they were called upon to satisfy.

Romanticism produces a reign of eclecticism

Nonetheless, the coming of romanticism did not leave the situation unaffected. The romantic passion for the Middle Ages produced in some areas, chiefly of northern Europe but also in the United States, a Gothic revival, which reached its height about the middle of the nineteenth century. As the Gothic revival was indicative of a renewed regard for the past, there was no reason why, prompted by the widened cultural sympathies inherent in the romantic spirit, nineteenth century architects should not assimilate also the Romanesque, Byzantine, Egyptian, Chinese, and Moorish forms of construction. This they actually did with the result that in the last quarter of the nineteenth century there was a reign of architectural eclecticism which is without parallel in the history of mankind. In spite of this maddening confusion, classicism retained a general ascendancy, thereby proving that its roots were sunk deep in western consciousness.

Classicism and eclecticism superseded

Not till the turn of the century did a movement appear in favor of making an entirely new start by the development of architectural principles expressive of the new age and its vast mechanical resources. Then only was eclecticism challenged and the long reign of classicism terminated. That story, however, in which the United States for the first time plays an important role, belongs to the twentieth century.

Section V

Revolution and Democracy (*Continued*)

2. AGE OF THE WORLD WARS

34 THE DIPLOMATIC PRELUDE TO WORLD WAR I: TRIPLE ALLIANCE AND TRIPLE ENTENTE

BISMARCK'S LEAGUE OF THE THREE EMPERORS

WE ARE NOW prepared to undertake a systematic account of European foreign policy in order to show how, motivated by a nationalism and an imperialism becoming ever more frenzied, it issued in the catastrophe of World War I. As our starting-point we may choose the situation resulting from the Franco-German War of 1870-1871. The newly created German empire replaced France as the leading continental power. For the time being at least its prestige was immense and all its neighbors awaited with anxiety the unfolding of its foreign policy.

The emergence (1871) of the German empire creates a new situation

The official ruler of the new Germany was Emperor William I. Such, however, was the authority enjoyed by his chancellor, Prince Bismarck, owing to his having been the successful architect of German unity, that he exercised an undisputed sway over German foreign and, for that matter, over German domestic affairs as well. Bismarck was not long in disclosing his hand. He believed that his country, more than all else, needed time to recover from the upheaval connected with the unification process and that the necessary preliminary to a healthy consolidation of the German empire was a long peace.

Bismarck, in control of German foreign policy, desires peace

The only probable immediate disturber of the peace was France which, as much because of the bare fact of its defeat as because of its loss of Alsace-Lorraine, nursed the sentiment of revenge. Bismarck, therefore, applied all his skill to bring about the diplomatic isolation of his western neighbor. His thought was that France would prove dangerous only in case she succeeded in finding a helper, an ally.

Bismarck tries to isolate France

With regard to Great Britain the circumspect chancellor was at ease because the island-power was at that time holding aloof from continental affairs on the assumption that its interests lay wholly outside of Europe. It maintained what was currently called "a splendid isolation." Italy, too, Bismarck could dismiss from the reckoning because Italy was relatively weak and, besides, did not border on Germany. He fixed his attention on Russia and Austria-Hungary. Only in case France won the close friend-

Bismarck regards Russia and Austria-Hungary as the only likely allies of France

ship of either of them would she care to risk a war with her Rhenish neighbor.

His plan

With this situation in mind Bismarck set to work to attach both Russia and Austria-Hungary to Germany. He succeeded so well that in 1872 the rulers of the three empires met and in the following year signed an agreement, called the League of the Three Emperors, in which they promised to work for peace and, if war threatened, to take counsel together "to determine a common course of action."

The League of the Three Emperors runs into a snag (1875)

However, an agreement yoking together Austria and Russia was of a precarious nature and almost certain to go by the boards the moment the Turkish question was mooted between them. Both states had for generations entertained, with regard to the Ottoman empire, ambitious and conflicting projects which, though often adjourned because of the pressure of other interests, had an uncomfortable habit of making a periodical reappearance. In 1875 there was precipitated the Bosnian crisis, of which we have heard. At once it aligned Russia and Austria-Hungary on opposite sides. And when, in 1877, Russia went to war with the Ottoman empire, the Hapsburg government looked on with a disapproval which was promptly converted to alarm when Russia won a brilliant victory and imposed on the sultan the Peace of San Stefano.

Checkmated at the Congress of Berlin (1878), Russia sulks

Since Great Britain took the Russian successes even more to heart than Austria, the two aggrieved governments by acting together were able to force the tsar to a revision of his San Stefano treaty at a congress held at Berlin (1878). Russia, getting less than she considered her just due, was outraged, blamed her mid-European friends, Germany as well as Austria, for her discomfiture, and grumblingly withdrew from cooperation with them.

End of the Three Emperors' League

To be sure, three years later, in 1881, Russia became alarmed at her isolation and renewed the Three Emperors' League. However, it never again achieved a genuine heartiness and in 1887 was permitted to expire. For three years more Bismarck tied Germany alone to Russia by a slender treaty thread, the so-called Reinsurance treaty. Therein he bound himself not to support Austria, should that power launch an attack against Russia. On his dismissal from office in 1890 this thread, too, snapped abruptly. Germany and Russia as well as Austria and Russia had severed company.

CREATION OF THE TRIPLE ALLIANCE

The German-Austrian alliance of 1879

In view of the fact that, on the heels of the Congress of Berlin, Russia and Austria seemed to have become hopelessly estranged, the Iron Chancellor took in 1879 a momentous step. He concluded an alliance between Germany and Austria of a strictly defensive character. By its terms each party was to aid the other in case it was attacked by Russia.

Two years later occurred an incident destined to bring an important accession to the Austro-German partnership: France and Italy engaged in a diplomatic clash over the Mediterranean. France, already in possession of Algeria, in 1881 seized Tunis, nominally an Ottoman province, though really an independent state. Having herself cast a covetous eye on Tunis, Italy resented the French action but was too weak to venture on an appeal to arms. However, so great was the indignation of Italy that her government turned to Germany for support. As Bismarck would not hear of a treaty with Italy which did not include Austria, there was concluded in 1882 the Triple alliance of the three central European powers. Italy joins the German-Austrian alliance

The Triple alliance was subject to renewal at five-year intervals. It was defensive in character, which means that it did not become effective till an attack had been launched on one of the three contracting parties. In reasonably plain language it indicated Russia and France as possible disturbers of the peace and therefore operated to draw these two malcontents together. Defensive character of the Triple alliance

THE FRANCO-RUSSIAN DUAL ALLIANCE CULMINATES IN THE TRIPLE ENTENTE

Radically dissimilar in political organization, the absolute monarchy of the tsar and the democratic French republic hesitated a long time before joining hands and fortunes. Finally, in 1890, they entered on negotiations which by 1894 had ripened into a military convention with the usual obligations of a defensive alliance. The Franco-Russian alliance (1894)

Thus, before the close of the century Europe fell into the two opposed camps of the Triple and Dual alliances, which maintained a delicate and perilous balance of power, with Great Britain swinging between them in the role of a wandering comet attached to neither system. The Triple and the Dual alliance

The British governments of the time, Conservative and Liberal alike, held the view that the two alliances dividing Europe had crystallized over purely continental matters which interested Great Britain remotely, if at all, since she was a colonial power pursuing objects lying beyond the confines of Europe. Hence the "splendid isolation," which became a confirmed item of her policy. However, granting that the two alliances were immediately concerned with problems pertaining to Europe, the five powers involved had alike embarked on a policy of expansion or imperialism. Consequently, whenever any one of them launched a forward movement in Africa or Asia or the Balkan peninsula, it very naturally turned for support to its allies, since it was sure to meet with nothing but ill-will from its rivals. Thus imperceptibly the two systems extended their influence till they took in the whole world. Theory on which Britain maintained a "splendid isolation"

Britain
disturbed by
the Russian
expansion
into China
Presently Great Britain discovered that her isolation was injurious to the overseas interests which she had mainly at heart. She was particularly disturbed by Russia, which in the nineties, following her discomfiture in the Balkan peninsula, had directed her surplus energies toward Asia and, more especially, toward China. Around 1900 it seemed that the tsar might eventually absorb Manchuria and acquire a dominating position at Peking. Anxiously considering this danger, the London cabinet at last resolved to back Japan as the state even more deeply concerned than Great Britain in blocking the Russian advance.

The Anglo-
Japanese
alliance
of 1902
In 1902 Great Britain and Japan signed an alliance. It did not promise Japan help in case the mikado came to blows with the tsar; but it did affirm that the moment a European power came to the aid of Russia Great Britain would take the side of Japan. We have noted elsewhere how under these circumstances Japan was encouraged to meet the Russian challenge and by defeating Russia in 1904-1905 ended, at least for the time being, the Russian threat.

Britain seeks
to check
Russia by an
agreement
with Ger-
many
Even before Great Britain was made more secure in the waters of the Pacific by the Japanese alliance, she had resolved to terminate her isolation on the continent of Europe and to this end keenly scanned the situation. Since she regarded Russia as her leading competitor, she quite naturally turned, first of all, to Russia's European neighbor, to Germany. On more than one occasion she suggested to the German foreign office that the two countries come to an agreement. Some ten years had passed since Bismarck had been dismissed from the chancellorship and the direction of German policy had become the jealously guarded prerogative of Emperor William II and his advisers. They met the British proposal with the counter-demand that Great Britain become a party to the Triple alliance. As the British did not wish to assume the peculiarly continental responsibilities of this combination, the negotiations were broken off.

Britain
concludes an
entente with
France, 1904
Rebuffed by Germany, Great Britain turned to France and in 1904 signed a treaty with that government. It was not an alliance but an understanding of the kind diplomacy designates with the French word, entente. The purpose of the treaty was to remove all immediate grounds of misunderstanding between London and Paris. Accordingly, its articles regulated certain disputes of long standing touching Newfoundland, Madagascar, and Siam. But the core of the document dealt with northern Africa. Ever since 1882 the British had occupied Egypt to the disappointment and disgust of the French, who had long coveted the Nile basin for themselves. The republic now promised to end its complaints, in fact to leave Egypt wholly in British hands, provided the British in return acknowledged the special interests of France in Morocco. In sum, Britain pledged support of the French project to acquire Morocco.

COUNT CAVOUR. After an engraving.
(Culver Service)

GIUSEPPE GARIBALDI.
(Bettmann Collection)

PRINCE BISMARCK. After a painting by Lenbach. (Bettmann Collection)

GENERAL VON MOLTKE. After a painting by Lenbach. (Bettmann Collection)

Morocco was an independent state inhabited by warlike Mohammedan tribes. Its independence did not hinder the two contracting powers from disposing of it in a manner corresponding to their interest. More important to them than its independence was its "backwardness," which sufficed to qualify it as a proper meal for the imperialist appetite.

Morocco an independent state

Let us repeat that the treaty of 1904 was not an alliance but an understanding which aimed at settling the numerous disputes existing between Great Britain and France. But Germany inevitably looked upon the new arrangement with concern. The situation was further complicated by the flamboyant personality of Emperor William II. Though his private aim, like that of every other ruler, was peace, his public speeches often created the opposite impression. Indubitably his self-esteem and instability projected an intangible element of nervousness into the European situation.

William II projects his impetuous personality into the situation

At about this time, too, the Germans began to build a navy. In 1898 the Reichstag passed the first Navy Bill. Two years later it was followed by a second Navy Bill, which provided for an ambitious building program covering more than a ten-year period. Thus Germany belatedly but vigorously made a bid for sea-power.

Germany develops a navy

Sea-power was sought and possessed in varying degree by every imperialist state. However, Great Britain had long specialized in this department and owed to it the unchallenged control of the waters of the earth. Though it was permissible in British eyes for Germany to have a navy, it was not permissible to have a strong navy, a navy which might eventually prove a danger to the traditional British ascendancy. In measure as the German navy grew, the British increased their own war fleet but were deeply irritated on account of the heavy financial burden put upon them.

Ill-will caused in Britain by Germany's naval program

The effect of the naval competition engaged in by Britain and Germany was to create an atmosphere of suspicion and ill-will in both countries. By the beginning of the twentieth century this murky atmosphere had found permanent lodgment in the two foreign offices. It was in all probability the decisive factor in frustrating the efforts made at that very time by the better disposed elements of the two governments to come to an understanding.

The German navy divides Britain and Germany

The announcement of the Anglo-French entente of 1904 made the situation more acute as between Germany and both her western neighbors. Moreover, France had put herself technically in the wrong by failing to observe the usual courtesy of communicating the treaty to Berlin. A great colonial prize—Morocco—was attributed to France and Germany was supposed to have nothing to say in the matter.

Germany irritated by the disposal (1904) of Morocco

With the purpose of forcing France into the path of negotiations the kaiser ostentatiously paid a visit to the sultan of Morocco in March, 1905, and assured that potentate of his interest in his continued independence. The demonstration produced a crisis which shook Europe to its depths. The upshot was that a conference of the powers, held at Algeciras in Spain in January, 1906, debated the Morocco problem.

The conference affirmed the sovereign status of the sultan, but at the same time declared that France had special interests in his dominions. Precisely this was the thesis of the French diplomats, who had invented it for no other reason than to effect thereby a gradual penetration of the country of the Moors. Germany was defeated at Algeciras because Great Britain had stood by France and, without adding a word to the treaty of 1904, had given to the entente the character of an alliance.

William II sulked and twice (in 1908 and 1911) reopened the question. On both occasions the Franco-British front remained unbroken. The successive crises were at length brought to an end when France reluctantly declared (1912) her readiness to offer Germany territorial compensation in the region of the French Congo. However—and this is the main point to be noted—the victory in this disturbing conflict fell to France. Casting to the winds all further hypocritical pretense touching the continued independence of Morocco, she now (1912) added it, except for a northern coastal strip assigned to Spain, to her African empire.

As soon as France and Great Britain had begun to co-operate diplomatically, the French cabinet did its best to promote better relations between Great Britain and Russia. Why should not an amicable arrangement dispose of the abundant inflammable matter heaped up between the two powers, one the ally, the other the friend of France? Under gentle pressure from Paris the Russian and British governments gradually drew together; and although there were some issues between them which resisted adjudication, they did in 1907 come to terms at least over their conflicting interests in central Asia.

The most important articles of the Anglo-Russian treaty of that year referred to Persia, which both powers had in the past attempted to draw within their respective spheres of influence. Persia was, like Morocco, free and independent but "backward." Again, like Morocco, it was a Moslem community; indeed its Mohammedanism was the essence of its backwardness. In substance Great Britain and Russia partitioned Persia, Russia being assigned the northern section, Great Britain the southern. A central area they left, for the present at least, to its legal ruler, the shah.

We note again that the treaty of 1907 was in form no more than an entente; but it had the effect of drawing France, Great Britain, and Russia into a diplomatic partnership. The partnership became known as the Triple entente and from the moment of its creation operated as a counterweight to the Triple alliance of Germany, Austria, and Italy.

In this manner were the six European powers split into two hostile, armed camps. Rarely after 1907 did they look upon a diplomatic incident which might arise as the occasion for a friendly exchange of views. Rather did each of the opposed groups seize upon the novel event as a welcome occasion for the display of temper and the assertion of prestige.

Europe split into two opposed camps

GERMANY, THE OTTOMAN EMPIRE, AND THE BALKAN PENINSULA

Germany's failure to participate in the appropriation effected among Russia, France, and Great Britain of such valuable properties as Egypt, Morocco, and Persia prompted her to increased activity in the direction of the one "backward" territory which seemed reasonably accessible to her, the Ottoman empire. Her impotence, revealed at Algeciras, was due to the circumstance that she could not make her influence felt across the seas against the will and pleasure of Great Britain. Britannia, who ruled the ocean, made Germany poignantly aware that she was a land power. On land, however, she carried indubitable weight. In view of this situation the Berlin government determined to concentrate its expansionist energies more narrowly on the Ottoman empire, the only "backward" area in all the world which, with the aid of its ally, Austria-Hungary, was accessible by the land-route.

Reasons why German attention swung to the Ottoman empire

If the Ottoman empire was an opportunity, it was an opportunity beset with many perils. Let us once more recall the stages of Ottoman decay. When, in the seventeenth century, the realm of the sultan first manifested its feebleness, it was its immediate neighbors, Austria and Russia, who took advantage of the situation. Each pushed forward along the line of least resistance, Austria by the course of the Danube and its tributaries, Russia by following the coast of the Black sea.

Stages of the appropriation of Turkey: Austria and Russia

Then in the nineteenth century France and Great Britain, both of them Mediterranean powers, showed an interest in the north-African provinces of Turkey. These, owing to the feeble grip of Constantinople, had already effectively become independent. In 1830 France landed in Algeria and began the conquest of that province destined to serve as the nucleus of a vast African dominion. In 1881 France rounded off Algeria to the east by seizing Tunis. The very next year, in 1882, Great Britain occupied Egypt, still nominally a part of the Ottoman state although practically independent under a native ruler, the khedive.

France and Britain appropriate the north-African territories of Turkey

In this way four great powers engaged in driving entering wedges into the Turkish mass until it looked as if its final division among the four expectant heirs would not be long delayed. Indeed Russia, the most impatient of the group, repeatedly broached the issue of partition. But as she invariably indicated that she regarded Constantinople and the

The Russian proposals of partition regularly rejected

straits as her proper share, the rest drew back, unwilling to see the empire of the tsar establish itself at this highly strategical point.

In consequence of this refusal Russia more than once (the Crimean War of 1854-1856; the War of 1877-1878) angrily took matters into her own hands, only to be cheated of her prize, not by the defensive strength of Turkey, but by the action of the European states. By the Treaty of Paris of 1856 as well as by the Treaty of Berlin of 1878 they reaffirmed the closing of the straits (the Bosporus and Dardanelles) to the warships of all the powers. In spite of its equalitarian ring, the closure was decreed solely because it operated as the most efficacious means of checkmating the Russian designs. It worked out in this way because the moment the tsar should venture to force the sea passage at Constantinople, he would be breaking international law and drawing the fire of united Europe.

Chief obstacle to the Russian advance on Constantinople the closing of the straits to her warships

We may agree that what chiefly retarded the carving up of the Ottoman empire in the second half of the nineteenth century was the mutual jealousies of the guests assembled for the feast, coupled with their resolution that the hungriest of their number, the tsar, was not to have the portion on which he had set his heart. Meanwhile another factor had arisen to complicate the situation. In the Balkan peninsula the subject nationalities had also become aware of the sultan's weakness and had rebelled against his rule. We have recounted how by gradual stages they emancipated themselves from Moslem tutelage and won their freedom. Before long they made it clear that they would not rest content till they had driven the sultan from all the Balkan provinces which he still held.

The Balkan states enter the game

The Balkan provinces remaining in the sultan's hands after the Congress of Berlin and coveted by his small Christian neighbors were, in the main, three, Albania, Bosnia, and Macedonia; and each offered a problem of its own. Albania, the land of the oldest of the Balkan peoples, was inhabited by contentious mountain clans so backward in civilization that it was doubtful whether they could ever be brought to establish an effective union. Albania seemed therefore fairly to invite seizure by its more advanced neighbors.

The three objectives of the Balkan states: (1) Albania

Bosnia, a territory inhabited by Serbs, had by a fateful decision of the Congress of Berlin (1878) been given to Austria-Hungary for "occupation and administration." While this was not formal ownership, everyone familiar with diplomatic practice knew that Bosnia would henceforth have to be listed as a Hapsburg possession. Nonetheless, the sultan remained technically the sovereign of Bosnia, while Serbia, cheated of its national hopes, never ceased to look with longing across the border toward its lost Bosnian brothers.

(2) Bosnia

As for Macedonia, the Berlin Congress dealt with it even more rudely

than with Bosnia. It was torn from the Big Bulgaria planned by Russia (3) Macedonia
and restored it to the "red sultan," Abdul Hamid II.

Thus the Balkan peninsula after 1878 reproduced in miniature the
disturbed picture afforded by the great powers in relation to the whole A second,
of the Turkish realm. The expectations of the great powers were directed minor group
principally at the vast Ottoman properties lying outside Europe; the small of heirs
Balkan states with no less eagerness set themselves the more modest goal
of appropriating the diminishing assets of the sultan's remaining Balkan
estate, i.e., Albania, Bosnia, and Macedonia.

It was into this welter of contentious projects that Italy and Germany
plunged as soon as their unification enabled them to take their place be- Emperor
side the older powers. Leaving Italy to one side for the moment, we shall William II
concentrate on Germany, which with its great economic and military takes a personal inter-
mass was bound to produce a very noticeable displacement in the troubled est in the
waters of the near east. Hardly had Emperor William II come to the Ottoman
throne when, in 1890, he paid a visit to Abdul Hamid II at Constanti- empire
nople in order to make a personal examination of possible openings for
Germany in the sultan's dominion.

There had by that time been worked out a successful technique for
gradually bringing a backward area under imperialist direction. Long The
practiced by such older powers as France and Great Britain, it consisted approved
in gaining, as a first step, a general social influence at the court of a imperialist
technique
foreign ruler in order gently to extort from him a series of economic
concessions. Among these would be the working of mines or the construction of public works, such as bridges, harbors, and railways. If, on
the heel of these activities, bankers should put in an appearance with
the offer of ready money to the spendthrift monarch at an attractive
interest rate, he was sure to awaken at some not too distant morning
to find himself bound hand and foot as effectively as ever Gulliver had
been by the swarming Lilliputians.

By this well-established procedure German diplomats and businessmen,
following the kaiser's visit, made a nest for themselves at Constanti- German
nople. Carefully surveying the situation, they finally concentrated on Asia attention
Minor, commonly called Anatolia, as the most promising field of action. concentrates
on Anatolia
Anatolia, almost incredibly backward because of Turk ignorance of even
the rudiments of modern economics, had very alluring potentialities from
a colonial standpoint. But before its mineral and other riches could be
developed it would have to be provided with an up-to-date system of
communications.

GERMANY AND THE BAGDAD RAILWAY

The Germans project a system of communications: the Bagdad railway

With this in mind a group of German financiers obtained a concession to construct a railway from Constantinople eastward to Angora. When this was ready, they acquired the right to build an extension to Konia, in central Asia Minor; and no sooner had they reached Konia than they recognized that it would be both logical and necessary to carry the line eastward all the way across the Euphrates to the city of Bagdad on the Tigris. From Bagdad it might ultimately be extended down the river to the Persian gulf and so open up a greatly shortened route to India and the Asiatic points beyond.

Objections against the Bagdad railway raised by the other powers

It was in 1899 that a German company received the first charter from the sultan to build what came to be known as the Bagdad railway. Owing to difficulties of one sort or another connected with this first concession, the project hung fire for a number of years. In 1903 a second charter removed all obstacles, and the construction of the line began in earnest. Immediately some of the powers, which had long taken jealous notice of the negotiations, were aroused to the pitch of protest. They had themselves followed an identical course in dozens of instances, but that did not hinder them from registering heated moral indignation as soon as they were convinced that Germany had achieved a notable advantage. An enormous agitation centered around the German design which, starting modestly in Anatolia, grew till it cast its shadow eastward all the way to the ancient valley-land of Mesopotamia.

The particular objections of Great Britain and Russia

Among the great powers it was, more particularly, Great Britain and Russia which showed resentment toward the Bagdad railway project. Great Britain feared for the security of India, always a source of grave anxiety; Russia dreaded the traversing of the Bosporus with an east-west artery of communication which would, in the long run, almost inevitably lead to a German political hegemony at Constantinople.

The Bagdad railway a factor in bringing to life the Triple entente

Undoubtedly it was this common alarm over the Bagdad route which helped to draw the two long obstinately opposed countries together. In 1907 they signed, as we are aware, the Russo-British entente. It dealt with Persia and breathed no word about the unwelcome railway, which was only just getting started and which it would manifestly take many years to bring to completion. Nonetheless, the German advance into the near east was a strong subconscious factor in the novel friendship between London and St. Petersburg. Added to the friendship already existing between London and Paris as well as between Paris and St. Petersburg, it produced the Triple entente.

THE OTTOMAN CRISES FOLLOWING THE REVOLUTION OF 1908

Even with Europe broken into Triple alliance and Triple entente the two groups might not have plunged into war in 1914 as they did, had it not been for the extraordinary succession of earthquakes which rocked the crazy Ottoman empire to its foundations. The first of the Ottoman disturbances was the domestic revolution of 1908, by virtue of which Turkey became a constitutional monarchy and passed into the hands of the party of the Young Turks. This has already been treated, together with some of the domestic consequences. It now becomes our task to trace the effect of the revolution on the already poisoned relations of the Triple alliance and Triple entente.

The successive crises of the Ottoman empire after 1908 raise the European temperature to fever heat

The Young Turk revolution was only a few months old when, on October 5, 1908, the Viennese cabinet startled the world with the announcement of the annexation of Bosnia and its minor adjunct of Herzegovina. The Austro-Hungarian foreign minister at the time was Aehrenthal. He was moved to take the step because he feared that the ambitious Young Turks would be inspired to make use of the sultan's merely theoretical sovereignty in order to bring the two Serb provinces once more under Ottoman rule. Aware of the advisability of a preliminary understanding with Russia, he had, in September, 1908, held an interview with the Russian foreign minister, Isvolski, at Buchlau in Moravia, as a result of which Isvolski agreed not to oppose the annexation if Austria would lend support to Russia's demand for a modification of the agreement shutting her warships from the straits.

Austria annexes Bosnia (1908) after an imperfect understanding with Russia

But Isvolski was balked by his own partners, France and Great Britain, who were unwilling to concede to Russia the particular advantage she sought. When, a few weeks after Buchlau, Aehrenthal went ahead just the same, Isvolski was indignant and joined France and Britain in a spirited protest. The immediate danger to peace did not, however, come from the Triple entente. It arose from Serbia, which was so enraged by the Austrian act that she looked upon war as the only adequate response. In case the Triple entente went the length of backing Serbia, an Austro-Serb conflict was inevitable. This in its turn would almost certainly develop into a general upheaval.

The annexation protested

In the ensuing controversy the Austrian contention was that, since the Hapsburg monarchy had been in actual possession of Bosnia for thirty years, the annexation was a mere formality. To this argument the Serbs refused to concede any weight because they were in the grip of the strongest national emotions. Looking on Bosnia as theirs on national grounds, they had never ceased to hope for the end of the Austrian occupation. Instead of the end there now loomed, because of the snapping

The Serb emotional crisis

of the tenuous thread of Turkish sovereignty, the permanent incorporation in the Hapsburg monarchy.

So open became the Serb preparations for war that the worst was
feared until Britain and France, feeling that the Bosnian issue was, after
all, too slight a stake on which to risk an appeal to arms, ceased to encourage the Serbs. Russia, more deeply concerned, proved more stubborn.
At length in March, 1909, St. Petersburg, on receiving a sharp note from
Austria's ally, Germany, also accepted the annexation and notified the
kingdom of Serbia to expect no aid from it. Thereupon the little state,
completely isolated, informed Vienna of its submission and solemnly
promised to discontinue its agitation in behalf of Bosnia.

The Bosnian crisis relieved (March, 1909)

A tremendous crisis had gripped Europe—a crisis which was relieved
but not terminated by the acceptance of the Austrian act. And hardly
was this particular incident closed, when another and still another storm
broke over the tormented dominion of the Young Turks. In 1909 the
Albanians rose to claim that measure of autonomy to which they thought
they were entitled. Then, while the Turk armies were still locked in battle
with the vigorous Albanian mountaineers, Italy suddenly pounced on the
remaining African province of the Ottoman empire, Tripoli, in order to
add it to its colonial domain.

The uninter-rupted suc-cession of Ottoman crises

ITALY AND THE OTTOMAN EMPIRE

The war of 1911 loosed by Italy against Turkey requires an exposition
of Italian policy. We have repeatedly noted that when, in 1881, France
appropriated Tunis, the Italians reacted so violently against this seizure
that the government gravitated toward Berlin and Vienna and with
their co-operation formed the Triple alliance. In the very next year (1882)
Egypt was occupied by Great Britain. That left for eventual seizure
along the north-African coast only Morocco, an independent sultanate,
and Tripoli, officially a province of Turkey but really in possession of
its own lawless desert tribes.

Italy fails to share in the appropria-tion of the north-Afri-can coast

Around the year 1900 the government of France developed the ambitious project to acquire Morocco. It did not fail to note that, as a necessary preliminary, it would have to come to terms with Great Britain as
well as with its immediate Mediterranean neighbors, Italy and Spain.
How it bought the consent of Great Britain is laid down in the famous
Anglo-French entente of 1904. To Spain at the same time was conceded
a narrow Moroccan strip opposite its own shores. There remained Italy,
and France from the inception of its Moroccan plan had thought of
Tripoli, a sun-scorched desert lying between Tunis and Egypt, as a suitable reward in return for Italian consent to the absorption of Morocco.

France offers compensa-tion for Morocco to Britain, Spain, and Italy

Beginning negotiations in 1900, the two Latin sisters had by 1902 come to a comprehensive agreement. Not only did Italy accept Tripoli in exchange for Morocco, but she gave an undertaking not to regard herself as obligated to fight with her allies, Germany and Austria, in an aggressive war against France. As Italy at the same time remained in the Triple alliance, indeed solemnly renewed the alliance in this very year (1902), the question may be raised how Italy regarded her contradictory responsibilities. The only possible answer is that, in the event of war, she intended to join the side that offered the greater inducements. *The Franco-Italian treaty of 1902*

The bearing of the Italian attitude on the European diplomatic situation will escape no watchful eye. It signified that the Triple alliance, although continuing to make a brave show before the world, was, after 1902, a leaky vessel. Italy had made a secret arrangement by which she could at her pleasure desert her allies. *Italy has a foot in either camp*

It was under these circumstances that Italy in September, 1911, fell upon the Ottoman empire. She saw France at that moment finally devouring the Moroccan dish and at the same time the Young Turks so embarrassed by the fiery Albanian revolt that it seemed almost like flying in the face of providence not to act. Besides, she had Tripoli, as it were, already in her pocket, for, in addition to the promise of France, she had at one time or another received the pledge of every power of Europe that Tripoli should eventually be hers. *Italy concludes (1911) that the time has come to take Tripoli*

Swooping down on the Tripolitan coast with her warships and transports, she engaged in a struggle with the native Arab tribes, who received only meager support from weak and distant Constantinople. By the autumn of 1912 the Young Turks recognized that they would have to yield. In a treaty signed at Lausanne in Switzerland they resigned their Tripolitan claims to the kingdom of Italy. Pending the execution of the treaty, they permitted Italy to hold and administer Rhodes and the Aegean group of twelve islands, called the Dodecanese. As conquered Tripoli, rebaptized Libya by its new masters, really belonged, not to Turkey but to its own desert people, their subjugation became the expensive undertaking of the following years. *Italy acquires title to Tripoli (1912)*

THE BALKAN WARS OF 1912-13

Even yet we have not come to the end of the Young Turk woes. Encouraged by the domestic disturbances of the Ottoman empire which the war with Italy had greatly intensified, the governments of the four small Christian states whose boundaries touched on Macedonia and Albania began negotiations with a view to the conquest of these territories or as much of them as they might succeed in getting in hand. The four Christian states were Greece, Bulgaria, Serbia, and Montenegro, both the last-named of the same, that is, of Serb nationality. However, the heavy em- *Greece, Bulgaria, Serbia, and Montenegro plan to seize Macedonia* barrassments of the Turks were not the only reasons prompting them to strike. Shortly before the Italian war was brought to a close, the Turks had placated the Albanian rebels by the offer of an autonomous Albania with boundaries which included a liberal slice of Macedonia. To this arrangement the outraged neighbors of Macedonia, accustomed to look on that province as their eventual property, were resolved never to submit. Finally, they were secretly encouraged to resort to arms by all-powerful Russia, which, without engaging to share in the enterprise, promised diplomatic support. It was with the heartening feeling that the benevolent eye of the great white tsar was upon them that in October, 1912, the four allied states declared war on the sultan and advanced upon his territories.

The victorious Bulgars lay siege to Constantinople

Whether because Turkey had been drained of its resources and was completely exhausted or because its armies were scattered over too broad a front to be effective, the allies immediately scored a succession of startling victories. The Bulgarians, driving southward, scattered the Ottoman forces and obliged them to take refuge behind the defenses of Constantinople. The war was hardly more than a month old when they laid siege to the famous city on the Golden Horn.

Success of the allies

The successes of the allies of the Bulgars were hardly less striking, for by the time the Bulgars had reached the outposts of Constantinople, the Serbs and the Greeks had occupied all Macedonia. Tiny Montenegro did its bit by slashing its way into northern Albania.

In May, 1913, the Turks agree to cede all their Balkan territory except Constantinople

In their surprise and distress the Turks appealed for help to the European powers, which agreed to assemble a conference at London to consider the case. As a preliminary measure the powers required the combatants to arrange a truce. When the peace terms offered the Turks were rejected, the war was renewed in the spring of 1913. But not for long: in May the utterly exhausted Ottomans agreed to surrender all the territory they still possessed in the Balkan peninsula with the exception of Constantinople and a narrow adjoining strip of territory. To all intents the cry echoing through all the Christian ages was realized: the Turks had been expelled from Europe!

The Ottoman territory ceded collectively

Then, just as everybody expected the martial excitement to die down, the Balkan pot boiled up and over once again. The new outbreak was due to the fact that the four allies, because they had been more successful than they had hoped, could not agree on the division of their profits. Turkey had surrendered to them collectively by the peace not only the coveted Macedonia but the province of Thrace as well, almost up to the gates of the Turk capital.

For a moment it had even looked as if the allies might acquire Albania too. But with regard to Albania the powers assembled at London interposed an Olympian veto. To this decision they were persuaded, in part at least, by the fact that the Albanians had recently shown their mettle by wresting autonomy from the Turks. In any case they held their shield over the last of the Balkan nationalities to seek liberation. In a formal announcement they declared their purpose to erect a free Albania with a boundary to be fixed after the necessary preliminary studies had been made.

The powers agree to set up an independent Albania

Even with Albania excluded from the spoils, the allies found themselves in possession of so much more territory than they had expected that they could come to no agreement on their respective shares. After futile negotiations they proceeded from words to blows. The new struggle is called the Second Balkan War. In it two of the allies, Greece and Serbia, combined against Bulgaria because Bulgaria could not make up its mind to be content with Thrace and to leave Macedonia in Greek and Serb hands.

A new war (1913) over the division of the spoils

Rumania now entered the struggle, in spite of the fact that it had not taken part in the First Balkan War. Stirred to jealousy by the success of its neighbors, the government of Bucharest had demanded territorial compensation. Finally, in order to make sure of receiving it, Rumania joined Serbia and Greece against their Bulgar enemy.

Rumania sides with Greece and Serbia

The union of three against one ended the war before it was well under way. Caught between the fresh Rumanian army coming from the north and the Greco-Serb forces advancing from the west and south, the Bulgarians were quickly struck to their knees. They humbly sued for peace which was concluded at Bucharest on August 10, 1913. Of course Serbia and Greece divided the disputed Macedonia between them without paying the least attention to the arguments of an ethnical nature advanced by Bulgaria. Rumania had to be conciliated by Bulgaria with the surrender of a strip of Bulgar land adjoining the Dobruja.

Peace of Bucharest

With three of its neighbors united to plunder prostrate Bulgaria, the last and fourth neighbor, the Turks, put in an appearance. They asked and received an extension of their narrow Constantinopolitan hinterland as far as the city of Adrianople. It was not much of a gain for the Turks, but it took away some of the sting of their recent defeat.

The Turks, too, improve their position

If the crisis precipitated by the two Balkan wars closed with a happy and elated Greece, Serbia, Montenegro, and Rumania, it left behind a deeply embittered Bulgaria. The Balkan animosities had not in the least diminished. There were storms ahead.

Embittered Bulgaria

THE OUTBREAK OF WORLD WAR I
(1914)

Feverish increase of armaments and attendant unrest

THE PROTRACTED OTTOMAN and Balkan crisis was attended by almost convulsive efforts on the part of every great state to increase its military and naval forces. More particularly, Russia, Germany and France took steps to be better prepared for a conflict they were coming to regard as inevitable. In case they or any other government made an effort toward better understanding, they were jeered by the jingo section of their press which fed its readers with a ceaseless savage vituperation of its country's enemies. Even so there were not lacking gestures and actions which gave hope to the optimists. Prominent among these was the fact that during the Balkan wars of 1912-1913 Great Britain and Germany had so far forgotten their animosities that they had worked together to effect a settlement. For the moment at least they showed themselves firmly resolved not to come to blows over the antics of the small states of the southeastern peninsula.

The growing rage of Serbia against Austria

But this was not the attitude of Austria and Russia, both of whom took the antics of one of these states, Serbia, most seriously. Ever since the Austrian annexation of Bosnia in 1908 Serbia had not ceased to occupy the European limelight. Its self-importance, already great, was immeasurably increased by its victories in the Balkan wars and the resulting territorial acquisitions. But its exasperation with Austria, instead of declining with success, was fed by new grievances. For Austria had been foremost among the powers in saving Albania from the dismemberment with which Serbia threatened it in its passionate resolve to reach an outlet to the sea.

The Serb nationalist propaganda

Quite openly Serbia fixed its hope on some future war which would topple Austria from its eminence. However, as that event was necessarily indefinite, the country found immediate relief for its vast indignation in secret societies charged with carrying nationalist propaganda among the Bosnian and other Serb subjects of the Hapsburg monarchy.

The aggression of Serbia backed by Russia

Should this secret Serb propaganda be vigorously prosecuted for a period of years, it would with mathematical certainty undermine the foundations of the Austrian state. However, when Vienna protested to Belgrade against these activities, its complaints were treated dilatorily. Little Serbia dared take this course in the face of a great power for the single reason that its propaganda policy enjoyed the backing of St. Petersburg. Nor did Russia omit to add the assurance that it would not desert a kindred Slav people in case of a renewal of the Bosnian crisis. On the surface, the relations between Austria and Serbia were being subjected to an unendurable strain; below the surface the strain involved the two great powers, Austria and Russia, and, through them, their respective partners of the Triple alliance and Triple entente.

Into this tense situation there crashed, like a clap of thunder, the news that on June 28, 1914, the heir to the Austrian throne, the archduke Francis Ferdinand, and his wife had been murdered as they were driving through the streets of Sarajevo, the capital of Bosnia. The assassin, a young Bosnian nationalist, Gavrilo Princip by name, had at a street corner stepped out of the crowd and fired two bullets, each of which found its destined mark. His deed, as everybody knows, unleashed World War I.

> Murder of the heir to the Austrian throne (June 28, 1914)

THE REMOTE AND THE IMMEDIATE CAUSES OF THE WAR

Confronted with the outbreak of World War I, which, because it all but wrecked civilization, released a passionate discussion as to its origin, let us at the very outset make a distinction. There are remote causes of the war which go back for generations and are tied up with some of the most characteristic developments of Western civilization; and there are immediate causes which lie very much nearer the surface and are more easily traceable. Let us consider the remote causes first. They are for the serious student the real and effective causes and fall much more heavily into the scales than the immediate causes, in spite of the importance attached to the latter by the general public.

> Distinction between the remote and immediate causes of World War I

To anyone versed in the processes of history it must be indisputable that such an epochal event as World War I could not have sprung from other roots than from the spirit and forms assumed by changing civilization itself. It is a correct appreciation of this fact which defines the struggle as a grave, perhaps a fatal crisis of our civilization. Since this book has, in effect, made Western civilization its central theme, the forces and conditions which co-operated to produce the catastrophe of 1914 have been repeatedly indicated. However, they have not yet been explicitly enumerated. Let us attempt to do that now, remembering at the same time that it is useless to signalize one of these conditions as more important than any other. They all had to be contemporaneous and intermingle in an indistinguishable complex to bring about or, as we more commonly say, to "cause" the war.

> The remote, that is, the real causes of World War I

We have learned that, ever since the Reformation, Europe has been a congeries of competitive, sovereign states. That means that, in spite of a

measure of unity based on a body of international law and an ever-grow-
ing mass of common practices, each state was a law unto itself and felt
free to pursue its selfish interest by every means at its disposal, including
war. Consequently, there always hung over Europe the threat of war
which periodically exploded into actual war. From this dangerous situation there was no escape except through the abandonment of unlimited
sovereignty.

The real causes: (1) Europe a body of competitive sovereign states

The sovereign states had, since the French Revolution, come to rest
more and more on the sentiment binding together all members of the
same state and called patriotism. When divided or oppressed peoples,
who had not yet achieved their own political state, cultivated a similar
sentiment, it was commonly called nationalism. Patriotism and nationalism, praiseworthy in themselves and even necessary if the states founded
on this sentiment were to survive, frequently led to an exaggerated form
of self-worship. We may call this exaggeration ultra-nationalism. It manifested itself by an intolerant and offensive attitude toward every rival
national group.

The real causes: (2) Exaggerated nationalism

As soon as a national state experienced the impact of the Industrial
Revolution, it sought to appropriate backward areas in order to exploit
them in its own interest. A national state embarking on this policy heartened itself with the theory of its civilizing mission. Minimizing its expectation of material advantages, it proclaimed the need of carrying its particular brand of culture to the brown or black or yellow brothers of
Africa and Asia in order to rescue them from their deplorable barbarism.
Admitting that a certain generous missionary impulse was often present
in these imperialistic enterprises, we cannot escape the conclusion that
imperialism was largely born of a hunt for profits and the love and pride
of power.

The real causes: (3) Imperialism

The imperialism, which, as just indicated, was tied up with nationalism, was, in its turn, vastly intensified by the search, on the part of bankers and company promoters, for profitable investments abroad. With the
usual selfishness of monied men the investors demanded that their ventures be protected by the armed forces of the home government. Such
action was resented not only by the exploited country but also by the
suspicious and jealous European rivals.

The real causes: (4) Export of capital

Since each power looked on war as a legitimate tool of policy, it desired to be as strong as possible on both land and sea. Hence constantly
increasing armies and navies; and, by the same token, growing expenditures, involving in their turn heavy and ever heavier taxation and a
national debt assuming fabulous proportions. From steadily mounting
armaments there inevitably issued an alarm and tension which destroyed
the confidence necessary for kindly, courteous intercourse among neighbors.

The real causes: (5) Vast, competitive armaments

The desire for security had led first, to alliances in the event of war, and, around 1907, to the bifurcation of Europe into the two hostile camps of the Triple alliance and Triple entente. Ever since the rise of international law in the seventeenth century the agency best suited to promote the cause of peace had been what was currently called the concert of Europe. This was the name given to a method of informal co-operation among the great powers to the end of bringing their differences to an accommodation. The domination of Europe by two rival groups, both armed to the teeth, undermined the concert by prompting the rivals to convert every issue that arose into an occasion for manifesting prestige. Besides, under the two-group system it would suffice for a single power recklessly to resolve on war in order, through the ramifications of the treaties, automatically to involve all the rest.

The real causes: (6) The concert of Europe replaced by the division of Europe into two hostile groups

All of the above factors taken together operated to undermine the good will preached by a thousand associative agencies of civilization, such as commerce, religion, science, and the arts, and to replace good will with its opposite, with suspicion, fear, and hatred. This psychological consequence of all the other forces at work in the world can hardly be overstated. It alone suffices to explain why in July, 1914, the powers flew at each other's throat in a panic indistinguishable from emotional insanity.

The real causes: (7) The diseased European mind

As to the immediate causes of the war, they have to do with the murder of the Austrian heir apparent and the developments that sprang from this root. As soon as the Sarajevo tragedy had led to a general and unique cataclysm, each side clamorously asserted its own innocence while doing its best to fasten the blame on its opponents. Germany and Austria pointed to Russia as the originator of the war and presently found France and Great Britain hardly less culpable on the ground that they had encouraged the Russian action.

The Austro-German thesis as to who caused the war

The members of the Triple entente, on the other hand, placed the blame on Germany so exclusively that they practically implicated Austria only in the role of willing tool. It was the entente thesis which, largely because of the control by the entente of the world's news agencies and cable lines, captured outside opinion. Germany's sole guilt or, what amounts to the same thing, the kaiser's sole guilt, became an article of faith, which deepened with every year the war lasted. By the time the war ended the belief had become so firmly established in the minds of Germany's opponents that they wrote it triumphantly into the treaty of peace, called the Treaty of Versailles.

The entente thesis that Germany was the immediate cause of the war

However, as soon as the war was over, it became possible to review the facts in a mood emancipated from the propaganda activities of the combatants. For the first time, too, the actual facts became known, owing to the writings of diplomats and politicians eager to claim a share in the great events which had occurred or desirous of defending themselves

The postwar review of the immediate causes

against disparaging charges. Far more important than these personal apologetics, the state archives were thrown open and innumerable official documents bearing on international relations were communicated to the public. While these frequently afforded an insight into the decisions of the chancelleries as they fluctuated from hour to hour during the July crisis of 1914, in some cases they went much farther and permitted a study of the foreign policy pursued by a given power for several decades previous to the great catastrophe. It was decidedly contrary to custom for such publications to be put forth by European governments. Owing to the circumstance that the monarchies of Russia, Austria-Hungary, and Germany were replaced in 1917-1918 by revolutionary governments which wished to proclaim their complete breach with the past, the customary reserve was abandoned and the public admitted to a knowledge of the most secret dispatches and reports.

All countries open their archives With St. Petersburg, Vienna, and Berlin putting their diplomatic cards, as it were, on the table, London and Paris were in self-justification obliged to do the same, with the total result that never since the formation of the European system of states has a similar opportunity been afforded for exact knowledge of the development, intensification, and violent resolution of a crisis of the immediate past.

Blame for the war still a controversial subject From the existence of this immense body of authentic materials touching the outbreak of the war, it might be concluded by the general reader that the special students of the subject were enabled to come to substantial agreement on the facts. That is far from being the case, in part owing to the persistence, even among scholars, of an unbalanced state of mind regarding the war, in part owing to the contradictory interpretations, which, in the case of anything so fallible as a human document, are unavoidable. It is, therefore, proper that the reader should know that the distribution of blame in connection with the outbreak of the war is still a controversial subject.

Reigning opinion in favor of a distributed responsibility Nonetheless, an immense advance has been made. The declaratory statements of 1914 issued from both camps have been set aside as worthless and the theory discredited that any one power, be it Germany or Russia, was exclusively the immediate cause of the war. Scholars of good standing are now unanimously of the opinion that all five powers immediately involved, Austria, Russia, Germany, France, and Great Britain, must assume some measure of responsibility. They differ, and differ vigorously, as to the relative share of each government in the catastrophe; but they stand together in favor of a guilt distributed among all the powers instead of a guilt monopolized by one. With the decks thus cleared we may take up the July events in the light of the present state of our information.

THE DIPLOMATIC CRISIS OF JULY, 1914

The Austrian heir apparent and his wife were murdered by a Bosnian youth of Serb nationality who acted under the direction of a terrorist society in Serbia, commonly called the Black Hand. The society was, to a large extent, made up of Serbian army officers and its most influential member was no less a person than the head of the Intelligence Division of the Serbian General Staff. Although it is certain that the Serbian government somehow gained knowledge of the plot, the Black Hand alone planned and executed it.

The archduke murdered by a Bosnian Serb

Immediately after the assassination the Austrians instituted an inquiry into its preliminaries. This put them in possession of evidence incriminating the propagandist societies of Serbia as well as a number of government employees, but it did not disclose all the ramifications of the conspiracy. Nonetheless, they resolved to publish their charges and at the same time signally to humiliate the little state.

The Austrian investigation of the plot

At 6 P.M. on July 23, Count Berchtold, the Austro-Hungarian foreign minister, presented a drastic ultimatum to Belgrade. It demanded that the Serbian government disavow and suppress all propaganda activities directed against Austria, that it take judicial proceedings against Serb subjects connected with the plot, and that it permit Austrian representatives to take part in the investigations. To give the ultimatum a particularly severe character a reply was demanded within forty-eight hours.

The Austrian ultimatum of July 23

When the Serb government presented its answer two days later (July 25), it accepted most of the Austrian demands but rejected the really decisive one, that is, Austrian collaboration in the investigations to be conducted on Serbian soil, on the ground that this would be an infringement of Serbian sovereignty. The Austrians at once declared the answer unsatisfactory and broke off diplomatic relations. Even before handing over her note, Serbia, expecting the worst, ordered the mobilization of her army.

The unsatisfactory Serb answer to the Austrian ultimatum

On receiving the Serbian answer, Austria began mobilization and, three days later, followed this move with the irreparable step of a declaration of war (July 28). In the hope of keeping Russia from feeling alarm for her own safety, the Austrian mobilization was limited to a number of army corps on the southern, that is, on the Serbian border.

Austria declares war against Serbia

There cannot be the least question that the Austrian policy aimed from the start at war with Serbia and only in part in revenge for the Sarajevo murder. What spurred Count Berchtold on to war was the conviction which had for years been growing in Vienna that Serb nationalist propaganda was slowly undermining the foundations of the Hapsburg monarchy, and that nothing would put an end to it short of a harsh

Austria did not proceed against Serbia without first getting (July 5) German support

lesson administered to the indeed small but lusty and expanding kingdom. Even before formulating the ultimatum Berchtold had communicated with his German ally and on July 5 had received a promise of support for any action against Serbia which Austria might consider necessary for her safety.

The German calculation in giving support to Austria

In thus pledging support Emperor William II and his chancellor,
Bethmann, reckoned with an Austrian punitive expedition into the Slav
kingdom. They did not want, and Austria did not want, a general European war. Both Vienna and Berlin foresaw that a general war might
follow, depending on how the entente took the punishment of Serbia.
But they hoped that the war might be avoided by the recognition, even
on the part of Russia, that Serbia had put herself in the wrong and would
have to pay the penalty.

Russia puts her whole weight behind Serbia

In calculating thus Austria and Germany made a grave mistake, for
Russia from the first refused to entertain a humiliation of Serbia which
went the length of war and invasion. St. Petersburg avowed an affection
for the Serbs on the ground of common Slav affinities. Much more decisive, however, as an explanation of Russian policy was the fact that
under the conditions obtaining in Europe in 1914 the safety and independence of Serbia were tied up with Russian self-interest. The tsar had
reason to fear the Austro-German influence at Constantinople, which,
with the straits, he looked on as one of the keys to the Russian house. In
this region Austro-German prestige and power had in recent years been
steadily advancing. Should they now become dominant at Belgrade too,
they would make themselves felt without interruption from Berlin to
Bagdad and shatter for good the ancient dream of the tsars to straddle
at some not too distant day the waters of the Bosporus.

The Russian foreign min-ister won over to the plan of mo-bilization

These fears may have been exaggerated but they were not groundless.
At any rate Nicholas II and his foreign minister, Sazonov, acted on them
without delay. As early as July 25, and before the expiration of the two-
day Austrian ultimatum, they ordered certain military measures of a preparatory nature. They hoped by this gesture to persuade Austria to adopt
a milder attitude toward Serbia. Unfortunately they also encouraged their
own military authorities to clamor for more sweeping measures. Sazonov
stoutly withstood this militarist pressure till, on the evening of July 28,
he was informed of the Austrian declaration of war against Serbia. Therewith his nervousness completely got the better of him and he offered no
opposition when the Russian chief of staff told him he was about to visit
the tsar to ask for an order of mobilization against Austria.

To this demand the pacific but feeble and vacillating Nicholas acceded
on July 29. But before the order could be carried out he canceled his consent. On the next day Sazonov called in person on the tsar and wrested

a renewed approval from the agitated ruler. The new, the second order called for general mobilization against both Austria and Germany. Before Nicholas had time again to change his mind, the order was, at about 6 P.M. of July 30, put upon the wires at St. Petersburg. At the signal the army was mobilized for war throughout the vast Russian realm.

Russian general mobilization ordered, July 30

That in the eyes of military men everywhere general mobilization—but not partial mobilization—signified war admits of no doubt. When in 1892 the French and Russian chiefs of staff exchanged views on the alliance they were shaping they set this opinion down in writing. And Nicholas II and his military advisers, including Sazonov himself, had no other view of the significance of their act.

"Mobilization means war"

It is not likely that the Russians would have moved so decisively and swiftly if they had not received assurance of support from their French ally. That the French ambassador, Paléologue, from the beginning of the crisis put his country unreservedly on Russia's side is certain. But it is difficult to say how far he was authorized in this action by his superiors at Paris. While the French government, which to an unusual extent was directed by the energetic president of the republic, Poincaré, seems to have considered war inevitable, it was anxiously averse to having Russia appear as the aggressor. Poincaré was emphatic in the expression of his desire that, in the event of Russia's mobilizing, she keep her action secret as long as possible in order to afford the opportunity of throwing the odium of the prior mobilization on Germany.

French undercover support of Russia

This was good policy not only from the point of view of public opinion throughout the world but more particularly with regard to Great Britain. Let us recall that since 1904 France had had an entente with Britain which did not in itself obligate the two powers to give each other support in such a crisis as the one which was now agitating Europe. However, becoming after 1904 steadily more intimate, the two governments had conducted naval and military conversations looking forward to possible concerted action in the future. The climax of this association was reached on November 22, 1912, when Sir Edward Grey, the British foreign minister, put his name to a letter in which he took what cannot be interpreted other than as a personal pledge to bring his country into a war at the side of France in case of an unprovoked attack upon that country.

The commitment of Britain to France culminates in the declaration of November, 1912

It must be clearly understood that the British parliament, which alone had the right to declare war, was not bound by this document and that both parliament and public opinion would have to be won over to the French side before Britain would enter an European struggle in aid of her neighbor across the channel. Furthermore, nothing short of the conviction of the complete innocence of France in connection with the outbreak of war would enlist the British parliament and people on the French side. Fully aware of this, the French government, in sharp con-

The French government assures Great Britain of its peaceful intentions

tradiction to its provocative attitude at St. Petersburg, never ceased to assure London of its love of peace.

Germany operates on the theory of a "localized" war

On turning now to Germany, every consideration of her role in the July drama must begin with the consent she gave, on July 5, to whatever the Austrians might resolve to do in order to abate the nuisance which Serbia had become. This has been called the German blank-check handed to Vienna. The kaiser himself later called it a noose into which he had thoughtlessly thrust his head. William II and Bethmann, his chancellor, held to the theory of a localized Austro-Serbian war which need not become a general action. They clung hopefully to "localization" until they became reluctantly convinced that Russia's attitude made this policy impossible.

Germany's changed plan after July 28

Then, but not till July 28, the German government dropped "localization" and, filled with sudden alarm by Russia's preparatory military measures, took a new stand. On the one hand, it warned Russia not to proceed to general mobilization and, on the other hand, it brought strong pressure to bear on Vienna to placate St. Petersburg with a more conciliatory attitude. An adjustment of the conflicting Austro-Russian views was to be brought about by "direct conversations" between the two foreign offices.

Failure of the German plan

Both German actions proved vain. Berchtold stubbornly ignored Berlin's representations till it was too late; and St. Petersburg, in view of Vienna's intransigence, went on with its policy of armament. With waxing suspicion driving calm and common sense from every foreign office, events now moved with ungoverned precipitation to the fatal order of general mobilization issued by Russia in the late afternoon of July 30.

The German mobilization order of August 1

Considering the Russian mobilization to mean war, Germany met it in the precise way the Russian military authorities foresaw. Learning of the order at noon on July 31, the kaiser informed the tsar that he would mobilize in his turn unless Russia rescinded her action within twelve hours. When Russia replied on the next day that the movement could not be stopped, at 5 P.M. on August 1 Germany decreed mobilization and followed it with a declaration of war.

French mobilization ordered on August 1

It was in keeping with the consistent support which Paléologue, the French ambassador, gave Sazonov that he was able to inform the Russian foreign minister some hours before this official rejected Germany's last warning that the French government authorized him to make the declaration that it would fully meet the obligations of its alliance. In accordance with this pledge France mobilized her army at 4:45 P.M., August 1, at approximately the same hour as Germany.

By this time Austria had already taken similar action: at noon of July 31, some eighteen hours after Russia, she called her army into the field.

In sum, following the Russian initiative, the mobilization orders of the other powers came with the swiftness of successive discharges from an automatic pistol. The dreaded war of the two hostile groups of powers had begun. Austrian mobilization ordered on July 31

All eyes now turned to Great Britain. What would she do in the present circumstances? During the crisis precipitated by the Austrian ultimatum of July 23, Sir Edward Grey had maintained a vacillating attitude. Without doubt he desired to avoid war. On the other hand, in the terrible storm threatening Europe he did nothing to discourage Russian mobilization. He may even be considered to have encouraged Sazonov by refusing to put any pressure upon him. His viewpoint and that of his closest advisers in the foreign office was that the Triple entente must be maintained at all costs and that to desert Russia in the present action would produce a resentment fatal to the recent Anglo-Russian friendship. Sir Edward Grey's indirect encouragement of Russia

Sir Edward Grey undertook a number of actions in favor of peace, all of which for one reason or another came to nothing. His most hopeful proposal was "direct conversations" between Austria and Russia, which, though obstinately delayed by Berchtold, might have been effective if sufficient time had been afforded and Russia had not snapped the thread by her mobilization order. When this precipitated a continental war, in which Germany and Austria faced Russia and France, the British foreign minister found himself importuned by the entente, more particularly by France, to come in on their side. Britain importuned to join Russia and France

The appeal of France threw Sir Edward into a quandary, for he did not conceal from himself that he had become committed to Paris by his letter of November 22, 1912, with its cautious personal pledge. On the other hand, he had never failed to make it clear to his French friends that his government had assumed no obligations and that the last word belonged to parliament. Sir Edward was therefore obliged to take the issue to the people and their representatives, and these ultimate judges, bewildered by a conflict originating in a Balkan quarrel and only remotely involving the interests of Great Britain, exhibited a strong disinclination to be pushed into the maelstrom. Sir Edward Grey obliged to carry the issue of Britain's participation in the war to parliament

At this juncture the German military machine entered the scene and by its action put an end to British indecision. Obliged to fight on two fronts, the German General Staff was very anxious to join issue with France in the west before Russia could release her vast man power against the German eastern frontier. The Germans calculated that their one chance of success in the face of the heavy numerical odds against them was to overcome France first and afterward to make the effort to stem the Russian tide. General Schlieffen, a former chief of staff, had long before 1914 worked out a plan carrying his name, in accordance with which the German army was to pour swiftly across the lowlands The German plan to attack France via Belgium

of Belgium, instead of wasting precious time in forcing its way over the difficult hills and past the mighty fortresses of the French border.

The viola-
tion of Bel-
gian neutral-
ity arouses
Britain to
declare war
on Germany,
August 5

On August 2, as soon as mobilization was under way, the German government requested Belgium to grant an unmolested passage through that country. When Belgium indignantly rejected this demand, Germany on August 4 committed an act of war against Belgium by sending troops across the frontier. The flagrant violation of Belgian neutrality, of which Germany was one of the guaranteeing powers, released a spontaneous indignation throughout the world. In Great Britain the violation gave rise, in addition, to the alarm lest the Germans establish themselves on the Belgian coast, where the British had never been willing to see a great power gain a foothold. Almost magically every trace of hesitation to enter the conflict disappeared; and Sir Edward Grey found himself supported by an enthusiastic parliament and people when, on August 5, the government moved to declare war on Germany.

Italy de-
clares her
neutrality

The feverish attention of the world now swung to Italy. As a member of the Triple alliance, she was in some quarters expected to be automatically sucked into the vortex on the Austro-German side. Such expectations were deceived. As we are aware, as early as 1902 she had given a secret engagement to France by which she greatly weakened the ties binding her to Austria and Germany. In the agony which came over Europe in 1914 the Italian government resolved to act solely in accordance with the dictates of self-interest. Its first step in pursuit of this policy was to proclaim its neutrality.

Japan serves
an ultima-
tum on
Germany,
August 17

Japan followed a different course from Italy, but it was no less inspired by purely selfish considerations. The empire of the mikado had ever since 1902 been bound by a treaty to Great Britain. It provided for co-operation in the Pacific ocean but did not include an European war. Japan was therefore under no obligation to enter the struggle. However, Germany was established on the Chinese coast in the province of Shantung; and Germany with her hands full in Europe would not be able to defend her valuable concession at Kiaochow. It would prove an easy conquest. On August 17 the mikado served an ultimatum on the kaiser, which was promptly followed by a declaration of war.

Once more
the deep-
lying causes
of the war

In this way the ultimatum presented to Serbia in connection with the assassination of the heir to the Austrian throne precipitated, in the course of ten hectic days, the struggle known as World War I. Once more let it be said, it is a short view to explain its outbreak on the basis of the moves made on the diplomatic chessboard of Europe between July 23 and August 2. At best these moves may be said to have caused the war *at that particular moment*. That it was prepared decades and generations before in the womb of Time is the long view which alone is worthy of every serious student of history. Seen thus, it is less a momentary madness of diplomacy than a plunge into disaster by our civilization owing to the growth of certain unfortunate trends which neither the peoples nor their leaders possessed the will or wisdom to bring under control.

Meanwhile a blaze had been started which spread until its fierce glare lighted Europe, the colonial areas of Asia and Africa, and all the highways of the ocean. In August, 1914, the actual situation was this: Germany and Austria stood shoulder to shoulder against Russia, France, Great Britain, and Japan, not to mention the small states of Serbia and Belgium. Italy declared herself neutral. So did the United States. So did the small powers of Europe and the numerous American republics. For the moment at least they were no more than singed by the vast conflagration. But before each neutral state the anxious question loomed: Could it escape the raging flames or would they prove uncontrollable and burst through every barrier that might be erected against them?

The situation in August, 1914

36 THE WAR AND THE PEACE (1914-1919)

Limited purpose of this chapter

IT IS HARDLY necessary to say that it will be impossible in a book of this scope to do more than call attention to a few leading facts and aspects of World War I. Important matters of great and legitimate concern will have to be resolutely excluded from consideration. There will be no description either of the instruments which have revolutionized warfare on land and water, such as the giant gun, the scouting and bombing airplane, the trench-bomb, the tank, poison gas, and the submarine, or of the altered tactics and strategy imposed upon generals and admirals by the new tools of destruction. Only scant mention will be made of the outstanding personalities of the various nations, the conspicuous and fast-shifting leaders in the field and council-chamber. Nor will it be possible to treat the heated domestic politics of each warring state, including such matters as its pro- and anti-war groups, the search for revenue to meet the vastly increased expenses, and the measures of economic reorganization for war production on a titanic scale. Our plan goes no farther than first, to enumerate the main areas of the prolonged ferocious struggle, together with the leading factors which determined the outcome, and second, to define and interpret the peace terms which the victors dictated to the vanquished.

THE WAR ON THE WESTERN FRONT

The Germans march through Belgium to defeat France before Russia becomes threatening

When Germany broke the neutrality of Belgium, in spite not only of the certainty of adding Great Britain to her enemies but also of the opprobrium with which she was sure to be visited, she disclosed the extreme importance she attached to the swift defeat of France. France once disposed of, Germany would turn upon Russia, which country, owing to its unwieldy bulk, the German General Staff supposed would get slowly under way and therefore not prove immediately threatening. Being convinced that the French would concentrate on the Alsace front, the Germans planned to surround them by executing an enormous flank attack through Belgium and northern France. This advance was bravely resisted by the small Belgian army supported by the strong forts along the Meuse as well as by the English and French troops hurrying up to stem

716

the tide. But, conducted with superior numbers and equipment, it broke for a while through every obstacle. Not till the Germans were almost within sight of Paris were they stopped by a direct frontal attack combined with a flanking movement which threatened to envelop their right wing.

The ensuing battle, lasting several days (September 5-10), is famous as the battle of the Marne. The Germans, beaten, had to retreat to the Aisne, where they entrenched. Having failed to trap the French army, they had lost the campaign; and though by way of compensation they succeeded in holding almost the whole of Belgium and a valuable industrialized area of northern and eastern France, they would thenceforth be in serious danger the moment their enemies became strong enough to attack in their turn. The Germans, halted at the Marne (September 5-10), fail to carry out their plan

This theoretic peril of the Germans, enhanced by the great distance which separated them from their source of supplies in Germany, was in practice greatly reduced by their resort to trench warfare. Adopted by one side, it had, perforce, to be adopted also by the other. Both sides dug themselves in, forming an immense zigzagging and heavily fortified battle line stretching for six hundred miles all the way from the sea at Nieuport (Belgium) to the Alps on the German-Swiss border. The resort by both sides to trench warfare

During the next three years first one side and then the other undertook an offensive with the purpose of breaking through the powerful system of underground defenses. Some of these attacks were conducted with military resources which threw into the shade everything ever heard of up to this time. Among the attacks, to select two outstanding instances, were the offensive of the Germans, in the spring of 1916, against the fortress of Verdun, and that of the British and the French, in the summer of that same year, along the Somme river. Failure of repeated efforts by both sides to break through

Generally speaking, the various offensives proved as costly as they were futile and the battle front remained substantially unchanged until March, 1918. For almost four years the military situation on the western and decisive front was deadlocked. The four-year deadlock

THE WAR ON THE EASTERN FRONT

Exactly as the German supreme command had miscalculated the Franco-British resistance in the west with the result that the German advance was stopped at the Marne, so it indulged in a wrong assumption as to the mobilization of Russia. The German rush toward France was, as we have seen, predicated on the probable slow advance of the Russian army. The Russian army, however, conducted its mobilization not only with unexpected speed but with enormous masses as well and undertook, The unexpectedly swift drive of the Russians into Germany and Austria-Hungary while the German army was sweeping on to Paris, to drive across the east-European plain into Germany and Austria.

The Germans turn the Russian advance into a rout at Tannenberg
So great was the Russian momentum that the Germans were obliged to retire before it from East Prussia and the Austrians from eastern Galicia. Not till they had drawn reinforcements from their army in France did the Germans succeed in stopping the invasion of their territory. At Tannenberg (August 26-September 1) they turned the too precipitate Russian advance into East Prussia into a disastrous rout. Hindenburg, the German commander, followed up his victory by crossing the Russian boundary into Poland.

The Russians in Austria
The Austrians, however, in their sector had no such success as the Germans and continued to give way until the Russians threatened the forts of Cracow in western Galicia. Cracow may be conceived as the outermost bastion of Vienna, the Austrian capital.

The successful Austro-German offensive of 1915 against Russia
Thus matters stood on the eastern front as the first winter came to an end. In May, 1915, the Austrians and Germans made a combined offensive on a vast scale. It pushed back the Russians at every point along the extensive battle front and ended in their complete defeat. Not only did the central powers now drive far into Russia but they succeeded in so severely crippling the Russian equipment by the destruction and capture of war material that the great Slav empire began to show signs of approaching exhaustion.

Russia's last offensive (1916)
True, the Russians staged an unexpected come-back by engaging, in the summer of 1916, in a partially successful offensive against Austria conducted by General Brusilov. But thereafter the army showed little fight, partly through deepening discouragement and partly because of the civil break-up behind the battle line, the usual accompaniments of defeat in the field.

The Russian revolution of March, 1917, obliges the tsar to abdicate
The war had, in the first instance, led to a great outburst of patriotism and unified Russia as it unified and solidified, through the same patriotic sentiment, every other fighting country. However, the political discontent which had produced the revolution of 1905 was still astir under the surface; and when the Russian defeats followed in rapid succession, the angered public laid the blame on the incompetence and corruption of the tsarist regime. In March, 1917, an uprising took place in Petrograd (as St. Petersburg had been officially renamed) which immediately gathered such momentum among both civilians and soldiers that the tsar, deserted by his people, was obliged to abdicate.

As soon as the absolute system crashed to the ground, the question arose whether it would be succeeded by a moderate middle-class or by a radical socialist government. The first arrangement to be effected was a compromise, certain middle-class groups co-operating with a moderate wing of the socialists. The new government stood by its allies and pledged itself to keep Russia in the war. Through the summer of 1917 the compromise ministry struggled on, becoming ever less bourgeois and ever more radical. At last, in November, it was overthrown by the extreme socialists, known under the party label of Bolsheviks and committed to a program of communism.

The government seized by the Bolsheviks (November, 1917)

On becoming Bolshevik, the Russian government fell under the direction of two fiery spirits of great organizing powers, Lenin and Trotsky. Interested pre-eminently in carrying through a thoroughgoing economic revolution, they resolved to take Russia out of the war by making peace with Germany. Under the circumstances they were at the mercy of the enemy and had to accept the peace which Germany ruthlessly imposed at Brest-Litovsk in March, 1918.

The Bolsheviks determined to make peace

By virtue of the treaty of Brest-Litovsk Russia renounced title to its vast western borderland, including Finland, the Baltic provinces (Estonia, Livonia, Courland), Lithuania, Poland, and the Ukraine. All these regions, with the partial exception of the Ukraine, represented conquests effected by Russia since the days of Peter the Great. Again with the exception of the Ukraine, which was inhabited by so-called Little Russians, the ceded territories were inhabited by a great variety of nationalities, but only to a small extent by Russians. Their separation from the former tsarist empire was therefore a grave political but hardly a national loss.

Losses imposed by the Peace of Brest-Litovsk (March, 1918)

An obvious drawback of the method here adopted of treating each battle front in turn is that it fails to bring out the close connection of events in the east and west. The campaigns on these two fronts and on all fronts whatever should, especially if military enlightenment is sought, be studied as a unit. Fighting in the east constantly affected the situation in the west and vice versa, as will appear by glancing back once more, for the purpose of illustration, to 1914. The Franco-British forces won the decisive battle of the Marne, but their victory was largely due to the unexpected invasion by Russia of East Prussia and to the consequent diversion by Germany of troops destined for the western front to her eastern marches.

Close interdependence of the fighting fronts

THE WAR ON THE SOUTHEASTERN FRONT

This intimate concatenation of events throughout the areas of combat should be borne in mind as we turn next to trace the course of events on the Balkan front. The war, though beginning in the Balkans as a conflict between Austria and Serbia, assumed at once so overshadowing an importance on the western and eastern fronts that the Balkan front sank into relative insignificance. However, an unbroken succession of

The less important southeastern front

fresh developments kept drawing the attention of the world back to the southeast.

It signified a vast extension of the struggle on the southeastern front when in November, 1914, the Ottoman empire sided with the central powers. The entrance of this state into the war was due to the trust which the Young Turks, the political masters of the Ottoman empire, put in the vigor of Germany. In August, 1914, they signed an alliance with Germany from which they expected security against Russia, the power they traditionally feared and hated. Three months later the Turks, who had been almost uninterruptedly at war since the Italian attack of 1911, once more drew the sword.

The Ottoman empire joins (November, 1914) the central powers

The entrance of weak but far-ruling Turkey into the war put a changed face on the situation in the Balkans and, for that matter, throughout the east. Russia, in particular, was hard hit, for the Bosporus and Dardanelles were immediately closed to the supply ships of the entente. In consequence, the empire of the tsar was unable to receive the military equipment of which it stood in need. As it was largely owing to this circumstance that it was overwhelmed in the campaign of 1915, we have another proof of the close interdependence of events on all the fighting fronts. It was to break the intolerable barrier at the straits and establish the sorely needed contact with Russia that her allies, France and Great Britain, undertook their first Balkan campaign.

The entrance of Turkey into the war closes the Dardanelles

In February, 1915, a Franco-British squadron suddenly attacked the Dardanelles with the purpose of silencing the Turkish forts and forcing a passage to Constantinople and thence to the Black sea. On losing in this hazardous enterprise several large battleships, the allies radically changed their plans. They landed troops, colonials from Australia and New Zealand for the most part, on the western shore of the Gallipoli peninsula, with the object of taking the forts of the Dardanelles from the rear. All summer this campaign continued at ruinous cost, only to be acknowledged a failure and to be given up at the coming of winter.

Failure of the allies to force their way (1915) through the Dardanelles

What gave the Gallipoli enterprise the finishing blow was a new and important development in Serbia. A recognized minor area of conflict, the little Slav kingdom was not seriously threatened by the Austrians till December, 1914, when an attempted Austrian invasion was victoriously repulsed. Almost a year later, in October, 1915, Serbia was obliged to face a second and more massive invasion. Strengthened by a German force and led by a German general, the Austrians concentrated on the Danube opposite Belgrade. This spectacle so encouraged Bulgaria, which, since the loss of Macedonia in the Second Balkan War of 1913, burned with a consuming hatred of Serbia, that the Bulgars formally joined the central powers.

A concerted attack on Serbia draws (1915) Bulgaria into the war

There now took place a double offensive against Serbia, the Austro-

Germans pushing southward from the Danube, while the Bulgarians attacked Serbia from the east, that is, in the Vardar valley. The entrance of Bulgaria into the war was a commanding event, because it planted the central powers in the heart of the Balkan peninsula. And when Serbia was now overrun, together with Montenegro and most of Macedonia and Albania, the longed-for, unimpeded connection between Berlin and Constantinople was at last made perfect. The crushing of Serbia

Thus the year 1915 proved a prosperous one for the central powers and particularly for Germany, since it brought the realization of a compact middle Europe under German direction extending from the North sea to the Dardanelles. The only offset for the Franco-British forces was the occupation of the Greek city of Salonica, at the head of the Aegean, and the successful establishment there of a military base strong enough to save southern Macedonia from the central allies. The allies maintain a foothold in the Balkan peninsula at Salonica

From Salonica it was possible, on the one hand, to bring political pressure to bear upon the kingdom of Greece and, on the other hand, to prepare a future offensive against Bulgaria. In spite, however, of a very heavy pressure, Greece refused at first to join the entente. She resented the unsolicited occupation of Salonica and resisted the dictation of the western powers for two years. Greece resists the pressure of the allies

The submission of Greece to the entente took place in 1917. By that time the remaining Balkan power, Rumania, had passed through a disastrous experience to be presently related. The whole history of the war goes to show that the small powers of the Balkans, so deeply involved in some of the main issues of the struggle, could not remain neutral. But to choose sides was a very delicate matter because it was far from clear which side would prove victorious. And yet life itself depended on picking the winner, for these small governments were no more than pawns in the game of the great powers and were sure to be crushed if they crossed the path of an irresistible moving force. Obliged to choose sides, the Balkan states find it hard to make a decision

For their part, the two opposed European groups recognized the value of the accession to their respective sides of a Balkan combatant and hotly bid against each other at every Balkan court and capital. It was in response to the play of these difficult countercurrents that the Ottoman empire and Bulgaria, in 1914 and 1915 respectively, joined the central powers. Rumania ranged herself on the side of the entente allies in 1916. Greece, though only under military duress, did the same, as we have just seen, in 1917. Distribution of the Balkan states among the two fighting groups

It was in August, 1916, that Rumania threw in her lot with the allies. As the Austro-Germans had for some time been expecting the event, they met the Rumanian attack with a counteroffensive, crushingly defeated their new foes, and all but completely occupied their territory. In the winter of 1916-1917 the central powers were apparently more Crushing defeat of Rumania, 1916 securely entrenched in the Balkans than ever. The only cloud on the Balkan horizon was the allied front firmly maintained at Salonica.

THE WAR ON THE SOUTHERN OR ALPINE FRONT

Italy joins the entente powers (May, 1915)

A last European front remains to be listed, the southern or Alpine front created when Italy terminated the neutrality proclaimed by her at the outbreak of the war. In April, 1915, she signed a treaty with the Triple entente (the Treaty of London), whereby she was promised enormous territorial advantages at the conclusion of peace; and in May of the same year she declared war on her former ally, Austria.

Advance of the Italians in 1916 followed by defeat in 1917 at Caporetto

The struggle between Italy and Austria took the form of an Italian offensive along the Italo-Austrian mountain border. Slow Italian advances in this difficult terrain culminated in the capture of the city and fortress of Gorizia in the summer of 1916. In the autumn of 1917, however, the gains made were again lost and, in addition, much Italian territory given up when the Austrians, supported by German troops, broke through the Italian lines at Caporetto. They captured many men and much equipment and were not brought to a halt till they had reached the line of the Piave river, northeast of Venice.

Recovery of Italy

In the spring of 1918 Italy was a source of grave anxiety to the entente which, however, the events of the summer and autumn of that year scattered to the winds by revealing the recovered spirit and striking power of the Italian troops.

MINOR FIGHTING FRONTS

Conflict areas outside Europe: (1) Asia Minor invaded by Russia

At this point, though chiefly concerned with Europe, we must at least indicate the leading conflict areas outside the European continent. The diminished Ottoman empire of the twentieth century was largely Asiatic, embracing Asia Minor, Syria, Mesopotamia, and Arabia. In all these provinces the vast struggle raged, the main feature being an attack by Russia and Great Britain upon the shaking Ottoman house. Russia made her forward thrust from the Caucasus into Asia Minor and conducted it, on the whole, victoriously until her collapse at home in 1917.

Conflict areas outside Europe: (2) Mesopotamia and Syria

Great Britain followed two separate and converging lines of penetration: the first led from the Persian gulf to Bagdad in Mesopotamia; the second from the isthmus of Suez into Palestine and Syria. In spite of multiple difficulties and occasional grave setbacks these two British offensives continued steadily for four years. At last in 1918 they were crowned by a succession of victories which resulted in the total collapse of the Ottoman state.

Inevitably, too, every German colony was at least a potential fighting area. However, owing to the small German forces abroad and their inability to receive reinforcements on account of the British control of the seas, most of the colonies fell with little resistance into the lap of the allies. The German concession in China, Kiaochow, was taken by the Japanese in 1914 after a campaign lasting a few weeks.

Conflict areas outside Europe: (3) Kiaochow

Besides Kiaochow, the Germans offered resistance only in German Southwest Africa and in German East Africa. As the forces they could mobilize in these colonies were small, they were quickly worn to a shadow in guerilla fighting. It is a notable circumstance that the work of winning these areas was done less by the British themselves than by the British colonial forces of South Africa.

Conflict areas outside Europe: (4) Africa

THE SEA FRONT

Having enumerated the main fighting areas on land, we must now turn to take account of the sea. Perhaps, when all is said, the sea front was the greatest of all the fighting fronts. In any case, it was the most decisive. The dominating factor in the situation was Great Britain's control of the world's seaways by means of her overwhelming naval forces.

Sea power the decisive factor in the war

The British fleet at once drove the German fleet and merchant shipping from the ocean; it gradually captured all those German merchantmen which, surprised by the declaration of war, failed to reach a safe port; and it pursued and finally destroyed such armed German raiders as undertook to prey upon the enemy commerce.

The British fleet controls the seas

At the same time the British established a long-distance blockade of the German coasts in order to cut off Germany from all transoceanic supplies. Then, in order to make the blockade thoroughly effective, the masters of the sea undertook to regulate and control neutral commerce, above all, the commerce of Holland, Norway, and all the regions immediately adjacent to Germany. Inevitably, also, they turned a sharp eye on the neutral United States of America, the greatest producer of raw products in the world.

The British blockade Germany and control neutral commerce

To break this obstruction of the indispensable channels for food and war materials Germany had a gambler's chance in the mysterious and as yet untried weapon of the submarine. She declared, in her turn, the British coast in a state of blockade and attempted to make good her threat against vessels seeking British ports by means of a fleet of under-sea boats. However, while the British blockade of Germany was wholly effective because no merchant vessel, neutral or otherwise, could pass into the North sea without being detected by the British guard-ships, the German blockade of the extensive British coasts was of the hazardous, hit-and-run variety.

The Germans answer the British blockade with the submarine campaign

The submarine imperils human lives

Carried through by means of the submarine, the German blockade necessitated, in order to be even partially effective, the submarine's sinking its merchant prize, since it was out of the question to bring the prize safely some hundreds of miles to a German port. However, to sink a ship with its cargo had the bad feature of imperiling the lives of passengers and crew, for the submarine, hardly more than a toy, though a toy with a sting, was unable, through lack of room, to take its captives on board. The commander of the submarine had nothing better to offer the captured crew than the uncertain chance of getting to shore in lifeboats.

The battle of Jutland, 1916

Only once did the German fleet enter into action in the hope of breaking the British strangle-hold. There followed on May 31, 1916, the battle of Jutland, in which the British lost more ships and men than the Germans but drove the enemy fleet back to its base at Helgoland. In spite of German claims of victory, the battle of Jutland left the British in more absolute control of the seas than before.

HOW THE UNITED STATES WAS DRAWN INTO THE WAR

The United States proclaims neutrality

Over the blockade and submarine situation the United States was drawn into the struggle. When the war broke out, the great American republic at once declared its neutrality. With this aloofness the citizen body was for a long time satisfied, although public sentiment from the first favored the entente. Many factors contributed to this state of mind, most conspicuously perhaps the indignation aroused by the outrage done by Germany to Belgium in seizing and holding the little land in an iron military vise.

Neutral rights overridden by both Great Britain and Germany

Once under way, the war made itself felt in America at innumerable points, chiefly through the ramifications of commerce. It was plain that Great Britain was determined by her measures of control to make the United States sell goods exclusively to her and to her allies; and it was just as plain that Germany was minded to have her share of American articles. Purposing with deadly intensity to injure each other, the two powers tried to regulate sea-borne trade according to their interest, and instituted their respective blockades. Unquestionably the measures of both combatants were illegal from the point of view of international practice. They signified a serious encroachment on the rights of neutrals and therefore also on those of the United States.

President Wilson protests against the measures of both countries

Protesting against the illegal measures of both belligerents, President Wilson began a lively exchange of diplomatic notes with London and Berlin. From the first, however, the notes exchanged with Germany had a special edge, absent in the case of Great Britain, because Germany's breaches of the sea law, involving the use of the novel weapon, the sub-

CLEMENCEAU. French statesman. (Lens & Letters)

LLOYD GEORGE. British statesman. (Lens & Letters)

WOODROW WILSON. Former President of the United States. (Lens & Letters)

WINSTON CHURCHILL
Three Lions

BENITO MUSSOLINI
Keystone View

JOSEPH STALIN
Keystone View

FRANKLIN D. ROOS
Three Lions

ADOLF HITLER
Keystone View

marine, imperiled American lives and thereby stirred the sentiment of humanity, already aroused over the invasion of Belgium.

The diplomatic argument was still being conducted in rather general terms when there occurred an event which sharply defined the issue between Germany and the United States. On May 7, 1915, a German submarine torpedoed and sank without warning the British liner *Lusitania*, drowning over a thousand men, women, and children, more than a hundred of them of American nationality. The indignation in the United States was so intense that the American government passed immediately from discussion to command and insisted that the submarine conform to established humanitarian rules. As obedience to these rules could not be reconciled with the free use of the submarine, the United States demanded, in substance, that Germany end forthwith the unrestricted employment of its too indiscriminately destructive tool. To this pressure the German government yielded; and though there were occasional transgressions of the conditions laid down by the United States, a precarious peace was maintained till January 31, 1917.

The "Lusitania" incident causes the United States to insist on the restricted use of the submarine

On that January day the German government published a declaration notifying the neutral world of its determination to resort once more to the unrestricted use of the submarine. The British octopus grip, continued for over two years, had begun to tell in the reduced production of Germany and in the progressive starvation of her people. It was on these grounds that the German government sought to justify the use of the only tool in its possession capable of terminating the British blockade. President Wilson promptly broke off diplomatic relations and on April 6, 1917, the Congress of the United States declared war on Germany.

On the resumption of the free use of the submarine the U. S. declares war, April, 1917

At this juncture it becomes necessary to set forth the motives and program with which the United States entered the war two and a half years after the struggle had begun. Owing to the small attention paid in the United States to affairs in Europe, the bewilderment over the sudden conflagration of 1914 was extreme. Accordingly, the neutrality promptly proclaimed by President Wilson not only met the wishes of the American people but expressed the undeniable fact that the explosion resulting from the clashing interests of the Triple alliance and the Triple entente in the Balkan peninsula was no concern of the Washington government.

American opinion, bewildered by the war, approves at first of neutrality

During the ensuing months and years the more enlightened section of the public took pains to inquire into the causes of the outbreak and slowly came to the conclusion that the war was due to a chain of rivalries and rancors reaching back for generations and involving every sort of bitter contention over markets, raw products, colonies, and military and naval establishments. This thinking minority consequently concluded that what was needed was a radical change of system, and began the discussion of

A liberal American minority dreams of a better world

a new, an idealist program to be adopted by Europe and the world on the termination of hostilities.

At the same time a corresponding body of liberal-minded men raised its head in every country of Europe, prepared to advocate a similar program. As the liberals of Great Britain and France could freely exchange ideas with their spiritual relatives of the United States, these three groups gradually merged into something like a single body of opinion. In the circumstances the united liberal intelligentsia came to the conclusion that, since the happy new order could not be instituted till the war was over, the immediately desirable event was the early defeat of Germany.

In measure as American liberal opinion clarified it found a spokesman in the country's political head, President Woodrow Wilson. He commanded an eloquence of the written and spoken word which could raise the mass of men, at least for the time being, to the level of his own high views. When the United States entered the war, President Wilson fired the enthusiasm of his people by a ringing indictment of the autocratic government of Germany. At the same time he voiced his continued good will toward the German people and pledged his country to the pursuit of unselfish ends. From time to time, in further illustration of his position, he made additional declarations. They culminated, on January 8, 1918, in a peace program of Fourteen Points.

The Fourteen Points included, among other matters, the abolition of secret diplomacy, the freedom of the seas, the reduction of armaments, the redrawing of the map of Europe along national lines, and the creation of a League of Nations as a guarantee against a repetition of the current disaster by the transformation of the prevailing international anarchy into a regulated system of law and order. President Wilson's clarion pronouncements appealed to European as well as to American idealism and unified liberal opinion the world over as it had never been unified before. Slowly a Wilsonian peace began to outline itself, very different from the predatory kind with which the world was only too familiar. While it aimed at curbing Germany, it was not concerned with revenge and punishment. Its main purpose was to go to the bottom of things by bringing the greedy imperialism of the great powers and the ruinous nationalist rivalries of the great and small states alike under the control of a world conscience and a world law.

TOTAL COLLAPSE OF THE CENTRAL POWERS

With refreshed spirits the allies resumed the war on the entrance into it of the United States. In 1917 the American participation hardly caused a ripple for the reason that unprepared America had first to get ready. Besides, the defection of Russia from the allied ranks in this same year broke the iron ring around Germany and greatly relaxed the pressure brought to bear on her.

The next campaign, however, the campaign of 1918, proved decisive. It began in March with a supreme effort by the German command to break down French and British resistance on the western front before the Americans could arrive on the scene in overwhelming numbers. For three months the Germans battered the allied lines, achieving considerable success but failing in the main purpose of breaking through to Paris.

The German offensive of the spring of 1918

In their hour of greatest need the allies unified their command as they had not before succeeded in doing. They put a Frenchman, Marshal Foch, in supreme control; and presently, in July, they assumed the offensive in their turn. The next months brought the most ferocious fighting which the war, from first to last unexampled in ferocity, had witnessed. Irresistibly the French and British, reinforced by ever-increasing masses of Americans, drove forward against the enemy lines. Foot by foot and mile by mile they pushed the Germans back until it was clear that the foe would have to abandon the invaded districts of Belgium and France.

The successful allied offensive of the summer of 1918

The outlook for Germany was already becoming somber when, through occurrences on the other fronts, it settled into the blackness of night. In the late summer of 1918, the British began to apply their final pressure upon the Turks in Syria. It resulted in the complete rout of the Turks and the utter breakdown of Turk resistance.

Defeat of Turkey (September, 1918)

Simultaneously the allies found themselves at last strong enough to move against Bulgaria from their Salonica base. In September, 1918, they crushed the Bulgarian forces with a few well-directed blows and obliged Bulgaria, unable to get support from Austria and Germany to steady its panicky cohorts, abjectly to sue for peace. Thus, following Turkey, Bulgaria was eliminated from the struggle.

Defeat of Bulgaria (September, 1918)

Inevitably the Austrian morale was badly shaken by these disasters in the immediate Austrian rear. A loosely knit state, the polyglot Hapsburg monarchy was, after four devastating years of storm, beginning to go to pieces. The soldiers at the front refused any longer to obey their officers and, abandoning their positions, started for home.

The Hapsburg monarchy falls apart

As soon as the Italians became aware of this disorderly retreat, they resumed their offensive. Thereupon the tottering political fabric of Austria-Hungary settled into complete collapse. The house of Hapsburg was deposed; the various nationalities merged in the composite state declared their independence; and the war ended on this front with an armistice, signed November 4, 1918, that left the Italian army in complete control of the situation.

The armistice of November 4, 1918, puts the Italians in control

These events, taken in connection with their own losing struggle on

the western front, obliged the Germans to sue for peace. In those autumn
weeks of 1918, while blow after blow was being delivered by the allies
on every war front, the shaken government of the kaiser slowly crumbled
to destruction. The first measure revealing a changed situation at Berlin
was that the opposition groups of the Reichstag took over the government and opened negotiations with President Wilson. They could not
maintain themselves, however, against the aroused and angered masses.
In an uprising on November 9 the people overthrew the imperial regime
and set up a republic.

Overthrow of the kaiser and procla-mation of a republic, November, 1918

It was the Social Democrats who led the insurgent masses and who
now took over the government with the solemn pledge of restoring peace
to the land. William II was unable to resist the storm. On November
10 he abandoned his defeated army and fled to neutral Holland.

Flight of the kaiser

After a prolonged exchange of notes between the German government
and President Wilson, who acted as the spokesman of the victorious
allies, the president's peace program as developed in numerous addresses
but, more particularly, in the Fourteen Points was, with a reservation by
Great Britain touching the freedom of the seas, accepted as the basis for
the general peace. Over and above the president's original program, the
Germans assumed the obligation to compensate the entente for all losses
suffered by civilians through Germany's action on land and sea and from
the air.

The prelimi-nary peace terms dic-tated by President Wilson

With these preliminaries settled, Marshal Foch, on November 11, 1918,
dictated the armistice which brought the colossal struggle to a close. By
its terms the Germans were obliged to fall back from Belgium and France
to the east bank of the Rhine. They were, besides, required to surrender
such vast quantities of war material that they would be unable under any
conceivable circumstances to renew the fighting. By an enormous co-
ordinated effort the resistance of the central powers had been broken and
the victory won. What would the peace bring?

The armistice of Novem-ber 11, 1918

THE PARIS PEACE CONFERENCE: IDEALISM VS. REALISM

The peace! Plainly it was as important as the war. In fact the war
would have proved a mere orgy of destruction if the peace did not
undertake vigorously to grapple with the evils which had afflicted the
world long before the war began and which were the real causes of the
war. And first in this connection let us note that, owing to the completeness of the allied triumph and the impotence of the vanquished, the
peace would be dictated by the victors. The four enemy states had become negligible: Austria-Hungary had disappeared from the map; the
Ottoman empire and Bulgaria were crushed and all but annihilated;

Owing to the exhaus-tion of the vanquished, the peace would be a dictated peace and Germany, disarmed on November 11 and passing through the throes of a revolution, might plead the protection of the Fourteen Points, but was without the power to enforce consideration for her views.

At the time when the long and terrible struggle came to an end, twenty-five states, great and small, were joined together as allies or associates against Germany. Therefore, as soon as Paris had been agreed on as the place of meeting, representatives of all these states wended their way to the French capital to take part in the great congress which was to bring a topsy-turvy world back to civilized order. All these agents would be permitted to present the viewpoint of their respective governments and would of course receive a polite hearing. The decisions, however, would be taken by the great powers, five in number, Great Britain, France, Italy, Japan, and the United States. At an early date the Japanese announced that they would take no part in discussions not affecting the far east. There remained, therefore, the Big Four, and, in accordance with immemorial usage, their representatives would always reserve the last word to themselves. *The peace would be shaped by the great powers*

When on January 18, 1919, the peace conference was called to order, it was at once dominated by the four Olympian figures of Clemenceau (France), Lloyd George (Great Britain), Orlando (Italy), and Wilson (United States). Much of what they might do would depend on their personal temper and outlook. However, let us not delude ourselves by imagining that they were free agents. They represented, in each instance, a carefully elaborated government program and would have to give ear to the opinions and sentiments of the respective publics they served. *The four men who represented the four leading powers were not free agents*

This latter consideration is particularly important, for the masses of the victor countries, in distinction from the enlightened minorities, were possessed by a war psychosis which filled them with a lively spirit of revenge. When an unexampled triumph suddenly ended the long agony of four years, all the remaining barriers of self-control were swept away by a savage exultation. This is the atmosphere in which the Big Four worked at Paris. It was the unhappy but inevitable by-product of the protracted war. The Big Four may have yielded too readily to this atmosphere, but they did not create it. *The peace congress dominated by a savage war psychosis*

No sooner had the Paris conference opened its doors than it became apparent that the peace which President Wilson had outlined in the Fourteen Points and which had been conceded to Germany as a basis of discussion would meet with resistance. Its most formidable opponent was the general war psychosis already mentioned. It reached its frenzied peak in the very city of the conference and destroyed the mental equilibrium of the delegates. Something akin to a hunger for raw meat came over them, prompting the rejection of the Fourteen Points as irrelevant ideal- *The idealism of the Fourteen Points brushed aside* ism. At best the plenipotentiaries gave them a hollow lip-service. Almost unanimously they declared themselves in favor of the political realism which had always ruled the relations of European states and, consequently, in favor of satisfying to the best of their ability the nationalist and imperialist appetites of the countries they represented.

During the long struggle these appetites had been in hot debate among the respective foreign offices and had finally led to secret agreements. In these were specified the territorial and economic advantages each power expected to receive as its particular reward at the conclusion of the war. All the victorious powers, with the single exception of the United States, had become involved in these dark deals. Under the unchecked influences obtaining after the victory they were, in effect, deposited on the conference table at Paris to serve as a set of counterproposals to the Wilsonian program. Could the two tendencies, the American and the European, be harmonized? Could the new idealism, represented by Wilson, be brought into agreement with the stark, old-fashioned realism championed by Clemenceau, Lloyd George, and Orlando?

The imperialist designs of the victor states laid down in secret treaties

For the better understanding of the nature and gravity of this issue it is necessary to take a closer view of the secret treaties. Signed, sometimes between two, sometimes among three and more powers, these very numerous documents had been buried in the darkest recesses of the respective national archives. They suddenly ceased to be secret, however, when in 1917 the Russian Bolsheviks gave the copies they discovered in the archives of Petrograd to the world.

The secret treaties disclosed by the Russian Bolsheviks

The Bolsheviks were moved to take the action they did by sheer malice. Having abandoned the war, they had sacrificed the benefits promised to tsarist Russia for its part in the struggle. At the same time it pleased these radicals, who were resolved to found a new society resting on communism, to disclose the base plotting in which the capitalist societies engaged behind a mist of idealist professions.

Reason for the action of the Bolsheviks

The rapacity revealed by these documents of state was indeed startling. One of the chief bones of contention among all European states had long been the Ottoman empire. In the secret treaties Turkey was completely parceled out among the four European allies, Great Britain, France, Russia, and Italy. If any portion was overlooked, it was for the sole reason that it was worthless or inaccessible.

Partition of the Ottoman empire

Japan, not admitted to the Ottoman feast, was by another treaty rewarded first, with the German leases in China, and second, with the island possessions of Germany in the Pacific ocean north of the equator. The remaining German colonies were by still other treaties divided among France, Great Britain, and the three British dominions of South Africa, Australia, and New Zealand.

Division of the German colonies

Of Germany proper France was to recover Alsace-Lorraine, lost in 1871, and to receive besides the whole left bank of the Rhine either in full possession or under cover of some arrangement assuring political control.

The territory given to France

Italy, as we have learned, had refused to join the allies till they lavishly baited the hook in the Treaty of London of 1915. That Italy was promised such fragments of Austria as the Trentino and the city of Trieste, which were genuinely Italian, goes without saying. But she was given, besides, the southern Tyrol, which was German, and Istria, which was preponderantly South Slav.

The territory given to Italy

Russia, it is perhaps hardly necessary to note, was not represented at Paris. Its communist government had broken off relations with the allies; or, to put it no less correctly, in view of the incompatibility manifested by both sides, the allies had broken off relations with the Bolsheviks. Alarmed at the subversive propaganda issuing from Moscow and Petrograd, the western nations had closed to Russia every avenue of trade and intercourse which they commanded. Indeed they had drifted into a relation with the revolutionary land indistinguishable from war. Russia was therefore quietly ignored when the distributions to be effected under the secret treaties came up for discussion.

Russia, having deserted the entente, was not represented at Paris

The self-elimination of Russia did not hinder the other powers, Great Britain, France, Italy, and Japan, from insisting each one on its pound of flesh. They stood shoulder to shoulder against President Wilson, champion of the Fourteen Points. In view of the fact, however, that Wilson, as representative of the United States, was strong in himself, and further, because he had the liberal, if minority, opinion of the world behind him, his opponents found it necessary to compromise. True, they stood stubbornly by the arrangements of the secret treaties; at the same time they considered it politic not to proceed to an open repudiation of the Wilsonian program.

The other beneficiaries of the secret treaties resolve to cash in on them

THE IDEALIST VICTORY: THE LEAGUE OF NATIONS

In these circumstances President Wilson had not been long in Paris before he saw that he would have to make concessions to the fierce egotism of his associates. Undoubtedly their private arrangements greatly disconcerted him. But since they would not abandon them, he considered it advisable first, to try to mitigate some of the worst provisions; and second, to trade his acceptance of the rest for the particular passion of his heart, a world league of peace to be called a League of Nations. By means of the new world league, processes of judicial conciliation were, if not on the present occasion, at least thereafter to replace a rapacious

By compromise action Wilson gets the League of Nations

imperialism and to ban forever the scourge of war. The League of Nations is and remains the outstanding historical action of the Paris conference. What is more, it is in literal truth the child of Wilson's loins.

In April, 1919, the Covenant or constitution of the League was com-

Criticism of the Covenant of the League

pleted and presented to the world. It goes without saying that so great an innovation was subjected to abundant criticism. People of a conservative and nationalist outlook thought that the Covenant went much too far in conferring power on an institution of an international scope. Men of a liberal persuasion, on the other hand, contended that the League was a makeshift affair insufficiently endowed with authority. It is probable that President Wilson had nothing more in mind than to sow a seed capable of developing into a lusty plant in the coming years.

The two leading institutions of the League were an Assembly and a

The League of Nations has an Assembly and a Council

Council. The Assembly was the general body wherein all states which were members of the League were represented. In the Assembly each state was equal to every other state and cast a single vote. The Council was a smaller and far more important body. As sketched in 1919 it was to be composed of five permanent members, one each from the United States, Great Britain, France, Italy, and Japan, together with four members elected annually by the Assembly, that is, nine in all.

The Council, which was to meet normally four times a year, could

The functions of the Council

be summoned, in addition, in any pressing emergency. With the least possible delay it was to act as a body of conciliators the moment a dispute arose which threatened war. As peace was its great concern it was authorized to formulate plans for the reduction of armaments. It was also to attempt to abate the evils which had arisen from the private and competitive manufacture of guns and munitions.

A very serious responsibility fell on the Council in connection with

The Council as guardian of the mandate system

the system of mandates. Under this system the colonies taken from Germany, as well as many of the provinces appropriated from the Ottoman empire, were not considered to be the property of the powers to which they were assigned but possessions held in trust for the League, to which an annual report was due touching their administration.

The seat of the League was established at the city of Geneva in Swit-

Geneva seat of the League

zerland. There the Assembly was to hold its annual meetings and there a permanent bureau or Secretariat was set up to dispatch current business. The small, mobile Council did not have to come together at Geneva. It was privileged to meet wherever it pleased.

Since the chief purpose of the League was to settle disputes among

The International Court

nations without recourse to war, it was necessary to supplement the Assembly and Council, which had a consultative and legislative character, with a court of justice. This, too, was outlined in the Covenant,

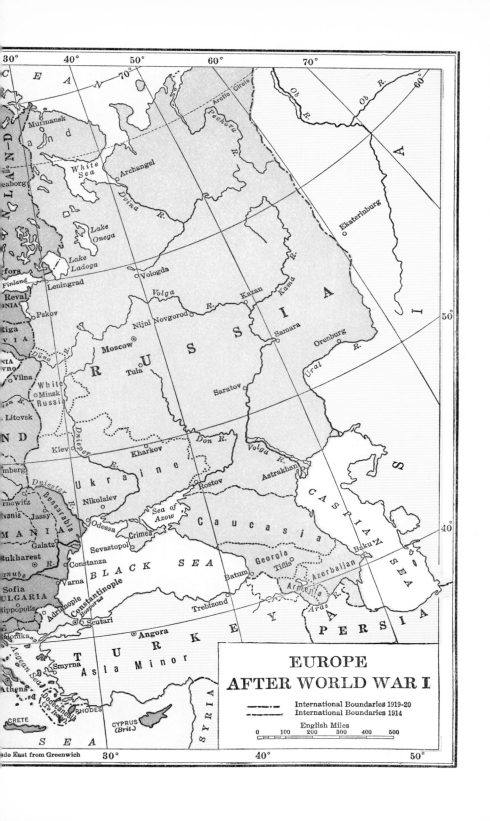

EUROPE
AFTER WORLD WAR I

International Boundaries 1919-20
International Boundaries 1914

English Miles
0   100   200   300   400   500

although its details were left for later elaboration. The world court was established, not at Geneva, but at The Hague, capital of the Netherlands.

THE TREATY OF VERSAILLES

With the League of Nations out of the way, the path was cleared for the treaty of peace with Germany. Besides the five great powers with which we are familiar, twenty states, not rated as powers, had joined in the war against the Teutonic empire. The adjustment of the often conflicting claims among this mass of victors was no easy matter. However, on May 7, 1919, the completed treaty was presented to a German delegation called for that purpose to Versailles. The Germans were told that no discussion was to be allowed. They might, however, communicate in writing their objections to the terms submitted. Such counterproposals as they offered were rejected as fast as they were made, until, weary of further interchange, the conference ordered the Germans to sign without delay on pain of renewal of the war.

A German delegation summoned (May, 1919) to Versailles to sign the treaty prepared by the victors

To this curt ultimatum the German government responded with a last-minute submission. On June 28, in a formal session held at Versailles in the famous palace of Louis XIV, where the German empire had been proclaimed in 1871, the document which registered its demise received the signature of vanquished and victors. By a no less remarkable coincidence the day marked the fifth anniversary of the historic pistol shot which killed the Austrian archduke and which had ever since filled the world with its deafening echoes.

Signing of the Treaty of Versailles on June 28, 1919

The Treaty of Versailles was an elaborate document of 80,000 words. Its severity makes it outstanding among treaties hitherto imposed as the result of a successful conflict. It declared Germany solely responsible for the war (Article 231) and justified its harsh measures on this ground.

Harsh character of the Treaty of Versailles

Taking up the main divisions of the treaty, let us consider first the territorial penalties. In the west Germany was obliged to give back Alsace-Lorraine to France. In the east she handed over the bulk of the two provinces of Posen and West Prussia to the resuscitated state of Poland. Belgium acquired Eupen and Malmédy. The territory of Memel, ceded to the victors, was afterwards given to Lithuania. The city of Danzig at the mouth of the Vistula was set up as a free state.

The territorial losses imposed on Germany

In addition, a number of regions were designated as plebiscite areas. Such were two zones of Schleswig on the Danish border, two zones in eastern Prussia, and the district of Upper Silesia with its invaluable coalfields. In these areas it was left to the inhabitants to decide by vote whether or not they wished to remain in the German communion.

The plebiscite areas

In another important coal region, that of the Saar, on the French

border, the coal mines were given to France outright in compensation
for the French mines destroyed in the war. Politically the Saar was put
under a commission responsible to the League of Nations with the understanding that the inhabitants would, after fifteen years, have the privilege
of determining their ultimate fate by a popular vote.

*Disposition
of the Saar*

Finally, the German colonies in Africa, Asia, and the Pacific ocean
were distributed among Great Britain, France, Belgium, the Union of
South Africa, Australia, New Zealand, and Japan, not as owners in full
sovereignty, it is true, but under the mandate system of the League of
Nations. This gave the League a right of supervision. The supervision
did not alter the fact that the colonies were allocated to the conquerors.

*Distribution
of the Ger-
man colonies*

An important section of the treaty dealt with the disarmament of
Germany. Germany agreed to dissolve her army and to surrender to the
allies her whole military and naval equipment. This signified by specific
tabulation her battle fleet, her submarines, her heavy artillery, her machine guns, her munitions, and her airplanes. A great power was rated
great in European affairs by reason of its army and navy and in approximate proportion to their size. Although this was not what historians
usually wrote in their books, it was what every diplomat knew. The purpose behind the disarmament measures of the Paris diplomats is therefore clear: it was to drop Germany from the list of the great powers.

*The dis-
armament
clauses of
the treaty
and their
purpose*

Once stricken from the list of powers, Germany was to be kept permanently out of that select company. This was to be achieved by the
limitation of her army to 100,000 men recruited by voluntary enlistment.
Universal compulsory service was abolished in order to deprive the army
of potential reserves. Above all, the German army was not to have the
characteristic equipment of the machine age and was obliged to renounce
the use of heavy artillery, tanks, poison gas, and airplanes. By the same
line of thought the navy was held to a limited tonnage of small-type
warships and was forbidden to own or build submarines.

*Size and
equipment
of the army
and navy
exactly
prescribed*

Since these regulations might not suffice for the end in view, Germany
was obliged to destroy the war harbor at Helgoland, which guarded the
North sea coast, and was prohibited from maintaining any fortifications
or stationing any soldiers on the left bank of the Rhine or in a zone
fifty kilometers wide on the right bank. This broad belt of territory toward France was completely demilitarized. Along her eastern frontier
she might maintain a few small and ineffective fortresses. In short, she
was to be open to invasion from every side and unable to defend herself
when invaded.

*Imposition
of a de-
militarized
Rhine zone
and of open
frontiers*

The most immediately harassing articles of the treaty dealt with reparations. In the armistice agreement of November 11 Germany had consented to accept responsibility for all damages suffered by the civilian
population of the allies due to her aggression. Elastically interpreted,

*Reparations:
indemnities
in kind*

this could be made to mean whatever the victors desired. They therefore saddled Germany with an enormous program of indemnities. She was at once to hand over all her merchant ships of 1600 tons and over together with immense quantities of cows, bulls, stallions, mares, sheep, coal, and dyestuffs.

When the plenipotentiaries came to the money indemnity to be imposed, they at once gave their imagination free rein. Unable at the moment to fix a limit, they resolved to call for an immediate payment of 20,000,000,000 gold marks and to adjourn the naming of the final sum to May 1, 1921.

Reparations: the money indemnity

All the complicated problems connected with indemnification were entrusted to a Reparation Commission to be established on German soil. In effect the Reparation Commission undertook to manage Germany as a bankrupt estate in the interest of the creditors.

The Reparation Commission

Grimly determined to get all the advantages the treaty allowed them, the allies did not overlook military coercion as a means for collecting reparations. They occupied with their armed forces the area west of the river Rhine together with three important bridgeheads on the east bank opposite the cities of Mainz, Coblenz, and Cologne. The cost of the occupation was charged to Germany. It was to continue for fifteen years and might be extended if Germany should fail to meet the financial obligations imposed on her. In case of such default, the victors asserted the privilege of occupying additional territory.

The military coercion clauses of the treaty

Although there were many other articles in the treaty, each of which canceled some property or treaty right of Germany within or without her political boundaries, enough has been said to make clear that, in addition to being stricken from the list of the great powers, she was, as far as lay with the victors, to be drained of her economic resources in the present and threatened with a continuation of the drain through an indefinite future.

The treaty imposes economic exhaustion

THE TREATIES WITH AUSTRIA, BULGARIA, HUNGARY, AND TURKEY

With the acceptance of the Treaty of Versailles by Germany, President Wilson and the other leading dignitaries went home. Delegates with full powers took their places and proceeded to draw up treaties with the remaining enemies, Austria, Hungary, Bulgaria, and Turkey. In connection with the treaties to be drawn up with these enemy powers, it was necessary to trace the boundaries and determine the international obligations of the many new states that had sprung up from the ruins of the ancient empires of the Hapsburgs and Romanovs. All this was very troublesome and obliged the peace conference to continue its sessions for over a

Heavy, additional labors of the peace conference

year after the completion of the Treaty of Versailles. The procedure in each case was modeled after that adopted toward the Germans. The treaty was drawn up by the victors according to their pleasure. When it was ready, the agents of the vanquished power were summoned and ordered to sign without demur.

The first of this lesser group of states to be called before the bar of the victors was Austria. Post-war Austria had shrunk to a small republic of German nationality. It had about 6,000,000 inhabitants, of whom little short of 2,000,000 lived in the single city of Vienna. The Austrian delegates were summoned to St. Germain, near Paris, and there on September 10, 1919, set their names to the document laid before them.

By the terms of the Treaty of St. Germain Austria was disarmed like Germany and along identical lines. She was required to pay a reparation bill of an amount to be determined at a later time. As a sum of any sort turned out to be beyond her strength, no indemnity was ever assessed.

The new republic was the outcome of the Hapsburg overthrow and of the victory of the principle of nationality. In accordance with this principle Austria had in November, 1918, proclaimed her union with Germany. Not only did the peace conference veto this act but it forbade the union of Austria and Germany until permission had been given by a unanimous vote of the Council of the League of Nations. For the present at least Austria was to remain an independent German republic dwelling in the shadow of her greater sister.

Regarding the states which had arisen on the Hapsburg ruins, Austria was obliged to recognize their independence within such boundaries as the plenipotentiaries saw fit to draw. These new creations were Czechoslovakia, Yugoslavia, and Poland. She was, of course, also obliged to accept the cessions of territory with which Italy and Rumania had been liberally favored.

Bulgaria was next in line. At Neuilly, another Paris suburb, she signed in November, 1919, the treaty prepared for her by the conference. Like the other defeated states she was obliged to accept military control, to pay an indemnity, and to suffer severe economic losses. Her army was restricted to 20,000 men and the indemnity fixed provisionally at 2,000,-000,000 gold francs.

More painful to the pride of Bulgaria were the losses of territory imposed on her. She had joined Germany and Austria in 1915 because she wished to win back Macedonia, to which she had, on purely nationalist grounds, at the very least as good a claim as Serbia and Greece. Yet these two neighbors had appropriated the whole of Macedonia after the Second Balkan War (1913). In consequence of the disastrous defeat of Serbia in the campaign of 1915, Bulgaria was able to occupy Macedonia till her

Marginal notes:

Austria, a republic of German nationality

The Treaty of St. Germain

Austria forbidden to join Germany

Austria obliged to recognize the new states

The Treaty of Neuilly offered to Bulgaria

In addition to the disputed Macedonia, Bulgaria suffers other territorial losses

own overthrow in 1918. At Neuilly not only was Macedonia lost again but Bulgaria was punished with fresh cessions of territory to her two leading enemies, Serbia and Greece. Among these new losses that of Thrace, which went to Greece, was particularly grievous because through Thrace Bulgaria had enjoyed direct access to the Aegean sea.

The signing of the treaty with Hungary had to be delayed, owing to violent domestic disturbances in that fertile mid-Danubian realm. As soon as the Hapsburg dynasty had been deposed, Hungary, following the fashion of the hour, became a republic. Proclaimed by middle-class elements, the republic assumed a moderate character. In March, 1919, however, a group of radicals or "reds," who were inspired and financed by Russia, overthrew the bourgeois republic and replaced it with a purely proletarian regime. The vicissitudes of Hungary after the war

Thereupon, with the blessing of the peace conference, Rumania took the warpath against this social-economic anomaly in central Europe and in the month of August made an end of it. When the Rumanian army retired, having done its work, the reactionary group of agrarian magnates, which had always dominated Hungary in the past, again assumed control of the state. The short-lived communist republic

Agents of this government were invited to Paris and in January, 1920, signed at a palace near Versailles the Treaty of Trianon. The new treaty was closely modeled on its predecessors in the matter of disarmament, military control, indemnities, and economic servitudes. The army was not to exceed 35,000 men. The territorial losses imposed were tremendous. The Treaty of Trianon

Large sections of the former kingdom of Hungary were handed over to the three neighbors, Rumania, Czechoslovakia, and Serbia. To be sure, the transferred areas were preponderantly inhabited by nationals of the country to which title was given. Nonetheless, there were many Hungarians on the soil of the surrendered territories. Even Austria gained a strip of western Hungary inhabited by a German population (Burgenland). By these vast reductions Hungary shrunk to less than half of her former size and to a little under 9,000,000 inhabitants. The territorial losses imposed on Hungary

The last state to hear from the peace conference was Turkey. This was because the Turkish problem was a knotty one and caused much dissension among Great Britain, France, and Italy, the three powers who reserved its settlement to themselves. The situation would have been easier if tsarist Russia had not disappeared from the scene, thus making impossible the execution of the secret treaties elaborated during the war. By these treaties the tsar was to get Constantinople and the straits, the goal of Russian longing for well over a century. With Russia gone Bolshevik it was necessary to find another solution for this strategic area. The partition of Turkey presents difficulties

After long discussion the three powers resolved to try the experiment of converting the straits area into an International Zone, subject to their common rule. As for the remainder of the Ottoman empire, they took

The revised partition plan of Britain, France, and Italy
over, each one for itself in either open or veiled possession, such areas as seemed economically desirable. Great Britain indicated Mesopotamia with southern Syria (Palestine) as the territory of her choice; France marked off a French sphere in northern Syria and southeastern Anatolia; and Italy reserved southwestern Anatolia (Adalia) to her uses.

Because the three allies wished to employ Greece as a spearhead against

Smyrna with hinterland assigned to Greece
a possibly recalcitrant Turkey, they assigned the rich city of Smyrna with its hinterland to this small Balkan power. There was very little left of the former Ottoman empire after these liberal subtractions had been made, and that little was sure to be taken away as soon as the victors, themselves still groggy from their exhausting struggle, should have recovered their normal self-assurance.

When the news of the proposed dismemberment of their state reached

The power in Turkey seized by the nationalists
the Turks in Anatolia, they again took up arms. Or rather they found an inspired leader in Mustapha Kemal, to whose summons to die like men rather than be sold like cattle they enthusiastically responded. The representatives of the meek sultan summoned to Paris duly signed the Turkish treaty submitted to them at the suburb of Sèvres in August, 1920. But when they brought the treaty home, they found that the sultan and his government no longer counted and that the power had been seized by Kemal and his followers, inflamed with a fierce nationalist spirit.

Of all the peace treaties drawn up at Paris the Treaty of Sèvres, which

Rejection of the Treaty of Sèvres
was the severest of all, was the only one that was never executed. It succumbed, as we shall see, to the aroused resistance of the Turkish will-to-live and led in due time to the negotiated Treaty of Lausanne (1923) which conceded to Mustapha Kemal's republican Turkey a free and independent status.

37 THE GERMAN REPUBLIC; THE EXECUTION OF THE TREATY OF VERSAILLES; THE REPARATIONS ISSUE

DURING WORLD WAR I the attention of Europe became focused on a single object to a degree perhaps never before experienced. As if by a kind of universal hypnosis, all eyes were fixed on the breathless, titanic struggle of the belligerents. But no sooner had the peace negotiations begun at Paris than the events particular to the separate countries and regions of which Europe was composed again surged to the front, demanding the consideration which was their due. Even the lofty demigods assembled in the French capital to reorganize a war-shattered world were moved to look about them with unconcealed anxiety: toward Russia, for instance, whence a communist propaganda of extraordinary intensity radiated over the Western world; or toward the many new and perilously frail political growths, such as Finland, Latvia, Estonia, and Poland, just springing to life along the western rim of Russia; or toward that ancient and apparently incurable center of confusion, the Balkan peninsula.

With the war's end many centers of disturbance rise into view

FORMATION OF THE GERMAN REPUBLIC

Undoubtedly, however, the chief source of anxiety for the peace delegates assembled at Paris was Germany, agitated with a revolution of which no one could foresee the end. The republic proclaimed at Berlin on November 9, 1918, was a creation of the Social Democrats. The day after its birth Emperor William II abandoned his army to take refuge in neutral Holland, and two days later (November 11) representatives of the new German republic signed the armistice agreement which brought the war to a close.

A leading center of anxiety is Germany

During the following months exhausted and defeated Germany looked more like a madhouse than an ordered civilized society. The Social Democrats had seized the power, and much depended on their courage and intelligence. Unfortunately they were not a united party, for they had during the war split into a majority and minority group. The minority group was radically inclined and sought contact with the still more

The Social Democrats weakened by splitting into a majority and a minority group

radical group of the Communists, who, indoctrinated by the forceful propaganda emanating from Russia, were firmly set on creating an exclusive government of the workers. After wavering for a few weeks, the Minority Socialists actually abandoned their more conservative brethren, threw in their lot with the Communist extremists, and unloosed a civil war which repeatedly tinged the pavements of Berlin with blood.

The middle classes rally to the Majority Socialists

It was chiefly because the middle classes lined up behind the Majority Socialists that this group was able to win out and rescue Germany from the sweeping bolshevism which the radicals desired to impose. The Majority Socialists favored a mild, evolutionary, not an uncompromising, revolutionary program. They bade the middle classes emerge from the holes in which they had been hiding since the proclamation of the republic and take their accustomed places in the social order. In fact, they established a working alliance between themselves and the moderate elements of the citizenry which stabilized the situation. It followed that when, on January 19, 1919, the elections for the National Assembly took place, the extremists of both the Right and the Left failed signally to muster the strength of the combined middle parties.

The Weimar National Assembly ruled by moderate, not extreme opinion

The National Assembly came together, not in the disturbed German capital, but in the quiet little town of Weimar in the heart of Germany. Its Right was made up of the irreconcilables of the old regime, its Left of the groups (Communists and Minority Socialists) which faced toward Moscow. In the middle of the house sat the moderates, distributed among several parties which reflected opinions either of a socialist or a liberal, democratic character. It was these middle groups which agreed on co-operation and therefore ruled the Assembly. By their union they were able to beat down repeated revolutionary outbreaks in various communist-tinged industrial centers and to give the republic a democratic constitution.

The Assembly accepts, under duress, the Treaty of Versailles

Nonetheless, the allied moderates in control at Weimar faced a very difficult situation. As the army, on flowing back from France, had been dispersed, the Assembly had no reliable force at its disposal. More, however, than on armed support its success would depend on the peace treaty which the victors were preparing at Paris and which they disdainfully refused to discuss with the vanquished. When the document was at last received, it caused the Assembly to give vent to a passionate protest. In the end, on being threatened with a resumption of the war, the Assembly authorized the representatives it had dispatched to Paris to submit. On June 28, 1919, the Treaty of Versailles received the signature of victors and vanquished.

Before taking up the main matter of this chapter—the problems that rocked Europe in connection with the execution of the Treaty of Versailles—we may advantageously dispose of the constitutional labors of the Weimar Assembly. Completed in the course of the summer, the new constitution, a very democratic document, was on August 14 declared to be the law of the land. The chief executive was a president, elected for a seven-year term by popular vote. The suffrage was extended to every person, male or female, over twenty years of age. Under the president and appointed by him was a cabinet of ministers responsible to the parliament or Reichstag. Besides the Reichstag, elected by the people, there was a second, less important chamber, called the Reichsrat, which represented the eighteen states making up the federated commonwealth (Reich). The eighteen component states, which were required to be republics like Germany itself, were not given all the local powers which had formerly characterized the German constitutive units. In a word, republican Germany was endowed with a more centralized constitution than that of its imperial predecessor.

Germany made a republic with a democratic constitution

For the next few years it looked doubtful whether the new constitution or indeed whether Germany itself would survive. There were repeated outbreaks on the part of the disappointed communist elements; and when these radicals had been put down, the monarchists of the extreme Right arose in their turn. It will be agreed that the republic was loaded with a heavy liability when it was obliged to accept the dictated peace of Versailles. Nor was its standing among its own people improved by the necessity it was under of kowtowing to innumerable entente commissions dispatched to Germany to carry out the many punitive stipulations incorporated in the treaty.

The republic confronted with many difficulties

THE EXECUTION OF THE TREATY OF VERSAILLES

The most striking event immediately following the acceptance of the treaty was the assembling under the control of enemy boards of the warships, merchant vessels, artillery, airplanes, tanks, machine guns, and other equipment which Germany had forfeited to the end either of dispatching them to the victor countries for distribution or of destroying them in immense repeated holocausts. More distressing still were the boundary commissions which, on the one hand, chipped important areas from Germany for transfer to its neighbors, and, on the other, superintended the several plebiscites which were to decide whether the nation would suffer still further amputations. The first plebiscite occurred in the two Schleswig zones. By virtue thereof the northern zone went to Denmark, while the southern chose to abide by Germany. In East Prussia both plebiscite districts (Allenstein and Marienwerder) chose by an all but unanimous vote to remain in Germany rather than be incorporated in Poland.

The surrender of equipment and territory; the two Schleswig plebiscites; the two East Prussian plebiscites

By far the largest as well as the most valuable plebiscite area was
Upper Silesia. Disturbed conditions in this region caused the postponement of the vote till March, 1921, when the population by a substantial
majority decided for Germany. As the allies, more particularly France,
were resolved that this rich mining and industrial area should not go
intact to Germany, they insisted on dividing it between Germany and
Poland in such a way that the overwhelming preponderance of its coal
and zinc mines was handed over to the resuscitated Polish state.

In order to make sure of Germany's acquiescence in the above-recited
measures, the allies had provided in the treaty for the military occupation
of the left bank of the Rhine together with three bridgeheads on the
right bank opposite the cities of Cologne, Coblenz, and Mainz. But,
more particularly, the stationing on German soil of allied troops amounting to an army of 75,000 men was intended to insure the ready acceptance of the penalties of the treaty and especially the payment of whatever reparations might be assessed against the defeated power.

THE REPARATION ISSUE

It will be remembered that the total reparation sum was not named
in the Treaty of Versailles because the victors were too far apart in
their figures to reach an agreement. In consequence, a Reparation Commission was appointed and charged with studying the problem to the
end of presenting the bill on which its members had reached an agreement by May 1, 1921. On this commission the United States was to be
represented; but as the Senate of the United States refused to ratify the
Treaty of Versailles, the American representative had to be withdrawn,
thus leaving the work to the four remaining members, representing
Great Britain, France, Italy, and Belgium.

The Senate
of the
United
States re-
jects the
Treaty of
Versailles
because tied
up with the
League of
Nations

The adverse action of the Senate was not due to opposition to the
Treaty of Versailles but to the League of Nations integrally merged
with it. The Republican minority of the Senate, led by Senator Lodge of
Massachusetts, maintained that the Covenant and, more particularly,
Article 10, which guaranteed the territorial integrity of all the League
members, constituted an infringement of the sovereignty of the United
States in that it obliged the country to wage war without the authorization of Congress. President Wilson, on his return to America, vigorously
denied this and other related charges but was unable to carry out the
public campaign by which he planned to bring the issue to the people
because he was incapacitated by a sudden attack of illness. Even so, he
could have had the two-thirds majority for the treaty required by the
constitution, had he been willing to accept the reservations proposed by
the opposition. Refusing to compromise, he lost the battle with the

Senate. A year later, by the presidential election of November, 1920, he lost also the battle with the people, for the Democratic candidate, whom he sponsored, was defeated by the Republican candidate, Warren G. Harding. Doubtless the Republican triumph was due as much, and more, to the general disillusionment following the war as to wide opposition to the League of Nations. Nonetheless, the League of Nations was in the resulting popular chill tacitly consigned to the grave. But not so the Treaty of Versailles, or at least its substance, for in a separate treaty of peace concluded with Germany in 1921 (the Treaty of Berlin) the United States insisted on receiving all the rights and privileges stipulated in the earlier treaty.

The withdrawal of the United States from the League of Nations greatly contributed to the instability of the post-war world. Immediate evidence was supplied on the resignation of the American representative from the Reparation Commission. It signified the extinction of the only moderating voice in that body, for the United States, having renounced its claim to reparations, was in a position to insist on Germany's being assessed, not vindictively but in strict accord with its capacity to pay. When on May 1, 1921, the Germans were presented with their bill, the Commission named as Germany's indebtedness the wholly irrational figure of 132,000,000,000 gold marks. In one of their many preparatory conferences the allied governments had agreed that whatever the sum Germany might be assessed, its distribution should take place in such a way that France would receive 52 per cent of the total, Great Britain 22 per cent, Italy 10 per cent, Belgium 8 per cent, while the slender remainder was to be divided among the many lesser allies.

The allies present the reparations bill (May 1, 1921)

In order to meet the annual payments imposed on Germany in connection with the reparations settlement, the government, already drained of its gold by the earlier assessments of the victors, printed paper money to sell on foreign markets for whatever it might bring. Before long the value of the unconscionably multiplied paper mark began to decline so rapidly that, hardly more than a year after the inauguration of the payment plan, the government was obliged to appeal to the Reparation Commission for a moratorium. A moratorium means a respite from payment; and a respite, if granted, signified that the allies would have to forgo an expected and much-needed income. Accordingly, the German appeal precipitated a crisis. Indeed, crisis followed crisis over the reparation issue for the next ten years and kept Europe in a turmoil by putting an intolerable burden on the processes of peaceful intercourse and exchange.

Already in 1922 Germany asks for a moratorium

Germany's request for a delay not only told the world that Germany was bankrupt but presently revealed that the two leading creditors were no longer of one mind. Great Britain wished to grant Germany a moratorium, France did not. This was not because Great Britain was magnanimous and France vindictive, but because the two countries were in an entirely different position. Great Britain, needing to revive its industries, wanted the profitable German market restored as soon as possible. France, on the other hand, having had her northeastern provinces shot and stamped to ruin during the war, wanted them restored with the least possible delay. The liability of Germany for this restoration had been laid down in the treaty and had been acknowledged by Germany herself. The French expectation was that, beginning with 1921, German payments would be set flowing toward France at a greatly accelerated rate. And here, with the flow no more than started, Germany demanded a halt! The exasperated French were convinced that their neighbors were acting in bad faith. Vehemently they threatened them with the occupation of further territory, a punishment which, in accordance with the Treaty of Versailles, the allies were free to inflict in case of a "voluntary" German default.

France, unsupported by Britain, rejects the moratorium plea

The French prime minister at the time was Poincaré. During a long and energetic career he had become the leading spokesman of French nationalism. In December, 1922, Poincaré's representative on the Reparation Commission, supported by the representatives of Italy and Belgium, declared that in his view Germany had "voluntarily" defaulted. Although the British representative refused to take this position, on January 11, 1923, French forces, supported by Italian and Belgian "token" contingents, entered the rich industrial area of the Ruhr in order to collect, under duress, the reparations which Germany, according to Poincaré, was willfully withholding. The Ruhr constituted one of the greatest coal and industrial areas of the world and was the heart of economic Germany. This must be kept in mind if the ensuing crisis is to be understood.

French troops seize the Ruhr to collect reparations by force (January, 1923)

Great Britain's refusal to concur in the French action encouraged Germany to declare it illegal. Ruhr government and factory officials, as well as the workers, were exhorted from Berlin to balk the French designs by a policy of passive resistance. Against their first plan of a small body of experts supervising the Ruhr industries and turning the profits into the French treasury, the French were obliged to bring an ever larger body of troops across the Rhine in order to set the recalcitrant Germans to work under military compulsion. The German government at Berlin, for its part, did its best to sustain the spirit of resistance by promising to pay wages and salaries to all workers whom the French might dismiss for disobedience or sabotage.

The Germans resort to passive resistance

The mad and ruinous Ruhr episode alarmed a breathless world till August, 1923. By that time the Germans were at the end of their tether, and made an abject submission. The government had paid the heavy bills of passive resistance by running off more and still more paper marks from the printing presses until it took a million and, finally, many tens of millions of marks to buy an American dollar, which in pre-war days had been quoted at a little more than four marks. To be sure, the value of the mark had begun to shrink as far back as the outbreak of World War I and the process had continued uninterruptedly since the peace. The precipitate downward plunge, however, the descent into Avernus, was due to the passive resistance of 1923. By the summer of that year, with the national treasury bankrupt and all individual savings wiped out, Germany had become a nation of paupers. In addition, since the exchange of goods could not be conducted with a useless currency, business was at a standstill and the whole population threatened with starvation.

Submission of Germany (August, 1923) and accompanying bankruptcy

With the Ruhr invasion post-war Europe reached its lowest ebb. Out of the distressing situation there gradually rose the conviction that the question of reparations must be removed from the heated atmosphere of politics by referring it to a body of economic experts. Even France came to this conclusion on discovering that the Ruhr occupation cost the French treasury more than it produced. A committee of experts, on which American representatives consented to act unofficially in the role of umpires, met at Paris in the early months of 1924 and devised a plan which was put into effect in the following summer. It is usually called the Dawes plan from the American, Charles G. Dawes (afterward vice-president), who headed the American delegation. Under the Dawes plan France agreed to withdraw from the Ruhr, and Germany received an international loan to enable her to re-establish her currency on a gold basis. A new reparation program was drawn up by which Germany's annual payments were appreciably reduced. There followed a considerable financial and economic pick-up not only in Germany but throughout the world. Before the end of the year the beaten country had started on the way to recovery.

The Dawes plan comes (1924) to the rescue of Germany

THE ISSUE OF FRENCH SECURITY

On this recovery the French government and people looked with somewhat mixed feelings. They argued that a strengthened Germany would inevitably attempt to strike off the shackles of Versailles and in the process might resume the ancient feud with its western neighbor. Against this eventuality France desired to be made secure by a system of international guarantees.

The French demand for security

Far from being raised for the first time in 1924, the issue of French security went back to the peace conference of five years before. At the instance of Clemenceau, the vigorous spokesman of his country at the

Paris meeting, security had been actually incorporated in the Treaty of Versailles by means of pledges given by Great Britain and the United States to come to the assistance of France the instant that Germany should make a warlike move. When the Senate of the United States repudiated the Treaty of Versailles, this pledge went aglimmering, and not only so far as the United States was concerned. It was canceled for Britain, too, owing to the provision that it was not to bind one of the pledging powers without binding the other.

French security originally incorporated in the Treaty of Versailles

Deeply disappointed, France undertook to look for security elsewhere. She returned to the system of military alliances, morally discredited though it was by the recent war, and attached to herself, one after the other, the many neighbors of Germany. Before the war she had cultivated the friendship of Russia as the best means of holding Germany in check. Now that Russia had gone Bolshevik, the Slav power was not available for French purposes and was replaced in the French system by three German border-states, Belgium, Poland, and Czechoslovakia. Even Rumania and Yugoslavia, although they nowhere touched on Germany, were ultimately incorporated in the French security system.

The French turn for security to the system of military alliances

It may be interposed at this point that France had helped establish the League of Nations and that the purpose of the League was to preserve peace by adjudicating national differences without resort to arms. Why not rely on the League for security? To this question France answered that the young League was an experiment and might prove too feeble to procure its ends. Hence France refused to place faith in it and went her own way by renewing the system, invented as far back as Richelieu and in full operation in 1914, of surrounding Germany with a ring of iron.

France refuses to have faith in the League of Nations

When the adoption of the Dawes plan led temporarily to a somewhat better feeling between France and Germany, it occurred to some leading Frenchmen that a more effective method of obtaining security than through either the League of Nations or a military ring of Germany's neighbors would be through an accommodation with Germany herself. The leading spokesman of this group was Aristide Briand, a prominent liberal and frequent member of the ministry, usually in the post of minister of foreign affairs. Briand's idea was echoed by Gustav Stressemann, the German foreign minister, and, following a friendly exchange between the two men, culminated in October, 1925, in a conference of all the leading powers in order to lend its support to the contemplated Franco-German rapprochement. The conference took place in Locarno in Switzerland and led to the signing of five important treaties.

The Locarno conference of 1925

The first four treaties were contracts between Germany, on the one hand, and France, Belgium, Poland, and Czechoslovakia respectively, on the other, whereby the signatories pledged themselves to settle all disputes between them by arbitral methods. More important by far was the fifth Locarno treaty, for it dealt with French security. It was arranged among Germany, France, Belgium, Italy, and Great Britain and put the Franco-German and the Belgian-German boundaries, as drawn in the Treaty of Versailles, under the collective guarantee of the five signatories. Than this it is difficult to conceive of any purely contractual arrangement that could have done more for French security. There followed a marked improvement in the political tone of Europe, joyfully hailed by men of good will as the Locarno spirit. While the brightened prospect was only too soon again obscured, it deserves to be recorded that, by the affirmation of the will-to-peace by victors and vanquished, Europe's characteristic post-war gloom was for one brief moment dispersed. *The Locarno treaties*

A logical consequence of the Locarno agreements was the admission of Germany to the League of Nations. It took place in September, 1926. Germany was accorded a permanent seat in the Council alongside of Great Britain, France, Italy, and Japan. While the permanent seats were thus increased to five, the nonpermanent seats, which the Assembly of the League had the right to fill by election, were also increased. Originally four, they had already been increased to six. In 1926 they were raised to nine and in the course of the next few years to eleven. It cannot be said that this increase in the representation of the small states improved the prospects of peace. The Council, and the Assembly no less, were from the first dominated by the great powers and that situation never changed so long as the League lasted. *Germany admitted (1926) to the League of Nations*

THE INTER-ALLIED DEBTS

A matter which profoundly troubled France and which in the French mind was inextricably tied up with German reparations was its debt to the United States, contracted during the war. All the allies without exception had in this connection received loans in substantial but varying amounts from the United States. Great Britain and France, in their turn, had made loans to their weaker allies, such as Italy, Rumania, and Serbia. All these obligations of the allies toward one another constituted an intricate web of accounts currently covered by the term inter-allied debts. Inasmuch as the debts had been contracted in a common cause, the opinion was frequently voiced after the war that the fairest manner of getting them out of the way would be by universal mutual cancellation. *The inter-allied debts and the European opinion in favor of their cancellation*

The stumbling-block to cancellation was the United States. The Washington government took the stand that it had made bona fide loans to the European states to an amount of over $10,000,000,000, and that in the coming time it would not, like them, receive German reparations. The three principal debtors of the United States were Great Britain, which owed over $4,000,000,000; France, which owed almost exactly $4,000,000,000; and Italy, which owed about $2,000,000,000. These sums the United States intended to get back, though the government indicated its readiness to remit a varying but substantial part of the interest charge, proportioned in every instance to the debtor country's "capacity to pay." There was a unanimous pained outcry from the borrowers on this ultimatum, but in the end they came to terms. Beginning with Great Britain, they signed between 1923 and 1929 debt settlements with the United States whereby they agreed to make annual payments over a period of sixty-two years.

The United States obliges its European debtors to make debt settlements

Although the United States held to the theory that the debts which the European states owed Washington had nothing to do with reparations, in actual fact the two items were inseparable. For only in measure as the debtors of the United States should receive payments from Germany would they be in possession of sums they could transmit to the United States; and in case Germany defaulted to the allies, it was as self-evident as the multiplication table that the allies would at once default to the United States.

The tie-up between reparations and the allied re-mittances

As the Dawes plan of 1924 was no more than an emergency measure, another international conference took place in 1929 to make final disposition in regard to the total reparation bill and the annual payments by which it was to be discharged. Once again a neutral American, Owen D. Young, acted as general chairman, and when the new plan had been worked out, it received his name. By the Young plan the total reparation bill was cut down to about $8,000,000,000, one-fourth of the original figure, and the German annual payments, owing to the addition of interest charges, hovered around $500,000,000 for a period of fifty-nine years. In return for accepting the Young plan Germany was offered the evacuation of the Rhineland. Accordingly, on German adherence having been secured, the allied troops took their departure (1930), and German soil was at last free after a twelve-year foreign occupation.

The Young plan of 1929 and the evacuation of the Rhineland in 1930

END OF REPARATIONS AND INTER-ALLIED DEBTS

The liberation of the Rhineland was the only one of the many happy expectations raised by the Young plan that was ever realized. For, in the very year of the Young plan (1929), an economic depression stole like a creeping paralysis through all the countries of the world. Its causes have been endlessly debated without having to date brought the quarreling experts to agreement. Doubtless the high tariffs were a factor by which, owing to the prevailing nationalism, every state, large and small, tried to exclude from its markets the products of its neighbors. The uninterrupted flow of inventions also figured, since they brought about, on

The world depression beginning in 1929, makes reparation payments impossible

the one hand, a vast overproduction of goods and, on the other, a reduction of workers till the unemployed throughout the civilized world constituted an army swollen to fantastic proportions. The annual reparation payments made by Germany under the Dawes plan of 1924 had, in the main, been made possible by large-scale borrowing in the money market of the United States. With the depression of 1929 this borrowing was abruptly cut off. The result was that by 1931 Germany was in such distress that her creditors had perforce to concede her a moratorium.

It was the beginning of the end, for the economic depression deepened from year to year. In 1932 another international conference, held at Lausanne, recognized that the whole reparations' structure had been erected on a prospective world prosperity which had completely vanished. The disillusioned conference offered to reduce the remaining German indemnity to an almost invisible figure, provided the United States would accept a proportional slashing of its war debts. Although the United States refused, most allies at once ceased paying anything to the United States on the ground, convincing at least to themselves, that they were not receiving anything from Germany. By 1934 all the allies, with the single exception of Finland, had followed the same course. *A conference at Lausanne practically cancels reparations (1932)*

The upshot was clear: While the reduced reparations of 1932 and the inter-allied debts as negotiated in the twenties did not lose their legal character, they were to all intents wiped off the slate of international accounting. With the year 1929 the world entered on an economic crisis, from which it had recovered, only partially if at all, when World War II broke out in 1939 and unceremoniously swept the once so cantankerous issue of reparations and inter-allied debts into the dust-bin of history. *Burial, with reparations, of the inter-allied debts*

38 THE PEACE MOVEMENT: PARTIAL SUCCESSES AND FINAL FAILURE OF THE LEAGUE OF NATIONS

WITH THE CLOSE of the war Europe and the world in general entered on a period of disillusionment. In spite of many brave attempts to restore hope and confidence and the occasional appearance of a rift in the black bank of overhanging clouds, disillusionment and its child, discouragement, stubbornly persisted. The causes that gave them birth are not far to seek. Grave political disturbances continued after the peace in innumerable places; the vast masses of demobilized soldiers, whom the economic organism of their respective countries could not at once absorb, created a distressing problem of unemployment; and the general misery and unrest were prolonged and deepened by the tariff barriers with which nationalism, intensified by the war, made it its business everywhere to reduce and cut off international commerce.

However, should the foremost reason for the post-war pessimism be sought, it might be identified with the failure to realize the new international order, which the liberal elements had so confidently prognosticated as the upshot of the ferocious struggle. In spite of high-sounding pronouncements, the Paris treaties in effect consecrated the traditional order based on nationalism and imperialism, thereby projecting a postwar world indistinguishable in its main aspects from its pre-war prototype.

STRUCTURE OF THE LEAGUE OF NATIONS

Nonetheless, there was an international novelty. Out of the Paris wreck of his plans President Wilson had salvaged the League of Nations and around it gathered the hopes of the disappointed idealists. Cautiously nursed into strength, the international League might yet prove the little David sent to slay the towering nationalist Goliath.

True, the League was not a super-state, a world government. It was no more than a free association of independent polities, each of them jealously intent on guarding what it considered its most precious jewel, its sovereignty. Nevertheless, its constitution, called Covenant, assigned to

The universal post-war disillusionment

Disillusionment due in the main to collapse of idealist hopes

Hope centers in the League of Nations

750

the League important international functions. Among these the two out-
standing ones were first, the prevention of war and second, the reduc-
tion of armaments. In the present chapter we shall examine not only
how the League of Nations discharged these two major and a number of
related minor purposes but also how the whole peace movement fared be-
tween the end of the war and its final collapse two decades later.

Leading
purposes of
the League:
(1) Preven-
tion of war;
(2) Reduc-
tion of arm-
aments

The League began life under the serious handicap of the abstention of
that country whose chief executive was largely responsible for its exist-
ence. When the people of the United States reacted against their wartime
experience by slowly disentangling themselves from the affairs of Europe,
they made a beginning, or the Senate acting for them made a beginning,
by rejecting the Treaty of Versailles, not because of its over-severe and
punitive character, but because of the international obligations implicit
in the League of Nations. As, for different reasons, communist Russia
and defeated Germany also figured among the absentees, the League was
not universal. As originally constituted, it looked suspiciously like the
perpetuated association of the European victors.

Important
absentees
from the
League
roster

On beginning operations in 1920 the League had a roster of forty-three
members. With subsequent additions, among them a number of van-
quished states, the membership reached into the fifties and gradually
came nearer to a true universality. In 1926 it even invited Germany to
membership, although in 1933, with the advent to power of Hitler, Ger-
many again withdrew. In the same year Japan also resigned, the two
withdrawals marking an ominous turn in the fortunes of the League.
The entrance in 1934 of Russia into the League seemed to some enthusi-
asts of the cause to counterbalance the two defections. But it did not alter
the fact that the League structure was badly shaken.

The shift-
ing member-
ship of the
League

We learned in an earlier chaper that the League operated with a small
Council, a large annual Assembly, and a permanent Secretariat located at
Geneva, which we may designate as the League capital. A permanent
court, called the Court of International Justice and located at The Hague,
served as the judicial arm of the League.

Main
institutions
of the
League

An important department of the League was the International Labor
Organization, instituted in recognition of the fact that "the relations of
capital and labor are a matter of international concern." The I.L.O.
operated through an annual Labor Conference and a permanent Secre-
tariat at Geneva, called the International Labor Office. A very spirited
body, the I.L.O. adopted in the course of its annual sessions many rec-
ommendations dealing with female and child labor, night work, unem-
ployment, and similar interests connected with the steadily expanding
world of industry. These recommendations were forwarded to the mem-
ber states, who might or might not adopt them according to their pleas-
ure. The Labor Office proved particularly valuable in the capacity of a

Machinery
and func-
tions of the
International
Labor Or-
ganization
(I.L.O.)

labor-research bureau. It assembled and published much important information dealing with the many problems in this troubled modern field.

It is a simple, verifiable fact that the League in its various departments
The League a going concern from the day it started lost no time in getting started. The Council met at least four times every year to deal with the agenda prepared by the Secretariat, and the annual meeting of the Assembly, which occurred in September, regularly attracted wide attention. Admittedly the actions of the League frequently disappointed its followers and invited the scorn of its opponents. But as it also scored many successes, it is fair, before discussing its failures, to take some account of its numerous positive achievements.

ACHIEVEMENTS OF THE LEAGUE

The achievements of the League were not all on the same level. In
The humanitarian services of the League addition to its two above-indicated main purposes, the League was intrusted with certain humanitarian services which it discharged with conspicuous success. Such services were the international traffic in women and children and the hardly less vicious traffic in opium and other similar drugs. Furthermore, the post-war confusion gave birth to many problems of an international scope which the League, the only effective international body in existence, promptly took under its wing. Thus it supervised the repatriation of 400,000 prisoners of war, belonging to twenty-six different nationalities. Again when, at the close of the war between Greece and Turkey, the question arose of who was to supervise the exchange of populations provided for in the Treaty of Lausanne (1923), the League assumed this responsibility. By the successful handling of these and similar cases, minor perhaps but pressing, the League conclusively proved that by the operation of forces characteristic of our time the world had become an international unit, and that an association of its kind could no longer, without grave loss to humanity, be dispensed with.

Even in one of its two main and most difficult functions, the peaceful
The League adjudicates many disputes among lesser sovereign states adjustment of disputes among sovereign nations, the League scored a number of impressive triumphs. When in 1920 Sweden and Finland quarreled over the ownership of the Åland Islands lying between them in the Baltic sea, the League stepped in and, through its Council, awarded the islands to Finland with the provision that they were never to be fortified. Again, when Lithuania forcefully appropriated Memel (1923), the League took the matter under consideration, and, while accepting the result of Lithuanian violence, obliged the Kaunas government to rule Memelland's overwhelmingly German population in accordance with a statute guaranteeing the inhabitants a liberal measure of autonomy. Still another case: In 1925 a Greek attack on Bulgaria was stopped by the threat of an economic boycott. As a final instance let us take the seizure

(1932) by Peru from Colombia of the border province of Leticia. By its timely interference the League not only prevented war but brought about the peaceful restitution of Leticia to Colombia.

FAILURES OF THE LEAGUE

In turning now to the failures of the League in its mediatory function between contentious states, we are struck by the fact that the failures occurred whenever one of the parties to a dispute was a great power. That would seem to indicate that the League lacked the political and military resources to bring adequate pressure to bear upon a state of great-power rank. Its strength lay largely in the moral realm and, as the great powers were instinctively aware, could be defied by them with relative impunity. Instances of their defiance multiplied ominously with the passing of the years, as the record eloquently reveals.

The League unable to coerce a great power

In 1920 Poland seized Vilna by force of arms, thereby separating it from Lithuania, to which state it had been accorded by treaty. It may be interposed that Poland, although a large state, was not exactly a great power. But Poland on the occasion in question had the backing of France, and with French support was able to avert the interference of the League. Accordingly, in spite of frantic appeals by Lithuania to Geneva, Poland quietly incorporated Vilna in its territory.

Failures of the League: The seizure of Vilna by Poland

Another failure of the League occurred when a dispute arose (1923) between Italy and Greece over the murder on Greek soil of several Italian members of an Albanian boundary commission. Italy at once demanded a large indemnity and, to enforce a quick compliance, occupied the Greek island of Corfu. When the League attempted to intervene, Italy refused to present itself at the League bar. While the issue did not lead to war, war was averted not by the action of the League but because Italy accepted the mediation of its "equals," Great Britain and France, and because Greece in the end reluctantly met the Italian demand for indemnity.

Failures of the League: Italy, to enforce its demand on Greece, occupies (1923) Corfu

Then, in 1931, Japan openly flouted the League, and presently there followed actions by Italy and Germany which showed that, under its existing powers, the League could not enforce respect for treaties or prevent the consequence of their infraction, even when the consequence was war. It was in September, 1931, that Japan, finally and fully resolved to increase its own scanty natural resources by getting hold of those of Manchuria, undertook forcefully to take over this rich Chinese province. China promptly appealed to the Secretariat at Geneva against the breach of the peace, particularly outrageous because committed by one League member against another. When the League Council met to consider the case, it appointed a commission of inquiry which, after a long delay,

Failures of the League: Japan appropriates (1931) Manchuria

made an indecisive report. Even before the report was ready a group of Manchurian leaders, acting on Japanese inspiration, issued a proclamation of Manchurian independence. Following this step, they drew up a constitution in which the now independent Manchuria was renamed Manchukuo and the office of chief executive conferred on Henry Pu Yi, who had been deposed as emperor of China when China became a republic (1912). Of course Henry Pu Yi and the whole Manchukuo regime along with him were but puppets manipulated by hidden Nipponese hands.

Japan in 1933 presses on into China proper

In the year following the creation of Manchukuo, Japan pressed on into the north-China province of Jehol and incorporated it with Manchukuo. Since China was at the time enfeebled by civil war, its leading political figure, Generalissimo Chiang Kai-shek, proceeded cautiously and let himself be drawn into negotiations with Japan. Doubtless, too, he hesitated to go to war because of his hope that the League of Nations would intervene to stop the invader. But as this body contented itself with investigations and its members did not go beyond an expression of liveliest sympathy, Chiang Kai-shek found himself facing the enemy without support. This situation encouraged Japan to pass gradually from roundabout and concealed to open and undisguised aggression.

In the year 1937 began the interminable undeclared war between Japan and China

Accordingly, in 1937 Japan sent an army into the north-China province of Hopei, within which lay the old imperial capital of Peking and the great port of Tientsin, thereby inaugurating an undeclared war against its apparently unresisting victim. The outrageous act put an end to the long submissiveness of Chiang Kai-shek's government, established at the new Chinese capital of Nanking. Chiang boldly brought into the field the small, relatively modern army he had been laboring to create and, for a time at least, he had an indignant, united China behind him. Even the powerful Chinese communists lent him their support. Nonetheless, Chiang was not strong enough to stop the well-equipped Japanese and, on being forced to retire from Nanking, established his government in distant, inland Chungking. The invaders followed their Manchurian pattern by setting up at Peking a puppet regime manned by traitorous Chinese collaborators. So patently that no one could any longer fail to see, the Japanese program now stood disclosed as the reduction of the immense bulk of China to a humble Japanese protectorate. To this shame the at last fully awakened Chinese resolved never to submit with the result that, although the efficiently armed Japanese could drive their underarmed opponents before them almost at will, they were unable to occupy the whole vast empire and could not bring the war to a successful close.

It was doubtless the egregious failure of the League to oblige Japan to submit to its control that inspired Italy to follow in Japan's footsteps. In the year 1922 the Italian government had been converted into a dictatorship under Benito Mussolini, and this fascist leader had from the first declared in favor of expansion in the Mediterranean, habitually designated by him in the ancient Roman style as *mare nostrum,* our sea. Biding his time, he at last, in 1935, launched a war against the African kingdom of Ethiopia, which he saw in the light of a valuable addition to the scorched, unproductive deserts constituting Italy's African dominion. The emperor of Ethiopia, Haile Selassie, repeating the procedure followed by China four years before, appealed to the League for help and got a much better reception than did Chiang Kai-shek. Italy was closer at hand than Japan and was distinctly vulnerable through the command of "our sea" by the fleets of the two leading members of the League, Great Britain and France. In these circumstances the League was emboldened unambiguously to stigmatize Italy as the aggressor and for the first time since its existence to call down on the offender the severest measures at its command. These, laid down in Article 16 of the Covenant, imposed an economic embargo, under which it was supposed by the authors of the Covenant that the country so penalized would promptly collapse. But the collapse, chiefly because of the many cracks in the embargo, did not occur; Italy resolutely went on with its campaign; and in the course of the spring months of 1936 drove Haile Selassie into flight and appropriated his territory. The most sustained attempt the League ever made to prove its effectiveness became the occasion of its most resounding fiasco.

Failures of the League: Italy conquers Ethiopia (1935-36)

The successive disasters of the League were not lost on Nazi Germany, which raised its fearsome head in Europe when Adolf Hitler became German chancellor on January 30, 1933. Since from his first plunge into German public life Hitler had made the shame of the Treaty of Versailles the central and abiding theme of his oratory, it was a reasonable assumption that with his advent to power he would attempt to break the shackles it imposed on German armament. After secretly inaugurating appropriate preparatory measures, he decreed, in March, 1935, universal compulsory military service and, a year later, boldly dispatched German troops into the demilitarized Rhineland. The shock administered to Europe was tremendous. However, apart from indignant words and frantic gestures, neither the League of Nations nor France, the state most immediately concerned, took action. The French government hesitated to resort to arms without the assured support of Great Britain, and Great Britain was at the moment too alienated from France to lend an ear to her impassioned plea. With the two leading members of the League at loggerheads, the League, as so often on lesser occasions, was hamstrung. Let it not remain unnoticed, however, that the German action fell clearly within the competence of the League, since the demilitarization of the Rhineland was a main feature of the system the League had

Failures of the League: Nazi Germany reoccupies (1936) the Rhineland

been fashioned to uphold. Its failure to accept responsibility was additional proof, if proof were needed, that it had neither the power nor the will to fulfill its primary avowed function, which was to preserve the peace.

FAILURE TO BRING ABOUT DISARMAMENT ON LAND

The League slow to meet its self-assumed obligation to reduce armaments

A function of the League secondary only to that of preserving peace was, in the precise wording of the Covenant, "the reduction of national armaments to the lowest point consistent with national safety"; and it should not be overlooked that its failure to make headway with this particular purpose provided Hitler with the excuse before the bar of public opinion for his unilateral correction of the Treaty of Versailles. The dilatory treatment by the League of its disarmament obligation sprang from the fact that its creation had not diminished by a hair the jealousy and suspicion that for centuries had ruled the relations of the European states. So long as this poisonous atmosphere prevailed, the great powers, always the determining factor in every question of international scope, would approach the reduction of armaments issue with the greatest caution and hesitate to the point of paralysis before assuming any restrictive obligation. Each government contended, and perhaps believed, that its existing forces on land, sea, and in the air were no larger than was compatible with its safety and that reduction should be reserved to its neighbors who were, it was as plain as a church steeple, without exception monstrously over-armed.

The hollow draft of the Preparatory Commission

Possessed by this monumental bias, the members of the League were understandably slow to attack the thorny issue. Not till 1925 did they go so far as to appoint a Preparatory Commission charged with shaping a draft which might serve as guide to a full-dress Disarmament Conference. Sea armaments were excluded from its deliberations because, as we shall presently hear, the naval problem had been taken up by the relatively small number of naval powers on their own initiative. As soon as the Preparatory Commission began its labors, it discovered that armament reduction had so many sides to it and involved so many matters of dispute that it took all of six years to bring the draft to completion. And even then, owing to heated, unadjustable differences, the document was a mere outline, a frame without contents. To fill in the contents was left to the full Conference; but what chance, may we ask, was there of a large assembly of delegates agreeing on controversial military details which had defied solution by a small, hand-picked group of specialists?

The World Disarmament Conference met at long last at Geneva in

February, 1932. Finding nothing in the draft to set their teeth into, the leading delegates were prompted to make vainglorious proposals of their own, which were critically picked to pieces by the rest of the membership and contemptuously thrown aside. Only in a fresh session following a long adjournment did the Conference get down to business by attempting exactly to specify first, the permissible size of each nation's army, and second, the permissible expenditure of each army on war material. At once a loud outcry over figures made itself heard on every hand but sank to silence presently before the single clamorous divergence between France and Germany. France now as always wanted security, which, so far as armament was concerned, meant superiority; Germany, harping on the defenselessness to which it was condemned by the Treaty of Versailles, demanded equality. It was the inability of the Conference to bring France and Germany to any kind of accommodation that exploded the whole undertaking. The fruitless meetings had continued for a year and a half, when a new German government brought them dramatically to an end. In January, 1933, what was still left of German democracy was swept from the stage by Hitler's assumption of power. He continued to permit the German delegates to participate in the Geneva debates until October, 1933, when, convinced that the equality which was his consistent demand would never be granted, he withdrew Germany from the Conference and followed this act a few days later by withdrawing it from the League as well. The whole disarmament project now fell to the ground, although, it is true, the Conference did not finally give up the ghost till two years afterward.

Insurmountable differences among the participants wreck the Disarmament Conference

ATTEMPT TO BRING ABOUT A LIMITATION OF NAVIES

It remains to follow up this story of the fiasco of disarmament on land with the parallel fiasco of naval disarmament. The latter was perhaps even more disappointing than the former since it had made an auspicious beginning and had raised a justified hope. The proposal for a limitation of navies did not emanate from the League of Nations but from a non-League state, the United States of America, which launched the project almost immediately after the close of the war.

Limitation of naval armament initiated by the United States

The United States took the initiative in this matter for a number of reasons. First, it was about to embark on a shipbuilding race with the only other two naval powers of any importance, Great Britain and Japan. Since the race would be very expensive, it was the part of prudence to try to set limits to it by a three-cornered agreement. A second reason for action was that the Washington government wished to show that, in spite of its abstention under public pressure from the League of Nations,

Reasons for the initiativ of the United States

it was ready to do its bit to promote the cause of world peace, which the League was supposed to have mainly at heart.

At the invitation of the United States the conference on limitation of navies took place in Washington in 1921-1922. In addition to the three great naval powers already mentioned, two lesser naval powers, France and Italy, were also invited to attend. While it was found impossible to come to terms on a plan of limitation for all categories of fighting vessels, it was an undeniable achievement that at least an agreement was reached on so-called capital ships, i.e., battleships and battle-cruisers. The agreement consisted in retaining for a period of ten years a fixed ratio in capital ship tonnages among the five negotiating powers. The ratio was put at the following figures: Great Britain 5, the United States 5, Japan 3, France 1.67, Italy 1.67.

Having inaugurated a limitation in the most expensive department of shipbuilding, the five powers continued to negotiate with a view to holding a later conference on the remaining classes of naval craft, on cruisers, submarines, and destroyers. Such a conference was duly called at Geneva in 1927, but it failed because the United States and Great Britain could not agree on the number or kinds of cruisers each should be permitted to have.

There followed another conference at London in 1930, at which Great Britain, the United States, and Japan consented to prolong the Washington ten-year agreement of 1922 for five years, that is, to 1937. France and Italy, however, refused to renew their particular commitment to the Washington agreement and began a naval race of their own in the Mediterranean. In addition to the five-year prolongation of their Washington agreement, the three leading naval powers reached an agreement on the tonnage to be allowed to each in the hitherto disputed categories of cruisers, destroyers, and submarines. Unfortunately a so-called escalator clause weakened the arrangement by permitting the signatories to exceed their tonnage in any category, if in the opinion of any one of them its national security appeared endangered by the new constructions of any non-signatory.

Such harmony as was achieved at London was rudely broken in 1934 when Japan advised the United States and Great Britain that she would not renew the London agreement when it expired, except on the basis of full naval equality. On being sternly refused this concession, Japan announced her intention to resume complete freedom of action in 1937. There were further halting negotiations among the powers and especially between Great Britain and the United States, but they had little significance. Plainly, every nation regarded national security as an issue of such supreme importance that it would not submit to limitations imposed by considerations of the common good.

Terms of the Washington agreement of 1921-22

Failure of the Geneva naval conference of 1927

The relatively successful London conference of 1930

All naval agreements gradually disavowed

In 1935 the rapidly deteriorating naval situation was complicated by a new factor. Germany and Russia, which had thus far been negligible as naval powers, entered the competition. The upshot of the various differences and rivalries was the most extravagant expenditure for naval preparedness ever recorded in history.

Unchecked competitive building of navies

THE RELAPSE INTO ANARCHY

By the time this anarchic situation had resulted from the unsuccessful attempt to restrict naval competition, the failure of the Geneva Disarmament Conference had brought about a wild scramble for preparedness on land. Following its departure (1933) from the Conference, Germany began to rearm without regard to the restrictions of the Treaty of Versailles and, as we have already learned, in 1935 announced the fact to the world by decreeing compulsory universal military service. This was all the provocation the other states needed to begin a feverish competition involving every known variety of deadly weapon. Unmistakably the peace movement had expired and the League of Nations had lost the little international authority with which it had been endowed and which it had exercised to the best of its ability but with tragic lack of success as to its main designated purposes. There followed even more feverish negotiations than before directed to the piling up of bilateral and multilateral non-aggression pacts in the hope of holding fast to a vanishing security. Completely dominating the situation, however, was the gradual consolidation of Italy, Germany, and Japan into an aggressor block. The outstanding details of the new confusion, which led directly and inescapably to a new World War, will have to be reserved to a final pre-war chapter, while we have a look at the striking domestic developments in the leading European states and follow this survey with a glance at the particular problems of the many small and generally new states of east-central Europe, of the Balkan peninsula, and of the Arab world.

General preparednes the curtain-raiser to World War II

39 RUSSIA GOES COMMUNIST

THE TRIUMPHANT BOLSHEVIKS

The Bolshevik victory of November, 1917

IN CHAPTER 36, which deals with World War I, we took account of the Russian revolution of March, 1917, and showed how by November of the same year it had taken on an extremely radical character under the energetic direction of the returned exile, Lenin. This extraordinary man had long headed the majority group of the Russian Socialist party, which carried the label Bolshevik (which means *majority*) and was dedicated to the realization of the Marxian program in its most uncompromising form. Since Bolshevism, reduced to its essence, was a thoroughgoing communism, we shall follow the practice of the Bolsheviks themselves and refer to them henceforth as communists. In this chapter we shall review the enormous disturbances in the midst of which the communist regime came to birth, define and clarify its principles, describe its leading institutions, and set forth the trials, failures, and triumphs that attended the execution of its program through the more than two decades that preceded the outbreak of World War II.

Lenin relies for success on the soviets of soldiers and workers

The leader of the Bolshevik revolution was Vladimir Ilyich Ulyanov, who in the course of his long conflict with the tsarist government had adopted the alias of N. Lenin, which became so inseparably attached to him that it has supplanted his true patronymic. To escape police persecution he had settled in 1900, when he was thirty years old, in Switzerland and, except for a brief visit to his native land during the revolution of 1905, he remained abroad till summoned back by the new and greater revolution of 1917. He arrived with the conviction developed by years of concentrated study that capitalism was evil incarnate and that the only effective way to get rid of it was by violent overthrow. This was also the view of a number of able associates, among whom the most outstanding was a man of Jewish stock destined to become famous as Leon Trotsky, although this, too, was merely an alias adopted in the days of the absolute tsar to put the police off his track. It was Lenin's great merit to have promptly decided, on arriving at Petrograd, that the most dynamic elements of the revolutionary upheaval were the spontaneously created *soviets,* or councils of soldiers, workers, and peasants. It was to them that he made his appeal and through them that he rose to the position of leader and master. To the slogan, "All power to the soviets," he successfully in November, 1917, overthrew the provisional government, devoted to a program of compromise, and proclaimed the unqualified dictatorship of the proletariat.

In strict accord with their doctrine, the Bolshevik rulers promptly seized the factories, banks, insurance companies, and other privately owned businesses and made them the property of the state. At the same time they invited the peasants to drive out the landlords and take over the mansions, woods, and grain fields of the legal owners. The execution of this sweeping policy of confiscation carried with it the murder of thousands of members of the former ruling classes, the nobility and bourgeoisie. Other thousands called themselves fortunate if they succeeded in saving their lives by escaping to foreign countries. The order went forth that the groups hitherto in command must be wiped out that the path might be cleared for a classless society of equals. *The confiscation of private businesses and estates*

These confiscatory violences threw the country into indescribable confusion. In order to give its undivided attention to the domination of this chaos the Bolshevik government resolved to abandon its allies—the war, we must remember, was still going on—and come to terms with Germany. Accordingly, in March, 1918, Trotsky, acting as government plenipotentiary, signed the Peace of Brest-Litovsk, which imposed on Russia the loss of a broad belt of western borderland. Since on surrendering to the allies some six months later Germany was obliged to renounce the Treaty of Brest-Litovsk, we may disregard its details, which never became effective. *The Bolsheviks make peace with Germany, March, 1918*

Outraged by Russia's desertion, the western allies turned sharply against the Bolsheviks, resolved to overthrow them by every means at their disposal. However, fully occupied at the time with the war, they were obliged to adjourn action till by November of the Brest-Litovsk year they had disposed of their last and most powerful enemy. They then adopted toward Russia a two-pronged policy consisting, first, of helping with supplies the numerous counter-revolutionary movements that had sprung up in the country, and second, of direct support of these movements by seizure of such ports of entry as Murmansk and Archangel on the White sea, Vladivostok in Asiatic waters, and Odessa and other points on the Black sea. *The western allies make war on Russia*

To the existing domestic turmoil there was thus added both a civil and a foreign war, with the former much more pressing than the latter, since Russia's former allies were too exhausted by the long struggle against Germany to give more than halfhearted attention to the war they launched against the Bolsheviks. Besides, with the termination of the war in the west the liberal sections of society in each allied country had recovered their power of speech and clamorously insisted on withdrawing *The Bolsheviks obliged to wage (a) a civil and (b) a foreign war*

from the Russian adventure. Consequently the Bolsheviks could afford
to treat the peripheral invasions lightly and to concentrate on the counter-revolutionary risings in their midst. Here were the immediate enemies
who needed imperatively to be crushed if the communist regime was to
survive.

The counter-revolutionary movements came to birth in four or five
widely separated areas of the vast expanse of Russia. They materialized
in the form of so-called White armies, under the leadership of former
tsarist generals. The Bolsheviks, who at the beginning had no armed
forces at their disposal, were obliged to improvise a Bolshevik, that is,
a so-called Red, army and to do so without delay. The difficult task was
intrusted to Trotsky, as commissar of war, and Trotsky, not hitherto
suspected of administrative talents, made a surprising success of his
undertaking. Appealing to the revolutionary and patriotic fervor of his
countrymen, he succeeded in the course of a single year in bringing together a force of several hundred thousand men which made up for its
inadequate equipment by its fanatic zeal. One after another of the White
armies were beaten and dispersed until by the spring of 1920 the civil
war had ceased to be a pressing peril. In the face of this unexpected turn
of affairs Great Britain and France, who alone among the allies had exhibited any genuine anti-Bolshevik vigor, reluctantly withdrew from the
scene.

A tragic episode of the bitter struggle must find a place in the record.
The former imperial family, consisting of Nicholas II, his wife, one son,
and four daughters had been transported for safekeeping to a distant
town in the Ural mountains. When in July, 1918, the town was threatened by a White army, the local soviet was seized with panic and hurriedly lined up the seven captives in the dark cellar of their temporary
shelter before a Red firing-squad and shot them.

Nonetheless, the Bolsheviks were not spared a very serious and costly
foreign war. It was launched against them by their immediate western
neighbor, Poland. The Polish state, risen from the dead in consequence
of the allied victory of 1918, desired an extension of its territory eastward
at the expense of Russia. The Polish ruling classes were excited by the
memory of a distant time when their country extended all the way from
the Baltic to the Black sea, and they resolved to utilize the troubles in
Russia to realize as far as possible this insubstantial dream. Accordingly,
in May, 1920, a Polish army invaded the Ukraine and pushed all the way
to its capital, Kiev, before the Red army, taken by surprise, could be
brought into action. Thereupon the Poles were forced into a disorderly retreat which did not end till Warsaw was in sight. Here the Poles, with the
powerful help of France, made a successful stand and crowded the Red
army back until both combatants came to a pause from sheer exhaustion.

The
Bolsheviks
win a
double
victory

Execution
of the
imperial
family,
July, 1918

The Russo-
Polish war
of 1920-21

Negotiations followed which in March, 1921, led to the Peace of Riga. Although by this treaty the boundary issue was compromised, the Poles got more than on strictly nationalist grounds they had any justification to claim. The Russians were worsted, but accepted their defeat with the mental reservation so usual in these circumstances of reopening the question on a later, more favorable occasion.

The peace with Poland may properly be associated in our minds with an accommodation on the part of Russia with a number of adjoining states, all products, like Poland, of the post-war upheaval. Finland, Latvia, Estonia, and Lithuania had set up independent governments immediately after the outbreak of the Russian revolution. Not only did the Bolsheviks lack the means to suppress these governments but they were restrained from action by the principle of national self-determination which at this time was a vigorously asserted article of their political philosophy. They therefore in the year 1920 signed treaties with these former dependencies whereby they acknowledged the sovereignty of each within mutually acceptable boundaries.

Russia acknowledges the independence of Finland, Latvia, Estonia, and Lithuania

CREATION AND CHARACTER OF THE UNION OF SOVIET SOCIALIST REPUBLICS (U.S.S.R.)

So long as they were occupied with the absorbing civil struggle the Bolsheviks adjourned the systematic reorganization of the country and relied on hurriedly improvised institutions to sustain their cause. The main improvisation was the Red army, in the astonishing success of which they naturally took an immense pride. A second, hardly less important improvisation was the Cheka. This was a secret state-police, endowed with power to arrest, punish, and execute all individuals suspected of enmity to the regime. The Cheka was intended to spread terror through the length and breadth of the land and, after destroying outright the leaders of the opposition, to reduce their humbler followers to a quaking silence. No statistics on its operations have ever been published, but it may be safely assumed that its executions ran into the thousands and tens of thousands. Of sole importance to the ruling group was the fact that it achieved its purpose and produced an at least superficially pacified Russia.

The earliest institutions: Red army and Cheka

No sooner had the Bolsheviks gained this relative security than they set about the permanent organization of their state. By the early twenties it had achieved the features which we shall now make it our business to set forth. Seven distinct national groups were recognized as settled on Russian soil, and each group was organized as a separate soviet socialist republic, that is, as a republic administered by a soviet or council of deputies. The association of the seven constituent republics

The federated Union of Soviet Socialist Republics (U.S.S.R.)

(a decade later the number had increased to eleven) was called the Union of Soviet Socialist Republics, abbreviated as U.S.S.R. Among the constituent republics the disparity in size and importance was enormous, since the single Russian Soviet Socialist Republic embraced about ninety per cent of the area and about seventy per cent of the population of the U.S.S.R. It thus came about that, in spite of the avowed purpose of the Bolsheviks to eliminate nationalism, the U.S.S.R. could not be kept from taking on from the first something of the character of a Russian national state, and this tendency in the years that followed grew rather than diminished.

The successive layers of soviets

The top governing body of the U.S.S.R. was called the Union Congress of Soviets. A schematic presentation of the total Bolshevik structure exhibits immediately below the supreme Union Congress of Soviets the Congresses of the seven constituent republics; below them the lesser regional soviets; and finally, below the last-named, the soviets of the towns and villages constituting the primary governing units. Since the Union Congress of Soviets crowning this heap of underlying soviets was far too large and unwieldy a body to govern directly, it delegated its power to a Union Central Executive Committee, and this in turn intrusted the practical work of government to a tight little ministry called the Union Council of Commissars. Since elective processes were employed in connection with all the above-mentioned bodies and since the franchise for the basic town and village soviets was conceded to all but known enemies of the regime, the system had on the surface a fairly democratic character.

Control exercised by the Communist party

The surface appearance was, however, belied by the facts. No political party other than the Communist party was permitted to exist. Its membership, small and hand-picked at first, was gradually enlarged till it came to embrace about three million persons. Even at this maximum figure it amounted to no more than some two per cent of the population. The all-important purity of the membership roster was guaranteed by periodic purges of the wavering or indolent elements. The Communist party was instructed to look on itself as an intellectual élite, whose business it was so thoroughly to rule the press, the radio, and the movies and so completely to dominate the electoral and administrative machinery that none but communist opinions and purposes should have a standing throughout the land.

Role of the Politburo

It follows that neither the Russian government nor Russian society was free in a democratic sense but under the domination of a powerful, relatively small oligarchy organized as the Communist party. And since the Communist party was under the control of a supreme political committee of nine members, the famous *Politburo,* we are justified in thinking of the Politburo as the outstanding political agency of the new state. It was this committee that formulated the major policies of the party and then imposed them on the official government. Government and party, theoretically separate, were for all practical purposes identical.

The continued domination throughout the land of both party and government had in the first instance been secured by the two provisional institutions, the Red army and the secret police. While given presently a permanent character, they passed, in the course of time, through important transformations. After its victory over the Whites the Red army was made permanent on the basis of what was substantially universal compulsory military service. Before long it became the world's largest standing army, which an untiring government did its best to supply with the most modern and effective implements of war. The secret police, originally called Cheka, was reorganized under another name but with the same authority over the civilian population and the same purpose of spreading terror. It became known by the initial letters of its new title *GPU* (pronounced Gay-pay-oo). Because of the evil reputation it rapidly gained, it went in 1934 the way of the Cheka, but as it continued to operate under still another name, we may conclude that the Bolshevik regime did not achieve a position where it felt secure without the help of a secret state police operating outside the law. The chief supports of both party and regime: (1) Red army; (2) secret police

In the year 1936 the Union Congress of Soviets, which, we have learned, was theoretically the highest source of authority in the U.S.S.R., adopted a new constitution. It introduced some changes which clarified the relation among the complicated elements of the administration; more notably it extended the amount and kinds of personal property the individual citizen might possess under the communist regime. But as it made no alteration in the essential structure of the state and, above all, none in the underlying communist theory, it was a delusion to regard the new constitution, as happened in some liberal western quarters, as marking a visible inching in the direction of western democracy. The constitution of 1936

LENIN SUCCEEDED BY STALIN

The overshadowing figure of the Russian world from the first moment of the Bolshevik seizure of power was, beyond all possibility of dispute, Lenin. It was his rule, in effect a dictatorship, that saw the regime through its early crises and endowed it with the institutions which we have described and under which it became a going concern. As early as 1922 Lenin's health began to give way under the strain of his labors and, although he was relieved of some of his burdens, he never recovered his strength, and died in January, 1924. An avowed atheist, he was accorded by his atheist partisans what in older periods of history would have been called divine honors by having Petrograd re- Death (1924) and apotheosis of Lenin named Leningrad after him and by the exhibition of his embalmed body in a glass-topped coffin within a specially constructed mausoleum beside the Kremlin walls.

Bitter struggle and ultimate triumph of Stalin

It was generally expected in the outside world that Lenin would be succeeded by Trotsky, Lenin's commissar of war and organizer of the Red army. More influential, however, within the Communist party than Trotsky was its Secretary General, Joseph Stalin, and in the end it was he and not Trotsky upon whom the mantle of Lenin descended. Since there were other aspirants to this honor besides Stalin and Trotsky, it was only after a bitter and prolonged struggle that Stalin won out. His name, too, exactly as in the case of Lenin and Trotsky, was an alias, an admirably appropriate alias we may add, for it signifies "man of steel." As self-contained, silent, and tough a character as any that has appeared in history, Stalin gradually crowded his rivals out of all the key positions and appropriated them to himself and his most-trusted followers. More especially he assumed Lenin's post of chairman of the Politburo. This done, he rendered his adversaries completely impotent by having them expelled from the Communist party. When they thereupon tried to effect a come-back by conspiring against him, he rid himself of them altogether by a succession of bloody purges. By 1937 the original nucleus of revolutionaries who had gathered around Lenin and proudly proclaimed themselves Old Bolsheviks had ended their existence before Red firing-squads. From this fate Trotsky alone was saved by his escape from Russia in 1929. Thenceforth a fugitive in a hostile world, he was at last in Mexico, in 1940, silenced in his turn by an assassin's knife. Long before this exit of his most unrelenting foe, Stalin had become the undisputed successor of Lenin, the second master and dictator of the U.S.S.R.

THE ECONOMIC POLICY OF THE U.S.S.R.

Marxism essentially an economic program

In now turning from government to economics we may begin by reminding ourselves that Marxism, of which Russian communism was an attempted realization, was projected in the first place as a purely economic program. Its purpose, according to its prophets beginning with Marx, was the creation of a society of equals living in the midst of a material abundance which its proponents might feel free to proclaim an earthly paradise. This happy condition was to be achieved by the abolition of private enterprise and profit, coupled with the appropriation and operation under state control of the means of production. Individualist, competitive capitalism, which may be thought of as having reached its apex as a world development just before and after 1900, was to be replaced by collective, equalitarian communism.

Toward this goal of plentiful, equally distributed goods Lenin and his associates had moved from the very first day of their rule. However, during the period of the civil war they had made as good as no progress, for, although they took over the land and the industries, they were unable to work them advantageously, owing to the reigning chaos. Production both of foodstuffs and industrial articles dropped far below the tsarist levels; the railroads and other means of communication, which had been permitted to run down during the war, almost ceased to operate; and in crushing evidence of the alarming general economic disintegration, the country was swept by a famine that in its worst year was calculated to have carried off some five million people. *The economic crisis that followed the Bolshevik victory of 1917*

The crisis was met by Lenin, who now revealed himself as that unusual phenomenon, a doctrinaire with an elastic mind, by a compromise. While reserving the major industries and the public utilities for state operation, he abandoned the ruling theory sufficiently to permit a certain amount of private industry and private trade in the hope of thereby encouraging individual enterprisers to restock the empty markets. Above all, since food was the prime demand of the hour, the peasants were to be stimulated to grow more foodstuffs by the privilege of selling their surplus for their private advantage. The mixed system of public and private enterprise was called the New Economic Policy, or NEP for short. *Lenin's compromise, the NEP*

While the NEP proved a success by seeing Russia through the worst disorder incidental to a too-sudden change of regime, it was repulsive to the collectivist spirit of communism. Collectivism calls not only for the abolition of the profit system in every one of its many forms, it demands besides an economic plan directed from a single center and applicable to the total territory of the state. Therefore, even while the NEP was in operation, careful preliminary studies were inaugurated to replace it with a program that conformed in every respect with communist principle. When it at length was ready, it was cast in the comprehensive form of a Five Year Plan and started on its career in October, 1928. *Abandonment of the NEP in 1928*

The Five Year Plan (called afterward the First Five Year Plan) concerned itself primarily with the increase of production in two directions. In industry there was to be a rapidly mounting output of coal, iron, steel, oil, and heavy machinery, that is, of so-called capital or production goods. Consumers' goods, that is, articles of immediate use, though desirable, were felt to be less urgent and were adjourned to a later period. In agriculture, which had thus far proved acutely disappointing, foodstuffs were to be made more plentiful by resort to a new and sweepingly revolutionary system of production. *The First Five Year Plan concentrates on machine industry and agriculture*

Let us dispose of the industrial program first. Spurred by a popular enthusiasm kept at high pitch by the amazingly effective propaganda of the Communist party, the production of the enumerated raw materials and of heavy machinery not only generally met but in many instances exceeded the projected figures of the plan. Transportation, which from the first had been one of the biggest headaches of the new rulers, proved the outstanding failure. On the whole, however, the industrial effort must definitely be called a triumph, for at the end of the five-year term Russia, hitherto almost wholly an agrarian society, had made enormous strides toward industrialization. This was clearly indicated by the production records of 1934, in which year three-fourths of the wealth produced in the Soviet Union was industrial and only one-fourth agricultural.

The agricultural program of the First Five Year Plan was, if not more important, far more startling than the industrial program. While the land had, at the outbreak of the revolution, been declared to belong to the state, it had in practice been seized by the peasants and treated by them as their private property. Then, by encouraging the peasants to grow grain for private profit, the NEP had been instrumental in producing a large body of well-to-do peasants, clearly set off from their impoverished fellows and known as *kulaks*. Private profit and kulaks were so opposed to communist equalitarian theory that the First Five Year Plan undertook systematically to socialize agriculture, thus bringing agriculture under the same close control by the state as industry.

The socialization of agriculture was to be brought about by the establishment of (1) collective farms, and (2) state farms. The state farms represented, in the main, an attempt to bring into use through government initiative and management vast stretches of unused or abandoned land. Much more significant were the collective farms. A collective farm (or *kolkhoz*) was created by uniting a variable number of peasant holdings and obliging the peasants to work the enlarged unit co-operatively. As for the kulaks, whom the rulers hated and resolved to get rid of, they were given the choice either docilely to submit to being merged with their poorer neighbors in the collectives or to be put to work in immense convict gangs on the public roads and in the dark forests of the arctic north. In either case they ceased to exist as a social class.

In spite of sporadic resistance by armed bands of kulaks, the program was carried out with such unflinching rigor that by the conclusion of the first five-year period the collectives represented almost three-fourths of the total seeded area of the U.S.S.R. Since in that year (1933) the state farms embraced ten per cent of the cultivated land and individual holdings had been reduced to a paltry fifteen per cent (with every prospect of quickly dwindling to zero), we may assert that collectivization had become the reigning agrarian system. Parallel with collectivization and indispensable to its success went a program of agricultural mechanization. As an indication of the considerable headway made in

The remarkable industrial achievement

The plan aims at the socialization of agriculture

Formation of collectives; liquidation of the kulaks

Agricultural successes and failures

this respect we may take account of the increased output of tractors. Their number grew in the five-year span from thirty-five thousand to well over two hundred thousand. While it is true that the grain harvest in these years did not quantitatively come up to expectations, there was nonetheless a definite increase in the total returns, which the government might fairly advertise as the earnest of greater achievements in the future. Livestock increases were not pushed in the First Plan and livestock inventories fell considerably short of even pre-war levels. Thus, in spite of the happily effected collectivization, agriculture in the most comprehensive sense of the term still had many serious obstacles to overcome.

So general and justified was the satisfaction felt over the results of the First Five Year Plan that the government promptly followed it up with the Second Five Year Plan. This ran from 1933 through 1937 and at its expiration was succeeded by the Third Five Year Plan, inaugurated on January 1, 1938. Of these later plans the purpose was not only to outdo the advances already effected in respect of industrialization and collectivization but also to make good the failures and omissions of Plan I. These later blueprints therefore laid special emphasis on transportation, electrification, and consumers' goods. And again the successes scored astonished the world, if not the hard-working, confident communists. On the eve of World War II the U.S.S.R. had outstripped every country throughout the earth, except the United States of America, as a producer of industrial goods. An inevitable consequence was a process of rapid urbanization. Large and even giant cities were becoming as characteristic of Russia as of its older industrial rivals. And, owing to a very high birth rate, the village population, instead of diminishing, also increased so that the census of 1939 showed a total of 170,500,000 inhabitants.

The success of the three plans raised to something akin to frenzy the enthusiasm with which Stalin was universally regarded. Had the economic miracle not been effected under his sure and undeviating guidance? It certainly had; and there was something else which only now stood clearly revealed. At the bottom of the ferocious clash between Stalin and the Old Bolsheviks, led by Trotsky, had been this very issue of Russia's economic self-realization. Stalin's rivals, and particularly Trotsky, were imbued with the idea of world revolution and wished to employ Russia as the battering-ram for beating down the still towering gates of capitalism. Much less swayed by theory than they, much more distinctly native than international, Stalin had taken the position that Russia must not be sacrificed in dubious battle but permitted to seek its own safety first by concentrating all its energies on realizing the perfect socialist order within its own boundaries. If at the time the Third

The Second and Third Five Year Plans

Triumph of Stalin's policy of socialism in one state

Five Year Plan went into action there were still any doubters touching this central issue, they must have been reduced to silence by the mighty economic edifice to which innumerable specialists had laid their hands but of which Stalin was without the least question the supreme builder.

RELIGION AND EDUCATION

As Marxism is a materialist philosophy and opposed to supernaturalism in every form, the Bolsheviks had no sooner seized power than they fell upon the Russian Orthodox church. All church property, including houses of worship, monasteries, and lands, was confiscated and title thereto vested in the state. Concomitantly church and state were completely divorced and the church was referred for support to the voluntary contributions of the worshipers. Many of the confiscated edifices were torn down, others were converted into social clubs. A limited number were conceded to congregations of twenty or more applicants for religious use. Such congregations agreed to find the priest's living, and the priest himself agreed to limit his activity to the service of the altar. The historical organization of the Orthodox church with its priests and bishops culminating in a patriarch was not destroyed but under the indicated pressures shriveled till it was hardly more than the shadow of its former self. The same may be said of Judaism, Mohammedanism, and the various Protestant denominations that existed within the boundaries of the U.S.S.R. They were not suppressed but, regarded with disfavor by the organs of government and actively denounced by the propagandists of the Communist party, they were smitten with the same blight as their Orthodox rival.

The Orthodox church is stripped of its possessions and divorced from the state

The official teaching of the Communist party in the religious area of thought is atheism. Not only has the party since its rise to authority proclaimed this, its faith, but in 1929 it imposed on the state a constitutional amendment which forbade the propagation through Russia of any doctrine of religious import other than atheism. The communist theory is that religion is an invention of the capitalists put out by them as an opiate to keep the common people in a state of drugged indifference to the real issues of life, which revolve exclusively around material well-being. As the chief instrument for carrying on its campaign the Communist party brought into existence so-called godless societies, which made it their business and delight to pour a devastating ridicule on all worship, whether Christian, Jewish, or Moslem. However, they did not succeed in completely smothering the religious congregations. Not only have they survived but, following the outbreak of World War II, they seem even to have scored a modest recovery.

The Communist party holds to atheism

The proper substitute for religion in communist eyes is education.

Accordingly, education received the uninterrupted attention of the Bolshevik rulers from the day of their victory. The educational situation taken over from their tsarist predecessors was lamentable in the extreme. Two-thirds of the men and seven-eighths of the women of the country were illiterate. An inevitable concomitant of this condition was a grave deficiency of both schools and teachers. The Bolsheviks at once proclaimed the right to education of every worke> and worker's child. While schooling was conceived as an enterprise of national scope, the control was wisely decentralized and put, in the main, in the hands of the local authorities. Buildings were competitively erected in villages and towns and teachers developed by teachers' institutes so that rapid progress was made. By the time the Third Five Year Plan was inaugurated in 1938, accommodations, sometimes ultra-modern, sometimes grossly defective, had been provided for the whole childhood population of Russia. Even the adults had to so considerable an extent received belated instruction that eighty per cent of the population could now be recorded as literate. The law provided for a seven-year minimum of school attendance but at the same time indicated the gradual universal addition of a term of years devoted to vocational training. Looking forward to a completely mechanized world, the U.S.S.R. wanted every citizen, male and female alike, to be put in at least rudimentary command of present-day tools and machines.

Establishment of universal education

But official attention was not limited to primary education. Secondary schools, approximately equivalent to our American high schools, were abundantly provided and the whole system crowned with universities, engineering schools, and professional institutes of every conceivable kind. While the Communist party made much of the obligation of the state to create a common-school education for the masses in order to enable them to participate intelligently in the bountiful life with which they were going to be endowed, at the same time the party did not fail to recognize the equal obligation of government to provide a steadily increasing body of every variety of specialist to keep the complicated social machinery in good running order. There is every reason to believe that these higher institutions of learning achieved an impressive level of competence.

Ample provision made for higher education

FOREIGN POLICY AND THE THIRD INTERNATIONAL

Identified with communism, which promulgated a program of world revolution, the Bolsheviks thought of their 1917 success as the beginning of a movement which would not come to a stop till it had made the circuit of the globe. In dedication to this wide prospect they assembled at Moscow in 1919 an international gathering of communists which organized itself as the Third International. It will be recalled that the

First International, a short-lived affair (1864-1874), was called into being by Marx himself. It was followed in 1889 by the Second International, which broke on the rocks in the storms of World War I and which, although laboriously put together again when the war was over, never regained its former vigor. Since the Moscow gathering was violently opposed to the mild evolutionary program to which both the First and the Second Internationals subscribed, it would have done well, instead of labeling the organization it created the Third International, to have named it frankly the First Communist International. However, owing to the connection of Marx in body or spirit with the two earlier organizations, they wished to present their renewed effort as the historical continuation of the two predecessors that had so manifestly sailed under the banner of the socialist patron-saint. Just the same, in common parlance the Third International has been generally designated the Communist International, or Comintern for short.

As the Comintern was founded to overthrow all existing social orders and bring about a universal communist society, it was regarded with an aversion not far removed from horror by the rest of the world. And since it had been called into being by the communist government of Russia and had set up its central office at Moscow, the view obtained that it was the active agent of the U.S.S.R., nay more, that it was in plain fact nothing other than Russia's department of foreign affairs. The Russian government itself denied this allegation and insisted on the separateness and independence of the Comintern. But the claim failed to convince, in view of the circumstance that practically every revolution of radical import that broke out anywhere in the world was guided by Russian agents and financed by Russian funds. The Russian agents may well have been dispatched not by Russia but by the Comintern, but this would still not account for the Russian funds. As the Comintern enjoyed no revenues, the monies put to work abroad could not possibly have come from anywhere save the treasury of the U.S.S.R.

The year 1921 brought a turning-point in the relation between Russia and the rest of the world. Lenin had adopted the New Economic Policy, and an essential feature of his revised orientation was to revive Russia's moribund trade with its neighbors. None of them, however, would listen to proposals for a trade agreement without the promise on the part of Russia to curb the incessant communist propaganda that radiated from the Comintern. With Lenin set on getting exchange started again, the desired engagement was given and agreements with both the large and little states of Europe followed in rapid order. They marked the first step in the drawing-together of two violently opposed worlds, but the hesitant approach was neither ingenuous, sincere, nor stable. The promised separation between the Russian

Creation (1919) of the Communist International (Comintern)

The Comintern generally considered the foreign department of the Russian government

Cautious acceptance of Russia by the rest of the world

government and the Comintern was more apparent than real, and the existence in every noncommunist country of a lively Communist party which took its orders from Moscow and never ceased a destructive activity expressively called "boring from within," kept the governments thus harassed perpetually on tenterhooks. Nonetheless, a rapprochement between Russia and its neighbors took place, attended by intermittent flare-ups of angry accusation and counteraccusation. In due time the negotiated commercial agreements were followed by that formal recognition of the hitherto outlawed Russian government which by long international practice alone signified acceptance into the comity of nations. Germany led the way by a treaty of recognition signed in 1922. When Great Britain and Italy followed in 1924, the remaining European countries could no longer hold out and signed within the year. The faraway United States was the last country to fall in line, for it did not perform the same act of courtesy toward the U.S.S.R. till 1933.

When in the course of the twenties Stalin became the dominating influence in Russia, the relationship between the U.S.S.R. and the rest of the world underwent further improvement. Since the main significance of the victory of Stalin over Trotsky and the Trotsky following was that the systematic build-up of the Russian economy took precedence over world revolution, Stalin was minded to stimulate commercial exchange with Russia's neighbors and to this end still further to limit, though from opportunism rather than principle, the activities of the Comintern. Of this softened attitude the best evidence was furnished by his drawing closer to the League of Nations. In the original view of the Bolsheviks the League was a weapon expressly forged by the western capitalist democracies to destroy communism, and they damned it in unbridled language. By 1929 the U.S.S.R. had swung around sufficiently to permit a representative to sit in on the preparatory disarmament sessions, and three years later went so far as actually to take part in the Geneva Disarmament Conference. Thus committed to an inclined plane, it failed to excite particular surprise when in 1934 it tobogganned right into the inner sanctuary of the League and was made welcome with both membership and a permanent seat on the Council.

The U.S.S.R. joins (1934) the League of Nations

Already by that time a significant change of weather had taken place throughout Europe, for in 1933 Hitler had assumed power in Germany. The savage denunciations of communism in which he at once indulged filled Stalin and his associates with alarm, and they undertook to strengthen themselves against a probable attack by a closer connection with Germany's western neighbors. In 1935 they signed with France a treaty of mutual assistance. It looked stronger on paper than it proved to be in fact, for republican France remained suspicious of the U.S.S.R.

Stalin tries in vain to forge a league of mutual security

and hesitated to commit itself to a policy looking toward war without the support of Great Britain. Great Britain in its turn preferred to wait on events. Litvinov, Stalin's commissar for foreign affairs, became the ardent advocate of a pact of mutual security among the powers threatened by an aggressive Germany, but his pleas fell on deaf ears. In 1936 Hitler put an end to the neutralization of the Rhineland by occupying it militarily. The year before, Dictator Mussolini had invaded Ethiopia with a view to its conquest and, not long after, Japan resumed more audaciously than ever the encroachments on China it had begun in 1931. These and a dozen other incidents indicated that Europe had entered on a crisis which, deepening with each passing year, would lead with deadly fatality to another world war. The prolonged tension preliminary to its outbreak belongs to general European history and will receive attention in a later chapter (Chapter 44).

40

ITALY GOES FASCIST

ALTHOUGH ITALY FOUND herself on the side of the victors at the conclusion of World War I, the strain of the long conflict on this poorest and weakest of the great powers had been so terrible that the country was visited with a moral and economic crisis that shook it to its foundations. Industry and commerce were disorganized, the currency became increasingly and perilously inflated, and unemployment and hunger prevailed in town and country. *Italy's post-war plight*

The result was social and moral unrest whipped into action by various radical bodies. The Italian Social Democratic party, Marxist and evolutionary in principle, had a violent left or Syndicalist wing, which went beyond Marx by advocating "direct action" as the only sure cure for existing ills. It will be seen at once that the Syndicalists were mentally and emotionally close to the Russian Bolsheviks. Logically enough, some of them were moved to found a Communist party, which made public affirmation of its extreme revolutionary faith by joining the Third or Moscow International. The several revolutionary groups, each according to the measure of its radicalism, stimulated strikes and practiced a destructive sabotage in the factories and on the farms. In sporadic instances they prompted the workers to seize and operate, or try to operate, industrial plants, and the peasants to expropriate the landlords. *Unrest stimulated by various groups of radicals*

The spectacle of their country in process of gradual disintegration stirred many people, chiefly of the middle and professional classes, to come to the rescue of their inherited institutions. Irrespective of the political party to which they belonged, we may designate them collectively as nationalists and agree that it was they who had been chiefly responsible for pushing Italy into the war. The Paris Peace Conference, according to them, had flagrantly repudiated most of the golden promises by which in 1915 the allies had lured Italy into the war and had pushed the late-comer around like a stepchild. To the disappointment caused by their failure to get all the territorial spoils to which they felt they possessed a claim was now added a passionate indignation over the domestic chaos precipitated by the radical agitators. *The nationalists: their grief and disappointment*

National
resistance
gives birth
to an asso-
ciation
called fascio

Spontaneously, here and there nationally minded men formed associations to offer resistance to their adversaries and commonly designated
such a resistance association a *fascio*. The word acquired special overtones from the fact that it derived from the Latin *fasces,* the name for
the ax and rods associated in olden times as a symbol of authority with
the consul, the chief Roman magistrate. Tied into a compact bundle,
ax and rods spoke to present-day Italian patriots primarily of the necessity of union but also of the magnificence and far-flung might of Rome.
The fasces must be supposed to carry a somewhat similar message to us
in distant America, for they are pictured on the reverse of our common-
est silver coin, the dime.

To develop its highest potentialities a popular movement must succeed in finding an audacious and magnetic leader. That chance befell
the Fascist movement, for it was still in its infancy when Benito Mussolini put himself at its head. Born in 1883, the son of a radically minded
blacksmith in a small village of hilly Romagna, Mussolini had had a
peculiarly stormy career. Even as an adolescent he had joined the revolutionary or Syndicalist section of the Social Democratic party, and
throughout early manhood he had never ceased playing the turbulent
agitator by busying himself with the founding of unions and the foment-
ing of strikes. To escape military service, which he abominated because
imposed by a government he despised, he escaped to Switzerland, where,
between periods of grinding labor as a mason, he attended lectures at
the universities of Lausanne and Geneva. On his return to Italy at the
age of twenty-three he submitted to the unescapable military training
and then, resuming his agitator's role, combined it with the work of a
militant journalist. So outstanding were his services in this department
that in 1912 he was promoted to the editorship of the official socialist
newspaper, *Avanti!* (Forward!). It was published at Milan, the leading
center of Italian industry and consequently a focal point of the radical
influences abroad in the land.

Mussolini was holding this editorial post when World War I broke
out in 1914. It made a different man of him, for almost overnight he
was converted into a flaming patriot. By temperament and habit an
agitator, he now directed his energy to the entrance of Italy into the
war on the side of the allies, and because his program ran contrary to
the pacifist policy of the Social Democratic party, he was promptly
ejected from both party and editorship. When, some months later, Italy
joined hands with the allies, the former socialist volunteered for service
and fought in the trenches till he was wounded in 1917 and honorably
discharged. When on the return of peace Mussolini's former friends, the
radicals, began their socially disruptive activities, he reacted to their
conduct in the spirit of an offended nationalist and with the least pos-

sible delay bent his dynamic energies to the organization of the rising Fascist movement. The whole startling reversal affords an insight into his character of the greatest importance. Although a man of uncommon mental endowment, he was not dominated by ideas or systems of thought, save insofar as they could be utilized as tools to serve his consuming will, his untamed aspiration to power. And to make this egotistic aspiration respectable, as much in his own eyes as in the eyes of his countrymen, he represented it as a struggle not for his personal aggrandizement but for that of the nation.

The tactics Mussolini imposed on his Fascist followers were simple: they were ordered to meet every act of violence with greater violence. Owing to the better discipline and equipment of the Fascist bands, they gradually drove their opponents, the Socialists and Communists, from their positions in the city and village administrations and forcibly took over their party headquarters. So catching was the enthusiasm that attended their success among nationalistically inclined men, and especially youths, of the middle classes that Fascist combat units sprang up as if by magic all the way from the Alps to the tip of Sicily. All through the period of 1921-1922 a veritable civil war, in its essence a class war, raged up and down the peninsula.

Spread and success of the Fascist movement

By the autumn of 1922 the fighting Fascist bands, usually called Black Shirts from the single article of apparel they all shared, had gained complete mastery. Not only had they by that time driven their immediate opponents, the Socialists and Communists, to cover but they had included in their destructive fury the legally established labor unions, the main source of radical energy. Either the labor unions were broken up entirely or they were transformed into their Fascist equivalents. In the long-drawn-out, ferocious struggle the Italian government had been as scrupulously neutral as the referee in a prize fight. It assumed this extraordinary attitude because, owing to the many parties represented in the Chamber of Deputies, the successive ministries were regularly coalition ministries, in which one opinion exactly canceled the other. It need hardly be expressly said that a government of this sort could not possibly achieve the self-confidence proper to a genuinely functioning regime.

Neutrality and feebleness of the Italian government

In view of this paralysis of government Mussolini, in whose eyes the one unforgivable sin was indecision, resolved to act. In October he ordered his Fascist legions to march on Rome and from his Milan headquarters unceremoniously demanded by wire that the feeble ministry resign. There followed a nervous moment, during which war between the government and the Fascists hung in the balance. It passed when King Victor Emmanuel, in his capacity of constitutional sovereign, sent for Mussolini and asked him to head a new ministry.

The march on Rome (October, 1922) and the collapse of the government

THE SHAPING OF THE FASCIST SOCIETY AND REGIME

The earliest and fundamental Fascist enactments

When Mussolini became prime minister by an act of force, he was already, in effect, the Italian dictator. But his dictatorship would remain somewhat in the nature of a prophecy till it had been organized in detail. This work he began by obliging a cowed parliament to vote him full powers for a year. The concession permitted him, as a first step, to fascisticize the administration by turning all opposition elements out of office. Then he had the docile parliament pass an electoral law by which the party that polled a plurality of the national vote should be rewarded with a two-thirds membership in the lower house, that is, be transformed into a majority party. By virtue of this stipulation the elections of 1924 put the Fascist party in complete legislative control. A veritable flood of hallmarked Fascist enactments followed. Strikes to enforce economic demands were forbidden; the press was subjected to the strictest surveillance; "seditious persons" (meaning opponents of the regime) were exposed to arbitrary arrest and indefinite confinement; local officials were no longer to be freely elected but, in the interest of a tightened centralization, appointed by the government; and, as a crowning measure, all political parties, except the Fascist party, were dissolved.

The solidly Fascist parliament of 1928 completed the dictatorship

With this comprehensive spade-work done the government in 1928 ordered new elections. They resulted in a Chamber of Deputies which was solidly Fascist because no other than the Fascist party had been permitted to present candidates. Thenceforth any law the prime minister chose to offer was passed at his nod. With the threads of administration from village to province and from province to capital converging in Mussolini's hands and with the parliament content to serve as his rubber stamp, the dictatorship was complete. The king was still the head of the state and the constitution continued in nominal existence, but every trace of that liberalism and democracy which had once been celebrated as the soul of the constitution had taken flight.

Reorganization (1926) of the Fascist party and its identification with the state

Two years before the sweepstake elections of 1928 the reigning Fascist party had given itself a new constitution dictated by the ruling spirit of consolidation. By its articles the secretaries of the local or basic fascios were subordinated to a provincial secretary and the provincial secretaries in their turn to a national secretary called Secretary of the Party. The whole elaborate structure was crowned by a supreme governing body called the Fascist Grand Council and made up of some twenty-five outstanding party figures. Perpetual chairman of the Grand Council was, of course, Mussolini, under the title *Il Duce* (The Leader). With Mussolini serving also as head of the government the identity of party and government became as clearly a feature of the Fascist system as we have found it to be of the Communist system in Russia. In spite of divergences of principle and goal, the two systems were organizationally identical in that they were both totalitarian. And what is totalitarianism? No better definition can be given than the one supplied by Mussolini himself: "All in the State, nothing outside the State, nothing against the State."

The Fascist party was intrusted with very important functions. One of them was to diffuse, and keep diffusing, its spirit through all official-dom from the lowest customs' collector to the highest cabinet minister. Even more important, if that were possible, was the task of plying the masses of the people with an unremitting propaganda in behalf of the Fascist measures and ideology. Since the party was in exclusive posses-sion of the resources of press, cinema, and radio, it was in the most fortunate conceivable position to fill the eyes, ears, and minds of the public throughout the days of the week and the hours of the day with the stereotyped arguments and the terse, explosive slogans embodying the Fascist faith. In the passionately pursued purposes of the Fascist party we cannot fail to detect an unmistakable analogy to the dynamic missionary role assigned in Russia to the Communist party.

The Fascist party as the supreme propaganda agency

For still another resemblance of the Fascist to the Communist system we may turn to its use of symbols and ritual. The rods and ax, which gave the party its name, have already been mentioned. They were sten-ciled, together with Mussolini's heavy jaw and knitted brows, on every available wall in Italy. In roaming through town or countryside one could no more get away from that scowling visage than one could in Russia from the multiple pictured images of Lenin and Stalin. When Fascists met in the streets, they saluted each other in the ancient Roman manner with the right arm outstretched; but far and away their most impressive public demonstration was staged by the ubiquitous Fascist bands which, following the victorious march on Rome, had been as-sembled into a national Fascist militia. The militia's most striking article of dress continued, as from the beginning, to be the black shirt and tasseled fez of the individual member. When he and his fellows thus attired marched to stirring military music and under fluttering banners down the street, they heartened themselves by chanting the quickening party anthem *Giovinezza* (Youth) and at its close affirmed their primal loyalty by bursting into savage, disordered shouts of *Duce! Duce!*

Symbols and rituals as a means of propaganda

Since a system with so highly wrought a mythology depended for its perpetuation on the capture of the nation's youth, the Fascists supple-mented the regular system of education in the primary and secondary schools with an educational system of their own. For boys from eight to fourteen years of age they established the *Balilla,* a kind of boy-scout organization; from the Balilla the boys passed into the *Avanguardia*

The youth organiza-tions as training schools for Fascism

(Advance Guard), to which they remained attached from the age of fourteen to the age of eighteen; on graduating from the Avanguardia they became *Giovani Fascisti* or Young Fascists, passing thence after three years into the regular Fascist militia. As soon as this comprehensive training had taken root it was decreed that none but its graduates should thenceforth be eligible to membership in the Fascist party, thereby securing to this highest directive institution the greatest attainable measure of moral coherence and mental uniformity. The girls were not so systematically indoctrinated, but they were not neglected. Gathered into *Piccole Italiane* for those under twelve years of age and into *Giovani Italiane* for those over twelve, they were physically hardened by appropriate athletic exercises and imbued with the confident spirit and nationalist teachings of the party.

Sharp distinction between Socialist and Fascist labor unions   The reader will recall that when, in the course of the civil war of 1921-1922, the Fascists attacked the Socialist labor unions, they spared them whenever they consented to become Fascist unions, commonly called Fascist syndicates. They were so named because they represented an Italian variation of syndicalism which had been evolved by a certain Edmondo Rossoni and was sharply opposed in some of its basic principles to current Socialism. Thus, Rossoni's syndicalism rejected the class-warfare doctrine of Marx and accepted the capitalist class as a necessary factor in production. Again, its ultimate goal was to replace parliamentary representation, based hitherto in Italy and everywhere else on geographic political units, with a representation based on economic units of occupational classes.

Mussolini couples Rossoni's syndicalism with totalitarianism   Since Mussolini, a former workingman, believed in the rights of labor, always provided they were not magnified into a right of revolution, he bestowed his blessing on Rossoni's Fascist syndicates. He was clear in his mind, however, that they must be balanced by syndicates of employers and that both kinds of syndicates must be unequivocally subordinated to the state. Let us never forget that since his conversion to an intensive patriotism he had completely broken away from the theory that the state exists for the benefit of its citizens—that was the essence of nineteenth century liberalism—in favor of the directly opposite view that the citizens exist for the benefit of the state. This was the recently-born totalitarian doctrine which had many spokesmen in the Europe of his day but none more impassioned than Mussolini. What from an economic angle the omnipotent state demanded above all else was a close partnership of employers and employees to the end of sustaining society and the state by an unintermitted flow of production.

In 1926 these economic ideas and speculations found expression in a comprehensive law. It created thirteen confederated Fascist syndicates, six of employers, six of employees, and one of lawyers, doctors, and other professionals. Each syndicate was to have provincial and local sub-divisions and, through them, to be nation-wide. All thirteen were put under the direction of a special Minister of Corporations (who, at least at first, was Mussolini himself), and to them belonged the sole right of drawing up collective contracts between the two production partners. Strikes and lockouts were alike forbidden, and conflicts between employers and employees were referable to special labor courts, from whose decision there was no appeal. A Charter of Labor that followed defined the rights of labor in a fairly liberal spirit. Sunday was made a legal holiday; every worker was conceded an annual vacation with pay; and the state promised, and presently enacted, a broad social-insurance policy. A separate but co-operating institution, called *Dopolavoro* (After Work) undertook to provide vacation trips at greatly reduced rates and to furnish besides, throughout the year, a stimulating variety of recreational and cultural facilities.

Creation of syndicates of employers and employees and publication of a Labor Charter

By these measures the state began to take on a syndicalist or corporative structure. The process was quickened by supplementary enactments till, in the course of the thirties, the old form of parliamentary representation by geographic districts and universal suffrage was replaced by corporative representation, with the right to vote limited to corporation members. While this, taken by itself, already signified a sharp decline in the freedom of elections, the decline went much farther. The reshaped Chamber of Deputies, although no longer called by that name, was in its new form made up of four hundred corporation members, and the list of the candidates for office was in last resort drawn up by the Grand Council of the Fascist party. In consequence of this control by the Grand Council, the only right that remained to the individual voter consisted in voting yes or no on the Council list. In the several elections that took place the list was overwhelmingly endorsed and the boast trumpeted to the world that Italy had become the first modern state to adopt a corporative (or occupational) form of representation. But the boast was hollow, for, born in chains, the new representative system lived in chains and furnished no acceptable evidence regarding its feasibility, let alone its superiority to the usual geographic system.

The former parliament replaced by representatives of the corporations

FASCIST DOMESTIC POLICY

The domestic effort of the Fascist party was directed, first, to recovery from the destructive effects of war and revolution, and second, to the increase by every possible means of the country's productive capacity. The foremost consideration of the recovery program was the annual budget. At the time the Fascists seized power, the budget had been for years out of balance to the tune of some billions of lire, and consequently

the national currency had never ceased dropping in value. By drastic
Earliest
economic
efforts of the
Fascists: a
balanced
budget and
restored
railways reduction of expenditures as well as by new taxes, the annual deficit
had already by 1925 been converted into a surplus. This success enabled
the government not only to return to the gold basis but to peg the slipping lira at nineteen to the dollar, a very considerable improvement on
previous quotations. What, after the budget, called most loudly for
restoration was the national railway system. Its equipment had been
allowed to become unbelievably dilapidated and, in spite of this neglect
of upkeep, its annual deficit ran into hundreds of millions of lire. A few
years of unrelenting effort sufficed to bring the service back to normal
(and soon beyond normal), to hold the trains to an accurate time sched-
ule, and to wipe out the devastating deficit. True, when the world depression of the thirties reached Italy, the achievements here recorded
were, at least in part, again canceled, but Mussolini could comfort himself with the thought that all the countries round about had been smitten
with an identical blight. However, when in 1935 he wantonly invaded
Ethiopia, with the evil consequences to his budget that war never fails
to bring, he could not, twist as he would, avoid having the fresh phase
of decline laid at any door save his own.

Mussolini's second domestic purpose, a vastly increased flow of pro-
Industrial
develop-
ment: sub-
stantial and
insubstantial
achieve-
ments duction, he had even more at heart than plain and prosaic recovery.
But here he faced an incurable lack of natural resources. Coal, iron,
copper, zinc, and oil simply did not exist in any but unimportant, scattered deposits in the peninsula, and their importation put such industrial
development as might be based on them at a fatal disadvantage compared with more happily situated countries. The one chance offered to
make up at least for the absence of coal was to capture the power residing in the numerous streams that poured steeply from the Alps and the
Apennines. On this prospect the government fastened with such concentrated purpose that a hydroelectric development followed in which
in the course of a decade Italy surpassed every other European country.
Moreover, by its means an industry normal to the peninsula, the silk
and rayon industry, expanded till it outdistanced all immediate rivals.
Even the machine, locomotive, automobile, and shipbuilding industries
experienced a notable growth; but since they were based on imported
raw materials, their cost was so high that it was only by means of a prohibitive tariff that they could be sold at a profit even on the closed
Italian market. Agreed that the Fascists never wearied of devising ways
and means to overcome existing difficulties, they learned to their sorrow
that they could not circumvent nature.

A much more encouraging record was established in agriculture because here nature had not been niggardly. And yet she had not been
lavish either, at least not in the degree commonly supposed on the

strength of the praises sounded through the ages of the beauty of the Italian landscape. The amount of land available for agriculture is cruelly reduced by the broad and towering backbone of the Apennines. However, the available land is reasonably fertile, and under vigorous Fascist stimulation its yield registered a remarkable improvement. If we recall that, owing to the dense population of Italy, a variable percentage of its foodstuffs had regularly to be imported, we shall not fail to celebrate the Fascist increases as a far from negligible triumph. After a few campaigns, which the party propagandists with their war obsession blatantly advertised as "the battle of wheat," "the battle of rice," and so forth, the wheat harvest rose by some seventy per cent, while the returns on rice, oats, and corn averaged a fifty per cent increase. The most spectacular single achievement in the area of agricultural enterprise was the draining of the Pontine Marshes between Naples and Rome. These extensive, poisonous swamps, which had defied all curative efforts for centuries, were successfully cleared for the plow and settled with some tens of thousands of peasant-farmers, each provided with a cottage and plot of ground. *The notable agricultural development*

If more space were available, account might be taken of the extraordinary expansion of the Italian merchant marine and the tourist trade. They were both pushed by liberal government subsidies. Subsidies are a normal feature of a planned economy, such as that of Fascist Italy, and some kind of planned economy is a logical product of totalitarian doctrine. *A planned economy and totalitarianism*

THE LATERAN ACCORD

Of the many domestic issues confronting the Fascist regime none was more pressing than the fifty-year-old quarrel with the Catholic church which sprang from the seizure of Rome, the papal capital, in September, 1870, by the kingdom of Italy. Ever since that event the pope had regarded himself as "the prisoner of the Vatican" and had refused to have any dealings with what he denounced as the usurping Italian government. But while the quarrel may be fairly viewed as an Italian domestic issue, it also, owing to the international character of the papacy, passed far beyond the domestic frame. Hence this setting of it off as a separate division of our story. *The Roman question a leading domestic issue*

No sooner had Mussolini become prime minister than he resolved to leave no stone unturned to reach a settlement with the pope. While he was, let us agree, no better than a nominal Catholic, he was, as a statesman, impressed with the indestructible power of the Catholic church and the consequent advisability of having it enlisted for rather than against his state. He therefore opened secret negotiations with the reigning pope, Pius XI, who, together with many members of the college of cardinals, had himself come round to the view that the time had arrived *Agreement between Mussolini and the pope reached on February 11, 1929* to end a conflict which, with the passing of the years, had become barren and unprofitable. Even with this inclination to treat on the part of both contestants, there existed so many points of difference that it took years to reach an accommodation. At last, however, it was effected and on February 11, 1929, signed in the form of three separate documents, not at the Vatican but at the pope's second palace in Rome, the Lateran.

The Lateran Accord: the political and the financial settlement

The three documents constitute what was officially called the Lateran Accord and incorporate, first, a political treaty, second, a financial settlement, and third, a religious concordat. By the political treaty the pope renounced his claims to the city of Rome and accepted it as the capital of the kingdom of Italy. In return Italy agreed to the creation of a separate state to be called the Vatican City, which was to be under the complete ownership and sovereign jurisdiction of the Holy See. The fact that the new creation comprised barely one hundred acres with less than a thousand inhabitants and was therefore the tiniest state in the world did not in any way detract from its exalted status. It followed that the person of the pope was declared sacred and inviolable and his power freely to send and receive ambassadors placed beyond dispute. In further witness of his sovereignty he was accorded the right to issue his own coinage and postage stamps and to operate a wireless station for unchecked communication with the outside world. So much for the political treaty: by the financial settlement which supplemented it and put it beyond recall, the pope accepted the sum of approximately $100,-000,000 as an indemnity for his territorial renunciation.

The Lateran Accord: the Concordat

The religious concordat enumerated the very considerable concessions the Italian government made to Catholicism and its traditional claims. The Catholic religion was acknowledged as the sole religion of the state, which undertook to maintain the already previously assumed obligation of paying clerical salaries. The appointment of archbishops and bishops was declared to pertain to the Holy See with the single reservation that the appointee must not be an active opponent of the Fascist government. While civil marriage, a conquest of the unification movement, was retained, religious marriage was accepted as possessing an identical validity in the eyes of the law. Perhaps the most important concession of all made by the state was that religious instruction by teachers approved by the bishops should henceforth be obligatory in both elementary and secondary schools.

MUSSOLINI'S FOREIGN POLICY A FIERY NATIONALISM AND IMPERIALISM

At once on taking over the government Mussolini revealed his purpose to revamp not only Italy's domestic policy but its foreign policy as well. There was to be an abrupt end of the feebleness by reason of which, according to patriot opinion, the country had been deprived of its fair share of the booty available for distribution among the victors after the war. He had been established in office only a few months when he reasserted Italy's claim to the Greek islands of Rhodes and the Dodecanese. The occasion was furnished by the negotiations which followed Kemal Pasha's victory over the Greeks and which culminated in the Treaty of Lausanne (1923). In the Treaty of Sèvres, dictated by the Paris Peace Conference in 1920 to the defeated Turks, Italy had been required to relinquish the islands in order that they might be given to Greece, to which on purely nationalist grounds they belonged. But when in the war that then broke out between Greece and Kemal's renovated Turkey the Greeks were not only beaten but crushed and the Treaty of Sèvres became a scrap of paper, Mussolini rescinded the surrender of his predecessor in office and insisted on having the islands reassigned to Italy. Thereupon with the least possible delay he proceeded to convert them into a fortified naval base.

Mussolini reasserts (1923) Italy's claim to Rhodes and the Dodecanese islands

It was a clear indication of his program to do his utmost to strengthen Italy's position in the Mediterranean, which his Fascist propagandists from this time on made a practice of designating "our sea." The next event in this area was the murder in August, 1923, on Greek soil, of four Italian members of a commission charged with drawing the boundary between Greece and Albania. It has already been related (p. 753) how Mussolini promptly demanded a huge indemnity from Greece and to enforce his claim occupied the Greek island of Corfu. Although in the end he accepted a settlement and withdrew from Corfu, we should not fail to take account of the fact, and concede it the significance which is its due, that the mediator between Mussolini and the Greeks was not the League of Nations, which Mussolini openly flouted, but the Council of Ambassadors, on which two "equal" powers, France and Great Britain, played the leading role.

Mussolini squeezes (1923) the Greeks for an indemnity

The next incident in which Mussolini figured carries the name of Fiume and exhibited him in a somewhat milder light. This north-Adriatic port, in bitter dispute between Italy and Yugoslavia throughout the Paris Peace Conference, had in a belated agreement signed in 1920 been declared an independent free city. When the agreement failed to work satisfactorily, Mussolini proposed to Yugoslavia that the free city be divided between them, Fiume proper to go to Italy, Port Baros, Fiume's eastern suburb, to Yugoslavia. In January, 1924, the proposal was incorporated in a treaty and for once Mussolini had achieved a settlement without the theatrical fanfare that usually attended his public appearances.

Mussolini acquires Fiume (1924)

Nonetheless, the acquisition of Fiume signified a strengthening of his

Adriatic position; and control of the Adriatic, an arm of the Mediterranean laid envelopingly along the eastern coast of Italy, was an indispensable preliminary to an enlarged Mediterranean role. Consequently Mussolini now fastened his attention on the Adriatic coastland opposite Italy, on Albania. This state had received recognition from the Paris Peace Conference, but its illiterate and primitive inhabitants were unable successfully to operate it. The government passed from one adventurer to another till in 1925 it was appropriated by a tribal leader, Ahmed Zogu by name. Three years later Ahmed Zogu proclaimed himself king under the title Zog I.

Pursing the policy, implicit in his seizure of control, of putting an end to the domestic chaos and endowing his people with at least a minimum of civilized organization, King Zog soon learned that he required foreign capital and foreign experts, and from what country was he more likely to get them than from Italy, just across the narrow strait of Otranto? Ever on the lookout to magnify his power, Mussolini met the Albanian needs in the way that might have been expected, in the only too familiar imperialist way. In return for repeated loans for such improvements as roads and harbors and for the creation of an army indispensable for the maintenance of order among the ever rebellious tribesmen, Italy acquired a right of supervision which by stages expanded into complete economic, financial, and military control. By the early thirties the too-trusting King Zog grew alarmed and began to offer resistance to the systematic Italian encroachments. To no avail, since by withdrawing financial support and dispatching, by way of warning, a few warships to the Albanian coast the Italians could always enforce compliance to their wishes. The situation became a diplomatic comedy, on which at length, in April, 1939, Mussolini resolved to ring down the curtain. He occupied the country with an army, before which King Zog made a precipitate exit by flight and his whole insubstantial regime disappeared overnight. The episode closed—for the moment—with the annexation of Albania by Italy.

Even before the piecemeal appropriation of Albania had been completed, Mussolini embarked on and carried through the most considerable adventure of his career, the conquest of Ethiopia. It was in 1934 that he let his attention swing to this independent African kingdom which, under its emperor, Haile Selassie, was, like Italy itself, a member state of the League of Nations. What mainly drew Mussolini's gaze to this, in current imperialist language, "backward" community was its rumored wealth of natural resources coupled with its exposed position between the two Italian colonies, Eritrea and Somaliland, which gripped it tightly in a pincers' hold. He was not in the least original, in fact he merely copied established imperialist technique when, by way of curtain-raiser to his proposed conquest, he precipitated a number of border clashes between Italian and Ethiopian troops. They led to accusation and counteraccusation, followed by the appeal of the alarmed Haile Selassie to the League of Nations. Since Mussolini treated evasively the successive proposals of the League for an amicable adjustment, their only effect was somewhat to put off the outbreak of war. When in October, 1935, the Duce's carefully elaborated preparations were complete, he gave the word of command and his armies moved into Ethiopia from the two pincers' ends, Eritrea and Italian Somaliland.

The flagrant breach of peace stirred the League of Nations to the sternest measures it had thus far in its existence ever taken to bring a **The** wrongdoer to terms. The Council unambiguously designated Italy the **conquest** aggressor, and the Assembly invoked against her its most serious sanc- **effected,** tions as defined by Article 16 of the Covenant. By virtue thereof the **May, 1936** League decreed that its members should break off all financial and economic relations with the offending country. It was generally supposed that the embargo would prove so disastrous that it would force Italy to her knees; and not improbably it would have done so, had its imposition of nonintercourse been strictly enforced. That was, however, far from the case, and Italy, though gravely handicapped by her inability to get all the supplies she needed, with a kind of fanatical resolution proceeded with her Ethiopian campaign. A disapproving world rejoiced when, not long after the invasion had begun, it was abruptly halted by the coming of the rainy season. Resumed in January, 1936, it was in May crowned with complete success by the capture of the capital, Addis Ababa. Emperor Haile Selassie effected his escape to Great Britain, the Italian flag was raised over his palace, and in witness of his deposition King Victor Emmanuel, at of course Mussolini's instigation, added to his Italian title that of emperor of Ethiopia.

Not to be overlooked is the humiliation suffered through this epi- sode by the League of Nations. In the face of the accomplished victory **The** there was nothing for it to do but shamefacedly lift the economic em- **drawing-on** bargo it had decreed. From this time on the reigning world-confusion **of a new** deepened steadily, driving forward inexorably to a new world explosion. **world war** But this story, with Italy's share therein, is reserved to the chapter dealing with the outbreak of World War II.

41 GERMANY GOES NAZI

ONCE MORE THE FEEBLE GERMAN REPUBLIC

The republic rides the waves safely for a decade, 1919-1930

THE GERMAN REPUBLIC, proclaimed in November, 1918, and fortified by the Weimar constitution of the following year, had the support of the majority of the people and of a majority of the members of the Reichstag. The Reichstag majority was a coalition majority composed of three parties, the Majority Socialists, the Centrists (Catholic party), and the Democrats (with whom some other bourgeois groups usually collaborated). While the government was frequently changed and many chancellors (heads of the ministry) came and went, there was not lacking a certain measure of stability, since what we may call the middle parties always at a pinch joined to preserve the republic. Not to be overlooked, however, was the injection from the first of a novel and ominous element of violence into German public life. It stemmed in the main from oath-bound groups of fanatical nationalists, who repeatedly went the length of assassinating an outstanding republican official. Nonetheless, for the decade (1919-1930) when the moderate parties commanded a majority in the Reichstag the republic was safe.

Two irreconcilable opponents, Nationalists and Communists

Two parties were from the first wholeheartedly opposed to the republic. They were the Nationalists of the extreme right and the Communists of the extreme left. If the republic had not been loaded with an intolerable sum of burdens, it might quite possibly have weathered the attack of these two groups of opponents and have retained sufficient popular support indefinitely to prolong its existence.

The economic confusion reaches a climax in a runaway currency inflation

The burdens laid on the republic resulted from an exhausting war ending in a crushing defeat and should logically have been charged by an enlightened opinion to the vanished imperial government. However, human beings are superficial reasoners and invariably blame for their hardships the government they happen at the moment to have. We may broadly classify the hardships suffered by the German people as economic and psychological. As the economic sufferings leap more readily to view, let us take them first. Exhausted like every other country by the war, Germany was drained of its little remaining wealth by the extravagant demands of the victors for reparations. In so far as they involved direct money payments they were chiefly settled by recourse to an inflated currency. This assumed fantastic proportions on the occupation in 1923 of the industrial region of the Ruhr by the French. When by the end of that year it took two trillions of marks to buy an American dollar and the currency had become useless for even the simplest business transaction, it had with all the values attached thereto to be repudiated and a new currency to be improvised, based on nothing more substantial than the very uncertain faith that the government would somehow muddle through.

The psychological hardships of the German people were those usual to a defeated group and came to expression in the Treaty of Versailles. **Popular** Not only was the treaty uncommonly severe, it was loaded with many **resentment** purely vindictive humiliations which it was the obligation of the republi- **directed** can government to accept without resistance or complaint. In the cir- **against the** cumstances it was inevitable that the government should appear to its **republic** own people in the light of an agent or tool of the victors. Although these victors had cheered the replacement of the empire with the republic and had affirmed their lively interest in its survival, they could not have done more to render it odious to the Germans themselves than they did when they carried through the many harsh articles of the treaty with the enforced co-operation of the republican government.

As we have seen in Chapter 37, in treating the execution of the Treaty of Versailles, the outlook for the republic became somewhat brighter in **The** 1924. By that year a new currency had replaced the useless mark and **economic** had somewhat lessened the despair connected with a runaway inflation. **improve-** At the same time the reparations bill was reduced to some extent by the **ment after** so-called Dawes plan and Germany was granted an international loan **1924** to give its new currency the necessary security. Finally, the departure of the French from the Ruhr did its bit toward improving the general situation. An industrial boom followed, which, as it happened, coincided with a boom of world-wide dimensions. The cheerful prospect generated so much confidence that Germany was able to borrow enormous sums abroad, chiefly from the bankers of the United States. With this borrowed money it succeeded not only in meeting the reparation payments imposed on it under the Dawes plan but also in so increasing its industrial output and absorbing its idle workers that its total domestic situation registered a considerable improvement.

The improvement lasted till 1929, with the result that for a period of five years the republic gained perceptibly in strength and that its two **Ebert** unbending opponents, the Communists and Nationalists, somewhat lost **succeeded** ground. The statement holds good, in spite of the victory won by the **(1925) as** Nationalists in the presidential election of 1925. The first president of the **by Field** republic was Friedrich Ebert, a Majority Socialist and former saddler **Marshal** from Heidelberg, who, a sober spirit free from offensive partisanship, **Hindenburg**

gave acceptable service from 1919 till his death in 1925. For the new election which, as the constitution required, was by popular vote, the Nationalists put up the seventy-seven-year-old hero of the war, Field Marshal Hindenburg. Although he was elected by many patriot votes not
strictly identified with the Nationalist party, it was generally expected
that, as a man of conservative sympathies, he would lend himself to the
overthrow of the republic. He did nothing of the sort. On the contrary,
he showed no hesitation in co-operating with the republican coalition
and thus actually strengthened the republic by putting his immense personal prestige behind it.

A new decline in the fortunes of the republic began in 1929 and pro-

ceeded with extraordinary precipitation. In that year began an economic
crisis which, on hitting the United States in October, was swiftly magnified into a world-wide panic. In Germany, as everywhere else, business
failures multiplied and the ranks of the unemployed, who had to be supported, no matter how meagerly, out of the public purse, swelled rapidly
to three and, finally, to six million. That was bad enough. It was from an
international viewpoint even worse that, when the money market of the
United States was abruptly and tightly closed to German borrowings,
Germany could not find the credits to continue its reparation payments
and the allies, with Germany defaulting to them, found themselves unable to meet the payments they owed the United States. We have already
treated this phase of the economic crisis of 1929 and noted that it led,
ultimately, to a complete breakdown of the whole complicated reparation
issue.

RISE AND TRIUMPH OF THE NATIONAL SOCIALISTS (NAZIS)

The evil political consequence of the economic crisis, which became

graver with each succeeding year, was that the republic lost most of the
credit which its not inconsiderable successes in the immediately preceding period had accumulated. The voters drifted in steadily increasing
numbers into one or the other of the irreconcilable oppositions. Already
by the autumn of 1930 there was a justified fear that either the Communists or the Nationalists, both of them believers in and practicers of
violence, would stage a rising and take over the government. Although
in the end it was not the Communists but the Nationalists who overthrew the republic, it was not the existing Nationalist party, made up of
landowners (Junkers), industrialists, and bureaucrats, which turned the
trick. The success fell to a new-risen body of nationalists who had the
acumen to combine with a fervent nationalism a social program alluring
alike to the impoverished small bourgeoisie and to the harassed, starving

workers. It was by reason of this double program that they called themselves National Socialists, abbreviated in ordinary usage to Nazis.

Even with their alluringly baited program the Nazis might not have got very far, had they not found a fanatically inspired leader, capable of holding an audience spellbound by his promise of the delivery of his people from the yoke of the Versailles dictate—the expression by which he habitually characterized the treaty of that name—and of abundant work and bread for all. This was Adolf Hitler. Born in a village of Upper Austria in 1889, Hitler had at an early age gone to Vienna with the plan of becoming an architect but was too lacking in educational fundamentals to be acceptable to the Imperial Academy of Fine Arts. He had been obliged to pick up an uncertain living by various kinds of lowly work, chiefly that of house-painting. By a diet of exciting newspaper reading focused on the disturbing racial problems of Austria-Hungary, he developed into a fervent German nationalist, passionately opposed to the international doctrine of socialism and to the Jews, to whom, in his view, socialism owed its existence and who served as the agents of its universal diffusion.

By the time World War I broke out, Hitler had transferred his residence from Vienna to Munich and, although an Austrian citizen, joined the German army as a volunteer. He served creditably in the field for the duration of the struggle without, however, rising higher than a corporal. On the dissolution of the army after Germany's defeat he resolved to open a new career for himself by turning politician. He had again settled in Munich, where with a handful of like-minded men he founded the National Socialist party, dedicated, as we have seen, to radical domestic reform coupled with a fiery, mystical nationalism. He had won over no more than an inconsiderable following when he resolved to overthrow the republic. It was the year 1923, the darkest year of the whole post-war period, owing to the occupation by the French of the Ruhr and the attendant astronomical inflation of the German currency. However, the government was strong enough to crush the uprising, which from its place of origin came to be known as the beer-cellar *putsch*. Arrested and tried, Hitler was sent for a year to prison, where he employed his leisure to write his depressingly verbose but highly revealing autobiography, *Mein Kampf* (My Battle).

In spite of the economic recovery which got under way in 1924, Hitler's National Socialists made a slow but steady advance, spreading from Munich to practically all other sections of Germany. Then, with the economic collapse of 1929-1930, the Nazi centers or cells multiplied so rapidly that in the Reichstag elections of 1932 the party gained a representation larger than that of any competing group. More than to any other single factor it owed this startling success to its frankly fighting char-

Hitler a nationalist fiercely adverse to socialists and Jews

Failure of Hitler's first attempt at revolution, the beer-cellar "putsch" of 1923

Rapid growth of Nazism following the depression of 1929-1930

acter. Precisely like the Communist party in Russia and the Fascist party in Italy, the Nazi party was an organization animated by the spirit of violence and domination; and, precisely as in the case of Lenin and Mussolini, it is difficult to decide whether the vast following ultimately won by Hitler was owing to his special genius for organization or to the revolutionary ardor which a generation of thwarted youth put at his disposal. Very likely, in all three instances, the two factors had to meet to give rise to the marching hordes of passionately intent Communists, Fascists, and Nazis.

The young people swarming into the party were organized as a militia wearing, in place of a uniform, a brown shirt with a red armband carrying a black swastika. Colloquially called Brown Shirts, they were organized in groups named *Sturm Abteilungen,* or S.A. for short. In addition to marching purely to make a propagandist public display, the S.A. served such practical purposes as safeguarding the meetings of the party and breaking up those of the other parties, especially the Social Democrats and Communists. A smaller and more select militia body wore black shirts and was called *Schutz Staffeln,* or, commonly, S.S. Theirs was the more distinguished task of serving as bodyguards to the party heads and blindly carrying out whatever orders wherewith they might be charged.

The swastika affixed to the armband of the S.A. and reproduced on the militia banners and on the proclamations with which the party flooded the country carried a mystic import. Supposed to be of remote Aryan origin, it proclaimed that the National Socialists stood for an Aryan Germany and that they were resolved to eliminate non-Aryans, meaning Jews, from German politics, art, and science. It need hardly be pointed out that Aryan is a term of so uncertain a meaning that none but professional word-jugglers are likely to use it. Although an Aryan group of peoples has undoubtedly figured in history, it has in the course of the ages been so widely dispersed that it can no longer be securely located anywhere. It is therefore extremely disputable to what extent the Germans or any other European group have Aryan blood in their veins. And if the extent could be ascertained, it would be impossible to determine with even approximate precision its human or cultural significance. Putative Aryans, who were taught to consider themselves a superior race, the Nazis held it to be their bounden racial duty to get rid of the inferior and alien Jewish element in their midst.

In the period of 1930-1932 the dwindling republican parties made a last stand. That it was a desperate stand is proved by the fact that when, in 1932, President Hindenburg's seven-year term expired, they made him, a professional soldier, their candidate and re-elected him to office against Adolf Hitler, running on the Nazi ticket, and Ernst Thälmann, the Communist candidate. It was a deceptive victory, for the president, who had

---

The two private Nazi militias of S.A. and S.S.

The swastika symbolizes the blindly adopted Aryan faith

supported the republicans as long as they commanded a majority in the Reichstag, drew away from them as soon as their influence had declined beyond recovery. A landowner or Junker by birth, Hindenburg was, after all, a convinced conservative and abandoned the republicans the moment this course was warranted by their minority representation in parliament. After experimenting hesitantly and unsuccessfully with two upper-class chancellors of nationalist persuasion, he took, in January, 1933, the decisive step of conferring the chancellorship on Hitler, as representing the largest single party in the Reichstag.

The steady Nazi advance brings Hitler to the chancellorship in January, 1933

Unable in his turn to rule without a majority, Hitler in March, 1933, called for new elections. Marvelously organized for propaganda purposes, the Nazis conducted a campaign of frenzied activity, not scrupling, when the occasion served, to resort to the violence which was the essence of their creed. In the new Reichstag the Nazis commanded a small majority.

Hitler wins the election of March, 1933

It was the end of the republic. The republican flag was at once replaced with the old imperial flag of black, white, and red, with the conspicuous addition of the swastika, emblem of the new Aryan nationalism. Then, on April 1, the Reichstag delegated its powers to Adolf Hitler for a period of four years. Thus made dictator, he considered the republican regime to have come to an end and gave the state delivered into his hands the official name of the Third Reich. According to the Nazi philosophy of history the empire they brought into existence had had two predecessors: the medieval empire (the Holy Roman Empire) and the Bismarckian empire of 1871-1918.

Hitler replaces the republic with the Third Reich

Without the least delay the dictatorship threw itself on its opponents to the end of completely removing them from the national political scene. Its leading enemies were the Marxists, whether Communists or Socialists, and the Jews, of whatever party. The outstanding representatives of these groups were arrested and herded by hundreds and thousands in concentration camps, where they were subjected to a course of starvation and torture spitefully calculated to break their spirit. Other hundreds and thousands, representing the highest level of the country's intelligentsia, escaped to other lands. It was a persecution paralleled only in Russia in 1917, and was by no means limited to Jews, for a large proportion of the exiles as well as the victims of the concentration camps ranked by Nazi definition as Aryans. In last analysis the crime of the enemies of the regime was their unwillingness to give up the thousand-year-old Christian culture of the west with its teachings of love and brotherhood for the primitive Nazi creed of "blood and soil" coupled with the practice of a brutal coercion against all opponents of their system.

Atrocious persecution of Marxists and Jews

Since the labor unions were without exception infected with Marxist doctrines, they were dissolved and their funds appropriated by the state.

Thereupon the whole body of German workers, over twenty million in
number, were gathered into a single labor union under a particularly
coarse and unrestrained Nazi leader, Dr. Ley. The merger was celebrated
by Hitler as the first step toward the realization of a national, as distinct
from an international, socialism.

A similar tendency toward elimination of divisive forces and in favor
of solidarity manifested itself in every department of public life. The
measures taken in regard to political parties were peculiarly illuminating
in this respect. All parties of Marxist inspiration were forcibly dissolved;
the others, under pressure, dissolved themselves. Only the Nazi party remained. In the Third Reich there was room for no more than a single
party, under a head called *Führer* or Leader.

When it came to the question of the shape to be given the Third
Reich, the same spirit ruled. The republic, like the empire before it, had
been a federal state, although somewhat more tightly cemented than its
predecessor. The Nazis set up as their goal a centralization as close as
that of France, but moved toward it with a measure of caution. Their
first step was to abolish the *Landtage* or legislative assemblies of the component German states; their second, to reduce the states themselves to
mere administrative divisions of the Reich. While they may be said to
have moved systematically toward the total abolition of the political entities of Prussia, Bavaria, Saxony, Baden, and the other states from which
united Germany had historically arisen, they never quite brought the task
to completion.

The ideology or system of political thought that underlay the reshaping of Germany was identical with that of Italian Fascism. Like the
Fascists, the Nazis proclaimed the totalitarian state, which exists for its
own sake and to which the actions of the individual citizen must in all
circumstances be subordinated. The totalitarian state is consciously and
sharply opposed to the democratic state, with its inalienable individual
rights of free speech, free press, and freedom of assembly. These traditional democratic liberties were sweepingly and on principle rejected by
the totalitarians.

In spite of the double claim of their party name, the Nazis, from the
first hour of their assumption of power, proved themselves much more
national than socialist. True, they promptly began reducing the swollen
figure of the unemployed till, after a few years, they could boast that all
that were left of the unemployed mass inherited by their regime were
the unemployable. The feat was overwhelmingly due to their, at first
secretly, and at last openly, rearming, and only to a smaller extent to a
comprehensive program of public works. Conceding that public works
are an acceptable remedy for public distress, they cannot, except for propaganda purposes, be represented as a novel variety of socialism. In 1936

All German workers gathered into a single union

Abolition of all parties save the Nazi party

Historical federalism replaced by centralization

Nazi ideology is totalitarian

Economic revival based on rearmament, public works, and a Four Year Plan

Hitler inaugurated, in manifest imitation of the Russians and with more than the usual fanfare associated with all his acts, a Four Year Plan. Its declared aim was to render Germany economically self-sufficient. While this was impossible, owing to the country's inadequate endowment with the raw materials indispensable for a modern industrial economy, certain successes could be and were achieved. There took place, for one thing, a more intensive use of the immediately available resources and, for another, the development, with the aid of chemists and other scientists, of synthetic substitutes (*Ersatz*) for the rubber, oil, cotton, wool, etc., for which Germany was dependent on foreign lands. This was no small advantage in view of the open drive of the regime toward war, for war would put an end to importation, and without home-grown substitutes war, the insatiable consumer of every variety of equipment, was an impossibility.

It was Hitler's hesitation to realize the socialist features of the party program that, in June, 1934, barely a year after his establishment, led to a plot being spun against him by a group of radically-minded district leaders. The brain of the movement was Ernst Röhm, head of the S.A. However, Hitler was on the alert and by the quick, relentless action of himself and his chief supporter, Hermann Göring, disposed of the insurrection by the summary execution of a hundred, possibly of several hundred, persons. It was one of those "purges" which characterized the Communist regime in Russia and which would seem to be inseparable from dictatorial systems. Shortly after, the secret police or *Geheime Staatspolizei,* which under its abbreviated title of *Gestapo* struck terror into all hearts, came more vigorously to the front under its cold-blooded, murderous chief, Heinrich Himmler. The Gestapo, employing thousands of agents and engaged in undercover activity in every town and village of the land, saw to it by methods peculiar to itself that there was no repetition of the June uprising.

The "purge" of June, 1934, and the rise of the Gestapo

In the summer of 1934 President Hindenburg died at the advanced age of eighty-six. Never possessed of a distinguished intelligence, he had been failing in mind as well as in body during recent years. On his death, Hitler abolished the presidential office and merged its powers with those of the chancellorship. To mark his increased dignity he adopted the title of *Reichsführer,* or Realm Leader. However, his preference ran to the earlier, simpler title of chancellor, as which he continued to be addressed, except insofar as his party members chose to address him as Führer.

Hindenburg succeeded (1934) in the presidency by Hitler

THE NAZIS AND RELIGION

Since the Nazis approached every issue of public and private life from the totalitarian angle, they made the same approach to religion. From their totalitarianism stemmed their most voluble governmental slogan, of *Gleichschaltung,* which has been usually englished as co-ordination but is better rendered as uniformity. It was under the inspiration of Gleichschaltung that they created a uniform state directed by a uniform party under a uniform leader—associated creations of an unwavering political logic. With this criterion as their guide, it was not surprising that, when they turned their attention to religion, they should have been deeply irritated by the diverse and confused situation that met their gaze and that, in spite of its having been handed down from a relatively distant past, they should have determined to correct its irregularities with the strong medicine of Gleichschaltung.

Ever since the Reformation Germany has been approximately two-thirds Protestant and one-third Catholic in population. While the Catholics had always been, and still were, a united body, the Protestants were not only Lutheran and Calvinist (though preponderantly Lutheran) but were, besides, organized into more than a score of separate state churches. Strict totalitarian theory demanded the merger of all Christian denominations, of even the Catholics and Protestants, to the end that the new Germany be bound together in a single faith. However, even the most enraged Nazi fanatic was obliged to recognize that in this particular matter the theory dashed itself to pieces on the facts. The Hitler crew therefore resolved to accept the Catholic-Protestant schism as, for the present at least, incurable and to treat with each main group separately to the end of getting it as completely as possible under the thumb of the state.

Taking the Catholics first, we note that Hitler had been in office only a few months when he signed in July, 1933, a concordat with the pope. In return for the Catholic clergy's pledging itself not to meddle in politics, it was permitted, over and above the free exercise of its religious activities, to conduct schools and maintain youth groups, which in their turn were pledged not to pursue political aims. As the bulk of German boys and girls were organized as Hitler Youth and the entrance into this nation-wide organization was soon made obligatory, conflicts between the two rival youth organizations were inevitable. On the Catholic press's reporting the frequent encounters and the Catholic priesthood's denouncing the government that permitted and even, on occasion, encouraged them, the offending newspaper would be confiscated and the offending priest penalized. This would produce an indignant protest from the local bishop or even from the pope with the result that the controversy repeatedly waxed so hot that a complete breaking-off of relations seemed to lie just ahead. However, that final step was always avoided on the ground, we must assume, that, in spite of an irreconcilable division of principle and the perpetual imminence of religious war, each side drew

[margin notes]

Totalitarian logic demands religious uniformity

The Nazi approach to the German religious situation

The concordat with the pope does not do away with conflicts between church and state

sufficient advantage from an uncomfortable *modus vivendi* to refrain from exchanging it for an open breach.

Having with the passing of the centuries grown tolerant of each other, the Protestant sects would never have moved toward the fusion Nazi theory demanded, except for a small Nazi element among them. This element, extremely nationalist in outlook, viewed with disfavor the Old Testament as a national Jewish document and wished to replace it, or at least to supplement its employment in the service, with religious writings of German origin. In line with this emphasis the members of this group called themselves *German* Christians, and Hitler, although a Catholic (insofar as he was anything) and not immediately concerned with Protestant affairs, gave them his blessing because of their nationalism. As the obsessed believer in uniformity, he convinced himself that only under the direction of the German Christians could the Protestant amalgamation be carried out. Opinion among the Protestant clergy in general was fluid and uncertain. While a majority favored amalgamation, a vigorous protest based on doctrine and tradition never ceased to make itself heard against the Hitler-favored sect of German Christians. When the issue was submitted for decision to the Protestant electorate, the German Christians, with the powerful support of the government, carried the day and a united church was set up under a head entitled Reichbishop. But substantial groups of pastors together with their congregations refused to join the new national church. Of these protesters the most unbending was Pastor Niemöller, who had been a submarine commander in the First World War. When the recalcitrant clergymen were punished with arrests and prison sentences, they became martyrs, and their cause grew stronger than ever. Enlivened with numerous clashes, the struggle, far from being brought to a triumphant close by the government, continued up to the outbreak of World War II, when it was blanketed by the din of arms.

Partial success and final failure of the attempted merger of all Protestants

More than any other area of German life and thought, religion emerged with credit from its struggle with totalitarianism. Admitting that there was some yielding by sections of both the Catholic and the Protestant clergy, a vigorous resistance never ceased to manifest itself not only against the flat uniformity of Gleichschaltung but even more against the idea that religion is the servant of the state and must submit to the role of willing tool.

Both Catholics and Protestants reject state domination

A curious religious aberration of the period may not be overlooked because it shows that the Nazi revolution awakened folk memories that were thought to have been buried beyond recall. A handful of what we must consider to be mental freaks advocated a backward leap over fifteen hundred years of Christian civilization in order to tie up again with the original German paganism, in which Woden and Thor, with the

The Neo-pagan movement

assistance of an omnipotent but elusive Fate, ruled the destinies of man. Hitler was too good a politician to commit himself to a religion so far removed from the understanding of the common man, but that he was secretly attracted to it is proved by the favors he heaped upon Neo-paganism's leading champion, Alfred Rosenberg. In 1937 the Führer awarded to this pagan "philosopher," who was also a leading exponent of the dubious doctrine of Aryanism, the country's highest honor, the National Prize.

THE NAZI FOREIGN POLICY

Core of Hitler's foreign policy is piecemeal cancellation of the Treaty of Versailles

During the years of intensive agitation preceding his advent to power Hitler pledged himself to the repudiation of what on his tongue was always the Dictate of Versailles. The progressive scrapping of the treaty may therefore be represented as the substance of his foreign policy. However, this was not at once made clear to the world, for he permitted the German delegation dispatched to the Disarmament Conference at Geneva to share in the deliberations till October, 1933, before he withdrew it. When he then at the same time withdrew Germany from the League of Nations, his antagonism to everything associated with Versailles became undisguisedly manifest. Consequently a grave apprehension seized on Europe and the world. It was intensified, first, by the frenzied domestic agitation of the Nazis in behalf of uniformity, and second, by the spread of Nazi doctrines into neighboring territories inhabited by people of German speech but not incorporated in the Reich. The areas more immediately affected were Danzig, Austria, and the Saar, and the happenings therein at this time need to be carefully set forth, since they made a measurable contribution to the deepening general nervousness.

The Free City of Danzig becomes Nazi in sentiment

By the Treaty of Versailles Danzig was made a free, that is, a self-governing, city but was incorporated economically in Poland. The arrangement caused friction from the start because Danzig was overwhelmingly German in population. Consequently, the Danzigers never ceased hoping that they would ultimately win their way back to the fatherland, and no sooner had the extreme Nazi nationalism become a swollen stream in Germany than it flowed across the border and invaded the Free City. As early as May, 1933, the Danzig Nazis won the municipal elections and became the majority party in the government. The alarm in Poland over this turn of affairs was great, especially as it hinted at a probable early intervention in behalf of the Danzigers on the part of Hitler. Because in this youthful period of his ascendancy his relationship with the western powers was still on a hardly better than war footing, he resolved to be conciliatory toward Poland and signed (January, 1934) with her a ten-year nonaggression pact. This proved so reassuring to the Polish government that a kind of truce was effected between Warsaw and Berlin with the result that the jittery Danzig issue to all intents disappeared from the German-Polish agenda till the eve of the new World War. Then indeed it reappeared with a vengeance and became the match that set fire to the house.

From the moment of its birth in the revolution of 1918 the reduced republic of Austria loomed as a major German problem. Although its population was solidly German, it had been forbidden by the Paris peace-makers to carry out that union with its sister-republic with the proclamation of which it had begun its existence. Nevertheless strong nationalist elements in both countries continued to hope for ultimate fusion or, as the German phrase ran, for *Anschluss*. In the circumstances, Nazi opinion gained an early footing in Austria and led to the formation of a party of Austrian Nazis. In July, 1934, this group staged a rising in Vienna which, after an early success culminating in the murder of the head of the government, Chancellor Dollfuss, fizzled out. The fiasco was due to the failure of Hitler to lend the expected support of German troops; and Hitler's failure was in its turn due to the action of Mussolini. Full as yet of suspicion of the young Nazi movement and booking the spread of German influence in Austria as an Italian loss, Mussolini promptly mobilized an army on the Austrian frontier. In the face of this threat Hitler backed down, and the Austrian government under continued Catholic party control regained command of the situation. Since the Catholic party was anti-Nazi and did not again lose command of the government, the relations between Austria and Germany remained strained till Hitler ended the conflict by the seizure of Austria in March, 1938—one of the several curtain-raisers, as we shall hereafter learn, to the subsequent world tragedy.

Nazi opinion spreads to Austria and causes an Austro-German conflict

As for the Saar, this was, as we know, an important coal-producing area on the French border which was detached from Germany by the Treaty of Versailles and handed over for a period of fifteen years to the guidance of the League of Nations. In January, 1935, the fifteen years were up, and a referendum was instituted by the League, by the terms of which the inhabitants were invited to signify whether they wished to re-join Germany, be absorbed by France, or continue under the League. They left no doubt as to their sentiment, since an overwhelming majority voted to return to the fatherland. While the Saar referendum was a triumph for Germany, it should not be forgotten that it was carried through by the League of Nations and that it stands out conspicuously on the credit side of that debatable body.

The Saar plebiscite of 1935 a German victory

We come now to the main theme of this section, to wit, Hitler's piecemeal repudiation of the Treaty of Versailles. His first measure, taken soon after his domestic victory, was secretly to rearm, but not so secretly that the whole diplomatic world was not fully aware of it. Then, in

March, 1935, when he thought he was strong enough to risk the conse-

Hitler's first measures of repudiation of Versailles

quences, he took his first step in the open by announcing his rejection of the military restrictions of Versailles. At the same time he put an end to secret rearmament by publicly proclaiming the resumption by Germany of universal military service. While there were murmured protests by the former allies, there was no adverse action and, thus encouraged, the Führer continued with mounting assurance on his way. If France and Great Britain had presented a solid front against him, he would without any doubt have been obliged to beat a retreat. Moreover, had they unitedly asserted themselves, they would have been on the firmest theoretical ground imaginable, since they would have been doing no more than upholding international law as laid down in a treaty to which every state in the world, great and little, had subscribed.

So far, however, were France and Great Britain from the close co-

Great Britain abets Hitler by authorizing a German navy and a German air force (1935)

operation which alone would have brought Hitler to a halt, that not only did they visibly drift more and more apart but Great Britain in particular on more than one occasion actually abetted the lawbreaker. Thus, for instance, in June, 1935, the London government signed an agreement with Germany by which it went so far as to become Hitler's accomplice in wrecking the Versailles edifice. By this agreement Germany was permitted to construct every kind of naval craft it pleased, provided that the German total tonnage never exceeded thirty-five per cent of the total British tonnage. At the same time Britain accepted a German proposal, according to which a German air force, forbidden by Versailles, was not only authorized but permitted to be brought to an approximate level with the air force of its nearest neighbors.

The inability of France and Great Britain to see eye to eye encouraged

The leveling of Versailles clears the way for unrestrained aggression

Hitler to continue his profitable game. In March, 1936, he boldly sent troops into the Rhineland. It will be remembered that the Rhineland had been demilitarized by the Treaty of Versailles and was then held under allied military occupation till 1930. Since that year there had been neither allied nor German troops in this strategically crucial area till Hitler's act of 1936 brought it again within the German military dominion. Again war threatened and again Great Britain refused to stand shoulder to shoulder with its Gallic neighbor. It was therefore hardly an occasion for astonishment that in January, 1937, the Führer took another audacious step: he repudiated the war-guilt clause of the Versailles document. Unchecked by a cowed Europe, he henceforth considered himself a free agent and embarked on a course of unrestrained aggression. By this policy he was drawn closer and closer to the similarly inspired states of Japan and Italy, with the result that among them they produced a succession of incidents that set the stage for the outbreak on September 1, 1939, of the new World War. In a later chapter we shall review these exciting concatenated events and follow them through to the dread catastrophe.

Our concluding remark on Nazi foreign policy is reserved to Russia. When Hitler set up his Nazi system, he did so in conscious opposition not only to western democracy but also to eastern, that is, Russian communism. In the years covered by this chapter the development of his own Nazi system gradually assumed the character of an unbridled denunciation of these two contemporary ideologies. Consequently, it was inevitable that, should he ever resolve to measure strength with one, he would in the long run be obliged to measure strength also with the other. In view of this fatality it is curious to observe that in *Mein Kampf* he solemnly warned against a war on two fronts as the certain destruction of Germany.

Hitler's war bound to become a war of two fronts

42

TWO CONTINUING DEMOCRACIES:

FRANCE AND GREAT BRITAIN

Democracy loses ground but is far from being a lost cause

IN THE LIGHT thrown, in the immediately preceding chapters, on the post-war behavior of Russia, Italy, and Germany it will have to be admitted that the democratic seed so freely cast abroad by the propaganda of World War I fell often on stony soil. The impression will be deepened by the chapter following the present one and dealing with the many small states of east-central Europe and the Balkan peninsula. Nonetheless, no greater mistake could be made than to regard democracy as a lost cause even in Europe, where its flag came down in so many areas. An impressive group of small states, representative of the most advanced form of Western civilization, never wavered in their attachment to the democratic system, and as they lay within the cultural orbit of the two leading western powers, France and Great Britain, both of which remained unbrokenly faithful to the same system, it continued to stand like a tower, even though its base was threateningly washed, on one side, by the rising stream of communism and, on the other, by the equally menacing fascist flood.

A group of small states faithful to democracy

The group of small states that continued to fly the banner of democratic liberalism embraced the two kingdoms of the Netherlands, Belgium and Holland, the three Scandinavian kingdoms of Denmark, Norway, and Sweden, and the Alpine republic of Switzerland. Slowly to tell off their names brings up the picture of communities which from a social, moral, economic, or any other viewpoint take their place among the soundest and most thriving societies to be encountered anywhere over the face of the earth. In Chapter 32 we traced the political development of these states up to 1914 and pointed out the leading problems wherewith each was confronted. Owing to the tremendous dislocations produced everywhere by the war and therefore also in the group under consideration, their domestic problems in the post-war period frequently took on an extremely acute form. The foremost cause of this turn of affairs was that, no more than any of their neighbor states, whether large or small, were they spared the formation among them of parties representing the two distinct but equally uncompromising oppositions to democracy, communism and fascism. In no case, however, did they permit these adverse pressures to deflect them from the democratic path to which they had committed themselves in the course of the nineteenth century.

Small polities with limited resources, these states naturally looked to their two strong, like-minded neighbors for support. Had not France and Great Britain also remained attached to the democratic system, which in point of fact owed its very existence to their initiative, it may be assumed that neither Belgium and Holland nor the three Scandinavian kingdoms could have survived the communist-fascist assault. Indeed it is not likely that even Switzerland, the oldest republic in all Europe, could have withstood the totalitarian tidal wave, had not France and Great Britain stood up courageously to meet its main impact. It is therefore not only proper but imperative that we give our concentrated attention to the two strongholds on whose sustained resolution hung the fate of democracy in Europe, and possibly throughout the world.

France and Great Britain the main strongholds of democracy

FRANCE

Reconstruction, Reparations, and National Finance

It was a coalition government of center and rightist parties, called the National Bloc, that successfully carried France through the devastating war. Great therefore was the prestige of its leaders, of Georges Clemenceau who, as prime minister, had led the republic from darkness to light, and of Raymond Poincaré, who had served as president during the five agonizing campaigns the war lasted. When in November, 1919, general elections were held, a grateful country gave the National Bloc a decisive victory; but when, early in the following year, the new chambers met to elect a president to succeed Poincaré, whose term was about to expire, they rejected with the not unfamiliar caprice of popular bodies, the too-masterful Clemenceau for a parliamentarian of long standing who had made fewer enemies. The defeat was felt as a slap in the face by the octogenarian leader, and he retired from public life.

Clemenceau and Poincaré, leaders of the National Bloc

Patriotically uplifted, the revised National Bloc ministry conceived its primary task to be the reconstruction of the war-torn departments of the east and northeast, and it floated loans on a huge scale in order to bring about their restoration in the shortest possible time. With such admirable energy was the reconstruction pushed that in the course of the next few years many thousands of new homes and factories were erected; and when in subsequent elections the National Bloc lost its ascendancy to other party alignments, the amazing tempo of the rehabilitation enterprise was in no respect relaxed. Within a decade the whole comprehensive program by whose application entire cities rose from the ground, with the necessary complement of houses, schools, and churches, had been

The chief peace task was to rebuild the devastated areas

brought to completion. A much-remarked feature of the work were the up-to-date factories, fitted with the latest and most efficient machines and drawing their motive power from the war-damaged coal-mines returned to improved operation and from numerous hydroelectric installations of the most advanced model. Industrial output reflected these multiplied facilities and brought to France an era of prosperity and full employment at a time when the rest of the world was passing through a depression caused by its inability to find work for the discharged soldiers the peace had returned to civil life.

The French calculation in regard to the immense outlay incurred by the recovery program was that it would presently be made good by the reparations due from Germany. But these, as we have learned, were not even exactly specified till two years after the Treaty of Versailles had become international law, and when they were at last imposed they proved so onerous that after little more than a year Germany sued for a moratorium. We have also learned how the National Bloc, laboring under the financial strain of the vast reconstruction enterprise, easily convinced itself that Germany was willfully withholding payment, and how, lifting Poincaré with his "strong man" reputation earned during the war to the premiership, roundly applauded his resolve to collect the lagging reparations by seizure and exploitation of the Ruhr. Unfortunately for the National Bloc the Ruhr turned out to be an unprofitable experiment. Not only was the net return of the occupation insignificant but the vast political disturbance it produced at home and abroad alike injured French credit and precipitated a disastrous decline in the value of the franc. The disappointment of the country found expression in the elections of 1924, in which Poincaré was defeated by his opponents, united in the Left Cartel, and was obliged to resign.

The new premier, Edouard Herriot, faced a deteriorating financial situation which he failed to improve. Nor did the ministries that followed him in rapid succession achieve a better result. Mounting annual deficits raised the national debt to the alarming figure of three hundred billion francs, and the currency continued uninterruptedly on its downward course. By 1926 the franc (normally worth about twenty cents) was valued at about two cents, and fear of impending bankruptcy became so general that a combination of Right and Left parties demanded the return of Poincaré, the recently discarded "strong man," and docilely voted the new taxes and administrative economies that he proposed in order to arrive at a balanced budget and to restore the country's shattered credit. In lively acclaim of his success Poincaré was hailed as "the Savior of the Franc," for he brought back this apparently doomed coin to twenty-five to the dollar, that is, to four cents. In distinction from his earlier ministry this second ministry of the thickset, dynamic little man

The lagging reparations are met by the invasion (1923) of the Ruhr

The bad French financial situation causes a mounting debt and the decline of the franc

was an unqualified success, largely because there emanated an authority from him which gave the centrifugal parliamentary system an indispensable center of stability and calm.

Fascist Leagues and the Popular Front

Evidence of this authority was supplied when Poincaré in 1929 was obliged to retire from office, owing to ill health. Immediately the old fiscal troubles returned attended by the former dizzy succession of ministries. And now, more and more, a protest against the intolerable parliamentary confusion began to make itself heard. While it came from practically every social level, it reached its noisiest expression in a group of reactionary leagues animated by either royalist or fascist sentiments. On their growing bolder and staging public demonstrations, such as in Italy and Germany had preceded the rise of Mussolini and Hitler, they threw so great a scare into the parties which, despite programmatic differences, were solidly devoted to the maintenance of free institutions that they merged in a Popular Front in order at all costs to save the republic. It was in 1935 that the Popular Front came into existence by the pledge of the Radical Socialists (in spite of their name an old-fashioned liberal party), the Socialists, and the Communists to stand shoulder to shoulder in the coming elections. When these took place in the following year, the Popular Front captured a majority of the deputies, and for the first time a socialist, Léon Blum, became premier with supporting ministers from his own party and from the Radical Socialists, but not from the Communists. This last party was willing to help elect anti-fascists to the Chamber of Deputies but not to serve in the government at their side.

The rise of fascism produces a republican concentration called the Popular Front

Not all the great expectations aroused by the coming to power of the compactly democratic Popular Front were destined to be realized. Léon Blum was an honorable, well-intentioned literary dilettante who lacked the inner fire alone capable of making men of diverse opinions pull together at the same cord. He suppressed the various fascist leagues, of which the *Croix de Feu* was the most threatening, but they promptly popped up again under another name. His greatest success was in the realm of working-class legislation. The revolt of the workers against the bourgeoisie had at the very moment of Blum's accession to power taken the novel and extravagant form of "sit-down" strikes, and nothing less than sweeping measures of worker relief would persuade the protesters to evacuate the factories they had occupied. Laws were accordingly spread on the statute books suggestive of the contemporary New Deal in the United States. They established a forty-hour week, holidays with pay, the right of collective bargaining, and sent the at least temporarily satisfied strikers back to work.

Many laws favoring the workers passed by the Popular Front

Then, with these achievements to the socialist premier's credit, the
Failure of the Popular Front many-headed serpent of finance raised its head and, as so often before, proved the undoing of the government. Blum depreciated the gold content of the franc in the hope of increasing French exports and balancing the budget, but these happy effects failed to materialize. After hardly a year in office, he was forced to resign and was followed by Chautemps. The new premier was a Radical Socialist and, as such, was supported by the Popular Front. He had a certain success in fiscal matters, for he gave up the struggle, long ago abandoned by Great Britain, the United States, and the other competitors for world trade, to keep his country on the gold basis and permitted the franc to find the less than three-and-a-half-cent level which was its competitive worth. In April, 1938, he was succeeded by another Radical Socialist, Daladier, whose personally conservative slant caused him to look for support rather to the parties of the Right than to the Popular Front. This once so enthusiastically greeted democratic combination consequently disintegrated.

France faces the impending European crisis It was during Daladier's first year of rule that there took place Hitler's march into Austria and the crisis over the Sudetenland. With these resounding breaches of the peace, foreign affairs completely crowded domestic concerns from the minds of Frenchmen. It is this hypnotic shift of attention that explains why in April, 1939, the parliament practically abdicated by granting Daladier's cabinet the power, for eight months, to rule by decree. The measure owed its passage to a general anticipation of war, which, some six months later, actually burst upon a tense world.

The weakness of French democracy is the parliamentary system This swift review of French parliamentary vicissitudes imposes a summarizing conclusion on French democracy. There can be no doubt that the republic with its guaranteed liberties of the individual enjoyed the cordial attachment of the vast majority of the citizen body. The revealed and recognized weakness of the republic lay in the parliament, and the weakness of the parliament was the large number of parties that com·posed it. Never did it happen that a single party by itself embraced a majority of the deputies. It followed that ministries were regularly constituted by a coalition of parties, or by what the French called a bloc. And it also followed that the moment some particularly contentious issue arose, the bloc went to pieces, the ministry fell, and a new bloc had somehow to be fashioned for the support of a new ministry. Government in these circumstances was in perpetual flux and dangerously unstable. Everything considered, there is less reason to be struck with the visible and alarming growth of fascist and communist oppositions, which fed on this grave confusion, than to wonder at the continued devotion of city and country to a democratic system scarred with so glaring and apparently so incurable a defect.

Foreign Policy

The ministries that rose and fell in rapid succession over the domestic problems might lead us to suspect that foreign policy was exposed to the same fluctuating treatment as public finance. However, this was far from the case, because foreign policy was overwhelmingly shaped by the single issue of the relation of France to Germany, and in this matter all Frenchmen, and consequently all ministries, were in substantial agreement. French foreign policy followed a rectilinear, undeviating course which summed up as the search for security against German attack. This policy, stemming from a set national frame of mind, has already been discussed in the chapter on reparations but may profitably be reviewed and amplified in this chapter dealing with the country's total post-war situation.

Foreign policy reveals a steady purpose

At the Paris Conference, Prime Minister Clemenceau, acting for France, had succeeded by numerous punitive articles written into the Treaty of Versailles in getting what looked like an abundant security against his country's historical eastern foe. A crowning measure in this connection was his obtaining from Great Britain and the United States a pledge to come to the assistance of France the moment Germany should make a hostile move against her. However, when the Senate of the United States repudiated the Treaty of Versailles, this particular feature of French security evaporated, and not only so far as the American republic was concerned. It evaporated also for Great Britain, since by the terms of the pledge it was binding for both or for neither. Consequently France, deserted by the two English-speaking powers, turned to a number of small states surrounding Germany, to Belgium, Poland, and Czechoslovakia, and in the immediate post-war period concluded defensive alliances with them. As Czechoslovakia was a member of the so-called Little Entente, it was not difficult somewhat later to draw also Yugoslavia and Rumania, although they did not border on Germany, into the French security system. Its form and nature indicated a return to the pre-war diplomacy of surrounding Germany with a ring of steel.

The search for security in the post-war period

Concerned with strengthening the hand of France in every direction, French diplomacy did not overlook the League of Nations. True, in a realistic spirit, it assessed the League's power at a low value, but it did not fail to see that the League's annual meeting might be utilized as a sounding-board for reaching and influencing world opinion. Not even the rather dour and tight-buttoned Poincaré neglected to make use of the League in this way; and when, in 1924, Herriot of the Left Cartel succeeded Poincaré, in accordance with the less narrowly nationalistic and more broadly European outlook of the typical liberal, he considerably

France and the League of Nations

expanded the role hitherto played by France at Geneva. He dispatched as French delegate to the League, as Poincaré had done before him, the man who more than any other Frenchman had from the first made it his business to sing the praises of the new world organization. This was Aristide Briand; and Briand was able to give his devotion to the League and peace a very special character by his unusual oratorical gifts.

The Locarno interlude of 1925

The result was that peace got a hearing, which not only was a welcome relief in a world deafeningly echoing with every variety of strife, but also blew some of the murk out of the atmosphere enveloping Franco-German relations. Consequently direct negotiations began to be spun between Paris and Berlin which by 1925 led to the signing of the five Locarno treaties. Of these by far the most important one put the Franco-German and Franco-Belgian boundaries, as laid down in the Treaty of Versailles, under the combined guarantee of France, Belgium, Germany, Great Britain, and Italy. The document signified nothing less than a second and, on this occasion, voluntary acceptance by Germany of its revised western boundary. The novel good will it evidenced among all the signatories reached a logical culmination in the admission in the following year of Germany to the League of Nations, coupled with the award of a seat in the governing body, the Council.

Reasons why Franco-German relations were not effectively improved

Hailed as the beginning of a new era in the relations between France and Germany, Locarno proved to be a mirage that dissolved almost as soon as it was glimpsed. Or, call it a hoax that Briand and his German counterpart, Stresemann, sprang on the world in their understandable longing to give a respite to hate: a hoax—for if we now inquire whether any of the fundamental causes of the resentment and suspicion animating the two neighbors had been removed, we shall find nothing whereon we might rest our case. France was not by a hair's breadth made more secure by the paper pledge of Locarno nor was Germany relieved of any of the Versailles disabilities that reduced her to a third-rate power. After, as before Locarno, Europe from the Atlantic to the Bosporus clung to its bad habit of breeding new, while stubbornly nursing its old, quarrels; and, as though that were not enough, the rancorous reparation problem, even after its revision (1924) by the Dawes committee, suspended a sword over France and Germany, over Europe and the world. When with the economic crisis of 1929 black clouds gathered in the sky of country after country, reparation payments were again halted; and this time (1932), with the general consent of Germany's creditors, including France, they were, together with the equally vexatious inter-allied debts, practically abolished.

While the fiasco of the two interwoven debts may be regarded as a blessing in disguise, this construction cannot possibly be put on the fiasco

of the Geneva Disarmament Conference which followed on the heels of
the annulment of reparations. Granted that the Conference failed because
sovereign states could not be persuaded to let the decision over their
means of defense be taken out of their hands, it is yet true that at the
center of the Geneva deadlock were the irreconcilable positions of France
and Germany. To underscore the hopelessness of any accommodation,
Chancellor Hitler, who had recently come to power, in October, 1933,
withdrew Germany from the Conference and, for good measure, from
the League as well. At the same time he began to rearm without regard
to the restrictions of Versailles and, failing to be halted in his earliest
breaches, repeated them on a larger scale with each new year.

Failure of
the Dis-
armament
Conference
and the rise
of Hitler

Nothing short of the firmly consolidated front of France and Great
Britain could have put a stop to this deliberate work of wreckage, but
France and Great Britain were no longer in agreement. The final opportunity to throw themselves across Hitler's path occurred in March, 1936,
when the Führer terminated the neutrality of the Rhineland by occupying it with his troops. To this provocation Great Britain responded with
a mild note of protest, and France, isolated, did not feel strong enough
to interpose with a call to arms. The remainder of the Versailles disabilities now fell as a matter of course. The only questions that remained for Frenchmen and Britons to turn over and over in their minds
was when Hitler's aggressions would stop and to what excess they would
have to go before the two estranged governments would forget their
differences and, renewing their former partnership, challenge the relentless forward thrust of the Nazi dictator.

Hitler's suc-
cess due to
the failure of
France and
Britain to
remain
united

While the rapid succession of breath-taking incidents that preceded the
outbreak of World War II are reserved to a later chapter, we may not,
in closing this sketch of French foreign policy, overlook a measure undertaken by France, which, when it came to a test, proved as unavailing
as all the other enumerated measures of security. The dominantly bourgeois society of France had been very reluctant even to give diplomatic
recognition to communist Russia and therefore showed very little inclination to revive an alliance which had constituted the leading item of
French policy before World War I. However, the alarm spread by the
rise of Hitler modified the French attitude and in 1934 persuaded the
Paris government to contract a defensive alliance with the great Slav
power. In many quarters this tie-up was considered as at last definitely
providing the security France had these many years been pursuing. But
this proved not to be the case, because no real confidence ever developed
between the fixedly capitalist government at Paris and the government
at Moscow, unalterably suspicious of capitalism. There was much talk in
both centers about their committing themselves, and all nonaggressor
states as well, to a league of general security, but the talk never solidified

The Franco-
Russian
alliance of
1934 fails
to become
effective

into action. The Franco-Russian alliance, and the general security movement along with it, ranks as another, and the last, of the futile attempts
to halt the world's downward plunge into war.

GREAT BRITAIN

Politics and Legislation

A parlia-
mentary
novelty:
the Labor
party
Older by a century than the democratic tradition of France was that
of Great Britain. In the post-war period it also proved itself stronger,
especially at the core of the system, the parliament. Having never known
any other than the two-party system, the British parliament was spared
the confusion from which the French parliament suffered, and not only
since the war's end, by reason of its multiple-party system. British
Liberals and Conservatives had patriotically united in 1914 to wage the
war but at the coming of peace promptly resumed their independence.
However, they faced a novelty in the coming to the front of a new
party, the Labor party. In the elections of 1922 it won a greater representation in the Commons than the Liberals, and in the elections of the
following year it made sufficient additional gains to deprive the Conservatives of the majority they had hitherto enjoyed. With no one of
the three parties in sole parliamentary command Ramsay MacDonald,
leader of the Labor party, undertook to form the first Labor cabinet in
British history on the strength of a tacit understanding with the Liberals
that they would support him so long as his proposals did not collide
with their most cherished beliefs. In these circumstances the Labor government was unable to push its own socialist measures and won no
honor either with its followers or with the country. Accordingly, it was
snowed under in the elections of 1924, which returned the Conservatives
to power with a thumping majority.

The Labor-
ites supplant
the Liberals
as the
leading
opponents
of the Con-
servatives
After governing for the full parliamentary period of five years, the
Conservatives in the elections of 1929 lost so many seats that the situation of 1923 was repeated with none of the three parties commanding a
majority. For the second time therefore Ramsay MacDonald undertook
to form a Labor ministry, which again was so dependent on Liberal
support that it led the same makeshift existence as its predecessor and
ignominiously quit office in 1931. In all subsequent elections the Conservatives won so decided a victory that Great Britain was ruled by a
Conservative cabinet through all the critical years immediately preceding the outbreak of World War II. From a purely parliamentary
angle we may designate as the outstanding development of the post-
war years the decline of the Liberals almost to the vanishing point
and the attendant rise of the Labor party to the position of chief opponent

of the usually dominant Conservatives. Plainly the middle classes, once the main strength of the Liberals, had in large part gone over to the Conservatives, while such of them as did not do so rallied to the Labor party because of its more vigorous opposition to Tory rule. The upshot of these changes may be represented as a swing-back on the part of the voters to the two-party system so dear to British tradition.

This consideration for the past, this healthy respect for continuity, manifested itself also in many legislative fields, for instance, in Insurance Legislation. True, Insurance Legislation went no farther back than the first decade of the twentieth century, when the Liberals under the leadership of Lloyd George established the most advanced insurance system that had been thus far devised. It had been created in response to the cry for social justice that was sweeping the world and, more particularly, the industrial nations, and in a surprisingly short time rallied British opinion solidly behind it. Consequently, in spite of the diminished national returns resulting from a world-wide depression, Insurance Legislation was in the twenties repeatedly extended and, often enough not on Liberal or Labor, but on Conservative initiative. Another area of legislation that profited from this same impulse to move forward on established lines concerned the suffrage. Three nineteenth-century bills, of 1832, 1867, and 1884 respectively, registered the stages by which the originally extremely narrow British suffrage had been gradually widened. All that still remained to be done after the war was to make the suffrage universal, and this was effected by a bill of 1918 followed by another bill ten years later. The two bills together gave the right to vote to men and women alike on their arriving at the age of twenty-one.

Let it not be imagined, however, that Great Britain was so traditionbound that it did not experience the impact of the anti-democratic parties which were at this time raising their heads throughout the world. A Communist as well as a Fascist party came into existence and conducted a noisy agitation in behalf of their respective creeds without however gaining more than a negligible following. While the Communists, in Britain as everywhere else, took their cue from Moscow, the Fascists accepted the leadership of an erratic young nobleman, Sir Oswald Moseley, who looked for inspiration to Mussolini and Hitler. The small success both movements achieved furnishes the best evidence that can be adduced of the country's solid attachment to the democratic faith.

Healthy political continuity evidenced by: (1) Insurance Legislation; (2) Universal suffrage

The unimportant role played by Communists and Fascists

The Serious Economic Crisis

Human society being ever subject to change, and our modern society to very rapid change, situations have inevitably resulted from this tendency which have defied treatment by past methods, no matter how elastic. Such a situation in Britain's case developed in the realm of foreign trade and produced general dismay and bewilderment. Not only did British post-war trade fail to return to the pre-war volume, it obstinately lingered considerably below that level. Many causes were assigned for the phenomenon, the most usual being the decline of the purchasing power of an impoverished world and the new economic nationalism which prompted most countries to surround themselves with unscalable tariff walls. With trade failing, the number of the unemployed workers grew till two million was not an unusual figure for those who had to be kept alive by unemployment benefits. Many were the remedies propounded by scholars and politicians to overcome the two interlocking evils, with what gradually developed as the Conservative remedy enjoying particular consideration because the Conservative party exercised an all but uninterrupted control of the government.

Decline of foreign trade and consequent unemployment

The Conservatives began unsystematically with measures to remove some particular economic grievance, for instance, dumping. By dumping was meant the cutthroat practice of neighbor countries of throwing their excess goods on the free British market, if need be at a loss. Accordingly, as early as 1921 parliament passed an anti-dumping act. With each succeeding year the Conservatives became more and more inclined to back away from free trade and to resort to a protective policy with the result that free trade versus protection waxed in importance till it became the liveliest issue of the successive elections. When in 1931 the Conservatives won an overwhelming victory at the polls, they viewed it as a popular mandate to impose their policy and passed a comprehensive, though moderate, tariff law. Nonetheless, it proclaimed in trumpet tones the end of the free-trade policy, which had been in force for eighty years and under which the country had achieved its nineteenth century economic eminence.

Surrender of free trade, adoption of protection

A strictly related action was the abandonment (September, 1931) of the gold standard. Therewith the pound fell about twenty-five per cent and cheapened British goods to that extent for foreign purchasers. But it cannot be said that the evils these measures were intended to cure disappeared, although they may, for a time at least, have been mitigated. It may be, and should be held in mind as a point of reference, that loss of trade and growth of unemployment have resulted from world-wide changes which no unilateral action on the part of Great Britain can effectively alter and which may have arrived to stay.

Abandonment of the gold standard

Ireland, India, Egypt

Three countries, Ireland, India, Egypt, had proved themselves outstanding British trouble-spots before World War I. It therefore behooves us to inquire how their relations to Great Britain developed after the peace.

Ireland. We learned in Chapter 29 of the considerable improvement of the Irish situation brought about in the second half of the nineteenth century, especially in agriculture, by the elevation of the hitherto dependent peasants to the status of freeholders. Even the political or Home-Rule agitation had been brought to a successful head, for in 1914, on the very eve of World War I, a bill, giving the lesser island a considerable measure of autonomy, had become law. However, in view of the absorbing national crisis, its application was suspended. A small body of extreme nationalists called *Sinn Fein* (the Gaelic expression means We Ourselves) had never ceased denouncing the Home Rule Bill and demanding complete independence. At Eastertide, 1916, the Sinn Feiners, still no more than a handful, staged an uprising in Dublin which the British government firmly and speedily suppressed.

The Easter rising of 1916

The effect on the Irish people of the thwarted rebellion, sharply followed by the execution of its leaders, was extraordinary. They passed into the Sinn Fein ranks in such numbers that, when the post-war elections of December, 1918, took place, a solid delegation of Sinn Fein representatives issued from the polls. Instead of reporting at London to take their seats in the British parliament, the delegates went straight to Dublin and set up an independent Irish republic. The inescapable consequence was a war between the rebels and the British government which lasted three years. Since such an Irish armed force as could be organized went into hiding and conducted a struggle of the guerilla kind, it could not be suppressed in its entirety and the British government, still in the hands of the war-time premier, Lloyd George, was obliged to have recourse to negotiations. The result was the treaty of December 6, 1921, which, while it did not concede independence, recognized an Irish Free State to be ruled by its own parliament and to enjoy all the privileges of dominion status.

Recognition of the Irish Free State by the treaty of December 6, 1921

From the thus-constituted Irish Free State six counties of the province of Ulster, Protestant and Unionist in sympathy, were expressly excluded. Nothing short of military coercion would have succeeded in merging these descendants of Scotch and English colonists in the same political entity with the Catholic Celts. The British government was therefore under irresistible pressure to organize the six counties as a separate state under the name of Northern Ireland with a parliament of its own and its own capital, Belfast. The continued union with Great Britain, which was for the Ulstermen the very heart of their quarrel with their fellow islanders of the south, was firmly maintained by the right to send elected representatives to the parliament at Westminster.

Simultaneous creation of Northern Ireland

Great as was the nationalist triumph represented by the creation of

the Irish Free State, it fell short of the outright independence demanded
by an extreme Sinn Fein group headed by Eamon De Valera. This
leader declared the treaty of 1921 inacceptable because it contained a
number of articles, largely, it is true, formal in character, which recorded
the continued submission of Ireland to Great Britain. Among these
figured the oath of allegiance to the British king required of the members of the Dail, as the Irish parliament was called, and the acceptance
at Dublin of a governor general to represent the king's person. However,
far and away the gravest objection registered by De Valera against the
treaty was that it did not include the six northern counties geographically
inseparable from the rest of the island.

De Valera,
in control
after 1932,
aims at
complete
independ-
ence
For the first decade of its existence the Irish Free State remained in
control of the moderate Sinn Feiners and the quarrel with Britain was
not renewed. However, in 1932 De Valera's party won a majority of the
seats in the Dail and De Valera himself became the head of the government under the title of president of the executive council. In the
course of the next few years he abolished the oath of allegiance to the
British king as well as the office of governor general and made further
show of his independence by conducting a tariff war with Great Britain.
This, however, when it became manifest that it hurt Ireland more than
its more powerful neighbor, was in 1938 brought to an end by mutual
consent. It accorded well with the whole spirit of De Valera's rule that
he issued (1937) a new constitution which replaced the constitution of
1922 and restored to Ireland its old Gaelic name of Eire. When it also
declared Eire to be a completely independent and sovereign state embracing the legally distinct southern and northern sections, this challenge
was quietly ignored by Great Britain in the assurance that De Valera
lacked the power to make it effective.

India. The most important development in India in the generation
The India
Act of 1919
the first
concession
to Indian
nationalism
before World War I was the growth, together with other features borrowed from Western civilization, of a confused kind of nationalism.
The confusion was due to the many peoples, languages, cultures, and
religions historically at home in the immense peninsula and the consequent inability of the inhabitants to agree on anything more substantial
than their aversion for the British ruler and their desire to transfer
political control at the earliest possible moment from his hands to their
own. Fully aware of this sentiment, the British undertook to dull its
edge, and in 1919, immediately after the war, passed an India Act which
permitted a modest participation on the part of the natives in both the
central and the provincial government of the vast dominion. That the
play given to self-rule by this act was very slight becomes clear when
we note that the police, the law and the courts, the army, and foreign

affairs remained the exclusive prerogative of the chief British agent, the viceroy.

The outcry against this derisory measure of home rule was universal and spurred the Indians to more intense agitation. Recognizing the need of organization if they were to make their criticism effective, they formed a country-wide association to which they gave the name of National Congress and which met periodically to clarify and define its aims. Although the National Congress invited the participation of the Moslem population as well as of every other native group, it took shape chiefly as an association of Hindus. Invincibly suspicious of the Hindus, the Moslems were moved to form their own Moslem League, which was as anti-British in principle as the National Congress but which weakened the common cause by cultivating a sense of political and religious separateness. Moreover, the existence of two opposition groups enabled the British to play off one against the other, Moslems against Hindus. The British enjoyed another advantage which is often overlooked but should never be forgotten. Some six hundred princes, in control of one-third of the Indian area and population, maintained in their respective states a purely autocratic regime formally guaranteed to them by the British government. The six hundred autocrats required the continuance of British rule to assure their own continuance, abominated the self-rule campaign of the National Congress and the Moslem League, and rigorously excluded the agents and propaganda of these organizations from their dominions.

National Congress and Moslem League

In the course of the twenties the Indian political atmosphere became so heavily charged with the smoke of battle that it was often impossible to get a clear picture of what was going on beneath its pall. However, one thing was manifest, to wit, that Indian opinion, offended by the insignificant concessions of the Act of 1919, was now demanding nothing less than the dominion status recently accorded to Ireland. An advanced section of opinion, no longer content with dominion status, even went farther and declared itself unwilling to accept any settlement short of complete independence. Inevitably the lively dispute made its regular appearance on the agenda of the National Congress, and the vacillation of the members was revealed by their declaring themselves on one occasion in favor of the dominion position, on another in favor of separation.

Dominion status versus independence

Each position had its peculiar implications of which every Indian was consciously or subconsciously aware. Dominion status was a grant which the British under continued pressure might conceivably make; independence they would resist with all the military resources at their disposal. This distinction, in view of the population's being systematically deprived of arms, was of capital importance. However, counting perhaps even more than its lack of weapons was its settled pacifist temper, or at least the settled pacifist temper of the Hindu majority. This signified an in-

The traditional Hindu pacifism embodied in Mohandas Gandhi

herent disinclination to every kind of warfare, including the prospective struggle with their unloved masters. At this point there was injected into the situation a personality very difficult for the Western mind to understand, Mohandas Gandhi. By making himself the mouthpiece of the voiceless Hindu millions, he became the dominant figure of the National Congress, and the indecision we have noted in its choice between dominion status and independence was a direct reflection of the Hindu leader's own indecision. That his opponents taunted him with what they called his political opportunism left him unaffected, for he declared himself swayed by a single guiding principle—the traditional pacifism of the Hindu people to which he belonged.

Gandhi, champion of civil disobedience

This unwavering central faith Gandhi coupled with habits of prayer and simple living which invested him in the eyes of the people with the quality of sainthood and caused them to confer on him the title *Mahatma,* the Great Soul. We may sum up his preachment directly to his people and indirectly to the whole war-ridden world in the simple ethical concept of non-violence. Specifically, in the pending issue with Great Britain he refused categorically even to consider a resort to arms. In its place he recommended a procedure he sometimes called non-co-operation, sometimes civil disobedience; and on two occasions he manifested his opposition to the government by urging the faithful to adopt this passive measure. Thereupon a considerable percentage of the population gave great annoyance to the British by refusing to pay taxes and performing similar obstructionist acts. But the administration refused to be intimidated and in each case the Mahatma, satisfied with the alarm he had created, called off the campaign.

British concessions culminate in the India Act of 1935

In the face of these constant and waxing discontents, the British concerned themselves with earnest intensity with their mitigation. London dispatched several parliamentary commissions to probe the situation on the ground, and more than once it summoned representatives of all the Indian parties to the British capital for a round-table discussion. In the hope of keeping Indian unrest within bounds it was officially announced that when the full information, which was the aim of these several investigations, had been assembled, a new India Act might be expected, embodying a greatly enlarged measure of home rule. It was not till 1935 that this new act was put through parliament and not till two years later that the ground had been sufficiently cleared in India itself for the Indian government to start giving it effect.

Main features of the new India Act

Let it be conceded at once that the new plan contained self-governing provisions far in excess of anything old-fashioned Tory imperialists had thus far considered permissible. However, it fell so far short of what even the most moderate elements of the National Congress and the Moslem League proclaimed their minimum demand that it was greeted with groans and hisses. The Act set up an Indian federation composed, on the one hand, of eleven provinces, into which the territory hitherto directly subject to Great Britain was divided, and, on the other hand, of the territories of the six hundred native princes. The eleven provinces were endowed with governments elected by a strictly limited electorate and given considerable powers of a purely local character; the six hundred princes were confirmed in their inviolate autocracy. The central government remained in the hands of the viceroy, who continued to be responsible to the Secretary of State for India in London and was left in unchallenged control of defense, foreign affairs, customs, and similarly crucial matters. Moreover, he could, when an emergency arose, suspend the new constitution. And indeed, hardly had anything more than a beginning been made with the new machinery, when, on the outbreak of World War II, the emergency was declared to have arrived and the Act was shelved "for the duration." So far as, following this abrupt turn, the Indian people continued to make themselves heard, they still clamored for either dominion status or independence with the cry for independence tending more and more to drown out the alternative cry.

Egypt. While the demise of the Ottoman empire in the trail of World War I freed the khedive of Egypt from the last remnant of dependence on his former overlord, the sultan, his dependence on Great Britain, dating from the conquest of Egypt by that power in 1882, remained unchanged. Nonetheless, with the coming of peace in 1918, Britain faced a difficult situation in the Nile valley. The nationalism of the Egyptians, dating from the last quarter of the nineteenth century, had waxed in intensity during the war and found numerous spokesmen who set their goal at nothing less than independence. The British did not seal their ears to this agitation any more than they did in the similar cases of Ireland and India. Recognizing that the days of the old-type autocratic imperialism had departed, they were willing to go far, in their own eyes dangerously far, to satisfy the demand for self-government. However, there were certain reserved rights which they were resolved under no circumstances to give up. In fact, unless they were prepared to surrender the whole idea and set-up of empire, the two outstanding items of which were India and the Mediterranean approach to it commonly called the British life-line, they would inescapably have to retain some kind of military and naval control in Egypt and, particularly, at the absolutely crucial link between the Mediterranean sea and the Indian ocean, the Suez canal.

Egyptian independence balked by the necessities of empire

Everything that happened in Egypt between World War I and II turned around the essential incompatibility of the Egyptian and British positions. There were murders, riots, even insurrections. They periodically

The issue in the open following the British declaration of 1922

precipitated a crisis between the two countries, but through every disturbance the British clung to the plan of somehow arriving at an accommodation which would placate the Egyptians without incurring the sacrifice of a single item of their indispensable imperial requirements. As early as 1922 they took a bold step along this road by investing the khedive with the title of king and declaring Egypt to be an independent sovereign state. When at the same time they announced that this sovereign Egypt would have to make full recognition of Britain's military prerogatives deriving from the need of securing its communications, the issue between the paramount power and its restless dependency was brought to a focus and was thenceforth contested with open visor.

The compromise treaty of 1936

In our next chapter, under the heading Egypt, some of the developments attending this often violent conflict are given attention and the story carried to the treaty of 1936, in which, in return for a few concessions that flattered Egyptian self-esteem, the British wrested from the Moslem kingdom full recognition of the reserved rights they had never ceased demanding. The consequence was that when World War II broke out in 1939, Britain was better prepared than during the earlier struggle to control the Mediterranean sea, using Egypt as its leading base.

The British Commonwealth of Nations

The dominions gain recognition of their independence at Paris in 1919

The by all odds most significant development within the British empire in the pre-war period had been the transformation of the colonies, which were prevailingly white and European in population, into self-governing dominions. When Great Britain declared war on Germany in 1914, the self-governing dominions without exception promptly aligned themselves at her side. The action revealed that in the hour of Britain's peril Canada, Australia, New Zealand, and South Africa were moved by an instinctive attachment to the mother-country far more coercive than the formal bond of law. In the exhausting struggle that followed, all the dominions alike lavishly contributed men and supplies to the common cause and were welcomed as equals by the allied powers. Consequently, when the Peace Conference took place, the dominions dispatched representatives to Paris who won recognition of the essential independence of their respective countries by signing the peace treaties in their own name and by accepting the invitation to join the League of Nations as charter members.

This advance in international status was effected not only with the consent but at the very instance of Great Britain. The dominion movement had been nursed into existence by the mother-country and, on its passing the nursery stage, had been given adult consideration by almost annual meetings, called Imperial Conferences, of the premiers of the dominions with the premier of Great Britain. The purpose of the meetings was, in the main, to lay down the principles by which the relations of the consultants were henceforth to be governed. Taking on a more liberal character from year to year, they culminated in 1926 in the following declaration of equality: "Great Britain and the dominions are autonomous communities within the British empire, equal in status, in no way subordinate one to another . . . though united by a common allegiance to the Crown and freely associated as members of the British Commonwealth of Nations." Five years later the declaration was enacted into law by the British parliament under the name of the Statute of Westminster. It leaves no doubt as to the full independence and sovereignty of the dominions, subject to nothing more tangible than a common allegiance expressed by the symbol of the Crown.

Formal creation (1926-31) of the British Commonwealth of Nations

43

THE STATES OF EAST-CENTRAL EUROPE, THE BALKAN PENINSULA, AND THE ARAB WORLD AFTER WORLD WAR I

EAST-CENTRAL EUROPE

The eight states of east-central Europe

WE HAVE LEARNED how, at the close of World War I, there sprang up along the western marches of Russia five new states: Finland, Estonia, Latvia, Lithuania, and Poland. At the same time the defeated Austro-Hungarian monarchy went to pieces and was replaced by the three so-called succession states, Austria, Hungary, and Czechoslovakia. Since Yugoslavia and Rumania also profited territorially from the demise of the Hapsburg dominion, they too are often, and properly enough, listed as Austrian succession states. However, in existence before the war began and definitely planted in the Balkan world, they will be treated in the following, the Balkan section of this chapter. In this section, devoted to east-central Europe, we shall give attention, in the order named, to the five Russian offspring, Finland, Estonia, Latvia, Lithuania, and Poland, and to the three Austro-Hungarian heirs, Czechoslovakia, Austria, and Hungary—eight states in all.

They are born under the stars of nationalism and democracy

All these eight states owed their existence to the creative energy of nationalism. As the war which gave them birth also popularized democracy, it befell that they all adopted very democratic constitutions and proudly proclaimed themselves republics. Thus introduced to an expectant Europe, they seemed to confirm the entente contention that the war had been fought for the double purpose of bringing freedom to small, oppressed nationalities and of preparing the world for universal democracy.

Democracy yields to dictatorship

From the start of their independent career they were, without exception, confronted with the gravest difficulties. They were loaded with debts resulting from the war; overrun for years by the armies of friend and foe, they were in a pitiable state of economic exhaustion; they were afflicted with irreconcilable divisions among their component social and racial groups; and they were agitated by the vagaries of a fluctuating currency. The result was that the democratic constitutions broke down and that, with the two notable exceptions of Finland and Czechoslovakia, they were obliged to resort to a dictatorial regime. True, in some in-s⸱ances the parliament was not abolished, but, whether it was abolished or retained, authority was monopolized by a single individual, whose announced purpose was to hold the country together on terms satisfactory to himself and the social group to which he belonged.

Finland

Beginning our review of this chain of states with its northernmost member, with Finland, we note that Finland is a sober, northland country of lakes and forests, whose inhabitants, called Finns, are liberally intermingled with Swedes along the coast. On effecting their liberation from Russia, the Finns created a republic with a president and a legislature of a single house chosen by universal (male and female) suffrage. Owing to the nearness of communist Russia, Finland never ceased to experience a powerful communist agitation. This, as usually happens, gave birth to a counter-vailing fascist movement. The government protected itself against communism by outlawing propaganda in its behalf. Then, by suppressing (1933) a rising fascist party, it indicated its determination to pursue a middle course and to preserve to the best of its ability the democratic system. In spite of the high measure of political and economic stability which the country achieved, there lay a peril that nothing could remove in the mere fact of its resting under the threatening shadow of the vast mass of Russia. *Finland a resolute democrati republic*

Estonia and Latvia

We may treat Estonia and Latvia together because, although inhabited by different peoples, Ests and Letts respectively, they were small neighboring republics which quickly recognized that, in order to live at all, they would have to co-operate both politically and economically. This accordingly they did, thereby adding measurably to their strength. They were, however, so harassed by the conflicting agitation of communist and fascist extremists in their midst that in 1934 both of them suspended their democratic constitutions and submitted to one-man rule. *Estonia and Latvia submit to dictatorship*

Estonia had a population of a little over 1,000,000, Latvia a little under 2,000,000. The few inhabitants and the limited extent of the two states denoted a feebleness which made their prolonged existence exceedingly doubtful. On an earth ruled more and more by vast aggregations like Russia and the United States, states such as Estonia and Latvia, although born only yesterday, convey the impression of time-worn anachronisms. *These tiny states an anachronism*

Lithuania

The quarrel with Poland over Vilna

Lithuania, with little more than 2,000,000 inhabitants, could not but raise similar doubts regarding its permanence. Even sooner than in Estonia and Latvia its democratic constitution gave way to a dictator. No other course was possible in view of the perilous situation which ensued when neighboring Poland in 1920 seized the city and district of Vilna. On Russia's making peace with Lithuania this region had been accorded to the new state and been duly incorporated in its domin-ion. Although Lithuania did not fail promptly and clamorously to re-port the injury done it by Poland to the League of Nations, it received no help from that quarter. The upshot was that it declared a state of war (without war's actuality) to exist between itself and its powerful tor-mentor and that it strengthened itself for the conflict by resorting to one-man rule. Down to practically the eve of World War II Lithuania and Poland maintained a condition of all but complete nonintercourse.

How Lithuania acquired Memel (1923)

As if the quarrel with Poland were not a sufficient cause of anxiety, Lithuania converted another neighbor, Germany, into an enemy by it-self resorting to violence and seizing the city and district of Memel. This region had been lopped off from Germany by the Treaty of Ver-sailles. The victor powers were still considering how to dispose of it when Lithuania took it over (1923) by an armed invasion. Accepting the accomplished fact, the Paris treaty-makers contented themselves with obliging Lithuania to concede a large measure of autonomy to the pre-dominantly German population of Memel. The inevitable clashes that followed between the Memellanders and the Lithuanian government at Kaunas stirred an excitement in Germany which did not particularly matter so long as Germany remained weak but would matter a great deal should Germany ever again recover her strength.

Poland

Two Polish acquisitions: the Corridor and Polish Upper Silesia

The largest and potentially strongest of all the new east-central states was Poland. Favoring reborn Poland at the expense of beaten Germany, the victors in the war gave the new state considerable territory, not all of it, to quote from President Wilson's Fourteen Points, "indisputably Polish." Most notable among the acquisitions of Poland from Germany were the so-called Corridor, a narrow tongue of land along the lower Vistula separating the mass of Germany from the German province of East Prussia, and the important industrial region that on its cession received the name of Polish Upper Silesia. Poland was further favored by the incorporation of the great port of Danzig in its customs system.

However, as Danzig was "indisputably German," it was permitted to organize itself politically as a Free City under the supervision of the League of Nations. Here, as in the case of Memel, danger was sure to show its head the moment Germany again became a great power.

Dissatisfied with the eastern or Russian boundary accorded them by the Paris Peace Conference, the Poles went to war (1920) with Russia and, on making peace after a partially successful struggle, acquired a not inconsiderable belt of territory inhabited by White Russians and Little Russians (Ukrainians). The inclusion both to the east and to the west of non-Polish minorities had the drawback of impairing the nationalist character of the Polish state. Totaling about 30,000,000 inhabitants, it aspired to be regarded as a great power, but as over twenty per cent of the population was not of Polish nationality, Poland was not so strong in fact as it looked on paper. *The Russian acquisitions of Poland*

Beginning life as a republic with a very democratic constitution, Poland experienced so many difficulties that the government was often incapable of taking any positive measures. To get rid of systematic obstruction in the parliament the Polish war hero, Marshal Pilsudski, in 1926 seized the power and made himself if not the declared, at least the virtual dictator, for, although he did not abolish the parliament, he left it without authority. Following Pilsudski's death ten years later, a group of army officers belonging to the inner Pilsudski ring continued the marshal's system of extraconstitutional, essentially military control. *Poland becomes (1926) an undercover military dictatorship*

Czechoslovakia

South of Poland, extending in a long and narrow east-west mass, lay the most important of the Austrian succession states, Czechoslovakia. It was a Slav state, to form which two closely related Slav groups, the Czechs and Slovaks, joined company. There were, however, important minorities of Magyars (Hungarians), Little Russians (Ukrainians), and, above all, Germans within the boundaries as drawn at Paris. The last-named group numbered well over 3,000,000 out of a total population of 14,000,000 and was strengthened in its national consciousness by compact settlement in a region called Sudetenland, which bordered immediately on Germany. Fortunately, under the guidance of the philosopher-statesman, Thomas Masaryk, who became the first president of the Czechoslovak republic, a liberal policy was adopted toward the minorities, which tempered their resentment against the ruling group. To President Masaryk and Eduard Beneš, who succeeded Masaryk in 1935, must also be given credit for keeping the other internal divisions, such as those between agrarians and industrialists, between Catholics and Socialists, from taking on an extremist character. Consequently Czecho- *Peoples composing the Czechoslovak state* slovakia, alone among the states in the heart of Europe, was able to operate uninterruptedly as a political democracy.

A rich state with a balanced economy
The exceptional stability of Czechoslovakia was greatly promoted by the circumstance that it was composed of the most populous and wealthy provinces of the former Hapsburg monarchy, wherein agriculture and manufacture were in healthy balance. A busy population of farmers made the country almost self-supporting in the matter of food, while a prosperous industry built on the region's abundant resources of coal and iron enabled it to supply the purely agricultural states which bordered it on the east and southeast with machine-goods in exchange for the foodstuffs in which it happened to be deficient.

Czecho-slovakia aligned with the Little Entente and France
Together with the two Balkan states, Yugoslavia and Rumania, Czechoslovakia as early as 1920-1921 formed the political combination that became known as the Little Entente. The three partners joined fortunes in order to hold fast to the advantages won by the war, especially against Hungary, the likeliest disturber of their common peace. As France was equally eager to retain the eminence it owed to the Paris treaties, the members of the Little Entente, as individuals, however, and not as a group, entered into a defensive alliance with the French republic.

Austria

Unhappy Austria: the economic crisis
We are aware that the Austrian remnant which issued from the crucible of the war voted to join Germany but was forbidden to do so by the Peace Conference. Accordingly, it became constituted as a small German republic made up of a group of beautiful but infertile Alpine provinces, such as the Tyrol, Salzburg, Styria, etc., attached to the former capital of the Hapsburg empire, the teeming metropolis of Vienna. The economic and political difficulties of the young republic were so enormous that it was at once thrown into a turmoil from which it did not emerge for even a moment throughout the period of its existence. To take the economic difficulties first, they sprang in the main from the fact that highly industrialized Vienna was unable to draw the foodstuffs it needed from the relatively unproductive mountain areas which made up the bulk of the state and that the poor upland population could not afford to buy the Viennese manufactures. This lack of balance occasioned a chronic economic crisis attended by an even sharper financial crisis. The two related crises might have been solved if Austria had been permitted to form a customs union with Germany, but this step, which the government was at the point of taking in 1930, was blocked by the victor powers on the ground that it would inevitably lead to the forbidden political union.

As great as the economic turmoil and inseparable from it was the political turmoil. The workers of industrial Vienna were banded together in the Social Democratic party, which acquired and steadily maintained control of the municipal government. The provincial or Alpine governments, on the other hand, were in the hands of the Catholics, organized as the Christian Socialist party. As for the federal government shared by capital and provinces, although it was immediately after the revolution under socialist control, it tended more and more to fall to the Christian Socialists, who waxed strong in measure as the conservative Catholic peasants developed a settled aversion for the radical workers of the capital. When, around 1930, a large section of the youth of both city and country was seduced by the violent nationalist doctrines imported from Nazi Germany, the position of the Catholic government at Vienna became so shaky that it resorted for its preservation to the extremist measure that had become almost prescriptive in this part of Europe: it set up a dictatorship.

Unhappy Austria: the political crisis

The leading figure of the Christian Socialist party after 1930 was Engelbert Dollfuss. It was he who, in the capacity of chancellor, took the first step toward dictatorship when he abolished the democratic constitution under which the republic had begun its existence. Looking toward a totalitarian regime like that of his admired friend, Mussolini, he resolved to abolish all parties save his own. The Austrian Nazi party was as yet too feeble to offer open resistance to this measure but the Social Democrats, firmly seated in the Viennese city hall, were a different matter. To smash them, Dollfuss resorted in February, 1934, to civil war and issued victorious from the short and bloody struggle. His success did not hinder the Nazis from trying to wrest the power from him by a sudden rising. They managed in July, 1934, to take over a few public buildings, from which they were again ousted before the sun had set. They did, however, before giving up, succeed in murdering their hated enemy, Dollfuss.

Austria a Christian Socialist (Catholic) dictatorship

The successor of Dollfuss as head of the Christian Socialist party, Schuschnigg, boldly maintained his predecessor's totalitarian system, but it brought neither surcease of the chronic economic misery nor domestic peace. The whole course of events since 1918 pointed to the absorption of Austria by Germany as the almost certain outcome of the interminable Austrian agony as soon as Germany would be strong enough to leap the barrier raised by the Treaty of Versailles. Already at the time of the unsuccessful Nazi putsch of 1934 it was generally supposed that Hitler would cross the border to steady his faltering Austrian cohorts. He held back on that occasion; but four years later (1938) his power in Germany and Europe had been so greatly fortified that he marched down the Danube right into Vienna without a shot being fired to stop him.

The fated absorption of Austria by Germany

Hungary

The heavy
territorial
losses of
Hungary

The reduced Hungary of the Paris Peace Conference was a state of about 8,000,000 people, of whom some ninety per cent were of Magyar nationality. So eager were the victor powers to clip off from historical Hungary such territories as were inhabited by Slovaks, Rumanians, and Yugoslavs that they overshot the mark and, for good measure, handed over approximately three million Magyars to their vindictive neighbors. Territorially Hungary was whittled down to less than half its former size. These reductions and the Magyar resolve to get them back became the factor overshadowing all others in the country's post-war period.

Hungary's
post-war
vicissitudes

Immediately on its defeat in 1918 Hungary presented the picture of a madhouse. The semi-socialist republic which first emerged could not maintain itself and was succeeded by a fanatic communist regime which tried to link up with communist Russia. When this was overthrown by an army dispatched to Budapest by the Rumanian government, it was months before the plundering invaders agreed to go home and give Hungary back to its inhabitants. The succession of savage disorders produced a violent conservative rebound, which brought the landlord class, traditionally in control, back into power. As might have been expected, these feudal magnates, who had learned nothing from the recent disasters, re-established the ancient constitution. This called for a king to crown the feudal pyramid who could not well be any but a Hapsburg prince. However, as the restoration of this family was emphatically vetoed by the Little Entente, the Hungarian parliament was obliged to content itself with appointing a member of the ruling class, Admiral Horthy, to the post of regent. Czechoslovakia, Rumania, and Yugoslavia, which made up the Little Entente, had alike profited from Hungary's defeat and formed an armed guard around their diminished and angry neighbor to see to it that he nowhere broke bounds.

Hungary a
reactionary,
fascist
state

The political control exercised by the landlord class gave the Hungarian government a strictly reactionary character. The rulers refused even to consider the reduction of the great estates to the end of creating a larger and happier landholding peasantry. So uncompromisingly backward-looking and at the same time nationalist were they that they drove the socialists and communists into hiding, maintained a strict press censorship, and repeatedly tampered with the franchise to suit their class interest. In sum, the regent and the clique from which he sprang conducted a regime of the dictatorial fascist type. It was therefore natural for it to cultivate, in the course of the thirties, intimate relations with Mussolini's Italy and, a little later, with Hitler's Germany. This was the situation when under the impact of the growing aggressions of the two dictators the world once again plunged into war.

THE BALKAN PENINSULA

In turning to the Balkan peninsula our minds at once stir ominously with memories of the interminable troubles which in the nineteenth century converted it into a witch's cauldron and caused it to play a leading part in the breathless events that culminated in the world explosion of 1914. When, four years later, the victorious powers met at Paris to mend the shattered universe, they gave a kindly nod to those Balkan states that had rallied to their side. These were Yugoslavia, Rumania, and Greece. Albania, too weak to engage in war, had during the struggle disappeared from view and so at least had not aroused any special animosity. Bulgaria and Turkey, however, as allies of the Central Powers, had been active enemies and were handled accordingly in the respective Treaties of Neuilly and Sèvres. While the servitudes of Neuilly against Bulgaria were enforced to the letter, those of Sèvres against Turkey were not, for the reason that the Turks responded to the Sèvres challenge with a war of independence. By coming out on top in this contest they obliged the allies to concede them (1923) the vastly better terms of the Treaty of Lausanne. In running over the post-war situation in the Balkans we shall follow the above-indicated order and treat first, the victors and then, the vanquished—a total roster of six states.

List of the six Balkan states to be here reviewed

A generalization already offered in connection with our review of the eight states of east-central Europe invites repetition in connection with the six Balkan states that follow. Starting on their post-war career as democracies, they were unable to support a popular regime and, some sooner, some later, transformed themselves into open or imperfectly disguised dictatorships. Plainly, therefore, dictatorship and not democracy was the style to which continental Europe overwhelmingly conformed in the period between the First and Second World Wars.

Their democracy yields to dictatorship

Yugoslavia

In the year 1917, at the moment of the lowest ebb of their war fortunes, representatives of the three Yugo- or south-Slav nations of the Serbs, the Croats, and the Slovenes made an alliance by which they agreed, when the victory had been won, to set up a state to be known as the Kingdom of the Serbs, Croats, and Slovenes, under the reigning Serbian dynasty. No sooner was the war concluded than this triune creation was proclaimed and amply rewarded for the services rendered

Creation (1918) of the kingdom of the Serbs, Croats, and Slovenes by its component elements to the allied cause with the assignment to it of liberal portions of the defunct Austro-Hungarian empire. Thus favored, it embraced, besides former Serbia, its core, the additional regions of Montenegro, Bosnia, Croatia, Dalmatia, Carniola, and other scattered territories for which it is necessary to consult a detailed map. In area the kingdom came to a little less than 100,000 square miles with a population of about 15,000,000. Of these a little less than one-half were Serbs, while one-third were Croats and Slovenes. The Serbs were therefore the preponderant element, which fact, added to their long and heroic fighting record against the Turks, inclined them unduly to lord it over their Croat and Slovene brothers.

The explosive Macedonian problem

While there were minority groups of Magyars, Germans, and Rumanians within the Yugoslav boundaries, they constituted a problem of little consequence compared with that of a kindred Slav people, the Macedonians. In Chapter 30 we treated of Macedonia and defined its people as south-Slavs who felt themselves more closely related to the Bulgars than to the Serbs, but who, in consequence of the defeat of Bulgaria in the Balkan wars of 1912-1913, were, in large part, incorporated in victorious Serbia. Although Bulgaria, on joining the Central Powers in 1915, had snatched Macedonia from Serbia, it was at the Paris Peace Conference obliged to restore it to Serb ownership. Resolved to make the inhabitants confessed Serbs, the government at Belgrade aroused a resistance which took the form of an undeclared war of the most lawless conceivable form. Of course, without help from across the border, from sympathetic Bulgaria, the rebellious Macedonians could not long have sustained their cause. The help, only too readily given, lifted the issue from the domestic to the foreign level and kept the two neighbor states perpetually embroiled. After a decade of bootless bickering they at length saw the advantage of an accommodation. Although the Macedonian question thereupon lost something of its edge, it never ceased to poison the relations between Yugoslavia and Bulgaria and to cause them to look on each other with wrath and suspicion in their hearts.

The unsolvable domestic issue: centralization versus federalism

Grave as was the issue of Macedonia, a still graver one arose over the kind of organization to be given the newborn state. A party of centralizers, chiefly Serbs, wanted a compact, unitary government with all authority emanating from the capital city of Belgrade. Opposed to them were the federalists, who insisted on the retention of a broad autonomy by the component provinces. The leader of the federalists was a fiery, erratic Croatian, Stefan Radich by name. When the constituent assembly was captured by the centralizers and a unitary constitution drawn up by them (1921), Radich urged his parliamentary following, and all good Croatians besides, to ignore it. The absence of the Croatians from the parliament greatly impaired its authority, and efforts were repeatedly made, especially by King Alexander I, a man of energy and initiative, so to modify the constitution as to make it acceptable to the insurgents. Not only did the efforts prove vain, they even dug deeper the chasm between the two parliamentary parties and the peoples they respectively represented. At last occurred the to-be-expected and characteristic Balkan denouement. When, on a June day of 1928, the debate in the parliament had reached a height of bitterness never before attained, a Serb deputy drew a pistol and, discharging it wildly at the massed Croatians, succeeded in killing three and wounding several more. Among the dead was Croatia's leader and idol, Stefan Radich.

This savage event drove the Croatians to the verge of revolt and persuaded the king to go into action in the role of *deus ex machina*. In January, 1929, he abolished the constitution, suppressed all parties, and made himself dictator. However, a Serb in blood and mind, he could think of no workable solution that did not take the unitarian line. He therefore, by royal decree, abolished the ancient historical provinces of Serbia, Croatia, Bosnia, Macedonia, etc., as too deeply lodged in the breasts of his subjects, and replaced them with nine departments or *banats,* determined solely by noncommittal geographical features. In further evidence of his consolidating intentions he decreed the official name of the state no longer to be the Kingdom of the Serbs, Croats, and Slovenes, but simply Yugoslavia. When a year or two later he published a constitution, it turned out to be a hoax insofar as any diminution of his dictatorship was concerned. Driving by such measures the Croats farther and farther from the throne, he prepared an end for himself that it would not have taken a prophet to foretell. In October, 1934, he went to France to pay his leading ally a visit of courtesy. No sooner had he landed at Marseilles than, as his automobile was proceeding to the City Hall, he was shot and killed by a young man who leaped out of the holiday crowd and jumped upon the running board. The assassin was at once trampled to death by the bystanders. The subsequent investigation clearly established that he was the emissary of a band of leagued terrorists recruited from the two estranged provinces of Croatia and Macedonia. Alexander was succeeded by his eleven-year-old son, Peter II, in whose name a regency took over the government. Although it made occasional gestures of reconciliation toward the Croats, it never succeeded in closing the rift that had opened between them and their Serb kin.

The foreign policy of Yugoslavia took shape when it joined the Little Entente and made an alliance with France. This meant just one thing: Yugoslavia was determined at all costs to maintain the Paris treaties. Apart from a sharp lookout in the direction of such close neighbors as

The dictatorship of King Alexander and his assassination (1934)

Yugoslavia's foreign policy

Hungary, Bulgaria, and Albania, its main concern was with Italy. We have noted the conflict over the port of Fiume, which Italy coveted and finally got. Although Italy also demanded at the peace table the coastal province of Dalmatia, it had to content itself with the single town of Zara and a few outlying strategic islands. When, later, under Mussolini, Albania was reduced to an Italian protectorate, Yugoslavia loudly beat her breast and asked the world to note her consequent imprisonment within the upper-Adriatic sea. But nobody paid particular attention, as Mussolini's star had risen and was still rising over these waters.

Rumania

Rumania fared very well in the aftermath of the war, for, in addition to certain minor territories, she acquired Transylvania from Hungary to her west and Bessarabia from Russia to her east. This more than doubled her pre-war area and brought her population to 18,000,000, of whom about 14,000,000 were Rumanian nationals. The more considerable minorities with which she had to deal were 1,500,000 Magyars in ceded Transylvania and 1,000,000 Ukrainians (Little Russians) in Bessarabia. In spite of these considerable figures of non-nationals, the Rumanians were undoubtedly the preponderant element in both the provinces in question.

Territories acquired by Rumania as a result of the war

Ever since Rumania had shaken off the Turkish yoke, its most disturbing issue had been that of the land. It was, in the main, held in large estates by a relatively small body of landlords, who for centuries had exploited a teeming population of serfs. An act of the year 1864 put an end to serfdom, but since no measures, at least no adequate measures, were taken to convert the liberated serfs into freeholders, they became agricultural laborers on the estates of their former masters and were no better off, economically, than before. By repeatedly rising in revolt in the last half of the nineteenth century, they made known their settled purpose of acquiring land of their own. In view of the control of the government by the landed magnates, their enemies, their efforts were regularly balked till Rumania joined the allies in World War I. In order to win wholehearted peasant support, the government then made promises which, on the return to peace, it proceeded loyally to carry out. By separate laws for the Old Kingdom and the two major acquisitions of Transylvania and Bessarabia the great estates were broken up, but not on identical terms. In the Old Kingdom, where the landlords enjoyed greater authority, they were treated more tenderly, and the permissible maximum estate was fixed at 1500 acres; in Transylvania and Bessarabia, on the other hand, the maximum estate could not surpass 300 acres. In all three cases the bulk of the arable land was acquired,

The great estates broken up for distribution among the landless peasants

though not without compensation to the owners, by the state and was distributed on easy terms among the landless laborers, transforming them in this manner into small independent proprietors.

It deserves particular notice that the solution of the land problem adopted by the Rumanians was in the sharpest conceivable contrast to the sullen refusal of the Hungarians to tamper with the traditional inequalities. The effect of the reform legislation was quick to put in an appearance. Under the vigorous leadership of Dr. Julius Maniu the peasant freeholders were organized into a National Peasant party, which presently swept the elections and became the dominant party in the Rumanian parliament. In 1928 Maniu became prime minister and announced a program so liberal and western in spirit that Rumania seemed on the point of transforming itself into the most democratic state in the peninsula. But the happy prospect was not to be realized, owing to the intervention of the self-willed king. The National Peasant party and its projected reforms

It was in the previous century, in 1866, that Rumania had acquired its ruling dynasty in the person of Carol I of the house of Hohenzollern-Sigmaringen, related, as the name indicates, to the reigning house of Prussia. Carol was an intelligent, circumspect ruler who, in a long reign (1866-1914), contributed notably to the modernization of his backward country. He was succeeded by his colorless nephew, Ferdinand I, who lived through the social transformation just recounted without leaving a trace of his personal impression on it. The rulers: Carol I and Ferdinand I

On Ferdinand's death in 1927 he should have been succeeded by his son, Carol, but was not because Carol had been guilty of such extravagant misbehavior that he had been banished from the country and debarred from the throne. Accordingly, on Ferdinand's death Carol's five-year-old son, Michael, became king under a regency, toward which Maniu, when he became prime minister, developed a profound distrust. Therefore, when Carol, tiring of his banishment, made (1930) a dramatic return to his country by airplane, he was heartily welcomed by Maniu and restored to the throne. Inescapably the new dispensation demoted the boy-king to his former post of crown prince. It took only a few months for Maniu to discover his radical mistake. Not only did Carol II refuse to give up his unsavory personal habits, he crowded the disillusioned Maniu out of office and in order to rid himself completely of ministerial tutelage established a veiled dictatorship. Succession of Rumania's evil genius, Carol II

But, with or without Maniu, Carol was not destined to wear his crown in ease. There came to birth at this time a virulently fascist, anti-semitic party, calling itself the Iron Guard, which the king tried in every way to crush, but without success. The Iron Guard was Nazi-influenced and pro-German, while Carol, attached to the Little Entente and allied with France, was necessarily pro-French. The tug of war between him and Rise of the fascist Iron Guard the fascist fanatics went on with varying fortunes to the end of the thirties, by which time it had become plain to every clear-thinking person in or outside Rumania that the outcome depended not on the local contestants but on the resolution of the vast fascist-democratic crisis that was convulsing Europe.

Greece

Greece, tempted by the offer of Smyrna, engages in war

By the Paris treaties Greece was liberally endowed with territorial increases at the expense of defeated Bulgaria and Turkey. She was even conceded the city of Smyrna in Asia Minor, together with its rich hinterland, on the understanding that she would render commensurable service to a group of victor powers who nursed the plan of carving up Turkey into spheres of influence. The powers involved in this crude project were Great Britain, France, and Italy. As their own troops were too war-weary and rebellious to be safely launched on the proposed enterprise, they bethought themselves of the Greeks, who were so late in getting into the war that, still fresh at its close, they manifested a positive hunger for the fray.

Defeat of the Greeks followed by the Treaty of Lausanne (1923)

Once again let us take note that the Turks were so outraged by the Treaty of Sèvres, coolly submitted to them for signature by the victorious allies, that under the leadership of the dauntless Mustapha Kemal they resumed the war. Thereupon the allies loosed on them their Greek bloodhound, kept in reserve for this very eventuality. The result was a Greco-Turk war which, begun in 1920, ended two years later with the crushing defeat of the Greeks, culminating in their ejection from the coveted Smyrna salient. At this point Great Britain intervened in behalf of its Greek agent, and the humiliated Paris conferees agreed to withdraw the Treaty of Sèvres and discuss a new settlement with representatives of victorious Turkey. The deliberations resulted in the Treaty of Lausanne (1923), by which the allies, giving up their plan of sharing Turkey as their prize, conceded to the resuscitated state the undivided possession of Anatolia (Asia Minor), proclaimed by the Kemalists as the inviolate home of their people.

The ceaseless domestic flux leads to dictatorship

Not only did the Smyrna hopes of the Greeks dissolve into thin air in consequence of their defeat but their government became so discredited that, owing also, it is true, to a dozen lesser reasons, it entered on a period of tumultuous fluctuations that cover the whole span between the First and Second World Wars. Immediately on the trail of the Smyrna rout the reigning sovereign, Constantine I, was deposed and the monarchy replaced with a republic. Since the republic failed to work smoothly, it was in practice usually dominated either by a military junta or an individual military usurper. By 1935 it had so generally lost the favor of a capricious public that a plebiscite re-established the deposed dynasty in the person of Constantine's son, George II. But the return of the monarchy did not bring a return to constitutionality for, even though the king reigned, it was still a dictator, open or hidden, who governed. In 1936 General Metaxas, who had long been hovering in the background, stepped to the front and, seizing the power, promptly organized Greece as a totalitarian corporative state on the general model of Italy.

In spite of the uninterrupted domestic turmoil, Greece on the whole pursued a pacific foreign policy following its one disastrous gamble of 1920-1922. It even took the lead in an attempt, by means of periodic meetings of representatives of all the Balkan states, to create a healthier Balkan atmosphere. Unfortunately, the by no means inconsiderable improvement brought about was diminished and finally eliminated altogether by the stealthy progress of the international tension resulting from the increasing aggressions of Mussolini's Italy and Hitler's Germany. *Greece pursues a chastened foreign policy after 1922*

Throughout the period here considered the Greek people continued to bemoan the occupation by Great Britain of the Greek island of Cyprus and of Greek Rhodes and the Dodecanese group by Italy. Their fixed view was that these islands, though momentarily held by Mediterranean powers with navies strong enough to occupy them, would by the unrelenting pressure of nationalism be ultimately united with the Greek homeland. *Greece expects to acquire Cyprus, Rhodes, the Dodecanese*

Albania

As it was the youngest, Albania was also, and by far, the weakest of the Balkan communities. Not born till the very eve of World War I, it had completely disappeared from view during that disaster, not again to raise a timid head till the cessation of hostilities in 1918. At the Paris Peace Conference both Italy and Yugoslavia advanced claims to Albania, which the leading statesmen, with President Wilson at their head, refused to allow. Instead, they gave their blessing to the plan of a patriot group to bring Albania back to life under a strictly native government. *Albania reconstituted as an independent state by the Paris Conference*

When a native government had been set up, its difficulties were found to be immeasurable. Albania is a country of steep, barren mountains, good only for feeding goats and cattle, and of a few valley floors, moderately serviceable for the growing of grain. Its primitive inhabitants, barely numbering 1,000,000 souls, were, as late as 1918, still loosely organized in tribes which lived by the barbarous code of the blood-feud. Since they had only recently adopted an alphabet and a written language, they were afflicted besides with an all but universal illiteracy. A final disastrous feature was to be found in their religious differences. About sixty per cent of the people were confessed Mohammedans, while the remainder were Christians, divided between the Roman Catholic and the Greek Orthodox faiths. *Its innumerable drawbacks*

No sooner had the Albanians, thus cruelly handicapped, acquired a government of their own than it was seen that they could not operate it in the democratic manner which it was the declared intention of their Paris spokesmen to adopt. The power was seized by a succession of adventurers, among whom a tribal chief, Ahmed Zogu, coming to the front in 1925, proved himself the most daring. Three years later, Ahmed persuaded himself that it would solidify his position to proclaim Albania a kingdom. He accordingly did so, adopting for himself the title of Zog I. An energetic man who thoroughly knew his country and understood at least its most immediate needs, he laid down an extensive program of road-building, an administrative service calculated to reach the remotest mountain villages, and a system of justice whereby the primitive blood-feud was to be replaced by a more civilized procedure.

Ahmed Zogu transforms Albania into a kingdom (1928)

For even these modest reforms the self-exalted king required tax returns which his impoverished and habitually lawless people were neither willing nor able to supply. In addition he required expert officials of a caliber simply not to be encountered within the boundaries of the state. Reluctantly but inescapably, Zog had to appeal for capital and guidance to the outside world and, as Italy was close at hand and acknowledged by the other powers to have a special interest in this near neighbor, it was Italy that answered the king's call for help. In return for subsidies in ever larger amounts conceded to King Zog, the Italians acquired economic, financial, and military advantages that, before many years had passed, constituted a virtual protectorate. In Chapter 40, dealing with Fascist Italy, it was related how Mussolini tightened his hold from year to year till he had Albania completely in his grasp. At length, in April, 1939, he dispatched an army to Tirana, the Albanian capital, before which King Zog sought safety in precipitate flight. It was the end of Albania, for by proclaiming Victor Emmanuel king of the conquered country, Mussolini virtually annexed it to Italy.

How Italy gradually took over Albania

Bulgaria

Shorn of important areas by the Paris Conference, defeated Bulgaria nursed a passionate resentment against its triumphant neighbors, Yugoslavia, Rumania, and Greece. Each of these three had been endowed with some territory to which, on nationalist grounds, Bulgaria felt it had an indefeasible claim. Of these lost areas the most important was Macedonia, in dispute since the Balkan Wars of 1912-1913 between Yugoslavia and Greece, on the one hand, and Bulgaria, on the other. In recently dealing with Yugoslavia (p. 828) we considered the Macedonian problem and have just one significant detail to add at this point. The disturbers of the Macedonian peace were not so much present as former

Bulgaria nurses the usual resentment of a defeated state

residents of Macedonia, who had been so greatly outraged by the latest partition (1919) of their homeland between Yugoslavia and Greece that, abandoning it, they migrated across the border into sympathetic Bulgaria. Some 200,000 strong, they resorted to every device evolved through the ages by restless exiles to effect their return.

The most powerful weapon of their devising was the Internal Mace- *Once again* donian Revolutionary Organization, called IMRO for short. While the *and for the* IMRO was chiefly recruited from among the exiles, it had also a numer- *last time,* ous following among the Macedonian stay-at-homes, and it was this com- *Macedonia* bination of outsiders and insiders that explains its effectiveness. This manifested itself, according to the immemorial creed of groups of this nature, by savage acts of arson and murder along the Yugoslav frontier. The lively protests forwarded by the government at Belgrade to the government at Sofia failed for a long time to bring about a change, since Bulgaria showed an understandable reluctance to employ force against the Macedonian refugees who had sought shelter under its roof. But when, after a decade and more of constant embroilment not only with Yugoslavia but also its other neighbors, Bulgaria realized that the IMRO was a barrier to even the most rudimentary understanding with them, it brought the IMRO leaders, who had developed the manners and morals of unqualified gangsters, under control with the result that its relations with its neighbors, without precisely becoming friendly, registered a measurable improvement.

Owing to the grave internal difficulties with which Bulgaria was beset, its government, like that of every other Balkan state we have passed in *The* review, continued throughout the period here considered to be rocked *peasant* like a ship in a storm. On the defeat of Bulgaria in 1918 its king, Fer- *rule of* dinand I, was obliged to abdicate and was succeeded by his son, Boris *Stambolisky* III. Boris was young, but intelligent and circumspect, and lent himself *overthrown* earnestly to the role of balance-wheel among the numerous parties that *by associated* vied with one another for the control of the government. Since Bulgaria *urban* was largely a land of peasants, a powerful peasant party led by Alex- *groups* ander Stambolisky exercised rule in the early years of Boris's reign till it was overthrown (1923) by an urban party of middle-class merchants and shopkeepers strengthened by the professional intelligentsia. That Stambolisky was murdered in the course of the conflict was the no more than usual concomitant of these transfers of power.

With the familiar exaggeration of politics, the adherents of the middle-class parties henceforth denounced the peasants as communists, while the *Party feroc-* peasants returned the compliment by calling their adversaries fascists. *ity leads* Doubtless there were not lacking in the distraught land a genuine fascist *inevitably to* and a genuine communist sentiment, especially the latter, owing to the *dictatorship* nearness of communist Russia and the vigorous propaganda emanating from the Third International. In 1934 the army officers injected them-selves into the situation by sweeping the stage free of all rivals and setting up a dictatorship. The very next year, however, King Boris, who had never ceased to play the part of mediator, ousted the officers and became dictator himself. Apparently, it was the only available escape from an intolerable situation. Accepted by the mass of his subjects, the king still held unchallenged sway when Hitler's invasion of Poland rang in a new era.

Turkey

The Treaty of Sèvres replaced by the Treaty of Lausanne

We have heard, in treating of Greece a few pages back, how the Greeks let themselves be used by the allies to carry out the partition of Turkey as laid down in the Treaty of Sèvres of 1920, and how, on encountering the resistance organized by the heroic Mustapha Kemal, they were disastrously beaten. Not only did they have to surrender their claim to the coveted Smyrna, but the powers who had hounded the Greeks on were obliged to disavow the Treaty of Sèvres and, an amazing decline from their earlier dictatorial arrogance, to negotiate a new treaty, which from its place of signature received the name of the Treaty of Lausanne (1923).

The new Turkey, limited to Anatolia, is essentially Asiatic

The independent Turkey which emerged from the Lausanne document, was, if so sweeping a statement is ever justified, the handiwork of a single individual, Mustapha Kemal. Identified with the province of Anatolia, better known in the west as Asia Minor and sentimentally cherished by the Turks as their homeland, Kemal's Turkey freely renounced all claims not only to its former Christian dependencies of the Balkan peninsula but also to the Arab-inhabited lands around the eastern bend of the Mediterranean. These renunciations marked the final passing of the Ottoman empire, which had been so unconscionable a time a-dying, and its replacement, so far as the Turks were concerned, with a diminished, nationally constituted Asiatic Turkey. However, since the crucial straits of the Bosporus and the Dardanelles, together with the city of Constantinople (called Istanbul by the Turks), were left in Turkish possession, the new Turkey, though essentially Asiatic, still maintained an European foothold. This did not keep the level-headed Mustapha Kemal from recognizing that its center of gravity now lay irrevocably in Asia. Consequently, rejecting ancient and far-famed Constantinople as his capital, he raised the obscure little town of Ankara (Angora) in the heart of Anatolia to this honor.

Nonetheless, the inclusion of Constantinople and the straits within Turkey added immensely to the country's international importance. So little was this fact overlooked by the western powers who negotiated the Treaty of Lausanne that they prepared a special regime for this area and were strong enough to impose its acceptance on the Turks. By a supplementary enactment called the Convention of the Straits, Turkey was obliged to demilitarize a narrow strip of coast on either side of the Bosporus and Dardanelles and concede the free passage through them to the ships of all nations. But the demilitarization clause did not stick. In 1936, at a conference held at Montreux in Switzerland, Kemal was able to persuade his fellow signatories to cancel it and to grant him the right to fortify this strategic area to his heart's content.

The demilitarization of the straits, imposed in 1923, withdrawn in 1936

As soon as Turkey's independence had been secured, the National Assembly at Ankara, presided over by Kemal, proclaimed Turkey a republic and named its honored leader as the first president. At the same time it elaborated a constitution which provided for a parliament of a single house and made display of other liberal features. In the interest of unity, however, these were, generally speaking, ignored, thus enabling the president, with the all but unanimous consent of his people, to exercise an effective dictatorship. Even before the republic had been formally proclaimed, the National Assembly made as complete as possible an avowal of its breach with the monarchical past by abolishing the sultanate and sending the former ruling-family into exile. By abolishing, a year later, the caliphate also, it broke as emphatically with the Turkish religious past, for let it not be forgotten that the sultan of the former Ottoman empire was also the caliph of the Moslem world and regarded by virtue of this office as the successor of the prophet Mohammed, much as the pope is held by Roman Catholics to be the successor of Christ. To renounce the caliphate meant, therefore, not that the Turks were going to renounce their religion but that, devoted to the intense nationalism of their rebirth, they gave up every pretension to exercise rule over Mohammedan believers outside their boundaries.

Turkey becomes a republic and abolishes sultanate and caliphate

What President Kemal had mainly at heart was a vast economic, financial, judicial, and social revolution in the course of which Turkey should be transformed from an almost unbelievably backward oriental society into a westernized community, prepared to take its place at the side of the most advanced nations of the Atlantic seaboard. It was to carry through this plan that he accepted the dictatorship which his immediate associates, dismayed by the enormous difficulties of his undertaking, fairly forced on him. Thus sustained, he set about his task with a tireless but also cautious energy in order not to arouse unnecessary opposition. With westernization as the objective, Turkey would, first of all, have to rid itself of its inherited legal system. This was done by the elaboration of civil, penal, and commercial codes selected at will from existent European models. In the religious field, the abolition of the caliphate was seen as only a beginning since the goal ultimately aimed at came to be complete

Kemal's goal: Turkey's complete westernization

religious toleration. Consequently, Islam, which in the original republican constitution had been declared to be the religion of the state, was, on second thought, denied this honor and all religions given an equal standing before the law.

As enthusiastic Europeanizers, the circle about the president was eager to promote education. This was a difficult undertaking, first, because of the all but universal illiteracy of the Turks, and second, owing to the lack of funds and teachers. Nonetheless, a comprehensive plan was laid down and sufficient schools erected and teachers trained appreciably to raise the educational level of the people. A wise concomitant measure was to abandon the intricate Arab alphabet, which the Turks had centuries ago taken over from their Arab neighbors, and to replace it with the Latin alphabet. The change was calculated by Kemal's experts to save several years' elementary schooling; and, as it was made obligatory also for newspapers and every form of print, the new alphabet became a general benefit as well.

A characteristic oriental evil, the low status of women, was attacked in numerous enactments. Polygamy was abolished and civil, that is, state-registered marriage, imposed in place of religious marriage. Women were given the vote and presently made eligible for public office, including the National Assembly. In line with this advance they were encouraged to adopt western dress and to throw away that symbol of cloistered womanhood, the veil. The parallel enactment for men was the order to abandon the picturesque fez and turban for the vulgar, undistinguished hat. Need we remind ourselves that westernization is a utilitarian, not an esthetic movement?

Since there were no capital accumulations in the society of impoverished peasants that Turkey essentially was, the state undertook to promote industry, agriculture, and communications, thereby committing itself to a form of state socialism. Progress was slow on these terms, but President Kemal was violently opposed to the importation of foreign capital with its inescapable accompaniment of political dependence.

Overlooking no feature characteristic of Western civilization, the reformers ordered the people to take on family names, a practice which had not thus far figured in the tradition of the orient. At the request of the Assembly, Kemal himself adopted the surname Ataturk, meaning Father of the Turks. Heaped with every conceivable honor, he died in 1938 and was succeeded in the presidency by his friend and collaborator, Ismet Inonu.

THE ARAB WORLD

Egypt

The Arab lands, the detachment of which from Turkey was accepted by Mustapha Kemal at Lausanne, were Arabia, Syria, and Mesopotamia. He also renounced any claim his country might be conceived to have to Egypt, even though it had been reduced to less than a shadow by the forcible seizure effected by Great Britain in 1882. At the war's close Great Britain was therefore in a position to make whatever arrangements she pleased in that ancient land. The war, ostensibly fought for the liberation of small nations, had aroused the nationalist fervor of the native population to such a pitch that a nationalist party had been formed which demanded complete independence. Unwilling to make this extreme concession, the British in 1922 recognized Egypt as "an independent sovereign state" with certain reservations giving Great Britain a preferred position, more particularly in regard to the Suez Canal. The ruler of Egypt, the former khedive, now took the title of king and issued a parliamentary constitution.

Britain and Egypt arrive (1922) at a temporary settlement

This settlement failed to satisfy the great majority of the Egyptians and disturbances, repeatedly culminating in violent outbreaks, marked the succeeding years. At length in 1936 a new treaty was signed with Great Britain which did not in any substantial way diminish the latter's hold. It did, however, contain the guardian country's promise to support Egypt's application to membership in the League of Nations. When, in 1937, the application was favorably acted on by the League, that once august body had already been shorn of much of its prestige.

The settlement of 1936 and Egypt's admission to the League of Nations

Arabia

As for Arabia, Syria, and Mesopotamia, they, too, hardly needed the express renunciation of Lausanne, since they had been freed from Ottoman rule in the course of the war, in part through their own action, in much larger part through the intervention of France and Great Britain. While the fighting was still going on, the two western powers had signed agreements with each other and with the native rebels in regard to the ultimate disposal of these lands. As might be expected, difficult and rancorous negotiations took place at Paris in 1919 before a settlement could be arrived at.

Rancorous negotiations over the remaining Arab lands

By the terms of the settlement, only one region was made completely independent. This was the Arabian coastal area of the Hedjaz, embracing the two Mohammedan holy cities of Mecca and Medina. The local sheik, Hussein by name, was acknowledged ruler under the more honorable title of king. Hussein did not last very long, for in 1925 he was driven out of the Hedjaz by a rival sheik, Ibn Saud, who, a valiant warrior, succeeded in the course of a few years in bringing almost the whole of the vast Arabian peninsula under his single scepter. Not only did Ibn Saud, as an independent sovereign, succeed in making himself a towering political factor throughout the near east, but his notable achievement lent spurs to the Arab national movement wherever Arabs dwelt.

The Arab areas which, in distinction from Arabia, did not achieve independence were the states that Great Britain and France carved out of Syria and Mesopotamia. The latter region, comprising the river valleys of the Tigris and Euphrates, went in the main to Great Britain, which rebaptized it Iraq and provided it with a measure of self-government. Syria went in the main to France, which chose to divide it into a larger dependency, called Syria, and a smaller, called Lebanon. Southern Syria, however, was handed over to Great Britain, which split it into two zones, a coastal zone more or less identical with ancient Palestine and a desert zone beyond the Jordan river called Transjordan. We thus have four or, if we count Syria and Lebanon separately, five Arab dependencies distributed between Great Britain and France. They did not, however, let it be noted, receive these dependencies in absolute possession but rather in trust, since all were designated as mandates at Paris and declared to be subject to supervision by the League of Nations.

Throughout the area under consideration in this section, the outstanding phenomenon has been the growth of Arab nationalism. While, exactly as with the Turks, it pursued in the main a political objective, it also, again as with the Turks, though with much more restraint, contemplated the capture of the cultural benefits of Western civilization. As the Arabs had once had a flourishing civilization of their own which, although in decline, was still alive, it is impossible to foresee how far they will make themselves over in the western image. Be that as it may, it is safe to prophesy that they will never cease from struggling to cast off the political tutelage of their western overlords.

Iraq and Transjordan

In point of fact the control of both the overlords, France and Britain, experienced a considerable decline in the period between World Wars I and II. As already noted, Great Britain from the start granted Iraq a measure of autonomy under a son of King Hussein of the Hedjaz. This prince was presently made king and by 1930 had persuaded the mandatory power to concede the independence of Iraq with reservations similar to those imposed on independent Egypt. Two years later Iraq was admitted to the League of Nations, an act considered the equivalent of a guarantee of sovereignty. In Transjordan, essentially a desert area inhabited by culturally retarded nomad Arabs, the national sentiment made but slow headway, with the result that Great Britain has been hardly, if at all, obliged to modify her over-all control.

Syria

The French, who in acquiring Syria got possession of what was culturally the most advanced area of the whole Arab world, fell into a veritable briar bush. Like the Egyptians, the Syrians promptly demanded independence and would be content with nothing less. Although unwilling to go so far, their French masters were obliged to make concessions comparable to those the British made to the Egyptians. Not only did their offer fail to win acceptance, but the debate that followed repeatedly led to such violent outbreaks that the French army had to be brought into action before order was restored. In 1936 the occupying power made its most determined effort to arrive at a compromise by the proffer of a treaty of alliance and friendship which granted independence subject to certain military and economic privileges reserved to France. The Syrians rejected liberation on these imperfect terms, and the seesaw between governors and governed continued without let-up. It seems reasonable to predict that the establishment of peace in Syria (and neighboring Lebanon as well) waits on French withdrawal from the scene.

Failure of France and the Syrians to come to terms

Palestine

More even than the French in their section of Syria the British ran into trouble in the section of Syria allotted to them and identical with historical Palestine. The taproot of the clamorous Palestinian strife was the promise Great Britain made in the famous Balfour Declaration of 1917 to establish in Palestine "a national home for the Jewish people." Although originally the land of the Jews, Palestine had many centuries ago passed into other hands and was at the time of the Paris Conference overwhelmingly populated by Moslem Arabs. No sooner had Palestine been assigned to Great Britain than the government undertook to make good its promise by inviting the Jews of Europe and America to create the appropriate agencies for the systematic re-occupation of the ancient home of their people.

Britain carries out the Balfour Declaration of 1917

The resultant immigration enjoyed the advantage not only of the large-scale financial backing of European and American Jewry but also of the utilitarian and scientific mentality the colonists brought with them from their several countries of origin. Land was liberally bought from the

The Arabs
protest
against
immigration
and land
purchase

Arabs by Jewish companies, and immigrants settled thereon so rapidly and in such numbers that the native Arabs became alarmed and protested with steadily waxing energy, first, against the pace of settlement, and second, against the Jewish land purchases, which were declared to be reducing a portion of the natives to landless laborers. To these complaints the Jews responded by pointing with pride to the prosperous condition of the areas taken over by them and by the vehement insistence that colonization be permitted to continue in accordance with the Balfour commitment.

The conflict
enters the
stage of
violence

In 1929 occurred the first country-wide upflare of Arab violence against the Jews. It was not suppressed by the British police and military till several hundred combatants had been killed and wounded on both sides. Practically every year after the first excess there took place an outbreak of rioting on a larger or smaller scale. The mandatory power attempted to moderate Arab resentment by limiting immigration and at times by even stopping it altogether. But already national and religious passions had been aroused to such a pitch in both parties to the conflict that the voice of reason could no longer make itself heard. In 1936 the wild excesses reached a climax and led to a thoroughgoing investigation of their source and origin by a British parliamentary commission dispatched to the scene.

The
partition
proposal
of 1937

The upshot of the investigation was that the British government in 1937 brought forward a proposal, based, as the preamble declared, on the conviction that the Arab and Jewish positions were absolutely irreconcilable. By that time the population had grown considerably since the mandate had been taken over, and there then lived in Palestine some 400,000 Jews and some 1,000,000 Arabs. By the terms of the proposal Palestine was to be divided into a northern state of the Jews and a southern state of the Arabs, with a neutral area between embracing Jerusalem, Bethlehem, and other Holy Places and retained under continuing British administration. The plan aroused such violent protests from both sides that it was withdrawn and another, less radical, accommodation substituted; but before this could be submitted to the House of Commons for approval, World War II broke out and obliged the government to adjourn further discussion till the return of peace.

The British
empire and
oil

A closing word of caution has reference to oil. The Palestinian harbor of Haifa is at the delivery end of the pipe-line that runs from Mosul in Iraq. It may be accepted as certain that every solution of the problem of Palestine contemplated by the British government has made and will continue to make the Haifa oil its primary consideration.

44 THE OUTBREAK OF WORLD WAR II
(1939)

WE HAVE REPEATEDLY taken account of how, by certain acts committed by Japan, Italy, and Germany in the course of the thirties, these three states had defined themselves to the world as an aggressor group. However, there was in the beginning no collaboration among them, each proceeding proudly on its own sovereign initiative. The absence of any original understanding was clearly brought out when, on the rising of the Austrian Nazis in 1934, they failed to get the expected help of Hitler for the single reason that Mussolini forbade the Anschluss by mobilizing an army at the Brenner pass. Two years later the situation had changed completely. Mussolini had launched his Ethiopian war, for which he so pressingly needed German support that he signed a treaty with Hitler by which the two dictators agreed to bring their foreign policies into the greatest possible accord. It was the first step toward the creation of an intimacy on which Mussolini himself presently hung the descriptive label of the Rome-Berlin axis.

Japan, Italy, and Germany at first uncommitted to each other

When in the same year of 1936 Germany and Japan signed an anti-Comintern pact (to which Italy shortly afterward gave its adherence), the axis was strengthened by a new link and became the Rome-Berlin-Tokyo axis. The anti-Comintern pact, it should expressly be said, was directed, so far as its language went, not against Russia but against the Third International, not against a state but against a political program. By the above-mentioned measures the three aggressor states had by 1937 become a closely co-ordinated group, if not yet, strictly speaking, military allies. And that they were drawing together in conscious opposition to the rest of the world was further emphasized by the fact that by this same year they had all three formally withdrawn from the League of Nations, for in 1937 Italy took the step that Japan and Germany had already taken in 1933.

Formation of the Rome-Berlin-Tokyo axis

In this manner the concert of the powers was, precisely as in the period preceding the outbreak of World War I, split sharply in two, and every incident of international scope that arose thereafter was certain to widen the breach between the three non-League powers, on the one hand, and the three League powers of Great Britain, France, and Russia, on the other. Far and away the leading incident of this divisive nature was the

The concert of the powers split sharply in two

Spanish revolution, which broke out in 1936 and needs to be closely examined not only for its own sake but also because of its disruptive effect on the international situation.

SPAIN

The mounting internal difficulties of Spain

In Chapter 32 we brought the history of Spain down to the outbreak of World War I in 1914. Spain promptly declared its neutrality, to which it clung throughout the struggle. However, opinion was sharply divided within the country regarding the war, and hardly had peace been proclaimed when a bumper crop of troubles put in an appearance: the labor agitation throughout the land, but especially in the prevailingly industrial province of Catalonia, became feverish and relieved itself by violence and riot; the ancient petition of Catalonia for autonomy developed into a clear-cut demand for separation; a rising wave of republicanism threatened to undermine the throne of the Bourbon king, Alfonso XIII; and self-willed military juntas, a curse inherited from the protracted civil wars of the nineteenth century, lurked in the background eager to quell every form of radicalism with cannon and grapeshot. Clear evidence of the growing instability was the endless succession of ministries installed at Madrid to wrestle with the desperate confusion.

Defeat of Spain by the Riffs and the dictatorship of Primo de Rivera (1923)

Then, when the Moroccan tribes of the Riff rose in rebellion and, in 1921, under the elusive and swift-moving chieftain, Abd-el-Krim, destroyed a Spanish army, the national discontent flamed to the skies and prompted a leading member of the military clique, General Primo de Rivera, to bring it under control before it had mushroomed into revolution. In 1923 Primo swept the constitution into the dustbin and, with the consent of Alfonso XIII, made himself dictator after the fashion recently set by his Latin neighbor, Mussolini. Primo's rule lasted seven years and was attended at first by a measure of success, more apparent than real however, since if he somewhat reduced the by now habitual lawlessness, it was solely by using the army as a police force. What probably more than any other one thing moved him to undertake his coup d'état was, as already indicated, Spain's unhappy war with the Riffian tribes, and here he was favored by fortune. In a thoughtless moment Abd-el-Krim declared war on France, which thereupon made common cause with Spain, and between them the two states reduced the Riff to order and brought about the surrender of its spirited tribal chief (1926).

The monarchy replaced by a republic (1931)

But beneath the surface all the old discontents continued to smolder so that Primo himself at last recognized that his mission had failed, threw up the sponge, and resigned (1930). More stubborn than his general, the king tried to go on with the dictatorship, but after an agitated year had to placate an aroused nation by restoring the constitution. All

DENSITY AND GROWTH
OF POPULATION IN
EUROPE

SCALE OF MILES

0   100   200   300   400   500

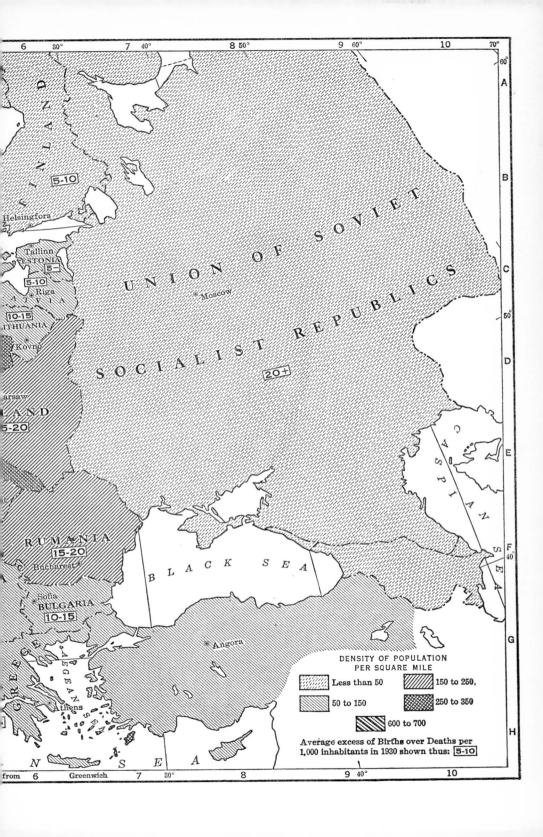

UNION OF SOVIET

SOCIALIST REPUBLICS

Moscow

20+

FINLAND

5-10

Helsingfors

Tallinn
ESTONIA
5-

Riga
LATVIA
10-15

LITHUANIA

Kovno

Warsaw

POLAND

15-20

RUMANIA

15-20

Bucharest

Sofia
BULGARIA

10-15

GREECE

Athens

A E G E A N

S E A

N

BLACK   SEA

Angora

A S I A

CASPIAN SEA

DENSITY OF POPULATION
PER SQUARE MILE

Less than 50   150 to 250,

50 to 150   250 to 350

600 to 700

Average excess of Births over Deaths per
1,000 inhabitants in 1930 shown thus: 5-10

from 6   Greenwich   7   30°   8   9   40°   10

issues had by now merged into a single issue, monarchy versus republic, and when the first free, nation-wide elections were held, the result was a republican landslide. Two days later the king left the country and the republic was formally proclaimed (April, 1931). In order to provide the new government with a constitution, elections for a constituent assembly took place and once again the nation avowed its faith in the new order by returning an overwhelming majority of republican delegates.

The constitution shaped by this assembly and completed before the year was out was a very democratic instrument. It provided for a uni-cameral legislature, or cortes, to be elected by universal (male and fe-male) suffrage, and a president to be elected for a six-year term by an electoral college composed of the members of the cortes plus an equal number of popularly chosen electors. The liberalism of these arrangements was not surprising nor, when the thoroughly democratic complexion of the constituent assembly is considered, was there reason for astonishment over the articles by which the country renounced the most deeply imbedded features of its past and brought itself abreast of advanced modern opinion. The new constitution separated the church from the state, established complete freedom of religion, and, taking education out of the hands of the clergy, made it the exclusive prerogative of the state. By a succession of trenchant measures, and overnight as it were, the Catholic church lost the dominating position it had held in Spanish society and culture since the distant days of Ferdinand and Isabella.

The republic provided with a liberal constitution

Feeling that its work of renovation was as yet incomplete, the constituent assembly, after winding up the particular task for which it was summoned, continued to sit as a legislature and framed a series of laws intended to fortify the revolutionary enactments of the constitution. Thus, not only was all church property nationalized, that is, declared to be the property of the state, and all church schools closed, but an issue was attacked which had long been held to be the greatest single economic evil from which the country suffered, the great estates. By a sweeping measure the large, individually-owned landed properties, on which rested the wealth and prestige of the nobility, were confiscated, practically without compensation, with a view to their distribution among the landless peasantry. In thus laying the groundwork for a renovated Spain the cantankerous Catalonian issue could not be overlooked. Consequently, a bill was passed giving that restless and semi-foreign province the autonomy it had never ceased to demand.

Education taken out of the hands of the clergy and the great estates confiscated

Then a reaction set in. In accordance with what would seem to be a law of human nature it always does. In the parliamentary elections of 1933 there was a distinct swing to the right, and the unobstructed reign of radical republicanism was over. The government, in order to function at all, had not only to rest chiefly on the middle, or center, parties but,

before long, it found itself obliged to placate the Right by giving it a
measure of representation in the cabinet. To this threat the alarmed Left
responded with an avalanche of strikes and in scattered instances with
the burning of churches and monasteries. In preparation for new elections set for February, 1936, all the Left parties (Republicans, Socialists,
Syndicalists, Communists) formed a Popular Front and emerged from
the polls with a small majority.

Swing to
the right
met by
formation
of a Popular
Front
(1936)

By now, fear and suspicion had become the very air men breathed,
and the outbreak of civil war was momentarily expected. It came on
July 17, when the troops in Morocco raised the banner of revolt and
under the prompting of their officers were joined by most of the garrisons in Spain itself. In expectation of just such a mutiny, the government had sent the most conspicuous military leaders into exile. One of
them, General Francisco Franco, had been dispatched to the Canary
Islands. On hearing of the action of the troops in Morocco, he flew
thither by airplane and, taking over the command, transferred them to
Europe and became the head and front of the rebellion.

The army
revolt of
July, 1936

Deprived of its military arm, the republican government stared into a
black abyss. However, by superhuman efforts it improvised a Popular
Militia of workers and thereby saved from seizure the capital, Madrid,
and the industrial province of Catalonia, all-important because of its
ability to manufacture the implements of war. The essential nature of
the struggle now stood revealed before all the world. The army, representing the reactionary forces of church, nobility, and capitalist enterprise, was identified with fascism, whereas the republic stood for democracy, with an unmistakable leaning toward its more radical forms. This
confrontation of two diametrically opposed political doctrines drew the
attention of close and distant neighbors to the struggle and attracted volunteers from practically every country of the world to both contesting
parties.

The civil
war a con-
test between
fascism and
democracy

Much more important for the final outcome than these trickles of support was the course of action the great powers would decide to follow.
And here a striking difference at once appeared, for the two aggressor
states, Italy and Germany, fascist in temperament and sympathy, gave
all the help they could spare to General Franco, acknowledged champion
of a common cause, while Great Britain and France, from fear of the red
communist thread in the texture of Spanish democracy, stood aloof.
Russia alone among the anti-axis powers recognized the complete identity of its interest with that of the republic.

Attitude to
the civil war
of the great
powers

It was this international situation that decided the struggle. Distrust-
ful of the Spanish republic, France and Great Britain contented themselves with playing the embarrassed spectators of its long agony. Italy
and Germany, on the other hand, supplied General Franco with military

equipment and men (under the transparent pretense that they were "volunteers"), and in far greater quantity than Russia, which, on account of its great distance from the scene, could not get into convenient touch with the republicans. In spite of drawbacks the common people of Spain, insufficiently furnished with the instruments of war but drawing ever renewed strength from the well of liberty at which they drank, made a magnificent resistance. Not till January, 1939, did their main stronghold, brave Barcelona, fall. Madrid continued the losing fight a little longer, but in March was captured in its turn. The war came to an end with Franco and fascism in unchallenged possession.

The victory of General Franco and fascism, 1939

Among the first acts of the victors was to rescind all the vigorous reform legislation of the republic, more particularly the measures that canceled the privileges of the Catholic church and ordered the confiscation of the vast estates of the grandees. At the same time a thoroughgoing reorganization of Spain was carried through with Mussolini's Italy as model. A party, called the Falangist party, was set up in imitation of Mussolini's Fascist party and given the same monopolistic political position. Franco, of course, became the Falangist head and at the same time was acknowledged sole responsible chief of the state, under the Spanish equivalent of the word for leader, *Caudillo*.

Franco's regime modeled on Mussolini's

FATAL CONSEQUENCES OF THE SPANISH CIVIL WAR

Long before the Spanish civil war ended in a sweeping fascist victory, it had been demonstrated to the two fascist powers of Italy and Germany that democratic France and Great Britain were not prepared unreservedly to commit themselves either in behalf of the general democratic cause or of the imperiled status quo in Europe. It was Italy and Germany which had disturbed the status quo in the first place and which nursed more or less openly avowed plans to disturb it still more gravely in the future. Booking Franco's triumph as their triumph, they threw aside such cautions as had hitherto restrained them and impetuously pressed forward on the path of conquest. More particularly was this true of Hitler, who, after having contented himself in his uncertain beginnings with playing a supporting part to the older Mussolini's lead, now more and more assumed the lead himself in the swelling knowledge of his far greater striking power.

Franco's victory encourages Mussolini and Hitler

At this point a reminder of the strangely warped personality of Adolf Hitler is in order. Instead of being complicated and unfathomable, as some have declared it to be, it is simplicity itself as soon as we become aware that it owes its peculiar twist to its possessor's rejection of the nobler faculties of man, the faculties of mind and heart, in order to feed and magnify the purely animal faculty of will. With his nature thus nar-

rowed to a single passion Hitler lived for no other end than power, and
was bound to drive on and on along the power path until stopped by
some greater power than his own. Starting his public career with the
suppression, by the use of every weapon known to tyranny, of every
German will opposed to his, he provided for the continued elimination
of opponents by an all-powerful secret police, the Gestapo, and by its
prisons of nameless suffering and horror, the infamous concentration
camps. Himself an intemperate fanatic, he drew to himself individuals
of an identical mental stamp, and in those months in which he took the
final steps preliminary to a new world-struggle held counsel mainly with
three associates: the cold-blooded Himmler, chief of the Gestapo and of
the blindly subservient S.S. guards; Goebbels, the slippery and freely
prevaricating minister of propaganda; and Ribbentrop, the foreign minister, who believed that might alone ruled the earth and that right was
only a word. Inspired and counseled in this manner, the Führer inaugurated a series of aggressions which we shall now pass in review and
which ended by plunging the world into the gigantic struggles of World
War II.

GERMANY ANNEXES AUSTRIA

Since it was by his loud beating of the nationalist drum that Hitler
made his dictatorship acceptable to his people, he directed the earliest
measures that went beyond the casting-off of the shackles of Versailles
to the addition to the re-constituted Reich of German groups and regions
lying beyond its boundaries. Owing to accidents of history of both remote
and recent date, there were many of these detached regions, Austria
being easily the foremost. We have in Chapters 41 and 43 taken note of
how a Nazi party sprang up in Austria on the heels of the movement in
Germany, and how as early as 1934 it tried to seize the power at Vienna.
The putsch failed, and Hitler, on the lookout from across the border,
was reluctantly constrained to withhold his hand. Four years later, in
February, 1938, he considered the occasion favorable for a new assault on
Austrian independence and began action by inviting or, more correctly,
abruptly ordering Chancellor Schuschnigg to meet him at his Bavarian
mountain chalet near Berchtesgaden, just across the Austrian border.

As the result of an agitated meeting drawn out far into the night, the
Austrian premier was obliged to accede to the admission of a representation of Austrian Nazis into his cabinet. This sufficed to terminate the
exclusive Catholic party control which was the Schuschnigg system and
which was as totalitarian in principle as Hitler's own. In these circumstances the Austrian government became hopelessly split between
Schuschnigg and the chief Nazi cabinet member, Seyss-Inquart, and
since in their conflict Hitler from across the border backed Seyss-In-

quart, it was he who won out. On March 11, 1938, this agent of the Führer forced Schuschnigg to resign and, assuming the chancellorship himself, inaugurated his rule by inviting Hitler to send troops into Austria, nominally to preserve order but really to effect at long last that attachment (or *Anschluss*) of the lesser to the greater German state which had been a ceaselessly agitated political issue ever since the break-up of the Hapsburg monarchy in 1918.

As the German soldiers marched down the Danube valley, wildly cheered by the inhabitants, Hitler, who attended his army, must have expanded with a deep inner satisfaction, for he was returning to the country of his birth, which he had never ceased to claim for an eventual Greater Germany. On March 14, at Vienna, he proclaimed the end of Austria as a separate state and experienced on that occasion the further pleasure of noting how Europe, though profoundly shaken by his daring stroke, viewed it, nonetheless, with folded arms. True, France and Great Britain lodged a formal protest at Berlin, but failed to follow up their words with deeds. They were, however, sufficiently alarmed to restore their one-time close partnership by initiating conversations between their respective general staffs which looked forward to the co-ordination of their armed forces in the event of war. The word went the round at Paris and London that Hitler should not be permitted to spring such another surprise. Yet that was precisely what he did do, for, with no more delay than is required to recover breath after a brief exertion, the Führer prepared to attack the next victim on his list, neighboring Czechoslovakia.

The incorporation of Austria silently accepted by France and Great Britain

GERMANY ANNEXES THE SUDETENLAND

Czechoslovakia shared with the Reich a long boundary line, along which dwelt some 3,500,000 Czechoslovak citizens of German nationality. Since they resided in the main along the Sudeten mountains, they were called Sudeten Germans, and the area they inhabited Sudetenland. Exactly as in the case of the Austrians, the furious Nazi nationalism effected an early lodgment among them in the form of a Nazi party, which presently badgered the government at Prague with a demand for self-government. Following Hitler's resounding triumph in near-by Austria, the Nazi party succeeded in gathering into its fold the larger part of the Sudeten Germans and, thus strengthened, insisted on the grant of autonomy without further delay. So deafeningly did the Berlin radio, operated by Propaganda Minister Goebbels, echo the demand that the government of President Beneš became alarmed and opened negotiations with the complainants. The voice of Goebbels left no doubt in the president's mind that, should he refuse to deal with the Sudetens, he

The Sudeten Germans and their demand of home rule

would with deadly certainty draw down Hitler's thunder on his head. Faced with this prospect, he naturally inquired of his allies, France and Russia, whether they were prepared to see him through his pressing troubles. Both acknowledged their obligation to give him their support, but France in particular insisted that every effort should first be made to avoid war by conceding to the Sudetens the home rule for which they were clamoring.

The hesitant attitude of France was due to Great Britain, which was under no treaty obligations to Czechoslovakia and which strongly objected to being drawn into a general war by an action taken on the sole responsibility of its ally, France. Prime Minister Chamberlain was cool to the predicament of Czechoslovakia because it lay beyond the range of Britain's immediate interests, and also because he was of the opinion that there was some justice in the Sudeten claim. If by its satisfaction the war clouds that had gathered over Europe would be again dispersed, he was willing to bring pressure to bear on the Slav state, regardless of the injury it might suffer from his action. In short, Chamberlain was for placating, nominally the Sudetens, but really Hitler with a policy of concession that his opponents sneeringly called "appeasement" and that has left a stain on the reputation he had earned by a long life of public service. His error, for he certainly was in error, lay in his radical misjudgment of Hitler, whom he took to be a man governed, like himself, by reason and not a tormented soul in the grip of an irrational will.

With Britain committed to appeasement the issue entered a new phase, wherein Hitler openly replaced the Sudetens in the argument and, encouraged by Britain's tacit support, repeatedly stepped up his demands on the government at Prague. In September he boldly shifted his claim from Sudeten autonomy to self-determination, equivalent in its consequences to separation, and when the Czechoslovak government, its patience exhausted, replied with mobilization, the so-dreaded general war was brought within a burning fuse's length of explosion. But again Chamberlain strained every nerve to avoid the catastrophe by extinguishing the fuse. He twice flew to Germany for a personal interview with Hitler, only to find that the insatiable Führer had increased his demands beyond what even the appeasing prime minister was prepared to urge the Czechoslovak government to accept. It was the last-minute intervention with Hitler by his partner, Mussolini, that saved the situation. The Duce persuaded his fellow dictator by telephone call from Rome to submit the issue to a conference of the responsible heads of Germany, France, Italy, and Great Britain. Accordingly, on September 29, 1938, Hitler, Mussolini, Daladier, and Chamberlain held a momentous meeting in the city of Munich, and when it was concluded, Hitler had been handed the

Great Britain adopts a policy of "appeasement"

The Sudeten crisis ends in the Munich surrender of September 29, 1938

Sudetenland with no further concession on his part than to conduct a somewhat less precipitate seizure than he had originally threatened.

With the four Olympians in agreement, there was nothing for feeble Czechoslovakia to do but unresistingly to permit Germany to take over the extensive Sudeten borderland. Nor was that the end of calamity: two other neighbors of Czechoslovakia, Poland and Hungary, their appetite aroused by the German success, put in an appearance with a demand for a seat at the feast and had perforce to be placated, Poland by the cession of the coal district of Teschen, Hungary by a long strip of southern Slovakia. Weakened by these amputations and deserted by its allies, Czechoslovakia was doomed to disintegrate. In order to quiet the complaints of its two eastern provinces of Slovakia and Ruthenia, they were granted the autonomy they asked for, with the result that what was left of the once well-integrated state assumed the form of a loose federation. *Czechoslovakia transformed into a loose federation*

However, even the liberal autonomy with which they were endowed failed to satisfy the Slovakian and Ruthenian diets, and with Hitler's consent they, on March 14, 1939, declared their independence. It was not the resolute President Beneš who witnessed these latest disasters, for he had resigned his post and left the country on the heels of the Munich verdict. On the very day of the Slovakian and Ruthenian declarations of independence, Hacha, the timid successor of Beneš, was summoned to Berlin, and there, under pressure which can be left to the imagination, agreed that what was left of the former flourishing state should become a part of Germany under the title of Protectorate of Bohemia and Moravia. Although provision was made for the retention by the Protectorate of its own government, it is plain that it became for all practical purposes a German province. *The Protectorate of Bohemia and Moravia absorbed by Germany, March 14, 1939*

MEMEL AND DANZIG

To these head-over-heel developments the rest of Europe had nothing to say. Having abandoned Czechoslovakia on the fateful Munich occasion, the two western powers were obliged to look on at its destruction in a stunned silence. But Hitler's crest swelled higher than ever. Within a week following the absorption of Bohemia-Moravia he notified Lithuania that he expected it to hand back the Memel territory it had appropriated at the close of World War I: and cowed Lithuania promptly complied. Thus were the German borderlands incorporated bit by bit in the Greater Germany constituting Hitler's nationalist dream until only Danzig remained outside, politically a self-governing city but economically incorporated in the state of Poland. *Memel recovered March, 1939*

Some years before, Danzig had come into the control of the local

Nazi party and was now clamoring vociferously for its reintegration with Germany. In approaching Poland about Danzig Hitler could therefore rest his case on the principle of self-determination. But closely tied up with Danzig was the more complicated issue of the Corridor. This area, fully incorporated in Poland by the Treaty of Versailles, cut off the province of East Prussia from the rest of Germany. Consequently, when in April, 1939, the Führer formulated his demands on Poland, he asked not only that Poland consent to the return of Danzig to the Reich but also that the Reich be granted an extraterritorial east-west highway and railway line across the Corridor, in other words, a narrow German corridor across the broader Polish one. On May 5 Poland rejected this double demand, and the situation became deadlocked.

Great
Britain and
France give
Poland their
unqualified
support

It may be doubted that the government at Warsaw would have taken the firm stand it did, if, in sharp contrast to what had happened in the case of Czechoslovakia the year before, Great Britain and France had not encouraged the Poles to stand up against Hitler and given solemn commitments to come to their aid in case Germany answered with a call to arms. Both western powers were of one mind on the issue, but Britain rather than France took the lead because Prime Minister Chamberlain had got over his delusion about Hitler and now reacted strongly against his former policy of appeasement. Even before Hitler in April had dispatched his demands to Warsaw, Chamberlain, certain that Germany's next move would be against its eastern neighbor, had joined Prime Minister Daladier of France in a public statement to the effect that Poland enjoyed their inalterable united backing. Shortly after, but still before the Führer had communicated his precise proposals to the Poles, Britain solemnized the obligation it had assumed toward the Slav state by a formal alliance. Essentially, therefore, the deadlock between Germany and Poland was a deadlock between Germany and the two western powers, and inevitably the thought rose to the surface in all three cabinets: What about the great unpledged eastern neighbor of Poland, what about Russia?

THE RUSSO-GERMAN NONAGGRESSION PACT

Russia
courted
by both
Germany
and the
two western
powers

Throughout the spring and summer months of this frenziedly agitated year the Polish-German issue hung fire, while the three main contestants hotly wooed Russia in their respective interests. If at this point we let our attention swing to Russia and give due consideration to its total position in the world, noting particularly the policy it had been recently pursuing, we shall incline to the opinion that its choice would be swiftly made and land it with all its resources and unspent energy in the camp of the western allies. And yet this did not happen for reasons which, although not publicly avowed, are easily deducible from the actual, as distinct from the ideological, Russian situation. The clear-sighted dictator of the U.S.S.R. would without doubt reckon Nazi Germany to be the more dangerous enemy, but never for a moment would he think of capitalist France and Great Britain in the light of friends. Moreover, being a consummate realist, sentiment would not figure in his calculations, and what alone would weigh with him would be the measurable material advantages with which the rival contestants angled for his favor.

We need not follow the protracted bargaining at Moscow, of which little became public knowledge beyond the fact that it was dark and devious. The crux of the matter in all probability was that France and Britain either would not or could not grant to Russia that security along the vulnerable Baltic coast line which Stalin insisted would not be his short of the surrender to him of the control of Finland, Latvia, and Estonia. An accommodation with Germany, on the other hand, meant that Russia would be at least temporarily guaranteed against attack, and that, with the coming war confined to the west, the U.S.S.R. would conserve its strength while the three fighting powers would be slowly exhausting themselves to a point which would leave the U.S.S.R. the arbiter of the situation. The upshot was that Russia dumbfounded the whole western world when on August 23, 1939, it signed a nonaggression pact with Germany, by the terms of which it was agreed that in case either of the contracting parties was attacked the other would remain neutral. From subsequent events it is reasonably safe to conjecture that Russia was won over by additional inducements, among them the promise of a free hand in the Baltic states of Finland, Latvia, and Estonia, as well as a solid slice of Poland, should that country come into German hands.

The Russo-German nonaggression pact of August 23, 1939

The treaty of August 23 was a diplomatic triumph for Hitler. He might now hope that, in view of the inability of France and Britain to come at once and directly to the aid of Poland, they would abandon that state as twelve months before they had abandoned Czechoslovakia. If this was his expectation, he met with disappointment, for, promptly on hearing of the Russo-German pact, the two western powers in the most explicit manner confirmed their original intention of standing by their Slav ally. Hitler might now, in order to avoid war, have backed down in his turn, but that was contrary to his headstrong, reckless nature. On consulting his general staff he was apprised that Poland could be completely crushed in a matter of weeks. This, then, he resolved to do with the further thought in mind that when, with his foot on prostrate Poland, he would urge the western powers to call off a war which was not directed against them, they would see the reasonableness of his

France and Great Britain resolutely stand by Poland

statement and make peace. The war was undoubtedly a hazard, but no worth-while success, he might argue, is ever achieved without risk.

As always in crises of parallel dimensions, there were some last-minute attempts, especially on the part of Britain, to turn the Führer from his purpose. They were bound to fail, and in the early dawn of September 1, 1939, the first elements of the German army crossed the Polish border. The answer of France and Great Britain was to dispatch an ultimatum to Berlin calling for an immediate German withdrawal; and when no action followed, on September 3 they came to the support of their ally by declaring war on the invader. Thus, with a breathless world as spectator did the curtain rise on the vast tragedy recorded in history as World War II.

Hitler invades Poland, September 1, 1939

45

WORLD WAR II (1939-1945)

THIS HISTORY, conceived as and titled A History of Europe from the Reformation to the Present Day, did not fail to take note of events contemporary with our starting point by which its scope was extended beyond Europe to the newly disclosed continents of Asia and America. We were made aware not only that these vast regions straightway became a stake in the savage power conflict among the European states but also that, by a development which, in the perspective of the centuries, proved to be of far greater significance, they attracted European trade and colonization. By these activities a movement was inaugurated which, by gathering strength with each passing generation, was bound to promote the assimilation of the invaded areas to the pattern of thought and action familiar to the readers of this book as Western civilization.

The expansion of Europe and of its civilization

The following up of these leads during the centuries after the Discoveries necessitated our recording developments of vast importance with which it may be permitted summarily to refresh our memory. We took account of the uninterrupted increase of trans-oceanic trade and colonization, of the outbreak of waxingly ferocious wars over these related interests among the bitterly competitive European powers, of the emergence of vigorous colonies of settlers in both North and South America (though not in Asia), and, finally, of the throwing off by these colonists in the late eighteenth and early nineteenth century of the yoke of their respective mother countries and of their stepping forth as independent sovereign communities.

Leading consequences of Europe's advance into the non-European world

Of these resolute new-world infants the former British colonies, lifted from the font as the United States of North America, reached a vigorous manhood considerably in advance of the former Spanish and Portuguese colonies to their south. However, both groups alike soon found themselves reluctantly sucked into the European power system. This followed inescapably from the fact that vastly improved communications, due to such startling inventions as the steamboat, the railroad, the telegraph, and the telephone, had the effect of so greatly shrinking distance that the once remote countries of the western hemisphere were brought into a formerly unimaginable proximity to Europe's vital energy. If we now further note

How inventions began to contract the world

855

that in the wake of their eager penetration by European traders the ancient Asiatic empires of the eastern hemisphere were also drawn closer to Europe and were, besides, gradually honeycombed with Western science and technology, we are confronted with a global situation which, as the nineteenth century merged into the twentieth, filled every intelligent observer with a lively sense of a world-wide transformation.

World union foreshadowed

Of this transformation the central and outstanding significance was that all the peoples of the earth were in process of being drawn within the framework of a single culture. Indefinitely continued, this process could have no other issue than that the once narrowly bounded Western civilization should extend its geographic range until it had become universal and that the once stubbornly distinct states scattered over the earth's surface should be obliged, despite a settled reluctance to give up their historical isolation, to enter upon negotiations looking to some kind of international association. In its essence such an association, if ever realized, would be a reflection of the common civilization at which through the slow-grinding action of the mills of Time they had arrived.

The League of Nations (1919), first fruit of the emerging world sentiment

When the unappeased and apparently unappeasable divisions among the European powers precipitated World War I, small enlightened groups of men throughout the world, shaken to their marrow by the blazing conflagration, became convinced that an organization pledged to the preservation of peace and unity could not any longer be put off. By their combined influence the first step in this direction was taken, and as soon as hostilities had ended, the League of Nations was set up. Unfortunately the League was not endowed with sufficient authority to impose peace on resolute violators. Consequently, the unreconciled quarrels of the great powers led to the outbreak of World War II, which is the point to which our narrative had been carried with the close of the preceding chapter.

Content of the three concluding chapters of this book

It is therefore the war itself, extending from 1939 to 1945, which is treated in this chapter. The next chapter undertakes to point out the most recent advances of our Western civilization and should serve to clarify its general character at the moment of its entering on its culminating universal phase. The third and final chapter of this concluding group of chapters concerns itself with the postwar period, which at the time of writing covers the five-year stretch from 1945 through the first nine months of 1950. Unavoidably held to a selective treatment, our exposition will revolve mainly around the renewal of the effort made at the close of the earlier world conflict to create a world federation dedicated to amity and peace. Our leading purpose will be to set forth the reasons why the new federation proved itself to be as feeble as, and even feebler than, its predecessor, and why, in spite of a few minor advances toward a general pacification on the part of the victors in the war, they have shock-ingly and disastrously failed to agree on the terms on which they are willing to bring the struggle to a close and, at long last, to end the racking agony of World War II.

In the course of the developments traced by the three final chapters of this book a change in the distribution of organized political power has occurred which is impossible to exaggerate: Europe, mother and nurse of Western civilization, has been deposed from its more than one-thousand-year-old rule! By the year 1950 it requires a blind man not to see that after the monstrous scourging of the late and, let us not forget, still continuing war there remain only two world powers, the United States of North America and the Union of Soviet Socialist Republics, identical on the score of authority with the single state of Russia. And now let us not fail to note that these two remaining and solely dominating powers lie outside the historical bounds of Europe. With the amazing transformation of the world picture represented by this novelty a general history which, like the present one, has from the outset focused attention on Europe and traced a political and cultural development, which after ten centuries culminated in the unforeseeable event of Europe's abdication in favor of America and Asia, comes to its logical conclusion. *(margin: Europe loses its leadership to America and Asia)*

From World War II onward a general history must inescapably embrace the whole globe and accept as its leading concern the adjustment to the ruling global viewpoint of the approximately fifty states still rated as separate sovereign units. With its acceptance of World War II as its starting point, it will be obliged, by way of introduction to its global theme, to trace the numerous influences and agencies which have co-operated to shape the new and revolutionary world-embracing approach. Passing on from there, the general history fashioned according to the indicated, vastly broadened viewpoint will then take up the current tragic world discord, the solution of which is beyond human penetration and rests with the inscrutable fates. To this vast subject matter, co-extensive with the globe itself, the present history, concerned with and dedicated to the vanished primacy of Europe, cannot either profitably or logically be extended. *(margin: A general history dedicated to the primacy of Europe ends with the loss of that primacy)*

In now taking up World War II three preliminary statements will help to clarify the writer's procedure. The first refers to the uniquely devastating destruction wrought by both sides; the other two define the unavoidably selective treatment imposed by the overwhelming mass of events constituting the unabridged record of the world-encircling conflict. *(margin: Three statements pertinent to the author's procedure)*

As to the first statement, it calls attention to an aspect of the war of which every reader is almost frighteningly aware and of which he is never for a moment permitted to lose consciousness: the warfare of World War II was mechanized warfare. While this was already true of World War I, the degree of mechanization in the later conflict was on so much vaster a scale as to give the earlier struggle the look of an apprentice job. It follows that the decision in isolated combats, and by so much more in sustained campaigns, depended on the total weight of armor the opponents were able to discharge against each other. Here lies the explanation of Hitler's sweeping early successes. He had for years been piling up the modern mechanized implements of war and fell with them on opponents who either did not have them or had them in insufficient quantities. The novel tactic he was able to employ received the startlingly descriptive name of *Blitzkrieg*. Plainly and unarguably the need both of Hitler's actual and of his potential opponents was to bring their own war output, first, abreast of his, and finally, so far beyond it that by the blitzkrieg in reverse they would be able to smother him and his armament under the overwhelming mass of their own.

Of the two selective procedures which will characterize—and limit—our story of the war, the first is a fairly obvious one, since it is imposed by the self-evident necessity of reducing our narrative to the outstanding and decisive actions, that is, to a presentation of the war in bare, skeletal form. Our second selective procedure will consist in making more of the American participation in the struggle than a strictly objective treatment would justify. Far from being prompted by an ill-judged and inflated patriotism, the American emphasis stems from the fact that this book has from the start been directed to the American college student who, while bowing to the necessity of a painfully contracted account of the world-shaking struggle, may yet in all fairness demand to have his country's participation in the greatest war of history set forth with sufficient detail to bring it into clear intelligibility.

We have learned that the war began on September 1, 1939, with the invasion of Poland by the German armies and that on September 3 Great Britain and France met their obligation to their Slav ally by declaring war on Germany. Two weeks later, when Poland was already tottering, Russia invaded Poland from the east to secure a share of the Polish spoils in accordance with the German-Russian neutrality treaty of August 23. When, toward the end of September, diplomatic representatives of Germany and Russia sat down to partition Poland between them, Polish resistance had, except for a few pockets, come to an end militarily. Dominant in eastern Poland, Russia automatically became dominant also throughout the eastern Baltic, and without more ado compelled the small states of Latvia, Estonia, and Lithuania to accept her control. On attempting to enforce an identical submission on Finland, the Moscow rulers were rebuffed and, on November 30, levied war on this recalcitrant little country. Thus ended the year 1939.

The first notable event of the year 1940 was that the Finns, realizing the hopelessness of their struggle, on March 13 submitted to their great Slav adversary. A month later, on April 9, Germany sprang her second blitzkrieg by invading Denmark and Norway and effecting their complete occupation before the month was out. And hardly had the two Scandinavian states been converted into a vast outer bulwark of the Reich when, on May 10, the blitzkrieg was discharged for the third time by the simultaneous invasion of Holland, Belgium, Luxemburg, and France. It was a success as swift as it was general. The Dutch army surrendered on May 15, with the Belgian army following suit two weeks later. The British army, which had rushed to the aid of the Belgians, was obliged to fall back to the coast at Dunkirk, where it made a memorable stand until it was evacuated to the homeland at the price of the total loss of its equipment.

More startling even than these successes was the knockout blow administered to France. The French had anticipated and prepared for a defensive campaign to be sustained by a vast system of border fortifications, called the Maginot line. When the German blitz broke through the French defenses at Sedan and then plunged westward all the way to the coast, the French campaign was completely disrupted. Resistance broke down at point after point and ended altogether when, on June 22, France abandoned the war by signing an armistice with Germany. The victor country was left in occupation of the northern half of France, while a French government, submissive to Germany, was set up in the provincial city of Vichy with the famous warrior, Marshal Pétain, at its head.

In the hope of a belated advantage to be gained for himself from the fall of France, Dictator Mussolini, on June 10, declared war on the defeated country (and of course also on its ally, Britain) and, by an armistice signed with France some two weeks later, was empowered to occupy a narrow French Alpine zone adjoining the Italian border.

Great Britain behind the protective ditch of the English channel was logically Hitler's next victim. But either because he was seized with indecision or, more probably, because he lacked the appropriate equipment of airplanes and ships, the Führer hesitated. More than six weeks passed before he embarked (August 8) on a program which aimed at reducing the island kingdom by bombardment from the air. Great damage to cities attended by heavy loss of life followed without shaking English resolution. Presently the Royal Air Force, called the R.A.F. for short, developed fighter planes which, handled by expert pilots, successfully destroyed or turned back the German bombers. In exasperation Hitler switched, in September, from daylight to night bombing, for which the British were

Blitzkrieg against Denmark and Norway, April, 1940; against Holland, Belgium, France in May

France yields to Germany in June, 1940

Italy declares war on France and Britain on June 10

Failure of the attempt to reduce Britain from the air

ill-prepared, owing to lack of anti-aircraft artillery. However, this and every other deficiency was by dogged determination made good; the German attack gradually weakened; and early in the following year was to all intents abandoned. Britain had stopped the German march of conquest.

Meanwhile, through the plunge of the Italians into the war, the Mediterranean had become an area of conflict. On September 13, 1940, an Italian army, assembled in Libya, invaded Egypt and, a month later, another Italian army invaded Greece. But neither of these offensives prospered. The Italian advance into Greece had hardly begun when the Greeks successfully turned it back and pursued the routed enemy all the way into Italian-held Albania. As for the British, it was not until their forces had been assembled in superior number at strategically selected points that they resorted to the offensive in their turn. On December 11 they fell upon the Italian army which had crossed the Egyptian border and annihilated it.

An event of September 27 may not be omitted from the record, is indeed important enough to merit a separate paragraph. On that day the three aggressor states of Germany, Italy, and Japan signed a close military and economic alliance. Thus ended the year 1940.

On April 6, 1941, a British army entered Addis Ababa, the capital of Ethiopia, thereby in effect sounding the knell of the Italian African empire. However, the colony of coastal Libya remained an obstacle to the British advance from Egypt, not because the badly shaken Italians developed unexpected strength but because Hitler sent a large tank force, the so-called *Afrika Korps,* across the Mediterranean to help them out. A checkered North-African campaign followed with the British thrusting repeatedly into Libya, only to be driven back on each occasion to their starting point in Egypt.

On the very day (April 6), on which the British completed their conquest of Ethiopia, Germany opened an attack of the by-now familiar blitz variety against Yugoslavia and Greece. She took this course because only through the Balkans could she come to immediate grips with her British foe in the Mediterranean area. Yugoslavia was quickly overrun, as was also Greece, together with the highly strategic island of Crete. By virtue of this German drive the Balkan peninsula as well as the whole eastern Mediterranean Sea became a secondary but still exceedingly important theater of combat.

But a vaster and far more significant theater than either the Balkans or the Mediterranean rose into view to the startled surprise of the whole world when on June 22, 1941, Hitler, unwilling to concede to the Russians the Dardanelles, which they named as the price of their continued partnership, broke with them and launched an invasion of Russian territory. With this eastward push the ever widening conflict was extended to embrace the enormous stretches of eastern Europe and northern Asia included within the Union of Soviet Socialist Republics. Sharply on the heel of this assault, Hungary, Rumania, and Finland declared war on the U.S.S.R., thereby revealing themselves as satellite states of the Nazis. All through the summer and autumn the drive into Russia by Germany and its dependents continued, marked by an uninterrupted advance in the teeth of stubborn Russian resistance. By the time winter arrived the invaders, on the one hand, were laying siege to an all but completely enveloped Leningrad and, on the other, had pushed to within sight of the towering spires and cupolas of Moscow. However, while gravely threatening these two leading cities of the enemy, they could not quite break through to their goal and take over these absolutely vital enemy centers.

At this point the third aggressor power, Japan, decided that the time had come to enter the constantly broadening struggle by launching an attack on the United States of America. However, before this event can be brought into intelligible focus the attitude of the United States government and people to the war calls for examination.

Japan decides to enter the war

HOW THE UNITED STATES WAS DRAWN INTO THE WAR

The outbreak of the war found the government of the United States committed to a policy of non-participation by a Neutrality Act passed by Congress in 1937. It owed its passage to an isolationist sentiment which had steadily deepened in the country, especially in the Middle West, in consequence of the heaped disappointments attendant on the aftermath of World War I. In the hope of keeping the country from ever again being drawn into the implacable animosities of Europe, the Neutrality Act went the length of forbidding the sale of munitions to any and every country engaged in war. It was through the sale of munitions to Great Britain and her allies by our money-minded manufacturers that Congress persuaded itself that the United States had been sucked into World War I.

The U. S. committed to neutrality at the outbreak of the war

Immediately on the outbreak of the new war President Franklin D. Roosevelt made up his mind that the states attacked by Hitler would, in order to survive, have to be supplied with American arms, and patiently set about weakening the Neutrality Act with the view to its final total removal from the statute book. Public opinion, alarmed and outraged by Nazi aggression, came vociferously to his support and enabled him to push through Congress a succession of measures which, while gradually nullifying the Neutrality Act, at the same time cleared the ground for the eventual entrance of the United States into the war on the side of the tottering democracies.

Movement to emasculate the Neutrality Act launched by President Roosevelt

Of these presidential preparatory measures it will suffice to enumerate three. (1) The so-called Cash-and-Carry Act, adopted November 4, 1939,

Three
measures by
which the
U. S. pre-
pared to
replace
neutrality
with par-
ticipation
permitted belligerents to buy munitions in the United States, provided they paid spot-cash for them and carried them home in their own ships. (2) Besides thus relaxing the rigors of the Neutrality Act in the interest of the embattled democracies, the President made himself the impassioned advocate of home preparedness. From his vigorously sounded alarm over the terrors of the German military machine there resulted in September, 1940, the Selective Service Act, which for the first time in history summoned the people to arms in time of peace. That the mobilization might reach as impressive an effectiveness as possible Congress in successive bills authorized expenditures to the tune of $17,000,000,000 for the most up-to-the-minute equipment for warfare on land, sea, and in the air. (3) Before long, with the rapid exhaustion of British credit, the Cash-and-Carry Act failed to fulfill its purpose of supplying Britain with the enormous mass of arms it needed to sustain the struggle. Consequently, the President moved on to the advocacy of direct aid, which then, under the elastic name of Lend-Lease, in March, 1941, became the law of the land.

The mag-
nitude of
Lend-Lease
It is no more than the bare truth to say that Lend-Lease put the total resources of the United States at the disposal, first, of Great Britain and, later, of all countries at war with the aggressor powers of Germany, Italy, and Japan. An initial appropriation of $7,000,000,000 manifested the more-than-readiness of Congress to take over the role for which the President had cast the country and which he popularized with the picturesque phrase of "arsenal of democracy." Let it be here noted by anticipation that the American munificence continued to be poured out through the following years and that by the time the war ended Lend-Lease had soared to the fabulous figure of $50,000,000,000. Of this immense contribution to the common war-chest 65 per cent was channeled to Great Britain, 23 per cent to the U.S.S.R.

Growing
friction
between
Japan and
the U. S.
because of
Japan's at-
tempt to
conquer
China
While these measures of financial support undoubtedly augured the ultimate plunge of the United States into the conflict, more immediately contributory to that result was the growing friction with Japan. This Asiatic island-power had in the year 1937 embarked on a war of conquest against its mainland neighbor, China, but, though driving deep into Chinese territory, had not been able to bring its invasion to a successful termination. The western powers, and especially the United States, had never ceased to encourage by the grant of credit and weapons the head of the Chinese government, Generalissimo Chiang Kai-shek, in his resistance to the vastly superior armed might of Japan. Then, when on the outbreak of World War II the European powers became so absorbingly involved with one another at home that distant Asia sank to a level of secondary importance, the Tokyo government achieved a relative freedom of action and was moved to embark on a policy of vast ambition directed at nothing less than the complete mastery of eastern Asia.

Since Japan to its misfortune (and sorrow) was only skimpily endowed with natural resources, it was clear that it could not commit itself to so headlong a policy of expansion without the assurance of an uninterrupted flow of such indispensable military commodities as gasoline, oil, scrap-metal, steel, and machine tools from the only country capable of furnishing them, the United States. This flow the Washington government, as soon as the extravagant ambitions of Japan became apparent, undertook sharply to reduce with consequent vehement remonstrances on the part of the Nipponese. When negotiations, which became ever more exacerbated, brought no agreement, war loomed as the unavoidable outcome and on December 7, 1941, duly exploded by way of a lightning stroke delivered by the Mikado's enraged government. On that day a wave of almost two hundred airplanes suddenly pierced the morning haze over Pearl Harbor in the Hawaiian Islands to release their bombs on the American fleet lying quietly at anchor without adequate or at least adequately functioning protection.

Japan ends negotiations by an air attack on Pearl Harbor, December 7, 1941

The inflicted damage was shattering: some eight battleships and a large number of airplanes lined up like sitting ducks on a nearby airfield were either totally destroyed or put indefinitely out of commission. Electrically aroused by the terrific blow, the United States, promptly joined by Great Britain, declared war on Japan the next day. Three days later, obedient to their tripartite pact of the previous year, Germany and Italy answered with a declaration of war against the United States. Therewith the struggle had achieved its widest expansion: it had become global, with Germany, Italy, and Japan constituting one party to the world-embracing conflict and the remaining major powers of Great Britain, Russia, and the United States the other.

The U. S. declares war on Japan. The war becomes global

Simultaneously with its surprise attack on the fleet of the United States at Pearl Harbor, Japan launched its long-prepared offensive against the adjoining Asiatic territories. Notwithstanding the stiff defense put up by the insufficient American army in the Philippines, following a memorable last stand in the Bataan peninsula the islands fell to the invaders. At the same time a powerful Japanese army drove down the China coast and, after capturing British Hong Kong, pressed on with amazing speed through the all but impenetrable jungles of Burma and the Malay peninsula to the great British naval base at Singapore. Hopelessly isolated, Singapore capitulated on February 15, 1942.

Japan conquers the Philippines and the Asiatic coast from Hong Kong to Singapore

It was now the turn of the Dutch East Indies. Between January and March, Sumatra, Borneo, Celebes, Java, Bali, Timor, and the northern coast of New Guinea were overrun with a speed that left the allied world aghast.

Conquest of the Dutch East Indies

It did not seem at all unlikely that the ever forward-pressing Japanese would next extend their operations to Australia and India, when two blows

fell from the recovered United States navy which effectively canceled
their plans. In May, 1942, a heavy concentration of Japanese vessels in the
Coral Sea, intended to cover a descent on Australia, was signally defeated;
a month later an even larger Japanese fleet was turned from an attempted
landing operation on Midway Island by the loss of four aircraft carriers
together with their invaluable complement of airplanes.

> The Japanese advance halted by two naval victories by the U. S.

With these two capital victories the offensive in the Pacific began to
pass to the United States, which single-handed and without allied aid,
except for that of Australia, took over the war in this largest of the world's
oceans. With the crushing double blow to enemy naval power, the plan
could now be entertained of again wresting their island conquests from
the Japanese; and the first step toward its fulfillment was taken when the
navy, spearheaded by regiments of specially trained marines, undertook to
capture the Solomon Islands by a hazardous landing operation on Guadalcanal.

> The offensive passes to the U. S. First operation at Guadalcanal

THE OFFENSIVE PASSES TO THE ALLIES IN THE
THREE MAIN THEATERS

Simultaneously with the seizure of the offensive in the Pacific by the
American navy as evidenced by the attack on Guadalcanal, the offensive
in northern Africa passed to the troops of Great Britain supplemented
by those of the United States and, most amazing of all, it passed also
to the invaded, hard-pressed Russians. However, these last two happy
turns of fortune did not occur until after a succession of deeply dis-
heartening events in the earlier months of the 1942 season.

> In the course of the 1942 campaign the offensive passes to the allies

Let us take the African theater first. We recorded on p. 860 how the
early British rush of victory over the Italians was checked on Hitler's
dispatching the Afrika Korps to the support of his demoralized ally.
Under the command of a German, General Rommel, the united German-
Italian forces succeeded, in the spring of 1942, in severely defeating the
British and driving them back into Egypt. At El Alamein, not far from
the great port-city of Alexandria, the retreating forces at length made a
stand and dug themselves in. Here at Alexandria, through many months,
they assembled every kind of military equipment, more particularly the
latest and most powerful type of armored tank. Then, when in October
a calculated superiority of weapons had been attained, the British under
General Montgomery launched an attack of such violence that it all but
crushed their stunned opponents. Only by precipitate flight westward
across the parched and burning desert did Rommel save the remnant of
his troops and their equipment.

> Egypt: the decisive British victory at El Alamein, October, 1942

While making ready for the stroke at El Alamein, British headquarters
had taken counsel with its American counterpart and together the two

staffs had resolved to combine with the El Alamein offensive a landing
in force on the African coast in Morocco and Algeria. With remarkably
exact timing this action was sprung on the surprised Nazis in November
under the supreme command of an American, General Eisenhower. In
almost the turning of a hand an army of British and Americans to the
number of several hundred thousand men was landed on the coast and
entrusted with the task of pushing eastward with a view to snuffing out
between them and the westward-marching British under General Montgomery the remnant of Rommel's Afrika Korps together with such reinforcements as had been rushed to its support across the Mediterranean.
By the time the Christmas bells of 1942 rang out their message of good
cheer around the world this operation had gone forward so auspiciously
that its ultimate success had become assured.

British-American invasion of North Africa, autumn, 1942

In turning next to Russia, we observe that the early months of the
year 1942 unloaded a fresh crop of perils on that harassed country, for
in June the Germans, mustering their as yet unexhausted reserves,
launched their second offensive. It was aimed in a southerly and southeasterly direction, led to the capture of the great fortress of Sebastopol in
the Crimea, and was not stopped until it had reached the industrial city
of Stalingrad on the Volga River. But there, following uninterrupted
fighting of the grimmest conceivable sort, the invaders were so weakened
that in the month of November the steadily strengthened Russians were
able to launch a counter-offensive. It made irresistible headway and ended
in a strangling envelopment of the enemy. Long before the calendar year
had run its course, it had become apparent to all the world that the Russians had scored an immense victory, although it was not until February
2, 1943, that the beaten remnant of a once magnificent German army
vanished from the scene by laying down its arms.

The second invasion of Russia (1942) ends disastrously for Germany at Stalingrad

THE ALLIED OFFENSIVE OF 1943 IN THE
THREE MAIN THEATERS

The successes gained by the allies toward the end of 1942 inspired
them to follow up their advantage with redoubled energy. But before
detailing their achievements on the three main scenes of action, it is
indispensable to take account of an event which cannot be too brilliantly
highlighted. In February, 1943, the vastly enlarged air forces of Britain
and the United States began a devastating "round-the-clock" bombing
of Germany and German-occupied Europe. The action proved that the
allies had gained air supremacy and could plan and execute at will a
campaign directed at the systematic destruction of communications and
industrial centers essential to the feeding of the German military machine.

The "round-the-clock" bombing of Germany begins February, 1943

In the course of this and the two following years these vital nuclei suffered tremendous losses, and, with the deepening of the savagery inseparable from every prolonged struggle, the bombardment from the air was aimed before long not merely at the industrial installations but at the urban residential areas as well. Hardly a German town, great or small, escaped the rain of ruin and by the time the war came to an end many scores of them had been substantially reduced to rubble. At the same time the allies, now relatively safe from German bombardment, were able greatly to intensify their own production of war materials. Especially was this true of the United States, which by the close of the year here treated was pouring out more war goods than its own allies and Germany put together.

Adoption of obliteration tactics against German cities

In attending first, among the three offensives, to the landing undertaken in the Pacific theater at Guadalcanal, we note that this turned out a hard nut to crack and that it occupied the Americans many weary months. The conduct of the war on this vast sheet of water had been entrusted to the efficient hands of General MacArthur and Admiral Nimitz, who proceeded energetically and systematically but without immediate spectacular results. A main effort was directed at picking off Japanese merchant shipping and destroying such elements of the weakened enemy navy as still ventured to show themselves. Only then, with the command of the sea fully assured, a campaign of "island-hopping" was inaugurated, which, after Guadalcanal had at last been securely occupied, was directed at Tarawa in the Gilbert Islands. By the Gilbert route, which lay far to the north of the original Japanese line of island conquest, the possibility was opened up of an attack on the Japanese homeland which by outflanking the main Japanese position would be relatively free from enemy interference (see map opp. p. 869). But the year 1944 had been rung in before an attack of this outflanking kind could be seriously considered.

From Guadalcanal to the Gilberts. American "island-hopping"

The developments in the Russian theater that followed on the heels of the German catastrophe at Stalingrad were of so sweeping a nature that it is hardly possible to overstate their importance. In measure as their victory stimulated the courage of the Russians it depressed their opponents, who, while continuing to offer stubborn resistance, were nevertheless forced to fall back at every point of the enormously extended battle line stretching all the way from the Baltic to the Black Sea. Space is lacking to do more than summarize the extraordinary gains of the uninterruptedly advancing Russians. In the course of the year under consideration (1943) they completely freed the once hard-beset cities of Leningrad and Moscow from enemy pressure. They then drove on to recapture the strategic centers of Kharkov, Smolensk, and Kiev, thereby liberating an immense segment of their country from the invader. So irresistible was the momentum with which they drove forward that it became manifest to every informed

The striking Russian successes of 1943 toward liberating their territory

observer that in the next year's campaign they would sweep the enemy completely out of what the people, still nursing their ancient religious inheritance, acclaimed as "Holy Russia" and spill over into the unholy country of the enemy.

The most striking events of the 1943 campaign, at least in western eyes, occurred in what began as an African affair and ended up in Italy. The successful landing in Morocco and Algeria of British-American forces in the late autumn of 1942 was, as has been duly noted, co-ordinated with the pursuit of the defeated Afrika Korps of General Rommel by the British. The two advances were steadily pressed throughout the winter of 1942-43 and resulted in squeezing the as steadily retreating Germans into the French North-African province of Tunisia. By early May, after desperate fighting by the Germans to retain this, their last African foothold, the broken remnants of their forces surrendered to their conquerors. In the spring of 1943 British-American pressure drives the enemy out of Africa

By this victory a path was cleared across the Mediterranean for a direct attack on the Italy of Dictator Mussolini, master of what was doubtless the weakest of the three aggressor regimes. The first phase of the new advance was a descent on the island of Sicily. Launched in July, it was proceeding according to plan when an event at Rome delivered, or seemed to deliver, the whole peninsula into the hands of the invading British and Americans. On July 25 the Fascist Grand Council at Rome, panic-stricken by the invasion of Italian soil, ousted Dictator Mussolini from control and appointed a soldier, Marshal Badoglio, chief of state in Mussolini's stead. The invasion of Sicily brings the downfall of Mussolini, July 25, 1943

On this evidence of collapse the Italian field army began to lay down its arms until to all intents it was the German auxiliaries alone who continued to offer resistance. Consequently, when, on September 3, the allies leaped the strait of Messina to the Italian mainland, they met with little opposition until they approached the great port of Naples. By effecting a landing to the south of Naples along the coast of Salerno they obliged the Germans to abandon the city, which they then triumphantly entered on October 1. By that time Judgment Day had come for Mussolini's Italy, for, five days after the allies had reached the Italian mainland, Marshal Badoglio reduced the fast-fading Italian military action to zero by bowing to the enemy demand for unconditional surrender. The allies invade the Italian mainland. Unconditional surrender of Italy

But this did not mean the end of the war in Italy. The German High Command resolved to maintain Italy as a fighting front with a view to holding as large a contingent of British and Americans as possible in the peninsula. By the bold airplane raid of a German crew Mussolini, confined by the Badoglio government in an Italian prison, was liberated and carried to Lombardy, where he set up a rebel Fascist regime and continued the war as best he could, but feebly enough, at the side of his German rescuers. Assailed by superior numbers, the Germans yielded Slow northward push of the allies against stubborn German resistance

ground slowly. At the ancient monastery of Monte Cassino, a powerful natural fortress half-way between Naples and Rome, they held up the allied advance until May of the following year. In June, 1944, Rome was taken and Florence two months later. By that time the war had reached its final phase through an attack on Germany itself. In the face of this last and decisive development the Italian theater sank to so negligible an importance that we may dismiss it from further consideration.

THE FINAL CAMPAIGNS OF 1944 AND 1945: DEFEAT AND SURRENDER OF GERMANY AND JAPAN

The two lines of attack on Japan

The capture of the Gilbert Islands in 1943 marked the starting point of an outflanking sweep of advance against the Nipponese enemy which owed its origin to the planning genius of General MacArthur and Admiral Nimitz. The program called for the successive occupation of the Marshall Islands, the Carolines, and the Marianas (Saipan) as bases of support for a direct air attack on the Japan homeland by the ever farther-ranging American bombers. Then, in October, 1944, by one of the boldest strokes of the whole war a landing was effected in the Philippines on the island of Leyte. To prevent it the Japanese risked their last naval reserves, only to have them annihilated by the superior skill and gun-power of their opponents. The winning of Leyte signified the opening of a second line of air attack on Japan (see map opp. p. 869) and, as the Americans were by now in undisputed command of the sky, their latest-model bombers, the B-29 superfortresses, were able to carry destruction to the leading industrial and population centers of the enemy.

Russia effects the surrender of the German satellites. Invasion of Germany begun

As foreshadowed by the Russian successes of 1943, the expulsion of the Germans from Russian territory was completed in the campaign of the following year and the invasion of enemy territory inaugurated with the most amazing results. The new fighting season was still young, when Russian troops, fighting on the northern front of the immense battle line, entered former eastern Poland, which ever since the treaty of partition with Germany of 1939 they had never ceased to regard as their own; in March, 1944, their southernmost army crossed the river Pruth into Rumania; and in August of the same year their northern army outdid this triumph by being the first to set foot on German soil by lunging forward into the province of East Prussia. The extremely important fruit of these accumulated victories was the collapse and surrender of Germany's little satellites. Already by September, 1944, Finland had abandoned the war by signing an armistice with a Russian plenipotentiary. In the same month Rumania bowed itself out of the war and, shortly after, Bulgaria, swamped by a sudden floodlike invasion, followed suit. Next to be swept

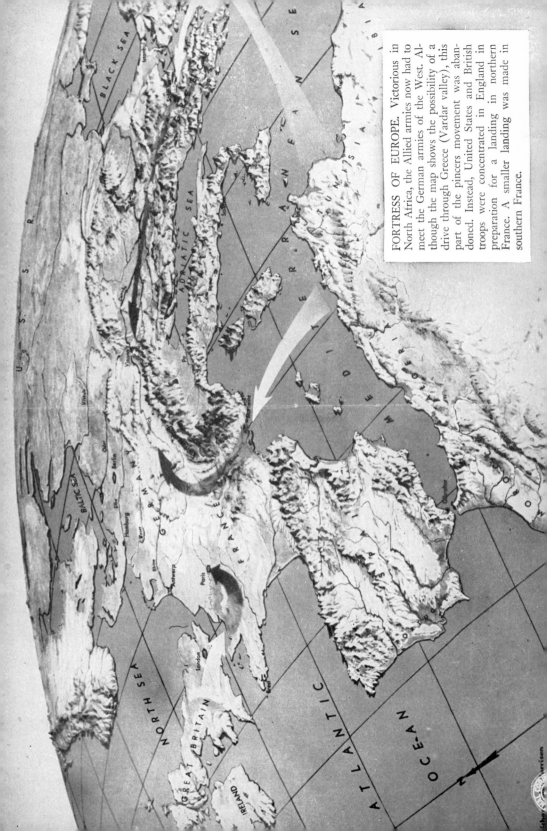

EUROPEAN THEATER

OF OPERATIONS

Quebec
19 AUG 1943
1 SEPT 1944

London
10 JUNE 1944

ashington

Yalta
4 FEB 1945

AMERICAN

THEATER

MEDITERRANEAN

Malta
30 JAN 1945

PERSIAN

Casablanca
15 JAN 1943

THEATER OF

Cairo
23 NOV 1943

Teheran
28 NOV

GULF

OPERATIONS

COMMAND

MIDDLE EAST

CENTRAL AFRICA

THEATER

S

THEATERS OF OPERATIONS. The Combined Chiefs of Staff was the agency created to co-ordinate the pooling of effort and resources of the United States and Great Britain in the attempt to defeat Germany, Italy, and Japan. The Combined Chiefs proposed the operations to be undertaken, allocated the resources of the two nations accordingly, defined Theaters of Operations (as shown on this map), and recommended the Allied Commanders for these theaters. The Combined Chiefs met periodically, usually with their Chiefs of State, in the International Conferences, here shown.

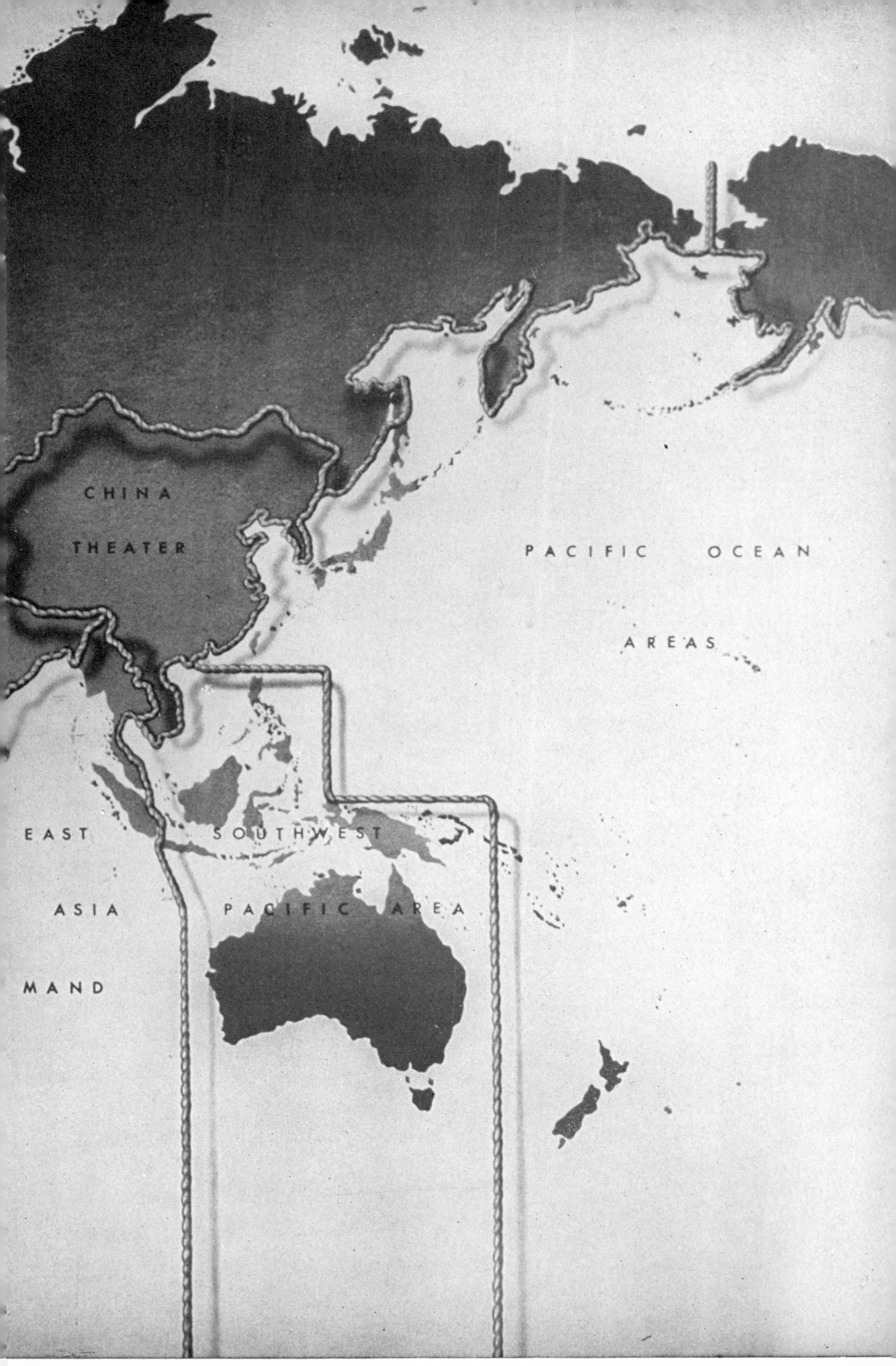

CHINA
THEATER

PACIFIC   OCEAN

AREAS

EAST   SOUTHWEST

ASIA   PACIFIC   AREA

MAND

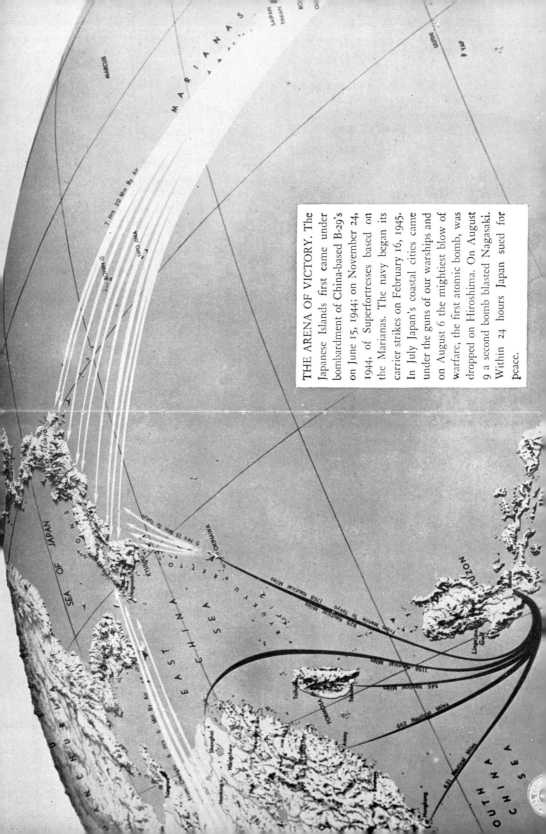

THE ARENA OF VICTORY. The Japanese Islands first came under bombardment of China-based B-29's on June 15, 1944; on November 24, 1944, of Superfortresses based on the Marianas. The navy began its carrier strikes on February 16, 1945. In July Japan's coastal cities came under the guns of our warships and on August 6 the mightiest blow of warfare, the first atomic bomb, was dropped on Hiroshima. On August 9 a second bomb blasted Nagasaki. Within 24 hours Japan sued for peace.

clear of the Nazi armies were Yugoslavia and Greece, the former by a thrust of the onrushing Russians, the latter by a British landing operation from the Mediterranean Sea. Before the close of the year the Balkan peninsula in its entirety had fallen under allied control.

Magnificent as was the Russian achievement, it was dwarfed and over-shadowed by the long-awaited and long-prepared landing in force of the British and Americans in what the over-confident Germans called their unassailable "Fortress Europa." It befell on June 6, 1944, on the coast of Normandy, directly across the English channel, and its purpose was the establishment of a mobile western front, reproduction and counterpart of the onward-rolling eastern front of the Russians. The two closely co-operating fronts, it was planned, would then exert a pressure on the Germans squeezed between them, the inescapable consequence of which would be their ultimate strangulation.

The British-American landing on the French coast, June 6, 1944

The landing on the Normandy coast, which the Germans had attempted to make impregnable with innumerable protective devices, called for the most undaunted resolution on the part of the invaders, and the outcome hung for a while in the balance. As in the African campaign the supreme command had again been assigned to General Eisenhower, who had at his disposal several million British and American troops of every category known to modern warfare, together with token contingents from all the smaller allies. In their entirety the invading forces may be visioned as the united democratic world launched on a crusade to defeat and destroy, root and branch, an intolerable totalitarian tyranny.

General Eisenhower heads the invading armies

As regiment on allied regiment penetrated the Normandy coast, the German defense slowly crumbled. Before the end of June the port of Cherbourg had fallen to the allies; this success was followed in July by the capture of the coast towns of Caen and Saint Lô. Their front line thus broken, the Germans began a retreat which, after another month, took on some of the aspects of a total rout. Its dimensions were beyond the expectations of even the most sanguine allied partisan. When, unable longer to hold Paris, the Nazis abandoned it, the victors on August 25 entered the French capital amidst wild demonstrations of joy.

The German defense is breached. Fall of Paris

A few weeks later the Americans, driving forward posthaste, succeeded in setting foot on German soil. Here the enemy, taking advantage of the great fortification system called the West Wall, made a stand, and the speed of the allied advance was markedly slowed down. In December the Germans even plucked up courage to launch a counter-offensive through the Ardennes forest, which scored an alarming success until it was halted by the hurried dispatch of relieving troops by General Eisenhower. A month later the Germans had been pushed back to their starting point with the net result of the loss of men and supplies they could ill afford. In the "Battle of the Bulge," as the episode came to be

Stiffening of the German resistance. The "Battle of the Bulge"

known in the United States, the German army threw its last trump into the game—and lost.

Following this defeat the German armies under unrelenting pressure on the ground and from the air were steadily driven back to their final destruction in the heart of the Fatherland. On March 7, 1945, an American armored division crossed the Rhine over a bridge which by an unpardonable act of negligence the defenders had failed to destroy. Three weeks later additional crossings of the river had been effected, thereby enabling some two million men to co-operate in delivering the final blow. They encountered little difficulty, for the enemy forces without support from the Luftwaffe, which, owing to the lack of gasoline, was no longer able to send a single airplane aloft, were visibly disintegrating. Already by April several hundred thousand men had capitulated and other thousands laid down their arms with every fresh advance of their opponents.

The effect in Italy of the collapse in Germany was electric. The German army, which during the past year had been slowly falling back northward toward the Alps, now accelerated its retreat and on April 29 ended hostilities throughout the peninsula by bowing to the allied demand for unconditional surrender. Already on the day preceding this decisive event his fate had caught up with ex-Dictator Mussolini. On attempting to make his way to safety by crossing into neutral Switzerland, he was apprehended by violently anti-Fascist partisans, who, after shooting and stabbing him to death, brutally vented their spite on his dead body.

During the same winter and spring months of 1944-45 which had carried the western allies forward into broken Germany, the Russians continued their westward drive under the momentum of some five million men and their overpowering machine equipment. In January, 1945, they broke the stubborn German resistance at Warsaw and swept on triumphantly into Germany and Austria with Berlin and Vienna as their final objectives. The Baltic city of Danzig fell on March 30; Königsberg in East Prussia on April 8. In this same month the province of Silesia was overrun, culminating in the occupation of its capital, the city of Breslau. A greater triumph still, indeed a master triumph, was scored by the seizure on April 13 of the Austrian capital of Vienna with very feeble resistance on the part of the retreating Nazis. Berlin, on the other hand, did not yield without the stiffest kind of fighting directed by the fanatic Führer in person.

After crossing the last defensive barrier of Berlin, the river Oder, the Russians worked their way forward almost yard by yard until, on April 30, they had penetrated the suburbs of the city. On that very day, resolved not to fall alive into the hands of the enemy, Adolf Hitler, a

Crossing of the Rhine followed by the German collapse

The unconditional surrender of the German army in Italy. Exit Mussolini

The Russians press forward with Vienna and Berlin as their double objective

psychopathic madman from the first to the last day of his fatal ascendancy, committed suicide in his bomb-shattered chancellery. His last official act was to appoint Admiral Doenitz his successor. The single measure remaining for the admiral to execute was to offer the victors the unconditional surrender of his country. On May 7 the document ending the war in Europe was signed at General Eisenhower's headquarters near Reims in France.

Suicide of Hitler followed by unconditional surrender, May 7, 1945

The last of the three aggressor allies to crack was Japan. However, already by the time Germany fell, Japan had been bled to the edge of exhaustion. It will suffice to list some of the American successes that brought about this progressive enfeeblement. In January, 1945, United States forces began the re-conquest of the Philippine Island of Luzon and, a month later, had by an irresistible advance penetrated to its capital, Manila. The next forward step on this, the southern line of attack against Japan, was the island of Okinawa. Here the desperate Japanese put up so fierce a resistance that it took several months of the most savage hand-to-hand fighting before they were completely subdued.

The cracking of Japan. Capture of the Philippines and of Okinawa

Meanwhile, by the outer rim of advance, Japan had been made a directly accessible target through the capture in March, 1945, of Iwo Jima, an island only seven hundred and fifty miles from the capital city of Tokyo. At the end of May an official American report affirmed that fifty-one square miles of Tokyo's housing had been leveled to the ground. Paralleling this obliterating fury with similarly devastating discharges on Japanese airfields, convoys, merchant shipping, that is, on every form of transport and communication indispensable for effective warfare, the Americans caused the Japanese defenses slowly to crumble away. It will help to grasp the besieged country's precipitate decline to note that the loss of Japanese shipping alone was calculated at four million tons.

The destruction wrought by American bombing

The rain of destruction falling without let-up through the spring and summer months culminated on August 6, 1945, with the dropping on the industrial town of Hiroshima of the first atom bomb ever devised by the ingenuity of man. It flattened 60 per cent of the city, killed 78,000 people, and seriously injured as many more. A second atom bomb, dropped three days later on the seaport of Nagasaki, deepened the horror with which the world had received the news of the first bomb. The two novel exterminators of the life and works of man were produced by the government of the United States, which had enlisted for the enterprise the services of several scores of the country's most eminent scientists, together with a substantial quota of their British colleagues.

The finishing blow: the atom bomb dropped on Hiroshima, August 6, 1945

The Significance of the Event Cannot Be Exaggerated. A New Age, the Atom Age, Had Dawned on the World with Absolutely Unforeseeable Consequences for the Human Race.

Surrender
of Japan,
August 14,
1945

With the choice between obliteration and the unconditional surrender demanded by the enemy, Japan, on August 14, chose the less grim alternative. (It helped speed the Japanese decision that two days after Hiroshima the Russians had declared war on Nippon.) With the surrender of the last of the three aggressors there descended the final curtain on the most savage and ruinous war in the six thousand years of recorded human history.

The peace
settlement
discussed
among the
allies dur-
ing the
war

What now at once became the most urgent issue confronting the allied victors was the re-establishment of peace. It was an issue at least as important as the war and without the successful solution of which the late monstrous conflict would take rank as no better than a fresh link in a chain of world wars destined to continue to the total extinction of life on earth as the human race has known it. It hardly calls for express statement that the terms to be imposed on their defeated enemies had been under discussion among the victorious allies from practically the beginning of the struggle. Indispensably therefore we must take cognizance of these discussions, although it will meet our limited purpose to take note of only such decisions as were of outstanding importance.

The Atlantic
Charter
of August,
1941

The first of these decisions befell when, on August 14, 1941, following their meeting at sea, Prime Minister Winston Churchill of Great Britain and President Franklin D. Roosevelt of the United States issued what came to be called the Atlantic Charter. Since the United States had not yet at that time entered the war, the war aims of the two signatories had perforce to be painted in the idealistic terms which appeal to sober reflection and which in the past history of mankind have been regularly rejected as soon as sober reflection has been replaced by the unbalanced emotions of war. Accordingly, the Charter pledged the two chiefs of state to a program of international peace and justice, to the repudiation of territorial aggrandizement, and to the right of every people freely to choose the form of government under which it desires to live.

Twenty-six
nations
sign the
Atlantic
Charter

Four months later, in the wake of the Japanese attack on Pearl Harbor, the United States plunged into the conflict but, still committed in spirit to the Atlantic Charter, undertook to have it accepted as their fundamental position by all the countries at war with the aggressors. It thus came about that the accredited representatives of twenty-six nations met at Washington and on January 1, 1942, greatly extended the authority of the Charter by signing a declaration solemnly dedicating themselves to its idealistic program.

A year later Prime Minister Churchill and President Roosevelt met again at Casablanca in northwest Africa. The United States had by that time been at war for more than a year and its government in order to inspire its people to put forth their highest energy had systematically blown on their passions until they were on fire. The result was a Churchill-Roosevelt statement of January 24, 1943, which not only in effect canceled the Atlantic Charter but by imposing "unconditional surrender" on their enemies threatened them with total destruction by denying them the benefit of a negotiated peace. The European powers had been involved in war with one another for many centuries but regularly throughout that time they had, while continuing to fight, looked forward to an early accommodation. For this reason war had never failed to be attended by either open or secret negotiations. Casablanca was therefore an innovation of positively revolutionary scope, for it invited Germany, Italy, and Japan to fight on to their last man and bullet since the only alternative offered them was political extinction.

The Atlantic Charter supplanted by "unconditional surrender"

In November, 1943, Churchill and Roosevelt met Stalin at Teheran in Persia and had no difficulty in inducing him to accept the unconditional surrender formula. Other meetings at other places of either the heads of the three leading powers or of their leading ministers may in this shortened account be omitted in favor of the crucial agreement reached in February, 1945, at Yalta in the Crimea. In this document the top-level conferees, the Big Three, agreed that Germany should be partitioned into three zones of occupation, with restored France invited to take over a fourth zone to be carved from the zones allotted to Britain and the United States. It was further agreed to destroy German militarism root and branch, to disband the German army without leaving as much as the smallest nucleus for its reorganization, to dissolve and outlaw the Nazi party, and to hale the leading war criminals before a bench of victor judges. There were many additional articles of a severely punitive nature, but as if to balance them with a note of Christian grace the document culminated in a proposal enthusiastically acclaimed by a war-weary world to summon a conference at San Francisco to draw up a charter for a new League of Nations dedicated to world unity and peace.

The crucial Yalta decisions, February, 1945

Before taking up the San Francisco conference we note that it was not the first action by the victor powers looking forward to the restoration of a ravaged world. As early as November, 1943, at Washington, representatives of forty-four countries, calling themselves the United Nations, signed an agreement creating the United Nations Relief and Rehabilitation Administration, reduced for ease of reference to the letter formula of UNRRA. The treaty outlined a program for the relief of the suffering populations of the most war-harried regions of Europe and Asia and indicated the contributions to a common fund imposed on the respective

The United Nations sets up a relief organization, November, 1943

participants. The central thought was to provide the people of the most devastated countries with every conceivable necessity—food, clothing, footwear, medical supplies, rolling stock, live stock, and building materials. While its biggest beneficiaries were the Balkan countries together with White Russia and the Ukraine, by far the biggest contributor was the United States, which supplied over 60 per cent of the $4,000,000,000 distributed during the next four years. The distributed money and goods may be thought of as constituting a sort of world community chest, and the fact that its people were proud to be permitted to assume the major portion of this humanitarian service was proof of the warm fellow-feeling of relatively unscathed America for the victims of totalitarian war.

The San Francisco conference draws up the United Nations Charter, June 26, 1945

When on April 25, 1945, the San Francisco conference of the United Nations assembled as stipulated at Yalta, it based its discussions on a provisional charter elaborated at Dumbarton Oaks, near Washington, in October, 1944. Only the three leading powers, Great Britain, the United States, and the U.S.S.R., participated in the Dumbarton Oaks discussions under the undoubtedly correct assumption that a preliminary agreement among these three major powers would facilitate agreement when the general discussions got under way. A total of fifty nations was represented at San Francisco. After nine weeks of often sharp divergence of opinion they brought their deliberations to a close on June 26 with a document, called the Charter of the United Nations, intended to serve as the framework of a new world organization.

The Charter described

The Charter may be summarily described by enumerating its leading institutions. They are a General Assembly, in which every member nation, large or small, disposes of a single vote; a Security Council, in which Russia, Great Britain, the United States, France, and China have permanent seats and which exercises primary responsibility; an Economic and Social Council; an International Court; and a permanent Secretariat. It cannot be too strongly emphasized that power is centered in the Security Council which, although embracing, in addition to the five permanent members, six members elected by the General Assembly, each for a two-year period, is so constituted that any one of the five permanent members may exercise the veto right against a measure of which his country disapproves. This so-called Great Power veto has proved the gravest kind of stumbling block, since it enables any one of the five outstanding powers to annul the operation of the Charter at will. The first meeting of the General Assembly convened at London in January, 1946. Its most notable action was to set up its permanent headquarters at New York.

In July, 1945, a month after the happily concluded labors over the new international organization, the heads of the three leading victor powers held a meeting at Potsdam, near Berlin, to draw up the first indispensable agreements regarding conquered Germany. It was no longer the original

Big Three who had shaped allied policy during the war. The death of President Roosevelt on April 12 had promoted Harry S. Truman to the headship of the United States and, while the British premier, Winston Churchill, participated in the early Potsdam sessions, he was replaced before the conference ended by Clement R. Attlee, whom the victory at the polls of the Labor party had raised to the head of the government. Stalin, however, with the unshaken security of a successful totalitarian chieftain, continued to represent Russia.

The Potsdam conference of July, 1945

The main business of the meeting was to give effect to the terms of Yalta by confirming the border lines of the four occupation zones of Germany and by agreeing on the military, economic, and political directives by which Germany was to be ruled until such time as the victors should see fit to bring the war to a formal close by a treaty of peace.

Potsdam lays down the rules for German control

However, although peace was adjourned to an indefinite future, the meeting underscored the superior alertness of the Moscow delegates, since Russia, and Russia alone, won its complete territorial objectives at Potsdam. For Britain and the United States gave their approval, doubtless to their later considerable regret, to the annexation by the Soviets, first, of the German city of Königsberg together with a substantial East Prussian hinterland, and second, of the territory of Poland east of the so-called Curzon line and substantially identical with the area secured by Russia in the partition treaty signed with Germany in 1939. It was further stipulated that for this loss Poland should be compensated by the cession of all German territory east of a line drawn along the Oder and Neisse rivers. Included in this cession was the right granted Poland of ruthlessly driving the ten million German residents from their homes and farmlands without even a pretense at compensation. The wretched expellees were peremptorily ordered to be on their way to western Germany, abandoning all their belongings save such clothing and household goods as they could carry on their backs.

Stalin secures the full territorial demands of Russia and Poland

Before adjourning, the three heads of state authorized the formation of a council of their foreign ministers charged to draft peace treaties for Italy, Finland, Rumania, Yugoslavia, Bulgaria, and Hungary. By this measure peace talks, although strictly limited in scope, were at least inaugurated and, after long and bitter haggling brought in February, 1947, to a conclusion which, even so, left many perilously contentious issues unsettled. As for a general peace settlement, embracing the two leading enemy powers, Germany and Japan, even its prospect has at the time of this writing, which is more than five years after Potsdam, practically evaporated. It is this diplomatic stalemate and the terrifying world-wide tension attending it which will be treated in Chapter 47.

Peace treaties with Italy and minor powers agreed on February, 1947

46 LEADING CULTURAL TRENDS OF THE TWENTIETH CENTURY

Expansion of Western civilization on two levels

ALTHOUGH THE purpose of this book was at the outset declared to be to set forth the sociopolitical developments of Europe since the Reformation, it was at the same time stated that the sociopolitical developments were so closely linked with the parallel cultural developments that in the interest of a better understanding of the former the latter would have to be at least broadly indicated. Accordingly, each main sociopolitical period of this book has been followed by a chapter dealing with the period's leading cultural trends. We have now reached the point where the carrying out of this plan imposes the presentation of the leading cultural trends of the twentieth century. However, before launching on this enterprise, it will help our understanding of this most recent phase of Western civilization to cast a rearward glance over the whole movement since its beginning. In this perspective view it will appear at once as a movement of continuous expansion on two distinct levels, one physical or geographical, the other mental or spiritual.

Main stages of expansion on the physical level

Let us take the physical expansion first. Western civilization originated within the relatively limited area of western Europe dominated by the Latin Christian church and did not pass beyond these bounds during the many centuries embraced by the period conventionally called the Middle Ages. When, with the coming of the Renaissance, the Voyages of Discovery disclosed hitherto unknown continents, Western civilization with relative ease and speed brought the sparsely inhabited Americas within its scope. However, it got no farther at first in Asia than an occasional foothold because Asia was a populous continent endowed with several vigorous civilizations of its own. Then, toward the close of the seventeenth century, Tsar Peter the Great opened Russia to west-European influences with the result that after some generations the whole vast Russian empire embracing eastern Europe and northern Asia fell under the western spell. With the immensely multiplied communications of the nineteenth century not only the manufactured products but also the characteristic ideas and institutions of the west were diffused over all the remaining continents or parts of continents that had thus far escaped Western influences, over Africa, Australia, and southern Asia. Wherewith we have arrived at the twentieth century, by which time what had started out over a thousand years before as a movement of civilization within the narrow boundaries of western Europe had overrun, or was on the point of overrunning, the last outposts of the earth.

Far more important than this widening of the physical empire of Western civilization was its mental or spiritual expansion. Throughout its protracted childhood, identified with the Middle Ages, it possessed a markedly religious and supernatural character, impressed upon it by Christianity as institutionally shaped by the Roman Catholic church. The church's teaching was that the highest knowledge, indeed the only knowledge worth acquiring, was knowledge of religious truth as revealed in the attested articles of the Christian faith. True, beginning with the rise of scholastic philosophy in the eleventh century, a modest role in the assembling of knowledge was conceded also to our reasoning faculty called *ratio* in the learned Latin medium of the period. However, in case a conflict arose between reason and faith, it was reason and not faith that was required to give way. *[margin: First stage of expansion on the mental level]*

Even with this brake applied to reason, secular as distinct from religious knowledge made considerable headway in the Middle Ages, as the development in such fields as geography, mathematics, and physics suffices to prove. Nonetheless, the path was not cleared for the unhampered advance of secular learning until the authority of the Catholic church had been impaired by the Renaissance and Reformation. Then, when in the course of the seventeenth and eighteenth centuries, the Reformation churches in their turn lost much of their hold on their followers, religiously unchecked advantage could be taken of the new and immensely fruitful scientific method that had taken shape under the guiding hand of Galileo and other daring spirits of his time. This scientific method became crucial for the whole subsequent development, since by its progressive application to every division of the study of nature and of man, it led to the accumulation of a constantly increasing body of highly specialized knowledge touching every conceivable human interest. The close of the nineteenth century revealed that the scientific movement, far from having slackened its pace, was, more eagerly than ever, pressing forward to new horizons. *[margin: Later stages of mental expansion]*

In now taking up the most recent or twentieth century phase of Western civilization we begin with the assertion that the momentum acquired along its two-level expansion showed no sign of a diminishing vigor. Its physical diffusion had, as we approach the middle of the century, become so general that it had outstripped and replaced all rival civilizations and now reigned supreme around the globe. It was no more than the bare truth to declare that Western civilization had entered on its *[margin: Western civilization has entered its Universal phase]* final, its Universal phase. At the same time, it had gone on accumulating knowledge at a faster rate than ever before, and of this knowledge much was of so startling a kind that it had cast doubt on many of the earlier propositions that had come to be regarded as rock-ribbed, fundamental, scientific truths. The resulting fluid situation suggested that we may be poised on the threshold of an entirely new understanding of the world.

Adoption of a selective procedure

It is this latest body of scientific discoveries that has affected Western civilization in every one of its numerous expressions, in government, law, medicine, economics, social relations, and of course also in literature, music, and the Fine Arts. In our proposed review of this most recent phase we shall not make the palpably hopeless attempt to cover all these fields. Fortunately some of them have already been covered, for in the course of the immediately preceding chapters we have taken account of the forms of government, the economic practices, and the class relations that obtain in the contemporary world. And we have also given attention to the movement looking forward to increased international co-operation, a certainly vastly significant aspect of a civilization that now rules universally.

Our inquiry directed to science and the arts

It is therefore hardly necessary to apologize for limiting the present inquiry to two fields: (1) science, and (2) the arts. We shall want to know something of the recent advance in the natural as well as the so-called social sciences and we shall want to record the reaction to our expanded state of knowledge registered by the arts. If the reader should demand a fuller justification of this selective procedure, let him recall that so much store has throughout the ages of mankind been set by science and the arts that the practice has very generally prevailed of evaluating a civilization by its achievement in these fields alone. Admitting that the practice is narrow, it is nonetheless certain that it yields insights of the greatest importance for the inquiring mind.

PHILOSOPHY

Late differentiation between science and philosophy

By way of introduction to the recent developments in the field of science a word may be conceded to philosophy. It is an entirely reasonable concession, since originally science and philosophy were held to constitute a single body of knowledge. It was only in the seventeenth century, scientifically forever notable because it saw the elaboration of an effective scientific method, that the two fields began to be clearly differentiated. A hundred years later their separation had become complete, scientist and philosopher going each his own specialized way.

The occasion for the separation may be presented in the following terms: Leaving the Greeks to one side, philosophy began its existence in close association with theology, from which it took over the main problems constituting its subject matter. These problems consisted in finding proofs acceptable to the human reason for the dogmatic assertions of theology touching such matters as God, the soul, immortality, and freedom of the will. In dealing rationally with these issues the philosophers, beginning with the great scholastics, such as Thomas Aquinas, and continuing through the impressive file of moderns from Descartes to Kant and Hegel, erected imposing metaphysical systems by which they made a valuable contribution to our spiritual culture but by which they added as good as nothing to the body of proved and positive knowledge. Philosophy took over its earliest problems from theology

It followed that, compared with the natural scientists, who were piling practical, utilizable discovery on discovery, their former associates, the philosophers, gradually lost standing. Larger and ever larger social groups became convinced that our sensory and intellectual equipment was insufficient to solve the problems posed by philosophy and that, thus handicapped by nature, we were deceiving ourselves in thinking that we could provide the issues stemming from religion with a solid rational foundation. Inevitably some restless and imaginative thinkers continued to occupy themselves with the traditional subject matter of philosophy, so deeply relevant to man's place in the universe, but they could not hinder the decline in prestige of a reflective activity which the revised opinion of mankind had come to consider unprofitable. Philosophers lose caste in comparison with scientists

By the beginning of the twentieth century it seemed to many observers, especially if they boasted a scientific background, that philosophy was moving toward its setting. If the expectation turned out to be premature, it was because revivals in ever new combinations of all the philosophies of the past continued to be put forth. There appeared an unbroken succession of professed novelties, whereof the novelty consisted largely in clothing old matter with a new verbal garment. Among them figured a New Aristotelianism, a New Scholasticism, a New Rationalism, and a New Kantism. Twentieth century philosophies lack originality

Among re-orientations of a more original kind may be noted an American variety, called pragmatism, of which Professor John Dewey became the leading exponent. At the present time pragmatism boasts friends—and vigorous enemies as well!—in every American center of learning. The two most notable features of pragmatism are: first, its frank abandonment of the search for final answers to such inscrutable problems, taken over from theology, as God and immortality; and second, its adoption of the method of the natural sciences for the solution of the much more modest problems with which it is content to wrestle. These problems derive from our immediate experience as social beings and include such matters as the moral and esthetic values appropriate to a demo- Pragmatism, an American philosophy cratic and industrial society and the educational program calculated to bring the wide variety of talents possessed by the pupils of our schools to their fullest unfolding.

The prospects of pragmatism

The enemies of pragmatism have argued that by giving up the lofty ground staked off by the famous philosophers of the past it has ceased to be philosophy and has identified itself with sociology. The taunt will not prove withering if pragmatism should make headway with the circumscribed problems it has set itself and if, to crown its efforts, it should succeed in weaving its conclusions into that fresh synthesis of man and nature of which our distracted world stands in such sore need.

THE NATURAL SCIENCES

Multiplication of the natural sciences by specialization

Continuously increased in number by progressive specialization ever since the early nineteenth century, the natural sciences have recently experienced further multiplication by merger at their borders of closely related sciences. Thus astrophysics, biochemistry, and physiological chemistry, to mention only a few of these combinations, have won a place for themselves among the most fruitful fields of current cultivation. Of course, no attempt will be made here to list the long file of these specialties, old and new, with a view to cataloguing their respective achievements. Our purpose is strictly limited; we shall sample the recent discoveries in a few random fields and pass on thence to the profound revolution in our thinking brought about by a novel series of fundamental concepts.

X-ray and radioactivity

It is to a physicist, Roentgen, that we owe the discovery of the X-ray, and to Madame Curie and her husband the discovery of radium and the earliest experiments in radioactivity, a field of enormous promise which as yet has barely been staked off. Radium and X-ray have been factors in the recent upsurge of medicine, especially remarkable in its subdivision of surgery. Other factors of surgical advance have been greatly improved anesthetics and antiseptics. Add a continuous refinement of the instruments of surgery and we get some notion of how it came about that present-day surgery has achieved its astonishing daring and precision.

Endocrine glands; chromosomes and genes; vitamins

A novel science stemming from biochemistry, itself a novelty, is endocrinology. It deals with the structure and function of the hitherto mysterious glands of internal secretion called ductless or endocrine glands. Patient investigation has yielded invaluable information touching their extraordinary services. We now have the assurance that the pituitary gland affects physical growth, the suprarenal gland the action of the heart, and the thyroid gland the development of both body and mind. From their imperfect functioning arises a great variety of physical and mental disorders which may be corrected by an artificial preparation of the particular secretion that is found to be lacking. Another mystery that through intense laboratory pursuit has become steadily less mysterious has to do with chromosomes and genes, now recognized as determining elements in sex and heredity. No less important are the vitamins which we absorb with our food and a just balance among which has been found to be indispensable for health and well-being. The vitamins have been identified by letters from A to G and the dietary service each renders has been experimentally determined.

Outstanding are the achievements in the broad field of chemistry, and especially in organic chemistry, which set itself the task of producing organic substances synthetically and, beginning with synthetic alcohol and synthetic indigo, has beaten a path to a veritable world of wonders. We get a faint glimpse of that world by noting what has been done with the humble cottonseed, which originally was rated as pure waste. Literally scores of synthetics are now derived from cottonseed, including smokeless powder, photographic films, salad oil, felt, and soap. Organic chemistry filiates by natural expansion into commercial chemistry, and the two partners have evolved the almost innumerable synthetics (commonly called plastics) which have been and are now more than ever engaged in revolutionizing the tools of industry and the conveniences of living. Intoxicated by a dream of unlimited gadgets (and profits equally unlimited), commercial chemists by extravagant newspaper and radio advertisement dangle before a hypnotized public the prospect of a practically effortless human future. Even rubber and oil can now be produced artificially, although still at a relatively high cost.

The wonders of organic chemistry include an endless variety of synthetics

When all is said, the most impressive feature of the intricate and intermingled advances of twentieth century science has been the formulation of a number of basic concepts of absolutely revolutionary import. Three of them belong to the border world of physics and chemistry: the quantum theory, the theory of relativity, and a group of theories regarding the structure and nature of the atom. Admitting that they require specialists fully to grasp them, laymen should experience no difficulty in compassing at least their main implications.

Three basic revolutionary concepts

The quantum theory, propounded by the German physicist, Max Planck, declared that energy does not radiate in continuous waves, as had been universally held, but that it is released in particles or bundles which he called *quanta*. This theory carried unrest into the whole scientific tradition, which was not quieted by the verdict of Planck's most eminent successors to the effect that the waves are particles and the particles waves. The issue remains open because the ultimate physical reality is still to be specified: is it a particle or is it a wave?

(1) The quantum theory

An even heavier blow was administered to scientific tradition by the theoretical physicist, Albert Einstein. In 1905 he published his theory of Special Relativity and followed it in 1915 with his theory of General Relativity. While both of them are beyond the understanding of the untrained amateur, it may give some idea of the turmoil they created to say that the Special theory affirmed the equivalence of mass and energy, while the General theory demonstrated that Newton's celebrated laws, rated as the undebatable constants of modern science, were, if not erroneous, an incomplete statement of the phenomenon of gravitation. By asserting that all motion is relative to the observer, the Einsteinian theory disposed of the absolutes of Newtonian physics, such as time, space, and length, and exhibited them as variables because dependent on the position of the observer. Einstein accepted as the one constant in nature the velocity of light. And this remaining constant, it may be pointed out, has recently met with challengers.

(2) Einstein's theory of relativity

We now turn to the recent theories regarding the atom, and by way of beginning note that already early in the nineteenth century chemists held the view that the ultimate constituent elements of matter were invisible particles called atoms. Some ninety distinct atoms have thus far been identified: oxygen, hydrogen, carbon, nitrogen, etc. Then, toward the end of the nineteenth century, the suspicion was aroused that even the invisible atoms were not irreducible substances but compounded of still more minute particles.

Atoms long considered as the ultimate substance

An exciting investigation into the constitution of the atom followed in which numerous scientists of all the nations of the world took part. The story proceeds from climax to climax, with perhaps the most important contributions made by Lorentz, Rutherford, and Bohr. It was presently possible to propound a theory of the atom which pictured it as a nucleus, called proton, charged with positive electricity, around which revolved a variable number of negatively charged particles called electrons. In the light of this theory the atom resembled a tiny solar system, wherein the nucleus was the sun and the electrons the revolving planets.

(3) The atomic theory

The continued study of the revolving electrons has brought to light that, individually at least, they do not behave according to a set pattern or "law." That means that their behavior is unpredictable and cannot be dealt with on the hitherto axiomatic principle of cause-and-effect. The best we can do for their behavior is to refer it to a principle of probability.

The behavior of the electrons unpredictable

When we bracket this startling challenge of the hitherto basic principle of causality with the conceded reduction of matter to mere waves of energy, we would seem to have arrived at the threshold of an entirely new scientific (and philosophic) era. In any case it is clear that the purely mechanical interpretation of the world of matter projected in the period of the Enlightenment and accepted as its established framework throughout the nineteenth century will have to be thoroughly revised, if not entirely discarded. To what new understanding of the universe the continued study of atomic energy will ultimately lead is unpredictable, but it is certain that it will engage the attention of scientists in an ever expanding degree. An alarming, immeasurable power is about to be put at the disposal of mankind, which without better self-control than our species has exercised in the past may very conceivably make of this power a thing of unimaginable evil. This prospect could not have been more poignantly brought home to the world than through the devastating effects of the dropping of the first atom bomb on Hiroshima in Japan in August, 1945. *Implications of the atomic theory*

To this exciting but also gravely disturbing story of our expanding knowledge may be added as the final touch the incredible expansion of the universe of matter. Let us recall that until only a few centuries ago men arrogantly assumed that the earth, for the entirely sufficient reason that it was the habitat of their lordly selves, was the center of creation. Copernicus put an end to this delusion and degraded the earth to a relatively unimportant tributary of the sun. Therewith the sun acquired a majesty which it long retained, even though astronomers became aware of larger and far more brilliant suns that made their appearance nightly in the heavens. Within the last few generations greatly improved instruments have enabled astronomers to perform amazing feats: they have with steadily increasing accuracy measured the speed of light; they have computed the size of many of the more distant stars; they have determined the chemical constitution of the stars; and they have by photographic means detected the existence of star clusters so remote that they remain invisible through the most powerful telescopes. *The amazing feats of modern astronomy*

The result has been an expansion of the universe that passes comprehension. We now know our sun to be a rather minor luminary among millions of suns associated together in a single system or galaxy named, because of the silver streak it makes across the sky, the Milky Way. And our particular galactic universe of the Milky Way is but one of an uncounted number of such universes located in the remote recesses of space. Their distance from our earth is ungraspable by the mind, as will at once be admitted on learning that one of these photographically detected galaxies exists at a distance so great that it requires 170,000,000 of our calendar years for its light, traveling at the rate of 186,000 miles a second, to reach our earth. Such immensities of space contract our poor planet to an invisible speck in an apparently unbounded universe and completely bury from view the self-inflated inhabitants of that speck, tirelessly coursing around a somewhat larger speck, indispensable to these same inhabitants as the sole source to them of light, heat, and life itself. *Our Milky Way galaxy and the galaxies beyond it*

THE SOCIAL SCIENCES

The social sciences adopt the method of the natural sciences

In our survey of the cultural trends of the nineteenth century (Chapter 33) we learned that the followers of the social sciences were so impressed with the amazing triumphs of the natural sciences that they resolved to adopt the method of the natural sciences in the hope of giving the studies dealing with man and society the same precision and validity as those dealing with nature.

The social sciences still in the fact-finding stage

We also learned on that occasion that the social sciences did not succeed in this purpose and therefore did not rise above their original experimental character. In the new, the twentieth, century the situation remained unaltered, although the social scientists employed, if anything with increased ardor, a method as close to that of the natural sciences as the different character of their studies permitted. Immense bodies of data were assembled both by energetic individuals and by co-operating research groups bearing upon economics, government, social classes, primitive cultures, and the various human races, and these data could in many cases be reduced to important generalizations; but propositions of the certainty and sweep of those formulated by the physicists, chemists, and biologists have conspicuously failed to put in an appearance. If the social scientists continue to be buoyed up with what must often seem to them to be an unwarranted hope, their optimism may be attributed to their having at least made available a vast amount of suggestive information or, as we may put it, of raw material dealing with every known phase of man and society. The social sciences are still in the fact-finding stage.

The recent advance in psychology

In one social science, psychology, so great an advance was made in the twentieth century that in the eyes of many scholars psychology has taken the lead over all its sister studies. This success sprang from the determination of a group of advanced psychologists to regard the brain and the nervous system, and not a mysterious inner consciousness, as the instrument of bodily and mental control and to subject to laboratory experiment and exact measurement the reactions of the nervous system to external physical stimuli.

The strictly material psychology called behaviorism

The result was a physiological psychology based on stimulus and response and liberated as far as possible from such concepts of its metaphysical past as consciousness, sensation, and will. The most sweeping rejection of these older concepts occurred in the United States under the leadership of John B. Watson. He propounded a strictly material psychology which became known as behaviorism. Widely accepted at first, it tended later to lose its vogue on the ground that it excessively simplified the problems which were its concern. Nonetheless, it registered, if

THE PARIS OPERA HOUSE. Erected in the second half of the nineteenth century, it exhibits the unbroken domination in architecture of the Italian Renaissance.

THE CHICAGO DAILY NEWS BUILDING. The solid massiveness of this twentieth-century steel structure proclaims the revolt against the classical tradition and the triumph of a new architectural form.

THE BURGHERS OF CALAIS. The tribute by the French sculptor, Rodin (d. 1917), to the heroic defenders of Calais obliged to surrender (1347) to the English. (Musée Rodin)

PORTRAIT OF THE POSTMAN
ROULIN. By the Dutch modernist,
Van Gogh (d. 1890). (Courtesy of
Museum of Fine Arts, Boston)

SELF-PORTRAIT BY THE FRENCH
PAINTER, CÉZANNE (d. 1906). The
most influential of the post-impression-
ists. (Culver Service)

THE REHEARSAL. By the French modernist, Degas (d. 1917). (Culver Service)

THE GUITAR PLAYER. By the Spanish modernist, Picasso. (Courtesy of the Chicago Art Institute)

in an extreme form, the tendency of the most recent psychological studies to regard man as a machine and to observe and classify the responses of the animal-machine to physical stimuli.

The interest aroused by a psychology productive of tangible results led to the penetration of hitherto neglected realms of the mind. A Viennese physician, Sigmund Freud, whose specialty was the diseases and phobias of the mind, became the founder of psychoanalysis. He laid particular emphasis on the instinctive and unconscious element within us and on the always subtle and often determining effect of the unconscious on our conscious life. Freud, founder of psychoanalysis

Since Freud tended to reduce his findings to an uncompromising doctrine, variants of psychoanalysis began to appear, of which that of Jung of Zurich is perhaps the most important. Instead of proving a setback, the many variations have served to increase the vogue of psychoanalysis, which has recently become so great that it has assumed some of the unattractive aspects of a fad. Nonetheless, psychoanalysis, which, when directed to the study and cure of abnormal mental behavior is commonly called psychiatry, has, although still in its infancy, become so solidly established as to take rank with the older social sciences. Psychiatry

The importance and present wide popularity of psychology are evidenced by the many subdivisions to which it has given rise. Thus social psychology concerns itself with group behavior and has promoted a better understanding of politics by showing the essentially nonrational action of crowds. Animal psychology has yielded results of considerable relevance for human psychology; and child psychology, by giving us expert information on the mental processes of the child, has greatly affected educational theory and practice. Social psychology; animal psychology; child psychology

THE ARTS

In turning to the arts for information regarding their contribution to contemporary civilization, we may well begin by referring to the somewhat artificial nature of the distinction commonly made between the higher and the lower arts, the so-called Fine Arts and the crafts. Every art is the process of making or doing something, and the maker or doer deserves the flattering name of artist whenever he achieves a convincing expression of his purpose. Failure, so much more common than success, classifies him as a would-be artist, a botcher and bungler. Artificial distinction between the Fine Arts and the crafts

We may, however, agree that there enters a more imaginative intention as well as a fuller command of the appropriate technical means into the making of a poem or a statue than, say, into the making of a table or the fashioning of a bracelet. For this reason a hierarchy of the arts has been recognized, and the arts which are the expression of an exceptional mental Why the Fine Arts rank above the crafts and emotional endowment enjoy a particular esteem. Outstanding among these are literature, music, painting, sculpture, and architecture.

Art both a social and an individual activity

We shall readily convince ourselves that an examination of the present drift of the arts will throw important light on the current phase of Western civilization if we keep in mind that the practice of an art, because the artist is an integrated member of a group, is fundamentally a social activity. Within every artist dwells the social consciousness of his group associates, which therefore inevitably comes to expression in his handiwork. However, this transfusion with his environment does not hinder the artist from making, in addition to a social, a highly individual contribution with his production. In fact, in a purely esthetic sense the individual element is so indispensable that it frequently receives exclusive consideration on the part of historians and critics of the arts. But for students of civilization, like ourselves, those features of an art in which the age mirrors its tendencies are unquestionably of superior importance.

Contemporary art rebellious and experimental

When we turn to contemporary expression in the arts as a means of penetrating to the drift and purpose of our age, we soon discover that each art repeats with the technique and accent peculiar to itself the message of all the others. And this message, succinctly put, is revolt against the past joined with the passionate resolve to set forth something novel and unique. In short, the arts in our time have to an unparalleled degree become experimental.

The sweeping character of contemporary revolt

It may at once be interposed that revolt is not an unusual frame of mind, since every generation reacts sharply against its predecessor. However, the revolt of the arts in our day is on a different plane. First, it is more violent in character than any previously reported revolt; and second, it aims its hostile shafts at the art output not merely of the immediate but also of the more distant past. Finally, the distaste expressed for the past is directed at both the inherited form and the inherited matter.

This sweeping character attributable to science and the machine

So sweeping an insurrection cannot be accounted for except on the ground of a fundamentally altered outlook on life. And that the outlook has been revolutionized becomes clear as soon as we recall the vast new stores of knowledge amassed by the natural and the social sciences. True, these stores had been in process of accumulation ever since the Renaissance and are responsible for all the important changes in artistic expression effected since the Middle Ages. It is undeniable, however, that the spiritual implications of the fresh accumulations were slow in penetrating the human consciousness, which has always loved to protect itself against innovation with the mummy-cloths of tradition; and it is also patent that the most revolutionary discoveries and changes are of very recent date. Granted that we have had with us those children of science, the machines, for over a hundred years, it remains a fact that the universalization of the machine has only now reached the extent which brings us into contact with it at every moment of our existence, absolutely obliging us to conform our lives to its rule.

The artist is an artist by virtue of his having a more sensitive organization than his fellow men, and when he says or something within him says, "This is a machine age," he realizes much more than express trains, automobiles, turbines, and airplanes. He realizes the reign of power and speed and their steadily increasing sway over man. At the same time he responds sympathetically or, as is also possible, antipathetically to the vast social and political changes which have recently taken place; he sees new approaches to age-old problems, such as food supply, population, poverty, and disease; he is aware of new possibilities of co-operation among groups within a nation and among the various nations themselves; and finally, he senses, in advance of the common run of mankind, the possible advent of an entirely new spiritual and moral outlook. *The sensitive response of the artist to the modern forces*

To the delicately organized artist it is clearer than to other men that the contemporary world has moved far away from the ages of the past, of which, nonetheless, it is admittedly the heir. It is from this descent of the present from the past that the conservatism stems which has always characterized the mass of men and which prompts them to look upon the artistic products carrying the imprint of the past as unapproached masterpieces. Assembled in libraries, museums, and private repositories, they exercise such tyrannical authority that they lay chains about the limbs of the living generation of artists. Therefore, the cry of the moderns became, Away with these shackles! And simultaneously there took shape in their hearts the plan to give birth to an art as vital and novel in matter and form as the dynamic society of which they were a part. *The masses dominated by tradition, which the artists reject*

Music

To illustrate these often contradictory and unclarified tendencies, let us take up music. There are "schools" of modern music in every country as, for instance, the school of Respighi in Italy, the school of the Six in France (of which Honegger and Milhaud are the outstanding members), the school of Schönberg in Austria, the school of Hindemith in Germany, the school of Stravinsky in Russia. In consequence of the savage upheavals of our age, many of these founders have long since abandoned the country of their birth and carried their talents to hospitable America. In America, too, in both North and South America, promising and richly diversified musical movements have come to the *The many "schools" of modern music* front. To focus for a moment on the United States, a highly interesting experimental activity is associated with such names as Aaron Copland, Roger Sessions, George Gershwin, and John Carpenter.

The common denominator of the new schools

Each of these schools differs in some particulars from every other, and each individual within a school insists on his right to stamp and color his work with his own personality. But all these schools and all these individuals have this in common—they are in some fashion in revolt against the music of the past, particularly against the more recent romantic past, represented by such composers as Chopin, Schumann, Schubert, and Wagner. For the highly subjective and idealist utterance of these men they would substitute an objective account of man's situation in nature and society with full consideration given to the dominant machine. Instead of blushing for this symbol of our time as a shameful birth, as did the prudish Victorians, they are proud of it and would fain reflect the intoxicating power it has conferred on our generation in the dynamism and strong pulsations of their compositions.

Revolt against the melody, harmony, and tonality of the past

Specifically, the schools agree in spurning melody, at least in the form in which it has been employed by the masters of Western music since its medieval beginnings. They are inclined to regard this traditional melody as sentimental feebleness and unworthy of strong-willed men living among the whirr of motors and the throb of pistons. Even our basic diatonic scale, with its octave of thirteen equal semitones, has come in for criticism because its limited range is charged with putting a check on the invention of new tone configurations. In sum, the moderns may be said to have discarded the melodic theme and the practice of varying, dissecting, and harmonizing it according to an elaborate set of rules, in favor of a new musical language which operates with exotic rhythms and the strident tones of novel instruments like saxophones.

Popularity and significance of jazz

Quite patently this shift in the means of expression accounts for the diffusion of jazz. Of Africo-American origin, jazz is an almost exact translation into music of the crudeness, the angularity, and the insistent beat of the machine. It is a point in favor of this American product that it comes direct from the masses and that the intelligentsia looks at it somewhat askance. Once taken over and accommodated to the new means of expression already captured, it may be expected to make an important contribution to our present-day musical resources.

Architecture

In turning, next, to architecture we may remind ourselves that we are appealing to the most universal and necessary of the arts. Let us, by way of preliminary, throw a backward glance at medieval architecture in order to acquaint ourselves with a simple and logical situation in the building realm which is in the sharpest conceivable contrast with the disorderly and chaotic situation which obtained some seven centuries later around the year 1900. The Middle Ages were dominated by Christianity and feudalism, from which it follows that these were the two interests the period took deeply to heart. Consequently, the Middle Ages built two original kinds of structure and only two—the church and the castle, each representing a perfect adaptation of form to function.

The Middle Ages credited with two original structures: the church and the castle

In the nineteenth century, a period that commanded material resources beyond even the wildest imaginings of our medieval ancestors, men raised countless monuments to interests which only casually held their attention, such as museums, urban tenements, city halls, railroad stations. The result was that their imagination remained unstimulated and they were content to erect their buildings according to the preference entertained for this or that historical style. They said to the architect who, as the graduate of a professional school, knew the monuments and styles of all the ages of the past and was at the same time commercially eager to please, that they should like a "colonial" residence, or a "Renaissance" museum, or a "Gothic" house of worship. Consequently, the towns throughout the western area, but especially in the United States, became cluttered with structures representative of every known form of architectural expression through the ages. The pompous array indicated an insecure, eclectic taste which, to our own undoing, we unhappily possessed the means to indulge. An eclectic taste usually passes for cultivation but is essentially no taste at all. Its diffusion proved our lack of artistic seriousness and accounted for the architectural chaos that reigned throughout the Western world.

The nineteenth century architectural chaos due to eclecticism

Around 1900 a change occurred. We became aware of our eclectic muddle and ashamed of it. It is clear that we Americans are an industrial and commercial people, for whom the part of life that deeply matters revolves around the axis of business. About business we are in earnest, and in the twentieth century gradually worked out for factories, office buildings, and those vast commercial structures called stores a plan which marks a return to the medieval urge of accommodating form to function. In buildings of this kind our best architects have now given up the folly of decking them with the borrowed plumage of Greek column and cornice or of Gothic arch and tracery. They oblige the structure publicly to proclaim in brick-and-stone or steel-and-concrete the exact purpose which it serves. Such close correspondence between idea and fulfillment again makes architecture functional; and with functional architecture we have re-established contact with first principles, with honesty and simplicity.

Since 1900 architecture has again become functional

The architectural awakening has been helped by the development,

in structural steel, of a wholly new building medium. It is steel which
has made possible the outstanding feature of American architectural
evolution, the skyscraper. The early skyscrapers were still nothing more
than monstrously enlarged editions of Venetian or Florentine palaces.
It is a witness to the birth of a truly modern sense of form that recent
skyscrapers with set-backs at stated heights have entirely broken away
from tradition and neither pretend to be nor are anything more than a
felicitously varied but always solid geometric mass set in a firm steel
frame.

The reign of structural steel

However, since the skyscraper owed its existence in the first instance
to the high rental value of land, it is destined to become obsolete as soon
as our society, taking advantage of our enormously accelerated means of
communication, abandons our present urban concentration in favor of a
deeper penetration of the countryside. This is the thesis of our leading
American architect, Frank Lloyd Wright, who has constructed a large-
scale model of the countrified city of the future which he calls Broadacre
City. Wright's idea has aroused more attention in Europe than in
America, probably because the skyscraper, as foreign to European urban
requirements, was never accepted there. Nonetheless, in Europe as well
as in America, a strict functional simplicity is the dominating trend. The
statement holds in both continents not only for business buildings but
also, in constantly increasing measure, for private residences and those
clustered city rookeries called apartments.

Is the skyscraper already obsolete?

Possibly our changing civilization will achieve before long a similar
artistic seriousness touching the many other features making up the
modern town. Our abundant talk about town-planning points in that
direction. In any case it will only be when we have recognized that the
modern town is the child of the machine and that architecture must
express a perfect accommodation of its aspirations to this basic fact that
the art, which is only just emerging from the stage of revolt against an
outmoded inheritance, will come to express itself in dynamic, free, and
modern terms.

Architecture and town-planning

Painting

In describing modern art as engaged in adjusting itself to the machine,
another aspect of the problem should not be overlooked. Side by side
with *submission to the machine* goes *revolt against it* and against the
whole overelaborate civilization which the machine symbolizes. Many
artists, disturbed beyond endurance by our cluttered material existence
and our overnumerous social distractions, have reverted to earlier, less
complicated phases of our culture, particularly to the Middle Ages; and
some have even gone back all the way to primitiveness and savagery,
which stress emotion and instinct as against our contemporary exaltation

Another aspect of modern art is revulsion against the machine

of thought and will. The passion for an Africa-derived jazz, which, in speaking of music, we connected with the machine, may with perhaps even greater justification be referred to this relapse into an earlier world of feeling. In all likelihood a more penetrating consideration of modern music than we have attempted would have to concern itself quite as much with the revulsion against some of the present-day aspects of life as with the attempt to digest them.

This state of affairs in the arts, this alternate acceptance and rejection of our current civilization, is well illustrated by painting. As we learned in Chapter 33, during the last quarter of the nineteenth century painting was dominated by a form of realism identified with a special technique called impressionism. Originating in France, it had swept everything before it until there slowly set in against it the inevitable reaction. The leader of the reaction was a stubborn individualist by the name of Paul Cézanne (1839-1906). He objected to the blurred colors and broken forms of impressionism on the ground that clear color and definite form had always constituted the fundamentals of the painter's art. In admirable still-life arrangements of fruits, cups, and bottles he disclosed the value of sharp geometric pattern, and in numerous landscapes and portraits he reverted to the classical ideal of expressive drawing and design. His work met with little attention from his contemporaries, and he died before more than a few disciples had rallied to his cause.

Impressionism and Cézanne's revolt against it

Cézanne's pioneering was reinforced, but with a different emphasis, by Van Gogh and Gauguin. Vincent Van Gogh (1853-1890) stemmed from the world of Dutch art but so resolutely went his own way that in the works of his last and most individual period he resembles no one but himself. Van Gogh was tormented by an emotional intensity that at times passed completely out of control. He sought an outlet for his overcharged feelings in a rendering of the objects engaging his attention— flowers, trees, fields, men and women—so spontaneous and vital that the original seemed to become the copy and the copy the original. While his art was in the highest degree subjective, he had to resort to objective means for conveying his inner agitation and found them in a vivacity of color and a vibration of surface which have perhaps never been equaled.

The emotional intensity of Van Gogh

Paul Gauguin (1848-1903) delighted in flat color patterns suggestive of the rich effects of medieval glass or oriental textiles. Disturbed by a contentious mechanical civilization for which he had no taste, he migrated to the South Sea Islands, among the primitive inhabitants of which he found the subject matter best suited to his taste. His non-naturalistic canvases, exhibiting the land, water, and people of the Pacific, communicate by their deep color masses and their ritual hush an entrancing air of timeless peace.

Gauguin excels in rich color patterns

Unre-
strained
experimen-
tation

In the course of the first decade of the twentieth century the hold of impressionism had become so shaken that almost overnight it disappeared. There followed a period of wild experimentation which has continued to the present day. While some painters followed the trails blazed by Cézanne, Van Gogh, and Gauguin, others went off in other directions too numerous even to list in such a sketch as this. Suffice it to name the movements called cubism and expressionism, although it is by no means easy to define them with any degree of accuracy because each practitioner tended to give them a particular slant.

Cubism and
expression-
ism

Cubism was an attempt to resolve an object or human figure into its underlying geometric elements, which are always present, though not immediately visible. The result was a structural pattern which no longer more than suggested the object it was intended to represent. If cubism may not improperly be referred to Cézanne as its source of origin, expressionism may with equal justification be referred to Van Gogh. In any case expressionism is a subjective, emotional form of art, which, going in its later followers far beyond Van Gogh, takes little or no account of objects as they exist in nature and concerns itself solely with rendering the impression they have made on the artist's mind and heart.

Picasso,
the tireless
experi-
menter

The name most completely expressive of the impetuous experimentation of recent decades is that of the Spaniard, Picasso (b. 1881), who settled in Paris in 1903. Picasso has worked in more "manners" than any painter of whom we have record. His talent is great, but it is at least open to question whether it can in the long run maintain its integrity if it remains always in flux and never achieves a confident equilibrium.

The other
arts tell
an identical
tale

We could go on to trace the revolt against the past and the new beginnings of sculpture, literature, and the various crafts, but considerations of space forbid. The reader may be assured that a similar state of things will be found to prevail and that sculptors, writers, and able craftsmen are, either as friends or as foes of the machine, engaged in coming to terms with the forces ruling the age in which we live.

THE OUTLOOK

Backward
glance over
the road
traveled by
Western
civilization

Therewith we have arrived at the point where we may be expected to offer a concluding reflection on the most recent phase of Western civilization. We have in this book followed Western civilization from its small, self-contained medieval beginnings and have become aware of the enormous energies it has in recent centuries devoted to material betterment through such agencies as commerce, industry, finance, and administration. The developments that followed gave rise to grave social problems, among which we have had frequent occasion to note the conflicts between capitalism and socialism, between nationalism and internationalism, be-

PEOPLES OF EUROPE

SCALE OF MILES

0   100   200   300   400

The stippled areas in each country
denotes a mixed people.

tween Christianity and innumerable philosophies of doubt. At the same time new knowledge with regard to the literally limitless forces of nature has swept over us like a tidal wave and put at our service for the satisfaction of our daily wants the painless work of millions and millions of mechanical horses. And now let us take our stand on the summit of the present moment and ask: What of the future?

This is a legitimate question for a student of civilization to ponder, provided it is done in a purely speculative manner, free from all dogmatism of prediction. A large majority of men and women, especially of the younger generation, will, in response to the very lively conviction of their hearts, be prompted to answer without hesitation touching this issue of the future that the future will be greater and more magnificent than the past. With such an instinctive affirmation they would be expressing first, the healthy faith in life which stirs in most of us, especially in the period of youth, and second, the conviction, born of an age of steadily advancing knowledge, that mankind has put its feet upon the ladder of "progress" and is mounting "onward and upward" to an ever loftier destiny.

What of the future?

Progress, let us record in this connection, has been the faith and watchword of the West ever since the coming of the machine and of the science on which the machine rests. But are we justified in trusting blindly to progress, to this faith born of science and the machine? Agreeing that science will increasingly add to our control of nature until we may, in the end, succeed in wielding the scepter of Jove and the trident of Neptune, will the innumerable machines, though they be as serviceable as the spirits of Aladdin's lamp, give inner worth to us as individuals together with that measure of security, as members of a group and nation, which are the necessary concomitants of the "good life"?

Our modern faith, progress, springs from science and the machine

But what is meant by the good life? Although not identifiable as an original Christian ideal because concerned too much with this house of sin, the earth, it has nonetheless drawn its strength from the Christian teaching of the sonship of all men under God and the associated teaching of peace and brotherhood as man's divinely appointed goal. Yet ever since science and the machine have become the dominating factors of our civilization, there has been a vast intensification of struggle, and with our recent fatal entrance on an era of World Wars the good life has become an increasingly obscured and diminishing prospect. Ever since the shock of the first of these wars, warners have arisen who, while joyfully welcoming knowledge and its fruits, boldly affirm that knowledge by itself may lead us to annihilation.

Will science and the machine bring us the "good life"?

Men concerned with human welfare, followers, therefore, not of the natural but of the social sciences, have been particularly energetic in raising their voice in admonition. Prominent among them are writers like H. G. Wells in England and J. H. Robinson, John Dewey, and Charles A. Beard among ourselves. The great desideratum in their eyes is that we bring our social studies, and among them our ethics and esthetics, abreast of the movement of science. Only in this way can we make sure that the resources of science, which in the World Wars were manipulated for the destruction of the human race, shall be dedicated to its preservation and improvement. According to these same critics it would be both stupid and cowardly not to face the disequilibrium projected into the world by an expansion of material power out of all proportion to our existing means of social control. They are neither professional pessimists, these men, nor deluded peddlers of petty, private nostrums. They are champions of human intelligence and proclaimers of the proved resourcefulness of man, that animal of many inventions. And while they acknowledge the existence of a crisis, they urge us to prove our worth by facing and solving it.

A history which, like the present one, holds that Western civilization is an individual entity born under particular conditions some twelve or thirteen hundred years ago and still engaged in organically unfolding itself, comes logically to a stop with the current stage of its unfinished evolution. We have proposed to call this latest phase the Universal phase, because Western civilization, no longer confronted with any serious rivals, is on the point of taking possession by peaceful and warlike means alike of the whole round earth.

While universalization represents a spectacular and unique triumph, does it in itself offer the guarantee of a nobly directed and illustrious future? Thus again and from another angle the question of the future forces itself on our attention. And again a group of warners, different from those named above, has been at pains to point out that our culture, in being distributed over brown and yellow peoples, over the Orient and the Antipodes, runs the risk of being spread so thin as to be sapped of its vigor and significance. An upholder of this view is Oswald Spengler, who in his *Decline of the West* maintains that a civilization is a biological cycle which, after passing through a definite succession of phases, completes its round and disappears. Arnold J. Toynbee in *A Study of History,* which is an impressive comparative study of all civilizations whereof we have knowledge, comes, though on different grounds from Spengler, to an essentially identical conclusion. Spengler and Toynbee can summon to their support two famous historians of the Greco-Roman civilization, Gibbon and Mommsen. They both bear witness that the civilization of which they mastered the stages in a life of devoted study entered at last a Universal phase attended by enfeeblement and death.

But a truce to prophecy! For us, the living, it should and must suffice that the prospect before us is more brilliant than any which ever lured into the unknown our adventuring forefathers. If the dangers which confront us on every hand are great, so also is the challenge to that virile zest which is life's earliest and most noble gift. Let us then march forward with the assurance that, commanding courageous hearts and wakeful minds, there is no need to fear.

The command laid on the living generation

47

THE POSTWAR WORLD (1945-1950)

The ruling issue of the postwar world is the "cold" war

THIS CONCLUDING chapter will touch only lightly on the events of the five years 1945-50. Crucial, complicated, and innumerable, the events of these years belong unarguably to the Global History which, following the view expounded in the Foreword of this book, takes its start with the termination of the History of Europe, its more narrowly bounded forerunner. However, an introduction to its global successor which undertakes to define the ruling issue at the outset of the global period may reasonably be conceded to this volume and is here offered as its concluding word. This ruling issue is the "cold" war between West and East, more specifically between the United States and the Soviet Union.

Basic character of the power struggle

The power struggle among states is as old as history. Its uninterrupted presence in the history of Europe since the Reformation has made up much of the substance of the present work. As an unfailing factor in every political crisis, it gave proof of the existence among the European states of a contentious and divisive tendency which, though occasionally quieted and buried from sight, was nevertheless always there, and time and again and often on the slightest provocation exploded in the savage frenzy of war.

Usual pattern of the power struggle was a coalition against an aggressor

There happily existed, however, a check upon these destructive outbursts in the common civilization in process of slow unfolding among the European states from as far back as the Middle Ages. One of the leading tenets of this civilization was that peace and amity defined the desirable relationship among the member states of the expanding culture to which they had all contributed and in which they all took a lively pride. It follows that wars were always conducted with a view to bringing them to a close at the earliest possible moment on mutually acceptable terms. The usual form taken by war throughout the period treated in this book was for a state aiming at greater power than it momentarily possessed to commit an act of aggression against a weaker neighbor. When the attack could not be successfully resisted by the intended victim, adjoining states would form an alliance in the victim's support. They did so because the victory of the aggressor threatened to disturb an existing desirable balance among the states constituting the European community, whereas the victory of the allies, which in the long run never failed to eventuate, would serve to restore the balance and bring about the resumption of the interrupted processes of peace.

Now, the novel and profoundly bewildering situation resulting from the victory of the anti-aggressor alliance of World War II was that, although the victors had not only defeated the three aggressors but had completely eliminated them as factors in the power situation, they were unable to reach an agreement as to the terms on which they were prepared to bring the conflict to a close and re-establish the passionately desired reign of peace. This surprising turn of affairs was due to developments with which the preceding chapter has made us in part familiar. When the fighting ended with the unconditional surrender of Germany and Japan, the power situation obtaining throughout this history had undergone a revolutionary change through the displacement of the several long-established European powers by the two giant non-European survivors, Russia and the United States.

The victorious coalition of World War II refuses to make peace

That fact by itself would not necessarily have made an agreement on the terms of peace impossible. However, the two survivors did not live within the framework of a common civilization or, to put it in the most unambiguous language, in an identical world of thought and feeling. Consequently, they were unable to see eye to eye in regard to their future political, economic, and intellectual association. The United States, a colonial projection of Western civilization, was determined to perpetuate its cherished inheritance with no more than the inevitable minor modifications imposed by never-resting social change. The Soviet Union, on the other hand, passionately rejected the European tradition in every area of human activity. In its place it was resolved to bring to the fullest possible realization a newly devised sociopolitical system called communism. While this system was to be applied first to Russia, it was later to be imposed, by persuasion if possible but, if necessary, by force on the rest of the world. True, it had been evolved not by Russian but by west-European thinkers under the dominant influence of Karl Marx. However, the Russian followers of Marx, led by Nicolai Lenin, had with their emphasis on the dictatorship of the proletariat given it so uncompromising a twist that the west-European followers of Marx refused to accept the Leninist variant of their teaching as the true word of the master. To mark the cleavage that had ensued they called themselves socialists in sharp distinction from their Russian communist relatives.

Unbridgeable ideological cleavage between the United States and Russia

From the October day of 1917 when the communists, at that time commonly called Bolsheviks, seized power in Russia, they never permitted the least doubt to arise as to the world-embracing character of their program. Again and again in authoritative official utterances they declared that, while for the time being they were engaged with establishing their system in its country of origin, in Russia, they would never cease from the effort of carrying it, as the Messianic character of their doctrine dictated, to all the peoples of the earth. In evidence of this flaming ambition they set up for propaganda purposes a Communist International association, called Comintern for short. Liberally supplied with funds from the Russian treasury, the Comintern, with offices at Moscow, made it its business to stir up communist revolt in every country of Europe, Asia, and America. However, neither Lenin, nor Stalin after him, was averse to striking a milder tone, in case such soft-pedaling of their program gave promise of furthering their cause. They were aware that there was a group in every country which took the communist promise of economic abundance and sociopolitical equality seriously and which by its insistence on keeping open a channel of communication between the West and the foreshadowed Russian paradise would invaluably promote the planned world revolution.

Russian communism aims from the first to girdle the globe

In order to strengthen the hand of all such voluntary helpers the men of the Kremlin were prepared to have recourse to double talk. They therefore let it be understood that, contrary to the official party line, it was quite possible for the two opposed systems to live side by side in peace. This studied blunting of the more usual unvarying hostility had sufficient success to bring about the diplomatic recognition of revolutionary Russia by state after state of the anti-communist world until only the United States stood aloof. When, on the election in 1932 of Franklin D. Roosevelt to the presidency, one of his earliest acts was to follow the precedent set by the European governments, the circle of anti-communist states extending a hand of welcome to an apparently reconciled opponent was complete. The advantage to the Kremlin of the access thus gained to all the lands of the earth can hardly be exaggerated. Enjoying full recognition, Russia could cast herself in the profitable role of wolf in sheep's clothing. She could for public consumption bleat alluring messages of unity and brotherhood, and simultaneously, under cover of diplomatic immunity, pursue her inalterable purpose of digging and gnawing away at the solid supports of Western civilization.

The Russian bear dons sheep's clothing

The association of the United States and the U.S.S.R., thus renewed, was carried over into the war which broke out in 1939, and presently, owing to the alarm created by Hitler's overwhelming victories, led to a definite drawing together of the two countries. In its course the remaining suspicions of the tricky salesmen of communism tended to vanish. At war after 1941, with Germany as well as with Japan, the government and people of the United States were roused to wild enthusiasm by the spectacle of the magnificent resistance of the Russian army to

Russian resistance to Hitler releases a vast American enthusiasm the German invasion drive. Neither the official Washington spokesmen nor the newspapers and magazines that echoed the Washington sentiments could find words adequate to their admiration of the bold front presented by the Russians to the common enemy. Hardly had Congress voted Lend-Lease to help equip the nations united to oppose the Hitler march of triumph when Russia was generously showered with American tanks, airplanes, trucks, and every other conceivable form of war equipment. Consequently, such mental reservations as still persisted were thrown to the winds, with the result that the speedily completed formal alliance was floated on a broad tide of unreserved good will.

When in these circumstances the nations allied against Italy, Germany, and Japan opened discussions regarding the peace to be imposed on their enemies, Russia enjoyed such favor that the likelihood was great she would be accorded every advantage she might claim as her due. As we are aware, the really significant negotiations were not conducted among the many nations, large and small, united against the aggressors, but solely among the Big Three, Great Britain, the United States, and the Soviet Union. And from the first the Soviet Union enjoyed an immense advantage not only because of the prestige gained through its stalwart conduct of the war but also because it knew precisely what it wanted. Never for a moment did it waver in the pursuit, first, of desirable territorial additions and, second, of political advanced positions helpful to the spread of that communist evangel which was ever on its mind. Britain and the United States, on the other hand, having in the Atlantic Charter foresworn territorial gains, were chiefly concerned with strengthening the inherited ideology of Western civilization with its most recently evolved and crowning feature of a world league dedicated to the maintenance of world peace. *Unflagging pursuit of territorial and ideological advantages by Russia*

It was at the Yalta conference of February, 1945, and six months later at Potsdam that these divergent purposes were first definitely brought into the clear. Stoutly opposed in deed and principle to a world league hailed as the happy fulfillment of European tradition, Stalin and his associates of the Politburo agreed at last to join it. They did so, however, only after they had assured themselves that the veto right attributed by the Charter to the permanent members of the Security Council could always be wielded like the ax of an officially accredited executioner to kill off any objectionable measure brought forward in that body. *The mental reservation with which Russia joined the United Nations*

But that is not the whole story of the Russian acceptance of the United Nations. In payment for their purely paper concession the Russians demanded and obtained the following roster of substantial material benefits: total absorption of Latvia, Estonia, and Lithuania; an immense slice of eastern Poland; a smaller slice of eastern Germany (the Königsberg

area); and essential control of the broad rim of states—Poland, Czechoslovakia, Yugoslavia, Albania, Hungary, and Rumania—lying between
themselves and central Europe. True, this control was not granted in clear
and unambiguous terms. Rather it was offered under cover of a pious
declaration to the effect that these border states were to set up their
renovated governments on the basis of free, democratic elections. However, since the Russians occupied these war-enfeebled countries with a
triumphant army, and since, moreover, they had from the birth of their
state piled up a veritable mountain of evidence that they were unscrupulous opportunists, it was an act of naïve folly to expect that they would
honor the democratic commitment. In point of fact they did not honor it;
and by the electoral trickery of which they were past-masters they
promptly took over the enumerated border states as Russian dependencies,
thereby throwing their considerable weight into the communist scales.

Nor are we even yet done with the sour brew concocted at Yalta and
Potsdam. On Germany's acceptance of unconditional surrender there remained Japan to be dealt with. At the time of the Yalta meeting the Soviet
Union was still at peace with Japan; and the United States, which was
carrying the sole responsibility for the defeat of the Nipponese, was understandably anxious to bring the Russian army into action against an enemy
in partial possession of a country, China, well beyond the reach of American ground forces. Again Stalin held back to wait and see how far the
soliciting Americans would go to win him over. Even to his exacting eyes
what was finally dropped into his lap must have looked like celestial
manna: the southern half of the island of Sakhalin, the Kurile Islands, and
a sum of political and territorial rights in China that conferred essential
control of the great industrial province of Manchuria. A smudge on the
good name of the United States that may not be overlooked was involved
in the Chinese stipulations. China, a wartime ally of the United States, was
obliged by the action of that ally to surrender important sovereign rights
without even the pretense of a previous understanding.

These various settlements serve to point up the radical distinction between the attitude of Russia and that of the two English-speaking governments touching the shape of the postwar world. Familiar with the tradition of power politics and dedicated to that system from the start of their
government, the Russian plenipotentiaries at Yalta and Potsdam were
determined to employ the achieved victory to secure as strong a postwar
position against Britain and the United States as sharp diplomatic practice could obtain. Britain and the United States were manifestly the only
power rivals still in the field; and before many months had passed it
became clear that Britain had been so weakened by the exhausting struggle
through which it had gone that it was the United States alone that
needed to be reckoned with.

Concessions to Russia in reward for joining the United Nations

Concessions to Russia for entering the war against Japan

Russian policy shaped by considera-tions of power

Against this starkly realist approach by the Russians to current and future problems, the United States and Great Britain comported themselves as if they entertained no doubt that the age-old, war-breeding power struggle had come to an end to be replaced at long last by the peaceful settlement of all conflicts arising among nations through the instrumentality of the United Nations. By joining the peace league, however reluctantly, and by vociferously lauding communists in and out of season as congenitally committed peace-lovers, the Soviet Union succeeded in convincing the United States and Great Britain of its good intentions. A further factor in the outlook of the two English-speaking nations was their belief that the planned stripping of Germany and Japan of every vestige of politico-military power would of itself serve as the solid guarantee of the triumph of their peaceful purposes. The strange fact must be accepted that President Roosevelt and the idealist group that surrounded him persuaded themselves that the Germans and the Japanese were the only peoples addicted to war, and that by keeping them in subjection, if not permanently, at least until they had been "reformed" under the instruction of their democratic conquerors, the other peoples, their neighbors, would be set free to indulge their inborn pacifist natures. It seems not to have occurred to these high-minded dreamers, or to have occurred to them only in passing flashes, that by furthering the expansion of Russian power far beyond the Russian national boundaries they were putting themselves, and the war-shattered states of western Europe as well, at the mercy of their unduly magnified ally.

Mistaken calculations of Britain and the United States

And that brings us to the issue of Germany as it took shape at Yalta and Potsdam. On bowing to unconditional surrender Germany ceased to exist, and on then being partitioned among the three victors, with France thrown in for good measure, was consigned to the unrestricted dominion of its four masters. The sector allotted to Russia embraced what was left of eastern Germany after the amputation, in favor of Poland and Russia, of all the territory east of the Oder-Neisse line. That remainder comprised the area between the Oder and the Elbe along the Elbe's northern course and extended deeply westward of the Elbe farther south. In this region it actually approached to within one hundred miles of the Rhine. At the approximate center of this Russian-held territory lay the country's former capital, Berlin. Completely enveloped by Russian military might, Berlin could be strangled at a nod, and almost certainly would have been, had the Russians not made a concession which they were unable to refuse. Berlin, ex-capital of the crushed foe, was the symbol of the common victory and logically called for shared occupation by the four victors. Reluctantly, therefore, the Russians had to agree to divide the town into four zones of occupation, the zones of the three western powers embracing

Germany partitioned among four victor powers; shared occupation of Berlin the western sections of the city, the zone of Russia, almost as large as the other three put together, embracing the eastern sections.

Promptly on winning the war, the United States and Britain demobilized their armies, leaving behind in Germany hardly better than a token force. In striking distinction from this trustful action, the Russians kept their armies at full war-footing both in their sector of Germany and in the ring of satellite states. Then only, that is, in the course of the winter of 1945-46, did the western governments begin to awaken to the realization that they were facing an old-fashioned power situation of the kind they thought they had seen the last of with the setting up of the United Nations. Dating from that first postwar winter, even a military amateur could figure out that the Russians would have only to give marching orders to their troops to push the reduced allies out of their sectors and seize all Germany. If this did not happen, it was because Russia herself was too exhausted by the long war to begin a new struggle without an intervening period of recovery and, more probably still, because Stalin and the Politburo, in view of the unbelievable disintegration of Germany, counted on such a tidelike sweep of despairing sentiment that the inhabitants of the eastern and western sectors alike would as of one accord turn to the communist faith as the only available prospect of some kind of continuing civil order.

With alarming speed incident now followed on the heel of incident, bringing home to the western governments their grievously erroneous appraisal of Russian policy. While many people, especially among the responsible policy-makers in high office, were slow to revise their judgment, the common people in every country took little time to convince themselves that the Russians, instead of joining in the promotion of the hoped-for universal pacification, were set on maintaining and, if possible, deepening the existing postwar confusion.

It will have to suffice us to list a scant selection of these negative acts. One of the many delusions harbored by the advocates of a united world was that, with war's end, there would follow a free movement of ideas, goods, and people across the dividing line between the communist and the democratic communities. The precise opposite occurred. And, everything considered, the Soviet Union was, after all, but following the policy laid down by its founders when, with unwavering determination, it rejected the one-world directive of the West and insisted instead on its own separate and undiluted communist world. Fearing the attractiveness to the Russian people of western visitors, with their alluring layout of desirable factory products and their eager advocacy of the freedoms of democracy, the Kremlin rulers systematically choked off both material and spiritual exchanges between themselves and the West until for all practical purposes they came to a dead stop. With observer on observer on or near the scene

Britain and the United States demobilize; Russia remains at full military strength

Rapid piling up of evidence of a settled Russian hostility

The Russians drop an Iron Curtain between East and West

crying out the startling news, it presently crystallized in the picturesque expression that the communists had dropped an Iron Curtain between themselves and the non-communist world.

Another particularly enlightening incident was the Russian reaction to the proposed control of the atom bomb. This devastating weapon was the most pressing problem which on the opening of their sessions faced the United Nations. Taking the lead as the only country possessed at the time of the death-dealing novelty, the United States declared its readiness to hand over its laboriously acquired scientific knowledge to all the world and to destroy its existing stock of bombs, provided the United Nations would set up a commission with complete authority over the manufacture of the inhuman invention and with the right of inspection everywhere and at any time. Authorized universal inspection, it will at once appear, was the gist of the proposal. When the Russians, with a violence of speech that had become habitual with them, uncompromisingly rejected the inspection feature, the whole project fell through. This tragic upshot brought home to all but the most stubbornly self-deluded partisans of a united world that the Russians were resolved not to surrender the tiniest particle of their national sovereignty in the interest of world order and that, unbendingly hostile to the central concept of the United Nations, they had accepted membership for no other purpose than to paralyze its work with their ever-ready veto.

The Russians reject the United Nations' control of the atom bomb

If we now turn to the Russian procedure in regard to the treaties that would have to be concluded in order to bring the war to a close, we face another complex of events that serve to throw a clarifying light on Moscow's secret designs. After taking advantage of every delaying action in its bag of diplomatic tricks, the Soviet Union did at last permit peace treaties to be drafted with Italy, Rumania, Bulgaria, Hungary, and Finland, and to have them signed and sealed in a solemn ceremony at Paris in February, 1947. But no amount of persuasion employed by the western powers succeeded in bringing their eastern ally to take as much as the first probing step toward the fashioning of a settlement with Germany and Austria. Concealing the reason for their action behind a riot of crooked words, the Russians revealed it in a form as legible as print to anyone skilled in looking beneath the political surface. The domination of Germany and Austria had been from the beginning, and thereafter remained, a main item of the Soviet plan of world rule; and since this domination could not be wrested from the other victors in the war by means of a treaty negotiated among equals, the Russians preferred to have no treaty at all in order thus to perpetuate the appalling chaos of Germany. It was their well-reasoned assurance that the denial of a settlement to this crucial European area would in the long run inescapably draw it into the communist fold.

The Russians block every move looking toward a German and Austrian treaty of peace

The allies
incited to
vengeful re-
pression by
the revela-
tion of the
Nazi
infamies

This systematic obstructionism gradually induced a change of attitude toward conquered Germany on the part of the three western occupying powers. They had invaded Germany on fire with the passions of war, which then blazed to the sky on their learning at first hand of the horrors associated with the infamous concentration camps of the Nazis. Their immediate furious reaction was the determination to destroy every vestige of German military might and so gravely to cripple the German economy as to make it impossible for the country in any conceivable future again to wage war. Consequently, they were more interested in punishing Nazis than in rehabilitating the shattered civil administration and in reviving the arrested labors of farm and factory. German life sagged to worse than a standstill with the national currency inflated to worthlessness and the population exchanging its last possessions in the black market for food and cigarettes. As a uniquely modern note it is worthy of mention that the humble cigarette, although officially forbidden to the Germans, became through the invasion of the black market by the cigarette-loaded American soldiers the only commercial contact between conquerors and conquered.

The western
allies moved
to revise
their
German
policy

It was not until late in the year 1946 that the steady refusal of the Russians to co-operate in reviving the economic life of Germany prodded the western powers to initiate measures of their own. A cautious start was made with the plan to merge the British, American, and French zones into a single economic unit and, although two years passed before the hesitant proposal became a reality, the mere debate attending the project relit a spark of courage among the dejected inhabitants. A measure more immediately contributory to business revival was a currency reform by which the worthless marks were replaced by new marks which the three sponsoring governments agreed to insure against devaluation.

The west-
ern allies
authorize
a German
constitutive
assembly to
draw up a
German
federal
constitution

Fully aware at last that, unless they were prepared to hand Germany over to the Russians, they would have to make a positive bid for German favor, the western powers were spurred to take the earliest steps directed to giving back to the Germans some of the functions of government. The three governments, and Russia as well, had from the outset agreed among themselves to fashion none but a decentralized Germany and had, accordingly, divided the country into sixteen states with very arbitrarily drawn boundaries, five of them in the Soviet sector. Each state had then been provided with a rudimentary local government. When some kind of unification of the eleven states (called *Länder*) embraced within the three western sectors could not any longer be postponed, a constituent assembly, composed of selected delegates from the local legislatures, was authorized to meet at Bonn on the Rhine to draw up a provisional German constitution. A strictly federal instrument resulted, which established a bicameral legislature made up of a house of the people (*Bundestag*) and a house of the Länder (*Bundesrat*). The President of the Republic, endowed with largely ceremonial duties, was to be elected by the house of the people, augmented for the occasion by an equal number of delegates from the legislatures of the Länder. The effective head of the government was the Chancellor, who was to be elected by the popular house and to be responsible to it. Since this took considerable time, it was not until September, 1949, that the new government was formally installed with Bonn as its provisional capital. The idea of returning to the former capital, Berlin, had to be abandoned, since Berlin lay in the Russian sector and was not available. While the authority of the new national government remained subject to restraint and regulation by the three sponsoring powers, it could not be denied that a step had been taken toward the political rehabilitation of Germany which proved gratifying to at least the moderate, middle-of-the-road element of the population.

Simultaneously with this initiation of constructive action in Germany, the Washington government, at last persuaded of the fixed Russian purpose unflinchingly to extend its sphere of influence, adopted a policy of open resistance to communist advance wherever it threatened the stability of the democratic world. Outstanding among the trouble spots along the communist-democratic borderline were Greece and Turkey. On the collapse of the Nazis the British had invaded Greece from the sea and had set up a conservative government, culminating in the recall of the self-exiled monarch, King George. Thereupon an exasperated body of communists withdrew into the northern mountains and with the active support of the communist neighbor states, Yugoslavia, Bulgaria, and Albania, waged guerrilla warfare on the Athens government. Too feeble to quash the rebels by their own efforts, King George's ministers requested and received British support until the financially-exhausted socialist government of Britain was obliged to discontinue its aid. However, before retiring from the scene, it persuaded the United States to step into its shoes with the result that in March, 1947, President Truman made the sensational announcement before Congress of his readiness not only to take over Britain's role in Greece but also to assume the much broader responsibility of defending the democratic world wherever it was threatened by communist aggression.

The communist revolt in northern Greece

The first application of what came to be called "the Truman doctrine" was to be made, the President went on to declare, to Greece and Turkey. He requested of Congress a grant of $400,000,000 to provide these two countries with needed economic and military help. Turkey was included in the measure because Russia had recently made proposals to Turkey which, if accepted, would have put Constantinople under the fire of Russian guns; for the culminating item of the Soviet demands was the shared control of the Dardanelles. Pre-eminently the British, but in hardly

President Truman comes to the support of Greece and Turkey (1947)

less degree all the remaining free nations, became panic-stricken at the prospect of Soviet might projected into the Mediterranean. President Truman therefore did not hesitate to extend the protective embrace of the United States to Turkey as well as to Greece.

The Marshall Plan announced on June 5, 1947

American action in behalf of these two east-Mediterranean countries proved to be only a beginning. Since there was not a single European state, large or small, that was not imploring Washington for similar aid against the communist menace, directed from either within the country or from without, and since Congress could not, without becoming recalcitrant, be asked for funds in an endless succession of bills, the government elaborated a plan which went far beyond the original design of the European petitioners to obtain money for the relief of a pressing immediate situation. It was on June 5, 1947, that Secretary of State Marshall made public announcement of the far-reaching new program. Its broad purpose was to promote world-wide economic recovery by means of a multi-billion grant-in-aid to the European countries to be spread over a number of years and to be paralleled by the vigorous self-help of every subsidized beneficiary. As a universal welfare project of mutual character, the Marshall plan was submitted to the approval not only of the western democracies but of the eastern communist bloc as well. But under advice from Moscow, indistinguishable from a command, the offer to include the communist states in its operation was contemptuously rejected. Accordingly, under the name of the European Recovery Plan (E.R.P.), its scope was limited to the nations of the western world.

The Marshall Plan culminates in the Atlantic Defense Pact

There followed a busy interchange among all western European states over the by no means simple issue of giving the Marshall plan practical effect. One of the earliest results of the economic hopes it excited was to kindle enthusiasm for tighter politico-military bonds in the always possible event of a Soviet attack. In this manner a project for west-European union took shape which, with the inclusion, as purely military members, of Canada and the United States, by April, 1949, expanded into the Atlantic Defense Pact. By its terms an armed attack on any one of the parties was to be accounted an attack on all. But how about the expensive re-armament of its members, without which the pact would be no better than a pasteboard front? This in the unanimous opinion of the impoverished European countries would have to come from the United States. Once more, therefore, Washington was obliged to loosen its purse-strings, and in the autumn of 1949 made its first billion-dollar contribution to the arming of its Atlantic partners. How many more billions would have to follow in the next few years was anybody's guess.

It would be altogether false to say that it was these stiffened defense measures that first prompted the Soviet Union to adopt an impassioned hostility toward the west, since never, following the common victory, had it done other than thwart and denounce its allies at every turn. A fair objective appraisal of the situation would be that, on the disclosure of a vigorous western resistance policy, the Soviet board of strategy at Moscow merely vastly intensified its long-practiced bitter opposition. At the height of the war, in the year 1943, to be exact, the Soviet Union had made a supreme concession to its western allies by suppressing the communist propaganda agency, the Comintern. Four years later, in manifest angry reaction to the Truman doctrine and the Marshall plan it reactivated it in a somewhat altered form and with the changed name of the Cominform.

The Soviet Union revives its earlier propaganda agency under the name of Cominform

While the satellite ring of buffer states had been communized promptly on the cessation of hostilities, they were now purged of every lingering "bourgeois" and "liberal" element and tied in a solid block of opinion to the communist mother-country. Particularly illuminating in this respect is what happened in Czechoslovakia. As culturally closest to the west of all the border states, Czechoslovakia had, as a concession to its past, been permitted to retain a mixed government of communists and non-communists. In February, 1948, the Russians made an end of this twilight condition by carrying out a sweeping purge of the west-inspired elements of the government and by forging Czechoslovakia into a stout link in the unbroken communist chain of border states.

Russia forces Czecho-slovakia to conform to the communist pattern (1948)

In Yugoslavia, however, there was a slip-up. Here the proclaimed darling of Moscow, Marshal Tito, had on the expulsion of the Germans been put in absolute charge and had set up a government of impeccable communist mold. In these circumstances it was with the liveliest surprise that the news was received in the west that in June, 1948, Tito had been publicly branded a traitor by the Cominform. Although the details of the clash between him and his former patrons at Moscow must await later clarification, it is already clear that Tito and his immediate following of nationalist-minded Yugoslavs have balked at yielding the unquestioning subservience demanded by the lord of the Kremlin. Rumors have occasionally been wafted over the Iron Curtain which report the determination of the Soviet Union to snuff out the recalcitrant Tito by dispatching against him his satellite neighbors, Bulgaria, Hungary, and Rumania; but at this writing no positive action of this nature has yet developed.

Marshal Tito of Yugoslavia declared a traitor by the Cominform (1948)

All the same, there has been action, and very bitter action, at several points along the line where democratic and communist opinion meet. These cases reveal the precarious state of the world's peace and call for the closest scrutiny. From the year 1946, when the wartime alliance of the western powers with the Soviet Union definitely fell apart, it was customary to speak of the resulting tension as a "cold" war. The phrase alarmingly defined the situation, especially as it carried the implication

The hostile
relations
between
East and
West assume
the character
of a "cold"
war

of a "hot" war in the unpredictable future. It may be accepted as certain that no state in the world desired the "cold" war to be thus transformed; nevertheless, the defense-minded West and the offense-minded East were now facing each other with the determination at all costs to cling to their respective positions. In these circumstances an outbreak at any one point of the globe-encircling area of contact might easily lead to that general conflict, to World War III, which everybody dreaded but which everybody was aware hung suspended over the nations like a flaming sword.

Suppression
of the
rebellion
of the
Greek
communists
(1949)

The first of these explosions which, though limited in area as it was, contained the threat of spilling uncontrollably over its boundaries occurred in northern Greece. We have heard of the revolt instigated by the Greek communists upon King George's being seated on his throne. Conducted by small bands, it would quickly have collapsed without the support of the three communist border states of Yugoslavia, Bulgaria, and Albania. On the pouring into Greece, in accordance with the Truman doctrine, of American military equipment, the rebels at once became hard-pressed but would hardly have been wiped out as soon as they were but for the breach between Tito and Stalin. In consequence of his quarrel with his Kremlin overlord, Tito discontinued his support of the Greek guerrilla bands, which thereupon were either captured or scattered by King George's regulars. In the course of the year 1949 the Greek border issue was, at least to outward appearances, liquidated.

The
precarious
hold of the
three
western
powers on
their Berlin
sectors

Here was a western success but, before it could be definitely so scored, Moscow inaugurated an aggression in Germany, that is, at the most sensitive point of the whole long line of East-West tension. It can with complete assurance be interpreted as a spiteful counterblast to the measures recently adopted by the three western powers looking toward the economic and political unification of their respective German zones. In consequence of the trustful attitude of Britain and the United States toward Russia at the time the war ended, they had been content to leave Berlin within the Russian sector of Germany, with a limited zone of the former capital allotted to each of them as well as to their belated associate, France. It is a fact hard to believe but nevertheless true that the three western powers concluded no written agreement with their eastern partner guaranteeing them control of a system of highways and railroads across the one-hundred-mile stretch of Soviet territory that separated Berlin from its western sources of supply.

Consequently, a more precarious foothold than the one Britain, the United States, and France held in Berlin can hardly be imagined. The unsentimental Russians were of course aware of it from the first, for they had planned it that way. However, not till June, 1948, when their rage over the measures of the three powers in behalf of German rehabilitation overflowed, did they resort to their legally unrestricted authority in order to squeeze their former allies out of Berlin. In that month they instituted a highway, waterway, and railway blockade, which put a complete stop to trade and travel between western Berlin and its regular supply centers in western Germany. American ingenuity and daring proved equal to this infamous attempt to starve Berlin into surrender to the blockaders. With British support, the United States government organized a dramatic and spectacular air-lift which succeeded in supplying the Berliners with at least the main necessities of life. The resounding achievement obliged the Soviet tricksters to make public acknowledgment of the defeat of their ignoble scheme by terminating the blockade some eleven months after its imposition.

The Russian blockade of Berlin defeated by the Anglo-American air-lift (1948-49)

Simultaneously with the Berlin squeeze play, the Russians instituted a second measure aimed at the hostile West, and with this they achieved an indisputable success. From the first day of the occupation of their German zone they were resolved to get the backing of a German political party; and since the German communist party was weak and the German socialist party strong, they forced a fusion of the two which took the name of the Socialist Unity party. With considerable confidence they looked forward to a similar merger of communists and socialists throughout western Germany in the hope of thus providing themselves with a general German tool for that control of the whole country to which they never ceased to aspire. However, the setting up by the western powers of a German Federal Republic with a democratically flavored constitution so effectively checked the Russian drive that the Kremlin was obliged to lower its sights and content itself with the organization of eastern Germany as a hallmarked satellite state. They therefore prompted their agents of the Socialist Unity party to draw up a constitution for the Russian zone in strict conformity with Russian views. The document arranged for a president with largely ornamental authority and a prime minister with powers substantial enough, so far as the patient paper is concerned on which they were recorded, but incapable of standing up against a growled blast from the Russian bear. By autumn, 1949, this puppet government was established with its seat in east Berlin. It glowered fiercely at its western counterpart, which glowered back with all the ferocity its essentially tame character enabled it to simulate. Thus was there created a perfect setting for a future civil war.

The Russians set up (1949) a German satellite state in their zone

To win this foreseeable civil war the ever purposeful Russians at once began the preparations indispensable for victory. By an article of the Potsdam agreement the four victor powers were forbidden to establish any German military force whatever: Germany was to remain completely disarmed. With their habit of blandly ignoring every assumed obligation that no longer served their purpose, the Russians now set up a German

The
Russians
create a Ger-
man army
under the
deceptive
name of a
police force

federal police force, which at this writing is reported to have swollen to
sixty thousand men and to be still growing. Called a police force, it was
uniformed, organized, and drilled like any professional army and was,
in addition, equipped with the most up-to-date weapons its Russian
sponsor was able to supply. The lively protest of the western powers
against this breach of a solemnly signed treaty was disdainfully dismissed.
But did these powers do anything to meet the Russian threat, or did they
authorize their ward, the German Federal Republic, to take appropriate
counter-measures? At least to date they have done nothing, on the declared ground that the German Federal Republic was deliberately founded
by them as a weak state with the policing power expressly denied to the
central authorities and attributed exclusively to the component Länder.
Perhaps the United States, but hardly Britain and France, will agree to
revise this fatal decision before it is too late.

The
ideological
war em-
braces Asia

It will not be disputed that for the states and peoples identified with
Western civilization the area of conflict with the communist ideology of
the greatest significance is the ancient continent of Europe. However,
the two opposed ideologies became involved in mortal combat all around
the globe; and of this circumstance a comprehensive study of their
antagonism would be obliged to present a detailed account. From so
sweeping a survey the author is dispensed by reason of the limits he set
himself at the beginning of this chapter. Nonetheless, to illustrate the
round-the-globe rivalry of the two hostile systems it will be necessary to
extend our view beyond Europe to at least Asia, and to take note briefly
of events in Iran and, at greater length, of events in China and the Far
East.

The intense
Russian
interest
in Iran

Iran, formerly called Persia, borders on the north on Russia and the
Caspian Sea. As it is extraordinarily rich in oil (which Europeans in general call petroleum), it has for a long time attracted the attention of
Russian industrialist interests. For an even longer time it has drawn the
far more intent gaze of the Russian governing circles, since it lay between the landlocked Russian interior and one of the several warm-
water ports, toward which these circles from as far back as the age of
Tsar Peter I have reached out. When shortly after the beginning of the
twentieth century, the British succeeded in practically monopolizing the
oil resources of Iran, the Russian desire to share in this exploitation was
intensified by both industrial hunger and nationalist envy.

Then, in the course of World War II, the Soviet Union obtained a
military foothold in northern Iran, to which it was resolved to cling as
a means of gaining access to the Iranian riches. Pledged to its wartime
allies to withdraw its troops six months after the close of hostilities, the

Kremlin did indeed fulfill this obligation, but only after having extracted a promise from the hard-pressed Teheran government to admit it to a share in its precious fuel stores. The promise has not yet—five years after its delivery—been met; and there for the moment the matter rests. But does anyone imagine that the Kremlin has forgotten it? This question is convincingly answered by asking another: Has the use of oil by industrial nations grown greater or less since the end of the war?

The friction between Russia and Iran is bound to continue

The problem of China in the contemporary world is composed of so many distinct and complicated elements that it would require nothing short of a volume to do them justice. The inadequacy of the brief digression to which we are here restricted is therefore freely admitted. In earlier pages mention has been made of Japan's attempted conquest of China which, begun in 1931 and intensified after 1937, was still in vigorous progress when Japan collapsed in 1945 under American attack. The drawn-out and exhausting struggle in defense of the Chinese Republic was conducted by the Nationalist party, the Kuomintang, under its head, Generalissimo Chiang Kai-shek. Chiang was steadily pushed back by the much better armed invaders and would almost certainly have succumbed, had he not been liberally furnished with supplies of every kind by the United States. The defeat of the Japanese, followed by the withdrawal of their armies, liberated China with almost miraculous suddenness and opened the happy prospect of its return to peace and unity under the nationalist leadership of Chiang Kai-shek.

The war against Japan conducted by Chiang Kai-shek

It was not to be. In the course of the civil disturbances created by World War I and its equally agitated aftermath, a communist party had been organized which the conservative and traditionalist Chiang had been able neither to conciliate nor to destroy. When the Russians occupied Manchuria in 1945, in accordance with the Yalta agreement, they not only made direct contact with their Chinese brethren in the communist faith but also transferred to them the immense military stores of the captured Japanese arsenals. The leader of the Chinese communists was the able and devoted Mao Tse-tung, who at the time was a responsible Chinese patriot and not yet the fanatically indoctrinated communist he apparently afterwards became. Commanding an army equipped with the Japanese spoils, Mao felt no need of any longer subordinating himself to Chiang, whose rule he abhorred not only because of its conservatism but also, and more deeply, because it was honeycombed with corruption. From chance clashes between the two rival armies there gradually flared up a full-scale civil war, in which Mao was so steadily successful that by the end of 1949 he had driven his opponents out of the city of Canton, their last foothold on the Chinese mainland. With the remnant of his

Chinese civil war follows the defeat of Japan

forces, Chiang retired to the island of Formosa, where he was safe, at least for the time being, since Mao possessed no navy and no more than a rudimentary air force.

Chiang loses the full sup-port of the United States Although the defeat of the nationalists resulted, in the main, from the incorrigible corruption of their officials coupled with their failure to proclaim a program of reforms possessed of mass appeal, a factor not to be overlooked was the loss of full American support. Such support had gone to the Generalissimo in magnanimous abundance as long as he was engaged in fighting the common enemy, the Japanese. However, the long wartime intimacy had bred a growing exasperation with Chiang among the staff of the Department of State at Washington. These officials had for years been pressing him to reach an accommodation with Mao and the communists, advice which for reasons springing from his nationalist viewpoint he had refused to take. In punishment for his stubbornness the United States government so drastically cut supplies to him that he could, and not without some show of reason, lay his defeat at the hands of Mao (whom *his* backers, the Russians, never let down) to the American default.

The victorious Mao signs an alliance with Moscow (1950) A China dominated by a native Communist party was from a partisan American viewpoint bad enough; but it was made worse, much worse, by what followed. Mao Tse-tung had through the freely-given aid of the Soviet Union become so deeply indebted to it that, when on the retreat of the last beaten nationalist remnant to Formosa, the master of the Kremlin invited Mao to Moscow for a conference, he was quick to accept. The result of prolonged negotiations was in the spring of 1950 announced as a close Russo-Chinese alliance, and doubtless such it was. But it may also be safely assumed that it carried something of that satellite subordination the Kremlin never fails to impose.

Liberated Korea occupied by Russian and American forces Thrusting southward from the Asiatic mainland into the waters between Japan on the east and China on the west is the peninsula and state of Korea. Originally a dependency of China, it was, when Japan on its Europeanization adopted an imperialist policy, pried loose from China in a victorious war. However, only following a second and far fiercer war over its ownership with tsarist Russia, did it pass in the year 1910 into the keeping of the Mikado. In one of their preliminary discussions during World War II regarding the disposition to be made of Korea after Japan had been beaten, the Big Three had agreed that it should ultimately be set up as an independent state. Since this could not be promptly brought about on the collapse of Japan, a provisional arrangement was adopted, by the terms of which the country was to be occupied by American and Russian troops with the 38th degree of latitude serving as the line of division between their respective spheres.

In their zone of North Korea the Russians at once set to work in their familiar manner to ready the country for incorporation in their system. They dropped an Iron Curtain along the 38th degree of latitude; they set up a communist government and administration; they saturated the largely illiterate population with the slogans of their faith; they organized an army which they trained under Russian officers and equipped with Russian weapons of the latest model. In the face of this openly separatist procedure, the plan with which the occupation had begun of having the two wartime allies work out an administration for a united Korea had to be abandoned. There remained nothing for the Americans to do but to help the South Koreans organize a government in their half of the country on American, that is, democratic lines. In due course a South Korean army began to take shape. While it received some training and equipment from its American sponsors, no attempt was made to bring its effectiveness abreast of that of its North Korean counterpart. Matters standing thus, the Russians proposed that both powers bring their military occupation to a close and permit the two Koreas to function, each according to its nature. The only precaution the government of the United States took to provide abandoned South Korea with the protection it so obviously needed was to have it elected to membership in the United Nations.

Russia organizes and arms North Korea as a communist state

Before going on from here it will be advisable to return to the postwar plan, of which President Roosevelt made himself the enthusiastic champion, to put an end to power politics and its recurrent, ever more devastating wars by means of a universal league of peace. A nobly inspired project, it was greeted with applause around the globe; but it miscarried in practice, because, although every existent state, whether large or small, flocked to its banner, the adherence of the Soviet Union was motivated solely by the design to defeat every proposal for united action which did not serve its ideological ends. The consequent paralysis at the topmost level of the United Nations assured the perpetuation of power politics, which then, by the elimination (through the grinding war) of the western European states as great powers, took the form of an unconcealed antagonism between the United States and the U.S.S.R.

The idealist purpose of the United Nations defeated by the Soviet Union

When this antagonism loomed so large that it could not any longer be blinked, the United States was moved to take a bolder though, in accordance with its political character, still timidly wavering stand. The Soviet Union, on the other hand, having from its origin resolved

How
Russian
totalitarian-
ism operates
ultimately to impose its system on the whole world, had at no time departed from its purpose. Back in the days of Lenin it had brought the unwilling Russian people under the communist yoke by means of a governmental tyranny expressively labeled totalitarianism. The word signifies the total control of the country's inhabitants through measures of which the following may be considered the most decisive. (1) The individual rights, so highly cherished in the west, of free speech, assembly, religion, and election were derided and denied. (2) Only one party, the Communist party, was permitted to exist, agitate, and offer candidates for election to office. (3) Both the formulation and execution of policies were exclusively reserved to a central governing committee, the Politburo, and its masterful head. (4) An omnipotent police at its pleasure arrested and punished with incarceration, exhausting service in hundreds of slave labor camps, and outright death every open or suspected critic of the system. The totalitarian setup made possible an unflinching line of political action unattainable by any western country with its frequent change of leadership due to free discussion and free elections. Equally ominous, a pattern of aggression of universal applicability could be elaborated by the all-powerful Politburo. Concealed though that pattern might be under a cloak of deceptive phrases, it would nonetheless disclose itself to every clear-sighted student of the public scene who had taught himself to distinguish between mendacious verbiage and rock-bottom facts.

Let us now examine this pattern of aggression. By the year 1950, which is as far as this review of the two contending ideologies reaches, the The Russian
pattern of
aggression
and its suc-
cessive stages Soviet pattern of aggression presented the following outstanding features. Since the inhabitants of every country of the world were overwhelmingly in favor of peace, each forward movement plotted by the Soviet Union was preceded by a clamorous propaganda campaign which endlessly rang the changes on this strongest surviving hope of despairing mankind. The propaganda then turned the spotlight on the Soviet Union, naming it as the dedicated upholder of world peace and mounting to a climax with the denunciation of the western "capitalist" and "imperialist" democracies as the incurable instigators of war. To clinch the argument, the aggression about to be sprung by the Soviet Union was then by anticipation attributed to a western country, preferably to the United States. With the tireless clamor of the radio and press services of Russia and its satellites, attention was kept focused on the false charge. Characteristically too, since the charge was consciously false, its propounders resorted to a savagely virulent abuse in the hope of thus covering up its hollowness. They brazenly called the democracies, and again preferably the United States, plotters of evil, warmongers, pliant tools of Wall Street—to mention only a few of the milder epithets employed. In moments of simulated, red-hot indignation terms

like assassins, murderers, sons of Belial broke on the patient air with a torpedo-like detonation.

Nor was the shabby defamation limited to the orbit of the communist world. In every country of the West there was to be found a communist party with sometimes a numerous and sometimes a quite feeble body of adherents. Regardless of size, it followed what was called the party line and servilely echoed the Moscow propaganda by denouncing the democracies as evil-minded warplotters and singing the praises of the totalitarian states as the sworn apostles of peace. To these communist parties of the West would come the order from Moscow to call public meetings, if possible under the aegis of prominent non-communist citizens in order to screen from view the actual communist promoters. Such a meeting would regularly culminate in the offer of resolutions petitioning the western states to abandon their aggressive plans and follow the shining lead of peace-loving Russia.

The communist parties of the western states echo the charges of Russia

When, in the course of the winter 1949-50, all the above-enumerated manifestations put in an appearance—a round-the-world propaganda campaign in behalf of peace initiated by the Soviet Union, a chain of public peace meetings in the West summoned by communist leaders hiding behind misguided fellow-travelers, a doorbell-ringing campaign by fanatic party members for signatures to a world-wide, Moscow-prompted peace petition—when all these symptoms steadily accumulated with the advancing spring of 1950, they should infallibly have apprised the western democracies that an act of aggression was about to be committed somewhere along the immense Russian perimeter. But either because their governments were even now not persuaded of the undeviatingly aggressive character of Russian policy or because of a certain lack of resolution inherent in their liberal ideality, they were completely taken by surprise when on June 25, 1950, the army of North Korea crossed the 38th degree of latitude with intent to conquer the brother state of South Korea.

Prompted by Russia, North Korea attacks South Korea on June 25, 1950

In spite of the complete unexpectedness of the attack, President Truman acted with the greatest dispatch by sending troops to the aid of the South Koreans and by submitting the wantonly provoked crisis to an emergency meeting of the Security Council assembled at Lake Success on Long Island. That body at once found North Korea guilty of breaking the peace and ordered the immediate withdrawal of its troops from the invaded territory. Nine of the eleven members of the Council voted for the resolution; one member, Yugoslavia, abstained from voting; the remaining member, Russia, was absent. Six months before, in a huff over the refusal of the Council to replace the representative of Nationalist

The action of the United States and the Security Council of the United Nations

China with a Chinese communist delegate, the Soviet Union had instituted a boycott of the supreme governing body of the United Nations. Because of this fortunate circumstance the Security Council was able to designate North Korea as guilty of aggression without having its action quashed by the invariable Soviet veto. More conclusive evidence that it was the Soviet Union, and the Soviet Union alone, that prevented the United Nations organization from fulfilling its avowed purpose of preserving the peace cannot be imagined.

The war in Korea from June 1950 to April 1951

From the Communist aggression of June, 1950, to this writing some nine months later Korea has been the focal point of world interest on both the military and the political level. The military fluctuations have held the breathless attention of the world. In the early weeks of the invasion the North Koreans drove rapidly forward, since they had only the ill-equipped South Koreans to deal with. Although United States troops were hurried to Korea from Japan, weeks passed before they could be built into an effective fighting force by reinforcements from America and by such contingents as other members of the United Nations felt moved to contribute. Consequently, the thin defensive ranks had been almost pushed into the sea before the arrival of fresh elements enabled them to end their retreat. A vigorous offensive under General MacArthur, named supreme commander by the United Nations, then swept the enemy out of South Korea. Pursuit of him into North Korea unhappily prompted communist China to rush to his aid. In a Chinese offensive conducted with overwhelming numbers the United Nations army was disastrously beaten back. Not till some months had passed, that is, not till the end of March, 1951, could MacArthur report that his lines had been stabilized in the vicinity of the 38th parallel and that the long see-saw had ended in a kind of stalemate.

Vain attempt to conclude the war by action of the United Nations

On the political side the Korean war was centered in the United Nations, where divided counsels were quick to put in an appearance. While the small Soviet block of states never ceased to voice violent opposition to the organization's action, other member states, especially of Asia, waxed lukewarm and advocated appeasements of the communist opposition. Under their pressure communist China was invited to send a delegate to Lake Success with a view to initiating peace negotiations. But when this agent of Mao Tse-tung insisted on having all of his master's demands and, above all, the admission of Red China to the Security Council, accepted even before discussions began, the majority refused to bow to this peremptory and humiliating condition and the delegate withdrew in a huff. When in April MacArthur countered by insisting on open war with China, President Truman relieved him of his command.

BIBLIOGRAPHY

THE AUTHOR of a history of Europe addressed to young men and women beginning their study in this field is not concerned with setting forth an exhaustive bibliography. The teaching experience which he may be assumed to have gathered before writing his history has apprised him that the majority of his readers will vigorously resist every attempt to lure them beyond their daily assignment and that, instead of venturing beyond the text, they would welcome a substantial reduction of its pages.

Happily, however, the author has also gathered from classroom experience that an alert and intelligent minority will be eager to arrive at a fuller understanding of this or that person or event than is afforded by the brief treatment characteristic of a historical manual. It is for this minority that the present bibliography has been drawn up. But, while the readers whom the author has in view are youthfully alert, they are not, or at least not yet, professionally minded and consciously headed for the graduate school and a Ph.D. in history.

With the needs of interested beginners exclusively in mind the author has adopted the following plan. He will, first of all, under the heading *General Bibliography* list a number of aids serviceable for an attack on the total field embraced by his book. This *General Bibliography* he will follow with forty-five *Chapter Bibliographies,* to which he prefers to give the less pretentious designation of *Reading Lists,* and by which he believes desirable additional light will be thrown on the material treated in the successive chapters.

In pursuit of this strictly limited plan the author has been guided by a number of criteria which in his own defense as well as for the enlightenment of his readers it is advisable to set forth:

1. He has attempted to make his selections conform to the educational level of students in the introductory course in European history.

2. Recognizing the incomparable freshness of original material, he has included some sources, but only such as seemed suitable for beginners and as were readily accessible.

3. In listing secondary works he has concentrated on what in his opinion rate as spark-plug books, that is, volumes which, having literary as well as historical merit, make easy and pleasurable reading.

4. He has been careful to include a fair proportion of biographies on

the proved psychological ground that young minds turn with instinctive zest to the lives of famous and heroic individuals.

5. He has listed a number of historical novels, plays, and poems which, although works of the imagination and not strictly history, have the merit of re-creating the atmosphere of a particular period of the past or of bringing back to life some historical movement or character.

GENERAL BIBLIOGRAPHY

Bibliographical Aids. G. M. Dutcher, H. R. Shipman, S. B. Fay, A. H. Shearer, and W. H. Allison, *Guide to Historical Literature* (1931); *The Cambridge Modern History* (14 volumes). Each volume of the *Cambridge Modern History* carries a rich bibliography.

Atlases. W. R. Shepherd, *Historical Atlas* (7th ed., 1929); C. Goode, *School Atlas;* Rand, McNally & Co., *Atlas; Cambridge Modern History Atlas.*

Source Readings. J. H. Robinson, *Readings in European History;* J. H. Robinson and C. A. Beard, *Readings in Modern European History;* The University of Pennsylvania, *Translations and Reprints;* H. Webster, *Readings in Medieval and Modern History.*

General Histories. *Cambridge Modern History* (14 volumes); W. L. Langer, *An Encyclopaedia of World History;* C. J. H. Hayes, *Political and Cultural History of Modern Europe* (2 volumes); H. E. Barnes, *The History of Western Civilization* (Vol. II); C. P. Higby, *A History of Modern Europe* (2 volumes); C. D. Hazen, *Europe Since 1815;* J. Schapiro, *Modern and Contemporary European History;* F. L. Benns, *Europe Since 1914;* W. C. Langsam, *The World Since 1914;* J. E. Gillespie, *Europe in Perspective: 1815 to the Present;* Bertrand Russell, *A History of Western Philosophy.*

General Works on Economic History. H. E. Barnes, *An Economic History of the Western World;* C. Day, *A History of Commerce;* E. Osgood, *History of Industry;* F. A. Ogg, *Economic Development of Europe.*

Encyclopedias. *Encyclopaedia Britannica* (14th ed., 1929); *New International Encyclopedia; Dictionary of National Biography.*

Magazines Devoted to Current Events. *Current History* (monthly); *Foreign Policy Association Reports; Life; Time; News Week.*

READING LIST FOR CHAPTER I

(Concerning History in General and This History in Particular)

H. E. Barnes, *The New History and the Social Studies;* J. H. Robinson, *The New History: Essays Illustrating the Modern Historical Outlook;* F. M. Fling, *The Writing of History;* J. T. Shotwell, *An Introduction to the History of History;* E. M. Hulme, *History and Its Neighbors.*

READING LIST FOR CHAPTER 2

(The First or Medieval Phase of West-European History)

J. W. Thompson and E. N. Johnson, *An Introduction to Medieval Europe, 300-1500;* D. C. Munro and R. J. Sontag, *The Middle Ages, 395-1500;* C.

Stephenson, *Medieval History;* H. Pirenne, *Medieval Cities: Their Origins and the Revival of Trade;* H. Pirenne, *Economic and Social History of Medieval Europe;* S. Baldwin, *Organization of Medieval Christianity* (Berkshire Studies); C. Day, *A History of Commerce;* G. G. Coulton, *Medieval Panorama;* E. Power, *Medieval People* (sketches of people representative of the various classes); W. S. Davis, *Life on a Medieval Barony* (picture of a typical feudal community); J. H. Randall, *The Making of the Modern Mind.*

READING LIST FOR CHAPTER 3

(The Second or Renaissance Phase of West-European History)

H. S. Lucas, *The Renaissance and the Reformation;* J. E. Gillespie, *A History of Geographical Discovery;* C. Day, *A History of Commerce;* R. S. Rait, *Life in a Medieval University;* G. F. Young, *The Medici;* F. Schevill, *A History of Florence;* H. Gardner, *Art Through the Ages;* G. Vasari, *Lives of the Most Eminent Painters, Sculptors, and Architects.*

Sources. F. Schevill, *First Century of Italian Humanism;* B. Cellini, *Autobiography;* N. Machiavelli, *The Prince.*

Fiction. G. Eliot, *Romola* (Florence in the Renaissance); E. G. Bulwer-Lytton, *Rienzi* (the struggle of the Roman people against the feudal barons); V. Hugo, *Notre-Dame de Paris* (Paris during medieval and Renaissance times); D. Merejkowski, *The Romance of Leonardo da Vinci;* C. Reade, *The Cloister and the Hearth* (western Europe in the time of Erasmus); W. Scott, *Quentin Durward* (France under Louis XI); Mrs. Hicks Beach, *A Cardinal of the Medici.*

READING LIST FOR CHAPTER 4

(The European States on the Eve of the Reformation)

H. S. Lucas, *The Renaissance and the Reformation;* E. F. Henderson, *Short History of Germany;* H. D. Sedgwick, *Spain, a Short History of Its Politics, Literature, and Art;* C. Headlam, *France;* W. E. Lunt, *History of England.*

READING LIST FOR CHAPTER 5

(The German Reformation to the Peace of Augsburg, 1555)

H. S. Lucas, *The Renaissance and the Reformation;* P. Smith, *Age of the Reformation;* E. Emerton, *Desiderius Erasmus of Rotterdam;* P. Smith, *The Life and Letters of Martin Luther;* A. C. McGiffert, *Martin Luther;* E. Armstrong, *The Emperor Charles V* (2 volumes); D. B. W. Lewis, *Charles of Europe;* J. T. McNeill, *Makers of Christianity.*

Sources. D. Erasmus, *In Praise of Folly.*

Fiction. W. S. Davis, *The Friar of Wittenberg;* M. Roberts, *In the Olden Time* (the peasant war in Germany).

READING LIST FOR CHAPTER 6

(The Spread of the Reformation to the Scandinavian Countries and to Switzerland)

H. S. Lucas, *The Renaissance and the Reformation;* P. Smith, *Age of the Reformation;* R. N. Bain, *Scandinavia: A Political History of Denmark, Norway, and Sweden from 1513;* S. M. Jackson, *Huldreich Zwingli;* W. Martin, *History of Switzerland.*

READING LIST FOR CHAPTER 7

(The Strengthening of the Reformation Under the Leadership of Calvin and the Counter-Reformation of the Catholic Church)

H. S. Lucas, *The Renaissance and the Reformation;* P. Smith, *Age of the Reformation;* F. C. Palm, *Calvinism and the Religious Wars;* W. Walker, *John Calvin;* A. W. Ward, *The Counter-Reformation;* B. Kidd, *The Counter Reformation;* P. Van Dyke, *Ignatius Loyola;* E. Vacandard, *The Inquisition: A Critical and Historical Study of the Coercive Power of the Church.*
Fiction. J. Oxenham, *The Hawk of Como* (life in 16th century Italy).

READING LIST FOR CHAPTER 8

(Spain Under Emperor Charles V and His Son, Philip II: Her World Eminence and Her Decay)

H. S. Lucas, *The Renaissance and the Reformation;* P. Smith, *Age of the Reformation;* E. D. Salmon, *Imperial Spain;* H. D. Sedgwick, *Spain;* R. B. Merriman, *Rise of the Spanish Empire;* E. Armstrong, *The Emperor Charles V* (2 volumes); D. B. W. Lewis, *Charles of Europe;* M. A. S. Hume, *Philip II of Spain;* D. Loth, *Philip II of Spain.*
Fiction. F. M. Crawford, *In the Palace of the King* (Philip II and Don John); G. Slocombe, *Don John of Austria.*

READING LIST FOR CHAPTER 9

(Tudor England: From the Accession of Henry VIII to the Death of Elizabeth)

E. P. Cheyney, *A Short History of England;* W. E. Lunt, *History of England;* F. Seebohm, *Oxford Reformers* (John Colet, Erasmus, and Thomas More); F. Hackett, *Henry VIII;* J. Neale, *Queen Elizabeth;* L. Strachey, *Elizabeth and Essex;* S. Zweig, *Mary, Queen of Scotland and the Isles;* L. F. Salzman, *England in Tudor Times, an Account of Its Social Life and Industries;* M. and C. H. B. Quennell, *A History of Everyday Things in England* (Vol. II, 1500-1799); D. Hartley and M. M. Elliott, *Life and Work of the People of England, 16th Century* (a pictorial record from contemporary sources); H. D. Traill, *Social England* (Vol. III).
Sources. T. More, *Utopia;* F. Roper, *Life of More;* R. Chambers, *Thomas More.*

Fiction. S. L. Clemens, *The Prince and the Pauper* (adventures of a boy prince); J. Bennett, *Master Skylark* (Elizabeth, Shakespeare, and others); M. Baring, *Robert Peckham;* W. Scott, *Kenilworth* (Time of Elizabeth); C. Kingsley, *Westward Ho!* (Drake and the Armada); M. Anderson, *Elizabeth the Queen* (drama); M. Anderson, *Mary of Scotland* (drama).

READING LIST FOR CHAPTER 10

(The Revolt of the Netherlands and the Founding of the Dutch Republic)

H. S. Lucas, *The Renaissance and the Reformation;* P. Smith, *Age of the Reformation;* J. E. Barker, *Rise and Decline of the Netherlands;* J. L. Motley, *Rise of the Dutch Republic* (3 volumes); R. Putnam, *William the Silent;* C. Wedgwood, *William the Silent;* D. Ogg, *Europe in the Seventeenth Century;* C. Day, *A History of Commerce.*

Fiction. H. R. Haggard, *Lysbeth, a Tale of the Dutch* (story of a burgher family in the time of William the Silent, 1544-1574); A. Dumas, *The Black Tulip* (William III); I. Zangwill, *The Maker of Lenses* (Spinoza).

READING LIST FOR CHAPTER 11

(The Reformation and the Civil Wars in France)

H. S. Lucas, *The Renaissance and the Reformation;* C. Headlam, *France;* F. Hackett, *Francis I;* P. Van Dyke, *Catherine de Medicis;* R. Roeder, *Catherine de' Medici and the Lost Revolution;* F. C. Palm, *Calvinism and the Religious Wars;* W. Besant, *Coligny;* P. F. Willert, *Henry of Navarre and the Huguenots in France;* J. B. Perkins, *Richelieu and the Growth of French Power;* D. Ogg, *Europe in the Seventeenth Century;* J. R. Boulenger, *The Seventeenth Century* (survey of French history and culture).

Fiction. B. Runkle, *The Helmet of Navarre* (period of Henry of Navarre); A. Dumas, *The Three Musketeers* (period of Richelieu); *Twenty Years After* (period of Mazarin); R. Sabatini, *Bardelys the Magnificent* (Louis XIII, Richelieu, rebellion in Languedoc); S. J. Weyman, *Under the Red Robe* (Richelieu).

READING LIST FOR CHAPTER 12

(The Thirty Years' War)

S. R. Gardiner, *Thirty Years' War, 1618-1648;* C. Wedgwood, *The Thirty Years' War;* D. Ogg, *Europe in the Seventeenth Century;* E. F. Henderson, *A Short History of Germany;* C. R. L. Fletcher, *Gustavus Adolphus;* T. A. Dodge, *Gustavus Adolphus: A History of the Art of War from Its Revival after the Middle Ages to the End of the Spanish Succession War;* M. Goldsmith, *Christina of Sweden.*

Fiction. Z. Topelius, *The King's Ring* (Gustavus Adolphus); D. Defoe, *Memoirs of a Cavalier* (Thirty Years' War, 1632-1638).

READING LIST FOR CHAPTER 13

(Leading Cultural Trends in the Period of the Reformation and Counter-Reformation)

General. P. Smith, *A History of Modern Culture* (Vol. I, The Great Renewal, 1543-1687); J. R. Boulenger, *The Seventeenth Century;* G. N. Clark, *The Seventeenth Century;* L. Thorndike, *A Short History of Civilization.*

Art, Music. H. Gardner, *Art Through the Ages;* F. Kimball and G. H. Edgell, *A History of Architecture;* G. H. Chase and C. R. Post, *A History of Sculpture;* T. Craven, *Men of Art;* C. G. Hamilton, *Outlines of Music History;* G. Grove, *A Dictionary of Music and Musicians.*

Literature. J. Macy, *The Story of the World's Literature;* W. V. Moody and R. M. Lovett, *A History of English Literature;* W. A. Neilson and A. H. Thorndike, *A History of English Literature;* K. Francke, *A History of German Literature as Determined by Social Forces;* G. Northup, *An Introduction to Spanish Literature;* W. A. Nitze and E. P. Dargan, *A History of French Literature;* R. Garnett, *A History of Italian Literature.*

Philosophy. A. K. Rogers, *A Student's History of Philosophy;* W. Durant, *The Story of Philosophy;* J. H. Randall, *The Making of the Modern Mind;* E. S. Haldane, *Descartes, His Life and Times.*

Science. W. T. Sedgwick and H. W. Tyler, *A Short History of Science;* R. J. Harvey-Gibson, *Two Thousand Years of Science;* P. Lenard, *Great Men of Science, a History of Scientific Progress;* J. H. Fahie, *Galileo, His Life and Work;* W. W. Bryant, *Galileo.*

Discovery, Commerce, Industry, International Law. J. E. Gillespie, *A History of Geographical Discovery;* L. B. Packard, *The Commercial Revolution;* C. Day, *A History of Commerce;* J. N. Figgis, *From Gerson to Grotius;* H. Vrieland, *Hugo Grotius.*

READING LIST FOR CHAPTER 14

(The Stuarts and the Puritan Revolution)

E. P. Cheyney, *A Short History of England;* W. E. Lunt, *History of England;* S. R. Gardiner, *The Puritan Revolution;* G. M. Trevelyan, *England under the Stuarts;* H. Belloc, *Charles I, King of England;* C. H. Firth, *Oliver Cromwell;* T. Carlyle, *Life and Letters of Oliver Cromwell;* O. Airy, *Charles II;* H. D. Traill, *William III;* H. D. Traill, *Social England* (Vol. IV); M. and C. H. B. Quennell, *A History of Everyday Things in England* (Vol. II); D. Hartley and M. M. Elliott, *Life and Work of the People of England, 17th Century;* S. Pepys, *Diary* (*Everybody's Pepys,* abridged and edited by O. F. Morshead); J. Evelyn, *Diary* (contemporary, like Pepys, and ranking as a source).

Fiction. W. Scott, *The Fortunes of Nigel* (time of James I); *Rob Roy* (time of the Jacobite rising of 1715); C. Stratton, *Robert the Roundhead* (the Puritan Revolution); B. M. Dix, *Hugh Gwyeth* (Cavalier and Roundhead); A. T.

Quiller-Couch, *The Splendid Spur* (time of Charles I); D. Defoe, *A Journal of the Plague Year* (1664-65); J. Drinkwater, *Mr. Charles, King of England* (drama).

READING LIST FOR CHAPTER 15

(The Ascendancy of France Under Louis XIV)

L. B. Packard, *Age of Louis XIV* (Berkshire Studies); C. Headlam, *France;* A. Tilley, ed., *Modern France; a Companion to French Studies;* Voltaire, *Age of Louis XIV;* C. Day, *A History of Commerce;* L. B. Packard, *The Commercial Revolution* (the work of Colbert); L. Bertrand, *Louis XIV;* C. Hugon, *Social France in the Seventeenth Century* (manners and customs of the times); D. Ogg, *Europe in the Seventeenth Century* (general history of Europe); J. R. Boulenger, *The Seventeenth Century* (survey of French history and culture); G. N. Clark, *The Seventeenth Century* (survey of European society and culture).

Sources. G. Masson, *Selections from the Letters of Madame de Sévigné.*

Fiction. A. Dumas, *The Black Tulip* (Louis' invasion of the Netherlands); *Vicomte de Bragelonne* (period of Louis XIV).

READING LIST FOR CHAPTER 16

(Baltic Affairs: The Rise of Russia and the Decline of Sweden)

F. Nowak, *Medieval Slavdom and the Rise of Russia* (Berkshire Studies); S. Platonov, *History of Russia;* W. A. Phillips, *Poland;* R. Dyboski, *Outlines of Polish History;* F. Schevill, *A History of the Balkan Peninsula* (Russia and the Ottoman empire); S. Graham, *Peter the Great;* M. Jones, *Peter, Called the Great;* G. Kaus, *Catherine, the Portrait of an Empress;* K. Anthony, *Catherine the Great;* Voltaire, *Charles the Twelfth;* R. N. Bain, *Charles XII and the Collapse of the Swedish Empire.*

Fiction. H. Sienkiewicz, *The Field of Glory* (John Sobieski, 1682-1683); H. Sienkiewicz, *With Fire and Sword; The Deluge; Pan Michael* (the border struggles of Poland and Russia); M. Bowen, *King-at-arms* (Charles XII and Peter); D. Merejkowski, *Peter and Alexis, the Romance of Peter the Great;* J. Porter, *Thaddeus of Warsaw* (partition of Poland, 1794-1800).

READING LIST FOR CHAPTER 17

(German Affairs: The Rise of Prussia and the Rebirth of Austria)

E. F. Henderson, *A Short History of Germany;* G. M. Priest, *Germany Since 1740;* F. W. Longman, *Frederick the Great;* W. F. Reddaway, *Frederick the Great and the Rise of Prussia;* T. Carlyle, *Frederick the Great;* C. L. Morris, *Maria Theresa, the Last Conservative;* J. F. Bright, *Joseph II;* S. K. Padover, *The Revolutionary Emperor* (Joseph II); G. Brunn, *The Enlightened Despots* (Berkshire Studies); C. Day, *A History of Commerce.*

Fiction. C. Major, *A Gentle Knight of Old Brandenburg* (Frederick William I, father of Frederick the Great); M. E. Seawell, *Lively Adventures of Gavin Hamilton* (Seven Years' War); L. Mulbach, *Frederick the Great and His Court.*

READING LIST FOR CHAPTER 18

(Great Britain and France in the Eighteenth Century)

W. E. Lunt, *History of England;* C. G. Buffington, *The Second Hundred Years' War* (Berkshire Studies); C. G. Robertson, *England under the Hanoverians;* H. Robinson, *The Development of the British Empire;* F. Parkman, *A Half Century of Conflict; Montcalm and Wolfe;* H. D. Traill, *Social England* (Vol. V); A. S. Turberville, *English Men and Manners in the Eighteenth Century;* J. B. Botsford, *English Society in the Eighteenth Century;* M. and C. H. B. Quennell, *A History of Everyday Things in England* (Vol. II); D. Hartley and M. M. Elliott, *Life and Work of the People of England, Eighteenth Century;* J. Morley, *Sir Robert Walpole;* Lord Rosebery, *William Pitt;* G. R. Gleig, *Life of Robert, Lord Clive;* C. Headlam, *France;* P. Gaxotte, *Louis the Fifteenth and His Times;* G. B. Malleson, *Dupleix;* H. Sée, *Economic and Social Conditions in France during the Eighteenth Century;* L. Ducros, *French Society in the Eighteenth Century;* P. Russell, *The Glittering Century;* C. Stryienski, *The Eighteenth Century.*

Fiction. W. M. Thackeray, *Henry Esmond* (England about 1690-1715); *The Virginians* (about 1750); W. Scott, *Waverley* (time of the Stuart rebellion, 1745); S. J. Weyman, *Queen's Folly* (time of Queen Anne); B. Tarkington, *Monsieur Beaucaire* (time of Beau Nash); H. Fielding, *Tom Jones* (contemporary fiction, about 1750); O. Goldsmith, *The Vicar of Wakefield* (contemporary fiction, about 1766).

READING LIST FOR CHAPTER 19

(Leading Cultural Trends Between 1648 and 1789)

General. P. Smith, *A History of Modern Culture* (Vol. I, The Great Renewal, 1543-1687; Vol. II, The Enlightenment, 1687-1776); L. Thorndike, *A Short History of Civilization;* R. B. Mowat, *The Age of Reason;* P. Russell, *The Glittering Century.*

Science. W. T. Sedgwick and H. W. Tyler, *A Short History of Science;* P. Lenard, *Great Men of Science, a History of Scientific Progress;* W. W. R. Ball, *A Short Account of the History of Mathematics;* C. Singer, *A Short History of Medicine;* G. S. Brett, *Sir Isaac Newton;* B. Jaffe, *Crucibles, the Lives and Achievements of the Great Chemists;* P. Mantoux, *The Industrial Revolution in the Eighteenth Century.*

Philosophy. A. K. Rogers, *A Student's History of Philosophy;* F. Thilly, *A History of Philosophy;* W. Durant, *The Story of Philosophy.*

The Enlightenment. D. Mornet, *French Political Thought in the Eighteenth Century;* K. Martin, *French Liberal Thought in the Eighteenth Century;* A. Sorel, *Montesquieu;* J. Morley, *Voltaire;* A. Maurois, *Voltaire;* J. Morley, *Rousseau;* J. Morley, *Diderot and the Encyclopedists;* L. Say, *Turgot;* H. J. Laski, *Political Thought in England from Locke to Bentham;* H. Higgs, *The Physiocrats;* J. Rae, *Life of Adam Smith.*

Art. H. Gardner, *Art Through the Ages;* F. Kimball and G. H. Edgell, *A History of Architecture;* G. H. Chase and C. R. Post, *A History of Sculpture;* T. Craven, *Men of Art.*

Literature. J. Macy, *The Story of the World's Literature;* W. V. Moody and R. M. Lovett, *A History of English Literature;* W. A. Neilson and A. H. Thorndike, *A History of English Literature;* K. Francke, *A History of German Literature as Determined by Social Forces;* W. A. Nitze and E. P. Dargan, *A History of French Literature.*

READING LIST FOR CHAPTER 20

(The French Revolution, 1789-1799)

E. Lowell, *The Eve of the French Revolution;* H. A. Taine, *The Ancient Regime;* L. Ducros, *French Society in the Eighteenth Century;* H. Sée, *Economic and Social Conditions in France during the Eighteenth Century;* L. R. Gottschalk, *The Era of the French Revolution;* L. Madelin, *The French Revolution;* A. Mathiez, *The French Revolution;* L. Madelin, *Men of the French Revolution;* L. Gershoy, *French Revolution;* H. Béraud, *Twelve Portraits of the French Revolution;* P. F. Willert, *Mirabeau;* L. R. Gottschalk, *Jean Paul Marat: A Study in Radicalism;* L. Madelin, *Danton;* H. Belloc, *Robespierre;* S. Zweig, *Marie Antoinette.*

Fiction. A. Dumas, *The Queen's Necklace* (1784-85); *Taking of the Bastille* (1789); *La Comtesse de Charny* (1792); *Le Chevalier de la Maison Rouge* (1793); C. Dickens, *A Tale of Two Cities;* V. Hugo, *Ninety-three;* R. Sabatini, *Scaramouche;* W. S. Davis, *The Whirlwind;* A. France, *The Gods Athirst;* F. Gras, *The Reds of the Midi; The Terror; The White Terror* (lower class viewpoint).

READING LIST FOR CHAPTER 21

(Napoleon Bonaparte and the French Empire, 1799-1815)

L. R. Gottschalk, *The Era of the French Revolution;* L. Madelin, *Consulate and Empire;* R. B. Mowat, *The Diplomacy of Napoleon;* P. Guedalla, *The Hundred Days;* P. Kircheisen, *Napoleon;* H. A. L. Fisher, *Napoleon;* E. Ludwig, *Napoleon;* A. Fournier, *Napoleon the First;* J. McCabe, *Talleyrand;* S. Zweig, *Joseph Fouché;* P. Guedalla, *Wellington;* W. C. Russell, *Horatio Nelson;* G. M. Priest, *Germany Since 1740;* G. S. Ford, *Stein and the Era of Reform in Prussia;* E. C. Corti, *The Rise of the House of Rothschild* (picture of Napoleonic Era).

Fiction. L. Tolstoy, *War and Peace* (ranks among the greatest historical novels); S. J. Weyman, *The Traveler in the Fur Cloak* (French occupation of Germany); F. B. Austin, *The Road to Glory* (young Napoleon); R. Sabatini, *The Snare* (the War in the Spanish Peninsula).

READING LIST FOR CHAPTER 22

(The Conservative Reaction and the Revolutionary Movements that Undermined It, 1815-1830)

F. B. Artz, *Reaction and Revolution, 1814-1832;* C. K. Webster, *The Congress of Vienna;* A. May, *The Age of Metternich* (a brief account); S. Cecil, *Metternich;* H. Du Coudray, *Metternich;* W. P. Cresson, *Diplomatic Portraits* (Alexander I, Napoleon, Castlereagh, Metternich); H. D. Sedgwick, *Spain;* E. F. Henderson, *A Short History of Germany;* M. Karpovich, *Imperial Russia,* 1801-1917 (Berkshire Studies); W. A. Phillips, *Poland.*

Fiction. E. W. Underwood, *The Penitent* (Alexander I); J. Verne, *Michael Strogoff, the Courier of the Czar* (Russia in Siberia, mid-nineteenth century); A. Dumas, *The Count of Monte Cristo;* V. Hugo, *Les Misérables* (1815-1848).

READING LIST FOR CHAPTER 23

(The Reign of Louis Philippe (1830-1848) and the Revolutions That Followed His Overthrow in 1848)

C. Headlam, *France;* G. L. Dickinson, *Revolution and Reaction in Modern France;* J. Lucas-Dubreton, *The Restoration and the July Monarchy;* J. M. S. Allison, *Monsieur Thiers;* H. A. L. Fisher, *Bonapartism;* A. L. Guérard, *French Civilization in the Nineteenth Century;* C. E. Maurice, *The Revolutionary Movement of 1848-1849;* E. F. Henderson, *A Short History of Germany;* B. King, *A History of Italian Unity* (2 volumes); G. F. H. and J. Berkeley, *Italy in the Making, 1846-1848;* G. M. Trevelyan, *Garibaldi and the Making of Italy;* L. Leger, *History of Austria-Hungary.*

Fiction. G. Meredith, *Vittoria* (1848, Italy); A. Dumas, *La Vendée* (1832).

READING LIST FOR CHAPTER 24

(Great Britain from 1815 to the Second Reform Bill, 1867)

J. A. R. Marriott, *England Since Waterloo;* G. M. Trevelyan, *British History in the Nineteenth Century;* W. E. Lunt, *History of England;* G. Slater, *The Making of Modern England;* P. Guedalla, *Wellington;* C. Seymour, *Electoral Reform in England, 1832-1885;* H. D. Traill, *Social England* (Vol. V); G. D. H. Cole, *A Short History of the British Working Class Movement, 1789-1848;* J. Morley, *Life of Richard Cobden.*

Fiction. J. Austen, *Pride and Prejudice; Emma;* E. Gaskell, *Cranford;* C. Dickens, *Dombey and Son; David Copperfield; Bleak House;* W. M. Thackeray, *The Newcomes* (Early Victorian Age); *Vanity Fair.*

READING LIST FOR CHAPTER 25

(The Industrial Revolution)

F. A. Ogg, *The Economic Development of Modern Europe;* F. C. Dietz, *The Industrial Revolution* (Berkshire Studies); E. Osgood, *History of Industry;* F. S. Marvin, *Century of Hope;* W. B. Kaempffert, *Popular History of*

Invention (2 volumes); E. W. Bryan, *The Progress of Invention in the Nine-teenth Century;* A. P. Usher, *Industrial History of England;* G. A. Trevelyan, *British History in the Nineteenth Century;* R. E. Prothero, *English Farming, Past and Present* (4th ed., 1927); J. L. and B. Hammond, *The Rise of Modern Industry;* S. and B. Webb, *History of Trade Unionism;* C. J. H. Hayes, *British Social Politics* (1913); J. H. Clapham, *The Economic Development of France and Germany, 1815-1914;* H. W. Laidler, *History of Socialist Thought;* O. Rühle, *Karl Marx, His Life and Work;* Karl Marx, *Capital;* F. Engels, *Socialism, Utopian and Scientific.*

Fiction. Mrs. D. M. Craik, *John Halifax, Gentleman* (1780-1834); B. Disraeli, *Coningsby* (1832-1840, politics); *Sybil* (1837-1842, labor conditions); C. Dickens, *Oliver Twist; Hard Times;* G. Eliot, *Felix Holt, the Radical* (about 1832); P. Bentley, *Inheritance* (social changes brought about by machinery); C. Kingsley, *Alton Locke* (workingmen of the 1840's).

READING LIST FOR CHAPTER 26

(The Rise of Napoleon III and the Unification of Italy)

H. A. L. Fisher, *Bonapartism;* P. Guedalla, *The Second Empire;* A. Forbes, *Napoleon the Third;* F. A. Simpson, *Louis Napoleon and the Recovery of France, 1848-1856;* A. L. Guérard, *French Civilization in the Nineteenth Century;* B. King, *A History of Italian Unity;* J. A. R. Marriott, *Makers of Modern Italy;* P. Orsi, *Cavour and the Making of Modern Italy;* E. Cesaresco, *Life of Cavour;* G. M. Trevelyan, *Garibaldi and the Thousand;* S. Barr, *Mazzini: Portrait of an Exile.*

Fiction. F. M. Crawford, *Saracinesca; Sant'Ilario; Don Orsino; Corleone* (Italy, 1865-1900).

READING LIST FOR CHAPTER 27

(The Unification of Germany and the Fall of Napoleon III)

E. F. Henderson, *A Short History of Germany;* G. M. Priest, *Germany Since 1740;* F. Schevill, *The Making of Modern Germany;* M. Smith, *Bismarck and German Unity;* J. A. R. Marriott and C. G. Robertson, *The Evolution of Prussia;* J. W. Headlam, *Bismarck and the Foundation of the German Empire;* W. H. Dawson, *The German Empire;* C. G. Robertson, *Bismarck;* R. Sencourt, *Napoleon III.*

Fiction. A. Daudet, *Monday Tales* (Franco-German War); E. Zola, *The Downfall* (Franco-German War).

READING LIST FOR CHAPTER 28

(Italy, France, Germany, and Austria-Hungary to the Outbreak of World War I)

Italy. B. King and J. Okey, *Italy Today;* F. M. Underwood, *United Italy;* B. Croce, *A History of Italy, 1871-1915;* W. Parsons, *The Pope and Italy.*

France. A. Tilley (ed.), *Modern France;* E. M. Sait, *Government and Politics in France;* R. Recouly, *The Third Republic;* H. Stannard, *Gambetta;* A. L. Guérard, *French Civilization in the Nineteenth Century.*

Germany. R. H. Fife, *The German Empire between Two Wars;* W. H. Dawson, *The German Empire;* H. Lichtenberger, *Germany and Its Evolution in Modern Times;* L. L. Snyder, *From Bismarck to Hitler: Background of Modern German Nationalism.*

Austria-Hungary. H. W. Steed, *The Hapsburg Monarchy;* J. Redlich, *Emperor Francis Joseph of Austria;* G. Drage, *Austria-Hungary* (a descriptive analysis).

Fiction. M. B. Whitney, *The Torchbearers* (political parties in Italy, 1898-1900).

READING LIST FOR CHAPTER 29

(Great Britain from the Second Reform Bill (1867) to the Outbreak of World War I)

W. E. Lunt, *History of England;* G. Slater, *The Making of Modern England;* G. M. Trevelyan, *British History in the Nineteenth Century;* H. Robinson, *Development of the British Empire;* J. A. Williamson, *Builders of the Empire;* E. Wingfield-Stratford, *The Victorian Aftermath* (to 1914); H. D. Traill, *Social England* (Vol. V); P. Guedalla, *Palmerston;* J. Morley, *Life of W. E. Gladstone;* W. P. Hall, *Mr. Gladstone;* L. Strachey, *Eminent Victorians; Queen Victoria;* A. Maurois, *Disraeli;* H. Spender, *The Prime Minister, Lloyd George.*

Fiction. J. Galsworthy, *Forsyte Saga.*

READING LIST FOR CHAPTER 30

(The Russian and Ottoman Empires from the Congress of Vienna (1815) to the Outbreak of World War I)

Russia. M. Karpovich, *Imperial Russia, 1801-1917* (Berkshire Studies); S. Platonov, *History of Russia;* G. Vernadsky, *A History of Russia;* D. S. Mirsky, *Russia, A Social History;* A. Rambaud, *The Expansion of Russia;* M. Essad-Bey, *Nicholas II, Prisoner of the Purple;* R. Fulop-Miller, *Rasputin, the Holy Devil;* R. K. Douglas, *Europe and the Far East.*

Turkey and the Balkan States. W. Miller, *The Ottoman Empire;* C. N. E. Eliot, *Turkey in Europe;* F. Schevill, *A History of the Balkan Peninsula;* W. M. Gewehr, *The Rise of Nationalism in the Balkans, 1800-1930* (Berkshire Studies); J. A. R. Marriott, *The Eastern Question;* L. Sergeant, *Greece in the Nineteenth Century;* H. W. Temperley, *History of Serbia;* T. W. Riker, *Making of Roumania.*

Fiction. I. Turgenev, *Fathers and Sons* (clash of imported European and native opinion in Russia).

READING LIST FOR CHAPTER 31

(The Partition of Africa Preceded by an Analysis of Foreign Policy as Practiced by the Great Powers)

D. E. Owen, *Imperialism and Nationalism in the Far East;* J. W. Swain, *Beginning the Twentieth Century;* R. J. Sontag, *European Diplomatic His-*

tory, 1871-1932; P. T. Moon, *Imperialism and World Politics;* H. A. Gibbons, *The New Map of Africa* (1900-1916); *The New Map of Asia* (1900-1919); H. L. Hoskins, *European Imperialism in Africa;* H. H. Johnston, *The Opening Up of Africa;* J. S. Keltie, *The Partition of Africa;* H. M. Stanley, *How I Found Livingstone;* H. Feis, *Europe, the World's Banker, 1870-1914.*

READING LIST FOR CHAPTER 32

(The Lesser States of Europe from the Congress of Vienna (1815) to the Outbreak of World War I)

General. F. A. Ogg, *The Governments of Europe.*

Spain. H. D. Sedgwick, *Spain.*

Portugal. H. M. Stephens, *Portugal.*

Switzerland. W. Martin, *History of Switzerland;* H. D. Lloyd, *A Study of Swiss Democracy;* J. M. Vincent, *Government in Switzerland.*

Netherlands. G. Edmundson, *History of Holland;* A. J. Barnow, *Holland under Queen Wilhelmina.*

Belgium. R. C. K. Ensor, *Belgium;* E. Corti, *Leopold I of Belgium.*

Scandinavia. R. N. Bain, *Scandinavia: A Political History of Denmark, Norway, and Sweden from 1513 to 1900;* G. Lundbörg, *Sweden, Its People and Industries;* K. Gjerset, *History of the Norwegian People.*

READING LIST FOR CHAPTER 33

(Leading Cultural Trends of the Nineteenth Century)

Science. W. T. Sedgwick and H. W. Tyler, *A Short History of Science;* C. Singer, *A Short History of Medicine;* H. S. Williams, *The Story of Nineteenth Century Science;* F. S. Marvin, *The Century of Hope;* A. Geikie, *Founders of Geology;* J. C. Brown, *The History of Chemistry;* R. Vallery-Radot, *Life of Pasteur.*

Biology, Evolution. W. A. Locy, *Biology and Its Makers;* H. F. Osborn, *From the Greeks to Darwin;* G. A. Dorsey, *The Evolution of Charles Darwin.*

Philosophy, Religion. J. H. Randall, *The Making of the Modern Mind;* A. H. Silver, *Religion in a Changing World;* W. Barry, *The Papacy and Modern Times;* C. Dawson, *Religion and the Modern State.*

Literature. W. V. Moody and R. M. Lovett, *A History of English Literature;* W. A. Neilson and A. H. Thorndike, *A History of English Literature;* W. A. Nitze and E. P. Dargan, *A History of French Literature;* D. S. Mirsky, *A History of Russian Literature.*

Art. H. Gardner, *Art Through the Ages;* F. J. Mather, *Modern Painting;* T. Duret, *Manet and the French Impressionists;* T. Craven, *Men of Art.*

Music. C. Grove, *A Dictionary of Music and Musicians;* N. H. Dale, *Famous Composers;* D. Ewen, *From Bach to Stravinsky.*

READING LIST FOR CHAPTER 34

(The Diplomatic Prelude to World War I: Triple Alliance and Triple Entente)

B. E. Schmitt, *Triple Alliance and Triple Entente* (Berkshire Studies); S. B. Fay, *The Origins of the World War* (Vol. I); W. L. Langer, *European Alliances and Alignments, 1871-1890; Diplomacy and Imperialism, 1890-1905;* R. B. Mowatt, *The Concert of Europe;* G. L. Dickinson, *The International Anarchy, 1904-1914;* C. Seymour, *The Diplomatic Background of the War, 1870-1914;* R. J. Sontag, *European Diplomatic History, 1871-1932;* J. W. Swain, *Beginning the Twentieth Century;* E. M. Earle, *Turkey, the Great Powers, and the Bagdad Railway.*

READING LIST FOR CHAPTER 35

(The Outbreak of World War I, 1914)

S. B. Fay, *The Origins of the World War* (Vol. II); B. E. Schmitt, *The Coming of the War* (two volumes); H. E. Barnes, *The Genesis of the World War;* A. Fabre-Luce, *The Limitations of Victory;* M. Montgelas, *The Case for the Central Powers;* E. Grey, *Twenty-five Years, 1892-1916.*

READING LIST FOR CHAPTER 36

(The War and the Peace, 1914-1919)

The War. C. J. H. Hayes, *A Brief History of the World War;* A. F. Pollard, *A Short History of the Great War* (a British account); L. Stallings, ed., *The First World War: A Photographic History;* B. H. Liddell Hart, *The Real War;* F. H. Simonds, *History of the World War* (5 volumes); C. Seymour, *Woodrow Wilson and the World War;* W. Millis, *The Road to War, America 1914-1917;* T. E. Lawrence, *Revolt in the Desert* (revolt of the Arabs against the Turks); H. D. Lasswell, *Propaganda Technique in the World War.*

The Peace. A. P. Scott, *An Introduction to the Peace Treaties;* I. Bowman, *The New World, Problems in Political Geography;* E. M. House and C. Seymour, *What Really Happened at Paris;* E. J. Dillon, *The Inside Story of the Peace Conference;* K. F. Nowak, *Versailles;* H. M. Hyndman, *Clemenceau;* S. Huddleston, *Poincaré, A Biographical Portrait;* H. Begbie, *The Mirrors of Downing Street.*

Memoirs. D. Lloyd George, *War Memoirs;* W. Churchill, *World Crisis;* R. Poincaré, *Memoirs;* E. von Ludendorff, *My War Memories, 1914-1918;* P. von Hindenburg, *Out of My Life.*

Fiction. M. Anderson and L. Stallings, *What Price Glory?* (drama); Sherwood, *Journey's End* (drama); E. M. Remarque, *All Quiet on the Western Front* (a German record); H. G. Wells, *Mr. Britling Sees It Through;* S. Zweig, *The Case of Sergeant Grischa* (military red tape versus human fate); J. H. Beith, *The First Hundred Thousand* (England).

READING LIST FOR CHAPTER 37

(The German Republic; the Execution of the Treaty of Versailles; the Reparation Issue)

F. L. Benns, *Europe Since 1870;* W. C. Langsam, *The World Since 1914;* F. P. Chambers (and others), *This Age of Conflict;* I. Bowman, *The New World, Problems in Political Geography;* M. Baumont, *The Fall of the Kaiser;* E. Luehr, *The New German Republic;* H. G. Daniels, *The Rise of the German Republic;* G. P. Gooch, *Germany;* H. Quigley and R. J. Clark, *Republican Germany;* J. M. Keynes, *The Economic Consequences of the Peace* (the first penetrating analysis of the disastrous effects of German reparations); T. R. Ybarra, *Hindenburg, the Man with Three Lives;* R. Recouly, *The Third French Republic;* S. Huddleston, *Poincaré.*

READING LIST FOR CHAPTER 38

(The Peace Movement: Partial Successes and Final Failure of the League of Nations)

F. L. Benns, *Europe Since 1870;* W. C. Langsam, *The World Since 1914;* F. P. Chambers (and others), *This Age of Conflict;* S. P. Duggan, *The League of Nations: The Principle and the Practice;* P. J. N. Baker, *The League of Nations at Work;* C. K. Webster, *The League of Nations in Theory and Practice* (1933); R. B. Mowat, *A History of European Diplomacy, 1914-1925;* M. O. Hudson, *The World Court* (1921-1931); G. N. Barnes, *A History of the International Labour Office;* F. K. Simonds, *The Great Powers in World Politics;* S. Madariaga, *Disarmament* (by the chairman of the disarmament committee); D. P. Myers, *World Disarmament* (good survey); N. Angell, *The Great Illusion* (the case for pacifism).

READING LIST FOR CHAPTER 39

(Russia Goes Communist)

Benns, Langsam, Chambers, as given for Chapter 38; L. Trotsky, *History of the Russian Revolution;* G. V. Vernadsky, *The Russian Revolution, 1917-21; Lenin, the Red Dictator;* W. H. Chamberlin, *The Russian Revolution, 1917-1921; Collectivism, a False Utopia;* S. Graham, *Stalin;* I. D. Levine, *The Man Lenin; Stalin;* M. G. Hindus, *Humanity Uprooted; Red Bread;* S. N. Harper, *Making Bolsheviks; The Government of the Soviet Union;* E. Lyons, *Assignment in Utopia;* S. and B. Webb, *Soviet Communism.*

READING LIST FOR CHAPTER 40

(Italy Goes Fascist)

Benns, Langsam, Chambers as above; G. A. Borgese, *Goliath: The March of Fascism;* H. Finer, *Mussolini's Italy;* B. King, *Fascism in Italy;* G. Salvemini, *Under the Axe of Fascism;* H. A. Steiner, *Government in Fascist Italy;* H. W. Schneider, *Making of the Fascist State;* H. W. Schneider and S. B.

Clough, *Making Fascists;* T. E. Moore, *Peter's City: An Account of the Origin, Development, and Solution of the Roman Question.*

READING LIST FOR CHAPTER 41

(Germany Goes Nazi)

Benns, Langsam, Chambers as above; R. H. Lutz, *The German Revolution;* H. Levy, *Industrial Germany: A Study of Its Monopoly Organizations;* R. T. Clark, *The Fall of the German Republic;* A. Hitler, *Mein Kampf* (autobiography); K. Heiden, *Hitler; A History of National Socialism;* I. L. Kandel, *The Making of Nazis;* D. Miller, *You Can't Do Business with Hitler;* F. L. Schuman, *The Nazi Dictatorship;* F. L. Neumann, *Behemoth: The Structure and Practice of National Socialism;* H. Rauschning, *The Revolution of Nihilism;* Dodd, W. E. Jr. and M. (eds.), *Ambassador Dodd's Diary, 1933-1938.*

READING LIST FOR CHAPTER 42

(Two Continuing Democracies: France and Great Britain)

Benns, Langsam, Chambers as above.
France. W. R. Sharp, *The Government of the French Republic;* R. W. Hale, *Democratic France: The Third Republic from Sedan to Vichy;* R. Cahill, *Economic Conditions in France;* W. MacDonald, *Reconstruction in France;* S. Huddleston, *Poincaré;* S. Roberts, *History of French Colonial Policy* (2 vols.); A. Werth, *Which Way France?*
Great Britain. E. H. Carr, *Great Britain: A Study of Foreign Policy from the Treaty of Versailles to the Outbreak of the War, 1939;* G. A. Greenwood, *England Today: A Social Study;* W. I. Jennings, *Cabinet Government;* A. L. Lowell and H. D. Hall, *The British Commonwealth of Nations;* A. Siegfried, *England's Crisis;* D. R. Gwynn, *The Irish Free State;* M. K. Gandhi. *The Story of My Experiments with Truth;* E. Emerson, *Voiceless India;* J. Nehru, *Toward Freedom: An Autobiography;* V. Chirol, *The Egyptian Problem;* T. R. Feiwel, *No Ease in Zion;* E. Main, *Palestine at the Crossroads.*

READING LIST FOR CHAPTER 43

(The States of East Central Europe, The Balkan Peninsula, and The Arab World after World War I)

Benns, Langsam, Chambers as above.
East Central Europe. M. W. Graham, *New Governments of Eastern Europe;* T. W. Atchley, *Finland;* A. Bihlmans, *Latvia in the Making;* R. Dyboski, *Outlines of Polish History;* R. Machray, *Poland, 1914-1931;* G. Humphrey, *Pilsudski;* L. Pasvolsky, *Economic Nationalism of the Danubian States;* C. Hamilton, *Modern Austria;* P. W. Slosson, *The Problem of Austro-German Union;* F. A. Eckhart, *Short History of the Hungarian People;* C. Holland, *Czechoslovakia: The Land and Its People.*
The Balkan States. H. F. Armstrong, *The New Balkans;* M. W. Graham, *The New Governments of Central Europe;* C. A. Beard and G. Redin, *The Balkan Pivot: Yugoslavia;* G. Ellison, *Yugoslavia;* J. Swire, *Albania: The*

Rise of a Kingdom; J. Buchan (ed.), *Bulgaria and Roumania;* C. V. Clark, *United Roumania;* D. Mitrany, *The Land and the Peasant in Rumania;* J. S. Rouček, *Contemporary Roumania and Her Problems;* W. Miller, *Greece;* A. J. Toynbee, *The Western Question in Greece and Turkey;* A. J. Toynbee and K. Kirkwood, *Turkey;* W. Miller, *The Ottoman Empire and Its Successors;* F. Schevill, *History of the Balkan Peninsula;* Halidah Adib, *Turkey Faces West;* H. E. Wortham, *Mustapha Kemal of Turkey.*

The Arab World. E. W. P. Newman, *Great Britain in Egypt;* G. Young, *Egypt;* L. Stein, *Syria;* A. Granovski, *Land Settlement in Palestine;* E. P. McCallum, *The Nationalist Crusade in Syria;* F. F. Andrews, *The Holy Land under Mandate* (2 vols.); H. A. Foster, *The Making of Modern Iraq;* D. G. Hogarth, *Arabia.*

READING LIST FOR CHAPTER 44

(The Outbreak of World War II, 1939)

Spain. W. B. Harris, *France, Spain, and the Riff;* J. McCabe, *Spain in Revolt, 1814-1931;* E. A. Peers, *The Spanish Tragedy, 1930-1936;* J. Ortega y Gasset, *Invertebrate Spain;* V. Sheean, *Personal History* (illuminating picture of the Riffian Revolt).

For the Hitler aggressions of 1938-1939 see Reading Lists under Austria, Czechoslovakia, Germany, and Poland. The best presentations available at the present time are given by the following general histories: F. L. Benns, *European History Since 1870;* W. C. Langsam, *The World Since 1914;* F. P. Chambers (and others), *This Age of Conflict.*

READING LIST FOR CHAPTER 45

(World War II, 1939-1945)

Benns, Langsam, Chambers as given in preceding chapter. Winston S. Churchill, *The Second World War:* Vol. I, *The Gathering Storm,* Vol. II, *Their Finest Hour;* H. S. Commager, *The Story of the Second World War;* Dwight D. Eisenhower, *Crusade in Europe;* William L. Langer, *Our Vichy Gamble;* Gilbert Cant, *The Great Pacific Victory: From the Solomons to Tokyo;* S. E. Morison, *History of the United States Naval Operations in World War II;* C. P. Romulo, *I Saw the Philippines Fall;* R. E. Sherwood, *Roosevelt and Hopkins: An Intimate History;* The War Reports of General of the Army George C. Marshall, General of the Army H. H. Arnold, Fleet Admiral Ernest J. King.

READING LIST FOR CHAPTER 46

(Leading Cultural Trends of the Twentieth Century)

Philosophy. A. K. Rogers, *A Student's History of Philosophy;* W. Durant, *The Story of Philosophy;* J. Dewey, *Reconstruction in Philosophy;* H. W. Schneider, *A History of American Philosophy.*

Science. W. T. Sedgwick and H. W. Tyler, *A Short History of Science;* H. H. Newman and others, *The Nature of the World and of Man;* E. E. Slosson and O. W. Caldwell, *Science Remaking the World;* E. E. Slosson,

Creative Chemistry; B. Jaffe, *Crucibles, the Lives and Achievements of the Great Chemists;* P. de Kruif, *Microbe Hunters; Men Against Death;* B. Harrow, *From Newton to Einstein;* J. Jeans, *This Mysterious Universe;* H. E. Barnes, *The New History and the Social Studies;* H. E. Barnes (ed.), *The History and Prospects of the Social Sciences;* J. H. Robinson, *The Mind in the Making: The Relation of Intelligence to Social Reform.*

Psychology. B. Low, *Psycho-analysis: A Brief Account of the Freudian Theory;* C. J. Jung, *Contributions to Analytical Psychology.*

The Arts. H. Gardner, *Art Through the Ages;* D. M. Robb and J. J. Garrison, *Art in the Western World;* T. Craven, *Modern Art: the Men, the Movements, the Meaning* (1934); C. Bell, *Since Cézanne* (1922); J. Gordon, *Modern French Painters;* F. J. Mather, *Modern Painting;* J. Meier-Graefe, *Vincent van Gogh;* A. M. Rindge, *Sculpture;* L. Mumford, *Sticks and Stones;* H. R. Hitchcock, *Modern Architecture;* Frank Lloyd Wright, *When Democracy Builds;* G. Grove, *A Dictionary of Music and Musicians;* D. Ewen, *From Bach to Stravinsky;* R. Rolland, *Musicians of Today* (1928); I. F. Stravinsky, *Stravinsky: an Autobiography.*

Philosophy of History. C. A. Beard (ed.), *Whither Mankind;* C. A. Beard, (ed.), *Toward Civilization;* H. G. Wells, *The Salvaging of Civilization: the Probable Future of Mankind;* A. H. Silver, *Religion in a Changing World;* A. E. Haydon (ed.), *Modern Trends in World Religion;* A. J. Toynbee, *A Study of History,* abridged edition by D. C. Somervell; F. S. C. Northrop, *The Meeting of East and West.*

READING LIST FOR CHAPTER 47

(The Postwar World, 1945-1950)

B. Souvarine, *Stalin: A Critical Survey of Bolshevism;* N. Timasheff, *The Great Retreat: The Growth and Decline of Communism in Russia;* P. Meyer, *The Soviet Union: A New Class Society;* D. Shub, *Lenin: A Biography;* W. Lippmann, *The Cold War: A Study in U. S. Foreign Policy;* W. H. Chamberlin, *The European Cockpit;* A. Koestler, *The Yogi and the Commissar* (A Personal Account of Russian Communism); D. J. Dallin, *The Real Soviet Russia;* R. Crossman (ed.), *The God That Failed* (A Confession by Six Communists and Communist Sympathizers); J. Steinberg, *Verdict of Three Decades* (Condemnation of Communism by a Group of Former Believers).

INDEX

Index by John Askling

EUROPE IN 1914

SCALE OF MILES

0 100 200 300 400 500

Capitals are shown thus: ◎

Longitude 1   West   2   3   4   **Longitude** 5   East

POATES CORP., N.Y.